SUPREME HEADQUARTERS ALLIED
EXPEDITIONARY FORCE
EVALUATION AND DISSEMINATION SECTION
G-2 (COUNTER INTELLIGENCE SUB-DIVISION)

# THE
# GERMAN POLICE

Prepared jointly by M.I.R.S. (London Branch) and E.D.S.
in consultation with the War Office (M.I. 14(d))

E.D.S./G/I0

April 1945

"In the coming war we shall fight not only on land, on sea, and in the air. There will be a fourth theatre of operations—the Inner Front. That front wil decide on the continued existence or the irrevocable death of the German Nation."

These were HIMMLER's words in September, 1937, and the Inner Front which he predicted is that which his police forces are now ordered to maintain to the last. To continue the fight on that front, even beyond the duration of actual hostilities, is undoubtedly the task HIMMLER has allotted to the German Police in conjunction with the SS.

In the EDS series of Basic Handbooks on German para-military formations and related subjects, this handbook—together with that on the Allgemeine SS—may well be described as the most important. It not only deals with organisation, administration and functions, but also attempts, by underlining the fundamental difference between the Allied and the Nazi concepts of "Police," to throw some light on the difficult problem of distinguishing those German Policemen who can, those who might, and those who should not be employed by an occupying Power. The citizen of a democracy knows the Police only as the servant and guardian of the people, and since a democratic government carries out the policies desired by the popular majority, it needs no deliberately created force to maintain its power. The Nazi dictatorship has never been bound by the will of the people ; the will of the Leader alone is both the law and the aim of the Totalitarian State. In such a State the Police is the instrument of oppression in the hands of its leaders.

Allied Armies in the course of their advance into German territory will as in the past, encounter the field forces of the German Police ; knowledge of their organisation and background is therefore an operational necessity.

In areas occupied by Allied troops the task of stamping out opposition and subversive activities will arise. The Nazi Police, the SS, and the intelligence services controlled by the two organisations will undoubtedly form the nucleus of resistance movements.

Finally, in the period of occupation, control and administration, it will be found necessary to render powerless, and to bring to justice, many dangerous and guilty members of the German Police. Even after the process of neutralisation and selection, the secure employment of the existing German Police machinery will be facilitated by an insight into its workings, and an understanding of its domination by the Nazi Party.

This handbook has therefore been compiled with the aim of providing an intelligence background for each of these three stages in the subjugation of Germany.

# THE GERMAN POLICE

## Table of Contents

**Foreword**

## PART ONE : HISTORY AND EVOLUTION OF THE GERMAN POLICE

## PART TWO : THE HIGH COMMAND OF THE GERMAN POLICE

**A. HEINRICH HIMMLER**

**B. HIMMLER'S IMMEDIATE REPRESENTATIVES**

## PART THREE : REGIONAL ADMINISTRATION AND THE POLICE

## PART FOUR : THE ORDNUNGSPOLIZEI

**A. HIGHER ORGANISATION AND GENERAL STRUCTURE OF THE ORPO**

# B. THE REGULAR UNIFORMED POLICE

## I. General Introduction

## II. Ordinary Branches

### (a) Schutzpolizei Schupo des Reiches

### (b) Schutzpolizei der Gemeinden

### (c) Gendarmerie

### (d) Kolonialpolizei

### (e) Wasserschutzpolizei

### (f) Feuerschutzpolizei

## III. Technical Auxiliary Branches

### (g) Feuerwehren

### (h) Luftschutzpolizei

### (j) Technische Nothilfe

# PART EIGHT : UNIFORMS AND PERSONAL DOCUMENTS

# ANNEXES

INDEX OF SUBJECTS

# FOREWORD

This Handbook attempts to present as complete a study on the German Police as possible. It should be pointed out, however, that no book can hope to deal exhaustively with subject matter of such magnitude, and to answer completely all questions that might arise. The German Police is not a static organisation, and the Nazis were still in the process of re-modelling both German administration and the German Police when war broke out. Since then wartime necessities have brought about a large number of further changes rendering the task of preparing a complete and up-to-date study even more difficult.

The main facts concerning the development of the German Police during the past twelve years are given in PART ONE of the text, but a number of lesser details of an historical nature appear throughout. PARTS TWO, THREE, FOUR and FIVE describing the organisation, functions and methods of the German Police should be considered as a whole, and for a better understanding of its organisation the two charts (in German and English) at the end of the book should be consulted. PART SIX, dealing with Legal Aspects, does not by any means constitute a complete study of the laws and regulations affecting the German Police ; it is a simple guide for laymen in the maze of legal details which exist in Germany, giving at the same time a number of definitions of legal terms that will constantly be encountered in connection with the German Police. PART SEVEN gives an outline of the principal features of the German Civil Service as far as this concerns the personnel of the Police. Comparative tables of Police ranks shown at the end of PART SEVEN should facilitate the understanding of that Part. Descriptions of Police uniforms and identity documents are given in PART EIGHT.

Strength estimates are not generally included owing to the difficulty of arriving at any reliable results.

All available details on identified Police headquarters and units within Germany and German-occupied territory are listed in the various Annexes, but facts referring to the German Police headquarters in occupied countries are not dealt with exhaustively. Even with regard to the headquarters inside Germany it should be understood that none of the Annexes can be completely up-to-date. Owing to Allied bombing, the manpower shortage and other exigencies of war, changes in addresses and personalities occur constantly. For this reason the number of personalities included in the book has been kept to a minimum. In order to find a given Police headquarters use should be made of the Gazetteer of German-towns and Police headquarters (Annexe K). Throughout the Annexes the liberation of formerly occupied countries and the conquest of Germany by the Allies have been ignored for purposes of compilation.

German official terminology and abbreviations have been used throughout the book, unless otherwise stated, and reference should be made to the list of abbreviations and to the Index of Subjects appearing at the end of the book.

Sources used include a great many German manuals, periodicals, telephone books, correspondence files, official orders, and other documents, as well as interrogations of PW and other intelligence reports. As far as is known, no single comprehensive German book on the Police exists, partly owing to the complicated nature of the subject matter, and partly to its confidential details.

The following MIRS publications have been incorporated into this book in revised forms and are therefore superseded :

MIRS/OCC-CI/1/44    *Gestapo* Headquarters in Greater Germany (see Annexe F).

MIRS/OCC-CI/2/44    SD (Security Service) Headquarters in Greater Germany (see Annexe H).

MIRS/OCC-CI/5/44    Headquarters of the *Kripo* (Criminal Police) in Greater Germany (see Annexe G).

MIRS/OCC-CI/10/44    Police.Schools in Germany (see Annexe J).

MIRS/OCC-CI/12/44    *Staatliche Polizeiverwaltungen* in Greater Germany (see Annexe C).

MIRS/OCC-CI/15/44    Higher Administrative and Police Authorities in Greater Germany (*Landes- und Höhere Polizeibehörden*) (see Annexe B).

MIRS/OCC-CI/28/44    The *Gestapoamt* (Amt IV of the RSHA) (see text, Part Five, Section B).

# Part One

# HISTORY AND EVOLUTION OF THE GERMAN POLICE

## 1. German Police before 1933

The German Police force is probably the most powerful organisation of its kind in the world. It is also the most ruthless—the operations of the *Gestapo* furnish ample evidence of that fact.

It is the purpose of this Part to trace the development of the German police, during the eleven years of the Nazi régime, from a number of loosely organised groups without central authority into a disciplined machine whose principal function is to maintain Nazi rule over the German people.

When the National Socialists obtained power on 30th January, 1933, there was no over-all police authority in Germany. The country was divided into *Länder* (states), as it had been under the monarchy and under the Weimar Republic, and each state had control of the police units (*Landespolizei*) within its own area.

These various police groups, being largely independent of one another and without a definite relationship, had their own individual systems of administration, pay, uniforms, and even their own legal codes.

Neither the Versailles Treaty nor the Weimar Republic changed the provincial nature of the German police, although the Weimar Constitution provided for financial control of the police by the Reich Minister of the Interior. Thus, by refusing to approve appropriations for the police force of a certain *Land*, the Minister could exercise a modicum of restraint upon a particular group. Otherwise, however, the *Länder* continued to administer their own police units.

Earlier attempts to unify the police force in Germany met with strong opposition from the States, especially from Catholic Bavaria, which traditionally feared encroachment on her rights by the more powerful and Protestant Prussia.

## 2. Gleichschaltung (Co-ordination and Assimilation)

To implement their plans, the National Socialists needed a uniform German administration and a strong, united police force rigidly controlled by the central government. But they could not immediately arrogate to themselves the powers of the various police agencies within the entire country, as they had to fight the still existing opposition of the other political parties, the church groups, the trades unions and various State interests.

With the police to aid them, the Nazis could more quickly subdue opposition groups, but at the time of the *Machtübernahme* (advent to power) they could not afford to upset the organisation of the police. They did, however, take immediate steps to change its personnel.

The first few months after the *Machtübernahme* were known as the period of *Gleichschaltung*, i.e. the assimilating and co-ordinating of all organisations in accordance with the changes which had taken place in the Reich government itself.

During that period all the governments of the *Länder* were taken over by the Nazis, and with them all the executive positions controlling the Police (Ministers of the Interior of the States, etc.). These newly appointed executives in turn began immediately a ruthless purge within their regions, to remove all the lesser members of the

Police who had been in any way connected with a republican or democratic party, or whose loyalty towards the ·Nazi cause was open to question. Such men were mostly replaced by " *Alte Kämpfer*" ("Old fighters" for Nazism) whose loyalty was beyond all shadow of doubt. Thus the police forces were nazified simultaneously from above and below. In addition, large numbers of the SA and SS were temporarily employed as auxiliary police.

## 3. Political Police : Birth of the Gestapo

The first important steps towards an organisational change in the German Police system were taken in the field of the *Politische Polizei* (Political Police)—known in Prussia as the *Staatspolizei* or *Stapo*—a limited force of which had been permitted in the Weimar period. The powers of this force, however, had been as strictly curtailed as its numbers and funds.

A " Secret State Police " existed neither under the Monarchy nor under the Weimar Republic and Germans had not become as they have to-day " mere Police Objects."

The National Socialists had not failed to study the technique of the Secret Police systems in other totalitarian states, and they were quick to seize upon and expand such an obvious weapon of repression as a Political Police organisation.

Above all they studied the exploitation of fear, transforming it into their most potent political weapon, and reducing mass and individual terrorism to a fine art.

They also saw the advantages of controlling and utilising the activities of *Auslandsdeutsche*, for Germans abroad clearly could not be neglected by the new régime.

Prussia, Germany's most militaristic state, was the first to establish an official secret police, though there are grounds for believing that the *Braunes Haus* (Party Headquarters) in Munich was the setting for the earliest conferences on the subject.

GÖRING, as, Prime Minister of Prussia, and in control of the Prussian police, was out to increase his personal power as much as possible, and it is also known that RÖHM, chief of the then politically powerful SA (Storm Troops), aspired to a large measure of control over this new police system.

*Die Geheime Staatspolizei* (*Gestapo* or Secret State Police) which replaced the former Prussian Political Police was officially established by GÖRING on 26th April, 1933.

GÖRING retained· the title of Chief of the *Gestapo* but delegated the active direction of this organisation to *Oberregierungsrat* DIELS, who until then had been in charge of the section for the Observation of Communism in the Reich Ministry of the Interior.

Thus the *Gestapo* emerged as a Prussian institution, and even to-day it is not technically a Reich organisation, though the question is now purely academic, since according to the Reich Decree of 17th June, 1936 (see para. 6) and the HIMMLER decree of 26th June, 1936 (see para. 7) the *Gestapo* forms part of the Reich Security Police.

Shortly after the *Machtübernahme* HIMMLER had become Commander of the Political Police in Bavaria, having with him HEYDRICH, then

Political Police Chief in Munich. But, far more important, HEYDRICH was also chief of the *Sicherheitsdienst des Reichsführers-SS (SD d RFSS—* Security Service of the Commander in Chief of the SS), and therefore again subordinate to HIMMLER in the latter's capacity as *Reichsführer-SS* (Commander in Chief of the SS).

The importance and influence of the SD in the early history of the formation of the *Gestapo* cannot be overestimated. It already formed the nucleus of a *Gestapo* since its exclusive mission was to spy upon the activities of the members of the National Socialist Party.

Thus a scientifically organised *Party* intelligence service was at hand to form the basis of a similar intelligence system run on government lines. The party SD was to continue as a separate entity, but it became indissolubly allied with the Secret State Police, all the personnel of the former, and to a large extent that of the latter, being drawn from the SS.

The most important executive arm during the early stages of the development of the *Gestapo* was the *Schutzpolizeiabteilung z.b.V.* (Safety Police Unit for Special Assignments), which subsequently became the *Polizeigruppe GENERAL GÖRING.* It consisted of selected officers and was commanded by Police Major WECKE. This unit was the nucleus of the present *Fallschirm Panzer Division HERMANN GÖRING* of the Luftwaffe.

The *Schutzpolizeiabteilung z.b.V.* was made up of uniformed squads and detachments, whose members wore a silver-embroidered brassard on the left lower sleeve to show that they were at the special disposal (*zur besonderen Verwendung*, abbr. *z.b.V.*) of GÖRING, and thereby, of his new police force, the *Gestapo.*

## 4. HIMMLER becomes Deputy Chief of the Gestapo

HIMMLER, casting an envious eye from his headquarters in Munich on GÖRING'S new Prussian Secret Police, was not to be outdone in the competition for personal power. As Commander in Chief of the SS, who above all was responsible for the life and safety of the Führer, and as ultimate Chief of the SD, whose espionage system enabled him to obtain a hold on all the other prominent members of the Party, he felt that he should have some say in the formation of a secret police.

But nearly a year passed before HIMMLER managed to realise his desire. During that time he had gradually but purposefully obtained control of the political police forces of all the *Länder* except Prussia, and held the title of *Politischer Polizeikommandeur der Länder* (Political Police Commander of the German States).

In the spring of 1934 HIMMLER brought several Prussian *Gestapo* officials under his sway, and "discovered" a plot against GÖRING, thus seemingly proving the inefficiency of the Prussian *Gestapo*. In typical Nazi style, therefore, HIMMLER forced GÖRING's hand, and the latter appointed him deputy chief of the Prussian *Gestapo* in place of DIELS, who was dismissed.

At the same time HIMMLER retained his posts as head of the political police forces of the other German States, and in that way managed as deputy chief of the *Gestapo* to become more powerful than his chief.

His first care was to purge the police of all officials suspected of a lukewarm attitude towards the régime. Then he rapidly replaced the dismissed officials by members of the SS, thus starting the amalgamation of the SS and the Police, which was to find its full expression some two years later.

## 5. Centralisation of Government and its effect on the Police

The first step towards centralised control was taken on 30th January, 1934, exactly one year after the *Machtübernahme*, when the decree for the reconstruction of the Reich (*Gesetz über den Neuaufbau des Reiches*) was published.

Article 2 of this law laid down that the sovereign rights of the *Länder* (States) were to be transferred to the Reich. All State governments were henceforth subordinated to the central Reich Government, including, of course, the police forces of each State. Thus one of the major aims, one of the major necessities of the National Socialist Party was achieved.

This sweeping development did not, however, produce any obvious change in the routine conduct of police work. In fact a subsequent ordinance dated 2nd February, 1934, stated that the execution of those sovereign rights transmitted to the Reich by Article 2 should remain in the hands of the States, which would act on behalf of the Reich Government in those cases where the latter did not choose, in a general or particular sense, to make full use of its rights under the new act. This left the central Government freedom of choice in the absorption of police functions, and it is this freedom which is responsible for the complicated structure of the German Police system and for the anomalous conditions under which the German Police operates to-day.

Outwardly, the *Länder* retain their individual control, but the real power is centred in Berlin.

A definite step in the unification and centralisation (*Verreichlichung*) of the police was the creation of the **Kasernierte Landespolizei** (*Lapo* or militarised barrack police), which was trained and equipped as infantry.

Prussia had already taken the lead in this matter and by a decree of 26th March, 1933, had established a number of *Landespolizei-Inspektionen* (Police Inspectorates) "with the object of preparing and implementing defensive measures directed against internal strife."

The Prussian example was followed by the governments of the other *Länder*, and finally, by a decree published on 29th March, 1935, the entire administration of the *Landespolizei* was handed over to the Reich Ministers of the Interior and of Finance for co-ordination.

This decree was speedily followed by additional legislation, which ordered that, as from 1st April, 1935, the combined *Landespolizei* formations of all the State governments should be taken over by the Reich.

With the introduction of national conscription in March, 1935, the majority of the men in the "*Lapo*" were drafted into the Army where they formed a useful nucleus of well-trained, well-disciplined soldiers.

Some continuity in the structure and purpose of the *Landespolizei* formations is to be seen in the barrack police battalions and regiments of to-day.

Attention was then directed to the question of the **Gemeindepolizei** (Municipal Police). The reorganisation of the *Staatliche Polizei* (State Police Forces) in the States had already produced a certain degree of uniformity, but there existed substantial differences in the sphere of the *Gemeindepolizei*, not merely between State and State but even between one area and another in the same State.

Prussia again took the lead by tightening up the position of her own Municipal Police, and raising them to the status of State Police. And in a decree issued on 25th October, 1935, the Reich and

Prussian Minister of the Interior laid down various principles covering the entire administration of this section of the Police.

A particular innovation was the creation of a *Chef der Gemeindepolizei* (Chief of Municipal Police), whose duty it was to unify and direct all municipal police activities in the various towns throughout the Reich.

The German Police Officials Law of 24th June, 1937, gave a new title to this body—*Schutzpolizei der Gemeinden* (Municipal Protection Police). The unification of this group with the State *Schutzpolizei* or *Schutzpolizei des Reiches* (Reich Protection Police) was further extended by various decrees which laid down, among other things, that in larger centres of population the Municipal Police were to be commanded by Police Officers, the area command being classed as a *Kommando der Schutzpolizei* (if commanded by a Major) or as a *Schutzpolizeidienstabteilung* (if commanded by a captain or lower ranking officer).

## 6. Appointment of a Chef der deutschen Polizei

The process of centralisation reached its peak on 17th June, 1936. On this date, HITLER created a new post, that of *Chef der deutschen Polizei* (Chief of the German Police) in the Reich Ministry of the Interior.

The man selected to fill this all-important position of supreme head of the Police forces of the Reich was HIMMLER, already, as we have seen, Commander of the SS and, more notoriously, deputy Chief of the *Gestapo*.

The law of 30th January, 1934, had already transferred State and police sovereignty from the *Länder* to the Reich, and this organic shift of power was now considerably strengthened by the appointment of a supreme police dictator who happened also to be one of the most powerful men in the Government and in the Party.

His position and responsibilities are clearly defined by the new decree : as *Reichsführer SS und Chef der Deutschen Polizei im Reichsministerium des Innern* HIMMLER was made directly responsible to the Ministry of the Interior. He was, therefore, in the exercise of his Police office, both the representative of the Reich Minister of the Interior, and the representative of GÖRING, the Prime Minister of Prussia. The position of Prussia as a distinct entity within the structure of the Reich should be noted.

As Commander in Chief of the SS, however, HIMMLER was directly responsible to HITLER alone, the Supreme Commander of the SS, and was, therefore, in a position to circumvent the authority of FRICK, the Minister of the Interior.

HIMMLER's status is made clear in a decree issued by the Reich and Prussian Minister of the Interior dated 15th May, 1937, which states in unequivocal terms that there is no difference in the authority for any ruling, whether it bears the signatures of officials in the Ministry of the Interior or whether it is issued by HIMMLER's office.

In either case it is a **Ministerial decision.**

## 7. Reorganisation of the Police under HIMMLER

HIMMLER lost no time in employing his new powers. His first task was to determine the division of functions within the Reich Police. A decree was therefore issued on the 26th June, 1936, entitled "*Geschäftsverteilung im Geschäftsbereich des Chefs der Deutschen Polizei*" (Division of Duties in the Office of the Chief of the German Police.)

This divided the police into two principal branches :
  (*a*) *Ordnungspolizei* (*Orpo* or Regular Police)
  (*b*) *Sicherheitspolizei* (*Sipo* or Security Police).

Into the *Ordnungspolizei* went all the existing branches of the Uniformed Police such as the *Schutzpolizei* (Protection Police) and the *Gendarmerie* (Rural Police) plus the *Verwaltungspolizei* (Administrative Police). The new *Sicherheitspolizei* was made up by the *Reichskriminalpolizei* (*Kripo*— Reich Criminal Police) and the *Geheime Staatspolizei* (*Gestapo*—Secret State Police).

Whatever doubts might have remained regarding the duties of this or that branch of the Police were completely dispelled by this decree which listed in detail the respective duties of the two principal divisions of the Police.

*SS Oberst-Gruppenführer und Generaloberst der Polizei* Kurt DALUEGE and *SS Obergruppenführer* Reinhard HEYDRICH (then only *SS-Gruppenführer*) were appointed heads of the *Ordnungspolizei* and the *Sicherheitspolizei* respectively.

The local and central direction of the police throughout the Reich was not disturbed by these innovations, but the superficial character of local administration was further emphasised by the creation of certain high police officials to supervise the regional forces of the *Orpo* and *Sipo* and act as their authoritative liaison officers with the local Governments as well as the central police departments in Berlin. To each *Wehrkreis* (Military District), therefore, were assigned an *Inspekteur der Orpo* (Inspector of the *Orpo*) and an *Inspekteur der Sipo* (Inspector of the *Sipo*).

They were appointed by a decree dated the 20th September, 1936.

Their tasks included co-operation with the Nazi Party *Gauleiter*, with the Commander of the *Wehrkreis* and with the administrative authorities of the Province or State to which they were appointed.

Unless bound by special instructions from the Head of the *Sipo* or *Orpo*, the *Inspekteure* are expected to carry out the requirements of the local Government Administrators.

In addition, HIMMLER appointed three General Inspectors for the *Ordnungspolizei*, viz :—

  (*a*) *Der Generalinspekteur der Schutzpolizei des Reiches*
  (*b*) *Der Generalinspekteur der Gendarmerie und der Schutzpolizei der Gemeinden*
  (*c*) *Der Generalinspekteur der Polizeischulen.*

In the course of the following years, further General Inspectors were created. (See para. 28.)

The principal duty of these General Inspectors is to bring forward proposals for the effective development of their respective branches, and generally maintain a careful check on the performance of duties.

A further step towards unification resulted from the edict of 25th June, 1936, which also prescribed the wearing of the same uniforms by the whole of the Police Force, and the adoption of standard rank titles and badges.

## 8. Höhere SS und Polizeiführer (Superior SS and Police Commanders)

Not content with these new measures, and doubtless having in mind the importance of the rapidly expanding Army, HIMMLER later created another type of high Police official.

In each of the *SS-Oberabschnitte* (main territorial divisions of the SS in the Reich corresponding with the *Wehrkreise* or Military Districts into which Germany is divided) there existed already an *SS*

*Führer* (Leader of the SS forces in that District). It was, therefore, a simple and logical step to place this *SS Führer* at the head also of the Police.

*Die Höhere SS und Polizeiführer* (*HSSPf* or Superior SS and Police Commanders) as they were called, were the direct and personal representatives in each *Wehrkreis*—and later on, during the War, in all occupied territories—of HIMMLER himself, the Commander-in-Chief of the SS and of the German police. In addition the HSSPf acted as HIMMLER's principal liaison officers with the *Wehrkreis* commanders, and other higher regional authorities.

### 9. New Organisation of the Sipo—General

Other measures directed towards the unification of the German Police concerned the new *Sicherheitspolizei* (Security Police), the more powerful of the two main branches of police laid down by HIMMLER on 26th June, 1936.

The first was a decree published on 10th July, 1936, which empowered officers of the *Gestapo* (Secret State Police) and *Kripo* (Criminal Police) which together constitute the *Sipo* (Security Police), to conduct their activities in any part of the Reich independently of the area covered by their bureaux.

This decree revived in fact the provisions of a still-born law of the 21st July, 1922, which had provided for a central Criminal Police Department responsible to the Reich Minister of the Interior, and represented in the *Länder* by similar departments. The Central Office was to lay down common principles of action, and its officers and those in the allied provincial offices were to be empowered, by virtue of this office, to exercise their functions in any part of the Reich. This law, however, was never promulgated in the Reich owing to opposition by the States.

### 10. New Organisation of the Gestapo

The incorporation of the re-moulded Political Police into the new organisation of the Secret State Police was clearly the next step.

On the 20th September, 1936, a new decree made the *Gestapo-Amt* (Office) in Prussia responsible for the duties of the Political Police Commanders in all the States of Germany.

On the 1st October, 1936, a further decree closed the gap completely by stating that the Political Police forces were to be called *Geheime Staatspolizei* (Secret State Police).

The creation of a network of *Gestapo* head offices and subsidiary offices, *Stapoleitstellen* (Regional Headquarters) and *Stapostellen* (Sub-regional Headquarters) throughout the Reich followed as a matter of course.

The *Gestapo* functioned for nearly three years before its position was defined by law. Though decrees dated 28th February, 1933, and 8th March, 1934, sanctioned the practice of protective custody, and a ruling of the Prussian Court on 2nd May, 1935, stated that the Secret State Police were not subject to judicial control, the fundamental legal basis on which the power of the *Gestapo* reposes is the famous Prussian (*not* Reich) Law of 10th February, 1936, entitled *Gesetz für die Geheime Staatspolizei* (Law concerning the Secret State Police).

This law, which consists of ten brief clauses, is so framed as to allow the very widest span of action to the Secret State Police; it is, in fact, nothing more than legal camouflage for unbridled police despotism of the most ruthless and sweeping nature.

The essence of the decree is contained in the seventh clause, which is barely three lines long. It states that decisions in *affairs conducted by the Gestapo may not be re-examined by the Judiciary*. This means in effect that persons may be arrested and imprisoned without just warrant or cause. It also means that persons tried and found "not guilty" in court, may be re-arrested by the *Gestapo*, the most famous example of this kind being the case of Pastor NIEMÖLLER.

In the course of their duties officers of the *Gestapo* may also invoke the co-operation of all types and branches of the local Police, whose personnel then enjoy the same legal protection as the *Gestapo* personnel.

Instructions for the application of this law, issued on the same date, i.e. 10th February, 1936, laid down in greater detail the functions and attributes of the *Gestapo*. Some of these are as follows:

(a) Measures instituted by the *Gestapo* are equally effective in all parts of the Reich.

(b) The *Gestapo* is the controlling authority for Political Police information.

(c) The *Gestapo* controls and supervises all State concentration camps.

The local *Gestapo* office is kept informed by all State, provincial and local authorities, including even the Ministers of the Interior of the *Länder*, of all important political moves and speeches.

It is interesting to note that according to the law of the 10th February, 1936, the Chief of the *Gestapo* is the Prime Minister of Prussia (i.e. GÖRING). Technically, therefore, HIMMLER has never been, and is not even to-day, Chief of the *Gestapo*, though in effect this technicality is of no real importance—except possibly to GÖRING.

### 11. New Organisation of the Kripo

As the *Kriminalpolizei* or *Kripo* (Criminal Police) now forms part of the *Sicherheitspolizei* it is important to mention at this point the unification, parallel to that of the *Gestapo*, which was effected in the organisation of the *Kripo*.

The principal changes were set out in a series of decrees affecting the officials, the duties, the reporting and the detective services of the Criminal Police.

The Prussian *Landeskriminalamt* (State Criminal Police Department) became the *Reichskriminalpolizeiamt* (*RKPA*—National Headquarters of the Reich Criminal Police).

The activities of the Criminal Police throughout Germany now radiate from a network of *Kriminalpolizeileitstellen* (Criminal Police Regional Headquarters). These were, until 1943, attached to the National Police Administrations in their respective localities. They act as channels for passing instructions and reports from the central Criminal Police Department to the local Police stations in their area.

These local stations collect and classify crime statistics, and forward appreciations of local criminal activity; their operations in fact resemble those of any well ordered criminal police organisation. Any comparison, however, between the German *Kripo* and the criminal police of the democratic countries must take into account the wide powers of "preventive arrest" enjoyed by the *Kripo*, comparable only to those vested in the *Gestapo*.

### 12. Final Concentration of the German Security Forces

One of the most important changes in the history

of the Police was the linking up of the *Sipo* with the *Sicherheitsdienst* (Security Service) *des Reichführers-SS* (SD d. RFSS), the most powerful intelligence and counter-intelligence unit of the Nazi Party.

The decree issued by the Reich Minister of the Interior on 11th November, 1938, made the SD officially responsible for the control of all persons, activities and events which might interfere with the dominance of the National Socialist idea. It stated :—

"The *Sicherheitsdienst* of the RFSS, as the Party and Reich Government organisation, has to carry out important tasks ; in particular it must assist the Security Police (i.e. the *Gestapo* and the *Kripo*). The SD is consequently active on behalf of the Reich and this demands close and intelligent co-operation between the SD and the officials of the General and Interior Administration."

The two branches of the *Sipo*, therefore, emerging from the 1936 reorganisation of the Police as new instruments of power, were now joined, i.e. ultimately dominated and controlled, by the SD. The consolidation of that control, finally placing the *Gestapo* and *Kripo* completely in the hands of the SD, was achieved by a decree of 23rd June, 1938, ordering the enrolment of all *Sipo* personnel in the ranks of the SS, if they were not already members.

The combined *Gestapo*, *Kripo*, and SD came to be known as the " *Staatsschutzkorps*,"—an unofficial Nazi term signifying the combination of forces for the " protection of the State." In terms of organisation the process was expressed in 1939 by the merging of the *Hauptamt Sicherheitspolizei* in the Reich Ministry of the Interior with the *SS-Sicherheitshauptamt*.

Together they formed the *Reichssicherheitshauptamt* (*RSHA* — National Department of Security), the *SD-Hauptamt*, the *Gestapoamt* and the *Reichskriminalpolizeiamt* becoming parts of this new creation.

In 1944 HIMMLER took the final step in the seizure of complete police power by taking away practically all functions of Military Intelligence from the Armed Forces and handing them over to the SD. Controlling all political and military intelligence, the net of the SD has thus been thrown over the entire population and Armed Forces of Germany and German-occupied Europe, and even extends—through all German agents with missions of sabotage and espionage against the Allies—into territories beyond HIMMLER's actual jurisdiction.

# Part Two

# THE HIGH COMMAND OF THE GERMAN POLICE

## A. HEINRICH HIMMLER

### 13. HIMMLER's Early Career and the Rise of the SS

Any description of the organisation of the German Police in its present-day form must start with the career of Heinrich HIMMLER, *Reichsführer-SS und Chef der deutschen Polizei* (*RFSS u Ch d Dt P*—Commander-in-Chief SS and Commander-in-Chief of the German Police). He is not only the leader of the German Police today, but he is the real dictator of Germany.

HIMMLER was born in 1900 and served for a brief period in the last war, attaining the rank of *Fahnenjunker* (Officer cadet). Afterwards he studied agriculture in Munich and unsuccessfully tried his luck in various types of business, including chicken farming. For a time he was also a clerk in an artificial manure factory.

He joined the original Nazi Party and became standardbearer to RÖHM, chief of the SA, the Nazi Party Brownshirted Stormtroopers. Later on, he was secretary to Gregor STRASSER and took part in the HITLER beerhall-putsch of 1923.

On revival of the Party in 1925, after it had been banned and HITLER had been imprisoned, HIMMLER for a while conducted the affairs of the Party *Gau NIEDERBAYERN* as *Geschäftsführer*. Later on he became deputy *Gauleiter*, first of that *Gau* and afterwards of *Gau OBERBAYERN* (Munich).

In 1926 HIMMLER was made one of the original members of the *Reichsleitung der NSDAP* (National Socialist Party Directorate). It is also noteworthy that during the important years from 1926–1930, when the Party was campaigning throughout the country in order to regain lost ground, HIMMLER held the position of *stellvertretender Reichspropagandaleiter* (Deputy Propaganda Chief of the Party).

In 1927 HITLER appointed him deputy leader of the SS, then a subdivision of the much more powerful SA. It seems to be characteristic of HIMMLER that repeatedly throughout his career he has begun as deputy leader of an organisation, and in a short time managed to work his way into the leading position. Thus in 1929 we find him appointed by HITLER as *Reichsführer-SS*.

At that time the SS, HITLER's small bodyguard, consisted of only 270 men, but by 1933 HIMMLER had increased this prætorian guard to roughly 50,000.

Their prestige was greatly advanced by the blood purge of the SA on 30th June, 1934, when the SS became independent of the Brownshirted Stormtroopers. The increase in powers of the SS was further accelerated by the emergence of the *Waffen-SS* (Armed SS).

At the beginning of the war the SS consisted of approximately 300,000 men, but the number of the members of the *Allgemeine-SS* (General SS) is now much smaller owing to the fact that many of its members have transferred into the *Waffen-SS*, the Police and the Armed Forces, or are employed as Concentration Camp guards.

The power of the SS, however, has still further increased, due to the enrolment of hundreds of thousands of men into the *Waffen-SS*, and owing to the fact that members of the SS today hold thousands of executive positions, not only in the Police, but in all branches of the Party, the German administration, business, industry, and official and private life in general. (The Basic Handbook of the SS, EDS/G/8, should be consulted.)

### 14. HIMMLER's Career in the Nazi Government

In 1933 HIMMLER became Chief of the Bavarian Political Police and in 1934 Deputy Chief of the Prussian *Gestapo* which later expanded into the *Gestapo* of today, spreading its tentacles over the whole of Germany and later, over Occupied Europe.

In June, 1936 HITLER created the new position of C-in-C of the German Police in the Reich Ministry of the Interior, and appointed HIMMLER to this post, thus making him *Reichsführer-SS und Chef der Deutschen Polizei*.

In 1939 HIMMLER was appointed *Reichskommissar für die Festigung des Deutschen Volkstums* (Reich Commissioner for the Strengthening of Germanism). As such he is responsible for the re-settlement of *Volksdeutsche* ("racial" Germans) —from the Volga, the Black Sea, Transylvania, Wallachia, etc.—in newly acquired territory, such as the *Reichsgaue* Wartheland and Danzig-Westpreussen, which had been taken from Poland, and were, prior to 1939, comparatively thinly populated by Germans.

This task is performed through the *Volksdeutsche Mittelstelle*, an office closely associated with the SS High Command and largely staffed by SS personnel.

Since the beginning of the war HIMMLER has acquired the positions of *Generalkommissar für die Innere Verteidigung* (Commissioner General for Internal Defence) and of *Generalbevollmächtigter für die Verwaltung* (G.B.V.—General-Plenipotentiary for Administration).

In this latter capacity he has under his supervision the Ministry of the Interior, the Ministries of Education, Church Affairs, and Space and Planning (*Raumordnung*), thereby controlling almost the entire bureaucratic machine of the Reich and its subordinate regional administrations. For some time the Ministry of Justice also belonged to this sphere of influence until THIERACK was appointed Reich Minister of Justice.

A major increase in HIMMLER's power occurred in August, 1943, when he was appointed *Reichsinnenminister* (Reich Minister of the Interior) succeeding Dr. FRICK, who became Reich Protector of Bohemia-Moravia. Until then HIMMLER had manœuvred himself more and more into a leading position within the Ministry; but even though he found ways and means of circumventing the authority of his superior, FRICK was still technically his chief. From August, 1943 on, however, he was not only in fact, but also in name, the chief of Germany's Inner Affairs.

This development of his power came to a climax after the attempt on HITLER's life on 20th July, 1944, when HIMMLER succeeded *Generaloberst* FROMM as *Chef der Heeresrüstung und Befehlshaber des Ersatzheeres* (Chief of Army Equipment and Commander of the Training Army). He is, therefore, Commander in Chief of all Home Forces.

Thus, while the *Führer* concerned himself more and more with military affairs, HIMMLER became the ruling power in Germany itself.

As HIMMLER rose to power the SS High Command and its executives increased their power likewise, and gradually superseded government agencies in many if not in all respects.

As outlined in PART ONE, the *Reichsführung-SS* absorbed step by step the functions of the *Hauptamt Sicherheitspolizei* (National Department of the Security Police), until finally, in 1939, the latter department was officially merged with the *SS-Sicherheitshauptamt der Reichsführung-SS* (Reich Headquarters of the SD, i.e. the Security Service) to form the *Reichssicherheitshauptamt* (*RSHA*—National Department of Security).

Thus the SS established its extra-legal status within the German administration in general and specifically in the German police, over which HIMMLER himself wields absolute power.

# B. HIMMLER'S IMMEDIATE REPRESENTATIVES

## 15. Central Control of the Police

HIMMLER exercises close control over his vast police empire through three chief assistants in Berlin, each in charge of one primary phase of police work, These are :—

(a) *Chef der Ordnungspolizei* (Chief of the Regular Police), who is in charge of the *Hauptamt Ordnungspolizei* (National Department of Regular Police).

This position is held today by *SS-OGF, General der Waffen-SS und General der Polizei.* Alfred WÜNNENBERG, who in 1943 succeeded *Generaloberst der Polizei SS-Oberst-Gruppenführer* Kurt DALUEGE.

(b) *Chef der Sicherheitspolizei und des SD des RFSS* (Chief of the Security Police and the Security Service of the Commander-in-Chief of the SS), who is in command of the *Reichssicherheitshauptamt* (National Department of Security).

The present holder of this position is *SS-OGF, General der Polizei, Staatssekretär* Dr. Ernst KALTENBRUNNER. His predecessor in both appointments was *SS-OGF* Reinhardt HEYDRICH, who was killed by Czech patriots in 1942, at a time when he also held the position of Deputy Reich Protector of Bohemia-Moravia.

(c) *Chef des Hauptamts Haushalt und Bauten* (Chief of the Department of Budget and Buildings), whose office has now been taken over by the *SS-Wirtschafts- und Verwaltungshauptamt* (*WVHA*—the SS Economic and Administrative Department).

Nothing definite is known about the manner in which this amalgamation has taken place, but it is known that the man in charge of the WVHA, *SS-OGF, General der W-SS* Oswald POHL, also holds the rank and function of a *Ministerialdirektor* (rank of *Generalleutnant* in the Administration) in the Reich Ministry of the Interior. It therefore appears almost certain that this man is the Chief of the *Hauptamt Haushalt und Bauten*, which is part of that Ministry.

Under him are the two *Ämter* belonging both to the Ministry of the Interior (Office of the *Chef der Deutschen Polizei*) and the SS-WVHA. They are :

*Amt Haushalt*, identical with *Amtsgruppe A* of the WVHA, whose chief is not known, and

*Amt Bauten*, identical with *Amtsgruppe C* of the WVHA, whose chief is *SS-Gruppenführer, Generalleutnant der W-SS* Dr. Ing. KAMMLER.

*Amtsgruppe A* has offices at Munich and Fürstenberg (Mecklenburg). *Amtsgruppe C* has an office at Berlin-Lichterfelde West, Schlossstr 60. Both *Amtsgruppen* may have offices in other regions, but if so, they have not been identified.

## 16. Regional Control of the Police through HSSPf

Regional control of the Police is exercised by HIMMLER through the *Höhere SS- und Polizeiführer* (Superior SS and Police Commanders). These posts are a National Socialist innovation, and according to reliable evidence the office wa created as early as 1937 at a time when HIMMLER, FRICK and GÖRING (the last in his capacity as *Präsident des Ministerrates für die Reichsverteidigung*—President of the Ministerial Council for National Defence), doubtless envisaged the possibility of war and the consequent need to strengthen the machinery of civil defence and internal security by appointing a personal representative of the Chief of the SS and Police with wide executive powers—a " little HIMMLER "— in each *Wehrkreis* (Military District or Armed Forces Corps Command). There are grounds for the assertion that this was a secret innovation and that the creation of this important office was not made known to the German public until shortly after the outbreak of hostilities.

Before the war the system of HSSPf was conceived as a " shadow " police organisation, their activities being limited to certain eventualities. On the outbreak of war, however, all police forces and formations in each *Wehrkreis* were subordinated to an HSSPf.

There are three categories of Superior SS and Police Commanders :—

(a) HSSPf installed in each of the eighteen *SS-Oberabschnitte*, which are almost identical with the eighteen *Wehrkreise* in Greater Germany. (This includes *Wehrkreis* Böhmen-Mähren, the former Protectorate.)

Since the *Wehrkreis*, i.e. the area over which an HSSPf has jurisdiction, is not identical with any administrative subdivision of Germany, the HSSPf is accredited *t*o each higher administrative authority whose territory belongs partly or completely to that *Wehrkreis*. This is expressed in the title of an HSSPf. For example, the bulk of *Wehrkreis IV* (i.e. *SS-Oberabschnitt* ELBE) consists of *Land* Sachsen, plus parts of the surrounding administrative regions. Therefore the title of the HSSPf in Dresden reads as follows :

" *Der HSSPf bei den Reichsstatthaltern und Oberpräsidenten in Sachsen, den Provinzen Halle-Merseburg, im Sudetengau, in Schlesien und in Thüringen im Wehrkreis IV.*"

Another good example is the HSSPf *im Wehrkreis XIII* (*SS-Oberabschnitt MAIN*), whose territory mainly consists of Northern Bavaria, plus the *Regierungsbezirk* Karlsbad of the *Reichsgau* Sudetenland and a few odd *Landkreise* of other German *Länder*. His title therefore reads :

" *Der HSSPf beim Bayrischen Staatsministerium des Innern und bei den Reichsstatthaltern in Baden, im Sudetengau, in Thüringen und in Württemberg im Wehrkreis XIII.*"

(b) HSSPf outside Greater Germany, but in territory populated by people considered " Nordic and Aryan," and therefore organised into *SS-Oberabschnitte*.

There are three such *SS-Oberabschnitte* :—
*SS-Oa NORD* (Norway).
*SS-Oa NORDWEST* (Holland).
*SS-Oa OSTLAND* (Baltic Countries).

The titles of these HSSPf are somewhat simpler than those located inside Germany because there is only one Higher Administrative Authority in occupied territory, namely the *Reichskommissar*. For example the title of the HSSPf in Holland reads as follows :

" *Der HSSPf beim Reichskommissar für die besetzten Niederländischen Gebiete.*"

(c) HSSPf in other occupied areas such as the *General Gouvernement*, Serbia, Greece, France, and the various Russian sectors. Virtually all these territories are already liberated, or about to be liberated by the United Nations, and little attention need therefore be paid to this group of HSSPf.

In Italy the German police administration is slightly different. Since the BADOGLIO Armistice in September, 1943, between the Italians and the Allies, *SS-OGF, Gen. d W-SS* Karl WOLFF has been installed in the German held part of the country as *Höchster SS- u. Polizeiführer*. He is HIMMLER'S representative and military plenipotentiary for all Italy with Headquarters at Verona.

WOLFF is the immediate superior to the *HSSPf Adriatische Küste* (Adriatic Coastal Zone) at Trieste and possibly also to one or two other HSSPf established for the Western and Central parts of Northern Italy. This, however, is not confirmed, and it is possible that WOLFF himself may administer these parts of Italy as HSSPf, his title as *Höchster-SSPf* merely expressing that he is the superior of one other HSSPf, namely the one located at Trieste. In addition, several SSPf (see para. 18 below) are known to be established in Italy.

WOLFF is also *Chef des Persönlichen Stabes* (Chief of HIMMLER's Personal Staff) and was, until recently, HIMMLER's representative at the *Führerhauptquartier*, i.e. the OKW (The Armed Forces High Command).

A situation similar to the one described above for Italy existed in the Ukraine, where until summer, 1944, *SS-OGF Gen. d. Pol.* Hans PRÜTZMANN was known as *Höchster-SSPf*, administering that territory himself like any other HSSPf, but being, at the same time, superior to another HSSPf, namely the HSSPf *Schwarzes Meer* (Black Sea) at Odessa—who has now moved to Tarnow (Tarnava) in Transylvania.

### 17. Powers of the HSSPf

The principal functions of the HSSPf today are to ensure smooth co-operation between the regional SS and Police Offices and the local military and civil authorities, and, in the event of an emergency, to take over command of the combined SS and Police forces in his area.

As senior responsible police official representing Headquarters in Berlin the HSSPf has a seat on the Defence Committee set up by the *Ministerrat für die Reichsverteidigung* (Ministerial Council for National Defence) in each *Reichsverteidigungsbezirk* (Reich Defence Region). These Defence Regions were originally identical with the *Wehrkreise*, but as a result of the decree of 17th November, 1942, they are now identical with the 42 Party *Gaue* in Greater Germany (see list of *Reichsverteidigungskommissare* in Annexe B).

The Superior SS and Police Commanders are also HIMMLER's representatives with the *Wehr-*

*macht* and work in close co-operation with the Acting Corps commanders, who are the military chiefs and commanding Generals of the *Wehrkreise*. Collaboration between these two high commanders in each area has become more and more important, because, since about June, 1943, " volunteers " have been drafted regularly and at an accelerated pace, partly through *Wehrmacht* channels, into the *Waffen-SS*, instead of into the regular Army, Navy or Air Force.

The forces at the disposal of the HSSPf include the *Allgemeine-SS Standarten* (Regiments)—i.e. the part-time voluntary members of the SS—units of the *Waffen-SS* in the local garrison and *Waffen-SS* depot units, all branches of the Regular Police (*Orpo*) and security police (*Sipo*) and the forces of the Security Service (SD).

An HSSPf usually holds the rank of *SS Gruppenführer und Generalleutnant der Polizei*. He has, as principal advisers and members of his staff, the Regional Commander of the *Sipo* and SD (BdS or IdS : see para 90), the Regional Commander of the *Orpo* (BdO : see para. 30), the *Stabsführer* (Chief of Staff) of the *Allgemeine-SS*, and any other official who may be nominated for a specific task.

In occupied territory the HSSPf may also command the units of the *Waffen-SS* if they are not under direct *Waffen-SS* or Army Command. For example, the HSSPf in Norway, *SS-Obergruppenführer, General der Polizei* Wilhelm REDIESS was appointed HIMMLER's special representative at the Norway Headquarters of the Army General Staff, and presumably commands the *Waffen-SS* units in Norway.

Two other recent incidents strikingly illuminate the growing potentialities of the post *Höhere-SS und Polizeiführer*.

*SS-OGF, General der Polizei und der Waffen-SS* Erich von dem BACH-ZELEWSKI, formerly HSSPf in *Wehrkreis VIII* (*SS-Oberabschnitt SÜD-OST*) and later HSSPf in several Eastern occupied territories, was recently appointed Commander in Chief of all German forces in the Warsaw sector, thereby commanding not only all SS, *Waffen-SS* and Police Forces, but the forces of the *Wehrmacht*, including even the *Luftwaffe*.

One day later, *SS-OGF, General der Polizei, NSKK-OGF* Hermann HÖFLE, the HSSPf of *Wehrkreis XI* (*SS Oberabschnitt* MITTE) was appointed Commander in Chief of all German forces in Slovakia. Hitherto SS and Police Forces employed at the front have always been under the command of Army or Air Force Generals : now, for the first time *Wehrmacht* forces have come under the command of SS and Police Generals.

### 18. SS-und Polizeiführer

Certain occupied territories such as the *General Gouvernement*, Norway, the Baltic countries, and other Eastern and Western territories (many, of course, having since been liberated by the Allies), are known as *Reichskommissariate*. In a *Reichskommissariat* all Police and SS forces are commanded by an HSSPf, with his assistant BdO and BdS. Most of the *Reichskommissariate* are again administratively subdivided into *Generalkommissariate*, and in these areas the Germans have established *SS- und Polizeiführer* (SSPf—SS and Police Commanders). As subregional executives these men combine full SS and Police command in their areas, and come under the HSSPf responsible for the entire territory.

Under the HSSPf of the Government General at Krakau for example, there exist, or existed,

SSPf in Lublin, Radom, Warsaw, Lemberg and Krakau.

An SSPf has, as his chief assistants and members of his staff, a *Kommandeur der Orpo* (Subdistrict Commander of the Regular Police) and a *Kommandeur der Sipo und des SD* (Subdistrict Commander of the Security Police and the Security Service) ; and these two offices are discussed in para. 32 and para. 93 respectively.

Thus, in the organisation of his staff as well as in his functions, the SSPf is a smaller scale version of the HSSPf.

# Part Three

# REGIONAL ADMINISTRATION AND THE POLICE

## 19. Dual Nature of the Police System

The direct chain of command which leads from HIMMLER, as Chief of German Police, through his immediate representatives, to the Police Forces, has been outlined in PART TWO. Side by side with this chain of command there exist channels of Police administration, based on Germany's general administration.

In para. 5 it was explained that the various German *Länder* were compelled by a decree of 1934 to surrender their *Hoheitsrechte* (sovereign rights) to the Reich, but were empowered by the Reich Government to execute these rights on its behalf. The authorities of the *Länder* and their subdivisions were therefore left in a position to administer and implement the decrees and directives of the Reich Ministers. This included responsibility for administrative Police routine.

The result of the 1934 decree was a complex hierarchy formed by the administrative officials of the *Länder*, outwardly functioning as though the Reich were still a collection of semi-independent States, but in fact subject at all times to the powerful influence of the Reich authorities. For the purpose of dealing with the administrative Police routine some of these officials, in addition to their ordinary functions are, ex officio, police administrators. In this capacity they are known as *Polizeibehörden* (Police Authorities), or sometimes as *Polizeiaufsichtsbehörden* (Police Supervisory Authorities).

**These Authorities administer the Ordnungspolizei side by side with the direct representatives of the central SS and Police autocracy.**

The dual nature of this system is at times puzzling to the student of German affairs; indeed German writers themselves admit its anomalies and hint at a future simplification.

## 20. General Administrative Authorities

The ordinary regional administration of Germany today is the most complicated and least uniform of any country; it varies with every part of the Reich. Greater Germany itself—excluding the Protectorate and the Government General—is divided administratively into 15 *Länder* (the traditional States) and 11 *Reichsgaue* made up of territory annexed by Germany since 1933, and directly subordinate to the Reich Government.

(*Note.*—The pre-1918 Prussian Provinces, e.g. Posen and Westpreussen, were not reincorporated into Prussia.)

The German administration is headed by the *Reichsminister des Innern* (Reich Minister of the Interior), i.e. HIMMLER.

Under him the senior executive official of each *Land* or *Reichsgau* is the *Reichsstatthalter* (Reich Governor) who is the direct representative of the *Reichsregierung* (Reich Government) and thus of HITLER himself.

Under the *Reichsstatthalter* each *Land* is administered by its own Government, known as the *Landesregierung* or *Staatsverwaltung*, while in the *Reichsgaue* the *Reichsstatthalter* is the direct head of the *Staatliche Verwaltung* which administers the affairs of the *Reichsgau*.

## 21. Administration in the Länder and Reichsgaue

The administrative organisations of the *Länder* and *Reichsgaue* are as follows :—

### (i) Land Preussen

In Prussia a *Preussische Staatsregierung* (Prussian State Government) exists in name only, as all ministerial positions are merged with the corresponding posts in the *Reichsregierung*. Since, therefore, the Prussian Ministry of the Interior is now completely merged with the Reich Ministry of the Interior—as shown in the title " *Reichs und Preussischer Minister des Innern* " (R u Pr M d I)—the Prussian Provinces are directly controlled by the *Reichsinnenminister* (HIMMLER).

There are 14 Prussian Provinces, each headed by an *Oberpräsident* (Provincial Chief Administrator).

Each Prussian Province is again divided into several *Regierungsbezirke* (Administrative Districts), each headed by a *Regierungspräsident*. There are, at the present time, 35 Prussian *Regierungsbezirke* (See Annexe B).

In addition to the 14 *Oberpräsidenten* there are three administrators who also rank as Prussian *Oberpräsidenten*, bringing the total to 17. They are :—

The *Stadtpräsident* of Berlin (City President, or Chief Administrator for Greater Berlin).

The *Reichsstatthalter* of Thüringen, in his capacity as · superior of the *Regierungspräsident* of the semi-independent Prussian *Regierungsbezirk* Erfurt.

The *Reichsstatthalter* of *Land* Oldenburg and *Hansestadt* Bremen, in his capacity as superior of the *Regierungspräsidenten* of Osnabrück and Aurich.

*Note.*—On the 1st April, 1944, the Prussian *Provinz* Sachsen was divided into two Provinces:—
*Provinz* Halle-Merseburg (the former *Regierungsbezirk* Merseburg) and
*Provinz* Magdeburg (the former *Regierungsbezirk* Magdeburg).

Similarly, the *Provinz* Hessen-Nassau was divided into :—
*Provinz* Kurhessen (the former *Regierungsbezirk* Kassel), and
*Provinz* Nassau (the former *Regierungsbezirk* Wiesbaden).

These four new Provinces consist each of only one *Regierungsbezirk*, and the *Stellvertreter* (Deputy) *Oberpräsident* of each of these Provinces has the rank and function of an acting *Regierungspräsident*.

The *Regierungsbezirke* Osnabrück and Aurich properly belong to the Province of Hannover, and as far as can be ascertained, still continue to do so, but administratively they have, since the 1st April, 1944, been separated for the time being from the province Hannover in order to bring them into accord with the borders of the *Reichsverteidigungsbezirke* (Reich Defence Regions).

Similar reasons may have existed for splitting the provinces of Sachsen and Hessen-Nassau.

### (ii) Land Bayern

Before 1933, Bavaria consisted of 8 *Regierungs-*

*bezirke*, but today it consists of only 5, owing to the fact that in two instances two former *Regierungsbezirke* have been combined into one, while one *Regierungsbezirk*, the Bavarian Exclave Rheinpfalz, has been included for administrative purposes in the *Reichsgau* Westmark for the duration of the war.

### (iii) Land Sachsen

Saxony formerly consisted of 4 *Regierungsbezirke*, which were dissolved at the end of 1942. Their functions were centralised and taken over by Saxony's Ministry of the Interior.

### (iv) Land Baden

Baden is divided into 4 *Landeskommissariate* (comparable in some respects to *Regierungsbezirke*) to which must be added 2 *Landeskommissariate* in the *Zivilverwaltungsgebiet* (Civil Administration Region) of Alsace, which are administratively attached to Baden.

### (v) The other Länder

The remaining *Länder* are not divided into *Regierungsbezirke* but directly into *Kreise* (see below).

### (vi) The " Austrian " Reichsgaue

The seven *Reichsgaue* Wien, Oberdonau, Niederdonau, Salzburg, Kärnten, Steiermark and Tirol-Vorarlberg cover the former Austria plus some border regions of former Czechoslovakia and Jugoslavia. (Until shortly after the *Anschluss* Austria was frequently referred to as the " Ostmark." This designation, however, has now been dropped entirely in favour of the term " *die Donau und Alpengaue*," in order to exclude any perpetuation of the idea of an independent Austria).

These 7 *Reichsgaue* are not subdivided into *Regierungsbezirke*. The *Reichsstatthalter* has the functions of a *Regierungspräsident* and delegates duties connected with this office to his deputy, who thereby becomes Acting *Regierungspräsident*.

### (vii) Reichsgaue Sudetenland, Danzig-Westpreussen and Wartheland

Each of these three *Reichsgaue* is subdivided into three *Regierungsbezirke*.

### (viii) Reichsgau Westmark

The *Reichsgau* Westmark is subdivided into the Bayerische Pfalz or Rhein-Pfalz (Rhenish Palatinate), the Saarland and *Zivilverwaltungsgebiet* Lothringen (Civil Administration Region of Lorraine).

Below the level of *Regierungsbezirke* or the level of the smaller *Länder* all Germany (the old Reich as well as the newly acquired territories) is divided into *Land- und Stadtkreise* (rural and urban districts corresponding to American counties) headed by a *Landrat* (Rural Councillor) or an (Ober-) *Bürgermeister* (Mayor) respectively.

## 22. Police Authorities (Polizeibehörden)

As explained in para 19 certain officials of the regional administrative system have the additional task of administering their local *Orpo* Forces, and are known in this capacity as *Polizeibehörden* (Police Authorities).

A number of decrees determine which officials shall constitute the *Polizeibehörden* in each territorial division of Germany. Police Authorities are classified in descending order, as follows :—

| | |
|---|---|
| *Höhere Polizeibehörden* | Higher Police Authorities, also referred to by their pre-1933 name of *Landespolizeibehörden* (State Police Authorities). |
| *Kreispolizeibehörden* | District Police Authorities. |
| *Ortspolizeibehörden* | Local Police Authorities. |

In addition to these authorities who, ex officio, administer Police affairs, there are other authorities staffed by full-time Police officials. These are the *Staatliche Polizeiverwaltungen* (HQs of the National Police Administration) and they are classified as :—

| | |
|---|---|
| *Besondere Polizei Behörden* | Special Police Authorities. |

Such Police Headquarters are established in almost all larger towns, where they combine the functions of the *Kreis-* and *Ortspolizeibehörden*. They are the backbone of the administrative system of the *Ordnungspolizei*.

These four categories of Police Authorities are discussed in the next two paragraphs.

## 23. The Higher, District and Local Police Authorities

### (i) Höhere Polizeibehörden

The higher Police Authorities in the various administrative areas of Germany are as follows :—

| Administrative Areas | Höhere Polizeibehörden |
|---|---|
| Prussia, Bavaria, *Reichsgaue* Sudetenland, Danzig - Westpreussen and Wartheland. | The *Regierungspräsidenten* (total 49). |
| Sachsen, Württemberg, Baden, Thüringen, Oldenburg, Braunschweig. | The *Innenministerien* (Ministries of the Interior). |
| Mecklenburg | The *Staatsministerium, Abteilung Inneres* (Ministry of State, Department of Internal Affairs). |
| Hessen, Anhalt, Lippe | The *Reichsstatthalter*, acting through the *Landesregierung* (State Government). |
| Schaumburg-Lippe ... | The *Landesregierung*. |
| Hamburg ... ... | The *Reichsstatthalter*, acting through the *Staatsverwaltung* (State Administration). |
| Bremen | The *Regierende Bürgermeister* (Governing Mayor) |
| The *Reichsgaue* Westmark, Wien, Niederdonau, Oberdonau, Salzburg, Steiermark, Kärnten and Tirol-Vorarlberg | The *Reichsstatthalter*, through his *Stellvertreter* (deputy) who acts as *Regierungspräsident*, head of the *Staatliche Verwaltung*. |

### (ii) Kreispolizeibehörden

The *Kreispolizeibehörden* (District Police Authorities) are controlled by the appropriate *Höhere Polizeibehörden*.

In a *Landkreis* (Rural District) the *Landrat* functions as *Kreispolizeibehörde* ; in a *Stadtkreis* (Urban District formed by a large town) it is the *Bürgermeister* or *Oberbürgermeister* (Mayor), or where applicable (see para. 24) the *Staatliche Polizeiverwalter*. The area under the jurisdiction of a *Kreispolizeibehörde* is called a *Kreispolizeibezirk*.

The *Kreispolizeibehörden* in turn supervise and control the *Ortspolizeibehörden*.

### (iii) Ortspolizeibehörden

These Local Police Authorities, consist in the main of the *Bürgermeister* of smaller towns and rural communities or the *Oberbürgermeister* of larger towns (cf. *Kreispolizeibehörden*).

In those towns and cities which have a *Staatliche Polizeiverwaltung* (see para. 24 below), the *Staatliche Polizeiverwalter* (National Police Administrator) assumes most of the functions of the *Ortspolizeibehörden* (see para. 81 on the *Verwaltungspolizei*).

In certain exceptional instances the authority of the *Ortspolizeibehörden* rests with such Police Officials as the following :

| Areas | Ortspolizeibehörden |
|---|---|
| Those of the *Preussische Ostprovinzen* (Prussian Eastern Provinces) in which several *Landgemeinden* (Rural Communities) are combined into one *Amtsbezirk*. | The *Amtsvorsteher* (the chief administrator) |
| Those parts of the *Regierungsbezirke* Schneidemühl, Frankfurt/Oder and Liegnitz (excluding the towns) which, before 1918, belonged to the Province Posen | The *Polizeidistrikt-kommissar* (Police District Commissioner) |
| The provinces Rheinland and Westfalen. | The *Amtsbürgermeister* |
| The province Hannover and Helgoland | The *Landrat* (Rural Subdistrict Councillor) |
| Cases where the police authority does not rest with the *Bürgermeister* in the newly incorporated *Ostgebiete* (Eastern Districts) | The *Amtskommissar* (Commissioner) |

The area under the jurisdiction of an *Ortspolizeibehörde* is known as an *Ortspolizeibezirk*.

All the above mentioned Police administrations rank as Regional Authorities in that they constitute chains of command, channels of reporting and administrative authorities for routine police work.

They are for the extent of such police work technically subordinate (*sachlich unterstellt*) to the Headquarters of the Chief of the German Police, and it depends on the matter in hand whether their orders will be issued by the *Hauptamt Ordnungspolizei* (National Department of Regular Police) or the *Reichssicherheitshauptamt* (National Department of Security) as will be discussed in PARTS FOUR and FIVE.

### 24. The Special Police Authorities

*Besondere Polizeibehörden* (Special Police Authorities) are the *Staatliche Polizeiverwaltungen* (see para. 79 *et seq.*). They are established in larger towns and cities and combine the police functions of an *Ortspolizeibehörde* with those of a *Kreispolizeibehörde* in the *Stadtkreis*.

Thus the official in charge, the *Staatlicher Polizeiverwalter* (National Police Administrator) takes the place of the appropriate administrative official described in the previous paragraph.

According to their relative importance and personnel strength, the *Staatliche Polizeiverwaltungen* are classified as follows :—

#### (a) Polizeipräsidien

Headed by a *Polizeipräsident*, and divided into four categories, viz :—
(i) *Sonderklasse* (Special Category), existing only in Berlin, Hamburg and Wien.
(ii) *Grosse Polizeipräsidien* (large).
(iii) *Mittlere Polizeipräsidien* (medium).
(iv) *Kleine Polizeipräsidien* (small).

#### (b) Polizeidirektionen

Headed by a *Polizeidirektor*.

#### (c) Polizeiämter

Divided into two categories, viz :—
(i) Branch Offices of (a) or (b) above, and controlled by (a) or (b). These are headed by a *Polizeirat*.
(ii) Independent *Polizeiämter*, controlled by the local *Landrat*. These are headed by a *Polizeirat* or *Polizeioberinspekteur*.

A list of all *Staatliche Polizeiverwaltungen* in Greater Germany with their street addresses, personalities and other details is given in Annexe C.

For both technical and personnel matters, the *Staatliche Polizeiverwaltungen* are subordinate (*personell und fachlich unterstellt*) to the *Chef der Ordnungspolizei* (WÜNNENBERG).

In those instances, however, where their tasks are in the field of the *Sicherheitspolizei*, they are subordinate for technical, but never for personnel matters to the *Chef der Sicherheitspolizei und des SD* (KALTENBRUNNER).

*NOTE.*—**Police Administration in Berlin**

Berlin is a special case ; here the functions of the *Höhere Polizeibehörden*, in addition to the *Kreis- und Ortspolizeibehörden*, are combined in the person of the *Polizeipräsident*. The latter is equal in rank to a Prussian *Regierungspräsident* in the same way as the *Stadtpräsident* of Berlin is equal in rank to the Prussian *Oberpräsident*.

Thus Berlin's administration has a double nature. It is at once a *Landesverwaltungsbezirk* (State Administrative District) and a *Selbstverwaltende Körperschaft* (Autonomous Administrative Body), like a *Regierungsbezirk*.

As a *Landesverwaltungsbezirk* Berlin then assumes the exceptional position of including the functions of a *Provinz*, a *Regierungsbezirk*, a *Kreispolizeibezirk* and an *Ortspolizeibezirk*.

It should be noted that Berlin has several, probably twenty, *Bezirksbürgermeister* (District Mayors).

### 25. Conclusion

Thus we see that the *Polizeibehörden*, which are manned either by regional administrative officials acting ex officio or by full-time police officials, constitute the administrative and partly the command channels of the *Orpo*. The manner in which this system works in practice is discussed throughout PART FOUR (*Orpo*) especially in the Section dealing with the *Verwaltungspolizei* (Administrative Police).

On the other hand the branches of the *Sipo* and SD, as their designation *Sonder- oder Fachpolizei* (Special or Technical Police) suggests, are in theory, if not always in practice, completely divorced from this regional system of administration. They have their own chains of command and their own administrative machine.

We are faced therefore today in the German police with certain chains of command which are direct and independent and others, which, though ultimately subject to the same central control, are interlocked with the remnants of a regionally dispersed system of state and local administration.

The complexity of this system, which may well be said to confuse even German officials themselves, might easily prove a means of creating difficulties for an Allied occupation government. It might even serve to cover up details which would otherwise be inconveniently revealing.

# Part Four

## THE ORDNUNGSPOLIZEI

### A. HIGHER ORGANISATION AND GENERAL STRUCTURE OF THE ORPO

#### 26. General

All Police activities concerned with the maintenance of order and the protection of public safety are today combined in the *Ordnungspolizei* (Regular Police), abbreviated *Orpo*.

A literal translation of the word *Ordnungspolizei* would be " Police for the maintenance of Law and Order." Throughout this book the word *Ordnungspolizei* is for simplicity translated as " Regular Police," but this does not imply that those branches of the German police which do not belong to the *Orpo* are irregular, wartime, or part-time services.

In an analysis of the *Orpo* the complete centralisation of this body of fully militarised and armed policemen must constantly be kept in mind.

The regular uniformed German policeman, his functions, powers and status in the community can hardly be compared with his so-called equivalent in the Western countries. The *Orpo* is far more a Military Force of the Interior than an organisation of public servants.

The Allies, therefore, must exercise extreme caution in the employment of any members of the *Orpo*. Their reliability is, to say the least, highly doubtful and the character and past history of each man needs close scrutiny as to former Party affiliation, SS-membership, pre-Hitler service in the police, and individual record.

Only the most careful weeding out and the most rigorous individual investigations of German police personnel down to the patrolman on the suburban street corner will leave the occupation authorities with a dependable German police force.

#### 27. The Orpo HQ (Hauptamt Orpo)

The *Orpo* Headquarters, officially known as the *Hauptamt Ordnungspolizei* (National Department of Regular Police) are in Berlin. They form part of the Office of the *Reichsführer-SS und Chef der Deutschen Polizei*, in the Reich Ministry of the Interior.

The *Hauptamt Ordnungspolizei* is headed by Alfred WÜNNENBERG (*Chef der Ordnungspolizei*). Originally that position had been held by *SS-Oberst-Gruppenführer, Generaloberst d. Pol.* Kurt DALUEGE until his habitual heavy drinking came to be considered too serious an interference with his official duties. In 1943, therefore, HIMMLER decided that the rudder of the *Hauptamt Orpo* was to be placed into steadier hands, but as a jealous guardian of the " reputation " of his organisation, he quietly shelved DALUEGE for " reasons of health " without ever publicly and officially ousting him from his position. As a result of this face-saving technicality DALUEGE is still, in name, Chief of the *Hauptamt Orpo* with WÜNNENBERG appearing only as *Chef der Ordnungspolizei m.d.F.b. (mit der Führung beauftragt,* i.e. charged with the conduct of affairs).

The *Hauptamt Ordnungspolizei* is divided into seven *Ämter*—consisting of three main divisions (I, II, III) and four lesser bureaux (IV, V, VI, VII)—which specialise in various functions of the *Ordnungspolizei*.

These *Ämter*, given with what are believed to be the official German numbers, are as follows :

#### I. Das Kommandoamt

The *Chef des Kommandoamtes* (Chief of the High Command or Operational Headquarters of the Regular Police) since November 1944 is *SS-BF Genmaj. d. Pol.* FLADE. He replaced *SS-BF Genmaj. d. Pol.* Anton DIERMANN. The *Kommandoamt* consists of three *Amtsgruppen*, each containing several *Ämter* (bureaux)—also called *Gruppen* (Groups)—as follows :—

*Amtsgruppe I*

*Ämter :*—

| | |
|---|---|
| *Verwendung* | Employment |
| *Organisation* | Organisation |
| *Wirtschaft* | Finance, Pay, etc. |
| *Bekleidung und Verpflegung* | Clothing and Rations |
| *Reichsverteidigung und Luftschutz* | Defence of the Reich and Air Raid Protection |
| *Feuerschutzpolizei* | Fire Protection Police |
| *Ausbildung* | Training |
| *Körperschulung* | Physical Training |
| *Nachrichtenverbindungswesen* | Signals and the Police Communications network |
| *Kraftfahrwesen* | Motor Transport |
| *Waffen und Gerätewesen* | Police Ordnance and Equipment |

*Amtsgruppe II*

*Ämter :*—

| | |
|---|---|
| *Personalangelegenheiten* | Personnel |
| *Weltanschauliche Erziehung* | Ideological Indoctrination |

*Note.*—The Publication " *Politischer Informationsdienst* " (Political Information Service) issued by the *Chef der Ordnungspolizei* was formerly published by the *Amt Weltanschauliche Erziehung*.

Some time between 10th March and 1st July, 1941 the title of this publication was changed to " *Mitteilungsblätter für die Weltanschauliche Schulung der Ordnungspolizei* " (Information for the Ideological Indoctrination of the Regular Police).

The Publishing Office is now listed as *Gruppe* instead of *Amt Weltanschauliche Erziehung*.

This publication can be compared to a similar one issued to the Armed Forces entitled : " *Mitteilungen für die Truppe* " (Information for the Armed Forces). Its contents are of the usual morale-building type and are designed for the lowest level of understanding.

| | |
|---|---|
| *Veterinärwesen* | Veterinary Service |

*Amtsgruppe III*

| | |
|---|---|
| *Amt Sanitätswesen* | Medical and Hygienic Services |

## 11. Das Amt Verwaltung und Recht

The *Amt Verwaltung und Recht* (Office of Administration and Judicial Matters) originally handled all budget, legal and administrative affairs (see III below). It is headed by *SS-GF Ministerialdirektor* BRACHT.

It consists of three *Amtsgruppen* each of which contains several *Ämter* (or *Gruppen*) as follows :—

### Amtsgruppe I

*Ämter :—*

| | |
|---|---|
| *Verreichlichung der Polizei* | Unification and Centralisation of the Police |
| *Haushaltswesen* | Budget and Economy |
| *Dienststrafrecht* | Official Police Disciplinary and Penal Code |
| *Deutsches Polizeibeamtengesetz* | Legal Code of the German Police Officials |
| *Personalangelegenheiten der Polizeiverwaltungsbeamten* | Personnel questions of the Police Administrative officials |
| *Besoldung und Versorgung* | Pay, Allowances and Pensions |

### Amtsgruppe II

*Ämter:—*

| | |
|---|---|
| *Allgemeine Organisation der Polizei* | General Organisation of the Police |
| *Allgemeines Polizeirecht* | General Police Law |
| *Theaterpolizei* | Police functions regarding places of entertainment (theatres etc.) |
| *Feuerpolizei* | Fire Police |
| *Gewerbepolizei* | Police controlling handicrafts and trades |
| *Meldewesen* | Police Registry and Reports |
| *Volkskartei* | The National Population Register |
| *Straftilgung* | Annulment of penalties |
| *Verkehrspolizei* | Traffic Police |

### Amtsgruppe III

*Ämter :—*

| | |
|---|---|
| *Unterkunftswesen der Polizei* | Quartering and billetting of the Police |

## III. Das Wirtschaftsverwaltungsamt

The war has brought about an enormous increase in the administration and supply problems of the Police.

The creation of field units and the constant flow of replacements for the home front from the Police Reserve added to the work of the *Kommandoamt* and the *Amt Verwaltung und Recht*. It appears that, some time in 1943, a new office, the *Wirtschaftsverwaltungsamt* (Office for the Administration of Budget and Supply) was added to the *Hauptamt Orpo* to deal with some of this extra work. The name of this new Bureau, as well as other pieces of evidence, indicate a close relationship between the *Wirtschaftsverwaltungsamt* of the Police and the *SS-Wirtschafts- und Verwaltungshauptamt* (WVHA), another manifestation of the ever-increasing tendency towards amalgamation of the Police with the SS.

It is of interest to note that the *Hauptamt Orpo* was damaged in an air raid in February 1914, and that as a result three of the *Amtsgruppen* of the *Wirtschaftsverwaltungsamt* were temporarily housed with one of the WVHA offices in Berlin-Lichterfelde West, Unter den Eichen 126.

The *Wirtschaftsverwaltungsamt* is headed by *SS-Obergruppenführer, Generalleutnant der Waffen-SS und Polizei* August FRANK. It consists of the *Amtschef* and the following five *Amtsgruppen :*

### Amtsgruppe I

| | |
|---|---|
| *Bekleidung und Verpflegung* | Clothing and Rations. |

### Amtsgruppe II

| | |
|---|---|
| *Kassen und Besoldungswesen* | Finance and Pay. |

### Amtsgruppe III

| | |
|---|---|
| *Unterbringung* | Quartering and Billeting. |

### Amtsgruppe IV

| | |
|---|---|
| *Versorgung und Recht* | Allowances, Pensions and Legal Matters. |

### Gruppe Pers.

| | |
|---|---|
| *Personal* | Personnel |

The four lesser bureaux are as follows :—

**IV. Das Amt Technische Nothilfe** (Bureau of the Technical Emergency Corps). At Berlin-Steglitz, Birkbuschstrasse 18.

Headed by *SS-GF Genlt. d. Pol.* Willy SCHMELCHER.

**V. Das Amt Feuerwehren** (Bureau of Fire Brigades). At Berlin, Lindenstrasse 40-42.
Headed by *Genmaj. d. Pol.* SCHNELL.

**VI. Das Kolonialpolizeiamt** (Bureau of the Colonial Police). In Berlin, Hegelplatz 2.

Headed until the middle of 1944 by *SS-OGF Gen. d. W-SS u. d. Pol.* Karl von PFEFFER-WILDENBRUCH, who was also *General-Inspekteur d. Polizeischulen* (see next paragraph).

**VII. Das Amt Technische SS und Polizeiakademie** (Bureau of the Technical SS and Police Academy). In Berlin-Zehlendorf, Potsdamer Chaussee.

Headed by *SS-BF Genmaj d. Pol. Professor Dr.* H. GERLOFF.

## 28. The Inspectorates in the Hauptamt Orpo

The *Hauptamt Orpo* also includes the following Inspectors who supervise the activities of the *Orpo* and are directly responsible to its head :—

*Der General-Inspekteur der Schutzpolizei des Reiches* (Inspector General of the Reich Protection Police).
    *SS-GF Genlt. d. Pol.* Georg SCHREYER.

*Der General-Inspekteur der Gendarmerie und der Schutzpolizei der Gemeinden* (Inspector General of Rural Police and of Municipal Protection Police).
    This position was held by *SS-OGF Gen. d. Pol.* Jürgen von KAMPTZ, until he was made BdO Italy some time in 1944.

*Der General-Inspekteur der Polizeischulen* (Inspector General of Police Schools).
    Also known as *General-Inspekteur für das Ausbildungswesen* (Inspector Gen. of Training). Until the middle of 1944 this office was held by *SS-OGF, Gen. d. W-SS und d. Pol.* Karl von PFEFFER-WILDENBRUCH, who was also Chief of the *Kolonialpolizeiamt* (see previous paragraph).

*Der General-Inspekteur der Feuerschutzpolizei und*

*Feuerwehren* (Inspector General of the Fire Protection Police and of the Fire Brigades).

This office is now held by *SS-BF Genmaj. d. Pol.* RUMPF, who succeeded *SS-GF Genlt. d. Pol.* Dr. Ing. MEYER.

This appointment is also known as the "*Inspekteur für das Feuerlöschwesen für Stadt und Land*" (Inspector of all Urban and Rural Fire Fighting Forces). The re-naming probably took place in 1939 when the *Feuerschutzpolizei* was instituted and the *Feuerwehren* came more or less under the control of that organisation.

*Der General-Inspekteur für das Sanitätswesen* (Inspector General of Police Medical Services).

It is not exactly known who holds this position at present. *SS-OGF, Prof. Dr.* Ernst R. GRAWITZ may possibly combine it with his position as *Reichsarzt der SS und Polizei*.

*Der Inspekteur für das Nachrichtenwesen* (Inspector of Signals).

This office is held by *Genmaj. d. Pol.* SCHLAKE.

*Der Inspekteur für Weltanschauliche Schulung* (Inspector for Ideological Indoctrination).

This office was held until 1942 by *SS-OF* Dr. Joachim CAESAR. It was subsequently vacant for a considerable period, but it is possible that it was held for a time by *SS-GF Genlt. d. Pol.* Adolf Th. E. von BOMHARD.

On 1st January 1944, an *Inspekteur für die gesamte Weltanschauliche Erziehung in der SS und Polizei* (Inspector for all Ideological Indoctrination of SS and Police) was appointed, the position being given to SS-BF Ernst FICK, who is directly subordinate to the *SS Hauptamt.*.

*Der Inspekteur der Wasserschutzpolizei* (Inspector of the Waterways Protection Police).

This office with Headquarters at Kiel was founded on 15th September 1943 by order of the *RFSS u Ch d Dt Pol. SS-BF Genmaj. d. Pol.* KRUMHAAR was appointed to this post. On 1st July 1944 he was succeeded by *Oberst der Schupo* Ernst SCHRÖTER, and the office moved to Berlin, N.W.7, Unter den Linden 74.

In addition the following Inspectorates exist :—

*Inspektion für das Kraftfahr- und Verkehrswesen* (*Jn K*—Inspectorate of M/T and Traffic Control).

*Inspektion für Waffen und Geräte* (*Jn WG*—Inspectorate of Arms and Equipment).

*Inspektion für die Luftschutzpolizei und den Luftschutzeinsatz* (*Jn L*—Inspectorate of Air Raid Protection and Air Raid Protection Police).

*Inspektion für das Veterinärwesen* (*Jn Vet*—Inspectorate of Police Veterinary Services).

## 29. Establishments controlled by the Hauptamt Ordnungspolizei

The following institutions and schools are under direct administration and supervision of the *Hauptamt Orpo* :—

*Das Staatskrankenhaus der Polizei* (Government Hospital for the Police)

In Berlin. Also several other sanatoria and convalescent homes for policemen.

*Die Staatliche Lehr- und Versuchsanstalt für Polizeihunde* (Government Institute for Police Dog Training and Research)

Berlin-Grünheide.

*Die Polizei-Offizier-Schule* (Police Officers' School)

In Berlin-Köpenick.

*Die Polizei-Offizier- und Schutzpolizei-Schule* (Police Officers' and Protection Police School)

In Fürstenfeldbruck, Bavaria.

*Die Schutzpolizei-Schulen* (Protection Police Schools)

In Berlin, Hellerau bei Dresden, Heidenheim, Bottrop, Köln, München, Königshütte, Frankfurt a/M, Hamburg, Porlitz, Pelplin and Gnesen.

*Die Polizei-Schule für Leibesübungen* (Physical Training College for Policemen)

In Berlin-Spandau.

*Die Technische Polizei-Schule* (Technical Police School)

In Berlin.

*Die Kraftfahr-Schule* (M/T School)

In Dresden.

*Die Wasserschutzpolizei-Schule* (School for Waterways Protection Police)

Formerly in Stettin, now at Lauterbach/Rügen.

*Die Polizeireit-Schulen* (Police Cavalry Schools)

In Rathenau (Mark Brandenburg) and Bendzin (Upper Silesia.)

*Die Kolonialpolizei-Schule* (School for Colonial Police)

In Oranienburg. Also known as *Schule für den auswärtigen Einsatz* (School for Service Abroad).

*Die Sanitätsschule beim Staatskrankenhaus der Polizei* (Medical School at the Government Hospital for the Police)

In Berlin.

*Die Polizei-Ski-Schulen* (Police Schools for Ski-training)

In Oberjoch (Allgäu), Sudelfeld (Upper-Bavaria) and Kitzbühel (Tyrol).

*Die Gendarmerie-Schulen* (Schools for Rural Police)

In Hildesheim, Suhl, Bad Ems, Freiburg (Br.), Deggingen (Württemberg), Wien-Mödling, Hollabrunn (N/D), and Fraustadt.

*Die Polizei-Akademie für Luftschutzführung* (Police Academy for ARP Tactics)

In Oranienburg. This school was originally called *Polizei-Schule für Luftschutzführer* (Police School for ARP officers), and was then in Berlin-Schöneberg.

## 30. Regional Control : Befehlshaber der Ordnungspolizei

As previously explained, the highest Commander of the Orpo in each *Wehrkreis* is the *Befehlshaber der Ordnungspolizei* (Commander of Regular Police, abbr. *BdO*).

HIMMLER originally installed these men as *Inspekteure der Ordnungspolizei* (*IdO*) in which capacity they were charged with supervising and co-ordinating all activities of the various branches of the Regular Police in their region. Only in emergencies were they to take actual command of all the forces under them.

Subsequently however, many war-time and political problems forced HIMMLER to concentrate Police power in the hands of a small number of trusted followers. In this process all the *Inspekteure der Orpo* were, in Oct., 1943, elevated to the position and status of *Befehlshaber der Orpo* (*BdO*).

They are today in full charge of all *Orpo* activities within their military district, and are within their *Wehrkreis* **direct representatives of the Hauptamt Orpo.**

A BdO is also the representative of the *Orpo* on the staff of the HSSPf, the Regional Chief of **all** Police and SS work. In the absence of the HSSPf, the BdO becomes the independent chief in the *Wehrkreis* as far as questions pertaining to the *Orpo* are concerned.

To what extent the BdO and above them the HSSPf will encroach upon the powers of the Corps Commander of each *Wehrkreis* is a matter of speculation. It must however be remembered that the BdO in occupied countries bordering Germany have often been in complete charge of large scale anti-partisan and anti-guerrilla warfare. In fact entire campaigns have been waged by fully militarised *Orpo* forces under their regional Commanders. Thus, while the HSSPf must be viewed as a regional "little HIMMLER," the BdO is his field commander.

Special tasks of the BdO are :—

(*a*) The supervision of basic and advanced training.

(*b*) The supervision of tactical Police and ARP Training.

(*c*) The supervision of the advanced technical training of Police Officers of all branches of the *Orpo*.

(*d*) The co-ordination of defensive preparations (*Reichsverteidigung*) in so far as they pertain to the work of the Orpo.

(*e*) Training of all auxiliary formations of the *Orpo* for ARP and similar war-time tasks.

It is not known whether the offices of all BdO are organised in a uniform manner, but the office organisation of the BdO in Paris can probably be considered as typical. It was organised in accordance with the basic pattern of a *Schutzpolizeikommando* (see para. 39) as follows :—

| | |
|---|---|
| *Adjutantur* | Central Office |
| *Abt. Ia* | Plans, training and operations |
| *Abt. Ib* | Supply and equipment |
| *Abt. Ic* | Control of French police forces<br>Counter-intelligence<br>Security of zone of communications |
| *Abt. II* | Personnel and welfare |
| *Abt. Registratur* | Documents and files |
| *Abt. K* | M/T (*Kraftfahrwesen*) |
| *Abt. LS* | ARP (*Luftschutz*) |
| *Abt. N* | Communications ; signals intelligence (*Nachrichten*) |
| *Abt. Feuerschutzpolizei* | Fire-fighting |
| *Abt. SAN* | Medical services (*Sanitätsdienste*) |
| *Abt. WE* | Ideology (*Weltanschauung*) ; party charities. See also next paragraph |
| *Abt. IV* | Cashier ; bookkeeping and accounting ; quarters and buildings |

*Abt. III* did not exist in France. Apparently the number was reserved for one of the sections now known by letters or names. In other countries *Abteilung III* was definitely identified, sometimes attending to certain aspects of recruiting for the field forces of the police, sometimes handling a variety of other subjects. No fixed conclusion can therefore be drawn concerning this *Abteilung*.

It should also be mentioned that *Abteilung SAN* (Medical Services) sometimes appeared as *Abt. IV B*, and in other places *Abteilungen* numbered between V and VIII were reported. Thus while the basic plan for the office of a BdO is standard, a certain amount of variation according to local requirements must be expected.

A full description of the organisation of the BdO Paris will be found in Annexe A.

According to the example of the office of the BdO in Paris, the filing system used in the offices of the BdO is the same as that used in all *Staatliche Polizeiverwaltungen* (National Police Administration). It is based on the *Einheitsaktenplan* (*EAPl*—Uniform Filing System), which was issued in 1934. For further details see para. 80 in the Section on *Verwaltungspolizei*.

### 31. Police Indoctrination Officers

In connection with the BdO a special type of officer deserves mention, the *Polizei-Schulungsleiter* (Indoctrination Officer of the Police). It appears that there is one assigned to the staff of each BdO.

Not very much is known about his function, but he seems to be charged with the supervision of morale and with National-Socialist education of the Regular Police personnel in the area of the BdO, to whose staff he is assigned.

He is comparable to the NSFO (*National-Sozialistische Führungsoffizier*—National Socialist Indoctrination Officer) of the *Wehrmacht*.

*Polizei-Schulungsleiter* are known to have existed since 1943. They are, like the NSFO, another striking indication of the endeavour of the Party to "nazify" and "fanaticise" all Germans.

Ten of these *Polizei-Schulungsleiter* have been identified so far. Their ranks range from *SS-Hauptsturmführer* (Captain) to *SS-Obersturmbannführer* (Lt. Colonel). Three of them come directly from the staff of the *SS-Hauptamt*. The names of those identified appear in Annexe A under the list of personalities mentioned in connection with the offices of the *Befehlshaber der Orpo*.

### 32. Kommandeure der Orpo

In the *Generalkommissariate*, which are sub-districts in certain occupied areas, there exist subregional Commanders of the *Orpo* known as *Kommandeure der Ordnungspolizei* (KdO). These should not be confused with the *Kommandeure der Schutzpolizei* (see para. 38), who are local Commanders of the forces of the Protection Police.

A *Kommandeur der Orpo*, as noted in para. 18 (q.v.), is a member of the staff of the SSPf in the particular sub-district. For this area he commands all *Orpo* forces in the same manner as his superior, the BdO, does for the entire occupied territory.

In the course of the war a number of these KdO have also been identified inside Germany, where they do not serve under an SSPf. Apparently they are established wherever there is need for local coordination of all *Orpo* forces, especially the forces of the urban and rural police.

Other reports mention an official known as the *Stabsoffizier der Orpo* at the office of the *Regierungspräsident* or similar higher police authority, who attends to such coordination and liaison in an allotted area. It is not clear whether or not *Stabsoffizier der Orpo* is simply another name for *Kommandeur der Orpo*. (See also para. 38 on the *Stabsoffizier der Schupo*).

### 33. The two categories of the Orpo

The *Ordnungspolizei* has two primary functions, carried out by two categories of police :—

Firstly, the duties usually connected with the concept of Police—but on a "German scale"—such as maintaining order, directing traffic, protecting the public safety, etc. This work is done by *Polizeivollzugsbeamte* (Regular Uniformed Police, literally Police executive officials).

The Regular Uniformed Police are discussed fully in Section B (paras 34–77).

Secondly, the administrative police work which in other countries would be done by civilian clerks. This is handled by the *Verwaltungspolizei* (Administrative Police), whose members are known as *Polizeiverwaltungsbeamte*, and may or may not wear uniform. Where, however, in a small locality, the same man discharges the duties of both the above classes of official, he will undoubtedly be in uniform at all times.

The Administrative Police are treated in Section C (paras. 78–86).

# B. THE REGULAR UNIFORMED POLICE

## I

## General Introduction

### 34. Branches and Functions

The High Command of the Regular Uniformed Police is the division known as the *Kommandoamt* (literally Command Headquarters) in the *Hauptamt Ordnungspolizei*. All chains of command in the entire network of Uniformed Police officials lead back to this Office.

The following are the different types and duties of the Uniformed Police :—

(i) Ordinary Branches of the Regular Uniformed Police :

| | |
|---|---|
| *Schutzpolizei (Schupo) des Reiches* | Reich Protection Police |
| *Schutzpolizei (Schupo) der Gemeinden* | Municipal Protection Police |
| *Gendarmerie (Gend.)* | Rural Police |
| *Kolonialpolizei* | Colonial Police |
| *Wasserschutzpolizei* (SW) | Waterways Protection Police |
| *Feuerschutzpolizei (FP or FS Pol.)* | Fire Protection Police |

(These branches are discussed under II, paras 38—61)

(ii) Branches of the Regular Uniformed Police known as *Technische Hilfspolizeien* (Technical Auxiliary Police) :

| | |
|---|---|
| *Feuerwehren* | Fire Brigades |
| *Luftschutzpolizei (LS Pol.)* | Air Raid Protection Police |
| *Technische Nothilfe (TN or Teno)* | Technical Emergency Corps |

(These branches are discussed under III, paras 62—75)

In addition there are auxiliary services to the Regular Uniformed Police, falling into the following two categories :—

*Sonderpolizeien* (Special Police)

*Hilfspolizeien* (Auxiliary Police)

These services, discussed under IV, paras 76, 77, are not integral parts of the *Orpo*, but they are frequently called upon to assist branches of the *Orpo* in the execution of their duties.

### 35. Militarisation of the Regular Uniformed Police.

The regular *Schutzpolizei* and the *Gendarmerie* are no Nazi innovations, although a centralised command as it exists today was not known prior to 1936.

The *Schutzpolizist* or *Schupo*, as he is called in Germany, roughly represents to the German public what a " Bobby " means to the Londoners, or a " Cop " to the New Yorkers.

A *Gendarm* can be compared in some respects to a rural policeman in England and to a State Trooper in America.

The important difference is, however, that the German *Schupos* and Gendarmes are **thoroughly militarised.** Even under the Republic they were always looked upon as a military body although the Nazis have, of course, enormously increased the emphasis on this aspect of German Police life.

Prior to World War I uniformed policemen were usually recruited from among ex-Service men who had finished their term of military service and were looking for civil service employment. Similarly, the *Gendarmerie*, who in rural districts used to tour their areas on horseback, were usually taken from former members of cavalry units in the Army.

This trend continued under the Weimar Republic for a twofold reason. The Versailles Treaty compelled the Germans to reduce their regular Army to one hundred thousand men : many who had made up their minds to become professional soldiers thus found themselves without employment. By placing these men in the Police Forces the States, who then administered the Police, not only solved one aspect of their unemployment problem, but also built up in the shortest possible time a military instrument with which to combat what they considered the enemies of the republican régime within the Reich, namely the extremist parties of the Left and Right.

This was undoubtedly favoured by the leading men in the *Reichswehrministerium* (the Ministry of War of that period), who saw in this militarisation of the Police a means of building up a large cadre which would some day be available for the organisation and expansion of a powerful German Army.

The Nazis were not slow in speeding up this development. From 1933 on, intensified regular infantry training with all types of weapons became routine for the Police. A great deal of time was spent on familiarising the men with the use of automatic weapons, and it was not long before instruction in the use of armoured vehicles and heavy weapons also appeared on their training schedule.

Thus when, beginning in 1935, the *Reichswehr* was expanded it is estimated that the Police was able to supply the newly created *Wehrmacht* with some 60,000 well-trained men, mostly of NCO and Officer calibre.

Finally in 1941, the Police was made subject to the military law of the SS, and the courts of the SS became known as *SS- und Polizeigerichte* (SS and Police Tribunals).

### 36. Nazification of the Regular Uniformed Police

This last-mentioned fact introduces another aspect of the Regular Uniformed Police of today ; the thorough nazification of the system.

It has already been mentioned (PART ONE) that right from the beginning the Nazis conducted a long-lasting purge of the Police, as indeed they did in every sphere of German life. In the course of this process they expelled all policemen who were in any way compromised as members of a former Democratic or other Opposition party, or who seemed otherwise suspicious to them.

If the number of dismissed members of the Police forces was not as large as one might have expected, this was primarily due to the fact that, even under the Liberal Republic, owing to their background as ex-Service men, the bulk of German policemen leaned politically towards the Right. Indeed, a high percentage of them professed strong Nazi sympathies, even as early as the nineteen twenties.

All the vacancies created by the Nazis in the ranks of the Police were of course filled with loyal followers of the Party, many of whom had been unemployed for a considerable period of time and were now anxious to share in the spoils and get themselves good jobs. This new enrolment may not have amounted to much in the beginning, but when the Police transferred many of its men to the expanding Army in 1935, large numbers of Party members, mostly taken from the SS, entered the ranks of the Police as replacements. Furthermore, when HIMMLER took over control of the German Police, he saw to it that all the leading positions were given to members of his own clan, the SS, and ever since, members of the *Waffen-* and *Allgemeine-SS* have been given preference among applicants for police posts, virtually to the exclusion of all others.

Since, however, it remained technically impossible to replace with SS personnel all existing members of the police forces, pressure was brought to bear upon them to enter the *Allgemeine-SS*. Indeed, membership of the SS became inevitable for officers and advisable, to say the least, for NCO's of the Uniformed Police ; a majority, doubtless, entered the SS without objection or compunction.

In some cases this process was rendered even more complete by the automatic enrolment into the *Allgemeine-SS* of all Police personnel who had previously been members of the Nazi Party. In the course of such enrolment, they received SS ranks equivalent to their Police ranks.

As a result of this development the influence of the SS within the ranks of the Regular Police increased rapidly and drastically. In Vienna, for instance, it is reported that well over 50 per cent of the *Orpo* are members of the *Allgemeine-SS* : higher percentages are likely to exist in Germany proper.

### 37. Effects of the War on Police Personnel

Of late, the process of placing members of the SS into the Police may have somewhat slowed down. With the outbreak of war policemen of the age classes 1901 and younger were sent into the field, where they formed various police combat units.

An *SS Polizeidivision* was formed within the framework and under the auspices of the *Waffen-SS*. This unit participated in practically all campaigns since the beginning of the war. In addition, other field units, such as SS Police Battalions and Regiments were formed (see para. 40) and sent to the front lines, where they suffered heavy losses. Thus, while most of the younger and middle-aged policemen were fighting at the front, replacements had to be found for them at home. For this purpose a *Polizei-Reserve Korps* was formed in order to draft into the Police Service men who had been rejected by the Armed Forces as too old or physically unfit. Today a large percentage of the Regular Uniformed Police in Germany consists of *Polizeireservisten*.

The average age of these men is between 45 and 50. They are drafted for the Police through the normal recruiting channels of the Armed Forces. Since they are not professional policemen, but only drafted to do police work for the duration, they will return to their civilian occupations after the war, with the exception of those who might wish to be transferred to the active ranks of the peacetime police.

Some of those men who were purged in 1933 and 1934 may possibly have been recalled to service, but it is not possible to determine to what extent this process has taken place. Even if some members of the Police should not sympathise with the Nazis, they certainly would not dare to show their sympathies in public since they, more than any other group of Germans, are watched and spied upon by the SD, *Gestapo* and Party zealots. In any event, it may be said with certainty that even today a large majority of German policemen are fully reliable from HIMMLER'S point of view.

The process of nazification of the German Police was further advanced by the formation or absorption of such present day branches of the *Orpo* as the *Wasserschutzpolizei, Luftschutzpolizei, Kolonialpolizei* and *Technische Nothilfe.* These organisations are either Nazi innovations or else they did not previously exist in their present form. They are discussed later.

# II

# Ordinary Branches

## (a) SCHUTZPOLIZEI (SCHUPO) DES REICHES

### 38. Command of the Schupo

The *Schutzpolizei des Reiches* (Protection Police of the Reich) is the " executive police branch " (Uniformed Police) in those larger towns and cities where *Staatliche Polizeiverwaltungen* (National Police Administrations) have been established.

The Uniformed Police force under each National Police Administration Headquarters is commanded by a *Kommandeur der Schutzpolizei* (Commander of the Protection Police), who is executive assistant to the *Polizeiverwalter*, the local head of the National Police Administration. The *Polizeiverwalter* may be either *Polizeipräsident, Polizeidirektor*, or *Polizeirat* (see para. 24). He wields disciplinary powers over the *Kommandeur der Schutzpolizei* and decides on all police actions. In the absence of the *Polizeiverwalter* command is exercised by his deputy, who does not, however, exercise disciplinary powers over the *Kommandeur*.

The tactical methods to be employed are decided on by the *Kommandeur* independently of the *Polizeiverwalter*, who has no authority over that decision. The *Polizeiverwalter* nevertheless has the power to cancel his original order for police action, and thereby retains some measure of control over the powers of the *Kommandeur*.

Liaison between the *Kommandeur der Schupo* of a city and the *Befehlshaber der Orpo* in the *Wehrkreis* is carried out through a *Stabsoffizier der Schupo* (Staff Officer of the Protection Police), who is attached to the Office of the *Regierungspräsident* or similar *Höhere Polizeibehörde*, to whom he is responsible for the conduct of the work of the *Schupo* in his area.

These *Stabsoffiziere der Schupo*, one from each *Regierungsbezirk*, smaller *Land* or *Reichsgau*, may be advisory members of the staff of the *Befehlshaber der Orpo* in the *Wehrkreis* (Military District), in which their governmental sub-areas are located. The highest supervisory authority of the *Schupo des Reiches* is the *General-Inspekteur der Schutzpolizei des Reiches* in the *Hauptamt Orpo*.

### 39. Local Organisation of the Schutzpolizei

The Headquarters of the *Kommandeur der Schutzpolizei* is organised in the same manner as the office of the BdO (see para. 30). The local *Schupo* forces under the *Kommandeur* are known as a *Schutzpolizeikommando* (*Schupo* Command), and fall into two categories.

First there are those policemen who serve in *Polizeireviere* (Precincts or Wards), direct traffic and patrol a regular beat. This service is called *Einzeldienst* (single service), and members of this branch are organised into *Schutzpolizeigruppen* (Groups), *Schutzpolizeiabschnitte* (Sections) and *Schutzpolizeireviere* (Precincts or Wards).

One *Revier*, made up of some 20–40 policemen, is normally established for every 20,000 to 30,000 inhabitants. Five or more *Reviere* make up one *Abschnitt*, and three to five *Abschnitte* one *Gruppe*, though only Berlin, Hamburg and Vienna are large enough to have *Schutzpolizeigruppen*.

Secondly, the *Kommandeur der Schutzpolizei* is responsible for the employment of large formations of uniformed Police at demonstrations, in air raids and emergencies of all kinds, for which purpose there exist the *Kasernierte Polizeieinheiten* (Barrack Police Units). These are organised into *Kompanien* (Companies), formerly called *Hundertschaften*. Wherever there are several companies under one *Staatliche Polizeiverwaltung* they are permanently organised into Police Battalions. Otherwise companies are usually independent, but for action in one specific area (e.g. *Regierungsbezirk* or *Wehrkreis*), the higher officers, such as the *Stabsoffizier der Schupo* or the *Befehlshaber der Orpo*, may temporarily combine the Barrack Police within their territory into Police Battalions and Regiments.

These units, largely made up of the younger age classes, are far more thoroughly militarised in appearance and equipment than those serving in the *Einzeldienst*, and may be employed at any time as regular infantry, for which purpose they have at their disposal all the necessary weapons and equipment.

The main tasks of these regular barrack *Schupo* units are as follows :

(*a*) To provide guards for Party meetings and other " festive occasions." (In this function they co-operate with the SS.)

(*b*) To deal with internal unrest in unison with Nazi Party formations.

(*c*) To maintain order during and after air raids, and to prevent looting.

(*d*) To maintain normal traffic control after any major disturbance or catastrophe.

The Barrack Police units may be regarded as an outgrowth of the former *Landespolizei* (*Lapo* or militarised barrack police), already discussed in para 5.

### 40. Barrack Police Units in the Field

With the outbreak of war, the need for fully militarised units became more acute, and continued to increase as additional territory was occupied and police functions had to be extended.

The new wartime duties of the Barrack Police include the guarding of lines of communications in occupied territory, the patrolling and safeguarding of guerrilla-infested areas, task force operations against partisans, and the general maintenance of law and order in co-operation with SS or Army formations and other security organisations.

Additional units of Barrack Police were therefore created by incorporating *Polizeireservisten* (Police Reservists) into this branch to form further police battalions. The personnel of these units includes therefore large numbers of ex-Service men, ex-policemen and pre- and post-conscription year classes.

Thus the constantly increasing need for police in occupied territory has brought about the re-establishment of a body of police both at home and abroad, which is almost indistinguishable from its predecessor, the fully militarised *Landespolizei*.

The gradual organisation of these units into regiments as a result of their wartime duties followed their increasing adaptation to purely military functions.

During the occupation of Austria in 1938 approximately 120 to 150 Motorised Barrack Police *Hundertschaften* were mobilised and available for action within 6 hours. Such companies or combined *Marschgruppen* (March groups) as were employed were fully equipped for field service with the regular Armed Forces.

Beginning with the Polish campaign *Polizeikompanien* were combined into and committed to action as *Polizei-Bataillone*. Each of these battalions, however, still belonged to a particular town or rather *Staatliche Polizeiverwaltung*, and the *Polizeipräsident* was responsible for their pay and supply as well as for their reinforcements. There were 84 of these original *Polizei-Bataillone*, each consisting of about 550 men, organised into a HQ and 4 companies.

In 1941 conditions in the Balkans began to make it necessary for regimental staffs to be set up in order to control a larger area where several police battalions were dispersed. Eventually regular and permanent *Polizei-Regimenter* were created, first in Russia, then in other Eastern and South-Eastern areas, until all the original 84 Battalions were organised into 28 Regiments (numbered 1–28) of 3 Battalions each. At the same time the Battalions were renumbered in the orthodox way, i.e. I, II and III within each regiment, retaining however, in addition, the original Arabic numbers which they held as independent battalions.

In the course of the war, as the need for additional police field units increased, further police regiments were formed. They were called *Polizei-Schützen-Regimenter* and received numbers from 30 onward, 38 being the highest identified number.

Since March, 1943, all the above police units have been renamed *SS-Polizei-(Schützen)-Regimenter* and *SS-Polizei-(Schützen)-Bataillone*. This change of designation falls in line with the amalgamation of Police and SS forces. Moreover, the change of name may well indicate that it has been found expedient for the police field formations to draw on the supplies of the SS rather than continue the cumbersome system of obtaining all supplies through the units' home stations. But it must be emphasised that these Battalions and Regiments are **not Waffen-SS units** and should not be confused with the components of the *SS-Polizeidivision* of the *Waffen-SS*, now known as the *(Waffen-)SS-Polizei-Panzer-Division*. *SS-Polizeiregimenter* and *-Bataillone* are rather **integral formations of the Police** and their men are not all SS members.

While the *Waffen-SS* was more and more diluted by forcibly conscripted youths, by "racial" Germans and by various types of foreigner, the SS-Police units remained to a much larger extent homogeneous.

Many of them are among the most nazified, fanatical and brutal German field units. Their participation in "punitive" actions has made them the terror of Norway, Poland, Yugoslavia, Greece, Czechoslovakia and Italy.

Certain other types of police field formation, staffed by *Volksdeutsche* and non-Germans, with German officers and NCO's, deserve mention. There were upwards of 100 *Schutzmannschaftsbataillone* (*Schumabataillone*) composed of Ukrainians and Baltic elements. These battalions were numbered in a separate system, thus duplicating many numbers which had been used before for the original police battalions. They were used all over occupied Russia, especially the Central and Southern sectors. But in the face of Russian advances many of them proved to be most unreliable : for this reason a considerable number were disbanded, their personnel being probably used for forced labour in Germany.

In Yugoslavia the police formed *Hilfspolizei-Regimenter* (*Hiporegimenter*), which were at the beginning of 1944 re-named *Polizei Freiwilligen-Regimenter*. Five of them were identified in Serbia (*Pol. Freiw.-Rgt. 1-5 Serbien*), and 5 others in Croatia (*Pol. Freiw. Rgt. 1-5 Kroatien*).

In Italy six *Polizei-Freiwilligen-Bataillone* have been identified (*Pol. Freiw. Btl. 1-6 Italien*). In addition there are certain Czech police units in Italy called *Regierungstruppen* ; they are believed to be numbered I to XII. Their personnel appears to come from the Protectorate police and is composed of Sudeten Germans and other volunteers. Each of the 12 *Truppen* is of about battalion strength. Mention should also be made in this connection of considerable forces of the Italian Fascist Army, who, though not belonging to the police or SS, are operating under the HSSPf in Italy.

A table of organisation (War Establishment) of a typical Barrack Police Battalion, and the Order of Battle of identified *SS-Polizei-Regimenter* and *Bataillone* is given in Annexe E.

## 41. Polizei-Wachbataillone

There is another type of *Kasernierte Polizei* which is strictly a wartime innovation and must not be confused with the Barrack Police units discussed above,—namely the *Polizei-Wachbataillone* (Police Guard Battalions) organised by *Wehrkreise*. Their principal task is to maintain order and to direct and re-route traffic in bombed-out areas.

About 4 to 5 such battalions exist in each *Wehrkreis*. They are designated by Arabic numbers and by the Roman numeral of the *Wehrkreis*. e.g., 4. *Polizeiwachbataillon VI,/Köln*.

These units are almost exclusively composed of civilians of post-conscription age classes, who have been drafted into the police as *Polizei-Reservisten* for the duration of the war. The average age in the battalion named above was reported to be 52, the oldest man in the unit being 58.

Only the officers and cadre are trained policemen; the rest are draftees who receive only short, basic police training.

There are 3 to 4 companies per battalion, 2 to 3 platoons per company, and 4 sections (US squads) per platoon. The total strength of a battalion ranges from 350—500 men.

These *Polizei-Wachbataillone* are constantly kept on the alert for duty in case of air raids. They are not motorised, but receive the necessary vehicles from the *Schupo-Kommando* of the town where they are located. Their armament consists of rifles and a few light machine guns. In contrast to the other barrack police units they cannot be considered fully-fledged infantry because of their poor training and high average age. One of these battalions was sent into the front line near Aachen and completely wiped out within a day.

## 42. MT Columns

The following paragraphs (42—46) deal with other units which are components of a *Schutzpolizeikommando*.

The first of these are the *Kraftfahrstaffeln* (MT Columns), which are organised into :—

*Kraftfahrbereitschaften* (MT Detachments)
*Motorisierte Verkehrsbereitschaften* (Motorised Traffic Detachments)
*Verkehrsunfallbereitschaften* (Road Accident Detachments).

The *Kraftfahrbereitschaften* take care of all duty travel as well as of the maintenance of all motor transport vehicles assigned to their *Schupo* command.

The *Motorisierte Verkehrsbereitschaften* were created in 1937 for the direction and supervision of traffic in the larger cities. Originally 51 units of this kind were formed, but it must be assumed that after the occupation of Austria in 1938, and again after subsequent conquests, additional units were created to operate in the newly acquired territories.

For the execution of their duties they have at their disposal patrol vehicles, staff cars and motor cycles with and without sidecars. Personnel of the *Motorisierte Verkehrsbereitschaften* are usually employed as small patrols, but in special instances entire detachments may be used. The strength of a full detachment consists of 48 men (known as a 4/4 unit). As local conditions demand, fractions of that figure may make up smaller, but still autonomous, detachments, such as units of 12, 24, or 36 men (referred to as 1/4, 2/4 or 3/4 units respectively).

As this service called for a considerable numbe of especially well-trained motor cyclists, a high percentage of its personnel was taken from the ranks of the *Nationalsozialistische Kraftfahrkorps* (NSKK—National Socialist Motor Corps). For an Order of Battle of the *Motorisierte Verkehrbereitschaften der Schutzpolizei* see Annexe D.

The *Verkehrsunfallbereitschaften* (Road Accident Detachments), sometimes known as *Verkehrsunfallkommandos* (Road Accident Squads) also have at their disposal special cars and trucks in order to perform all tasks which arise in connection with traffic accidents. These accident detachments are established in the larger *Staatliche Polizeiverwaltungen* in towns of 200,000 inhabitants and above. Their strength is largely dependent on local conditions, but will, in most instances (with the exception of Berlin, Vienna and Hamburg) range from 10 to 20 men.

It should be noted that all vehicles of the German Police carry the *Kennzeichen* (Insignia) "Pol" preceding the licence number on the licence plate.

## 43. Verkehrskompanie (mot.) z.b.V.

In November, 1941, the *Reichsführer-SS und Chef der Deutschen Polizei* created a *Motorisierte Verkehrskompanie z.b.V.* (Motorised Traffic Company for Special Employment) to perform functions essential to the prosecution of the war.

This unit is charged with the supervision of wartime traffic in the Reich, excluding the Protectorate *Böhmen und Mähren* and the *General-gouvernement*.

Its duties include :

(*a*) Supervision of all measures ordered for the preservation of tyres.

(*b*) Supervision of the lawful use of vehicles operated under special wartime licences.

(*c*) Supervision of maintenance of vehicles in the interest of public safety.

(*d*) General supervision of traffic as well as any additional police duties necessitated by extraordinary wartime conditions.

The *Verkehrskompanie* is under the direct command of the *Reichsführer-SS und Chef der Deutschen Polizei*, who, in the original decree instituting the organisation, placed special emphasis on its importance.

It consists of specially trained police personnel, and is organised into five *Züge* (Platoons) each of which is assigned to a specific area. Following is a list of the platoons, with names and definitions of their areas.

| No. and Headquarters of Zug (Platoon) | Platoon Area known as | Covers territories of :— | |
|---|---|---|---|
| | | Wehrkreis | HSSPf and BdO |
| 1. Posen | OST | I | Königsberg (Pr) |
| | | VIII | Breslau |
| | | XX | Danzig |
| | | XXI | Posen |
| 2. Berlin | MITTE | II | Stettin |
| | | III | Berlin |
| | | IV | Dresden |
| 3. Hannover | NORD | VI | Münster |
| | | IX | Kassel |
| | | X | Hamburg |
| | | XI | Hannover |
| 4. Stuttgart | SÜD | V | Stuttgart |
| | | VII | München |
| | | XII | Wiesbaden |
| | | XIII | Nürnberg |
| 5. Wien | SÜDOST | XVII | Wien |
| | | XVIII | Salzburg |

## 44. Signals Columns

The *Polizei-Nachrichtenstaffeln* (Police Signal Columns) are responsible for Police communications, all of which are maintained at readiness throughout the twenty-four hours of the day. Both the radio and telephone nets are divided into trunk lines and secondary circuits.

The communications control headquarters is the Police wireless station in Berlin, which represents the centre of all principal Police trunk lines in Germany. For control of the borders, the *Orpo* has at its disposal *Grenzfunkstellen* (Frontier Wireless Stations).

In the largest towns and on highways the *Orpo* owns and operates exceptionally well-equipped mobile transmitters and receivers which are handled by the *Nachrichtenbereitschaften* (Signal Squads). Radio communication lines are further supplemented by an inter-urban and road network of two-way channels over permanent stations. All equipment (largely manufactured by *Telefunken* and AEG) is qualitatively at least equal to that of the German Armed Forces. Thus the *Orpo* has at its disposal what may perhaps be termed the best and densest net of police radio communications in the world, surpassed—as to efficiency though not as to coverage and density—only by the communication lines owned by the *Sipo* and SD.

The *Orpo* wireless network is linked with the system of universal stations, which is composed of permanent propaganda, military, police, railway, postal and naval centres for transmitting, receiving and monitoring. Police signals personnel therefore is trained to co-operate with all these other wireless stations.

Alongside its own telephone wires, the *Orpo* also operates its own teletype system composed of both above-ground open-wire lines and overland cable lines.

Its central exchange is the *Reichsvermittlungsstelle (Rvst.)* in the *Hauptamt Orpo*. Other exchanges, known as *Leitvermittlungsstellen (Lvst.)*, are located at the offices of the BdO and the headquarters of the *Staatliche Polizeiverwaltungen*, which have locally their own teletype lines connecting them with the headquarters of the *Gruppen-und Abschnitts-kommandos* and with the individual *Reviere* of their city or town. Most of these exchanges are also connected with the teletype net operated by the German Postal Authorities. Thus the *Orpo*, in addition to its own networks, may avail itself of the government-owned general telephone and teletype net, enjoying highest priority.

For further details on German Police communication lines see paras. 94 and 95.

As part of the field forces of the Police there exist *SS-Polizei-Nachrichtenkompanien* (SS-Police Signals Companies). 49 have been identified, some as component units of *SS-Polizei-Regimenter*, others as Signals units of the Police in occupied countries (see Annexe E).

## 45. Mounted Police Troops

Until April, 1941, mounted detachments were known as *Reitstaffeln*, but were later renamed *Polizei-Reiterstaffeln* (Mounted Police Troops).

The *Reiterstaffel* is the basic unit of the Mounted Police regardless of numerical strength. According to need, *Reiterstaffeln* are either in existence as autonomous mounted units or are combined into mixed detachments with the regular *Schutzpolizei*. The following combined detachments were known to exist in 1938 :—

Mounted Detachments in Berlin, Königsberg, Stettin, Breslau and Gleiwitz, where there are always three detachments combined under one command.

Mixed Detachments in Frankfurt a.M., Bochum, Düsseldorf, Halle and Magdeburg, composed of two-thirds mounted and one-third foot police.

Mixed Detachments in Tilsit, Elbing, Schneidemühl, Oppeln, Erfurt, Kassel, Koblenz and Aachen composed of one-third mounted and two-thirds foot police.

Mixed Detachments in Wiesbaden composed half of mounted and half of foot police.

In the Ukraine, a *Polizei-Reiter-Regiment*, composed of locally recruited *Volksdeutsche*, was in operation. Two or three *Polizei-Reiter-Abteilungen* (Battalions) were also identified on L of C duties in Russia.

## 46. Other Units of the Schutzpolizeikommando

The **Sanitätsdienst** (Medical Service) operates under the *Polizei-Ärzte* (Medical Officers of the Police), who have their own *Sanitätsstellen* (Medical and First Aid Posts).

The **Veterinärdienst** (Veterinary Service) operates under *Polizeiveterinäroffiziere* (Veterinary Officers of the Police). In addition to the care of horses and dogs used by the Police, they are charged with the combatting of animal epidemics and the inspection of meat and other animal products.

The **Motorisierte Überfallkommandos** (Motorised Riot Squads) are established in every town which has a *Staatliche Polizeiverwaltung*. They are kept in readiness at all times and are used for prompt assistance in case of any type of emergency which may arise in a larger city. The number of such squads depends on the size of the town.

These riot squads, equipped with light, armoured high-speed cars mounting revolving MG turrets, are known to have been brought from Germany to Denmark, Holland and Belgium to quell larger demonstrations. Units from Austria have been dispatched to Slovenia to track down partisans and stamp out guerrilla strongholds, and to act independently on such duties as the patrol of roads leading through mountain passes.

Such commitment leaves no doubt as to the character of these units. A cursory survey of their personnel suggests that it continues to be composed of younger SS-men rather than of reservists.

For more effective supervision of urban and rural traffic, and especially for the enforcement of speed laws, the *Schutzpolizei des Reiches* (as well as the *Schutzpolizei der Gemeinden* and the *Gendarmerie*) employ **Zivilstreifen** (Patrols in Plain Clothes, abbr. *Zstr*).

These patrols may operate on foot (*ZStrF— Fusszivilstreifen*), on bicycles (*ZStrR—Radzivil-streifen*) or motorised (*ZStr mot.—Motorisierte Zivilstreifen*). Vehicles are, if necessary, supplied by the NSKK.

Employment of these patrols is decided on by the *Kommandeur der Schutzpolizei* (in the case of the *Gendarmerie* by the *Hauptmannschaftsführer*). Each patrol consisting of more than one man is headed by a *Streifenführer* (Patrol leader).

## 47. NSKK Assistance to the Schupo

The Regular Uniformed Police is assisted in its duties in many instances by Party Organisations.

The *NSKK* **Verkehrsdienst** (Traffic Control Service) has assumed the function of an auxiliary police force, because of the increase in military traffic and the drain on the regular Police personnel as more and more of the latter were called to the colours of the *Waffen-SS*, the *Wehrmacht* and the Police Field Units.

It appeared for the first time in this role when the bulk of the German Army was moved from the East to the West following the conclusion of the Polish campaign. Identified units of this type include :

*NSKK Verkehrsstandarte* (Traffic Control Regiment) Wien
*NSKK Verkehrsstaffeln* (Battalions) Berlin and Hamburg
*Verkehrskompanie* Lemberg
*NSKK Polizeiverkehrskompanie* on the Eastern Front.

When the need arose these units were sent bodily into front line service.

These units were also engaged in **Verkehrserziehungsdienst** (Traffic Educational Service) especially under wartime conditions, by means of films, exhibitions and the posting of road warning signs.

In its capacity as **Verkehrshilfsdienst** (Road Aid or Traffic Assistance Service), the NSKK posts square white signs in blue frames from 6 kilometres to 8 kilometres apart along all main roads. The centre of these signs shows a red dial with the insignia of the NSKK above and a red cross below. The signs are illuminated, and indicate the nearest telephone by which the *NSKK-Zonenführer* (Road

Zone Controller) may be called. It is the latter's duty, in case of accident, to arrange for a doctor, for police assistance, for ambulance, tows, and similar services, including even funeral vehicles.

This service is mainly an accident reporting system organised in road zones. For instance, the *NSKK Motorgruppe* HESSEN reported in 1942 that its unit directed 525 call posts. The area of this regional command at the time was divided into 35 zones, and the *Motorgruppe* served 30 main roads, and 2,650 kilometres of secondary roads.

In addition to the above functions the NSKK is charged with the **Transportkontrolle des Motorisierten Transportes der Kriegswirtschaft** (Cargo Inspection Service of Motorised Wartime Transport). Drivers of commercial vehicles have to obtain permits from a special NSKK official (*Fahrbereitschaftsleiter*) for journeys exceeding certain distances, details of which are fixed regionally. This NSKK official is also responsible for proper utilisation of vehicles, ·as well as for the efficient employment of the most suitable means of transport. In the interests of maximum economy he will also provide cargo for the return trip.

As a logical adjunct to these functions the *Reichsverkehrsblatt* (Official Traffic Regulations Gazette), dated 10th June, 1944, entrusts the NSKK exclusively with the testing of applicants for, and the issue of, drivers' licences. Similarly the certificate for operation of producer gas driven vehicles (*BB-Schein or Betriebsberechtigungsschein*) is only issued by the NSKK, under the direction of the *Verwaltungspolizei* (Administrative Police).

For further details on the NSKK, reference should be made to the Basic Handbook EDS/G/3 in this series.

## 48. HJ Assistance to the Schupo

The other Party organisation assisting the Regular Uniformed Police is the *HJ-SRD* (*HJ-Streifendienst*) a local patrol service instituted by the Hitler Youth Organisation. It started in 1934 as a junior police organisation controlling activities of the members of the HJ, in a manner comparable to American or British MPs checking the conduct of their Service men, but its scope has since widened.

The service is particularly concerned with carrying out the provisions of the *Reichspolizeigesetz zum Schutze der Deutschen Jugend* (Reich Police Law for the protection of German Youth) of 1943. This law imposes many restrictions on boys and girls in Germany, such as prohibiting smoking, drinking, public dancing, etc.

By now, however, the HJ-SRD has been extended into a semi-military organisation supervised and commanded by SS personnel. A board of HJ and SS leaders considers individual applications for service in the SRD, applying the rigorous standards of the *Allgemeine-SS*. In the SRD today are combined all the various tasks of a supplementary SS and Police force. In that capacity SRD personnel operate in close collaboration with the police authorities including the *Gestapo*. Indeed the SRD may be considered a major problem for Allied occupation forces as its 14-16 year old members are of the most dangerous and unscrupulous Nazi type. For instance, they have been extensively used as raiding squads and as informers ; in Poland the SRD is even known to have furnished execution squads.

A branch of this organisation is known as the *Schnellkommando* or *Rollkommando* (Mobile Emergency Squad), a motorised patrol which is at the constant disposal of the German Police. It is kept in readiness to assist or take the place of the Regular Police in any emergency, especially in the case of air raids and *Grossfahndungen* (see para. 124. Further details on this subject may be found in the publication EDS/G/5, Basic Handbook on the HJ Movement).

## (b) *SCHUTZPOLIZEI DER GEMEINDEN*

### 49. Organisation of the Schutzpolizei der Gemeinden

In those communities of more than 2,000 inhabitants in which a *Staatliche Polizeiverwaltung* has not been established, the executive Police functions of the *Orpo* are carried out by units of the *Schutzpolizei der Gemeinden* (Municipal Protection Police).

Their local administrative Chief is the *Bürgermeister* (Mayor) or *Oberbürgermeister* (Lord Mayor). In communities of less than 2,000 inhabitants the executive Police authority rests with the *Gendarmerie* (Rural Police). It is planned to extend the Police authority of the *Gendarmerie* to all communities below 5,000 inhabitants, but up to the present time this has only been achieved in the newly annexed territories such as the *Reichsgaue*, and in a few communities of the old Reich. Statistics of 1942 mention that *Gemeindepolizeiverwaltungen* (Municipal Police Administrations) exist in 1,338 municipalities of over 5,000 inhabitants, all of them without *Staatliche Polizeiverwaltungen*. Of these :

5  have over 100,000 inhabitants
22  have between 50,000 and 100,000 inhabitants
591  have between 10,000 and 50,000 inhabitants
720  have between 5,000 and 10,000 inhabitants

In the larger municipalities without *Staatliche Polizeiverwaltungen* the *Schutzpolizei* is headed by a *Stabsoffizier der Schupo* and the unit is known as a *Kommando der Schutzpolizei* (the same term as for the *Schupo des Reiches*). In small communities the officer in charge of the *Schupo* is a Captain or Lieutenant, and his unit is known as a *Schutzpolizei-Dienstabteilung* (*Schupo* Service Detachment).

Prior to the formation of a unified *Schupo der Gemeinden* considerable variation existed in the police organisation in different areas and even in adjacent townships, but now a number of decrees regulate and co-ordinate the strength of these units (in relation to the population), uniformity of rank, pay, replacement, and training all over the Reich.

Although members of the *Schutzpolizei der Gemeinden* are technically municipal civil servants, they were made subject to the same regulations of the Reich Authorities as the members of the *Schutzpolizei des Reiches*. As a matter of fact the personnel of the *Schupo der Gemeinden* is taken exclusively from personnel of the *Schupo des Reiches*, and one of the decrees states that members of the *Schupo des Reiches* can be transferred to the *Schupo der Gemeinden* and vice versa, or from one community to another without the individual's consent.

Thus very little difference exists today between the *Schupo der Gemeinden* and the *Schupo des Reiches*.

### 50. Command of the Schutzpolizei der Gemeinden

The activities of all units of the *Schupo der Gemeinden* are supervised by the *Generalinspekteur der Gendarmerie und der Schutzpolizei der Gemeinden*.

Below him the units of the *Schupo der Gemeinden* are under the command and supervision of the *Befehlshaber der Orpo* in the particular *Wehrkreis*.

The heads of the local *Kommandos der Schutzpolizei der Gemeinden*, who hold ranks from *Major der Schutzpolizei* upwards, and who are known as *Stabsoffiziere*, are directly responsible to the Higher Police Authorities (*Regierungspräsidenten*, etc.) of the area. In addition they may be advisory members on the Staff of the *Befehlshaber der Orpo*.

The heads of the *Schutzpolizei-Dienstabteilungen* in communities of over 5,000 inhabitants are subject to the supervision of the *Stabsoffiziere der Schutzpolizei* attached to the Higher Police Authorities. These officers represent the *Schupo-Dienstabteilungen* at the Headquarters of the *Regierungspräsident*, etc. as well as on the Staff of the BdO of the *Wehrkreis*. In communities of less than 5,000 the *Schupo-Dienstabteilungen* are subject to supervision by the Commanders of the *Gendarmerie* who are attached to the Headquarters of the *Regierungspräsidenten* or other Higher Police Authorities.

Otherwise, units of the *Schupo der Gemeinden* are organised in much the same way as units of the *Schupo des Reiches*, except that they are smaller, not so elaborately equipped, and are directly at the disposal of the Mayor of the town instead of the *Polizeiverwalter*.

## (c) *GENDARMERIE*

### 51. Gendarmerie : General

The *Gendarmerie* constitutes the uniformed police in the open country, and in communities of less than 2,000 inhabitants. It has been planned to extend the field of action of the *Gendarmerie* to all communities up to 5,000 inhabitants, but so far this has only been achieved in certain parts of the country (see para. 49).

The principal difference between the *Gendarmerie* and the *Schutzpolizei* is that, owing to the nature of the territory in which they serve, the members of the *Gendarmerie* in addition to their ordinary functions as *Polizeivollzugsbeamte* (Police Executive Officials) are also trained and equipped to " help and advise " the rural population in matters of general administration, and in the manifold dealings which in Germany concern the "authorities," and all too frequently the police.

The individual *Gendarm* who makes his daily tour of duty on foot, bicycle, motorcycle or on horseback is very often the only representative of the government in his small area in direct and constant touch with the population. His office is in his home, where he maintains files and where he is reached by telephone or sometimes only by messenger. This wider scope of the *Gendarmerie* is expressed in its entire organisation which, of necessity is more decentralised than that of the *Schupo*, but by no means less militarised.

Two main categories of the *Gendarmerie*, which are discussed in following paragraphs, must be distinguished :—

The *Gendarmerie des Einzeldienstes* (" Single Service " Gendarmerie).

The *Motorisierte Gendarmerie* (Motorised Gendarmerie) or *Gend.* (*Mot.*).

### 52. Gendarmerie des Einzeldienstes

The smallest unit of the *Einzeldienst* is the *Gendarmerie-Einzelposten* (Single Post), consisting of only one *Gendarm* assigned to a thinly populated area. More densely populated country districts which include larger villages have *Gendarmerie-Posten* manned by several *Gendarmen*, and led by a *Gendarmerie Hauptwachtmeister* or *Meister* (senior

NCO). Several *Gendarmerie-Einzelposten* are organised to form a *Gendarmerie-Gruppenposten* (Group Post) headed normally by a *Gendarmerie Meister*. The latter, however, does not exercise full command over the men of the *Einzelposten* within his district, as they retain a fair amount of independence to enable them to cope with strictly local matters.

This partial independence in no way conflicts with the centralisation of the German rural police. It does, however, stress the particular status of the individual *Gendarm*, who exercises a considerable amount of control over the population in his district, in which he constitutes the immediate representative of the law, both as " adviser " and as " *Staatsgewalt*," the strong arm of the regime.

All the members of the *Gendarmerie* in a *Landkreis* constitute a unit termed a *Gendarmeriekreis* and led by a *Gendarmeriekreisführer* whose rank is normally that of a *Gendarmerie-Bezirksleutnant* or *Oberleutnant*.

The *Gendarmerie-Kreis*, which is headed by a *Gendarmerie-Oberleutnant*, should have a minimum strength of about 40 men. In matters pertaining to the *Gendarmerie*, the *Gendarmeriekreisführer* is also the police advisor to the *Landrat* (Rural Councillor or Executive) and as such is responsible to him for the execution of locally issued orders affecting the *Landkreis*.

If a *Landkreis* covers a larger than average area the *Gendarmeriekreis* may be subdivided into *Gendarmerieabteilungen* consisting each of a number of *Gendarmerieposten* of all sizes, such as regular *Posten*, *Einzelposten* and *Gruppenposten*, and commanded by a *Gendarmerie-Abteilungsführer*.

A *Gendarmerie-Abteilung* comprises, on the average, from 15 to 20 men. However, special conditions such as a dense network of *Gendarmerie* stations in the vicinity of large cities, in industrial regions or near the National frontier may necessitate the formation of stronger *Abteilungen*.

Several *Gendarmeriekreise* form a *Gendarmeriehauptmannschaft* with an average of 140 to 150 men, commanded by a *Major* or a *Hauptmann* (Captain) *der Gendarmerie*, who, in turn, is subordinate to a *Kommandeur der Gendarmerie* (Commander of Rural Police) of the *Regierungsbezirk* or similar Higher Police Authority.

The *Kommandeur der Gendarmerie*, who also represents the *Gendarmerie* of his *Regierungsbezirk* on the staff of the *Befehlshaber der Orpo* at *Wehrkreis* Headquarters is responsible to the latter for all *Gendarmerie* activities within his district. The *Kommandeur der Gendarmerie* and all units subordinate to him are furthermore supervised by the *General-Inspekteur der Gendarmerie und der Schutzpolizei der Gemeinden* in the *Hauptamt Orpo* of the *Reichsministerium des Innern*.

A special branch of the *Gendarmerie* is the *Hochgebirgs-Gendarmerie* (Mountain Gendarmerie). It was created in August 1941 and is, in the main, organised along the same lines as the regular *Gendarmerie*. Its personnel, however, undergoes special training for duty in Alpine regions and as mountain guides. *Gendarmerie-Posten*, situated in mountainous areas of more than 1,500 metres (about 4,500 ft.) in altitude, are referred to as *Gend. Hochgebirgsposten*.

Recent developments as well as public utterances by German leaders clearly indicate that these mountainous regions may be expected to be turned into strong centres of resistance for regular, as well as guerrilla warfare. The territories policed by the *Hochgebirgsgendarmerie*, therefore, become of special interest to Allied advancing and occupying armies. The following areas policed by these units as mapped out in the decree of 1941 should be noted in this connection :—

*Reichsgau* Salzburg.
*Reichsgau* Tirol-Vorarlberg.
*Reichsgau* Steiermark (including Untersteiermark).
*Reichsgau* Kärnten (including Südkärnten and Krain).
*Gend. Kreise* Gmünden, Kirchdorf a.d. Krems, Vöcklabruck and Steyr of the *Reichsgau* Oberdonau.
*Gend. Kreise* Scheibbs, Lilienfeld, Neunkirchen and Wiener-Neustadt of the *Reichsgau* Niederdonau.
*Gend. Kreise* Füssen and Sonthofen of the *Reg. Bezirk* Schwaben.
*Gend. Kreise* Garmisch, Bad Tölz, Miesbach, Rosenheim and Berchtesgaden as well as the *Gend. Abt.* Traunstein of the *Gend. Kreis* Traunstein of the *Reg. Bezirk* Oberbayern.
*Gend. Zug* Neumark (Distrikt Krakau).

## 53. Landwacht and Stadtwacht

In January, 1942, the *Landwacht* (Auxiliary Rural Police) was set up by DALUEGE, then Chief of the *Orpo*, to assist the *Schutzpolizei der Gemeinden* and, especially, the *Gendarmerie*.

Its members are mainly recruited from *SA-Wehrmannschaften* (Germans between the ages of 18 and 65 not otherwise mustered, but provided with basic military training by the Nazi Party Storm Troops) and ex-Service men of the last war. While recruits for the *SA-Wehrmannschaften* are conscripted under an Emergency Service Decree, enlistment for the *Landwacht* was originally voluntary and on a part-time basis, only later developing into compulsory service.

Military training is provided by the SA and personnel of the *Landwacht* are not uniformed, wearing only a white armband with the inscription " *Landwacht*." They are issued with light arms such as pistols, rifles, etc.

The *Landwacht* is responsible to the Chief of the Regular Uniformed Police, *SS-Obergruppenführer* WÜNNENBERG and through him to HIMMLER. The present commander of the entire German *Landwacht* is *SS-Obergruppenführer* Friederich ALPERS, State Secretary, Forester General, and a member of GÖRING'S Economic Council.

When on duty, the *Landwacht* are under the orders of the Police and *Gendarmerie* and are attached to their regular police posts.

Even though the *Landwacht* was instituted at a period of increasing delinquency in rural areas, its present primary concern is the supervision of the activities of almost 12 million foreign workers, prisoners of war, and those " anti-social " German elements employed or residing in rural districts. Under prevailing conditions it is obvious that a strong network, such as is represented by the *Landwacht*, has become necessary to cover the entire Reich.

The formation of the *Landwacht* was kept secret by the Germans for over a year. It was never mentioned until the beginning of 1943, when a similar organisation, the *Stadtwacht* (Auxiliary Urban Police) was created ; the *Stadtwacht* was also derived from the *SA-Wehrmannschaften*. Its function is to assist the *Schutzpolizei des Reiches* in cities in the same manner as the *Landwacht* is at the disposal of the *Schutzpolizei der Gemeinden* and *Gendarmerie* in the country.

In October, 1943, HIMMLER issued a decree for the expansion of both the *Stadtwacht* and the *Landwacht*. Whereas previously only those Germans who were not members of other Nazi Party organisations were subject to service with the urban or rural guard formations, the new edict made every German, regardless of affiliation, liable to be called up.

The tremendous and rapid growth of these organisations necessitated their sub-division into three classes :—

(a) *Aktive Stadt-* or *Landwacht :* personnel of this category are liable to do duty for extended periods of time. They are constantly at the disposal of the police and subject to immediate call. Not included are members of the ARP and similar passive defence services.

(b) *Reserve I :* includes personnel who, because of their civilian or official occupations, are not immediately available for duty, but may be called in on special occasions.

(c) *Reserve II :* includes all personnel who, owing to the special importance of their occupations, are available for police duty in extreme emergencies only, e.g. *Grossfahndungen* (National Searches).

As preparations for Nazi resistance and for guerrilla warfare within Germany are rapidly accelerated, militarisation of these auxiliary police formations is reaching its peak.

On 18th October, 1944, HIMMLER announced the formation of a "*Volkssturm*" (People's Militia) under the auspices of the SA to include all able-bodied men from 16 to 60 years of age not so far members of the Armed Forces. Under existing circumstances the difference between such newly formed field units and the similarly organised auxiliary police forces of the *Stadt- und Landwacht* will become increasingly smaller and indeed negligible.

For further information on the *SA-Wehrmann-schaften*, *Stadtwacht* and *Landwacht* see publication EDS/G/1 (SA of the NSDAP).

## 54. The Motorised Gendarmerie

In the heyday of their power, the *Sturm Abteilungen* (*SA*—Storm Troops) included a special shock formation, the *Feldjägerkorps*. It was comparable to a military provost corps and was apparently to act as such in the event of war.

Its great defect—the fact that it was an SA organisation recruited only from established Nazi Party members and not from regular conscripts—brought about its eventual eclipse after the 1934 purge of the SA. Finally, on 1st April, 1935, the *Feldjägerkorps* was dissolved. Some of its units were transferred bodily to the new *Kasernierte Polizei*, replacing the *Landespolizei*, which was incorporated into the newly created *Wehrmacht*. Other *Feldjägerkorps* units went to form the *Motorisierte Gendarmerie* (Motorised Gendarmerie), abbr. *Gend. (Mot.)*. The men exchanged their SA badges for the standard police insignia and badges of rank. This was a change of some political importance, marking still more clearly the then declining power of the SA and the growing confidence of the régime in the regular Police forces from which all "undesirables" had been removed ; it meant, too, an influx of 100 per cent. Nazi units into the most militarised branches of the Police.

A decree issued on 30th June, 1937, by the RFSS u Ch d Dt Pol i RM d I declared the newly created *Motorisierte Gendarmerie* to be a "special service branch of the *Gendarmerie* operating throughout the entire territory of the Reich, with the control of traffic both on *Landstrassen* (First class roads) and on the *Autobahnen* (National Highways) as its main function."

Differing from the regular *Gendarmerie*, the *Motorisierte Gendarmerie* are *Kasernierte Einheiten* (Barrack Units), and are organised along purely military lines into *Motorisierte Kompanien* (Companies) and *Motorisierte Züge* (Platoons). Like the regular *Gendarmerie*, however, they are subordinate to the *Kommandeur der Gendarmerie*, who is attached to the *Höhere Polizeibehörde* (*Regierungspräsident*, etc.) of the area.

Apart from patrolling the highways, the duties of the *Motorisierte Gendarmerie* comprise the reporting of all accidents, the rendering of First Aid, the apprehension of stolen vehicles, the reporting to their administrative authorities on the state and condition of roads and on the need for new traffic signs ; for the last-mentioned functions, see also paragraph 47 above on the NSKK *Verkehrshilfsdienst*.

In the interest of more effective supervision of the *Reichsautobahnen*, *Reichsautobahnen-Kommandos* (*RAB Kdos*) were created in October, 1941. These units are furnished by the *Motorisierte Gendarmerie*, the strength of each consisting of 5 *Gendarmen* and 1 *Kommandoführer* (squad leader). They are equipped with 1 patrol car and 2 motor cycles with sidecar.

On special occasions, the *Motorisierte Gendarmerie* may be employed to perform tasks outside their normal sphere of duty. While they generally operate in small patrols, they may, in emergencies be committed in full strength as units. The *Gendarmerie* officers will determine whether any need exists for such *Grosseinsätze* (Total commitments). In such instances, a request must be made to the Higher Police Authorities which administer the unit. Whenever entire units or component parts of units are to be employed on special tasks for more than three days, approval must be obtained from the *Reichsführer-SS und Chef der Deutschen Polizei*.

The authority of the *Motorisierte Gendarmerie* extends throughout the entire Reich and is not bound by the political boundaries within the country. The only exceptions are the areas of those cities in which are located *Staatliche Polizeiverwaltungen ;* there the authority of the *Gend. (mot.)* is restricted to the *Reichsautobahnen* passing through the city limits.

Men selected for the *Motorisierte Gendarmerie* are trained in the following special centres :

> *Gend. Schule* Suhl
> *Gend. Schule* Deggingen
> *Gend. Schule* Fraustadt
> *Gend. Schule* Hollabrunn

In the ordinary course of events and with the necessary vacancies, members of the *Motorisierte Gendarmerie* are, after approximately 5 to 6 years service, transferred into the *Gend. Einzeldienst*.

## 55. Organisation of the Motorised Gendarmerie

The *Motorisierte Gendarmerie* is organised on the basis of a so-called 3/3 unit containing 108 men and 3 officers. Such basic units can be subdivided into 1/3 units (36 men and 1 officer), or 2/3 units (72 men and 2 officers), or extended into overstrength 4/3 units (144 men and 4 officers), and will then function as independently operative units. In 1937 a total of 42 units were created and organised as follows :—

Two 4/3 *Bereitschaften*, also termed *Motorisierte Gend. Abteilungen*—4 officers and 144 men each.

Twelve 3/3 *Bereitschaften*, also termed *Gend. Kompanie mot.*—3 officers and 108 men each.

26

Eighteen 2/3 *Bereitschaften*, also termed *Kleine Gend. Kompanie mot.*—2 officers and 72 men each.

Ten 1/3 *Bereitschaften*, also termed *Gend. Züge* (platoons) *mot*—1 officer and 36 men each.

By 1942, a great number of additional units had been formed to police Austria and other newly-acquired territories. By that time, the term *Bereitschaft* had been dropped, and the term *Gendarmerie-Abteilung (mot)* had been replaced by *Verstärkte (Verst.*—reinforced) *Gendarmerie-Kompanie (mot)*. A corps of 66 units with a total personnel of 5,931 officers and other ranks was formed. This new organisation includes the following units :—

Three 4/3 *Verst. Gend. Komp. (mot.)* of 4 officers and 144 men each.

Twenty-four 3/3 *Gend. Komp. (mot.)* of 3 officers and 108 men each.

Thirty-one 2/3 *Kl. Gend. Komp. (mot.)* of 2 officers and 72 men each.

Eight 1/3 *Gend. Züge (mot.)* of 1 officer and 36 men each.

It must be borne in mind that the units and strengths mentioned above are valid only for 1942 and it must be assumed that a number of additional units have since been formed and are now in operation.

An Order of Battle arranged according to *Wehrkreise* (Military Districts) of all identified units of the *Motorisierte Gendarmerie* will be found in Annexe D.

Since the *Motorisierte Gendarmerie* is a fully militarised and mobile formation, its importance increases in the light of the present trend to prepare the Police forces for their employment in National Defence and resistance inside Germany. Indeed, since the outbreak of war, large numbers of *Motorisierte Gendarmerie* personnel have been incorporated into *Feldgendarmerie* units (Army Military Police) and as such are attached to divisions, corps and armies of the Field Forces.

*Motorisierte Gendarmerie* units furthermore are being sent to the zones of communications immediately adjacent to the theatres of operations and to occupied territories, to assist other Police formations in traffic control, as well as in the prevention of sabotage and partisan warfare.

From 70 to 80 *Gendarmerie-Züge (mot.)*, i.e. platoons of the normal strength of 1 officer and 36 men, have been identified in Russia and Italy. In addition, two *Gendarmerie-Bataillone (mot.)* are known to exist, one of them having been identified in France.

The *Motorisierte Gendarmerie* is armed with carbines, pistols and machine pistols. Its weapons and equipment are supplied and maintained by the special *Waffenmeistereien der deutschen Polizei* (Ordnance and Maintenance Shops) which serve all branches of the German Police. A table of weapons and vehicles, and a list of the locations of the *Waffenmeistereien* will be found in Annexe D.

A definite system of licence plate numbers for all vehicles of the *Motorisierte Gendarmerie* with special numbers assigned to each regional headquarters as well as to each category of vehicles has been set up. The tabulation of these licence numbers for the original 42 units (i.e. not to include the units added in 1942 and later) will be found in Annexe D.

It can be assumed that similar numbering systems exist for police licence plates of *all* police vehicles.

## (d) KOLONIALPOLIZEI

### 56. HIMMLER's plans for a Colonial Police

From the very beginning the Nazi government took great interest in fanning the smouldering ashes of German colonial aspirations. This is demonstrated by the fact that in 1936 certain units of the *Schutzpolizei* were charged with the continuation of the colonial tradition.

Thus the *Schutzpolizei* of Bremen was selected to perpetuate the ghost of the police force of former German South West Africa, the *Schutzpolizei* of Kiel was to serve as a reminder of Kamerun (Cameroon) and the *Schutzpolizei* of Hamburg was identified with the memories of Kiautschau.

These traditional units were distinguished with the *Kreuz des Südens* (Southern Cross) worn on the left sleeve.

In January, 1941, the Nazis began to take some interest in the Italian campaign in North Africa, and HIMMLER therefore founded the *Kolonialpolizei* (Colonial Police) and instituted the *Kolonialpolizeiamt* (Bureau of the Colonial Police) within the *Hauptamt Ordnungspolizei*. The purpose of this newly founded bureau was, in the words of the decree, " the uniform preparation and eventual employment of the *Ordnungspolizei* in future German Colonies and Mandates."

The *General-Inspekteur der Polizeischulen* (Inspector General of the Police Schools), *Generalleutnant der Polizei* von PFEFFER-WILDENBRUCH, was appointed chief of the *Kolonialpolizeiamt*, and held this position until the middle of 1944.

A *Kolonialpolizeischule* (Colonial Police School) was established at Oranienburg near Berlin. Since intimate cooperation with the Nazi Party was regarded as essential, the *SS-Kolonialpolitische Schulungshaus* (SS Colonial Political Institute) at Ladenburg near Berlin, as well as the *Führerschule der Sicherheitspolizei* (Officers' School of the Security Police) in Berlin-Charlottenburg furnished a considerable part of the training of the Colonial Police.

In addition to the courses given in Germany, specially selected SS and police officers were sent to the Italian Colonial Police College at Tivoli, near Rome, for special training.

Personnel of the police selected for any of the colonial training courses were returned to their units or stations after completion of their schooling, but were hopefully earmarked for colonial service at some future date. A small number of them are reported to have made their appearance in North Africa in 1942 and 1943. It can, therefore, be said that the Colonial Police has never been much more than a name.

Just how far the Nazis progressed in their plans for future colonial splendour is immaterial, but, at any rate, the very existence of the *Kolonialpolizei* is indicative of the thoroughness of Germany's preparations for, and former confidence in the outcome of the war and the attainment of her colonial aspirations. It may, therefore, be added with some satisfaction that by now the *Kolonialpolizeiamt* and its staff have probably for the most part been disbanded. If it is still lingering on in any form at all, it is certainly on a most insignificant scale and with no great prospects for the future.

### (e) WASSERSCHUTZPOLIZEI

### 57. The Wasserschutzpolizei : General

The Regular Uniformed Police includes among

its duties the control of inland waterways and harbour traffic.

Following an agreement of 21st January, 1937, between the RFSS u Ch d Dt Pol and the *Reichsverkehrsministerium* (Ministry of Transport), HIMMLER took over on 1st March, 1937, the responsibilities of the existing *Schiffahrtspolizei* (Water Traffic Police) and *Hafenpolizei* (Harbour Police), whose tasks were henceforth to be discharged by a branch of the Regular Uniformed Police, i.e. the *Wasserschutzpolizei* (Waterways Protection Police).

Subsequently a decree of 26th July, 1937, declared the Waterways Protection Police to be a " special service branch of the *Schutzpolizei*, with the official abbreviation " SW." It is not quite clear why the abbreviation " SW " was used instead of " WS." The most plausible explanation is that the *Wasserschupo* is—unlike the *Feuerschupo*—considered an integral part of the *Schupo* and may originally have been known as *Schutzpolizei (Wasser)*. In connection with ranks the abbreviation " WSchP " is often used, e.g. in " *Hauptmann d. WSchP.*"

From the point of view of the invading Allied forces, the SW, patrolling the rivers and canals of Germany, may well be regarded as a military formation.

The SW is part of HIMMLER's widespread system and must, therefore, also be reckoned with as a potentially troublesome source of disaffection in territory under Allied control, representing as it does an effective instrument available to the Nazis; its posts and vessels on German waterways could easily become vantage points and escape channels for a future underground movement.

## 58. Organisation of the Wasserschutzpolizei

The principal task of the SW is to maintain law and order on waterways, in harbours and in harbour approaches. Its units are at the disposal of the local authorities, who may at all times call upon them for technical assistance. They may also act in certain circumstances on behalf of the *Sipo* (Security Police).

The *Wasserschutzpolizei* is organised into the following units :—

| | |
|---|---|
| *Gruppenkommandos* | Group Commands. |
| *Kommandos* ... | Commands. |
| *Abschnitte* ... | Sectors. |
| *Reviere* ... | Brit.—Wards : U.S.—Precincts. |
| *Revier-Zweigstellen* | Revier Branches. |
| *Stationen* ... | Stations. |
| *Wachen* ... | Squads. |
| *Fliegende Wachen* | Patrols. |
| *Posten* ... | Posts. |

These units are located wherever their duties require and in a strength commensurate with the size and importance of their areas. Their organisation is highly flexible : not all levels necessarily exist in each area, and there is little regularity. A *Kommando* may not include any *Abschnitte*, but may instead have only a number of independent *Reviere* and *Stationen*, some of them not further subdivided, others consisting of two, three or more *Wachen* or *Posten*, etc.

*Wasserschutzpolizei Kommandos* were also established in occupied territories for patrol duty in ports and on inland waterways.

Higher administrative authorities such as *Oberpräsidenten* of the Prussian Provinces, *Innenminister* of the *Länder*, BdO of the *Wehrkreise* or the Headquarters of the *Staatliche Polizeiver-*

*waltungen* (National Police Administration Headquarters) are responsible for the Police on the rivers and waterways in or nearest their area. Such offices include a special section, *Abteilung Wasserschutzpolizei*, as part of the Headquarters of the Staff Officer or Commander, as the case may be, of the *Schutzpolizei*, who controls the *Wasserschutzpolizei* administratively through this section. In special emergencies he may assume direct command.

The highest supervisory authority rests since 15th September, 1943, with the *Inspekteur der Wasserschutzpolizei* (Inspector of the Waterways Protection Police). *SS-BF, Genmaj. d. Pol.* KRUMHAAR held this position until 1st July, 1944, when he was succeeded by *Oberst d. Schupo* Ernst SCHRÖTER. Simultaneously the office was moved from Kiel to Berlin N.W.7, Unter den Linden 74.

For their actual police duties, these units are subordinated to the local authorities, and perform police functions within their field at the request of those authorities. They will, for instance, exercise revenue control at the order of the regional Finance and Customs office by boarding ships and barges and searching for contraband and black market goods, or they will instruct their patrols to check unauthorised fishing at the request of the local Fishery and Game Police.

The *Wasserschutzpolizei* operates in patrols of varying types. Alongside the waterways, foot and bicycle patrols are used wherever they are deemed sufficient, but, when needed, motor vehicles are also available.

On the waterways the *Wasserschutzpolizei* employs boats of all types, but mostly small *Hafenboote* (patrol craft). Larger SW units have *Streckenboote* (long-range boats) at their disposal, most of which are capable of performing coastal and even sea patrols.

The submerged part of the hulls of these craft is painted black or red, their waterline is marked in white and the upper hull is painted grey.

All boats fly the *Reichsdienstflagge* (official Reich Government Service flag), and have the designation of their home station painted on the stern and the word " *Wasserschutzpolizei* " together with an arabic numeral painted on the bows. This numeral is the serial number of the craft as registered with the particular *Staatliche Polizeiverwaltung* regardless of the vessels' Station or *Revier*. In addition, each boat carries on its bow another number, assigned to it by the Ministry of the Interior.

The personnel of the SW units is made up of Police NCOs (*Oberwachtmeister, Revieroberwachtmeister, Hauptwachtmeister* and *Meister*) and Police Officers (*Revier-Leutnant, Oberleutnant, Hauptmann, Major* and *Oberstleutnant*). Two administrative officers (*Pol. Inspektor* and *Pol. Assistent*) are usually included in the personnel of an *SW Kommando*.

Large Headquarters like Stettin or Bremen have a Major as their highest ranking officer, and only *SW Gruppe* Hamburg is commanded by an *Oberstleutnant* (Lt.-Col.). It is, however, possible that in wartime SW ranks have been raised beyond the limits of the peace-time establishments (U.S.—T/O).

## 59. Related and Auxiliary Units

Close cooperation exists between the *Wasserschutzpolizei* and the *Marine-Küstenpolizei* (Naval Coastal Police, abbr. MKP). The personnel of the MKP may be drawn from the Waterways Protection Police and an agreement to this effect was reached on 26th April, 1940, between the OKM (High Command of the Navy) and the *RFSS u Ch d Dt Pol*, in which the terms of employment of officers and men of the *Wasserschutzpolizei* as *Marine-Küstenpolizei* are laid down.

Before D-Day, units of MKP operating motorboat patrols were stationed at points along the entire coast line of occupied Europe from northern Norway to the Bay of Biscay.

Their duties include the inspection of all fishing vessels, the control of small craft movement and of sailing permits and the pursuit of smugglers, deserters and fugitives. MKP units are under the orders of *Küsten- und Hafenüberwachungsstellen* (Coastal and Port Authorities).

Members of the SW serving in the MKP are temporarily classed as naval personnel and are subect to naval regulations. The MKP has regular *Marinesoldaten* (naval soldiers or marines), who in most cases are under the supervision of SW personnel entrusted with these duties because of their special police experience.

The ranks of the MKP are *Wehrmacht* terms with the words " *der MKP* " added (e.g. " *Maat, Feldwebel der MKP* "). The MKP is commanded by its own officers and its employment is directed by the naval commander of the area in which it operates.

The NSKK has established *NSKK-Motorbooteinheiten* (Motorboat Units) which operate on Germany's main rivers, waterways and lakes, e.g. the Danube and the Rhine. They function as auxiliaries to the *Wasserschutzpolizei*, assisting in the control of traffic and maintenance of a permanent patrol service. Some of these NSKK units are of regimental size (*Motorbootstandarten* 1, 3, and 4 have been identified), but most of them are *Motorbootstürme* (Companies).

In larger ports the *Wasserschutzpolizei* is also reinforced by special units of the *Allgemeine-SS* who are at the disposal of the Chiefs of the Coastal *SS-Oberabschnitte NORDWEST, NORDSEE, OSTSEE* and *NORDOST*. These units are known as *SS-Hafensicherungstruppen* (Port Security Troops). They patrol the waterfronts and major ports in cooperation with Police authorities and the *Sicherheitsdienst*, especially during and after air raids.

## (f) FEUERSCHUTZPOLIZEI

### 60. Organisation of the Feuerschutzpolizei

Before 1933 fire protection and fire fighting in Germany were the concern of two organisations. Larger cities had professional Fire Brigades, whose members were municipal civil servants ; smaller towns and villages maintained voluntary fire brigades. At no time was fire fighting considered a Police function.

The Nazis, soon after their advent to power, changed this concept by subordinating the existing fire brigades to the *Ortspolizeibehörden* (Local Police Authorities). Later on, the administration of fire brigades was also subordinated to the *Höhere Polizeibehörden*, and, since the latter are directly under the Reich Government, control was completely centralised.

Shortly after the outbreak of war, on 27th September, 1939, a *Feuerschutzpolizei* (Fire Protection Police, abbr. FP) was created by the Reich Government in agreement with the Chiefs of the Army and Air Force (BRAUCHITSCH and GÖRING). All larger German cities were ordered to organise Fire Protection Police forma-

tions and to transfer their former Fire Brigades into the new organisation.

Some German towns, however, which had professional fire fighting services, were not called upon to form units of the *Feuerschutzpolizei*. In such instances the old Fire Fighting Brigades continued to exist.

The members of the new *Feuerschutzpolizei* were termed *Polizeivollzugsbeamte* (police executive officials), just as are the members of the *Schupo*, and were made subject to all laws and regulations governing the officials of all other branches of the Reich Police.

The controlling bureau of the FP and its organisational apex is the *Amt Feuerschutzpolizei* of *Amtsgruppe I* in the *Kommandoamt* of the *Hauptamt Ordnungspolizei* (see para. 27).

All units of the FP in the entire Reich are supervised by the *General-Inspekteur der Feuerschutzpolizei und Feuerwehren* (Inspector General of the Fire Protection Police and Fire Brigades) who reports directly to the Chief of the *Orpo* on the state of training of personnel and on technical details of equipment. He also makes recommendations and submits observations on new methods and developments of fire fighting to the Chief of the *Orpo* (WÜNNENBERG).

Regionally the FP, like all other branches of the *Orpo*, is controlled by the *Befehlshaber der Orpo* of each *Wehrkreis* to whose staff is attached a *Stabsoffizier* (Staff Officer) of the *Feuerschutzpolizei* serving as specialist and technical adviser.

Locally the *Feuerschutzpolizei* is administered by the (*Ober-*) *Bürgermeister* of the town, but it is known that in towns with a *Staatliche Polizeiverwaltung* a considerable amount of the administration rests with the *Polizeipräsidien, -direktionen* and *-ämter*. In any case, all expenses of the *Feuerschutzpolizei*, including those for the purchase and maintenance of equipment, are borne by the community. Personnel matters are handled directly by the Reich Ministry of the Interior, i.e. the *Kommandoamt* in the *Hauptamt Orpo*, and in certain instances by the Higher Police Authorities, but never by the Mayors of the towns where *Feuerschupo* units are stationed.

The decision whether a town has to form a *Feuerschutzpolizei* unit does not only depend on the number of inhabitants, but on certain characteristics and conditions of the locality such as the type and volume of a town's industrial activity, its buildings and constructions, its potential exposure to air raids, etc.

The local chief of the FP is the *Kommandeur der Feuerschutzpolizei*, who is responsible for the organisation and the operation of the entire unit stationed in the municipality. He allots operational areas to the various subsections of his unit, and issues orders concerning fire prevention. At least in the larger towns the *Kommandeur der Feuerschutzpolizei* is tactically subordinate to the *Kommandeur der Schupo*.

Subsections of the local *Feuerschutzpolizei* are called *Abschnittskommandos* (District Commands) and *Feuerwachen* (Fire-fighting Detachments). In Berlin, Hamburg and Vienna, several *Abschnittskommandos* form a *Gruppenkommando*.

The smallest unit called out by a regular alarm is known as a *Feuerlöschzug* (fire-fighting platoon). It consists of two to three trucks carrying about ten to twelve men. There are normally several *Züge* allotted to each *Feuerwache*.

One *Feuerwache*, as a rule, covers an area of several *Polizei-Reviere* (Police Wards or Precincts), but wide variations exist, depending on the constructional characteristics and the layout of the town and immediate vicinity.

The FP has its own teleprinter and alarm systems.

A list of the towns in which units of the FP are known to exist is given in Annexe D.

### 61. Military Aspects of the FP

In addition to their normal functions, it is the duty of officials of the *Feuerschutzpolizei* to take action and exercise full police powers in matters outside their specific technical sphere, whenever officials of the *Schupo* or *Gendarmerie* cannot be reached. In the light of this fact it is of greatest importance to keep in mind how thoroughly centralised and militarised the *Feuerschutzpolizei* has become under the Nazi regime. It would, therefore, be misleading to treat it as a parallel to organisations of equivalent functions in democratic countries or to forget that, just like every other branch of the German police, the FP must be regarded as an instrument of Nazi power.

The *Feuerschutzpolizei* has even been organised into larger units as field formations. There exist several *Feuerschutzpolizei-Abteilungen* (*mot*), i.e. motorised battalions, of which Nos. 3 to 7 have been identified. There are also various *Feuerschutzpolizei-Regimenter*; those identified are given in Annexe E.

These units are fire-fighting shock troops. The *Feuerschutzpolizei-Regiment SACHSEN*, for instance, operated in France and at Rotterdam with advance units of the *Wehrmacht* in order to prevent any possible " scorched earth " policy by the retreating Allied Forces. Towards the end of 1941, when an advance into the Caucasus by the German Army seemed imminent, the *Regiment SACHSEN* was again held in readiness to save the Russian oil wells for the Reich war effort.

Units of this regiment were also stationed at Ploesti in Rumania, when the oilfields were bombed in 1944 by the American Air Forces.

# III

## Technical Auxiliary Branches

### 62. Status of the Technische Hilfspolizeien

So far the various ordinary branches of the Regular Uniformed Police have been discussed. As previously noted, however, these are augmented in many instances by the *Technische Hilfspolizeien* (Technical Auxiliary Police Services), who, for the most part have been created as a direct result of the war and are an integral part of the *Orpo*.

While even the regular police had to find some replacements for its personnel of younger age classes among the *Polizeireserve*, the *Technische Hilfspolizeien* had to resort almost exclusively to the employment of *Polizeireservisten*.

Thus, personnel of the *Technische Hilfspolizeien* are not necessarily professional members of the police. They have, however, in many instances, become full-time police personnel for the duration of the war. Thereafter most of them will return to their civilian occupations, although it may be expected that some will try to transfer to the active ranks of their branch of the Police.

It should be especially noted that members of the *Feuerwehren* (see below) are in many instances not full-time members of the Police, but are merely called away from their civilian occupations for duty whenever the need for their services arises. Their status, therefore, very closely resembles that of the ordinary *Hilfspolizeien* (Auxiliary Police) which will be discussed in greater detail in para. 77; but they are nevertheless officially termed *Technische Hilfspolizeien*.

The *Technische Hilfspolizeien* include the *Feuerwehren* (Fire Brigades), the *Luftschutzpolizei* (ARP Police), and the *Technische Nothilfe* (Technical Emergency Corps). These organisations are discussed in detail below under (g), (h) and (j) respectively.

### (g) FEUERWEHREN

### 63. Organisation of the Feuerwehren

As noted in para. 60 above, in September, 1939 most of the former *Berufsfeuerwehren* (Professional Fire Brigades) were incorporated as units into the newly-created *Feuerschutzpolizei*. In all communities where no units of the FP were established the *Berufsfeuerwehren* were transferred into the already existing or newly formed *Freiwillige Feuerwehren* (Voluntary Fire Brigades).

While many of the municipal *Feuerwehren* were thus absorbed by the *Feuerschutzpolizei*, it was deemed preferable in some localities to retain the well-established and smoothly functioning *Feuerwehren*, partly in place of, partly as an auxiliary to the *Feuerschutzpolizei*.

It would, of course, be erroneous to assume that such *Feuerwehren* as continued to exist, retained their former independence. Like every other organisation in Nazi Germany, they too were completely coordinated, centralised and militarised throughout the Reich. Accordingly they are now classified as *Technische Hilfspolizei*, and have therefore become directly subordinated to the *Ordnungspolizei*.

Four categories of this organisation must be distinguished :

(1) *Freiwillige Feuerwehren* (Voluntary Fire Brigades).
(2) *Pflichtfeuerwehren* (Compulsory Fire Brigades).
(3) *Werkfeuerwehren* (Factory Fire Brigades).
(4) *HJ-Feuerwehrscharen* (Fire-fighting platoons of the Hitler Youth).

Any community or municipality which was not compelled by decree of the Reich Minister of the Interior to establish a unit of the *Feuerschutzpolizei* is instead required to form a fire brigade which must be trained and equipped to combat fires and meet other emergencies caused by fire in its area.

As a rule, such units were, and frequently still are, formed on a voluntary basis. In places where voluntary enlistment does not suffice, the authorities (*Bürgermeister* or *Landrat*) may establish a *Pflichtfeuerwehr* by drafting personnel for service in the fire brigade.

Wartime manpower shortage especially went far in depleting the ranks of the voluntary fire brigades, and the authorities had to resort more and more to the employment of *Pflichtfeuerwehren* to fill the gaps.

In areas comprising mainly small villages where the formation of individual fire brigades would constitute a distinct hardship and waste of manpower, the *Kreis* authorities (*Landrat*) may organise one fire brigade for several villages or for an entire *Landkreis*. Organisations of this kind are known as *Feuerschutzverbände* (Fire Protection Groups) and do not in principle differ from regular *Freiwillige* or *Pflichtfeuerwehren*.

Even though a unit of the *Feuerschutzpolizei* may already exist in a town, the *Ortspolizeibehörde* (Local Police Authority, e.g. the Mayor) may decide that it is inadequate to meet all contingencies, and may therefore supplement the

*Feuerschutzpolizei* by a *Freiwillige* or *Pflicht-feuerwehr* or both. While such auxiliary fire brigades retain administrative independence, they are for all tactical purposes operationally attached to the *Feuerschutzpolizei*, and for training and employment subordinated to the direction of the local commander of the *Feuerschutzpolizei*.

Recruits for both the *Freiwillige* and *Pflicht-feuerwehren* must, in addition to the required minimum physical qualifications, be known to be " at the disposal of the National Socialist State at all times and without reservations." They may not be drawn from the personnel of either the *Technische Nothilfe* (Technical Emergency Corps), the Red Cross, or a *Werkfeuerwehr* (see below). Except for these limitations, all Germans between the ages of 17 and 65 are eligible for the *Freiwillige* and *Pflichtfeuerwehren*.

At the age of 60 members of the *Pflichtfeuerwehr* are placed in the Reserve where they remain informed of all matters pertaining to fire-fighting and fire protection so that they can be recalled in the event of an emergency.

### 64. Command of the Feuerwehren

Individual units of both *Freiwillige* and *Pflichtfeuerwehren* are headed by a *Wehrführer* (contingent leader) who is appointed by the *Ortspolizeibehörde*.

Each *Kreis* has a *Kreisführer* and below him several *Unterkreisführer* of the *Freiwillige Feuerwehr*. On the level of the *Regierungsbezirk* there is a *Bezirksführer* (District Commander) and on the staff of a BdO in each *Wehrkreis* an *Abschnitts-inspekteur der Freiwilligen Feuerwehr* (Regional Inspector of the Voluntary Fire Brigades).

*Bezirksführer* are appointed by the Higher Administrative Authorities (e.g. *Reg. Präs.*) with the consent of the *Reichsführer-SS und Chef der Deutschen Polizei* (HIMMLER). They supervise and command the activities of all voluntary fire brigades within their respective districts, co-ordinate their activities and issue general directives concerning training and employment.

In the case of the *Pflichtfeuerwehren* the functions, appointments, and offices of the *Kreisführer*, *Bezirksführer*,˙ and the *Abschnittsinspekteur* are non-existent. On those levels (*Kreis*, *Regierungs-bezirk*, and *Wehrkreis*) all compulsory fire brigades are tactical units of the *Feuerschutzpolizei*, attached and subordinated to the latter.

The highest supervisor for the entire Reich is the *General-Inspekteur der Feuerschutzpolizei und Feuerwehren* (Inspector General of the Fire Protection Police and Fire Brigades) already mentioned in paras. 28 and 60. His office is also referred to as that of the *Inspekteur für das Feuer-löschwesen für Stadt und Land* (Inspector of all Urban and Rural Fire-fighting Forces).

The highest Headquarters of all fire-fighting brigades in Germany is the *Amt Feuerwehren* (Bureau of Fire Brigades), which is *Amt V* in the *Hauptamt Orpo*. This bureau does not, however, control the *Feuerschutzpolizei*, whose highest Headquarters is in the *Kommandoamt* of the *Hauptamt Orpo* (see paras. 27 and 60).

It should be noted that before the incorporation of the *Feuerwehren* into the *Orpo* the bureau responsible for them as their highest Headquarters was known as the *Reichsamt Freiwillige Feuer-wehren* (National Bureau of Voluntary Fire Brigades).

### 65. Werkfeuerwehren and HJ-Feuerwehrscharen

In wartime, with increased fire hazards due to air raids, *Werkfeuerwehren* (Factory Fire Brigades) have rapidly gained in importance. To all intents and purposes, they resemble the *Frei-willige* or *Pflichtfeuerwehren* : just as the latter are organised by a village or rural sub-district (*Kreis*), the *Werkfeuerwehren* are established by the management of industrial factories, etc., and are staffed by their employees.

The decision as to the formation of *Werkfeuer-wehren*, however, is not left with the individual management of a factory. Instead, the Higher Administrative Authorities (e.g. the *Reg. Präs.*) in conjunction with the Reich Ministry of the Interior and the *Luftschutzdienststelle* (local ARP Headquarters) in the *Reichsgruppe Industrie* (National League of Industry, an obligatory association of all industries) determines where *Werkfeuerwehren* are to be established. In addition, a factory desiring to organise a *Werkfeuerwehr* may seek the approval of the above mentioned authorities by filing a request through the local ARP unit, also notifying the *Ortspolizeibehörde* or *Staatliche Polizeiverwaltung*.

Each unit of the *Werkfeuerwehr* must consist of at least 18 members and must be equipped with a minimum of one power-driven pump.

These organisations exist in manufacturing concerns such as munitions factories and synthetic oil plants. They are much the same as the ARP units which similar undertakings in England have organised for the protection of their property.

To counter the manpower shortage within the ranks of the *Feuerschutzpolizei* and *Feuerwehren* at a time of increased wartime fire hazards, the *Hitler Jugend* (Hitler Youth Organisation) founded the so-called *HJ-Feuerwehrscharen* (HJ Fire Fighting Platoons). Normally, they are organised as components of a *HJ-Bann* (Regiment), a local unit of the HJ.

A *HJ-Feuerwehrschar* consists of approximately 50 youths and is divided into 3 *Kameradschaften* (Squads).

The *Feuerwehrscharen* are equipped and trained by the local *Feuerschutzpolizei*, *Pflichtfeuerwehr* or *Freiwillige Feuerwehr*, as the case may be. They then operate under the direct command of the local chief of the respective organisation.

Larger localities may have more than one *Feuerwehrschar*, according to particular local needs. In other towns where no *Feuerwehrscharen* have been formed, the local HJ Headquarters may detail boys from the HJ-SRD (*Streifendienst*) for fire-fighting duty. For further information on the SRD as a police auxiliary force, see para. 48.

### 66. Maintenance of Fire Services

All expenses of the Fire Protection Services, whether it be the *Feuerschutzpolizei*, the *Frei-willige* or *Pflichtfeuerwehren*, or the *HJ-Feuer-wehrscharen*, are met entirely by the local community. In the case of *Werkfeuerwehren*, the factories which organise them share some of the burden with the community.

Only for the maintenance of the *Feuerwehr-schulen* (Fire Brigade Schools) of the *Länder* and *Provinzen* does the Reich Government contribute half of the expenses, the remaining half being covered by the *Länder* and *Provinzen*. An exception to this financial arrangement is one *Reichsfeuerwehrschule* in Eberswalde ; this school is fully under the control of the national Government and its expenses are paid entirely by the Reich.

For purely technical matters the fire fighting organisations rely on the specialised knowledge of an association of technicians known as the *Reichsverein Deutscher Feuerwehringenieure* (*RDF-*

National League of German Fire Protection Engineers).

## (h) LUFTSCHUTZPOLIZEI

### 67. Original Air Defence Measures : the RLB

Before the outbreak of war, preparations for air raid protection in Germany were controlled by the *Reichsluftschutzbund* (*RLB*—Reich Association for Air Raid Protection). This organisation had the character of a private institution but was, of course, sponsored and supported by the Nazi Party, the Reich Government, the Military and, in particular, the Air Force.

After the Polish campaign, the organisation obtained a semi-official status when the authorities of the general administration as well as those of the police were directed to co-operate closely with the RLB.

A year later the RLB was completely taken over by the *Reichsminister der Luftfahrt und Oberbefehlshaber der Luftwaffe* (*RM d L u Ob d L*—Reich Minister for Aviation and C-in-C of the GAF) GÖRING, who is in supreme command of all active air defences, such as A.A. and barrage balloons.

The President of the RLB was then officially appointed *Inspekteur des Selbstschutzes im Reichsministerium der Luftfahrt* (Inspector of Civilian Passive Air Defence in the Reich Air Ministry). Similarly in the *Luftgaue* (Administrative Districts of the GAF) *RLB Gruppenführer* were appointed to cooperate with the regional Command Headquarters of the Army, the Air Force, and the Police.

The organisation attained the character of a *Hilfspolizei* (Auxiliary Police), when the police were ordered to delegate official authority to the RLB members as regards the inspection of buildings, black-out, erection of air raid shelters and " *Entrümpelung* " (i.e. removal of inflammable scrap material from buildings, a compulsory precaution against fire).

Work in the RLB is largely unpaid and part-time. It is divided into *Gruppen* (Groups), *Untergruppen* (Sub-groups), *Ortsgruppen* (Local Units) and *Reviere* (Wards).

### 68. Institution of the Luftschutzpolizei

Up to that time the *Sicherheits- und Hilfsdienst* (*SHD*—Security and Assistance Service) formed the professional nucleus of all defensive ARP services and as such was responsible for the execution of all major tasks arising in emergencies caused by air raids. It consisted of full-time members with the status of auxiliary policemen.

After the first 1,000 bomber raid by the RAF on Cologne, on 30th May, 1942, the SHD proved completely incapable of coping with any such major emergency. It was at that time that the *Luftschutzpolizei* (Air Raid Protection Police) was instituted and placed under the direct command of HIMMLER. Thus it became a branch of the *Ordnungspolizei* in general and a *Technische Hilfspolizei* (Technical Auxiliary Police) in particular.

The newly created organisation became the professional air raid protection service, responsible for rescue and repair work, demolition, decontamination, and a large share of the fire-fighting. The nature of its work necessitated, of course, very close co-operation with the *Feuerschutzpolizei* and the *Technische Nothilfe*. As a result of these developments two distinct types of ARP service must now be recognised. One is the full-time service of the *Luftschutzpolizei* ; the other is the part-time service of various auxiliary organisations (discussed in the next paragraph) as well as the network of house and block wardens.

In the main the *Luftschutzpolizei* has taken over all the functions and personnel of the SHD, reinforcing them with the personnel of the *Technische Nothilfe*. It therefore includes the following full time services, formerly branches of the SHD or TN :—

*Feuer- und Entgiftungsdienst* (Fire-fighting and decontamination service)—abbreviated *F.u.E.-Dienst*. This service in particular is still frequently referred to by the obsolete term " SHD," the service from which it has developed. Personnel is trained mainly by the *Feuerschutzpolizei*.

*Instandsetzungsdienst* (Repair, demolition and rescue services)—abbreviated *J-Dienst*.

This service includes emergency engineering as well as bomb-disposal work. It was originally furnished by the *Technische Nothilfe* and has been derived from the *Luftschutzdienst* of that organisation (See para. 74).

*Luftschutzsanitätsdienst* (Medical and First Aid Service)—abbreviated *San-Dienst*.

*Luftschutzveterinärdienst* (Veterinary First Aid Service).

*Fachtrupps* (Specialised technical squads).

These units are charged with the repair of damaged gas and water mains, electrical installations, sewers, drains, and smaller water ducts ; they have developed out of the *Bereitschaftsdienst* of the TN (See para. 74).

It must be noted that the *Luftschutzpolizei* in its capacity as a *Technische Hilfspolizei* has been created as a technically specialised supplement to the regular police. Its personnel is therefore not entitled to take independent action.

Thus, in the event of air raids, the Regular Police takes full charge of all ARP operations and directly determines the employment and commands the forces of the *Luftschutzpolizei*. Through the latter, it controls all the various auxiliary ARP services. At no time does the *Luftschutzpolizei* assume the independent power of arrest ; however, co-operation with the regular police is so close that no problem arises out of this lack of authority.

As a consequence of this auxiliary character of the *Luftschutzpolizei*, its members are not subject to the jurisdiction of the *SS- und Polizei-Gerichte* (SS and Police Tribunals) unless they are simultaneously members of the Regular Police or any branch thereof.

Most men of the *Luftschutzpolizei* are recruited from the *Polizeireserve* and are, therefore, not professional police personnel. On 1st June, 1942, when the SHD was incorporated into the *Luftschutzpolizei*, its entire personnel, not previously holding any police status, was bodily transferred into the *Polizeireserve*.

Officers of the *Luftschutzpolizei* are trained at the *Polizeiakademie für Luftschutzführung* (Police Academy for ARP Tactics) at Oranienburg, formerly known as the *Polizeischule für Luftschutzführer* at Berlin-Schöneberg.

As a result of an increasing manpower shortage, women are now being employed to replace men in the *Luftschutzpolizei*. Directives have lately been issued to accelerate this process in order to free as many men as possible for active field service.

As the air war intensified, mobile ARP field

units were formed, which could be quickly transported from one place to another, wherever they were needed. Originally they were known as *SHD Abteilungen (mot)*, but are now called *LS Abteilungen (mot)*. Approximately 50 such battalions have been identified. Some of them have even appeared behind the front in Russia and at Ploesti in Rumania, where they were employed to save strategic targets from destruction.

### 69. Auxiliary ARP formations

The *Luftschutzpolizei* is assisted in its functions by various auxiliary ARP organisations such as :—
*Werkluftschutzdienst* (Factory ARP Services).
*Werkschutzpolizei* (Factory Protection Police).
*Selbstschutz* (Self-Protection Service).
*Erweiterter Selbstschutz* (Extended Self-Protection Service).
*Luftschutzwarndienst* (ARP Warning Service).

The **Werkluftschutzdienst** is organised in all larger and war-essential plants by the *Reichsgruppe Industrie* (National League of Industry—an obligatory association of all industries) according to instructions from the *Reichsluftfahrtministerium*. It is formed and supervised by the management of each factory and staffed by the workers and employees.

The **Werkschutzpolizei** is found in most of those factories which have also organised a *Werkluftschutzdienst*. It is organised to provide for " maximum " protection of industrial plants and workers. Employees are conscripted for this service and are registered with the *Luftschutzpolizei* which is operationally in charge of the organisation.

While the *Werkschutzpolizei* was originally created, not for ARP purposes, but for the protection of factories and workers in general, e.g. against sabotage and theft, it does now take an active part in ARP work. The organisation—or at any rate its key personnel—is believed to be identical with the *SS-Werkspolizei* (SS Industrial Police), the officers being under the command of the *Führer* of the *SS-Oberabschnitt* in which they function.

At this point it should also be noted that the *Werkfeuerwehren* (Factory Fire Brigades), discussed in para. 65, cooperate tactically with the *Werkluftschutzdienst* and the *Werkschutzpolizei*.

The **Selbstschutz** might well be termed the basis for all civilian ARP activities. It includes air-raid wardens, block · wardens, roof spotters, and all other essential civilian ARP workers, not unlike those in Allied ARP organisations but more thoroughly militarised, as might be expected in Nazi Germany.

The **Erweiterter Selbstschutz** is organised in all official buildings, hotels, restaurants, department stores, theatres, and other public and semi-public buildings where large crowds congregate. As in the case of the *Selbstschutz* its members are conscripted from among the employees of the buildings concerned.

The function of the **Luftschutzwarndienst** is to observe approaching enemy planes and to place the threatened population on the alert—along similar lines to the Observer Corps in the U.K. Increased Allied air attacks, however, have caused this organisation to become largely obsolete. Most of · its former functions are now performed by specialised German Air Force personnel with the remnants of the civilian *Luftschutzwarndienst*, including women and juveniles, merely assisting and supplementing the technically trained and specially equipped Air Force personnel.

*Werkluftschutz, Selbstschutz, Erweiterter Selbstschutz* and *Luftschutzwarndienst* are also referred to as the services of the *Luftschutzbereitschaftsdienst* (Air Protection Emergency Service). Service in these organisations is compulsory, but on a part-time basis and unpaid except for certain small reimbursements covering meals and expenses. Today many *Ost-Arbeiter* (foreign workers, including PW from the Eastern occupied territories) are pressed into service in these auxiliary ARP organisations. Some of the *Schutzmannschaftsbataillone* (para. 40) have also been identified performing ARP duties and guard duties after air raids in Germany.

All civilian auxiliary ARP services discussed above are supervised and trained by the RLB. That organisation, still advisory agency for all civilian ARP services, is itself now supervised by the *Luftschutzpolizei*, so that the entire system of German ARP services is effectively centralised and co-ordinated, while at the same time reaching down into the smallest sector of the community. It is under complete control of the Regular Police whose technically specialised agency for ARP work is the *Luftschutzpolizei*.

It has previously been pointed out that the *Luftschutzpolizei* and its auxiliaries do not possess regular police powers : the complete control of all these services by the *Orpo*, however, makes this efficiently militarised organisation a useful and constantly available tool of the German police.

Lately the term *Luftschutzpolizei* has to some extent come to be an all-inclusive designation of all Police and auxiliary police forces whenever these are employed during and after air raids. Thus the *Schutzpolizei, Feuerschutzpolizei*, and *Technische Nothilfe* are all referred to as " *Luftschutzpolizei* " whenever they are functionally employed in that capacity.

The *Luftschutzpolizei* is assisted in the discharge of its duties by various volunteer Party formations, e.g. the *SA Katastrophen-Stürme* (Emergency Companies). These and similar units are specially trained under the SA command, but are not necessarily composed entirely of SA men, and serve less as police units than as ARP squads engaged in clearance of debris, traffic regulation and fire watching. The German press stresses the special training these units receive, and the important role they play in Allied air raids.

*SS Industrieschutzmannschaften* (Industrial Safety Crews) are described as cadres of SS Officers, who are in charge of employees of plants and serve as liaison officers with the various forces of the *Orpo* which are concerned with fire-fighting and air-raid precautions.

## (j) TECHNISCHE NOTHILFE

### 70. Scope of the Technische Nothilfe

The *Technische Nothilfe* (Technical Emergency Corps), often referred to as *Teno* and officially abbreviated TN, is a Technical Auxiliary Police formation of the *Ordnungspolizei* (Regular Police). It is a corps of engineers, technicians, and skilled and semi-skilled specialists in construction work, public utilities operation, communications, metal salvage, and other related fields. As engineer corps of the German Police the TN is to-day one of the principal agencies in combatting the effects of Allied air raids.

The TN has been called upon to remove mines, clear fields of fire, repair roads, restore communications, repair electrical installations, dismantle plants and boilers in factories, build bridges, demolish damaged buildings, as well as to perform many other tasks of demolition and restoration made necessary by natural catastrophes and the war.

The Armed Forces have made extensive use of the TN. Its field formations have been attached to the Army and Air Force ever since the annexation of Austria. As a rule TN Battalions, known as *Technische Bataillone* or *Abteilungen* are attached to an Army Group, sending *Technische Kommandos* (Technical Detachments) to lower formations. In Russia all *Technische Abteilungen* were controlled at the highest Headquarters by a *TN-Einsatzgruppe* (Group Command).

On occasions fully armed members of the TN have been assigned to defensive positions in the field and even been employed as reinforcements for depleted infantry units. TN field units have also been assigned to police formations in occupied territories to assist in the rebuilding of public utilities and other installations.

The depot for the TN field formations is the *Ersatz-Abteilung der Technischen Nothilfe* in Köln-Dünnwald.

*TN Abteilungen* are formed on a *Landesgruppe* basis, and are therefore designated each by the same Roman numeral as its parent *Landesgruppe*. Thus, *TN Abteilungen* I, III, IV, V, VI, VIII, IX, X and XIII have been identified.

A *TN Abteilung* generally consists of five companies, each again sub-divided into specialist sections such as :—

*Bautrupp* (Construction Section).

*Rohrtrupp* (Pipeline Section).

*Leitungstrupp* (Electrical Circuit Section).

*Wasserwerktrupp* (Waterworks Maintenance Section).

*Krantrupp* (Crane Section).

*Brücken- u. Schleusentrupp* (Bridges and Water Locks Section).

In army rear areas, TN units are allotted to the HSSPf who, as their commander, may employ them for tasks of a technical nature. Allied Armies now fighting on German soil will, therefore, even before the phase of occupation, encounter TN forces as part of the units under the command of HSSPf of Germany proper. In addition it should be borne in mind that a considerable proportion of the senior officers of the TN hold high ranks in the SS and German Police.

Thus the TN is to-day a problem both for Allied operational intelligence and for Allied occupation counter-intelligence.

### 71. History of the TN

The *Technische Nothilfe* was instituted in 1919 under the auspices of *Generaloberst* von SEECKT, the founder of the old *Reichswehr*. It was originally meant to be just what its name implies— a technical organisation to be used in emergencies.

During the first years of the Weimar Republic when violent political strikes, instigated by the extremist parties of the Right and Left, shook the life of the country, the TN kept public utilities and essential industries running. Thus, although its character was distinctly that of a strike-breaking organisation, it served the democratic parties then in power.

Between 1925 and 1930, during the period of pseudo-prosperity, the TN lost much of its importance, without ever ceasing to exist.

In 1930 the TN introduced a gas and air protection service and enlarged its *Bereitschaftsdienst* (Emergency Service Branch) into an organisation equipped to fight natural catastrophes.

This offspring of the *Bereitschaftsdienst* was called *Hilfspionierdienst* (Auxiliary Engineer Service).

When HITLER came to power, any strike-breaking organisation lost its raison d'etre. But rather than dissolve the TN, the Nazi Party decided to remodel it completely and use it as a tool for its own ends. It became a " *Machtmittel des Staates zur Beseitigung öffentlicher Notstände,*" i.e. a powerful tool of the Government to deal with public emergencies.

Thus, in 1934, the TN was converted into a fully-fledged Party formation. Its National Headquarters and apex was named the " *Reichsamt Technische Nothilfe* " (RATN—National Department of the TN).

In March, 1935 the Reich Minister of the Interior FRICK referred to the TN as a *Hilfsformation der Polizei* (Auxiliary Formation of the Police Force). The year 1936 saw the opening of the *TN Reichsschule* (TN National Academy) in Belzig, Mark Brandenburg, which was to train TN officers between the ages of 30 and 55 ; its head in 1943 was *Hauptbereitschaftsführer* HUGENDUBEL.

The year 1937 marks a big step towards the centralisation of the TN and its complete incorporation into the Police. It became a *ständiges technisches Hilfsorgan der Polizei* (permanent technical auxiliary corps of the Police). To its chief was given the title " *Chef der TN* " and the National Headquarters which he commanded was made part of the *Hauptamt Ordnungspolizei* and as such called " *Amt Technische Nothilfe* " (*Amt TN*—Department of the TN). The original designation *Reichsamt Technische Nothilfe*, however, is still officially used by the TN.

In March, 1939, members of the TN were given the right to carry sidearms and firearms. In June of the same year, the TN Law was made public. It laid down as basic function of the TN to render technical assistance in the following three fields :—

(a) Keeping essential public utilities operating under all circumstances.

(b) ARP work.

(c) Dealing with major emergencies.

This law also changed the organisation from a *Verein* (membership association) to a *Körperschaft des öffentlichen Rechtes* (a legal, registered, state-controlled corporation).

In 1941, WEINREICH, its C-in-C, became first *Generalmajor* and later *Generalleutnant der Polizei*.

In 1942, the TN was placed under the *SS-und Polizeigerichtsbarkeit* (SS and Police Jurisdiction and Disciplinary code).

### 72. Membership, Strength, and General Organisation

Members of the TN must, because of their functions as a *Technische Hilfspolizei*, be completely reliable from the Nazi point of view. They must be Germans or " racial " Germans and " must be able to prove that they are loyal to the National Socialist State." For example, no one who has been expelled from the Nazi Party can be accepted by the TN.

The majority of members of the TN (known as *Nothelfer*) are men over military age (45–70). They joined the organisation voluntarily, but can no longer withdraw at will. *Notdienstpflichtige* (persons required to serve in an emergency on the home front) can at any time be assigned to the TN.

Only the key positions in higher headquarters are filled by full-time TN officers. The ordinary

34

*Nothelfer* serves only in his TN capacity when called up in an emergency.

In addition a provision is made under which specialists, both within and outside the TN, may be appointed *Sonderführer* (specialist officers) for the execution of particularly responsible tasks. Such *TN Sonderführer* may be granted any TN rank for the duration of the war. This provision points clearly to the possibility of further infiltration into the TN of SS and Party men wishing to conceal their past activities.

The strength of the TN is difficult to estimate but will hardly exceed 200,000 men. The Germans reported that by 1939, 105,154 TN men had at one time or another been employed; and that in the first twenty months of the war 150,000 *Nothelfer* had worked at 7,500 places in the *Heimatgebiet* (Greater Germany).

Many TN members will have joined the Armed Forces, but on the other hand the organisation will undoubtedly have recruited new members compulsorily.

In occupied countries the Germans have created organisations similar to the German TN such as the " *Secours Technique* " in France, the " *Teknisk Nodhjelp* " in Norway, or the " *Technische Nodhulp* " in the Netherlands. In Eastern Europe and the Baltic, the population was pressed into emergency units known as " *Pioniermannschaften* ".

The *Technische Nothilfe* is organised from two different points of view. It has a regional organisation and chain of command leading from the National Headquarters to its *Landesgruppen, Bezirksgruppen*, and *Ortsgruppen*. This form of organisation may best be described as " vertical." According to its various functions and purposes, however, the TN is also sub-divided on all levels into *Dienste* (services), which is to say that it is organised in units trained and equipped to perform a specific technical task. This structure is best termed a " horizontal " one. In following paragraphs both forms of organisation are described.

### 73. Vertical Structure of the TN

At the top of the vertical structure of the TN comes its highest agency, the *Amt Technische Nothilfe* in the *Hauptamt Orpo*.

The *Amt TN* is located at Berlin-Steglitz, Birkbuschstrasse 18; Tel. 791101.

The *Chef der TN* (C-in-C of the TN) exercises his authority over the subordinated *Landesgruppen, Bezirksgruppen*, and *Ortsgruppen* through the *Amt TN*, which consists of his personal staff and several sections, as follows :—

#### Personal Staff of the C-in-C

| | |
|---|---|
| *Chef der TN* (C-in-C of the TN) | SS-GF, Genlt. d. Pol. SCHMELCHER (since end of 1943) |
| *Stellvertretender Chef der TN* (Deputy C-in-C of the TN) | Genlt. d. Pol. Th. SIEBERT (reported dead Sept., 1944). |
| *Chefadjutantur* (Chief Adjutant's office) | *Hauptbereitschaftsführer* Walter TROSCHKE |
| *Persönlicher Adjutant* (Personal Adjutant) | *Gemeinschaftsführer* PROBST |
| *Pressestelle* (Press Office) | *Hauptbereitschaftsführer* FISCHER |
| *Bild-und Filmstelle* (Pictures and Film Office) | *Hauptbereitschaftsführer* Dr. KRÖNCKE |
| *Inspekteur* 1 (Inspector 1) | *Landesführer* FORNONI |
| *Inspekteur* 2 (Inspector 2) | *Landesführer* Dr. RÖTHENMEIER |

*Note.*—On 17th January, 1943, *Landesführer* JÖNECKE, founder and chief of LG Donau, was appointed *Chef des Stabes* (C of S) *Amt* TN, a post not previously accounted for in the Headquarters structure.

### Amt I
#### Chefamt (Bureau of the C-in-C)

| | |
|---|---|
| Chief of Bureau | *Genlt. d. Pol. Th.* SIEBERT |
| *TN Feldeinsatzführer* (Commander of TN Employment in the Field), also known as *General Insp. für den auswärtigen Einsatz* (General Inspector for Employment Abroad) | *Landesführer* Dr. ETMER |
| *Allgemeine Chefangelegenheiten* (General Affairs of the Chefamt) | *Hauptbereitschaftsführer* Dr. KRÖNCKE |
| *Gruppe A : Einsatz, Organisation* | (Employment and Organisation Branch) |
| *Gruppe B : Ausrüstung* | (Equipment Branch) |
| *Gruppe C: Aufklärung, Weltanschauliche Erziehung, Kräftenachschub-Erfassung, Erhaltung.* | (Branch for Enlightenment, Indoctrination, Replacements and Maintenance of Establishment) |
| *Gruppe D : Ausbildung* | (Training Branch) |

### Amt II/III
#### Personal- und Rechtsamt (Personnel and Legal Bureau)

| | |
|---|---|
| Chief of Bureau | *Bezirksführer* MALICKE |
| *Gruppe II : Personalien* | (Personal Records Branch) |
| *Gruppe III: Rechts- und Versicherungsangelegenheiten* | (Legal and Insurance Matters Branch) |
| *Führerverwaltung* (Officers Administration) | *Hauptbereitschaftsführer* Walter TROSCHKE |

### Amt IV
#### Haushalts- und Verwaltungsamt (Budget and Administration Bureau)

| | |
|---|---|
| Chief of Bureau | *Landesführer* RAMTHUN |
| *Gruppe Haushalt und Finanzwesen* | (Budget and Finance Branch) |
| *Gruppe Verwaltung und Beschaffung* | (Administration and " Procurement " Branch) |
| *Gruppe Prüfwesen* | (Audit and Control Branch) |

### Amt V
#### Abnahmeamt

| | |
|---|---|
| Chief of Bureau | *Gen. d. Pol. a.D.* OSSWALD |

It is not quite clear what the functions of this office are. It probably deals with the testing and checking of technical equipment and of installations before they are accepted by the TN from the manufacturers and again before the TN hands them over to the Army, Air Force, Police or other authorities after completion of their work. The proper translation, perhaps would be " Contract

Acceptance Bureau" or "Bureau of Technical Specifications and Tests."

The highest territorial command of the TN is the *Landesgruppe* (LG—district group unit). *Landesgruppen* coincide with the territorial boundaries of the *Wehrkreise* (Armed Forces Military Districts) and each *Landesgruppe* carries the Roman numeral of the corresponding *Wehrkreis*. In addition to the *Landesgruppen* there are the *TN Befehlsstellen* (Command Areas) Oberschlesien, General Gouvernement, Niederlande, and Norwegen.

At the head of each *Landesgruppe* is the Commander (*Führer der Landesgruppe*).

Under the commander, a *Stabsführer* (C of S) appointed by the *Amt TN* is charged with the overall administrative direction of the *Landesgruppe*. He may, in addition, take over the conduct of certain *Einzelsachgebiete* (Special Sub-sections). In general, however, such sub-sections are directed by specialists (*Sachbearbeiter*) who, with their staffs, work out technical problems arising in the administration of the *Landesgruppe*.

Purely administrative as well as financial matters are in the hands of a *Verwaltungsführer* (administrative officer) and his staff. In addition to this directing staff of the *Landesgruppe*, the Headquarters includes of course such additional personnel as draughtsmen, technical employees and clerks.

*Bezirksgruppen* (BG—sub-district group units), each commanded by a *Führer der Bezirksgruppe*, sometimes form the intermediate echelon between *Landesgruppen* and *Ortsgruppen*. As with the *Landesgruppe*, the various sub-sections in the BG Headquarters are handled by specialists and all administrative and financial matters by the *Verwaltungsführer*. These officials, however, are not necessarily full-time personnel.

The *Ortsgruppen* (OG—local units) are the basic units for TN activities. They should not be confused with the Nazi Party *Ortsgruppen*.

1,500 *TN Ortsgruppen* are said to exist in Germany. In addition there are an unidentified number of smaller local TN groups known as *Zweigstellen* (branches) or *Untergruppen* (local sub-units) of the *Ortsgruppen*. Functionally each *Ortsgruppe* is divided into various *Dienste* (services), which are dealt with below in the discussion of the TN horizontal structure.

At the head of each *Ortsgruppe* stands the *Ortsführer* (local unit commander). The designation *Ortsführer* (H) indicates that in this capacity he is a full-time (*hauptamtlich*) TN official.

All local business matters arising within the *Ortsgruppe* are handled by the *Sachwalter* (specialised sub-section official) who is a full-time employee of the *Ortsgruppe*. He in turn is assisted by a number of honorary *Stabsgehilfen* (staff assistants) who handle such matters as recruiting and training, administration and auditing, and medical and legal aid.

In *Ortsgruppen* with gas and air raid protection schools, heads of such schools are members of the OG staff.

## 74. Horizontal Structure—the TN Service Branches

To accomplish the various tasks with which the TN is charged it is horizontally organised into *Dienste* (Service Branches). Four of these exist in every *Ortsgruppe*, viz :—

    *Technischer Dienst*
    *Luftschutzdienst*
    *Bereitschaftsdienst*
    *Allgemeiner Dienst*

The *Dienste* are organised as follows :—

*Schar*, 8–15 men.
*Kameradschaft*, 2–4 *Scharen*, 25–50 men
*Gemeinschaft*, 2–4 *Kameradschaften*, 50–100 men
*Gefolgschaft*, 2–4 *Gemeinschaften*, 100–200 men
*Bereitschaft*, 2–4 *Gefolgschaften*, 200–400 men
*Hauptbereitschaft*, several *Bereitschaften*, 400–1,000 men.

When actively employed, however, the *Dienste* are divided into *Züge* (Platoons) and *Trupps* (Sections). This apparent overlapping of subsections can best be explained by the fact that the *Scharen*, *Kameradschaften*, etc. are administrative entities, whereas *Züge* and *Trupps* are functional units.

The **Technischer Dienst** (Technical Service Branch, abbr. TD) is employed in important factories and public utility works when sabotage or natural catastrophes interfere with their operation and the employees are unable to cope with the situation. The factory supervisors themselves regulate the employment of the TN personnel. According to its tasks, the TD consists of :—

*Betriebstrupps*, who specialise in electric, gas, water, sewage, and drains work
*Fachreservetrupps* who are the reserve group for the same type of work as the *Betriebstrupps*
*Leitungstrupps*, sections which work on lines and circuits. These are sub-divided into *Hochspannungstrupps* (high tension sections), *Rohrtrupps* " Gas " (gas pipeline sections), and *Rohrtrupps* " Wasser " (water pipeline sections).

The strength of *Betriebstrupps* depends on local needs ; that of the *Leitungstrupps* on the extent of local lines. *Betriebstrupps* are trained as replacement personnel for specialised tasks in factories ; the *Leitungstrupps* are trained for the maintenance and repair of lines and circuits.

Generally speaking, only experts who have been trained for the particular task are used in the TD. Public utilities and industrial installations requiring TD personnel must inform the Headquarters of the TN as to their exact requirements. The working organisation of the TD is not rigid and will be modified according to the nature of the work in hand. Sub-units are kept to a minimum and complicated chains of command are avoided.

The **Luftschutzdienst** (Air Raid Protection Service Branch, abbr. LD) of the TN was originally created with the specific function of organising, training, and maintaining the *Instandsetzungsdienst* (JD—Repair, Demolition and Rescue Services). However, in 1942, the *Instandsetzungsdienst* was incorporated into the *Luftschutzpolizei* and is now an integral part of that organisation. While, therefore, its personnel is still derived from the ranks of the TN, its training and employment are now under the command of the Air Raid Protection Police.

In detail, the special functions of the JD include removal of traffic obstructions, particularly difficult rescue work, furnishing of temporary shelters, bomb disposal work and emergency demolitions in case of large scale fires or collapsing buildings.

The **Bereitschaftsdienst** (Emergency Service Branch, abbr. BD) deals with natural catastrophes and consists of motorised *Bereitschaftszüge* (mot. *BZ*—emergency platoons), equipped with special motor vehicles developed by the *Amt TN*, and auxiliary motorised *Bereitschaftszüge* equipped as completely as possible.

These platoons are composed of *Bereitschaftstrupps*, which are sub-divided as follows :

    1 *Führer* (Leader)

36

1 *Führerstellvertreter* (Assistant Leader)
2 *Arbeitsgruppenführer* (Detail Leaders)
2 *Arbeitsgruppen* (Details) of 8 men each
2 *Kraftfahrer* (Drivers)
2 *Melder* (Messengers).

The Headquarters locations of BZ are situated so that they are in or near danger areas. The BD. also takes on the duties of the *Instandsetzungsdienst* (Utilities Maintenance Service) in those locations where the *Luftschutzpolizei* (ARP police) is not equipped to perform repair services.

The **Allgemeine Dienst** (General Service Branch, abbr. AD) includes all the TN men who are not in the specialised *Dienste* listed above and represents a general reserve, including, however, the following special units :—

Signal Platoons
*Sprengtrupps* (demolition sections)
*Musik- und Spielmannszüge* (band platoons)·
*Parktrupps* (motor maintenance sections)
*Lichtzüge* (searchlight platoons).

All men who are available only for limited service or who are members of the Armed Forces, as well as all *TN Verfügungsreserve* (*TN VR*—Active Reserve), are part of the AD. *Nothelferanwärter* (candidates for TN membership) are also organised as part of the AD.

### 75. Future Significance of the TN

The full potentialities of the TN for the future can be pictured only by considering the combination which arises now that the TN field units, retreating with the Armed Forces into the Reich, are merging with the TN units of the home front.

From preceding paragraphs it will be clear that the TN field units have a wide range of technical experience, while the home front units must, in their specialist capacity, have become thoroughly familiar with the working details of all essential industries as well as with the precise locations of industrial installations, public utilities, water mains, gas mains, sewers, telephones, etc.

When these two elements of the organisation combine forces on an inner German front, their danger as a synchronised team must be fully reckoned with.

As the Allied Armed Forces continue to narrow the ring around Germany, the TN will undoubtedly be charged with the transfer of vital machinery to the safer areas in the interior of the Reich. As the " safer areas " too are overrun by the Allied advance, it would be only logical for the Nazis to call upon the TN to dismantle and hide some of this machinery for use later by the already clearly foreshadowed underground movement.

The TN, officered largely by SS personnel, will then be ready to spring into action as a thoroughly " nazified " technical shock-formation of industrial saboteurs.

Considering the TN in this light, therefore, Allied occupation forces need to pay close attention to this efficiently devised and powerful weapon of the Nazis. Indeed, a knowledge of, and careful control over the TN might assist the Allied forces considerably in countering the sabotage preparations of German resistance movements.

# IV

## Auxiliaries to the Regular Uniformed Police

### 76. Sonderpolizei

Certain categories of uniformed police in Germany are not an integral part' of the *Ordnungspolizei*. They do not therefore come under the jurisdiction of the *Hauptamt Orpo*, although their duties are similar to those of the *Ordnungspolizei*. They are known under the general term of *Sonderpolizei* (Special Police), and include :—

The *Bahnpolizei* (State Railway Police) with its branches, the *Bahnschutzpolizei* (Railway Protection Police)—and the *Reichsbahnfahndungsdienst* (Railway Criminal Investigation Service)
The SS-*Bahnschutz*
The SS-*Postschutz* (Postal Guards)
The SS-*Funkschutz* (Radio Installation Guards)
The *Bergpolizei* (Police for the Supervision of Mines)
The *Deichpolizei* (Dam and Dyke Police).

The **Bahnpolizei** is maintained by the *Deutsche Reichsbahn* (State Railways), and is primarily subordinated to the *Reichsverkehrsministerium* (RVM—Ministry of Transport). When, however, the *Bahnpolizei* exceeds its technical specialised functions in order to assume some of the duties of the *Ordnungspolizei*, it acts under the command of the *Reichsführer-SS und Chef der Deutschen Polizei*. Specific instructions are then transmitted by the Chief of the *Ordnungspolizei* through the *Kommandoamt* of the *Hauptamt Orpo*, " in agreement with the *Reichsverkehrsministerium*." In such instances, personnel of the *Bahnpolizei* are accorded the status of *Hilfspolizei* (see next para.).

In special emergencies which necessitate the employment of *Bahnpolizei* for general police tasks the *Reichsverkehrsministerium* will, upon request of the *Orpo*, place the *Bahnpolizei* at the disposal of the RFSS u Ch d Dt P for combined employment with units of the *Orpo*. To facilitate cooperation between the *Reichsverkehrsministerium* and the Police the *Reichsverkehrsministerium* appoints a *Verbindungsreferent* to establish liaison with the RFSS.

In addition *Reichsbahnangestellte* (employees of the State Railways), such as stationmasters, conductors and engineers, have been entrusted with Police power on trains.

The **Postschutz** and **Funkschutz** function under the *Reichspostministerium* and their primary duty is to guard property belonging to the Postal and Broadcasting authorities. The **Bahnschutz** similarly functions under the railway authorities. (See paras. 122 f.f.).

Most of the branches of the *Sonderpolizei* are today closely affiliated with and to a large extent taken over by the SS. It becomes evident, in fact, that although the outward appearance of these branches of Police, as well as the bulk of their duties, are of an *Orpo* nature, their real significance is predominantly of a security police character. They are, therefore, discussed later in greater detail in connection with the *Sicherheitspolizei* and the SD. The *Bergpolizei* and *Deichpolizei*—which come under the *Reichswirtschaftsministerium* (RWM—Ministry of Economics)—are discussed in para. 86 in connection with the *Verwaltungspolizei*.

### 77. Hilfspolizei

The *Hilfspolizei* (Hipo—Auxiliary Police) consists of various auxiliary services—largely recruited from Nazi Party formations (*Gliederungen*)—which may be called upon to assist the Regular Police on a part-time basis. They have been discussed in various places in preceding parts of this book.

The *Sonderpolizei*—discussed in the previous paragraph—which is staffed by full-time personnel, should not be confused with the various types of

*Hilfspolizei.* At times, however, members of the *Sonderpolizei* may be appointed *Hilfspolizisten* and will then assist the Regular Police in their functions.

The most important category of the *Hilfspolizei* is formed by the *Landwacht* and the *Stadtwacht* (Rural and Urban Guards), recruited mainly from among the *SA-Wehrmannschaften*. When on duty as Auxiliary Policemen, they wear an arm-band, usually white with the black inscription " *Hilfspolizei.*" For further details see para. 53.

Other Services sometimes given the status of *Hilfspolizeien* are :—

| | |
|---|---|
| *NSKK-Verkehrsdienst* | Traffic Control Service of the NSKK (National Socialist Motor Corps). See para. 47. |
| *NSKK-Verkehrserzie-hungsdienst* | NSKK Traffic Educacation Service. See para. 47. |
| *NSKK-Verkehrshilfs-dienst* | NSKK Road Aid Service. See para. 47. |
| *NSKK Transportkon-trollen des motorisierten Transportes der Kriegs-wirtschaft* | NSKK Cargo Inspection Service of Motorised Wartime Transport See para. 47. |
| *HJ-SRD (Hitler Jugend Streifendienst)* | Hitler Youth Patrol Service. See para. 48. |
| *HJ-Feuerwehrscharen* | Fire Fighting Platoons of the Hitler Youth. See para. 65. |
| *Werkluftschutz* | ARP Services in factories consisting of *Werkpolizeien* — Industrial Police. See para. 69. |
| *Werkschutz or Werk-polizei* | Industrial Police. See para. 69. |
| *Selbstschutz* | Self-protection Service. See para. 69. |
| *SA-Katastrophenstürme* | Emergency Companies. See para. 69. |
| *SS-Industrieschutzmann-schaften* | Industrial Safety Crews. See para. 69. |

## C. THE ADMINISTRATIVE POLICE

### 78. Verwaltungspolizei : General

Even before the foundation of the German Reich in 1871, the Police was a powerful factor in the administration of both Prussia under STEIN and HARDENBERG, and Austria under METTERNICH. Thus for a century and a half the tradition has existed which makes Germany a " *Polizeistaat,*" a country controlled and governed by the Police. Today the Police in the Third Reich is immeasurably more powerful and closer to the life of the individual than is the case in England or the United States.

The present-day German concept of " Police " is, as becomes apparent from those branches discussed so far, extremely wide. On the administrative side also it will be seen that the German Police does not attend merely to the great volume of paper work connected with its regular duties of maintaining order and protecting public safety, but. has in addition taken over a great many administrative functions, which in other countries are performed by purely civilian clerical staffs. In Germany it is the *Verwaltungs-polizei* (Administrative Police) which handles these duties.

While personnel of the other branches of the *Orpo* are referred to as *Polizeivollzugsbeamte* (Police Executive Officials), members of the various sections of the *Verwaltungspolizei* are called *Polizeiverwaltungsbeamte* (Police Administrative Officials). They are not necessarily uniformed. As a rule, they are men of older age classes and many of them may have risen to their administrative positions after having completed a stretch of service as *Polizeivollzugs-beamte.* At any rate, since the Nazis came to power, these men, too, are more or less militarised. Even if they do not always wear uniforms, they have normally had some military training and experience in the past, and are now frequently " combed out " and conscripted.

The *Verwaltungspolizei* is a branch of the *Orpo,* as are all the branches previously discussed in this part. The apex of its command structure, however, is not *Amt I,* the *Kommandoamt* in the *Hauptamt Orpo,* as is the case with all ordinary branches of the Regular Uniformed Police, but rather *Amt II, Amt Verwaltung und Recht* (Bureau of Administration, Law and Legal Affairs).

The *Staatliche Polizeiverwaltungen* throughout Germany are the local centres where most of the duties and functions of the *Verwaltungspolizei* are performed. The organisation of the *Verwal-tungspolizei* within the *Staatliche Polizeiverwal-tungen* has been standardised throughout Germany. Its wide scope is indicated by the list, in the next paragraph, of the various divisions within each *Polizeiverwaltung.*

### 79. Standard Organisation of a Staatliche Polizeiverwaltung

The Administrative Police within a *Staatliche Polizeiverwaltung* are organised into 5 principal sections (*Abteilungen*) and a *Sekretariat* consisting of three bureaux, viz :—

1. *Präsidialgeschäftsstelle* (P)
(Office of the Chief of the *Polizeiverwaltung*).
2. *Polizeikasse* (Ka)
(Office of the Police Cashier).
3. *Polizeirechnungsrevisor* (Rv)
(Office of the Police Auditor and Controller).

The five principal sections are organised as follows :—

#### Abt. I (Abt. W)
#### Wirtschaftsabteilung (Financial Administration)

This section deals with :—

*Haushalts- und Rechnungswesen* (Budget, Bookkeeping and Accounting)

*Besoldungsangelegenheiten der Beamten, Ange-stellten und Lohnempfänger* (Pay of Officials, Clerks and others on the Police payroll)

*Versorgungsangelegenheiten* (Allowances, Allotments and Pensions)

*Wirtschaftsangelegenheiten der Schutzpolizei—Bekleidung, Verpflegung, Unterkunft* (Budget matter of the Protection Police such as Uniforms, Subsistence and Billets).

#### Abt. II
#### Passwesen, Ausländerpolizei, Meldewesen, Wehrer-satzwesen (Passports, Control of Foreigners, Police Registration, Recruiting of the Armed Forces)

This section deals with :—

*Durchführung der Passvorschriften* (Execution of Passport Regulations)

*Ausländerpolizei—Überwachung, Aufenthalts-erlaubnis und -verbot usw* (Supervision and Registration of Foreigners, issue and refusal of permission to reside, etc.)

*Meldewesen, Meldevorschriften, Melderegister* (Police Registration Regulations, forms, etc.)

*Volkskartei* (National Population Register)

*Wehrersatzwesen—Wehrerfassung, Wehrstamm-rollen, Musterung* (Registration of Recruits for the Armed Forces and other Police assistance in the call-up of age groups)

*Staatsangehörigkeitssachen* (Matters of citizenship)

*Zeugnisse und polizeiliche Bescheinigungen* (Attestations and Police Certificates)

*Durchführung der Nürnberger Gesetze und Juden-gesetze* (Nürnberg Racial Discrimination and anti-Jewish Laws)

*Auswanderungswesen* (Emigration)

*Namen, Namensänderungen, Titel* (Names, changes of name, titles).

## Abt. III

### Verkehrs-, Wasser-, und Feuerpolizei (Traffic, Waterways and Fire Police)

This section deals with :—

*Verkehrspolizeiangelegenheiten — Strassen, und Strassenordnung, Verhalten im Verkehr und Ver-kehrsregelung, und Zulassung zum Strassenverkehr* (Roads, Road Control and anything connected with Traffic Police, such as street permits for vehicles)

*Ausstellung von Führerscheinen* (Issue of Driving Licences, with the assistance of the NSKK ; see para. 47)

*Fahrlehrerwesen* (Supervision of Driving Instruction)

*Genehmigungspflichtiger Beförderungsverkehr* (Licences for Taxis, Buses and other Commercial vehicles)

*Feuerpolizeiliche Vorschriften* (Fire Police Regulations and Preventive measures)

*Wasserpolizeiliche Vorschriften* (Water Police Regulations)

*Enteignungsangelegenheiten* (Confiscation and Expropriation)

## Abt. IV

### Gewerbepolizei (Administrative Police for the control of Trade Establishments and their licences.)

This section is the competent authority for the handling of matters pertaining to Trades and Licences on the basis of the *Reichsgewerbeordnung* (a code of Reich decrees governing the licensing of trades and crafts). It deals with the following matters :—

*Preisüberwachung* (Enforcement of Price Control)

*Lichtspiel und Theaterwesen* (Supervision of theatres and cinemas)

*Ausstellung von Wandergewerbescheinen und Reiselegitimationskarten* (Licences for Pedlars and Commercial Travellers, Travel Permits)

*Regelung der Sonntags- und Festtagsruhe und von Lustbarkeiten* (Supervision of Sunday peace, curfew hours for places of entertainment)

*Überwachung der Gewerbebetriebe, der Fremden-heime und Gaststätten* (Supervision of trades, hotels, inns and restaurants)

*Wirtschaftswerbung, Sammlungen* (Supervision of Advertisements and Street Collections)

*Schutz Nationaler Symbole* (Protection of National Symbols and Emblems).

## Abt. V

### Strafverfügungen, Amtshilfesachen, Gesundheits-, Lebensmittel und Veterinärpolizei (Regulations on punishable offences, Welfare matters, Health, Food and Veterinary Police.)

This section deals with :—

*Polizeistrafrecht* (Police Courts, Penal Code and Police Regulations)

*Amtshilfesachen* (Inter-Office Assistance)

*Polizeiverwaltungsgesetz und Polizeistrafver-fügungen* (Police Administrative Code and Penal Orders)

*Verwaltungszwangsverfahren* (Compulsory Administration, i.e. Receivership, Condemnation, Administration of Confiscated Property, and other compulsory proceedings)

*Volks-, Vieh- und Betriebszählungen usw* (Census of Population, Cattle, Commercial and Industrial Establishments)

*Polizeiliche Mitwirkung in Fürsorge und Wohl-fahrtsangelegenheiten* (Police Assistance in Public Welfare)

*Gesundheits- und Lebensmittelpolizei, Medizinal-personen, Apothekerwesen, Heilmittel, Handel mit Giften, Badewesen, Leichen, Bestattungen* (Health and Food Administration, Supervision of Doctors and Nurses, Pharmacists, Trade in Drugs and Poisons, Inspection of Public Baths, Regulations regarding Corpses and Funerals)

*Überwachung des Verkehrs mit Lebensmitteln* (Supervision of Trade in Foodstuffs)

*Tierseuchen, Schlachtvieh- und Fleischbeschau* (Animal Epidemics, Inspection of Slaughter Houses and Meat)

*Waffen- und Jagdwesen* (Fire-arms and Hunting Licences)

### 80. Records and Documents

Like the German Armed Forces, the *Staatliche Polizeiverwaltungen* use a uniform filing system for all records—the *Einheitsaktenplan* (Standard Filing System, abbr. EAPl). This system was instituted on the 9th November, 1934.

A representative condensation of the system, tabulated in ranges of numbers according to subject headings, will be found in annexe C. The complete carding key has not been reproduced as it consists of a series from 1,000 to over 10,000. This most voluminous bureaucratic system goes into great detail with specific filing numbers for such subjects as signal whistles and the training of police horses.

One of the functions of the *Verwaltungspolizei* is the supervision of the security classification system of civil documents and publications. In detail, the classifications in use are :—

*Nur für den Dienstgebrauch (NfdD)* or
*Nur für deutsche Behörden (NfdB)* : For official use only.

This classification is the equivalent of " Restricted."

*Vertraulich (Vertr.)* : Confidential.

*Geheim (Geh.)* : Secret.

*Geheime Kommandosache (Geh KdoS)* : Literally " Secret command matter." The equivalent of this classification would be slightly below our " Top Secret," approximating to "Secret and Registered." It is used for documents pertaining only to command and operational matters for highest headquarters.

*Geheime Reichssache (Geh RchS)* : Secret matter relating to national affairs. Its approximate equivalent would be slightly higher than our "Top Secret." It is used for matters of major national or diplomatic importance and is comparatively rare.

While these are the official classifications for German police documents, others may occasionally be found. Such unofficial classifications as "*streng vertraulich*" (strictly confidential), or other variations and combinations do occur, but they are, as a rule self-explanatory.

## 81. Police Duties carried out by Local Authorities

It is noteworthy that even in towns with a *Staatliche Polizeiverwaltung* not all matters of police administration are handled by these authorities. A limited number of police functions is left to the municipalities, i.e. to the Mayor or Lord Mayor and his office. These duties are referred to as *Restpolizeiliche Aufgaben* ("residual police tasks").

The jurisdiction of both national and local authorities (*Staatliche Polizeiverwaltung* and *Gemeindepolizeibehörde*) has been regulated in Prussia in a set of decrees dated 31st March, 1938 and entitled "*Verordnung über die sachliche Zuständigkeit der Staatlichen Polizeiverwaltung in Preussen*" (Decree concerning the jurisdiction of the National Police Authorities in Prussia). Similar decrees have been issued in the other *Länder*.

A system of this kind leads inevitably to a certain amount of over-lapping and duplication, but the following fields of action are clearly defined as the responsibility of the *Gemeindepolizeibehörden* (Police Authorities of the Municipalities) :—

*Baupolizei* (Police in charge of enforcement of the Building and Construction Code).

*Feld- und Forstpolizei* (Field and Forest Police).

*Naturschutz* (Protection of plants and animal life).

*Feuerpolizei* (Fire Police), as far as their activities are affected by the Building and Construction Code.

Certain aspects of the *Gewerbepolizei*.

*Gesundheits-, Veterinär- und Lebensmittelpolizei* (Health, Veterinary and Food Administration) unless in certain cities the Reich Ministry of the Interior has specifically transferred these functions to the *Staatliche Polizeiverwaltung*.

*Marktpolizei* (Police for the Supervision of Public Markets and Fairs), which includes in its duties the examination of cattle and meat.

*Wasserpolizei* (Waterways Police), not to be confused with the *Wasserschutzpolizei* (Water ways Protection Police, discussed in para. 57, et seq).

*Wege- und Strassenpolizei* (Road Police), which concerns itself with the maintenance, illumination and cleaning of streets.

*Bergpolizei* (Police for the Supervision of Mines).

*Jagdpolizei und Fischereipolizei* (Police administering hunting and fishing rights).

*Wohnungspolizei* (Police for the supervision of Buildings, Tenements, Residential Houses and other Dwellings).

*Obdachlosenpolizei* (Police for the supervision of the Homeless and Vagrants).

*Schulpolizei* (Police for the supervision of Schools and School Attendance).

Other functions which may have been added to the authority of the *Gemeindepolizei* by special decree.

Most of the above functions are discussed in later paragraphs.

Only larger communities have a special staff of *Gemeindeverwaltungspolizeibeamten* (Municipal Administrative Police Officials) to attend to the above listed duties. In medium sized and smaller communities all these administrative police functions are handled by the personnel of the regular civil municipal administration. In addition, in localities without a *Staatliche Polizeiverwaltung*, the same personnel take care of those administrative activities which in cities with *Staatliche Polizeiverwaltungen* are assigned to the staffs of the *Polizeipräsidien, -direktionen* or *-ämter*. (See also paras. 24, 79.)

## 82. Police Registration

Of the many varied activities of the *Verwaltungspolizei* some must be particularly emphasised. Among the most important, from the Allied occupation and Counter-Intelligence point of view are *Meldewesen* (Police Registration) and the *Volkskartei* (National Population Register).

Registration of the population has always been compulsory in Germany since the last century. Using the existing laws as a basis for an even more rigid control, the Nazi government remodelled and reinforced previous provisions, in decrees issued in 1938 and 1940. Thus, for instance, the new edicts ordered all Germans to register with the police within three days of any change of residence. Foreigners were governed by the same decree, but their registration had to take place within 24 hours.

The basis of this police registration is a certificate from the appropriate police authority giving the place of former residence and stating that the particular person was registered there until his or her change of residence. The certificate is called the *Abmeldeschein* (Certificate of change of Residence). In return, on re-registering, the registrant receives his new *Meldeschein* (Certificate of Residence), which shows that he is properly registered in the new locality. In order to keep the authorities fully informed, all persons are required to advise the police even if they only move within their own community. In that case a new *Meldeschein* is not issued, but an entry as to the change of address is made on the existing certificate of residence.

Duplicates of all *Meldescheine* and *Abmeldescheine* are forwarded to the regional *Finanzamt* (Internal Revenue Office) concerned. That office then turns them over to the *Statistische Reichsamt* (Reich Bureau of Statistics) in Berlin. There they are used primarily for statistical and census tabulations, but it may be assumed that the duplicate certificates of registration can be found on permanent file with that office.

As a development of this registration, the Police keep alphabetical *Melderegister* (card file registers) of all residents in the community. The office maintaining this register is called the *Einwohnermeldeamt* or *Einwohneramt* (Bureau of Population Registry). The individual records are called *Personenregisterkarten* (Personal Registration File Cards).

The colour of the *Personenregisterkarte* is white for men and blue for women. The personal data contained on the card include the registered per-

40

son's name, date of birth, place of birth, marital status, religion, race, occupation, nationality and citizenship, military status and criminal record. Additional information found on this card includes name, date of birth, place of birth and religion of the registered person's parents, husband or wife and parents-in-law. Further remarks refer to possession of a passport and licences for weapons, hunting, driving or piloting.

Unmarried juveniles living with their father or mother are listed on the Registration Card of the parent. They obtain their own Personal Registration Card when they come of age, marry or take up their own residence.

On the reverse side of the Personal Registration card are recorded the address and any subsequent changes of address.

Foreigners who do not take up permanent residence in a German community, but who intend to stay in the Reich only for a short period, are issued with a *Passbegleitschein* (Supplementary Paper to the Passport) instead of a *Meldeschein*. This *Passbegleitschein* shows the exact route of travel, and must be shown by the foreigners wherever they stay overnight or whenever requested by the authorities to identify themselves.

A special **Ausländerkartei** (Card Index for foreigners) is kept by the *Ausländerpolizei* (Police handling all matters regarding non-Germans) ; the *Ausländerpolizei* is represented at all *Polizeibehörden* and it is part of the *Verwaltungspolizei*. This file is divided into *Ausländerkartei A* and *Ausländerkartei B*.

*Ausländerkartei A* contains a card for every foreigner residing for any long period within the area of the particular *Kreispolizeibehörde*. The file is arranged alphabetically according to surnames. Four colours (green, yellow, blue and red) are used to indicate certain groupings of nationalities. Each nationality within the group is again designated by a number ranging from 1 to 12. Thus, the names of citizens or subjects of each country are kept on cards coloured and numbered according to a combination which will identify each card unmistakably as belonging to a definite country. (A chart showing this scheme of registration of foreigners will be found in Annexe C.)

Included in this system of registry are all residents of Germany who come under the categories *Staatenlos* (stateless), *Juden* (Jews) and *Volksdeutsche* (" Racial " Germans). *Volksdeutsche* are divided into the categories of *Volkslisten* I, II, III. Those " racial " Germans who were born in Greater Germany but resided abroad were entered as members of *Volksliste I*, and carry blue personal identity cards. Others, who expediently remembered their Germanic origins after, for example, the German occupation of Poland and Slovenia, applied to have their names entered in *Volksliste II*. They also carry blue identity cards. A third group, who were " converted " into Germans without having been consulted, were lumped together in *Volksliste III*. This last group receives citizenship on probation and carries green identity cards with the remark " *Staatsangehörigkeit auf Widerruf* " (Citizenship subject to cancellation). In special instances, members of *Volksliste III* may be advanced to List II, after having proved their National Socialist loyalties. Similarly *Volksdeutsche* of List II may graduate into List I as a special honour. For further details on the identity cards designating members of the *Volksliste* see section on personal documents.

*Ausländerkartei B* contains all cards of foreigners which have been removed for any reason from *Ausländerkartei A*. Thus, foreigners, for instance, who have become full German citizens are still carried in this file.

Under the Nazi regime, registration of foreigners and most matters within the sphere of the *Ausländerpolizei* can no longer be regarded as purely administrative police functions. Thus, while the mere clerical registration has remained the duty of the *Ausländerpolizei*, all executive tasks, investigations and prosecutions have become the concern of the *Sipo* and the SD. In most instances, the *Ausländerpolizei* is then simply informed of any action taken or to be taken, so that it may keep administrative records up to date.

## 83. Population Registers : the Volkskartei

In their perfection of the complete regimentation of the German people, the Nazis found the system of registration described above insufficient. It was especially inadequate for the administration of National Conscription. Since, under the existing system, registration cards were merely filed alphabetically, according to surnames, the call-up of certain age classes for conscription necessitated an extremely complicated routine of paper work. As a remedy, the Nazi government introduced the *Volkskartei* (National Population Register) on 18th January, 1939. In this register file cards of all males and females between the ages of 5 and 74 are arranged according to age classes, i.e. according to groups of individuals born in the same calendar year.

These files contain the most detailed personal information, such as year, day, month and exact place ` of birth, full occupational qualifications, schooling, training, academic degrees, present and former residences, nationality, place of employment, foreign travel and residence, knowledge of foreign languages and service in the Armed Forces, foreign services or Reich Labour Service. Registration cards for German women contain such additional information as experience in office work, housekeeping, science, factory work, nursing, Red Cross service, number of children under 15 years still living at home, and other such data as indicate a woman's availability for any kind of war work in the widest sense of the term.

Index Cards of the *Volkskartei* are brown for men and green for women. Cards for Jews are marked by black index tabs. All registrants working in the field of maintenance of Public Health are indicated by white, those holding drivers' licences by red, and those not in possession of an *Arbeitsbuch* (working pass) by blue tabs.

The *Volkskartei* is not kept in one central location, but is regionally distributed. In the larger towns it is kept by the *Staatliche Polizeiverwaltungen* (National Police Administrations), i.e. the *Polizeipräsidien*, the *Polizeidirektionen* and *Polizeiämter*. Where these do not exist the local sections of the *Volkskartei* are entrusted to the office of the *Bürgermeister* of the community, but duplicate cards of the entire district are kept in the office of the *Landrat*, the Chief of the *Landkreis*.

The *Volkskartei* will undoubtedly be one of the major aids available locally to the Allied occupation authorities. Its importance can hardly be overrated. When the Allied military administrators are looking for information concerning individual Germans, the *Volkskartei* will present them with a complete record of the whereabouts, past and present activities and qualifications of every inhabitant. Even though the Germans admit that because of manpower shortage these records have not always been kept up to date during the latter stages of the war, the basic records of the adult population may still be considered almost complete. This may be assumed to be true although further entries in each *Volkskartei* were reported suspended in September, 1943.

Since this national register is the fundamental record of all administrative work concerning the entire population, it is unlikely that the Nazis will make an attempt to destroy it in order to prevent its falling into Allied hands. From past experience the assumption seems justifiable that the methodical German mind will hesitate at the idea of burning such a bureaucratic masterpiece as the *Volkskartei*.

Should, however, parts of the *Volkskartei* be destroyed either by Nazi demolition squads or by Allied attacking forces, the occupation authorities will be able to locate duplicate and similar registers in various other German indexes. Thus, for instance, the Administrative Police of every city, town, or village maintains a very extensive card file of the population as an aid to the allotment of ARP duties, while the regional *Arbeitsämter* (National Employment Offices) keep complete files of all employable Germans and have added to these records a file of all locally available foreign labourers. The *Finanzämter* (National Internal Revenue Offices) also maintain complete population files, necessary for the control of tax levies.

At all Headquarters of the Nazi Party, records are kept, not only of all Party members, but of all Germans residing within the area of the particular Party Headquarters. A separate record is kept of those who have been rejected by the Party. These indexes are especially thorough, since the population included in them is under the constant supervision of the Nazi Party block warden. In addition, minute membership records, and files of those not admitted to membership, are kept at the local Headquarters of all Nazi Party formations (SA, SS, NSKK, etc.) and affiliates. Thus, for example, all practising physicians and surgeons are recorded at the Headquarters of the *NS Ärzte-Bund* (*NSÄB*—National Socialist Medical League).

A great number of indexes of this kind are, of course, maintained by the various Headquarters of the *Sipo* and SD. These, however, will be discussed in greater detail in the sections dealing with *Gestapo*, *Kripo* and SD.

A less obvious but extremely useful population index is maintained by both the Lutheran and Roman Catholic Churches, as well as smaller religious communities permitted in Germany such as Old Catholics. Since the first two mentioned Churches include more than 90% of the entire German population, and since their records still list those former members who have left the Church voluntarily or under Nazi pressure, these files are very nearly complete. As a last resort they will certainly remain available to the Allies for any intention on the part of the Churches to destroy their records before Allied occupation may be completely discounted.

Another index maintained by the *Verwaltungspolizei* is the *Hausregister*, a register of all buildings within each district. Cards of this index are white. On top of each appear the names and addresses of the owner and superintendent, followed by the names and occupations of each individual tenant. Names of former tenants

are crossed out, but remain legible. The House Registration file is kept in alphabetical order, arranged by street names with the houses in each street in numerical order.

The above list of German administrative registers should certainly not be regarded as exhaustive. An attempt to compile a complete list would lead too far into the jungle of German administrative routine. But the instances given may serve as a guide to the various sources available for building up an index—either general or local—of the German population.

## 84. Supervision of Trade

Another section of the *Verwaltungspolizei* which merits separate mention is the *Eichamt* (Bureau of Weights and Measures). All tradesmen, shopkeepers and other business establishments using scales, measures or containers of a specified size must submit these once a year to the *Eichamt* to have them checked. The inspectors and other officials working in this office and its subsidiaries are members of the *Eichpolizei*.

The control of prices in Germany rests with the *Reichskommissar für die Preisbildung* (Reich Commissioner for Price Control)—*SS-Brigadeführer Staatssekretär* Dr. Hans FISCHBÖCK, whose office is a subsection of the office of the *Beauftragte für den Vierjahresplan* (Authority for the Four-Year Plan, i.e. GÖRING). The general administration of Price Control is regionally carried out by the network of *Preisüberwachungsstellen* (Price Control Bureaux), with only a small staff at their disposal. For the close supervision of prices and the enforcement of price ceilings and regulations they depend upon the assistance of the *Verwaltungspolizei*. As will be clear from para. 79 above, the Administrative Police supervise almost all phases of business activity: they inspect weights and measures, issue business licences, supervise the quality of goods for sale, check the proper sale of products earmarked for a particular purpose, and, in general, keep strict guard over all commercial activities. This constant insight into matters of business and manufacture makes the *Verwaltungspolizei* well qualified to enforce regulations of the price-control authorities to prevent violation of such regulations and to investigate black-market activities whenever the *Preisüberwachungsstellen* call for such intervention.

The *Gewerbepolizei* (Police for the Control of Crafts and Trades), as a branch of the *Verwaltungspolizei*, executes these functions of market and price control in close cooperation with the price-control authorities.

## 85. Censorship

In pre-Hitler Germany, the Administrative Police used to exercise all normal functions of censorship of mail, press, radio and films. This was known as *Polizeizensur* (Police Censorship).

Under the Nazi regime the scope of this police function has increased tremendously both in volume and in importance. It has, indeed, become a powerful means of oppression in the hands of the Reich Government and of the Nazi Party. It is obvious, therefore, that censorship in Germany can no longer be regarded as a purely administrative function. For this reason it has for the most part been taken out of the hands of the Administrative Police, which merely retains some of the clerical tasks of censorship. The important political and repressive police functions connected with censorship are now in the hands of the *Sipo* and the SD in cooperation with the

German Postal Authorities : this is fully discussed in para. 106.

Censorship of the press, radio and films takes place at the very source of the material to be censored. The responsible agency is the *Ministerium für Volksaufklärung und Propaganda* (Ministry of Public Enlightenment and Propaganda) headed by Dr. GOEBBELS. Once a film or other medium of public entertainment has been approved by the Ministry, it becomes the duty of the local police to accord it full protection.

In some instances of local entertainment the Administrative Police still retain a certain voice of authority, but even so all major decisions are made by the competent representative of the *Sipo* or the local Nazi Party Chief and his staff. Intervention by the *Orpo* will occur only when public safety and order are threatened.

### 86. Other Specialised Functions of the Administrative Police

The **Baupolizei** (Building and Construction Code Enforcement Police), listed above as one of the municipally controlled branches of the *Verwaltungspolizei*, supervises the execution of action called for in directives concerning construction and maintenance of buildings. These directives are issued by the Ministries of Finance, Labour and Health, as well as by the authorities charged with fire prevention. Plans giving prescribed details for all building projects in Germany must be submitted to the *Baupolizei* for approval before construction work may be started.

This field of police activity also includes the granting of all building permits in accordance with legal restrictions concerning siting, construction, area, height, architectural exterior, and street-space. Prospective builders are guided in the drawing up of their plans by *Baupolizei-ordnungen* (Building Regulations) published locally. By means of these regulations the police control even the style of modern edifices. When actual construction begins, execution of the work is again checked through systematic inspections by the *Baupolizei*. Special emphasis is placed on proper ventilation, sanitation, and the elimination of fire hazards.

The personnel of the **Feld- und Forstpolizei** (Field and Forest Police) consists of the professional *Feld- und Forsthüter* (Field and Forest Guards) and belong to the so-called *Niedere Polizei-vollzugsdienst* (Lowest Grade Police Executive Service). These men are usually not uniformed and can be identified only by an official cap and an armband with the Police Badge. They come under the administration of the municipal police authorities, and their pay, equipment and clothing are covered by the municipality. Normally they are not equipped with rifles, but they can obtain permits for the possession of arms, " in case they require them," from the regular police authorities. The principal function of the *Feld- und Forst-polizei* is the prevention of forest fires, lumber thefts, damage to legally protected plants and animals, and unlawful entry into municipal property or other restricted areas. In these duties they are assisted by the *"Ehrenfeldhüter"* (Honorary Field Guards), who are appointed to perform these duties on a voluntary, unpaid and part-time basis.

The **Wasserpolizei** (Waterways Police) must not be confused with the *Wasserschutzpolizei* (Waterways Protection Police). The local *Wasserpolizei* agency is also referred to as *Wasserstrassenamt* (Bureau of Waterways). It administers smaller rivers and waterways graded as second and third class, and is responsible for the maintenance of law and order on those waterways and in their vicinity. Under the jurisdiction and inspection of the *Wasserpolizei* are, furthermore, reservoirs, ponds, aqueducts and watermains, the inspection of drinking water being an especial responsibility. The Waterways police in addition determines the local water tax and fixes and administers the water rights, such as the drilling of wells. It also issues all licences and permits for the use of waterways under its jurisdiction.

The *Wasserpolizei* is one of the branches listed above as the responsibility of the municipal Police Authorities.

The protection of municipal as well as private property in some localities is delegated to **Nachtwachmänner** or *Nachtwächter* (Night Watchmen), who may be employed either by the municipality or by private detective agencies, e.g. the *Wach- und Schliessgesellschaften* (Guard and Property Protection Companies). The watchmen need not be uniformed, but usually wear at least uniform caps. The uniform emblem of most of the employees of these private companies consists of two crossed keys.

Night watchmen are, on special occasions, entrusted with the execution of limited police functions. Whenever they need to be armed they must obtain weapon permits from the Regular Police. As a result of the growing manpower problem, the Police avails itself to an increasing extent of the auxiliary services of these *Nachtwachmänner*. On the island of Sylt, for instance, members of the *Wach- und Schliessgesellschaft* are employed as regular defence guards along the coast in cooperation with Police, Army and Air Force Units. At this point, it should be noted that employees of such protective agencies are not exempt from the latest conscription into the *Volkssturm* (People's Militia) along with all other males from 16 to 60 years of age.

The *Verwaltungspolizei*, together with the municipal police, is charged with the performance of certain duties concerning road maintenance, street cleaning and street illumination. A substantial part of the actual execution of such work is, however, delegated to and is the full responsibility of property owners in accordance with numerous German laws and city ordinances. Thus the main function of the **Wege- und Strassenpolizei** is to ensure that the responsible owners of property adjacent to thoroughfares take care of their required share of the above duties. The larger tasks of street cleaning, sanitation, and collection of garbage are covered in most German towns and cities by municipal sanitation departments or, in some instances, by contracting with chartered companies.

In mining regions a special **Bergpolizei** (Police for the Supervision of Mines) has been established. It is classified as one of the *Sonderpolizeien* and its administration is the responsibility of the municipal authorities. Among the primary functions of this branch of the Police were originally the supervision of essential safety devices and of suitable working conditions, as well as the control of the miners from a labour point of view. Under the Nazis, however, the *Bergpolizei* has become an administrative auxiliary to Party and Police agencies responsible for the prevention and prosecution of sabotage in the mines and hostile acts by miners, especially foreign or forcibly recruited labourers. As a result of this development, the *Bergpolizei* has become closely linked with the *Sipo* and the SD. The *Bergpolizei* will therefore be discussed later under the Kripo.

The **Obdachlosenpolizei** (Police for the Supervision of the Homeless and Vagrants) is another municipally controlled branch of the Administrative Police. In peacetime, it provides emergency shelters for the homeless, administers asylums, and cooperates in such matters with various types of charitable organisations. The *Obdachlosenpolizei* is authorised to requisition private houses and public accommodation if no other shelter for the needy can be found.

In wartime, as a consequence of damage to dwellings by air raids, the responsibilities of the *Obdachlosenpolizei* have increased enormously. During and after the last war, when the housing shortage in Germany was not nearly so acute as it is today the *Obdachlosenpolizei* set up local *Wohnungskommissionen* (Commissions to provide tenements) as authorities empowered to requisition the necessary billets and dwellings. These commissions were able to compel people who lived in large houses or flats to take in sub-tenants for an indefinite period of time. A similar service, but on an immeasurably larger scale, functions today. Thus, the quartering of bomb-victims and refugees from zones of operations is to a considerable extent handled by the *Obdachlosenpolizei* in co-operation with the Nazi Party, Party Formations, the *Wehrmacht* and the German Red Cross, as well as with civil administrative authorities.

The municipal administration in coastal areas includes the **Deichpolizei** (Dam and Dyke Police), classified as a *Sonderpolizei*. Its functions are the inspection and protection of such coastal installations as dams, dykes, locks and water works. Most of its duties, however, are of a purely administrative and supervisory nature. Whenever the small executive forces and facilities at the disposal of this service prove inadequate, the *Landrat, Polizeipräsident*, or Higher Police Authority may supplement them by regular police forces, members of the *Technische Nothilfe*, or other auxiliary formations. These services are then referred to as *Erweiterte Deichpolizei* (Reinforced Dyke Police).

# PART FIVE

## THE SICHERHEITSPOLIZEI AND THE SD

## A. HIGHER ORGANISATION AND GENERAL STRUCTURE OF THE SIPO AND SD

### 87. Development of the Sipo and SD

The development of the German Police system into a repressive totalitarian force upholding the Nazi régime has already been outlined in PART ONE of this book. Again, PART FOUR included a detailed discussion of the way in which the Nazis applied their principles of concentration, centralised control, and intensified militarisation to the *Orpo*. However radical these changes may appear, the most significant developments in the German Police since the Nazi advent to power were not those affecting the *Orpo*, but those which took place in the evolution of the *Sipo* and SD. These most typical Nazi creations, devised by HIMMLER and his late assistant HEYDRICH, have in effect become the strongest weapons of coercion at the disposal of the present rulers of Germany.

In PART ONE the development of the *Sipo* and SD was traced through the years from 1933 until 1939 when it culminated in the establishment of a combined central headquarters, the RSHA in BERLIN. It may be useful to recapitulate briefly this development. In 1933 under GÖRING's aegis, the Prussian Political Police had been transformed into the *Gestapo*. About the same time HIMMLER succeeded in establishing himself as the head of the Political Police in all the other *Länder* and finally in 1934 his intrigues gained him the control of the Prussian *Gestapo* itself. In 1936 he became Commander in Chief of the German Police, combining this position with that of Commander in Chief of the SS. In this new capacity he then formed the *Sicherheitspolizei* (*Sipo*—Security Police) as a new branch of the German Police, by linking the *Gestapo* (Secret State Police) with the *Kripo* (Criminal Police). He simultaneously re-organised and re-modelled both these branches, extended their jurisdiction over all of Germany and in matters of personnel established extremely close ties with the SS. Finally, in 1939 both these branches were merged with the *Sicherheitsdienst des Reichsführers SS* (SD—Security Service of the C-in-C of the SS), the intelligence system of the SS and Nazi Party. Thereby HIMMLER empowered the SD to establish its extra-legal status within the Government and the Police, although the SD never ceased to be a **Party rather than a Government organisation.** It may be true to-day that a number of the lower members of the SD, agents and others, are nothing but mercenary opportunists, but originally all SD personnel was drawn exclusively from the most reliable and fanatical members of the SS, and this certainly still holds good for the bulk of the SD, especially its executives.

It must constantly be emphasised that the *Sipo* and SD by no means restrict themselves to activities generally regarded as being within the scope of a Police organisation. Any attempt to equate the functions of the *Sipo* and SD with those of the police forces of democratic countries would be completely misleading. As the following pages will show, the influence of the *Kripo*, *Gestapo* and SD extends into every phase of German private and public life. *Kripo*, *Gestapo* and SD, though three distinct services, must to-day be regarded as one force. Inside Germany each still maintains its own system of regional and lower headquarters, which, however, function in each *Wehrkreis* under the supervision of one common head, the *Befehlshaber* (or *Inspekteur*) *der Sicherheitspolizei und des SD*. Abroad, in occupied territories, the three services appear in combined units, known as *Einsatzkommandos*. There may be friction between the three branches; there may be indications that *Kripo* and *Gestapo* personnel resent the dominating position of the SD within the combined force; there may even be reasons to believe that *Kripo* and *Gestapo* men might turn against each other, especially if encouraged from without. Nevertheless, the predominant fact is that at present the three services together constitute a single striking force forged and wielded by the leading Nazi clique as an instrument to strengthen and perpetuate their power.

HITLER and HIMMLER have always aimed at a fusion of Government and Party, with the Party as the ruling element. That amalgamation was never fully realised, but in the *Sipo* and SD, acting under a unified command and staffed by men who are almost exclusively members of the SS, this Nazi aim has been most nearly achieved. It is significant that *Kripo*, *Gestapo* and SD together are in Nazi circles unofficially called the "*Staatsschutzkorps*" (Combined Force for the Protection of the State) and that this repressive Police organisation is ominously directed to find its guiding policy in the "principles of the SS." Furthermore, in 1944, the *Sipo* and SD acquired supervision of virtually all German military intelligence forces at home and abroad. Thus in HIMMLER's grasp converge the threads of a system of political control which, blindly loyal to the Nazi regime, dominates the lives of all Germans within the Reich and all inhabitants of German occupied territory. It must therefore be expected that this rigidly controlled organisation will remain the hard core of a desperate movement of resistance to the Allied destruction of National Socialism.

### 88. The National Headquarters of the Sipo and SD

*Der Chef der Sicherheitspolizei und des SD* (Chief of the Security Police and the SD) is at present *SS-OGF, General der Polizei, Staatssekretär Dr.* Ernst KALTENBRUNNER, who succeeded HEYDRICH after the latter was shot by Czech Patriots in 1942. He is the highest commander of the two branches of the *Sipo*, viz. the *Geheime Staatspolizei* (*Gestapo*) and the *Kriminalpolizei* (*Kripo*), as well as of the SD, and is responsible only to HIMMLER, the *Reichsführer-SS und Chef der Deutschen Polizei*. His Headquarters is the *Reichssicherheitshauptamt* (RSHA—National Department of Security), the combined National Headquarters of *Sipo* and SD.

The RSHA, responsible under KALTENBRUNNER for the control of the *Kripo, Gestapo* and SD, consists of eight *Ämter* (Bureaux), whose offices were formerly located in or near Berlin, but are now widely scattered. Nevertheless the RSHA should be regarded as a single department rather than a collection of separate offices. It incorporates within its structure the old *Gestapoamt* (Headquarters of the *Gestapo*), the *Reichskriminalpolizeiamt* (Headquarters of the *Kripo*) and the former *SD-Hauptamt* (Headquarters of the SD), but the work of the three branches of the RSHA is to-day so closely connected that it is in many instances impossible to draw a clear line separating their functions and duties.

The official description of the functions of the *Ämter* in the RSHA is as follows :—

| | |
|---|---|
| *Personal* (Personnel) | *Amt I* Under *SS-GF* Erwin SCHULZ |
| *Organisation, Verwaltung und Recht* (Organisation, Administration and Law) | *Amt II* Until some time ago under *SS-SF* SIEGERT, who is believed to have been succeeded by *SS-OSBF* HAENEL. The Chief of *Amt II* appears to be subordinate to the Chief of *Amt I* |
| *Deutsche Lebensgebiete* (Spheres of German Life) | *Amt III* Under *SS-BF* OHLENDORF. This Bureau is the successor to the old SD-*Hauptamt* |
| *Gegnererforschung und Gegnerbekämpfung* (Investigation and combatting of Opposition) | *Amt IV* Also known as the *Geheime Staatspolizeiamt* (abbr. *Gestapa*). Under *SS-OGF* MÜLLER, who is probably also Deputy *Chef der Sipo und des SD*. |
| *Verbrechensbekämpfung* (Combatting of Crime) | *Amt V* Also known as the *Reichskriminalpolizeiamt* (RKPA) until recently under *SS-GF* NEBE who disappeared after the attempt on Hitler's life on 20th July, 1944. |
| *Ausland* (Foreign Countries) | *Amt VI* Under *SS-BF* SCHELLENBERG |
| *Weltanschauliche Erforschung und Auswertung* (Ideological Research and its Exploitation) | *Amt VII* Until recently under *SS-OF* Dr. SIX who is reported to have been succeeded by *SS-OSBF* DITTEL |

*Militärisches Amt*
(MI Bureau)

*Note.*—This Bureau was added to the RSHA in June, 1944. It is closely affiliated with and dominated by *Amt VI* and it too is headed by *SS-BF* SCHELLENBERG. As far as is known, however, the *Militärisches Amt* is still an independent Bureau within the RSHA and has not been incorporated into *Amt VI*.

Most of the offices of *Ämter* I, II, III, IV and VII, were located in Berlin in the blocks formed by Wilhelmstrasse and Prinz-Albrecht-Strasse, generally known as Prinz-Albrecht-Strasse 8–9 and Wilhelmstrasse 100–109. *Amt V* was located in Berlin in the blocks known as Werderscher Markt 5–6 and Oberwallstrasse 14–16. The offices of *Amt VI* are in Berlin-Wilmersdorf, Berkaerstrasse 32–35. It is known that in the course of the heavy Allied air attacks on Berlin, 1943/44, most of these buildings were severely damaged

and many of the offices were evacuated to other locations in Berlin and vicinity. Certain offices even moved to Mecklenburg, Silesia, Munich and Vienna. Thus a great number of addresses exist to-day, each giving the location of one or other of the sections or sub-sections of the above Bureaux. Since many of these addresses are only of a temporary nature it has not been considered advisable to list them in this book.

### 89. Functions of the RSHA Bureaux

The functions of **Ämter I** and **II** are administrative, with *Amt II* now probably subordinated to *Amt I* under SCHULZ. Existing evidence suggests that they are concerned with the personnel, organisation and administration of the combined *Sipo* and SD although it is known that *Amt VI* retains a considerable measure of autonomy in the administration of its SD personnel and agents abroad.

**Amt III** directs the principal functions of the SD inside Germany and is the control Headquarters for all SD *Leitabschnitte*, *Abschnitte*, *Hauptaussenstellen* and *Aussenstellen* in the Reich. But it also functions abroad where it is represented by *Abteilung III* in an *Einsatzkommando* and in the office of a BdS. The main task of *Amt III* is the collection, by open and secret methods, of information concerning all events and tendencies liable to affect the maintenance of Nazi power at home and abroad. It supervises all " spheres of German life " (*deutsche Lebensgebiete*) and gathers intelligence for the control of all religious, cultural, and economic activities, but especially for the suppression of anti-Nazi elements.

As indicated above, **Amt IV** is the designation of the *Gestapoamt* (*Gestapa*), both titles being still in use. It is mainly concerned with investigating and crushing any opposition to the Nazi régime. For this purpose it controls a vast network of Headquarters of various sizes, known as *Leitstellen*, *Stellen*, *Aussendienststellen* and *Aussenstellen* of the *Gestapo*. It may be said that to a large degree *Amt III* supplies the information used by *Amt IV* as basis for its measures against anti-Nazi elements, although by no means all *Amt III* material is passed for repressive action to the *Gestapo*. Since the dissolution of the former *Abwehr-Amt* the *Gestapo* took over from Military Intelligence all counter-espionage work, and combined it with their similar activities in the political field. This absorption of military counter-espionage caused a complete reorganisation within *Amt IV* some time in the summer of 1944. Further details of the old and new organisation and the activities of *Amt IV* and the *Gestapo* will be discussed in paras. 96–108.

**Amt V**, which is also known as the *Reichskriminalpolizeiamt* (RKPA), is the national Headquarters of the *Reichskriminalpolizei* (*Kripo*, Criminal Police), controlling the network of criminal police offices, the *Kripo-Leitstellen*, -*Stellen*, -*Aussendienststellen* and -*Aussenposten*. The RKPA developed out of the old *Preussisches Landeskriminalamt* (Prussian Criminal Police Headquarters), whose functions consisted only of the combatting of crime in the normal sense of the term. The RPKA, however, under the Nazi régime, has not only expanded the concept of " combatting " to include " prevention " in the most ruthless sense ; it also plays an important part in the investigation and prosecution of what are to-day called " political crimes," but would formerly have been regarded at the most as venial offences. The line dividing cases of interest to the *Gestapo* and those within the field of the *Kripo* has in many instances become rather vague.

Co-operation between *Amt* IV and *Amt* V is therefore extremely close. A detailed discussion of the German Criminal Police and of *Amt* V, its organisation and tasks will be found in paras. 109 ff.

Closely connected with the activities and functions of *Amt* III are those carried out by **Amt VI**, which mainly deals with espionage, sabotage and subversion in occupied and enemy countries. Within this Bureau are concentrated, therefore, the foreign intelligence and the sabotage services of the SD, which, since June, 1944, were reinforced by the military intelligence and sabotage services of the former *Abwehr* (Military Intelligence), now known as the *Militärisches Amt*.

**Amt VII** was added to the RSHA in 1940. It was derived from the *Auslandswissenschaftliches Institut* (Institute for " Research " in Foreign Countries), whose former chief, *Dr.* SIX, was until recently in charge of *Amt* VII. This Bureau maintains close liaison with the Reich Foreign Office in Berlin and probably also with *Genmaj. Prof. Dr.* Karl HAUSHOFER's Geopolitical Institute in Munich. *Amt* VII deals mainly with occupied and satellite countries and is concerned with the preparation of political warfare material and the conduct of ideological supervision, especially in the academic field. The result of the bureau's research is then made available to the RSHA and to the Foreign Office, and possibly also to other official agencies. The SD, including *Amt* III, and brief notes on *Amt* VI, *Amt* VII, and the *Militärisches Amt* is further discussed in paras. 127 ff.

A special independent Section in the RSHA, directly subordinated to the *Chef der Sicherheitspolizei und des SD*, is the **Attaché-Gruppe**. This Section was founded in August, 1942, to combine all functions connected with the work of the *Polizei Attachés* (Police-Attachés) at German Embassies and Legations in neutral and satellite states. Attachés of this kind are, or were, established in Madrid, Rome, Lisbon, Tokio, Zagreb, Athens, Bucharest, Budapest, Sofia, Paris, Bratislava (Pressburg), Ankara, Buenos Aires, Stockholm, Berne and Copenhagen, where they acted as HIMMLER's representatives\*. In the original decree it was pointed out that the *Attaché-Gruppe* in the RSHA was formed as an independent unit in order to concentrate in one section all work of *Ämter* I, II, IV and VI concerning the Police-Attachés and to administer the personnel and technical affairs of the Attachés and their assistants. The section is also instructed to attend to social and technical matters arising from the presence of foreign Police-Attachés accredited to the German Government. The chief of the Attaché-Gruppe is *SS-SBF Dr.* PLOETZ.

## 90. Schools controlled by the RSHA

The following training schools are directly subordinate to and administered by the *Reichssicherheitshauptamt* :—

| | |
|---|---|
| *Führerschule der Sicherheitspolizei und des SD* (Training School for Officers of the Security Police and the SD) | At Berlin-Charlottenburg |
| *Kriminalfachschule* (Criminology College) | Attached to the above |
| *Sicherheitspolizeischule* (Security Police School) | At Fürstenberg |
| *SD Schule* (SD School) | At Bernau, near Berlin. Also reported as Sipo and SD-School |
| *Funkschule* (W/T School) | At Castle Grünberg, near Nepomuk/Protektorat |
| *Schiess-Schule* (Weapon Training School) | At Zella-Mehlis |
| *Sportschule* (Sports Training School) | At Pretzsch/Elbe |
| *Grenzpolizeischulen* (Frontier Police Schools) | At Aken, near Dessau and Pretzsch/Elbe |
| *Schule der Sicherheitspolizei und des SD* (School of the Security Police and SD) | At Prag |

According to the latest reports the schools at Pretzsch are said to have been moved to Fürstenberg.

## 91. Regional Control : Befehlshaber (Inspekteure) der Sipo und des SD

Like the *Ordnungspolizei*, whose highest commander in each *Wehrkreis* is the *Befehlshaber der Orpo*, the *Sicherheitspolizei* and SD are commanded in each *Wehrkreis* by the *Befehlshaber (Inspekteur) der Sicherheitspolizei und des SD* (Commander or Inspector of the Security Police and the Security Service of the C-in-C of the SS). The BdS or IdS is directly responsible to the HSSPf of the *Wehrkreis*, on whose staff he is the representative of the *Sipo* and SD. In the absence of the HSSPf the BdS or IdS assumes final authority in all matters concerning the *Sipo* and SD within the *Wehrkreis* or area. He is also, through the HSSPf, responsible for liaison between the *Sipo* and SD on one hand and the civil authorities, Nazi Party and *Wehrmacht* Headquarters and Internal Defence Authorities, on the other.

When these officers were first appointed in 1936, they were given the title and function of an *Inspekteur* (Inspector) *der Sipo und SD*, abbreviated IdS or IdSPuSD. As in the *Orpo*, however, further concentration of power was deemed necessary in many regions, and *Inspekteure* in occupied territories and in *Wehrkreise* close to the national frontier, such as Austria, Alsace-Lorraine and others, where partisan activities were increasing, were therefore raised to the status of *Befehlshaber* (Commanders) *der Sicherheitspolizei und des SD*, abbreviated BdS or BdSPuSD. The distinction between IdS and BdS is, however, only of minor significance. A BdS has at all times complete command over his forces and supervises the state of training, preparedness, equipment and methods of the units under his command. The IdS normally has only supervisory functions, but he is empowered in case of extreme emergency to assume complete command. As Allied troops advance into German territory, this state of emergency will undoubtedly be considered to exist, rendering the actual difference between a BdS and an IdS one of small consequence, if indeed such a difference has not already disappeared. In the following parts of the book and especially in the Annexes the abbreviation BdS is, therefore, used frequently regardless of whether the latest reports on a particular city give the Office as that of a *Befehlshaber* or *Inspekteur der Sipo und des SD*.

Whenever the *Gestapo*, SD and *Kripo* are

\* In Lisbon and Tokio these men are known as *Polizeiverbindungsführer*.

assigned a combined operation, the BdS or IdS assumes full command over the united forces in the *Wehrkreis* in order to co-ordinate their actions. He may in addition, whenever necessary, request assistance from the *Orpo*. In occupied territory these commanders are known to have led such combined forces in large scale actions against guerrilla and partisan formations.

Special attention should be paid to the tendency to increase constantly the power of the BdS at the expense of the Regional Headquarters of *Gestapo* and *Kripo* (*Leitstellen*), and of the SD (*Leit-Abschnitte*). These Regional Headquarters, discussed more fully later, were originally set up in a *Land*, *Reichsgau* or *Wehrkreis* to control the activities of their respective branches within their area, and especially to exercise a large amount of co-ordinating and directing power over the sub-regional Headquarters, the *Stellen* of *Gestapo* and *Kripo*, and *Abschnitte* of the SD. Since 1941, however, the authority of the Regional Headquarters over the sub-regional Headquarters has been constantly reduced. The name *Leitstelle* or *Leitabschnitt* is still retained, but in power and functions the *Leitstellen* and *Leitabschnitte* may now almost be regarded as juxtaposed to, rather than superior to the *Stellen* and *Abschnitte*, executive power having gradually been transferred to the Office of their BdS or IdS, which has by now become the central authority of the *Sipo* and SD in the *Wehrkreis*. This development is, of course, in line with the constant endeavour to unify and centralise power within the German Police, and to eliminate conflicting and over-lapping authority within the field of action of the Regional Headquarters.

## 92. The Headquarters of the BdS

At present the organisation of the Office of a BdS is mainly known from examples found in occupied or formerly occupied areas such as France. There, the BdS Headquarters was organised into 7 *Abteilungen* (Sections) parallel to *Ämter* I to VII of the RSHA in Berlin. Thus **Abteilungen I and II** of the BdS Headquarters in France dealt largely with organisation, personnel, general administration and legal affairs, like *Amt* I and *Amt* II in the RSHA. However, certain contingencies are apt to arise in occupied territories which would not occur in the area controlled by a corresponding office inside the Reich. For instance, *Abteilung* I in France maintained liaison with the French Police, but in Norway this duty is carried out by a sub-section of *Abteilung* VI.

Like its parent *Amt*, **Abteilung III** watches over German " spheres of life." In this connection the section investigates the economic trends and political feelings of the population towards the German army of occupation in particular and Nazi Germany in general. Constant reports of such findings are made to the parent Amt in Germany. Economic matters in occupied territories are of vital concern to this section, and sabotage of these interests, or even lack of co-operation, in foreign countries can easily be interpreted as falling within the jurisdiction of *Abteilung* III. In this connection documentary evidence indicates that in the course of this " protection " of Reich economic welfare, the material interests of the *Sipo* and SD are frequently permitted to overshadow those of the German people, or even of the German Government.

In occupied countries, as the section handling matters of interest to the *Gestapo*, **Abteilung IV** concerns itself mainly with counter-espionage and the crushing of all resistance groups. Its

sub-divisions correspond generally to those of Amt IV in the RSHA. Special attention is paid by *Abteilung* IV to such elements as Communists, Jews, Freemasons, and members of Rotary Clubs.

**Abteilung V** is the section representative of Amt V of the *Reichskriminalpolizeiamt* in Berlin. It handles criminal matters, but to-day the distinction between ordinary crime and political offence is often rather vague. Black-market investigations are frequently handled by this section in conjunction with *Abteilung* III, as indicated above. Like all agencies of the *Kripo*, *Abteilung* V is also concerned with *Fahndung* (Search for Wanted Persons), which includes search for escaped PW.

Like Amt VI in Berlin, **Abteilung VI** is in many instances closely connected with the activities and functions of *Abteilung* III, but this section, by the very nature of its interest in foreign political intelligence is more or less separated from the other sections, and for a long time its existence was virtually unknown to the rest of the *Sipo* and SD personnel.

In conformity with the relationship between the other RSHA *Ämter* and the corresponding *Abteilungen* abroad, it seems probable that **Abteilung VII** has a twofold function. On the one hand it collects information concerning Nazi interests and local trends abroad, in order to report them to its parent office ; on the other hand, it makes use of the results of " research " given in reports from *Amt* VII in Berlin as a guide in spreading the Nazi gospel outside the Reich borders, especially in educational circles.

The example of BdS offices encountered in France shows that the BdS has some connection with the *Einwanderungszentrale*, the Central Office dealing with repatriation of " Racial " Germans. It is known that the SS deals with the *Umwandererzentralen* in the East through the medium of the SD, so it appears likely that some BdS Headquarters also have a section or sub-section concerned with resettlement matters.

Whereas the Office organisation of all BdS in occupied territories seems to follow more or less the plan outlined above, the organisation of the Office of the BdS or IdS inside Germany is probably on a smaller scale, because much of the actual work is done by the separate Headquarters of the *Gestapo*, *Kripo* and SD. Since the BdS in Germany handles all personnel questions for the three organisations, *Abteilung* I is probably fairly large, but it is doubtful whether *Abteilung* II operates on any extensive scale. *Abteilungen* III, IV and V, inside Germany, are certainly much smaller than in occupied territories because all executive functions are directly handled by the separate *Gestapo*, *Kripo* and SD Headquarters. *Abteilung* VI almost certainly does not exist, and the same may also be true of *Abteilung* VII. All this can only be surmised at the present time until documents showing the organisation of a BdS or IdS Headquarters inside Germany have become available.

## 93. Kommandeure der Sipo und des SD

As in the *Orpo*, we also find in the *Sipo* and SD under certain circumstances Sub-District Commanders who within the areas under their jurisdiction exercise command over all three Services, the *Gestapo*, the *Kripo* and the SD. These are known as *Kommandeure der Sipo und des SD* (KdS or KdSPuSD).

KdS are found in those occupied territories which are known as *Reichskommissariate* and which are divided into Sub-Districts called

*Generalkommissariate.* As explained in para. 18, Police Forces in a *Generalkommissariat* are under the command of an SSPf (Sub-District Commander of SS and Police). The KdS is the representative on his staff for *Sipo* and SD affairs and therefore holds the same position on a smaller scale as his superior, the BdS, does for the whole occupied territory.

In the course of the war, as more and more countries were overrun by the German Army, the *Sipo* and SD were ordered to take charge of security police duties in the newly occupied regions. This included such special tasks as the tracking down of subversive elements, the taking of hostages and the prompt rounding up of Jews and Freemasons. For this purpose mobile task forces, known as *Sipo* and SD *Kommandos* and *Einsatzkommandos* were formed to operate under officers called *Kommandeure der Sicherheitspolizei und des SD*. Each of these units was assigned a certain area. After the initial period of occupation they usually became more and more static, setting up Headquarters in the largest town of the area with parts of the unit, known as *Teilkommandos*, established as outposts in smaller towns. The organisation of these *Kommandos*, *Einsatzkommandos* and *Teilkommandos* is largely the same as the one previously described for the Headquarters of a BdS in an occupied country. Thus, whereas inside Germany the *Gestapo*, *Kripo* and SD have their separate static Headquarters and their separate chains of command, in occupied countries they appeared in combined Headquarters with a much greater degree of unity between the various *Abteilungen*. KdS and their (*Einsatz-*) *Kommandos* were established in France, for example, at Angers, Bordeaux, Chalons s/Marne, Dijon, Limoges, Lyons, Marseilles, Montpellier, Nancy, Orleans, Paris, Poitiers, Rennes, Rouen, St. Quentin, Toulouse and Vichy.

As one after the other of these occupied territories was liberated by the Allies many of these *Einsatzkommandos* again became mobile, at first establishing Headquarters closer to the Reich borders and finally even setting up their offices inside the Reich.

As the military situation in Germany deteriorates the presence of these *Kommandeure* within the Reich itself will become even more logical. Indeed, evidence already exists that a KdS has been established in Reichenberg (former Czech territory) to take over and unify the work of the formerly separate *Gestapo*, *Kripo* and SD Headquarters.

In addition, *Kommandeure der Sipo und des SD* have existed for several years inside Greater Germany where combatting of partisan activities made a local concentration of *Sipo* and SD power necessary. *Kommandeure* of this kind were established in Veldes/Krain and Marburg/Untersteiermark, former Yugoslav territory which was annexed by Germany.

## 94. Sipo and SD Communications : Radio

From the very beginning the SS and the Police considered communications to be a matter of the utmost importance. They owe a considerable part of their power to their control of communications, which they expanded enormously after the " Advent to Power " in 1933. It is not surprising, therefore, that the training of Police signals personnel and the quality of their equipment have always been of the highest order, invariably surpassing those of the *Wehrmacht* or Civil Authorities ; thus, many Police W/T and R/T operators are capable of remarkably high speed transmitting and receiving over protracted periods.

They are trained in such establishments as the *Funkschule der Sipo und des SD* (W/T School of the *Sipo* and SD) at Castle Grünberg in the Protectorate, the *Schupo-Nachrichtenschule* (Protection Police Signal School) at Eilenburg, the *Polizeischule für Nachrichtenhelferinnen* (Police School for Women Signals Operators) at Erfurt and the *SS-Funkschule* (SS Signals School) at Unna.

The basic system of German Police wireless transmission is the " *Polfunk*," a dense network of immobile W/T stations situated all over Germany and controlled by the Central Wireless Station in Berlin (*Hauptfunkstelle Berlin*). This network is made up of *Leitfunkstellen* (Regional Control Wireless Stations) and *Nebenleitfunkstellen* (Branch Wireless Stations) of which there are one or two in every *Wehrkreis*. The (*Neben-*)*Leitfunkstellen* each have a number of smaller *Funkstellen* (Sub-Stations) working with them. There is also a large number of small transmitting stations, known as *Gendarmeriefunkstellen* (Rural Police Wireless Stations), located in the mountainous country of former Austria.

The *Polfunk* system is operated by the *Orpo*, but is at the disposal of all branches of the German Police. The *Kripo* makes extensive use of it for *Fahndungen* (Searches for Wanted Persons) and for other investigations ; a noun code issued by the *Internationale Kriminalpolizeiliche Kommission* (IKPK—International Criminal Police Commission) is employed. For details of the *Polfunk* network and the IKPK noun code see Annexe F.

The *Sipo* and SD also have their own network of immobile W/T stations, but this is not nearly so extensive as the *Polfunk*. Very few of its stations are in Germany proper, the majority being established in occupied territories, especially in Norway and the East ; the reason for this is probably the comparatively poor and uncertain communications in those countries.

It is interesting to note some of the instructions which are issued to *Sipo* and SD personnel with regard to this radio network. For instance, it is specifically stated that wireless is only to be used where no teleprinter or other means of communication are available, or where the message concerned is addressed to a limited number of recipients. Messages of high security classification, such as " *Geheime Reichssache* " (Top Secret), can be sent by wireless only in an emergency or if no other means of communications are available, and must of course be sent in code. At no time may messages received by wireless be re-transmitted to the final recipient over ordinary postal telephone lines ; the recipient may only be told over the telephone that there is a message for him. Further instructions state that wireless messages should contain no more than 20 typewritten lines and must be in telegraphic style, omitting all reference to file numbers or any other identification. Other details concerning the *Sipo* and SD wireless network, and the full text of the German instructions are given in Annexe F.

The *Sipo* and SD also own a considerable amount of mobile two-way wireless equipment of excellent quality which they can, if need be, supplement by similar high quality transmitting and receiving gear held by the *Orpo* as well as by various other para-military organisations. The NSKK, the HJ and the SA maintain signals units of their own which are well equipped, though their personnel is probably not as highly trained as that of the SS and Police.

For high speed W/T transmissions the German Police is reported to make considerable use of

" *Hellschreiber* " apparatus (high speed radio teletype).

## 95. Telephone and Teletype

. For long-distance communications the *Sipo* and SD use mainly underground single-wire or multi-wire telephone and teletype channels, each wire carrying a multi-load of anything from 5 to 12 circuits. It is not certain whether these lines are owned and maintained by the *Sipo* and SD or whether they are rented from the postal authorities, but as the maintenance of an independent network, spread all over Germany and some of the occupied countries as well, would mean an enormous expenditure of money and manpower, it is more likely that the lines are merely rented and actually belong to the regular postal network. Recently captured documents stressing the importance of security and warning all *Sipo* and SD personnel against the use of telephone and teletype when transmitting classified information in plain language, seem to bear out this assumption.

For local, short-distance communications, however, the *Sipo* and SD undoubtedly possess lines of their own. Those lines, partly telephone and partly teletype, connect for instance many *Grenzpolizeiposten* of the *Gestapo* with the controlling *Grenzpolizeikommissariat*, or *Kriminalreviere* with the local *Kripo* Headquarters. It is believed that many of these lines are scrambled.

No documents showing the location and inter-connections of *Sipo* and SD telephone lines have come to hand up to the present time, but an original German list of August, 1941, plus several amendments up to 1943 have yielded details of the *Sipo* and SD teletype network (see Annexe F).

This network not only connects the main Headquarters of the *Sipo* and SD, but its branch-lines also reach the various regional and district offices. Direct teletype lines provide connections with the private residences of HITLER and HIMMLER, the Foreign Office, the Reich Ministry of the Interior, and the Headquarters of HIMMLER's Personal Staff. Other teletype lines are extended to the Concentration Camps and the *Volksgerichtshof* (People's Court) as well as to the Headquarters of the Military Districts and the *Gestapo* Frontier Police Posts.

It must be assumed that a number of new lines have since been added, probably extending branch lines down to most, if not all of the lower echelons of the *Sipo* and SD as well as to the branch offices of the *Militärisches Amt* (M.I. Bureau).

Complete control of all the German Police communications networks is a necessity for the Allies, since it will mean control over the most dangerous potential source of opposition which the Occupying Forces are likely to encounter. In this connection it is significant that, according to a number of sources, HIMMLER's forces are collecting lightweight and mobile signal equipment of all types, including lorry driven wireless transmitters and field receiving sets. Depots for such equipment are reported to be located near Concentration Camps (e.g. Oranienburg).

The networks of the *Gestapo*, *Kripo* and other German Police services, when fully controlled, would also constitute a most useful system of inter-communication between the various Allied regional Headquarters and other military units.

# B. GEHEIME STAATSPOLIZEI

## 96. The Gestapo Headquarters, Amt IV of the RSHA

Amt IV of the RSHA is also known as the *Geheime ·Staatspolizeiamt (Gestapa)*, the original *Gestapo* Headquarters. It deals with the investigation and elimination of all political opposition to the Nazi State. The *Gestapo* receives much of its material and direction for its action from the *Sicherheitsdienst*, but in addition the *Gestapo* joins the SD in the " observation " of the German population, maintaining a great many files and a network of agents of its own. As one of the three branches of the *Staatsschutzkorps* (the " Combined Force for the Protection of the State," consisting of the *Gestapo*, SD and *Kripo*) the *Gestapo* is responsible for those measures—so characteristic of Nazi Police principles—which are euphemistically termed " *Präventivmassnahmen staatsabträglicher Handlungen* " (measures for the prevention of acts which might be harmful to the Reich). The implications of such vague terms are obvious, and they become even more striking when considered in the light of the official rights and privileges bestowed upon the *Gestapo*.

*Gestapo* decisions are not subject to, or limited by, any revision by the ordinary Judiciary (see para. 10). Furthermore the *Gestapo* may call upon the services of all other police branches in Germany and Occupied Territories and issue orders and directives to them ; in the German terminology, the *Gestapo* is " *weisungsberechtigt gegenüber allen anderen Zweigen der Polizei.*" Thus, the *Gestapo* has assumed unlimited powers, and serves the Nazi State as an efficient tool for the ruthless suppression of all dissenters.

*Amt* IV, the Headquarters of all *Gestapo* activities, is a vast and intricate organisation reflecting in its structure the widespread interests and functions of the Secret State Police. Up to the summer of 1944, *Amt* IV was sub-divided into several, probably 6, *Gruppen* (Sections), lettered from A to F. Shortly before the attempt on HITLER's life in July, 1944, the *Abwehr* (Military Intelligence) was dissolved and *Amt* IV of the RSHA took over most of the functions of M.I. Section III dealing with counter-espionage. This caused a complete reorganisation of *Amt* IV and, according to latest indications, it now consists of two *Gruppen* only, IV A and IV B.

·*Gruppe* IV.A now covers most of the functions of the former *Amt* IV of the RSHA. In *Gruppe* IV B the counter-espionage activities of the former *Abwehr* are combined with the supervision of foreigners and the control of passports, visas and other identity papers.

Like the· other *Ämter* of the RSHA, *Amt* IV is organised into *Gruppen* (Sections, e.g. IV A), *Referate* (Sub-Sections, ·e.g. IV A 1) and *Hilfsreferate* (Sub-Sectional Units, e.g. IV A 1 a). In detail *Amt* IV appears to be organised as shown in the next paragraph.

*Note.*—Headlines marked by an asterisk (*) were not contained in the main source, but were taken from other German papers.

## 97. Structure of Amt IV

The official heading of *Amt* IV of the RSHA is *Gegner-Erforschung und Bekämpfung* (Investigation and Combatting of Opposition ; it is organised as follows :—

### Gruppe IV A

#### IV A 1
#### * Opposition

**IV A 1 a**

| | |
|---|---|
| *Kommunismus, Marxismus und Nebenorganisationen (Nationalkommittee " Freies Deutschland ") in Deutschland, den besetzten Gebieten und auch im Ausland* | Communism, Marxism and affiliated organisations (National Committee " Free Germany ") in Germany, occupied territories and foreign countries |
| *Rundfunk-Verbrechen* | Violation of broadcasting regulations |
| *Illegale kommunistische und marxistische Propaganda* | Illegal communist and marxist propaganda |
| *F e i n d p r o p a g a n d a —durch Flugblätter und A u s l a n d s e n d u n g e n— und deren Verbreitung* | Enemy propaganda— through leaflets and foreign broadcasts— and its dissemination |
| *B a n d e n u n w e s e n in Deutschland, der Untersteiermark und Oberkrain* | Hostile guerrilla units in Germany and the annexed portions of Northern Yugoslavia |
| *Deutsche und verbündete Kriegsgefangene in Sowjetrussischer Gefangenschaft* | German and satellite Prisoners-of-War in Soviet captivity |

**IV A 1 b**

| | |
|---|---|
| *Reaktion* | Reactionary movements |
| *Opposition* | Opposition |
| *Liberalismus* | Liberalism |
| *Legitimismus* | Monarchism |
| *Pazifismus* | Pacifism |

| | |
|---|---|
| *Heimtückeangelegenheiten* | Treacherous acts, spreading of rumours, etc. |
| *Zersetzung der Wehrmacht und Miesmacherei* | Undermining of the morale of the Armed Forces, grumbling |
| *Defaitismus* | Defeatism |
| *Unzufriedene Wehrmachtsangehörige in Deutschland, auch in Kriegsgefangenschaft und deren Angehörige* | Discontented members of the Armed Forces in Germany, also those in enemy captivity, and their next-of-kin |

#### IV A 2
#### * Sabotage

**IV A 2 a**

| | |
|---|---|
| *Sabotageabwehr und -Bekämpfung* | Prevention and combatting of sabotage |
| *Politische Attentate* | Political assassinations |
| *Politische Pass- und Ausweisfälschungen* | Forgery of passports and identity papers, for political purposes |
| *Terroristen* | Terrorists |
| *Syndikalisten* | Syndicalists |

**IV A 2 b**

| | |
|---|---|
| *Fallschirmagenten* | Parachute agents |
| *Funkspiele* | Radio interference, jamming |

#### IV A 3
*Abwehr* (Counter Intelligence)

**IV A 3 a**

| | |
|---|---|
| *Gesellschaftsspionage* | Combatting of espionage in society |

* See note, para. 96

| | | | |
|---|---|---|---|
| *Fahrlässiger Landesverrat* | Treason through negligence, careless talk, etc. | | |

<table>
<tr><td>Fahrlässiger Landesverrat</td><td>Treason through negligence, careless talk, etc.</td></tr>
<tr><td>Spionage</td><td>Combatting of political espionage</td></tr>
</table>

**IV A 3 b**

| | |
|---|---|
| *Wirtschaftsangelegenheiten in Deutschland, den besetzten Gebieten, im Verkehr mit dem Ausland und umgekehrt (siehe auch unter Amt III)* | Economic matters in Germany and the occupied territories, trade with foreign countries (see also under Amt III of the RSHA) |
| *Wirtschaftsspionage* | Combatting of espionage |
| *Surveillance in der Schweiz* | Surveillance activities in Switzerland |
| *Devisenvergehen* | Transgressions of foreign exchange regulations |

**IV A 3 c**

| | |
|---|---|
| *G r e n z a n gelegenheiten, kleiner Grenzverkehr und Grenzzwischenfälle* | Frontier Control, local border traffic and frontier incidents |

**IV A 3 d**

| | |
|---|---|
| *Abwehr über Nachrichtenverkehr* | Signals and Communications counter - intelligence (monitoring, censorship, etc.) |
| *Verstösse gegen den Nachrichtenverkehr* | Illegal Communications traffic |

*(IV A 3 d incorporates Section III N of the former Abwehr-Amt.)*

### IV A 4

**\* *Weltanschauliche Gegner* (Ideological Opponents)**

**IV A 4 a**

| | |
|---|---|
| *Katholizismus und Protestantismus, Sekten, sonstige Kirchen, Freimaurer in Deutschland und den besetzten Gebieten* | Catholicism and Protestantism, sects, other religious bodies, freemasons, in Germany and in the occupied territories |
| *Grundsätzliche Angelegenheiten, auch im Ausland* | Basic problems at home and abroad |

**IV A 4 b**

| | |
|---|---|
| *J u d e n, Emigranten, Volks- u n d Staatsfeindliche Vermögensangelegenheiten, Aberkennung d e r Reichsangehörigkeit, im Inland, den besetzten Gebieten und Ausland* | Jews, emigrés, Enemy and Opposition Property, taking away of Reich citizenship, at home, in the occupied territories and abroad |

### IV A 5

**\* *Sonderfälle* (Special Cases)**

**IV A 5 a**

| | |
|---|---|
| *Schutzdienst* | Protective Service (for leading Party and Government personalities) |
| *Sonderaufgaben* | Special duties |
| *Asoziales Verhalten gegen Evakuierte* | Unfriendly attitude towards evacuees |
| *Deutsche Arbeitsbummelanten* | German work-dodgers |
| *Gemeinschaftswidriges Verhalten* | Anti-social behaviour |

**IV A 5 b**

| | |
|---|---|
| *Parteiangelegenheiten und Presse* | Party Affairs and Press |

### IV A 6

**\* *Karteien und Fahndung* (Card Indexes and Search for Wanted Persons)**

**IV A 6 a**

| | |
|---|---|
| *Kartei und Personalakten* | Card Index, Personal Dossiers (Probably the central index of the RSHA) |
| *Auskunft* | Information |

**IV A 6 b**

| | |
|---|---|
| *Schutzhaft* | Protective custody (Concentration Camps) |

**IV (?)**

| | |
|---|---|
| *Ausländische Arbeiter u n d fremdländische Kriegsgefangene* | Foreign workers and prisoners-of-war |
| *Fluchtabsichten u n d Fluchten ausländischer Arbeiter in Deutschland und den besetzten Gebieten (siehe auch Amt V)* | Escapes and attempts to escape by foreign workers in Germany and the occupied territories (see also Amt V of the RSHA) |
| *Unerlaubte Briefvermittlung* | Illicit transmission of mail to and from foreign workers |
| *Arbeitsverweigerung der Ausländer* | Refusal to work by foreigners |

*Note.*—The number of this *Hilfsreferat* is not clear. From a comparison with the structure of some outposts of the Gestapo one would expect it to be IV A 6 c or possibly IV A 1 c. The original Gestapo document from which this tabulation was mainly taken listed the number as IV 8, but this seems more likely to be due to an error or a mutilation in transmission.

## Gruppe IV B

### \* Abwehrangelegenheiten (Military Counter Intelligence)

**IV B 1**

**\* Western Europe, English-speaking countries, Scandinavia**

**IV B 1 a**

| | |
|---|---|
| *Frankreich, Belgien* | France, Belgium |

**IV B 1 b**

| | |
|---|---|
| *Holland, England, Nordamerika, Kanada* | Holland, England, North America, Canada |

**IV B 1 c**

| | |
|---|---|
| *Dänemark, Norwegen, Schweden, Finnland* | Denmark, Norway, Sweden, Finland. |

**IV B 2**

**\* Eastern Europe**

**IV B 2 a**

| | |
|---|---|
| *Ostgebiete, sowie Sowjet Union* | Eastern territories, and Soviet Union |
| *Weissruthenische, ukrainische Emigration, Vertrauensstellen* | White Ruthenian and Ukrainian emigration, confidential agents |

**IV B 2 b**

| | |
|---|---|
| *General Gouvernement* | Government General (Poland) |

**IV B 2 c**

| | |
|---|---|
| *Protektorat, Slovakei* | Protectorate, Slovakia |

\* See note, para. 96

## IV B 3
* Southern and South-eastern Europe, Africa and South America

**IV B 3 a**

| | |
|---|---|
| *Balkan mit Ungarn und Rumänien, Bulgarien, Türkei, Ferner Osten* | Balkans, including Hungary and Roumania, Bulgaria, Turkey, Far East |

**IV B 3 b**

| | |
|---|---|
| *Schweiz, Italien, Spanien, Portugal, Afrika, Süd-Amerika* | Switzerland, Italy, Spain, Portugal, Africa, South America |

*Note.*—All the above sub-sections of *Gruppe* B (IV B 1 a to IV B 3 b) deal with matters which were, until summer 1944, handled by *Abwehr* III, a section of the former Military Intelligence dealing exclusively with security and counter espionage. *Abwehr* III had separate sub-sections watching over security in the German Army, Navy and Air Force. Other sub-sections of *Abwehr* III dealt with the security and protection of German industries, especially of civilian establishments connected with the Armed Forces, the combatting of enemy intelligence services and their deception for strategic purposes, security in PW camps, compilation of statistics for security instruction, and the supervision of public communications, which included censorship. All but the last-mentioned item are now handled by the above sub-sections of IV B. Communications and censorship are dealt with in IV A 3.

### IV B 4
* *Passangelegenheiten* (Passport Matters)

**IV B 4 a**

| | |
|---|---|
| *Passwesen* | Passports |

**IV B 4 b**

| | |
|---|---|
| *Ausweiswesen, Kennkarten* | Identity papers, identity cards |
| *Ausländerpolizei* | Registration and Control of Foreigners |

**IV B 4 c**

| | |
|---|---|
| *Zentrale Sichtvermerkstelle* | Central Office for Issue of Visas |

## 98. The former structure of Amt IV

Before the reorganisation, the structure of *Amt* IV presented a more complicated picture. No single document revealing the old organisation has been found, but a fair amount of information on it has been extracted from various sources. Since many documents coming to hand at the present time still refer to the old organisation of *Amt* IV, it has been considered advisable to reproduce it. All the functions of the old *Amt* IV are retained in the new structure, and details known about the old organisation may also help to clarify the present system.

Wherever information is derived from PW and other reports, this is indicated by the use of such phrasing as " it is reported." If documentary evidence itself was insufficient but certain conclusions could be drawn from the general structure, the item is marked thus †. It must be remembered, however, that this tabulation of the former *Amt* IV is neither complete nor correct in all its details. There may have been a number of additional sections and sub-sections, the existence of which did not become known, while others which are listed may actually have dealt with a much wider field than could be gathered from the available documents. Since the German terms given in the next paragraph are not in all cases known to be official, they are given in brackets after the English definition.

Just before the reorganisation in summer, 1944, *Amt* IV appears to have been organised as follows :

### Gruppe IV A
#### † Sabotage—Security—Opposition

#### IV A 1
† Treason—Sabotage

**IV A 1 a**
High treason and acts of sabotage committed by Germans
Possible sub-divisions :
Communists and Marxists
Social-Democrats and Trades Unionists
Other Left-Wing subversive elements

**IV A 1 b**
Enemy sabotage and enemy propaganda
Possible sub-divisions :
Sabotage through agents and parachutists, dropping of forged papers, ration cards, etc.
Propaganda through leaflets and broadcasts, jamming of foreign broadcasts (*Gegenfunkspiele*)

**IV A 1 c**
Sabotage by foreigners (especially foreign workers and PW)

#### IV A 2
† Open Terrorist Attacks, Forgeries

**IV A 2 a**
†Search for wanted terrorists, identification of evidence (*Fahndung, Erkennungsdienst*)
This may include a central card index, known as IVA—PA, of persons wanted in connection with terrorism

**IV A 2 b**
†Arms—High Explosives (*Waffen—Sprengstoffe*)

**IV A 2 c**
Central Bureau for combatting forgeries, for political reasons, of passports and identity papers (*Zentralstelle zur Bekämpfung der politischen Pass- und Ausweisfälschungen*)
Dealing with forgery, theft, and illegal use of identity papers.

#### IV A 3
Right-Wing Opposition, Subversive Activities and Treacherous Acts
(*Reaktion, Widerstandsbewegungen, Opposition, Heimtückeangelegenheiten*)

This sub-section seems to have been the Right-Wing counterpart to IV A 1 above. It may have had separate sub-divisions for the *Deutsch-Nationale Partei* (German Nationalist Party) and for other Right-Wing political bodies of the Weimar period, such as the *Junkers, Stahlhelm, Zentrum, Deutsche Volkspartei*, etc. Other activities include dismissed or penalised officials (*Gemassregelte Beamte*) and disgruntled members of the Nazi Party. All these activities are now dealt with by IV A 1 b under the new organisation of the *Gestapo Amt*.

#### IV A 4
Personal security of prominent members of the Government and the Nazi Party (*Schutzdienst*)
Possible sub-divisions :—
Investigation of assassinations.
Train control (Zü = *Zugüberwachung*).
Mail control (Pü = *Postüberwachung*).
Special investigations.

* See note, para. 96     † See above

## Gruppe IV B
### † Ideological Opponents (Weltanschauliche Gegner)

Whereas the opponents mentioned in IV A are active enemies of Nazism, IV B dealt with people who by reason of their spiritual, intellectual or racial background take a negative attitude towards the régime. Although they are less likely to obstruct Nazism openly they are just as vigorously prosecuted and checked by the *Gestapo*.

### IV B 1
#### Roman Catholic Church

Supervision of the Roman Catholic Church, R.C. clubs and organisations, religious orders, Catholic Press, etc.

### IV B 2
#### Protestants

Protestants and other religious sects, their clergy, press, clubs, charitable institutions, etc.

This *Referat* was at times reported to deal with political supervision of the press, but this seems rather to have been handled normally in *Referat* IV C 3.

### IV B 3
#### Freemasons and Lodges

A document from a Regional Headquarters of the *Gestapo* mentions this *Referat* as having dealt also with emigrés. It is, however, more likely that such work was handled by IV B 4 a or b.

### IV B 4
#### Jews

This *Referat* probably dealt with those activities which, under the new organisation, are handled by the *Hilfsreferat* IV A 4 b, such as Jews, emigrés, enemy and opposition property, taking away of Reich Citizenship.

IV B 4 a (?)

IV B 4 b (?)

IV B 4 c

Seizure of property belonging to enemy and opposition groups. (*Einziehung von Volks- und Staats- (Reichs-) feindlichen Vermögen*).

## Gruppe IV C
### Central Registry

### IV C 1
#### Central Registry

This *Referat*, sometimes known as IV C—PA, disseminated information and rendered reports to other *Referate*, offices of the *Gestapo* and other specific persons. It also checked applications for visas, passports and other identity papers against the files.

### IV C 2
#### Protective Custody (*Schutzhaft*)

Transfer of persons into concentration camps (*Einweisung in Konzentrationslager*), release, if any, from concentration camps, and treatment after release.

This *Referat* maintained its own card index, known as the *Schutzhaftkartei*, showing the names of all those who are, or ever have been in protective custody. It is not clear whether this section also handled the political supervision of concentration camps through the Political Commissars.

*Note.*—IV C 1 and 2 formed the "*Zentralkartei des RSHA*" (Central Card Index of the RSHA), which became IV A 6 in the new numbering system.

### IV C 3
#### (Files of printed matter)

Pictures, magazines and foreign newspapers.

Documentary evidence exists that this *Referat* dealt with the prohibition of foreign magazines and newspapers and the ban on indecent books and papers (*Ausländische Druckschriften, Photo-Akt-Werke*). It is possible that it was concerned generally with *Gestapo* supervision of the press.

### IV C 4

Reported to have dealt with control of members of the Party and its formations.

This *Referat* dealt more with the general supervision of Party personnel than with the investigation of subversive activities by disaffected members as covered by IV A 3.

## Gruppe IV D
### Foreigners

This Gruppe dealt mainly with the investigation and prosecution of anti-Nazi underground movements among foreigners in the Reich and occupied countries.

### IV D 1
#### Czechs and Slovaks

(*Protektoratsangelegenheiten, Tschechen im Reich*)

### IV D 2
#### Poles

(*Gouvernementsangelegenheiten ; Polen im Reich*)

IV D 2 a (?)

IV D 2 b (?)

IV D 2 c

Identified as having dealt with matters relating to medals and decorations worn by Poles.

### IV D 3
#### Enemy Aliens (*Staatsfeindliche Ausländer*)

### IV D 4

People from occupied territories, other than Czechs and Poles.

This probably included Danes, Norwegians, Dutch, Belgians, French and Balkan Peoples.

IV D 4 a (?)

IV D 4 b (?)

IV D 4 c (?)

IV D 4 d (?)

IV D 4 e

Frenchmen

This *Hilfsreferat* recovered the personnel files from the Sureté Nationale and set them up in Berlin in January, 1943. They were used to provide political information concerning French citizens and persons who resided in France up to 1940, their citizenship status, their political activities and other details.

IV D 4 e also collected and disseminated information concerning French Trade Unions, clubs, newspapers and magazines.

The file is maintained independently of the Central Card Index of the RSHA, which was kept in *Referat* IV C 1 and IV C 2 (see above). It can be assumed that IV D 4 a, b, c and d recovered similar files for the countries they dealt with.

† See above

## Gruppe IV E
### Counter Espionage, Political and Economic Control

This Gruppe, dealing with counter espionage, was subdivided according to the countries involved. Gruppe IV E may also have dealt with the political control of concentration camps through the Political Commissars, but this has not been definitely established.

*Gruppe* IV E published its own Gazette, reporting on discoveries about enemy Secret Service organisations (*Feind Nachrichtendienst ;* ND) and on the search for wanted enemy agents. This publication, entitled "*Mitteilungsblatt der Gruppe* IV E," was issued on the 15th of each month.

### IV E 1
Counter Espionage along the German Frontiers
Direction of counter espionage work of the *Grenzpolizei* (Frontier Police).

### IV E 2
Economic and Political Control of Trades
Possibly also handled liaison with *Arbeitsämter* (Labour Bureaux).

IV E 2 a
Imports
A file found with this number concerned the limited free importation of goods by members of the Armed Forces.

IV E 2 b
Exports

IV E 2 c (?)

IV E 2 d
Security of industrial establishments (*Industriesicherung*), liaison with and control of Industrial Police (*Werkschutz*) and private detective agencies (*Bewachungsgewerbe*).

### IV E 3
Counter Espionage : France, Belgium, Switzerland.
A large amount of work by this *Referat* was devoted to the control of former members of the French Foreign Legion—regardless of their citizenship—upon their entry into the Reich, especially with regard to their possible membership of the French Secret Service. For this purpose, as well as for the purpose of handling their resettlement or expatriation, a Central Card Index of former members of the Legion was maintained in this *Referat*, in cooperation with the *Stapoleitstelle* Karlsruhe. In 1940 and 1941 a special camp for returning legionnaires, the *Durchgangslager* (Transit Camp) in Kislau, was set up and close cooperation maintained with the Frontier Police in order to catch all legionnaires who entered the Reich.

### IV E 4
Counter Espionage : English-speaking Countries and Northern Europe (England, USA, Sweden, etc.).
Owing to its connections with Great Britain and the U.S., counter espionage against supporters of de Gaulle was also handled by IV E 4 rather than IV E 3.

### IV E 5
Counter Espionage : the East (Russia, Poland, Finland).

### IV E 6
Counter Espionage : the South.
(Czechoslovakia, Balkans, Hungary, Italy, Spain and S. America).

## Gruppe IV F
### Border Control of Civilians—Grenzpolizei

Identity papers, passports, visas, control of foreigners upon entry into the Reich, and similar subjects.

### IV F 1
Civilian "*Passeure.*"
Smugglers, smuggling of persons, letters and information across the borders.

### IV F 2
Control of legal border traffic.
Visas, papers, passports (*Passangelegenheiten*) where espionage is not suspected ; local border traffic (*kleiner Grenzverkehr*).

### IV F 3
General prosecution of wanted persons.
Possibly included cases of refusal to serve in the Labour Service and the Armed Forces, desertion, self-mutilation and other crimes against Germany's war effort. (*Kriegsfahndung, Sonderfahndung, Fahnenflucht, Überläufer, Zersetzung der Wehrkraft, Selbstverstümmelung*).

### IV F 4
Registration of civilian foreign workers upon entry into the Reich (*Ausländerüberwachung— Ausländerzentralkartei*)
This *Referat* assigns the foreign workers to industry, possibly in cooperation with the *Arbeitsämter* (Labour Bureaux).

## 99. Other possible sections of Amt IV

One other section should also be mentioned, although there is no documentary proof of its actual existence in the RSHA, viz. *Gruppe* IV N (*Nachrichten*—communications and information). In view of the fact that a sub-section IV N appears in almost all documents describing the inner organisation of out-stations of the *Gestapo* it is quite likely that a similar section exists in *Amt* IV of the RSHA.

There are a number of other designations of sub-sections which occur frequently in the lower echelons of the *Gestapo*, but it is not at all certain whether these designations are also used in *Amt* IV. It may, however, be worth while to enumerate those which are most frequently encountered, namely :—

IV G *Gefangenen - Transporte* (Transport of prisoners)

IV H Nazi Party and Affiliated Organisations

IV J *Juden* (Jews and Concentration Camps, Card Index of Jews—see also IV A 4)

IV K *Kirchenwesen* (Churches and Sects—see also IV A 4)

IV M *Freimaurer* (Freemasons : see also IV A 4)

IV P *Presse* (Press—see also IV B 2 and IV C 3, in the former structure)

IV R *Russenangelegenheiten* (Russian PWs and Civilians)

IV S *Schutzdienst* (Security of prominent people, sometimes also including investigation regarding Nazi Party members, combatting of homosexuals, etc.—see also IV A 5)

It was also reported at one time that the *Gestapo* had a section known as IV RW (for *Reichswehr*), dealing with the collection of dossiers on prominent members of the German Armed Forces. This section was said to have been created as early as 1933 to collect data on personalities of the *Reichswehr* and to have expanded and continued its functions under the original designation even after the *Reichswehr* had been transformed into the *Wehrmacht* in 1935. No documentary proof, however, of the existence of such an office in the RSHA has come to hand. There is not much doubt that the Party, and in particular the SS, keep a close check on personalities of the Armed Forces, but if a special office for this purpose exists within the framework of the German Police it seems more likely that it would be connected with *Amt* III of the RSHA and the organisation of the SD.

## 100. Functions of the Gestapo

The main functions of the *Geheime Staatspolizei* are "prevention," detection and prosecution of political crimes as defined by the Nazis. It has been previously pointed out that the *Gestapo* interprets its mission in the widest possible sense of the word; basically, however, it concerns itself with the following types of "crime" or any expedient elaboration of them.

(Interpretations rather than exact translations have been given in the right hand column, and in view of the difference between the Nazi and Allied systems of government, the word "Gesetz" has been translated as "decree" rather than as "law").

| | |
|---|---|
| *Landesverrat gem. ¶¶ 88 –93 RStGB (Reichs-Strafgesetzbuch)* | Treason according to articles 88–93 of the Reich Penal Code |
| *Hochverrat gem. ¶¶ 80– 87 RStGB* | High Treason (treason aimed at the overthrow of the German Government) according to articles 80–87 of the Reich Penal Code |
| *Weitere im RStGB enthaltene Tatbestände wie öffentliche Beschimpfung des Staates* | Other crimes mentioned in the Reich Penal Code, such as public libel and slander of the Government |
| *Öffentliche Beschimpfung der Partei und ihrer Gliederungen* | Public libel or slander of the National Socialist Party and its formations, e.g. the SS, SA or NSKK |
| *Aufruhr* | Riots or incitement to rioting |
| *Verletzung der Wehrpflicht und der Wehrkraft* | Contraventions of the Conscription Law and offences against Germany's war potential |
| *Unterlassung der rechtzeitigen Anzeige von Verbrechen des Hochverrats, des Landesverrats usw.* | Failure to make a prompt report of any indications of high treason and treasonable acts, etc. |
| *Feindliche Handlungen gegen befreundete Staaten* | Hostile acts against friendly nations |
| *Verbrechen und Vergehen in Beziehung auf die Ausübung staatsbürgerlicher Rechte u.a.* | Crimes and offences against the exercise of citizens' rights and privileges |
| *Zuwiderhandlungen gegen das Gesetz gegen heimtückische Angriffe auf Staat und Partei und zum Schutz der Parteiuniformen vom 20. Dez 34* | Offences against the decree of 20 Dec 34 dealing with treacherous attacks on the Government and Party, and Protection of Party Uniforms |
| *Zuwiderhandlungen gegen das Gesetz zum Schutze von Bezeichnungen der NSDAP vom 7. Apr 37* | Offences against the Decree of 7 Apr 37 for the Protection of Party Designations |
| *Zuwiderhandlungen gegen das Gesetz zum Schutze der nationalen Symbole vom 19. Mai 33* | Offences against the Decree of 19 May 33 for the Protection of National Symbols |
| *Zuwiderhandlungen gegen das Gezetz zur Abwehr politischer Gewalttaten vom 4. Apr 33* | Offences against the Decree of 4 Apr 33 for the Prevention of Political Terrorism or Acts of Violence |
| *Zuwiderhandlungen gegen das Gesetz gegen Verrat der deutschen Volkswirtschaft vom 12. Juni 33* | Offences against the Decree of 12 Jun 33 against Treason towards the German Economic System |
| *Zuwiderhandlungen gegen auf Grund der Verordnung des Reichspräsidenten zum Schutz von Volk und Staat vom 28. Februar 33 getroffene Massnahmen* | Offences against any of the Statutes or Ordinances based on the Presidential Decree of 28 Feb 33 for the Protection of Nation and Government |
| *Zuwiderhandlungen gegen das Gesetz über die Einziehung kommunistischen Vermögens vom 26. Mai 33* | Offences against the Decree of 26 May 33 covering the Expropriation of Communist Property |
| *Zuwiderhandlungen gegen das Gesetz zur Gewährleistung des Rechtsfriedens vom 13. Okt 33* | Offences against the Decree of 13 Oct 33 for the Protection of the Judicial Administration |
| *Zuwiderhandlungen gegen das Gesetz gegen die Neubildung von Parteien vom 14. Juli 33* | Contraventions of the Decree of 14 Jul 33 against the Formation of new Political Parties or Factions |
| *Zuwiderhandlungen gegen das Gesetz gegen Wirtschaftssabotage vom 1. Dez 36* | Offences against the Decree of 1 Dec 36 against Economic Sabotage |
| *Zuwiderhandlungen gegen das Gesetz über die Devisenbewirtschaftung (Devisengesetz) vom 12. Dez 38* | Offences against the Statutes of 12 Dec 38 dealing with the Administration of Foreign Exchange (Foreign exchange Regulations and Restrictions) |
| *Zuwiderhandlungen gegen :—* | Offences against :— |
| *(a) die Verordnung über den Warenverkehr vom 18. August 39* | (a) the Ordinance of 18 Aug 39 for the Control of Goods and Trade |
| *(b) die Verordnung über die Wirtschaftsverwaltung vom 27. August 39* | (b) the Ordinance of 27 Aug 39 establishing German Economic Administration |

| | |
|---|---|
| (c) die Verordnung zur vorläufigen Sicherstellung des lebenswichtigen Bedarfs des deutschen Volkes vom 27. August 34 | (c) the Ordinance dated 27 Aug 39 covering provisionally defined Priorities to provide for the Essential Needs of the German People (Food, Consumer Goods, Fuel, etc.) |
| (d) die zu den 3 vorerwähnten Verordnungen ergangenen Durchführungs- und Ergänzungsverordnungen | (d) any other ordinances which were issued as directives and supplements to the three preceding ordinances |
| Zuwiderhandlungen gegen die Verordnung über ausserordentliche Rundfunkmassnahmen vom 1. Sept 39 | Offences against the Ordinances of 1 Sep 39 covering extra-ordinary measures relating to Wireless Transmitting and Receiving |
| Zuwiderhandlungen gegen die Grenzzonenverordnung vom 2. Sept 39 | Offences against the Ordinances of 2 Sep 39 for the Protection of the German Border Regions and Internal Customs Zones |
| Zuwiderhandlungen gegen die Verordnung über die Behandlung von Ausländern vom 5. Sept 39 | Offences against the Ordinance of 5 Sep 39 dealing with the Treatment of Foreigners (PWs, Non-German workers, etc.) |
| Zuwiderhandlungen gegen die Verordnung gegen Volksschädlinge vom 5. Sept 39 | Offences against the Ordinances of 5 Sep 39 against the Enemies of the People (Anti-social Elements, as defined by German decrees) |
| Zuwiderhandlungen gegen die Verordnung zur Ergänzung der Strafvorschriften zum Schutze der Wehrkraft des deutschen Volkes vom 25. Nov 39 | Offences against the Ordinance of 24 Nov 39 supplementing the Penal Regulations for the Protection of Germany's war effort |
| Zuwiderhandlungen gegen die Polizeiverordnung zum Schutze der nationalen Symbole und Lieder vom 5. Jan 40 | Offences against the Police Ordinance of 5 Jan 40 for the Protection of National Symbols and Songs |

## 101. Gestapo Interpretations of the Law

Certain acts, hostile to the government and the people, are considered political crimes in any country ; they need no further discussion. But whereas, according to the democratic conception of justice, such offences are clearly defined and graded from misdemeanours to crimes by a precise legal code and a corresponding set of precedents, Gestapo procedure is based on the unlimited interpretation of the above-listed " political crimes." Its guiding principles seem to range from opportunist expediency to a rather musty mysticism.

Thus, the Gestapo adds to the more conventional concept of treason and high treason any action, planned or executed, and even any opinion, suspected or expressed, which it considers dangerous or inconvenient to the Nazi Party, any of its formations or leading personalities, its uniforms and insignia, and its ritual or traditions. Nor does " guilt " in the eyes of the Gestapo stop with the committing or planning of such " crimes." Passive sympathy with a political " offence "

often suffices to effect intervention by the Secret State Police.

The next step of repression is made possible by the way in which the Nazis have deliberately blurred and mixed together the concepts of Government, State, Nation, People and Party, and infused fictitious interests into the resulting politico-national creation. The safeguarding of such interests may then be construed as including an unlimited number of " crimes " ranging from communist activities, agitation or sympathies to offences against the privilege of German citizenship and the " honour of the German Race," and even beyond that, to mere dislike of German folklore, songs, art or any other form of " Kultur."

To the crime of transmission, publication, and general spreading of anti-Nazi propaganda is added mere listening to " illegal " broadcasts, perusal of enemy or opposition leaflets, or reading of banned literature.

Acts which elsewhere would be considered minor economic or financial infractions of the law are in Germany crimes against the Government and the people and as such become the concern of the Gestapo. This category is stretched to cover a list of crimes ranging from offences against foreign exchange and currency regulations and hoarding of goods listed as essential down to any communication or transaction with elements regarded as non-German or anti-Nazi. A peasant who, without a permit, slaughters a pig is prosecuted as vigorously as somebody accused of " harbouring thoughts unworthy of a German."

The use of a thin cloak of legality was only a convenient pretence and was never guided by considerations of justice. The Statutory regulation issued to amplify the Prussian Decree of 10 Feb 36 (see also para. 10) in effect authorised HIMMLER to take measures necessary for the preservation of security and order, even exceeding the limits previously defined by law. Not content with the mock-interpretation of a so-called legal code, the Gestapo could thus proceed to supplement the law by any extra-legal action it considered necessary. Subsequently, a HITLER proclamation of 22 Oct 38 removed even theoretical limitations, such as they were, by pointing to the " unwritten law " of Germany as expressed in " the will of the Party Leader." The proclamation stated bluntly that " every means adopted for the purpose of carrying out the will of the Leader is considered legal even though it may conflict with existing statutes and legal precedent "; the Gestapo had received its unlimited " hunting licence." Thus, long after the body had been buried, even the ghost of " Government by Law " departed from the German scene.

As may be seen from the foregoing, Gestapo methods have passed through three stages of evolution—undefined interpretation of the law, unchecked supplementing of the legal code, and authorised violation of statute and precedent. The Gestapo is now in a position to apply the methods of these three successive stages of " justice " separately or in any convenient combination, and since it is in no way subject to veto, review, or advice by the Judiciary its powers have become absolute and unlimited both in theory and in practice.

## 102. Regional Organisation of the Gestapo

In paragraph 3 it was mentioned that the Geheime Staatspolizei is a Nazi development of the former Staatspolizei, the Political Police which existed in Prussia under the Weimar Republic. A political police was formed in Germany as early as 1914 when it consisted of three branches. The first branch, known as *Staatspolizei*, dealt with the combatting of any plots against the Emperor and the Government. The other two branches of the political police handled censorship and the political supervision of clubs, societies and parties. With the establishment of a republic under the leadership of liberal parties in 1919 any strict censorship and any supervision of parties by the Police were abolished and the only remaining branch of the Political Police was the *Staatspolizei* protecting the Government against plots and treasonable attacks by extremists. In 1933 the Nazis took over this organisation, completely remodelled it and renamed it the *Geheime Staatspolizei*. The regional offices, however, retained the old name in their designations and are thus still known as *Staatspolizei-Leitstellen* (*Stapo-LSt*), *Staatspolizei-Stellen* (*Stapo-St*), *Staatspolizei - Aussendienststellen* (*Stapo - AuDSt or Stapo - ADSt*) and *Staatspolizei - Aussenstellen* (*Stapo - AuSt or Stapo - ASt*). It must be remembered, however, that despite this difference in usage the term *Staatspolizei* (*Stapo*) today simply means *Geheime Staatspolizei* (*Gestapo*).

A **Stapo-Leitstelle** is usually established at the seat of a *Wehrkreis* (Military District), or at the administrative capital of a Prussian province or one of the larger German *Länder* or *Reichsgaue*. At present there are 21 *Stapo-Leitstellen* in existence in Greater Germany, including Bohemia-Moravia. As a rule, the Chief of a *Stapo-Leitstelle* has the rank of an *Oberregierungs- und Kriminalrat* (official approximately equal to a Lt.-Col.). He is the political adviser to the *Reichsstatthalter* or Prussian *Oberpräsident*. He cooperates closely with this high administrative official as well as with the authorities of the *Wehrmacht* and Party, which are normally located in the same town.

A **Stapo-Stelle** is established at the seat of a Prussian *Regierungsbezirk* or smaller German *Land* or *Reichsgau*. According to the most recent information there are 30 such *Stellen* in existence at the present time. The Chief of a *Stapo-Stelle* usually holds the rank of *Regierungs- und Kriminalrat* (approximately equal to Major), and is the political adviser to the *Regierungspräsident*, or similar authority in the *Land* or the *Reichsgau*.

*Stapo-Stellen* are **not** subordinate to *Stapo-leitstellen*. They function independently and no executive orders as from a higher to a lower echelon are issued by a *Leitstelle* to a *Stelle*. Since, however, *Stapo-Stellen* may be located within the larger administrative area of a *Leitstelle*, many instances of overlapping and duplication of functions may arise. In the interests of greater efficiency and uniformity of procedure, therefore, the *Leitstelle* may sometimes send directives and memoranda to the *Stellen* within its territory but, in doing this the *Leitstelle* acts as a coordinating, not as a directing agency. An arrangement of this kind may seem rather vague and involved, and contrary to the usual clear-cut conception of a chain of command. It is, therefore, worth while quoting the no less complicated German terminology defining this relation :—

" *Die Staatspolizeileitstellen üben gegenüber den anderen Staatspolizeistellen des Leitstellenbezirkes gewisse Leitbefugnisse aus, und haben für die Koordinierung des staatspolizeilichen Einsatzes der im Leitstellenbezirk zusammengeschlossenen Staatspolizeistellen zu sorgen. Übergeordnete Instanzen gegenüber den Staatspolizeistellen ihres Bezirkes sind die Staatspolizeileitstellen nicht.*"

In this connection it must be pointed out that 8 of the above mentioned 30 *Stapostellen* are completely independent. Their work is not subject to any coordination by a *Leitstelle* and instructions are issued directly to them from the RSHA.

*Stapo-Leitstellen* and *Stapo-Stellen* are therefore completely self-contained units authorised to take any independent action they may deem necessary. They handle all *Gestapo* matters in their immediate area, i.e. in the *Orts- und Kreispolizeibezirk* in which they are located. In addition they supervise all *Gestapo* activities in the larger area which is administratively controlled by the governmental Headquarters of their location. For this purpose they have established a considerable number of branch offices within the *Regierungsbezirk*, *Land* or *Reichsgau*. These branch offices are known as **Stapo-Aussendienststellen** (or **Stapo-Aussenstellen**). The actual difference between these two types of office has not as yet been fully ascertained, but it may be assumed that a *Stapo-Aussendienststelle* will be found in the larger towns and in districts of greater potential *Gestapo* activity. In addition an *Aussendienststelle* is known to have a number of lesser branch offices and outposts at various places within its area, whereas an *Aussenstelle* has no such subordinate agencies.

It is important to note that both *Stapo-Aussendienststellen* and *Aussenstellen* are not self-contained independent offices, but rely for the conduct of their work on orders and directives from the *Stapo-Stelle* or *Stapo-Leitstelle* in whose area they are located.

A number of *Stapo-Stellen* have been officially down-graded to the status of *Aussendienststellen* for the duration of the war. Among the reasons given for this development is the increasing manpower problem, which has affected the *Gestapo* to the same extent as other branches of the German Police, although while available personnel decreases, its functions and responsibilities are constantly growing. In particular, many of the leading personalities of the *Gestapo* were sent to occupied territories. By the reduction of a number of the *Stapo-Stellen* to the size and strength of *Aussendienststellen*, some of their former executive members and lesser personnel were freed for service in those conquered and infinitely more troublesome areas. It seems probable, however, that offices thus down-graded have retained much of their former independence ; they are, for example, still expected to perform the same functions as when they were *Stapo-Stellen*. Furthermore, the down-graded *Stapo-Stellen* were all located in places which are the seats of a *Regierungspräsident* or a similar higher administrative authority with the Chief of the *Stapo-Stelle* as the political adviser to such authorities ; it seems a reasonable assumption that the chief of the new *Aussendienststelle* still performs this advisory function, even though he must depend on orders from higher *Gestapo* authorities.

All *Gestapo* offices are under the supervision, and in certain previously explained instances, under the direct command of the *Befehlshaber* (*Inspekteur*) *der Sipo und des SD*. While, however, the BdS or IdS is responsible for an area coinciding with the regional administration of the Armed Forces, i.e. the *Wehrkreis*, the territory assigned to *Stapo-Leitstellen* and *Stapo-Stellen* follows mainly the historical administrative system of *Länder*, *Reichsgaue*, *Provinzen*, *Regierungsbezirke*, etc. This inconsistency further complicates the administration : *Stapo-Stellen*, for instance, may come under the supervision or command of a different BdS from the one controlling their responsible *Stapo-Leitstelle*. Conditions of this kind have probably gone far to bring about the gradual increase in the power of the BdS in comparison with that previously exercised by the *Leitstelle* (see para. 91).

227 *Stapo-Aussendienststellen* have been identified in Greater Germany, whereas the identity of only 4 *Stapo-Aussenstellen* has been established. Latest evidence makes it appear that *Aussenstellen* as a rule are not found inside Germany and that the normal classification of a *Gestapo* branch office is that of an *Aussendienststelle*.

In addition 10 *Gestapo* Headquarters of unknown classification have been identified. These, too, are most likely *Aussendienststellen*. Furthermore 6 *Aussendienststellen* are known to have existed, but are, at present, suspended. This brings the total of identified *Gestapo* branch offices to 247. None of the above figures include any of the *Gestapo* Headquarters in occupied territories other than Bohemia-Moravia, nor are the Headquarters of the *Gestapo*-operated *Grenzpolizei* (see para. 105) included.

Further details about all identified *Stapo-Leitstellen, -Stellen, -Aussendienststellen* and *-Aussenstellen*, such as location, address, telephone number, personalities, branch offices and chain of command will be found in Annexe F.

### 103. Internal Organisation of Gestapo Headquarters

Regional Headquarters of the *Gestapo* more or less reflect the organisation of *Amt* IV in the RSHA on a smaller scale, but the numbering system for sub-sections used in the various Headquarters did not, until recently, coincide with that employed in the parent *Amt*.

The original sections in regional headquarters within Greater Germany seem to have been as follows :—

Section I   Office Administration and Personnel.

Section II  Divided into *Abteilungen* A, B, C, etc., with *Referate* 1, 2 and 3 in the same manner as *Amt* IV of the RSHA. Thus, for example, II A 3 would deal with the same subject matters as *Referat* IV A 3 in the RSHA.

Section III Liaison with the *Abwehr* (Military Intelligence), and matters of espionage and counter espionage. Administration of *Grenzpolizei* (Frontier Police).

Wartime requirements seem to have produced a large number of local changes and modifications, so that the inner structure of individual *Stapo* Regional Headquarters began to show considerable variations. It now appears, however, that a further reorganisation of the inner structure of many *Stapo-Leitstellen* and *Stapo-Stellen* has taken place with the object of bringing them into line with the newly organised *Amt* IV of the RSHA. Under this new scheme Section I continues to handle Administration and Personnel, but Sections II and III have been abolished. Instead a Section IV has been formed, with sub-sections reflecting the new organisation of Section IV A of the parent *Amt* in Berlin. Section IV B of *Amt* IV is not represented in the regional *Gestapo* Headquarters, since its functions are still handled, regionally, by the offices of the old *Abwehr* (e.g. *Abwehrstellen*, abbr. *Ast*, etc.).

Thus, the section designations in regional *Gestapo* Headquarters do not contain an " A," *Hilfsreferat* IV A 1 a of the RSHA, for example, being represented regionally by a sub-section VI 1 a.

It cannot be stated with certainty at present whether this reorganisation has taken place in all regional Headquarters of the *Gestapo* in Greater Germany. German admiration of uniform bureaucratic methods certainly makes this tendency to unification appear a logical and likely development, but experience shows that such processes take a long time, and the older system may still be encountered in some instances.

On the other hand, the inner organisation of *Gestapo* headquarters in occupied territories always followed closely the original pattern of *Amt* IV of the RSHA. In contrast to the organisation within Greater Germany, the *Gestapo* in occupied countries does not, as a rule, function in independent headquarters, but forms part of combined *Sipo* and SD units, such as the office of the *Befehlshaber der Sipo und des SD* or of *Sipo* and *SD-Kommandos*.

These combined *Sipo* and *SD* command headquarters are divided into seven *Abteilungen* (sections) similar to the *Ämter* (Bureaux) of RSHA, numbered I–VII.

Within this organisation *Abteilungen* I and II handle matters of administration and personnel for all the other sections, and *Abteilung* IV deals with *Gestapo* affairs exclusively.

Following the reorganisation of *Amt* IV in the RSHA, a parallel reorganisation of *Abteilung* IV appears to have taken place in all *Kommandos*, which therefore now conform to the pattern described above for the *Gestapo* Headquarters within Germany.

Minor differences, such as those for example, which arise from the problems peculiar to occupied territory, must naturally be expected, but the typical example of *Abteilung* IV in a *Sipo* and SD *Kommando*, given in the next paragraph, illustrates clearly the uniformity with the *Amt* IV pattern, which may be said to prevail largely throughout the system of *Gestapo* Headquarters both in Germany and abroad.

### 104. Specimen Organisation of Abteilung IV in an Einsatzkommando

The following tabulation shows the divisions of *Abteilung* IV in the *Sipo* and SD *Einsatzkommando* Luxemburg.

#### IV 1
Opposition

IV 1 a

| | |
|---|---|
| *Linksbewegung* | Left Wing Movements |
| *Kommunismus, Marxismus u n d Neben-organisationen* | Communism, Marxism and related organisations |
| *Illegale und Feind-propaganda* | Illegal and enemy propaganda |
| *Rundfunkverbrechen* | Violation of broadcasting and receiving laws |
| *Widerstandsbewegungen* | Resistance movements |
| *Rückwanderer* | Re-migration |

IV 1 b

| | |
|---|---|
| *Rechtsbewegung* | Right Wing Movements |
| *Reaktion, Opposition, Liberalismus, Heim-tücke (soweit nicht IV 1 a zuständig)* | Reactionary Movements, opposition, Liberalism, Sabotage (in so far as it is not handled by IV 1 a) |
| *Illegale Abwanderung* | Illegal emigration |
| *Zwangsgelderhebung* | Collection of Blackmail |
| *Homosexualität* | Homosexuality |

59

| | |
|---|---|
| *Gemassregelte Beamte* | Reprimanded Officials |
| *Absiedlung* | Removal from residence |

**IV 1 c**

| | |
|---|---|
| *Ausländische und inländische Arbeiter* | Foreign and Native workers |
| *Bummelanten* | Vagrants |
| *Gemeinschaftswidriges Verhalten (unerwünschter Verkehr mit Soldatenfrauen, Verbotener Umgang mit Kriegsgefangenen)* | Behaviour detrimental to the community (Undesirable relations with soldiers' wives, illegal relations with Prisoners of war) |

## IV 2
### Sabotage

**IV 2 a**

| | |
|---|---|
| *Sabotage, Attentate* | Sabotage and Assassinations |
| *Erkennungsdienst* | Identification of criminals |
| *Waffen, Sprengstoff* | Weapons, Explosives |
| *Politische Fälschungen* | Political forgeries |

**IV 2 b**

| | |
|---|---|
| *Gegenabwehr* | Counter Intelligence |
| *Fallschirmagenten* | Parachute agents |
| *Gegenfunkspiele* | Wireless interference and jamming |

## IV 3
### Abwehr (Counter Intelligence)

**IV 3 a**

| | |
|---|---|
| *Spionageabwehr* | Counter espionage |

**IV 3 b**

| | |
|---|---|
| *Wirtschaftsangelegenheiten* | Economic matters |
| *Industriesicherung* | Safeguarding of industries |
| *Werkschutz* | Protection of factories |
| *Bewachungsgewerbe* | Commercial Guard Services |

## IV 4
*Weltanschauliche Gegner* (Ideological opponents)

**IV 4 a**

| | |
|---|---|
| *Politische Kirchen* | Political Religious Communities |
| *Sekten und Freimaurer* | Sects and Freemasons |

**IV 4 b**

| | |
|---|---|
| *Juden und Emigranten* | Jews and Emigrés |

## IV 5
*Sonderfälle* (Special cases)

**IV 5 a**

| | |
|---|---|
| *Schutzdienst* | Protective Service |
| *Dauerdienst* | Permanently maintained Protective Service |
| *Sonderaufträge (Zugüberwachung, Postüberwachung, Behandlung der anonymen und pseudonymen Schreiben)* | Special Missions (Supervision of trains, supervision of mails, dealing with anonymous writing and writing under a pseudonym) |
| *Spezialaufträge* | Special assignments |
| *Illegaler Nachrichtenverkehr* | Illegal signal communications |

**IV 5 b**

| | |
|---|---|
| *Partei, Presse* | Party, Press |

## IV 6
*Fahndung* (Barriers and Searches for wanted persons)

**IV 6 a**

| | |
|---|---|
| *Kartei, Personenakten* | Card Index, Personal Dossiers |

| | |
|---|---|
| *Auskunft* | Information |
| *Ausländer* | Foreigners |
| *Ausländischer Schriftverkehr* | Foreign correspondence |
| *Eindeutschung von Polen* | Germanisation of Poles |

**IV 6 b**

| | |
|---|---|
| *Haftkontrolle* | Detention Control |
| *Schutzhaft* | "Protective" Custody |
| *Transportangelegenheiten* | Matters of Transport |

**IV 6 c**

| | |
|---|---|
| *Allgemeine Fahndung* | General Search for wanted persons |
| *Kriegs- und Sonderfahndung* | Wartime and special searches for wanted persons |
| *Wehr- und Arbeitsdienstpflichtentziehungen* | Evasion of labour and military service |
| *Fahnenflucht* | Desertion |
| *Überläufer* | Deserters to the enemy |
| *Zersetzung der Wehrkraft* | Undermining the war effort |
| *Selbstverstümmelung* | Self-inflicted injuries |

**IV 6 d**

| | |
|---|---|
| *Passangelegenheiten* | Passport matters |
| *Sichtvermerke* | Visas |

## 105. The Grenzpolizei

A Decree of 8 May 37 placed the responsibility for the security of the German frontiers with the Chief of the Security Police, acting on behalf of the Reich Minister of the Interior. Under this decree the *Gestapo* took charge of frontier control and, for this purpose, formed a new specialised branch, the *Grenzpolizei* (Frontier Police).

This special arm of the *Gestapo* operates through **Grenzpolizei-Kommissariate** (Frontier Police Commissariates ; abbr. *Grekos*), situated at key points along the Reich frontiers as well as along such borders as those between Germany and the Government General. 70 such *Grenzpolizei-Kommissariate* have been identified. These regional Headquarters are on the same level as *Stapo-Aussendienststellen*, but they deal only with the control and supervision of the frontiers. The strength of a *Kommissariat* is usually between 10 and 25 men. Like the *Stapo-Aussenstellen*, *Grekos* are controlled by the nearest *Stapo-Stelle* or *Stapo-Leitstelle*, which has a special section (IV 3 c, known under the old numbering system as III C) dealing exclusively with the *Grenzpolizei*. In *Amt* IV of the RSHA matters dealing with the actual work of the *Grenzpolizei* are mostly concentrated in the corresponding *Hilfsreferat* IV A 3 c.

*Grenzpolizei-Kommissariate*, in turn, establish their own branch offices in roads and railways crossing the frontier within the area under their jurisdiction. These branch offices are known as **Grenzpolizeiposten** (Frontier Police Outposts ; abbr. *Grepos*). The strength of a *Grepo* varies greatly, according to the volume of traffic handled. Many of these outposts are staffed by only two or three men and may operate only during certain hours of the day ; others, located at key-points on main roads or railways, may employ 12 or more officials. 34 *Grepos* have been identified.

Some *Grenzpolizei-Kommissariate* are known to have formed special units called *Fliegende Kommandos* (Flying Squads). Exact details concerning these units are not known, but it is obvious that highly mobile patrols must serve to reinforce and tighten control of the German frontiers. They are equipped with staff cars and their personnel may be drawn from the regular staff of the *Kommissariate*. Instructions contained in an original document indicate that the *Fliegende Kommandos* are employed to check and supervise the activities of the regular customs officials of the Reich Finance Administration.

The main function of the *Grenzpolizei* is to supervise all persons crossing the international frontiers of Germany and to establish the identity of such persons by checking passports and other identity papers. *Amt* V of the RSHA, i.e. the *Kripo*, issues a monthly *Fahndungsbuch des Deutschen Reiches* (German Book 'of Wanted Persons), which lists all Wanted Persons such as escaped prisoners of war, common criminals, perpetrators of political " crimes," runaway foreign workers and escaped inmates of Concentration Camps. In addition to this book the *Grenzpolizei* receives copies of the " *Deutsche-Kriminal-Polizeiblatt* (Official Gazette of the German Criminal Police), which resembles the *Fahndungsbuch* but consists merely of several pages as opposed to a large book. This gazette is published whenever a supplement to the *Fahndungsbuch* is thought necessary. The *Grenzpolizei* must see that none of the persons thus listed escapes from Reich territory and the clutches of the German Police.

The *Grenzpolizei* does not deal 'with Wanted Persons after they have been arrested. If the prisoner is guilty of an ordinary crime, he, or she, is handed over to the nearest *Kripo* Headquarters ; if accused of a political or military crime or of espionage he is passed on to the *Gestapo*. All further investigation and prosecution then becomes the task of the branch concerned.

There are two other border control organisations, the **Zollkontrolle** or **Zollpolizei** (Customs Control) and the **Verstärkter Grenzaufsichtsdienst** (*VGAD*: Reinforced Frontier Control), which are both classified as *Sonderpolizei* (Special Police) and come under the authority of the *Reichsfinanzministerium* (RFM : Reich Ministry of Finance). Their respective duties are to exercise customs control over passenger and goods traffic and to provide an armed patrol service all along the borders. However, under the Decree of 8 May, 1937, the *Gestapo*, and through it the *Grenzpolizei*, is given authority to override the powers 'of the Reich Ministry of Finance on matters of border control and to issue orders and directives to the *Zollkontrolle* and the VGAD. Close cooperation therefore exists between these two services and the *Grenzpolizei*. It is reported, for instance, that the *Grenzpolizei* does not normally carry out any personal searches. Persons suspected of espionage or sabotage are as a rule handed over to the Customs Control officials who, ostensibly acting in their normal capacity, carry out a search and report the results to their colleagues of the *Grenzpolizei*. If necessary, action is then taken by the Frontier Police : the suspects are detained and handed over to the *Kripo* or *Gestapo*, according to circumstances. These Customs Control officials are Civil Servants stationed like the Frontier Police at all principal frontier crossings.

The VGAD, a strongly militarised organisation whose cooperation with the Frontier Police consists especially in the task of apprehending wanted persons all along the borders of Germany, is a Nazi innovation. It made its first appearance during the occupation of Austria and was undoubtedly planned in anticipation of war. Since then the VGAD has greatly expanded and some of its units are attached to the Armed Forces as guards for operational and rear areas.

The *Zollkontrolle* and VGAD are in practice closely controlled by the *Gestapo* as far as their functions and tactical employment is concerned, although they are administered by the Reich Finance Authorities. Their cooperation with the *Gestapo* is directed and controlled by three *Generalinspekteure* (Inspectors-General) known as :

*Generalinspekteur* I  (*Ost*- East) in Posen

*Generalinspekteur* II  (*Südost*—South-east)  in Dresden

*Generalinspekteur* III (*West*) in Koblenz

These *Generalinspekteure* are attached to *Amt* IV of the RSHA and are responsible for liaison with the Reich Ministry of Finance.

Another organisation for the protection of frontiers made its appearance in the West in the latter part of 1944. It is known as the **Grenzschutz** (Frontier Protection Service). Its personnel is recruited from Customs Officials, but the organisation was taken away from the control of the Finance Authorities and incorporated into the *Sipo*.

The *Grenzschutz* is organised in companies (of approximately 100–120 men), platoons and sections. It operates by patrols and fixed posts ; house-searches may also be carried out. The *Grenzschutz* is authorised to fire on anyone who resists or attempts to escape. It is to assist the Army in securing the frontier known as the " *Vordere Sperrlinie West*," which does not necessarily coincide with the Army front line. The *Grenzschutz* is an independent organisation belonging to the *Sipo* and is therefore not subordinate to the Army, which cannot call upon its assistance except in emergencies. The men of the *Grenzschutz* are ordered not to leave their posts without orders from their superiors, except when the Army moves its own front line further to the rear.

## 106. Postüberwachungsdienst (Postal Censorship)

In democratic countries censorship of letters does not exist in peace-time. Even in war-time such intrusions into the private rights of the individual are at best regarded as a necessary evil and limited to safeguarding information that might be of use to the enemy, but in Germany such considerations of civil liberties are no longer permitted to interfere with measures for the maintenance of Nazi power. Postal censorship has therefore become a regular police function.

It is a widely known fact that such censorship, based on the 1933 Decree for the Protection of People and Government, was put into operation immediately after the Advent to Power. Details of the early organisation of this control, however, are not available. As previously mentioned (in para. 85) some of the functions of censorship may originally have been carried out by the *Verwaltungspolizei* in cooperation with the postal authorities, but the system has, since 1933, expanded so enormously that censorship can no longer be regarded as an administrative function ; it has become instead a powerful instrument for the subjugation of the German people.

Theoretically certain limitations on the power of the censorship have been imposed, but they are neutralised by so many clauses open to almost any interpretation that it seems futile to discuss them. In practice censorship by the German Security Police is limited only by the machinery and personnel at its disposal. In order to " legalise " a purely extra-legal function of this kind German

Police authorities again stress the principle of crime prevention and point to the responsibility of the *Staatsschutzkorps* for protecting the German People against all political and criminal attacks.

Three types of censorship of communications must be distinguished : inside Germany and occupied countries, to and from foreign countries and to and from the Armed Forces. All three types include the control of every means of communication, postal censorship being, of course, the largest and the most important task.

Originally the Police took over only the censorship inside Germany and occupied countries and there are reasons to believe that this merely took on the form of " snap checks " against specific persons who were politically or otherwise suspected. On 30 June 1938, it was decreed (MBliV—*Ministerialblatt für die innere Verwaltung*—p. 1087/38) that the sole authority for official violation of the privacy of personal communications rests with the *Geheime Staatspolizeiamt* and, through it, with the *Stapo-Leitstellen*. This decree was amended on 19 Mar. 1943 giving the same authority to the *Reichskriminalpolizeiamt* and the *Kripo-Leitstellen*, but pointing out the technical difficulties which are in the way of postal and other censorship against specific persons. It appears, therefore, that no large-scale machinery was set up inside the country to control all mail and other private communications. Man-power shortage in war-time has probably added to the difficulties and has most likely forced the *Kripo* and *Gestapo* to limit themselves to the control of a relatively small amount of letters and to specific instances only.

Mail to and from foreign countries is censored at the *Auslands-Briefprüfstellen* (Censorship offices for Foreign Mail) which were as far as can be ascertained set up and controlled, until the summer of 1944, by the former *Abwehr*, the Military Intelligence. Thirteen of these offices have been identified, 6 of them located in the old Reich, one in Austria and the others in occupied countries. They control 100 per cent of the letters and telegrams to and from foreign countries. It is not clearly established, yet it is likely, that the *Gestapo* and the *Kripo* in the absence of any censorship machinery of their own also made use of these *Briefprüfstellen*, by indicating specific cases for observation and report.

Up to summer, 1944, *Briefprüfstellen* were centrally controlled by Section III N of the old *Abwehr*. When the latter was dissolved, Section III N was taken over by *Amt* IV of the RSHA and was, under the new organisation of *Amt* IV, merged with the *Hilfsreferat* IV A 3 d. Thus, at least since June, 1944, censorship of mail and telegrams in Germany, with the exception of military mail, is completely in the hands of the *Gestapo*, which set up for this purpose an office known as the *Zentrale für die Auslands-Briefprüfstellen* (ZABP—Central Censorship Office). This office, and under it the local censorship offices, report or hand over to the local *Gestapo* and *Kripo* headquarters any suspicious material. They also comply with the directives and specific requests of the central and regional HQ of the *Gestapo* and *Kripo*.

Military mail in Germany is not dealt with by the censorship discussed above but by the Army field post organisation, which has separate agencies directly maintained by the military authorities. Since, however, the functions of the *Abwehr* (Military Intelligence) have been almost completely taken over by the RSHA, it is probable that the *Sicherheitspolizei* now exercises some sort of control over military mail also. Practical experience and documentary evidence, however, seem to indicate that censorship of letters written by members of the German Armed Forces is not very rigid or effective, and in many instances information contained in letters violates the basic rules of military security.

## 107. Concentration Camps

The ruthless methods of the Nazi Police are most apparent in the workings of the Concentration Camps, where the *Gestapo* imitation of the Inquisition rises to its climax. As already explained the Nazi interpretation of the term *Schutzhaft* (protective custody) means the temporary or permanent detention of persons a large proportion of whom have never been legally tried or sentenced by a Court of Law. Protective custody has also been extended to include persons who have served their term of imprisonment according to the sentence awarded by a Court, but are further detained by order of the *Gestapo* (Secret State Police, the *Kripo* (Criminal Police), the SD (Security Service) or the *Geheime Feldpolizei* (Secret Field Police). It is in the *Konzentrationslager* (officially abbreviated in Germany by the letters KL, but popularly referred to as KZ— Concentration Camps) that such persons are detained.

Actual detention orders appear to be issued as follows :—

(a) The *Kripo* handles cases involving *Berufs- or Gewohnheitsverbrecher* (Professional or Habitual Criminals).

(b) The *Gestapo* deals with all " political " criminals.

(c) The *Geheime Feldpolizei* (GFP—Secret Field Police), as sister organisation of the *Gestapo* within the Armed Forces, may in some instances, through the *Gestapo*, submit civilians as well as soldiers for detention.

It is not likely that the SD issues direct detention orders. Instead that branch probably submits its findings to the Gestapo with a recommendation for the subject's removal to a Concentration Camp.

To effect the release of an inmate from a Concentration Camp, approval must be obtained from the *Gestapo* and *Kripo*, and the SD is almost certainly consulted as well.

The number of Concentration Camps in Germany and occupied countries has risen constantly and runs into hundreds at the present time. All available information on them, especially on their administration and chain of command, has been published in E.D.S./G/6 : " German Concentration Camps." Within the scope of the present book it is only possible to mention briefly the links between the Concentration Camps and the various branches of the German Police.

In paragraph 2, sub-para. 4, of the statutory regulation amplifying the decree regarding the Secret State Police, issued 10 Feb 1936, it is stated that the *Gestapo-Amt* is entrusted with the administration of the Government Concentration Camps. The bulk of the Concentration Camp guards, however, were not drawn from the *Gestapo* or any other German Police branch, but were recruited from the *Allgemeine-SS* and became known as the SS *Totenkopf-Verbände* (SS-Death's Head Units), notorious for their ruthlessness and brutality. Their Chief, *SS-OGF* Theodor EICKE was made *Inspekteur der Konzentrationslager* (Inspector of Concentration Camps) and as such was directly responsible to HIMMLER. It was stated in 1940 that this *Inspekteur* and his office were in charge of all direction and administration of the camps. In 1941 EICKE, took command of the *Waffen*-SS Panzer Division " *Totenkopf*," and was succeeded as *Inspekteur* of the KL's by *SS-GF, Genlt. d. W-SS*, Richard GLÜCKS. (EICKE was killed on the Eastern Front in 1943.)

As the war progressed and the manpower shortage in Germany became more acute, the SS realised the great value of the slave labour held in Concentration Camps; the exploitation of this labour naturally entailed an increasing amount of administrative work for the SS. All the economic administration of SS and Police was, from 1941 on, concentrated in the *Wirtschafts- u. Verwaltungshauptamt* of the SS (SS-WVHA—SS Economic and Administrative Department), which among other Offices took over the *Hauptamt Haushalt und Bauten* (Department of Budget and Buildings) of the Police.

In 1942 the office of *Inspekteur der Konzentrationslager* was abolished and its functions transferred to the WVHA; GLÜCKS became Chief of *Amtsgruppe D, Führung und Verwaltung der Konzentrationslager* (Supervision and Administration of KL's) in the WVHA.

It appears that since then all administrative and economic matters concerning Concentration Camps have been handled by *Amtsgruppe* D. Further details concerning the WVHA and its link with the Concentration Camps will be found in E.D.S./G/8, " The *Allgemeine* SS."

This change in the administration of the Camps leaves to the *Gestapo* merely the supervision of KL inmates and political control over the KLs. Exact details are not known and it is likely that even this responsibility for political control is shared with the SD. This control appears to be exercised through the Political Commissar in each camp, who according to reports, is a member of the political section of the *Stapo(-Leit-)stelle* in whose area the Concentration Camp is located.

### 108. The Secret Field Police.

At the outbreak of war the OKW organised a police force, the *Geheime Feldpolizei* (GFP— Secret Field Police), to serve with the Armed Forces. It was conceived as a counterpart to the *Gestapo*,—which furnished much of the GFP's executive personnel—and was principally designed to carry out security work in the field, as the executive agent of the Security Department (*Abwehr*, or Section Ic) of the *Wehrmacht*.

The *Geheime Feldpolizei* should not be confused with the *Feldgendarmerie* (mentioned in para 55) which corresponds to the British or American Corps of Military Police, and is concerned solely with disciplinary matters within the Armed Forces.

Since the GFP is primarily a military organisation it will only be mentioned briefly in so far as it comes within the scope of this handbook.

The German GFP Field Manual defines the principal functions of the GFP as follows :—

(a) The prevention and discovery of espionage and other offences against security in the German Armed Forces as well as of all other military or civilian tendencies and actions within the zone of operations, which may be hostile to the Nazi State. Special emphasis is placed on the prevention and prosecution of sabotage, demoralising propaganda and rumour-mongering. This work includes the control of identity papers, travel permits and supervision of all civilian movement in forward and rear areas.

(b) The prevention of civilians from joining in an action against the occupying forces.

(c) The execution of all security measures within forward and rear zones of operation. The GFP also acts in an advisory capacity to all officers dealing with military intelligence and security.

(d) The recording of persons suitable to act as agents.

(e) The execution of all Security Police tasks not within the field of action of the *Feldgendarmerie* (Military Police).

(f) The briefing of all military HQ and the issuing of directives on questions affecting military security.

(g) All other functions of military intelligence in co-operation with, and according to instructions from, MI HQ and officers.

The Secret Field Police, however, have never had jurisdiction over matters within the field of the *Sipo* and SD. Like the *Gestapo*, the Secret Field Police may arrest civilians without court orders. They may also arrest personnel of the Armed Forces, but in such instances are directed to obtain the formal consent of the soldier's superior officer whenever possible. In cases of emergency, the GFP may call on the services of the *Feldgendarmerie*.

The GFP maintains close co-operation at all times with the Ic/AO (*Abwehroffizier*—CI Officer) of the Intelligence Section of the Armed Forces and with all units and Headquarters. As a rule one *Gruppe* (group) of the GFP is attached to each Army and Air Fleet, but detachments of this group may be assigned to lower echelons.

Personnel of the Secret Field Police are furnished with identity papers which enable them to enter any military building, pass through any barrier of restricted area and to use all military channels of communications and transport as well as all billeting and supply facilities.

Most of the executive personnel and officers of the GFP are furnished by the *Gestapo*, although some have been drawn from the *Kripo* and even from various branches of the *Orpo*. The remainder of the Secret Field Police personnel, however, is recruited to some extent on a less selective basis from regular Army and Air Force units. Theoretically all members of the GFP are chosen for special qualifications such as knowledge of languages and travel experience abroad and for ability to deal with people. In practice, however, it is reported that GFP personnel is of rather poor calibre.

Originally co-operation between the *Gestapo* and the GFP was strongly emphasised, but the importance of the GFP has gradually dwindled in proportion to the growth of power of the combined *Sipo* and SD. Since the GFP was dependent for its funds, equipment and facilities on the Military Intelligence Department of the OKW it was never able to compete with the vastly superior resources of the RSHA.

The original clause denying the GFP jurisdiction over matters within the field of the *Sipo* came to be interpreted so generously in favour of the RSHA that the GFP was in practice deprived of much of its power.

Finally, during the course of 1942, most of the functions as well as the units of the GFP were officially taken over by the *Sipo* and SD, and the remaining units of the GFP were reduced to a small field security corps of the Armed Forces. Personnel of the GFP transferred to the *Sipo* and SD who had not previously been members of the SS, received SS ranks equivalent to their former position and the GFP insignia worn on shoulder straps were removed.

Thus, like most of the other agencies and

functions of military intelligence, the *Geheime Feldpolizei* is now largely controlled by HIMMLER's police system. Not only are the Armed Forces now dependent on the *Sipo* and SD for their intelligence information (see para. 137), but at the same time HIMMLER is enabled to keep a close watch over the activities of Army Personnel.

# C. THE KRIPO

## 109. Criminal Police : General

It has been pointed out that the *Geheime Staatspolizei* is in every respect a Nazi innovation. On the surface it might not appear true to say the same of the *Kriminalpolizei* (*Kripo*—Criminal Police). Functionally such an organisation has long existed in Germany, as in all other countries, but a good deal of its organisation was left to the various *Länder* and even to individual police authorities, who established, according to local needs, headquarters and agencies for combatting crime. As a rule these offices worked in close co-operation with the *Staatliche Polizei* (State Police) or *Gemeindepolizei* (Municipal Police). Upon more careful study, however, it becomes apparent that the German Criminal Police of today cannot simply be regarded as a continuation of the former agencies for the investigation and prosecution of common crime. In official publications the Nazis clearly state that the fulfilment of the tasks of the Criminal Police can no longer be the responsibility of a number of independent, decentralised headquarters.

The *Gestapo* was charged with the ruthless suppression of all opposition and dissension in order to preserve and strengthen the power of the Nazi State and the Party Machine. In a parallel fashion the *Kripo* was called upon to become a guardian of the national " strength " as interpreted by the Nazis. Its task in general remains the combatting of " ordinary " crime, but again it must be remembered that the interpretation of the word " crime " has been adapted to suit Nazi ideas. Just as the *Gestapo* has become the agency for the prevention of political and so-called political acts opposed or inconvenient to the Nazi state, so the *Kripo* deals in an increasing measure with the prevention of crimes considered to be a menace to the German " People," i.e. to the Nazi regime. Thus, the *Kripo* has become the second branch of the *Staatsschutzkorps* (Combined Force for the Protection of the State, consisting of the *Gestapo*, the *Kripo*, and the SD).

## 110. Functions of the Kripo

The principal functions of the Criminal Police in any country are the discovery, investigation and prosecution of crime ; theoretically these are also the functions of the German Criminal Police as will be seen from the breakdown of *Amt* V given later. A general picture of *Kripo* functions is given in the following official German outline of the work of the RKPA in Berlin :—

   (i) Standardisation of criminological methods and equipment ;

   (ii) Application of the results of research and experience in the field of crime detection and prevention ;

   (iii) Criminological training of all officials ;

   (iv) Policy and legislation ;

   (v) Centralisation of the machinery of identification, registration, surveillance and searches for wanted persons ;

   (vi) Maintenance of central indexes for all categories of criminals ;

   (vii) Actual intervention in important criminal cases.

But the Germans themselves make it very plain that it would be completely misleading to regard the Kripo as an ordinary Police Force for combatting crime ; this is merely *one* of the functions of the German Criminal Police.

As previously mentioned the Kripo has become one of the three branches of the " *Staatsschutzkorps.*" As such it must make it its duty to protect not merely public safety in the face of crime, but beyond that, to strengthen and safeguard the German " Nation " as conceived by the National Socialist régime.

To endow the German Criminal Police with the necessary powers to carry out these functions the Nazis have emphasised the importance of crime prevention : this means that in addition to the discovery and arrest of criminals, the *Kripo* tracks down and even detains *potential* criminals. The *Gestapo* had received its unlimited " hunting licence " on the theory of the " unwritten law "; the Kripo derived its extra-legal powers from the flexibility of the term " *Verbrechens-Vorbeugung* " (Crime Prevention). In the hands of a democratic government the theory of crime prevention is sound and justifiable, and is closely linked with social improvements. To assume that the term can be applied in a similar manner to Germany would be dangerously misleading, for the Nazis, with their usual sense of propaganda values, have readily adopted a word connoting progress and humanitarian measures as a cover for totalitarian Police power. Thus a term which, under democracy represents educational reform and social reconstruction, in Germany stands for Concentration Camps, enforced sterilisation and ruthless persecution or even elimination of innocent, but, to the Nazis, undesirable people.

In order to devise a practicable theory of crime prevention the Nazis have constantly had recourse to pseudo-scientific biological and racial myths fashioned to suit their intentions. According to their philosophy the " *Untermenschentum* " (i.e. the dregs of humanity) " the diseased bloodstream within the German People," must be segregated. To this end, Chemistry, Biology and Medicine have been distorted by the German Criminal Police to provide grounds for ascribing criminal tendencies to members of entire " racial " groups or minorities. Armed with these doctrines the new German Criminal Police takes its place beside the *Gestapo* to deal with elements regarded as anti-social by the Nazis, but not dealt with as political " criminals " by the Secret State Police. Indeed, to the unity of purpose between these two branches of the *Staatsschutzkorps* is added close co-operation and an interchangeability of personnel. Men of the *Kripo* and *Gestapo* receive fundamentally the same training and are united by their common membership of the SS. Instances are even known where officials hold simultaneously positions in both *Gestapo* and *Kripo*. A practical example of the close relationship between the two branches of the *Sipo* is given by captured *Kripo* reports on the political morale of the population in Lorraine (*Lageberichte*). Even though reports of this kind would obviously be within the jurisdiction of the *Gestapo*, they were in these instances drawn up by the local *Kripo* headquarters. Clearly the *Kripo* could not possibly discharge such functions, had it not at its disposal a system of Police observers, spies and informers very similar to that of the *Gestapo*.

Perhaps most typical of the new conception of *Kripo* functions is the emphasis placed on the importance of those *Kripo* officials whose work brings them closest to the population, namely the Criminal Police officials in the *Reviere* (precincts or wards). Directives state that such an official is to be shifted as little as possible ; he must become familiar with all persons residing within his area ; he must study their habits and observe every detail of their behaviour. He is also directed to employ a maximum number of unofficial informers among the most " trustworthy " of the population. In addition he is ordered to work in constant liaison with the officials of the NSDAP, the *Blockleiter* and the *Zellenwalter* (Nazi Party Block and Cell Wardens). Obviously a system of spies and informers of this kind by far exceeds all normal needs for combatting crime ; it shows clearly the true character of the *Kripo* as partner of the *Gestapo* in the service of the Nazi régime.

## 111. Organisation of Amt V of the RSHA

In 1936, in order to align the Criminal Police branch with the centralised organisation of the newly-created *Sicherheitspolizei*, HIMMLER combined those sections of the Reich Ministry of the Interior which handled Criminal Police matters with the *Preussisches Landeskriminalamt* (Prussian State Criminal Police HQ) to form the *Reichskriminalpolizeiamt* (RKPA), which then became part of the *Hauptamt Sicherheitspolizei*. In 1939 the RKPA was included into the newly-formed *Reichssicherheitshauptamt*, where it became *Amt V, Verbrechensbekämpfung* (Combatting of Crime). Thus *Amt V* is today the head office of the entire Criminal Police organisation in Germany. It was located in Berlin C 2 at Werderschermarkt 5-6, but has, as a result of Allied air attacks moved partly or completely to other locations.

*Amt V* is divided into *Gruppen* (Sections) designated by capital letters, e.g. *Gruppe V A : Kriminalpolitik und Vorbeugung* (Crime Investigation Policy and Crime Prevention). There are four regular *Gruppen* lettered A—D, but additional sections may have been established. Thus, for instance, the existence of Section F, probably for finance, has been confirmed, but it need not follow that there is a *Gruppe* E.

Each *Gruppe* is divided into a varying number of *Referate* (sub-sections) designated by Arabic numerals ; for example, *Referat* V B 1 handles *Kapital*-

*verbrechen* (Capital Crimes). The *Referat* may again be divided into any number of *Hilfsreferate* (sub-sectional units) designated by small letters ; for example, V B 1 c indicates the *Reichszentrale für Vermisste und Unbekannte Tote* (Central Reich Bureau for missing persons and unidentified corpses).

In the tabulation given in the next paragraph an attempt is made to show the internal structure of *Amt V*. This breakdown of functions and offices is not available in toto in any original document, but has been assembled from a number of German documents and other sources. Whenever there was a high degree of probability but no absolute proof that a sub-section existed, the sub-section in question has been marked with an asterisk(*). If information concerning some of the sections and sub-sections could not be tabulated, an explanatory paragraph indicating the degree of reliability of the information has been added instead. While this tabulation can be regarded as a conclusive overall picture of the organisation of *Amt V*, it cannot, of course, lay claim to absolute accuracy or completeness. Wherever possible the original German phraseology has been preserved. At the same time an attempt has been made to combine an accurate translation with an interpretation of functions wherever this seemed necessary.

It should be noted that before the incorporation of the Criminal Police into the RSHA in 1939 the *Reichskriminalpolizeiamt*, used a different system of designation for its sections and sub-sections. The *Gruppen* (Sections) then referred to as *Abteilungen*, were designated by Roman numerals, ranging from I—III ; the *Referate* were designated by the Roman numeral of the *Abteilung* followed by a capital letter indicating the *Referat* : for instance, I A was the *Referat* handling most of the internal administration. The Hilfsreferate (sub-sectional units) were designated by the addition of an Arabic numeral, thus for instance I A 3 indicated the sub-sectional unit handling registry and administrative office routine. Since it is highly improbable that any application of this system will still be encountered except perhaps in documents of purely historical interest this obsolete numbering system has not been included.

## 112. Structure of Amt V

The official heading of *Amt V* of the RSHA is *Verbrechensbekämpfung* (Combatting of Crime) ; it is organised as follows :—

### *Geschäftsstelle* (Administration Office)

| | | | |
|---|---|---|---|
| *Personalangelegenheiten* | Personnel matters | *Dienstbetrieb der Amtsgehilfen* | Routine for office employees |
| *Innerer Geschäftsbetrieb* | Internal office organisation | *Dauerdienst* | Roster for 24 hour duty |
| *Geschäftsverteilungs- und Aktenplan* | Distribution of work and standard filing system | *Fernschreiber* | Teleprinter room |
| *Raumbedarf und Verteilung* | Assignment of office space | | |
| *Registratur* | Registry | | |
| *Kanzlei* | Secretariat | | |

In general the *Geschäftsstelle* contains all those sections dealing with the immediate administration of personnel and office routine. The more important and long range aspects of administration and personnel, however, have been shifted to *Ämter* I and II following the reorganisation of the *Reichssicherheitshauptamt*.

## V A 1

*Rechtsfragen, Internationale Zusammenarbeit, Kriminalforschung* (translated below)

### V A 1 a

| | |
|---|---|
| *Rechtsfragen* | Legal Matters |
| *Recht und Gesetzgebung im Arbeitsbereich der Kriminalpolizei* | Law and legislation on Criminal Police matters |
| *Grundsätzliche Fragen* | Matters relating to policy |
| *Kontrolle der Reichskriminalpolizei* | Control of Reich Criminal Police |
| *Veröffentlichungen* | Publications |
| *Dienstvorschriften* | Official manuals and publications |
| *Vordruckwesen* | Forms and printed matter |
| *Belohnungen an Privatpersonen | Rewards to private individuals |
| *Rechts- und Kriminalpolitik | Legal and criminal investigation policy |
| *Strafrecht | Penal Law |
| *Strafverfahren | Penal procedure |
| *Lehrfilme | Training films |
| *Amtliche Nachrichten | Dissemination of official messages and reports |
| *Kriminalpolizeiliche Sonderfragen | Special problems of the Criminal Police |
| *Wissenschaftliche Sonderfragen | Special scientific problems |
| *Auskunfterteilung | Information Service |

This *Hilfsreferat* probably handles such matters as the investigation of applications to serve in the Armed Forces or evasions of such service. It may submit its findings to the Police authorities interrogating suspected evaders. For this purpose files may be kept in *Hilsreferat V A 1 a* for *Charakterkundliche Gutachten* (Character References), but it is believed that the bulk of such references is kept in V A 4 (see below).

### V A 1 b

| | |
|---|---|
| *Internationale Zusammenarbeit* | International Collaboration |
| *Auslandsdienst* | Matters regarding foreign countries |
| *Internationale Kriminal-polizeiliche Kommission* (IKPK) | International Criminal Police Commission |
| *Auslandskontrolle* | Control of matters regarding foreign countries (extradition etc.) |
| *Verkehr mit dem Ausland* (*Briefverkehr*) | Relations with foreign countries (Probably includes correspondence) |
| *Übersetzungsstelle* | Translations |
| *Dolmetscherdienst* | Interpreter Service |
| *Ausländerbesuch* (*Gegebenenfalls Beteiligung an Dienststellen*) | Visits of foreigners and, where arising, their participation in work at Police HQ) |
| *Festnahme von Ausländern | Arrest of foreigners (see also V A 2) |

This *Hilfsreferat* may contain a great number of other sections not specifically mentioned above, but handling work of a similar nature. It may be assumed that, especially in wartime, co-operation between the German Criminal Police and the corresponding Police branches of the various satellite nations has considerably increased the work in this direction.

### V A 1 c

| | |
|---|---|
| *Kriminalforschung* | Criminal Research |
| *Kriminalbiologie* | Criminal Biology |
| *Statistik* | Statistics |
| *Statistische Erfassung von Plünderungen* | Statistics of looting and plundering |
| *Polizeiliche Kriminalstatistik* | Crime Statistics |
| *Kriminalität der Ausländer usw.* | Crimes committed by foreigners etc. |
| *Archive* | Archives |
| *Bücherei* | Libraries |
| *Prüfung von fachwissenschaftlichen Kripo-abhandlungen | Examination of specialised scientific Kripo appreciations and treatises |
| *Kriminologie | Criminology |
| *Kriminalistik | Criminalistics |
| *Kriminalrassenkunde | Research into racial theories of criminology |
| *Kriminalberatung | Advice in criminal matters |
| *Auswertung alles eingehenden Forschungsmaterial des In- und Auslandes | Exploitation of detailed research material received from home and abroad |

*Hilfsreferat* V A 1 c, in line with its interest in criminology and racial studies, also deals with such subjects as criminal biological *Sippenforschung* (study of heredity and eugenics). It also appears to co-operate in the investigation of suicide or attempted suicide, but in such instances will probably work in conjunction with the *Kriminaltechnisches Institut* (see Gruppe V D). It also seems likely that V A 1 c deals with the statistical, documentary and theoretical aspects of such matters, leaving the *Kriminaltechnisches Institut* to do the actual scientific research and analysis.

In addition, this *Hilfsreferat* is reported to handle certain aspects of *polizeiliche planmässige Überwachung* (systematic and routine Police supervision).

## V A 2
*Vorbeugung* (Prevention)

### V A 2 a

| | |
|---|---|
| *Vorbeugungsmassnahmen gegen Berufs-, Gewohnheits- und Triebverbrecher* | Preventive measures against professional, habitual and pathological criminals. |

### V A 2 b

| | |
|---|---|
| *Vorbeugungsmassnahmen gegen Asoziale, Prostituierte und Zigeuner* | Preventive measures against anti-social elements, prostitutes and gypsies |
| *Reichszentrale zur Bekämpfung des Zigeunerunwesens* | Central Bureau for the suppression of gypsies |

*Hilfsreferat* V A 2 b deals with police measures against prostitution, the availability of gypsies for military service, their admission to state schools, and their employment in peace and war-time industry. It is known that in several instances reports on the arrest of foreigners were handled by V A 2, but this probably does not indicate a shift

* See **para. 111**

of functions from *Hilfsreferat* V A 1 b to V A 2. Instead it seems that such reports are made to V A 2 in conjunction with that section's measures against so-called anti-social elements, here applied to undesirable foreigners.

## V A 3

*Weibliche Kriminalpolizei* (Criminal Police— Women's branch)

| | |
|---|---|
| *Organisation und Einsatz* | Organisation and employment |
| *Reichszentrale zur Bekämpfung der Jugendkriminalität* | Central Reich Bureau for combatting juvenile delinquency |
| *Jugendarrest* | Arrest of juveniles |
| *Jugendstrafrecht* | Juvenile Penal Code |
| *Polizeiliche Jugendschutzlager* | Police reformatory and penal camps for juveniles |

It appears that all matters of juvenile delinquency are handled by V A 3. The subject matter dealt with in this Referat is almost unlimited. It includes such items as arrest of juveniles for violation of traffic and railway regulations, transfer of youths into *Polen-Jugendverwahrlager* (Internment Camps for Polish youths) and many other related matters. It furthermore deals with collaboration between the Police and the Hitler Youth in matters of juvenile delinquency.

## V A 4

It appears that this Referat has been added to the organisation of *Amt* V at a comparatively late date. Its official designation is not known at present, but its functions seem to be the following:—

| | |
|---|---|
| *Polizeiliche An- und Abmeldung* | Registration with the Police on taking up or giving up residence |
| *Standesamtliche Mitteilungen und deren Auswertung* | Information (personal, marital and family status) from the civil registrars, and its exploitation |
| *Jahrgangsregister Erfassung* | Register of age groups Collation |

These *Hilfsreferate* may contain extensive files and character references (see also V A 1 a), and as a result they supply the necessary information for controlling bombed-out people and other persons making forced or voluntary changes of residence

## Gruppe V B
### Vollzugmässiger Einsatz des Reichskriminalpolizeiamtes
### (Executive Work of the RKPA)

### V B 1

*Kapitalverbrechen* (Capital Crimes)

**V B 1 a**

| | |
|---|---|
| *Reichszentrale zur Bekämpfung von Kapitalverbrechen* | Central Reich Bureau for combatting capital crimes (see also VB 1b) |
| *Mord und Totschlag* | Homicide and manslaughter |
| *Raub und räuberische Erpressung* | Robbery and robbery with blackmail |
| *Roheitsdelikte* | Crimes involving cruelty |
| *Wilderei* | Unlawful hunting and fishing |

**V B 1 b**

| | |
|---|---|
| *Reichszentrale zur Bekämpfung von Kapitalverbrechen* | Central Reich Bureau for combatting capital crimes (see also VB 1a) |
| *Brandstiftung und Explosionen* | Arson and explosions |
| *Verkehrsunfälle und Betriebsunfälle* | Traffic and industrial accidents |
| *Katastrophen* | Disasters |
| *Nachrichtensammelstelle für Munitions-Sprengstoff und Waffendiebstähle* | Section collecting reports on the theft of munitions, explosives and weapons |

**V B 1 c**

| | |
|---|---|
| *Reichszentrale für Vermisste und unbekannte Tote* | Central Reich Bureau for missing persons and unidentified corpses |

**V B 1 d**

| | |
|---|---|
| *Reichszentrale zur Bekämpfung internationaler und interlokaler Taschendiebe* | Central Reich Bureau for combatting international and inter-urban pickpockets |

**V B 1 e**

| | |
|---|---|
| *Reichszentrale zur Bekämpfung reisender und gewerbsmässiger Einbrecher* | Central Reich Bureau for combatting travelling and professional burglars |

### V B 2

*Betrug* (Fraud)

**V B 2 a**

| | |
|---|---|
| *Reichszentrale zur Bekämpfung der reisenden und gewerbsmässigen Betrüger und Fälscher : allgemeiner Betrug* | Central Reich Bureau for combatting travelling and professional frauds and forgers : general fraud |
| *Reichszentrale zur Bekämpfung von Kunstwerkfälschungen* | Central Reich Bureau for combatting art forgeries |

**V B 2 b**

| | |
|---|---|
| *Reichszentrale zur Bekämpfung der reisenden und gewerbsmässigen Betrüger und Fälscher : Betrug in der Wirtschaft* | Central Reich Bureau for combatting travelling and professional frauds and forgers : fraud in business and industry |
| *\*Bekämpfung der Kriegswirtschaftsdelikte* | Combatting crimes against wartime economy (see also V B 2 and Gruppe V Wi) |

*Hilfsreferat* V B 2 b seems to have been greatly expanded as a result of wartime conditions. It now combats to a considerable extent black market operations and illegal slaughtering of livestock (*Schwarzschlachtungen*) as well as violations of price control.

**V B 2 c**

| | |
|---|---|
| *Reichszentrale zur Bekämpfung von Betrug : Korruption an und bei Behörden* | Central Reich Bureau for combatting fraud : bribery and corruption of Government officials |

This Bureau deals with all categories of fraud, corruption and embezzlement by government authorities, as well as in public corporations. Thus, for instance, V B 2 c also prosecutes accused officials and leading personalities in the armament industry.

* See para. 111

67

**V B 2 d**

| | |
|---|---|
| *Reichszentrale zur Bekämpfung des Glücks- und Falschspiels* | Central Reich Bureau for combatting games of chance and fraudulent gambling |

**V B 2 e**

| | |
|---|---|
| *Reichszentrale zur Bekämpfung v o n Geld, Wertpapier- u n d Briefmarkenfälschungen* | Central Reich Bureau for combatting forgeries of currency, securities and postage stamps |

**V B 2 f**

This *Hilfsreferat* has probably been added to the organisation of *Gruppe B* since the outbreak of war. Its functions are closely related to those of V B 2 b. Its field of action probably centres on :—

| | |
|---|---|
| *Bekämpfung der Verstösse gegen die Kriegswirtschaftsbestimmungen* | Combatting violation of statutes governing wartime economy (see also Gruppe V Wi) |

## V B 3

| | |
|---|---|
| *Sittlichkeitsverbrechen* | (Offences against Public Morality) |

**V B 3 a**

| | |
|---|---|
| *Reichszentrale zur Bekämpfung unzüchtiger Bilder, Schriften und Inserate* | Central Reich Bureau for the suppression of obscene pictures, books and advertisements |

**V B 3 b**

| | |
|---|---|
| *Reichszentrale zur Bekämpfung d e s internationalen Mädchenhandels* | Central Reich Bureau for combatting international white slave traffic |
| *Zuhälter* | Pimps |
| *Kuppler* | Procurers |
| *Erpresser auf heterosexueller Grundlage* | Blackmailers on a heterosexual basis |

**V B 3 c**

| | |
|---|---|
| *Reichszentrale zur Bekämpfung von Rauschgiftvergehen* | Central Bureau for combatting traffic in illegal drugs |

**V B 3 d**

| | |
|---|---|
| *Reichszentrale zur Bekämpfung der Homosexualität und Abtreibung* | Central Reich Bureau for combatting homosexuality and abortion |

**V B 3 e**

| | |
|---|---|
| *Reichszentrale zur Bekämpfung von Sittlichkeitsdelikten und Triebverbrechen* | Central Reich Bureau for combatting offences against morality and pathological sex crimes |

This *Hilfsreferat* also handles the investigation and prosecution of so-called *Rassenschändung* (" Pollution of the German Race "), i.e. sexual relations between Germans and " non-Aryans." It furthermore maintains the central card index of pathological criminals (*Zentralkartei der Triebverbrecher*).

## Gruppe V C
### Kriegsfahndung und Fahndung (Wartime search and general search for wanted persons)

**V C 1**

| | |
|---|---|
| *Kriegsfahndung* | (War-time Search for Wanted Persons) |

**V C 1 a**

| | |
|---|---|
| *Fahndung nach Fahnenflüchtigen und bei unerlaubter Entfernung von Angehörigen der Wehrmacht, der Waffen-SS, der SS- und Polizeibataillon, des RAD, der Organisation Todt einschl. des Wehrmachtgefolges* | Searches for deserters and for men absent without leave, from the Armed Forces, the W-SS, the SS-Police battalions, the Reich Labour Service, the Todt organisation ; also employees of the Armed Forces |
| *Erfassung Dienstpflichtiger, die sich schuldhaft der Zustellung des Gestellungsbefehls entziehen* | Arrest of persons subject to military service who are guilty of dodging the call-up order |
| *Bekämpfung der Begünstigung Fahnenflüchtiger aus nicht politischen Motiven durch Angehörige* | Combatting of the assistance of deserters by their relatives if the motives are non-political |
| *Mitwirkung bei der Aufklärung von Straftaten unbekannter Fahnenflüchtiger* | Assistance in the solution of crimes committed by unidentified deserters |
| *Karteimässige Erfassung der in das Ausland geflüchteten Fahnenflüchtigen und Dienstpflichtigen* | Maintenance of card files of deserters and other persons subject to military service who have escaped into foreign countries. |

**V C 1 b**

| | |
|---|---|
| *Kriegsfahndungszentrale* | Central Bureau for the war-time search for Wanted Persons |
| *Fahndung nach flüchtigen Kriegsgefangenen und abgeschossenen Feindfliegern* | Search for escaped Prisoners of War and baled-out enemy airmen. |
| *Vorbeugung gegen Kriegsgefangenenfluchten* | Preventive measures against escapes by Prisoners of War |
| *Fluchtmittel und -wege von Kriegsgefangenen usw. (Nicht: Fluchthilfsorganisationen, Vorbeugung gegen Arbeitsflucht)* | Methods and routes of escape of Prisoners of War etc. (Not to include : organisations aiding the escape of prisoners, preventive measures against escape of foreign labourers) |
| *Bahn-, Strassenverkehrs- und Riegelfahndung, Kontrollbefugnis Polizei/Wehrmacht* | Search on railways, on highways and at barriers ; authority for control of Armed Forces by Police |
| *Sonderfahndungsplan der Sicherheitspolizei und des SD (Alarm- und Einsatzpläne der KPStellen. Alpha-, Beta- und Grossfahndung)* | Special search system of the Security Police and Security Service (Alarm and operational plans of the Kripo-Stellen ; Alpha-, Beta-, and Grossfahndung) |
| *Nachrichtenmittel der Kriminalpolizei* | Signals and communications equipment of the Criminal Police |

Originally *Referat* V C 1 with its *Hilfsreferate* a-f was made up of the *Reichserkennungsdienstzentrale* (Central Identification Bureau) in addition to the *Fahndung*. Since the Indentification Bureau, however, had to work in extremely close liaison with the *Kriminaltechnisches Institut* (KTI—Criminological Institute) for many of its investigations, numerous instances arose of duplication and overlapping of functions. To remedy this situation, and at the same time, to save man-power, the functions of the *Reichserkennungsdienstzentrale* were merged with the KTI, and will be discussed in further detail in *Gruppe* D below.

The *Kriegsfahndungszentrale* was originally contained in *Hilfsreferat* V C 2 k, (q.v.) but with the steadily increasing tasks which fell on this sub-section as the war continued, it underwent important changes and was expanded enormously. In 1942 it was shifted to *Referat* V C 1. This particular change may possibly have been decided on in anticipation of the transfer of the *Reichserkennungsdienstzentrale* out of *Gruppe* V C into *Gruppe* V D.

Among the less obvious functions of V C 1 b is liaison and co-operation of the *Kripo* with units of the NSKK (National Socialist Motor Corps), and other Party formations.

## V C 2

*Polizeiliche Fahndungsmittel* (Means employed by the Police in the search for Wanted Persons)

| | |
|---|---|
| *Grundsätzliche Fragen der Kriminalpolizeilichen Fahndung* | Policy with regard to *Kripo* searches for Wanted Persons |

**V C 2 a**

| | |
|---|---|
| *Reichshandschriftensammlung (Politisch und Kriminal)* | Central graphological collection (Political and Criminal) |

This *Hilfsreferat* probably handles the extensive campaigns conducted in Germany against the authors and passers of chain letters.

**V C 2 b**

| | |
|---|---|
| *Kriminalpolizeiliche Personenakten* | Criminal Police collection of personal dossiers |

**V C 2 c**

| | |
|---|---|
| *Sammlung und Auswertung ausländischer Nachrichten und Fahndungsblätter* | Collection and exploitation of reports and Wanted Persons lists received from abroad |
| *Reichsspitznamen- und Merkmalskartei* | Central files of nicknames and distinguishing marks |

**V C 2 d**

| | |
|---|---|
| *Geschäftsstelle des Deutschen Kriminal Polizeiblattes* | Publishing Office of the Criminal Police Gazette |

**V C 2 e**

| | |
|---|---|
| *Zentrale Fahndungskartei* | Central files of Wanted Persons |

**V C 2 f**

| | |
|---|---|
| *Reichszentrale für das Erfassungswesen* | Central Reich Bureau of registration and identification |

**V C 2 ?**

| | |
|---|---|
| *Deutsches Fahndungsbuch* | German Book of Wanted Persons |

**V C 2 ?**

| | |
|---|---|
| *Aufenthaltsermittlungsliste* | List of individual residences and personal whereabouts |

**V C 2 g ?**

**V C 2 h ?**

**V C 2 i ?**

**V C 2 k**

As explained under V C 1 b, *Hilfsreferat* V C 2 k formerly contained the *Kriegsfahndungszentrale*, and some of the functions may still be carried out by this sub-section, but exact details are not available. In certain instances it seems that this sub-section deals with searches for Wanted Persons on the German Railway system.

## V C 3

**V C 3 a**

| | |
|---|---|
| *Diensthundewesen der Sicherheitspolizei, Einsatz von Hunden zur Fährtensuche, zum Auffinden von Minen und zum Aufstöbern von Personen* | Police dogs of the Security Police, employment of dogs for the following of traces, for the detection of mines and for the discovery of persons |

**V C 3 b ?** — ?

**V C 3 c**

| | |
|---|---|
| *Erfassung aller im Reichsgebiet polizeilich in Erscheinung getretenen Chinesen* | Control of all Chinese who have become subjects of police attention in Reich territory |

*Referat* V C 3 is probably a later addition to *Amt* V. Apart from the details above, it seems to handle the listing of illegal products and merchandise as well as the names and addresses of their manufacturers and distributors. Among the lists kept and issued by V C 3 for instance, are those of illegal drugs for purposes of birth control and abortion. This work (possibly done by V C 3 b) has perhaps been added to the *Gruppe* handling *Fahndung*, because, in a wider sense, it deals with the search, identification and apprehension of makers of and dealers in all types of illegally manufactured goods.

## Gruppe V D
### Kriminaltechnisches Institut der Sicherheitspolizei
### (KTI—Criminological Institute of the Security Police)

### V D 1

*Spuren- und Personenidentifizierung* (Identification of Traces and Persons)

**V D 1 a (1)**

| | |
|---|---|
| *Identifizierung daktyloskopischer Spuren und Abdrücke* | Identification of fingerprints and traces |
| *Einzelfingerabdrucksammlung* | Library of single fingerprint records |

**V D 1 a (2)**

| | |
|---|---|
| *Identifizierung von Werkzeugen, Schuhwerk, Tierfährten, Zähnen, usw., und deren Spuren* | Identification of tools, footwear, animal tracks, teeth etc., and their imprints |

**V D 1 a (3)**

| | |
|---|---|
| *Identifizierung von Schusswaffen und Munition* | Identification of firearms and ammunition |

**V D 1 b (1)**

| | |
|---|---|
| *Zehnfingerabdruckzentrale* | Central library of ten-finger print records |

**V D 1 b (2)**

| | |
|---|---|
| *Personenfeststellungszentrale* | Central bureau for tracing and identifying of persons |

### V D 2

*Chemisch-Physikalische und Biologisch-Naturwissenschaftliche Untersuchungen* (Chemical, physical, biological and botanical Research and Analysis)

**V D 2 a**

| | |
|---|---|
| *Brand- und Explosionsuntersuchung* | Investigation of arson and explosions |

**VD2b**

| | |
|---|---|
| *Materialuntersuchung und Vergleich* | Comparative analysis of materials |

**VD2c**

| | |
|---|---|
| *Giftausmittlung* | Analysis of poisons |

**VD2d**

| | |
|---|---|
| *Biologisch - Naturwissenschaftliche Untersuchungen* | Research and analysis in the field of the natural sciences |

Among other matters, this *Referat* handles the analysis and identification of blood-groups, blood types, sperms, etc., also of dust, dirt and ashes.

It should be noted that *Referate* V D 1 and V D 2 now cover all the interests of the former *Reichserkennungsdienstzentrale* (see also V C 1 above).

### VD3
*Dokumentenuntersuchung*
(Scientific examination of documents)

**VD3a**

| | |
|---|---|
| *Urkundenprüfung—Fälschungen* | Examination of documents—forgeries |

**VD3b**

| | |
|---|---|
| *Schriftvergleich—Hand-, Druck- und Maschinenschriften* | Comparative graphology—handwritten, printed and typewritten documents |

This *Referat* conducts such work as the analysis of inks, pencils and stamps, the interpretation of blacked-out or erased writing, and the reading of matters written in invisible ink (see also *Reichshandschriftensammlung* V C 2 a above).

### VDW
*Technische Werkstätten*
(Technical Workshops and Laboratories)

| | |
|---|---|
| *Lichtbildstelle* | Photolaboratory and files of photographs |
| *Zeichen- und Abformstelle* | Drafting, copying, plaster casts, etc. |
| *Mechanische Werkstätten* | Workshops and laboratories |

The collection of photographs in the *Lichtbildstelle* probably also contains files of trade marks, samples of materials, and other matter useful for the identification of stolen property. Formerly this collection was maintained by *Hilfsreferat* V C 1 e, which ceased to exist when the *Reichserkennungsdienstzentrale* was abolished and its functions taken over by the KTI.

### Gruppe V F

This *Gruppe* was not originally part of *Amt* V, but appears to have been added later. Its exact functions and details of its organisation are not available, but documentary evidence seems to indicate that among its functions are payment of fees and rewards as well as of extraordinary expenses. The existence of two *Referate* within this *Gruppe*, namely V F 1 and V F 2, has been definitely established. V F 1 seems to deal in particular with payment of fines and possibly also of damage and insurance claims in case of accidents. *Referat* V F 2 may handle the payment of special fees, awards and expenses incurred in the course of actions such as searches and raids.

At first glance the letter F designating this Gruppe does not seem to fit into the organisation of *Amt* V, but it may have been chosen to indicate that this department handles *Finanzen* (Financial matters).

(*Note* : No reference to a sub-section V Wi 1 was made in the document.)

### Gruppe V Wi

### Wirtschaftsverbrechen—(Criminal acts against the National Economy)

A recently received document mentions the existence of a Gruppe V Wi, which may have been formed to cope with increasing economic offences during wartime. Whether this section has been added as an independent Gruppe to those already existing in Amt V is not known. It is possible, however, that it represents either an expansion of, or a substitute for, Hilfsreferate V B 2 b and V B 2 f.

**V Wi 2**

| | |
|---|---|
| *Verstösse gegen die Bewirtschaftungsvorschriften* | Violations of the decrees governing economic matters |
| *Schleich- und Tauschhandel* | Blackmarket and illegal bartering |
| *Diebstahl und Unterschlagungen von Bezugsberechtigungen* | Theft and embezzlement of purchasing permits |

**V Wi 3**

| | |
|---|---|
| *Verstösse gegen die Preis-, Devisen-, Zoll- und Steuervorschriften* | Violations of regulations governing prices, foreign exchange, customs and taxes |

**V Wi 4**

| | |
|---|---|
| *Korruption in der Wehrmacht, beim RAD, bei der OT und sonstigem Wehrmachtsgefolge, sowie bei der SS und Polizei* | Corruption in the Armed Forces, the RAD, the OT and other formations with the Armed Forces as well as in the SS and the Police |

**V Wi 5**

| | |
|---|---|
| *Korruption bei staatlichen und kommunalen Behörden, bei der NSDAP und innerhalb der Wirtschaft* | Corruption in national and local authorities, in the Nazi Party and in business and industry |

**V Wi 6**

| | |
|---|---|
| *Kaufmännischer Betrug, Erfinderschutz, alle gewerblichen Angelegenheiten und Fälschungen von Bezugsberechtigungen* | Fraud in business, protection of inventors' rights, all trade matters and forgeries of purchasing permits |

Certain items in the foregoing tabulation of *Amt* V, namely the IKPK, the Female Criminal Police, the *Reichszentralen* and the files maintained by the *Kripo* and the scientific institute, deserve amplification. They are dealt with in the next five paragraphs.

## 113. International Criminal Police Commission

In order to prosecute international criminals, an International Criminal Police Commission was created in Paris in 1923. It was originally known as the Commission Internationale de la Police Criminelle, but after 1940 the Nazis managed to dominate the Commission and moved its headquarters first to Vienna and later to Berlin. Reinhard HEYDRICH became its first German President. After his death, KALTENBRUNNER succeeded him, and it was agreed that the Chief of the *Sipo* would in future also hold the position of President of the *Internationale Kriminalpolizeiliche Kommission* (IKPK). Until recently the Vice-Presidency of the Commission was held by *SS-GF, Genlt. d. Pol.* Artur NEBE, who was also head of *Amt* V of the RSHA. *SS-SF Dr.* Karl ZINDEL is the chairman of the IKPK and the former Police Vice-President of Vienna, *Dr.* Bruno SCHULTZ, is its permanent Secretary. The latter is at the same time the Treasurer of the Commission, as well as Chief Editor of the publication " *Internationale Kriminalpolizei*," a technical journal issued in five languages. In 1944 *Regierungsdirektor Dr.* DRESSLER was appointed *Generalsekretär* of the IKPK. It is not quite clear whether he thus replaces SCHULTZ.

German personnel employed by the Commission are administered by *Ämter* I and II and receive directives for their work from *Amt* V of the RSHA.

The commission maintains extensive files of international crimes and criminals, and their photographs and fingerprints. These collections are located in the *Internationales Büro* (IB—International Bureau) under the Chief of the *Reichskriminalpolizeiamt*.

At present the Headquarters of the IKPK are located at Berlin-Wannsee, Am Kleinen Wannsee 16 ; these offices are linked with the *Sipo* telephone and teleprinter network.

From the preceding outline it is evident that the use of the term " international " is misleading since the IKPK is completely dominated by the German Police. At present the activities of the Commission are probably concerned with the control of the Criminal Police Departments in the various satellite nations.

## 114. Female Criminal Police

The *Weibliche Kriminalpolizei* (WKP—Female Criminal Police) has always been in existence, but it was reorganised towards the end of 1935. Its main functions have been shown in the preceding tabulation of *Amt* V : in more detail its functions are as follows :—

(i) General assistance in crime detection.

(ii) The registration and supervision of children and female minors, who are exposed to criminal and immoral influences. (This comes under the heading of general crime prevention).

(iii) Initiation of educational and welfare measures for persons whose cases become known to the *Kripo*.

(iv) The handling of all incoming reports on children and female juveniles, and in certain instances adults.

(v) Assistance on all criminal investigations, especially in questioning and searching children, minors, and in some instances female adults.

(vi) Assistance in Kripo activities pertaining to crime prevention among women in general.

The WKP forms a separate office within *Kripo-(Leit-)Stellen* (Regional and sub-regional *Kripo* Headquarters) which is exclusively under female direction. These *Sonderdienststellen* (Special Offices) are directly subordinate to the Chief of the *Kripo-(Leit-)Stelle* and are not attached to any other department within the headquarters. A WKP office is usually headed by a *Kriminalkommissarin* or by an acting " *Leitende Beamtin* " (Directing Woman Officer).

The original decree explaining the functions of the WKP specifically points out that its personnel may also be employed in cases which are really under the jurisdiction of the *Gestapo* and the *Orpo*. Beyond that women in the service of the *Kripo* may, on their own initiative, submit their observations and experiences to the interested departments of the *Gestapo*.

Personnel of the WKP are not issued with a uniform, but wear civilian clothes. They are unarmed, but are trained in the handling of weapons.

A directive states that, in addition to their regular police functions, the WKP shall in some instances take the place of, or assist the various welfare organisations, especially in localities where Party organisations such as the *NS-Volkswohlfahrt* (National Socialist Welfare Organisation), or the Hitler Youth Movement are incapable of reaching every member of the population.

## 115. Reichszentralen (Central Reich Bureaux)

The existence and function of *Reichszentralen* (Central Reich Bureaux) have been shown in the previous tabulation of *Amt* V of the RSHA. These Bureaux have been established to enable the *Reichskriminalpolizeiamt* to cope with the great variety of Criminal Police activities with a higher degree of efficiency. While a centralised treatment of Criminal Police matters is essential in the lower echelons of the *Kripo*, the opposite, namely a logical division of this complicated work is desirable at the Reich Headquarters. In particular, the *Reichszentralen* in their functions of combatting " all anti-social " elements are charged with a twofold task : to collect all information on their specialised fields of activity and to carry out research on such material with a view to its practical application by the lower *Kripo* headquarters, to whom the results of research are disseminated.

In special instances, where a criminal operates over a wide area covered by more than one Regional Headquarters of the Kripo the competent *Reichszentrale* is fully authorised and even required to take an active and executive hand in his apprehension. For this purpose the *Reichszentralen* maintain a staff of executive officials consisting of highly trained Criminal Police personnel. The number of personnel employed by each *Reichszentrale* varies according to the importance of the work handled.

The *Reichszentralen* fit into the pattern of *Amt* V of the RSHA and details of each one will be found in para. 112. A *Reichszentrale* has been identified as dealing with matters under each of the following broad headings (designations in brackets refer to the section of *Amt* V concerned) :—

Gypsies (V A 2 b)
Juvenile delinquency (V A 3)
Capital crimes (V B 1 a and b)
Missing persons (V B 1 c)
Pickpockets (V B 1 d)
Burglars (V B 1 e)
General fraud and Art forgeries (V B 2 a)
Industrial fraud (V B 2 b)
Bribery and corruption (V B 2 c)
Gambling (V B 2 d)

Forgeries of money (V B 2 e)
Obscenity (V B 3 a)
White slave traffic (V B 3 b)
Drug traffic (V B 3 c)
Homosexuality and abortion (V B 3 d)
Sex crimes (V B 3 e)
Registration and identification (V C 2 f)

## 116. Files maintained by the Criminal Police

The preceding tabulation of the organisation of *Amt* V makes it apparent that many of the sections and sub-sections maintain extensive files and card indexes. No attempt has been made here to present a complete list of these files ; not only is their number almost unlimited but many of them are the same as those maintained by the Criminal Police organisation of any country. Nevertheless the existence of a few of the more important files should be mentioned.

Perhaps the most extensive file maintained by the German Criminal Police, and at the same time that of greatest interest for counter intelligence purposes is the *Zentrale Fahndungskartei* (Central file of Wanted Persons). Its value would be further increased if used in connection with the *Reichsspitznamen und Merkmalskartei* (Central files of nicknames and distinguishing marks) and the *Aufenthaltsermittlungsliste* (List of residences and personal whereabouts) as well as the various files of fingerprints and the collection of handwritings. Beyond that, the Criminal Police maintains files of all types of professional criminals (*Verbrecherkartei*) arranged according to the 182 different categories of crimes, according to a report of 1939. Many of these files may be of interest ; they list for instance all professional criminals formerly or at present detained in concentration camps. Also included are a number of inmates committed to such camps for "political" crimes. Duplicates of these records are held by the Reich Ministry of the Interior.

In 1940 two additional specialised Indexes were started by the Police and probably maintained, at least in part, by the *Kripo*. The *Ermittlungsstelle für Seeleute* (Office for tracing seamen) located in Hamburg and a *Zentralkartei der Auslandsdeutschen* (Central card index of Germans abroad). The latter remained in the offices of the *Auslandsorganisation der NSDAP* (AO—Organisation for Germans in Foreign Countries) in Berlin-Wilmersdorf, Westfälischestrasse 1, but special officials of the *Einwohnermeldeamt* (Office for the Registration of Residents) were ordered to maintain these records.

The *Weibliche Kriminalpolizei* maintains an index of all juveniles who have in any way come in contact with the police. This file is known as the *Jugendlichenkartei* (Card Index of Juveniles), and is located at the *Sonderdienststellen* of the WKP. In order to facilitate handling, yellow tabs are used for potential criminals, purple tabs for Jewish children, and black tabs for gypsies.

## 117. Scientific Institutes of the Security Police

The **Kriminaltechnisches Institut der Sicherheitspolizei** (KTI, also KTJ—the Criminological Institute of the Security Police) was founded late in 1938 for the purpose of handling technical and scientific investigations essential for the discovery and solution of crimes. It gradually became so important that it was later incorporated into *Amt* V of the RSHA as the independent *Referat* V D. The Institute is headed by *SS-Standartenführer Dr.* HEES. Its offices are located in the main building of the *Reichskriminalpolizeiamt* at Werderscher Markt 5–6 in Berlin, though,

according to the latest information *Referat* V D 1 (Identification of traces, imprints and persons) and *Referat* V D 3 (Examination of documents) were temporarily transferred to Grambow, near Schwerin, Mecklenburg, late in 1943.

The Institute has at its disposal 27 laboratories equipped with the most modern type of apparatus for experiments and research in all branches of criminology, and its staff consists of a number of highly trained scientific experts. The functions of the KTI necessitate specialised departments such as laboratories for the identification of arms and ammunition, every aspect of graphological study and comparison, every means of determining the causes of fires, explosions and other acts of sabotage, as well as detailed chemical and biological analysis of blood, dust and dirt, and every possible clue which might lead to the apprehension of a criminal.

The KTI was also given the task of equipping and organising *Kriminaltechnische Untersuchungsstellen* (KTU—Criminal Research Branches) at all *Kripo-(Leit-) Stellen*. For this purpose special training courses were instituted by the KTI. The intensity of these courses can be judged by the fact that it took three years to train forty-three specialists. The courses consist of six weeks of lectures, practical work and experiments and admit 2–3 officials at one time ; by the end of 1942 they were most probably discontinued for the duration of the war, but by that time specialists for KTU's had been supplied to all the then existing *Kripo- (Leit-) Stellen*, with the exception of the following 12 :

| | | |
|---|---|---|
| Augsburg | Frankfurt/O | Weimar |
| Darmstadt | Saarbrücken | Wilhelmshaven |
| Dessau | Schneidemühl | Würzburg |
| Erfurt | Schwerin | Zwickau |

In addition to training its own personnel the KTI also provides lectures for all members of the *Kripo* and possibly even for members of the other branches of the German Police. For this purpose the Institute prepares charts, pictures and training films.

Late in 1942 the *Reichserkennungsdienstzentrale* (Central Reich Bureau for the identification of criminals) was abolished and its functions were taken over by the KTI ; a logical development, since its work could not be efficiently carried out without the aid of the KTI. (For further details see *Referat* V C 1 in the previous tabulation of *Amt* V.)

It should be pointed out that the close co-operation between all branches of the German Police is again underlined by the fact that the KTI serves not only the *Kripo* but the *Gestapo* and the *Orpo* as well.

An additional agency in the service of crime prevention and detection is the **Kriminalbiologisches Institut der Sipo** (Institute of Criminalbiology of the Security Police). A central office of this kind has existed in Germany since 1937. Even earlier, however, in 1924, a collecting station of Criminal biological data had been established in Straubing/Bavaria and later in München by *Ministerialrat Prof. Dr.* VIERNSTEIN. The science of criminal biology was then further developed by the former *Staatssekretär* in the Reich Ministry of Justice *Dr.* FREISLER, who stressed especially its application in cases of juvenile delinquency.

In December, 1941, the *Kriminalbiologisches Institut der Sipo* was established and became part of the *Reichskriminalpolizeiamt*. Its offices are located with the KTI at Werderscher Markt 5–6 in Berlin ; its staff consists of a number of doctors and medically trained personnel. The specific functions of the Institute are as follows—

(i) To maintain indexes of all anti-social and criminal " family groups " in Germany.

(ii) To segregate according to the principles of criminal biology all juveniles who are regarded as harmful to society, and who " necessitate " Police action in the interests of crime prevention.

(iii) To establish an observation office in co-operation with the *Reichsgesundheitsamt* (National Health Bureau) in order to compile records from the point of view of criminal biology.

(iv) To take part in research into the heredity of the German people, and act in an advisory capacity to the National Health Bureau.

Wherever deemed necessary advisory personnel trained by the Institute may be attached to regional *Kripo* Headquarters.

Throughout Germany *Kriminalbiologische Sammelstellen* (Collecting stations of information in the field of criminal biology) have been established. By October, 1942, according to a document, such stations had been formed in the following towns :—

| | | |
|---|---|---|
| München | Köln | Leipzig |
| Freiburg | Berlin | Halle |
| Münster | Königsberg | Graz |

It seems that many of the functions of the Institute to some extent overlap those of *Gruppe V D*, the *Kriminaltechnisches Institut*. Whether the Institute of Criminal Biology has been attached to or incorporated into the KTI is not known and there are no documentary indications for a development in that direction. Nevertheless, it seems safe to assume that the two institutes, if separate, maintain that close co-operation which the nature of their work necessitates.

The **Kriminalmedizinisches Zentralinstitut der Sicherheitspolizei** (Central Institute of Criminal Medicine of the Security Police) was formed in September, 1943, and incorporated into the *Reichskriminalpolizeiamt*. Its functions are :—

(i) Training of replacements for the medical personnel of the SS and Police (this apparently does not include the *Waffen*-SS).

(ii) Scientific research and experiment in criminal medicine.

(iii) Direction and exploitation of all research by other scientific criminal institutes in medical matters.

(iv) Direction in all matters regarding criminal medicine within the *Sipo*.

(v) Medical examination of criminal cases of interest to the Police.

(vi) Training of *Kripo* personnel to deal with problems of criminal medicine.

Personnel trained by the Institute may be sent to the *Kripo-(Leit-)Stellen* as branch representatives or attached to the *Kriminaltechnische Untersuchungsstellen*. The functions of the *Kriminalmedizinisches Institut* may also be delegated to faculties of criminal medicine existing at various universities.

The directors of any of the Criminal Institute branches established at the (*Leit-*) *Stellen* must be professors of criminology.

As in all the other scientific institutes of the *Sipo* the *Kriminalmedizinisches Institut* serves the *Gestapo* as well as the *Orpo*, and close co-operation is maintained with all branches of the German Police.

## 118. Development of the Kripo Regional Network

The Nazi policy of taking over existing Police organisations in Germany and superimposing new structures has been discussed in detail in PARTS ONE and THREE of this book. With regard to the regional organisation of the Criminal Police in Germany this policy resulted in the simultaneous existence of three systems of Criminal Police control until a complete reorganisation of the *Kripo* was ordered by HIMMLER in 1943. For a clearer understanding of the present organisation a brief outline of the previous system follows.

Headquarters of the Reich Criminal Police were established in most towns containing corresponding headquarters of the *Gestapo*. The *Kripo-(Leit-) Stellen* (Kripo Regional and Sub-regional Headquarters) have, since their establishment in 1936, been directly subordinate to the *Reichskriminalpolizeiamt*, but for administrative purposes, they were, until Oct 1943, attached to the *Staatliche Polizeiverwaltungen* of their respective localities. Their offices were therefore located in the *Polizeipräsidien, Polizeidirektionen*, or *Polizeiämter*. For this reason *Kripo Leitstellen* and *Kripo-Stellen* would only be found in towns having a *Staatliche Polizeiverwaltung*, and the local *Polizeipräsident* or *-direktor* was at the same time the " *Chef* " of the *Kripo-(Leit)-Stelle*. Under him the senior *Kripo* official, known as the *Leiter* (Chief), was in charge of the actual work and received orders and technical directives from the RKPA.

*Staatliche Polizeiverwaltungen* to which no *Kripo-(Leit-)Stellen* were allotted formed their own sections devoted exclusively to Criminal Police functions, known as *Staatliche Kriminalabteilungen* (or, in Bohemia-Moravia, *Regierungskriminalabteilungen*). These were, unlike the *Kripo-(Leit-) Stellen*, directly subordinate to the *Polizeipräsident, Polizeidirektor* or *Polizeirat* and had only a functional connection with the RKPA and the Reich Criminal Police.

In localities without a *Staatliche Polizeiverwaltung*, the *Gemeindepolizei* (Municipal Police) took charge of all Criminal Police functions through its own Criminal Police sections known as *Gemeinde-Kriminalpolizei-Abteilungen*. The size of these headquarters depended largely on local requirements and they varied considerably ; at one end of the scale were specialised offices, and at the other end *Kripo* matters were handled *ex- officio* by a *Gendarm*. These *Gemeinde-Kriminalpolizei-Abteilungen* were supervised by the *Leiter* of the nearest *Kripo-(Leit)-Stelle*.

Obviously this administrative dependence and organisational confusion between *Reichs-, Staatliche* and *Gemeinde-Kriminalpolizei* was opposed to Nazi principles of centralisation and unification ; accordingly in a decree of 7 Sep 1943, HIMMLER ordered a far-reaching reorganisation which completely separated the Criminal Police from the *Staatliche* and *Gemeinde-Polizeiverwaltungen*, and incorporated all Criminal Police Headquarters into the structure of the *Reichskriminalpolizei*.

As a result of this reorganisation *Kripo-Leitstellen* and-*Stellen* were made independent headquarters within the chain of command of the *Sicherheitspolizei*, and the *Leiter* of the *Kripo-(Leit)Stelle*, formerly subordinate, at least administratively, to the local *Polizeiverwalter*, now merely submits routine reports to him.

All former *Staatliche Kriminalabteilungen* and *Gemeinde-Kriminalpolizei-Abteilungen* with an establishment of 10 or more officials were, by this decree, transformed into *Aussendienststellen* of the *Reichskriminalpolizei*. As such they are now directly subordinate to the *Kripo-(Leit-)Stellen* in their particular area. *Abteilungen* of fewer than 10 Criminal Police officials became *Aussenposten* (literally Outposts) of the nearest *Kripo-(Leit)-Stelle* or *Aussendienststelle* (Branch Office). As a general rule it appears that there were usually 10 or more *Kripo* officials in communities of over 50,000 inhabitants, and less than ten *Kripo* officials in towns of less than 50,000 inhabitants. It must be pointed out, however, that this proportion is not based on an original directive or regulation, but has been arrived at as a result of comparative research in a large number of individual instances ; it should therefore be regarded merely as a general guide allowing of variations wherever local conditions, such as a concentration of essential industries, proximity to the frontier, or the number of foreign workers, necessitate the establishment of an *Aussendienststelle* rather than an *Aussenposten*.

For financial and economic administration (*Wirtschaftliche Betreuung*) the *Kripo* are now dependent on the nearest *Stapo-(Leit)-Stelle*. Appointments to and dismissals from the service, however, have become the responsibility of the *Leiter* of each *Kripo-(Leit-)Stelle*.

## 119. Regional Organisation of the Kripo

**Kripo-Leitstellen** are usually established at the seats of larger German *Länder* or *Reichsgaue* or at the administrative capitals of Prussian Provinces. The head of a *Leitstelle* usually holds the rank of an *Oberregierungs- und Kriminalrat*.

Just before the War a *Kripo-Leitstelle* employed between 150 and 250 persons. These figures may have been somewhat reduced since that time, but on the whole there is no reason to believe that the average number has undergone a substantial change. At present there are 22 *Kripo-Leitstellen* in existence in Greater Germany. Their functions are as follows :

(i) Study of information received, and its application to local Kripo problems.

(ii) Maintenance and compilation of statistics ; publication of a *Meldeblatt* (Official Gazette) furnishing of reports and expert opinions ; general advice on criminal matters.
To discharge their advisory functions properly, *Kripo-Leitstellen* maintain *Kriminalberatungsstellen*, which are offices furnishing information and assistance to the public in all criminal matters. Beyond that the *Kriminalberatungsstellen* supplement the work of the newspapers, films, and wireless in the education and propaganda tasks of enlightening the public as to the danger of criminal and " asocial " elements.

(iii) Supervision of all specialised and technical equipment ; standardisation of all routine administrative matters, supply, equipment and training. Special emphasis is placed on cooperation between sections and proper liaison with other agencies.

(iv) Serving as a message centre for all incoming reports and information, as well as a collecting centre for ten-fingerprint records. All material of this nature not concerning the particular district is forwarded to the *Reichskriminalpolizeiamt*.

(v) Taking action in all cases of more than ordinary importance which go beyond the territory and responsibility of one of the lower Kripo headquarters including *Kripo-Stellen*.

The Nazi concept of the function of the Criminal Police, however, includes far more than the above list of tasks, which must not be regarded as final or exhaustive. The close relationship of *Kripo* and *Gestapo* functions, already discussed, must constantly be stressed. In cooperation with the *Gestapo* the Criminal Police, through its *Leitstellen* and lower headquarters, may be called upon to discharge any additional duty regarded as necessary for combatting crime and " safeguarding the State."

*Kripo-Leitstellen* maintain the following files collating information essential to the work in their particular district :

Criminals and their crimes
Fingerprints (ten-fingers, single fingerprints, and palm prints)
Photographs of criminals (*Verbrecheralbum—* Rogues' Gallery)
Special distinguishing marks of criminals
Nicknames and aliases.
Missing Persons
Wanted Persons.

It is obvious that the larger cities present the most serious problem from the point of view of the Criminal Police. For this reason the *Kripo-Leitstellen* may attach officials of their staff to the local *Polizei-Reviere*. There they will work together with the officers and personnel of the *Orpo* in an attempt to carry the machinery of the Criminal Police down to the lowest possible echelon. In some instances local conditions have made it necessary for the *Leitstellen* to establish complete *Kriminalreviere* to function as specialised offices assisting the Regular Police ; in Hamburg a variation known as a *Kriminalhafenrevier* (Harbour Ward or Precinct of the Criminal Police) has been identified. It may be assumed that similar *Reviere* exist in other German harbour cities.

**Kripostellen** have been established at the seats of Prussian *Regierungsbezirke* or at the administrative capitals of smaller German *Länder* or *Reichsgaue* ; at present there are 44 *Kripostellen* in existence in Greater Germany. The head of a *Stelle* usually holds the rank of a *Regierungs- und Kriminalrat* or *Kriminaldirektor*. The average *Kripostelle* is believed to employ 80—120 men, the exact figure depending mainly on local needs.

The relationship between the *Kripo-Leitstellen* and *Kripostellen* is more or less the same as that between the equivalent offices of the *Gestapo*— the *Stapoleitstellen* and *Stapostellen*. *Kripostellen* are **not** subordinate to *Kripo-Leitstellen*. They function independently and no executive orders as from a higher to a lower echelon are issued by a *Leitstelle* to a *Stelle*. Since, however, *Kripostellen* are usually located within the larger administrative area of a *Leitstelle*, a great many instances of overlapping and duplication may arise, as the combatting of crime cannot be tied to any narrow regional limits or boundaries, and the tracking down of criminals can only be effective if a maximum of cooperation exists between the various regional Police headquarters. In the interests of greater efficiency and uniformity of procedure, therefore, the *Leitstelle* will frequently issue directives and memoranda to the *Stellen* within its territory. While this function of coordination, even sometimes of direction, is in principle the same as that encountered within the *Gestapo*, in practice the character of *Kripo* work, with a constant exchange of information, usually necessitates more detailed and frequent guidance on the part of the *Kripo-Leitstellen* than is exercised by the *Stapo-Leitstellen*. However, the *Kripo-Leitstelle* never functions as a superior Command Headquarters to the *Stelle*, and a large measure of independence given to *Kripostellen* is repeatedly stressed in German official publications as being necessary for the effective fulfilment of their functions.

*Kripostellen* maintain the same categories of files as the *Leitstellen*, but on a smaller scale and covering their immediate territories only. Whenever the information contained in these files is deemed insufficient the *Stelle* may call upon the more detailed data kept in the files of the *Leitstelle*. Similarly the *Kripostelle* may request the temporary attachment of additional personnel from the larger headquarters in special instances requiring large scale operations.

Since *Kripo-Leitstellen* and *-Stellen* exercise jurisdiction over wide areas, they are assisted in their duties by a considerable number of branch offices within the *Regierungsbezirk, Land* or *Reichsgau*. These branch offices, of which 698 have been identified in Greater Germany, are known as **Kripo-Aussendienststellen** and **Kripo-Aussenposten** (literally Outposts). These are not independent offices, but are controlled and directed by a *Leitstelle* or *Stelle*, which lays down the policy governing the conduct of their work and the execution of their duties.

The difference between the *Aussenposten* and the *Aussendienststelle*, as already mentioned, is mainly one of size. An establishment of more than 10 *Kripo* officials is called an *Aussendienststelle*, and an establishment of less than 10 an *Aussenposten*. The *Aussenposten*, which is thus the smallest regular Headquarters of the *Kripo*, may nevertheless be to some extent subordinate to an *Aussendienststelle* in that it may be directed to use the *Aussendienststelle* as a channel for communications with the superior (*Leit-)Stelle*.

Like the headquarters of the *Gestapo* those of the Criminal Police are subject to the supervision of the BdS (IdS) of the *Wehrkreis* in which they are located. As previously explained *Kripo-(Leit-)Stellen* were established along the lines of the regional administration of Germany, but the BdS on the other hand is responsible for an area coinciding with a *Wehrkreis* (*SS-Oberabschnitt*). Consequently the same difficulty arises for the *Kripo* as that already noted in the regional administration of the *Gestapo* : a *Kripostelle* may come under the supervision or command of a different BdS from the one controlling the responsible *Kripo-Leitstelle*. As a remedy for complications arising from this inconsistency, again following the pattern of the *Gestapo*, the powers of the BdS in relation to those of the *Leitstelle* have been gradually but consistently increased. In addition it should again be pointed out that regional discrepancies of this kind, which might be expected to hamper the organisation of the German Police, are compensated for by the closest possible liaison and cooperation between headquarters at all levels.

### 120. Internal Structure of a Kripo Headquarters.

The inner organisation of a regional *Kripo* Headquarters does not conform to a standard pattern nor is it identical with that of *Amt* V of the RSHA. Following the principle that maximum efficiency can best be achieved if the structure of each headquarters is adapted to local requirements, the *Leiter* of a *Kripo-(Leit-)Stelle* is empowered, within limits, to determine the most advantageous internal organisation of his particular office. The following basic structure will serve as an indication of the type of organisation likely to be encountered in all *Kripo* headquarters.

*Kripo* headquarters are usually sub-divided into 3 or more **Direktionen** (Directorates) each handling one type of *Kripo* activity. Each *Kriminal-Direktion* is designated by a Roman numeral (e.g. Direktion I), but in many instances the abbreviation K, followed by an Arabic numeral, is used, e.g. K 1, K 2. In one specific instance Direktion I is known to handle personnel and office organisation, Direktion II professional and habitual criminals and Direktion III amateur crimes and local activities of the Criminal Police. Each *Direktion* is again sub-divided into **Inspektionen** (Inspectorates) which as a rule are abbreviated by the letter K followed by a Roman numeral, e.g. K.I, K.II. Each *Inspektion* in turn consists of a varying number of **Kommissariate** each covering a specific field of crime.

As a rule *Kommissariate* are numbered consecutively throughout the entire headquarters, but in some instances they may be numbered from 1 onwards within each *Inspektion*. They are designated by an Arabic numeral preceding the letter K, e.g. 1.K, 9.K. In official language these are sometimes referred to as " *Erstes* K, *Neuntes* K, etc."

It must be emphasised again that this pattern is merely a guiding one. Even the numbering system and the abbreviations used may vary from one Headquarters to another. The schematic structure of a typical *Kripo-Leitstelle* in a large German city, as well as the organisational breakdown of the *Leitstellen* of Köln in 1941 and of Hannover in 1943, are given in Annexe G.

### 121. Search for Wanted Persons (Fahndung)

Originally the searches for Wanted Persons were conducted by the German Criminal Police as actions against individuals on warrants issued for each particular case (*Einzelfahndung*), an ordinary Police function carried out in any country. With the constant increase in the scope of Police activities under the Nazi régime, and especially since the outbreak of war, the method of the *Fahndung* in Germany has undergone fundamental changes, typical of the expansion of German Police power in general. To the already considerable number of persons wanted on political grounds have been added the ever increasing cases of fugitive foreign workers and prisoners of war as well as of German soldiers absent without leave or trying to desert. In coping with the problem the old system of the *Einzelfahndung* was found completely inadequate. It became technically impossible to issue individual warrants or to act in each case on an individual basis. To overcome these difficulties the *Kriegsfahndung* (Wartime Search for Wanted Persons) was inaugurated, making provisions for large scale actions, fully organised raids and systematic checks on the identity papers of all persons travelling on railways, roads and highways, crossing bridges or using ferries.

To control actions of this kind HIMMLER on 5th December, 1942, added the *Kriegsfahndungszentrale* (Central Bureau for the Wartime Search for Wanted Persons) to the RKPA as *Hilfsreferat* V C 2 k. Later the bureau was transferred to *Referat* V C 1 where it forms the *Hilfsreferat* V C 1 b, though parts of it are in *Hilfsreferat* V C 1 a. In V C 1 are now centred all functions necessary to direct the arrest or recapture of all foreigners, foreign workers, prisoners of war, baled out Allied flying personnel, foreign agents, spies and saboteurs as well as Germans trying to evade military service or deserting from the Armed Forces.

In the interest of greater efficiency in such searches the Criminal Police is authorised to drop the prosecution and investigation of minor crimes (*Bagatellsachen*) according to two unpublished directives by HIMMLER issued on 25th August, 1939, and 31st August, 1939, referring respectively to "*Entlastung der Staatlichen Kriminalpolizei*" (Order to relieve the Criminal Police of minor duties) and "*Entlastung der Geheimen Staatspolizei*" (Order to relieve the Secret State Police of minor duties).

Regionally the BdS (IdS) of each *Wehrkreis* supervises and co-ordinates all *Kriegsfahndung* activities. In cases involving the Orpo the BdO is also required to co-operate with the *Sipo*. The various regional headquarters of the *Kripo* are tactically in control of searches within their areas ; an exception to this rule appears in border districts where the *Gestapo* takes charge of all these functions (*Grenzfahndung*) but maintains constant and close co-operation with the *Kripo*, *Orpo* and Frontier Guard formations. For further centralisation and uniformity of *Kriegsfahndung* the *Beauftragter des RSHA für die Verhinderung von Gefangenenfluchten* (special officials of the RSHA for the prevention of the escape of prisoners of war) receive and collate all reports on matters of this kind.

To keep the agencies concerned up to date in all details necessary for the conduct of these searches the RKPA issues several specialised publications, the most important of which is the *Deutsches Fahndungsbuch* (Book of Persons Wanted by the German Police). The *Sonderausgabe zum Reichskriminalpolizeiblatt* (Special Edition of the Official Gazette of the German Criminal Police) also contains detailed descriptions of escaped Prisoners of War and other wanted persons.

## 122. Types of Fahndung

There are five different categories of the ordinary *Fahndung*, which are as follows :—

| | |
|---|---|
| *Bahnfahndung* | Search on Railways |
| *Strassenverkehrsfahndung* | Search on roads and at other traffic points |
| *Riegelfahndung* | Search at barriers |
| *Razzien* | Police Raids |
| *Grenzfahndung* | Search at frontiers (see previous para.). |

The **Bahnfahndung** is carried out by the *Bahnpolizei*, an organisation which has been in existence ever since the unification of the German railway system in 1920. All its members are employees of the *Deutsche Reichsbahn* and come under the supervision of the *Reichsverkehrsministerium* (RVM—Reich Ministry of Transport). On 17 July, 1928, an entirely new version of the *Reichsbahn-Betriebsordnung* (Railway Statutory Regulations) was passed.* It included for the first time a uniform Railway Police Code, equally applicable to all parts of the Reich. Thus the *Bahnpolizei* became—with the exception of the *Postschutz*—the first and only Police force operating before 1933 on a national basis under a central command with a uniform legal code.

The *Bahnpolizei* consists of part-time and full-time railway police officials. The part-time police officials are railway employees such as stationmasters, conductors, train personnel, guards on level crossings and others. In addition to their usual functions, they are responsible for the maintenance of law and order on railway property.

Full-time railway police officials are organised into two services, known as the *Bahnschutzpolizei* (Bzp — Railway Protection Police) and the *Reichsbahnfahndungsdienst* (RBFD — Railway Criminal Investigation Service). The *Bahnschutzpolizei* is a regular guard and patrol service.

Its members are uniformed and are usually armed with pistols and clubs. They patrol station platforms and trains where their task is the direct maintenance of law and order. The *Reichsbahnfahndungsdienst* was founded in order to combat corruption among railway personnel and to prevent and investigate the theft of goods and the embezzlement of funds held by the National Railways. Both services still function as originally conceived, but in the new system of *Fahndung*, they have, especially the *Reichsbahnfahndungsdienst*, assumed additional duties.

For this purpose the RBFD was afforded special powers in March 1943 following an agreement between the *RFSS und Chef der Deutschen Polizei* and the *Reichsverkehrsministerium* (Reich Ministry of Transport). Under this agreement the *Gestapo* and the *Kripo* may request the services of the *Bahnpolizei* to assist in the investigation of any political or other crime. Under such circumstances members of the RBFD, which is a *Sonderpolizei* (Special Police), acquire the status of *Hilfspolizei* (Auxiliary Police). While they still remain under the supervision and administration of the RVM they have now become operationally attached to the *Reichssicherheitshauptamt* and thereby assume regular Police powers of arrest and detention, confiscation and search. In matters of equipment and selection of personnel, the RVM must obtain the consent of the *Chef der Sicherheitspolizei und des SD ;* the latter is also responsible for the specialised training of personnel in Security Police functions and methods.

The regional chief of the RBFD is the *Fahndungsdezernent ;* one such official is located at each *Reichsbahndirektion* (National Railway Regional Headquarters). In all matters regarding the Security Police functions of the RBFD the *Fahndungsdezernent* receives his orders from the chief of the nearest *Kripo-(Leit-)Stelle* who maintains constant liaison with the *Reichsbahnfahndungsdienst* through a special member of his staff. The *Kripo* is also kept informed on all activities of the *Bahnpolizei* through this official.

The **Strassenverkehrsfahndung** is ordinarily carried out by formations of the *Orpo* in co-operation with such auxiliary formations as the NSKK *Verkehrshilfsdienst* (Road Aid or Traffic Assistance Service) and the NSKK *Transportkontrollen des Motorisierten Transportes der Kriegswirtschaft* (NSKK Cargo Inspection Service of motorised wartime transport). The local *Kripo* headquarters, however, while not directly in control of the activities of any of these formations, maintain close co-operation with them in all matters of wartime searches. For this purpose *Hauptamt* V in the National Headquarters of the NSKK, which controls all functions regarding *Fahndung* within the NSKK, maintains direct liaison with the RKPA. The existing network of call posts established by the NSKK in order to carry out their functions as a traffic aid and control organisation are of course extremely valuable in carrying out widespread searches. (For further details on the various NSKK Auxiliary Police formations see para. 47).

The *Verkehrskompanie (mot.) z.b.V.* (Motorised Traffic Company for special employment) has been discussed in para. 43. The nature and functions of this unit make it apparent that during special searches it may also be very usefully employed as a highly mobile patrol unit.

In order to tighten the network of Police searches even further the system of **Riegelfahndung** was instituted, whereby theoretical barriers, made up of *Riegelstellungen* (Barrier Points) and traversing Germany, were drawn up to prevent any person from

* Published in the *Reichsgesetzblatt*, Part II, page 541.

crossing these lines without having his papers and permits thoroughly examined. These barriers are the rivers Rhine, Oder, Vistula and Danube as well as the Kaiser Wilhelm (Kiel) Canal. To supplement these main lines of demarcation similar positions were established at other important river crossings and key points. These are known as *Zwischenriegel* (Intermediate Barriers). In addition it appears that Germany is divided into six large zones (Südost, Südwest, Nordost, Nordwest, Mitte and General Gouvernement) to facilitate police searches.

Another important method of capturing wanted persons is through the large scale **Razzien** (Police Raids) carried out by the *Orpo*. *Kripo* personnel usually take part as specialists in such raids to interrogate suspects. As in most other actions connected with the *Kriegsfahndung* formations of both Party and Wehrmacht may also assist.

Since the most difficult problems connected with *Fahndung* have been created by the large number of fugitive foreign workers, special *Auffangslager* (Reception Camps) were established in August 1943. While these camps are actually organised and maintained by the Labour Offices, the regional *Kripo* headquarters keep in constant touch with these installations. In addition the *Kripo* attempts to anticipate future sources of trouble especially wherever large-scale bombing has caused serious dislocation of industries employing foreign labour. In carrying out these functions the *Kripo* calls on the assistance of the RBFD, the *Bahnschutzpolizei* and the previously mentioned NSKK formations.

### 123. Sonderfahndung

So far the organisations and functions of the ordinary *Fahndung* and *Kriegsfahndung* have been discussed. In many instances, however, these measures have been considered inadequate. In such cases an extra-ordinary plan known as the *Sonderfahndungsplan der Sipo und des SD* (Special Search system of the *Sipo* and SD) is put into operation. This state of emergency may be declared to exist by any of the regional *Kripo* headquarters, or in frontier districts, by the equivalent *Gestapo* offices.

The *Sonderfahndung* is divided into three degrees of emergency :—

> *Fahndungsstufe Alpha*
> *Fahndungsstufe Beta*
> *Grossfahndung.*

The finer details distinguishing the three plans are not known. The main difference seems to be one of intensity, *i.e.* the number of personnel involved in the action. *Fahndungsstufe Alpha* is an alarm calling into action only the forces of the Security Police (*Sicherheitspolizeiliche Fahndung*). *Fahndungsstufe Beta*, the *Allgemeine Polizeifahndung* (General Police Search) involves personnel of all branches of the German Police augmented by civilians temporarily pressed into Police service.

*Grossfahndung* means not only mobilisation of all branches of the Police including all auxiliaries, Party Formations, Affiliated Organisations and whatever units of the *Wehrmacht* can be mustered, but actually interferes with almost every phase of normal activity in Germany. Among the organisations taking part in the General Search are the SA, SS, NSKK, NSFK, RAD, HJ, TN, *Feuerwehr*, *Stadt- und Landwacht* and Forestry Services. To illustrate the scope of the security problem as well as the intensity of a search of this kind the results of the first *Grossfahndung* conducted all over Germany from 6–20 March, 1943, may be of interest. The search was occasioned by the escape

of 43 British and Dominion airmen from a camp near Posen, but the arrests included the following :

| | | | |
|---|---|---|---|
| Escaped prisoners of war | ... | ... | 809 |
| Foreign workers who had left their assigned places of work | ... | ... | 8,281 |
| Other persons wanted by the Police | ... | 4,825 |

| | | | | |
|---|---|---|---|---|
| Total | ... | ... | ... | ... | 13,915 |

Recently the German Armed Forces have begun to play an increasing part in patrols and searches. In order to lessen the confusion resulting from the great variety of different organisations engaged in searches and patrols the OKW, the *RFSS und Chef der Deutschen Polizei*, the Reich Minister of Transport and the Chief of the NSKK agreed to form mixed patrols. Units of this kind are regulated by the *Kommandeure des Wehrmachtsstreifendienstes* (commanders of the *Wehrmacht* patrol service in each *Wehrkreis*) in agreement with the BdOs and the commanders of the *NSKK-Motorgruppen*.

### 124. Other Organisations taking part in Fahndung

The **SS-Bahnschutz** (Railway Guard) and the **SS-Postschutz** (Postal Guard), organisations similar to the *Bahnschutzpolizei* and serving the railway and postal authorities respectively, were formed by the SS, and in 1942 placed under the command of *SS-OGF* BERGER, the Chief of the *SS-Hauptamt* (SS Central Office). At the same time a related service, the **SS-Funkschutz** (Radio Installation Guard) was formed. Its functions are to guard all radio installations (such as the *Rundfunkhaus* in Berlin and other transmitters and power plants) to detect illegal wireless stations and even to track down listeners to illegal or foreign broadcasts. Ordinary policing of public property such as railways, postal and broadcasting installations would seem to be the task of the Regular Police. The fact that the SS has taken over many of these functions is yet another indication of its close connections with the *Kripo*, *Gestapo* and SD.

The **Hitler Youth** has also been placed at the disposal of the Police for carrying out Police Searches. Originally the *Hitler-Jugend-Streifendienst* was intended only for searches involving minors and concentrated its efforts on locating missing juveniles. As a result of the present man-power shortage, however, the Hitler Youth SRD is employed as an auxiliary force co-operating in regular Police searches.

For their specialised searches for missing juveniles the personnel department of the *Reichsjugendführung* (Reich Youth Directorate) issues a *Fahndungsblatt des Hitler-Jugend-Streifendienstes* (HJ-SRD Gazette of wanted persons). This publication appears approximately once a week and is distributed down to the lowest echelons. For additional information on the HJ-SRD see para. 48.

Another Party organisation assisting the Police in searches are the **SS-Bordschutzmannschaften** (Ship Board Security Crews). In compliance with a proclamation by *SS-OGF*, Karl KAUFMANN, Reich Commissioner for Ocean Navigation, all ships essential to Germany's war effort and manned partially or entirely by non-German crews are policed and supervised by *SS-Bordschutzmannschaften*. These units are assigned by the *Führer* of the *SS-Oberabschnitt* in which the port of departure is located. According to the proclamation these units are to " man anti-aircraft guns, assist the German officers on such vessels and provide security for the non-German crew members." Their relationship to the masters of such ships was not defined. Notwithstanding these alleged official functions, their real purpose probably lies in serving the *Sipo* and SD ; in particular they assist the *Kripo* by carrying the *Fahndung* on to the high seas, *e.g.* in the search for stowaways.

### 125. Forestry and Hunting Authorities

Headquarters of the *Forst- und Jagdschutz* (Forestry and Hunting Authorities) are spread over the entire Reich. They are under the command of GÖRING in his capacity as *Reichsforstmeister* (Reich Chief Forester). Regionally the Reich Forest administration has its main offices at the administrative headquarters of the *Länder* with branch offices situated throughout each Land. These administrative areas are called *Jagdgaue* (Hunting Districts). In most instances such branch offices follow the regional sub-divisions of the *Länder*, but local conditions may necessitate the creation of additional *Jagdgaue*. Each *Jagdgau* is headed by a *Gaujägermeister* (District Chief Forester) whose HQ is the *Stabsamt des Gaujägermeisters* (Staff Office of the District Chief Forester).

The main function of the Reich forest administration and its executive agencies is to combat illegal hunting (*Wilderei*) and to protect German forests. Personnel of the *Forst- und Jagdschutz* are trained by the nearest regional *Kripo* headquarters and cooperate closely with the Criminal Police. Under the Nazis, however, they have gained far more importance than their specific tasks would seem to warrant. Since personnel of the *Forst- und Jagdschutz* are armed and *Kripo*-trained they must be reckoned with not only as extra police agencies in forest areas, but also as an active aid to the *Sipo* and SD, and even beyond that as a possible nucleus for guerrilla bands in the most inaccessible parts of the Reich.

A tabulation of the regional organisation of the Reich Forest Administration will be found in Annexe G.

### 126. Police for the Supervision of Mines

As previously mentioned (para. 86) in connection with the *Verwaltungspolizei*, the *Bergpolizei* (Mines Police) under the Nazi régime took over the prevention and prosecution of sabotage in mining areas as one of its main functions. It has, therefore, except for administrative purposes, grown out of its original place within the *Verwaltungspolizei*, and a decree of 12 September, 1942, by the *Chef der Sipo und des SD* stresses the extremely close cooperation of the *Bergpolizei* with the *Kripo*, *Gestapo* and SD. According to this decree the *Gestapo* cooperates with the *Bergpolizei* in all investigations of sabotage and other treasonable political acts against the Nazi Party and Government, and the *Kripo* has taken over all other investigations within the sphere of action of the *Bergpolizei* which are not directly connected with the technical operation of the mines. Wherever such technical considerations enter into any of the cases treated by the *Sipo*, the *Bergbehörden* (Mining Authorities) and the *Bergpolizei* take part in the proceedings. In cases not involving anything of interest to the Security Police, the *Bergpolizei* may carry out the necessary investigations independently unless the *Sipo* specially desires to participate.

Details of the cooperation between *Bergpolizei* and *Sipo* are settled by the *Inspekteure* of the *Sipo* and SD according to local conditions.

A table of the *Bergbehörden* linking them with the responsible *Sipo* and SD HQ will be found in Annexe G.

# D. THE SICHERHEITSDIENST

### 127. Formation and Purpose of the SD

The Leaders of the Nazi régime always realised that their dictatorship could only be upheld by the scientific application of force implemented by the shrewd exploitation of the fear of force. The preceding chapters of this book have discussed many of the executive organisations which the Nazis employed to that end. The system, however, would have been incomplete without an efficient and unscrupulous intelligence agency to collect information in every sphere of German life, evaluate it and make it available to the executive branches of the German Police. An agency of this kind was developed by the Nazis in the *Sicherheitsdienst des RFSS* (SD—Security Service of the RFSS) which had been devised by HIMMLER as early as 1932. HIMMLER put this organisation under the direction of Reinhold HEYDRICH, in whose hands the SD grew into a highly efficient political intelligence system and later became the most effective instrument for suppression at the disposal of the Nazi régime. In a decree of 9 June, 1934, three weeks before the purge of the SA, all other intelligence organisations within the Nazi Party were dissolved and their members transferred to the SD which thereby became the sole political intelligence agency in Germany.

When HIMMLER, in 1936, became *Chef der Deutschen Polizei* and founded the *Sicherheitspolizei* by combining the *Gestapo* and the *Kripo* he made the chief of the SD, HEYDRICH, also *Chef der Sipo*, thereby indicating the close relationship which was to be established between the two organisations. This cooperation ran its course for two years without any official announcement until

FRICK (then Reich Minister of the Interior), apparently in an attempt to clarify and justify this union, published a decree on 11 November, 1938, which indicated clearly the important tasks of the SD in its capacity as the intelligence system serving Party and State, notably that of upholding the work of the *Sipo*.

Originally the central office of the SD was the *SD-Hauptamt*, also known as the *Sicherheitshauptamt der SS* (SS Department of Security) which formed part of the *Reichsführung SS* (SS High Command). On 27 September, 1939, the SD was officially linked with the *Sicherheitspolizei*, when a decree of HIMMLER combined the *Hauptamt Sicherheitspolizei* and the *SS-Sicherheitshauptamt* to form the *Reichssicherheitshauptamt* ; Reinhold HEYDRICH, who, as mentioned above, was already chief of both the former offices, became Chief of the RSHA and assumed the title of *Chef der Sicherheitspolizei und des SD*.

A year later *SS-BF Dr.* Werner BEST summed up the importance of the SD even more clearly than had been done before, when he stated : " The SD, finally, must investigate and explore thoroughly the background and activities of the great ideological arch-enemies of National-Socialism and of the German People, in order to make possible a determined and effective effort for the annihilation of those enemies."

The scope of the SD was further widened by a decree of 19 August, 1942, issued by the Reich Minister of Justice. This decree stated that the SD, by virtue of its character as the intelligence service for Party and State, had the special duty of reporting to the leading offices of the Government all popular reactions to official measures. The Minister of Justice, consequently, instructed the judiciary authorities to make available to the men of the SD all information required by them. Similarly it was made the duty of the SD personnel to brief the judiciary authorities. Thus the finishing touches were put to an intricate machinery for internal espionage. The SD, submitting information to the Police, the Judiciary and the whole complex of central and local Party and Government headquarters, attained a key position in the structure of the Nazi State. With its scientific approach and its practically unlimited use of agents and funds, the SD developed internal espionage to the highest degree, surpassing anything that ever existed in Germany before. The SD must therefore be expected to be, in some form, behind every Nazi effort to retain or regain complete control over any phase of German life.

The SD occupies two bureaux in the *Reichs-sicherheitshauptamt* : Amt III entitled *Deutsche Lebensgebiete* (spheres of German Life) and *Amt* VI entitled *Ausland* (Foreign countries). *Amt* VII, dealing with *Weltanschauliche Erforschung und Auswertung* (Ideological research and its exploitation) while not definitely proved to be part of the SD, is known to operate in practice under SD direction. Full-time members of the SD are invariably SS-men, enjoying the extra-legal status (*Sondergerichtsbarkeit*) of the SS, and because of the highly confidential nature of SD work they are selected for their proven loyalty to the Nazi régime and are carefully checked before being admitted to full membership of the SD. On the other hand, such a vast espionage system as the SD must inevitably make use of a large number of part-time agents and informers many of whom are merely mercenary opportunists without any real convictions of their own. These men are selected from all walks of German life and range from the local greengrocer to the most esteemed members of university faculties. In every factory and workshop SD agents watch their fellow-workers, employees and managers. In theatres the position of SD agent may be filled by the make-up man, the star, or the stage director.

Such persons may even serve the SD without their knowledge. It is characteristic that at various times in the development of the SD the term " *Volksmeldedienst* " (People's Denouncing Service) has been unofficially mentioned, indicating the endeavours of the SD to build up a system by which almost every German becomes an informer against his fellow-countrymen.

## 128. Nature and Importance of Amt III of the RSHA

The duties of the SD as an intelligence agency inside Germany are discharged by *Amt* III of the RSHA and its network of regional and local headquarters. The discussion of the SD in the following paragraphs will concern itself exclusively with the activities carried out by *Amt* III. These activities consist of the observation and investigation of political conditions and popular attitudes in all spheres of German life. Its general function is to keep the leaders of both Party and State constantly informed on the people's reaction towards all official measures ; to maintain a constant check on the fluctuations of the nation's morale ; and to uncover any sources of potential dissatisfaction, opposition, or underground movements. *Amt* III has, further, now taken over the study of all financial, agricultural, industrial and social trends in Germany and occupied territories, and even goes so far as to check many major

business transactions. In this connection it is important to remember that the SD was created as, and has always remained, a Nazi Party organisation. **The SD is not a Government agency.** SD directives constantly point out this special status and make it clear that the SD, as the intelligence organisation of the Commander in Chief of the SS serves both Party and State, but retains its independence from Governmental agencies. The SD is therefore placed in an ideal position to observe and report on the various departments of the Government and its leading personalities.

The nature of the SD makes it self-evident that its work must always be carried out in the closest co-operation with the *Sicherheitspolizei* and especially with the *Gestapo*. Personnel of the *Sipo* and SD may frequently even be transferred from one organisation to the other. This essential degree of liaison is achieved through the regional supervision of *Sipo* and SD work by the BdS (IdS) and central direction by the RSHA. Considering the official emphasis on co-operation between *Sipo* and SD it may at first seem surprising that the two organisations have remained separate. The answer is that an autonomous intelligence agency strengthens enormously HIMMLER'S grasp on all other organisations including the Police. Again, while the executive functions of the *Kripo* and *Gestapo* cannot, of course, remain unknown to the public, it is essential for maximum efficiency, that an intelligence organisation like the SD should remain hidden. The functional separation of *Sicherheitspolizei* and SD tends to safeguard that secrecy. The two organisations must, nevertheless, be studied together, for knowledge of the one without consideration of the other would give a distorted picture. Only in occupied territories where speedy action and immediate intervention may often be necessary, the scheme of separation gives way to combined *Sipo* and SD commands.

A discussion of the functions of the SD would include a large number of subjects already touched upon in connection with the *Gestapo* and *Kripo* but there is no general overlapping or duplication of activities between the *Sipo* and the SD ; the SD in Germany is not an executive organisation, it merely collects information which then provides the basis for executive action by the *Gestapo* and the *Kripo*.

The information gathered by SD agents is collated in *Lageberichte* (situation reports) which are forwarded from the Branch Offices to the Higher Regional Headquarters, where they are consolidated and finally passed on to the RSHA. These reports are issued periodically and deal with an unlimited range of topics covering every phase of German public and private life. They are among the most interesting documents issued by any German agency. In them is contained a complete and unbiassed picture of German public opinion and morale, and since they are written for the highest Nazi authorities only, they are free from propaganda and wishful thinking. These *Lageberichte* give a better insight into the sentiments of the Germans than can be found in any other source. From them can be gained an impartial account of popular sympathies, apathies and opposition to the Nazi régime as well as an accurate appraisal of the results of every Allied action. Thus, for instance, they discuss objectively popular reaction towards Allied bombing attacks as well as towards every official utterance by State and Party leaders. A complete collection of *Lageberichte* from all parts of Germany and the occupied territories would furnish detailed testimony of every fluctuation of public opinion throughout the years of Nazi dictatorship. But even fragmentary situation reports of individual sections of Germany will provide an almost infallible key to the political feelings and, thereby, to the potential attitude of the population in those areas towards the Allied armies of occupation.

## 129. SD Penetration of German Life

It is almost impossible to give an overall picture of *Amt* III interests but some instances of SD activities other than the more obvious investigation and observation of opposition groups are given here.

One of the most extensive fields covered by the SD is that of education, culture, religion and intellectual life in general. SD agents check the political attitude of every teacher whether in university or school ; they supervise the tendencies and development of every group of students; they make frequent and detailed reports on lectures and courses. For this purpose the SD has enlisted as its agents teachers, students and administrative personnel of every educational establishment, who for the sake of advancement—or safety—are willing to turn informer on their colleagues. All works of art, all artists, all public entertainers are constantly subject to the observation of the SD and must, for their existence, have the SD's approval. On the recommendation of the SD, for instance, long monthly lists of prohibited books, music, plays and other works of art are published. Similarly a close check is kept on all films, on radio programmes and on every form of propaganda and counter-propaganda.

The SD, however, is not only interested in the investigation of the medium, but to an even greater extent it watches the response of the public to such entertainments.

A study of SD reports on public morale and the effect of enemy propaganda will in fact, often suggest the most opportune line of propaganda to be applied to the German people. Thus it is known that on occasions where important members of Party or Government, such as GÖBBELS, make a speech the SD is notified in advance, and sends out all its observers and contacts who during the speech observe popular reaction in restaurants, hotels, and other public meeting places. Immediately after the speech they hand in their reports which are consolidated at the headquarters and passed on to *Amt* III in BERLIN. Only a few hours later the Government officials and especially the speaker have a minute report on their desks giving them the popular reaction towards the speech. In addition to routine surveillance of radio programmes and a constant hunt for listeners to foreign broadcasts, the SD itself has established an elaborate system for monitoring.

Among the problems regarded as most serious by the Nazis is political opposition within religious groups. The SD therefore constantly watches all church activities, studies every written document originating from the clergy and analyses the effect of sermons and religious services on the political opinions of the population. In the course of these investigations the SD attempts to utilise members of the church administration and the clergy itself as agents and informers against their own colleagues and their fellow members of the congregation.

In the legal field the SD watches popular reaction towards new laws or decrees, and attempts to discover any violations of them or any loopholes in their execution ; the SD may, as a result, suggest judicial changes or amendments.

In its investigation of decisions by the German military courts in France the SD is reported to have been frequently dissatisfied by the leniency of sentences. In many instances these courts followed regular legal procedure and either meted out the ordinary punishment for the offence or released arrested persons when sufficient evidence for conviction was not forthcoming. To stop this, pressure was brought to bear upon the authorities by the SD and repeated reports were sent to Headquarters in Germany. In December, 1941, probably as a result of this pressure, the German High Command issued a secret decree for combatting offences against the security of the Reich and the occupying forces, especially sabotage, espionage or any other activities of potential danger to the German forces of occupation ; this order was officially referred to as the *Nacht- und Nebel-Erlass* ("Night and Fog" Decree). It authorised the secret transfer to Germany of persons subject to trial ; thus, whenever prolonged legal procedure was expected, a lenient sentence seemed probable or the execution of a harsh sentence might create unrest among the population, the accused was, on the recommendation of the SD, secretly (*i.e.* "*bei Nacht und Nebel*") transferred to the Reich for further detention, trial or execution. Whenever enquiries were made concerning persons thus deported, information was flatly denied. Many victims of this order are still detained without ever having come up for trial, a number of them being held in concentration camps under the classification of "NN" inmates. In most cases, therefore, the independence of the military courts was in practice severely restricted. Even though many political offenders were dealt with in this manner, the SD sometimes even ordered the arrest or detention of persons immediately after they had been acquitted or released by the military or civil authorities. It is reported that since June, 1944, the SD, on orders from HITLER, no longer recommends the death penalty, but probably as a consequence of the man-power shortage, commits most offenders to forced labour.

In order to "complete their records" the SD also receive a detailed report whenever a soldier is either imprisoned or released. This contains detailed personal data, the reason for the arrest or the release as well as the unit or location to which the soldier has been sent after having served his sentence. These files enable the SD to keep a close check even on military personnel.

Every detail of German administration is followed and investigated by the SD. Administrative officials, including the leading personalities of Party and State and even of the *Kripo* and *Gestapo* are covered by the information system of the SD. The scope of SD activities in this connection is illustrated by a document of 1939 which under the classification "*Geheime Reichssache*" (Top Secret) gave an SD account of a desperate struggle for power between the German Foreign Office on one side and the Reich Ministry of Propaganda and the OKW on the other. The SD in this instance not only kept the detailed minutes of the progress of this internal competition, but utilised the information gained to strengthen its own position by playing off the two contestants against each other.

Since "racial" problems and questions concerning minorities have been pushed into the foreground of Nazi ideology the SD also takes an interest in these matters. In particular, it studies the effect of mass assignments of foreign workers and estimates their usefulness on the one hand, or disrupting influence on the other, in certain sections of the country and in particular industries. The SD supervises the working of the German resettlement policy as well as the forced evacuation and systematic persecution of " racial " groups. Thus, for instance, the SD submitted a lengthy report on the procedure for evacuating Jews from Alsace and on the public attitude towards that measure. In its " racial " functions the SD works in close liaison witht he *SS-Rasse- und Siedlungs-Hauptamt* (SS Race and Settlement Department)—which gives expert advice on the *SS-Fähigheit* (SS suitability) of men applying for SS membership, and with the *SS-Hauptamt Volksdeutsche Mittelstelle* (*Vomi*—Department for the Repatriation of " racial " Germans) and its *Unwandererzentralen* (Repatriation Offices) ; it also probably reports on the progress of Nazi attempts to link up as many of the " racial " Germans with the interests and activities of the Reich, at the same time checking the political reliability of the " new Germans." It is interesting to note that the post of *Reichskommissar für die Festigung des Deutschen Volkstums* (Reich Commissioner for the Strengthening of Germanism) is held by HIMMLER.

Censorship has already been discussed in para. 106. It is evident, however, that so important an instrument of political control would not be neglected by the SD. While the actual machinery of censorship is probably left entirely in the hands of the *Sipo* and to some extent of the *Militärisches Amt*, SD observations and reports may in many cases suggest to these agencies when and where censorship should be applied. Thus, SD agents may observe the effect of letters on their recipients. In other cases the SD may get hold of letters or learn of their contents through informers after such letters have been delivered and read. The SD would then recommend the *Gestapo*, *Kripo* or Military Intelligence either to take executive action or to continue observation by means of censorship. It has been reported that SD personnel in France received assignments of telephone, radio or telegram interception, control and censorship, but it is not known whether they operated independently or merely assisted the executive staffs of the other branches of the Police in their duties.

### 130. SD Economic Transactions

What is perhaps one of the most extensive fields of SD activities can be found in the various phases of German economic life. In many instances staffs of specialists have been formed into *Wirtschaftssonderstäbe* (Special Economic Staffs). Observation of economic matters has been tremendously expanded since the outbreak of war, especially in occupied territories. Detailed reports on industries and agriculture are submitted regularly to the RSHA, ranging from overall comparative studies of production, supply, and demand, to minute checks on the most insignificant farmhouse, resulting in the discovery of an undeclared sheep or of hoarded foodstuffs in the possession of a French farmer. Economic reports of the SD include potential purchases of large stores of supplies, methods of achieving better prices and more advantageous contracts and the possible application of extra-legal measures to force the sale of goods not otherwise intended for the market. A document even shows the SD to have suggested strictly illegal transactions recommending the purchase of goods from Spain and Portugal by agents in Switzerland, with the intention of diverting large quantities of such shipments while en route to their destination. Transactions of this kind are referred to as " *Tarngeschäfte*" (Camouflaged Transactions) and make use of such means as fraudulent bills of lading.

Documentary evidence indicates that the wealth of useful information collected in the economic sphere frequently leads the SD to yield to the temptation of putting its own interests and those of its personnel before those of the German government and people. For instance, an SD headquarters in France went to great lengths to prove the illegality of a planned purchase of coffee by a German Army agency, in order to confiscate the goods for its own benefit. In the course of correspondence concerning this particular transaction, it was specifically stated that the SD wished to prevent any other German headquarters from securing the goods in question.

Similarly it is not at all unusual for the SD to recommend seizure of black market goods in occupied territories and make generous disposition of the materials thus acquired to combined *Sipo* and SD units. In one particular instance the SD confiscated 3,000 Kilos of cocoa and allocated two-thirds of the total to an SS-Panzer division while the remaining one-third found its way into the private stores of *Sipo* and SD officials. 11,000 tins of sardines were distributed in roughly the same proportion. Such transactions, of course, occur mainly in the *Sipo* and SD combined *Kommandos* in occupied territories, but it would not be surprising to find the SD within Germany exploiting their inside knowledge of economic trends.

Government Agencies and Ministries have been instructed to co-operate to the fullest degree with the SD—" co-operation " being even officially interpreted to mean free access for the SD to all inside information collected by these agencies. The importance of liaison with the Headquarters of the *Reichsnährstand* (Reich Food Administration) the *Reichsverkehrsbehörden* (Reich Transport and Traffic Authorities) and the *Reichsministerium für Rüstung und Kriegsproduktion* (Reich Ministry for Armament and War Production) has been particularly stressed. The consequences and advantages to the SD of connections of this kind cannot be overestimated.

### 131. Organisation of Amt III of the RSHA

Like all RSHA Bureaux, *Amt* III is divided into *Gruppen* (Sections) ; there are four *Gruppen* in *Amt* III, designated by the capital letters A to D (e.g., *Gruppe* III A). Each *Gruppe* is divided into a varying number of *Referate* (Sub-sections) indicated by Arabic numerals (e.g., *Referat* III A 2). The *Referat* may again be divided into any number of *Hilfsreferate* (Sub-sectional units) designated by small letters, e.g., III C 1 e.

In the next paragraph an attempt has been made to show the internal structure of *Amt* III. Owing to the secret nature of this bureau the breakdown of functions and offices naturally cannot be found listed in any available German document or publication but has been assembled from various German documents and other sources. Often the information so derived cannot be regarded as final, but in such cases the degree of uncertainty has been indicated in explanatory notes, and a maximum number of examples has been given to throw additional light on the functions of the particular section or sub-section.

Some of the functions listed as belonging to *Amt* III in the RSHA have been actually identified only within equivalent offices in some regional SD Headquarters ; in such cases, however, the coincidence of several instances made it safe to assume that the system is a standard one and that it applies also to the parent *Amt*. This tabulation therefore can be regarded as an over-all picture of the organisation of *Amt* III without laying claim to absolute accuracy or completeness.

Whenever possible the original German phraseology has been preserved but at the same time an attempt has been made to combine accurate translation with an interpretation of functions wherever this seemed necessary.

## 132. Structure of Amt III

The official heading of *Amt* III in the RSHA is *Deutsche Lebensgebiete* (Spheres of German Life) ; it is organised as follows :—

### Geschäftsstelle (Administration Office)

| | |
|---|---|
| *Personalangelegenheiten* | (Personnel Matters) |
| *Geschäftsverteilungsplan* | (Distribution of Work) |
| *Geschäftsaktenplan* | (Standard Filing System) |
| *Statistik* | (Statistics) |
| *Geheimregistratur* | (Registry of Classified Documents) |

### Gruppe III A
### Gemeinschaftsleben Allgemein (General Community Life)

#### III A 1

*(Organisation der Arbeit* (Organisation of Work) also referred to as *Allgemeine Fragen der Lebensgebietsarbeit* (General Questions of *Amt* III work)

The work of this *Referat* is not known in detail. It may, however, be assumed that it concerns itself mainly with planning and recording the work carried out by *Amt* III in general. *Hilfsreferat* III A 1 c is known to be responsible for co-operation between SD and *Wehrmacht*. No other sub-sectional units have been identified.

#### III A 2

*Rechtsleben Allgemein* (General Legal Matters)

This *Referat* is reported to examine every new act or law, to collect suggestions and reports on laws and on their effects from all the regional SD headquarters, and to forward the results of such research to the *Reichsjustizministerium*. Its personnel as well as its agents are drawn mainly from the legal profession.

In addition to the more general functions *Referat* III A 2 seems to deal with specific cases of violations of the law. The SD will investigate such violations in order to report them to the *Gestapo* or *Kripo* for action. Particular topics which are known to have been investigated by III A 2 and which may give an idea of the wide scope of this *Referat* are :—

Political offences and violations of the law in general.
Popular attitude towards distinguishing emblems to be worn by Jews.
Attitude of Germans towards Jews.
Marriages between Germans and " Non-Aryans."
Protection of the honour of soldiers killed in battle.
Legal matters in connection with public collections.
Theft of mails.
Public and official corruption.
Forged ration coupons.
Illegal slaughter of livestock.
Investigation of claims.
Court decisions incompatible with Nazi ideas.
Protective Custody (*Schutzhaft*) and Concentration Camps.

#### III A 3

*Verwaltung Allgemein* (Administration in General)

This *Referat*, covering the investigation of administrative matters, has naturally a fairly close relation to III A 2. Many of its agents are ordinary citizens. Its duties include observing public reaction to various administrative offices and official actions as well as public opinion in general. It is furthermore reported that III A 3 also supervises all Police personnel, including even the *Kripo* and *Gestapo*. The importance of that function and the extent of the powers derived from it need not be explained or stressed. The *Hilfsreferat* of III A 3, while not specifically identified, are known to range at least from a to e.

A conclusive and exhaustive enumeration of the functions of III A 3 cannot, of course, be given. The following examples of special cases investigated by this *Referat*, however, may help to illustrate its general work :—

Simplification of administration.
Elimination of unnecessary recourse to higher Headquarters.
Lack of co-operation between various official agencies.
Behaviour of high ranking public officials, such as *Landräte*.
Attitude of officials towards the public.
Cancellation of pay and pensions to officials found politically unreliable.
Replacement of personnel in local offices (*Beamtennachwuchs*).
Deferment of officials from military service (*Uk-Stellung*).
The effects of military recruiting policy.
Effect of the distribution of duties and financial burdens on local communities.
Public attitude towards compulsory insurance for employees.
Family allowances for military personnel.
Fixing of responsibility for the investigation of acts of sabotage in mining areas.
Listening to foreign wireless stations.
Study of results of enemy air raids.
Surveillance of prisoners out on parole.
National Population Register (*Volkskartei*).

#### III A 4

*Allgemeines Volksleben* (General National Life)

This *Referat* deals with mass observation and its evaluation. The term " *Volksleben*," translated as " national life," includes all matters concerning both nation and Party. The *Referat* has almost unlimited scope in the surveillance of individual and community, of possible anti-Nazi tendencies, of the written and the spoken word. Investigations and spying of this kind are carried right into the ranks and Headquarters of the Nazi Party. A recent document shows that III A 4 was the *Referat* through which the SD collected information on an attempt by leading personalities to transport their families and possessions to the vicinity of the Swiss border. In addition, III A 4 investigates relations between the Party and the Armed Forces.

The following specific cases for which documentary evidence exists are listed to illustrate some of the activities of III A 4 :—

Observation of general morale (*Stimmung und Lage*).

Reception by the public of enemy leaflets and propaganda in general.

Rumours, political jokes and popular humour.

Rumours concerning discontinued payment of pensions for invalid veterans after the war.

Observation of the effect of mail on the morale of the troops.

Behaviour of leading personalities of the Party and State.

Blameworthy behaviour of soldiers' wives.

General attitude toward mass evacuations and ARP measures.

ARP daily reports.

Press comments and editorial opinion on court sentences.

Relations between Party and *Wehrmacht*.

The extent of the powers of this *Referat* is demonstrated even further by reliable reports of the existence of the sub-sectional unit III A 4 g (*Geheim*—secret) which is said to watch all leading personalities in the Nazi Party with the rank of *Kreisleiter* and above.

## III A 5

Co-operation between *Sipo* and SD with other Police and Government agencies : general problems of police law

This *Referat* was probably a later addition to III A, and its exact functions are not known. It is known, however, that requests for character references by the *Kripo* to Government agencies, liaison between the *Sipo* and the Postal authorities in matters of censorship, and written reports furnished by the *Sipo* and SD to local Police headquarters or to the Administrative Police on matters of Police registration and Police law in general are handled in this *Referat*. The following sub-sectional units are known to exist, but their actual interests cannot be accurately identified :—

III A 5 a  Possibly : SD supervision of co-operation between the *Sipo* and the general administrative authorities.

III A 5 b  Possibly : SD supervision of co-operation between *Gestapo* and other branches of the Police.

III A 5 c  Possibly : SD supervision of co-operation between *Sipo* and *Orpo*. Liaison with Administrative Police in matters of Registration.

III A 5 d  Possibly : SD supervision of co-operation between the *Sipo* and other branches of the Police in general.

A decree of the RSHA of September, 1943, ordered that all matters of Police law and registration affecting in some way the relationship between the German Police and other Government agencies were to be handled by the RSHA instead of by the *Hauptamt Orpo*. *Hilfsreferat* III A 5 c deals with these new functions. While this decree assigned certain supervisory duties of Police registration to III A 5 c, this change of procedure did not cause any new establishments of personnel or organisation within the *Staatliche Polizeiverwaltungen* and therefore does not affect the general picture of Police registration given in paragraph 82.

## Gruppe III B

## Volkstum und Volksgesundheit (Dealing with the German People and " the well-being of the German Race ")

### III B 1

*Deutsches Volkstum* (German " Racial Heritage ").

This *Referat* contains several *Ämter für Volkstumsfragen* (Bureaux for questions concerning the German " Racial Heritage "). Close liaison is probably maintained with the NSDAP *Hauptamt* (Main Bureau) *für Volkstumsfragen* and with the *Beauftragter d. NSDAP für alle Volkstumsfragen*. It is believed that III B 1 was intended to become an important office only after final German victory.

The sub-section was probably expected to observe all kinds of re-adjustment such as the settlement of Germans in newly-acquired territories. Reports indicate that III B 1 has made extensive plans for German expansion. In this connection HIMMLER's position as *Reichskommissar für die Festigung d. deutschen Volkstums* (Reich Commissioner for the Strengthening of Germanism) should be borne in mind.

### III B 2

*Fremdes Volkstum und Minderheiten* (Foreign " Races " and Minorities).

This *Referat* concerns itself with the relations between Germans and people of other nations as well as minorities within Germany. It is reported also that this *Referat* deals with the liquidation of Jews in Poland, the resettlement of Poles and their " Germanisation." *Hilfsreferat* III B 2 c is known to deal-with Italian workers in Germany. No details on other sub-sectional units are available. Among some specific cases known to have been dealt with by III B 2 are the following :—

Problems of racial policy (*Volkspolitische Fragen*)

Utilisation of foreign workers.

Specific questions of foreign labour, such as employment of Poles, Dutch, Russians.

Employment of Russian women for domestic help.

Distinguishing marks for foreign workers and their effect on the public.

### III B 3

*Rasse- und Volksgesundheit* (Health of the German Race and People)

This *Referat* usually deals with general aspects of national health rather than with specific technical and medical matters. It employs a considerable number of doctors as agents. The following specific examples of topics known to have been covered by III B 3 may help to clarify the functions of the sub-section :—

Reports on public health

Reports on medical aid given in schools

The effect of air raids on public health

Investigation of shipments of inferior X-ray equipment and drugs and chemicals to hospitals

Problems of immunisation

Euthanasia

Propaganda campaigns to popularise certain medical aids, such as Vitamins (*Vitamin-Aktion*)

Investigation of grants of additional rations.

This *Referat* appears also to be interested in the composition of the " Germanic " SS formations. Liaison is probably maintained with the *SS-Rasse- und Siedlungshauptamt* (SS Race and Settlement Dept.)

## III B 4
*Staatsangehörigkeit, Wanderung und Siedlung* (Citizenship, Migration and Settlement)

This *Referat* deals with such matters as the resettlement of families who have lived in non-German territories, but who have come under German jurisdiction as a result of the expansion of the Reich and are now regarded as Germans by the Nazis. Close liaison is probably maintained with the *Volksdeutsche Mittelstelle* (Vomi—Department for the repatriation of " racial " Germans) and its *Umwandererzentralen* (Repatriation Offices).

In a more general way this *Referat* also handles all questions of citizenship and naturalisation from the SD point of view.

## III B 5
*Innerpolitische Lage der besetzten Gebiete* (Political Conditions in Occupied Territories)

Few details are known about the workings of this sub-section, but among its main functions is the study of the attitude of the native population in occupied territories. It is further reported that the department has dealt with the exchange of students between Germany and occupied countries. Special courses were given to students from the Eastern territories by the *Ostministerium* (Ministry for Eastern Affairs) headed by Alfred ROSENBERG. Among the topics of interest to III B 5 is the attitude of the population toward Pan-Germanism.

## Gruppe III C
## Kultur (Culture)

### III C 1
*Wissenschaft und Hochschule* (Sciences and Higher Education)

The various sub-sectional units of this *Referat* are responsible for the supervision of universities, interesting themselves in the students as well as in the teachers. All scientists and scientific institutions come under its supervision and many of the agents of III C 1 are recruited from among the teaching staffs of universities. III C 1 also checks certain activities in secondary schools but the main interest is in universities, colleges and similar institutions.

The following specific subjects and *Hilfsreferate* have been definitely identified as coming under III C 1.

III C 1 a
Archives
Scientific studies
Superstitions, astrology and similar matters
? Replacements (*Nachwuchs*) of technical and scientific personnel

III C 1 b
Study of Oriental cultures

III C 1 c ? •

III C 1 d ?

III C 1 e
Supervision of university faculties and student bodies, fraternities, students' unions, etc.

### III C 2
*Erziehung, Religiöses Leben und Sport* (Education, Religious Matters and Sport)

The following *Hilfsreferate* are responsible for the observation and investigation of the subjects indicated :

III C 2 a
Schools
Teachers
Prohibition of certain plays etc. in schools

III C 2 b
Youth in general
Juvenile Delinquency
Camps, including disciplinary camps for juveniles
Military service for juveniles
Matters concerning the *Hitler Jugend*

III C 2 c
Sport

III C 2 d
Religious problems

This is one of the largest *Hilfsreferate* in *Amt* III, and its range of interests is almost unlimited. Among the specific problems which have been identified as concerning III C 2 d are the following :

Religious services, and their effect on the population
Memorial celebrations, and their effects
Observation of money collections for Church purposes
Assistance given by the Church to soldiers
Pastoral letters
Catholicism and Protestantism
Reports on the Clergy's attitude to political speeches
Propaganda among opposition Church groups
Rumours circulating among the Clergy.

### III C 3
*Kulturelles Leben* (Cultural Matters)

This *Referat* concerns itself mainly with the effect on the public of news, music, theatre, films, museums, buildings, monuments and art in general. The interest is, of course, not in culture and art as such, but rather in the investigation of artists from the Nazi point of view. A careful and detailed check is kept on all phases of cultural life and any anti-Nazi tendencies are immediately reported to the *Gestapo* or *Kripo*. To cover these varied topics thoroughly III C 3 has been divided into various sub-sectional units, some of which may be designated as follows :—

III C 3 a
Associations, clubs and similar organisations
Investigations of the employment of " undesirable racial groups " (e.g. Negroes) for public performances

III C 3 b
Cultural advancement in general
Strength through Joy (KdF—*Kraft durch Freude*) presentations
Lectures, public speeches and recitals
Studies of local history
National Socialist celebrations

III C 3 c
Public entertainment ; its effect on the audience

III C 3 d
Music—possibly also prohibited music

III C 3 e
Production and sale of art products
Investigation of inferior art
Approval for the erection and maintenance of monuments

III C 3 f
Theatre
Opera
Actors, singers, etc.
Probably also includes control of actors' and singers' salaries.

III C 3 g
Films
Newsreels
Propaganda films
III C 3 ?
Reports on compères (MC) and announcers.

## III C 4

*Allgemeine Propaganda—Presse, Schrifttum, Rundfunk* (Propaganda in general—Press, Literature and Wireless)

This *Referat* is the counterpart of III C 3 in the field of propaganda and literature.

III C 4 a
Press

Sub-divisions within this unit apparently provide for study of the theatre, films and music as discussed in the press. III C 4 also checks newspaper vendors and similar agencies, and determines the desirability of any newspaper and its contents.

III C 4 b
Literature
Books in general
Book clubs.

Collections of books for the Armed Forces (Rosenberg Bücherspende)
Libraries
Liaison with the *Reichsschrifttumskammer* (National Chamber of Literature).

III C 4 c
Wireless
Wireless reporting
Community wireless programmes
Investigation of listeners to foreign and illegal broadcasts
Monitoring of foreign wireless stations.

III C 4 d
Propaganda
Study of the effects and reception of propaganda
Weekly propaganda slogans
Propaganda literature
Public showcases exhibiting daily newspapers (*Pressekästen*)
Popular reaction to foreigners

One of the *Hilfsreferate* of III C 4—most probably III C 4 d—handles the sub-section's confidential reports and information.

## Gruppe III D

### Allgemeine Wirtschaftspolitik—General Economic Matters

This *Gruppe* deals with economic matters of all kinds, including agriculture.

III D has become extremely important because of its activities in occupied territories. It is reported that it is territorially divided into Gruppe D West and D Ost. In its investigations of black market and other illegal activities it has established itself as an economic control agency of tremendous scope. Documentary evidence indicates that in many instances it has by far exceeded its original mission and has entered into economic transactions to the definite advantage of its own personnel.

## III D 1

*Agrarpolitik, Forstwirtschaft und Ernährung* (Agricultural Policy, Forestry and Food Distribution)

This *Referat* deals with the investigation of every detail of agriculture and forestry, in particular :—

Violations of wartime economy regulations
Food production in general
Distribution of such foodstuffs as eggs, milk, bread, meat, vegetables and fruit
Control of livestock
Study of purchasing power (*Kauf und Kaufkraft*)
Allotment of food to occupying forces and to the population of occupied territories
Distribution of alcoholic beverages
Exploitation of the soil for agricultural purposes.

## III D 2

*Handel, Handwerk und Verkehr* (Trades, Crafts, Traffic and Communications)

This *Referat* studies and investigates the following activities :—

Distribution of fuel
Hoarding and black market activities
Distribution of manufactured products—fabrics, soap and shoes
Abuse of motor vehicles
Conditions of roads and highways
Motor traffic in general
Supervision of all trade organisations and clubs
Supply problems resulting from the closing down of shops, etc.
Supply of essential materials for the construction and maintenance of public air raid shelters
Control of hotels, inns and restaurants
Water and power supply
Employment and efficiency of telephone, telegraph and postal communications.

## III D 3

*Finanzwesen (Finance)*

This *Referat* studies and investigates the following activities :—

Financial and tax policy
Control of currency, dividends, banks, savings banks and stock-exchanges
Insurance
Supervision and regulation of prices (*Preisüberwachung, Preisgestaltung*)
Rumours concerning confiscation of property, freezing of bank accounts and inflation reports
Credit in industry and agriculture
Speculative sales of real estate; profits in general.

## III D 4

*Industrie und Energiewirtschaft* (Industry and Power Supply)

This *Referat* studies and investigates the following activities :—

Power supply and rates governing the supply
Mining
Production matters in general
Distribution and exploitation of raw materials
Specific industries such as metallurgy or the textile industry
Collection of salvage
Closing down of industries
Investigation of the distribution of contracts and orders
Administration of enemy industries and property.

## III D 5

*Arbeitseinsatz und Sozialwesen* (Employment of Labour and matters of Social Welfare)

This *Referat* has been greatly expanded by the

manifold problems arising from foreign labour ; it studies and investigates the following :—

Employment of foreign workers in Germany and their administration
Unemployment problems
Employment of women for national labour
Employment of PW
Employment of Party organisations such as the NSKK
Surveillance and discipline of foreign labour
Results of increased working hours
Results of wage ceilings
Slacking and absenteeism
Legal and illegal labour organisations
All matters of pay and salary
Housing conditions for workers

Social insurance and benefits
Working conditions in industry
Holidays for workers
Enforced savings and collections
Evacuation and resettlement of children
Benefits for next-of-kin of soldiers killed in action

### III D 6
*Kolonialwirtschaft* (Colonial Economic Policy)

Little is known about the functions of this *Referat*. In view of the present dwindling importance of German colonial aspirations it may be assumed that III D 6 is operating on rather a reduced scale, if at all.

*Note.*—Pa (*or PA*). The designation Pa (*Personalangelegenheiten*—Personnel) may be found in combination with any of the *Referate* and *Hilfsreferate* designations. It indicates that the subject matter relates to a person and can be found in the Personnel files of the particular section or sub-section. Thus, for instance, III C 1 Pa would refer to a particular member of the Clergy, and so on.

### 133. SD Files

The SD maintains a *Reichszentralkartei und Zentralaktenhaltung* (Central Reich Index and Central Files), to keep records of all incidents of administration, personnel, employment and similar business. Late in 1943 this central collection of records, previously located in Berlin, was moved to Wartenburg/Sudetengau, but recent unconfirmed reports indicate that it may have been transferred to Southern Germany. Similar collections of records on a smaller scale are maintained by the various SD headquarters in Germany and occupied territories.

It is also noteworthy that in December, 1942, *Sipo* and SD headquarters were ordered to collect and preserve all documents and reports which were no longer of practical value, but which might still be useful from the political and historical point of view. The order stated that a *Zentralarchiv* (Central Archives) *für Sipo und* SD was to be established, and that these collections of documents were to be permanently stored there. It is not known whether these archives have been started, but it is of interest from a CI point of view to note that collections of this kind are being made. The order specifically called for safe storage places to avoid destruction of such valuable documents as a result of Allied air attacks.

### 134. Regional Organisation of the SD inside Germany

The regional organisation of both *Gestapo* and *Kripo* follows to a certain extent the old administrative system of Germany, but since the SD was originally a branch of the SS it followed, in its early days, the old regional organisation of the SS into *Oberabschnitte* and *Unterabschnitte*. Gradually, however, as a result of its intimate connection with the *Sicherheitspolizei* the regional organisation of the SD was brought into line with that of the *Gestapo* and the *Kripo*, and its headquarters were consequently re-named **SD-Leitabschnitte** (SD Regional Headquarters) and **SD Abschnitte** (SD Sub-regional headquarters). At present 17 SD-*Leitabschnitte* and 27 SD-*Abschnitte* have been identified in Greater Germany. Finally, as the Party administrative and territorial system tended to be regarded as the guiding pattern for future German administration in general, areas controlled by SD Headquarters came to be defined in terms of Party *Gaue* and *Kreise*. This change emphasises the close link between the SD and the Party *Gauleiter*, *Kreisleiter*, and *Ortsgruppenleiter* on all routine matters.

As in the case of the *Gestapo* and the *Kripo* the regional headquarters of the SD were considered inadequate to consolidate the control of the Security Service down to the smallest unit of the community, so SD Headquarters established their own branch offices, viz. **SD-Hauptaussenstellen** and **SD-Aussenstellen,** for this purpose. Documents indicate that all regional and local SD headquarters resemble in their inner organisation the structure of *Amt* III of the RSHA, but, of course, on a smaller scale corresponding to the size of the office and local requirements.

SD- (*Leit-*) *Abschnitte* are usually established in the same localities as *Stapo-* (*Leit-*) *Stellen* in order to facilitate constant and close co-operation between the two services. Within their particular area the (*Leit-*) *Abschnitte* are responsible for the administration and direction of all SD activities. They receive their orders direct from, and report to the RSHA. At the same time they are subject to general supervision and co-ordination by the BdS (IdS) in their *Wehrkreis*. A BdS (IdS) is usually chosen from among the highest officials of the SD. It can therefore be assumed that the BdS (IdS), if only by reason of his personal contacts, stands closer to the SD than to the *Kripo* and *Gestapo*.

Each (*Leit-*) *Abschnitt* is headed by a *Leiter* (Chief). The chain of command from this chief of the regional headquarters to the BdS and finally to the RSHA is somewhat complicated by the fact that the SD as a Party organisation is also responsible to the appropriate *Gauleiter* (Party Regional Chief Executive) who is authorised to assign specific missions to the SD. The *Gauleiter's* expert adviser in all SD matters is the *Leiter* of the Regional SD headquarters. Indications are, however, that a good deal of the important SD work is made to by-pass the *Gauleiter*.

The relationship between SD-*Leitabschnitte* and *Abschnitte* is similar to that between the equivalent offices of the *Gestapo* and *Kripo*. SD-*Abschnitte* are not subordinate to SD-*Leitabschnitte* ; they are independent headquarters and no executive orders as from a higher to a lower echelon are issued by a *Leitabschnitt* to an *Abschnitt*, but, again as with the *Sicherheitspolizei*, the *Leitabschnitt* may frequently issue directives and memoranda to the various *Abschnitte* within its territory to ensure uniformity of procedure and to avoid overlapping. In certain instances the *Leitabschnitte* may also act as a collecting point for information to be passed on to the RSHA and to regional Headquarters. While in general the functions of both

*Leitabschnitt* and *Abschnitt* are the same, the *Leitabschnitt*, as the guiding and co-ordinating headquarters, probably maintains more extensive files and employs a larger staff.

The SD-*Hauptaussenstellen* and *Aussenstellen* are, like the corresponding *Kripo* and *Gestapo* branch offices, normally established in nearby localities. In the case of the SD, however, such branch offices have been identified even in towns where *SD-* (*Leit-*) *Abschnitte* are located. In these towns the (*Haupt-*) *Aussenstelle* deals with the local collection of intelligence to be passed on to the (*Leit-*) *Abschnitt* where the reports of all the lower headquarters in the region are evaluated, consolidated, and then forwarded to *Amt* III. Thus, regional and local activities are carried out in separate headquarters. It must be emphasised that the *Hauptaussenstellen* and the *Aussenstellen* (the difference between them being merely one of size) are definitely subordinate to the (*Leit-*) *Abschnitt* in their area. 56 SD-*Hauptaussenstellen* and 556 SD-*Aussenstellen,,* which exist at present, have been identified. In addition 1 *Hauptaussenstelle* and 17 *Aussenstellen* existed, but are known to have suspended operations. This brings the total of all identified SD-HQ in Greater Germany to 668.

A number of SD *Abschnitte* have been downgraded to become *Hauptaussenstellen* or *Aussenstellen* for the duration of the war (cf. similar developments in the *Gestapo*, para. 102). The main reason for these changes was the manpower problem created by the constantly growing responsibilities of the SD, especially in occupied territories. To meet the demand for personnel to work in these areas a number of regional headquarters in Germany had to be reduced in size, but documentary evidence indicates that such newly-formed *Hauptaussenstellen* continue to fulfil all the functions of the former *Abschnitt*. They are defined as *Meldeköpfe* (information collecting centres) for all the branch offices which were formerly subordinated to them. Reports received at the *Hauptaussenstelle* in its capacity of *Meldekopf* are not exploited by that office, but are collated and passed straight on to the RSHA. The term *Meldekopf* should not, however, mislead the reader into believing that these new headquarters are simply message centres ; they still have all the authority and responsibilities of the former *Abschnitt* towards the subordinate branch offices, which they continue to administer and direct.

The liberation of a considerable part of the formerly Nazi-occupied territories has begun to reverse this process of downgrading regional headquarters of the SD within Germany. As Allied forces approach the borders of the Reich security control within Germany is being constantly tightened and as a result, a number of SD offices have been restored to their original classification, size and importance—a trend facilitated by the influx of SD personnel from areas liberated by the Allies. It may be expected that changes along these lines will not only continue but will be accelerated.

In the discussion of the regional organisation of both *Gestapo* and *Kripo* the supervisory and even directing powers of the BdS were pointed out. In the case of the SD this control exists to an even greater degree, and in many instances the BdS may even assume full command of the SD ; where this is not the case he definitely supervises and co-ordinates the work of the various regional SD headquarters within his district. The BdS is therefore in constant touch with the *Leiter* of the (*Leit-*) *Abschnitte*.

## 135. The SD system of Agents

It is obvious that complete control of all sources of information, as practised by the SD, could not be exercised merely through the regional headquarters and branch offices which have been discussed in this paragraph. The *Sipo* has been shown to have a system of informers which reaches right into the individual household and it is not surprising, therefore, that the SD has developed a network of agents which is spread all over the country and functions as a system of listening posts for the regular SD headquarters. The nucleus of this organisation of agents is formed by a group of regular full-time and paid SD members. These are referred to as *hauptamtlich* (full-time) and are assisted in their functions by *ehrenamtlich* (Honorary, unpaid) members of the SD. These agents, both *hauptamtlich* and *ehrenamtlich*, direct the activities of the *Beobachter* (Observers) or *Vertrauensmänner* (Confidential Agents or " Contacts "). Finally, this more or less professional group is supplemented by a number of so-called *Zubringer* (Informers) who may be employed only temporarily to supply specific items of information. These are taken from all classes and professions to ensure that every detail of German life is covered.

Observers are chosen from among people who are extremely reliable politically ; they are assigned a particular field, as a rule one closely connected with their profession. They are charged with constant observation within that sphere and furnish periodical reports to the SD headquarters which employ them. Sometimes they may be called upon to keep a watchful eye on particular individuals. It is reported that *Beobachter* placed within factories and offices and indeed even within Party formations, including the SS, operate unknown to their employers or commanding officers. Theoretically the services rendered by observers are honorary, no payment being made to them except for expenses incurred during their duties, but it is known that in practice handsome commissions are frequently given. In one particular instance of large scale confiscations of blackmarket merchandise the agents were given 10% of the blackmarket price. Usually observers are selected by the chief of the SD headquarters among the larger group of *Vertrauensmänner* or *-leute*. These " contacts " are recruited only as and when required ; they are employed in great numbers and are generally used for the observation of individuals rather than of general trends. It is reported that as a rule suitable persons are suggested by the local headquarters of the NSDAP, then checked by the *Gestapo* ; finally they are subject to approval by the chief of the SD headquarters. The *Vertrauensmänner* receive their orders from, and report all their findings to a *Beobachter* and only in rare instances communicate directly with the SD headquarters. Both *Beobachter* and *Vertrauensmänner* are sworn in by the SD before they are permitted to carry out their duties, and card indexes are kept on personal data concerning them.

Regular SD agents are well protected by their organisation. Wherever possible their identity is kept hidden, and instances are known where certain reports have been withheld as a safety precaution, preventing any possible exposure of the informer. They are frequently given code numbers to cover their real identity ; a special numbering system serving as a cover for agents has been devised, but details of this system are not available. Judging by a French agent operating in Marseille, who, according to documents, was known under the file number AG-Me 66, it seems probable that agents are numbered consecutively and designated by the letters AG (*Agent*), followed possibly by an abbreviation denoting the locality in which they operate (e.g. Me probably stands for Marseille). It should be noted that the term *Agent* is only used for foreigners serving as agents for the SD and never for Germans. (Personnel records of agents in occupied territories are probably maintained by *Amt* VI.)

In addition to the various types of agent so far discussed, the SD make occasional use, especially in occupied territory, of anyone willing to sell information. These " collaborators " do not enjoy the same protection as the regular SD agents, and in some instances are known to have been " eliminated " when their usefulness had ceased.

## 136. Regional organisation of the SD in occupied territories.

As previously pointed out the *Sipo* and SD in occupied territories operate in combined commands; such headquarters are organised, along the same lines as the RSHA, in *Abteilungen* numbered from I—VII. Thus *Abteilung* III is the direct representative of *Amt* III in Berlin whose inner structure it more or less reflects. Sometimes the term Sparte (division) is used to indicate the functional breakdown, e.g., " Sparte Gestapo " for the section dealing with Gestapo (presumably equivalent to Abteilung IV).

The largest unit of this kind is the *Sipo* and *SD-Einsatzgruppe*, headed by a *Chef*. The *Einsatzgruppe* covers a very large area, probably an entire country; for instance, an " *Einsatzgruppe der Sicherheitspolizei und des SD Kroatien* " has been identified. The *Gruppe* is sub-divided into a varying number of *Sipo-und SD-Kommandos*, each headed by a *Kommandeur der Sipo und des SD*. In Southern France these units were referred to as *Einsatzkommandos*, and were headed by a *Kommandeur* or *Führer*. Apparently there is no difference in organisation between the *Kommandos* and *Einsatzkommandos*, but the latter were probably formed as mobile units for the total occupation of France, only later becoming static while retaining their original name. The size and scope of each *Einsatzkommando* no doubt varies according to local needs; a document of the middle of 1940 refers to two *Einsatzkommandos* with a combined strength of about 260 men, but the average strength of such a unit is about 70—80.

SD Headquarters in occupied territories may, if necessary, form branch offices corresponding to those discussed in the regional organisation of the SD in Germany, which are known as *Aussenkommandos* or *Aussenstellen* and are headed by a *Sipo* and SD Leiter.

For specific tasks *Sondereinsatzkommandos* (Special Duty Commands), *Sonderkommandos* (Special Commands), *Teilkommandos* (" Part " Commands) and *z.b.V. Kommandos* (Special Employment Commands) may be formed, according to need. Such units are frequently specialist in function and personnel; their existence is temporary, and dependent on the duration of their mission. For instance, *Sonderkommandos* are known to have been formed for the evacuation of Jews from their homes and their eventual shipment to Poland. The term *Sonderkommando* is, also reported to have been used to designate certain regular *Einsatzkommandos* in the East, sub-divisions of such units being similarly termed *Teilkommandos*. This usage may perhaps have arisen because the term *Einsatzkommando* had by then acquired too

static a connotation to be applicable to the more fluid Eastern front.

All *Sipo* and SD units operating in occupied territories are under the command and supervision of the appropriate BdS. Copies of all written communications and reports are also sent to the HSSPf. It appears that in occupied territories the connection between the SD and the Nazi Party is not nearly so closely maintained as it is in Germany and the combined *Sipo* and SD commands abroad have increased their power by remaining almost completely independent.

## 137. Foreign and Military Interests of the SD

The remaining three *Ämter* in the RSHA, *Amt* VI *Ausland* foreign countries), *Amt* VII *Weltanschauliche Erforschung und Auswertung* (Ideological Research and its exploitation), and the *Militärisches Amt* (MI Bureau) are closely linked with *Amt* III, but their spheres of influence are in the foreign and military fields. Except for the following brief outline they are not dealt with in this book.

As its designation " *Ausland* " indicates **Amt VI** (headed by SS-BF SCHELLENBERG) is the foreign branch of the SD intelligence system. Its work is mainly concerned with espionage, sabotage and subversion in territories not under the direct control of the Reich, so that its functions do not overlap those of *Amt* III, which, as has already been shown, only covers occupied territories where the Nazi Police are in full control.

Much of the information, however, needed by *Amt* VI for the successful execution of its main assignments must of necessity be collected in occupied territory by its agents, who must therefore work in co-operation with those of *Amt* III. In addition to this *Amt* VI maintains an extensive network of agents for espionage in every satellite, neutral, and hostile country; the information thus gained is sent back to *Amt* VI, where it is sorted and evaluated.

Offices of *Amt* VI have been established as *Abteilung* VI within many of the *Sipo* and SD headquarters in occupied territories. The officials of these lower echelons of *Amt* VI are subordinate to the HSSPf and to the BdS under him. Reports indicate, however, that in many instances a clear-cut chain of command and channel of communications cannot be maintained; frequently therefore, *Amt* VI representatives receive orders from, and submit reports to the main headquarters in Berlin without intermediaries. It should also be noted that officials of the *Sipo* and SD are intentionally left in ignorance about much of the work of section " *Ausland* " which may be done through their office.

**Amt VII,** under the title of *Weltanschauliche Erforschung und Auswertung* (Ideological Research and its Exploitation) was added to the RSHA in 1940. It developed from the *Auslandswissenschaftliches Institut* (Institute for " Research " in Foreign Countries). The Headquarters is located in Berlin/Grunewald, Delbrückstrasse. *Amt* VII operates in close liaison with the German Foreign Office in Berlin and probably also with the Geopolitical Institute in Munich. While it is not definitely confirmed whether *Amt* VII is an organic part of the SD, a study of its functions and operations indicates that in practice its work is always closely connected with, and frequently supplementary to that of the SD.

The general function of *Amt* VII is the collection of political warfare material to be used by *Sipo*, SD and other Party and Government agencies. *Amt* VII observes and investigates all institutes of learning and education, all scientific establishments and all literature and printed matter. Documentary evidence indicates, that in the course of its development *Amt* VII has increasingly deviated from its theoretical aim of merely exploiting ideological research for official propaganda purposes, and has joined the other agencies of the SD in gathering general information on activities in occupied territories and foreign countries for the work of combatting elements opposed to Nazi ideology and interests.

The regional branches of *Amt* VII, and probably also the main bureau in the RSHA, are subdivided into 3 *Gruppen* (sections) :—

VII A *Hochschule und Wissenschaft* (Universities and Scientific matters)

VII B *Schulwesen und Erziehungsfragen* (Schools and Problems of Education)

VII C *Schrifttum und Verlagswesen* (Literature and Publishing)

*Amt* VII was until recently under the direction of *SS-OF* Dr. SIX, who, accordance to reports, has been replaced by *SS-OSBF* DITTEL.

The **Militärisches Amt** was added to the RSHA as a result of the following development. Until the middle of 1944 the *Oberkommando der Wehrmacht* (OKW—the German High Command) operated its own Intelligence Services through the *Abwehr* (Military Intelligence). That meant the existence of two intelligence organisations in Germany : the *Sicherheitsdienst des Reichsführers-SS* as the political information service of the Party and State and the military intelligence system of the *Abwehr* operated by and for the Armed Forces exclusively. It would seem that functionally the two systems might well stand side by side without interfering with each other, and indeed originally their spheres did not seriously clash or overlap, but during the course of the war and especially as the military situation began to deteriorate, friction arose between them and gradually their former parallel existence gave way to opposition, competition and rivalry. The reason for this development may be found partly in the difference between the personnel of the two agencies. The SD was staffed by the most fanatical followers of the Nazi Party and its full time personnel was derived exclusively from the ranks of the SS. The *Abwehr* on the other hand was composed of German Staff Officers, many of whom had never favoured National Socialism except for political expediency ; in addition, their knowledge of military affairs and their access to inside information on the darker facts of the strategic position of Germany led many of them to take a more realistic, i.e. defeatist, outlook on Germany's future. The orthodox Nazi, in contrast, still believed in Germany's invincibility.

To this basic difference in outlook between the *Abwehr* and SD must be added certain practical and operational factors. The working machinery of the *Abwehr* had never reached a very high degree of efficiency and was perhaps tied by too much bureaucratic procedure. The SD on the other hand, newly risen to power, carried out its own aims and those of the SS with scientific ruthlessness and efficiency. As military conquests added foreign territories to the Reich the SD expanded in proportion and (through *Amt* VI) took over many functions of espionage and sabotage which ordinarily might be considered the responsibility of military intelligence and counter-intelligence. It is not surprising then that rivalry between *Abwehr* and SD, i.e. between the OKW and the Nazi Party, led to strife.

In June, 1944, the influence of the Party on military matters had reached a point which enabled the SD to cause the organisation of the *Abwehr* to be disbanded. Its offices became a bureau of the RSHA under the name of *Militärisches Amt* and the major part of its functions, as well as the funds allotted to them, were taken over by the SD. Under this new scheme the *Militärisches Amt* became closely associated with and perhaps actually attached to *Amt* VI under the command of *SS-BF* SCHELLENBERG.

This extension of SD power into fields far beyond its original scope as a political intelligence service underlines its significance to the Nazis as the carefully chosen, highly-trained and fanatically loyal nucleus of their whole vast system of control. If in the future that system is replaced by underground resistance to Allied occupation the central role will undoubtedly be played, again, by the SD.

# PART SIX

## LEGAL ASPECTS OF POLICE ACTIVITY

### 138. Introduction

Before 1933 the powers and duties of the German Police were clearly defined. Article 14 of the *Polizei Verwaltungsgesetz* (*PVG*—Prussian Police Administration Law) of 1 Jun 1931 stated that the Police were " to take, within the framework of existing laws, such measures as they deemed necessary to protect the community or any member thereof from all dangers threatening public safety and order." In addition, the Police authorities had to carry out the tasks assigned to them by special laws. In the Weimar Republic, which strove unsuccessfully to be a liberal state, this meant that the Police only took action when a crime had actually been committed, to ensure the maintenance of law and order. The Nazis, however, immediately after their advent to power set out to turn the Police into one of their principal instruments for disciplining the German people. To achieve this the organisation of the Police had to undergo drastic changes, and a new orientation of the principles underlying Police—especially Political Police—action had to take place. The Police was no longer simply an agency for maintaining public safety and order ; the so-called " *Nachtwächterphilosophie* " (literally : " the Night Watchman Idea ") was obsolete. The Nazi Police no longer adhered to such outmoded principles as " no punishment without law " or " no crime without law."

The Political Police philosophy of the Third Reich is based on the vague and flexible concept of " *Volk* " (the People), and the allegedly paramount need to protect it. The Nazi leaders have invested this *Volk* with a mystical ego which has elected to be governed by the State (i.e. the Nazi Party) and must therefore be protected (in reality, kept in check) by the political acumen of this Party State.

According to *SS-BF, Ministerialdirigent Dr.* Werner BEST, a leading legal authority in the SS and Police, the *Volk* is the real stuff of human life. It is an eternal, superhuman collective being, with a single mind, reproducing itself through the offspring of each succeeding generation. The *Volk* represents the highest scale of values in life ; consequently all fundamental concepts of human will and action, all individual standards of morality, must be subordinated to the aim of securing the permanence of the *Volk* and, if necessary, be sacrificed for it. Every influence working against this supreme standard of life is amoral. This philosophy implies that all creative human effort must spring from the activity of the *Volk* as a collective being, and Nazi Police law, therefore, is based on nothing more than the " sound instinct " of the German people, as expressed in the will of the Leader.

" Right," as *Dr.* FRICK, former Reich Minister of the Interior, remarked in 1933, " is that which serves the interests of the German *Volk*, wrong that which harms it." Having elaborated ad nauseam on this theme BEST, FRICK and other apologists of the Third Reich set out to prove by ponderous arguments that the bear must be strictly controlled by the keeper in the bear's own interest.

This task naturally required full liberty of action for the " keeper " and a subservient *Reichstag* obediently abrogated whatever constitutional limitations still remained to hamper that independence so necessary for the extension of German Police Power. The Police has become the whip in the hands of the German people's " keeper." The decree for the " Protection of People and State " (*Gesetz zum Schutze von Volk und Staat*) of 28 Feb 1933 states inter alia :

" Articles 114, 115, 117, 123, 124, 153 of the constitution of the German Reich are suspended for the time being. Therefore, it will be lawful to restrict personal liberties, freedom of speech and of the press, the right to associate and to assemble ; to violate the secrets of mail, telephone, and telegraph ; to search homes ; to confiscate and to restrict property rights— notwithstanding any legal limitations heretofore existing."

Even Metternich, who in his day controlled one of the most powerful and ruthless Secret Police forces in Europe, never went to the length of endowing his agents with the unlimited authority given to the *Sicherheitspolizei* in Nazi Germany. Under the present régime the *Kripo* (Criminal Police) may " in the interests of crime prevention " place under arrest habitual or professional law-breakers or other dangerous criminals " even if at the moment of arrest no concrete danger threatens." In fact any person suspected of asocial behaviour (as interpreted by the Nazis) is subject to incarceration.

The *Gestapo* has carried the use of this despotic power to an even higher degree of perfection, acting in anticipation of activities considered likely, by the *Gestapo*, to undermine the security of the *Volk*.

The real significance of this new philosophy, the " safeguarding of the *Volk*," is only too well known—*Gestapo* firing squads, Concentration Camps, beatings and torture, and the shadow of fear over the whole of Germany. The *Volk der Dichter und Denker* (Nation of Poets and Thinkers) has become a *Volk der Richter und Henker* (Nation of Judges and Hangmen).

While these sinister aspects of the German Police must be stressed, the routine side of Police work also requires consideration ; in the problem of eliminating the many dangerous Nazis from the German Police Forces it will be important to distinguish clearly the two sides of Police activity. The Police in Germany, as in any other country, must carry on the everyday tasks of supervision and protection of the public, and for this purpose bureaucratic organisation and machinery governed by definite laws are indispensable. Without any contradiction here to the above-quoted decree permitting the violation of civil liberties " notwithstanding any legal limitations heretofore existing," it is clear that in routine matters, the individual policeman, and even individual headquarters, must be guided by hard and fast regulations and laws ; the ordinary police executive official cannot be expected to act on so vague a principle as " the Will of the Leader." Thus while the system is operated and directed by Nazi motives, the individual member functions according to a routine fixed by Police law.

This distinction will be an important consideration when the Allies come to make use of the German Police system. Knowledge of the laws by which it functions will be necessary, so that they may, according to need, be kept in operation or revised ; it may also be of value in the indictment of those who have violated those laws.

### 139. Legislation governing Police Activities

Police laws in general (*Polizeirecht*) may deal with the organisation of the Police (*Polizeiverfassungsrecht*), regulate the terms of service of the Police official (*Polizeidienstrecht*), or lay down the duties of the Police and their execution (*Polizeiwirkungsrecht*, more usually called *materielles Polizeirecht*). Whereas *Polizeiverfassungsrecht* and *Polizeidienstrecht* have been, to a large extent, unified and centralised, no such unification has taken place as far as *materielles Polizeireoht* is concerned, but the PVG is for all practical purposes (although not technically) the basic codification of German Police laws.

Unless otherwise specified, the execution of all Police functions, is, according to the PVG, the responsibility of the *Ortspolizeibehörden* (Local Police Authorities). These authorities, the lowest level in the Police hierarchy, therefore originally carried out the general duties of the Police as stated in article 14 of the PVG (see para. 138) and performed those tasks assigned to the Police by the legislature of the Reich and of the *Länder* (States). Under the Nazis, however, the functions of these legislative bodies were in effect taken over by Nazi Government or, indirectly, by Nazi Party representatives, e.g. the *Reichsstatthalter* and *Gauleiter*.

No attempt is made in this book to discuss the numerous Police laws as they were published by the *Länder*. Certain *Reichsgesetze* (Reich Laws), however, form the basis for Police direction of many aspects of everyday life and give a clear outline of the functions and authority of the Police ; the most important are therefore listed in the ensuing paragraphs. The list is not meant to be either complete or systematic, and for legal details reference should be made to the relevant technical publications. To facilitate such reference correct German titles and dates of issue have been included in the discussion of the various laws and decrees.

The **Strafprozessordnung** (*StPO*—Code of Criminal Procedure) makes the Police responsible for investigating punishable offences and taking immediate measures for the prevention of any removal of evidence ; in cases in which death by unnatural causes is established or an unidentified body is found the Police must immediately render a report to the public prosecutor. The *Strafprozessordnung* also authorises the *Länder* to punish certain *Vergehen* by *Polizeiliche Strafverfügung* (Police Penal order).

*Note.*—The terms " *Verbrechen* " and "*Vergehen*" which appear, untranslated, throughout this part of the book, cannot be accurately translated, except perhaps by an approximation using such generic terms as " crime " and " offence " respectively. In effect it can only be said that the " *Verbrechen* " is more serious than the " *Vergehen*"

The **Gerichtsverfassungsgesetz** (General Judiciary Act) states that Police officials are assistants to the public prosecutor and as such are obliged to take orders from him. Under the Nazis, however, fundamental changes in the investigation and prosecution of crimes have taken place. Werner BEST speaks of " a reversal in the traditional distribution of tasks between Police and Prosecution." To increase its independence and power the Police has been emancipated completely from the hold which the public prosecutor's office formerly exercised over it ; today it is the public prosecutor who follows the suggestions of the Police in the initiation of criminal proceedings.

To facilitate this work it is important that the local Police authorities maintain *Polizeiliche Listen* (Police lists) as decreed by the *Runderlass* (*RdErl*—Circular Order) of 3 Jun 1940. These lists are alphabetical card indexes of law breakers and their offences ; the cards are in turn the basis of the *Polizeiliche Führungszeugnisse* (Police Certificates of Conduct) in which the Police attests to previous convictions or to the integrity of the bearer, as authorised by the *RdErl* of 27 May 1940.

According to Article 330c of the **Strafgesetzbuch** (Penal code) the Police may also, in connection with the punishment of offences, recruit the assistance of other citizens in case of emergency.

The Reich Laws invest the Police with the necessary authority to aid other public offices and officials in the fulfilment of their duties. For instance the Finance offices, according to article 424, *Reichsabgabenordnung* (Reich Statute on Taxes, Duties, etc.), and the Postal authorities, according to the *Postgesetz* (Postal Law) of 1871, may call on the Police for assistance.

Police responsibility for the interests and wellbeing of the public extends over a wide field. In various matters covered by the *Gewerbeordnung* (Industrial and Trade Code), for example, the Police are involved ; thus the erection or change of location of any installations causing disturbing noises near hospitals or schools must be reported to the Police.

According to an *Ausführungs Verordnung* (Regulatory Decree) to the *Mass- und Gewichtsgesetz* (Law relating to measures and weights) of 20 May 1936 all business establishments using scales, measures and containers of specified size, must submit such instruments once a year to the *Eichamt* (see para 84 *Verwaltungspolizei*) for inspection.

Other Police responsibilities include the licensing of entertainment by street performers, sale of papers, sale of alcoholic drinks ; the protection of the public against undesirable public spectacles (*RdErl* of 11 Mar 1942) ; compliance with the *Lichtspielgesetz* (Law governing the showing of films) ; the supervision of inns and restaurants as defined in the *Gaststättengesetz* (Law governing catering places) of 28 Apr 1930 ; the proper observance of holidays in accordance with the *Gesetz über die Feiertage* (Law governing holidays) of 27 Feb 1934 ; and compliance with curfew laws.

An important responsibility of the Police is the prevention of juvenile delinquency. Thus the *Polizeiverordnung* (*PolVO*—Police Decree) of 10 Jun 1943 charges the Police with protecting German youth from undesirable literature and films and with restricting their liberty of movement by such measures as keeping juveniles off the streets and prohibiting their admittance to bars and dance halls.

One of the more important tasks of the Police is the protection of public health. According to the *Gesetz über die Bekämpfung gemeingefährlicher Krankheiten* (Law to combat dangerous and infectious diseases) of 30 Jun 1900 and the VO (*Verordnung*) of 1 Dec 1938 the Police must take the necessary protective measures to prevent the spreading of contagious diseases.

Similarly, various health laws regulate the sale of food and call for rigid Police supervision and enforcement. Among these laws the most important ones are the *Lebensmittelgesetz* (Food Law) 17 Jan 1936, and the *Fleischbeschauungsgesetz* (Meat Inspection Law) of 29 Oct 1940.

Closely related to regulations of this kind are the *Schlachtviehverkehrs VO* (Cattle Trade Decree) of 27 Feb 1935, the *Viehseuchengesetz* (Law covering animal epidemics) of 26 Jun 1909, and the *Marktaufsichts VO* (Decree for Supervision of Fairs and Markets) of 20 Oct 1942.

Innumerable other aspects of daily life are of course subject to Police regulations, especially as a consequence of the broad powers granted under article 14 of the PVG. Thus, for instance, the Police is responsible for supervising working conditions, measures for accident prevention, control of child labour, sale of perishable food-stuffs, the inspection of warehouses, the enforcement of price regulations and the control of the sale of contraceptives. (See also *Verwaltungspolizei*, para. 81).

## 140. Legal Instruments of the Police

The legal and extra-legal powers of the *Sipo* and SD—or more particularly, of the *Gestapo*—have already been sufficiently emphasized (notably in paras. 10 and 100ff). Again, although those powers include the right to make use of all other branches of the Police, such co-operation is not dealt with here; the paragraphs following are chiefly concerned with Police activities which are closer to legal theory.

To carry out the general tasks of protecting the public against any threats to safety and order, as specified in article 14 of the PVG, the Police has at its disposal a number of legal instruments. These can be brought into operation against any person failing to conform with the requirements of the Police that every citizen maintain his property and regulate his actions in accordance with Police laws (*Polizeimässiger Zustand* and *Polizeimässiges Verhalten*). Any behaviour contrary to those laws (*Polizeiwidriges Verhalten* and *Polizeiwidriger Zustand*) constitutes a threat to public order invoking preventive or punitive measures. Accordingly persons whose actions cause a disturbance or danger (*Störer*) are answerable to the Police (*polizeipflichtig*), irrespective of whether or not the *Störer* is legally responsible for his actions; thus, children or mentally deranged persons are also *polizeipflichtig*. The owner is responsible for the *polizeimässige Zustand* of his property (*Sachen*, i.e. "things" as opposed to persons) whether he himself has caused a disturbance or not; the owner of a house is responsible for the removal of seditious inscriptions from the walls of his buildings if neither the perpetrator nor the instigator can be found.

Some of these legal instruments merely provide for Police instructions to the public, others authorise the Police to perform certain judicial functions by punishing minor transgressions of the law; the third group constitutes an interference with the freedom and property of the individual, and is therefore defined in greater detail by German legislation. The three groups are discussed briefly in the following paragraphs.

## 141. Police Orders and their Enforcement

*Polizeiverordnungen* (*PolVO*—Police orders) are legally defined in article 24 of the PVG. They are addressed to the public in general and must have a formal subject heading indicating the contents of the order, e.g. "*Polizei VO* concerning the Operation of Taxi-cabs." They must be dated, signed and properly published by the issuing Police authority. Pol.VO's may cover a wide field as long as they keep within the limits set by article 14 of the PVG. Any Police Authority in communities of more than 5,000 inhabitants may issue *Polizeiverordnungen*. Offenders may be punished with fines or imprisonment. The maximum penalty which may be imposed depends on the level of the Police authorities as set out in the following table:—

| Police Authorities | Maximum Fine or Imprisonment |
|---|---|
| *Ortspolizeibehörde* | 50 RM or One week |
| *Kreispolizeibehörde* | 100 RM or Two weeks |
| Higher Police Authorities | 150 RM or Three weeks |
| Reich Ministers | 150 RM or Six weeks |

The **Polizeiliche Verfügung** (Specific Police Order), defined in article 40 of the PVG, is addressed to an individual or a definite group of persons. It may be given verbally, in writing, or posted as a notice, or by means of signs. If given in writing the reasons for the *Polizeiliche Verfügung* must be stated, but otherwise no formalities are required. *Polizeiliche Verfügungen* are issued to deal with a particular situation; thus, a signal given by a traffic policeman to stop a vehicle, a telephone call from the local Police station ordering a shopkeeper to remove an offensive book from his shop window, the rejection of an application for a driver's licence are all examples of specific Police Orders.

*Zwangsmittel* (means of compulsion) is the generic term for the following methods at the disposal of the Police, to enforce compliance with a Police order:

| | |
|---|---|
| *Ersatzvornahme* | Performance by a third person |
| *Zwangsgeld* | Fine |
| *Zwangshaft* | Detention in default of payment of fine |
| *Unmittelbarer Zwang* | Application of force |

The term *Ersatzvornahme* may be illustrated in the following way. If a person fails to comply with a Police order, the Police may employ someone else to carry it out, and charge the expenses to the person who failed to act according to the order. The offender is in no way exempted from responsibility for any violation of the law connected with the case.

In cases of a minor offence or failure to comply with a Police order, the Police authority may impose a fine (*Zwangsgeld*). If the fine is not paid, detention of the person, i.e. *Zwangshaft*, may be ordered. It should be emphasised, however, that this detention does not represent a penal procedure, but is merely to be regarded as a method of compulsion.

The Police may only resort to the application of actual force (*unmittelbarer Zwang*) in circumstances specified in *Ausführungsbestimmungen* (Regulatory Instructions) to article 55 of the PVG. Actual force may be applied by the Police in various ways, such as the removal (*Wegführen*) of persons or *Sachen*, boxing, jiu-jitsu, handcuffing, the use of fire hoses, tear gas, rubber truncheons or other weapons, including fire-arms.

The regulations governing the use of weapons (**Waffengebrauch**) merit closer study. Policemen—unless under definite orders—may have recourse to weapons only in the lawful performance of their duty. Such use of weapons is authorised in the following circumstances:—

(i) in self-defence
(ii) to defend persons, or *Sachen*, whose protection has been entrusted to the Police
(iii) to break violent resistance to lawful orders
(iv) to arrest persons caught in the act of committing a crime or under serious suspicion of having committed a crime and attempting to escape arrest or identification
(v) to prevent a person escaping from prison or to apprehend a fugitive

Furthermore, the use of fire-arms or explosives

is, except in instances of self-defence, justified only if previous warning has been given. A crowd must be warned three times—the warning taking the form best suited to the circumstances. Challenges such as " *Halt, oder ich schiesse* " (Halt, or I fire) as well as " shots aimed in the wrong direction " are considered proper warning. At no time, except in self-defence, are fire-arms or explosives to be used against persons appearing to be juveniles. Persons attempting to evade arrest are only to be fired at if they have been found guilty of a crime or are highly suspect of having committed one. Thus, if a wanted murderer is arrested and attempts to escape, the policeman must not fire unless he is convinced of the man's identity as the murderer. Again, if a cyclist riding without cycle lamps attempts to escape arrest the Policeman must not make use of his fire-arms, since no crime has been committed. It should be noted in this connection that somewhat less stringent regulations apply to the *Grenzpolizei* (Frontier Police) and to Police executive officials guarding and escorting prisoners.

At this point it must again be stressed that these careful restrictions on the use of force are merely the theory ; in practice, of course, the Nazis have never been guided by such humane considerations. There are innumerable examples of the application of force by the Nazis when neither conditions nor legal grounds justified such action. Certainly persons labelled as political criminals and "offenders against the sound instinct of the people " are not treated according to the principles set down by German Police law. To take the most obvious example, the Nazis have long since shown that undesirables can most easily be disposed of " while trying to escape " from a concentration camp.

**Strafverfügungen** (Penal Orders) should not be confused with the previously discussed *Polizeiverfügungen*. The latter are specific Police orders dealing with a given situation : a *Strafverfügung*, on the other hand, is a penal measure against minor offences carried out by the Police authorities in order to lighten the work of the Judiciary. Offences involving a maximum fine of 150 RM or imprisonment for not more than two weeks may thus be prosecuted by the Police authorities directly. Instead of submitting the case to the court for trial the Police authority itself imposes the penalty by issuing a *Strafverfügung*. This penal order must be in writing and must state the case, the evidence, and the article of law invoked. The accused must be informed of his right to submit the case to the *Höhere Polizeibehörde* (Higher Police Authority) within two weeks or to the Civil Court within one week. If no recourse to such authority is taken within two weeks the order becomes final and may be executed three weeks after the date when it was served on the accused.

## 142. Restrictions on Rights of Property

The two most important infringements upon the citizen's property rights are :

> *Durchsuchung* (Search) and
> *Beschlagnahme* (Seizure)

The **Durchsuchung** (search) is applicable to private dwellings and other premises (*Haussuchung*) or to properties and persons. Entry into a dwelling for the purpose of a search is regulated by the *StPO* in Articles 102/111. A magistrate or, in an emergency calling for swift action (*bei Gefahr im Verzug*), the *Staatsanwaltschaft* (Prosecuting authority) or its assistant, the Police, may order a *Haussuchung*. The homes of persons suspected of having committed a crime may be searched in order to apprehend the criminal or to find evidence. Homes of unsuspected persons are subject to search only if there is sufficient reason to believe that a criminal or evidence of a crime may be found there.

*Haussuchung* at night is permissible only for the pursuit of a criminal caught in the act, " *bei Gefahr im Verzug*," (under the threat of imminent danger) or to effect the apprehension of an escaped prisoner ; night searches are however permissible on such premises as homes of persons under Police supervision, premises accessible to the public generally, premises known to be meeting places of criminals, storage places of goods obtained by criminal means, gambling places and houses of prostitution. Forced entry into dwellings at night-time is also dealt with by Article 16 of the PVG, and is authorised only when necessary to prevent danger to the public or to save the life of a person. The law defines night-time as comprising the hours from 9 p.m. to 4 a.m. from the 1 Apr to the 30 Sep, and the hours from 9 p.m. to 6 a.m. from the 1 Oct to the 31 Mar. However, entry into dwellings or premises during day or night-time is permissible under the authority granted by Article 14 of the PVG, or at the request of, or by permission of, the owner.

Persons suspected of having committed a crime may be searched according to Article 103 of the *StPO*. Whether that article is also applicable to unsuspected persons is open to argument, but decisions of the highest law courts (which are not, however, binding as in the UK or USA,) have been in the affirmative. Furthermore, search of persons or *Sachen* (property) is permissible under the authority granted by Article 14 of the PVG.

Under certain circumstances *Sachen* are subject to **Beschlagnahme** (seizure) by the Police. *Sachen* which are regarded as important for the investigation of a crime may be seized by the Police, and retained in temporary custody ; properties subject to confiscation (*Einziehungsstücke*) such as counterfeit money, or burglar's tools must be seized and retained. If a person refuses to surrender evidence or *Einziehungsstücke*, a judge may order the seizure of such properties. In addition the Police may seize properties in the event of an emergency (*Notstand*) under authority of Article 21 of the PVG, or in application of Article 14 of the PVG. Whenever a person is arrested, all property found on that person is automatically subject to seizure by the Police.

Under the pre-Hitler régime searches of a German home and permanent seizures or confiscations had to be ordered by the courts, as described above. The PVG, which is essentially a liberal law, provides for appeals against the decisions of the Police authorities, and entitles the citizen to payment of indemnity in case he suffers damage through Police action. Where an official has committed an illegal act on his own initiative he himself is to be held responsible ; where he acted in performance of his duties, the responsible authority must answer for him in an administrative court.

All these safeguards have, under the Nazi régime, been stripped of their significance by the immunity enjoyed by the German Police, and especially the *Sipo* and SD, in the ruthless execution of their duties. The Nazi leaders and Police authorities are known to cover up the illegal acts committed by their organisations, and the individual no longer dares to take legal action against the authorities. While the original safeguards of the individual's liberty and property were never legally abolished by the Nazi régime, the decree "for the Protection of People and State," in suspending certain clauses of the Weimar Constitution carried the powers of the Police to restrict individual and property rights far beyond the legal limits previously existing. The Police may now " in the interests of the nation " seize property and raid homes at discretion. In fact it can be said that all legal limitations of Police Power are in practice pushed aside ; persons and properties are subjected to searches indiscriminately, at the will of the Police, and homes are entered by force without legal grounds and at any time.

### 143. Restrictions on Personal Freedom

The liberal governments of pre-Hitler Germany introduced a set of minute regulations for the protection of certain individual rights and privileges, such as personal freedom, the sanctity of the home, and other safeguards of the liberty of the German citizen. Most of these legal guarantees of individual liberty have been suspended under the Nazi régime, and even those still officially existing are violated daily by the unscrupulous application of Police power. Raids, searches, arrests and detentions over long periods of time have become normal occurrences in the Third Reich. The following discussion of legally authorised infringements upon liberty does not therefore imply that any genuine limitations of present German Police power exist in practice, but merely indicates the machinery set up by law to regulate Police action, in the days when the German Police was a protective, and not an oppressive force.

The right of depriving people of their liberty (*Freiheitsentziehung*) has, under civilised constitutions, always been reserved for the judicial branch of the government. In Germany the *Strafprozessordnung* (*StPO*—code of criminal procedure) provides for restrictions of liberty in the following instances :

*Verhaftung* (arrest)—Articles 112, 114, 131, 230, 236 and 457 of the StPO.
*Vorläufige Festnahme* (arrest without warrant) —Article 127 of the StPO.
*Zwangsgestellung* (see below)—Articles 163 and 164 of the StPO.
*Vorführung* (compulsory appearance)—Article 51, 133, 134, 230, 236 and 457 of the StPO.

To authorise a **Verhaftung** (arrest) the issuing of a *Haftbefehl* (warrant) is required. It is signed by a judge and contains the exact personal data of the suspected person, the crime with which he is charged and the reason for his arrest. It may only be issued when a person is under serious suspicion and if there is danger of his escape or of his obscuring the evidence. If at all possible the suspect must be notified of the contents of the warrant, and must be brought before the judge not later than the following day.

If, after issue of a warrant, the suspect tries to prevent his arrest by fleeing or hiding, the judge or the public prosecutor may appeal to the public for assistance in his apprehension. This appeal to the public, known as a **Steckbrief**, contains a description of the criminal, the crime for which he is wanted and the prison to which he should be handed over. If a detained person escapes the Police Authority has the power to issue the *Steckbrief* without a preceding *Haftbefehl*.

**Vorläufige Festnahme** (arrest without warrant) may be effected by any citizen whenever a person is caught in the act of violating the law, if there is danger of his escape, or if he cannot be immediately identified. The Police have the additional right to arrest a person if, under circumstances which would normally call for the issue of a

*Haftbefehl*, the danger of his escaping or obscuring the evidence is too immediate for the longer process of issuing the warrant. If not released, the person arrested without warrant must be immediately taken before the judge, who may either issue a warrant or order his release.

**Zwangsgestellung** can only be paraphrased, as " taking a person, by force, to the police station." The grounds for such action are either suspicion that the person has committed a crime, or refusal by persons witnessing a punishable offence to identify themselves. The *Ordnungspolizei*, acting on the basis of their general Police power, may also take to the Police station any person who cannot be identified on the spot.

Law courts may order the **Vorführung** (compulsory appearance) of a person failing to comply with a summons to appear as the accused or as a witness. But the Police themselves—according to article 17 of the PVG—have a right to summon persons in cases involving the investigation of *Verbrechen* and *Vergehen*. The law states that in fixing time and date of the appearance, consideration should be given to the special circumstances of the person whose appearance has been ordered. The Police can in this manner enforce compliance with the summons, but cannot force the person involved to give testimony. Here again the wide gap between Police law and Nazi practice must be pointed out. It is a well known fact that the German Police under the Nazi regime, and especially the *Gestapo*, do not hesitate to employ any means, including torture, to obtain confessions or denunciations from political prisoners.

The Nazis soon added to the above provisions for restrictions on liberty ; their legal innovations were, characteristically, aimed at indefinite detention rather than at the immediate bringing to justice of the individual.

**Polizeihaft** (police custody) was introduced by the *Verordnung des Reichspräsidenten zum Schutze des deutschen Volkes* (decree of the Reich President for the Protection of the German People), published in the *Reichsgesetzblatt* (*RGBl.*—Reich Legal Gazette) of 4 Feb 1933, p. 35. This law is noteworthy in that it marks the first official departure of the Nazi regime from the police system of the old republic.

According to article 22 of the Verordnung any person may be held in Police custody who is suspected of a political crime, of having violated military secrecy, or of having committed *Verbrechen* or *Vergehen* involving the use of a weapon. The *Ortspolizeibehörde* is the competent authority to order and carry out Police custody. A copy of the order, stating reasons, must be handed to the person taken into custody, within 24 hours. The custody becomes arrest if the investigating judge orders criminal proceedings against the suspect. The suspect himself may appeal to the local judge, who decides whether the grounds for suspicion justify the custody. If the judge does not order arrest the Police custody terminates after three months.

**Vorbeugungshaft** (preventive detention) is similar to *Polizeihaft*, and is another Nazi innovation. It is the most severe of the measures known collectively under the title of *planmässige Überwachung* (systematic supervision). In pre-Hitler days *planmässige Überwachung* was employed against professional criminals, criminally inclined persons, and others who might endanger public safety. Persons of these categories were required to report to the local Police station at specific intervals, and certain prohibitions could be imposed upon them. They could, for instance, be prohibited from practising certain trades, entering parks or taverns, or leaving their homes at night. In case of non-compliance they could be punished or arrested. While, of course, retaining the existing procedure for its original purpose, the Nazis went a step further and created a new instrument of Police power, the *Vorbeugungshaft*. This preventive detention may be ordered by any *Kripo* headquarters, but, at least in theory, needs the approval of the *Reichskriminalpolizeiamt*. The period of the *Vorbeugungshaft* is spent in a concentration camp, and there is no limit to its duration. Prisoners may be released when they have thoroughly improved in the eyes of the authorities. Since persons who are considered as " *erblich belastet* " (inflicted with hereditary defects) cannot " improve," their release is as a rule not to be expected. *Vorbeugungshaft*, applied in the interests of what the Nazis call " crime prevention," and reinforced by the convenient theory of " hereditary defects," is clearly an ideal instrument for the removal of any form of opposition ; it has, of course, been unscrupulously exploited by the Nazis.

**Polizeiliche Verwahrung** (police detention), frequently called **Schutzhaft** (protective custody), was, as defined in article 15 of the PVG, a purely protective measure. Persons needing protection in their own interest (e.g. helpless, homeless or intoxicated persons, persons in danger or under threat),• as well as individuals causing trouble or liable to disturb the peace, especially cases of disorderly conduct, can be detained by the Police for a maximum of one day. Minors can be taken in charge and held pending their transfer to juvenile disciplinary institutes.

Out of this harmless measure, the Nazis by a mere turn of words, made a terribly powerful instrument of persecution. On the pretence that persons opposed to the new régime would arouse the wrath of the population against them to such an extent that they would need protection, the Nazis proclaimed that it was necessary to keep such persons in " safe places." Political enemies, Jews, Clergymen, and any " undesirables" against whom no possible charge could be made, became victims of the new application of *Schutzhaft* and went to fill the concentration camps. A Prussian Administrative Court was quick to state (2 May 1935) that a *Gestapo* order for detention in protective custody could not be challenged in a court of law, thereby stifling any attempt to see justice done.

### 144. Policeman and Citizen

In the foregoing discussion of legal theory and Nazi practice, the most striking aspect of the relationship between policeman and citizen is naturally that which concerns the actual machinery of repression. It is, however, on the legal theory that the emphasis of this section is placed ; the present paragraph deals therefore with the every-day activities of the ordinary policeman, not with the details of Nazi police tyranny. To the average German the policeman is the visible exponent of the authority of the country and the manner in which he performs his duties is indicative of the general attitude of the government. The individual policeman on the other hand, as the strong arm of the law, is of vital importance to those responsible for the peace of the community as well as to those anxious to perpetuate their power.

In the present context, more detail than was included in the earlier chapters on the lower organisation of the Police, can be given.

The most familiar example of the uniformed Police in everyday life is the traffic policeman at

road crossings and other places necessitating special control of traffic. He sees to it that the signals and speed laws are observed. In cases of minor violations he may issue a formal warning, or even exact a payment which is not considered a fine. If the offender refuses to pay, further measures are invoked against him. In these and other dealings with the public the policeman is instructed to be brief and to the point and should, at least in theory, be helpful to the public.

The most important link between the people and the authorities is the patrolman, the representative of law and order on the route assigned to him by his superiors. It is regarded as his responsibility—and is not a mere coincidence —that he should be well acquainted with the residents on his beat. Transfers of patrolmen from one *Revier* (ward or precinct) to another are, therefore, kept down to a minimum. His duties are extremely varied and extensive, and Police manuals give the following examples :—

To keep the rowdy, rough and indecent under observation ;

To protect the public against crimes, and to prevent accidents ;

To assist the helpless, the blind, the drunk and the homeless.

He watches the traffic and directs it, if necessary, and draws up reports in case of accidents. Persons selling tickets and goods, or offering their services in public places are required to show him their permits upon request ; the patrolman also checks the authorisation of public meetings, parades and demonstrations. In disputes between tenant and landlord he may intervene but leaves the decision to the courts. The patrolman plays a very definite role in criminal investigation ; if any violations of the law come to his knowledge, it becomes his duty to take all necessary measures. Thus, for instance, in the case of an anonymous denunciation, the patrolman, while not making any immediate arrests, investigates the matter in a way not injurious to the suspect. He may bring the case into the open only if at least one essential claim of the informer has been confirmed. If a crime has been committed, the patrolman must attempt to apprehend the criminal if possible at the scene of the crime. If that is impossible he must guard all evidence and place it at the disposal of the Criminal Police. For this purpose the patrolman always keeps in touch with the *Kripo* representative in his *Revier*.

In cases of minor infringements of the law the patrolman merely records the pertinent facts in his notebook. If the offence is more serious, a *Strafanzeige* (literally, penal report) has to be submitted. The *Strafanzeige* includes the policeman's ward number and file reference ; name, age, occupation and address of each person involved, i.e. offender, victim and witnesses ; reference to the law, article or order involved.

In case of theft or misappropriation, the *Strafanzeige* also includes the value of the property, and the list of articles held as evidence. In all instances a brief account of the case must be added. A higher administrative Police official then specifies the fine or punishment, and the offender is notified. If a particular case exceeds the jurisdiction of the Police, it is brought to the attention of the prosecuting authority.

Frequently the policeman is approached with complaints or requests by the people in his *Revier*. If he is unable to cope with them he refers them to the *Revier* Police station, where an administrative staff (*Innendienst*) is available to deal with the public. Such Police staffs interview persons willing to communicate their knowledge about crimes, take note of requests for the prosecution of minor offences, and deal with all persons who desire Police permits, wish to enquire about lost property, or are trying to trace a certain address. The size of such staffs and their equipment vary according to the level of the Police authority.

In large cities the intricate Police problems created by congested living conditions and housing require specialised Police administration. There, a separate building, the *Polizeipräsidium* or *Polizeidirektion* is the centre of police activities and is equipped with all the facilities necessary for the efficient working of a large organisation. The size of the area requires a sub-division into *Abschnitte* (sections) and *Reviere* (wards or precincts), and sometimes even further into *Revierzweigstellen* (precinct branch offices) and *Posten* (posts). In Berlin, Vienna and Hamburg, there are also *Gruppenkommandos*, i.e. command headquarters which direct the affairs of several *Abschnitte*. In lesser towns the system is the same, but on a simpler and smaller scale.

The *Revier* comprises a comparatively small area and is commanded by a commissioned officer usually of the rank of Captain or Lieutenant or, in wartime, by a *Revieroffizier* (defined in para. 147). He is responsible for the efficient working of the Police station, determines the route of the *Aussendienst* (outdoor patrol service), and makes certain that 24 hour duty is maintained. Official cars and motor cycles are usually available. In addition Police stations are equipped with a few cells, sufficient to accommodate the daily quota of drunks and culprits. Wherever the local requirements warrant it, *Polizeigefängnisse* (Police prisons) equipped with all modern safeguards have been established.

In the country the *Gendarm* is frequently the sole representative of the government in a wide area. He, perhaps even more than the patrolman in the city, is in the eyes of the population the undisputed authority. In many instances his office may be in his home, where he keeps his records and files. He may patrol his beat by foot, on bicycle, motorcycle, by car or on horseback. Often a police dog is his only assistant, and the capture of a prisoner may constitute a serious problem to him. In all official matters affecting the lives of the rural population the opinion and advice of the *Gendarm* is regarded as important.

In conclusion attention must be called to the basic difference between the German policeman and his British or American counterpart. While the latter is generally regarded as the friend and helper of the population, the German policeman is a faithful servant only to his superiors, and is constantly on guard against any sign of disloyalty or coolness toward the régime. He, therefore, watches over the proper display of flags and symbols, and the wearing of uniforms by authorised persons. He is trained to protect the leaders of the Party and of the State, and to guard them against insults and attacks by their enemies. The occupying authorities in Germany, aware of these facts, should make certain that every policeman they employ carries out his duties to the letter, and that his entire conduct takes cognisance of the fact that the Nazi rule is a thing of the past. Yet another aspect of the problem, worthy of emphasis, is that in a " Police State " such as Germany the citizen regards the policeman with awe and respect. Even in pre-Hitler days German children were trained by their parents to fear the policeman rather than to regard him as a friend. This attitude may be said to have become a German national characteristic; it tends to make the German citizen follow the example of the policeman even in matters not actually connected with Police power. This tendency has, of course, greatly increased under the Nazi régime, and has been purposely fostered in line with the Nazi " *Führer* Principle." The authority and rights (often self-assumed) of the individual policeman have increased proportionately with the general intensification of Police power. It may be regarded as significant that an ex-member of the German Police, when captured and interrogated by the Allies, seemed rather startled when the interrogator questioned the authority of the police to carry out certain illegal acts of oppression. His answer, to him apparently a complete justification, was simply " *Aber wir sind doch die Polizei* " (" But then we are the Police ").

# PART SEVEN

## THE PERSONNEL OF THE GERMAN POLICE

### 145. The German Policeman

Before the German Police can be regarded as an organisation useful to the Allied armies of occupation, the reliability of its members will require careful consideration. It seems most apt to preface the study of German Police personnel with a quotation from the Civil Service Law, which states that Police officials can be "relied upon to support the Nazi State unflinchingly." Nevertheless the summary dismissal as Nazis of all members of an organisation whose continued existence is indispensable would hardly provide a solution to the problems facing the Allies. German Police personnel will be required to help carry out the task of maintaining law and order and of policing their country. Although it will be necessary to make immediate decisions according to the local circumstances, some general guidance—by no means conclusive—as to the reliability of groups of officials within the various branches of the Police can be attempted. Past experience would indicate a need for extreme caution; in general it would seem better, when judging the degree of Nazi tendency in a German policeman, to follow the principle of "guilty until proved innocent," rather than the reverse.

The German Police, even in pre-Hitler days, tended to lean politically toward the Right. When the Nazis assumed power, therefore, they found that the Police showed a rather friendly attitude, and the subsequent purge of undesirables within the force resulted in the dismissal of a comparatively small percentage of officials; even of these many were later recalled to duty. Together with the thorough militarisation a process of "Nazification" (see para. 36) began to remodel the Police and eventually led to the virtual fusion of the Police and the SS. Indeed German official documents speak of the *Verschmelzung* (complete fusion) of the personnel of the German Police with the SS. For this final purpose a set of qualifications for membership in the SS has been defined and is known under the term "*SS Fähigkeit*." In spite of these drastic measures it cannot be categorically stated that all policemen have become fanatical Nazis, especially since it is known that a number of them waited until as late as 1938 or 1939 before joining the SS. Such personnel may be willing to cooperate with the Allies and might be put to use after careful scrutiny of their individual records.

Within the Regular Uniformed Police, in particular, those men who have become professional policemen since 1933 cannot be regarded as reliable from the Allied point of view, since they were either recruited from the SS or had to produce certificates of political reliability issued by the Nazi party. On the other hand, officials who served in the Police before 1933 (or in Austria before 1938) are not necessarily Nazis by conviction, and merit further attention as potentially useful personnel. Similarly *Polizeireservisten* (Police reservists) who are non-professional, wartime members of the Police cannot be condemned or accepted as a group, since they represent a cross-section of the entire population. (For further details on the members of the *Polizeireservekorps* see para. 37.)

Members of the *Verwaltungspolizei* are regular Civil Service personnel. They are part of the large and typical class of German bureaucratic officials who are distinguished by their literal approach to the execution of their orders. They are often servile in obedience and respect for their superiors, and they encounter the public with a cool and lofty attitude. Even under the Weimar Republic most of these officials were followers of the Right Wing or reactionary currents, because they resented the lowering of esteem suffered by their caste since the glorious days of the "Imperial and Royal Civil Service." But in spite of such retrospective regrets they were anxious to retain their positions and salaries under the Weimar Republic, which needed them as skilled personnel and did not indulge in purges of undesirables. These officials of the *Verwaltungspolizei* probably welcomed the Nazi regime, which revived and intensified the tendency to regard the masses as subjects, rather than free citizens with the rights of individuals and taxpayers. Beyond that the expansion of governmental functions and powers under the Hitler regime brought rapid advancement to many specialists in the service of the Police and created new jobs for a great number of formerly unemployed or badly paid German civilians. In other words, many of the members of the *Verwaltungspolizei* are guided by considerations of personal gain and prestige rather than political convictions; while it is probably true that such personnel are at present faithful servants of HIMMLER, it may be assumed that many of them will, if ordered, be ready to serve any government, and thereby retain their ranks and emoluments.

Members of the *Sicherheitspolizei* and the SD, on the other hand, must be regarded in a totally different light. Any effort on their part to co-operate "willingly" with the Allies will doubtless be rejected. The SD is an SS organisation and the *Sipo* has come to be completely dominated by the SS; personnel of the present-day *Sipo* who served in the Police of pre-Hitler days not only had to join the SS, but were subjected to very thorough indoctrination courses. Captured documents reveal that the programme of these courses was not limited to the constant reiteration of Nazi precepts, but familiarised the students with every possible means of *Gegnerbekämpfung* (Combatting of Opposition) ranging from investigation and propaganda to espionage and sabotage. In view of the ultimate meaning of *Gegnerbekämpfung*, the bulk of *Kripo* personnel cannot be regarded as politically reliable from the Allied point of view. However, the services of a small number of trained Criminal Police experts will inevitably be required; their personal records and careers would need to be checked with extreme caution in every instance. All information on the relationship between such personnel and the Nazi Party, in particular the SS, will be of value.

A recent document shows that as late as the middle of 1944 some *Kripo* officials of ranks ranging from major to colonel were still officially designated as *SS-Bewerber** (aspirants for SS membership). Since such men must either have tried to avoid membership in the SS as long as possible or have been considered unsuitable for the SS, certain inferences may be drawn as to their attitude towards the Nazi régime. This is, of course,

A

merely one example of many possible means by which the individual case can be investigated (e.g. personnel files, personal documents, membership dates and numbers).

In the case of the *Gestapo*, not even the most urgent need for skilled Police personnel would justify the employment of any of its members in the post-Hitler police force. The *Gestapo's* political record rules out the employment, by the Allies, of any German who has at any time been in the service of that organisation. Regular members of the SD are even more dangerous, since they have been chosen exclusively from among the most fanatical and ruthless SS personnel. Both *Gestapo* and SD members when interrogated after capture, frequently advance motives of material gain as an excuse for their membership and insist that they have never participated in any atrocities. Any such " post factum " apologies are almost certainly worthless ; it will probably be safest to regard personnel of both *Gestapo* and SD—even if they cannot actually be convicted of their crimes—as categorically disqualified from holding any public office in post-war Germany.

As a background for the control of the Police force in Germany and for the treatment of its members, the present chapter deals with the legal status, the careers and the pay of German Police personnel. Such details as can be given, without enumerating the many minute regulations on these subjects, are basic rather than exhaustive.

The ranks and titles used in the German Police are extremely varied and numerous. To avoid confusion and inaccuracies, no translations have been given, but the equivalent SS and Army (German, British and American) ranks have been listed in a comparative table of ranks instead (see para. 170). Furthermore, to convey a clear picture of the ranks used within each branch of the Police, a table of ranks grouped according to those branches has been added in the same paragraph. Reference to both tables will be of value in the reading of this chapter.

## 146. Legal Status

The personnel of the German Police is mainly composed of civil service employees whose legal status, training and careers vary according to the branch of Police to which they belong. As civil servants, however, all of them are subject to the following laws :

*Deutsches Beamtengesetz* (German Civil Service Law) of 26 Jan., 1937.

*Reichsdienststrafordnung* (Reich Civil Service Disciplinary Code) of 26 Jan., 1937 and

*Reichsbesoldungsgesetz* (Reich Civil Service Salaries Law) of 16 Dec., 1937.

Police officials in the narrower sense of the word, i.e. executive officials (*Vollzugsbeamte*) are governed by a set of special regulations laid down in the *Deutsches Polizeibeamtengesetz* (Civil Service Law for German Police officials) of 24 June, 1937.

The *Deutsches Beamtengesetz* regulates the relationship between the employee and the employer, states the duties of the civil servant and the consequences of failure to perform them ; it establishes the procedure for appointments and transfers, and lays down the regulations safeguarding the legal status of the official, the duration of his employment and various other matters. •

The *Reichsdienststrafordnung* provides for the following disciplinary penalties :—

*Warnung* (Warning).
*Verweis* (Rebuke).
*Geldbusse* (Fine).

*Gehaltskürzung* (Reduction in salary).
*Entfernung aus dem Dienst* (Removal from office).
*Kürzung des Ruhegehaltes* (Reduction in pension), and
*Aberkennung des Ruhegehaltes* (Forfeiture of pension).

The *Reichsbesoldungsgesetz* is dealt with later in this part in connection with Pay.

The most important provisions of the *Deutsches Polizeibeamtengesetz* are as follows : —

Every executive police official receives a certificate on appointment, containing the words " *unter Berufung in das Beamtenverhältnis*," which means that henceforth he will be subject to the conditions of civil service employment.

After having served as a *Beamter auf Widerruf* (literally, official on probation), he receives—if he meets certain legal requirements—an appointment for life. All lifetime-positions in the *Vollzugspolizei* (collective term for the Executive Branches of the Police) and the majority of posts in the *Verwaltungspolizei* (Administrative Police) are filled with members of the *Schutzpolizei* (Protection Police).

Police officials of the *Kasernierte Polizei* (Barracks Police) need special permission to marry, which must not be given to a man less than 26 years old. Police officials—usually up to the age of 27—can be required to live in Police billets.

*Polizeivollzugsbeamte des Reiches* (Reich Police Executive Officials) may be transferred to the *Gemeindepolizei* (Municipal Police) if placed in positions corresponding to those formerly held. Similarly, officials of the Municipal Police may be transferred to another municipality or to the Reich Police Service.

Certain regulations on the subject of the retirement age for *Polizeivollzugsbeamte* differ from those for other civil servants. Officers released or retiring from Police service may be given the honorary title of the next higher rank and the right to wear Police uniform.

A decree of 17 Oct, 1939 subjected all members of the *Sicherheitspolizei* and the SD and those members of the *Orpo* organised into units, to the jurisdiction of SS and Police Tribunals in all instances involving crimes (*Straftaten*) committed by them. A subsequent decree of 8 Aug, 1942 extended that *Sondergerichtsbarkeit* (Special Jurisdiction) to all members of the *Ordnungspolizei* and its auxiliary branches (*Hilfsverbände*). Under this decree personnel of the *Feuerwehren* (Fire Brigades) *Technische Nothilfe* (Technical Emergency Corps) and the *Luftschutzpolizei* (Air Raid Protection Police) are also to be tried by these tribunals, but only for crimes committed in uniform or in connection with official duties.

While the *Landwacht* is not regarded as a *Hilfsverband* under this decree, foreign units entrusted with Police duties in the annexed Eastern territory and in the Government General are considered as auxiliary branches of the Police.

*Polizei Verwaltungsbeamte* (Administrative Police Officials including such political appointees as *Polizeipräsidenten* and -*direktoren*) also come under the *Sondergerichtsbarkeit*, but members of the general internal administration, even though they may exercise Police functions (e.g. the *Bürgermeister* or the *Landrat*) are not included. On the other hand, the *Gefolge* (German personnel employed by the Police), as well as the Women's Auxiliaries, are subject to the SS and Police Tribunals.

For locations of the SS and Police Tribunals see E.D.S./G/8 : The *Allgemeine SS*.

## 147. Police Careers : NCOs in the Ordnungspolizei

In discussing qualifications, training and advancement of Police officials, it is advisable to follow the pattern set up by the Germans who, for the purpose of service careers, divide the Police into :—

*Ordnungspolizei,*
*Verwaltungspolizei,* and
*Sicherheitspolizei.*

The basic career in the *Orpo* is that of the **Schutzpolizei.** NCO Recruits for the *Schupo* are taken, if possible, from members of the *Waffen-SS,* formerly called SS Special Service Troops (*SS-Verfügungstrupper*), or from the Armed Forces ; they originally had to meet the following requirements :

German citizenship.
No previous convictions.
Good health (Wearers of glasses are rejected).
Minimum height of 5 feet 7 inches (1.70 m.).
Honourable discharge after two to five years' service in the Army, or four years in the *Waffen-SS.*
Age between 20 and 25 years.
Applicants must be single.
Passing of a physical and mental aptitude test.

Minimum requirements for the physical test are : 1,500 m. (1,650 yards) race in 6 minutes ; long jump, 4.15 m. ; throwing a handgrenade 32 m. The mental test, consisting of a written and oral examination, is considered as passed when the examiners are satisfied that the candidate will be able to perform his duties intelligently.

It is preferred that the applicant should hold at least one sports badge.

A former member of the Army must, in addition, have the following qualifications :

*Deutschgebürtige* or *artverwandte Abstammung* (of German birth or a " racial German ").
Membership of the NSDAP or one of its formations previous to his entry into the Army.
*SS-Fähigkeit* (SS-qualifications) ; this includes the passing of a thorough examination by SS doctors and dentists coupled with the findings of specialists in racial matters (*Rasse- und Siedlungshauptamt*) as well as an intelligence and general knowledge test.

An honourable discharge from military service, preferably as an NCO (*Unteroffizier d.Res.*).

At this point it must be stressed that the above listed specifications for membership in the Police are those originally set down for peace-time conditions. As a result of wartime manpower problems the standard of physical fitness has been drastically lowered and may by now, in many instances, be disregarded entirely. As most of the younger and physically fit men were drafted into the Armed Forces or sent into the lines as members of field units of the Police, older and, perhaps, in some cases even partially disabled Germans as well as foreigners or " Racial " Germans became acceptable and eventually even received priority as potential Police personnel. This development, however, should not lead to the faulty deduction that the standards of political reliability for any of the branches of the German Police, and particularly the *Sipo* and SD, have been lowered in a parallel manner.

After his admission to the *Schupo* the candidate receives training in Police companies and is sent on courses for *Schupo* candidates (*Schutzpolizeianwärterlehrgänge*).

The trainees are organised in companies. Advanced training takes place in separate courses. Specialists may be assigned to a Police cavalry school, ski school, M/T school, or a technical police school. For a list of Police Schools see Annexe J.

It should be noted that there are no privates in the German Police. A *Wachtmeister* (the lowest regular rank) with a good record may be promoted to *Oberwachtmeister* after 6 years service, and to *Revieroberwachtmeister* (or to *Zugwachtmeister* in the Police companies ; see rank tables, para. 170) after 7 years. During their first twelve years with the Police Force, enlisted personnel are appointed on a revocable basis. Thereafter they are promoted to *Hauptwachtmeister* and receive appointment for life provided they pass a special examination. Membership of the Nazi party and of its sub-divisions is added to the length of their police service and counts towards making up this 12 years service. After 16 years promotion to *Meister der Schutzpolizei* may take place. The retirement age which has, however, been suspended during the war is sixty for EM (Br. O.R.'s).

A *Meister der Schutzpolizei* who has shown above-average qualities, and who has attended a *Revier-*

| Rank | Paygroup * | Salary (in RM. per year) | Av. age of Appointment | Retirement age |
|---|---|---|---|---|
| *Rottwachtmeister* | 8c5 | 1536 | | |
| *Wachtmeister* | 8c4 | 1920 | 24 | 60 |
| *Oberwachtmeister* | 8c3 | 2040 | 29 | 60 |
| *Revieroberwachtmeister* | 8c2 | 2160–2340 | 30 | 60 |
| *Komp.-Hauptwachtmeister* | 8c1 | 2370 | | |
| *Hauptwachtmeister* | 8a | 2000–3000 | 35 | 60 |
| *Meister* | 7a | 2350–3500 | 40 | 60 |
| *Revierleutnant* | 5b | 2300–4200 | 42 | 60 |
| *Revieroberleutnant* | 4c2 | 2800–5000 | 45 | 60 |

\* See chart para. 164.

A2

*offizier* candidate school may become a *Revier-leutnant* and later a *Revieroberleutnant*. After having served in that grade for five years and having shown outstanding abilities he may be given the honorary rank of *Revierhauptmann*, but not before having reached the age of fifty.

The creation of the rank of *Revieroffizier* was designed to fill the gap left by the drafting of young Police officers to the Armed Forces and was to be an added incentive for experienced NCO's and Police reservists who were too old to qualify as commissioned officers. Since this is obviously a war-time measure, the *Revieroffiziere* are frequently referred to as *Kriegsoffiziere* (Wartime officers). As their titles show, they are meant to be in charge of a *Revier* (a Police Precinct or Ward).

The table on page 101 shows paygroups (see para. 164), average yearly basic salary in *Reichsmark*,** average age of appointment and age limit of the NCOs and *Revieroffiziere* of the *Orpo*.

The ranks of *Anwärter* and *Unterwachtmeister* have been omitted since they are preliminary stages preceding the appointment to *Rottwacht-meister*.

Members of the **Gendarmerie** start their career in the *Motorisierte Gendarmerie*, for which only *Wachtmeister* with 4 years' service—two in the army and two in Police companies—are eligible. After having served from 5 to 6 years in the motorised units they are tentatively transferred to the *Gendarmerie des Einzeldienstes* (Single Service) with the rank of *Bezirksoberwachtmeister z. Pr.* (*zur Probedienstleitung*—on trial) or *Hauptwachtmeister z.Pr.* depending on the total length of their previous service.

During the trial period they undergo a three months' course at a *Gendarmerie* school and may, either upon recommendation of the Police authority in charge of training or at their own request, go back to the *Schutzpolizei*. After the completion of the trial period and having passed another examination the Rural Policeman receives his assignment. Appointment for life in the rank of *Hauptwachtmeister der Gendarmerie* follows after a total of 12 years' service with the Police.

In all other respects the careers and ranks of the non-commissioned officers and *Bezirksoffiziere* of the *Gendarmerie* correspond to those of the non-commissioned officers and *Revieroffiziere* of the *Schutzpolizei*.

Ranks and careers in the **Wasserschutzpolizei** are identical with those of the *Schutzpolizei*. Special qualifications for an appointment are as follows: Maximum age is 26 years and 30 months experience at sea or on inland waterways is required. All NCOs are trained for a period of one year at the Waterways Protection School originally in Stettin, but moved August, 1944 to Lauterbach on Rügen.

The personnel of the **Feuerschutzpolizei** consists of former members of the professional fire-fighting organisations. Personal qualifications, ranks and careers are similar to those in the *Schupo*. All candidates for the force must attend special Fire Fighting schools.

The nucleus of the **Luftschutzpolizei,** created in 1942, was taken from the personnel of the SHD (Security and Assistance Service) who, up to that time, had formed the nucleus of all ARP services. Another part of the personnel, experienced in repair and demolition work, was drawn from the Technical Emergency Corps. The average age is believed to be 45. Members of the Air Raid Protection Police are full-time personnel drawn principally from the *Polizei-Reservekorps* and should not be confused with members of auxiliary organizations doing part-time service.

The general requirements for the **Technische Nothilfe** are the same as for candidates for the *Orpo*.

Note: A decree by HIMMLER promulgated late in 1943 assigned uniform ranks to the following *Technische Hilfspolizeien* (Technical Auxiliaries to the Police):

*Technische Nothilfe* (Technical Emergency Corps).

*Freiwillige Feuerwehren* (Volunteer Fire Fighting Brigades).

*Luftschutzpolizei* (Air Raid Protection Police). For old and new ranks see rank table, para 170.

### 148. Commissioned Officers of the Ordnungspolizei

Officers of the **Schutzpolizei** are primarily recruited from graduates of the *SS-Junkerschulen* (SS-officers schools) in Bad Tölz, Brunswick and Klagenfurt. It was intended that all officers should be drawn from this source, but because of the great demand for SS leaders in all branches of the administration and in the *Waffen-SS*, an indefinite number of commissions in the *Schupo* still remain open to members of other Nazi organisations.

These candidates from other organisations must have all the qualifications of the enlisted personnel (OR) ; in addition they must have had a secondary school education, and qualify as a candidate for commissioned rank. Every candidate has to apply for membership in the SS before starting his training.

Police training is given at the police training and police officers' schools located at Berlin-Köpenik and Fürstenfeldbruck (Bavaria).

Promotions to higher ranks depend on ability, efficiency and seniority. Every officer of the *Orpo* has to pass a written examination before he can become a *Hauptmann* (Captain). This examination not only includes Police subjects but national and world politics as well. Promotion from *Hauptmann* to *Major* is only granted after the candidate has successfully concluded a three months' course at a police officers' school. A special *Schule für Generalstabsausbildung der Ordnungspolizei* (School for General Staff Training in the *Orpo*) exists in Dresden.

For entry into the **Wasserschutzpolizei** a diploma testifying to the experience of the candidate at sea (*Seesteuermann auf grosser Fahrt*) is also required.

Officers for the **Gendarmerie** are taken from the officers' corps of the *Schupo*. Service in the motorised units precedes service in the *Einzeldienst*.

Officers' ranks in the **Feuerschutzpolizei** are identical with those of the *Schupo*. All officers must graduate from the Fire Fighting school for officers at Eberswalde.

The following table shows paygroups, yearly

---

** Note, until 1931 £1 was equal to RM 20.40, and $1 to RM 4.20 (or roughly 1 RM to 1/- or 25c.), a value which approximately corresponds to buying power. Before the outbreak of war, when German currency was already rigidly controlled £1 equalled approximately RM 12 and $1 approximately RM 2.50 (or 1 RM=1s. 8d. or 40c.). Actually the value of 1 RM in the free market was then already much lower and indications are that it will most likely after cessation of hostilities be fixed at an even lower level.

| Rank | Paygroup * | Salary (in RM. per year) | Av. age of Appointment | Retirement age |
|---|---|---|---|---|
| *Offiziere* (Commissioned Officers) of the Orpo : | | | | |
| *Leutnant* | 4e | 2400–4200 | 25 | 51 |
| *Oberleutnant* | 4e | 3400–4200 | 29 | 51 |
| *Hauptmann* | 3b | 4800–6900 | 34 | 51 |
| *Major* | 2c2 | 7700–8400 | 40 | 53 |
| *Oberstleutnant* | 2b | 9700 | — | 56 |
| *Oberst* | 1a | 12600 | — | — |
| *Generalmajor* | B7a | 16000 | — | — |
| *Generalleutnant* | B4 | 19000 | — | — |
| *General* | | No data available | | |
| *Generaloberst* | | No data available | | |
| *Sanitätsoffiziere* (Medical Officers) of the *Orpo* : | | | | |
| *Assistenzarzt* | 4e | 3400–4200 | 26 | — |
| *Oberarzt* | 4e | 3400–4200 | 27 | — |
| *Stabsarzt* | 3b | 4800–6900 | 30 | — |
| *Oberstabsarzt* | 2c2 | 7700–8400 | 38 | — |
| *Oberfeldarzt* | 2b | 9700 | 45 | — |
| *Oberstarzt* | 1a | 12600 | 50 | — |
| *Generalarzt* | B7a | 16000 | 50 | — |
| *Veterinäroffiziere* (Veterinary Officers) of the *Orpo* : | | | | |
| *Veterinär* | 4e | 3400–4200 | 26 | — |
| *Oberveterinär* | 4e | 3400–4200 | 27 | — |
| *Stabsveterinär* | 3b | 4800–6900 | 30 | — |
| *Oberstabsveterinär* | 2c2 | 7700–8400 | 38 | — |
| *Oberfeldveterinär* | 2b | 9700 | 45 | — |
| *Oberstveterinär* | 1a | 12600 | 50 | — |

\* See chart para. 164.

salary in *Reichsmark*, average age of appointment and age limit of the commissioned officers of the *Orpo*.

### 149. Women Auxiliaries of the Regular Police

The expansion of the German Police, especially with regard to communications, has brought about the employment of women on an ever increasing scale. These *Helferinnen* may be employed as telephone, teletype, and radio operators (*Nachrichtenhelferinnen*), or as stenotypists and for general office work (*Stabshelferinnen*), within the Reich as well as in the garrisons and police offices in the occupied territories. Girls and women of German (or related) blood are eligible, preference being given to those who have had previous office experience. The training lasts 6 months ; its main purpose is to familiarise the *Helferinnen* with the equipment they have to use. *Unter-führerinnen* (comparable to NCOs) have to pass a course at the *Polizeischule für Helferinnen der Ordnungspolizei* at Erfurt. *Führerinnen* (comparable but not equal in rank to officers) are appointed by the *Hauptamt Orpo* and are charged with the welfare and supervision of their subordinates. Legally the *Helferinnen* are *Gefolgschaftsmitglieder* (non Civil Service Personnel) and their pay (*Vergütung*) and all other conditions of employment are fixed by a *Tarifordnung* (Tariff Code ; see para. 156).

### 150. Verwaltungspolizei

Administrative Officials do not only make up that part of the *Orpo* known as the *Verwaltungspolizei*, they are also employed in all other branches of the Police wherever duties in connection with the Police's own administration have to be performed.

There exists, in addition to the *Verwaltungspolizei*, a *Verwaltungsdienst* of the *Orpo* and a *Verwaltungsdienst* of the *Sipo* in contrast to the *Vollzugsdienst* (Executive Service) of these branches.

The *Verwaltungsdienst* of the *Sipo* is therefore discussed together with the *Verwaltungsdienst* of the *Orpo* in the following paragraphs.

All Administrative Officials come under the provisions of the *Deutsches Beamtengesetz* (German Civil Service Law), but the *Polizeibeamtengesetz* (Law concerning Executive Police Officials) is not applicable to them. The authorities of the *Orpo* and *Sipo* have the right to lay down regulations governing qualifications and training of administrative officials employed by them.

It is certain that the members of the *Verwaltungsdienst* of the *Sipo* are just as devout followers of the Nazi régime as is the rest of the Security Police, which may not be true to the same extent of the administrative officials of the *Orpo*, many of whom may be in the first place bureaucrats and only secondly convinced Nazis.

The activities of the Administrative Service are many and varied, and range from messenger service to Senior Police Officials and high grade Civil Servants. German tables of organisation distinguish between the following groups of Administrative Officials :—

*Einfacher Polizeiverwaltungsdienst* — Lower Grade in the Police Administration.

*Mittlerer Polizeiverwaltungsdienst* — Intermediate Grade in the Police Administration.

*Gehobener Polizeiverwaltungsdienst* — Senior Grade in the Police Administration.

*Höherer Polizeiverwaltungsdienst* — Superior Grade in the Police Administration.

*Technische Polizeibeamte* (Technical Police Officials) also belong legally to the Administrative Branch. They will be discussed in para. 155.

### 151. Administrative Officials of the Einfacher Polizeiverwaltungsdienst

Personal qualifications for employment in the *Einfacher Polizeiverwaltungsdienst* (Lower Grade in the Police Administration) are as follows :

*Polizeidiensttauglichkeit* (Suitability for Police duties)

Age between 21 and 45

Membership of the NSDAP or one of the Party formations

Attendance of an elementary school (*Volksschule*) ; in doubtful cases passing of an examination set by the *Verwaltungspolizei*

*SS-Fähigkeit* is indispensable if the candidate is to serve in the *Sicherheitspolizei*, but is regarded as a desirable qualification in all branches of the German Police.

As a result of wartime manpower shortage many of the requirements for candidates for this branch have, however, been relaxed, as has previously been pointed out in connection with the Regular Uniformed Police.

Preference is given to *Schupo* members with 8 years' service for whom 80 per cent. of all openings are reserved. Training is given on the job and candidates hold the rank of *Amtsgehilfe auf Probe* (Office Help on trial) during a probationary period. After six months the "*auf Probe*" is dropped and in the case of *Schupo* members appointment for life is given after two years.

*Amtsgehilfen* act as messengers and are supervised by a *Botenmeister* (Head Messenger) who is also in charge of incoming and outgoing mail. *Hausmeister* (Caretaker or Building Superintendent) are responsible for the cleaning, lighting and heating of office buildings.

A *Botenmeister* or a *Hausmeister* may be promoted to *Betriebsassistent*, or if he has the necessary qualifications to *Vollziehungsbeamte* (an Official who collects fines imposed by the Police).

Officials employed in police prisons (*Polizeigefängnisbeamte*), also belong to the Lower Service, but constitute a group by themselves.

Promotions from the Lower Grade to the Intermediate Grade are only given in exceptional cases.

The following table shows ranks, paygroups, salaries and average age of retirement in the *Einfacher Dienst* :—

| Rank | Paygroup* | Salary | Retirement age |
|---|---|---|---|
| *Amtsgehilfe* | 10b | 1700–2400 | 65 |
| *Botenmeister* | 10b | 1700–2400 | 65 |
| *Hausmeister* | 10b | 1700–2400 | 65 |
| *Betriebsassistent* | 10a | 1759–2550 | 65 |
| *Vollziehungsbeamter* | 9 | 1800–2700 | 65 |
| *Pol. Gefängnisoberwachtmeister* | 9 | 1800–2700 | 65 |
| *Pol. Gefängnishauptwachtmeister* | 9 | 1800–2700 | 65 |
| *Pol. Gefängnisverwalter* | 7a | 2350–3500 | 65 |
| *Pol. Gefängnisoberverwalter* | 5b | 2300–4200 | 65 |

* See chart para. 164.

### 152. Administrative Officials of the Mittlerer Polizeiverwaltungsdienst

90 per cent. of all positions in the *Mittlerer Polizeiverwaltungsdienst* (Intermediate Grade) are reserved for members of the *Schutzpolizei des Reiches*. The *Gestapo* is an exception to this rule. Because of the confidential nature of the work only 50 per cent. of its administrative officials of the Intermediate Grade are drawn from the *Schutzpolizei*, the remaining half being made up of special civilian personnel.

Having done 12 months' preparatory service, all candidates for the *Mittlerer Polizeiverwaltungsdienst* must pass an examination and are then appointed *Polizeiassistent*. Candidates from the Lower Grade may be admitted in exceptional cases provided they are not more than 45 years old.

Civilian candidates for the *Mittlerer Dienst* have to meet the following requirements :—

*Polizeidiensttauglichkeit*

Age between 21 and 41

Membership of the NSDAP or one of the Party formations

Attendance at an elementary school, in doubtful cases passing of an examination set by the *Verwaltungspolizei*

Proficiency in shorthand

*SS-Fähigkeit* is required if the candidate is to serve in the *Sipo*

Training for a civilian candidate also lasts for 12 months and includes service with various Police Authorities. During that period civilian candidates are called *Polizeiassistentenanwärter* and draw a living allowance only. This period terminates with an examination for the Intermediate Grade. After passing the examination candidates are appointed *apl.* (*ausserplanmässig— supernumerary*) *Polizeiassistent* and receive a regular appointment after three more years.

Officials of the Intermediate Grade are in charge of the less difficult office duties.

Promotion from *Polizeiassistent* to *Polizeisekretär* is given whenever a vacancy occurs, according to a seniority list kept by the office of the *Reichsführer-SS und Chef d Dt Polizei*. In addition, length of membership in the Party, military decorations and number of children are considered. In the Security Police promotion to *Polizeisekretär* may take place after two years of service or in cases of outstanding merit after one year. Members of the SS must attend an *SS-Führerlehrgang* (Officers' training school) before promotion is granted.

*Polizeisekretäre* with above-average abilities may qualify for the post of *Obersekretär* on reaching the age of 40. In the Security Police the *Polizeisekretär* must serve three years in that rank before he can qualify for appointment to *Polizeiobersekretär*.

The following table shows ranks, paygroups, salaries, average age of retirement in the *Mittlerer Polizeiverwaltungsdienst* :—

| Rank | Paygroup* | Salary (in RM.—per year) | Av. age of Appointment | Retirement age |
|---|---|---|---|---|
| *Pol. Assistant* | 8a | 2100–2800 | 25–33 | 65 |
| *Pol. Sekretär* | 7a | 2350–3500 | 27–35 | 65 |
| *Pol. Obersekretär* | 5b | 2300–4200 | 38–45 | 65 |

\* See chart para. 164.

### 153. Administrative Officials of the Gehobener Polizeiverwaltungsdienst

Half of the posts in the *Gehobener Polizeiverwaltungsdienst* (Senior Grade) are reserved for the NCOs of the *Schupo* with at least 12 years of service; the remainder go to the few who are admitted from the Intermediate Service and to civilian candidates.

Candidates from the *Schupo* have to go through three years of preparatory service and have to pass two examinations. The *Kalkulator-Prüfung* to ascertain their knowledge of accountancy and financial administration, and the *Polizei Inspektorenprüfung*, which terminates the preparatory service. Upon successful completion of these examinations the candidate is given the title of *apl. Polizeiinspektor*.

A candidate from the *Mittlerer Polizeiverwaltungsdienst*, provided he is not more than 45 years old, may be admitted to the *Gehobener Polizeiverwaltungsdienst*, if he has shown outstanding abilities. Preparatory service, in that case, lasts two years and the *Kalkulator-Prüfung* is not required. Even after passing the *Polizeiinspektorenprüfung* (examination for the *Gehobener Polizeiverwaltungsdienst*), the candidate still holds his old rank until his final appointment as *Polizeiinspektor*.

Civilian candidates have to meet the following requirements :

*Polizeidiensttauglichkeit* (Fitness for Police duties)

Age for apprentices not over 17, for holders of a *Reifezeugnis* (certificate given to graduates of a *Mittelschule*, i.e. school immediately below university level) not over 30.

Membership of the NSDAP or one of the Party formations

Honourable discharge from the Reich Labour Service and the Army for holders of the *Reifezeugnis*

Possession of a *Reifezeugnis*, or attendance of a secondary school and advanced courses

Proficiency in shorthand

*SS-Fähigkeit* is required if the candidate is to serve in the *Sicherheitspolizei*.

The training period consists of an apprenticeship followed by the preparatory service, except for holders of the *Reifezeugnis*, who start immediately with the preparatory service.

The apprenticeship lasts for two years during which time the candidate is called a *Verwaltungslehrling* (Apprentice in the Administrative Service). He gets an allowance of RM. 50— per month in the first year and RM. 60— per month in the second. After completion of his apprenticeship a *Lehrling* has to do his Reich Labour Service and his Army Service, and is expected to leave the Army as a Reserve Officer Candidate.

The preparatory service lasts for 3 years, during which the candidate holds the rank of *Polizeiinspektoranwärter*. After having passed the *Kalkulator-Prüfung* and towards the end of his preparatory service the candidate attends a course at the Police School for Administrative Officials of the *Orpo* at München-Haar (Administrative Officials of the *Sipo*, however, go to Braunau).

After passing the *Inspektorenprüfung* he is appointed to *apl. Polizeiinspektor* and draws *Diäten* (Food and Lodging Allowance) until his final appointment as *Polizeiinspektor*.

Officials of the *Gehobener Polizeiverwaltungs-*

*dienst* are employed for difficult office work and are usually found in executive positions. Promotions are given according to ability and seniority. Detailed information is available only for the *Sipo*. There a *Polizeiinspektor* may be promoted to *Polizeioberinspektor* after 3 years, and to *Polizeirat* after an additional period of 2 years.

Aside from the officials mentioned a specialist group of officials, e.g. *Rentmeister*, is employed for the financial administration of the Police.

The following table shows ranks, paygroups, salaries, and average age of appointment and retirement in the *Gehobener Polizeiverwaltungsdienst* :—

| Rank | Paygroup* | Salary (in RM per year) | Av. age of Appointment | Retirement age |
|---|---|---|---|---|
| Pol. Inspektor<br>Pol. Rentmeister | 4c2 | 2800–5000 | 27–35 | 65 |
| Polizeioberinspektor<br>Polizeirechnungsrevisoren | 4b2 | 3000–5500 | 31–39 | 65 |
| Polizeioberrentmeister<br>Oberbuchhalter | 4b1 | 4100–5800 | | |
| Pol. Amtmann, Polizeirat,<br>Landrentmeister | 3b | 4800–7000 | 37–50 | 65 |
| Regierungs- und Kassenrat | 2c2 | 4800–8400 | | |

### 154. Administrative Officials of the Höherer Polizeiverwaltungsdienst

Requirements for the *Höherer Polizeiverwaltungsdienst* (Superior Grade) are only known in detail for the *Sicherheitspolizei*. It may, however, be assumed that requirements for the *Ordnungspolizei* are similar to those listed below :—

> *Polizeidiensttauglichkeit* and *SS-Fähigkeit*
> Membership of the NSDAP or of one of the Party formations
> Completion of labour and military service
> *Reifezeugnis*
> Passing of the Final Legal Examination (*Grosse Staatsprüfung*), i.e. candidates must be trained lawyers
> Pure German racial stock
> No criminal record.

Candidates are selected after a personal interview at the RSHA in Berlin. During the ensuing 12 months' training period those selected are called *Probeassessor*, and after successful completion of this period may receive an appointment as *Regierungsassessor*. Two years must elapse between the final Legal Examination and a regular appointment to *Regierungsrat*.

Advancement from the *Gehobener Polizeiverwaltungsdienst* into the *Höherer Polizeiverwaltungsdienst* is possible where exceptional ability warrants such a step. In the Security Police an *Amtsrat* in the Senior Grade may be promoted to *Regierungsrat* after 5 years, and *Regierungsamtmänner* and *Polizeiräte* may also be promoted to *Regierungsräte* if they have outstanding qualities and especially if they were lawyers prior to joining the *Sipo*. Further advancements are subject to existing vacancies and political reliability is, of course, an indispensable prerequisite.

*Polizeipräsidenten* (*Polizeidirektoren*) are *politische Beamte*, i.e. officials whose appointment is largely governed by political considerations.

Officials of even higher rank are in effect no longer regarded as Police officials but as high government officials who supervise the service, formulate policy and have over-all responsibility regarding Police matters. They in turn are responsible to the *Staatssekretär* or *Reichsminster* in whom the highest authority is vested.

The following table shows ranks, paygroups and salaries of officials in the *Höherer Polizeiverwaltungsdienst* :—

| Rank | Paygroup* | Salary (in RM.–per year) |
|---|---|---|
| Regierungsrat | 2c2 | 4800–8400 |
| Polizeidirektor | 2c1 | 4800–8800 |
| Oberregierungsrat | 2b | 7000–9700 |
| Regierungsdirektor | 1b | 6200–10600 |
| Polizeipräsident | 1a, 1b | 6200–12600 |

* See chart para. 164.

### 155. Technische Polizeibeamte

The technicians of the *Orpo* deal with the supervision and care of weapons, transport equipment, technical and optical instruments, signals equipment, anti-gas equipment, and fieldkitchens of the *Schupo*, *Kripo*, and *Gendarmerie*. They assist in the disposal of ammunition and explosives, found or confiscated by the Police, give instruction to other officials and are generally consulted on technical matters.

Candidates with at least 8 years' service in the *Schupo* are eligible if they have had previous experience as mechanics. They attend a two-year course at the *Polizeischule für Technik und Verkehr*, and, after an examination and further training at an ordnance depot they are appointed *Waffenmeister* and cease to be *Polizeivollzugsbeamte* (Police Executive Officials).

Promotion to *Waffenrevisor* depends on passing another examination. Legally all *Technische Beamte* are Administrative Officials, but the technicians of the *Orpo* come under the jurisdiction of the *Kommandeur der Schupo*.

The following table shows ranks, paygroups, salary and average age of appointment for *Technische Polizeibeamte* :—

| Rank | Paygroup* | Salary (in RM.—per year) | Av. age of Appointment |
|---|---|---|---|
| *Waffenmeister* | 5b | 2300–4200 | 35 |
| *Waffenrevisor* | 4c2 | 2800–5000 | 45 |
| *Waffenoberrevisor* | 4b1 | 4100–5800 | 50 |
| *Technischer Verwaltungsamtmann* | 3b | 4800–7000 | |

Less information is available about the *Technische Beamte* employed by the *Sipo*. Most of them seem to be in the service of the *Gestapo* and it may be assumed that in addition to performing similar duties as the technicians of the *Orpo*, they have to take care of the wireless, teletype and monitoring equipment at the disposal of the *Sicherheitspolizei*.

The following table shows ranks, paygroups and salary for *Technische Beamte* serving with the *Sipo* :—

| Rank | Paygroup* | Salary (in RM.—per year) |
|---|---|---|
| *Technischer Assistent* | 8a | 2100–2800 |
| *Technischer Sekretär* | 7a | 2350–3500 |
| *Technischer Obersekretär bei der Gestapo* | 5b | 2300–4200 |
| *Technischer Inspektor* | 4c2 | 2800–5000 |
| *Technischer Oberinspektor* | 4b1 | 4100–5800 |
| *Technischer Amtmann* | 3b | 4800–7000 |

### 156. Die nichtbeamteten Hilfskräfte or Gefolgschaftsmitglieder

The vast extension of Police activities and the strained manpower situation has led to the increasing employment of less experienced personnel who are used as clerks, typists, and drivers. Such personnel are not given the status of regular officials but are called *nichtbeamtete Hilfskräfte* (Employees with non-official status), or *Gefolgschaftsmitglieder* (non civil service personnel). Their qualifications, rights, duties, pay, etc., are regulated in various *Tarifordnungen* (Tariff codes), and the number of posts available is determined by the *Kassenanschlag* (Advance Expenditure Estimate).

The following general requirements have to be met by such personnel :—

German (or related) blood. (This also applies to the wife.)

German citizenship

No Police record

Education and training required for the position.

Those seeking employment with the *Kripo* as *Kriminalangestellte* must, in addition, be fit for Police duties (*Polizeidiensttauglichkeit*), meet the requirements of *SS-Fähigkeit*, and must not be less than 21 years or more than 40 years old. All data presented upon the application for the job is checked against information available in the NSDAP, SD and the *Strafregister* (Criminal Registry files). In all other respects the decision lies with the hiring authority.

### 157. Vollzugsbeamten of the Sicherheitspolizei

All designations of rank and position in the *Sicherheitspolizei* apply equally to both *Gestapo* and *Kripo*. The prefix *Kriminal-* in all these

* See chart para. 164.

ranks, e.g. *Kriminalrat*, should not therefore be permitted to create the impression that an official so designated must necessarily be a member of the Criminal Police.

It has been constantly stressed that membership in the SS has become almost necessary in all branches of the German Police and is by this time indispensable for all personnel of the *Sicherheitspolizei*. To complete this process of fusion of Police and SS special pressure seems to have been applied to members of the *Sicherheitspolizei* in October, 1943 to join the SS, if they had not previously done so. In order to be eligible they must, according to this order, meet the following requirements :

General *SS-Fähigkeit*

Membership in the NSDAP or one of its formations (SA, NSKK, HJ) on or before 30 Jan, 1933. Such membership is to be counted even if the official in question has since that time left such organisation honourably

or

Membership in the SS as a *fördendes Mitglied* (sponsoring patron) before 30 Jan, 1933

or

3 years of satisfactory service in the *Sicherheitspolizei* under the direction of the *Reichsführer-SS*.

Special additional membership to the SS may be granted by the *Reichsführer-SS* in person. As a rule, the SS rank conferred upon members of the *Sipo* corresponds to the rank then held by them in the Police. Those entering the *Sipo* preparatory service from professions other than the Police join the SS as *Staffelmänner* (ordinary SS men), and may gradually advance to corresponding higher SS NCO ranks as follows :

*Amtsgehilfen a. Pr.*
*Polizeiassistentenanwärter* } up to *SS-Unterschar-*
*Kriminalassistentenanwärter* } *führer*

*Polizeiinspektorenanwärter* } up to *SS-Haupt-*
*Kriminalkommissaranwärter* } *scharführer*

The ordinary tasks allotted to the *Sipo* are performed by the *Vollzugsbeamte der Sicherheitspolizei* (Executive Officials of the Security Police). They are either non-commissioned or commissioned officers and recent German publications in discussing their career (*Laufbahn*) use the following designations :—

*Unterführerlaufbahn* — Non - commissioned officers

*Führerlaufbahn des mittleren Dienstes*—Officers' Intermediate grade

*Führerlaufbahn des gehobenen Dienstes*—Officers' Senior grade

*Führerlaufbahn des leitenden Dienstes*—Officers' Superior grade

The above careers as well as all the details outlined in the succeeding paras. apply equally to the Kripo and the Gestapo.

## 158. The Unterführerlaufbahn in the Sicherheitspolizei

Candidates for the *Unterführerlaufbahn* in the *Sipo* must meet the following requirements (it should again be borne in mind that physical requirements may have been considerably relaxed as a result of the war) :—

German (or related) blood
Reich Citizenship
Political reliability
No criminal record—good conduct
*Polizeidiensttauglichkeit*
*SS-Fähigkeit*
Possession of at least one Sports Badge (SA or Reich Sports Badge)
Good education (good command of German in speaking and writing ; also shorthand and typing)
Passing of a classification test ascertaining the candidate's general background
Age between 18 and 35 (candidates from the *Schupo* up to 38)
Membership of the NSDAP or one of its formations
Preference is given to specialists and candidates with language qualifications.

The training period for candidates extends over one year during which they work in *Sipo* offices and attend a course at a *Kriminalfachschule* (specialist's school for Criminologists), concluding with *Fachprüfung* I (First Specialist Examination). During that probationary period candidates from the *Schupo* hold the rank of *Kriminalassistent z.Pr.* (*zur Probedienstleistung*—on trial) or *Kriminaloberassistent z.Pr.* depending on the length of their previous service.

Upon completion of the probationary period the candidate receives a regular appointment on an establishment (*Planstelle*) and the " z.Pr." following his rank is dropped.

Candidates from the Armed Forces or the Reich Labour Service with 12 years' service are called *Kriminaloberassistentenanwärter* during the probationary period and are appointed *Kriminaloberassistent* after having successfully passed the course at the *Sipo* School in Berlin-Charlottenburg.

A candidate from civilian professions receives training for twelve months and is then appointed *apl.* (*ausserplanmässig*—supernumerary) *Kriminalassistent*, i.e. he is added temporarily to an establishment without taking up a vacancy on it.

Normally a *Kriminalassistent* is promoted to *Kriminaloberassistent* when he has completed a total of 12 years of service. To make up this total, years of previous service with Party, Police or Administrative Authorities may be counted. The *apl. Kriminalassistent* is placed on establishment after 5 years, and may, after three more years' service, be promoted to *Kriminaloberassistent*.

The following table shows ranks, paygroups, salary and average ages of appointment and retirement for executive officials of the *Unterführerlaufbahn* :—

| Rank | Paygroup* | Salary (in RM.—per year) | Av. age of appointment | Retirement age |
|---|---|---|---|---|
| *Kriminalassistent* | 8c2 | 2160–2340 | 25–35 | 60 |
| *Kriminaloberassistent* | 7c | 2000–3000 | 28–38 | 60 |

\* See chart para. 164.

108

Civilian candidates serving as *apl. Kriminalassistenten* are paid a living allowance (*Diäten*) during their training period.

## 159. The Führerlaufbahn des mittleren Dienstes in the Sicherheitspolizei

Having passed an *SS-Führerlehrgang* (SS- Officers Training Course) a *Kriminaloberassistent* moves up to the *Führerlaufbahn des mittleren Dienstes* and is appointed *Kriminalsekretär*. After 3 years he may be promoted to *Kriminalobersekretär*, and after a further 3 years to *Kriminalinspektor* provided he passes an examination. Officials not belonging to the SS must pass a course in a *Führerlager* (Officer's Camp, where they receive SS training and indoctrination) before they can reach the grade of *Kriminalinspektor*.

The following table shows the ranks, paygroups, salary and average age of appointment and retirement for officers of the *Führerlaufbahn des mittleren Dienstes* :—

| Rank | Paygroup* | Salary (in RM.—per year) | Av. age of Appointment | Retirement age |
|---|---|---|---|---|
| *Kriminalsekretär* | 7a | 2350–3500 | 40–50 | 60 |
| *Kriminalobersekretär* | 5b | 2300–4200 | 45–55 | 60 |
| *Kriminalinspektor* | 4c2 | 2800–5000 | 45–55 | 60 |

## 160. Führerlaufbahn des gehobenen Dienstes in the Sicherheitspolizei

Candidates for the *Führerlaufbahn des gehobenen Dienstes* may either come from the intermediate grade or from other civilian professions. Both groups must have the following qualifications :—

*SS-Fähigkeit* and *Polizeidiensttauglichkeit*

Membership of the NSDAP or one of its subdivisions

Possession of the *Reichssportabzeichen* (National Sports Badge) and the *SA-Wehrabzeichen* (SA-Defence Training Badge)

Passing of an aptitude test to ascertain the general background of the candidate and his capacity for criminal police work. This test is set by the *Führerschule der Sipo* in Berlin-Charlottenburg

Candidates coming from other professions than the Police must, in addition, meet the following requirements :—

Between 18 and 35 years of age

Excellent performance of duties for at least two years following *Fachprüfung* I

3 months' work in the *Reichssicherheitshauptamt* under special supervision

Graduation (*Abitur, Reifezeugnis*) from a *Mittelschule* (Junior College) or from a *SS-Junkerschule*.

All Candidates receive their preparatory training by working under various authorities of the Security Police for a period of one to two years. Afterwards they go through a 9 months' course at the *Führerschule* which concludes with the " *Kriminalkommissar* " examination.

Civilian candidates hold the rank of *Kriminalkommissaranwärter* during the period of training and are appointed *Hilfs-*(Assistant) *kriminalkommissar*. Civilian candidates receive a food and lodging allowance (*Diäten*) after the examination. Appointment to a regular post (*Planstelle*) follows later and is preceded by a six months' trial period during which their designation is *Kriminalkommissar a.Pr.* (*auf Probedienstleistung*—on trial). Appointment for life is not given before the age of 27.

Candidates from the officer's intermediate grade are immediately assigned to the post of a *Kriminalkommissar* and are given the title of *Kriminalkommissar z.Pr.* (*zur Probedienstleistung*—on trial) during the 6 months' probation preceding their definite appointment to *Kriminalkommissar*. Until that time they draw their previous salary.

A *Kriminalkommissar* may be promoted to *Kriminalrat* after a period of five years, and to *Kriminaldirektor* after another five years. It should be pointed out that promotion in the SS may continue even though a man remains in the same rank in the Police or Administrative Service ; for example, a *Kriminalrat* may advance from *SS-Hauptsturmführer* to *SS-Sturmbannführer* without changing his rank in the *Sicherheitspolizei* (see comparative table of ranks, para. 170).

The following table shows ranks, paygroups, and average age of appointment for officers in the *Gehobener Dienst* :—

| Rank | Paygroup* | Salary (in RM.—per year) | Av. age of Appointment | Retirement age |
|---|---|---|---|---|
| *Kriminalkommissar* | 4c1 | 3900–5300 | 30 | 60 |
| *Kriminalrat* | 3b | 4800–7000 | 36 | 60 |
| *Kriminaldirektor* | 2d | 4800–7800 | 50 | 60 |

## 161. The Führerlaufbahn des leitenden Dienstes in the Sicherheitspolizei

The officials of the *Führerlaufbahn des leitenden Dienstes* are taken from the *gehobener Dienst* and it goes without saying that only dyed-in-the-wool party members will be taken into consideration to fill existing vacancies.

The *Kriminaldirektor* of the *Vollzugsdienst* (Executive Service) may become a *Regierungs- und Kriminalrat* after 5 years, and a *Kriminalrat*

* See chart para. 164.

who shows outstanding ability and leadership may after a period of 5 years be promoted directly to *Regierungs- und Kriminalrat*.

No material is available concerning the rules governing promotion to higher posts in the executive branch of the *Sipo*. It is stated in documents that these should be filled with " men of outstanding merit." It can be assumed there-fore, that political considerations, i.e. good con-nections with high SS-leaders, are deciding factors. The majority of officials making up the *Leitender Dienst*, however, are administrative officials who have been discussed in para. 154.

The following table shows ranks, paygroups, salary and average age of appointment and retirement of officers in the *Leitender Dienst* :—

| Rank | Paygroup* | Salary (in RM.—per year) | Av. age of Appointment | Retirement age |
|---|---|---|---|---|
| *Regierungs- u. Kriminalrat* | 2c2 | 4800–8400 | 52 | 60 |
| *Ob. Regierungs- u. Kriminalrat* | 2b | 7000–9700 | 52 | 60 |
| *Regierungs- u. Krim. Direktor, Reichskriminaldirektor* | 1b | 6200–10600 | — | 60 |

* See chart para. 164.

## 162. Weibliche Kriminalpolizei

Personal qualifications for admission to the *Weibliche Kriminalpolizei* are the following :—

Age between 23 and 30
German racial stock
Good health
Membership of the NSDAP or one of the Party formations
Experience in one of the following fields : Social welfare, law, economics, youth movement or nursing.

Training lasts from 1 to 2 years, depending on the education of the candidate, and consists of practical and theoretical schooling. An examina-tion (*Fachprüfung* I) has to be passed, after which the graduate is appointed *Kriminaloberassistentin*. The appointment, given on a revocable basis, becomes an appointment for lifetime after 5 years provided the official is 35 years of age.

During the training period candidates receive an allowance of about RM 140—per month, but they are paid according to the regular pay-scales for Police officials as soon as they receive a permanent appointment. From that time on they may be employed anywhere in the Reich. Ability and existing vacancies make it possible to advance to the following ranks : *Kriminal-sekretärin*, *Kriminalobersekretärin*, *Kriminalkom-missarin*, and *Kriminalrätin*.

*Nachrichtenhelferinnen* (signal auxiliaries) are used to a large extent by the Security Police and what has been said about the *Nachrichtenhelfe-rinnen* of the *Orpo* applies also to them (see para. 149).

## 163. SS Careers in the SD

Since the SD is a formation of the SS, the ranks held by its personnel are not those previously discussed in the *Sicherheitspolizei* and bear no relation to them. SD ranks and careers are strictly and at all times those of the SS. The SS ranks commensurate with the various SD functions are therefore given in the following table :—

| SD Functions | SS Rank |
|---|---|
| *Hilfskräfte* | SS-*Unter-* to SS-*Hauptscharführer* |
| *Geschäftsführer* (Office Chiefs of *SD-Aussenstellen*) | SS-*Hauptscharführer* to SS-*Untersturmführer* |
| *Sachbearbeiter* | SS-*Unter-* to SS-*Hauptsturmführer* |

| SD Functions | SS Rank |
|---|---|
| *Hilfsreferenten* (Sub-sectional unit chiefs of the RSHA) and *Abteilungsleiter* (Section chiefs in SD-*Leitabschnitte* and with the BdS) | SS-*Hauptsturmführer* and SS-*Sturmbannführer* |
| Chiefs of *SD-Abschnitte* and *Referenten* (Sub-section Chiefs in the RSHA) | SS-*Sturmbannführer* and SS-*Obersturmbann-führer* |
| Chiefs of *SD-Leit-abschnitte* and Chiefs of *Gruppen* (Sec-tions) in the RSHA | SS-*Obersturmbann-führer* and SS-*Standartenführer* |

Promotions of SD officials to the appropriate SS rank depend on definite prescribed periods of service in the Nazi Party and its formations, as well as in the SD or the Police. The following table defines such required periods of service :—

| Promotion to | Active Service in the Nazi Party (Years) | Active Service in the SD or the Police (Years) |
|---|---|---|
| SS-*Standartenführer* | 12 | 5 |
| SS-*Obersturmbannführer* | 10 | 4 |
| SS-*Sturmbannführer* | 8 | 3 |
| SS-*Hauptsturmführer* | 6 | 2 |
| SS-*Obersturmführer* | 4 | 1½ |
| SS-*Untersturmführer* | 3 | 1 |

The compulsory two years of service in the Armed Forces or the *Waffen-SS* are counted as active service in the Nazi Party.

## 164. Pay and Allowances

In pre-HITLER Germany Police officials were employed by the various *Länder* (States) and therefore subject to what were, very often, widely differing laws. It could happen, for instance, that a Policeman in Hamburg received very much more pay—or less, as the case may have been—than his colleague performing the same duties in München. HITLER, in his attempts to unify the German Police, decreed in 1937 that all Police officials were to be subject to the *Reichsbesoldungsgesetz* (Reich Civil Service Salary Act) and at the same time placed the *Polizei-vollzugsbeamte* (Executive officials) immediately under the control of the Reich Government. A similar step was taken in 1940 regarding the *Polizeiverwaltungsbeamte* (Administrative officials), thereby making all members of the Police *unmittelbare Reichsbeamte* (regular Reich officials). As a result, the following categories of pay and allowances for Police officials are now uniformly regulated :

*Besoldungsgruppen* (Pay Grades)
*Besoldungsdienstalter* (Pay Seniority)
*Wohnungsgeldzuschuss* (Lodging Allowance)
*Kinderzuschläge* (Allowance for Children)
Payments other than Salary
Pay for candidates for the Police and officials on probation
Reductions and Taxes
Pensions and Payments in case of Death.

Nevertheless, regulations concerning pay and allowances remain an inextricable maze and the scope of this book forbids more than a brief explanation of the basic terms. German Police Calendars published for the guidance of Police officials invariably include a pay chart (reproduced on page 112) in order to give a helping hand to the bewildered Policeman who desires to compute his salary.

Column one of this chart gives the pay grade for the various ranks. The appropriate pay grade for each rank has been shown in the tables of ranks and salaries which appear at the end of each paragraph on careers. Column two shows the number of the various *Tarifklassen* (Tariff Classes), and the bold lines across the chart indicate the limits of each separate class. It should be noted that in the majority of cases the *Tarifklasse* does not alter with the pay grade. For instance, a *Leutnant*—pay grade 4e—belongs to *Tarifklasse* V during his first 6 years of service in that rank, but after that period he moves up to *Tarifklasse* IV. These *Tarifklassen* determine the scale of allowances (*Wohnungsgeldzuschuss*, etc.) to which each rank is entitled. Certain reductions of the basic pay shown on this chart have been permanently fixed by law (see para. 167)*.

**Besoldungsgruppen** (Pay Grades) determine the salary of Police officials by stating the initial pay and the increases that are given bi-annually. They are consecutively numbered from 1 to 11 and are sub-divided by the addition of the small letters a, b, c, etc. (e.g. 2a, 2b). In some cases a further sub-division is made by adding a number after the small letter (e.g. 2c1, 2c2). In all, there are 30 pay grades (column 1 of the chart) determining the pay scales of posts with lifetime tenure. The lowest grade, 11, sets a rate of RM 1,600—annually for the first two years of service, and the highest, 1a, a rate of RM 8,400—for the same period. Upon receiving a regular appointment, or in the case of promotion, Police officials acquire

the pay grade of their new rank. If, for instance, a *Hauptwachtmeister* is promoted to *Meister*, he goes from pay grade 7c to pay grade 7a which determines the salaries of all *Meister*. Increases are provided for all officials of the Police with the exception of officers of General's rank and in the case of the Police Presidents of Berlin, Hamburg and Wien, whose salaries are fixed.

The **Besoldungsdienstalter** (Pay Seniority) determines the number of increases to which an official is entitled and starts from the day of his regular appointment. In the initial appointment it is identical with the length of service. On receiving promotion, however, the official changes his pay grade, but does not as a rule retain his previous pay seniority. In order to prevent an excessive increase in salary the *Besoldungsdienstalter*—while not entirely cancelled—is curtailed to a pay seniority ranging from 4–8 years, varying with each individual pay grade. For example, a *Polizeiinspektor* (pay grade 4c1) with a pay seniority of more than 6 years, drawing annually RM 3,600—if promoted to *Polizeioberinspektor* (pay grade 4b1) would not be entitled to a salary of RM 5,200—but owing to his new *Besoldungsdienstalter* will, in all likelihood, get paid according to column " after 2 years " and receive RM 4,400—a year.

Supernumerary (*ausserplanmässig*) personnel, candidates with previous civil service experience, and candidates discharged from military or labour service, get some credit for time served before receiving their regular appointment and their *Besoldungsdienstalter* is raised accordingly.

A **Wohnungsgeldzuschuss** (Lodging Allowance) is given to every Police official holding a regular appointment. The amount is determined by the following factors : size of the town where the official is employed and resides, pay grade, marital status and number of children. It ranges from RM 96 to RM 2,520 per annum. Unmarried Police officials without dependents receive a lower lodging allowance than is prescribed for their actual pay grade. Unmarried *Wachtmeister* belonging to the *Kasernierte Polizei* (Barrack Police) are not entitled to a lodging allowance, but become eligible as soon as they get married or are transferred to the *Einzeldienst* (Single Service).

*Örtliche Sonderzuschläge* (Special Local Allowances) amounting to 3 per cent. of the basic pay, are given to Police officials residing in places where economic conditions warrant such an allowance.

**Kinderzuschläge** (Allowances for children) are paid for all children of Police officials regardless of whether they are legitimate, adopted, foster, or illegitimate. The rates are RM 20 monthly for each child and an additional allowance (*Kinderbeihilfe*) of RM 10 is paid from the third child onward. *Kinderzuschläge* are only paid until the

---

* According to more recent information, German Police pay has been newly regulated and simplified by the RFSS u.Ch.d.Dt.Pol. under a decree of 9 Nov 1944, which states that the Police is to receive payment according to the **Einsatz Wehrmachtgebührnisgesetz** (EWGG—law governing Pay of the Armed Forces in the Field), as published in the *Reichsgesetzblatt* I, page 290. This decree states as reason for the new pay regulation that nowadays the employment of the Police is identical with that of the Armed Forces, and that their pay should therefore be the same. This fact is of particular interest because it confirms the military nature of all branches of the German Police, which has so frequently been stressed in the preceding chapters of this book.

In detail the new pay regulation decrees that all members of the German Police are to receive uniform Army Pay (*Wehrsold*), food and supplies, quarters, clothing, field allowances (*Frontzulage*) and medical care. The new regulation applies to all those members of the German Police who are entitled to receive the *SS-Soldbuch* (see paragraph 184), with the exception of the non-uniformed officials of the *staatliche Polizeiverwaltungs- und Wirtschaftsdienst*, the *Freiwilligen der Deutschen Polizei*, members of the *Schutzmannschaften* and of the *Hilfspolizei*, who will continue to receive pay according to previously existing regulations.

The details, pay charts and tariff classes of the new pay regulation would by far exceed the scope of this study. Any such tables, when actually used, will however include references to the previous tariff classes and the latter are therefore still useful. Furthermore, as was stated in the introduction to this chapter, the main purpose of this study of German Police pay is to enable the Allied occupation authorities to familiarise themselves with the regular and pre-war levels of pay, and it is of little practical importance to know the last minute privileges which the Nazi Government has decided to grant to Police personnel.

# ANNUAL BASIC PAY CHART
### in Reichsmark

| Pay Grade | Tariff Classes | Starting Pay | After 2 Years | After 4 Years | After 6 Years | After 8 Years | After 10 Years | After 12 Years | After 14 Years | After 16 Years | After 18 Years | After 20 Years | Tariff Classes |
|---|---|---|---|---|---|---|---|---|---|---|---|---|---|
| | II | | | | | | | | | | | | |
| | | 8 400 | 9 500 | 10 600 | 11 600 | 12 600 | | | | | | | II |
| 1b | III | 6 200 | 7 000 | 7 800 | 8 500 | 9 200 | 9 900 | 10 600 | | | | | |
| 2a | | 4 800 | 5 400 | 6 000 | 6 600 | 7 100 | 7 600 | 8 100 | 8 600 | 9 100 | 9 700 | | |
| 2b | | 7 000 | 7 500 | 8 000 | 8 500 | 8 900 | 9 300 | 9 700 | | | | | |
| 2c1 | | 4 800 | 5 300 | 5 800 | 6 200 | 6 600 | 7 000 | 7 400 | 7 800 | 8 200 | 8 500 | 8 800 | |
| 2c2 | | 4 800 | 5 200 | 5 600 | 6 000 | 6 400 | 6 800 | 7 200 | 7 500 | 7 800 | 8 100 | 8 400 | |
| 2d | IV | 4 800 | 5 200 | 5 600 | 6 000 | 6 400 | 6 800 | 7 200 | 7 500 | 7 800 | | | III |
| 2e | | 3 600 | 4 000 | 4 400 | 4 800 | 5 200 | 5 600 | 6 000 | 6 400 | 6 800 | 7 100 | 7 400 | |
| 3a | | 3 600 | 4 000 | 4 400 | 4 800 | 5 200 | 5 600 | 6 000 | 6 300 | 6 600 | 6 900 | 7 200 | |
| 3b | | 4 800 | 5 200 | 5 600 | 6 000 | 6 400 | 6 700 | 7 000 | | | | | |
| 3c | | 3 600 | 3 900 | 4 200 | 4 500 | 4 800 | 5 100 | 5 400 | 5 700 | 6 000 | 6 300 | 6 600 | |
| 4a | | 3 000 | 3 300 | 3 600 | 3 900 | 4 200 | 4 450 | 4 700 | 4 950 | 5 200 | 5 500 | 5 800 | |
| 4b1 | | 4 100 | 4 400 | 4 700 | 4 950 | 5 200 | 5 500 | 5 800 | | | | | |
| 4b2 | | 3 000 | 3 250 | 3 500 | 3 750 | 4 000 | 4 250 | 4 500 | 4 750 | 5 000 | 5 250 | 5 500 | |
| 4c1 | | 2 800 | 3 100 | 3 400 | 3 600 | 3 900 | 4 150 | 4 400 | 4 650 | 4 900 | 5 100 | 5 300 | |
| 4c2 | | 2 800 | 3 050 | 3 300 | 3 550 | 3 800 | 4 000 | 4 200 | 4 400 | 4 600 | 4 800 | 5 000 | |
| 4d | | 2 800 | 3 050 | 3 300 | 3 550 | 3 800 | 4 000 | 4 200 | | | | | IV |
| 4e | | 2 800 | 3 000 | 3 200 | 3 400 | 3 600 | 3 800 | 4 000 | 4 150 | 4 300 | 4 450 | 4 600 | |
| 4f | V | 2 400 | 2 600 | 2 800 | 3 000 | 3 200 | 3 400 | 3 600 | 3 800 | 4 000 | 4 200 | | |
| 5a | | 2 800 | 3 000 | 3 200 | 3 400 | 3 600 | 3 750 | 3 900 | 4 050 | 4 200 | | | |
| 5b | | 2 300 | 2 550 | 2 800 | 3 000 | 3 200 | 3 400 | 3 600 | 3 800 | 4 000 | 4 200 | | |
| 6 | | 2 400 | 2 600 | 2 750 | 2 900 | 3 050 | 3 200 | 3 350 | 3 500 | 3 600 | | | |
| 7a | | 2 350 | 2 500 | 2 650 | 2 800 | 2 950 | 3 100 | 3 200 | 3 300 | 3 400 | 3 500 | | |
| 7b | | 2 400 | 2 550 | 2 700 | 2 800 | 2 900 | 3 000 | 3 100 | 3 200 | | | | |
| 7c | | 2 000 | 2 100 | 2 200 | 2 300 | 2 400 | 2 500 | 2 600 | 2 700 | 2 800 | 2 900 | 3 000 | |
| 8a | | 2 100 | 2 190 | 2 280 | 2 370 | 2 460 | 2 550 | 2 640 | 2 720 | 2 800 | | | V |
| 9 | | 1 800 | 1 900 | 2 000 | 2 100 | 2 200 | 2 300 | 2 400 | 2 500 | 2 600 | 2 700 | | |
| 10a | | 1 750 | 1 840 | 1 930 | 2 020 | 2 110 | 2 200 | 2 290 | 2 380 | 2 470 | 2 550 | | |
| 10b | VI | 1 700 | 1 790 | 1 880 | 1 970 | 2 060 | 2 150 | 2 240 | 2 320 | 2 400 | | | |
| 11 | | 1 600 | 1 690 | 1 780 | 1 870 | 1 960 | 2 050 | 2 140 | 2 220 | 2 300 | | | |

child reaches the age of 16 unless it continues schooling or does not earn more than RM 40 a month. In these cases the allowance continues until the 24th year. In special cases where the child is incapacitated or education is interrupted by Reich labour service or military service, the allowance may be continued after the age of 24.

### 165. Payments other than salary

The salary of a Police official may also be augmented by various other payments. These may be reimbursements for expenses incurred, allowances for service outside Germany, payments to relieve temporary distress, and so forth. Some of the more usual ones are listed below :

The *Gehaltszuschuss (Vergütungszuschuss)* of RM 15 monthly is paid to Executive Police officials drawing less than RM 7,000 per annum. It is supposed to cover local fares, but its payment is continued even though the recipient enters the Armed Forces. Payment is stopped only on retirement.

The *Protektoratszulage* is paid to German Police officials and civilian employees (*Gefolgschafts-mitglieder*) serving away from home in Bohemia or Moravia. It ranges from RM 30 to RM 90 monthly for married personnel. Single persons receive about one half of that amount, but never less than RM 20.

The *Aufbauzulage* is the same as the *Protektorats-zulage*, but applies to the incorporated Eastern territories with the exception of the city of Danzig.

The *Gouvernementszulage* is paid to officials in Poland (*General-Gouvernement*) with monthly rates for married personnel ranging from RM 90 to RM 170, single persons receiving about half as much.

The *Bewegungsgeld* is an allowance of RM 30 monthly, paid to *Kripo* officials to cover expenses incurred while conducting investigations (visits to restaurants, bars, etc.).

A set of detailed regulations coming under the heading of *Reise- und Umzugskostenvergütung*, determine the reimbursements to be paid in case of official travel, or of expenses caused by the transfer of officials.

Temporary employment at another office requiring the official to leave his place of residence entitles him to a *Beschäftigungsvergütung*.

The *Dienstbereitschaftsgeld*—RM 20 per month— is paid to all officials of the *Gestapo*, the GFP (Secret Field Police), but not to any other *Sipo* or *Orpo* personnel. The *Gestapo* also has an allowance known as " *Gefahrengeld* " (danger money), amounting according to reports to RM 20 to 30 a month. It is not clear whether such an allowance is identical with the *Dienstbereitschafts-geld* or not. These extra allowances cause many candidates to choose *Gestapo* rather than *Kripo* service.

*Dienstkleidungszuschüsse* are given to officers who have to provide their own uniforms. Non-commissioned officers have their uniforms issued to them.

The *Einsatzbesoldung* entitles Police Reservists recalled to active Police duty to the same pay, allowances, etc. as regular Police officials. While serving with the police field forces, however, officials continue to draw their peacetime salary.

*Gehaltsvorschüsse* (Salary Advances) up to the amount of one month's pay may be granted to Police officials who need money due to extra-ordinary circumstances (serious sickness or death of a member of the family, wedding, etc.). Members of the *Sipo* may be given advances to buy SS uniforms. The advanced money must be repaid within 1, or at most, 2 years.

A similar purpose is served by the granting of *Beihilfen* (financial aid) in cases of death, illness, dental treatment or childbirth. The Police will contribute 60 to 80 per cent. of the expenses incurred.

*Unterstützung* (relief) is granted to persons finding themselves in a desperate economic situation through no fault of their own. Widows and orphans of Police officials may be granted a *fortlaufende Unterstützung* (continuous relief).

As a rule Police officials have no claim to a cash reimbursement for medical treatment since they are entitled to *freie Heilfürsorge* (free medical care). This includes :

Doctor's care
Supplying of medicines, artificial limbs, orthopædic and other aids
Dental care
Specialist's care
Hospital care
Recuperation in Police homes
Recuperation in spas and health centres
Special arrangements in cases of injury received in the course of duty.

To provide special medical care for German Police personnel a number of Police hospitals and health centres have been established. The most important ones of these are :

*Staatskrankenhaus der Polizei* in Berlin
*Polizeikrankenhaus* München
*Polizeikrankenhaus* Wien
*Polizeikuranstalt* Badgastein
*Polizeikuranstalt* Biesenthal
*Polizeikuranstalt* Karlsbad
*Polizeikuranstalt* Freienwalde
*Polizeikuranstalt* Lauterbach
*Polizeikuranstalt* Rohitsch-Sauerbrunn
*Polizeikuranstalt* Wiesbaden
*Polizeikuranstalt* Bad Rötenbach/Schwarzwald
*Polizeikuranstalt* Haus Gutenberg in Bad Schwalbach

It should be noted that the designation *Polizei-kurlazarett* has recently been substituted by official decree for *Polizeikuranstalt* ; in practice this sub-stitution may not in all cases have been made.

Members of a Police official's family receive a limited amount of free medical care.

In case of special *Urlaub* (leave) over extended periods of time all payments to Police officials are stopped. This does not of course apply to ordinary leaves, *Erholungsurlaub* (sick leave) or *Urlaub aus besonderen Gründen* (compassionate leave). During wartime ordinary leave is limited to 21 days a year at the most. If special leave is granted in the interest of the public, e.g. for special studies, etc., the official may draw his full salary for the first 6 weeks, and half his salary up to the 6th month.

### 166. Pay for Candidates for the Police and Officials on Probation

Before receiving a regular appointment candidates for positions in the German Police must, as a rule, undergo a period of preparation which may in turn lead to a supernumerary appointment (*ausserplanmässig*). During the initial stage of this employment pay depends on the candidate's occupation before joining the Police.

*Zivilanwärter* (Civilian Candidates) receive *Unterhaltszuschüsse* (living allowances) ranging from RM 110 to RM 140 monthly in the case of single persons, the amount depending on age and type of service. Rates for married personnel range from RM 125 to RM 200. No reduction under the *Gehaltskürzungsverordnung* (see para. 167) is made from these rates, but neither are provisions made for an increase in pay. Civilian candidates are entitled to an allowance for children, but not to any special local allowance. Preferential treatment is accorded to old Party members, not only in the distribution of jobs, but actually in the amount given in pay and allowances.

*Versorgungsanwärter* (candidates with previous civil service experience) receive payments (*Vergütungen*) amounting to 75 to 100 per cent. of what would be their starting salary if they held a regular appointment. They are entitled to all the additional allowances of a regular official, but are subject to the regulations concerning reduction of salary (see next para.).

Pay regulations for *Militäranwärter* (candidates who have served in the Armed Forces) are dealt with in a separate law of 20 Jan, 1940, but no detailed information concerning it is available.

The appointment to *ausserplanmässiger Polizeibeamter* represents the last step before receiving a regular appointment. This status is in many respects similar to that of the *planmässige* official, except that the position to which the man is appointed is not an integral part of the establishment, in which he works. The salary of supernumeraries—*Diäten*—is regulated in Annexe 5 of the *Reichsbesoldungsgesetz* and leads gradually up to the pay of a regular official.

The following is a pay table for Candidates for the Police and officials on probation :—

| Officials who, if holding a regular appointment, would be placed in pay grade :— | In the first 2 years (*Versorgungsanwärter* in the first year) :— | After 2 years (*Versorgungsanwärter* after the first year) :— | In the fifth year (*Versorgungsanwärter* in the fourth year) :— |
| --- | --- | --- | --- |
| 2c2 | 3 400 RM.—per year | 3 950 RM.—per year | 4 400 RM.—per year |
| 3a (2e), 3c and the *Kriminalkommissare* from 4c1 | 2 500 ,, ,, ,, | 2 900 ,, ,, ,, | 3 300 ,, ,, ,, |
| 4c2 and 4e | 2 000 ,, ,, ,, | 2 300 ,, ,, ,, | 2 600 ,, ,, ,, |
| 4f, 5, 7a, and 7b | 1 700 ,, ,, ,, | 1 950 ,, ,, ,, | 2 160 ,, ,, ,, |
| 7c, 8b | 1 500 ,, ,, ,, | 1 680 ,, ,, ,, | 1 850 ,, ,, ,, |
| 8b | 1 350 ,, ,, ,, | 1 430 ,, ,, ,, | 1 500 ,, ,, ,, |
| 9 and 10 | 1 300 ,, ,, ,, | 1 400 ,, ,, ,, | 1 500 ,, ,, ,, |
| 11 | 1 250 ,, ,, ,, | 1 300 ,, ,, ,, | 1 400 ,, ,, ,, |

The *Diätendienstalter* (*Diäten* seniority) corresponds to the *Besoldungsdienstalter* of the regular officials and starts with the appointment to *ausserplanmässiger Beamter*. *Versorgungsanwärter* receive credit for the amount of time they have spent in preparatory training whenever this exceeds one year. Service before the age of 20 always counts as preparatory service, even if the official concerned has been given a supernumerary appointment before reaching that age.

The amount of *Diäten* received by *Versorgungsanwärter* in their 5th year of service—civilian candidates in their 6th—equals the initial salary of a regular official in the corresponding pay grade. All supernumerary officials are entitled to a lodging allowance ; married personnel receive a higher allowance than unmarried.

### 167. Taxes and Reductions in Pay

The pay of civil servants is considerably reduced by three laws published in 1931 (1, 2 and 3 *Gehaltskürzungsverordnung*). These affect the basic pay, the lodging allowance and the special local allowance. Allowances for children and reimbursements of any kind are not subject to reduction. The aggregate reductions are approximately as follows :—

23 per cent. if monthly pay exceeds RM 1,000
22 ,, ,, ,, ,, ,, ,, RM 500
21 ,, ,, ,, ,, ,, ,, RM 250
19 ,, ,, ,, ,, ,, ,, RM 135
13 ,, ,, ,, ,, ,, ,, RM 125

The principal tax to be paid by the Police officials is the *Lohnsteuer* (tax on earnings) which serves as a basis for fixing the amount to be paid in *Kriegssteuer* (war tax) and *Wehrsteuer* (Defence tax).

The *Bürgersteuer* (citizen tax) is collected by the municipality and varies throughout the Reich. Very roughly it can be said that, depending on the size of his income, a German Police official has to part with from 15 per cent. to 45 per cent. of his earnings in reductions and taxes.

### 168. Pensions and Payments in case of Death

According to the *Deutsches Beamtengesetz* (German Civil Service Law) the retirement age is 65, but this provision has been suspended for the duration of the war. Retirement before that age is possible in cases where a disability prevents the official from performing his duties. *Beamte auf Lebenszeit* (Officials appointed for life) could, before the war, apply to retire after reaching the age of 62, without having to prove any disability.

A *Ruhegehalt* (pension) is paid to all civil servants from the day of their retirement until death. This is a fixed proportion of their *ruhegehaltsfähige Dienstbezüge* (that part of the salary which is recognised as the basis for the pension, i.e. basic pay as last drawn, plus lodging allowance and special local allowance, if any). The amount of the pension is determined by the length of *ruhegehaltsfähige Dienstzeit* (pensionable service) ; credit is given for every year of service which the official has completed after his 27th birthday. The years of service before that date count only if he was with the Armed Forces, in the Reich labour service, in the Executive service of the Police

114

(*Vollzugsdienst*), or if he was a full-time employee of the NSDAP.

The pension received by a civil servant after having served at least 1 year of *ruhegehaltsfähige Dienstzeit* amounts to 35 per cent. of his *ruhegehaltsfähige Dienstbezüge*, but must be not less than approximately RM 100 per month. This percentage rises proportionately with the length of service until, upon completion of his 65th year, an official is entitled to the maximum pension, i.e. 75 per cent. of his *ruhegehaltsfähige Dienstbezüge*. Where retirement has been caused by an accident suffered in the line of duty, however, the official is entitled to the pension according to his age and rank plus 20 per cent. In such cases, however, 66⅔ per cent. of the *ruhegehaltsfähige Dienstbezüge* is the minimum and 80 per cent. the maximum pension to be paid to the disabled official.

In case of the death of an official his heirs receive not only his salary for the month in which death occurred but also his salary for the 3 following months, as a lump sum. Further provision is made by the Civil Service Law for the widow and the orphans of a deceased civil servant in the form of *Witwengeld* (Widow's pension), which amounts to 60 per cent. of the pension which her husband drew or would have drawn if he had retired on the day of his death. The *Witwengeld* must not exceed 45 per cent. of the *ruhegehaltfähige Dienstbezüge* of the deceased. Children receive one fifth of the *Witwengeld*, or one third if the wife is dead. Regulations differ somewhat in cases where death occurred through an accident in the line of duty.

## 169. Der Kameradschaftsbund der Deutschen Polizei

The German habit of forming a *Verein* (association) whenever more than two people get together, found its expression in the numerous *Polizeivereinigungen* which had sprung up in pre-HITLER Germany. HIMMLER, eager to supervise the private lives of his followers, dissolved them all and authorised the *Kameradschaftsbund der Deutschen Polizei* as the sole association for Police officials. As a benevolent association, it has many features in common with similar organisations of civil servants throughout the world. The *Kameradschaftsbund* provides group insurance, maintains holiday homes, assists in emergencies and in general looks after the welfare of its members' and their families. What makes it, however, different from other organisations is the fact that in the words of HIMMLER's decree the *Kameradschaftsbund* " . . . is called upon to help . . . in carrying out ideological indoctrination within the Police, in close co-operation with the SS." *SS-OSBF, Oberstleutnant d. Schupo Dr.* ZWINGENBERG, chief of the *Gruppe Weltanschauliche Erziehung* in the *Kommandoamt* of the *Hauptamt Orpo*, was on 30 September, 1944 also appointed Chief of *Abteilung Weltanschauliche Erziehung* in the *Kameradschaftsbund*. It has, therefore, been found advisable to list the offices, holiday homes and schools of the *Kameradschaftsbund* as potential C.I. targets.

(i) *Geschäftsstellen* (Regional Offices) of the *Kameradschaftsbund* :—

| | | |
|---|---|---|
| Anhalt | ... ... | Dessau, Funkplatz 6 |
| Baden | ... ... | Karlsruhe i.B., Karlsstrasse 15 |
| Bayern | ... ... | München 2, Neuhauser Strasse 7/4 |
| Brandenburg | ... | Berlin W 35, Lützowstrasse 73 |
| Braunschweig/Gau Hannover... | ... | Braunschweig, Bohlweg 27 |
| Bremen | ... .·. | Bremen, Langenstrasse 19 |
| Danzig-Westpreussen | | Danzig, Kassubischer Markt 17/20 |
| Donau | ... ... | Wien 66, Müllnergasse 4 |
| Generalgouvernement | | Krakau, Aussenring 29 |
| Gross-Berlin | ... | Berlin W 35, Woyrschstrasse 32 |
| Hamburg/Gau Nordmark | | Hamburg 1, Beim Strohause 68 |
| Hessen | ... ... | Darmstadt, Hügelstrasse 31/33 |
| Hessen-Nassau | ... | Frankfurt a.M., Grüneburgweg 86 |
| Inn-Drau ... | ... | Wien 66, Müllnergasse 4 |
| Mecklenburg | ... | Bad Doberan, Rathaus Z.18 |
| Niederschlesien | ... | Berlin W 35, Lützowstrasse 73 |
| Oberschlesien | ... | Kattowitz-West, Moltkestrasse 65, 5.Pol.-Rev. |
| Oldenburg ... | ... | Oldenburg i.O., von-Finkh-Strasse 26 |
| Ostpreussen | ... | Königsberg (Pr.), Hans-Sagan-Str. 26 |
| Pommern ... | ... | Stettin, Moltkestrasse 9 |
| Reichsprotektorat Böhmen/Mähren | | Prag 19, General-Roettig-Strasse 14 |
| Rheinland ... | ... | Düsseldorf, Mackensenplatz, Pol.-Präsidium, Room 116-119a |
| Sachsen | ... ... | Dresden-A.1, König-Johann-Strasse 14 |
| Sachsen | ... ... | Weimar, Wörthstrasse 23 |
| Sudetenland | ... | Reichenberg, Liliengasse 4 |
| Thüringen ... | ... | Weimar, Bernhardstrasse 22 |
| Wartheland... | ... | Lobau, Kreis Posen, Hindenburgstr. 11 |
| Westfalen ... | ... | Bottrop, Osterfelderstrasse 30 |
| Westmark ... | ... | Saarbrücken, Cäcilienstrasse 9 |
| Wien | ... ... | Wien 66, Müllnergasse 4 |
| Würtemberg | ... | Stuttgart, Keplerstrasse 22 |

(ii) *Erholungsheime* (Sanatoria) of the *Kameradschaftsbund* :—

Polizeihaus " Kurmark," Potsdam-Babelsberg, Strasse der SA 33/34
Polizei-Erholungsheim " Erlenbruck " bei Hinterzarten im Schwarzwald
Polizei-Erholungsheim, " Haus am Fleesensee," Malchow, Mecklenburg
Polizei-Erholungsheim " Friedrich-Jeckeln-Hütte," Königskrug bei Braunlage (Harz)
Bootshaus Stettin (Ortsgruppe Stettin des Kameradschaftsbundes der Deutschen Polizei, Stettin, Moltkestrasse 9)
Polizei-Schi- und Wanderhütte Schöneck bei Plauen i. Vogtland
Polizei-Erholungsheim " Spitzingsee," Post Neuhaus bei Schliersee (Bayern)
Polizei-Erholungsheim " Heiligendamm," Bad Doberan
Polizei-Erholungsheim " Klausen " bei Bad Gleichenberg (Steiermark)
Ruderheim der Ortsgruppe Kalisch des Kameradschaftsbundes der Deutschen Polizei in Kalisch (Warthegau)

Ruderheim der Ortsgruppe Konin des Kameradschaftsbundes der Deutschen Polizei in Konin (Warthegau)

Polizei-Erholungsheim Zakopane (Bez. Krakau)

(iii) The following schools are owned by the Reich but administered by the *Kameradschaftsbund* under the direct supervision of the *Hauptamt Orpo* :—

Polizeischule für Schiausbildung " Kitzbühel," Kitzbühel, Nordtirol

Polizeischule für Schiausbildung " Am Oberjoch," Post Hindelang (Allgäu)

Polizeischule für Schiausbildung " Am Sudelfeld," Post Bayrischzell (Oberbayern)

Polizeischule für Schiausbildung " Witow " bei Zakopane (Gen.-Gouv.)

Polizeischule für Hochgebirgsausbildung Innsbruck

Höhenstützpunkt " Wiesbadener Hütte," Post Obervermunt/Silvrettadorf über Parthenen (Montafon).

## 170. Police ranks

The following table of comparative ranks is necessarily a compromise. In some instances it is virtually impossible to equate existing designations. This table has been based exclusively on German documents comparing various ranks and official careers. These enemy sources themselves frequently disagree or are unclear on the subjects of ranks of various services and their equivalents. For example, a number of police ranks is not equated by the Germans with one specific *Wehrmacht* or SS rank, but rather to a range of ranks depending on length of service.

British and U.S. equivalents have been entered as accurately as possible, but rather on a basis of grades than of functions.

Approximate equivalents are listed in the following order :

1. *Waffen-SS*
2. German Army
3. U.S. Army
4. British Army

Key to abbreviations :—

| | |
|---|---|
| *SchP* | *Schutzpolizei* |
| *Gend* | *Gendarmerie* |
| *FSchP* | *Feuerschutzpolizei* |
| *TN* | *Technische Nothilfe* |
| *LSPol* | *Luftschutzpolizei* |
| *VerwB* | *Verwaltungsbeamter* |
| *TechnB* | *Technischer Beamter* |
| *GemP* | *Gemeindepolizei* |
| *PolitB* | *Politischer Beamter* |

| Police Ranks | Approximate Equivalents |
|---|---|
| *Anwärter d. SchP. (Gend., TN.)* | *SS-Anwärter Grenadier*, etc. Pvt. Pte. |
| *Unterwachtmeister d. SchP. (Gend., TN., LSPol.)* | *SS-Mann Obergrenadier*, etc. Senior Private Senior Private |
| *Rottwachtmeister d. SchP. (Gend., FSchP., TN., LSPol.)* | *SS-Sturmmann, SS-Rottenführer Gefreiter, Ober-, Stabs-, Hauptgefr.* Pfc. |
| *Amtsgehilfe auf Probe (VerwB.)* | L/Cpl. |
| *Wachtmeister d. SchP. (Gend., FSchP., TN., LSPol.)* *Amtsgehilfe (VerwB.)* *Botenmeister (VerwB.)* *Hausmeister (VerwB.)* *Polizeiassistenten-anwärter (VerwB.)* *Kriminalassistenten-anwärter (Sipo)* | *SS-Unterscharführer Unteroffizier* Cpl. Cpl. |
| *Oberwachtmeister d. SchP. (Gend., FSchP., T.N., LSPol.)* *Ausserplanmässiger Polizeiassistant (VerwB.)* *Ausserplanmässiger Kriminalassistent (Sipo)* | *SS-Scharführer Unterfeldwebel* Sgt. L/Sjt. |
| *Revieroberwachtmeister d. SchP.* *Bezirksoberwachtmeister d. Gend. (FSchP.)* *Zugwachtmeister d. SchP. (Gend., TN., LSPol.)* *Polizeigefängnisoberwacht-meister (VerwB.)* *Betriebsassistent (VerwB.)* *Oberbotenmeister (VerwB.)* *Vollziehungsbeamter (VerwB.)* *Kanzleiassistent (VerwB.)* *Polizeiassistent (VerwB.)* *Regierungsassistent (VerwB.)* *Verwaltungsassistent (VerwB.)* *Kriminalassistent (Sipo)* *Technischer Assistent (Sipo)* | *SS-Oberscharführer Feldwebel* S/Sgt. Sjt. |
| *Kompaniehauptwacht-meister d. SchP. (mot. Gend.)* *Bereitschaftshauptwacht-meister d. TN. (LSPol.)* *Polizeigefängnishaupt-wachtmeister (VerwB.)* *Kriminaloberassistent (Sipo)* | *SS-Hauptscharführer Oberfeldwebel* T/Sgt. S/Sjt. |
| *Hauptwachtmeister d. SchP. (Gend., FSchP., TN., LSPol.)* | *SS-Stabsscharführer Hauptfeldwebel* First Sgt. C.S.M. |
| *Meister d. SchP.\* (Gend., FSchP., TN.)* *Polizeigefängnisver-walter\* (VerwB.)* *Polizeisekretär (VerwB.)* *Kanzleisekretär\* (VerwB.)* *Regierungssekretär\* (VerwB.)* *Kriminalsekretär\* (Sipo)* *Technischer Sekretär bei der Gestapo\** | *SS-Sturmscharführer Stabsfeldwebel* M/Sgt. R.S.M. |

*Note :* The SS equivalent of ranks marked with an asterisk (\*) can be either *SS-Sturmscharführer* or *SS-Untersturmführer.*

| Police Ranks | Approximate Equivalents |
|---|---|
| *Leutnant d. SchP. (FSchP.)* | *SS-Untersturmführer* Leutnant |
| *Revierleutnant d. SchP.* | 2nd Lt. |
| *Bezirksleutnant d. Gend. (FSchP.)* | 2nd Lt. |
| *Zugführer d. TN. (LSPol.)* | |
| *Veterinär d. Pol.* | |
| *Assistenzarzt d. Pol.* | |
| *Waffenmeister d. Pol. (TechnB.)* | |
| *Polizeigefängnisober- verwalter (VerwB.)* | |
| *Polizeiobersekretär (VerwB.)* | |
| *Regierungsobersekretär (VerwB.)* | |
| *Probeassessor (VerwB.)* | |
| *Polizeiinspektoranwärter (VerwB.)* | |
| *Ausserplanmässiger Polizeiinspektor (VerwB.)* | |
| *Kriminalobersekretär (Sipo)* | |
| *Hilfskriminalkommissar (Sipo)* | |
| *Kriminalkommissar zur Probedienstleistung (Sipo)* | |
| *Technischer Obersekretär b.d. Gestapo* | |
| *Kriminalbezirkssekretär (GemP.)* | |
| *Oberleutnant d. SchP. (Gend., FSchP.)* | *SS-Obersturmführer* Oberleutnant |
| *Revieroberleutnant d. SchP.* | 1st Lt. |
| *Bezirksoberleutnant d. Gend. (FSchP.)* | Lt. |
| *Oberzugführer d. TN. (LSPol.)* | |
| *Oberveterinär d. Pol.* | |
| *Oberarzt d. Pol.* | |
| *Waffenrevisor d. Pol. (TechnB.)* | |
| *Ministerialregistrator (VerwB.)* | |
| *Polizeiinspektor (VerwB.)* | |
| *Regierungsinspektor (VerwB.)* | |
| *Regierungsreferendar (VerwB.)* | |
| *Assessor (VerwB.)* | |
| *Polizeirentmeister (VerwB.)* | |
| *Kriminalinspektor (Sipo)* | |
| *Kriminalkommissar (Sipo)* | |
| *Technischer Polizei- inspektor beim Gestapo- amt* | |
| *Technischer Oberinspektor (Sipo)* | |
| *Hauptmann d. SchP. (Gend., FSchP.)* | *SS-Hauptsturmführer* Hauptmann |
| *Revierhauptmann d. SchP.* | Capt. |
| *Bezirkshauptmann d. Gend. (FSchP.)* | Capt. |

| Police Ranks | Approximate Equivalents |
|---|---|
| *Bereitschaftsführer d. TN. (LSPol.)* | |
| *Stabsveterinär d. Pol.* | |
| *Stabsarzt d. Pol.* | |
| *Stabsapotheker d. Pol.* | |
| *Waffenoberrevisor d. Pol. (TechnB.)* | |
| *Technischer Verwaltungs- amtmann d. Pol.* | |
| *Polizeirechnungsrevisor (VerwB.)* | |
| *Oberbuchhalter (VerwB.)* | |
| *Bezirksrevisor (VerwB.)* | |
| *Polizeioberrentmeister (VerwB.)* | |
| *Polizeioberinspektor (VerwB.)* | |
| *Regierungsoberinspektor (VerwB.)* | |
| *Regierungsassessor (VerwB.)* | |
| *Polizeiamtmann (VerwB.)* | |
| *Regierungsamtmann (VerwB.)* | |
| *Polizeirat (VerwB.)* | |
| *Kriminalkommissar* with more than three years' service *(Sipo)* | |
| *Kriminalrat (Sipo)* | |
| *Technischer Amtmann (Sipo)* | |
| *Kriminaloberinspektor (GemP.)* | |
| *Major d. SchP. (Gend., FSchP.)* | *SS-Sturmbannführer* Major |
| *Abteilungsführer d. TN. (LSPol.)* | Major |
| *Oberstabsveterinär d. Pol.* | Major |
| *Oberstabsarzt d. Pol.* | |
| *Oberstabsapotheker d. Pol.* | |
| *Landrentmeister (VerwB.)* | |
| *Polizeiamtmann* with more than three years' service *(VerwB.)* | |
| *Polizeirat* with more than three years' ser- vice *(VerwB.)* | |
| *Polizeioberamtmann (VerwB.)* | |
| *Amtsrat (VerwB.)* | |
| *Regierungsrat (VerwB.)* | |
| *Regierungs- und Kassen- rat*, Berlin *(VerwB.)* | |
| *Kriminalrat* with more than three years' ser- vice *(Sipo)* | |
| *Kriminaldirektor (Sipo)* | |
| *Regierungs- und Kriminalrat (Sipo)* | |
| *Oberstleutnant d. SchP. (Gend., FSchP.)* | *SS-Obersturmbann- führer* |
| *Oberabteilungsführer d. TN. (LSPol.)* | Oberstleutnant |
| *Oberfeldveterinär d. Pol.* | Lt.-Col. |
| *Oberfeldarzt d. Pol.* | Lt.-Col. |
| *Oberregierungsrat (VerwB.)* | |
| *Polizeidirektor (VerwB.)* | |
| *Oberregierungs- und Kriminalrat (Sipo)* | |

| Police Ranks | Approximate Equivalents | Police Ranks | Approximate Equivalents |
|---|---|---|---|
| *Oberst d. SchP. (Gend., FSchP.)* | *SS-Standartenführer, SS-Oberf.* | *Generalarzt d. Pol.* | *Generalmajor* <br> Brig. Gen. <br> Maj. Gen. |
| *Landesführer d. TN.* | *Oberst* | *Polizeipräsident* in Berlin, Hamburg, Wien *(VerwB.)* | |
| *Oberstveterinär d. Pol.* | Col. | *Ministerialdirigent (VerwB.)* | |
| *Oberstarzt d. Pol.* | Col., Brigadier | *Generalleutnant d. Pol.* | *SS-Gruppenführer* <br> *Generalleutnant* <br> Maj. Gen. <br> Lt. Gen. |
| *Regierungsdirektor (VerwB.)* | | *Ministerialdirektor (VerwB.)* | |
| *Ministerialrat (VerwB.)* | | *General d. Pol.* | *SS-Obergruppenführer* <br> *General* <br> Lt. Gen. <br> Gen. |
| *Polizeivizepräsident,* Berlin *(VerwB.)* | | *Staatssekretär (PolitB.)* | |
| *Polizeipräsident (VerwB.)* | | *Generaloberst d. Pol.* | *SS-Oberst-Gruppenführer* <br> *Generaloberst.* <br> Gen. |
| *Regierungs- und Kriminaldirektor (Sipo)* | | *Reichsminister (PolitB.)* | Field-Marshal |
| *Reichskriminaldirektor (Sipo)* | | | |

*Note :* Appointments of *Verwaltungsbeamte* from *Polizeipräsident (Polizeidirektor)* up are largely governed by political considerations.

| Police Ranks | Approximate Equivalents |
|---|---|
| *Generalmajor d. Pol.* | *SS-Brigadeführer* |

The following tables of ranks are arranged according to branches.

## (1) Vollzugsbeamte der Orpo
### (Executive Officials of the Regular Police)

| | Schupo (and Wasser-schutzpolizei | Gendarmerie | Feuerschutzpolizei | Teno (and Luftschutzpolizei) |
|---|---|---|---|---|
| **Männer :** | Anwärter | Anwärter | | Anwärter |
| | Unterwachtmeister | Unterwachtmeister | | Unterwachtmeister |
| | Rottwachtmeister | Rottwachtmeister | Rottwachtmeister | Rottwachtmeister |
| **Unterführer :** | Wachtmeister | Wachtmeister | Wachtmeister | Wachtmeister **Obervormann |
| | Oberwachtmeister | Oberwachtmeister | Oberwachtmeister | Oberwachtmeister **Scharführer |
| | Revieroberwachtmeister | Bezirksoberwacht-meister | Bezirksoberwacht-meister | |
| | Zugwachtmeister | Zugwachtmeister | Zugwachtmeister | Zugwachtmeister **Oberscharführer |
| | Kompaniehaupt-wachtmeister | Kompaniehaupt-wachtmeister | | Bereitschaftshauptwacht-meister**Hauptscharführer |
| | Hauptwachtmeister | Hauptwachtmeister | Hauptwachtmeister | Hauptwachtmeister **Haupt-scharführer |
| | Meister | Meister | Meister | Meister **Stabsscharführer |
| **Kriegs-offiziere :** | Revierleutnant *Polizeiobermeister | Bezirksleutnant | Bezirksleutnant | |
| | Revieroberleutnant *Polizeiinspektor | Bezirksoberleutnant *Gend. Inspektor | Bezirksoberleutnant | |
| | Revierhauptmann *Polizeioberinspektor *Polizeikommissar | Bezirkshauptmann *Gend. Oberinspektor | Bezirkshauptmann | |
| **Offiziere :** | Leutnant | | Leutnant | Zugführer **Kamerad-schaftsführer, **Gemeinschaftsführer |
| | Oberleutnant | Oberleutnant | Oberleutnant | Oberzugsführer **Gefolg-schaftsführer |
| | Hauptmann | Hauptmann | Hauptmann | Bereitschaftsführer |
| | Major | Major | Major | Abteilungsführer **Haupt-bereitschaftsführer |
| | Oberstleutnant | Oberstleutnant | Oberstleutnant | Oberabteilungsführer Bezirksführer |
| | Oberst | Oberst | Oberst | Landesführer |
| **Generale** | | Generalmajor d. Pol. | | |
| | | Generalleutnant d. Pol. | | |
| | | General d. Pol. | | |
| | | Generaloberst d. Pol. | | |

* Obsolete rank in the former *Gemeindepolizei* which might, however, still be encountered.

** Indicates former ranks of the TN.

## (2) Ärzte und Technische Beamte der Orpo
### (Medical Officers and Technicians of the Regular Police)

| Polizeiärzte | Polizeiveterinäre | Polizeiapotheker | Waffenmeister |
|---|---|---|---|
| Assistenzarzt | Veterinär | | Waffenmeister |
| Oberarzt | Oberveterinär | | Waffenrevisor |
| Stabsarzt | Stabsveterinär | Stabsapotheker | Waffenoberrevisor |
| Oberstabsarzt | Oberstabsveterinär | Oberstabsapotheker | Technischer Verwaltungsamt-mann d. Pol. |
| Oberfeldarzt | Oberfeldveterinär | | |
| Oberstarzt | Oberstveterinär | | |
| Generalarzt | | | |

| (3) **Verwaltungsbeamte**<br>(Administrative Officials) | | (4) **Vollzugsbeamte der Sipo**<br>(Executive Officials of the Security Police) |
|---|---|---|
| General Careers : | Special Careers : | |
| *EINFACHER DIENST* | | |
| *Amtsgehilfe auf Probe*<br>*Amtsgehilfe*<br>*Botenmeister*<br>*Hausmeister*<br>*Vollziehungsbeamter*<br>*Oberbotenmeister* | *Polizeigefängnisoberwachtmeister*<br>*Polizeigefängnishauptwachtmeister* | (Ranks marked with an asterisk (*), though obsolete, may still be encountered. They refer to the former *Gemeindekriminalpolizei*). |
| | | *EINFACHER DIENST*<br>(*Unterführerlaufbahn*) |
| *MITTLERER DIENST* | | |
| *Polizeiassistentenanwärter*<br>*Apl. Polizeiassistent*<br>*Polizeiassistent*<br>*Kanzleiassistent*<br>*Regierungsassistent*<br>*Verwaltungsassistent*<br>*Betriebassistent* | | *Kriminalassistentenanwärter*<br>*Apl. Kriminalassistent*<br>*Kriminalassistent*<br>*Kriminaloberassistent* |
| | | *MITTLERER DIENST*<br>(*Führerlaufbahn des mittleren Dienstes*) |
| *Polizeisekretär*<br>*Kanzleisekretär*<br>*Regierungssekretär*<br>*Polizeiobersekretär*<br>*Regierungsobersekretär* | *Polizeigefängnisverwalter*<br><br>*Polizeigefängnisoberverwalter* | *Kriminalsekretär*<br>*Kriminalbezirkssekretär**<br>*Kriminalobersekretär*<br>*Kriminalinspektor* |
| *GEHOBENER (MITTLERER) DIENST* | | *GEHOBENER (MITTLERER) DIENST*<br>(*Führerlaufbahn des gehobenen Dienstes*) |
| *Polizeiinspektoranwärter*<br>*Apl. Polizeiinspektor*<br>*Polizeiinspektor*<br>*Regierungsinspektor*<br>*Polizeioberinspektor*<br>*Regierungsoberinspektor*<br>*Polizeiamtmann*<br>*Regierungsamtmann*<br>*Polizeirat*<br>*Polizeioberamtmann*<br>*Amtsrat* | *Polizeirentmeister*<br>*Ministerialregistrator*<br>*Polizeirechnungsrevisor*<br><br>*Oberbuchhalter*<br>*Bezirksrevisor*<br>*Polizeioberrentmeister*<br>*Landrentmeister*<br>*Reg.- und Kassenrat, Berlin* | *Hilfskriminalkommissar*<br>*Kriminalkommissar zur Probe*<br><br>*Kriminalkommissar*<br><br>*Kriminaloberinspektor**<br><br>*Kriminalrat*<br><br>*Kriminaldirektor* |
| *HÖHERER (LEITENDER) DIENST* | | *HÖHERER (LEITENDER) DIENST*<br>(*Führerlaufbahn des leitenden Dienstes*) |
| *Probeassessor*<br>*Assessor*<br>*Regierungsreferendar*<br>*Regierungsassessor*<br>*Regierungsrat*<br>*Oberregierungsrat*<br>*Regierungsdirektor*<br>*Ministerialrat*<br>*Ministerialdirigent*<br><br>*Ministerialdirektor* | *Polizeidirektor*<br>*Polizeipräsident*<br>*Polizeivizepräsident, Berlin*<br>*Polizeipräsident, Berlin, Hamburg, Wien*<br><br>*Staatssekretär*<br>*Reichsminister* | *Regierungs- und Kriminalrat*<br>*Oberregierungs- und Kriminalrat*<br>*Regierungs- und Kriminaldirektor*<br>*Reichskriminaldirektor* |

(5) **Technische Beamte der Sipo**
(Technical Officials of the Security Police)

*Technischer Assistent*
*Technischer Sekretär bei der Gestapo*
*Technischer Obersekretär bei der Gestapo*
*Technischer Polizeiinspektor beim Gestapoamt*
*Technischer Oberinspektor*
*Technischer Amtmann*

# PART EIGHT
## UNIFORMS AND PERSONAL DOCUMENTS
### A. UNIFORMS

#### 171. General Introduction

The militarised nature of the German Police and the employment of some of its branches in the field and in occupied territories make it essential for intelligence purposes at the present stage of operations, that Police uniforms, ranks and insignia should be immediately identifiable. After the cessation of hostilities many, especially the Nazi-created branches of the German Police, will of course no longer be encountered in uniform, but even then the possession of any part of a Police Uniform may be valuable evidence of a man's identity.

It would be impossible to give details of all the variations which arise from the German's characteristic love of colourful costume, and this section aims merely at presenting the typical uniforms of the various Police branches as worn on duty in Germany, in occupied territory and in the field.

It must be pointed out that changes in style of uniform have occurred at frequent intervals and are still taking place. Sometimes our information on these changes is incomplete, sometimes wartime conditions, such as shortage of material and supply difficulties, make it unlikely that officially decreed changes are in practice carried out immediately—if at all—by all the personnel involved. Furthermore, in many instances units of one branch of the Police are employed by other branches; auxiliaries are added to the existing forces to take care of urgent wartime needs; and Party formations are called upon to assist regular Police personnel. All these factors tend to blur the lines of demarcation between the uniforms of the various branches.

For quick reference a comparative table of Police Uniforms is included at the end of this section. Annexe M gives illustrations of a representative selection of uniforms, ranks, insignia and emblems, as follows :—

*Figures :*
```
 1-  5  Shoulder straps of Generals and officials
         of equivalent rank
 6-  7  Collar patches of Generals and officials
         of equivalent rank
 8- 19  Shoulder straps of Officers
20- 22  Collar patches of Officers
23- 40  Shoulder straps of officials of Officers'
         rank
41- 45  Collar patches of officials of Officers' rank
46- 59  Shoulder straps of Senior NCO's and
         officials of equivalent rank
60- 68  Collar patches of Senior NCO's and
         officials of equivalent rank
69- 76  Service insignia
77- 81  Cap Badges
82- 86  Sleeve Insignia
87- 94  Types of Uniforms
95-101  Greatcoats and tunics
102-110 Headgear
111-122 Photographs of the Orpo in action, etc.
123-124 Photographs of Sipo and SD
```

#### 172. Terms used in connection with Uniforms

The following general notes and definitions will save repetition in the text.

##### (i) Rank and Arm of Service

All rank insignia are worn on the *Schulterklappen* (shoulder straps) and/or collar patches ;

certain other details of uniform vary from one group of ranks to another.

Generals and officials of generals' rank have gold embroidered cap badges, and gold edging or piping to the crown of their caps. Officers and officials of officer rank wear aluminium piping.

The word for " collar patch " is *Kragenspiegel* or *Litze*; the *Einheitslitzen* (standardised collar patches), described as being identical with the *Schupo* collar patches (light green on a grey background), were decreed in 1943 for all branches of the *Orpo* who previously wore collar patches peculiar to their branch. The old type may, however, still be encountered.

In January 1943 HIMMLER decreed that all Police collar patches were to be replaced by SS symbols of rank. Although this decree was cancelled two months later, high ranking officers are still found wearing SS collar patches.

##### (ii) Headgear

The following types of cap are in use :—

| | |
|---|---|
| *Tschako* | Shako. |
| *Schirmmütze* | Peaked cap |
| *Hausmütze, Feldmütze,* | Cloth cap, similar to a |
| *Schiffchen* | field or forage cap |
| *Bergmütze* | Peaked mountain cap (ski cap) |

The *Kokade* or *Tschakonationale* (National Cockade), in black, white and red, representing the national colours of Germany, is worn on every German Police cap. When worn on the Shako it is oblong in shape and framed with a silver cord. On the *Schirmmütze* and on the *Hausmütze* it is round, and has no corded edge.

In theory the above listed headgear was superseded in 1943 by the issue of a new design. Regulations describe this uniform headgear as a *Feldmütze mit Schirm* (peaked forage cap) which is to replace the various former caps of personnel stationed outside Germany. Discarded caps in the old styles are to be returned and will be re-issued to members of the Police inside Germany, where they will probably be worn until supplies are exhausted.

The new caps, which may have already been distributed, are described as being of a grey-green colour (navy-blue for the *Wasserschutzpolizei*). The badge on this new type of headgear is the police version of the *Hoheitsabzeichen* (National Emblem ; see below) worked in light grey together with the national cockade. This *Hoheitsabzeichen* will be worn on the cap by every branch of the *Orpo*, including the *Wasserschutzpolizei*, who formerly wore a different type of *Hoheitsabzeichen*, in gold.

##### (iii) Badges

In addition to the *Kokade* on the cap, the following *Abzeichen* (badges) require description. There are numerous versions of the *Hoheitsabzeichen* (National Emblem) which is worn in some form on nearly all German uniforms, but the basic design is a spread eagle over a *Hakenkreuz* (swastika). The police version of the *Hoheitsabzeichen** is a spread eagle over a swastika enclosed in a wreath of oak leaves. This design is worn by all members of the German Police on the cap and/or on the sleeve of the tunic. The

---

\* In the discussion of uniforms below, the term *Hoheitsabzeichen* should be taken as referring to the **Police version unless** otherwise stated.

cap badge is made of aluminium, and on the sleeve the emblem is embroidered in the distinguishing colour of the branch (see below), e.g. orange for the *Gendarmerie* or yellow for the *Wasserschutzpolizei*; generals wear gold emblems.

The *Altkämpferwinkel* (old Party Members' chevron), or *Ehrenwinkel* (Chevron of Honour), in silver and black, is worn on the right upper sleeve of the tunic by those who, on or before 30 Jan 33, were members of the NSDAP or one of its Formations or Affiliated Organisations.

*Runen* are traditional Teutonic emblems—originally runic letters—which are worn as flashes. The Police wear the well known *Sigrune* (⚡⚡); all Police who are members of the *Allgemeine SS* wear a *Sigrune* in white on green below the left breast pocket of the tunic.

### (iv) Distinguishing Colours

Each branch of the German Police has a distinguishing colour, which appears in the collar patches, in the shoulder strap background, in the piping of the cap and tunic and in the sleeve insignia; for example grey is the distinguishing colour for the *Verwaltungspolizei*.

### 173. Uniforms of the Schutzpolizei

The uniform of the *Schutzpolizei* consists of a green greatcoat with a brown collar, a green tunic with brown collar and cuffs, and green breeches or trousers. The officers' tunic and greatcoat are piped and faced in the colour of the branch of service.

On duty a green *Tschako* (for Other Ranks: U.S., Enlisted Men), or the *Schirmmütze* (for NCOs, usually) are worn; they bear the national cockade and the *Hoheitsabzeichen*, and have black leather chin straps. In summer a white uniform and a white cover to the *Schirmmütze* may be worn. The green *Hausmütze* (field or forage cap), worn by ORs, has the *Hoheitsabzeichen* woven in white rayon on a black background; this cap is usually worn in Police offices, but may also be seen in the field or at training camps.

The headgear for officers is distinguished from that for ORs by the white metal used in the *Hoheitsabzeichen*, the national cockade and the chin strap cords. Generals wear gold *Hoheitsabzeichen* and chin strap cords.

Steel helmets, of a dark grey-green, are worn in the field, on guard duty, and on raiding parties; they have the swastika on the right side and the *Hoheitsabzeichen* on the left.

Belts and Sam Brownes are of black leather with white metal buckles.

The distinguishing colour of the *Schupo des Reiches* is light green, that of the *Schupo der Gemeinden* wine red. Although by a HIMMLER decree of 1943 the colour of the collar patches of both the *Schupo des Reiches* and the *Schupo der Gemeinden* were made uniform, i.e. light green, the shoulder straps still provide a ready means for distinguishing the two services. It is also possible that the old wine red colour may still be encountered on the collar patches of the *Schupo der Gemeinden*.

Officers' shoulder straps are of aluminium cord on a background of the appropriate colour of branch of service; generals' epaulettes are in gold cords and braid.

*Hoheitsabzeichen* are worn on the left upper sleeve; for ORs they are light green or wine red according to the branch of service, and for officers they are in silver thread (or gold for generals).

The officers' greatcoat has a white metal belt, and the buttons of both tunic and greatcoat are

also white metal. Generals have gold belt and buttons. Shoes or riding boots are black.

Field units, i.e. Police battalions and regiments, wear a field grey uniform similar to that of the *Wehrmacht* but distinguished by dark green collar and cuffs, white metal buttons, and the *Hoheitsabzeichen* on the left sleeve, and on the cap or helmet. The number of the regiment appears on the middle of the shoulder straps.

The distinguishing colour of the *Verkehrspolizei* is bright red; it occurs in the collar patches and in the pipings of the cap, shoulder straps and tunic, as well as in the *Hoheitsabzeichen* on the left sleeve. The uniform itself is the same as that of the ordinary *Schutzpolizei*, except that the belt is brown.

In summer a white jacket may be worn with black trousers, brown shirt and black tie, and the *Schirmmütze* worn on duty has a white linen cover. The *Schirmmütze* has a brown band and a black chin strap (aluminium for officers). NCOs wear a gold metal *Hoheitsabzeichen* on the cap; the officers' *Hoheitsabzeichen* is in gold.

### 174. Gendarmerie Uniform

The uniform of the ordinary *Gendarmerie* is the same as that of the *Schutzpolizei*, except that the collar of the greatcoat, and the collar and cuffs of the tunic, are a much lighter shade of brown.

The distinguishing colour of the *Gendarmerie* is orange. Shoulder straps and collar patches are light brown with orange piping. Sleeve insignia showing the name of the *Bezirk* (area) in orange on a green background are worn on the left upper sleeve. Belts and Sam Brownes are brown.

The motorised *Gendarmerie* wear the same uniform, but their collars and cuffs are dark brown like the *Schutzpolizei*. They wear a light brown crash helmet, with a white metal *Hoheitsabzeichen*. Armlets, worn above the cuff, are in brown with the aluminium embroidered inscription "*Motorisierte Gendarmerie.*" The Bezirk is not indicated.

Personnel of the *Hochgebirgsgendarmerie* (Gendarmerie in the Alpine regions) wear the same green uniform, also with orange piping. The trousers are worn tucked inside the boots. The green *Bergmütze* (Ski cap) carries the national cockade and the *Hoheitsabzeichen* and has orange piping. The *Hoheitsabzeichen*, in orange, appears on the left sleeve, but the *Bezirk* is not indicated.

The officers' uniform has the same light brown collar and cuffs as that of the other ranks, but the shoulder straps and collar patches are of aluminium on an orange background.

The *Schirmmütze* for all types of *Gendarmerie* is green, and has a band of the light brown colour peculiar to the *Gendarmerie*. It bears the national cockade, aluminium *Hoheitsabzeichen* and orange piping. The green Shako has a light brown peak and crown, with national cockade, *Hoheitsabzeichen* and chin straps in aluminium.

### 175. Wasserschutzpolizei Uniform

The SW uniform consists of a navy-blue greatcoat, a reefer type (double-breasted) jacket and trousers. Blue denim trousers are often worn on duty.

The distinguishing colour of the *Wasserschutzpolizei* is yellow, appearing in the shoulder straps, and in the piping around the cuffs of the jacket.

Either the navy-blue *Schirmmütze* or the *Schiffchen* (field or forage cap) may be worn. The *Schirmmütze* for ORs bears the *Hoheitsabzeichen* in yellow metal, and has a black chin strap; the officers' *Schirmmütze* has gold chin strap cords (regardless of rank), the national cockade, and the

*Hoheitsabzeichen* in gold. The ORs *Schiffchen* also bears the yellow *Hoheitsabzeichen*, and has yellow piping on the crown. In summer a white linen cover may be worn over the crown of the *Schirmmütze*.

The *Hoheitsabzeichen*, embroidered in yellow (gold for officers), on a dark blue background, is worn on the left upper sleeve of the jacket, but not on the greatcoat. Similarly, only the cuffs of the jacket, not of the greatcoat, are piped with yellow.

Leather belts and boots are black.

All buttons of officers' uniform are gold. Officers wear a white metal belt with the greatcoat. The *Marine Küstenpolizei* wear the same uniform as the *Wasserschutzpolizei*, plus a yellow *Wehrmachtsbinde* (Armed Forces armband).

## 176. Feuerschutzpolizei Uniform

The old *Feuerwehren* wore black uniforms with carmine as their distinguishing colour in the piping of the tunic and around the cuffs. This uniform is probably still worn to some extent in wartime, although minor changes may have taken place as many of the former members of the *Feuerwehren* were incorporated into the *Feuerschutzpolizei*.

Officially the *Feuerschutzpolizei* wear the regular green uniform of the *Orpo*, but to what extent this uniform is actually worn—other than on special occasions calling for ceremonial dress—is not definitely known.

The *Schirmmütze*, bearing the national cockade and the *Hoheitsabzeichen* in white metal, is worn off duty. On duty a black steel helmet is worn, showing the *Hoheitsabzeichen* on the left side, and the *SS Rune* on the right.

The distinguishing colour is still carmine and appears in the piping of the *Schirmmütze*, in the background of shoulder and collar patches, and in the *Hoheitsabzeichen* worn on the left upper sleeve of the tunic.

Leather belts, Sam Brownes and boots are black.

The old black uniform will probably still be encountered. The green tunic and greatcoat are piped with carmine and the shoulder straps and collar patches have a carmine background. The tunic has black collar and cuffs, and the greatcoat a black collar. Black helmets are worn for service uniform, showing the *Hoheitsabzeichen* on the left side, and, if the wearer is a member of the SS, the *SS Rune* (flash) on the right. The *Hoheitsabzeichen*, embroidered in silver, is worn on the left sleeve of the tunic.

## 177. Luftschutzpolizei Uniform

As a result of its close connection with the *Luftwaffe* this branch of the *Orpo* wears the grey-blue Air Force uniform. Green armbands are worn on the left lower sleeve of the tunic, inscribed " *Sicherheits- u. Hilfsdienst* " in white lettering. The *Hoheitsabzeichen* appears on the left upper sleeve. The collar patches are the same as those worn by the *Schutzpolizei*, with the exception of the *Aufsichtsbeamten* (inspectors) who may still be found wearing the SS collar patches authorised in the obsolete HIMMLER decree (see EDS/G/8, Basic Handbook of the SS, for SS insignia). Black steel helmets are worn on duty.

The *Teno* furnishes the nucleus of the *Luftschutzpolizei*, i.e. the former *Sicherheits- und Hilfsdienst* ; such former TN men are reported to wear the grey-blue uniforms of the *Luftschutzpolizei*, probably with *Teno* emblems and insignia.

On the other hand, the *Instandsetzungsdienst* (*JD*—Repair, Demolition and Rescue Services)

although now part of the *Luftschutzpolizei* wear *Technische Nothilfe* uniform (see below).

## 178. Technische Nothilfe Uniform

The former TN uniform was blue, but this is practically obsolete, and *Teno* personnel now wear various types of uniform, depending on their employment. In the field *Teno* personnel wear the usual *Wehrmacht* field grey uniform, which is however in the style of the *Waffen-SS*, less the skull-and-crossbones on the cap. When actually attached to the Armed Forces TN personnel may, in addition, wear the *Wehrmachtsbinde* on the left upper sleeve, with the Gothic lettering " *Deutsche Wehrmacht* " woven in black thread on yellow linen.

When assigned for duty with the *Schutzpolizei*, TN personnel wear the green uniform of the *Schupo* with TN badges of rank.

The distinguishing colour of the TN is black and appears on the collar patches and shoulder straps. The collar patches of the tunic and greatcoat are bordered with a silver and black twisted cord, and bear the TN emblem, a white cogwheel on a black background. The badge on the left upper sleeve is the SS, not the Police, version of the *Hoheitsabzeichen*.

Within the TN, the four branches of the TN are distinguished by subsidiary service colours, blue for the *Technischer Dienst* (*TD*—Technical Service Branch), red for the *Luftschutzdienst* (*LD*—Air Raid Protection Service Branch), orange-yellow for the *Bereitschaftsdienst* (*BD*—Emergency Service), and green for the *Allgemeine Dienst* (*AD*—General Service).

The *SS-Hoheitsabzeichen* and the national cockade are worn on the *Feldmütze* and *Schirmmütze* ; officers wear silver chin strap cords on the cap. The cogwheel emblem is worn on the black collar patch above the TN symbol of rank. TN officers who are members of the SS may wear the SS flash on their collar patches in combination with the TN emblem.

Officers of the highest rank, i.e. *Chef der TN*, *Stellvertretender Chef der TN*, and *Landesführer* wear gold collar patches and shoulder straps, with gold cogwheel emblems. Their collar patches have a red background.

## 179. Hilfspolizei Uniforms

The *Landwacht* and the *Stadtwacht* acting as *Hilfspolizisten* (Auxiliary Police) may wear civilian clothes, with wide white armbands bearing the inscriptions " *Landwacht* " or " *Stadtwacht* " to differentiate them from other Auxiliary Police personnel, who wear armbands inscribed " *Hilfspolizei.*"

Members of the *Hilfspolizei* drawn from the ranks of the para-military formations may wear their own uniform when on duty.

## 180. Verwaltungspolizei Uniform

The greatcoat, tunic and breeches of the *Verwaltungspolizei* (Administrative Police) are of the same green as those of the *Schutzpolizei*. The collar of the greatcoat and the collar and cuffs of the tunic are brown. The distinguishing colour (*Hauptfarbe*) is grey, but in addition this branch wears a secondary colour (*Nebenfarbe*) which is red, though according to latest reports the *Nebenfarbe* has been abolished. The primary colour, grey, appears on the collar patches, in the background of the shoulder straps, and in the tunic and cap pipings of all officials regardless of branch. The secondary colour, red, appears in the upper backings of the shoulder straps.

The officers' uniform is identical with that of the *Schutzpolizei*, but the cuffs and tunics are piped with grey. The cap bears the *Hoheitsabzeichen*, an aluminium chin strap, and grey piping. The *Hoheitsabzeichen* is also worn on the left sleeve.

### 181. Uniforms of the Sicherheitspolizei and the SD

Members of the *Kripo*, *Gestapo* and SD usually wear plain clothes ; uniform is however worn on some occasions, the same type being worn by all three branches. It was originally black, underlining the close relationship of these branches with the *Allgemeine-SS*, but since the beginning of the war the black has, for ordinary duty, been replaced by field grey, of a shade considerably lighter than that of the army uniform. Brown shirts are usually worn with both the black and the grey uniform.

The black uniform of the SD is similar to the traditional black uniform worn by the *Allgemeine-SS*, with only one silver and black epaulette or shoulder strap, on the right. SS insignia of rank are worn on the collar patches. The *Schirmmütze* carries the skull-and-crossbones emblem instead of the national cockade. The caps of the other ranks have a black chin strap, those of the officers have silver cords, and generals wear gold cords.

The right collar patch of the grey tunic is plain black and the left collar patch bears the rank insignia for both other ranks and officers. (For SS insignia see EDS/G/8, Basic Handbook of the SS). Officers of high rank, i.e. from *SS-Standartenführer* upward, wear rank insignia on both collar patches. The shoulder straps of all ranks are black, and are identical with those worn by the *Waffen-SS* with field service uniform (in *Wehrmacht* field grey).

The swastika armband of the *Allgemeine-SS* is normally no longer worn by the *Sipo* and the SD, but may possibly still appear on ceremonial occasions. The silver and black *Altkämpferwinkel* (Old Party Members' chevron) is worn on the right upper sleeve of both black and grey uniforms.

Personnel of the *Sicherheitsdienst* may wear a black diamond patch, with the inscription " SD " in Gothic letters, over the left cuff. When worn on the black uniform, this is framed with a silver cord, but on the grey uniform the cord is usually omitted.

The caps carry the *Hoheitsabzeichen* and the skull-and-crossbones emblem of the SS, and have black chin strap cords for the other ranks and silver cords for all officers.

A decree of 28 Aug 1944 states that foreign auxiliaries from the East employed by the *Dienststellen* of the *Sipo* as *Wachmänner* guarding foreign prisoners are to wear field grey without any insignia. An armband inscribed with the words " *Im Dienst der Sicherheitspolizei* " (in the service of the Security Police) is to be worn on the right upper sleeve.

### Note.—Police Clothing and Supply Depots

It may be of interest to know the supply headquarters through which uniforms and similar equipment are furnished to the Police. The following list, dated February 1944, shows the various *Polizei-Bekleidungs- und Beschaffungsämter* (Police Clothing and Supply depots) and the areas they supply :—

*Pol. Bekleidungsamt* in Königsberg supplies :

| | |
|---|---|
| Königsberg | Elbing |
| Tilsit | Danzig |
| Memel | Gotenhafen |

*Pol. Bekleidungsamt* in Posen supplies :

| | |
|---|---|
| Posen | Thorn |
| Bromberg | Litzmannstadt |
| Graudenz | Leslau |

*Pol.-Bekleidungsamt* in Breslau supplies :

| | |
|---|---|
| Breslau | Kattowitz |
| Waldenburg | Sosnowitz |
| Oppeln | Troppau |
| Gleiwitz | |

*Pol.-Beschaffungsamt* in Berlin supplies :

| | |
|---|---|
| Berlin | Lübeck |
| Potsdam | Cuxhaven |
| Frankfurt/Oder | Hamburg |
| Stettin | Bremen |
| Wesermünde | Dessau |
| Magdeburg | Wilhelmshaven |
| Flensburg | Rostock |
| Kiel | |

*Pol.-Beschaffungsamt* in Weimar supplies :

| | |
|---|---|
| Halle | Kassel |
| Weissenfels | Weimar |
| Erfurt | Leipzig |
| Suhl | Braunschweig |
| Hannover | |

*Pol.-Beschaffungsamt* in Köln supplies :

| | |
|---|---|
| Münster | Wuppertal |
| Recklinghausen | Gladbach-Rheydt |
| Bochum | Köln |
| Dortmund | Aachen |
| Hamm | Darmstadt |
| Hanau | Offenbach |
| Wiesbaden | Giessen |
| Frankfurt a.M. | Mainz |
| Koblenz | Worms |
| Düsseldorf | Saarbrücken |
| Duisburg | Metz |
| Oberhausen | Luxemburg |
| Essen | |

*Pol.-Beschaffungsamt* in Nürnberg supplies :

| | |
|---|---|
| München | Karlsruhe |
| Nürnberg | Mannheim |
| Hof | Freiburg |
| Augsburg | Konstanz |
| Würzburg | Innsbruck |
| Regensburg | Strassburg |
| Ludwigshafen | Mülhausen |
| Stuttgart | |

*Pol.-Beschaffungsamt* in Prag supplies :

| | |
|---|---|
| Dresden | Aussig |
| Chemnitz | Brüx |
| Plauen | Karlsbad |
| Zwickau | BdO Prag |
| Reichenberg | |

*Pol.-Beschaffungsamt* in Wien supplies :

| | |
|---|---|
| Wien | Klagenfurt |
| Graz | Leoben |
| Linz | Marburg (Drau) |
| Salzburg | |

# B. PERSONAL DOCUMENTS OF THE GERMAN POLICE

## 182. General Introduction

In Germany, more than in any other country, the number and variety of documents issued to every member of the community is vast and constantly changing ; it also seems characteristic of the German that he can rarely be persuaded to part with a paper even though it has long lost its validity or its usefulness. The present discussion of German Police documents, while detailed, is by no means exhaustive.

The actual documents found on a member of the German Police will not necessarily accord with the specifications of the latest regulations ; normal administrative tardiness or war conditions may be grounds for the continued use, or revived validity of documents officially obsolete.

A decree of the RSHA, dated December, 1943, ordered all *Dienstausweise* (identity documents) expiring in December, 1943, to be provisionally extended until 30 April, 1944. Shortage of raw materials was given as the official reason for this regulation. Possibly the validity of such identity papers was extended even beyond that date and a new issue avoided. The details of the extension were to be indicated by a typewritten validity endorsement giving date, official signature and stamp of the responsible headquarters.

The main details of the personal identity papers carried by members of the German Police and its auxiliaries will remain more or less constant, and the typical examples discussed here may be of value as a guide to the exploitation of documents of the same or a similar type.

The detailed page by page descriptions in this section should be read in conjunction with the illustrations in Annexe M, to which reference is made throughout ; Annexe M is intended not only to show the outward appearance of these documents, but also to indicate the most important pages from which information may be extracted.

The present value, to the interrogator, of a knowledge of these documents, need not be stressed ; the future value lies in the probability that under an Allied occupation, when the German policeman has discarded his uniform, he may well be reluctant to part with his personal documents, and by retaining them, may preserve evidence of his past background and present degree of reliability.

The study of personal documents has a certain additional value, in the light it sheds on the administrative system of various organisations, the maintenance of their records and the routine followed in their personnel administration.

## 183. The Soldbuch

The *Soldbuch zugleich Personalausweis* (Paybook and Identity Document ; see Annexe M, Fig. 125) is by far the most important personal document carried by members of the German Police ; it is not only a paybook but also an extensive record of the bearer's personal history and career in the Police ; it therefore contains a great deal of information of intelligence value, such as identifications of field units, replacement units, schools, training courses, and locations of any units to which the bearer may have belonged. In addition a list of decorations received in the course of service may throw a helpful light on the bearer's enthusiasm in the Nazi cause. A *Soldbuch* is issued to every member of the German Police, and must be carried at all times for purposes of identification.

Entries in the paybook are made, dated and initialled, by the Administrative officer or the clerk of the bearer's unit, and German administrative thoroughness may be counted on to be of great assistance in the exploitation of such documents.

The *Soldbuch* has a green paper cover, showing the Police Badge (*Hoheitsabzeichen*) and the heading in black. It has 36 pages, containing the following details :—

|  | | |
|---|---|---|
| Page | 1— | Personal data<br>Rank and promotion<br>Bearer's unit (usually the replacement unit) and identity number as shown on his identity disc |
| Page | 2— | Personal data and description<br>Police stamp and details of the unit which issued the *Soldbuch*<br>Signature of the commanding officer of the issuing unit |
| Pages | 3–4— | Endorsement of any alterations, signed by the unit commander |
| Page | 5— | Personal data, next of kin, etc. |
| Page | 6— | Police authority of the holder's home station<br>Police replacement unit and location<br>Police field unit |
| Page | 7— | Awards and medals |
| Page | 8— | Combat experience (information listed on this page includes all units in which the owner may have served) |
| Pages | 9–34— | Information includes allotments of pay, allowances, medical treatment (also inoculations, vaccinations, etc.), any alterations and amendments, and details of furlough |
| Pages | 35–36— | Instructions on the handling, use and authority of the *Soldbuch*. |

## 184. SS-Soldbuch used by the Police

In June, 1944, the *Reichsführer-SS und Chef der Deutschen Polizei* decreed that the *Soldbuch* of the *Waffen-SS* was to be introduced as the official identity document for all members of the *Orpo*. In effect the book finally issued to the police was a variation of the *Waffen-SS Soldbuch* (see Fig. 126) adjusted for use by the *Orpo*. The decree specified that the members of the following Police branches were to be furnished with the new paybook :—

*Schutzpolizei*, including *Wasserschutzpolizei*

*Gendarmerie*

*Feuerschutzpolizei*

Administrative officials of the *Ordnungspolizei* (*Polizeiverwaltungsbeamte*)

*Polizeireserve*, including the *Luftschutzpolizei*

All full-time professional leaders of the *Teno* who are part of the establishment of the *Orpo*

Field units of the *Teno*

All full-time professional leaders of the *Freiwillige Feuerwehren* who are on the establishment of the *Orpo*

*Hilfspolizisten*

*Freiwillige der deutschen Polizei* (literally German Police Volunteers ; it is not clear to what class this refers)

Units of the *Schutzmannschaften*

For all these classes of official the *SS-Soldbuch* should replace the green Police *Soldbuch* (in the case of the *Luftschutzpolizei* it takes the place of the *Luftschutzdienstbuch*); it supersedes all older forms of identity paper. It is not, however, known to what extent this order has been carried out in practice and both the old and the new type of *Soldbuch* may still be found. Superseded *Soldbücher* which have been withdrawn are kept on permanent file among the owners' personnel records.

A special difference between the old Police *Soldbuch* and the new (SS) type is that the latter carries a paybook number and the man's registration number (*Wehrnummer*) on page 1. The paybook number should always be the same as that appearing on the bearer's identity disc. The *SS-Soldbuch* has a grey paper cover showing the SS emblem and the heading in black. The photograph and signature of bearer are on the inside of the cover page. The contents are similar to those of the green Police *Soldbuch*, except that Police replacement and field units and locations are noted on page 4 instead of on page 6 as in the green *Orpo Soldbuch*. Details of the contents of the *SS-Soldbuch* are as follows :—

Page 1—Number of *Soldbuch*
Name, rank and promotion
Bearer's unit and identity number as shown on the holder's identity disc
*Wehrnummer*

Page 2—Personal data, description and signature of bearer
Official stamp and details of unit by which the *SS-Soldbuch* was issued
Signature of the commanding officer of the above unit

Page 3—Endorsement of any alterations signed by the unit commander

Page 4—Home, Replacement and Field units and locations

Page 5—Awards and medals

Page 6—Combat experience

Page 7—Personal data, next of kin, etc.

Pages 8–14—Clothing record

Pages 15–18—Arms and equipment issued to bearer

Pages 19–21—Medical record (including inoculations, vaccinations, etc.)

Pages 22–23—Hospital record

Pages 24–25—Record of valuables in possession while in hospital

Pages 26–28—Dental record

Page 29—General entries

Pages 30–34—Pay entries

Pages 35–38—Leave or furlough

Pages 39–40—Instructions on handling, use and authority of *SS-Soldbuch*

### 185. Polizeidienstpass (Police Service Record)

In contrast to the *Soldbuch* the *Dienstpass* (see Fig. 127) is **not** an identity paper. It is approximately equivalent to the *Wehrpass* (German Army Service record). The *Dienstpass* is never carried on the person except when the holder is being transferred from one unit or headquarters to another. On arrival at his new unit he immediately hands in the *Dienstpass* which is then kept and maintained by the Personnel office for the duration of his service with that unit or head-

quarters. Only on final dismissal or retirement from Police service is the *Dienstpass* handed over to its owner for permanent retention.

It should be noted that the *Dienstpass* contains a number of details concerning the holder which will not normally be found in the *Soldbuch*, notably details concerning membership of the Nazi Party, its formations or affiliated organisations, including original date of joining and membership serial number. The intelligence value of such information is obvious; moreover it can be assumed that *Dienstpässe* have been provided for the majority of German Police personnel in spite of the fact that the previously mentioned decree introducing the SS type paybook, also abolished the *Polizeidienstpass*. However, these service records after their withdrawal were filed with each man's personal records at the various police headquarters and units.

The *Polizei Dienstpass* has a green paper cover, with the printed matter and the Police Badge in darker green. The fact that this is not an identity paper is indicated on the cover in green and red print. It contains 32 pages on green anti-erasure paper, each page watermarked with the police *Hoheitsabzeichen*.

The inside cover page contains instructions on the handling, use and authority of the *Dienstpass*. Other details are as follows :—

Page 1—Creed of the German Policeman

Page 2—Blank

Page 3—Personal data and description
Stamp of the *Polizeibehörde* and signature of the commanding officer

Pages 4–6—Personal data, including educational background and professional qualifications

Page 7—Details of membership of the NSDAP and all other Nazi party formations, giving date of joining and membership number
Party decorations held
Bearer's SS rank

Page 8—Details of *Reichsarbeits- und Wehrdienst* (Reich labour service and army service)

Pages 9–13—Record of police service with details of transfers, promotion and employment

Page 14—Training courses attended

Page 15—Combat experience

Pages 16–18—Medical record

Page 19—Decorations

Pages 20–27—Other entries

Pages 28–31—Endorsement of any alterations signed by the unit commander

Page 32—Details of retirement or discharge from service

### 186. Personal Documents of the Firefighting Services

The **Dienstausweis—Feuerwehrdienst** (Official Service Pass—Firefighting Services ; see Fig. 128) is a four-page folding pass of grey-blue glazed linen. The front cover bears the Police *Hoheitsabzeichen* and the name, rank and address of the bearer in black print. This pass may be carried by both *Feuerschutzpolizei* and *Feuerwehren*. Page 2 contains personal data, shows the issuing office with official stamp and signature, and defines the authority conferred by the pass ; page 3

126

contains validity endorsements (entered periodically); photograph and signature of bearer are on page 4.

The **Mitglieds-Ausweis Freiw. Feuerwehr** (Membership Card—Voluntary Fire Brigade; see Fig. 129) was probably used by the Fire Brigades at the time when they did not constitute a uniform and standardised organisation, but were merely local units. The card illustrated is therefore merely a sample of one of many existing types and probably has little more authority than the membership card of any ordinary association. This particular sample is printed in black on pink paper. The front cover shows the name and the date of birth of the bearer, the two inside pages (pages 2 and 3) are divided into squares, provided for monthly membership stamps. Page 4 is blank. *Mitgliedsausweise* of this kind may still be found as a concession to local traditions, but officially they have been superseded by the preceding service pass (see Fig. 128) since the *Freiw. Feuerwehren* have either been taken over by or attached to the *Feuerschutzpolizei*.

The **Ausweis der Feuerwehrscharen im HJ-Streifendienst** (Identity Card for members of the Fire-fighting Squads in the Hitler Youth Patrol Service; see Fig. 130) is used by those members of the *HJ-Streifendienst* (*SRD*—Hitler Youth Patrol Service) who have received fire-fighting training and are now qualified to serve as members of the *Feuerwehrscharen* (Fire-fighting Squads). It is a pink, four-page folding document. The front cover carries the heading and serial number of the *Ausweis*. Page 2 gives the name of the bearer, defines the authority of the *Ausweis*, and shows the issuing headquarters, with official stamp and signature. Page 3 contains personal data, the bearer's unit and his signature, and page 4 validity endorsements.

### 187. Personal Documents of the ARP Services

Officially, the **Luftschutzdienstbuch zugleich Personalausweis** (ARP Service Pass and Personal Identity Document; see Fig. 131) has been replaced by the *SS-Soldbuch*, following the decree of 9 Jun 1944 (see para. 184). Prior to this decree however it was carried by all members of the SD and possibly by other personnel connected with ARP Services. It was published by the Air Force High Command and issued by local ARP headquarters.

The cover is of blue paper with black lettering, and contains, on the inside, instructions on handling the *Dienstbuch*. Details on other pages are as follows :—

| Page | 1—Duties, rules and regulations |
| Page | 2—Photograph and stamp |
| Page | 3—Personal data and *Luftschutzort* (local ARP sector) |
| Page | 4—Personal data |
| Page | 5—Next of kin |
| Page | 6—Police order for ARP service and additional entries |
| Page | 7—Additional entries continued |
| Pages | 8–19—Entries on medical care, clothing and equipment, and pay |
| Page | 20—ARP training in peacetime |
| Pages | 21–22—Wartime ARP employment |
| Page | 23—Employment under enemy action or abroad |
| Page | 24—Injuries, accidents or serious illness incurred in the course of duty |
| Page | 25—Promotions |
| Page | 26—Decorations |
| Pages | 27–28—Furloughs |
| Page | 29—Discharge from ARP service |
| Pages | 30–31—Endorsements by unit commanding officer |
| Page | 32—Blank page |

Officials of the RLB who supervise civilian ARP measures carry the **Ausweis für RLB-Amtsträger** (Identity Card for Officials of the Reich Association for ARP; see Fig. 132). It is a four-page document made of grey-blue paper and the front cover is crossed by two green diagonal lines. Page 2 gives bearer's name and rank, the *Revier* in which he serves and defines his authority. Page 3 continues the definition of the bearer's authority and contains the official stamp and signature of the issuing office. Page 4 provides space for any special mission or authority assigned to the bearer by the police.

Ordinary members of the RLB carry the **Mitgliedsausweis-Reichsluftschutzbund** (Membership Certificate of the Reich Association for ARP; see Fig. 133). It is a light blue card with black print. The front shows the name, address, occupation and signature of the bearer, as well as the official stamp and signature of the headquarters and responsible officer. The reverse side shows receipt of membership dues.

The **Bescheinigung-Reichsluftschutzbund** (Certificate of the Reich Association for ARP; see Fig. 134) is issued to members of the RLB who have undergone specialised training, the course from which the bearer graduated being specified on the certificate. The front contains personal data and training qualifications, and the signature and stamp of the issuing office. The other side contains endorsements certifying courses attended.

### 188. Personal Documents of the Teno

Personnel of the *Teno* not part of the Field Units may, instead of—or in addition to—the Paybook, carry the **Ausweis-Technische Nothilfe** (Identity card of the *Teno*; see Fig. 135). It is a four-page folding document of grey-blue paper with black print. Page 1 contains personal data, and bears the signature and stamp of the issuing headquarters. Page 2 gives details of unit and civilian identity card, as well as the photograph and signature of bearer. Page 3 records the *Teno* and Police Unit or branch, and contains *Teno* unit entries. Page 4 shows details of training, qualifications, rank, promotions, decorations, employment and commitment.

The **Technische Nothilfe-Beitragskarte** (Receipt for membership dues; see Fig. 136) is carried in the *Teno Ausweis*; it is a light blue card printed in black. The front side shows unit, personal data, and the official stamp and signature of the issuing headquarters; the reverse is for the monthly receipt stamps.

The **TN-Unterführer-Ausweis** (Identity Card for NCOs of the *Teno*; see Fig. 137) is a six-page folding document of brown glazed linen. Details contained in the various pages are as follows :—

| Page (front cover) | 1—Personal data Official stamp and signature of issuing headquarters and officer |
| Page | 2—Photograph and signature of bearer Personal data TN Unit and TN decorations |
| Page | 3—Higher TN headquarters Promotions |

Page   4—Transfers
Additional information such as participation in training courses

Page   5—Validity endorsements

Page   6—Instructions regarding the *Ausweis*
(back cover)

### 189. Personal Documents of the Hilfspolizei (and Sonderpolizei)

The *Hilfspolizei-Dienstausweis* (Official Service Pass—Auxiliary Police ; see Fig. 138) may be issued to any member of the *Hipo* (*Hilfspolizeibeamter*). It authorises the bearer to exercise police authority and to carry firearms. It is a four-page folding document of blue glazed linen with black print ; details are as follows :—

Page   1—Police *Hoheitsabzeichen* and number
(front cover)   of *Ausweis*
Name and rank of bearer

Page   2—Personal data
Issuing headquarters and official stamp and signature

Page   3—Validity control stamps

Page   4—Photograph and bearer's signature.
(back cover)

It is not known whether the *Wehrmannschaftspass* (Identity Pass of the Internal Defence Formation ; see Fig. 139) is still generally issued. Originally it was carried by the *SA Wehrmannschaften* from which the *Stadt-* and *Landwacht* (Auxiliary Urban and Rural Police) were derived. It may be interesting to note that these units are responsible for a major part of the training given to the *Volkssturm*. The specimen illustrated was issued by the *Steirischer Heimatbund* and may be only one of a number of local variations of this type of document ; it has a green paper cover with black printing and contains 16 pages in black and white, showing the following information :—

Page   1—List of contents and the creed of National Socialism

Page   2—Photograph, signature and membership number of bearer, official stamp and signature of issuing officer

Page   3—Personal data

Page   4—*Wehrmannschaftsdienst* (Service in the Internal Defence Formations)

Page   5—*Überweisung von der HJ* (Transfer from the HJ)

Page   6—*Reichsarbeitdienst* (Reich Labour Service)

Page   7—*Aktiver Wehrdienst* (Active Military Service)

Page   8—*Wehrdienst im Beurlaubstand* (Military Service in a reserve or retired status—including the former Jugoslav Forces)

Page   9—*Beförderungen und Ernennungen* (Promotions and appointments)

Pages 10–11—*Nachweis über die Dienstbeteiligung in der Wehrmannschaft* (Record of the number of hours of actual duty in the Internal Defence Formations)

Pages 12–13—*Abmeldungen und Anmeldungen* (In and out registration with service headquarters)

Pages 14–15—Medical entries

Page   16—Instructions on the use of the *Wehrmannschaftspass*

Inside rear cover : Validity endorsements.

It seems probable that originally the only pass issued to members of the *Stadtwacht* was the **Ausweis—Stadtwacht** (Identity Pass—Auxiliary Urban Police ; see Fig. 140), but as a result of the previously mentioned decree of 9 June, 1944, they are now, as Auxiliary Police personnel, also furnished with the *SS-Soldbuch* (Fig. 126). They may also carry the *Hilfspolizei-Dienstausweis* (Fig. 132). Whether they retain the *Stadtwacht Ausweis* in addition is not known.

The *Ausweis* is a light blue paper card with the front showing the bearer's signature. The reverse side shows personal data, confers authority to exercise Auxiliary Police powers, and carries signature of the issuing officer.

The **HJ Streifendienst-Ausweis** (Identity Pass—Hitler Youth Patrol Service ; see Fig. 141) is a small light green paper card, printed on one side only, showing the name and rank of the holder and bearing the official stamp and signature of the issuing officer in black print. Since the SRD has by now taken on the character of a fully recognised auxiliary police force, its personnel may also be issued with the *Hilfspolizei-Dienstpass* (Fig. 138).

Members of the NSKK, units of which are frequently employed to assist the Regular Police in their functions, carry the **NSKK-Pass** (Identity Book of the National Socialist Motor Corps ; see Fig. 142), a light-brown book containing 24 black and white pages. The *NSKK Hoheitsabzeichen* appears on the cover and is superimposed on every page of the book. Details are as follows :—

Pages 1–2—Bearer's Unit
Photograph and signature of bearer
Description of bearer

Pages 3–5—Personal data

Pages 6–11—Registration with NSKK Service Units on arrival or departure

Pages 12–15—Promotions, appointments, transfers, etc.

Pages 16–17—Training courses

Pages 18–19—Miscellaneous entries

Pages 20–24—Receipt stamps for dues and insurance fees

The **Ausweiskarte—Bahnpolizei** (Identity Card—Railway Police ; see Fig. 143) was originally issued to personnel of the *Bahnpolizei* by the *Deutsche Reichsbahn* ; it is not known whether this identity card is still issued or whether it has been superseded by the SS Paybook (see para. 184). The *Ausweiskarte* is a small white card of glazed linen. The front shows the date of issue and duration of validity, the reverse side gives the name, rank and signature of the bearer, and carries the stamp of the issuing railway office.

### 190. Personal Documents of the Sipo and SD (and related branches)

The cover of the **SS-Soldbuch zugleich Personalausweis** (SS Paybook and Identity Document, issued to the *Sipo* and SD ; see Fig. 144) is light brown, with the heading in black print, and shows the SS emblem. The contents are similar to those of the *W-SS Soldbuch* (see para. 184). According to latest reports the grey *SS-Soldbuch* may have been substituted for the brown one.

The **Dienstausweis—Sipo und SD** (Identity Card of the Security Police and the Security Service ; see Figs. 145a and b) is a red glazed linen or paper card (10 × 7.3 cm). The paper card as illustrated has an intricate anti-erasure pattern of red and orange on a white background ; since the anti-erasure markings are so heavily concentrated, the general appearance of the paper is red. The *Ausweis* carries the photograph and signature of the bearer. The number of the *Ausweis* and the date of validity are printed in the right upper corner. The card also bears the official stamp and signature of the issuing office, i.e. *Chef der Sicherheitspolizei und des SD* (Chief of the Security Police and of the Security Service).

The *Dienstausweis* illustrated in Fig. 145a is carried by the following *Sipo* and SD personnel: BdS, IdS and KdS, and all *Gestapo* officials in their headquarters; all administrative and executive officials in the office of the *Chef der Sicherheitspolizei und des SD*, *Gestapo* officials in *Sipo* and SD schools. The same pass, but with the signature, "*Der Reichsführer SS u. Chef der Deutschen Polizei im Reichsministerium des Innern. In Vertretung,*" is carried by all HSSPf. The equivalent officials in the service of the *Kripo* carry the same *Ausweis*, but with a green diagonal line superimposed on the cover; SS personnel in the service of the SD carry the same pass with a white diagonal line instead of the green (see Fig. 145b).

The **Hausausweis** (Permit to enter an official building) is a white card with the heading in black print. It carries the photograph and signature of the bearer, the date of validity, and the signature and official stamp of the local office and its Chief.

The *Hausausweis* authorises the bearer to enter any particular building but does not endow him with any police or similar authority. It is issued to employees (not members) of the SD, e.g. clerks.

A similar *Ausweis* in yellow is issued to persons not employed by the particular headquarters, but who may have temporary business in the building. Validity is limited to the period specified on the *Ausweis*.

A decree of 28 Aug 1944 states that a special *Ausweis* is issued to foreign auxiliaries from the East employed as *Wachmänner* guarding foreign prisoners by the *Dienststellen* of the *Sipo* in the Reich. It is described as being 15 × 10.4 cm. in size, and is printed on anti-erasure paper. It carries a photograph of the bearer, is valid for a period of three months only, and is signed by the *Leiter* of the responsible *Stapo-(Leit)stelle*.

Since the SD is still officially a party organisation and not a police or government agency, SD Identity Documents are issued by the SS, and not by the police. Usually both the stamp of the *Reichsführer SS und Chef der Deutschen Polizei* and that of the *Chef der Sicherheitspolizei und des SD* appear on the **Ausweis—SS der NSDAP im Sicherheitsdienst** (Identity Card for NCOs of the SS of the NSDAP in the Security Service; see Fig. 146). The card is printed on red glazed linen. It shows the party membership number, date of birth, and the photograph and signature of the bearer. The document shown is that of an NCO.

The **Dienstmarke-Gestapo** (Identity Badge—Secret State Police; see Figs. 147 and 148) formerly known as *Erkennungsmarke* (Identity disc) serves as the official identification in all instances of executive action. Neither the *Dienstmarke* nor the *Sipo* and SD Identity papers may be carried when travelling abroad, even on official journeys.

The badge is oval, one side showing the words "*Geheime Staatspolizei*" and the serial number, the other the *Hoheitsabzeichen*. The number on the *Dienstmarke* corresponds with that on the *Dienstausweis*.

Officials of the *Grenzpolizei* carry the same identity badge as the *Gestapo*. The *Kripo* carry the same *Dienstmarke*, but with the inscription "*Kriminalpolizei*" instead of "*Geheime Staatspolizei.*"

Personnel of the SD carry the same *Dienstmarke* with the corresponding inscription. The reason for the change of name is that members of the *Sipo* and the SD are now in addition issued with an *Erkennungsmarke* similar to that of the Armed Forces and the *Waffen-SS*, which serves as an identification in case of accident or death. (Since this is recent information the captions of Figs. 147 and 148 of Annexe M could not be revised accordingly.)

The **Geheime Feldpolizei Ausweis** (Identity Pass—Secret Field Police; see Fig. 149) is carried by members of the GFP. The card is printed on lime-green glazed linen. The front of the card records the issuing headquarters, shows the name, signature, *Kennkarte* number and photographs (in uniforms and civilian clothes) of the bearer, and carries the official stamp, date and signature of issuing commander. The reverse of the card states the authority of the Secret Field Police and lists the regulations governing the certificate.

The **Reichsnetzkarte für Sipo and SD** (Reich Railway warrant for the *Sipo* and the SD) authorises journeys, free of charge, anywhere on the German railways.

The plain white document illustrated simply indicates that it is a "*Reichsnetzkarte für einen Beauftragten der Sicherheitspolizei*" (Reich railway warrant for an official of the Security Police). The omission of any mention of the SD on this paper may possibly be a security measure to hide the bearer's membership of that organisation since the warrants are probably produced at the request of ordinary railway control personnel.

Identity documents of the railway officials working with the *Reichsbahnfahndungsdienst* (RBFD) receive their pass from the *Chef der Sicherheitspolizei und des SD*. It is a service pass of white paper with a green diagonal line from the left top to the lower right corner (10 × 7.3 cm.). The paper shows the bearer's photograph and signature, service pass number, name and address, and carries the official stamp and signature of the issuing office; and also the bearer's authority to carry service weapons. The passes are valid for one year; they are numbered consecutively in one series for the entire territory of the Reich.

All entries must be typewritten and passes must bear the signature or stamp of the *Chef der Sicherheitspolizei und des SD*.

Each member of the RBFD also carries an identity disc of yellow metal (2 mm thick, 5 cm long and 3.5 cm wide). It shows the *Hoheitsabzeichen* on one side, and the inscription "*Reichsbahnfahndungsdienst*" and the number of the bearer's *Dienstausweis* on the other.

The VGAD works in close liaison with the *Sicherheitspolizei* in Frontier regions. It has, however, its own identity document, the **VGAD Personalbuch** (Personal Identification book of the Reinforced Frontier Control Service; see Fig. 150).

The *Personalbuch* has a light green paper cover and contains 28 pages of light green paper with black print. The following information is contained in the book:—

Pages 1–2—Photograph and signature of bearer (title page)

Pages 3–5—Personal data

Pages 6–7—Previous employment

Page 8—Decorations and recommendations

Page 9—Furloughs

Pages 10–20—Miscellaneous entries including medical record, pay and allowances

Pages 21–22—Special training courses
Pages 23–28—Miscellaneous entries

The **Dienstausweis — Reichsfinanzverwaltung** (Service Identity Card—Reich Finance Administration; see Fig. 151) is issued to auxiliary members of the *Zollgrenzschutz* (Frontier Control Service). It is a light green paper card, showing the bearer's photograph, signature and personal data on the front. The bearer's authority to carry service weapons, the date of expiry and the official stamp and signature of the issuing office, are shown on the reverse side.

### 191. Documents issued to the public by the Police

The **Berechtigungsschein** (see Fig. 152) is a permit issued by the *Wasserpolizeibehörde* (*Wasserstrassenamt*—Waterways Police) and entitles the bearer to operate a steam or motor vessel on specified rivers. It is a four-page folding document of grey glazed linen.

The **Deutsches Reich—Kennkarte** (Identity Card; see Fig. 153) is issued by the local police authorities to every German citizen born and residing in Germany proper and is the most important civilian identity document. All Germans not in military service who are over the age of fifteen must carry the *Kennkarte*. Only as a result of administrative dislocation and difficulties, mainly due to Allied air attacks, are exceptions made at present, and regulations relaxed so that other official or semi-official identity papers showing the bearer's photograph may be accepted as authoritative for the time being.

It is a four-page folding document of light grey glazed linen with black print, containing the following information :—

Page 2—Town of registration
   Identity number (*Kennummer*) which may provide the key to the National Population Registry number
   Date of expiry
   Personal data including profession, distinctive marks and control stamp (this stamp may be found on the back cover page).

Page 3—Bearer's photograph and signature, with official stamps
   Two fingerprints
   Date, stamp and signature of the issuing police authority

The **Ausweis der Deutschen Volksliste** (Blue certificate of registration for " Racial Germans ";

see Fig. 154) is issued to all " racial Germans " who were born in greater Germany but resided abroad ; they are entered as members of *Volksliste I*. Germans of *Volksliste I* are regarded as full citizens and enjoy all political and economic rights.

Those who expediently remembered their German origin after the German occupation of, e.g. Poland and Slovenia, had their names listed in *Volksliste II*, but also carry the blue identity card (see also para. 82).

The blue *Ausweis* is a four-page folding document showing the following :—

Page 2—Number of registration in the *Deutsche Volksliste* and statement of German citizenship, as well as personal data, including occupation or profession
   Official stamp and signature of the Police or Administrative official, usually the *Landrat*

Page 3—Photograph and signature of bearer and official stamp of issuing office.

Except for its colour the *Ausweis der Deutschen Volksliste* (Green certificate of registration for " Racial Germans "; see Fig. 155) is exactly the same as the preceding. It is issued to members of *Volksliste III*, which comprises those who were " converted " into Germans without having been consulted. Its bearers have received citizenship on probation (*Staatsangehörigkeit auf Widerruf*); this is usually indicated by a rubber stamp inscription on page 2 or 3 of the green card. Bearers are entitled to the economic, but not the political rights of the German citizen (see para. 82).

### 192. Registration on arrival or departure

The system of police registration and the various forms used were discussed in para. 82, under *Verwaltungspolizei*. The **Anmeldung bei der Polizeilichen Meldebehörde** (Police Registration on taking up Residence) which is shown in Fig. 156, is printed on thin white paper. It lists personal data, military service information, etc., in great detail. On the reverse side an extract from the official registration decree is given.

The **Abmeldung bei der Polizeilichen Meldebehörde** (Police Registration on leaving the district; see Fig. 157), which is printed on thin green paper, contains information similar to that in the *Anmeldung*, and the same extract from the registration decree is given on the reverse side.

### 193. Police Publications

The most important periodicals put out either by the Police or by other official agencies covering matters of Police interest are enumerated below :—

| 1<br>Title | 2<br>Issuing Agency | 3<br>Publisher | 4<br>Published | 5<br>Security Classification, if any |
|---|---|---|---|---|
| *Ministerialblatt des Reichs- und Preuss. Ministeriums des Innern*, also known as : *Ministerialblatt für die Innere Verwaltung* (MBliV.) | *Reichsministerium des Innern*, Berlin | Carl Heymanns *Verlag*, Berlin W 8, Mauerstr. 44 | Weekly | None |
| *Befehlsblatt des Chefs der Ordnungspolizei* | *Hauptamt Orpo*, Berlin | Carl Heymanns *Verlag*, Berlin W 8, Mauerstr. 44 | Weekly | None |
| *Befehlsblatt des Chefs der Sicherheitspolizei und des SD* | *Reichssicherheitshauptamt*, Berlin | *Preussische Verlags- und Druckerei GmbH*, Berlin | Weekly | " *Nur für Behördengebrauch* " |
| *Die Deutsche Polizei Ausgabe Ordnungspolizei* (combined for the duration of the war with the magazine " *Sport der Ordnungspolizei* ") | *Kameradschaftsbund der Deutschen Polizei* by order of the *RFSSuChdDtPol.* | Deutsche Kulturwacht Oscar Berger, Berlin Steglitz, Schützenstr. 7 | Twice monthly until 1 Jan., 1944 ; since then monthly | None |

130

| 1 | 2 | 3 | 4 | 5 |
|---|---|---|---|---|
| Title | Issuing Agency | Publisher | Published | Security Classification, if any |
| *Die Deutsche Polizei* <br> *Ausgabe Sicherheitspolizei und SD* | *Kameradschaftsbund der Deutschen Polizei,* by order of the *RFSSuChd-DtPol.* | *Deutsche Kulturwacht* Oscar Berger, Berlin Steglitz, Schützenstr. 7 | Twice monthly | None |
| *Kriminalistik (Monatshefte für die gesamte kriminalistische Wissenschaft und Praxis)* | *Chef d. Sipo u. d. SD* through RKPA by order of the *RFSS uChdDtPol* | *Kriminal-Wissenschaft und -Praxis Verlag* E. Jaedicke, Berlin N 54 Schwedter Str. 263 | Monthly; since end of 1943 six times a year | None |
| *Mitteilungsblatt des Reichskriminalpolizeiamts (Amtliche Beilage der "Kriminalistik")* | RKPA, Berlin | *Kriminal-Wissenschaft und -Praxis Verlag* E. Jaedicke, Berlin N 54 Schwedter Str. 263 | Monthly | " *Vertraulich* " |
| *Chef der Ordnungspolizei Besondere Anordnungen für die Versorgung* | *Kommandoamt im Hauptamt Orpo* | — | Weekly | None |
| *Deutsches Kriminalpolizeiblatt* | RKPA, Berlin | *Verlag und Geschäftsstelle des Deutschen Kriminalpolizeiblatts,* Potsdam, Kaiserstr. 3 | " *Nach Bedarf* " | " *Vertraulich* " |
| *Sonderausgabe zum Deutschen Kriminalpolizeiblatt* | RKPA, Berlin | *Verlag und Geschäftsstelle des Deutschen Kriminalpolizeiblatts,* Potsdam, Kaiserstr. 3 | " *Nach Bedarf* " | " *Nur für Deutsche Behörden bestimmt* " |
| *Deutscher Feuerschutz Amtliche Zeitschrift für das gesamte Feuerlöschwesen* | *Hauptamt Orpo* by order of the *RFSSuChdDt-Pol* | Brunnen-*Verlag,* Berlin | Monthly | None |
| *Mitteilungsblatt der Gruppe IV E (Gestapo Fahndung*—Counterespionage—also information about foreign, including enemy, intelligence services) *Note.*—This paper was undoubtedly re-named after June 1944, when *Gruppe* IV E changed its designation under the new organization of *Amt* IV | *Gruppe* IV E of the RSHA | RSHA, *Gruppe* IV E | Twice monthly | " *Geheim* " or " *Streng Vertraulich* " |
| *Meldung wichtiger staatspolizeilicher Ereignisse* | RSHA, *Amt* IV (*Gestapoamt*) | RSHA, *Amt* IV | Three times a week ? | " *Streng Vertraulich* " |
| *Meldung wichtiger kriminalpolizeilicher Ereignisse* | RHSA, *Amt* V (*Reichskriminalpolizeiamt*) | RSHA, *Amt* V | Daily | " *Streng Vertraulich* " |
| *Auslandslageberichte* | RSHA, *Amt* VI | RSHA, *Amt* VI | Periodically | " *Geheim* " or " *Streng Vertraulich* " ? |
| *Funkdienst* | RSHA, *Amt* VI | RSHA, *Amt* VI | Periodically | " *Geheim* " or " *Streng Vertraulich* " |
| *Meldungen aus dem Reich* (Limited distribution to HSSPf, IdS and BdS) | RSHA, *Amt* III | RSHA, *Amt* III | — | " *Geheim* " or " *Streng Vertraulich* " ? |
| " *Vorschriftensammlung für die Deutsche Polizei* " | — | *Verlag für polizeiliches Fachschriftentum,* Lübeck, Herderstr. 14 | — | None |
| *Mitteilungsblätter für die weltanschauliche Schulung der Ordnungspolizei* Formerly " *Politischer Informationsdienst* " | *Chef der Orpo Gruppe* " *Weltanschauliche Erziehung* " | *Hauptamt Orpo* | Twice monthly | " *Nur für den Dienstgebrauch innerhalb der Ordnungspolizei* " |
| *Das Schwarze Korps* | *Reichsführung-SS* | *Franz Eher Nachfolger GmbH,* Berlin SW 68, Zimmerstr. 88 | Weekly | None |
| *SS-Leithefte* | *Der Reichsführer SS, SS-Hauptamt* Berlin W 35, Lützowstr. 48/49 | *Buchgewerbehaus* M. Müller & Sohn, Berlin SW 68 | Monthly ? | None |

| 1<br>Title | 2<br>Issuing<br>Agency | 3<br>Publisher | 4<br>Published | 5<br>Security<br>Classification,<br>if any |
|---|---|---|---|---|
| *Mitteilungen über die SS- und Polizei-gerichtsbarkeit* | *RFSSuChdDtPol Hauptamt SS-Gericht* | *SS-Vordruckverlag* W. F. Mayr, Miesbach Bayern | Four times a year | *" Vertraulich "* |
| *Internationale Kriminalpolizei* | IKPK, Berlin | IKPK, Berlin | — | — |
| *Archiv für Kriminologie* | RKPA, Berlin | — | — | — |
| *Monatsschrift für Kriminalpsychologie* | RKPA, Berlin | — | — | — |
| *Aufenthaltsermittlungsliste* | RKPA, Potsdam, Am Kanal 45 | — | — | — |

Also : various technical magazines for Signals, M/T, ARP, Police Medical and Veterinary Services, Arms and Equipment, Sports.

Also : *Meldeblätter* of the various *Kripo-(Leit-) Stellen.*

| Title | Issuing Agency | Publisher | Published | Security |
|---|---|---|---|---|
| *Deutscher Reichsanzeiger und Preussischer Staatsanzeiger* | | *Geschäftsstelle des Reichs- und Preuss. Staatsanzeigers,* Berlin SW 68, Wilhelmstr. 32 | — | — |
| *Reichsgesetzblatt* | *Reichsministerium des Innern* | *Reichsverlagsamt* Berlin NW 8, Scharnhorststr. 4 | — | — |
| *Reichsministerialblatt (Zentralblatt für das Deutsche Reich)* | — | *Reichsverlagsamt* Berlin NW 40, Scharnhorststr. 4 | — | — |
| *Reichsverwaltungsblatt* | *Reichsministerium des Innern* | Carl Heymanns *Verlag* Berlin W 8, Mauerstr. 44 | — | — |
| *Deutsche Verwaltung* | — | — | — | — |
| *Der Gemeindetag* | — | — | — | — |
| *Reichsgesundheitsblatt* | *Reichsministerium des Innern* | *Reichsverlagsamt,* Berlin NW 40, Scharnhorststr. 4 | — | — |
| *Zeitschrift für Standesamtswesen* | — | — | — | — |
| *Ministerialblatt des Wirtschaftsministeriums* | *Reichswirtschafts-ministerium* | Carl Heymanns *Verlag,* Berlin W 8, Mauerstr. 44 | — | — |
| *Mitteilungsblatt des Reichskommissars ür die Preisbildung* | *Reichkommissar für die Preisbildung* | *Reichsverlagsamt,* Berlin NW 8, Scharnhorststr. 4 | — | — |
| *Reichshaushalts- und Besoldungsblatt* | *Reichsfinanz-ministerium* | *Verlagsbuchhandlung* Trowitzsch & Sohn, Berlin SW 68, Kochstr. 32 | — | — |
| *Verkündungsblatt des Reichsnährstands* | *Reichsministerium für Ernährung und Landwirtschaft* | *Reichsnährstand-Ver-lags-GmbH,* Berlin N 4, Linienstr. 139/140 | — | — |
| *Reichsministerialblatt der Reichsforst-verwaltung* | *Reichsforstamt* | *Verlag* Hans Braig, Berlin NW 7, Friedrichstr. 118/119 | — | — |
| *Verordnungsblatt der Reichsleitung der NSDAP* | *Reichsleitung der NSDAP* | *Zentralverlag der NSDAP* Franz Eher *Nachf. GmbH* Berlin SW 68, Zimmerstr. 87 München 13, Schellingstr. 39 | — | — |

The information contained in this chart is intended for quick identification of the basic fact
to cover details which appear in the text. It should especially be noted that in all instances
a varying degree of elaborate design no indication of this fact is given in the chart.

| Branches | SCHUTZPOLIZEI (Protection Police) | VERKEHRSPOLIZEI (Traffic Police) | GENDARMERIE | VERWALTUNGS-POLIZEI (Administrative Police) | WASSERSCHUTZ POLIZEI (Waterways Protection Police) |
|---|---|---|---|---|---|
| DISTINGUISHING COLOURS | Light Green (*Schupo d. Reiches*) Wine Red (*Schupo d. Gemeinden*) | Bright Red | Orange | Grey (primary colour) Red (secondary colour —now obsolete) | Yellow |
| SHOULDER STRAPS | **OR's (EM)** Brown (light green or wine red piping) **NCO's** Brown & aluminium (light green or wine red piping) **Officers** Silver (light green or wine red piping) Gold for Generals | Brown (bright red piping) Brown & aluminium (red piping) Silver (bright red piping) Gold for generals | Light brown (orange piping) Light brown and aluminium (orange piping) Silver (orange piping) Gold for generals | Brown (grey piping) Brown & aluminium (grey piping) Silver (grey piping) Gold for generals | Yellow Yellow & aluminium Silver (yellow piping) |
| COLLAR PATCHES | Light green (wine red patches for *Schupo d. Gemeinden* now obsolete) | Bright red | Orange | Grey | |
| GREATCOAT ... ... | Green | Green | Green | Green | Dark blue |
| TUNIC ... ... BREECHES ... ... | ,, ,, | ,, ,, | ,, ,, | ,, ,, | ,, ,, |
| CUFFS : GREATCOAT ... TUNIC ... ... | ,, Brown | ,, Brown | Light brown (brown for Mot.) ,, | ,, Brown | Dark blue (yellow piping) ,, |
| COLLAR : GREATCOAT ... TUNIC ... ... | ,, ,, | ,, ,, | ,, ,, | ,, ,, | Dark blue ,, |
| CAPS AND HELMETS (each piped with distinguishing colour) | (1) *Schirmmütze*—green *Tschako*—green Steel Helmet—grey green | (1) *Schirmmütze*—green *Tschako*—green | (1) *Schirmmütze*—green *Tschako*—green (2) *Bergmütze*—green Crash helmet (brown) for Mot. | (1) *Schirmmütze*—green *Hausmütze*—green | (1) *Schirmmütze*—dark blue *Schiffchen* (dark blue) |
| CAP BADGES ... | (1) *Schirmmütze* : Police badge National cockade Shako : police badge Steel helmet has swastika on Right and police badge on Left | (1) *Schirmmütze* : Police badge National cockade Shako : police badge National cockade | (1) *Schirmmütze* : Police badge National cockade Shako : police badge National cockade | (1) *Schirmmütze* : Police badge National cockade | (1) *Schirmmütze* : Police badge (yellow metal) |
| SLEEVE INSIGNIA ... | Left sleeve : Police badge (light green or wine red) | Left sleeve : Police badge (bright red) | Left sleeve : Police badge (orange and green) | Left sleeve : Police badge (grey) | Left sleeve : Police badge (yellow on dark blue) |
| ARMBANDS : | | | | | |

(1) *Schirmmütze*—peaked cap.      (2) *Bergmütze*—peaked ski cap.

# OLICE UNIFORMS

rman police uniforms. It provides an overall picture but does not attempt
the distinction between enlisted personnel (OR's) and officers is merely one of

| UERSCHUTZ-POLIZEI (Fire Fighting Police) | HILFSPOLIZEI (Auxiliary Police) | LUFTSCHUTZ-POLIZEI (Air Raid Protection Police) | TECHNISCHE NOTHILFE (Technical Emergency Corps) | SICHERHEITSPOLIZEI & SD (Security Police and Security Service) |
|---|---|---|---|---|
| nine | | | Black | |
| k (carmine ng) | | | Black | Black (identical with those worn by W-SS for all ranks) on grey uniform |
| k & aluminium mine piping) | | | Black & aluminium | On Right side only. Silver and black or silver according to rank on black uniform |
| er (carmine ng) | | | Silver | |
| y and carmine | | | Black (white cogwheel emblem) | **OR's (EM)** Right patch black (plain) Left patch black with rank insignia  **Officers** Right patch black (plain) Left patch black with rank insignia  (SS-Standartenführer and upwards wear rank insignia on both collar patches) |
| en or black | Green | Air Force grey-blue | Field grey, Blue, Green (when attached to Schutzpolizei) | Field grey or black |
| ,, | ,, | ,, | ,, | ,, |
| ,, | ,, | ,, | ,, | ,, |
| k (carmine ng) | ,, | ,, | ,, | ,, |
| ,, | ,, | ,, | ,, | ,, |
| ck | ,, | ,, | ,, | ,, |
| | ,, | ,, | ,, | ,, |
| hirmmütze—green lack iffchen (green or k) el helmet—black | (1) Schirmmütze—Tschako (green) | (3) Schiffchen—Air Force grey-blue Steel helmet—black or grey | (3) Schiffchen (colour as above) Steel helmet—black | (1) Schirmmütze—field grey or black |
| ice badge minium) el helmet has ice badge on Left SS emblem on ht | (1) Schirmmütze: Police badge (aluminium)  National cockade | Police badge (aluminium) | Hoheitsabzeichen (aluminium) Cogwheel emblem | Hoheitsabzeichen Skull-and-cross-bones emblem |
| t sleeve: Police lge (carmine) | Left sleeve: Police badge | | Left sleeve: Hoheits-abzeichen | Left sleeve: Hoheitsabzeichen (sometimes omitted) Left cuff: Black SD patch Right sleeve: Altkämpferwinkel (Silver and black chevron) |
| | Left arm: "Hilfspolizei" in black and white or "Stadtwacht" or "Landwacht" in black and white | Left cuff: "Sicherheits u. Hilfsdienst" in green and white | Left cuff: "Technische Nothilfe" in black and white or "Deutsche Wehrmacht" in yellow and black (when attached to Wehrmacht) | Left arm: Swastika armband (usually only on ceremonial occasions) |

(3) Schiffchen—forage cap.

# ANNEXE A

## POLICE HIGH COMMAND

**PART ONE :** OFFICE of the RFSS und CHEF der DEUTSCHEN POLIZEI im REICHSMINISTERIUM des INNERN

    (*a*) Hauptamt Ordnungspolizei (National Department of the Regular Police).

    (*b*) Reichssicherheitshauptamt (National Department of Security).

    (*c*) Amt Haushalt und Bauten (Department of Budget and Buildings).

**PART TWO :** REGIONAL POLICE COMMANDERS

    (*a*) List of HSSPf, according to Wehrkreis or Territory.

    (*b*) List of BdO, according to Wehrkreis or Territory.

    (*c*) List of BdS, according to Wehrkreis or Territory.

    (*d*) Organisation of the Office of the BdO France.

# ANNEXE A : PART ONE

## Office of the Reichsführer SS und Chef der Deutschen Polizei

## im REICHSMINISTERIUM des INNERN

**Address :** Berlin, SW 11, Prinz-Albrecht-Str. 8.
Telephone : 12 00 40.

**Chef :** Heinrich HIMMLER, also *Reichsminister d. Innern, M.d.R., Preuss. Stts. R. etc.*

### (a) HAUPTAMT ORDNUNGSPOLIZEI

**Address :** Berlin, NW 7, Unter den Linden 74.
Telephone : 12 00 34.

**Chef :** *SS-OGF, General der Waffen-SS u. General der Polizei* Alfred WÜNNENBERG (m.d.F.b.)

Nominal chief : *SS-Oberst-Gruppenführer, Generaloberst der Polizei* Kurt DALUEGE, *Pr. Stts. R., M.d.R.* (reported sick).

### I. DAS KOMMANDOAMT

**Chef :** *SS-BF, Genmaj. d. Pol.* FLADE.
Predecessors : *SS-GF, Genlt. d. Pol.* Otto WINKELMANN, *SS-BF, Genmaj. d. Pol.* Anton DIERMANN.

**Leiter der Amtsgruppe I :** *SS-BF, Genmaj. d. Pol.* GRÜN-WALD.

**Leiter der Amtsgruppe II :** *SS-SF, Oberst d. Gend.* GEIBEL.

**Leiter der Amtsgruppe III :** *SS-BF, Generalarzt d. Pol.* Dr. WENZEL.

**Gruppenleiter :** *Generalveterinär d. Pol.* Dr. KRIES.

**Untergruppenleiter, und Sachbearbeiter :** *SS-BF, Genmaj. d. Pol.* FISCHER.

*Obersten :* SCHMIEDEL. SCHLAKE. *SS-SF* STACH. *SS-SF* ZUPKE. *Oberst d. FSchP* GOLDBACH. *Oberstärzte d. Pol. :* *SS-SF,* Dr. HOFFMANN, Dr. SITTE. *Oberstleutnante :* ABESSER, JOASS, EGGEBRECHT, FREY, *SS-OSBF* HOHMUTH, JÖRSS, KRÖGER. Dr. KÜHHAS, PETERSDORFF, ROGALSKI, *SS-OSBF* SCHIERHORN, SCHRÖTER, *SS-OSBF* TREUKE, WAGNER. *Oberstlt. d. FSchP :* GUNDERLOCH, Dr. KALASS, SCHIKORR. *ORR.* RÖSSLER. *Oberfeldarzt d. Pol. :* *SS-OSBF,* Dr. FUCHS. *Oberstvet d. Pol. :* *SS-SF,* Dr. PFRAGNER. *Majors :* AURICH, BEZ, BORCHERT, *SS-SBF* BOURIER, BRÖSICKE, EBELING, FENSKE, FRISCHMUTH, GRAPPENDORF, HEINZ, *SS-SBF* LEHMANN, *SS-SBF* TREUKE, *SS-SBF* KROPP, *SS-SBF* STELZER. *Maj. d. FSchP :* SYMANOWSKI. *Regierungsräte :* DAMEROW, DIERSCHKE, Erich MÜLLER.

### II. DAS AMT VERWALTUNG UND RECHT

**Chef :** *SS-GF, Min. Dir.* BRACHT.

**Leiter der Amtsgruppe I :** *Min. R.* RHEINS.

**Amtsgruppe II :** *SS-BF, Min. Dirig.* Dr. BADER.

**Amtsgruppe III :** *Min. Dirig.* SCHEIDEL.

**Gruppenleiter :** *SS-OSBF, Min. R.* Dr. BRÖMSE. *Min. R.* Dr. GRUNEWALD. *Min. R. Frhr. von* HOHENASTBERG gen. WIGANDT. *Min. R. Dr.* KÄÄB. *Min. R.* MEINECKE. *Min. R.* MÖLLER. *Min. R.* POHLMAN. *Min. R.* REPPERT. *Min. R.* RHEINS. *Min. R.* SCHMIDT. *Min. R.* SCHOOR. *SS-SF, Reg. Dir.* Dr. DIEDERICHS (abg.). *ORR :* ENGEL-HARDT, GROTE, HERZOG, KLAPPER, KLEMM, Dr. KNY. *SS-SBF,* Dr. LÖCKER, OLISCHLÄGER. *O. Reg. Bau. R.* FRANK.

**Untergruppenleiter :** *Regierungsräte (RR) :* EVERS, DOOGS, FRITZSCHE (abg.) Dr. KASSEBEER, KOCHSKÄMPER, KÖPCKE, Fritz MEIER, MICHEL, Dr. NOACK, WETZEL.

### III. DAS WIRTSCHAFTSVERWALTUNGSAMT

**Chef :** *SS-GF, Genlt. d. W-SS- u. Pol.* FRANK.

**Amtsgruppe I :** *Bekleidung und Verpflegung.*

**Amtsgruppe II :** *Kassen-u. Besoldungswesen.*

**Amtsgruppe III :** *Unterbringung.*

**Amtsgruppe IV :** *Versorgung u. Recht.*

**Gruppe Pers :** *Personal.*

### IV. DAS AMT TECHNISCHE NOTHILFE

**Chef :** *SS-GF, Genlt. d. Pol.* Willy SCHMELCHER.

### V. DAS AMT FEUERWEHREN

**Chef :** *Genmaj. d. Pol.* SCHNELL.
**Gruppenleiter :** *Oberstlt. d. Schupo* KESSLER.
**Untergruppenleiter :** *RR. Dr.* SALAW.

### VI. DAS KOLONIALPOLIZEIAMT

**Chef :**

*SS-OGF, Gen. d. W-SS u. d. Pol.* Karl von PFEFFER-WILDENBRUCH (replaced middle of 1944 ; successor unknown).

### VII. DAS AMT TECHNISCHE SS- UND POLIZEI-AKADEMIE

**Kommandeur :** *SS-BF, Genmaj. d. Pol. Prof.* Dr. GERLOFF.

**Sachbearbeiter :**

*SS-SBF, Oberstlt.* SUCK, *Oberstlt.* BAUMANN, *Oberstlt.* FRAIN. *Majore :* HENSEL. *SS-SBF* KOHRS, SYMANOWSKI.

## DIE GENERAL-INSPEKTEURE

1. *Der General-Inspekteur der Schutzpolizei des Reiches* (Inspector General of the Reich Protection Police), *SS-GF, Genlt. d. Pol.* Georg SCHREYER.

2. *Der General-Inspekteur der Gendarmerie und der Schutzpolizei der Gemeinden* (Inspector General of Rural Police and of Municipal Protection Police), *SS-OGF, Gen. d. Pol.* Jürgen von KAMPTZ (replaced in 1944 : successor unknown).

3. *Der General-Inspekteur der Polizeischulen* (Inspector General of Police Schools), *SS-OGF, Gen. d. W-SS u. d. Pol.* Karl von PFEFFER-WILDENBRUCH (replaced middle of 1944 : successor unknown).

4. *Der General-Inspekteur der Feuerschutzpolizei und Feuerwehren* (Inspector General of the Fire Protection Police and of the Fire Brigades), *SS-BF, Genmaj. d. Pol.* RUMPF.

5. *Der General-Inspekteur des Sanitätswesen* (Inspector General of Police Medical Services), (possibly : *SS-OGF, Professor Dr.* Ernst R. GRAWITZ, *Reichsarzt der SS u. Polizei*).

6. *Der Inspekteur für das Nachrichtenwesen* (Inspector of Signals), *Genmaj. d. Pol.* SCHLAKE.

7. *Der Inspekteur für Weltanschauliche Schulung* (Inspector for Ideological Indoctrination of the Police Corps), *SS-BF,* Ernst FICK, also *Inspekteur für die gesamte Weltanschauliche Erziehung in der SS u. Polizei* (Inspector for all Ideological Indoctrination of SS and Police).

8. *Der Inspekteur der Wasserschutzpolizei* (Inspector of the Waterways Protection Police), *Oberst d. Schupo* Ernst SCHRÖTER. Predecessor : *SS-BF, Genmaj. d. Pol.* KRUMHAAR.

9. *Inspektion für das Kraftfahr- und Verkehrswesen* (*Jn K*—Inspectorate of M/T and Traffic Control).

10. *Inspektion für Waffen und Geräte* (*Jn WG*—Inspectorate of Arms and Equipment).

11. *Inspektion für die Luftschutzpolizei und den Luftschutzeinsatz* (*Jn L*—Inspectorate of Air Raid Protection and Air Raid Protection Police).

12. *Inspektion für das Veterinärwesen* (*Jn Vet*—Inspectorate of Police Veterinary Services).

## (b) REICHSSICHERHEITSHAUPTAMT

**Address :** Berlin, SW 11, Prinz-Albrecht-Str. 8.
Telephone : 12 00 40.

**Chef :** *SS-OGF, Gen. d. Pol. Dr.* Ernst KALTENBRUNNER.

### AMTSCHEFS

| | |
|---|---|
| **Amt I** (Personnel) : | *SS-GF, ORR.* Erwin SCHULZ. |
| **Amt II** (Organisation, Administration, Law) : | *SS-OSBF, ORR.* HAENEL. |
| **Amt III** (Spheres of German Life) : | *SS-BF, Genmaj. d. Pol,* OHLENDORF. |
| **Amt IV** (Investigation and combatting of opposition) : | *SS-OGF, Genlt. d. Pol.* MÜLLER. |
| **Amt V** (Combatting of Criminals) : | *SS-GF, Genlt. d. Pol.* NEBE (replaced since 20 July, 1944 ; successor unknown). |
| **Amt VI** (Foreign Countries) : | *SS-BF, ORR.* SCHELLENBERG. |
| **Amt VII** (Ideological Research and its application) : | *SS-OF, Prof. Dr.* SIX (replaced end of 1944: successor unknown). |
| **Militärisches Amt (Ml Bureau) :** | *SS-BF, ORR.* SCHELLENBERG. |

## (c) HAUPTAMT HAUSHALT UND BAUTEN

(absorbed by the *SS-Wirtschafts- u. Verwaltungs Hauptamt*)

**Chef :** *Min. Dir., SS-OGF, Gen. d. W-SS* Oswald POHL.

**Amt Haushalt** (identical with *Amtsgruppe* A of the WVHA) :
Offices at Munich, Fürstenberg/Meckl. and other places.

**Amt Bauten** (identical with *Amtsgruppe* C of the WVHA) :

Chef: *SS-GF, Genlt. d. W-SS Dr. Ing.* KAMMLER.

Offices at Berlin-Lichterfelde-West, Schloss-Str. 60 and other places.

# ANNEXE A : PART TWO
## REGIONAL POLICE COMMANDERS
### (a) HÖHERE SS- UND POLIZEIFÜHRER
#### (Listed according to Wehrkreis or Territory)

| Wehrkreis or Territory | Name | Title | Address |
|---|---|---|---|
| I | SS-GF, Genlt. d. Pol. JOST. Predecessor: SS-GF, Georg EBRECHT (Acting) | Der HSSPf beim Oberpräsidenten von Ostpreussen in Wehrkreis I. | Königsberg, Hindenburg-str. 11. Tel. 24126. |
| II | SS-OGF, Genlt. d. Pol. Emil MAZUW. | Der HSSPf beim Oberpräsidenten von Pommern, beim Reichsstatthalter in Mecklenburg und beim Oberpräsidenten von Brandenburg im Wehrkreis II. | Stettin, Falkenwalder Str. 96. Tel. 32790/91. |
| III | SS-OGF, August HEISSMEYER. | Der HSSPf beim Oberpräsidenten von Brandenburg im Wehrkreis III. | Berlin-Spandau, Radelandstr. 21. Tel. 375435, 375547. |
|  | SS-GF, Genlt. d. Pol. Kurt GOEHRUM (Pol. Präsident, Berlin). | Der HSSPf für die Reichshauptstadt, Berlin. | Pol. Präsidium, Berlin, C2, Alexander Str. 10. Tel. 510023. |
| IV | SS-GF, Genlt. d. Pol. Ludolf von AL-VENSLEBEN. Predecessor: SS-OGF, Ger. d. Pol. v. VOYRSCH. | Der HSSPf bei den Reichsstatthaltern und Oberpräsidenten in Sachsen, der Provinz Halle-Merseburg, im Sudetengau, in Schlesien und in Thüringen im Wehrkreis IV. | Dresden, Devrientstr. 2. Tel. 24866. |
| V | SS-OGF, General d. Pol. u. Genlt. d.W-SS Otto HOFMANN. | Der HSSPf bei den Reichsstatthaltern in Württemberg und Baden und dem Chef der Zivilverwaltung im Elsass im Wehrkreis V. | Stuttgart, Gerokstr. 45. Tel. 28041/43. |
| VI | SS-OGF, General d. Pol. Karl GUTEN-BERGER. | Der HSSPf bei den Oberpräsidenten von Westfalen, Hannover, der Rheinprovinz und beim Reichsstatthalter in Lippe und Schaumburg-Lippe im Wehrkreis VI. | Düsseldorf, Neues Pol. Präs. Tel. 10215. |
| VII | SS-OGF, General d. Pol. Karl Frhr. von EBERSTEIN. | Der HSSPf beim Bayrischen Staatsminister des Innern im Wehrkreis VII. | München 2, Ettstr. 4/II. Tel. 44405/07. |
| VIII | SS-OGF, General d. Pol. Ernst Heinrich SCHMAUSER. | Der HSSPf bei den Oberpräsidenten in Nieder- und Oberschlesien und beim Reichsstatthalter im Sudetengau im Wehrkreis VIII. | Breslau, Ebereschenallee 14 Tel. 82411. |
| IX | SS-OGF, General d. Pol. Josias Erbprinz zu WALDECK u. PYRMONT. | Der HSSPf bei den Reichsstatthaltern und Oberpräsidenten der Provinz Kurhessen, in Hannover, in Hessen, Reg. Bez. Erfurt, in Thüringen und in Westfalen und beim Bayrischen Staatsminister des Innern im Wehrkreis IX. | Kassel, Germaniastr. 1. Tel. 31913. |
| X | SS-GF, Genmaj. d. Pol. Graf Georg Henning, v. BASSEWITZ-BEHR | Der HSSPf bei den Reichsstatthaltern und Oberpräsidenten in Hamburg, in Oldenburg und in Bremen, in Hannover und in Schleswig-Holstein im Wehrkreis X. | Hamburg, 13, Harvestehuder Weg 12. Tel. 558055. |

| Wehrkreis or Territory. | Name. | Title. | Address. |
|---|---|---|---|
| XI | *SS-OGF, General d. Pol.* Rudolf QUERNER. Predecessor: *SS-GF, Genlt. d. Pol.* Hermann HÖFLE. | *Der HSSPf bei den Reichsstatthaltern und Oberpräsidenten von Hannover, in Braunschweig und Anhalt, in Lippe und Schaumburg-Lippe und in der Provinz Magdeburg im Wehrkreis XI.* | Braunschweig, Landtagsgebäude. Tel. 484041. |
| XII Also Westmark-Lothringen. | *SS-OGF, Genlt. d. Pol.* Josef STROOP. | *Der HSSPf bei den Reichsstatthaltern und Oberpräsidenten der Rheinprovinz, in Hessen, in der Provinz Nassau und in Baden und dem Chef der Zivilverwaltung in Luxemburg im Wehrkreis XII.* *Beim Reichsstatthalter in der Westmark u. Chef der Zivilverwaltung in Lothringen.* | Wiesbaden, Uhlandstr. 4–5. Tel. 28940/50. Metz, Bärenstr. 10. Tel. 3620/22. Saarbrücken, Scharnhorststr. 4. |
| XIII | *SS-OGF, General d. Pol. u. Genlt. d. W-SS* Dr. Benno MARTIN. | *Der HSSPf beim Bayrischen Staatsministerium des Innern und bei den Reichsstatthaltern in Baden, im Sudetengau, in Thüringen und in Württemberg im Wehrkreis XIII.* | Nürnberg. Polizeipräsidium Tel. 2951. |
| XVII | *SS-BF, Genlt. d. Pol.* SCHIMANA. Predecessor: *SS-OGF, General d. Pol.* Rudolf QUERNER. | *Der HSSPf bei den Reichsstatthaltern in Wien, in Ober- und in Niederdonau im Wehrkreis XVII.* | Wien, I, Parkring 8. Tel. R27575. |
| XVIII | *SS-OGF, Genlt. d. Pol.* Erwin RÖSENER. | *Der HSSPf bei den Reichsstatthaltern in Salzburg, in Kärnten, in Steiermark und in Tirol-Vorarlberg im Wehrkreis XVIII.* | Salzburg, Kapitelplatz 2. Tel. 2633/34. |
| XX | *SS-GF Genlt. d. Pol.* Friedrich KATZMANN. | *Der HSSPf beim Reichsstatthalter in Danzig-Westpreussen im Wehrkreis XX.* | Danzig, Opitzstr. 2. Tel. 23951. |
| XXI | *SS-GF, Genmaj. d. Pol.* Heinz REINEFARTH. | *Der HSSPf beim Reichsstatthalter in Posen im Wehrkreis XXI.* | Posen, Fritz-Reuter-Str. 2a. Tel. 6561. |
| Böhmen und Mähren. | *SS-GF, Genmaj. d. W-SS, SA-BF,* Karl Friedrich Graf v. PÜCKLER-BURGHANS. | *Der HSSPf beim Reichsprotektor in Böhmen und Mähren.* | Prag, IV, Czerninpalais. Tel. 093 |
| General Gouvernement. | *SS-OGF, General d. Pol.* Wilhelm KOPPE | *Der HSSPf beim Generalgouverneur in Krakau.* | Krakau, 20, Bergakademie. Tel. 15400. |
| Frankreich. | *SS-OGF, Genlt. d. Pol.* Karl Albrecht OBERG. | *Der HSSPf für den Bereich des Militärbefehlshabers in Frankreich.* | Paris, Boulevard Lannes 57. |
| Niederlande (SS-OA Nordwest). | *SS-OGF, Gen. d. Pol.* Hanns RAUTER. | *Der HSSPf beim Reichskommissar für die besetzten niederländischen Gebiete.* | Den Haag, Plein 1. Tel. 183250. |
| Norwegen (SS-OA Nord). | *SS-OGF, Gen. d. Pol.* Wilhelm REDIESS. | *Der HSSPf beim Reichskommissar für die besetzten norwegischen Gebiete.* | Oslo, Stortingetgebäude. |
| Dänemark. | *SS-OGF, Genlt. d. Pol.* Günther PANCKE. | *Der HSSPf beim Befehlshaber der deutschen Truppen.* | Copenhagen. |

| Wehrkreis or Territory. | Name. | Title. | Address. |
|---|---|---|---|
| Serbien | SS-GF, Dr. Hermann BEHRENDS. Predecessor : SS-GF, Genlt. d. Pol. MEYSZNER | Der HSSPf beim Militärbefehlshaber in Serbien. | Belgrad. |
| Ostland (SS-OA Ostland) | SS-OGF, General d. Pol. Friedrich JECKELN. | Der HSSPf beim Reichskommissar für das Ostland. | Riga. |
| Ukraine | SS-OGF, General d. Pol. Hans PRÜTZMANN (until summer 1944). | Der HSSPf beim Reichskommissar für die Ukraine. | Kiev, Jungfernstieg 10. |
| Black Sea | SS-OGF, General d. Pol. Richard HILDEBRANDT | — | Odessa ; later, in 1944, Tarnow (Tarnava ?), Transylvania. |
| Italy | SS-OGF, General d. W-SS. Karl WOLFF | Der Höchste SS u. Polizeiführer in Italien. | Verona. |
|  | SS-OGF General d. Pol. Richard HILDEBRANDT (Reported July, 1944 HSSPf Black Sea—see above). | Der HSSPf Verona. | Verona. |
| Adriatic Coastal Zone | SS-GF, Genlt. d. Pol. Odilo GLOBOCNIK | Der HSSPf Triest u. Adriatische Küste. | Trieste u. Fiume. |
| Hungary | SS-OGF, Genlt. d. W-SS. Georg KEPPLER. Replaced by SS-GF, Genlt. d. Pol. Otto WINCKELMANN. | Der HSSPf beim Befehlshaber in Ungarn. | Budapest. |
| Greece | SS-BF, Genmaj. d. Pol. FRANZ. | Der HSSPf beim Befehlshaber in Griechenland. | Athens. |
| Belgium and N. France | SS-GF, Richard JUNGKLAUS. | Der Wehrmachtsbefehlshaber u. HSSPf in Belgien u. Nordfrankreich. | |
| Croatia | SS-GF, Genlt. d. Pol. KAMMERHOFER. | Der Beauftragte des RFSS beim Befehlshaber der Deutschen Truppen in Croatien. | |

## (b) BEFEHLSHABER DER ORDNUNGSPOLIZEI
### (Listed according to Wehrkreis or Territory)

### WEHRKREIS I

**BdO :**
*SS-OF, Genmaj. d. Pol.* Helmut MUELLER
or *Genmaj. d. Pol.* FRANZ

**Address :**
Königsberg, General-Litzmann-Str. 86/88 and
Mitteltragheim 40.
Tel. 24206 34081

**C of S :**
*Oberstlt. d. Schupo* SCHROETER

**Sachbearbeiter :**
*Oberstlt. d. Feuerschupo* BRAUN
*Maj. d. Schupo* MURASCH
*Maj. d. Schupo* LOAKE
*Maj. d. Schupo* HABELT
*Hptm. d. Schupo* PAPENKORT
*POI.* PAPIN
*PI.* SCHIPP
*Oblt. d. Schupo* v. HELDEN
*Oblt. d. Schupo* ULRICH

**Pol. Schulungsleiter :**
*SS-SBF, Major d. Schupo* TIMM

### WEHRKREIS II

**BdO :**
*SS-BF, Genmaj. d. Pol.* Konrad RITZER

**Address :**
Stettin, Landeshaus Tel : 35231

**Sachbearbeiter :**
*Oberstlt. d. Schupo* KÜHL
*Oberstlt. d. Feuerschupo* ELFREICH
*Maj. d. Schupo* CHRISTOPH
*Maj. d. Schupo* FLEISCHER
*Maj. d. Lds. Pol. a. D.* KEMPF

**Adjutant :**
*Hptm. d. Schupo* GEFFROY

**Pol. Schulungsleiter :**
*SS-SBF Major d. Schupo* Karl KRÜGER

### WEHRKREIS III

**BdO for Mark Brandenburg :**
*Oberst d. Schupo* Dr. WOLFSTIEG

**Address :**
Berlin W 15, Kurfürstendamm 165/6   Tel :
928061

**Pol. Schulungsleiter :**
*OSBF d. W-SS d. R.* WOELFERT (or Wkr.
VIII)

**BdO für Reichshauptstadt Berlin :**
*Genmaj. d. Pol.* Erik von HEIMBURG

### WEHRKREIS IV

**BdO :**
*SS-GF, Genlt. d. Pol.* HITZEGRAD (transferred to Hamburg, successor unknown).

**Address :**
Dresden N 6, Königsufer 2
Tel : 52151

**Pol. Schulungsleiter :**
*SS-SBF, Major d. Schupo* HEYSE

### WEHRKREIS V

**BdO :**
*SS-BF, Genmaj. d. Pol.* WINKLER

**Address :**
Stuttgart, Mörikestr. 14
Tel : 28141

**Sachbearbeiter :**
*Major d. Schupo* MAUERMANN (from : PV.
Stuttgart)

**Pol. Schulungsleiter :**
*SS-SBF, Major d. Schupo* RÖSINGER

### WEHRKREIS VI

**BdO :**
*SS-BF, Genmaj. d. Pol.* SCHUMANN

**Address :**
Münster, Kaiser-Wilhelm-Ring 28
Tel : 41157

**Sachbearbeiter :**
*Oberstlt. d. Schupo* KLUPSCH
*Oberstlt. d. Schupo* WÖSSNER
*Oberstlt. d. FSchP. Dipl. Ing.* SENF (From :
FSchP. Düsseldorf)
*Oberst d. FSchP. Dipl. Ing.* ROESNER

**Pol. Schulungsleiter :**
*SS-SBF Major d. Schupo* WAGENER

### WEHRKREIS VII

**BdO :**
*Genlt. d. Pol.* Friedrich von OELHAFEN

**Address :**
München 27, Möhlstr. 26 or Ettstr. 2
Tel : 21641

**Pol. Schulungsleiter :**
*SS-SBF Major d. Schupo* SPRENGLEWESKI
(to : III/Pol. Regt. 19).

### WEHRKREIS VIII

**BdO :**
*SS-BF, Genmaj. d. Pol.* LIESSEM or *Genmaj.
d. Pol.* GRUSSENDORF

**Address :**
Breslau, Hohenzollernstr. 153 and Neumarkt
1/8
Tel : 22211, 22451

**Sachbearbeiter :**
*Oberstlt. d. Schupo* WOLLESSEN
*Oberstlt. d. Feuerschupo* GRIBOW
*Maj. d. Schupo* FRANZKE
*Maj. d. Schupo* MITTENDICK
*Maj. d. Schupo* LIEDKE
*POI.* GILLER

**Adjutant :**
*Hptm. d. Schupo* SCHILL

**Pol. Schulungsleiter :**
*OSBF d. W-SS d. R.* WOELFERT (or
Wkr. III)

### WEHRKREIS IX

**BdO :**
*SS-BF, Genmaj. d. Pol.* Karl HOFFMANN

**Address :**
Kassel, Wilhelmshöher Allee 13
Tel : 31155/57, 31294, 33978, 36560

**Sachbearbeiter :**
*Oberstlt. d. Schupo* SPONER
*Oberstlt. d. Feuerschupo Dr. Ing. u. OBauR.*
  FREIESLEBEN ;
*Maj. d. Schupo* OETTERT
*Maj. d. Schupo* HEINOLD
*Hptm. d. Schupo* HÖKEN
*Major d. FSchP. Dipl. Ing.* ISENBART
  (from : *FSchP.* Berlin)

**Pol. Schulungsleiter :**
*SS-SBF Major d. Schupo Dr.* POHL

## WEHRKREIS X

**BdO :**
*SS-GF, Genlt. d. Pol.* HITZEGRAD (former
  BdO Dresden)
Predecessor : *Genmaj. d. Pol.* LIESSEM (now
  in Breslau)

**Address :**
Hamburg 36, Feldbrunnenstr. 16
Tel : 354161

**Sachbearbeiter :**
*Oberstlt. d. Feuerschupo. Dipl. Ing.* DREWS
  (to *FSchP.* Köln)
*Oberstlt. d. Feuerschupo. Dipl. Ing.* STOLL
*Major* EBELING (To *Hauptamt Orpo*)

## WEHRKREIS XI

**BdO :**
*Genmaj. d. Pol.* KEUCK
Predecessor : *Genmaj. d. Pol.* BASSET (retired)

**Address :**
Hannover, Calenbergerstr. 29
Tel : 43464, 43636, 44221

**Sachbearbeiter :**
*Oberstlt. d. Schupo* BREYER
*Oberstlt. d. Feuerschupo* BANGE
*Major d. FSchP. Dipl. Ing.* EFFENBERGER
  (From : *FSchP.* Bochum)
*Maj. d. Schupo* PRANGE
*Hptm. d. Schupo a. D.* LAPPE
*Hptm. d. Gend.* STURMAT
*Hptm. d. Schupo* BUSCHHEUER
*Oblt. d. Schupo* PIRKLBAUER
*RevLt. d. Schupo* KRANZ
*Pl.* GAUDE

**Schulungsleiter :**
*SS-SBF* HECKMANN

## WEHRKREIS XII

**BdO :**
*Genmaj. d. Pol.* HILLE (former BdO
  Königsberg and Posen)
Predecessor : *Genmaj. d. Pol.* MASCUS (since
  5.1.44 BdO Nimwegen)

**Address :**
Wiesbaden, Paulinenstr. 7
Tel : 25840, 23337

**Sachbearbeiter :**
*Oberstlt. d. FSchP. Dipl. Ing.* NOEHL

## WESTMARK

**BdO :**
*Oberst d. Schupo* Maximilian Ritter von
  ZOTTMANN

**Address :**
Saarbrücken, Bismarkstr. 106
Tel : 22331

## WEHRKREIS XIII

**BdO :**
*Genmaj. d. Pol.* WILL or *SS-BF, Genmaj. d.*
  *Pol.* GRIPHAN

**Address :**
Nürnberg O., Siegener Str. 4
Tel : 42201

## WEHRKREIS XVII

**BdO :**
*SS-BF, Genmaj. d. Pol. Dr.* Kurt BADER or
  *SS-GF Genlt. d. Pol. Dr.* RETZLAFF

**Address :**
Wien I, Herrengasse 7
Tel : U 29560

**Sachbearbeiter :**
*Oberstlt. d. FSchP. Dipl. Ing.* KATTEN-
  STROTH
*SS-SBF, Oberst d. Schupo* ENDLER

## WEHRKREIS XVIII

**BdO :**
*Oberst d. Schupo* GRIEP
Predecessor : *SS-BF, Genmaj. d. Pol.* KNOFE

**Address :**
Salzburg, Kapitelplatz 2
Tel : 1300

## WEHRKREIS XX

**BdO :**
*Oberst d. Schupo* STREHLOW
Predecessors : *SS-BF Genmaj. d. Pol.* DIER-
  MANN
  *Genmaj. d. Pol.* von FALKOWSKI

**Address :**
Danzig, Reitbahn 4
Tel : 27604, 27605

**Pol. Schulungsleiter :**
*SS-SBF, Major d. Schupo* RAULIN

## WEHRKREIS XXI

**BdO :**
*SS-BF, Genmaj. d. Pol.* KNOFE

**Address :**
Posen, Fritz-Reuter-Str. 2a
Tel : 6561
Predecessor : *Genmaj. d. Pol.* HILLE (now
  BdO Wiesbaden)

**Pol. Schulungsleiter :**
*SS-SBF, Major d. Schupo Dr.* WIEKBERG

## WEHRKREIS BÖHMEN und MÄHREN

**BdO:**
*SS-BF, Genmaj. d. Pol.* DIERMANN (since
  April 44 *Chef d. Kdo. Amtes, Hauptamt Orpo*).
Predecessor : *SS-GF, Genlt. d. Pol.* RIEGE
  (Retired Jan. 44)

**Adjutant :**
*Hptm. d. Schupo* SCHMIDT

**Chef d. Stabes :**
*Oberst d. Schupo* MONTUA

**Sachbearbeiter Ia :**
Maj. d. Schupo KAUTSCH ; Ib : Maj. d.
Schupo WITTKE
II : Maj. d. Schupo GRITZBACH ; IVa :
Oberstlt. d. Lds. Pol. VALTIN
Uniformierte Protektoratspolizei : Oberstlt. d.
Schupo Dr. HARTMANN
Luftschutz : Maj. d. Schupo BOGS
Dtsche Gend. : Hptm. d. Schupo ROTHE-
BURGER
Nachr.-Führer : Maj. d. Schupo AMMAN
Feuerschupo : Oberstlt. d. Feuerschupo
GARSKI (to : FSchP. Berlin)
Amt Verwaltung und Recht : MinR. Frhr.
von PUTTKAMER
Polizei-Beschaffungsamt : PolR. KOLLMANN
Major d. FSchP. Dipl. Ing. MÖBIUS (to :
FSchP. Hannover)
Major d. FSchP. Dipl. Ing. HAASE

## GENERAL GOUVERNEMENT

**BdO :**
Genlt. d. Pol. BECKER

**Address :**
Krakau, Aussenring 3
Tel : 15420

**Sachbearbeiter :**
Maj. d. FSchP. Dipl. Ing. SOPP (from
FSchP. Frankfurt/M)
SS-SBF, Major d. FSchP. GABBERT (to :
FSchP. Memel)

## FRANKREICH

**BdO :**
Oberst d. Schupo Bodo von SCHWEIN-
ICHEN
Predecessor : Genmaj. d. Pol. SCHEER

**Address :**
Paris, Rue de la Faisandaie 49

**Adjutant :**
Oberlt. d. Schupo MOCKER

**Chef d. Stabes :**
Oberstlt. d. Gend. NIEMANN

## NIEDERLANDE

**BdO :**
Genmaj. d. Pol. MASCUS
Predecessor : Genlt. d. Pol. Dr. LANKENAU
Address : Den Haag, Pleinstr. 1
Tel : 183250/55

**Address :**
Nimwegen, Molenstraat 41

**Chef des Stabes :**
Oberstlt. d. Schupo MÜLLER ; Major der
Schupo ZIEHE

**Sachbearbeiter :**
PI. STEINKAMP

## NORWEGEN

**BdO :**
Genmaj. d. Pol. HÖRING

**Address :**
Oslo, Drammensveien
Tel : 43810/14

## SERBIEN

**BdO :**
Oberst d. Pol. MAY

**Address :**
Belgrad

## OSTLAND

**BdO :**
Genlt. d. Pol. JEDICKE

**Address :**
Riga

## UKRAINE

**BdO :**
Genlt. d. Pol. von BOMHARD

**Address :**
Rowno

## ITALIEN

**BdO :**
SS-OGF, Gen. d. Pol. Jürgen von KAMPTZ

## (c) BEFEHLSHABER or INSPEKTEURE DER SICHERHEITSPOLIZEI UND DES SICHERHEITSDIENSTES DES REICHSFÜHRERS-SS

(Listed according to Wehrkreis or Territory)

### WEHRKREIS I

**BdS or IdS :**
*SS-SF Oberst d. Pol. Dr.* Constantin CANARIS

**Address :**
Königsberg, Gen.-Litzmann Str. 3/7
Tel : 22537 (and T/P)

**Other Personalities :**
*SS-SBF* B. SOHST
*SS-HSF* H. BECKER

**Controlling :**
*Der Kommandeur der Sipo u. des SD in
BIALYSTOK : SS-SBF, RR Dr.* ALTEN-
LOH
Address : Nikolaistr. 15 (Erich-Koch-Str.)
Tel : 423/25 (and T/P)

### WEHRKREIS II

**BdS or IdS :**
*SS-OSBF, Reg. Dir.* SENS
Predecessors : *SS-BF General d. Pol.* NAU-
MANN, *SS-SF Oberst d. Pol.* WERNER

**Address :**
Stettin, Arndtstr. 30
Tel : 25621

**Other Personalities :**
*SS-OSBF Dr.* Max NEDWED
*SS-OSBF Dr.* Leopold SPANN
*SS-OSF* J. MÖRER
*SS-USF* W. HEIM
*SS-USF* R. POHL

### WEHRKREIS III

**BdS or IdS :**
*SS-BF Genmaj. d. Pol.* Erik von HEIMBURG
Predecessors : *SS-BF General d. Pol.* NAU-
MANN, *SS-OF, Oberst d. Pol. Dr.*
ACHAMER-PIFRADER

**Address :**
Berlin-Grunewald, Jagowstr. 16/18
Tel : 897731 (T/P and Polfunk)

**Other Personalities :**
*SS-OSBF Dr.* Robert SCHEFE
*SS-SBF* Hans HASSE
*SS-HSF* K. H. LANGENAU
*SS-HSF* Hermann EICHLER
*SS-HSF* G. LEPEK
*SS-OSF* P. ELBERS
*SS-OSF* P. WISSMANN

### WEHRKREIS IV

**BdS or IdS :**
*SS-SF, Oberst d. Pol. Dr.* Hans GESCHKE
(see also UNGARN)
Predecessor : *SS-OF Oberst d. Pol.* KLEIN

**Address :**
Dresden A24, Kaitzer Str. 30
Tel : 48197, 47967 (and T/P)

**Other Personalities :**
*SS-OSBF Dr.* Werner BRAUNE
*SS-OSBF* Hans HEINICHEN
*SS-OSBF* Ernst KAUSSMANN
*SS-OSF Dr.* EICHLER
*SS-USF* H. BROMME

### WEHRKREIS V

**BdS or IdS :**
*SS-OF Oberst d. Pol. Dr.* FISCHER

**Address :**
Stuttgart, Reinsburgstr. 32/34
Tel : 67651/53 (and T/P)
(See also Elsass)

**Other Personalities :**
*SS-SBF Dr.* Claus HÖGEL
*SS-HSF* Heinrich BERGMANN
*SS-HSF* C. WIRTH
*SS-USF* A. LEHMANN

#### Elsass

**BdS or IdS :**
*SS-OF Oberst d. Pol. Dr.* FISCHER

**Address :**
Strassburg, Otto Back Str. 10
Tel : 23761 u. 28308 (and T/P via *Stapo*)

**Other Personalities :**
*SS-SBF Prof. Dr.* Johannes STEIN
*SS-OSF* H. SCHLÜDE

### WEHRKREIS VI

**BdS or IdS :**
*SS-SF, Reg. Dir. Dr.* ALBATH
Predecessor : *SS-SF Oberst d. Pol. Dr.* BLUME

**Address :**
Düsseldorf, Kaiserswerth, Leuchtenberger
Kirchweg 73-75
Tel : 66151 (and T/P)

**Other Personalities :**
*SS-OSF* G. BOVENSIEPEN
*SS-OSF Dr.* H. SCHMID
*SS-USF* K. HARTUNG
*SS-USF* K. KÖDDERMANN
*SS-SBF* Hanns SEVERIT

### WEHRKREIS VII

**BdS or IdS :**
*SS-OF R. u. KD Oberst d. Pol.* Paul
SCHMITZ-VOIGT

**Address :**
München 22, Briennerstr. 43 (former address :
Wiedenmayerstr. 27/1)
Tel : 53218/19

**Other Personalities :**
*SS-OSBF Dr.* Werner KNAB
*SS-OSBF Dr.* Alfred TRENKER
*SS-SBF Dr.* Hans GADE
*SS-OSF* S. RANNER
*SS-USF Dr.* J. H. MITGAU

### WEHRKREIS VIII

**BdS or IdS :**
*SS-SF Oberst d. Pol.* BÖHME
Predecessors : *SS-SF Oberst d. Pol.* BIER-
MANN, *SS-BF, Oberst d. Pol.* SEETZEN

**Address :**
Breslau 18, Hohenzollernstr. 159
Tel : 82471 (and T/P)

**Other Personalities :**
*SS-HSF* K. PAHLEN
*SS-OSF* H. FIERING
*SS-OSF* H. KUNTE
*SS-OSF* W. POHL
*SS-OSF* H. TITZE
*SS-USF* F. HACKBUSCH

## WEHRKREIS IX

**BdS or IdS :**
*SS-SF, ORR Oberst d. Pol.* Otto BOVEN-SIEPEN (also listed as BdS Kopenhagen)
Predecessor : *SS-SF, Oberst d. Pol.* SEETZEN

**Address :**
Kassel, Kölnische Str. 112
Tel : 36607 (and T/P)

**Other Personalities :**
*SS-USF* W. SCHNEIDER

## WEHRKREIS X

**BdS or IdS :**
*SS-BF Oberst d. Pol.* Johannes THIELE

**Address :**
Hamburg 13, Badestr. 46 (formerly Hamburg 36, Kaiser-Wilhelm-Str. 46)
Tel : 553844 (and T/P)

**Other Personalities :**
*SS-OSBF* Hans HENSCHKE
*SS-SBF Dr.* Erwin DÖRNTE
*SS-SBF* Hans TESENFITZ
*SS-OSF* J. THOMAS
*SS-USF* K. BECKER
*SS-USF* F. SCHMOLL

## WEHRKREIS XI

**BdS or IdS :**
*SS-OSBF, ORR.* RAPP
Predecessor : *SS-OF Oberst d. Pol. Dr.* FUCHS

**Address :**
Braunschweig, Wilhelmstr. 21
Tel : 9080 (and T/P)

**Other Personalities :**
*SS-OSBF* Helmut BISCHOFF
*SS-OSF* A. KUSCHMANN
*SS-USF* P. LEMKE

## WEHRKREIS XII (including LUXEMBURG)

**BdS or IdS :**
*SS-SF Oberst d. Pol.* SOMANN
Predecessor : *SS-SF Oberst d. Pol. Dr.* ACHAMER-PIFRADER

**Address :**
Wiesbaden, Paulinenstr. 11
Tel : 28034 (and T/P)
(See also Lothringen-Westmark)

**Other Personalities :**
*SS-HSF* K. SCHÖTZ

**Controlling :**
*Kdr. d. Sipo und SD* Luxemburg : *SS-OSBF, ORR.* HARTMANN

### Lothringen-Westmark

**BdS :**
*SS-BF Genmaj. d. Pol.* DUNCKERN (P/W)

**Address :**
Metz, Bärenstr. 10
T/P

**Deputy :**
*SS-SBF RR Dr.* SCHWEDER

**Other Personalities :**
*SS-OSF* W. KLEMMER
*SS-OSF* F. MÖHLEN
*SS-USF* E. HORST

## WEHRKREIS XIII

**BdS or IdS :**
*SS-BF, Genmaj. d. Pol.* NAUMANN
Predecessor : *SS-OF, Oberst d. Pol.* KLEIN

**Address :**
Nürnberg, Pirkheimerstr. 14a
Tel : 52441 (and T/P)

**Other Personalities :**
*SS-OSBF* Josef GMEINER
*SS-USF* H. MOSANDL

## WEHRKREIS XVII

**BdS or IdS :**
*SS-BF Genmaj. d. Pol.* HUBER

**Address :**
Wien 50/IV, Theresianumgasse 18
Tel : U 46005 (and T/P)

**Other Personalities :**
*SS-HSF Dr.* F. MÜLLNER
*SS-USF* F. JOKSON
*SS-USF* F. REICHLEITNER

## WEHRKREIS XVIII

**BdS or IdS :**
*SS-BF Genmaj. d. Pol.* BRUNNER

**Address :**
Salzburg, Elisabethstr. 39
Tel : 6246 (and T/P)

**Other Personalities :**
*SS-OSBF* Adolf HOFFMANN
*SS-OSBF Dr.* Ernst WEINMANN
*SS-OSF Dr.* F. BERINGER

**Controlling :**
*Kdr. d. Sipo u.d. SD,* Marburg/Drau :
*SS-SBF, Krim. Dir.* STAGE or *SS-SF* LURKER

Address : Tegethoffstr. 34
Tel : 24/84 (and T/P, *Polfunk, Bildfunk*)

*Kdr. d. Sipo u.d. SD,* Veldes :
*SS-SBF, RRuKR* VOGT

Address : Parkhotel
Tel : 204/206 (and T/P)

## WEHRKREIS XX

**BdS or IdS :**
*SS-BF Genmaj. d. Pol.* Helmut WILLICH

**Address :**
Danzig, Neugarten 27
Tel : 21051 (and T/P via *Stapo*)

Other Personalities :
*SS-OSF* B. KUSCHEL
*SS-OSF* E. RASCH
*SS-OSF* O. WEBERSTADT


## WEHRKREIS XXI

**BdS or IdS :**
*SS-BF Oberst d. Pol.* DAMZOG
Predecessor : *SS-SF Oberst d. Pol. RDir.*
*Dr.* Hans GESCHKE

**Address :**
Posen, Fritz-Reuter Str. 2a
Tel : 6561 (and T/P via *Stapo*)

**Other Personalities :**
*SS-HSF* G. REISNER


## BÖHMEN und MÄHREN

**BdS :**
*SS-SF Oberst d. Pol. Dr.* Erwin (or Rudolf)
WEINMANN

**Address :**
Prag XIX, Kastanienallee 19
Tel : 70615, 70465 (and T/P via SD Prag)
Also : *Zentralamt für die Regelung der Juden-*
*frage in Böhmen und Mähren*, Prag XVIII,
Schillerstr. II
Tel : 71912, 71795
Controlling ; HQ Theresienstadt

**Other Personalities :**
*SS-OSBF* Heinrich BERGER
*SS-OSF* G. CLAVIEN
*SS-OSF* H. MEYER


## GENERAL GOUVERNEMENT

**BdS :**
*SS-OF Oberst d. Pol.* BIERKAMP
Predecessor : *SS-BF Genmaj. d. Pol. Dr.*
Eberhard SCHÖNGARTH

**Address :**
Krakau, Grotgera 1
Tel : 20080

**Other Personalities :**
*SS-OSBF ORR* SCHINDHELM
*SS-OSBF Dr.* Horst BARTH
*SS-SBF* Walter SCHENK
*SS-OSF* P. DOMINICK
*SS-USF* W. KÖNIG
*SS-USF* K. MISCHKE
*SS-USF* E. NEUMANN
*SS-USF* W. WALTHER

**Controlling :**
*Kdr. d. Sipo u.d. SD*, Krakau : *SS-OSBF*
*ORR Dr.* BATZ
Address : Pomorska 2 (Schlesienstr.)
Tel : 15030 (and T/P)
*Kdr. d. Sipo u.d. SD*, Lemberg : *SS-OSBF*
*ORR Dr.* TANZMANN (or WITISKA)
Address : Pelczynska 55-57 (T/P and *Polfunk*)
*Kdr. d. Sipo u.d. SD*, Lublin : *SS-OSBF*
*ORR Dr.* PÜTZ
Address : Universitätsstr. 3
Tel : 1920/24 (T/P and *Polfunk*)
*Kdr. d. Sipo u.d. SD*, Radom : *SS-OSBF*
*ORR* ILMER
Address : Kosziuskistr. 6 (Neue Gartenstr.)
Tel : 1306, 1339 (and T/P)

*Kdr. d. Sipo u.d. SD*, Warschau : *SS-OSBF*
*ORR Dr.* HAHN
Address : Str. d. Polizei 25
Tel : 80220 (T/P and *Polfunk*)


## NIEDERLANDE

**BdS :**
*SS-BF, Genmaj. d. Pol. Dr.* Eberhard
SCHÖNGARTH
Predecessors : *SS-BF Genmaj. d. Pol. Dr.*
HARSTER, *SS-OF Oberst d. Pol.* NAU-
MANN

**Address :**
Den Haag, Pleinstr. 1, or Binnenhof 7
Tel : 182540 (T/P and *Polfunk*)


## NORWEGEN

**BdS or IdS :**
*SS-SF Oberst d. Pol.* FEHLIS

**Address :**
Oslo, Viktoriaterrasse 5/7
Tel : 15801/09 (T/P and *Sipo und SD Funk*)

**Controlling :**
*Kdr. d. Sipo u.d. SD*, Bergen : *SS-OSBF*
*ORR Dr.* WEIMANN
Address : Ole Bullsplass 15
Tel : 18077/79, 18324/25 (T/P, *Sipo and SD*
*Funk*)
*Kdr. d. Sipo u.d. SD*, Drontheim : *SS-OSBF*
*ORR* FLESCH
Address : Kongensgate 26-28
Tel : 6505, 6325/26 (T/P, *Sipo and SD Funk*)
*Kdr. d. Sipo u.d. SD*, Stavanger : *SS-SBF*
WILKENS
Address : Egenesveien 17
Tel : 21595/97 (T/P, *Sipo and SD Funk*)
*Kdr. d. Sipo u.d. SD*, Tromsö : *SS-OSBF*
*ORR* POCHE
Address : Bankgate 13
Tel : 1019/20 (T/P, *Sipo and SD Funk*)


## DÄNEMARK

**BdS :**
*SS-SF Oberst d. Pol.* BOVENSIEPEN

**Address :**
Copenhagen, Shellhuset, Kampmannsgade
Vester Farimagsgade

**Deputy :**
*SS-SBF ORuKR Dr.* ZECHENTER

**Other Personalities :**
*SS-HSF* PR BETHMANN (Chief of *Abt.*
I & II—*Verwaltung*)
*SS-HSF* PAHL (Chief of *Abt.* III—*Sicher-*
*heitsdienst*)
*SS-SBF RR Dr.* HOFFMANN (Chief of
*Abt.* IV—*Stapo*)
*SS-SBF ORuKR Dr.* ZECHENTER (Chief
of *Abt.* V—*Kripo*)
*SS-HSF* DAUFELD (Vesterport) (Chief of
*Abt.* VI)
*SS-OSF Pol.* RAUTENBERG (*Abt.* I A)
*SS-OSF Pol.* PLODECK (*Abt.* I—*Organisation,*
*Dienststrafsachen*)
*SS-OSF Pol.* RATHJE (*Abt.* II A—*Besoldung,*
*Reisekosten, Unterstützungen, Beihilfen*)

*SS-USF apl. Pol.* SCHIEBER (*Abt.* II B—
*Unterkunftswesen*)

*SS-Hschaf* TA ZIEMANN (*Abt.* II C 2—
*Fernschreib- u. Fernsprechwesen*)

*SS-USF* TOS BOTOR (*Abt.* II C 3 u. II C 4
—*Kraftfahr- u. Waffenwesen*)

*SS-HSF* ARNOLD (*Abt.* III A—*Recht u.
Verwaltung in Dänemark*)

*SS-HSF Std. Rat* WÄSCHE (*Abt.* III B—
*Volkstumsfragen u. allg. polit. Fragen*)
(*Abt.* III C—*Kulturelles Leben*)

*SS-OSF* LITEL (*Abt.* III D—*Wirtschaft*)

*SS-HSF KR* HERMANNSEN (*Abt.* IV 1a-
*Linksbewegung, Dänische Gewerkschaften,
Deutsche Emigranten, Druckschriftensam-
melstelle*)

*SS-OSF KR* SCHWEITZER (*Abt.* IV 1b—
*Rechtsbewegung, Heimtücke, Dänisch-
nationalistische Widerstandsbewegung*)

*SS-Stabsscharführer* KS SCHRÖDER (*Abt.*
IV 1c—*Dänische Arbeiter im Reich, Bummel-
anten, Kriegsgefangene u. gemeinschaft-
widriges Verhalten*)

*SS-HSF KR* BUNKE (*Abt.* IV 2e—*Sabotage-
abwehr, Attentate, Waffen, Sprengstoffe*)
(*Abt.* IV 3b—*Wirtschaftsangelegenheiten,
Werkschutz, Industriesicherung, Bewachungsgewerbe*)

*SS-Oberkriminalrat* ELPERT (*Abt.* IV 3c—
*Spionageabwehr, Grenzangelegenheiten*

*Hauptmann* JAKOBSEN (*Abt.* IV/III—*Fern-
melde u. Postnachrichtendienst*)

*Major Dr.* SCHIERHOLT (*Abt.* IV/III—
*Vorsorglicher Geheimschutz auf milit.
Gebiet, allgem. Abwehrfragen u. Verbind-
ungsoff. zur Wehrmacht*)

*Major* MAYER PITON (*Abt.* IV/III-ABP
*Auslandbrief- u. Telegrammprüfstelle*)

*Hauptmann* JUSTUS (*Abt.* IV/III—*Mili-
tärische Abwehr in der Wirtschaft* " *Rüstungs-
wirtschaft* " " *Zivilwirtschaft* ")

*SS-HSF KR* BUNKE (*Abt.* IV 4a—*Politische,
Kirchen, Sekten, Freimaurer*) (*Abt.* IV
4b—*Juden, Emigranten*)

*SS-Stabsscharführer* KS KEETZ (*Abt.* IV
3r—*Registratur*)

*SS-HSF KR* HERMANNSEN (*Abt.* IV 5a—
*Schutzdienst, Überwachung, Sonderaufträge*)
(*Abt.* IV 5b—*Presseauswertung*) (*Abt.* IV
6a—*Politische Überprüfungen, Leumunds-
fragen, Auskünfte*)

*SS-USF* KS PREISSER (*Vesterport*) (*Abt.*
IV N—*Gegnernachrichtendienst*) (*Abt.* IV
6b—*Haftsachen, Schutzhaft, Arbeitserziehungslager*)

## OSTLAND
**BdS :**
*SS-OF Oberst d. Pol. Dr.* FUCHS
Predecessors : *SS-OF Oberst d. Pol. Dr.*
ACHAMER-PIFRADER, *SS-SF Reg. Dir.*
KONZINGER

**Address :**
Riga

**Controlling :**
*Kdr. d. Sipo u.d. SD in* Kauen, Minsk, Reval
Riga.

## SERBIEN
**BdS :**
*SS-OF Oberst d. Pol. Dr.* Emanuel SCHAEFER

**Address :**
Belgrad (T/P and *Polfunk*)

## UKRAINE
**BdS :**
*SS-SF Oberst d. Pol.* BÖHME
Predecessor : *SS-GF Genlt. d. Pol. Dr.*
THOMAS

**Address :**
Kiew, later Rowno (T/P)

**Controlling :**
*Kdr. d. Sipo u.d. SD in* Charkow, Dniepro-
petrowsk, Kiew, Nikolajew, Rowno (Luzk),
Shitomir, Tschernigow, Stalino, Simferopol

## FRANKREICH
**BdS :**
*SS-SF Oberst d. Pol. Dr.* KNOCHEN

**Address :**
Paris, Avenue Foch 72

**Ständ. Vertreter (Permanent Deputy) :**
*SS-OSBF* HENSCHKE

**Pers. Ref. d. BdS :**
*SS-OSF Dr.* SCHMIDT

**Controlling :**
*Kdr. d. Sipo u.d. SD in* Angers, Bordeaux,
Chalons-sur-Marne, Dijon, Nancy, Orleans,
Paris, Poitiers, Rennes, Rouen, St. Quentin ;
Limoges, Lyon, Marseille, Montpellier, Tou-
louse, Vichy.

## BELGIEN
**BdS :**
*SS-OSBF, ORR* EHLERS

**Address :**
Brüssel
(T/P and *Polfunk*)

## UNGARN
**BdS :**
*SS-SF, Oberst d. Pol. Dr.* Hans GESCHKE
(see also Wkr. IV)
*SS-OSBF ORR Dr.* AUINGER
*SS-OSBF ORR Dr.* BAUER
*SS-SBF ORR* SPRINZ

A 13

B 3

# (d) ORGANISATION OF THE OFFICE OF THE BdO, FRANCE

*(Geschäftsverteilungsplan für den Stab des Befehlshabers der Ordnungspolizei in PARIS)*

## ADJUTANTUR

| Sachgebiete | Sub-sections |
|---|---|
| Geschäftsstelle | Central Office |
| Kriegstagebuch | War Diary |
| Eingänge—offene u. VS—(Schriftwechsel, Reklamationen, usw.) | Incoming mail — ordinary and classified—(correspondence, claims, etc.) |
| Anordnungen für die Dienststelle des BdO. Stabsbefehle | BdO office directives. Staff orders |
| Vorbereitung von Dienstreisen | Arrangements for duty travel |
| Festlegung von Besprechungsterminen | Arrangements for conferences |
| Führung der persönlichen Listen des Stabes (Geburtstag, Wohnung, Fernsprechanschluss) | Keeping of personal data of staff members (date of birth, address, telephone number) |
| Stellung von Offizieren zu Veranstaltungen als Vertreter des Befehlshabers | Nomination of officers as representatives of the BdO at official functions, etc |
| Führung des Repräsentationsfonds | Funds for expenses at official functions |
| Kraftwagengestellung für den BdO Stab | Motor Pool for the staff of the BdO |
| Führung der Abwesenheitsliste vom Standort (Offz.) | List of Officers absent from the Garrison |
| Einladungen zu Veranstaltungen, Vorträgen usw | Invitations to meetings, lectures, etc |

## ABTEILUNG Ia

| Sachgebiete | Sub-sections |
|---|---|
| Aufbau und Einrichtung der deutschen Ordnungspolizei im Befehlsbereich | Organisation and establishment of the *Orpo* within the area of BdO, France |
| Aufgaben, Verwendung und Einsatz der unterstellten Einheiten | Tasks and employment of subordinate units |
| Führung von Stärkennachweisungen in der Schutzpolizei und Gendarmerie im Befehlsbereich | Strength returns of *Schupo* and *Gendarmerie* in the area of BdO France |
| Fertigung und Weiterleitung von Lage- und Tätigkeitsberichten | Compiling and forwarding of routine reports on situation and activities |
| Polizeitaktische fachwissenschaftliche Ausbildung sowie Fortbildung der Offiziere, Unterführer und Männer | Training in police tactics and methods; advanced training of Officers, NCOs and men |
| Waffen- und Schiessausbildung, Körperschulung sowie Durchführung sportlicher Veranstaltungen | Weapon Training and marksmanship; physical training; organisation of athletic meetings |
| Durchführung von Exekutionen | Executions |
| Verteidigungsmassnahmen und Verteidigungspläne, Schutz der Unterkünfte bei Unruhen. Einsatz zur Ergreifung flüchtiger Angehöriger feindlicher Flugzeugbesatzungen, Bekämpfung von Fallschirmabspringern, Luftlandetruppen | Defence measures and plans. Protection of billets during disturbances. Capture of fugitive enemy aircrews. Combatting of paratroop and airborne attacks |
| Einsatz zwecks Umsiedlung und Evakuierung | Duties in connection with forced population movements and evacuations |
| Überwachung von Gefangenen und Gefangenentransporte | Guarding of prisoners and prisoner transports |
| Gestellung von Begleitkommandos bei französischen Arbeitertransporten in das Deutsche Reich | Posting of guards for French labour transports to Germany |
| Ablösung, Verlegung bezw. Zurückziehung der unterstellten Einheiten aus dem Befehlsbereich | Relief, disposition or recall, of subordinate units from the area of BdO France |
| Durchführung von Massnahmen bei Besuchen des Führers und führender Persönlichkeiten des Staates und der Partei | Arrangements for visits of the Führer and other important personages of Government and Party |
| Paraden, Aufmärsche und Gestellung von Ehrenposten und Ehrenformationen | Parades, ceremonies, guards of honour |
| Zwischenfälle und Zusammenstösse mit Angehörigen anderer Verbände (Wehrmacht, Sicherheitspolizei, usw.) in Verbindung mit der Abt. II | Incidents and disputes with members of other organisations (*Wehrmacht, Sipo,* etc.)— in conjunction with Section II |
| Zoll- und Grenzpolizei | Customs and Frontier Police |
| Zusammenarbeit mit Wehrmacht, Sicherheitspolizei und Parteigliederungen | Co-operation with *Wehrmacht, Sipo* and Party formations |
| Feldpostangelegenheiten | Field Post |
| Weitergabe von Parolen | Issuing of passwords |
| Anfertigung von Zeichnungen. Beschaffung und Verwaltung der Karten | Preparation of drawings and overlays. Supply and Control of maps |

## ABTEILUNG Ib

| Sachgebiete | Sub-sections |
|---|---|
| Beschaffung und Verwaltung von Waffen, Munition und Gerät. Beutewaffen, Beutemunition und sonstiges waffentechnisches Beutegerät | Supply and control of arms, ammunition and equipment. Captured enemy material |

| Sachgebiete | Sub-sections |
|---|---|
| *Fahrräder, Gasmasken, Feldküchen, Beklei-dung, Ausrüstung und Verpflegung (in Ver-bindung mit Abt. IVa)* | Bicycles, gas masks, field kitchens, cloth-ing and equipment, rations—in conjunc-tion with Section IVa |
| *Beschaffung, Verwaltung und Benützung des Übungs-und Sport-geräts (in Verbindung mit Abt. IVa)* | Supply, control and use of sports equipment—in conjunction with Section IVa |
| *Truppenmässige Unter-bringung, Nachschub-wesen einschl. Betriebs-stoffversorgung (in Ver-bindung mit Abt. K)* | Billets; supplies, includ-ing fuel—in conjunc-tion with Section K |
| *Waffeninstandsetzungs-werkstätten* | Ordnance shops |

## ABTEILUNG Ic

| | |
|---|---|
| *Grundsätzliche Fragen in Ordnungspolizeilicher Hinsicht in Bezug auf :* | Basic problems of the Orpo concerning : |
| (a) *Abwehr* | (a) Military Intelli-gence |
| (b) *Französische Poli-zei* | (b) French Police |
| (c) *Französische Gen-darmerie* | (c) French Gendar-merie |
| (d) *Verkehrsmittel-schutz* | (d) Protection of ve-hicles |
| (e) *Verkehrspolizei* | (e) Traffic Police |

### Sachgebiet 1 :

| | Sub-section 1 : |
|---|---|
| *Überwachung der Bewaff-nung und Ausrüstung der französischen Poli-zei und Gendarmerie* | Supervision of arms and equipment used by the French Rural and Urban Police |
| *Kontrolle der Motorisier-ung der französischen Polizei und Gendarm-erie, Verkehrspolizei, soweit nicht vom Ab-teilungsleiter bearbeitet* | Control of the motorisa-tion of French Urban and Rural Police and Traffic Police (unless handled by Chief of section) |

### Sachgebiet 2

| | Sub-section 2 |
|---|---|
| *Abwehrangelegenheiten :* | Matters concerning Mili-tary Intelligence : |
| (a) *Sicherungsmass-nahmen zum Schutze der deutschen Ord-nungspolizei gegen-über Anschlägen, Sabotage und Spion-age* | (a) Security measures for the protection of the Orpo against attacks, sabotage and espionage |
| (b) *Auswertung des politischen Infor-mation-materials* | (b) Evaluation of poli-tical information |
| (c) *Behandlung von Verschluss-sachen* | (c) Handling of clas-sified material |
| *Aufsicht in truppenpoli-zeilicher Hinsicht über die Organisation :* | Police supervision of : |
| (a) *der französischen Polizei* | (a) French Urban Police |
| (b) *der französischen Gendarmerie* | (b) French Rural Police |
| *Stärken der französischen Polizei und Gendar-merie (in Verbindung mit dem BdS)* | Reports on strength of French Urban and Rural Police—in con-junction with BdS |

| | |
|---|---|
| *Überwachung des Ein-satzes geschlossener Verbände der franzö-sischen Polizei und Gendarmerie* | Supervision of the em-ployment of French Urban and Rural Police Units |
| *Aufsicht über die Schulen für die uniformierte französische Polizei und Gendarmerie* | Supervision of French Police Schools |
| *Aufsicht über die sonstige Ausbildung der unifor-mierten französischen Polizei und Gendar-merie in truppen-polizeilicher Hinsicht* | Supervision of other training of the French Police (Field Units) |
| *Verkehrsmittelschutz (Garde des Communica-tions), Schutz der Eisenbahnen, Wasser-strassen und wichtigen Verkehrs- und Versor-gungseinrichtungen* | Protection of means of transport and com-munication, e.g. rail-ways, waterways and other important lines of communication and supply |

### Sachgebiet 3 / Sub-section 3

| | |
|---|---|
| *Gesetzgebung betreffend die französische Polizei und Gendarmerie sowie den Verkehrsmittel-schutz (in Verbindung mit dem BdS)* | Legislation concerning French Urban and Rural Police and protection of means of transport and com-munication (in con-junction with the BdS) |
| *Dienstvorschriften der französischen Polizei und Gendarmerie* | Service regulations for French Urban and Rural Police |
| *Mitbeteiligung bei allen Rechtsfragen* | Participation in all legal questions |
| *Besonders zugewiesene Einzelfälle* | Special cases |

### Sachgebiet 4 / Sub-section 4

| | |
|---|---|
| *Durchsicht des Journals Officiel der französisch-en Regierung und der französischen Tages-presse* | Reading of the Official Gazette of the French Government and of the French Daily Press |
| *Anfertigung schriftlicher Übersetzungen für Abt. Ic* | Translations for Sec-tion Ic |
| *Mündliche Übersetzung bei Besprechungen mit französischen Dienststel-len, Anfertigungen von Besprechungsnieder-schriften* | Interpreting at confer-ences with French authorities, drawing-up of conference min-utes |
| *Tätigkeitsberichte* | Routine reports on acti-vities |
| *Besonders zugewiesene Einzelfälle* | Special cases |

## ABTEILUNG II

| Sachgebiete | Sub-sections |
|---|---|
| *Allgemeine Personalan-gelegenheiten der Schutzpolizei des Reiches und der Ge-meinden, sowie der Gendarmerie* | General personnel mat-ters of the Reich and Municipal Protection Police and of the German Gendarmerie |
| *Grundsätzliche Personal-angelegenheiten für die Offiziere, Unter-führer und Männer* | Basic personnel mat-ters (Officers, NCOs and men) |

## ABTELIUNG II—*continued*

| Sachgebiete | Sub-sections |
|---|---|
| *Führung von Polizeidienstpässen und Polizeidienstausweisen* | Police passes, service records and other personal documents |
| *Führung der Personalkartei* | Personnel file |
| *Urlaubsangelegenheiten* | Furloughs and leaves |
| *Dienststrafsachen der Offiziere, Unterführer und Männer, einschliesslich der unterstellten Einheiten* | Disciplinary matters concerning Officers, NCOs and men, including those of subordinate units |
| *Belohnungen, Belobigung* | Rewards, commendations |
| *Kriegsauszeichnungen, Waffenabzeichen und Verwundetenabzeichen des jetzigen Krieges. Polizeidienstauszeichnungen* | Decorations |
| *Dienstreisen, Erkrankungen* | Duty travel, sick register |
| *Führung der Abwesenheitsliste vom Standort* | Record of personnel absent from Garrison |
| *Todesfälle (Beisetzungsfeierlichkeiten)* | Deaths (funerals) |
| *Familienangelegenheiten (Ehescheidungen, Kinderfragen), Fürsorge der Offiziere, Unterführer und Männer. Notstands- und Unterstützungsgesuche* | Family matters (divorces, children), welfare for Officers, NCOs and men; applications for emergency allowances |

## ABTEILUNG REGISTRATUR

| Sachgebiete | Sub-sections |
|---|---|
| *Registrierung aller Verschluss-sachen* | Registration of all classified material |
| *Führung des Verschlusssachentagebuches* | Register for classified material |
| *Absendung der Verschluss-sachen* | Dispatch of classified material |
| *Ordnung aller Eingänge nach dem Aktenplan* | Sorting of all incoming mail according to the Standard Filing System |
| *Verwaltung der offenen und geheimen Akten des gesamten BdO Stabes* | Handling of all files, classified and unclassified of the BdO staff |
| *Einrichtung, Beschaffung und Verwaltung der Dienstbücherei* | Service library |
| *Anforderung von Dienst- und Druckschriften, Gesetz- und Verordnungsblättern, Zeit- und Fachzeitschriften, Heeres- und Luftwaffeverordnungsblättern* | Collection of Official Regulations and Circulars, Gazettes of the Reich Government, the Police, the Army and the Air Force |
| *Führung des Hauptbestandbuches* | Inventory records |
| *Inventarisierung sämtlicher Dienst- und Druckschriften* | Indexing of all Official Regulations and Circulars |
| *Belegsammlung über Dienst- und Druckschriften* | Collection of receipts for Official Regulations and Circulars |
| *Einrichtung und Verwaltung der R.-Pol.-Vordruckkontrolle* | Police forms and control |

## ABTEILUNG K

| Sachgebiete | Sub-sections |
|---|---|
| *Kraftfahrdienst in technischer und personneller Beziehung* | Technical and personnel aspects of M/T service |
| *Dienstaufsicht über die dem Stab des BdO zugeteilten Fahrer und Fahrzeuge* | Supervision of drivers and vehicles assigned to BdO staff |
| *Beschaffung und Verteilung von Kraftstoff für die in Frankreich eingesetzten Einheiten der Ordnungspolizei* | Procurement and distribution of fuel for *Orpo* M/T units stationed in France |
| *Abnahme neuer Fahrzeuge für Reichsministerium des Innern* | Taking over and inspection of new vehicles for the Reich Ministry of the Interior |
| *Revision aller in Frankreich eingesetzten polizeieignen Fahrzeuge* | Inspection of all Police vehicles in France |
| *Anforderung und Austausch von Kraftfahrern (in Verbindung mit Abt. II)* | Requests for, and exchange of, drivers—in conjunction with Section II |
| *Unfälle mit Dienstkraftwagen (Bearbeitung von Verkehrsunfällen)* | Accidents involving Police vehicles (handlings of traffic accidents) |
| *Dienststrafsachen des Kraftfahrtechnischen Personals (in Verbindung mit Abt. II)* | Disciplinary matters regarding M/T personnel—in conjunction with Section II |
| *Gutachtliche Stellungnahme zu Verkehrsunfällen der K.-Staffeln der Polizeibataillone* | Testimonials in case of traffic accidents of the M/T columns of Police Battalions |
| *Feuerlöscheinrichtungen für Pol. - Kraftfahrzeuge, Kraftwagenhallen und Einstellräume sowie Tankanlagen (in Verbindung mit Abt. F)* | Firefighting equipment for Police vehicles, garages and fuel dumps — in conjunction with Section F |
| *Luftschutz im Kraftfahr- und Verkehrswesen* | ARP for roads and traffic |

## ABTEILUNG LS

| Sachgebiete | Sub-section |
|---|---|
| *Durchführung des Luftschutzes für die im Bereich des Befehlshabers eingesetzten Polizeieinheiten (Ausbildung, vorbeugender Brandschutz durch Gestellung von Brandwachen, Geräte- pp. Beschaffung, Schutzräume, Verdunklung). Gestellung von Wehrmachthilfskommandos* | ARP for Police Units within the area of the BdO (Training, fire prevention measures —provision of fire guards and of equipment, air raid shelters, black-out) ARP assistance from Wehrmacht units |
| *Verbindung mit den zuständigen Wehrmachtstellen (Luftflotte, Luftgaukommandos, Militärbefehlshaber in Frankreich, Kommandant vom Gross-Paris)* | Liaison with the Wehrmacht (Air Forces, GAF District Commands, Military Commander France, Commandant of Greater Paris) |
| *Auswertung der täglichen Luftlagemeldung* | Evaluation of daily reports, on aerial activity |

| Sachgebiet | Sub-section |
|---|---|
| *Auswertung der Schadensfälle nach Luftangriffen* | Estimation of damage after air attacks |
| *Mitwirkung mit der Wehrmacht an der durch den Erlass des Oberbefehlshabers der Luftwaffe vom 4.6.42–LS Nr.2202/42—LA77—befohlenen Organisation (vornehmlich in den Betrieben, die im deutschen Auftrage arbeiten)* | Collaboration with the Wehrmacht in organising ARP (principally in those establishments working on German orders) according to the decree by the C-in-C of the GAF of 4/6/1942—LS Nr.2202/42—LA 77 |

## ABTEILUNG N

| Sachgebiete | Sub-sections |
|---|---|
| *Sicherstellung der Nachrichtenverbindungen der Ordnungspolizei* | Maintenance of Orpo signal communications |
| *Neueinrichtungen, Erweiterungen, Bedienung und Wartung von Nachrichtenanlagen der Ordnungspolizei* | New installations for, extensions to, and maintenance of *Orpo* signal stations |
| *Ortsfeste Drahtnachrichtenangelegenheiten* | Permanent telegraph and telephone installations |
| *Fernschreibnetz* | Teleprinter network |
| *Bewegliches Drahtnachrichtengerät* | Mobile telephone and telegraph equipment |
| *Ausrüstung und Ausbildung der beweglichen Nachrichten-Einheiten bei den im besetzten Frankreich eingesetzten Polizeieinheiten* | Training and equipment of mobile signal units of the Police in Occupied France |
| *Lautsprechgerät* | • Public loudspeaker systems |
| *Funkwesen* | W/T |
| *Organisation des Funkwesens, Funkbetrieb allgemein* | W/T Organisation ; general W/T matters |
| *Funkabwehr* | W/T (counter) intelligence |
| *Kurzwellenüberwachung* | Short-wave monitoring |
| *Durchführung der erforderlichen Massnahmen gegen Agenten-Funksender. Durchführung von grösseren Unternehmungen gegen Agenten-Funksender in Benehmen mit der Sicherheitspolizei und dem OKW* | Necessary measures against enemy agents using wireless. Wider operations in collaboration with the Sipo and Army Supreme Command against enemy agents using wireless |
| *Überwachung des französischen Funkdienstes. Überwachung und Kontrolle der Funk- und Fernsprechanlagen der französischen Polizei* | Supervision of French broadcasting stations. Supervision and control of French Police radio and telephone communications |
| *Festes Funknetz* | Permanent radio network |
| *Geheimschriftwesen der Ordnungspolizei* | Orpo cryptography |
| *Bewegliches Funkgerät* | Mobile radio equipment |
| *Film- und Bildwesen* | Motion pictures and photographs |

| | |
|---|---|
| *Ausbildung von Nachrichten-personal* | Training of signal personnel |
| *Personalangelegenheiten im Einvernehmen mit Abt. II* | Personnel matters—in conjunction with Section II |
| *Zusammenarbeit mit den Höheren Nachrichtenführern beim Militärbefehlshaber in Frankreich und beim Luftflottenkommando* | Collaboration with the Senior Signal Officers on the staff of the Military Commander in France and GAF HQ |
| *Bearbeitung bezw. Überwachung der Angelegenheiten des Nachrichtenverbindungsdienstes der Berufsfeuerwehren einschl. Feuerwehrregimenter im besetzten Frankreich. Überwachung und Sicherstellung der Nachrichtenverbindungen für die freiwilligen Feuerwehren im besetzten Frankreich* | Supervision of the signal communications of professional Fire Brigades, including Fire-Fighting Regiments in Occupied France. Supervision and maintenance of signal communications for the voluntary Fire-Fighting units in Occupied France |

## ABTEILUNG FEUERSCHUTZPOLIZEI

| Sachgebiete | Sub-sections |
|---|---|
| *Dienstaufsicht über die Berufs- und Freiwilligen Feuerwehren des besetzten Gebietes (Organisation, Personal, technische Einrichtungen und Ausrüstung, Ausbildung, Einsätze)* | Supervision of professional and voluntary Fire Services in Occupied France (Organisation, personnel, technical installations and equipment, training, employment) |
| *Dienstaufsicht über das Pariser Feuerwehrregiment (Personal, Kraftfahr- und Nachrichtenwesen, technische Einrichtungen und Ausrüstung, Löschwasserversorgung, Gasschutz, Ausbildung, Feuerpolizei, Luftschutzabteilung, Beaufsichtigung und Leitung des Einsatzes bei Luftangriffen)* | Supervision of the Paris Fire-Fighting Regiment (Personnel, M/T Signal communications, technical installations and equipment, water supply, anti-gas precautions, training, Fire Police, ARP, direction of employment during air attacks) |
| *Feuerpolizeiliche Überprüfungen lebenswichtiger und feuergefährdeter Betriebe* | Inspection by the Fire Police of essential installations, in particular those exposed to fire hazards |
| *Feuersicherheitliche Bearbeitungen im Rahmen des Luftschutzes (Überprüfung von Betrieben auf Luftschutzeinrichtungen, wie Feuerwehrgeräte und Löschmittel, Brandwachen, Feuerwehrkräfte und Löschwasserversorgung* | Fire prevention in connection with ARP (Inspection of Fire-Fighting equipment, Fire guards, water supply, at military and civilian establishments) |
| *Erstattung feuerwehrtechnischer Gutachten* | Expert opinions on fires, fire prevention, etc. |
| *Abnahme französischer Feuerwehrgeräte für deutsche Dienststellen* | Inspection of French fire-fighting equipment destined for German HQs |

## ABTEILUNG FEUERSCHUTZPOLIZEI—*contd.*

| Sachgebiete | Sub-sections |
|---|---|
| *Ausbildung von betriebseignen Feuerwehren deutscher Dienststellen* | Training of fire-fighting units belonging to German establishments |

## ABTEILUNG SANITÄTSWESEN

| Sachgebiete | Sub-sections |
|---|---|
| *Angelegenheiten des Sanitätsdienstes (Sprechstunden, Unterricht, Ausbildung) der Polizeiärzte und der Sanitäts-Beamten* | Medical Services (Office hours, instruction, training); Police Doctors and Health Officers |
| *Beschaffungen für den ärztlichen und zahnärztlichen Dienst. Heilfürsorge, Hygiene, Luftschutzsanitätsdienst* | Medical and dental supplies. Medical assistance, hygiene, ARP First Aid |

## ABTEILUNG WE

| Sachgebiete | Sub-sections |
|---|---|
| *Weltanschauliche Erziehung und Schulung. Auswertung des Schriftums* | Ideological indoctrination and training. Exploitation of printed matter |
| *Vorträge über Tagesfragen* | Lectures on current affairs |
| *Truppenbetreuung* | Police welfare |
| *KWHW (Kriegswinterhilfswerk)* | Wartime Winter Relief Work |
| *Spendensammlungen* | Collections for charity |

## ABTEILUNG IVa

| | |
|---|---|
| *Dienstaufsicht* | Office Administration |
| *Zahlungsanweisungen* | Money orders |
| *Verkehr mit Wehrmachtdienststellen* | Relations with Wehrmacht HQs |
| *Verbindungsführer für das Beschaffungsamt in Frankreich* | Liaison Officer with the Supply Office in France |

### Sachgebiet 1 — Sub-section 1

*Besoldung, Sondergebührnisse und Reisekosten* — Pay, allowances and travelling expenses

*Prüfung und Feststellung dieser Gebiete für Höhere SS und Polizei Führer, BdO - Stab, Kommandeur der Ordnungspolizei Paris, Aussenstellen und K.W.U. Stelle Westen* — Accounting for auditing for the HSSPf, BdO Staff, Commander of the *Orpo* in Paris, outposts and War Industries (Control Office " West ")

### Sachgebiet 2 — Sub-section 2

*Kassenleiter* — Cashier

*Geldempfang, Abrechnung, Betriebsmittelkontrolle, Postkontrolle und Aktenführung. Löhne und Sozialversicherung für Hilfskräfte* — Incoming money; accounts, inventory control, control of mail and files. Wages and social insurance for civilian employees

### Sachgebiet 3 — Sub-section 3

*Büromaterial (Dienststempel)* — Office supplies (Official rubber stamps)

*Zeitungen, Bücher, Karten, Gesetzblätter, Kraftfahr- Nachrichten- Luftschutz- und Sanitäts-wesen* — Newspapers, books, maps, official gazettes and printed matter concerning M/T, Signals, ARP and Medical affairs

### Sachgebiet 4 — Sub-section 4

*Verwaltung der Dienstgebäude und Offizierwohnungen. Geräte. Wäsche. Bausachen. Beschaffungen auf Requisition. Verpflegung (Lebensmittelmarken) Marketenderwaren* — Administration of office buildings and Officers' quarters. Equipment. Laundry. Building materials. Requisitioning. Provisions. (Ration Cards) Canteen supplies

### Sachgebiet 5 — Sub-section 5

*Heizung, Beleuchtung und Reinigung. Verbrauchsmittel. Bekleidung. Uniformbezugscheine. Instandsetzungsmaterial* — Heating, lighting and cleaning materials. Clothing. Uniform clothing coupons. Material for repairs

# ANNEXE B

## HIGHER ADMINISTRATIVE AND POLICE AUTHORITIES

PART ONE : GOVERNMENT
   (a) Government of the German Länder
       (including Prussian Provinces) and Reichsgaue
   (b) Regierungsbezirke

PART TWO : PARTY GAULEITER AND REICHSVERTEIDIGUNGSKOMMISSARE
   (RVK—Reich Defence Commissioners)

A

# ANNEXE B : PART ONE
# GOVERNMENT

## (a) GOVERNMENT OF THE GERMAN LÄNDER
### (Including Prussian Provinces) and Reichsgaue

### LAND PREUSSEN

**Reichsstatthalter**
Hermann GÖRING, acting for HITLER

**\*Ministerpräsident :**
Hermann GÖRING

**\*Staatsminister d. Innern**
Heinrich HIMMLER, also *Reichminister d. Innern, Reichsführer SS und Chef der Deutschen Polizei, Chef der Preuss. Polizei, Befehlshaber des Heimatheeres,* etc.

*These men also hold corresponding offices in the *Reichsregierung* (Reich Government) according to the principle of " personal union."

**Staatssekretär :**
*SS-OGF,* Paul KÖRNER, *Preuss. SttsR.*

**Ministerialdirektor :**
*Dr.* GRAMSCH

**Ministerialdirektor z.b.V. :**
Helmut WOHLTHAT, *Preuss. SttsR.* (Reported Head of German Economic Mission in Japan)

**Ministerialräte :**
BERGBOHM, DRAPE, LEGLER, v. NORMANN, *Dr.* KADGIEN, *Dr.* STEFFLER

Within *Land* Preussen each Province has its own administrative system as follows :

### Provinz Ostpreussen
**Address :**
Königsberg, Mitteltragheim 40B
Tel : 34081

**Oberpräsident :**
Erich KOCH, *Preuss. SttsR, Gauleiter* Party *Gau* Ostpreussen

**Deputy :**
*SS-BF, Dr.* HOFFMANN, *RPrs. b. OPrs.*

**Chief of Police Section :**
*BdO Wks.I—SS-OF, Genmaj.d.Pol.* Helmut MÜLLER, Section V

**Regierungsbezirke :**
Allenstein, Gumbinnen, Königsberg, Zichenau

### Stadt Berlin
**Address :**
Berlin, W8, Französische Str. 48
Tel : 110051

**Stadtpräsident :**
*Reichsminister Dr.* Joseph GOEBBELS, also *Gauleiter* Party *Gau* Berlin

**Vizepräsident :**
*Dr.* SCHAMVOGEL

**Chief of Police Section :**
*Pol. Präs., SS-GF, Genlt.d.Pol.* Kurt GOEHRUM

### Provinz Mark Brandenburg
**Address :**
Berlin, W35, Viktoriastr. 34
Tel : 218161

**Oberpräsident :**
*NSKK-GF,* Emil STÜRTZ, also *Gauleiter* Party *Gau* Mark Brandenburg

**Deputy :**
EBERHARDT

**Chief of Police Section :**
*BdO Wkr.* III—*Oberst d. Schupo, Dr.* WOLFSTIEG, Section IX

**Regierungsbezirke :**
Frankfurt/Oder, Potsdam

### Provinz Pommern
**Address :**
Stettin, Landeshaus
Tel : 35361

**Oberpräsident :**
*SA-OGF,* Franz SCHWEDE-COBURG, also *Preuss. SttsR, Gauleiter* Party *Gau* Pommern

**Deputy :**
*SS-OF,* ECKARDT, RPrs. Schneidemühl

**Chief of Police Section :**
*BdO Wkr* II—*SS-BF, Genmaj.d.Pól.* Konrad RITZER, Section V

**Regierungsbezirke :**
Köslin, Schneidemühl, Stettin

### Provinz Oberschlesien
**Address :**
Kattowitz, Hindenburgstr. 25
Tel : 34921

**Oberpräsident :**
*SS-OGF, SA-OGF,* Fritz BRACHT, *Gauleiter* Party *Gau* Oberschlesien

**Deputy :**
SPRINGORUM, RPrs.d.OPrs.
RR Dr. SCHWARZ, *Pers. Referent d. OPrs.*

**Regierungsbezirke :**
Kattowitz, Oppeln

### Provinz Niederschlesien
**Address :**
Breslau, Neumarkt 1–8
Tel : 22451

**Oberpräsident :**
*SS-OGF, Dr.* Karl HANKE, *Gauleiter* Party *Gau* Niederschlesien

**Deputy :**
*Graf* Otto v.d. SCHULENBURG, *RPrs. d. OPrs.*

**Chief of Police Section :**
*BdO Wkr.* VIII—*SS-BF, Genmaj.d.Pol.* LIESSEM, Section Ia

**Regierungsbezirke :**
Breslau, Liegnitz

### Provinz Magdeburg
(formerly Reg. Bez. Magdeburg in the Provinz Sachsen)

**Address :**
Magdeburg, Fürstenwallstr. 19/20 and Dompl. 3
Tel : 33891, 33881

**Oberpräsident :**
*Genlt.* Hans Georg v. JAGOW

**Deputy :**
*Dr.* OEHLER or v. BONIN

**Stabsoff. d. Schupo :**
*Maj. d. Schupo* MERCK (attached to the *OPrs.* in his capacity as *Regierungspräsident*)

**Kdr. d. Gend. :**
*Maj. d. Gend.* KINDLER (attached to the *OPrs.* in his capacity as *Regierungspräsident*)


## Provinz Halle-Merseburg

(formerly Reg. Bez. Merseburg in the Provinz Sachsen)

**Address :**
Merseburg, Schloss
Tel : 3861

**Oberpräsident :**
*Dr.* Robert SOMMER or Friedrich UEBELHÖR

**Deputy :**
v. ALT-STUTTERHEIM

**Stabsoff. d. Schupo :**
*Maj. d. Schupo* SCHRÖDER (attached to the *OPrs.* in his capacity as *Regierungspräsident*)

**Kdr. d. Gend. :**
*Maj. d. Gend.* NÜRRENBERG (attached to the *OPrs.* in his capacity as *Regierungspräsident*)


## Provinz Kurhessen

(formerly Reg. Bez. Kassel of the Provinz Hessen-Nassau)

**Address :**
Kassel, Schlossplatz 6
Tel : 24211

**Oberpräsident :**
*SA-SBF,* Erich Kurt v. MONBART or *SA-OGF,* PRINZ PHILIP v. HESSEN

**Deputy :**
*Dr.* Ernst BECKMANN

**Stabsoff. d. Schupo :**
*Maj. d. Schupo* SCHIMMEL
Deputy : *Hptm. d. Schupo* REINKE
} Attached to *OPrs.* in his capacity of *RPrs.*

**Kdr. d. Gend. :**
*Oberst d. Gend.* OVERBECK
Deputy : *Oberstlt. d. Gend.* FENSKI *or Maj. d. Gend.* DOMBROWSKI
} Attached to *OPrs.* in his capacity of *RPrs.*


## Provinz Nassau

(formerly Reg. Bez. Wiesbaden. of the Provinz Hessen-Nassau)

**Address :**
Wiesbaden, Luisenstr. 13
Tel : 59361

**Oberpräsident :**
Jakob SPRENGER, also *Reichsstatthalter Land* Hessen, *Gauleiter* Party *Gau* Hessen-Nassau

**Deputy :**
Otto SCHWEBEL


## Rheinprovinz

**Address :**
Koblenz, Wilhelmi Str. 5
Tel : S.Nr. 2301

**Oberpräsident :**
*Dr.* Nikolaus SIMMER.
Acting for *SS-OGF,* Josef TERBOVEN, at present *Reichskom.* in Oslo; also *MdR., Preuss. SttsR., Gauleiter* Party *Gau* Essen

**Deputy :**
*SS-OF,* DELLENBUSCH, *RPrs.d.OPrs., Preuss. ProvR.*

**Chief of Police Section :**
*BdO im Wkr.XII—Genmaj.d.Pol.* HILLE, Section IV

**Regierungsbezirke :**
Aachen, Düsseldorf, Koblenz, Köln, Trier, Sigmaringen (Hohenzollerische Lande)


## Provinz Schleswig-Holstein

**Address :**
Kiel, Schloss
Tel : 1384/87, 1365

**Oberpräsident :**
*SA-OGF,* Heinrich LOHSE, also *Preuss. SttsR, Gauleiter* Party *Gau* Schleswig-Holstein

**Deputy :**
*SA-SF* VÖGE, *RPrs.d.OPrs.*

**Chief of Police Section :**
*IdO—SS-OF* Paul LANGOSCH, *Pol. Präs.*
Predecessor : *Genmaj.d.Pol.* KRUMHAAR, Section VI

**Regierungsbezirk :**
Schleswig


## Provinz Hannover

**Address :**
Hannover, Calenberger Str. 29
Tel : 41221

**Oberpräsident :**
*SS-OGF,* Hartmann LAUTERBACHER, also *Gauleiter* Party *Gau* Süd-Hannover-Braunschweig

**Deputy :**
BREDOW, *RPrs.d.OPrs.*

**Chief of Police Section :**
*BdO im Wkr.XI—Genmaj.d.Pol.* KEUCK, Section I

**Regierungsbezirke :**
*Aurich, Hannover, Hildesheim, Lüneburg, *Osnabrück, Stade

*Regierungsbezirke* Aurich and Osnabrück are for the duration of the war under the *Reichsstatthalter* of Oldenburg and Bremen in his capacity as Prussian *Oberpräsident.*


## Provinz Westfalen

**Address :**
Münster, Schlossplatz 5
Tel : 24201

**Oberpräsident :**
*Dr.* Alfred MEYER, also *Gauleiter* Party *Gau* Westfalen-Nord, *Reichsstatthalter Land* Lippe (Detmold) and *Land* Schaumburg-Lippe, *MdR, ständ. Vertr. d. RM f.d. bes. Ostgebiete*

**Deputy :**
GOEDECKE, *RPrs.d.OPrs.*

**Chief of Police Section :**
*BdO im Wkr.VI—SS-BF, Genmaj.d.Pol.* SCHUMANN, Section XI

**Regierungsbezirke :**
Arnsberg, Minden, Münster

## Erfurt

(semi-independent Reg. Bez. of Prussia under Reichsstatthalter of Thüringen, in his capacity as Prussian Oberpräsident; for further details see Reg. Bez. Erfurt)

**Address:**
Erfurt, Regierungsstr. 73
Tel: S.Nr. 25131

**Regierungspräsident:**
*Dr. Otto WEBER, Thür. SttsR.*

**Vizepräsident (Deputy):**
*Dr. LAMBERT*

# LAND BAYERN

**Reichsstatthalter:**
*SA-OGF*, Franz Ritter von EPP, *Reichsleiter, Gen.d.Inf.a.D.*
München, 22, Prinzregentenstr. 7
Tel: 20209/10

**Ministerialrat:**
*SA-OGF*, SCHACHINGER

**Ministerpräsident:**
*SA-OGF*, Paul GIESLER
Ritter-von-Epp-Platz 2
Tel: 2893, 21641

**Staatsminister d.Innern:**
*SA-OGF*, Paul GIESLER, also *Staatsminister d.Finanzen, für Unterricht und Kultus und für Wirtschaft, Gauleiter* Party *Gau* München-Oberbayern
München, Theatinerstr. 21
Tel: 2893, 21641

**Ministerialdirektor:**
*Dr. MENSENS*

**Staatssekretär d.Innern:**
*SS-BF*, Hans DAUSER (?)
Predecessor: *SA-GF*, Max KÖGLMAIER
(Appointed *Präs. d. Bayer. Versich. Kammer* in München, July, 1944)

**Chiefs of Police Sections:**
*SS-OGF, Gen.d.Pol.* Karl Frhr. v. EBERSTEIN, VI (*Polizei im allgemeinen*), also HSSPf, *Wehrkr.* VII
*RDir.* Frhr. v. SCHWERIN, IV (*Bau-.Wasser-, Feuerpolizei, Energiewirtschaft*)

**Regierungsbezirke:**
Oberbayern (seat: München), Niederbayern-Oberpfalz (seat: Regensburg), Oberfranken u. Mittelfranken (seat: Ansbach), Mainfranken (seat: Würzburg), Schwaben (seat: Augsburg), Bayrische Pfalz (administered by *Reichsgau* Westmark for the duration of the war)

# LAND SACHSEN

**Reichsstatthalter und Führer der Sächsischen Landesregierung:**
*SA-OGF* Martin MUTSCHMANN, also *Gauleiter* Party *Gau* Sachsen

**Executive Assistant:**
*MinDir. Dr.* GOTTSCHALD, *Chef der Staatskanzlei* Dresden, A1, Schlossplatz 1
Tel: 24371
*RDir.* GRAEFE, *RDir. Dr.* KÄMPFE

**Minister d. Innern**
*Dr.* FRITSCH
Dresden, N6, Königsufer 2
Tel: 52151, 52251, 52051

**Chiefs of Police Sections in the Ministerium d. Innern:**
*ORR* WEICHELT, Chief of *Ministerbüro* (*Politische Polizei*)
*MinR.* SCHULZE, I (*Allg. Verwaltung*) and V (*Polizeiverwaltung und -Recht, Verkehr*)
*SS-GF, Genlt.d.Pol.* HITZEGRAD, VI (*Polizei Vollzug*—replaced, successor unknown
*MinR., Prof. Dr. Ing.* HAMMITZSCH, VIII (*Baupolizei*)

**Kdr.d.Gend.:**
*Oberst d. Gend.* KLEIN

**Regierungsbezirke:**
The four *Reg. Bez.* Dresden-Bautzen, Leipzig, Zwickau, and Chemnitz were dissolved in 1943 and their functions taken over by the *Innenministerium* of *Land* Sachsen

# LAND WÜRTTEMBERG

**Reichsstatthalter:**
*SS-OGF*, Wilhelm MURR, also *Gauleiter* Party *Gau* Württemberg - Hohenzollern
Stuttgart O, Richard-Wagner-Str. 15
Tel: 29044/45

**Staatssekretär:**
Karl WALDMANN

**Regierungsdirektoren:**
*Dr.* RITTER, SCHWENNINGER

**Ministerpräsident:**
*SA-OGF, Prof.* Christian MERGENTHALER
Stuttgart O, Richard-Wagner-Str. 15
Tel: 99111, 29741

**Innenminister:**
*SA-OGF, Dr.* SCHMID
Stuttgart-S, Wilhelm-Murr-Str. 6
Tel: 99111, 29741
Adjutant: *MinR. Dr.* GÖBEL, Personal Assistant to the Minister of the Interior
Deputy: *MinR. Dr.* DILL

**Chiefs of Police Sections in the Innenministerium:**
*SS-OGF, Gen.d.Pol., Genlt.d.W-SS* Otto HOFMANN, *MinDir.m.d.Leitung u. Bearbeitung d.Angelegenheiten d.Polizei* (Sections III A, B, C, D and E, *sowie Regelung u. Beaufsichtung d. Strassenverkehrs u. Feuerlöschwesens*) *beauftragt*. Also HSSPf, *Wehrkreis* V (Predecessor: *SS-GF, Genlt.d.Pol.* Kurt KAUL)
*LR* FEUER, III A (*Polizeidezernat*)
*Oberstlt.d.Schupo* STÜTZENBERGER, III B (*Schupo-Angelegenheiten*), *Stabsoff.d.Schupo*
*RuKR.* MUSSGAY, III C (*Politische Angelegenheiten*)
*Oberst d. Gend.* NIEDERMAYR, III D (*Gendarmerie-Angelegenheiten*), *Kdr.d.Gend.*
Deputy: *SS-OSBF, Oberstlt.d.Gend.* DORGERLOH
*ORuKR.* ELSNER, III E (*Kriminalreferat*)
*MinR.* EBERHARDT, V A (*Baupolizei*)
*MinR.* HAUG, *RV* (*Reichsverteidigung*—Reich Defence Section)

# LAND BADEN

**Reichsstatthalter:**
Robert WAGNER, also *Gauleiter* Party *Gau* Baden, *Chef der Zivilverwaltung* Elsass
Karlsruhe, Erbprinzenstr. 15
Tel: 4620/1

**Regierungsdirektor:**
(last reported as vacant)

**Ministerpräsident:**
*SA-OGF*, Walter KÖHLER, also Deputy *Gauleiter* Party *Gau* Baden
Karlsruhe, Ritterstr. 20
Tel: 4890

**Innenminister :**
SS-BF, Karl PFLAUMER
Karlsruhe, Schlossplatz 19
Tel : 7460/8
Deputy : *MinDir.* MÜLLER-TREFZER
*ORR Dr.* HERBOLD, Personal Assistant to the
· Minister
*SS-OF, Dr.* Paul Ludwig SCHMITTHENNER,
Minister without Portfolio

**Chiefs of Police Sections in the Innenministerium**
*RDir.* SCHNEIDER, *V A* (*Wehrmacht u.*
*Reichsverteidigungsangelegenheiten*)
*Oberstlt.d.Schupo* SPIEKER, V B (*Schupo*)
*Stabsoff.d.Schupo*
*Oberstlt.d.Gend. Dr.* HELD, V C (*Gend.*)
*Kdr.d.Gend.*
*MinR. Dr.* KELLER, III A (*Gewerbepolizei,*
etc.)

**Landeskommissariate :**
Freiburg, Karlsruhe, Konstanz, Mannheim, Mül-
hausen (*Zivilverwaltung* Elsass—Alsace Civil
Admin.), Strassburg (*Zivilverwaltung* Elsass).

## LAND THÜRINGEN

**Reichsstatthalter :**
SS-OGF, Fritz SAUCKEL, also *Gauleiter* Party
*Gau* Thüringen, *MdR.*
Weimar, Fürstenplatz 2 and Museumplatz 4
Tel : 6377, 2307/9

**Ministerialrat :**
(last reported as vacant)

**Ministerpräsident :**
SA-GF, Willi MARSCHLER
Weimar, Markt 15
Tel : 6141

**Chief of Innenministerium :**
SS-BF, Sttssekr. Dr. Walter ORTLEPP, SttsR.
Deputy : *Min.Dir., GehRR.* WALTHER

**Chiefs of Police Sections in the Innenministerium :**
*ORuBauR.* LANG, B (*Baupolizei,* etc.)
*RDir.* KLEINMAIER, C (*Wegepolizei,* etc.)
*ORR Dr.* SCHMIDT, P (*Polizei- u. ziviler*
*Luftschutz*)

## LAND HESSEN

**Reichsstatthalter and Führer d. Landesregierung :**
Jakob SPRENGER, also *Gauleiter* Party *Gau*
Hessen-Nassau and *Oberpräsident* of the
*Provinz* Nassau
Darmstadt, Neckarstr. 7
Tel : 4063
· Deputy : *Sttssekr.* Heinrich REINER

**Stabsamtsleiter :**
*MinR. Dr.* GROSS

**Chief of Police Section :**
*RDir.* STIEH, II (*Polizei*)

**Stabsoff.d.Schupo :**
*Oberstlt.d.Schupo* LESSING

**Kdr.d.Gendarmerie :**
*Major d. Gend.* BORSCHEL

## LAND MECKLENBURG

**Reichsstatthalter :**
SS-OGF Friedrich HILDEBRANDT, also
*Gauleiter* Party *Gau* Mecklenburg, RVK.
Schwerin i.M. Schlosstr. 9/11
Tel : 5026

**Regierungsdirektor :**
KLITZING

**Staatsminister :**
*Dr.* Friedrich SCHARF
Tel : 5051

**Chief of Staatsministerium, Abteilung Inneres :**
*MinDir. Dr.* STUDEMUND

## LAND OLDENBURG

**Reichsstatthalter :**
SS-OGF, Paul WEGENER, also *Rsth.* of
Bremen, *Gauleiter* Party *Gau* Weser-Ems
and *RVK* of Weser-Ems
Oldenburg, Adolf-Hitler-Platz and Ratherr-
Schulz-Str.
Tel : 4580

**Ministerpräsident and Innenminister :**
SA-BF, Georg JOEL, Adolf-Hitler-Platz
Tel : 6291

**Chief of Police Section in the Innenministerium :**
*MinR.* EILERS, C (*Polizei,* etc.)

**Kdr.d.Gend. :**
SS-OSBF, *Oberstlt.d.Gend.* GENZ

## LAND BRAUNSCHWEIG

**Reichsstatthalter :**
SA-OGF, Rudolf JORDAN, also *Gauleiter*
Party *Gau* Magdeburg-Anhalt, *Rsth.* of Anhalt

**Ministerpräsident and Innenminister :**
SS-OGF, KLAGGES,
Braunschweig, Bohlweg 38
Tel : 5800, 5809

**Personal Adjutant :**
SS-SBF, Peter BEHRENS

**Chief of Police Section in the Innenministerium :**
*LR* SIEVERS, Chief of Section III (*Polizei*),
also Chief of Section VI C (*Reichsverteidigungs-*
*angel.u.Militärsachen*)

**Kdr.d.Gend. :**
*Maj.d.Gend.* WITTZANG

## LAND ANHALT

**Reichsstatthalter and Führer der Landesregierung :**
SA-OGF, Rudolf JORDAN, also *Gauleiter*
Party *Gau* Magdeburg-Anhalt, and *Rsth.* of
Braunschweig
Dessau, Kavalierstr.
Tel : 3191

**Innenministerium :**
*MinR.* ACKERMANN

**Stabsoffizier der Schupo :**
*Maj.d.Schupo* ORTHMANN

**dr.d.Gend. :**
*Hptm.d.Gend.* KROKER

## LAND LIPPE

**Reichsstatthalter and Führer der Landesregierung :**
*Dr.* Alfred MEYER, also *Gauleiter* Party *Gau*
Westfalen-Nord, *OPrs.* of *Provinz* Westfalen
(seat : Münster) *Rsth.* of Schaumburg-Lippe
(seat : Bückeburg), Deputy Minister for
occupied Eastern Territories.
Detmold, Friedrichshöhe
Tel : 3407
Deputy : Adolf WEDDERVILLE

**Chief of Innenministerium :**
*RDir. Dr.* OPPERMANN

**Kdr.d.Gend. in Lippe und Schaumburg-Lippe :**
*Hptm.d.Gend.* PETZNICK

## LAND SCHAUMBURG-LIPPE

**Reichsstatthalter :**
*Dr.* Alfred MEYER, (See also *Land* Lippe)
Detmold, Friedrichshöhe
Tel : 3407

**Landespräsident :**
Karl DREIER, also *Regierungsvizepräs. Reg. Bez. Minden*
Bückeburg
Tel : 646/7

**Kdr.d.Gend. in Lippe u. Schaumburg-Lippe :**
*Hptm.d.Gend.* PETZNICK

## HANSESTADT BREMEN

**Reichsstatthalter :**
SS-OGF, Paul WEGENER, also *Rsth.* of Oldenburg, *Gauleiter* Party *Gau* Weser-Ems, and *RVK* of Weser-Ems
Deputy : *SA-OF,* Senator *Dr.* FISCHER
Bremen, Haus des Reiches
Tel : 22501

**Landesregierung (Senat) :**
*SA-OGF,* BÖHMCKER, also *Regierender Bürgermeister* (Governing Mayor)
Tel : 22501

**Innere Verwaltung :**
*SA-OF,* Senator *Dr.* FISCHER
Bremen, Contrescarpe 22/23
Tel : 22501
Deputy : KAYSER

## HANSESTADT HAMBURG

**Reichsstatthalter und Chef der Staatsverwaltung :**
*SS-u.NSKK-OGF,* Karl KAUFMANN, also *Gauleiter* Party *Gau* Hamburg
Hamburg, 13, Harvestehuder Weg 12
Tel : 445151
Deputy : *SS-GF,* Georg AHRENS, *Prs. Sttssekr.*

**Regierender Bürgermeister (Governing Mayor) :**
*Dr.* Karl Vincent KROGMANN

**Chiefs of Police Sections :**
*SS-GF, Genmaj.d.Pol.* Graf Georg HENNING BASSEWITZ-BEHR, Chief of Section III (*Polizei*)
*RViPrs. Dr.* BOCK von WÜLFINGEN, Chief of Section I (*Allg. Angelegenheiten, Reichsverteidigung,* etc.)
Deputy : *ORR* LUDWIG

## REICHSGAU WIEN

**Reichsstatthalter :**
Baldur v. SCHIRACH, also *Reichsleiter, Gauleiter* Party *Gau* Wien
Wien I, Ballhausplatz 2
Tel : 24520
Deputies : *SS-BF, RPrs. Dr.* DELLBRÜGGE, (for *Reichsgau* Wien)
*Bürgermeister* JUNG (for Stadt Wien)
Deputy : *SS-GF, Dr.* Hans BLASCHKE

**Chief of Police Section :**
*LtRDir. Dr.* KRAMER (Section I—*Allg. u. innere Angelegenheiten*)

## REICHSGAU KÄRNTEN

**Reichsstatthalter :**
*SS-OGF, Dr.* Friedrich RAINER, also *Gauleiter* Party *Gau* Kärnten
Klagenfurt, Arnolfplatz 1
Tel : 1701, 2701, 2191
Deputy : THIMEL

**Chief of Police Section :**
*RDir. Dr.* v. BURGER-SCHEIDLIN, Section I (*Allg. u. innere Angel.*)

**Kdr. d. Gend. :**
*Oberst d. Gend.* HANDL
*SS-OSBF, Oberstlt.d.Gend.* SCHINTLER

## REICHSGAU NIEDERDONAU

**Reichsstatthalter :**
*SS-OGF, Dr.* Hugo JURY, also *Gauleiter* Party *Gau* Niederdonau
Wien I, Herrengasse 11/13
Tel : 20520
Deputy : *RPrs. Dr.* Erich GRUBER

**Chief of Police Section :**
*LtRDir. Dr.* VOGEL, Section I (*Allg. u. innere Angelegenheiten*)

## REICHSGAU OBERDONAU

**Reichsstatthalter :**
*SS u. SA-GF,* August EIGRUBER, *Gauleiter* Party *Gau* Oberdonau
Linz, Landhaus, Stockbauer Str.
Tel : 26821
Deputy : *SS-BF, RPrs. Dr.* Günther PALTEN

**Pers. Asst. of the Rsth. :**
*RPrs. Dr.* SCHIELIN

**Chiefs of Police Sections :**
*RDir. Dr.* STÖGER, I (*Allg. u. innere Angelegenheiten*)
*ORR* WÖSS, Ia (*Innere Angelegenheiten*)

## REICHSGAU SALZBURG

**Reichsstatthalter :**
*SS-OGF, Gen.maj.d.Pol. Dr.* Gustav Adolf SCHEEL, also *Gauleiter* Party *Gau* Salzburg
Salzburg, Residenzplatz 1
Tel : 2541, 2471
Deputy : *RPräs. Dr.* Wolfgang LAUE

**Personal Assistant of the Rsth. :**
*GauOVwR.* HANSEL

**Chief of Police Section :**
*RDir.* DENGLER, I (*Allg. u. innere Angelegenheiten*)

## REICHSGAU STEIERMARK

**Reichsstatthalter :**
*SA-OGF, Dr.* Siegfried UIBERREITHER, also *Gauleiter* Party *Gau* Steiermark
Graz, Burg, Hofgasse 13
Tel : 83000

**Pers. Assistant of the Rsth. :**
*RR Dr.* JÄGER

**Adjutant :**
*SA-SBF, Dr.* RUMPF

**Chiefs of Police Sections :**
*LtRDir. Dr.* MAYRHOFER, Chief of Section I (*Allg. u. innere Angelegenheiten*)
*ORR Dr.* WÖHRER, Chief of Sub-section Ia (*Innere Angelegenheiten*)

**Kdr. der Gendarmerie :**
*Oberst d. Gend.* NOWOTNY

**Stabsoffizier d. Schupo :**
*Oberstlt. d. Schupo,* BELLEVILLE

## REICHSGAU TIROL-VORARLBERG

**Reichsstatthalter :**
*NSKK-GF, Okom.* Franz HOFER, also *Gauleiter* Party *Gau* Tirol-Vorarlberg
Innsbruck, Landhaus
Tel : 3600
Deputy : *RPrs. Dr.* HOFMANN, or *Dr.* KOCH

**Chief of Police Section :**
*RDir. Dr.* SCHULER, Section I (*Allg. u. innere Angelegenheiten*)

**Stabsoff.d.Schupo :**
*Maj.d.Schupo* LEIB (from *PV.* Berlin)

## REICHSGAU SUDETENLAND

**Reichsstatthalter :**
*SS-OGF*, Konrad HENLEIN, *Gauleiter* Party
*Gau* Sudetenland Reichenberg, Gymnasium-
str. 6
Tel : 3841/47
Deputy : *RPrs. Dr.* Friedrich VOGELER

**Personal Assistant of the Rsth. :**
*ORR.* MÄNNEL

**Chiefs of Police Sections :**
*LtRDir.* KELLNER, Section I (*Allg. u.innere
Angelegenheiten*)
*LtRDir.* FREMEREY, Section II (*Wirtschafts-
abt.*)

**Regierungsbezirke :**
Aussig, Eger, Troppau

## REICHSGAU DANZIG-WESTPREUSSEN

**Reichsstatthalter :**
*SS-OGF*, Albert FORSTER, also *Gauleiter*
Party *Gau* Danzig-Westpreussen
Danzig, Jopengasse 11
Tel : 23088
Deputy : *SS-BF, Dipl.Ing.* Wilhelm HUTH,
*RPrs.*

**Chief of Police Section :**
*RDir.* STUNTZ, Section I (*Allg.u.Innere Verw.*)

**Regierungsbezirke :**
Bromberg, Danzig, Marienwerder

## REICHSGAU WARTHELAND

**Reichsstatthalter :**
*SS-u.NSKK-OGF* Arthur GREISER, also
*Gauleiter* Party *Gau* Wartheland.
Posen, Felix-Dahn-Platz 17
Tel : 8241
Deputy : *SA-BF, RPrs.* August JÄGER

**Chief of Police Section :**
*RDir.* WEBER

**Regierungsbezirke :**
Hohensalza, Litzmannstadt, Posen

## REICHSGAU WESTMARK

**Reichsstatthalter :**
*Dr.* Robert LEY, also *Gauleiter* Party *Gau*
Westmark, *Chef der Zivilverwaltung* in Lothrin-
gen
Saarbrücken, Hindenburgstr. 15
Deputy : *RPrs.* BARTH
Dienstgebäude f. Polizei u. Gendarmerie
Saarbrücken, Hindenburgstr. 4/6

**Chiefs of Police Sections :**
*RViPrs.* BINDER, I (*Verwaltung*)
*RDir. Dr.* HEYDENREICH, Ia (*Allg.u.Innere
Angel.*)
*RDir.* SCHNARRENBERGER, Ia (*Elsass*)

**Kdr.d.Gend. :**
*Maj.d.Gend.* PÖCK
Deputy : *Hptm.d.Gend.* RENSTROENISCH

## PROTEKTORAT BÖHMEN und MÄHREN

**Reichsprotektor :**
*Reichsleiter Dr.* Wilhelm FRICK (Former *Reichsminister des Innern*)

**M.d.F.d.G.b. :**
*SS-Oberstgruppenführer, Generaloberst d.Pol.* Kurt
DALUEGE (reported ill)

**Staatssekretär :**
*SS-OGF, Dr.* Karl Hermann FRANK, *Staats-
minister*
Deputy : *MinR. Dr.* GRIES

**Generalinspekteur der Verwaltung :**
*RR Dr.* REICHMANN

**Chiefs of Police Sections :**
*BdO, SS-BF, Genmaj.d.Pol.* DIERMANN
*ORR* REISCHAUER, Section I, II (*Allgemeine-
und Kommunalverwaltung*)
*MinR. Dr.* RÖSSLER, Section I, III (*Bau-
polizei*, etc.)
*Gebietsführer* KNOOP, Section I, IV (*Staats-
jugend*)

**Stabsoffizier der Schupo :**
*Maj. der Schupo* KAUTSCH (?) also Ia office
of *BdO*

**Kdr. d. Gendarmerie :**
*Oberstlt. der Gend.* KREIKENBORN

## (b) REGIERUNGSBEZIRKE
## LAND PREUSSEN

### AACHEN
(Rheinprovinz)

**Address :**
Aachen, Theaterplatz 14
Tel : 27511

**Regierungspräsident :**
*SS-OF* Franz VOGELSANG

**Regierungsvizepräsident :**
FROITZHEIM

**Stabsoff. d. Schupo :**
*Maj. d. Schupo* SIEGMEIER

**Kdr. d. Gend. :**
*Oberst d. Gend.* OEMLER
Deputy : *Major d. Gend.* GRUNOW

### ALLENSTEIN
(Ostpreussen)

**Address :**
Allenstein, Frhr. v. Stein Str. 1
Tel : 3241/49

**Regierungspräsident :**
*Dr.* Karl SCHMIDT

**Regierungsvizepräsident :**
v. SCHELLER, *ständ. Stellvertreter d. RPräs.,*
Dirig. I

**Stabsoff. d. Schupo :**
*Major d. Schupo* BODENSTEDT

**Kdr. d. Gend. :**
*Oberstlt. d. Gend.* LUEG

### ARNSBERG
(Westfalen)

**Address :**
Arnsberg, Seibertzstr. 1
Tel : 241/3 and 341/6

**Regierungspräsident :**
EICKHOFF

**Regierungsvizepräsident :**
*Dr.* RUHS (*Wehrd.*)
Deputy : *Dr.* STIER

**Stabsoff. d. Schupo :**
Oberstlt. d. Schupo SAUPE

**Kdr. d. Gend. :**
Oberstlt. d. Gend. WEIGERT
Major d. Gend. WILKE

## AURICH
(Hannover)

—for the duration of the war under the RSth. of Oldenburg and Bremen

**Address :**
Aurich, Schlossplatz
Tel : 441

**Regierungspräsident :**
SA-BF Dr. LAMBERT
Deputy : KRIEGER

**Regierungsvizepräsident :**
Dr. IDE

**Stabsoff. d. Schupo**
Major d. Schupo SKISCHALLY

**Kdr. d. Gend. :**
Major d. Gend. BOLTE

## BERLIN

**Address :**
Berlin W 8, Französische Str. 48
Tel : 110051

**Pol. Präsident or Regierungspräsident :**
SS-GF, Genlt. d. Pol. Kurt GOEHRUM

**Pol. Vizepräsident :**
SCHOLTZ

## BRESLAU
(Niederschlesien)

**Address :**
Breslau, Lessingplatz
Tel : 22281 and 28898

**Regierungspräsident :**
Dr. Georg KROLL

**Regierungsvizepräsident :**
v. RUMOHR, ständ. Stellvertreter d. Präs.

**Stabsoff. d. Schupo :**
Major d. Schupo BRAU

**Kdr. d. Gend. :**
Major d. Gend. GIEBEL

## DÜSSELDORF
(Rheinprovinz)

**Address :**
Düsseldorf, Alte-Garde-Ufer 2
Tel : 36011

**Regierungspräsident :**
Dr. BURANDT

**Regierungsvizepräsident :**
Dr. KÄMMERER, ständ. Stellvertreter d. Präs., Dirig. I

**Stabsoff. d. Schupo :**
Major d. Schupo RIECK

**Kdr. d. Gend. :**
Oberstlt. d. Gend. KÖLLNER
Major d. Gend. HINZEMANN

## ERFURT

(Note.—Regierungsbezirk Erfurt is semi-independent and comes under the Reichsstatthalter of Thüringen in his capacity as Prussian Oberpräsident.)

**Address :**
Erfurt, Regierungsstr. 73
Tel : 25131

**Regierungspräsident :**
Dr. Otto WEBER, Thür. SttsR.

**Regierungsvizepräsident :**
Dr. LAMBERT

**Stabsoff. d. Schupo :**
Major d. Schupo SCHMIDT-HAMMERSTEIN
Deputy : Hptm. d. Schupo EHRENBERG

**Kdr. d. Gend. :**
Oberstlt. d. Gend. MEIER

## FRANKFURT a.d. ODER
(Mark Brandenburg)

**Address :**
Frankfurt, Regierungsstr. 23/26
Litzmannstr. 11
Tel : 2701/06, 2458/59

**Regierungspräsident :**
Heinrich REFARDT

**Regierungsvizepräsident :**
KOTHE, ständ. Stellvertreter d. Präs., Dirig. I (retired April, 1944)

**Stabsoff. d. Schupo :**
Major d. Schupo FUCHS, I

**Gend. Off. :**
Oberst d. Gend. WALTER
Oberstlt. d. Gend. SCHOLZ
SS-OSBF u. Oberstlt. d. Gend. KAHL
Major d. Gend. WITZMANN

## GUMBINNEN
(Ostpr.)

**Address :**
Gumbinnen, Königsplatz 1
Tel : 2253/54

**Regierungspräsident :**
Dr. Herbert ROHDE

**Regierungsvizepräsident :**
EICHHARDT, ständ. Stellvertreter d. Präs. (abg.)

**Stabsoff. d. Schupo :**
Major d. Schupo FABER

**Kdr. d. Gend. :**
Oberstlt. d. Gend. WALTER
Major d. Gend. MEINKE

## HANNOVER
(Hannover)

**Address :**
Hannover, Am Archiv 3, Archivstr. 2
Tel : 44221

**Regierungspräsident :**
SS-GF, Genmaj. d. Pol. Paul KANSTEIN

**Regierungsvizepräsident :**
Dr. BIERWIRTH

**Kdr. d. Gend. :**
Major d. Gend. BRUCHMÜLLER

## HILDESHEIM
(Hannover)

**Address :**
Hildesheim, Domhof 1
Tel : 2721—2730

**Regierungspräsident :**
Dr. BINDING

**Regierungsvizepräsident :**
Dr. BACKMEISTER, ständ. Stellvertreter d. Präs., Dirig. I

**Stabsoff. d. Schupo :**
Major d. Schupo BUCHHOLZ

**Kdr. d. Gend. :**
Major d. Gend. LEISTE

## KASSEL

Since early 1944 changed to Prussian Province Kurhessen ; for details see under Provinz Kurhessen in section (a).

## KATTOWITZ
### (Oberschlesien)
**Address :**
Kattowitz, Charlottenstr. 44
Tel : 34921
**Regierungspräsident :**
*Dr.* MÜLLER-HACCIUS
**Regierungsvizepräsident :**
*Dr.* KESSLER
**Kdr. d. Schupo :**
*Oberstlt. d. Schupo* BROCKMANN
**Kdr. d. Gend. :**
*Oberst d. Gend.* MATT

## KOBLENZ
### (Rheinprovinz)
**Address :**
Koblenz, Am Rhein 12
Tel : 2301
**Regierungspräsident :**
*SS-BF Dr.* Gerhard MISCHKE
**Regierungsvizepräsident :**
*Dr.* STRUTZ, *ständ. Stellvertreter d. Präs., Dirig. I, Stellvertreter d. RPräs. im BezVwg.*
**Stabsoff. d. Schupo :**
*Oberst d. Schupo* PUTZ
*Major d. Schupo* ARNIKE
**Kdr. d. Gend. :**
*Major d. Gend.* PALM

## KÖLN
### (Rheinprovinz)
**Address :**
Köln, Zeughausstr. 4
Tel : 220901
**Regierungspräsident :**
*SS-OF* Karl Eugen DELLENBUSCH *RPrs. d. OPrs.*
**Regierungsvizepräsident :**
*Dr.* BECKHAUS, *ständ. Vertreter d. Präs., Dirig. I*
**Stabsoff. d. Schupo :**
*Oberstlt. d. Schupo* BUCH
*Oberstlt. d. Schupo* v. HIRSCH
**Kdr. d. Gend. :**
*Major d. Gend.* BERGAUER

## KÖNIGSBERG
### (Ostpr.)
**Address :**
Mitteltragheim 40, Schönstr. 3
Tel : 34071 and 34081
**Regierungspräsident :**
ANGERMANN or
*SS-BF Dr.* Philip HOFFMANN
**Stabsoff. d. Schupo :**
*Major d. Schupo* KOPKA
**Kdr. d. Gend. :**
*Major d. Gend.* RUDAT

## KÖSLIN
### (Pommern)
**Address :**
Köslin, Strasse der SA 34
Tel : 2981 and 3211

**Regierungspräsident :**
*SS-BF* Emil POPP
**Regierungsvizepräsident :**
*Dr.* SCHROEDER
**Stabsoff. d. Schupo :**
*Major d. Schupo* FISCHER
**Kdr. d. Gend. :**
*SS-OSBF, Oberstlt. d. Gend.* GOEDE (*abg.*)

## LIEGNITZ
### (Niederschlesien)
**Address :**
Liegnitz, Schlossplatz 1
Tel : 1931'
**Regierungspräsident :**
*Dr.* BOCHALLI
**Regierungsvizepräsident :**
*Dr.* BEHR, *LR* (*k*)
**Stabsoff. d. Schupo :**
*Major d. Schupo* VOGELSÄNGER
**Kdr. d. Gend. :**
*Major d. Gend.* KREUTZAHLER

## LÜNEBURG
### (Hannover)
**Address :**
Lüneburg, Am Ochsenmarkt 3
Tel : 4058
**Regierungspräsident :**
*SS-BF* Fritz HERMANN, *RPrs.*
**Regierungsvizepräsident :**
v. KUSSEROW, *ständ. Stellvertreter d. Prs., Dirig. I u. III*
**Stabsoff. d. Schupo :**
*Major d. Schupo* HANISCH
**Kdr. d. Gend. :**
*Major d. Gend.* NILSSON

## MAGDEBURG

Since early 1944 changed to Provinz Magdeburg ; for details see under Provinz Magdeburg in section (a).

## MERSEBURG

Since early 1944 changed to Provinz Halle-Merseburg ; for details see under Provinz Halle-Merseburg in section (a).

## MINDEN
### (Westfalen)
**Address :**
Minden, Weserglacis 2
Tel : 1411/14
**Regierungspräsident :**
*Dr.* Graf Günther v. STOSCH
**Regierungsvizepräsident :**
*Landespräs.* Karl DREIER (*Landesregierung Schaumburg-Lippe*); *Dr.* RESCHKE, *LR. ständ. Stellvertreter d. Prs., Dirig. I, III; Dr,* ZACHER
**Stabsoff. d. Schupo :**
*Oberstlt. d. Schupo* BROCKE
**Kdr. d. Gend. :**
*Major d. Gend.* ZUTZ

## MÜNSTER
### (Westfalen)
**Address :**
Münster, Domplatz 1
Tel : 24451

**Regierungspräsident :**
Dr. RUHS (Wehrd.)
SA-BF Theodor FRÜNDT

**Regierungsvizepräsident :**
KLEIN, ständ. Stellvertreter d. Präs., Dirig. I

**Stabsoff. d. Schupo :**
Major d. Schupo BECK

**Kdr. d. Gend. :**
Oberstlt. d. Gend. Dr. BARFUSS

## OPPELN
(Oberschlesien)

**Address :**
Oppeln, Hafenstr.
Tel : 3311

**Regierungspräsident :**
SS-OF Dr. Herbert MELHORN
Predecessor : SS-BF Albrecht SCHMELT (retired March, 1944)

**Regierungsvizepräsident :**
WEHRMEISTER, ständ. Stellvertreter d. Präs.

**Stabsoff. d. Schupo :**
Major d. Schupo BEER (abg.)

**Kdr. d. Gend. :**
Oberstlt. d. Gend. SCHMIDT

## OSNABRÜCK
(Hannover).

—for the duration of the war under the RSth. of Oldenburg and Bremen.

**Address :**
Osnabrück, Braunauer Wall 18
Tel : 4171

**Regierungspräsident :**
Dr. Karl STÜBLER

**Regierungsvizepräsident :**
Dr. SCHULTZ, ständ. Stellvertreter d. Präs., Dirig. I
Dr. STÜHLER (abg. z. Rchskom. Den Haag)

**Stabsoff. d. Schupo :**
Major d. Schupo APELDORN

**Kdr. d. Gend. :**
Major d. Gend. BOOS

## POTSDAM
(Mark Brandenburg)

**Address :**
Potsdam, Spandauerstr. 32/33
Tel : 4051

**Regierungspräsident :**
SS-BF Graf Gottfried von BISMARCK-SCHÖN-HAUSEN

**Regierungsvizepräsident**
Dr. HONIG, ständ. Stellvertreter d. Präs.

**Stabsoff. d. Schupo :**
Oberstlt . WESTPHAL

**Kdr. d. Gend. :**
Oberst d. Gend. SPAETHEN
Major d. Gend. SCHÜLER

## SCHLESWIG
(Schleswig-Holstein)

**Address :**
Schleswig, Gottorpstr. 2
Tel : 2141

**Regierungspräsident :**
Otto HAMKENS (in Wartestand versetzt, March, 1944)

**Regierungsvizepräsident :**
Dr. RÖHRIG, ständ. Stellvertreter d. Präs., Dirig. Ia (retired March, 1944)

**Kdr. d. Gend. :**
Major d. Gend. DAHNKE

## SCHNEIDEMÜHL
(Pommern)

**Address :**
Schneidemühl, Danziger Platz 7
Tel : 2341 and 2351

**Regierungspräsident :**
SS-OF Paul ECKARDT

**Regierungsvizepräsident :**
DANZIG, ständ. Vertreter d. Präs., Dirig. I

**Stabsoff. d. Schupo :**
Major d. Schupo LABUDE (abg.)

**Kdr. d. Gend. :**
Major d. Gend. MÜLLER

## SIGMARINGEN

Note.—Reg. Bez. Sigmaringen, also known as the Hohenzollerische Lande, is semi-independent, but comes administratively under the Oberpräsident of the Rheinprovinz, seat Koblenz.

**Address :**
Sigmaringen, Karlstr. 13
Tel : 312/14

**Regierungspräsident :**
SS-BF Wilhelm DREHER

**Stellvertreter d. Präs. :**
v. REDEN, VwgDir. u. Dir. d. OVA u. VG Ltr. des GPA

**Gend. Oberaufsichtsbeamter :**
Hptm. d. Gend. SEELING

## STADE
(Hannover)

**Address :**
Stade, Adolf-Hitler-Platz 16
Tel : 3041

**Regierungspräsident :**
SA-BF Hermann FIEBIG

**Regierungsvizepräsident :**
Dr. POTTHOF, ständ. Stellvertreter d. Präs., Dirig. I

**Stabsoff. d. Schupo :**
Oberstlt. d. Schupo STOCKHOFE

**Kdr. d. Gend. :**
Major d. Gend. BÖHLKE

## STETTIN
(Pommern)

**Address :**
Stettin, Hakenterrasse 4
Tel : 25131

**Regierungspräsident :**
SS-OF, Paul ECKARDT (also RPrs. in Schneidemühl)

**Komm. m.d. Verwd. Reg. Präs. Stelle beauftr. :**
LR Dr. LOTZ, vom LRA Giessen

**Regierungsvizepräsident :**
TINCAUZER, ständ. Stellvertreter d. Präs.

**Stabsoff. d. Schupo :**
Oberst. d. Schupo PORATH
Major d. Schupo PERLING

**Kdr. d. Gend. :**
Major d. Gend. SCHWIEGER

## TRIER
### (Rheinprovinz)

**Address :**
Trier, Domfreihof 1
Tel : 4241

**Regierungspräsident :**
SIEKMEIER

**Regierungsvizepräsident :**
*Dr.* MALLMANN, *stand. Stellvertreter d. Präs.,
Dirig.* I u. III (retired April, 1944)

**Stabsoff. d. Schupo :**
*Oberstlt. d. Schupo* HARTMANN
*Major d. Schupo* BELOW

**Kdr. d. Gend. :**
*Oberstlt. d. Gend.* RIBSTEIN
*Major d. Gend.* CORNELIUS

## WIESBADEN

Since early 1944 changed to Prussian Provinz
Nassau ; for details see under Provinz Nassau in
section (a).

## ZICHENAU
### (Ostpr.)

**Address :**
Zichenau, Bahnhofstr.
Tel : 441—45

**Regierungspräsident :**
ROSSBACH

**Regierungsvizepräsident :**
EICHHARDT, *RViPrs.*

**Stabsoff. d. Schupo :**
*Major d. Schupo* BARTH

**Kdr. d. Gend. :**
*Oberst d. Gend.* KRAUSE

# LAND BAYERN

## OBERBAYERN

**Address :**
München, Maximilianstr. 14

**Regierungspräsident :**
*SS-BF* Franz MAYR

**Regierungsvizepräsident :**
*Dr.* DITTMAR (*abg.*)

## NIEDERBAYERN-OBERPFALZ

**Address :**
Regensburg
Tel : 2251

**Regierungspräsident :**
*SS-OF* Gerhard BOMMEL

**Regierungsvizepräsident :**
*Dr.* SIERP, *ORR* (*RMdI*) (*k*)

## PFALZ
### (see under Westmark)

**Address :**
Speyer, Maximilianstr. 5
Tel : 2411

**Regierungspräsident :**
WERNER

## OBER- u. MITTELFRANKEN

**Address :**
Ansbach
Tel : 2151

**Regierungspräsident :**
DIPPOLD

**Regierungsvizepräsident :**
HETZEL

## MAINFRANKEN

**Address :**
Würzburg

**Regierungspräsident :**
*SS-GF Dr.* Otto HELLMUTH

## SCHWABEN

**Address :**
Augsburg
Tel : 5842

**Regierungspräsident :**
*SS-u. SA-GF* Karl WAHL

**Regierungsvizepräsident :**
*Dr.* SCHWAAB

# REICHSGAU SUDETENLAND

## AUSSIG

**Address :**
Aussig, Schillerstr. 6
Tel : 3242/3249

**Regierungspräsident :**
*SS-OSBF Dr.* Oskar DENGEL

**Regierungsvizepräsident :**
*Dr.* Harry v. CRAUSHAAR

**Stabsoff. d. Orpo :**
*Oberstlt. d. Schupo* DÜNNEBIER

## EGER

**Address :**
Karlsbad, Prof. Rudolf-Lössl Str. 10
Tel : 2254—57, 3368-70

**Regierungspräsident :**
*SA-SF Dr.* Wilhelm SEBEKOVSKY

**Regierungsvizepräsident :**
MÜLLER

**Stabsoff. d. Schupo :**
*Oberstlt. d. Schupo* STERN

**Kdr. d. Gend. :**
*Major d. Gend.* MASCHLER

## TROPPAU

**Address :**
Troppau, Landhausg. 1
Tel : 221

**Regierungspräsident :**
Edler v.d. PLANITZ or
*SS-OF* ZIPPELIUS

**Regierungsvizepräsident :**
*Dr.* SCHÖNBERG

**Stabsoff. d. Schupo :**
*Oberstlt. d. Schupo* GRUNDIG

**Kdr. d. Gend. :**
*Major d. Gend.* JÄCKEL
*Hptm. d. Gend.* WECKAUF

# REICHSGAU DANZIG-WESTPREUSSEN

## DANZIG

(*Regierungsbezirk* Danzig is now merged with the office of the *RSth.*)

**Address :**
Danzig, Jopeng. 11
Tel : 23088

**Regierungspräsident :**
SS-OGF Albert FORSTER, *RSth.*, *Gauleiter* Danzig
Deputy : *SS-BF* Wilhelm HUTH

**Stabsoff. d. Schupo :**
*Major d. Schupo* FILZECK

**Kdr. d. Gend. :**
*Oberstlt. d. Gend.* WILCKE
*Deputy : Major d. Gend.* KÖHLER

## BROMBERG

**Address :**
Bromberg, Hermann-Göring-Str. 39
Tel : 2720–30

**Regierungspräsident :**
KÜHN

**Regierungsvizepräsident :**
*Dr.* MÜNZEL (*abg. nach* Luxemburg)
KÖHLER, *LR* (Offenbach)

**Stabsoff. d. Schupo :**
*Major d. Schupo* SCHIEMANN

**Kdr. d. Gend. :**
*Oberstlt. d. Gend.* BANDLIN

## MARIENWERDER

**Address :**
Marienwerder, Regierungsplatz 3
Tel : 2341/2347

**Regierungspräsident :**
Otto von KEUDELL

**Regierungsvizepräsident :**
*Dr.* SCHUMANN, *LR.* (vtrw.)

**Stabsoff. d. Schupo :**
*Oberstlt. d. Schupo* ROGGENBUCK

**Kdr. d. Gend. :**
*Major d. Gend.* KUHN

# REICHSGAU WARTHELAND

## HOHENSALZA

**Address :**
Hohensalza, Bismarckstr.
Tel : 2001

**Regierungspräsident :**
SS-BF Genmajor d. Pol. Dr. W. ALBERT

**Regierungsvizepräsident :**
*Dr.* PICKEL, *ständ. Vertreter d. Präs.*

**Stabsoff. d. Schupo :**
*Major d. Schupo* JONUSCHEIT

**Kdr. d. Gend. :**
*Oberst d. Gend. Dr.* GUDEWILL

## LITZMANNSTADT

**Address :**
Litzmannstadt, Gartenstr. 15
Tel : 14414

**Regierungspräsident :**
SS-SF Dr. Walter MOSER

## POSEN

**Address :**
Posen, Reichsring 5
Tel : 8181

**Regierungspräsident :**
*Dr.* Viktor BÖTTCHER, *SttsR.*

**Regierungsvizepräsident :**
*Dr.* RIEDIGER, *ständ. Stellvertreter d. Präs.*

**Stabsoff. d. Schupo :**
*Oberstlt. d. Schupo* DAMM

**Kdr. d. Gend. :**
*Oberstlt. d. Gend. Dr.* HELD
*Major d. Gend.* TEETZMANN

# SPECIAL CASES

## Länder or Reichsgaue which are subdivided into districts comparable to Regierungsbezirke

### BADEN and ALSACE

Subdivided into *Landeskommissariate*

| | |
|---|---|
| **Freiburg** | *Landeskommissär* Georg SCHWOERER |
| **Karlsruhe** | *Landeskommissär* DOLD |
| **Konstanz** | *Landeskommissär* Gustav WÖHRLE |
| **Mannheim** | *Landeskommissär Dr.* Gustav BECHTOLD |
| **Mülhausen** | |
| **Strassburg** | |

### REICHSGAU WESTMARK

Subdivided into :—

**Zivilverwaltungsgebiet Lothringen, seat Metz**
*RPräs.* Friedrich WENNER

**Saarland, seat Saarbrücken**
*RPräs.* BARTH

**Bayrische Pfalz (see Bayern), seat Speyer**
*RPräs.* WERNER

# ANNEXE B: PART TWO

## PARTY GAULEITER AND REICHSVERTEIDIGUNGSKOMMISSARE

### (RVK-Reich Defence Commissioners)

### BADEN

**Address :**
*Gauleitung* Baden *der NSDAP*,
Strassburg, Gauhaus, Pioniergasse 2–20
Tel : 29620

**Gau Area :**
*Land* Baden and the *Zivilverwaltungsgebiet* Elsass

**Gauleiter and RVK :**
Robert WAGNER, also *RSth. u. Chef d. Zivilverwaltung* in Elsass
Deputy *Gauleiter* : *Befehlsleiter* Hermann RÖHN
Acting for the RVK : *SS-BF* Karl PFLAUMER, Minister of the Interior of Baden

### BAYREUTH

**Address :**
*Gauleitung* Bayreuth *der NSDAP*,
Bayreuth, Maxstr. 2
Tel : 2651

**Gau Area :**
*Reg.-Bez.* Niederbayern and *Reg.-Bez.* Oberpfalz (seat Regensburg) and part of the *Reg.-Bez.* Ober- and Mittelfranken (seat Ansbach)

**Gauleiter and RVK :**
*SS-OGF, SA-GF* Fritz WÄCHTLER
Deputy *Gauleiter* : Ludwig RUCKDESCHEL
Acting for the RVK : *SS-OF* BOMMEL, also *RPrs.* of *Reg.-Bez.* Niederbayern-Oberpfalz (seat Regensburg)

### BERLIN

**Address :**
*Gauleitung* Berlin *der NSDAP*,
Berlin, W9, Hermann-Göringstr. 14
Tel : 110029

**Gau Area :**
*Reichshauptstadt* Berlin

**Gauleiter and RVK :**
*Dr.* Joseph GOEBBELS, also *Reichsminister für Volksaufklärung und Propaganda, Preussischer Oberpräsident* (Berlin ranks equal to the Prussian Provinces)
Deputy *Gauleiter* : *Befehlsleiter* Arthur GÖRLITZER

### DANZIG-WESTPREUSSEN

**Address :**
*Gauleitung* Danzig-Westpreussen *der NSDAP*,
Danzig, Jopengasse 10
Tel : 25641

**Gau Area :**
*Reichsgau* Danzig-Westpreussen

**Gauleiter and RVK :**
*SS-OGF* Albert FORSTER
Danzig, Jopengasse 11
Tel : 23088/89
Deputy *Gauleiter* : Gerhard SEEGER
Acting for RVK : *SS-BF* Wilhelm HUTH, also acting *RPrs.* of *Reg.-Bez.* Danzig.

### DÜSSELDORF

**Address :**
*Gauleitung* Düsseldorf *der NSDAP*,
Düsseldorf, Alte-Garde-Ufer 3
Tel : 10131

**Gau Area :**
Southern half of the *Reg.-Bez.* Düsseldorf

**Gauleiter and RVK :**
*SA-GF* Friedrich Karl FLORIAN
Deputy *Gauleiter* : *Hauptdienstleiter* Karl OVERHUES
Acting for the RVK : *Dr.* BURANDT, also *RPrs.* Düsseldorf

### ESSEN

**Address :**
*Gauleitung* Essen *der NSDAP*,
Essen, Friedrichstrasse 1 (Thomashaus)
Tel : 51661

**Gau Area :**
Northern half of the *Reg.-Bez.* Düsseldorf

**Gauleiter and RVK :**
*SS-GF* Joseph TERBOVEN
Deputy *Gauleiter* : *Hauptdienstleiter* Fritz SCHLESSMANN, also *RPrs.* Düsseldorf
Acting for the RVK : *Dr.* BURANDT, also *RPrs.* Düsseldorf

### FRANKEN

**Address :**
*Gauleitung* Franken *der NSDAP*,
Nürnberg 0, Schlageterplatz 1–5
Tel : 22081

**Gau Area :**
Southern half of the *Reg.-Bez.* Ober-und Mittelfranken (Seat Ansbach)

**Gauleiter and RVK :**
*SA-GF, Befehlsleiter* Karl HOLZ (k)
Acting for the RVK : DIPPOLD, also *RPrs.* Ansbach

### HALLE-MERSEBURG

**Address :**
*Gauleitung* Halle-Merseburg *der NSDAP*,
Halle-Saale, Rudolf-Jordan-Platz 1
Tel : 7111

**Gau Area :**
Identical with the Prussian Province Halle-Merseburg (former *Reg.-Bez.* Merseburg of the Province Sachsen)

**Gauleiter and RVK :**
*SS-OGF* Joachim-Albrecht EGGELING
Deputy *Gauleiter* : *Hauptdienstleiter* Georg TESCHE
Acting for the RVK : Friedrich UEBELHOER, also *OPrs.* Halle-Merseburg (formerly *RPrs.* of *Reg.-Bez.* Merseburg)

### HAMBURG

**Address :**
*Gauleitung* Hamburg *der NSDAP*,
Hamburg 36, Alsterufer 27 (Gauhaus)
Tel : 441061

**Gau Area :**
*Reichsgau u. Hansestadt* Hamburg

**Gauleiter and RVK :**
*SS-und NSKK-OGF* Karl KAUFMANN, also *Rsth.*
Deputy *Gauleiter :* Harry HENNINGSEN

## HESSEN-NASSAU

**Address :**
*Gauleitung* Hessen-Nassau *der NSDAP,*
Frankfurt/Main, Horst-Wessel-Platz,
Tel : 50011        Schliessfach 615

**Gau Area :**
*Land* Hessen (Oberhessen, Starckenburg und Rheinhessen), the Prussian Province Nassau, Stadtkreis Hanau and the *Landkreise* Hanau, Gelnhausen and Schlüchtern

**Gauleiter and RVK :**
Jakob SPRENGER, also *RSth.* of *Land* Hessen (seat Darmstadt), and *OPrs.* of the Province Nassau (seat Wiesbaden)
Deputy *Gauleiter : Befehlsleiter* Karl LINDER
Acting for the RVK : Otto SCHWEBEL, also *RPräs.* of *OPräs.* Province Nassau.

## KÄRNTEN

**Address :**
*Gauleitung* Kärnten *der NSDAP,*
Klagenfurt, Miesstaler Str. 1
Tel : 1701

**Gau Area :**
*Reichsgau* Kärnten, including the Oberkrain (comprising the *Landkreise* Krainburg, Radmannsdorf, Stein and Feldkirch)

**Gauleiter and RVK :**
*SS-OGF Dr.* Friedrich RAINER, also *Rsth.* and *Chef der Zivilverwaltung im besetzten Gebiete* in Krain und Südkärnten
Deputy *Gauleiter : Oberdienstleiter* Friedrich THIMEL
Klagenfurt—Arnulfpl. 1
Tel : 1701
Acting for the RVK : Ferdinand WOLSEGGER, also *RPrs.*

## KÖLN-AACHEN

**Address :**
*Gauleitung* Köln-Aachen *der NSDAP,*
Köln/Rhein, Claudiusstr. 1
Tel : 90451

**Gau Area :**
*Reg.-Bez.* Aachen und Köln

**Gauleiter and RVK :**
*SS-GF* and *NSKK-OGF* Joseph GROHÉ
Deputy *Gauleiter : Befehlsleiter* Richard SCHALLER
Acting for the RVK : *SS-OF,* Karl Eugen DELLENBUSCH, acting *RPrs. Reg.-Bez.* Köln

## KURHESSEN

**Address :**
*Gauleitung* Kurhessen *der NSDAP,*
Kassel, Humboldtstr. 8 1/2

**Gau Area :**
Prussian Province Kurhessen (formerly the *Reg.-Bez.* Kassel of the Prussian Province Hessen-Nassau), excluding the *Stadtkreis* Hanau and the *Landkreise* Hanau, Gelnhausen, Schlüchtern and the *Herrschaft* Schmalkalden

**Gauleiter and RVK :**
Karl WEINRICH or Karl GERLAND (acting)
Deputy *Gauleiter : Hauptdienstleiter* Max SOLBRIG
Acting for the RVK : *SA-OGF* Prinz Philip von HESSEN, *OPrs.* Province of Kurhessen, probably through *SA-SBF* Erich Kurt von MONBART, *RPrs.* (possibly *OBrs.*) of Kurhessen

## MAGDEBURG-ANHALT

**Address :**
*Gauleitung* Magdeburg-Anhalt *der NSDAP,*
Dessau, Seminarstr. 10
Tel : 3111

**Gau Area :**
*Land* Anhalt and Prussian Province Magdeburg (formerly *Reg.-Bez.* Magdeburg of the Prussian Province Sachsen)

**Gauleiter and RVK :**
*SA-OGF* Rudolf JORDAN, also *Rsth.* ot Braunschweig-Anhalt
Deputy *Gauleiter : Hauptdienstleiter* Rudolf TRÄUTMANN
Acting for the RVK : *Genlt.z.V.* Hans Georg von JAGOW, *RPrs.* (possibly *OPrs.*) of Magdeburg

## MAINFRANKEN

**Address :**
*Gauleitung* Mainfranken *der NSDAP,*
Würzburg, Adolf-Hitler-Str. 24a
Tel : 3561

**Gau Area :**
Identical with the *Reg.-Bez.* Mainfranken
*Gauleiter* and RVK : *SS-GF Dr.* Otto HELLMUTH, also *RPrs.* of Mainfranken
Deputy *Gauleiter : Hauptdienstleiter* Wilhelm KÜHNREICH

## MARK BRANDENBURG

**Address :**
*Gauleitung* Mark Brandenburg *der NSDAP,*
Berlin, W35, Kurmärkische Str. 1
Tel : 213625/26, 219641

**Gau Area :**
Prussian Province Mark Brandenburg except Greater Berlin

**Gauleiter and RVK :**
*NSKK-GF* Emil STÜRTZ, also *OPrs.* of Mark Brandenburg

## MECKLENBURG

**Address :**
*Gauleitung* Mecklenburg *der NSDAP,*
Schwerin i.M. Adolf Hitler Haus
Tel : 5191

**Gau Area :**
Identical with the *Land* Mecklenburg

**Gauleiter and RVK :**
*SS-OGF* Friedrich HILDEBRANDT, also *Rsth.* *Land* Mecklenburg
Deputy *Gauleiter : Hauptdienstleiter* Gerd von KOERBER

## MOSELLAND

**Address :**
*Gauleitung* Moselland *der NSDAP,*
Koblenz, Emil-Schüller Str. 18/20
Tel : 2261

**Gau Area :**
*Reg.-Bez.* Koblenz and Trier and the *Zivilverwaltungsgebiet* Luxemburg (*Landkreise* Esch, Grevemacher and Diekirch)

**Gauleiter and RVK :**
Gustav SIMON, also *Chef der Zivilverwaltung*
in Luxemburg
Deputy *Gauleiter* : *Befehlsleiter* Fritz RECK-
MANN
Acting for the RVK : *SS-BF Dr.* Gerhard
MISCHKE, also *RPrs.* in Koblenz

## MÜNCHEN-OBERBAYERN

**Address :**
*Gauleitung* München-Oberbayern *der NSDAP*,
München, 30, Prannerstr. 20
Tel : 12343

**Gau Area :**
*Reg.-Bez.* Oberbayern, except the *Landkreis*
Friedberg

**Gauleiter and RVK :**
Paul GIESLER, also *Bayrischer Minister-
präsident* and *Innenminister*
Deputy *Gauleiter* : Franz BUCHNER
Acting for the RVK : *SA-GF* Max KÖGL-
MAIER, *Staatssekretär im Bayr. Innen-
ministerium*

## NIEDERDONAU

**Address :**
*Gauleitung* Niederdonau *der NSDAP*,
Wien IX, Wasagasse 10 (offices partly in Krems)
Tel : A 19550/57

**Gau Area :**
*Reichsgau* Niederdonau and those *Kreise* of
the Protektorat which are included in the
Party *Gau* by the same name.

**Gauleiter and RVK :**
*SS-OGF Dr.* Hugo JURY, also *Rsth.* of Nieder-
donau
Deputy *Gauleiter* : *Hauptdienstleiter* Karl GER-
LAND
Acting for the RVK : *Dr.* Erich GRUBER,
*RPrs.*

## NIEDERSCHLESIEN

**Address :**
*Gauleitung* Niederschlesien *der NSDAP*,
Breslau 5, Eichhornstr. 2
Tel : 52161

**Gau Area :**
Identical with the Province Niederschlesien

**Gauleiter and RVK :**
*SS-OGF Dr.* Karl HANKE, also *OPrs.* of the
Province Niederschlesien

## OBERDONAU

**Address :**
*Gauleitung* Oberdonau *der NSDAP*,
Linz, Landhaus
Tel : 26821

**Gau Area :**
*Reichsgau* Oberdonau and those *Kreise* of the
Protektorat which are included in the Party
*Gau* of the same name

**Gauleiter and RVK :**
*SS-u.SA-GF* August EIGRUBER
Deputy *Gauleiter* : *Hauptdienstleiter* Christian
OPDENHOFF
Acting for the RVK : *SS-BF Dr.* Günther
PALTEN, also *RPrs.*

## OBERSCHLESIEN

**Address :**
*Gauleitung* Oberschlesien *der NSDAP*,
Kattowitz, Gauhaus
Tel : 36921/25

**Gau Area :**
Identical with the Province Oberschlesien

**Gauleiter and RVK :**
*SS-OGF, SA-OGF* Fritz BRACHT, also *OPrs.*
of the Province Oberschlesien

## OST-HANNOVER

**Address :**
*Gauleitung* Ost-Hannover *der NSDAP*,
Lüneburg, Schiessgrabenstr. 8/9
Tel : 4344/46

**Gau Area :**
Identical with the *Reg.-Bez.* Lüneburg and
Stade of the Province Hannover

**Gauleiter and RVK :**
Otto TELSCHOW
Deputy *Gauleiter* : *Hauptdienstleiter* Heinrich
PEPER
Acting for the RVK : *SS-BF* Fritz HERMANN,
also *RPrs.* of *Reg.-Bez.* Lüneburg

## OSTPREUSSEN

**Address :**
*Gauleitung* Ostpreussen *der NSDAP*,
Königsberg, Grosse Schlossteichstr. 7
Tel : 34085/88

**Gau Area :**
Identical with the Province Ostpreussen, possibly
including the Bialystok District

**Gauleiter and RVK :**
Erich KOCH, also *OPrs.* of the Province Ostpr.
Deputy *Gauleiter* : *Befehlsleiter* Ferdinand
GROSSHERR

## POMMERN

**Address :**
*Gauleitung* Pommern *der NSDAP*,
Stettin, Landeshaus (Eingang Schubertstr.)
Tel : 25781

**Gau Area :**
Identical with the Province Pommern

**Gauleiter and RVK :**
*SA-OGF*, Franz SCHWEDE-COBURG, also
*OPrs.* of the Province Pommern
Deputy *Gauleiter* : *Hauptdienstleiter* Paul
SIMON

## SACHSEN

**Address :**
*Gauleitung* Sachsen *der NSDAP*,
Dresden, A 1, Bürgerwiese 24
Tel : 24241

**Gau Area :**
Identical with the *Land* Sachsen

**Gauleiter and RVK :**
*SA-OGF* Martin MUTSCHMANN, *Rsth.* of
Land Sachsen

## SALZBURG

**Address :**
*Gauleitung* Salzburg *der NSDAP*,
Salzburg, Mozartplatz 8
Tel : 2541

**Gau Area :**
Identical with the *Reichsgau* Salzburg

**Gauleiter and RVK :**
*SS-GF, GenMaj.d.Pol. Dr.* Gustav Adolf
SCHEEL, also *Rsth.* of Reichsgau Salzburg
Deputy *Gauleiter* : *Hauptdienstleiter* Anton
WINTERSTEIGER
Acting for RVK : *Dr.* LAUE, also *RPrs.* of
Salzburg

## SCHLESWIG-HOLSTEIN

**Address :**
*Gauleitung* Schleswig-Holstein *der NSDAP*,
Kiel, Gauhaus, Jensenstr. 1
Tel : 8080

**Gau Area :**
Identical with the Province Schleswig-Holstein

**Gauleiter and RVK :**
*SA-OGF* Heinrich LOHSE, also *OPrs.* of the
Province Schleswig-Holstein
Deputy *Gauleiter : Befehlsleiter* Wilhelm SIEH
Acting for the RVK : *SA-SF* VÖGE, *RPrs.*
of Schleswig

## SCHWABEN

**Address :**
*Gauleitung* Schwaben *der NSDAP*,
Augsburg, Kornhausg. 4
Tel : 6631

**Gau Area :**
*Reg.-Bez.* Schwaben and the *Landkreis* Friedberg of the *Reg.-Bez.* Oberbayern

**Gauleiter and RVK :**
*SS-u. SA-GF* Karl WAHL, *RPrs.* of the
*Reg.-Bez.* Schwaben
Deputy *Gauleiter :* Anton MÜNDLER

## STEIERMARK

**Address :**
*Gauleitung* Steiermark *der NSDAP*,
Graz, Landhaus
Tel : 83000/113/200

**Gau Area :**
Identical with the *Reichsgau* Steiermark, including the *Zivilverwaltungsgebiet* Untersteiermark (*Landkreise* Cilli, Marburg, Murau,
Trifail, Pettau, Luckenburg and Rann, and
the *Stadtkreis* Marburg)

**Gauleiter and RVK :**
*SA-OGF* Dr. Siegfried UIBERREITHER, also
*Rsth.* and *Chef des Zivilverwaltungsgebietes*
Untersteiermark
Deputy *Gauleiter : Hauptdienstleiter* Dr. Tobias
PORTSCHY

## SUDETENLAND

**Address :**
*Gauleitung* Sudetenland *der NSDAP*,
Reichenberg, Peter-Dornhäuser Str. 2
Tel : 3753/57

**Gau Area :**
Identical with the *Reichsgau* Sudetenland

**Gauleiter and RVK :**
*SS-OGF* Konrad HENLEIN, *Rsth.* Sudetenland
Deputy *Gauleiter : Dienstleiter* Hermann NEU-
BERG
Acting for the RVK : *Dr.* Friedrich VOGELER,
*RPrs.* of Reichenberg

## SÜD-HANNOVER—BRAUNSCHWEIG

**Address :**
*Gauleitung* Süd-Hannover—Braunschweig *der
NSDAP*,
Hannover, Gaubefehlsstand, Schützenpl. 5
Tel : 44291–94

**Gau Area :**
Identical with the *Reg.-Bez.* Hannover (excluding
the *Landkreis Grafschaft* Schaumburg) and
the *Reg.-Bez.* Hildesheim and the *Land*
Braunschweig

**Gauleiter and RVK :**
*SS-OGF* Hartmann LAUTERBACHER
Deputy *Gauleiter :* August KNOP
Acting for the RVK : *SS-BF* Dr. Walter
ORTLEPP, *Thüringischer Innenminister* and
*Staatssekretär*

## THÜRINGEN

**Address :**
*Gauleitung* Thüringen *der NSDAP*,
Weimar, Adolf-Hitler-Str. 7
Tel : 6191

**Gau Area :**
Identical with the *Land* Thüringen, the *Reg.-*
*Bez.* Erfurt of Preussen and the *Landkreis*
*Herrschaft* Schmalkalden

**Gauleiter and RVK :**
Fritz SAUCKEL, M.d.R.
Deputy *Gauleiter : SS-BF* Heinrich SIEK-
MEIER, *M.d.R.*

## TIROL-VORARLBERG

**Address :**
*Gauleitung* Tirol-Vorarlberg *der NSDAP*,
Innsbruck, Landhaus (Erweiterungsbau)
Tel : 6311, 6331

**Gau Area :**
Identical with the *Reichsgau* Tirol-Vorarlberg

**Gauleiter and RVK :**
*NSKK-GF* Franz HOFER, also *Rsth.*
Deputy *Gauleiter : Befehlsleiter* Herbert
PARSON
Acting for the RVK : *Dr.* KOCH or *Dr.* HOF-
MANN, *RPrs.*

## WARTHELAND

**Address :**
*Gauleitung* Wartheland *der NSDAP*,
Posen, Schlossfreiheit 11/13
Tel : 8171, 1823/24

**Gauleiter and RVK :**
*SS-u. NSKK-OGF* Arthur GREISER, also
*Rsth.*
Deputy *Gauleiter : Befehlsleiter* Kurt SCHMALZ
Acting for the RVK : *SA-BF* August JÄGER,
*RPrs.* Posen, *Min Dir.* and *Ständiger Vertr.*
*d. Rsth.*

## WESER-EMS

**Address :**
*Gauleitung* Weser-Ems *der NSDAP*,
Oldenburg, Landtag, Adolf Hitler Pl.
Tel : 6171

**Gau Area :**
*Land* Bremen-Oldenburg and the *Reg.-Bez.*
Aurich and Osnabrück

**Gauleiter and RVK :**
*SS-OGF* Paul WEGENER, *Rsth.* (seat Bremen)
Deputy *Gauleiter : Befehlsleiter* Georg JOEL

## WESTFALEN-NORD

**Address :**
*Gauleitung* Westfalen-Nord *der NSDAP*,
Münster, Bismarckallee 5
Tel : 24271

**Gau Area :**
Identical with the *Reg.-Bez.* Münster and
Minden, the *Länder* Lippe and Schaumburg-
Lippe, and the *Landkreis Grafschaft* Schaum-
burg

**Gauleiter and RVK :**
Dr. Alfred MEYER, also *OPrs. d.* Provinz Westfalen (seat Münster) and *Rsth* Lippe (seat Detmold) and Schaumburg-Lippe (seat Bückeburg), and Deputy Minister for the Occupied Eastern Territories
Deputy *Gauleiter : Befehlsleiter* Peter STANGIER

### WESTFALEN-SÜD

**Address :**
*Gauleitung* Westfalen-Süd *der NSDAP,*
Bochum, Königsallee
Tel : 63401/07

**Gau Area :**
Identical with the *Reg.-Bez.* Arnsberg

**Gauleiter and RVK :**
*SS-GF* Albert HOFFMANN (*k*)
Deputy *Gauleiter : Hauptdienstleiter* Heinrich VETTER
Acting for the RVK : EICKHOFF, *RPrs.* of *Reg.-Bez.* Arnsberg (Bochum)

### WESTMARK

**Address :**
*Gauleitung* Westmark *der NSDAP,*
Neustadt/W., Str.d.13. Januar 1925
Tel : 3596

**Gau Area :**
*Reichsgau* Westmark, including the Bavarian *Reg.-Bez.* Pfalz, the Saarland and the *Zivilverwaltungsgebiet* Lothringen

**Gauleiter and RVK :**
*Reichsleiter Dr.* Robert LEY, also *Rsth.* of *Reichsgau* Westmark (seat Saarbrücken) and *Chef der Zivilverwaltung in* Lothringen (seat Metz) with

Wilhelm STÖHR as acting *Gauleiter* and RVK
Deputy *Gauleiter : SS-BF* Ernst Ludwig LEYSER
Acting for the RVK : BARTH, *RPrs.*

### WIEN

**Address :**
*Gauleitung* Wien *der NSDAP,*
Wien, I., Josef-Bürckel-Ring 3
Tel : 50560

**Gau Area :**
Greater Vienna

**Gauleiter and RVK :**
Baldur von SCHIRACH, *Rsth.*
Deputy *Gauleiter : Befehlshaber* Karl SCHARIZER
Acting for the RVK : *SS-OF* DELLBRÜGGE, also *RPrs.* and *Ständiger Stellvertreter d. Rsth.*

### WÜRTTEMBERG-HOHENZOLLERN

**Address :**
*Gauleitung* Württemberg-Hohenzollern *der NSDAP,*
Stuttgart, N., Goethestr. 14
Tel : 25935

**Gau Area :**
Identical with the *Land* Württemberg, including the Hohenzollerische Lande (*Reg.-Bez.* Sigmaringen)

**Gauleiter and RVK :**
*SS-OGF* Wilhelm MURR, also *Rsth.* Württemberg-Hohenzollern
Deputy *Gauleiter :* VOGT
Acting for the RVK : *Dr.* SCHMID, *Minister d.Innern,* Württemberg

# ANNEXE C

## NATIONAL POLICE ADMINISTRATION HQ

PART ONE :     POLIZEIPRÄSIDIEN.

PART TWO :     POLIZEIDIREKTIONEN.

PART THREE : POLIZEIÄMTER.

PART FOUR :    EINHEITSAKTENPLAN (Standard Filing System).

PART FIVE :     AUSLÄNDERKARTEI (System of Registration of Foreigners).

A

## POLIZEIPRÄSIDIEN

*Note.*—The capital letter in brackets after the name of the town indicates the official German classification of the individual *Polizeipräsidium* as follows :

(S) *Sonderklasse* (Special class).
(A) *Grosse* (Large).

(B) *Mittlere* (Medium size).
(C) *Kleinere* (Small).

### AACHEN (C)
**Address :—**
Polizeipräsidium, Kasernenstrasse 25.
Telephone : 27121.

**Nr. of Precincts :—**6.
(*Polizeireviere*).

**Personalities :—**
*Pol. Präs. :* SS-SF August FLASCHE.
*Vertr. :* RR ERDMANN.
*Kdr. d. Schupo :* Oberstlt. d. Schupo WASKOW ;
Maj. TRÖGER.
*Sachbearbeiter :* PR. RETHAGE, BEIER,
STÜTTGEN.
*Pol. Amtm. :* HAYN.

### AUGSBURG (C)
**Address :—**
Polizeipräsidium, Prinzregentenplatz 1.
Telephone : 3231

**Personalities :—**
*Pol. Präs. :* SS-BF, Genmaj. d. Pol. Wil.
STARCK (also commander of SS-Abschn. 32).
*Kdr. d. Schupo :* Maj. STAEB.

### AUSSIG (C)
**Address :—**
Polizeipräsidium, Bismarkstr. 4, 6, and 8.
Telephone : 2072, 2121.

**Nr. of Precincts :—**3.

**Personalities :—**
*Pol. Präs. :* SS-SF Dr. NUTZHORN ; Dr.
MICHELS.
*Kdr. d. Schupo :* Oberstlt. d. Schupo ILIAS.

**Subord. Office :—**PA. TEPLITZ-SCHÖNAU.

### BERLIN (S)
**Address :—**
Polizeipräsidium, C2, Alexander Str. 10.
Telephone : 510023.

**Nr. of Precincts :—**168.

**Personalities :—**
*Pol. Präs. :* SS-GF, Genlt. d. Pol. Kurt GOEH-
RUM, also HSSPf Berlin.
*Vizepräs. :* SCHOLTZ.
*Kdr. d. Schupo :* Genmaj. d. Pol. ERIK von
HEIMBURG, also reported BdO and BdS
BERLIN.
*Chef d. Stabes :* Oberst d. Schupo ABRAHAM.
*Kdr. FSchP. :* Genmaj. d. Pol. Dipl. Ing.
GOLDBACH.
*Leit. Polizeiarzt :* Oberstarzt d. Pol. Dr. JÜTT-
NER.
*Leit. Pol. Veter. Arzt :* SS-SF, Oberstvet. d. Pol.
Dr. BÖLLERT.
*Staatskrankenhaus d. Pol. ; BERLIN :* Ober-
feldarzt d. Pol. Dr. Walter VOIGT.
*Leitender Regierungsdirektor :*
KRETZSCHMAR, *Abt.* III.
*Regierungsdirektoren :*

| | |
|---|---|
| BOLZ | *Abt.* IV. |
| Dr. JENTZSCH | (*Wehrm.*). |
| Dr. KRAUSSOLDT | (*Wehrm.*). |
| TRITTEL | (*Wehrm.*). |

*Oberregierungsräte :*

| | |
|---|---|
| v. ABERCRON | *Abt.* I. |
| Dr. BRAILEAU | *PA* Wedding. |
| DIERIG | *PA* Charlottenburg. |
| GRUNDEY | *Präs. Geschäftsst.* |
| KRAATZ | *Abt.* III. |
| MEYER | *PA* Schöneberg. |
| v. MILLESI | *Abt.* IV. |
| Dr. MÜLLER-STOSCH | *PA* Lichtenberg |
| MUSSMANN | *PA* Pankow. |
| Dr. POLTROCK | *Abt.* V. |
| Dr. RHUMBLER | *PA* Mitte. |
| Dr. SCHUBERT | *PA* Wedding. |
| WOBBE | *PA* Neukölln. |
| ZIEDRICH | (*abg. zur Pol. Verw. Schule* München.) |

*Oberregierungs-u. Bauräte :*

| | |
|---|---|
| Dr. BERTRAM | |
| HERRMANN | *Abt.* III. |
| v. BOTH | *Abt.* III. |
| MARGRAF | (*ORBauR*). |

*Oberregierungs-u. Gewerberat :*

| | |
|---|---|
| FRITZ | *Abt.* IV. |

*Oberregierungs-u. Medizinalrat :*

| | |
|---|---|
| Dr. REDEKER | *Abt.* V. |

*Oberregierungs-u. Gewerbemedizinalrat :*

| | |
|---|---|
| Dr. GERBIS | *Abt.* IV. |

*Oberregierungs-u. Veterinärräte :*

| | |
|---|---|
| Dr. WUNDRAM | *Abt.* V. |
| Dr. LINDENAU | *Abt.* V. |

*Regierungsräte :*

| | |
|---|---|
| BATHE | *Abt.* III. |
| BEHRENS | *Abt.* V. |
| v. BERCKEFELDT | *Präs. Geschäftsst.* |
| Dr. BERINGER | *Abt.* IV. |
| BONDKOWSKI | *Abt.* IV. |
| Dr. Baron v. CEUMERN-LINDEN-STJERNA | (*Wehrm.*). |
| DEGNER | *PA* Charlottenburg. |
| FOLIE | *Abt.* IV. |
| HAUBRICH | *Abt.* I. |
| Dr. HORST | (*Wehrm.*). |
| Dr. KONHÄUSSER | *Abt.* IV. |
| Dr. LUGER | *Abt.* IV. |
| MEUSSER | *Präs. Geschäftsst.* |
| PFETZING | *Abt.* II. |
| PIEFKE | *Abt.* IV. |
| RUMPF | *Abt.* IV. |
| Dr. SCHNEIDER | *Abt.* II. |
| SCHROEDER | *Abt.* IV. |
| SCHULTE | *Abt.* III. |
| SIMONET | *PA* Mitte. |
| WESKAMP | *Abt.* II. |
| KLEINGEIST | *Pol.-Beschaff.-Amt.* |
| NOVOTNY | *PA* Schöneberg. |

*Regierungs-u. Bauräte :*

| | |
|---|---|
| PFEIL, MÖSENTHIN, PUSCHMANN | *Abt.* III. |

*Regierungs-u. Medizinalräte :*
Dr. HEUPEL, Dr. HEINMÜLLER.

*Regierungs-u. Kassenrat :*
BUSCH, *Ltr. d. Rechnungsamtes.*

*Regierungschemiker :*
Dr. WOLTER, *Leit. Chemiker.*

*Regierungsbauräte :*

| | |
|---|---|
| JURISCH, WINZER | *Abt.* III. |

*Regierungs-u. Gewerberat :*
RÖSSLER        *Abt.* IV.

*Gewerbemedizinalrat :*
Dr. BREITENBACH  *Abt.* IV.

*Medizinalräte :*
Dr. KRACHT, Dr. TREMBUR (*Gen. Arzt
a.D.*)        *Abt.* V.

*Regierungsveterinärräte :* (*Abteilung V.*)
Dr. ADAM, Dr. ADAMECK, Dr. BANSE,
Dr. BAUER, Dr. BERNSTORFF, Dr.
BROHMANN, Dr. DAASCH, Dr. DU-
MONT, Dr. MÜLLER, Dr. FLEISCH-
HAUER, Dr. FREITAG, Dr. GOERTZ,
Dr. GESCHEIDLEN, Dr. GÜNTHER,
Dr. HÄBERER, Dr. HEINE, Dr. HEN-
NINGFELD, Dr. HERRMANN, Dr.
HOCK, Dr. KEIL, Dr. KETTNER, Dr.
KIEDROWSKI, Dr. KRUG, Dr. KUSS-
MANN, Dr. KÖRKE, Dr. LIEBERT, Dr.
MOLLENHAUER, Dr. Hermann OTTO,
Dr. Fritz OTTO, Dr. PILWAT, Dr.
RÖSSLER, Dr. ROTHENSTEIN, Dr.
SCHÖNECK, Dr. SCHÖNWETTER, Dr.
SCHWARZ, Dr. TORMANN, Dr. TROST,
Dr. TÜRK, Dr. TUTZER.

*Veterinärassessor :*
Dr. HÖLZNER, Dr. SCHNEIDER
        *Abt.* V.

*Regierungsassessor :*
Dr. BRUNNER    *PA* Charlottenburg.

*Polizeiräte :*
| | |
|---|---|
| ANIKA | *Abt.* II. |
| ASSMUS | (*abg. z. Reichsm. f. Ern. u. Landw.*). (*Wehrm.*). |
| BALTZER | |
| BENKENDORFF | *Abt.* I. |
| BLAESE | *Abt.* II. |
| BLOCK | *Abt.* I. |
| BORSCHDORF | *Abt.* III KVA. |
| CALDERAROW | *Abt. Rechnungsamt.* |
| DEICKERT | *PA* Lichtenfels. |
| FIESSLER | *Abt.* I. |
| GIERKE | (*Wirtschaftsstelle West*). |
| GIESECKE | *Abt.* II. |
| GOEBBELS | *Abt.* II. |
| HARTMANN | *Abt.* I. |
| HEIN | *Pol. Gef.* |
| HERRMANN | *PA* Neukölln. |
| HOLLENBACH | (*Wirtschaftsstelle Ost*). |
| JAGOW | *PA* Pankow. |
| KLINGER | (*Wirtschaftsstelle Nord*). |
| KONZAK | (*Wirtschaftsstelle Mitte*). |
| KUCKENBURG | *PA* Charlottenburg. |
| KÜHLE | *Präs. Geschäftsst.* |
| KÜSGEN | *Abt.* II. |
| LANGSTEIN | *Abt.* II. |
| LEUTLOFF | (*Wirtschaftsstelle Süd*) |
| LIEBIG | *PA Mitte.* |
| MARSAL | *Abt.* II. |
| MERKEL | *Abt.* II. |
| MÜLLER-WICHARDS | (*abg. zum* BdO. Prag). |
| MUNK | *Abt.* III KVA. |
| Dr. PATZELT | *Abt.* II. |
| PORSCHIEN | *PA Schöneberg.* |
| REEDER | *PA Pankow.* |
| REYLÄNDER | *Abt.* III KVA. |
| ROLLIN | *Abt.* V. |
| SCHMIDT | *Pol. Rechn. A. f. ausw. Einsätze.* |
| SOMMERFELD | *Abg. Pol. Präs.* Reichenberg. |

| | |
|---|---|
| STERN | *Abt.* III KVA. |
| TIMME | *Abt.* II. |
| VOULLIEME | *PA* Lichtenberg. |
| WIESNER | *Abt.* III. |
| WILL | *Abt.* III. |
| Dr. WOLF | (*Wehrm.*). |

*Pol. Amtm. :*
| | |
|---|---|
| BARTELS | *PA* Pankow. |
| BEREITER | *PA* Charlottenburg. |
| BRUCKS | *Präs. Geschäftsst.* |
| GROSCH | *PA* Mitte. |
| GAUMER | *Abt.* III KVA. |
| GREMPEL | *Abt.* III. |
| KNOOP | *Abt.* II. |
| LAASCH | *PA* Schöneberg. |
| MUTKE | *Abt.* V. |
| RICHTER | *PA* Lichtenberg. |
| SCHOLZ | *PA* Wedding. |
| STAMM | *PA* Neukölln. |
| TEITGE | *Abt.* III KVA. |
| WEISS | *Abt.* II. |

Subord. Offices of *Polizeipräsidium* Berlin :
*Polizeiamt* (*PA*) Charlottenburg.
*Polizeiamt* (*PA*) Lichtenberg.
*Polizeiamt* (*PA*) Mitte.
*Polizeiamt* (*PA*) Neukölln.
*Polizeiamt* (*PA*) Pankow.
*Polizeiamt* (*PA*) Schöneberg.*
*Polizeiamt* (*PA*) Wedding.*

# BIALYSTOK

# BOCHUM (A)

**Address :—**
Polizeipräsidium, Uhlandstr. 35.
Telephone : 60661.

**Nr. of Precincts :—**9.

**Personalities :—**
*Pol. Präs. : SS-BF* Walter OBERHAIDACHER
(transferred to Dresden).
*Vertr. : RDir.* TIETJENS.
*Kdr. d. Schupo : Oberst d. Schupo* VOEL-
KERLING.
*Sachbearbeiter : PR.* KÄSS, SCHENKEL,
KEMPER, HERCHET, P*Amtm. v.* HÖNE.

**Subord. Offices :—**
*Polizeiamt* Herne/Westfalen.

# BRAUNSCHWEIG (B)

**Address :—**
Polizeipräsidium, Münzstr. 1.

**Nr. of Precincts :—**7.

**Personalities :—**
*Pol. Präs. : SS-BF* SCHMAUSER.
*Sachbearbeiter : ORR.* JÜRGENS, *ORR.*
GRÜNKORN, *RR.* MEISSNER, *RAmtm.*
BROCH.

**Subord. Offices :—**
*Polizeiamt Watenstedt*—Salzgitter (*Reichswerke*
HERMANN GÖRING).
*Leiter : RR.* MUSSBACH.

---

*On 1st Sept., 1944, *Polizeiämter* Schöneberg
and Wedding were dissolved. Personalities listed
under these two *Polizeiämter* have most likely
been transferred to other Berlin Police offices.

## BREMEN (B)

**Address :—**
Polizeipräsidium, Am Wall 200-206.
Telephone : 21411, 21511, 22211.

**Nr. of Precincts :—**30.

**Personalities :—**
*Pol. Präs. : SS-BF Genmaj. d. Pol.* SCHROERS.
Predecessor : *SS-OF* LUDWIG.
*Kdr. d. Schupo : Oberst d. Schupo* ZILLER.

## BRESLAU (A)

**Address :—**
Polizeipräsidium, Schweidnitzer Stadtgraben 5-7
Telephone : 22211.

**Personalities :—**
*Pol. Präs. : SS-BF* ULLMANN.
*Vertr. : RDir.* HAUKE.
*Kdr. d. Schupo : Oberst d. Schupo* CRUX (*abg.*),
*Maj. d. Schupo* LIEBMANN.
*Ltr. d. Pol. Kasse : PORm.* NOWACK.
*Sachbearbeiter : RR. Dr.* WEISS, *PAmtm.*
KALAUCH, *PR.* ELLE, MINTE, PAUKE,
MATTHES.

## BROMBERG (C)

**Address :—**
Polizeipräsidium, Potsdamer Str. 35.
Telephone: 2700.

**Personalities :—**
*Pol. Präs. : SS-OSBF* v. SALISCH.
*SS-OF* v. PROEK (*abg.*).
*RR. Dr.* ALEXNAT.
*RR.* SUDAU (formerly *Pol. Präs.* Litz-
mannstadt).

## BRÜX (C)

**Address :—**
Polizeipräsidium, Sterngasse 12.
Telephone : 526, 390.

**Nr. of Precincts :—**1.

**Personalities :—**
*Pol. Präs. : SS-SF, ORR.* WIESE.

## CHEMNITZ (B)

**Address :—**
Polizeipräsidium, Hartmannstr. 24.
Telephone : 22441, 33041.

**Personalities :—**
*Pol. Präs. : SS-OF* WEIDERMANN.
*RR.* MATHE; *RR.* SCHÜHLY.
*Kdr. d. Schupo : Oberstlt. d. Schupo* Fritz
BEYER.

## DANZIG (B)

**Address :—**
Polizeipräsidium, Karrenwall 6.
Telephone : 24141.

**Nr. of Precincts :—**7.

**Personalities :—**
*Pol. Präs. : SS-OF* STEIN.
*ORR. Dr.* MÜLLER.
*RR. Dr.* HANIK.
*ORR. Dr.* STURMINGER (formerly *Pol.
Dir.* Frankfurt/Oder).

## DARMSTADT (C)

**Address :—**
Polizeipräsidium, Hügelstr. 31/33.
Telephone : 7511/18.

**Personalities :—**
*Pol. Präs. : Oberst d. Schupo* GEPPERT.

## DESSAU (C)

**Address :—**
Polizeipräsidium, Wolfgangstrasse 25.
Telephone : 4151.

**Personalities :—**
*Pol. Präs. : NSKK-OF* TRIPPLER.
*RR.* HIRSELAND.
*Dr.* WALHEIM.

## DORTMUND (A)

**Address :—**
Polizeipräsidium, Adolf Hitler-Allee 1-3.
Telephone : 20821.

**Nr. of Precincts :—**24.

**Personalities :—**
*Pol. Präs. : SS-BF* ALTNER.
*Vertr. : NSKK-SF, RDir. Dr.* EILER.
*Kdr. d. Schupo : Oberst d. Schupo* STÖWE.
*Sachbearbeiter : RR.* DRIESSEN (*abg.*).
*RR.* RITTER KRIEGELSTEIN von
STERNFELD ; *PR.* ARNDT, STRENGE,
MARQUIS ; *POI.* ALBUSCHKAT,
BÄCKER, HELLKÖTER, LANGEMANN,
MEYER (*Wehrd.*), SCHWEPPER, SPIES,
WILMES.

## DRESDEN (A)

**Address :—**
Polizeipräsidium, Schiessgasse 7.
Telephone : 24831.

**Nr. of Precincts :—**26.

**Personalities :—**
*Pol. Präs. : SS-BF* Walter OBERHAID-
ACHER.
Predecessor : *SS-BF* PFLOMM (*abg.*).
*RDir. Dr.* HERRMANN ; *RDir. Dr.* SEILER
*RR.* MÜLLER.
*RR. Dr.* KUNZE.
*Kdr. d. Schupo : Oberst Dr.* WOLFSTIEG.

## DUISBURG (B)

**Address :—**
Polizeipräsidium, Düsseldorferstr. 161.
Telephone : 26301.

**Nr. of Precincts :—**17.

**Personalities :—**
*Pol. Präs. : NSKK-OF* Paul FOERSTER.
*Vertr. : ORR.* KAUFMANN.
*RA. Dr.* KIENEGGER.
*Kdr. d. Schupo : Oberstlt. d. Schupo* TIMAEUS.
*Sachbearbeiter : PR.* WEBER, FÖRSTER,
ERRENST, RUNNE.
*Ltr. d. Polizeikasse : PORm.* OPITZ.
*Pol. Rechn. Rev. POI.* HOECKE, *POI.*
KRIEGER.

## DÜSSELDORF (A)

**Address : —**
Polizeipräsidium, Mackensenplatz 4/5.
Telephone : 10215.

**Nr. of Precincts :—**19.

**Personalities :—**
*Pol. Präs. : SS-BF* KORRENG.
*Ständ. Vertr. : RDir.* SCHÜFFNER (to BdO
Nimwegen).
*Kdr. d. Schupo : Oberstlt. d. Schupo* FUCHS.
*Sachbearbeiter : RR. Dr.* MAIR (*abg.*).
*PR.* MAUBACH, GREISER, SCHIWECK.
*PAmtm.* KILIAN.

## ELBING (C)

**Address :**
Polizeipräsidium, Göringplatz 10.
Telephone : 2941.

**Personalities :—**
*Pol. Präs. : SS-SF* WICKE (now Wilhelmshaven).
Predecessor : *RR.* BLUME (auftrw.).
*RR.* KÖNIGSFELD.

## ERFURT (C)

**Address :—**
Polizeipräsidium, Meister-Eckehart-Str. 2.
Telephone : 25261.

**Nr. of Precincts :—**

**Personalities :—**
*Pol. Präs. : SS-SF* WICKE (now *Pol. Präs.* Wilhelmshaven)
*Vertr. : RR.* BLABUSCH (*Wehrd.*).
*Vtrw. : PR.* SCHREIBER.
*Kdr. d. Schupo : Maj. d. Schupo* WEHLOW.

## ESSEN (A)

**Address :—**
Polizeipräsidium, Büscherstr. 2.
Telephone : 44551.

**Nr. of Precincts :—29.**

**Personalities :—**
*Pol. Präs. : SS-BF* HENZE.
*Vertr. : RDir.* SCHROTH.
*RR. Dr.* SALZMANN.
*Kdr. d. Schupo : Oberst d. Schupo* KRAUSE.
Predecessor : *Oberst d. Schupo* SCHUSTER.
*Sachbearbeiter : PR.* GNÜGGE, GILFERT, BORGSCHULTE, BECKER, LAUING.
*Pol. Amtm.* ASSHAUER.
*Oberstlt. d. Lds. Pol.* SCHÜNZEL.

## FRANKFURT/Main (A)

**Address :—**
Polizeipräsidium, Hohenzollernanlage 9-11.
Telephone : 20015.

**Nr. of Precincts :—24.**

**Personalities :—**
*Pol. Präs. : SA-BF* Fritz STOLLBERG or BECKERLE.
*Vertr. : RDir. Dr.* SCHULZE.
*RR. Dr.* REICHELT ; *RR.* ENDRÖS.
*Kdr. d. Schupo : Oberst d. Schupo* GRIPHAN.
*Oberstlt. d. Schupo* HAMEL.
*Sachbearbeiter : PR. Dr.* AUERBACH, EHLE, WALTER, WIRSIG.

## FREIBURG/Breisgau (C)

**Address :—**
Polizeipräsidium, Adolf-Hitler-Str. 167.
Telephone : 5131.

**Personalities :—**
*Pol. Präs. : SS-OSF* HENNINGER.

## GLEIWITZ (A)

**Address :—**
Polizeipräsidium, Teuchertstr. 20.
Telephone : 3331.

**Personalities :—**
*Pol. Präs. : SS-OF Dr.* VITZDAMM.
Predecessor : *SS-BF Dr.* RAMSPERGER (now Kattowitz).

*Vertr. : RDir.* SCHADE.
*RR. Dr.* KIRCHNER.
*Kdr. d. Schupo : Oberst d. Schupo* v. TROTHA gen. TREYDEN.
*Ltr. d. Pol. Kasse : PORm.* GRETT.
*Sachbearbeiter : PR.* GOGOLIN, HASE.
*PR. Rev.* KARNER, GEHM.

**Subord. Offices :—**
*Polizeiamt* Beuthen.
*Polizeiamt* Hindenburg.

## GOTENHAFEN (Gdynia) (C)

**Address :—**
Polizeipräsidium, Hafenstr. 13.
Telephone : 2921.

**Personalities :—**
*Pol. Präs. : SS-OF* M. BRAND (formerly Graz).
Predecessor : *Dr.* MÜLLER.

## GRAZ (B)

**Address :—**
Polizeipräsidium, Paulustorgasse 8.
Telephone : 6010.

**Nr. of Precincts :—9.**

**Personalities :—**
*Pol. Präs. : SS-OF* RUST.
Predecessor : *SS-OF.* BRAND (now Gotenhafen).
*Sachbearbeiter : ORR.* TOLLOWITZ, *RR.* JANUSCH, *RR.* THENIUS, *RR.* SPINDEL-BRÜCK, *RR.* PETRISCHEK.

## HALLE/Saale (B)

**Address :—**
Polizeipräsidium, Dreyhauptstr. 2.
Telephone : 27751.

**Nr. of Precincts :—9.**

**Personalities :—**
*Pol. Präs. : SS-OF Dr.* VITZDAMM (now Gleiwitz).
*Vertr. : RR. Dr.* TSCHOCHNER.
*Sachbearbeiter : PR.* KELLERMANN, RISSMANN, OTTO.
*PAmtm.* GARTZ, SIPPEL.

**Subord. Offices :—**
*Polizeiamt* Merseburg.
*Leiter : RR.* SCHENK.

## HAMBURG (S)

**Address :—**
Polizeipräsidium, Dammtorstrasse 1.
Telephone : 351931.

**Nr. of Precincts :—**

**Personalities :—**
*Pol. Präs. : SS-BF* KEHRL.
*Kdr. d. Schupo : Genmaj. d. Pol.* ABRAHAM.
Predecessor : *SS-BF, Genmaj. d. Pol.* v. HEIMBURG.
*Ltr. d. Abt.* I : *RR.* BÖSE.
*Ltr. d. Abt.* II : *RDir.* JANNSEN.
*Ltr. d. Abt.* III : *ORR.* CLAUSEN (*Wehrd.*), KLEYBOLDT.
*Ltr. d. Abt.* IV : *RDir.* JANNSEN.
*Ltr. d. Abt.* V : *ORR.* MEYER.
*Ausbildungsltr : RR. Dr.* TOMEK (*Wehrd.*).
*K. Ltr. d. Abt.* III : *RR. Dr.* HEYERDIERKS

Pol Räte. : Abt. I : COLLIN.
            Abt. I : HEESCHEN.
            Abt. I : LAABS.
            Abt. I : SCHROEDER.
            Abt. II : JDEN.
            Abt. II : GROTH.
            Abt. III : DWENGER.
            Abt. IV : HARMS.
            Abt. V : PEIN.
            PA. Altona : GIESELER.

**Subord. Offices :—**
*Polizeiamt Altona.*
*Polizeiamt Harburg.*
*Polizeiamt Wandsbek.*

### HANNOVER (B)
**Address :—**
Polizeipräsidium, Hardenbergstr. 1.
  Telephone : 44361.

**Nr. of Precincts :—16.**

**Personalities :—**
*Pol. Präs. : SS-OSBF Dr. DEUTSCHBEIN
(auftrw.).*
*Vertr. : ORR. Dr. TEGETHOFF.*
*Kdr. d. Schupo : Oberstlt. d. Schupo HESKE.*
*Sachbearbeiter : RR. DIEKMANN.*
  *PR. :* UEBE, BEUTIN, WEBER, NAW-
OTNIK.
  *PAmtm.* FAUBEL

### INNSBRUCK (C)
**Address :—**
Polizeipräsidium, Südtiroler Platz 14/16.
  Telephone : 2640.

**Personalities :—**
*Pol. Präs. : SS-OSBF Dr. Hans DORNAUER.*
*RR. KEMPF.*
*RR. Dr. ODLAZEK.*

### KARLSRUHE (C)
**Address :—**
Polizeipräsidium, Karl-Friedrich-Str. 15.
  Telephone : 6093/95.

**Nr. of Precincts :— 8**

**Personalities :—**
*Pol. Präs. : SS-OF CLAASEN.*
*RR. Dr. FRANZ.*
*RR. KLEMM.*
*Kdr. d. Schupo : Oberstlt. v. d. MOSEL.*

### KASSEL (B)
**Address :—**
Polizeipräsidium, Königstor 31.
  Telephone : 35041.

**Nr. of Precincts :— 9**

**Personalities :—**
*Pol. Präs. : SS-BF, Genmaj. d. Pol. Lutz
WYSOCKI.*
  Predecessor : *SS-OF* v. PROECK.
*Vertr. : RR. Dr. MAIR.*
*Sachbearbeiter : PR. :* EBERHARDT, SCHU-
BERT.
  *PAmtm.* KRIESCH.

### KATTOWITZ (A)
**Address :—**
Polizeipräsidium, Hindenburgstr. 23.
  Telephone : 35961.

**Personalities :—**
*Pol. Präs. : SS-BF Dr. RAMSPERGER.*
*Ständiger Vertr. : RDir. NIEWIESCH.*
*Ltr. d. Schupo : Oberst d. Schupo HIMMEL-
STOSS.*
  *Oberstlt. d. Schupo* BROCKMANN.
*Ltr. d. Präs. Abt. : PAmtm.* STADE.
*Sachbearbeiter : RR.* HENNIG.
  *RR. Dr.* MATTHIEU.
  *PR. :* PUTTINS, RANOSCHEK, BUDER.

**Subord. Offices :—**
*Polizeiamt Königshütte.*

### KIEL (B)
**Address :—**
Polizeipräsidium, Blumenstr. 2.
  Telephone : 4300/7

**Personalities :—**
*Pol. Präs. : SS-OF, RDir.* Paul LANGOSCH.
*Vertr. : ORR.* SCHULZ.
*Kdr. d. Schupo : Oberstlt. d. Schupo* WIRTHS
*Sachbearbeiter : PR. :* MAUER, LÜTH,
TUCHTENHAGEN.
  *PAmtm.* MENNICKE.

### KOBLENZ (C)
**Address : —**
Polizeipräsidium, Kaiser-Wilhelm-Ring 47-51.
  Telephone : 2121.

**Personalities :—**
*Pol. Präs. : SA-BF* WETTER.
*Vertr. b. Abwesenh. d.*
*Pol. Präs. u. Kdr. d.*
*Schupo : Oberstlt. d. Schupo* STEFFEN.
*Sachbearbeiter : PR. :* GIESE, KLEINEVOSS.

### KÖLN (A)
**Address :—**
Polizeipräsidium, Krebsgasse 1- 3.
  Telephone : 210171.

**Nr. of Precincts :—25.**

**Personalities :—**
*Pol. Präs. : SS-OF* Alexander v. WOEDTKE.
  Predecessor : *SA-GF* HOEVEL.
*Vertr. : RDir.* DELIUS.
*Kdr. d. Schupo : SS-SF, Oberst d. Schupo*
DAUME (PW).
*Sachbearbeiter : PR. :* ACKER, HAMMER,
PALM, RÜMENAPF.
  *Pol. Amtm.* GLEISSNER.
*Ltr.d.Pol.Kasse: Pol.ORntmstr.* BORNEMANN.

### KÖNIGSBERG (B)
**Address :—**
Polizeipräsidium, General-Litzmann-Str. 3-7.
  Telephone : 34081, 24011.

**Nr. of Precincts :—12.**

**Personalities :—**
*Pol. Präs. : SS-OGF* SCHOENE (abg.)
  *SS-BF* DORSCH (m.d.F.d.G.b.)
*Vertr. : ORR. Dr.* BOEHM.
*Kdr. d. Schupo : Oberstlt. d. Schupo* SAPP.
*Ltr. d. Präs. Abt. : POI.* POPKEN.
*Ltr. d. Pol. Kasse : PORm.* PANSEN.
*Sachbearbeiter : ORR. Dr.* NESTMANN.
  *Pol. R. :* JÜLICH, KRAENZ, LOEPKE,
QUITTNAT, NICKLAUS.

## LEIPZIG (A)

**Address :—**
Polizeipräsidium, C4, Wächterstr. 5.
Telephone : 72321.

**Personalities :—**
*Pol. Präs. :* SS-BF, *Genmaj. d. Pol.* v. GROL-
MANN.
*RDir. Dr.* EBBEKE.
*RR. Dr.* BURGHARDT.
*Kdr. d. Schupo :* *Oberst d. Schupo* SORGE.

## LINZ/Donau (B)

**Address :—**
Polizeipräsidium, Mozartstr. 6.
Telephone : 26831.

**Nr. of Precincts :—**5.

**Personalities :—**
*Pol. Präs. :* SS-SF Dr. PLAKOLM.
*Sachbearbeiter :* ORR. Dr. HANSS.
*ORR. Dr.* BRUCKNER.
*RR., Dr.* PRINZ, MARKUT.
*RA.* SEREGELY.

**Subord. Offices :—**PA. Wels.
PA. Steyr.

## LITZMANNSTADT (A)

**Address :—**
Polizeipräsidium, Hermann-Göring-Str. 114.
Telephone : 25360.

**Nr. of Precincts :—**25.

**Personalities :—**
*Pol. Präs. :* SS-BF Dr. ALBERT.
*Kdr. d. Schupo :* *Oberst* DRESSLER.
*Vertr. :* *Oberstlt.* RÖSE.
*RDir.* WEGELER.
*RR.* MECKING.

**Subord. Office :—**PA. Pabianice.

## LUDWIGSHAFEN/Rhein (C)

**Address :—**
Polizeipräsidium, Wittelsbachstr. 3.
Telephone : 61911.

**Nr. of Precincts :—**6.

**Personalities :—**
*Pol. Präs. :* ANTZ.
*RR. Dr.* WODITSCHKA.
*Kdr. d. Schupo :* *Maj. d. Schupo* Paul STIER-
WALDT.

## LÜBECK (C)

**Address :—**
Polizeipräsidium, Grosser Bauhof 14.
Telephone : 25121.

**Nr. of Precincts :—**6.

**Personalities :—**
*Pol. Präs. :* *Oberstlt. d. Schupo* PETSCH
(*auftrw.*) or Walter SCHRÖDER.
*RR. Dr.* HOFBAUER (abg.).
*Abt. Ltr. :* PR. ANTON, LEONHARDT.
*Kdr. d. Schupo :* *Oberstlt. d. Schupo* PETSCH.
*Ltr. d. Präs. Abt. :* POI. SIEBELT.

## MAGDEBURG (B)

**Address :—**
Polizeipräsidium, Halberstädterstr. 2.
Telephone : 42841.

**Personalities :—**
*Pol. Präs. :* SS-BF BOLEK.
*Ständ. Vertr. :* SS-OSBF, ORR. Dr. GALASCH.
*Kdr. d. Schupo :* *Oberstlt. d. Schupo* HOPPE.
*Ltr. d. Präs. Abt. :* *Pol. Amtm.* MARKGRAF.
*Sachbearbeiter :* RR. Dr. SAUER v. NORDEN-
DORFF.
*RR.* BETHKE.
*PR., Dr.* QUENSTEDT, BAYERDÖRFFER,
JENICH, RIPKE, BRAUN.
*Funkleiter :* *Maj. d. Schupo* HAUCK.

## MAINZ (C)

**Address :—**
Polizeipräsidium, Klarastr. 4.
Telephone : 40171.

**Personalities :—**
*Pol. Präs. :* REICHARD.

## MANNHEIM (B)

**Address :—**
Polizeipräsidium, L6, 1.
Telephone : 35851.

**Nr. of Precincts :—**14.

**Personalities :—**
*Pol. Präs. :* SA-BF HABENICHT.
*ORR. Dr.* STÖCKL.
*RR. Dr.* NOWOTNY.

## METZ (B)

**Address :—**
Polizeipräsidium.

**Subord. Office :—**
PA Diedenhofen.

## MÜLHAUSEN (C)

**Address :—**
Polizeipräsidium.

**Nr. of Precincts :—**6.

**Personalities :—**
*Pol. Präs. :* SACKSOFSKY
*RR. Dr.* NEUGEBAUER.

## MÜNCHEN (A)

**Address :—**
Polizeipräsidium, 6 Ettstr. 2.
Telephone : 451.

**Nr. of Precincts :—**31.

**Personalities :—**
*Pol. Präs. :* SS-BF Hans PLESCH(K).
*ORR.* FELLNER.
*RR.* MAIERHOFER

## MÜNCHEN-GLADBACH-RHEYDT (B)

**Address :—**
Polizeipräsidium, Dietrich-Eckhardt-Str. 5/11.
Telephone : 23451.

**Nr. of Precincts :—**8.

**Personalities :—**
*Pol. Präs. :* SS-SF WEHRLE.
*Vertr. :* RR. FÖRSTER.
*Kdr. d. Schupo :* *Oberstlt. d. Schupo* BRUCH.
*Ltr. d. Präs. Abt. :* *Pol. Amtm.* PÖTZSCH.
*Sachbearbeiter :* PR. : BUSSE, Dr. GRUND-
WALD, SCHÖLL.

## MÜNSTER (C)

**Address :—**
Polizeipräsidium, Syndikatsplatz 2.
Telephone : 24011.

**Personalities :—**
*Pol. Präs. : SS-SF* Heinz MANGER.
*Vertr. : RR.* SCHLETTE.
*Ltr. d. Schupo :* Oberstlt. d. Schupo ZICKLAM
*Ltr. d. Präs. Abt. : POI.* JAHRENS.
*Ltr. d. Abt. I (W) : PR.* BLUME.
*Ltr. d. Abt. II u. V : PR.* WETTHAUER.
*Ltr. d. Abt. III u IV : PR.* KNUST.

## NÜRNBERG-FÜRTH (A)

**Address :—**
Polizeipräsidium, Ludwigstr. 36.

**Nr. of Precincts :—**21.

**Personalities :—**
*Pol. Präs. : Genmaj. d. Schupo* KUSCHOW.
*RDir.* HOLZ.
*RR. Dr.* DREXLER.
*RR.* STEIGLEDER.

**Subord. Office :—**
*PA.* Fürth.

## OBERHAUSEN (B)

**Address :—**
Polizeipräsidium, Adolf-Hitler-Platz 2.
Telephone : 24221.

**Nr. of Precincts :—**9.

**Personalities :—**
*Pol. Präs. : RDir. Dr.* WAGNER (*auftrw.*) or
*SA-SF* VETTER.
*Ständ. Vertr.: ORR.* HEUSON.
*ORR. Dr.* PUTZENGRUBER.
*Kdr. d. Schupo :* Oberstlt. d. Schupo TAUTE.
*Ltr. d. Präs. Abt. : Pol. Amtm.* WILLE.
*Sachbearbeiter : PR. :* BÜCHLER (*abg.*),
BERGHOFF.

**Subord. Offices :—**
*Polizeiamt* Mülheim/Ruhr.

## PLAUEN (C)

**Address :—**
Polizeipräsidium.

**Personalities :—**
*Pol. Präs. : SS-SBF Dr.* UHLIG.

## POSEN (B)

**Address :—**
Polizeipräsidium, Wilhelmplatz 17-18.
Telephone : 8161.

**Nr. of Precincts :—**10.

**Personalities :—**
*Pol. Präs. : SS-BF, Frhr.* v. MALSEN-
PONICKAU.
*ORR. Dr.* KRAUS, *RR., Dr.* TORGGLER,
*Dr.* POSTATNY.

## POTSDAM (C)

**Address :—**
Polizeipräsidium, Priesterstr. 11-12.
Telephone : 4151.

**Personalities :—**
*Pol. Präs. : SS-SF* v. DOLEGA-KOZIER-
OWSKI.
*Kdr. d. Schupo : Maj. d. Schupo* FUCHS.

*Ltr. d. Präs. Abt. : PR.* SEELIGER.
*Abt. Ltr. : PR.* KNORR.
*Ltr. d. Pol. Kasse : PRm.* FLEMMING.
*Ltr. d. Wirtsch Abt. : PR.* PIPER.

## PRAG (A)

**Address :—**
Polizeipräsidium.
Zentrale Prag I : Svetla Gasse 313.
Zentrale Prag II : Neuhofg. 455.
Zentrale Veitsberg : Lupaciusstr. 1065.

**Nr. of Precincts :—**17 (called Kommissariate).

**Personalities :—**
*Pol. Präs. : SS-GF* Willi WEIDERMANN.

## RECKLINGHAUSEN (A)

**Address :—**
Polizeipräsidium, Westerholter Weg 27.
Telephone : 4343.

**Nr. of Precincts :—**9.

**Personalities :—**
*Pol. Präs. : SA-GF* VOGEL.
*RDir. Dr.* ROSENDAHL (*abg.*).
*Vertr. : ORR. Dr.* ECKRIEDER, *RR. Dr.*
POHL.
*Kdr. d. Schupo :* Oberst d. Schupo GÖHRUM or
Oberstlt. LÜDERS.
*Ltr. d. Pol. Kasse : PORm.* WEGER.
*Sachbearbeiter : PAmtm.* ROLLMANN.
*PR.,* HEUSERS, KALTENBACH, SIEVERS
Head of *F. u. E. Dienst :* Oberstlt *Dr.* MANS-
KOPF.

**Subord. Offices :—**
*Polizeiamt* Bottrop.
*Polizeiamt* Gelsenkirchen.
*Polizeiamt* Gladbeck.

## REICHENBERG (C)

**Address :—**
Polizeipräsidium, Laufergasse 8.
Telephone : 3141.

**Nr. of Precincts :—**6.

**Personalities :—**
*Pol. Präs. : SS-OF* LEFFLER.
*RR. Dr.* HITSCHMANN.

**Subord. Offices :—**
*Polizeiamt* Gablonz.

## ROSTOCK (C)

**Address :—**
Polizeipräsidium, Reiferbahn (Finanzamt).
Telephone : 7271.

**Nr. of Precincts :—**6.

**Personalities :—**
*Pol. Präs. : SS-SF Dr.* SOMMER.

## SAARBRÜCKEN (B)

**Address :—**
Polizeipräsidium, Schlossplatz 3/5.
Telephone : 29261.

**Nr. of Precincts :—**6.

**Personalities :—**
*Pol. Präs. Dr.* DIETRICH.
Predecessor : *SS-BF* DIEHM.
*Vertr. : RR. Dr.* SAM.
*ORR. Dr.* GRAFE.

## SOSNOWITZ (B)

**Address :—**
Polizeipräsidium, Breslauerstr. 38.
Telephone : 61101-5 and 35593.

**Personalities :—**
*Pol. Präs. :*
Predecessor : *SS-OF* v. WOEDTKE (now Köln).
*Vertr. :* ORR. Dr. GOETSCH.
*Kdr. d. Schupo:* Oberstlt. d. Schupo BALKE.
*Sachbearbeiter :* PR. ; POHL, HECKMANN.
*PAmtm.* KRAFT.

## STETTIN (B)

**Address :—**
Polizeipräsidium, Augustastr. 47.
Telephone : 35231.

**Nr. of Precincts :—**16.

**Personalities :—**
*Pol. Präs. :* JAHN or *ORR.* GRUNDEY (from PV Berlin).
*Ständ. Vertr. :* ORR. Dr. BUECH.
*Kdr. d. Schupo :* Oberstlt. d. Schupo WOLFF.
*Ltr. d. Präs. Abt. :* PAmtm. NOEGGERATH.
*Ltr. d. Pol. Kasse :* PORm. SOMMER.
*Ltr. d. Wirtsch. Abt. :* PR. GRABOW.
*Sachbearbeiter :* PR. : HEYN, AULER.

## STRASSBURG (B)

**Address :—**
Polizeipräsidium.

**Nr. of Precincts :—**13.

**Personalities :—**
*Pol. Präs. :* SS-OF ENGELHARDT.

## STUTTGART (B)

**Address :—**
Polizeipräsidium, Adolf-Hitler-Str. 1.
Telephone : 22941.

**Nr. of Precincts :—**18.

**Personalities :—**
*Pol. Präs. :* SA-BF, Genmaj. d. Orpo a.D.
SCHWEINLE.
*RDir.* HAHN.
*RR.* HÖLLHUBER.

## WALDENBURG/Schlesien (C)

**Address :—**
Polizeipräsidium, Anlaufstr. 2.
Telephone : 1740.

**Nr. of Precincts :—**5.

**Personalities :—**
*Pol. Präs. :* SA-OSF MÄHLICH.
*Vertr. :* PR. SCHWETJE.
*Kdr. d. Schupo :* Maj. d. Schupo DUDLER (abg.)
*Ltr. d. Präs. Abt. :* POI. HELBIG.

## WEIMAR (C)

**Address :—**
Polizeipräsidium, Sophienstr. 8-10.
Telephone : 6341.

**Personalities :—**
*Pol. Präs. :* SS-SF Walter SCHMIDT
(formerly *Pol. Dir.* Jena).

## WEISSENFELS (C)

**Address :—**
Polizeipräsidium, Zeitzerstr. 2.
Telephone : 2202/04.

**Personalities :—**
*Pol. Präs. :* SA-OF SCHULZ-SEMBTEN.
*Vertr. :* RR. JEDDING.
*Kdr. d. Schupo :* Oberstlt. d. Schupo BÜSCHER (abg.).
*Ltr. d. Präs. Abt. :* POI. ZENKER.

**Subord. Offices :—**
*Zweigstelle* Zeitz.

## WESERMÜNDE (C)

**Address :—**
Polizeipräsidium, Wesermünde-Mitte, Am Hafen 15-17.
Telephone : 3000.

**Personalities :—**
*Pol. Präs. :* SA-GF BAUER (k.).
*Kdr. d. Schupo :* Maj. d. Schupo STARK.
*Ltr. d. Präs. Abt. :* POI. MUCK.

## WIEN (S)

**Address :—**
Polizeipräsidium, I., Schottenring 11.
Telephone : R 57500.

**Nr. of Precincts :—**89.

**Personalities :—**
*Pol. Präs. :* SS-BF Dr. GOTZMANN.
*Vertr. :* RDir. Dr. HEDRICH.
*Kdr. d. Schupo :* Oberst d. Schupo SCHUSTER.
*Adjutant :* Hptm. DEMUTH.
*C.O.S. :* Oberstlt. GRIFFAN.
*Chief of Abt. I :* Major WOERMANN.
*Chief of Abt. II :* Major KROEGLER.
*Chief of Abt. Lu :* Major WEISS.
*Chief of Abt. N :* Major DOMS.
*Gruppe Mitte :* Oberstlt. DENNICKE.
*Gruppe Süd :* Oberstlt. STAN.
*Gruppe Ost :* Oberstlt. SCHMUTTERER.
*Sachbearbeiter :* RDir. FIZTHUM.
*Oberregierungsräte (ORR)*

| | |
|---|---|
| Dr. AITZINGER | Dr. HERMANN |
| Dr. ALZNER | JUNOWICZ |
| Dr. BATTEK | KARCZOK |
| Dr. BORSCHKE | KLEINER |
| Dr. BÜNGERER | Dr. LANGENBERGER |
| Dr. DURST | Dr. MÜLLER |
| Dr. EMMER | NAVARRA |
| Dr. FISCHER | Dr. NIGEL |
| Dr. FUCHS | Dr. PETRI |
| Dr. GUTTENFELD | PFOB |
| Dr. HAAS | Dr. PHILP |
| Dr. HASSLINGER | SCHATTL |
| | Dr. SCHÜSSLER |

*Regierungsräte (RR)*

| | |
|---|---|
| ARNOSCHT | Dr. MALHEIM |
| Dr. BINDER | Dr. MANDIAK |
| Dr. BRAUCEK | Dr. MITTERMANN |
| Dr. FESSLER | Dr. PIWETZ |
| Dr. FRIEBEL | Dr. PORM |
| FUCKNER | Dr. PUTRICH |
| GENSER | Dr. QUIETENSKY |
| GREGER | Dr. ROEDER |
| Dr. HACKL | Dr. SCHMIDL |
| Dr. HÖLLHUBER | Dr. SCHULTHEISS |
| Dr. HOYER | Dr. SCHUPP |
| Dr. HUTTERER | Dr. SCHWEIGER |
| KASERER | SEKA |
| KLEMM | Dr. SPRINGER |
| Dr. KIEBA | Dr. STROUHAL |
| Dr. KRAUS | Dr. WALCHSHOFER |
| Dr. LEO | Dr. WEINZINGER |
| LOICHT | WICKE |
| Dr. LOOS | Dr. ZIMMERMANN |

*Regierungsassessoren (Reg. Ass.)*
Dr. GUTMANN      Dr. PAUMGARTNER
Dr. HEGER        Dr. RICHTER
Dr. JAKESCH

## WIESBADEN (B)

**Address :—**
Polizeipräsidium, Friedrichstr. 25.
Telephone : 59251, 59255.

**Nr. of Precincts :—**6.

**Personalities :—**
*Pol. Präs. : Frhr. v.* GABLENZ.
*RR. Frhr. v.* ZSCHINSKY.
*Kdr. d. Schupo : Maj. d. Schupo v.* COELLN.
*Sachbearbeiter : PR. :* GAUL, DOUGLAS,
KIRCHNER.
*PAmtm.* HORNBERGER.

## WILHELMSHAVEN (C)

**Address :—**
Polizeipräsidium, Hindenburgstr. 29.
Telephone : 5231.

**Nr. of Precincts :—**3.

**Personalities :—**
*Pol. Präs. : SS-SF* WICKE (transferred from
Elbing).
Predecessor : *SS-SF Dr.* RUST.
*ORR. Dr.* GRUBE.

## WUPPERTAL (A)

**Address :—**
Polizeipräsidium, Adolf Hitler-Str. 390.
Telephone : 21101.

**Nr. of Precincts :—**16.

**Personalities :—**
*Pol. Präs. : SA-GF* HINKLER, *MdR., Gaultr.
z. D.*
*Komm. m. d. Verw. d. Pol. Präs. Stelle beauftr. :
SA-BF* KRAHNE.
*RDir. Dr.* WAGNER (*abg.*) .
*PR.* GÜTTLER.
*Kdr. d. Schupo : Oberst d. Schupo* KEUCK (rep.
BdO of Wkr. XI).
*Sachbearbeiter : PR.,* BRUDER, GILBERT,
LINDEQUIST, *Dr.* ZIMMERMANN.
*Pol. Amtm.,* BÖHME, STROTKAMP.

**Subord. Offices :—**
*PA.* Remscheid, Solingen.

## WÜRZBURG (C)

**Address :—**
Polizeipräsidium, Ottostr. 1.
Telephone : 4703.

**Personalities :—**
*Pol. Präs. : SA-OF* WICKLMAYR.
*RR.* ENDRÖS (transferred to *Pol. Präs.*
Frankfurt/Main).

## ZWICKAU (C)

**Address :—**
Polizeipräsidium, Werdauerstr. 62.

**Personalities :—**
*Pol. Präs. : SS-SF* BECK.

# ANNEXE C: PART TWO
## POLIZEIDIREKTIONEN

### ALTENBURG

**Address :**
Polizeidirektion, Bei der Brüderkirche 1
Tel : 1096

**Personalities :**
*Pol. Dir. :* VOGEL

### BADEN-BADEN

**Address :**
Polizeidirektion, Sofienstr. 40
Tel : 1317, Ext. 24

**Nr. of precincts : 2**

**Personalities :**
*Pol. Dir. : SA-USF* MALLEBREIN

### BITTERFELD

**Address :**
Polizeidirektion, Röhrenstr. 17
Tel : 3444

**Nr. of precincts : 2**

**Personalities :**
*M.d.W.d.G.b. : RR.* MAINZ or *ORR. Dr.*
JEDDING
*Dezernent : PR.* LUCKENBACH
*Kdr. d. Schupo : Maj. d. Schupo* FYDRICH
*Ltr. d. Präs. Geschäftsst. : POI.* WARNECK

### BRÜNN

**Address :**
Polizeidirektion, Pahackystr. 6/8

**Personalities :**
*Pol. Dir. : Dr.* JUNGWIRT

### CUXHAVEN

**Address :**
Polizeidirektion, Friedrich Carl Str. 19
Tel : 2081

**Personalities :**
*Pol. Dir. :* (not filled)
*Kdr. d. Schupo : Maj. d. Schupo* ROTH

### ESSLINGEN

**Address :**
Polizeidirektion, Platz der SA
Tel : 16345

**Personalities :**
*Pol. Dir. :* PR DANGEL (k.)

### FLENSBURG

**Address :**
Polizeidirektion, Norderhofenden 1
Tel : 2590/2

**Personalities :**
*Pol. Dir. : SS-SF. Oberst d. Schupo* Hans
HINSCH
*Kdr. d. Schupo : Maj. d. Schupo* MEIER
*Ltr. d. Präs. Geschäftsst. : POI.* KOENIG

### FRANKFURT/Oder

**Address :**
Polizeidirektion, Wilhelmsplatz 20
Tel : 2775–6, 3959, 4746

**Nr. of precincts : 3**

**Personalities :**
*Pol. Dir. : SS-OSBF* BACHMANN
*Pol. Dir. (abg.) : ORR. Dr.* STURMINGER
(transf. to *Pol. Präs.* Danzig)
*Kdr. d. Schupo : Maj. d. Schupo* SCHMIDT
*Ltr. d. Präs Geschäftsst. : POI.* THÖNE
*Ltr. d. Wirtschaftsabt. : POI.* SCHULZE

### FRIEDRICHSHAFEN

**Address :**
Polizeidirektion, Friedrichstr. 87
Tel : 796

**Personalities :**
*Pol. Dir. : Dr.* SPIESS or HOCH

### GERA

**Address :**
Polizeidirektion, Stadthaus, Zeppelinstr. 4
Tel : 4526

**Personalities :**
*Pol. Dir. : Dr.* KOHLER

### GIESSEN

**Address :**
Polizeidirektion, Landgraf-Philipp-Platz 1

**Chief :** *Oberst d. Schupo* HELLWEGE-EMDEN

**Subord. Offices :**
*Polizeiamt* Friedberg-Bad Nauheim

### GOTHA

**Address :**
Polizeidirektion, Erfurterstr. 2.
Tel : 1621 .

**Personalities :**
*Pol. Dir. :* HERFURTH

### GRAUDENZ

**Address :**
Polizeidirektion, Königstr. 2
Tel : 1171

**Personalities :**
*Pol. Dir. : SS-SF* MEYER
*Vertr. Weise m. d. Verw. der Pol. Dir. Stelle
beauftr. : SS-SBF, Pol. R.* KAMMER (PV.
Gotenhafen).

### HAMM/Westfalen

**Address :**
Polizeidirektion, Göring-Str. 80
Tel : 1662/3

**Personalities :**
*Pol. Dir. : RR. Dr.* ROTMANN
*Vertreter : PR.* LEISE
*Kdr. d. Schupo : Maj. d. Schupo* STOLZEN-
BERG
*Ltr. d. Präs. Geschäftsst. : POI.* DEPPE

### HANAU

**Address :**
Polizeidirektion, Paradeplatz 2-4
Tel : 4056/8

**Nr. of precincts : 2**

**Personalities :**
*Pol. Dir. : SS-SBF* FEHRLE
*Ständ. Vertr. : Maj. d. Schupo* OBERESCH
*Kdr. d. Schupo : Maj. d. Schupo* OBERESCH
*Sachbearbeiter : POI.* RYBKA

## HEIDELBERG

Address :
Polizeidirektion, Rohrbacher Str. 11
Tel : 6151

Nr. of precincts : 4

Personalities :
*Pol. Dir. : RR.* KÄRCHER

## HEILBRONN

Address :
Polizeidirektion, Wienerstr. 4
Tel : 5255

Nr. of precincts : 3

Personalities :
*Pol. Dir. : SS-SF* D'ANGELO
*Kdr. d. Schupo : Maj. d. Schupo* KUHLEMANN

## HOF

Address :
Polizeidirektion, Pfarrgasse 1
Tel : 3456

Personalities :
*Pol. Dir. : SS-OSBF* SCHMITT, Emil

## IGLAU

Address :
Polizeidirektion

Personalities :
*Pol. Dir. : SS-SF* E. SLADEK

## JENA

Address :
Polizeidirektion, Felsenkellerstr. 25
Tel : 4841

Personalities :
*Pol. Dir. : PR.* SCHULZ (k)
Predecessor : *SS-SF* Walter SCHMIDT

## KAISERSLAUTERN

Address :
Polizeidirektion, Ritter-von-Epp-Str. 5
Tel : 390

Nr. of precincts : 3

Personalities :
*Pol. Dir. : Dr.* BEUSCHLEIN

## KARLSBAD

Address :
Polizeidirektion, Waldzeile 24
Tel : 3526

Nr. of precincts : 3

Personalities :
*Pol. Dir. : RR. Dr.* HANIK
*Kdr. d. Schupo : Maj. d. Schupo* RIECKHOFF

## KLAGENFURT

Address :
Polizeidirektion, St. Ruprecht Str. 5

Nr. of precincts : 1

Personalities :
*Pol. Dir. : Dr.* v. LICHEM
*Sachbearbeiter : RR. Dr.* v. VIVENOT
*RR. Dr.* SEEBACHER
*RR.* SCHUSTER-BONNOT

Subord. Office : *PA* Villach

## LEOBEN

Address :
Polizeidirektion, Kaiser-Josef-Park 3
(administered by *Landrat*)
Tel : 30

Personalities :
*Leiter : Dr.* KADLETZ (*Nebenamtl.*) LR

## LESLAU/Warthe

Address :
Polizeidirektion, Brückenstr. 3
Tel : 1062

Nr. of precincts : 3

Personalities :
*Pol. Dir. : SA-OF* WOLF
*Kdr. d. Schupo : Maj. d. Schupo* LESCHKE

## LUDWIGSBURG

Address :
Polizeidirektion, Vordere Schlosstr. 31
Tel : 4422

Personalities :
*Pol. Dir. : SS-OSBF* MEMMINGER

## LÜNEBURG

Address :
Polizeidirektion

## LUXEMBURG

Address :
Polizeidirektion

Personalities :
*Pol. Dir. :* GERTH

## MÄHRISCH OSTRAU

Address :
Polizeidirektion, Adolf Hitler Str. 24

Personalities :
*Pol. Dir. :* MERLER

## MARBURG/Drau

Address :
Polizeidirektion

Personalities :
*Pol Dir. : SS-OSBF Dr.* WALLNER

## MEMEL

Address :
Polizeidirektion, Fischerstr. 12
Tel : 2121

Nr. of precincts : 2

Personalities :
*Pol. Dir. : SS-OF* FISCHER-SCHWEDER
(abg.)
*Vertr. : PR.* STEINWENDER
*Kdr. d. Schupo : Maj. d. Schupo* GÜNTHER

## OFFENBACH

Address :
Polizeidirektion, Ludwigstr. 69
Tel : 80331

Nr. of precincts : 3

Personalities :
*Pol. Dir. : SA-OF* EICHEL
*Kdr. d. Schupo : Maj. d. Schupo* HOLTEY-
WEBER

## OLMÜTZ

Address :
Polizeidirektion

Personalities : *ORR. Dr.* POHL

## OPPELN

**Address :**
Polizeidirektion, Moltkestr. 43
Tel : 3451, Ext. 131

**Personalities :**
*Pol. Dir. : NSKK-OSF Dr.* HEIGL
*RA.* KONRATH
*Kdr. d. Schupo : Maj. d. Schupo* LANGE
(*auftrw.*)

## OSNABRÜCK

**Address :**
Polizeidirektion

## PILSEN

**Address :**
Polizeidirektion

**Personalities :**
*Pol. Dir. : OLR. Dr.* ECKOLDT

## PFORZHEIM

**Address :**
Polizeidirektion, Bahnhofstr. 24
Tel : 2323

**Personalities :**
*Pol. Dir. : Dr.* SCHNEIDER

## REGENSBURG

**Address :**
Polizeidirektion, Minoritenweg 1
Tel : 5251

**Nr. of precincts : 4**

**Personalities :**
*Pol. Dir. : SS-OSBF* PQPP
*RR.* MUSIL
*Kdr. d. Schupo : Oberstlt. d. Schupo* MEYER-
SPELBRINK

## SALZBURG

**Address :**
Polizeidirektion, Churfürststr. 1
Tel : 2521

**Personalities :**
*Pol. Dir : SS-OSBF Dr. v.* BRAITENBERG
*Vertr. : SS-SBF, RR. Dr.* PITTER
*RR. Dr.* BEGUS
*Ltr. Pol. Arzt. : SS-SBF, Oberstabsarzt d. Pol.*
*Dr.* W. REGER

## ST. PÖLTEN

**Address :**
Polizeidirektion, Linzer Str. 47
Tel : 601–605·

**Personalities :**
*Pol. Dir. : SS-OSBF Dr.* WITTMANN
*Sachbearbeiter : RR.* KIRCHL
*RR. Dr.* MERK

## SUHL

**Address :**
Polizeidirektion (administered by *Landrat*)
Tel : 2601/2

**Personalities :**
*Pol. Dir. : Landrat,* SETHE (*nebenamtl.*)
*Vertr. : Pol. Rat.* HUMPF (Tel : 2601/2)
*Kdr. d. Schupo : Hptm. d. Schupo* GIES

## THORN

**Address :**
Polizeidirektion, Stadtgraben 31
Tel : 2371/73

## 

**Personalities :**
*Pol. Dir. : SS-SF* GRAF (*auftrw.*)
*RR. Dr.* UNGER

## TILSIT

**Address :**
Polizeidirektion, SA-Strasse 67
Tel : 2991

**Nr. of precincts : 2**

**Personalities :**
*Pol. Dir. : SS-OSBF RR.* THIELER
*Kdr. d. Schupo : Maj. d. Schupo* KÄRNBACH
*Ltr. d. Präs. Abt. : Pol. OI.* LAMPRECHT
*Ltr. d. Gesch.St.* i. V. : *PR.* PELZNER

**Subord. Office :** *Zweigstelle* Ragnit

## TRIER

**Address :**
Polizeidirektion

## TROPPAU

**Address :**
Polizeidirektion, Johannesgasse 4
Tel : 66 and 82.

**Nr. of precincts : 2**

**Personalities :**
*Pol. Dir. : SS-SBF* PRUCHTNOW (k)
*k. Pol. Dir. z. OLR* Olmütz
Dr. POHL

## ULM

**Address :**
Polizeidirektion, Münsterplatz 47
Tel : 2151/301

**Personalities :**
*Pol. Dir. : SA-BF* HAGENMEYER
*Predecessors : SS-BF :* DREYER ; RICHTER

## WIENER NEUSTADT

**Address :**
Polizeidirektion, Adolf Hitler Platz 3
Tel : 1250/53

**Personalities :**
*Pol. Dir. : SS-OSBF Dr.* KITTEL
*RR. Dr.* ANDERSCH
*RR. Dr.* FESSLER

## WITTENBERG

**Address :**
Polizeidirektion, Tauentzienstr. 11
Tel : 3511

**Nr. of precincts : 3**

**Personalities :**
*Pol. Dir. : SS-OSBF* WICKERT
*Abt. Ltr. : PR.* WEIDNER
*Kdr. d. Schupo : Maj. d. Schupo* DALMANN
*Ltr. d. Präs.Geschäftsst. : POI.* HAGEMEISTER

## WORMS

**Address :**
Polizeidirektion, Ehrenburgerstr. 35
Tel : 4444

**Personalities :**
*Pol. Dir. : SS-OSBF* LÖW

## ZNAIM

**Address :**
Polizeidirektion (administered by *Landrat*),
Schillerstr. 4
Tel : 44, 476, 478

**Personalities :**
*Pol. Dir. : LR. Dr.* KOTTEK (*nebenamtl.*)

# ANNEXE C : PART THREE
## POLIZEIÄMTER

**ALTONA**

**Address :** Einunddreissigerstr. 66.
   Telephone : 421102.
**Subordinate to :** *Pol. Präs.* Hamburg.
**Chief :** *RA Dr.* ZIMMERMANN.

**BEUTHEN**

**Subordinate to :** *Pol. Präs.* Gleiwitz.
**Chief :** *PR* PRANG, *PR* SPROTTE.

**BOTTROP**

**Subordinate to :** *Pol. Präs.* Recklinghausen
**Chief :** *PR* WENGEL (K).

**(BERLIN)—CHARLOTTENBURG**

**Subordinate to :** *Pol. Präs.* Berlin.

**DIEDENHOFEN**

**Subordinate to :** *Pol. Präs.* Metz.

**EBINGEN**

**Subordinate to :** Local *Landrat.*
**Chief :** *POI* LAUTH.

**FRIEDBERG-BAD NAUHEIM**

**Subordinate to :** *Pol. Dir.* Giessen.
**Under** *Pol. Dir.* LUTTNER.

**FÜRTH**

**Subordinate to :** *Pol. Präs.* Nürnberg-
   Fürth.

**GABLONZ**

**Subordinate to :** *Pol. Präs.* Reichenberg.
**Chief :** *PR* BUCHARDI.

**GELSENKIRCHEN**

**Subordinate to :** *Pol. Präs.* Recklinghausen.
**Chief :** *RR Dr.* ALTMANN.
   *PR* UHL, NIEMEYER.

**GLADBECK**

**Subordinate to :** *Pol. Präs.* Recklinghausen.
**Chief :** *PR* BOETCHER.

**GÖPPINGEN**

**Subordinate to :** Local *Landrat.*
**Chief :** *PR* HAHN.

**HARBURG-WILHELMSBURG**

**Address :** Georgstr. 7.
   Telephone : 371001.
**Subordinate to :** *Pol. Präs.* Hamburg.
**Chief :** *PR* RÖHL.

**HEIDENHEIM**

**Subordinate to :** Local *Landrat.*
**Chief :** *PR* KÖHL.

**HERNE/Westfalen**

**Subordinate to :** *Pol. Präs.* Bochum.

**HINDENBURG**

**Subordinate to :** *Pol. Präs.* Gleiwitz.
**Chief :** *RR Dr.* KIRCHNER.
   *PR* SCHILL, GRZENDA.

**KEHL**

**Subordinate to :** Local *Landrat.*
**Chief :** *Dr.* PETRI (*LR.*)

**KÖNIGSHÜTTE**

**Subordinate to :** *Pol. Präs.* Kattowitz.
**Chief :** *PR* WITTIG.
   *POI* TETZNER.

**KONSTANZ**

**Address :** Lutherplatz 12.
**Nr. of precincts :** 2.
**Subordinate to :** Local *Landrat.*
**Chief :** *Dr.* KAUFFMANN (*LR.*)
   *(Kdr. d. Schupo)* : Oberstlt. d. Schupo TENN-
STÄDT.

**LAHR**

**Subordinate to :** Local *Landrat.*
**Chief :** STRACK (*LR.*)

**(BERLIN)—LICHTENBERG**

**Subordinate to :** *Pol. Präs.* Berlin.

**LÖRRACH**

**Subordinate to :** Local *Landrat.*
**Chief :** PETER (*LR.*)

**MERSEBURG**

**Subordinate to :** *Pol. Präs.* Halle/Saale.
**Chief :** *RR* Schenk.

**(BERLIN)—MITTE**

**Subordinate to :** *Pol. Präs.* Berlin.

**MÜLHEIM/Ruhr**

**Subordinate to :** *Pol. Präs.* Oberhausen.
**Chief :** *RR Dr.* MIRGEN.
   *PR* TRIPPE.

**(BERLIN)—NEUKÖLLN**

**Subordinate to :** *Pol. Präs.* Berlin.

**OFFENBURG**

**Subordinate to :** Local *Landrat.*
**Chief :** *Dr.* SANDER, (*LR.*)

**PABIANICE**

**Subordinate to :** *Pol. Präs.* Litzmannstadt.
**Chief :** *PR* SUDAU.

**(BERLIN)—PANKOW**

**Subordinate to :** *Pol. Präs.* Berlin.

**RASTATT**

**Subordinate to :** Local *Landrat.*
**Chief :** BAER (*LR.*)

**REMSCHEID**

**Nr. of precincts :** 6.
**Subordinate to :** *Pol. Präs.* Wuppertal.
**Chief :** *PR* BULA.

**REUTLINGEN**

**Subordinate to :** Local *Landrat.*
**Chief :** *PR* MANGOLD.

## SCHRAMBERG
**Subordinate to :** Local *Landrat.*
**Chief :** *POI* ELWERT.

## SCHWÄBISCH GMÜND
**Subordinate to :** Local *Landrat.*
**Chief :** *PR* FRANK.

## SCHWENNINGEN
**Subordinate to :** Local *Landrat.*
**Chief :** *PR* KELLER.

## SOLINGEN
**Nr. of Precincts :** 6.
**Subordinate to :** *Pol. Präs.* Wuppertal.
**Chief :** *RR Dr.* GÜTTLER.

## STEYR
**Nr. of Precincts :** 2.
**Subordinate to :** *Pol. Präs.* Linz/Donau.
**Chief :** *RR Dr.* PRINZ.

## TEPLITZ-SCHÖNAU
**Subordinate to :** *Pol. Präs.* Aussig.
**Chief :** *PR* DÖRING.

## TÜBINGEN
**Subordinate to :** Local *Landrat.*
**Chief :** *PR* BÜCHELER.

## TUTTLINGEN
**Subordinate to :** Local *Landrat.*
**Chief :** *POI* BURKART or ECKHARDT

## VILLACH
**Subordinate to :** *Pol. Dir.* Klagenfurt.
**Chief :** *RR Dr.* SCHUSTER-BONNOT.

## WALDSHUT
**Subordinate to :** Local *Landrat.*
**Chief :** *SS-SBF Dr.* ERNST (*LR.*)

## WANDSBECK
**Address :** Witthöfstr. 5–6.
 Telephone : 288851.
**Subordinate to :** *Pol. Präs.* Hamburg.
**Chief :** *PR* BOE.

## WATENSTEDT-SALZGITTER
**Address :** *Reichswerke* Hermann Göring.
**Subordinate to :** *Pol Präs.* Braunschweig.
**Chief :** *RR* MUSSBACH.

## WELS
**Nr. of Precincts :** 1.
**Subordinate to :** *Pol. Präs.* Linz/Donau.
**Chief :** *SS-HSF* MARKUT.

## ZELLA-MEHLIS
**Subordinate to :** Local *Landrat.*
**Chief :** *PR* SCHULZE.

## ZWEIBRÜCKEN
**Subordinate to :** Local *Landrat.*
**Chief :** *LR* KIEFER (*nebenamtl.*).

## RAGNIT
*Zweigstelle* of Tilsit.
**Chief :** *PI* KÜHNAPFEL.

## ZEITZ
*Zweigstelle* of Weissenfels/Sachsen.
**Chief :** *PR* UECKERT.

# ANNEXE C: PART FOUR

## UNIFORM FILING SYSTEM OF THE NATIONAL POLICE ADMINISTRATION HQ—AS APPLIED TO THE PROTECTION POLICE

### (Einheitsaktenplan für die Staatlichen Polizeiverwaltungen—Schutzpolizei)

*Note.*—The following list is a condensation of the *Einheitsaktenplan* as used in all German National Police Administration Headquarters, the offices of the BdO and the *Schutzpolizeikommandos*. The document which furnished the information tabulated below showed the application of the EAPl to the *Kommando der Schupo* in Vienna. Consequently it lists only those numbers which have any reference to the *Schupo* and its work.

It appears that the EAPl is divided up as follows :—

| | |
|---|---|
| 1000–5999 | Section I of a *Staatliche Polizeiverwaltung* (this includes the organisation and establishment, etc. of the *Schutzpolizei Kommando*). |
| 6000–6999 | Section II |
| 7000–7999 | Section III |
| 8000–8999 | Section IV |
| 9000–9999 | Section V |

Despite the fact that the examples in the tabulation below are restricted to those used by the *Schutzpolizei*, the following list may be helpful in the search for any specific files in an *Orpo* Headquarters.

| File No. | German Text | English Text |
|---|---|---|
| **(1000/5999)** | **Aufbau, Einrichtung, Technischer Dienst, Personalangelegenheiten, Ausbildung und Verwendung der Schutzpolizei** | **Organisation, Establishment, Technical Services, Personnel Training and Employment of the Protection Police** |
| 1000/1089 | *Aufbau und Einrichtung der Schutzpolizei. Geschichte und Tradition* | Organisation and establishment of the Protection Police. History and traditions |
| 1090/1099 | *Aussergewöhnliche Vorkommnisse in der Schutzpolizei* | Special occurrences in the Protection Police |
| 1100/1199 | *Personal-Stärken der Schutzpolizei* | Strength reports of the Protection Police |
| 1200/1299 | *Aufbau und Einrichtung des Revierdienstes und der Polizeireviere* | Organisation and establishment of the Precinct Service and Police Precincts (or Wards) |
| 1300/1399 | *Aufbau, Einrichtung und Dienstvorschriften der berittenen Schutzpolizei* | Organisation, establishment and service regulations of the Mounted Protection Police |
| 1400/1499 | *Aufbau und Einrichtung der Schutzpolizei Schulen* | Organisation and establishment of the Protection Police Schools |
| 1500/1599 | *Aufbau der Schutzpolizei-Kompanien* | Organisation of the Protection Police Companies (Barrack Police) |
| 1600/1699 | *Geschäftsführung, Dienstaufsicht, Schriftverkehr, Dienstbesprechungen* | Administration, routine supervision, correspondence, conferences (Includes communication with other branches and offices, such as the *Kripo, Gestapo, NSDAP, Wehrmacht*, etc.) |
| 1700/1799 | *Unterkunft, Verpflegung, Bekleidung, Ausrüstung.* | Billets, rations, clothing, equipment |
| 1800/1899 | *Waffen, Munition, Transporte von Polizeikörpern* | Arms, ammunition, transport for Police units |
| 1900/1999 | *Druckschriften, Dienstvorschriften, Kartenmaterial, zeichnerische Arbeiten* | Publications, service regulations, maps, drawings and overlays |
| 2000/2099 | *Aufbau und Einrichtung und Dienstvorschriften des Kraftfahrdienstes* | Organisation, establishment, and service regulations of M/T service |
| 2100/2199 | *Beschaffung, Bewirtschaftung und Betriebe der Kraftfahrzeuge. Einschliesslich Streifenboote für die Wasserschutzpolizei, Betriebstoffe der Kraftfahrzeuge, usw.* | " Procurement," administration and use of motor vehicles. Includes patrol vessels for the Waterways Protection Police, petrol for motor vehicles, etc. |
| 2200/2269 | *Nachrichtenverbindungswesen der Polizei* | Police signals communications |
| 2270/2279 | *Nachrichtenverbindungsdienst in Ausnahmefällen* | Signals communications in special circumstances |
| 2280/2299 | *Nachrichtenverbindungsdienst im zivilen Luftschutz* | Signals communications for civilian A.R.P. |
| 2300/2359 | *Fernsprechwesen und Telegrafenwesen* | Telephonic and telegraphic communications |
| 2360/2369 | *Fernschreibwesen* | Teletype communications |

| File No. | German Text | English Text |
|---|---|---|
| 2370/2399 | Polizeimeldeanlagen | Police Alarm System |
| 2400/2499 | Drahtloser Nachrichtenverbindungsdienst | Wireless communications |
| 2460/2469 | Geheimschlüsselwesen | Secret codes and ciphers |
| 2500/2599 | Scheinwerfer, optische Instrumente | Searchlights ; optical equipment |
| 2600/2699 | Aufbau und Einrichtung der Wasserschutzpolizei | Organisation and establishment of the Waterways Protection Police |
| 2700/2799 | Beschaffung, Bewirtschaftung und Betrieb für die Wasserfahrzeuge der Wasserschutzpolizei | " Procurement," administration and use of vessels of the Waterways Protection Police |
| 2900/2999 | Lichtbild und Film für schutzpolizeiliche Zwecke | Motion pictures and photographs for Protection Police purposes |
| 3000/3039 | Personalangelegenheiten. Einschliesslich Amt Recht, Amtsbezeichnungen, Urlaub, usw. | Personnel. Includes Bureau for Legal Affairs, ranks, leave, etc. |
| 3040/3054 | Zugehörigkeit der Schutzpolizeibeamten zur Berufs- oder sonstigen Organisationen | Membership of Protection Police personnel in professional and other organisations |
| 3055/3059 | Bekämpfung des Alkoholmissbrauchs in der Schutzpolizei | Combatting of drunkenness among the Protection Police |
| 3060/3069 | Bestimmung über Personalakten | Rulings on personnel files |
| 3070 | Beteiligung der Polizei am Winterhilfswerk | Participation of the Police in the Winter Relief Work |
| 3100/3199 | Laufbahn der Schutzpolizeibeamten, Wehrdienst, Abstammungen, Dienstausweise, Beurteilungen, Beförderungen, Bezeichnungen, usw. | Service careers of Schupo personnel ; military service ; racial background ; identity documents ; reports on personnel ; promotions ; ranks, etc. |
| 3200/3299 | Dienstzucht, Dienststrafen, Dienstentlassungen | Discipline, disciplinary measures, dismissals from the service |
| 3300/3399 | Belohnungen, Orden und Ehrenzeichen | Rewards, medals and decorations |
| 3400/3499 | Mitwirkung bei den vermögensrechtlichen Angelegenheiten der Schutzpolizei Beamten. Dienstreisen | Pensions, allowances, etc., for Protection Police personnel. Duty travel |
| 3500/3599 | Erkrankungen, Dienstunfälle, Todesfälle | Illness, accidents and death |
| 3600/3699 | Beamtenwohlfahrt, Seelsorge | General and spiritual welfare |
| 3700/3704 | Allgemeinbildender Unterricht für Schutzpolizeibeamten | General education for Protection Police personnel |
| 3900/3999 | Musikkapellen der Schutzpolizei | Military bands of the Protection Police |
| 4000/4610 | Ausbildung | Training. This category includes all branches of training and instruction—from ordinary weapon training to ideological indoctrination |
| 5000/5099 | Aufgaben des Revierdienstes | Duties of men serving on Precincts (Wards) |
| 5100/5199 | Ordnungspolizeilicher Vollzugsdienst im Ortspolizeibezirk und Einsatz der Schutzpolizei ausserhalb des Ortspolizeibezirks. Katastrophenschutz | Orpo Executive Service within the local Police district and employment of the Protection Police outside the limits of the local Police district. Protection against catastrophes. Includes such functions as protection of communication systems, Schupo co-operation with the Kripo, Gestapo, Fire Service, Technical Emergency Corps, German Red Cross, and organisations of the NSDAP. |
| 5200/5299 | Vorbereitende Massnahmen sowie Einsatz der Schutzpolizei zur Abwehr innerer Unruhen | Protective Police duties—employment of the Protection Police against riots, etc. |
| 5300/5399 | Verwendung von Reizstoffen bei der Polizei | Use of gas by the Police |
| 5400/5599 | Ziviler Luftschutz (Gesetzliche Bestimmungen, Schutzräume, usw.) | A.R.P. (statutory regulations, shelters, etc.) |
| 5600/5645 | Mitwirkung der Schutzpolizei bei der Strafverfolgung ; Zwangsmittel der Polizei | Participation of the Protection Police in implementing judicial sentences ; coercive measures by the Police |
| 5900/5999 | Mitwirkung der Schutzpolizei in Angelegenheiten der Präsidialgeschäftsstelle ; Verleihung in- und ausländischer Orden und Ehrenzeichen | Participation of the Protection Police in matters concerning Secretariat ; granting of national and foreign decorations |

| File No. | German Text | English Text |
|---|---|---|
| **(6000/6999)** | **Mitwirkung der Schutzpolizei in Angelegenheiten der Staatspolizei (Politische Polizei) und Abteilung II (Fremdenpolizei)** | **Participation of the Protection Police in matters concerning the Gestapo and Section II of the Administrative Police (Police for Control of Foreigners)** |
| 6000/6099 | *Verfassung, Freie Meinungsäusserung und Presse (Nationalfeiertage, Wahlen, Volksabstimmungen, Vertrieb von Druckschriften)* | Matters concerning the Reich Constitution ; freedom of the Press ; freedom of thought. This category includes national holidays, elections, and distribution of printed matter |
| 6100/6199 | *Vereinsrecht und Versammlungswesen* | Legal status and meetings of various organisations, including political parties |
| 6200/6299 | *Schutz des Staates, Kultur- und Wirtschaftspolitik (Judensachen, Kirchenverfassung ; Vierjahresplan, Boykott gegen Verkaufsstellen, usw., Sicherheitsdienst bei Arbeitseinstellungen, usw.)* | Upholding of the States' cultural and economic policies (Jewish and religious questions ; Four Year Plan, boycotts, guards for forced labour drafts) |
| 6300/6333 | *Verkehr mit Waffen, Munition ; Schiesssport* | Traffic in arms and ammunition ; shooting practice |
| 6500/6599 | *Meldewesen, Zeugnisse und Bescheinigungen auf Grund des Melderegisters. Ausländersachen* | Police Registry ; attestations and certificates connected with the Police Registry. Registration of foreigners |
| 6600/6699 | *Passvorschriften, Reichsangehörigkeitssachen, Auswanderungswesen. Angelegenheiten der exterritorialen Personen und Dienststellen sowie der Konsulate* | Passport regulations. Citizenship. Emigration. Persons and offices, including consulates, with extra-territorial rights |
| 6700/6799 | *Namen, Adelsprädikate, Titel* | Names (changes, aliases, etc.) ; titles, including those of the nobility |
| 6800/6899 | *Mitwirkung der Schutzpolizei in Angelegenheiten der Wehr- und Arbeitsdienstpflicht* | Police assistance in recruiting for the Armed Forces and the Reich Labour Service |
| **(7000/7999)** | **Mitwirkung der Schutzpolizei in Angelegenheiten der Abteilung III (Verkehr-, Feuer- und Wasserpolizei)** | **Participation of the Protection Police in matters concerning Section III of the Administrative Police (Traffic, Fire and Waterways Police)** |
| 7000/7099 | *Strassen ; Strasseninstandhaltung* | Roads ; Road maintenance |
| 7100/7199 | *Verkehrsregelung (Verkehrszeichen, Handel und Gewerbe an und auf der Strasse, Eisenbahnen, Strassenbahnen, Verkehrsunfälle, usw.)* | Traffic Rules and Regulations. This category includes traffic signs, hawkers and pedlars, railways, tramways, traffic accidents, etc. |
| 7200/7231 | *Verkehr in der Luft ; Flughäfen* | Regulation of Air Traffic. Aerodromes |
| 7270/7299 | *Fernsprech-, Fernschreibe- und Rundfunkwesen in materiellrechtlicher Hinsicht* | Telephone, teletype and broadcasting regulations |
| 7300/7399 | *Feuer- und Betriebssicherheit* | Safety from fire and accidents in industry |
| 7400/7499 | *Wasserschutzpolizei, Verkehr auf Wasserstrassen, Fischereiaufsicht, usw.* | Waterways Protection Police ; Supervision of fishing rights and other water traffic matters. |
| **(8000/8999)** | **Mitwirkung der Schutzpolizei in Angelegenheiten der Abteilung IV (Gewerbepolizei)** | **Protection Police participation in matters concerning Section IV of the Administrative Police (Police for the supervision of Trades and Crafts)** |
| 8000/8099 | *Gewerbepolizeiliche Bestimmungen, ambulanter Gewerbebetrieb, Preisüberwachung, Gast- und Schankwirtschaften* | Trade regulations, hawkers, price control, supervision of inns, public houses, etc. |
| 8100/8199 | *Theater, Lichtspiele, Lustbarkeiten, Bekämpfung von Schmutz und Schund* | Theatres, cinemas, public amusements ; combatting of pornography, etc. |
| 8150/8160 | *Schutz der Sonn- und Feiertage* | Sunday rest, holidays |
| 8200/8299 | *Gewerbeaufsicht* | Supervision of trades and crafts |
| 8231 | *Kinderarbeit in gewerblichen Betrieben* | Child labour in industry |
| 8240 | *Sonntagsruhe in Gewerbe und Handelsgewerbe* | Sunday rest in business and trade |
| 8250/8270 | *Unfallverhütung* | Protection against accidents in factories, etc. |

C18

| File No. | German Text | English Text |
|---|---|---|
| **(9000/9999)** | **Mitwirkung der Schutzpolizei in Angelegenheiten der Abteilung V (Strafverfügungen, Amtshilfe, Gesundheitspolizei, Veterinärpolizei, usw.** | **Participation of the Protection Police in matters concerning Section V of the Administrative Police (Regulations on Punishable Offences, Welfare Matters, Health, Food and Veterinary Police)** |
| 9000/9099 | *Polizeiverwaltungsgesetz, Zwangsgeldverfügungen, Strafverfügungen, Amtshilfe* | Police Administrative Law, fines, compulsory administration, assistance to other authorities and organisations |
| 9100/9199 | *Fürsorge und Wohlfahrtsangelegenheiten* | Welfare and Relief Work |
| 9105 | *Bekämpfung des Bettler- und Landstreicherunwesens* | Combatting of vagrancy |
| 9200/9299 | *Gesundheitspolizei* | Police for Health Affairs |
| 9200 | *Heilpersonen* | Supervision of doctors, dentists, midwives, etc. |
| 9210/9219 | *Apotheker und Apotheken* | Pharmacists, drugs, etc. |
| 9290 | *Leichenwesen* | Corpses, funerals |
| 9400/9499 | *Lebensmittelpolizei* | Police for supervision of foodstuffs |
| 9500/9599 | *Feld- und Forstpolizei, Natur- und Vogelschutz, Ungeziefer und Schädlingsbekämpfung, Jagdangelegenheiten* | Field and Forest Guards. Protection of plant and animal life. Combatting of pests. Hunting rights and permits |
| 9600/9699 | *Versicherungswesen* | Insurance |
| 9700 | *Fundwesen* | Lost Property department |

# ANNEXE C : PART FIVE

## AUSLÄNDERKARTEI

### (System of Registration of Foreigners)

### (a) ALPHABETICAL LIST OF COUNTRIES

—indicating colour and number of each country included in the Ausländerkartei.

(Use in conjunction with (b) )

| | Colour and Number | | Colour and Number |
|---|---|---|---|
| Ägypten | red (1) | Lettland | green (5) |
| Afghanistan | red (6) | Liberia | red (2) |
| Albanien | blue (9) | Liechtenstein | blue (9) |
| Amerika, Ver. St. von | red (3) | Litauen | green (6) |
| Andorra | blue (9) | Luxemburg | yellow (5) |
| Argentinien | red (5) | | |
| | | Mandschukuo | red (6) |
| Belgien | yellow (1) | Mexiko | red (4) |
| Bolivien | red (5) | Monaco | blue (9) |
| Brasilien | red (5) | | |
| Bulgarien | blue (1) | Nepal | red (6) |
| | | Nicaragua | red (4) |
| Chile | red (5) | Niederlande | yellow (6) |
| China | red (7) | Norwegen | green (7) |
| Costa Rica | red (4) | | |
| | | Palästina | red (9) |
| Dänemark | green (1) | Panama | red (4) |
| Danzig | green (2) | Paraguay | red (5) |
| Dominikanische Republik | red (4) | Peru | red (5) |
| | | Polen | green (8) |
| Ecuador | red (5) | Portugal | yellow (7) |
| Estland | green (3) | | |
| | | Rumänien | blue (4) |
| Finnland | green (4) | | |
| Frankreich | yellow (2) | San Marino | blue (9) |
| | | San Salvador | red (4) |
| Griechenland | blue (2) | Siam | red (6) |
| Grossbrittannien | yellow (3) | Sowjetunion (U.d.S.S.R.) | blue (6) |
| Guatemala | red (4) | Spanien | yellow (8) |
| | | Südafr. Union-Afrika | red (2) |
| Haiti | red (4) | Schweden | green (9) |
| Honduras | red (4) | Schweiz | blue (5) |
| | | | |
| Irak | red (6) | Tschechoslowakei | yellow (9) |
| Iran | red (6) | Türkei | blue (7) |
| Irland | blue (9) | | |
| Italien | yellow (4) | Ungarn | blue (8) |
| | | Uruguay | red (5) |
| Japan | red (8) | | |
| Jugoslavien | blue (3) | Vatikanstadt | blue (9) |
| | | Venezuela | red (5) |
| Kolumbien | red (5) | Vereinigte Staaten von Amerika | red (3) |
| Kuba-Mittelamerika | red (4) | Yemen | red (6) |

## (b) TABLE OF COLOUR-NUMBER SYSTEM

(Foreigners' Registration Cards)

| Colour | 1 | 2 | 3 | 4 | 5 | 6 |
|--------|---|---|---|---|---|---|
| GREEN | Dänemark | Danzig | Estland | Finnland | Lettland | Litauen |
| YELLOW | Belgien | Frankreich | Gross Britannien | Italien | Luxemburg | Niederlande |
| BLUE | Bulgarien | Griechen-land | Jugoslavien | Rumänien | Schweiz | Sowjetunion |
| RED | Ägypten | Afrika (i) | Ver. St. von Amerika | Mittel-Amerika (ii) | Süd-Amerika (iii) | Asien (iv) |

| Colour | 7 | 8 | 9 | 10 | 11 | 12 |
|--------|---|---|---|----|----|----|
| GREEN | Norwegen | Polen | Schweden | Staatenlos | Jude | Volks-deutscher |
| YELLOW | Portugal | Spanien | Tschecho-slovakei | Staatenlos | Jude | Volks-deutscher |
| BLUE | Türkei | Ungarn | Sonstige europäischen Staaten (v) | Staatenlos | Jude | Volks-deutscher |
| RED | China | Japan | Palästina | Staatenlos | Jude | Volks-deutscher |

(i) Liberia, Südafrikanische Union.

(ii) Costa Rica, Dominikanische Republik, Guatemala, Haiti, Honduras, Kuba, Mexiko, Nicaragua, Panama, San Salvador.

(iii) Argentinien, Bolivien, Brasilien, Chile, Ecuador, Kolumbien, Paraguay, Peru, Uruguay, Venezuela.

(iv) Afghanistan, Irak, Iran, Mandschukuo, Nepal, Siam, Yemen.

(v) Albanien, Andorra, Irland, Liechtenstein, Monaco, San Marino, Vatikanstadt.

# ANNEXE D

## ORDER OF BATTLE OF ORPO FORCES IN GERMANY

**PART ONE : MOTORISIERTE VERKEHRSBEREITSCHAFTEN DER SCHUPO**
(Motorised Traffic Control Detachments)

**PART TWO : GENDARMERIE (MOT.)**
(Motorised Gendarmerie)

    (a) Units and locations
    (b) Table of weapons and equipment of the Motorised Gendarmerie
    (c) Tabulation of Licence Plate Numbers of the Motorised Gendarmerie

**PART THREE : WASSERSCHUTZPOLIZEI**
(Waterways Protection Police)

    (a) SW Headquarters and Affiliated Sub-units
    (b) Alphabetical Index of SW Units by locations

**PART FOUR : FEUERSCHUTZPOLIZEI**
(Fire Protection Police)

**PART FIVE : LUFTSCHUTZPOLIZEI**
(Air-Raid Protection Police)

**PART SIX : TECHNISCHE NOTHILFE**
(Technical Emergency Corps)

    (a) O/B according to Landesgruppen (Wehrkreise) and Befehlsstellen
    (b) List of identified Senior Officers of the TN

**PART SEVEN : WAFFENMEISTEREIEN OF THE POLICE**
(Ordnance and Maintenance Shops of the Police)

# ANNEXE D : PART ONE

## MOTORISIERTE VERKEHRSBEREITSCHAFTEN DER SCHUPO
### (Motorised Traffic Control Detachments)

### (a) UNITS AND LOCATIONS
(as officially listed, end of 1942)

| No. | HQ of controlling Staatliche Polizei-verwaltung | Strength in official fraction form | Actual Strength | Cars | M/C Com-binations | M/C Solo | Total |
|---|---|---|---|---|---|---|---|
| 1 | Königsberg | 2/4 | 24 | 2 | 2 | 6 | 10 |
| 2 | Elbing | 1/4 | 12 | 1 | 1 | 3 | 5 |
| 3 | Berlin | | | | | | |
| | Gruppe Mitte | 4/4 | 48 | 4 | 4 | 12 | 20 |
| | Gruppe Ost | 4/4 | 48 | 4 | 4 | 12 | 20 |
| | Gruppe Süd | 4/4 | 48 | 4 | 4 | 12 | 20 |
| | Gruppe West | 4/4 | 48 | 4 | 4 | 12 | 20 |
| | Gruppe Nord | 4/4 | 48 | 4 | 4 | 12 | 20 |
| 4 | Potsdam | 1/4 | 12 | 1 | 1 | 3 | 5 |
| 5 | Stettin | 2/4 | 24 | 2 | 2 | 6 | 10 |
| 6 | Breslau | 3/4 | 36 | 3 | 3 | 9 | 15 |
| 7 | Gleiwitz | 3/4 | 36 | 3 | 3 | 9 | 15 |
| 8 | Magdeburg | 2/4 | 24 | 2 | 2 | 6 | 10 |
| 9 | Halle | 2/4 | 24 | 2 | 2 | 6 | 10 |
| 10 | Erfurt | 1/4 | 12 | 1 | 1 | 3 | 5 |
| 11 | Kiel | 2/4 | 24 | 2 | 2 | 6 | 10 |
| 12 | Hannover | 2/4 | 24 | 2 | 2 | 6 | 10 |
| 13 | Recklinghausen | 3/4 | 36 | 3 | 3 | 9 | 15 |
| 14 | Bochum | 3/4 | 36 | 3 | 3 | 9 | 15 |
| 15 | Dortmund | 3/4 | 36 | 3 | 3 | 9 | 15 |
| 16 | Kassel | 1/4 | 12 | 1 | 1 | 3 | 5 |
| 17 | Frankfurt a.M. | 3/4 | 36 | 3 | 3 | 9 | 15 |
| 18 | Wiesbaden | 1/4 | 12 | 1 | 1 | 3 | 5 |
| 19 | Koblenz | 1/4 | 12 | 1 | 1 | 3 | 5 |
| 20 | Essen | 3/4 | 36 | 3 | 3 | 9 | 15 |
| 21 | Wuppertal | 3/4 | 36 | 3 | 3 | 9 | 15 |
| 22 | Oberhausen | 2/4 | 24 | 2 | 2 | 6 | 10 |
| 23 | Düsseldorf | 2/4 | 24 | 2 | 2 | 6 | 10 |
| 24 | Duisburg | 2/4 | 24 | 2 | 2 | 6 | 10 |
| 25 | Gladbach-Rheydt | 1/4 | 12 | 1 | 1 | 3 | 5 |
| 26 | Köln | 3/4 | 36 | 3 | 3 | 9 | 15 |
| 27 | Aachen | 1/4 | 12 | 1 | 1 | 3 | 5 |
| 28 | Münster | 1/4 | 12 | 1 | 1 | 3 | 5 |
| 29 | München | 3/4 | 36 | 3 | 3 | 9 | 15 |
| 30 | Nürnberg | 3/4 | 36 | 3 | 3 | 9 | 15 |
| 31 | Augsburg | 1/4 | 12 | 1 | 1 | 3 | 5 |
| 32 | Ludwigshafen | 1/4 | 12 | 1 | 1 | 3 | 5 |
| 33 | Würzburg | 1/4 | 12 | 1 | 1 | 3 | 5 |
| 34 | Leipzig | 3/4 | 36 | 3 | 3 | 9 | 15 |
| 35 | Dresden | 3/4 | 36 | 3 | 3 | 9 | 15 |
| 36 | Chemnitz | 2/4 | 24 | 2 | 2 | 6 | 10 |
| 37 | Plauen | 1/4 | 12 | 1 | 1 | 3 | 5 |
| 38 | Stuttgart | 2/4 | 24 | 2 | 2 | 6 | 10 |
| 39 | Mainz | 1/4 | 12 | 1 | 1 | 3 | 5 |
| 40 | Darmstadt | 1/4 | 12 | 1 | 1 | 3 | 5 |
| 41 | Mannheim | 2/4 | 24 | 2 | 2 | 6 | 10 |
| 42 | Karlsruhe | 1/4 | 12 | 1 | 1 | 3 | 5 |
| 43 | Freiburg | 1/4 | 12 | 1 | 1 | 3 | 5 |
| 44 | Heidelberg | 1/4 | 12 | 1 | 1 | 3 | 5 |
| 45 | Hamburg | | | | | | |
| | Gruppe Ost | 3/4 | 36 | 3 | 3 | 9 | 15 |
| | Gruppe West | 3/4 | 36 | 3 | 3 | 9 | 15 |
| 46 | Bremen | 2/4 | 24 | 2 | 2 | 6 | 10 |
| 47 | Lübeck | 1/4 | 12 | 1 | 1 | 3 | 5 |
| 48 | Braunschweig | 1/4 | 12 | 1 | 1 | 3 | 5 |
| 49 | Saarbrücken | 2/4 | 24 | 2 | 2 | 6 | 10 |
| 50 | Dessau | 1/4 | 12 | 1 | 1 | 3 | 5 |
| 51 | Rostock | 1/4 | 12 | 1 | 1 | 3 | 5 |
| | Totals | | 1,380 | 115 | 115 | 345 | 575 |

# ANNEXE D : PART TWO

## GENDARMERIE (mot.)

## Motorised Gendarmerie

### (a) UNITS AND LOCATIONS

(as officially listed in 1942/43)

| Wehrkreis : | Location | Higher Administrative Authority | No. of men |
|---|---|---|---|
| I | Königsberg | *Reg. Präs.* Königsberg | 108 |
| | Allenstein | *Reg. Präs.* Allenstein | 72 |
| | Gumbinnen | *Reg. Präs.* Gumbinnen | 36 |
| | Zichenau | *Reg. Präs.* Zichenau | ? |
| II | Altdamm | *Reg. Präs.* Stettin | 72 |
| | Güstrow | Meckl. *Sttsmin., Abt. Inneres* | 72 |
| | Greifswald | *Reg. Präs.* Stettin | 36 |
| | Köslin | *Reg. Präs.* Köslin | 36 |
| | Schneidemühl | *Reg. Präs.* Schneidemühl | 36 |
| III | Schönewalde (Kr. Nieder-barmin) | *Reg. Präs.* Potsdam | 144 |
| | Frankfurt/Oder | *Reg. Präs.* Frankfurt/Oder | 36 |
| | Cottbus | *Reg. Präs.* Frankfurt/Oder | 72 |
| | Küstrin | *Reg. Präs.* Frankfurt/Oder | ? |
| IV | Wiederitzsch (Sachsen) | *Kreishauptmannschaft*—Leipzig | 108 |
| | Dresden | *Kreishauptmannschaft*—Dresden-Bautzen | 72 |
| | Chemnitz | *Kreishauptmannschaft*—Chemnitz | 72 |
| | Teplitz-Schönau | *Reg. Präs.* Aussig | ? |
| V | Stuttgart (Vaihingen a.d. Fildern) | *Min. d. Innern* (Stuttgart) | 108 |
| | Freiburg i. Br. | Badisches *Min. d. Innern* (Karlsruhe) | 72 |
| | Ravensburg | *Min. d. Innern* (Stuttgart) | 36 |
| | Schlettstadt (Elsass) | *Chef. d. Zivilverwaltung* Elsass | ? |
| VI | Duisburg | *Reg. Präs.* Düsseldorf | 108 |
| | Köln | *Reg. Präs.* Köln | 72 |
| | Münster (Hiltrup i.W.) | *Reg. Präs.* Münster | 72 |
| | Kamen i.W. | *Reg. Präs.* Arnsberg | 72 |
| | Detmold | *Rsth.* Lippe & Schaumburg-Lippe *Landesreg.* Lippe-Detmold | 72 |
| | Eupen | *Reg. Präs.* Aachen | ? |
| VII | Haar bei München | *Reg.* Oberbayern, *Abt. Gend.* (München) | 144 |
| | Traunstein | *Reg.* Oberbayern, *Abt. Gend.* (München) | 36 |
| | Kempten i.Allgäu | *Reg.* Schwaben, *Abt. Gend.* (Augsburg) | 36 |
| VIII | Breslau | *Reg. Präs.* Breslau | 108 |
| | Bunzlau | *Reg. Präs.* Liegnitz | 72 |
| | Troppau | *Reg. Präs.* Troppau | ? |
| | Hohenstedt | *Reg. Präs.* Troppau | ? |
| | Oppeln | *Reg. Präs.* Oppeln | 72 |
| | Kochlowitz | *Reg. Präs.* Kattowitz | ? |
| IX | Frankfurt/Main-Höchst | *Reg. Präs. beim O. Präs.* Wiesbaden | 108 |
| | Weimar | Thüring. *Min. d. Innern* (Weimar) | 108 |
| | Kassel-Niederzwehren | *Reg. Präs. beim O. Präs.* - Kassel | 72 |
| X | Lüneburg (Winsen/Luhe) | *Reg. Präs.* Lüneburg | 72 |
| | Neumünster | *Reg. Präs.* Schleswig | 72 |
| | Bremen | *Reg. Präs.* Aurich | 72 |
| XI | Wolfenbüttel | Braunschw. *Sttsmin. Abt. Inneres* | 108 |
| | Magdeburg | *Reg. Präs. beim O. Präs.* Magdeburg | 108 |
| XII | Bendorf/Rhein | *Reg. Präs. Koblenz* | 108 |
| | Mannheim | Badisches *Min. d. Innern* (Karlsruhe) | 108 |
| | Trier | *Reg. Präs.* Trier | 72 |
| | Lubeln (Lothringen) | *Chef. d. Zivilverwaltung* Lothringen | ? |

| Wehrkreis : | Location | Higher Administrative Authority | No. of men |
|---|---|---|---|
| XIII | Plan im Sudetengau (*später* Elbogen) | *Rsth.* Sudetenland | ? |
| | Zirndorf (b. Nürnberg) | *Reg.* Ober-u. Mittelfranken, *Abt. Gend.* (Ansbach) | 108 |
| | Würzburg | *Reg.* Unterfranken, *Abt. Gend.* (Würzburg) | 72 |
| | Schwandorf/Bayern | *Reg.* Niederbayern u. Oberpfalz, *Abt. Gend.* (Regensburg) | 72 |
| XVII | Wien-Purkersdorf | *Rsth.* Wien | ? |
| | Linz | *Rsth.* Oberdonau | ? |
| | Krems | *Rsth.* Oberdonau | ? |
| XVIII | Graz | *Rsth.* Kärnten | ? |
| | Klagenfurt | *Rsth.* Steiermark | ? |
| | Innsbruck | *Rsth.* Tirol-Vorarlberg | ? |
| | Lienz | *Rsth.* Kärnten | ? |
| | Markt Pongau | *Rsth.* Tirol-Vorarlberg | ? |
| | Feldkirch | *Rsth.* Tirol-Vorarlberg | ? |
| XX | Gotenhafen | *Reg. Präs.* Danzig | ? |
| | Bromberg | *Reg. Präs.* Bromberg | ? |
| | Strasburg | *Reg. Präs.* Marienwerder | ? |
| XXI | Posen | *Reg. Präs.* Posen | ? |
| | Pabianice | *Reg. Präs.* Litzmannstadt | ? |
| | Alexandrowo (Weichsel) | *Reg. Präs.* Litzmannstadt | ? |

## (b) TABLE OF WEAPONS AND EQUIPMENT OF THE MOTORISED GENDARMERIE

(as officially listed, end of 1942)

| Unit | No. of men | Carbines | Pistols (08) | Pistols (7.65) | MP's |
|---|---|---|---|---|---|
| *Gr. Gend.-Komp.* (*mot.*) | 144 | 144 | 144 | 148 | 18 |
| *Gend.-Komp.* (*mot.*) | 108 | 108 | 108 | 111 | 12 |
| *Kl. Gend.-Komp.* (*mot.*) | 72 | 72 | 72 | 74 | 9 |
| *Gend.-Zug* (*mot.*) | 36 | 36 | 36 | 37 | 6 |

| Unit | Staff cars | Trucks | Motor-cycles | Motor-cycles with sidecar |
|---|---|---|---|---|
| *Gr. Gend.-Komp.* (*mot.*) | 2 | 22 | 12 | 2 |
| *Gend.-Komp.* (*mot.*) | 1 | 15 | 8· | 1 |
| *Kl. Gend.-Komp.* (*mot.*) | 1 | 11 | 6 | 1 |
| *Gend.-Zug* (*mot.*) | 1 | 7 | 4 | 1 |

## (c) TABULATION OF LICENCE PLATE NUMBERS OF THE MOTORISED GENDARMERIE

(as officially listed, end of .942)

| | Unit | | | Sub-division of licence numbers according to type of vehicle | | | | |
|---|---|---|---|---|---|---|---|---|
| No. | HQ. | Unit Strength in Official Fraction Form | Assigned "Pol." Licence Nos. | M/C Solo | M/C Combination | Small staff cars | Trucks | Large staff cars |
| 1 | Königsberg | 3/3 | 701–730 | 701–708 | 710 | 711–722 | 727–729 | 730 |
| 2 | Allenstein | 2/3 | 731–760 | 731–736 | 740 | 741–749 | 758, 759 | 760 |
| 3 | Gumbinnen | 1/3 | 761–780 | 761–764 | 770 | 771–776 | 779 | 780 |
| 4 | Stettin | 2/3 | 781–810 | 781–786 | 790 | 791–799 | 808, 809 | 810 |
| 5 | Güstrow | 2/3 | 811–840 | 811–816 | 820 | 821–829 | 838, 839 | 840 |
| 6 | Greifswald | 1/3 | 841–860 | 841–844 | 850 | 851–856 | 859 | 860 |
| 7 | Köslin | 1/3 | 861–880 | 861–864 | 870 | 871–876 | 879 | 880 |
| 8 | Schneidemühl | 1/3 | 881–900 | 881–884 | 890 | 891–896 | 899 | 900 |
| 9 | Potsdam | 4/3 | 901–950 | 901–912 | 919, 920 | 921–938 | 945–948 | 949, 950 |
| 10 | Frankfurt (Oder) | 1/3 | 951–970 | 951–954 | 960 | 961–966 | 969 | 970 |
| 11 | Cottbus | 1/3 | 971–990 | 971–974 | 980 | 981–986 | 989 | 990 |
| 12 | Leipzig | 3/3 | 991–1020 | 991–998 | 1000 | 1001–1012 | 1017–1019 | 1020 |
| 13 | Dresden | 2/3 | 1021–1050 | 1021–1026 | 1030 | 1031–1039 | 1048, 1049 | 1050 |
| 14 | Chemnitz | 2/3 | 1051–1080 | 1051–1056 | 1060 | 1061–1069 | 1078, 1079 | 108) |
| 15 | Stuttgart | 3/3 | 1081–1110 | 1081–1088 | 1090 | 1091–1102 | 1107–1109 | 111 ) |
| 16 | Freiburg | 2/3 | 1111–1140 | 1111–1116 | 1120 | 1121–1129 | 1138, 1139 | 1140 |
| 17 | Ravensburg | 1/3 | 1141–1160 | 1141–1144 | 1150 | 1151–1156 | 1159 | 1160 |
| 18 | Duisburg | 3/3 | 1161–1190 | 1161–1168 | 1170 | 1171–1182 | 1187–1189 | 1190 |
| 19 | Köln | 2/3 | 1191–1220 | 1191–1196 | 1200 | 1201–1209 | 1218, 1219 | 1220 |
| 20 | Münster | 2/3 | 1221–1250 | 1221–1226 | 1230 | 1231–1239 | 1248, 1249 | 1250 |
| 21 | Arnsberg | 2/3 | 1251–1280 | 1251–1256 | 1260 | 1261–1269 | 1278, 1279 | 1280 |
| 22 | Detmold | 2/3 | 1281–1310 | 1281–1286 | 1290 | 1291–1299 | 1308, 1309 | 1310 |
| 23 | München | 4/3 | 1311–1360 | 1311–1322 | 1329, 1330 | 1331–1348 | 1355–1358 | 1359, 1360 |
| 24 | Traunstein | 1/3 | 1361–1380 | 1361–1364 | 1370 | 1371–1376 | 1379 | 1380 |
| 25 | Kempten | 1/3 | 1381–1400 | 1381–1384 | 1390 | 1391–1396 | 1399 | 1400 |
| 26 | Breslau | 3/3 | 1401–1430 | 1401–1408 | 1410 | 1411–1422 | 1427–1429 | 1430 |
| 27 | Bunzlau | 2/3 | 1431–1460 | 1431–1436 | 1440 | 1441–1449 | 1458, 1459 | 1460 |
| 28 | Oppeln | 1/3 | 1461–1480 | 1461–1464 | 1470 | 1471–1476 | 1479 | 1480 |
| 29 | Frankfurt (Main) | 3/3 | 1481–1510 | 1481–1483 | 1490 | 1491–1502 | 1507–1509 | 1510 |
| 30 | Weimar | 3/3 | 1511–1540 | 1511–1518 | 1520 | 1521–1532 | 1537–1539 | 1540 |
| 31 | Kassel | 2/3 | 1541–1570 | 1541–1546 | 1550 | 1551–1559 | 1568, 1569 | 1570 |
| 32 | Lüneburg | 2/3 | 1571–1600 | 1571–1576 | 1580 | 1581–1589 | 1598, 1599 | 1600 |
| 33 | Schleswig | 2/3 | 1601–1630 | 1601–1606 | 1610 | 1611–1619 | 1628, 1629 | 1630 |
| 34 | Oldenburg | 2/3 | 1631–1660 | 1631–1636 | 1640 | 1641–1649 | 1658, 1659 | 1660 |
| 35 | Braunschweig | 3/3 | 1661–1690 | 1661–1668 | 1670 | 1671–1682 | 1687–1689 | 1690 |
| 36 | Magdeburg | 3/3 | 1691–1720 | 1691–1698 | 1700 | 1701–1712 | 1717–1719 | 1720 |
| 37 | Koblenz | 3/3 | 1721–1750 | 1721–1728 | 1730 | 1731–1742 | 1747–1749 | 1750 |
| 38 | Mannheim | 3/3 | 1751–1780 | 1751–1758 | 1760 | 1761–1772 | 1777–1779 | 1780 |
| 39 | Trier | 2/3 | 1781–1810 | 1781–1786 | 1790 | 1791–1799 | 1808, 1809 | 1810 |
| 40 | Nürnberg | 3/3 | 1811–1840 | 1811–1818 | 1820 | 1821–1832 | 1837–1839 | 1840 |
| 41 | Würzburg | 2/3 | 1841–1870 | 1841–1846 | 1850 | 1851–1859 | 1868, 1869 | 1870 |
| 42 | Regensburg | 2/3 | 1871–1900 | 1871–1876 | 1880 | 1881–1889 | 1898, 1899 | 1900 |
| 43 | Kraftfahr u. Verkehrsschule Suhl | — | 500–700 | | | | | |

D5

# WASSERSCHUTZPOLIZEI
## SW—Waterways Protection Police

### (a) SW HEADQUARTERS AND AFFILIATED SUB-UNITS
(as officially listed, end of 1942)

*Note :* The area controlled is given in brackets wherever the designation of the SW headquarters is not self-explanatory.

### SW-GRUPPE HAMBURG
(Elbe from Lauenburg, part of the Kaiser-Wilhelm Canal and areas listed below)

**Controlling Authority :**
*Pol.-Präs.* Hamburg

**Subordinate units :**
*SW-Abschn.* A,
  *SW-Revier* 1
  *SW-Revier* 2
  *SW-Revier* 3
  *SW-Revier* Alster
  *SW-Revier* Cuxhaven
  *SW-Station* Brunsbüttelkoog
*SW-Abschn.* B,
  *SW-Revier* 5
  *SW-Revier* 6
  *SW-Revier* Branch Amerikahöft
*SW-Abschn.* C,
  *SW-Revier* 8
  *SW-Revier* 9
  *SW-Revier* 10
  *SW-Revier* 11

**Other Units :** *Luftschutzbefehlsstelle, Bootbereit-schaft, Technischer Betrieb.*

### SW-Kdo. ÖSTLICHE OSTSEE

**Controlling authority :**
BdO Königsberg

**Subordinate units :**
*SW-Revier* Königsberg
  *SW-Station* Pillau
  *SW-Wache* Lötzen
*SW-Revier* Tilsit
  *SW-Station* Labiau
  *SW-Wache* Klocken
*SW-Revier* Memel

### SW-Kdo. WEICHSEL

**Controlling authority :**
*Reichsstatthalter* Danzig-Westpreussen
*Kdr (d. Wasserschupo) Oberstlt.* Voss

**Subordinate Units :**
*SW-Revier* Danzig-Weichselmünde
*SW-Revier* Branch Danzig
*SW-Wache* Danzig-Neufahrwasser
*SW-Wache* Einlage
*SW-Wache* Dirschau
*SW-Revier* Elbing
*SW-Revier* Gotenhafen
*SW-Station* Thorn
*SW-Wache* Graudenz
*SW-Wache* Leslau
*SW-Station* Schröttersburg/Weichsel
*SW-Wache* Neuhof (Nowy-Dwor)

### SW-Kdo. WESTLICHE OSTSEE

**Controlling authority :**
*Pol. Präs.* Kiel, Holstenstr. 99
  Tel : 1384/87
*Kdr : Maj. d. Schupo* Onken

**Subordinate units :**
*SW-Revier* Rostock
*SW-Revier* Lübeck
  *SW-Station* Travemünde
*SW-Revier* Kiel
*SW-Revier* Flensburg

### SW-Kdo. ODER

**Controlling authority :**
BdO Breslau
*Kdr : Maj. d. Schupo* Kaiser

**Subordinate units :**
*SW-Ergänzungswache* Jast
*SW-Wache* Gleiwitz
*SW-Ergänzungswache* Brieg
*SW-Wache* Maltsch
*SW-Revier* Breslau
  *SW-Station* Cosel
  *SW-Wache* Glogau
*SW-Wache* Fürstenberg
*SW-Wache* Küstrin

### SW-Kdo. ELBE

**Controlling authority :**
*Ob. Präs. d. Prov. Sachsen,* Magdeburg, Auf dem Fürstenwall 3b.
  Tel : 35901
*Kdr : Maj. d. Schupo* Stucke

**Subordinate units :**
*SW-Wache* Leitmeritz
*SW-Wache* Aussig
*SW-Revier* Dresden
  *SW-Wache* Riesa
  *SW-Wache* Bad Schandau
*SW-Station* Dessau-Rosslau
*SW-Revier* Magdeburg
  *SW-Wache* Wittenberg
  *SW-Wache* Wittenberge (*Bez.* Potsdam)
  *SW-Wache* Hitzacker
*SW-Wache* Lauenburg
*SW-Wache* Braunschweig-Veltenhofen
*SW-Wache* Halle/Saale-Trotha
*SW-Wache* Salzgitter
*SW-Posten* Rothensee (*Post* Wolmirstedt)

### SW-Kdo. RHEIN

**Controlling authority :**
*Ob. Präs. d. Rheinprovinz,* Koblenz
*Kdr : Oberstlt. d. Schupo* Pietzker

**Subordinate units :**
*SW-Station* Strassburg
*SW-Wache* Hüningen
*SW-Wache* Breisach i.B.
*SW-Station* Karlsruhe
  *SW-Wache* Ludwigshafen a.Rh.
*SW-Posten* Mannheim
*SW-Wache* Heilbronn a.Neckar
*SW-Station* Mainz
  *SW-Wache* Nierstein a.Rh.
  *SW-Wache* Frankfurt a.M.
  *SW-Wache* Rüdesheim

## SW-Kdo. RHEIN (*continued*)

*SW-Station* Koblenz/Ehrenbreitstein
*SW-Wache* Bad Salzig
*SW-Wache* Neuwied
*SW-Station* Köln
*SW-Wache* Bonn
*SW-Wache* Düsseldorf
*SW-Station* Duisburg/Ruhrort
*SW-Wache* Emmerich
*SW-Wache* Wesel
*SW-Fliegende Wache* Lobith

## SW-Kdo. DONAU

**Controlling authority :**
*Reichsstatthalter* Wien

**Subordinate units :**
*SW-Revier* Wien
*SW-Revier* Branch Winterhafen
*SW-Wache* Krems
*SW-Revier* Linz
*SW-Wache* Engelhartszell
*SW-Wache* Passau
*SW-Station* Engerau
*SW-Station* Hainburg
*SW-Wache* Regensburg

## SW-Kdo. BODENSEE

**Controlling authority :**
*Württ. Innenminister*, Stuttgart

**Subordinate units :**
*SW-Station* Friedrichshafen
*SW-Station* Lindau
*SW-Station* Konstanz

## SW-Abschn. Kdo. STETTIN

(The Oder in Pommern, the Dammsche See, and the coastal waters around Rügen and areas listed below.)

**Controlling authority :**
*Pol. Präs.* Stettin

**Subordinate units :**
*SW-Revier* 1
*SW-Revier* 2
*SW-Station* Swinemünde
*SW-Station* Stralsund
*SW-Wache* Wolgast
*SW-Wache* Fiddichow
*SW-Schule* Stettin

## SW-Abschn. BREMEN

(Parts of the Weser, Hunte, Ems, Dortmund-Ems-Kanal, Leda, the Ems-Jade-Kanal and areas listed below.)

**Controlling authority :**
*Pol. Präs.* Bremen

**Subordinate units :**
*SW-Revier* 1
*SW-Revier* 2
*SW-Revier* Branch Bremen
*SW-Revier* Branch Bremerhaven
*SW-Revier* Wesermünde
*SW-Revier* Emden
*SW-Wache* Elsfleth
*SW-Wache* Nienburg
*SW-Wache* Oldenburg i.O.
*SW-Sd. Kdo.* Dörpen b. Papenburg a. Ems.

## SW-Abschn. BERLIN

(The Havelseen, parts of the Havel and areas listed below.)

**Controlling authority :**
*Pol. Präs.* Berlin

**Subordinate units :**
*SW-Revier* Baumschulenweg
*SW-Revier* Spandau
*SW-Revier* Berlin-Mitte
*SW-Wache* Eberswalde
*SW-Posten* Oranienburg
*SW-Posten* Wernsdorf

## SW-Revier WARTHE/NETZE

**Controlling authority :**
BdO Posen

**Subordinate units :**
*SW-Station* Posen
*SW-Station* Bromberg
*SW-Wache* Landsberg/Warthe
*SW-Wache* Usch (*Kr.* Schneidemühl)

## SW-Revier POTSDAM

(The Havel to its confluence into the Elbe, Ihle-Plauer-Kanal and areas listed below.)

**Controlling authority :**
*Pol. Präs.* Potsdam

**Subordinate units :**
*SW-Wache* Brandenburg a.H.
*SW-Wache* Rathenow
*SW-Wache* Genthin

## SW-Revier RECKLINGHAUSEN

(Rhein-Herne-Kanal, Lippe-Seitenkanal, Ems, Ems-Weser-Kanal, the Weser and areas listed below.)

**Controlling authority :**
*Pol. Präs.* Recklinghausen

**Subordinate units :**
*SW-Posten* Duisburg-Ruhrort
*SW-Wache* Essen-Dellwig
*SW-Wache* Henrichenburg
*SW-Wache* Münster, i.W.
*SW-Wache* Bevergern ü/Rheina
*SW-Wache* Minden i.W.
*SW-Wache* Anderten ü/Hannover
*SW-Wache* Dorsten i.W.
*SW-Wache* Meppen a. Ems

## SW-Kdo. IJSSELMEER
## SW-Kdo. NIEDERLANDE

**Controlling authority :**
BdO Nimwegen

**Subordinate units :**
*SW-Wache* Dordrecht
*SW-Wache* Delfzijl

## SW-Kdo. OSTLAND

**Controlling authority :**
BdO Riga

## SW-Flotille SERBIEN

**Controlling authority :**
*Mil. Befh. in Serbien*, Belgrad

**Subordinate units :**
*SW-Wache* Felico-Gradiste
*SW-Wache* Tekija

| Location | Designation and Affiliation | Address | Remarks |
|---|---|---|---|
| Alster | *SW-Revier* under *SW-Gruppe* Hamburg | Hamburg 21, Schöne Aussicht 39 Tel.: 34 1000 | |
| Amerikahöft | *SW-Revier* branch under *SW-Abschn.* B, Hamburg | Amerikastr. 2 Tel: 34 1000 | |
| Amsterdam | *SW-Kdo.* Ijsselmeer | | |
| Anderten über Hannover | *SW-Wache* under *SW-Revier* Recklinghausen | Hindenburgschleuse Tel: Hannover 56572 | |
| Aussig | *SW-Wache* under *SW-Kdo.* Elbe | Am Laden, Alte Hafenmeisterei Tel: 3448 | |
| Bad Salzig | *SW-Wache* under *SW-Station* Koblenz | Rheinbaden Allee Tel: Boppard 351 | Personnel and equipment probably from *SW-Station* Koblenz |
| Bad Schandau | *SW-Wache* under *SW-Revier* Dresden | | 1 Officer, 4 NCOs 1 *Hafenboot*. Continued existence uncertain |
| Baumschulenweg | *SW-Revier* under *SW-Abschnitt* Berlin | Verlängerte Baum-schulenstr. Tel: 631993 631994 | 5 Officers, 23 NCOs 3 *Hafenboote*, 1 *Streckenboot* |
| Belgrad | *SW-Flotille* Serbien under *Mil. Befh. Serbien,* in Belgrad | Decauska 12 Tel: 22 320 | |
| Berlin | *SW-Abschn.* under *Pol. Präs.* Berlin | Verlängerte Baum-schulenstr. Tel: 631993 631994 | |
| Berlin-Mitte | *SW-Revier* under *SW-Abschn.* Berlin | Berlin N 65, Westhafen, Zollspeicher Tel: 356541 (240) 350913 | |
| Bevergern über Rheina | *SW-Wache* under *SW-Revier* Recklinghausen | Tel: Hörstel 203 | 1 Officer, 3 NCOs 1 *Hafenboot* |
| Bonn | *SW-Wache* under *SW-Station* Köln | Fritz Schröder Ufer 3 Tel: 2230 | Personnel and Equipment probably from *SW-Station* Köln |
| Brandenburg a.H. | *SW-Wache* under *SW-Revier* Potsdam | Adolf-Hitlerstr. 31 Tel: 3067 | 1 Officer, 5 NCOs 2 *Hafenboote* |
| Braunschweig-Veltenhofen | *SW-Wache* under *SW-Kdo.* Elbe | Hafenstr. 14 Tel: Braunschweig 4330 | |
| Breisach i.B. | *SW-Wache* under *SW-Kdo.* Rhein | Zollamtsgebäude Tel: 249 | |
| Bremen | *SW-Abschn.* under *Pol. Präs.* Bremen | Überseehafen Tel: 84 221 | 13 Officers, 77 NCOs 2 *Hafenboote* 1 *Streckenboot* 1 PKW (automobile). Probably provides personnel and equipment for 2 Reviere and 1 Revier branch |
| Bremen | *SW-Revier* 1 under *SW-Abschn.* Bremen | Überseehafen Tel: 84 221 | Personnel and equipment probably from *SW-Abschn.* Bremen. |

| Location | Designation and Affiliation | Address | Remarks |
|---|---|---|---|
| Bremen | *SW-Revier* 2 under *SW-Abschn.* Bremen | Waterbergstr. Tel: 84 221 83 953 | Personnel and equipment probably from *SW-Abschn.* Bremen |
| Bremen | *SW-Revier* branch under *SW-Abschn.* Bremen | Europahafen Tel: 84 221 | Personnel and equipment probably from *SW-Abschn.* Bremen |
| Bremerhaven | *SW-Revier* branch under *SW-Abschn.* Bremen | Inselstr. 11 Tel: Wesermünde 3 006 | 5 Officers, 27 NCOs 1 *Hafenboot* |
| Breslau | *SW-Kdo.* Oder under BdO Breslau | Neumarkt 1-8 Tel: 22 451 | 5 Officers, 1 NCO 2 adm. Officers, 1 PKW |
| Breslau | *SW-Revier* under *SW-Kdo.* Oder | Gnesenerstr. 2 Tel: 22 751 23 911 | 4 Officers, 18 NCOs 2 *Hafenboote* 1 *Streckenboot* 1 Motor-cycle |
| Brieg | *SW-Erg. Wache* under *SW-Kdo.* Oder | Mühlendamm 10 Tel: 1232 | |
| Bromberg | *SW-Station* under *SW-Revier* Warthe/ Netze | Bollmanstr. 21 Tel: 3466 | 3 Officers, 6 NCOs 1 *Hafenboot* |
| Brünsbüttelkoog | *SW-Station* under *SW-Gruppe* Hamburg | Schleuse Tel: 256 | 2 Officers, 9 NCOs 1 *Streckenboot* |
| Cosel | *SW-Station* under *SW-Revier* Breslau | Eisenbahnstr. 1 Tel: 586 | 2 Officers, 7 NCOs 1 *Hafenboot* 1 Motor-cycle |
| Cuxhaven | *SW-Revier* under *SW-Gruppe* Hamburg | Lentzkai Tel: 2072 | 3 Officers, 10 NCOs 1 *Streckenboot* |
| Danzig | *SW-Kdo.* Weichsel under *Reichssth.* Danzig/Westpr. | Rennerstiftsgasse 7 Tel: 25 200 | |
| Danzig | *SW-Revier* branch under *SW-Kdo.* Weichsel | Schuitensteg 7 Tel: 28 291 | |
| Danzig-Neufahrwasser | *SW-Wache* under *SW-Kdo.* Weichsel | Lotsenweg 2 Tel: 35 070 (?) 28 467 (?) | |
| Danzig-Weichselmünde | *SW-Revier* under *SW-Kdo.* Weichsel | Festung 1 Tel: 28 467 25 293 | |
| Delfzijl | *SW-Wache* under *SW-Kdo.* Niederlande | | |
| Dessau | *SW-Station* under *SW-Kdo.* Elbe | Strasse d.SA 49 Tel: 4151 | |
| Dirschau | *SW-Wache* under *SW-Kdo.* Weichsel | Weichselstr. 4 Tel: 1481 | |
| Doerpen b. Papenburg | *SW-Sonderkdo.* under *SW-Abschn.* Bremen | Tel: 107 | |
| Dordrecht | *SW-Wache* under *SW-Kdo.* Niederlande | Merve Kade 22 Tel: 4133 | |
| Dorpat | *SW-Kdo.* Ostland under *BdO.*, Riga | Aurikusstr. 2 Tel: 72 | |
| Dorsten i.W. | *SW-Wache* under *SW-Revier* Reckling-hausen | Tel: 2127 | |

| Location | Designation and Affiliation | Address | Remarks |
|---|---|---|---|
| Dresden | *SW-Revier* under *SW-Kdo.* Elbe | König Albert Hafen Tel : 24111 (197) | 4 Officers, 15 NCOs 1 *Hafenboot* 1 *Streckenboot* |
| Duisburg-Ruhrort | *SW-Station* under *SW-Kdo.* Rhein | August Hirschstr. 19 Tel : 41 449 | 4 Officers, 16 NCOs 3 *Hafenboote* 1 PKW |
| Duisburg-Ruhrort | *SW-Posten* under *SW-Revier* Reckling-hausen | Am Hafenkanal, Ruhrschleuse Tel : 4320 | 1 NCO |
| Düsseldorf | *SW-Wache* under *SW-Station* Köln | Kornhausstr. 6 Tel : 24 601 | Personnel and equipment probably from *SW-Station* Köln |
| Eberswalde | *SW-Wache* under *SW-Abschn.* Berlin | Ruderklub, Wasser-torbrücke Tel : 2408 | |
| Einlage (Kr. Danzig-Land) | *SW-Wache* under *SW-Kdo.* Weichsel | Schleuse Tel : Schiewenhorst 61 | |
| Elbing | *SW-Revier* under *SW-Kdo.* Weichsel | Kraffohlsdorferweg 5 Tel : 4344, 2941 | 4 Officers, 12 NCOs 1 *Hafenboot* 1 *Streckenboot* |
| Elsfleth | *SW-Wache* under *SW-Abschn.* Bremen | Weserstr. 11 Tel : 377 | 1 Officer, 2 NCOs 1 *Hafenboot* |
| Emden | *SW-Revier* under *SW-Abschn.* Bremen | Nesserlanderschleuse Tel : 3 561 | 4 Officers, 12 NCOs 2 *Hafenboote* 1 *Streckenboot* |
| Emmerich | *SW-Wache* under *SW-Kdo.* Rhein | Am Wassertor 6 Tel : 2775 | Personnel and equipment probably from *SW-Station* Duisburg |
| Engelhartszell | *SW-Wache* under *SW-Revier* Linz | | Continued existence uncertain |
| Engerau | *SW-Station* under *SW-Kdo.* Donau | Wienerstr. 260 Tel : 42 | |
| Essen-Dellwig | *SW-Wache* under *SW-Revier* Reckling-hausen | Ankerstr. Schleuse III Tel : Bottrop 2622 | 1 Officer, 4 NCOs 1 *Hafenboot* 1 Motor-cycle |
| Felico-Gradiste | *SW-Wache* under *SW-Flotille* Serbien | | |
| Fiddichow | *SW-Wache* under *SW-Abschn. Kdo.* Stettin | Gr. Oderstr. Tel : 130 | |
| Flensburg | *SW-Revier* under *SW-Kdo.* Westliche Ostsee | Norderhofenden 23 Tel : 2590 | 3 Officers, 8 NCOs 1 *Hafenboot* 1 *Streckenboot* |
| Frankfurt a.M. | *SW-Wache* under *SW-Station* Mainz | Scharnhorststr. 22 Tel : 34973 | Personnel and equipment probably from *SW-Station* Mainz |
| Friedrichshafen | *SW-Kdo.* Bodensee under Württ. *Innenmin.,* Stuttgart | Seestr. 27 Tel : 2124 | 2 Officers, 1 NCO 1 PKW |
| Friedrichshafen | *SW-Station* under *SW-Kdo.* Bodensee | Seestr. 27 Tel : 2124 | 2 Officers, 7 NCOs 1 *Streckenboot* 1 *Hafenboot* |
| Fürstenberg | *SW-Wache* under *SW-Kdo.* Oder | Neue Brückenstr. 1 Tel : 312 | 1 Officer, 2 NCOs 1 *Hafenboot* |

| Location | Designation and Affiliation | Address | Remarks |
|---|---|---|---|
| Genthin | *SW-Wache* under *SW-Revier* Potsdam | Amtsstr. (Ausbau) Tel : 232 (Wasseramt) | |
| Gleiwitz | *SW-Wache* under *SW-Kdo.* Oder | Laband O.S. Schleuse Tel : 182 | |
| Glogau | *SW-Wache* under *SW-Revier* Breslau | Steinweg 2 Tel : 1341 | 1 Officer, 2 NCOs 1 *Hafenboot* |
| Gotenhafen | *SW-Revier* under *SW-Kdo.* Weichsel | Am belgischen Kai Tel : 1491 | |
| Graudenz | *SW-Wache* under *SW-Kdo.* Weichsel | Lehmstr. 12 Tel : 1380 | |
| Hainburg | *SW-Station* under *SW-Kdo.* Donau | | Continued existence uncertain |
| Halle-Saale | *SW-Wache* under *SW-Kdo.* Elbe | An d. Hansastr. Tel : 25 319 | 2 Officers, 5 NCOs 1 *Hafenboot* |
| Hamburg | *SW-Gruppe* under *Pol. Präs.* Hamburg | Burchardstr. 14 Tel : 34 1000 | 232 Officers, 61 NCOs 23 *Hafenboote* 2 *Streckenboote* Supplies, personnel and equipment for 3 *Abschn.*, 10 *Reviere* and 1 *Revier* branch |
| Hamburg | *Luftschutzbefehlsstelle* | Dalmannstr. Kaispeicher A Tel : 34 1000 | |
| Hamburg | *Bootsbereitschaft* under *SW-Gruppe* Hamburg | Worthdamm 47 (Schlageterkas.) Tel : 34 1000 | |
| Hamburg | *Technischer Betrieb* under *SW-Gruppe* Hamburg | St. Pauli Landungsbrücke, Brücke 5 Tel : 422027 | |
| Hamburg | *SW-Abschn.* A under *SW-Gruppe* Hamburg | Brooktor 4 Tel : 34 1000 | |
| Hamburg | *SW-Abschn.* B under *SW-Gruppe* Hamburg | Lübecker Ufer 1 Tel : 34 1000 | |
| Hamburg | *SW-Abschn.* C under *SW-Gruppe* Hamburg | Nehlstr. 23 Tel : 34 1000 | |
| Hamburg | *SW-Revier* 1 under *SW-Abschn.* A Hamburg | Bei den St. Pauli Landungsbrücken Tel : 34 1000 | |
| Hamburg | *SW-Revier* 2 under *SW-Abschn.* A Hamburg | Kehrwiederspitze Tel : 34 1000 | |
| Hamburg-Altona | *SW-Revier* 3 under *SW-Abschn.* A Hamburg | Landungsbrücke Altona Tel : 34 1000 | |
| Hamburg | *SW-Revier* 5 under *SW-Abschn.* B Hamburg | Entenwärder Tel : 34 1000 | |
| Hamburg | *SW-Revier* 6 under *SW-Abschn.* B Hamburg | Lübecker Ufer 1 Tel : 34 1000 | |
| Hamburg | *SW-Revier* 8 under *SW-Abschn.* C Hamburg | Breslauerstr. Tel : 34 1000 | |
| Hamburg-Finkenwärder | *SW-Revier* 9 under *SW-Abschn.* C Hamburg | Tankweg 7 Tel : 34 1000 | |
| Hamburg | *SW-Revier* 10 under *SW-Abschn.* C Hamburg | Nehlstr. 23 Tel : 34 1000 | |

B 2

| Location | Designation and Affiliation | Address | Remarks |
|---|---|---|---|
| Hamburg-Harburg | *SW-Revier* 11 under *SW-Abschn.* C Hamburg | Lauenbrucherdeich 14 Tel : 34 1000 | |
| Heilbronn a. Neckar | *SW-Wache* under *SW-Kdo.* Rhein | Alte Schleuse Tel : 2481 | |
| Henrichenburg | *SW-Wache* under *SW-Revier* Reckling-hausen | Mecklinghoeven bei Datteln i.W. Tel : Datteln 347 | 1 Officer, 3 NCOs 1 *Hafenboot* |
| Hitzacker | *SW-Wache* under *SW-Revier* Magdeburg | | 1 Officer, 2 NCOs |
| Hüningen | *SW-Wache* under *SW-Kdo.* Rhein | Weil a. Rh. 7 Tel : St. Ludwig 74 | |
| Jast (ü/Auschwitz) | *SW-Erg. Wache* under *SW-Kdo.* Oder | Tel : Imilien 30 | |
| Karlsruhe | *SW-Station* under *SW-Kdo.* Rhein | Honsellstr. 34 Tel : 8398 | 4 Officers, 14 NCOs 4 *Hafenboote* 1 PKW |
| Kiel | *SW-Kdo.* Westliche Ostsee under *Ob-Präs.* Kiel | Schloss Tel : 1384 | 5 Officers, 1 NCO 2 adm. Officers 1 PKW |
| Kiel | *SW-Revier* under *SW-Kdo.* Westliche Ostsee poss. with 2 *SW-Revier* branches | Wallstr. 42 Tel : 4 300 | 6 Officers, 28 NCOs 2 *Hafenboote* 1 *Streckenboot* |
| Klocken (Kr. Eich-niederung) | *SW-Wache* under *SW-Revier* Tilsit | Tel : Kukerneese 296 | 1 Officer, 2 NCOs 1 *Hafenboot* |
| Koblenz | *SW-Kdo.* Rhein under *Ob. Präs. d.* Rheinprovinz | Wilhelmstr. 3-5 Tel : 3201 | 3 Officers, 1 NCO 1 PKW |
| Koblenz/Ehren-breitstein | *SW-Station* under *SW-Kdo.* Rhein | Humboldtstr. 116 Tel : 3374 | 4 Officers, 12 NCOs 3 *Hafenboote* 1 PKW |
| Köln | *SW-Station* under *SW-Kdo.* Rhein | Hafen, Hansawerft Tel : 91 033 | 4 Officers, 16 NCOs 3 *Hafenboote* 1 PKW |
| Königsberg | *SW-Kdo.* Östliche Ostsee under BdO Königsberg | Weidendamm 34 Tel : 40 555/46 | 5 Officers, 1 NCO 2 adm. Officers 1 PKW |
| Königsberg | *SW-Revier* under *SW-Kdo.* Östliche Ostsee | Deutschordenring 53 Tel : 32 945 | 6 Officers, 28 NCOs 3 *Hafenboote* 1 *Streckenboot* (b.s.) |
| Konstanz | *SW-Station* under *SW-Kdo.* Bodensee | Hafenstr. Tel : 851 | 1 Officer, 7 NCOs 1 *Streckenboot* 1 *Hafenboot* |
| Krems | *SW-Wache* under *SW-Kdo.* Donau | Ruderklubgebäude Tel : 511 | |
| Küstrin | *SW-Wache* under *SW-Kdo.* Oder | Friedrichstr. 19 Tel : 612 | 1 Officer, 2 NCOs 1 *Hafenboot* |
| Laband | see Gleiwitz | | |
| Labiau | *SW-Station* under *SW-Revier* Tilsit | Rathaus Tel : 493 | 2 Officers, 7 NCOs 1 *Streckenboot* 1 *Segelschlitten* |
| Landsberg | *SW-Wache* under *SW-Revier* Warthe/ Netze | Dammstr. 27 Tel : 2529 | 2 Officers, 4 NCOs 1 *Hafenboot* |

| Location | Designation and Affiliation | Address | Remarks |
|---|---|---|---|
| Lauenburg | *SW-Wache* under *SW-Kdo.* Elbe | Elbstr. 116 Tel : 291 | |
| Leitmeritz | *SW-Wache* under *SW-Kdo.* Elbe | Lachswerder 11 Tel : 167 | |
| Leslau | *SW-Wache* under *SW-Kdo.* Weichsel | Richard-Wagnerstr. 3 Tel : 1356 | |
| Lindau | *SW-Station* under *SW-Kdo.* Bodensee | Segelhafen 2 Tel : 2107 | 1 Officer, 8 NCOs 2 *Streckenboote* |
| Linz | *SW-Revier* under *SW-Kdo.* Donau | Mühlkreisbahnstr. 2 Tel : 27 602 | |
| Lobith | *SW-Fliegende Wache* under *SW-Kdo.* Rhein | Am Wassertor 6 Tel : 2775 | |
| Lötzen | *SW-Wache* under *SW-Revier* Königsberg | Pionierstr. 1 Tel : 776 | 1 Officer, 2 NCOs 1 *Hafenboot* 1 *Segelschlitten* (Windsleigh) |
| Lübeck | *SW-Revier* under *SW-Kdo.* Westliche Ostsee | Hafenstr. 2 Tel : 25 121 | 4 Officers, 12 NCOs 3 *Hafenboote* |
| Ludwigshafen | *SW-Wache* under *SW-Station* Karlsruhe | Zollhof Tel : 61692 | Personnel probably from *SW-Station* Karlsruhe |
| Magdeburg | *SW-Kdo.* Elbe under *Ob. Präs. d. Prov.* Sachsen | Fürstenwallstr. 3b Tel : 35 901 | 5 Officers, 1 NCO 2 adm. Officers 1 PKW |
| Magdeburg | *SW-Revier* under *SW-Kdo.* Elbe | Alte Schiffswerft 1 Tel : 42841, 32880 (270) | 3 Officers, 12 NCOs 1 *Hafenboot* 1 *Streckenboot* 1 PKW |
| Maltsch | *SW-Wache* under *SW-Kdo.* Oder | Kohlenstr. 11 Tel : 115 | 1 Officer, 5 NCOs 1 *Hafenboot* |
| Mainz | *SW-Station* under *SW-Kdo.* Rhein | Am Winterhafen 21 Tel : 43 727 | 5 Officers, 16 NCOs 4 *Hafenboote* 1 PKW |
| Mannheim | *SW-Posten* under *SW-Kdo.* Rhein | Mühlauschleuse Tel : 35851 (116) | |
| Memel | *SW-Revier* under *SW-Kdo.* Östliche Ostsee | Norderhuk 5 Tel : 2 121 | |
| Meppen a. Ems | *SW-Wache* under *SW-Revier* Recklinghausen | Schleuse Tel : 554 | |
| Minden i.W. | *SW-Wache* under *SW-Revier* Recklinghausen | Schierholzstr. 28 Tel : 1425 | 1 Officer, 4 NCOs 1 *Hafenboot* 1 Motor-cycle |
| Münster i.W. | *SW-Wache* under *SW-Revier* Recklinghausen | Schiffahrterdamm 192 Tel : 40 322 | 1 Officer, 2 NCOs 1 *Hafenboot* |
| Nienburg | *SW-Wache* under *SW-Abschn.* Bremen | Jugendherberge Tel : 868 | |
| Nierstein | *SW-Wache* under *SW-Station* Mainz | Strasse d. SA. 80 Tel : 552 | Personnel probably from *SW-Station* Mainz |
| Neuhof (Nowy-Dwor) | *SW-Wache* under *SW-Kdo.* Weichsel | Bez. Zichenau Tel : 31 | |

| Location | Designation and Affiliation | Address | Remarks |
|---|---|---|---|
| Neuwied | SW-Wache under SW-Kdo. Rhein | Deichstr. 4 Tel: 4 208 | |
| Oldenburg i.O. | SW-Wache under SW-Abschn. Bremen | Am Stau 54 Tel: 4 208 | |
| Oranienburg | SW-Posten under SW-Abschn. Berlin | Schleuse Lehnitz Tel: 2177 | 2 NCOs |
| Passau | SW-Wache under SW-Kdo. Donau | Rathausplatz Tel: 2811 | |
| Pillau | SW-Station under SW-Revier Königsberg | Hindenburgstr. 1 Tel: 261 | 3 Officers, 12 NCOs 1 Hafenboot 1 Streckenboot (Bs) 1 Segelschlitten |
| Posen | SW-Revier Warthe/Netze under BdO Posen | Fritz Reuterstr. 2a Tel: 6561 | 3 Officers, 1 NCO 1 PKW |
| Posen | SW-Station under SW-Revier Warthe/Netze | Raiffeisenallee 8 Tel: 1421 | 3 Officers, 6 NCOs 1 Hafenboot 1 rowboat with outboard motor |
| Potsdam | SW-Revier under Pol. Präs. Potsdam | An d. Gewehrfabrik 6 Tel: 5944 4151 | 3 Officers, 13 NCOs 2 Hafenboote 1 Streckenboot |
| Rathenow | SW-Wache under Revier Potsdam | Hauptmann-Loeperstr. 104 Tel: 3276 | 1 Officer, 2 NCOs 1 Hafenboot |
| Recklinghausen | SW-Revier under Pol. Pr. Recklinghausen | Westerholterstr. 27 Tel: 4343 (195) | 2 Officers, 1 NCO 1 PKW |
| Regensburg | SW-Wache under SW-Kdo. Donau | Wienerstr. 18 Tel: 5251 (328) | |
| Riesa | SW-Wache under SW-Revier Dresden | Gröbaer Hafen Tel: 309 | 1 Officer, 2 NCOs 1 Hafenboot |
| Rothensee | SW-Posten under SW-Kdo. Elbe | Schiffshebewerk Rothensee, Baustoffprüfstelle Tel: Magdeb. 22938 (24) | |
| Rotterdam | SW-Kdo. Niederlande under BdO Nimwegen | Veerkade Tel: 39538 | (Kapitänleutnant JAKOBS) |
| Rostock | SW-Revier under SW-Kdo. Westliche Ostsee | Neue Werderstr. 32 Tel: 7271 | 3 Officers, 8 NCOs 1 Streckenboot 1 Hafenboot |
| Rüdesheim | SW-Wache under SW-Station Mainz | Albertistr. 3 Tel: 681 | Personnel and equipment probably from SW-Station Mainz |
| Salzgitter | SW-Wache under SW-Kdo. Elbe | Hafen d. Hermann-Göring Werke | 1 Officer, 5 NCOs 1 Hafenboot |
| Schröttersburg | SW-Station under SW-Kdo. Weichsel | Gillystr. 18 Tel: 1049 | |
| Spandau | SW-Revier under SW-Abschn. Berlin | Mertenstr. 140 Tel: 37 2594 | 4 Officers, 19 NCOs 3 Hafenboote 1 Streckenboot |
| Stettin | SW-Abschn. Kdo. under Pol. Präs. Stettin | Augustastr. 15 Tel: 25 231 | 8 Officers, 43 NCOs 5 Hafenboote 1 Streckenboot 1 PKW—supplies personnel and equipment for 2 Reviere |
| Stettin | SW-Revier 1, under SW-Abschn. Kdo. Stettin | Fürstenstr. 4a Tel: 35 231 | |

| Location | Designation and Affiliation | Address | Remarks |
|---|---|---|---|
| Stettin | *SW-Revier* 2 under *SW-Abschn. Kdo.* Stettin | Reiherwederhafen Tel: 33 764 | |
| Stettin | *SW-Schule* under *RdI* (*Hauptamt Orpo*) | Fürstenstr. 4a Tel: 35 231 (659) | 5 Officers, 55 NCOs |
| Stralsund | *SW-Station* under *SW-Abschn. Kdo.* Stettin | Seestr. 6 Tel: 2957 | 2 Officers, 7 NCOs 1 *Streckenboot* |
| Strassburg | *SW-Station* under *SW-Kdo.* Rhein | Rheinhafenstr. 5 Tel: 22 644 | |
| Swinemünde | *SW-Station* under *SW-Abschn. Kdo.* Stettin | Schiffahrtsgeb. Tel: 2785 | 3 Officers, 11 NCOs 1 *Hafenboot* |
| Tekija | *SW-Wache* under *SW-Flotille* Serbien | | |
| Thorn | *SW-Station* under *SW-Kdo.* Weichsel | Fischerweg 13 Tel: 1794 (?) | |
| Tilsit | *SW-Revier* under *SW-Kdo.* Östliche Ostsee | Schlachthofhafen Tel: 2 991 | 3 Officers, 10 NCOs 1 *Hafenboot* 1 *Streckenboot* |
| Travemünde | *SW-Station* under *SW-Revier* Lübeck | Vorderreihe 18 Tel: 600 | 2 Officers, 6 NCOs 1 *Streckenboot* |
| Usch (Kr. Schnei-demühl) | *SW-Wache* under *SW-Revier* Warthe/Netze | Tel: 22 | 1 Officer, 5 NCOs 1 *Hafenboot* |
| Veltenhofen | see Braunschweig-Veltenhofen | | |
| Wernsdorf bei Erkner | *SW-Posten* under *SW-Abschn.* Berlin | Schleuse Tel: 65 9259 | 2 NCOs |
| Wesel | *SW-Wache* under *SW-Kdo.* Rhein | Hafenstr. 46 Tel: 2190 | |
| Wesermünde | *SW-Revier* branch under *SW-Abschn.* Bremen | Hoebelstr. 7 Tel: 2 491 | 3 Officers, 13 NCOs 1 *Streckenboot* |
| Wien | *SW-Kdo.* Donau under *Reichsstatthalter*, Wien | Erzherzog Karl-Platz 4 Tel: R 48 087 R 47 402 R 43 457 | |
| Wien | *SW-Revier* under *SW-Kdo.* Donau | Erzherzog Karl-Platz 4 Tel: R 48 087 R 47 402 R 43 457 | |
| Winterhafen | *SW-Revier* branch under *SW-Kdo.* Donau | Wien, Freudenauer Hafengebäude Tel: R 41 570 | |
| Wittenberg | *SW-Wache* under *SW-Revier* Magdeburg | Schlosstr. 14-15 Tel: 3511 (24) | 1 Officer, 2 NCOs 1 *Hafenboot* |
| Wittenberge | *SW-Wache* under *SW-Revier* Magdeburg | Adolf-Hitlerstr. 196 Tel: 712 | 1 Officer, 2 NCOs 1 *Hafenboot* |
| Wolgast | *SW-Wache* under *SW-Abschn. Kdo.* Stettin | Schifferstr. 7 Tel: 486 | |

# ANNEXE D : PART FOUR

## FEUERSCHUTZPOLIZEI

### (Fire Protection Police)

The following is a list of towns in which units of the *Feuerschutzpolizei* are known to exist.

| | | | |
|---|---|---|---|
| Aachen | Flensburg | Königshütte | Posen |
| Augsburg | Frankfurt/M | Krefeld | Potsdam |
| Berlin | Frankfurt/O | Leipzig | Prag |
| Beuthen | Gelsenkirchen | Liegnitz | Regensburg |
| Bielefeld | Gleiwitz | Linz | Remscheid |
| Bochum | Görlitz | Litzmannstadt | Rostock |
| Bonn | Gotenhafen | Ludwigsburg | Saarbrücken |
| Brandenburg | Graz | Ludwigshafen | Salzburg |
| Braunschweig | Guben | Lübeck | Schwerin |
| Bremen | Hagen | Magdeburg | Sosnowitz |
| Bremerhaven | Halberstadt | Mainz | Stettin |
| Breslau | Halle | Mannheim | Stuttgart |
| Bromberg | Hamburg | Memel | Stralsund |
| Chemnitz | Hannover | Mülhausen | Strassburg |
| Danzig | Hindenburg | München | Thorn |
| Darmstadt | Innsbruck | München-Gladbach | Tilsit |
| Dessau | Insterburg | Münster | Wesermünde |
| Dortmund | Karlsruhe | Neumünster | Wien |
| Dresden | Kassel | Nürnberg | Wiesbaden |
| Duisburg-Hamborn | Kattowitz | Oberhausen | Wilhelmshaven |
| Düsseldorf | Kiel | Offenbach/M | Wittenberg |
| Elbing | Klagenfurt | Oldenburg | Wuppertal |
| Erfurt | Köln | Osnabrück | Zwickau |
| Essen | Königsberg | Plauen | |

# ANNEXE D: PART FIVE

## LUFTSCHUTZPOLIZEI

### (Air Raid Protection Police)

The following is a complete official list (Sept. 1944) of all towns where *Luftschutzpolizei* units are located.

| | | | |
|---|---|---|---|
| Aachen | Erfurt | Langeoog | Prag |
| Augsburg | Essen | Leipzig | Recklinghausen |
| Aussig | Flensburg | Leoben | Regensburg |
| Bamberg | Frankfurt/Main | Leverkusen | Rheinhausen |
| Bayreuth | Frankfurt/Oder | Liegnitz | Riesa |
| Berlin | Freiburg | Linz | Rostock |
| Bernburg | Friedrichshafen | Litzmannstadt | Saarbrücken |
| Bielefeld | Gleiwitz | Lötzen | Salzburg |
| Bielitz | Glogau | Ludwigshafen | Schönebeck |
| Bitterfeld | Görlitz | Lübeck | Schweinfurt |
| Bochum | Göttingen | Luxemburg | Siegen |
| Bonn | Gotenhafen | Mähr. Ostrau | Sosnowitz |
| Borkum | Gotha | Magdeburg | Stendal |
| Brandenburg | Graz | Mainz | Stettin |
| Braunschweig | Hagen | Mannheim | Steyr |
| Bremen | Halle/Saale | Marburg/Drau | St. Pölten |
| Breslau | Hamburg | Memel | Stralsund |
| Bromberg | Hamm | Metz | Strassburg |
| Bruck/Mur | Hannover | Minden | Stuttgart |
| Brünn | Heilbronn/Neckar | Mülhausen | Suhl |
| Brüx | Hildesheim | München | Swinemünde |
| Brunsbüttelkoog | Ingolstadt | München-Gladbach | Trier |
| Chemnitz | Innsbruck | Münster | Ulm |
| Coburg | Jena | Neuwied | Villach |
| Cottbus | Kaiserslautern | Norderney | Waldenburg |
| Cuxhaven | Karlsbad | Nordhausen | Weissenfels |
| Danzig | Karlsruhe | Nürnberg-Fürth | Wesermünde |
| Dessau | Kassel | Oberhausen | Westerland/Sylt |
| Diedenhofen | Kattowitz | Oldenburg/O. | Wien |
| Dortmund | Kiel | Olmütz | Wiener-Neustadt |
| Dresden | Klagenfurt | Oppeln | Wiesbaden |
| Düsseldorf | Koblenz | Oranienburg | Wilhelmshaven |
| Duisburg | Köln | Osnabrück | Wismar |
| Eberswalde | Königsberg | Peine | Wittenberg |
| Eger | Kolmar | Pillau | Würzburg |
| Eisenach | Krefeld | Pilsen | Wuppertal |
| Elbing | Kreuznach, Bad | Posen | Zwickau |
| Emden | Küstrin | Potsdam | |

ANNEXE D : PART SIX

# TECHNISCHE NOTHILFE
## (Technical Emergency Corps)

### (a) TN ORDER OF BATTLE
### (1942-43)

Listed by *Landesgruppen* (LG) and *Befehlsstellen* with component *Bezirksgruppe* (BG).

## LG. I : OSTPREUSSEN
**Address :**
Königsberg (Pr), Friedländer Wall 1
Tel. 45796

**Commander :**
*L.-F.* SCHRIEVER (in 42 probably EHRBAR)

**Components :**
BG. I Südost

**Commander :**
*m.d.F.b. Gf.-F.* POLKEHN

## LG. II : NORD
**Address :**
Stettin, Elisabethstrasse 35 (Polizeiunterkunft)
Tel. 36506

**Commander :**
*m.d.F.b. L.-F.* HERMANNS (in 42)

**Remarks :**
In Apr 44 *Oberabteilungsführer der TN und Maj. d. Sch.* LANGJAHR was in charge of the LG. SCHILLING has also been reported in this capacity.

## LG. III : BERLIN-MARK BRANDENBURG
**Address :**
Berlin-Steglitz, Leydenallee 70
Tel. 792266/67

**Commander :**
*L.-F.* SCHRÖDER

**Remarks :**
*Mot. BZ* " Kurmark," " Siemens," " Geheimrat Klingenberg " (last two from Berlin) were units of TN engaged in the Silesia flood, from this LG.

## LG. IV : OBERELBE
**Address :**
Dresden-A.1, Schlosstrasse 25
Tel. 27380

**Commander :**
*L.-F.* BUBAN

**Components :**
BG. IVa Sudetenland-Nord
Address : Reichenberg (Sudetenland), Andreasgasse 38
Tel. 3670
Commander : *M.d. vertretungsw. F.b. : Ka.-F.* WAGNER
BG. IVb Sachsen-West
Address : Chemnitz, Stadthaus, Falkeplatz 2
Tel. 23666
Commander : HB.-F. KEISELT
BG. IVc Halle-Leipzig
Address : Halle/Saale, Rathausstrasse 3
Tel. 36439
Commander : *B.-F.* RUDOLPH

BG. IVd Sachsen-Ost
Commander : *M.d.F.b. B.-F. Dr.* BREMER
OG 12 Wehlen

## LG. V : SÜDWEST
**Address :**
Stuttgart, Rheinsburger Strasse 107
Tel. 64800

**Commander :**
*Bez.-F.* OELKER (was *SS-SBF* Ernst OEKLER, *HB.-F* as *K. Führer* May 1941)

**Components :**
BG. Va Elsass
Address : Strassburg/Elsass, Ludwigshafnerstrasse 2
Tel. 20052
Commander : *Komm. m.d.F.b. (S)* BRENDOW
BG. Vb Baden
Address : Freiburg/Br., Adelshauser Strasse 4
Tel. 2925

## LG. VI : WESTFALEN-NIEDERRHEIN
**Address :**
Köln-Bayenthal, Bonnerstrasse 498
Tel. 91047 and 13351

**Commander :**
*L.-F.* PRÜSSNER

**Components :**
BG. VIa Niederrhein
Address : Düsseldorf, Ellerstrasse 116
Tel. 23898
Commander : *HB.-F.* VOLLMER (at present in the Armed Forces)
BG. VIb Westfalen
Address : Dortmund, Südwall 2
Tel. 28555
Commander : *Bez.-F.* BEIL (at present in the Armed Forces), *i.V.HB.-F.* SELLQUIST
BG. VIc Weserland
Address : Bielefeld, Ritterstrasse 27
Tel. 2990
Commander : *Gf.-F.* ROMANY

OG VI/16, Remscheid (May 1943). In charge : *Gf.-F.* SPÖHRER

## LG. VII : BAYERN-SÜD
**Address :**
München 23, Leopoldstrasse 61
Tel. 36 22 57

**Commander :**
*Bez.-F.* DÜLL

D18

## LG. VIII : SCHLESIEN

**Address :**
Breslau, Burgfeld 10
Tel. 58741/42

**Commander :**
L.-F. BERGER (in 1942) (in 1943 Waldemar
GEYER reported there)

**Components :**
BG. VIIIa Sudetenland-Ost
Address : Troppau, Adolf-Hitler-Ring 58
Tel. 373
Commander : *Komm. m.d.F.b. : B.-F.*
HEBERER

OG : Breslau, Lüben, Brieg, Sagan,
UG : Trebnitz, Frankstein, Grottkau, Haynau,
Löwenberg, Beuthen, Sprottau


## LG. IX : HESSEN-THÜRINGEN

**Address :**
Kassel, Georgenstrasse 6
Tel. 30208

**Commander :**
L.-F. HÖPKER

**Components :**
BG. IXa Thüringen-Erfurt
Address : Weimar, Geleitstrasse 3a, Eingang
Böttchergasse
Tel. 3240
Commander : *B.-F.* von ZASTROW


## LG. X : NORDWEST

**Address :**
Hamburg 11, Admiralitätsstrasse 56
Tel. 362052

**Commander :**
*Bez.-F. Dr.* MAACK (in 1942)

**Remarks :**
In 1943 L.-F. KOLLEYER reported there;
at the same time *Dr.* MAACK was mentioned
as *HG.-F.* in Pommern, but may still be
deputy for KOLLMEYER.

**Components :**
BG. Xa Hansestadt Hamburg
Address : same as above
Tel. 362051
Commander : *Bez.-F.* MAGNUS (at present
in the Armed Forces) *i.V.Gf.-F.* PAUL

BG. Xb Bremen
Address : Bremen, Rövekamp 12
Tel. 27500/1
Commander : *HB.-F.* CONDREIT


## LG. XI : MITTE

**Address :**
Hannover, Langemarckstrasse 14
Tel. Domsheide 25458

**Commander :**
*Bez.-F.* LANGJAHR (in 1942 ; in 1943 went to
LG II and was replaced by L.-F. SCHLÄGER

**Components :**
BG. XIa Magdeburg-Anhalt
Address : Magdeburg, Breiter Weg 86
Tel. 22965
Commander : *B.-F.* SCHULZE


## LG. XII : WESTMARK

**Address :**
Frankfurt/Main, Bockenheimer Landstrasse 21
Tel. 77777

**Commander :**
L.-F. WENZEL

**Components :**
BG. XIIa Saarpfalz
Address : Saarbrücken, Hohenzollernstrasse
45
Tel. 21113
Commander : *Komm. m.d.F.b. B.-F.* GRIM
BG. XIIb Moselland
Address : Koblenz, Nördl. Schloss-Eckbau
Tel. 3880
Commander : *Bez.-F.* WIERSS
BG. XIIc Lothringen
Address : Metz, Ritter-von-Schober-Strasse 8
Tel. 2869
Commander : *Komm. m.d.F.b. Gf.-F.* DICK
OG. 57 Bendorf


## LG. XIII : NORDBAYERN-EGERLAND

**Address :**
Nürnberg-A., Burgstrasse 15 (Fembo-Haus)
Tel. 20084/86

**Commander :**
L.-F. MEIER (at present at the front) *i.V. B.-F.*
ZIMMER

**Components :**
BG. XIIIa Egerland
Address : Karlsbad, Polizeidirection, Schlies-
fach
Tel. 353629
Commander : *Gf.-F.* LÖBERMANN


## LG. XVII : DONAU

**Address :**
Wien I, Gauermanngasse 4
Tel. B 21545

**Commander :**
*m.d. stellv. F.b. Bez.-F.* STAUSS (see also
LG. XVIII)

**Components :**
BG. XVIIa Wien
Address : Wien VII, Lerchenfelder Str. 1
Tel. B 21545 (same as LG.)
Commander : *Komm. m.d.F.b. Gf.-F.* BAKA-
LAR
BG. XVIIb Oberdonau
Address : Linz, Landstrasse 21
Tel. 23988
Commander : *B.-F.* LOHMAR (at present in
the Armed Forces), *komm. m.d.F.b. Gf.-F.*
SCHÜFFL
BG. XVIIc Niederdonau
Address : Wien I, Gauermanngasse 4
Tel. B21545 (same as LG.)
Commander : *B.-F.* KUNZIG (at present at
the front), *i.V. Gm.-F.* MAIRHOFER
*Befehlsstelle* Reichsprotektorat
Address : Prag XIX, Dr. Winter Strasse 2
Tel. 77355
Commander : *Komm.m.d.F.b.B.-F.* EICHNER
BG. Böhmen/Prag
Address : Same as above
Commander : Same as above
BG. Mähren/Brünn
Address : Brünn
Commander : *M.d.F.b. B.-F.* KROTSCHAK

## LG. XVIII : ALPENLAND

**Address :**
Salzburg, Chiemseegasse 6
Tel. 1789

**Commander :**
*Bez.-F.* STAUSS (see also LG. XVII)

**Components :**
BG. XVIIIa Steiermark
Address : Graz II, Morellenfeldgasse 8
Tel. 6187
Commander : *B.-F.* SCHMIDT
BG. XVIIIb Tirol-Vorarlberg
Address : Innsbruck, Sonnenburger Str, 15
Tel. 594
Commander : (post at present unfilled)
BG. XVIIIc Kärnten
Address : Klagenfurt, Adolf-Hitler-Platz 12
Tel. 2131
Commander : *HB.-F.* TAZOLL, Emil

## LG. XX : DANZIG-WESTPREUSSEN

**Address :**
Danzig, Stadtgraben 15
Tel. 21085

**Commander :**
*HB.-F.* KAMM, Willibald (also mentioned as
*Kdr.* of a *TN Abt.* in the East with the rank
of *SS-SBF*)
*i.V. B.-F.* HOFFMANN

## LG. XXI : WARTHELAND

**Address :**
Posen, Am Goethepark 3
Tel. 2469

**Commander :**
*L.-F.* SCHULZE

**Components :**
XXIa Wartheland-Ost
Commander : *M.d.F.b. HB.-F.* KUNA
(Reg. Bez. Litzmannstadt is part of Warthe-
gau-Ost)
OG. Ostrovo *Gf.-F.* BÖHMERT (Sep. 42)

## TN BEFEHLSSTELLE VIII A OBER-SCHLESIEN

**Address :**
Kattowitz, Heinzelstrasse 1

**Commander :**
*Bez.-F.* HAUST

**Components :**
BG. VIII A a Oberschlesien
Address : Oppeln, Nikoleistrasse 22
Tel. 3880
Commander : *M.d. vertretungsw. F.b. Gm.-F.*
NIETZEK

## BEFEHLSSTELLE GENERALGOUVERNE-MENT

**Full Name :**
*TN-Befehlstelle beim Befehlshaber der Ordnungs-
polizei im Generalgouvernement* Polen (TN
Command HQ under O.C. of Regular Uniformed Police in G.-G.)

**Address :**
Krakau, U1. Wloczkow 20 (TN Bereitschafts-
haus)
Tel. 23440

**Commander :**
*M.d. vertretungsw. F.b. Gf.-F.* SCHULER

**Remarks :**
A newspaper article mentions *Gf.-F.* von ZAST-
ROW as being at *TN Befehlstelle* Polen ; the
same article mentions *Bez.-F.* HÖLZLE as in
charge of *Befehlsstelle* Protektorat, which
did not exist in 1942.

## TN-BEFEHLSSTELLE NIEDERLANDE

**Address :**
Niederlande, Den Haag, Klatteweg 1

**Commander :**
*HB.-F. Dr.* BECK

## TN-BEFEHLSSTELLE NORWEGEN

**Address :**
Norwegen, Oslo, Drammensvejen 4

**Commander :**
*B.-F. Dr.* SCHMITZ

(Each name is followed by the rank or title in brackets, his function and unit.)

BAKALAR (*Gf.-F.*)
*Komm.m.d.F.b.*
BG XVIIa, Wien.

BECK (*HB.-F.*)
*Führer der Befehlsstelle* Niederlande

BEIL (*Bez.-F.*)
At present in the Armed Forces
BG VIb, Westfalen

BERGER (*L.-F.*)
*Führer der* LG VIII, Schlesien (1942)

BÖHMERT (*Gf.-F.*)
OG Ostrovo in LG XXI (Sep 42)

BREMER, Dr. (*B.-F.*)
*m.d.F.b.*
BG IVd, Sachsen-Ost.

BRENDOW (*Gf.-F.*)
*m.d.F.b.*
BG Va, Elsass

BUBAN (*L.-F.*)
*Führer der* LG IV, Oberelbe

CONDEREIT (*HB.-F.*)
BG Xb, Bremen

CURTZE (*L.-F.*)
Formerly *Führer der* LG X, Nordwest

DICK (*Gf.-F.*)
*Komm.m.d.F.b.*
BG XIIc, Lothringen

DÜLL (*Bez.-F.*)
*Führer der* LG VII, Bayern-Süd

EHRBAR (*L.-F.*)
*Führer der* LG I, Ostpreussen (after 42)
Also *Oberabteilungsf.* and *Major der Schupo*

EICHNER (*B.-F.*)
*Komm.m.d.F.b.*
*Führer der Befehlsstelle* Reichsprotektorat and
BG Böhmen/Prag

ETMER, Dr.
*Feldeinsatzf. der TN* and *Gen Inspekteur f.d.
auswärtigen Einsatz d. TN* of the RATN

FISCHER (*HB-F.*)
Head of the *Pressestelle* of RATN

FORNONI (*L.-F.*)
*Inspekteur* 1 of RATN

GEYER, Waldemar (*L.-F. ?*)
*Führer der* LG VIII, Schlesien (1943)

GRIM (*B.-F.*)
*Komm.m.d.F.b.*
BG XIIa, Saarpfalz

HAMPE, Erich
*Stellv. Chef der TN* (1939–40)

HAUST (*Bez.-F.*)
*Führer der Befehlsstelle* VIIIA Oberschlesien

HEBERER (*B.-F.*)
*Komm.m.d.F.b.*
BG VIIIa, Sudetenland Ost

HERMANNS (*L.-F.*)
*m.d.F.b.*
*Führer der* LG II, Nord (1942)

HOFFMANN (*B.-F.*)
LG XX, Danzig-Westpreussen (replacing temp.
KAMM)

HÖLZLE (*B.-F.*)
Reported incorrectly as in charge of *Befehlsstelle*
Protektorat in 1942 (when it was not yet in
existence)

HÖPKER (*L.-F.*)
*Führer der* LG IX, Hessen-Thüringen

HUGENDUBEL (*HB.-F.*)
Head of *TN Reichsschule* in Belzig (1943)

JÜNECKE
*Chef des Stabes des RATN* (appointed 17 Jan 43)
Formerly *Führer* of LG XVII, Donau

KAMM, Willibald (*HB.-F.*)
*Führer der* LG XX, Danzig-Westpreussen (at
present at the front)
Now *Kdr.* of a *TN Abt.* on the Eastern front
SS-SBF
*Dip. Ing.* Residence-Zoppot, Horst-Wesselstr. 43

KEISELT (*HB.-F.*)
BG IVb, Sachsen-West

KOLLMEYER (*L.-F.*)
*Führer der* LG X Nordwest (1943), MAACK may
be his deputy

KRÖNCKE, Dr. (*HB.-F.*)
Head of *Bild-und Filmstelle* (Pictorial and Film
Centre) and *Allgemeine Chefangelegenheiten*
(General Administrative Matters of the C-in-C)
of the RATN

KROTSCHAK (*B.-F.*)
*m.d.F.b.*
BG Mähren/Brünn

KUNA (*HB.-F.*)
*m.d.F.b.*
BG XXIa, Wartheland-Ost.

KUNZIG (*B.-F.*)
BG XVIIc, Niederdonau (at present at the
front)

LANGJAHR (*Bez.-F.*)
*Führer der* LG II, Nord (Apr 44)
Formerly (in 1942) *Führer der* LG XI, Mitte
*Major der Schupo*

LÖBERMANN (*Gf.-F.*)
BG XIIIa, Egerland

LOHMAR (*B.-F.*)
BG XVIIb, Oberdonau, (at present in the Armed
Forces)

MAACK, Dr. (*Bez.-F.*)
*Führer der* LG X, Nordwest (1942). May now
be deputy for KOLLMEYER. *F.d. Instand-
setzungsdienst d. LS-Ortes :* Hamburg
*Oberstlt. d. Schupo*
*Ingenieur*

MAGNUS (*Bez.-F.*)
BG Xa, Hansestadt Hamburg (at present in the
Armed Forces)

MAIRHOFER (*Gm.-F.*)
BG XVIIc, Niederdonau, replacing KUNZIG

MALICKE (*Bez.-F.*)
Head of II/III *Personal-und Rechtsamt* of the
RATN
*Maj. der Schupo*

MEIER (*L.-F.*)
*Führer der* LG XIII, Nordbayern-Egerland (at
present at the front)

NIETZEK (*Gm.-F.*)
*m.d. vertretungsw.F.b.*
BG VIII Aa, Oberschlesien

OELTER, Ernst (*Bez.-F.*)
*Führer der* LG V, Südwest
SS-SBF,
Residence-Frankfurt/M, Staufenstr. 30

OSSWALD
  *Gen.d.Pol. a.D.*
  Head of V. *Abnahmeamt* of the RATN

PAUL (*Gf.-F.*)
  BG Xa, Hansestadt Hamburg, replacing MAGNUS

POLKEHN (*Gf.-F.*)
  *m.d.F.b.*
  BG I Südost.

PROBST (*Gm.-F.*)
  *Persönlicher Adjutant* in RATN

PRÜSSNER, Fr.-Wilh. (*L.-F.*)
  *Führer der* LG VI, Westfalen-Niedershein
  *NSKK-OF*

RAMTHUN (*L.-F.*)
  Head of *Haushalts- und Verwaltungsamt* of the RATN (Bureau of Budget and Administration)

ROMANY (*Gf.-F.*)
  BG VIc, Weserland

RÖTHENMEIER, Dr. (*L.-F.*)
  *Inspekteur* 2 of the RATN
  *Oberst d. Schupo.*

RUDOLF (*B.-F.*)
  BG IVc, Halle-Leipzig

SCHILLING
  LG II, Nord (Apr 44)

SCHLÄGER (*L.-F.*)
  *Führer der* LG XI, Mitte (Mar 42)

SCHMELCHER, Willy (*B.-F. of SS*)
  *Chef der TN* (15 Oct 43)

SCHRIEVER (*L.-F.*)
  *Führer der* LG I, Ostpreussen (1942)
  *Oberst d. Schupo*

SCHROEDER (*L.-F.*)
  *Führer der* LG III, Mark Brandenburg

SCHMITZ (*B.-F.*)
  *Führer der Befehlsstelle* Norwegen

SCHMIDT (*B.-F.*)
  BG XVIIIa Steiermark

SCHÜFFL (*Gf.-F.*)
  *Komm.m.d.F.b.*
  BG XVIIb, Oberdonau, replacing LOHMAR

SCHULER (*Gf.-F.*)
  *m.d. vertretungsw. F.b.*
  *Führer der Befehlsstelle* Generalgouvernement

SCHULZE (*B.-F.*)
  BG Xa, Magdeburg-Anhalt

SCHULZE (*L.-F.*)
  *Führer der* LG XXI, Wartheland

SELLQUIST (*HB.-F.*)
  BG VIb, Westfalen, replacing BEIL

SIEBERT, Th.
  *Stellvertretender Chef der TN* and head of *Chefamt/I* of the RATN.
  *Genmaj. der Polizei*
  Reported dead September 44

SPÖHRER (*Gf.-F.*)
  OG VI/16, Remscheid (May 43)

STAUSS, Carl (*Bez.-F.*)
  *m.d.F.b.*
  *Führer der* LG XVII, Donau and LG XVIII, Alpenland

TAZOLL, Emil (*HB.-F.*)
  BG XVIIIc, Kärnten
  *Gold. Treuedienstehrenzeichen d. Partei* (11 December 42)

TROSCHKE, Walter (*HB.-F.*)
  *Chefadjutant* I and head of *Führerverwaltung* (officers' administration) of the RATN

VOLLMER (*HB.-F.*)
  BG VIa, Niederrhein, (at present in the Armed Forces)

WAGNER (*Ka.-F.*)
  *m.d.vertretungsw. F.b.*
  BG IVa, Sudetenland-Nord

WENZEL (*L.-F.*)
  *Führer der* LG XII, Westmark

WIERSS (*Bez.F.*)
  BG XIIb, Moselland

ZASTROW, von (*B.-F.*)
  BG IXa, Thüringen-Erfurt

ZIMMER (*B.-F.*)
  LG XIII, Nordbayern-Egerland, replacing MEIER.

# ANNEXE D : PART SEVEN

## WAFFENMEISTEREIEN DER DEUTSCHEN POLIZEI

### (as officially listed, end of 1942)

The following is a complete list of all *Waffenmeistereien* of the German Police, including those which were located in towns now liberated by the United Nations.

| | | | |
|---|---|---|---|
| Aachen | Elbing | Leipzig | Recklinghausen |
| Augsburg | Erfurt | Lemberg | Reval |
| Aussig | Essen | Leslau | Radom |
| Belgrad | Frankfurt a.M. | Linz | Riga |
| Berlin | Fürstenfeldbruck | Litzmannstadt | Rostock |
| Bialystok | Gladbach-Rheydt | Lublin | Saarbrücken |
| Bochum | Gleiwitz | Lübeck | Salzburg |
| Braunschweig | Graz | Magdeburg | Shitomir |
| Bremen | Halle | Mannheim | Simferopol |
| Breslau | Hamburg | Metz | Sosnowitz |
| Bromberg | Hannover | Mödling near Wien | Stalino |
| Brünn | Hildesheim | Mogilew | Stettin |
| Bunzlau | Innsbruck | Mülhausen | Strassburg |
| Charkow | Karlsruhe | München | Stuttgart |
| Chemnitz | Kassel | Minsk | Tilsit |
| Danzig | Kattowitz | Nikolajew | Waldenburg |
| Darmstadt | Kowno | Nürnberg | Warschau |
| Den Haag | Klattau | Oberhausen | Weimar |
| Dessau | Kiel | Oppeln | Wien |
| Dnjepropetrowsk | Kiew | Oslo | Wiesbaden |
| Dortmund | Klagenfurt | Plauen | Wilhelmshaven |
| Dresden | Koblenz | Posen | Wuppertal |
| Drontheim | Köln | Potsdam | Würzburg |
| Duisburg | Königsberg | Prag | Zwickau |
| Düsseldorf | Krakau | Regensburg | |

# ANNEXE  E

## FIELD UNITS OF THE ORDNUNGSPOLIZEI·(ORPO)

# ORDER OF BATTLE OF SS-POLICE REGIMENTS

*Note :* For an explanation of Arabic numerals see Text, para. 40.

## SS-Polizei Regiment 1

Component Bns :
I, II (3), III
Units of this regiment were identified in Narvik Nov 1941, Holland Jul 1943 and Eastern Poland Apr 1943. The regiment is reported to have moved to Yugoslavia some time later in 1943.

## SS-Polizei Regiment 2

Component Bns :
I, II, III
Located on the Eastern Front during the winter of 1943/44.

## SS-Polizei Regiment 3

Commander :
Oberst BOEHMER
Component Bns :
I (66), II (68), III (63? or 318?), Pol. Art. Abt.?
Located in Holland in 1944.

## SS-Polizei Regiment 4

Commander :
Oberst HANNIBAL
Component Bns :
I, II, III
Located in France in May 1943 and later on the Eastern Front.

## SS-Polizei Regiment 5

Commander :
Oberstlt. SCHWERTSCHLÄGER
Component Bns :
I, II, III
Located in Yugoslavia in spring 1944.

## SS-Polizei Regiment 6

Component Bns :
I (82), II (311), III (318)
Located in Russia Aug 1942—Mar 1943. Remnants of the regiment were reported leaving for Gdynia in Mar 1943.

## SS-Polizei Regiment 7

Component Bns :
I (302?), II, III
Located in Norway in Jul 1944.

## SS-Polizei Regiment 8

Commander :
Oberstlt. WEIS
Component Bns :
I (91), II (111), III (134)
Formerly located on the Central Sector in Russia. In Jun 1944 the 1st Bn was reported disbanding in Koblenz. The 3rd Bn was reported to be at the Nikolauskaserne in Zabern/Elsass in Apr 1944.

## SS-Polizei Regiment 9

Component Bns :
I, II, III
Formerly located on the Northern Sector, Russia. Regiment was reported disbanding in Saarbrücken in summer 1944.

## SS-Polizei Regiment 10

Commander :
Oberstlt. KELLNER
Component Bns :
I (45), II (303), III (314)
Regiment was reported on the Eastern Front in

1942/43 and in Italy in Jul 1944 after which it was supposedly disbanding in Saarbrücken in Aug 1944. Another report places it at Istria in Nov 1944.

## SS-Polizei Regiment 11

Commander :
Oberst SCHULZ (killed ; successor unknown)
Component Bns :
I, II (315), III (33?)
Located on the Eastern Front in Aug 1944.

## SS-Polizei Regiment 12

Commander :
Oberst MACHTAN
Component Bns :
I, II, III (105)
Located in Italy in Nov 1944. Units of this regiment variously reported in Bremen, Budapest and Verona during 1944.

## SS-Polizei Regiment 13

Commander :
Oberstlt. Hans FLECKNER
Component Bns :
I (6), II (85?), III (301? or 322?)
Located on the Central Sector in Russia, Aug 1942. Reported in Lublin, Sept 1943, in Northern Yugoslavia, Sept 1944. Former Bn 125 reported to belong to this regiment.

## SS-Polizei Regiment 14

Commander :
Oberstlt. BLEHER
Component Bns :
I (10), II (122), III (63 or 313)
Located in Holland and France during part of 1943 and 1944. Later reported in Yugoslavia in Jul 1944 and in Northern Italy in Nov 1944. Former Bn 51 reported to belong to this regiment. According to reports, this regt. is identical with the SS-Pol. Regt. GRIESE (see below).

## SS-Polizei Regiment 15

Commander :
Oberst BACH
Component Bns :
I, II (319?), III
Virtually destroyed in the Don Region in winter 1942/43. Was reformed at Ilowitz near Prag in Mar 1943 from drafts of various police training battalions. Regiment moved to Mysen, Norway in Apr 1943 for training. In Aug 1943 moved back to Germany and later on to Italy where it was still reported to be in Nov 1944.
(See also *SS-Pol. Regt.* 20 for details on II/15).

## SS-Polizei Regiment 16

Commander :
Oberstlt. GIESEKE
Component Bns :
I (305), II (306), III (310)
The regiment, or parts thereof, were reported on the Northern Sector in Russia, Aug 1942, in Holland, Feb 1943 and again on the Northern Sector in Russia in Apr 1944, with headquarters evidently at Riga.

## SS-Polizei Regiment 17

Commander :
Oberst BOCK

Component Bns :
I (42), II, III (69)
Located on the Northern Sector in Russia, Aug 1942. Regiment was reported to be in Warsaw, Mar 1944.

## SS-Polizei Gebirgs-Jäger Regiment 18

Commander :
Oberstlt. HOESL
Component Bns :
I (302), II (312), III (325), Geb. Art. Abt. (no Nr.)
Formed at Garmisch-Partenkirchen May-Jun 1942. In Northern Yugoslavia until Oct 1942. In Finland Dec 1942—Jul 1943. Was transferred to Greece in Aug 1943 where it was still reported to be in Aug 1944.

## SS-Polizei Regiment 19

Commander :
Oberst KOELBLINGER (replaced)
Component Bns :
I (72?), II, III
Located in Slovenia in Jan 1944. Moved to France in Apr 1944, to replace SS-Pol. Regt. 28, but was again reported in the area Laibach/Croatia in Sept 1944.

## SS-Polizei Regiment 20

Commander :
Oberst KUCHAR (?)
Component Bns :
I, II (56?), III
The regiment was reported in Czechoslovakia in Jul 1944 with headquarters at Prag. In November 1944 the regiment was identified in Bologna. Bn. III was committed to action as part of a Kampfgruppe " Bürger " consisting of II/15 and III/20 SS-Pol. Regt.

## SS-Polizei Regiment 21

Commander :
Oberst A. BERGER or Oberstlt. SALBEY (?)
Component Bns :
I (23), II (84), III
Located in Czechoslovakia in Jul 1944 with headquarters at Brünn ; also known as SS-Pol. Regt. Mähren

## SS-Polizei Regiment 22

Component Bns :
I, II, III (53)
Located on the Eastern Front 1942–1944.

## SS-Polizei Regiment 23

Commander :
Oberst d. Gend. BARDUA
Component Bns :
I, II, III
Located in Poland Aug 1942–Jun 1944.

## SS-Polizei Regiment 24

Component Bns :
I (307?), II (83?), III
The former Pol. Bn. 62 may also possibly belong to this regiment. Regiment has been located on Eastern Front 1942/44.

## SS-Polizei Regiment 25

Component Bns :
I (65), II (101?), III (67?)
The former Pol. Bn. 41 may also possibly belong to this regiment. The regiment was reported in Lublin in Aug 1942 and Oct 1943. In 1944 it was reported in Untersteiermark and Northern Yugoslavia.

## SS-Polizei Regiment 26

Commander :
Oberstlt. Georg WEISSIG
Component Bns :
I (255?), II (312), III (256)
Located in Norway in Aug 1942. Eastern Front 1943/44.

## SS-Polizei Regiment 27

Component Bns :
I (44?), II (253?), III (9?)
The 3rd Bn. was reported in Norway in Aug 1942 and the entire regiment identified there in summer 1944.

## SS-Polizei Regiment 28 (" Todt ")

Commander :
Oberst KOESTERBECK
Component Bns :
I (252), II (251), III (62?)
The former Pol. Bn. 69 may possibly belong to this regiment. The 1st and 2nd Bns. were reported in Norway in Aug 1942. In Aug 1943 the entire regiment was located in Holland and some time later moved to France where it was identified in summer 1944. Soon after replaced by SS-Pol. Regt. 19, and then identified in Upper Slovenia in Aug 1944.

## SS-Polizei Schützen Regiment 31

Commander :
Oberst HANNIBAL (trsfd. to SS-Pol. Regt. 4)
Component Bns :
I, II, III
Formerly located in Poland. Reported disbanding in Hamburg in Aug 1944.

## SS-Polizei Schützen Regiment 32

Component Bns : ?
Reported forming at Frankfurt/Main in Jun 1943.

## SS-Polizei Schützen Regiment 33

Commander :
Oberst d. Gend. KOELLNER.
Component Bns :
I, II, III.
Located on the Eastern Front 1943–1944. Engaged against partisans in the Narew triangle Jul-Sep 1943. Subordinated to the 5th Pz. Div. in the Dnieper Sector Sep 1943–Jan 1944. Under the 13 A.K. in Southern Poland (Rowno) Jan-May 1944.

## SS-Polizei Schützen Regiment 34

Component Bns :
I. II, III.
Located in Russia Jun 1944, Poland Aug 1944.

## SS-Polizei Schützen Regiment 35

Component Bns : ?
1st Coy was reported at Dubno, Poland, in Feb 1944. Regiment disbanded in Apr 1944.

## SS-Polizei Schützen Regiment 36

Component Bns :
I, II, III.
Located in Russia (Centre) in Mar 1944. Disbanding Nov 1944. (Abwicklungsstelle Berlin.)

## SS-Polizei Schützen Regiment 37

Commander :
Oberstlt. GIESEKE (trsfd. to SS-Pol. Regt. 16)
Component Bns :
I, II, III.
Formerly located in Russia. Disbanding at Breslau in Aug 1944.

## SS-Polizei Schützen Regiment 38
Commander :
  Oberstlt. WEISS.
Component Bns : ?
Forming at Sigisvara, Hungary, in Jul 1944.

The following regiments have been identified by name only and may possibly be identical with one of the known numbered regiments.

## SS-Polizei Regiment Alpenvorland
Identified in Northern Italy in Nov 1944.

## SS-Polizei Regiment Bozen
This regiment was formerly known as *Pol. Regt.* "Südtirol" and was re-named in Oct 1943. Located at Istria in Nov 1944.

## SS-Polizei Regiment Griese
Reported to contain three Bns plus one battery of artillery. An Oberst GRIESE was reported as C.O. of a Pol. Regt. on the Mediterranean Coast. Other reports state that this regt. is identical with *SS-Pol. Regt.* 14

## SS-Polizei Regiment Mähren
*SS-Pol. Regt.* 21 was identified in Sept 1944 under this name.

## SS-Pz. Gren. Brig. 49
This is known to be a W-SS unit but the fact that it receives replacements for its 2nd Bn from *Polizei Waffenschule* I, Hellerau near Dresden and from *Polizei Ersatzabteilung* Mährisch-Ostrau makes it worthy of mention here. The 2nd Bn has definitely been identified as a Police Bn and may be identical with *Pol. Bn. z.b.V.* which was formed at Dresden in spring 1944, and which is known to have been incorporated into *SS-Pz. Gren. Brig.* 49, moved to Denmark and later sent to France. In Aug 1944 the Brigade was renamed 26 *SS-Pz. Div.*, committed to action shortly thereafter and destroyed. The remnants were incorporated into 17. *SS-Pz. Gren. Div.* "Götz von Berlichingen."

## Polizei Reiter Regiment
Composed of *Volksdeutsche* from the Ukraine. Reported to have operated on the Central and Southern Sectors of the Eastern Front.

## Polizei Ausbildungs-Regiment Oranienburg
Identified in May 1943

# FEUERSCHUTZPOLIZEI-REGIMENTER
## Feuerschutzpolizei-Regiment Sachsen
Possibly also called *Feuerschutzpolizei-Regiment* 1. Located at Winsen a.d. Luhe in Aug 1942.

## Feuerschutzpolizei-Regiment Ost/West Flandern
A partly Belgian unit.

## SS-Niederländische Feuerschutzpolizei-Regiment in Holland
Possibly identical with *Feuerschutzpolizei-Regiment* 2 in Holland.

## Feuerschutzpolizei-Regiment Ostpreussen
Also known as *Feuerschutzpolizei-Regiment* 3. *Standortdienststelle* for a time at Königshütte/OS and later at Nürnberg-Zirndorf in Aug 1942 and at Schloss Kappenberg üb. Lünen/Westfalen in Mar 1943.

## Feuerschutzpolizei-Regiment Böhmen-Mähren
Located at Pilsen.

## Feuerschutzpolizei-Abt. (mot.) Ukraine*
Identical with *Feuerschutzpolizei-Abt.* (mot.) 4.

*Note: Latest reports state that all *Feuerschutzpolizei-Regimenter* were renamed *Feuerschutzpolizei-Abteilungen* (mot.), probably an indication of their irregular strength and size. 9 of these *Abteilungen* are reported to exist.

# ANNEXE E: PART TWO

## ORDER OF BATTLE OF SS-POLICE BATTALIONS

**Note.**—It is evident from the following tabulation that all battalions from No. 11 to No. 181 were numbered according to the Wehrkreise in which they were originally recruited. Thus, Nos. 11–19 were reserved for battalions from Wehrkreis I, Nos. 21–29 for Wehrkreis II, and so on. However, prior to the initiation of this system, certain Police battalions existed which are now believed to be disbanded. The numbers of these battalions, as shown at the bottom of the list, ranged from 1–210, but they were never duplicated in those battalions existing to-day. Present existing battalions with a number below 11 appear to be remnants of this former system.

There are three additional blocks of battalions which were formed at a later date from personnel available in various parts of Germany. They are numbered: 251–256, formed in winter 1940–41 for use in Norway and Holland; 301–320, formed in winter, 1940–41, most of them for use on and behind the Eastern Front; and 321–325, formed in July 1941, also for use in the East.

| Original Battalion | New Battalion and Regiment | Original Home-Station | Remarks |
|---|---|---|---|
| 2 | | Berlin | Reported in action on Russian Front 1941/2. |
| 3 | II/1 | Berlin | Identified at Baranowicze April 1943. |
| 6 | I/13 | Berlin | Located on Russian Front (central sector) 1942/3 and last identified at Eisenkappel, Yugoslavia, during 1944. |
| 9 | ?III/27 | Frankfurt/M. | Reported in Russia, Iglau and last at Kongsvinor, Norway, summer 1944. |
| 10 | I/14 | Berlin | Identified at Novo Mesto, Yugoslavia, September 1944, and believed in action on Italian Front. |
| 11 | | Wkr. I—Königsberg Area | Reported in action on Russian Front. |
| 13 | | Wkr. I | Identified in Bialystok area. |
| 22 | | Wkr. II—Stettin | |
| 23 | I/21 | Wkr. II | Assumed to be with Regt. in Czechoslovakia during 1944. |
| 32 | | Wkr. III | Located on Eastern Front. |
| 33 | ?III/11 | Wkr. III | Reported in action on S. Russia sector, August 1942. CO: Maj DALL (October 1942). |
| 41 | ?/25 | Wkr. IV—Leipzig, Dresden, Halle, Chemnitz | Reported in Poland (Lublin area) 1942/3. |
| 42 | I/17 | Wkr. IV | Identified in Warsaw, March 1944, and in Holland, late 1944. |
| 44 | ?I/27 | Wkr. IV—Leipzig, Halle | Reported in Oslo, July 1944. |
| 45 | I/10 | Wkr. IV—Aussig | Identified on Russian Front, August 1943; reported disbanding. |
| 51 | ?I/14 | Wkr. V—? Stuttgart | Reported in Elsass, October 1940. |
| 53 | III/22 | Wkr. V—? Mülhausen | Identified in Warsaw, December 1943. |
| 54 & 55 | | Wkr. V | Located in Elsass, October 1940; since disbanded. |
| 56 | ?II/20 | Wkr. V—? Stuttgart | Reported in Czechoslovakia, July 1944. CO: Maj STOETZER (September 1943). |
| 61 | | Wkr. VI—? Dortmund | |
| 62 | ?III/28 " Todt " | Wkr. VI—? Aachen | Located on Eastern Front; also reported part of Regt. 24. |
| 63 | ?III/3 | | Reported in Hamburg, August 1944; also believed part of Regt. 14 (see Bn. 313 and 318). |
| 64 | | Wkr. VI—? Münster | Identified in Belgrad, September 1942. |
| 65 | I/25 | Wkr. VI | Identified at Chelm, Poland, 1942/3. |
| 66 | I/3 | Wkr. VI | Identified at Tilburg, Holland, March 1944. CO: Maj VOLK. |
| 67 | ?III/25 | Wkr. VI | Reported in Lublin and The Hague, 1942/3. |
| 68 | II/3 | Wkr. VI—Rhineland-?Köln | Identified in Amsterdam, March 1944. |
| 69 | III/17 | | Located at Opatov, Poland, November 1943; also believed part of Regt. 28 " Todt." |
| 72 | ?I/19 | Wkr. VII—München | Reported at Annecy, France, July 1944. CO: Maj W. FISCHER (December 1943). |
| 74 | | Wkr. VII—?München | Reported in Elsass, October 1940. |
| 82 | I/6 | Wkr.VIII—Liegnitz,Oppeln, Kattowitz | Reported in action on Russian Front 1942, and remnants on way to Gdynia, March 1943. |
| 83 | ?II/24 | Wkr. VIII—Upper Silesia | Reported on Russian Front and at Sluzk, April 1944. |
| 84 | II/21 | Wkr. VIII—Holleschau | Identified in Brünn, Moravia, July 1944, also reported in connection with Pol. Regt. Mähren. |
| 85 | ?II/13 | Wkr. VIII—Kattowitz | Reported at Pliberk, North Jugoslavia, October 1943. CO: Maj OPPENBERG(?). |

| Original Battalion | New Battalion and Regiment | Original Home-Station | Remarks |
|---|---|---|---|
| 91 | I/8 | Wkr. IX—Frankfurt/Main | Reported disbanding at Koblenz, June 1944. |
| 93 | | Wkr. IX—?Kassel | |
| 101 | ?II/25 | ?Wkr. X | Reported in Untersteiermark, September 1944. |
| 102 | | Wkr. X—?Hamburg | |
| 103 | | Wkr. X—?Hamburg | |
| 104 | | Wkr. X | |
| 105 | III/12 | Wkr. X—?Bremen | Identified in Holland 1942/3, moved to Verona, Italy, during 1943 and reported in action on Italian Front. |
| 111 | II/8 | Wkr. XI—?Dessau | Reported in Koblenz, June 1944. |
| 112 | | Wkr. XI | |
| 113 | | Wkr. XI | |
| 121 | | Wkr. XII | Identified at Diedenhofen, April 1941. |
| 122 | II/14 | Wkr. XII—Metz | Identified in Holland, September 1942, and Laibach area during 1944 ; believed in action on Italian Front. |
| 123 | | Wkr. XII—?Echternach | |
| 124 | | Wkr. XII—Luxemburg | |
| 125 | ?/13 | | |
| 131 | | Wkr. XIII—Nürnberg | |
| 132 | | Wkr. XIII—?Nürnberg | Identified at Lodz, October 1943. |
| 133 | | Wkr. XIII—Würzburg | |
| 134 | III/8 | Wkr. XIII | Reported in Zabern/Elsass, April 1944. |
| 171 | | Wkr. XVII——?Wien | |
| 181 | | Wkr. XVIII—Salzburg | Located in Krain area. |
| 251 | II/28 " Todt " | Wkr. V—Deggingen | Identified in Holland, Aug 1943, and reported at Brezjan, Aug 1944 ; CO : Maj RICHTER (Oct 1942). |
| 252 | I/28 " Todt " | Wkr. XII—Wiesbaden | Located in Norway, Aug 1942, moved to Holland and last identified at Kranj, Aug 1944. |
| 253 | ?II/27 | Wkr. VII—Fürstenfeldbruck | Reported in Norway, March 1944. |
| 254 | | Wkr. I—?East Prussia | Identified in Amsterdam, Sept 1941, believed to be in Tilsit or Memel area later on. |
| 255 | ?I/26 | Wkr. IV—Aussig area | Located in Norway, summer 1941. |
| 256 | III/26 | ?Wkr. XVII or XVIII | Located in Norway, Aug 1942 ; reported moved to Italian Front 1943/4 ; CO : Maj OLSEN (Jan 1943). |
| 301 | ?III/13 | Wkr. VI—Bochum | Located on Central Sector in Russia 1940/1 (also see Bn. 322). |
| 302 | I/18 (Mtn.) | Wkr. VII—München | Identified at Athens, May 1944 ; CO : Maj BEHRENDS. Also reported I/7 located in Norway, June 1944. |
| 303 | II/10 | Wkr. X—Bremen | Located on Russian Front, summer 1943, and last identified in Saarbrüchen, Aug 1944. CO : Maj HASENPUSCH(?), Nov 1943. |
| 304 | | Wkr. IV—?Chemnitz | Reported on Eastern Front 1940/1, and employed in rear area duties. |
| 305 | I/16 | ?Hamburg or ?Berlin | Last identified on Northern Sector Russia with HQ at Riga, April 1944. |
| 306 | II/16 | Wkr. IX—?Frankfurt/M. | Summer 1941, mentioned in connection with Pol. Regt. Lublin ; reported at Riga, April 1944. |
| 307 | ?I/24 | Wkr. X—Lübeck | Located on Eastern Front and last reported at Poloyk, March 1944. |
| 308 | | Wkr. VI—?Duisburg | Located on Russian Front 1940/1 ; meanwhile disbanded—remnants to Bn. 32 and 307. |
| 309 | | Wkr. VI—?Köln | Located on Russian Front 1940/1. |
| 310 | III/16 | | Last identified at Riga, April 1944. |
| 311 | II/6 | Wkr. IX—Jena | Reported in action on Russian Front 1942 ; remnants on way to Gdynia, March 1943 ; CO : Maj KRÄSE (Jan 1943). |
| 312 | II/18 (Mtn.) or II/26 | Wkr. XVIII—Innsbruck | Reported as II/18 and identified at Lamia, Greece, Aug 1944. CO : Maj RECKLING (43). Also reported as II/26 in Norway, May 1943 ; CO : Maj REHBEIN (Feb 1943). |
| 313 | III/14 | Wkr. II—Schneidemühl | Identified in Holland, Sept 1942, and at Veliko Lascekocevje, Yugoslavia, Sept 1944 (also see Bn. 63). |
| 314 | III/10 | Wkr. XVII—Wien | Located on Russian Front 1942 ; reported disbanding in Saarbrücken during 1944. |
| 315 | II/11 | Wkr. III—Berlin | Located on Eastern Front-Radom area, Aug 1944 ; ?CO : Maj GEWEHR (Aug 1943). |
| 316 | | Wkr. VI—Bottrop-Oberhausen | On Russian Front 1940/1. |

| Original Battalion | New Battalion and Regiment | Original Home-Station | Remarks |
|---|---|---|---|
| 317 | | Wkr. VI—Renscheid | On Russian Front 1940/1. |
| 318 | III/6 | | Reported in connection with Pol. Regt. Mähren; also reported as III/3 believed to be in Hamburg, Aug 1944(?) (also see Bn. 63). |
| 319 | ?II/15 | Wkr. VI—Köln-Riehl | Reported at Aosta, Italy, Aug 1944; CO: Maj HARTEL. |
| 320 | | Wkr. III—Berlin | Reported on Eastern Front 1941. |
| 321 | | Wkr. VIII—Breslau | Reported on Eastern Front 1941. |
| 322 | ?III/13 | | Reported on Central Sector in Russia 1940/1 (also see Bn. 301). |
| 323 | | Wkr. I—Königsberg, Tilsit | Reported on Eastern Front 1941. |
| 324 | | Wkr. V—?Stuttgart | Reported on Eastern Front 1941. |
| 325 | III/18 (Mtn.) | Wkr. IV? | Identified at Athens, July 1944. |

The following Bns. are known to have existed but have since been disbanded :—

Nr. 1, 4, 5, 7, 8, 12, 14, 21, 25, 26, 31, 39, 43, 52, 71, 73, 81, 92, 98?, 106, 107, 120, 141, 144, 153, 161, 164, 172, 191, 192, 201, 202, 203, 204, 205, 206, 207, 208, 209 and 210.

## ANNEXE E : PART THREE

# T/O AND T/E (WAR ESTABLISHMENT AND WAR EQUIPMENT SCALE) OF A TYPICAL POLICE BATTALION (MOT.)

| | PERSONNEL Off. | Men | MP 9 mm. | LMG 7.92 mm. | SMG 7.92 mm. | LIG 75 mm. | PAK 37 mm. |
|---|---|---|---|---|---|---|---|
| *Befehlsstab* (HQ) ... ... ... | 4 | 12 | | | | | |
| *Sanitätsstaffel* (Medical Detachment)... | 1 | 6 | | | | | |
| *Nachrichten Zug* (Sig. Pl.) ... ... | 1 | 18 | | | | | |
| *\*Kradschützenzug* (M/C Pl.) ... ... | 1 | 34 | 4 | 3 | 1 | | |
| 3 *Pol. Kompanien* (Pol. Coys) each with 5 Off. and 145 men organised in 3 Rifle Pls. with 3 LMGs and 4 MPs each and 1 heavy Machine Gun Pl. with 4 HMGs and 1 MP ... ... | 15 | 435 | 39 | 27 | 12 | | |
| *\*Strassenpanzerwagenzug* (Armoured Car Pl.) ... ... ... ... | 2 | 15 | 2 | 4 | 4 | | |
| *\*Leichter Infanterie-Geschützzug* (Light Inf. How. Pl.) ... ... ... | 1 | 25 | 1 | | | 2 | |
| *\*Panzerjägerzug* (A/T Pl.) ... ... | 1 | 25 | | 1 | | | 3 |
| *Kraftfahrstaffel* (M/T Column) ... | 5 | 92† | | | | | |
| Total ... ... ... | 31 | 662 | 46 | 35 | 17 | 2 | 3 |

| Abbreviations | German | English |
|---|---|---|
| MP | *Maschinenpistole* | Sub Machine Gun |
| LMG | *Leichtes Maschinen-Gewehr* | Light Machine Gun |
| SMG | *Schweres Maschinen-Gewehr* | Heavy Machine Gun |
| LIG | *Leichtes Infanterie Geschütz* | Light Inf. How. |
| Pak | *Panzerabwehrkanone* | Anti-tank Gun |

\* Indicates units which may be attached from Regt.

† Plus drivers for M/C-Armoured Car-Light Inf. How- and A/T Platoons.

# ANNEXE E: PART FOUR

## SS POLICE SIGNALS COMPANIES
### (SS-Polizei Nachrichten-Kompanien)

| No. | Last identified Location | Operating with |
|---|---|---|
| 1 | Warsaw | |
| 2 | Lipke | |
| 3 | ?Berlin | |
| 6 | Recklinghausen | |
| 7 | Munich | |
| 11 | Minsk | |
| 12 | Warsaw | SS-Pol Regt 17 |
| 17 | Wkr. XVII | |
| 21 | Lipke (mot) | |
| 22 | Nimwegen | SS-Pol Regt 3 |
| 31 | Minsk | SS-Pol Schz Regt 31 |
| 32 | Lipke-Neumark | SS-Pol Regt 10 |
| 33 | Riga | |
| 34 | Biesenthal/Berlin | |
| 35 | Lipke | |
| 41 | Posen | |
| 42 | Returning to Reich | |
| 43 | ?Essegg | |
| 51 | N. Italy | SS-Pol Regt 15 |
| 52 | Neuntaubendorf | SS-Pol Schz Regt 33 |
| 61 | Recklinghausen | |
| 71 | Bielsk/Białystok | |
| 72 | Verona | SS-Pol Regt 14 |
| 81 | Kostopol | |
| 82 | Vorkdo. going to Wilna | |
| 83 | Sedziszow | |
| 91 mtn | Drontheim | |
| 101 | ?Athens | |
| 111 | ?France | |
| 112 | Minsk | |
| 121 | Brody | SS-Pol Regt 10 |
| 131 | Berlin | |
| 132 | ?France | ?SS-Pol Regt 14 |
| 171 | Laibach | ?SS-Pol Regt 14 |
| 172 | Mogilew | |
| 173 | ?Serbia | |
| 181 mtn | Veldes | |
| 201 | Norway | SS-Pol Regt 15 & 27 |
| 205 | Sarny | |
| 211 | Minsk | SS-Pol Regt 2 |
| 301 | ?Laibach | SS-Pol Regt 13 |
| 302 | Lemberg | SS-Pol Regt 10 |
| 304 | Budapest | |
| 305 | Kragujevac | |
| 306 | Lipke | SS-Pol Regt 11 |
| 307 | ?Russia | |
| 308 | Krakau | |
| 309 | Lublin | SS-Pol Regt 25 |
| 310 | Krakau | |

## DEPOT-UNITS OF POLICE FIELD FORMATIONS

### (MARCH 1943)

---

### * Pol.-Lehr. Batl.
(Pol. Training Bns.)

I—Dresden-Hellerau
II—Iglau (temporarily at Laon, France), now at Dresden-Moritzberg
III—Den Haag (believed to have moved into Reich, Autumn 1944)
IV—Maastricht (dissolved September 1943)

serving the following units :—

*Regts.-, Batls.- u. Abt.-Stäbe ohne Pol. Reiter Abt.* (Regt. and Bn. staffs except Pol. Cavalry Bn.)
*Pol. Kompanien* (Pol. Coys.)
*Schwere Pol. Komp.* (Heavy Weapon Coys.)
*Pol. Panz. Jäg. Komp.* (Anti-Tank Coys.)
*Pol. Geschütz Batterien* (Howitzer Dets.)
*Pol. Gebirgs Batterien* (Mtn. Howitzer Dets.)
*Nachrichten Züge u. Nachrichten Gruppen b.d. Pol. Batl. u. Pol. Art. Abt.* (Sigs. Pls. and Sigs. Sections of the Pol. Bn. and Pol. Arty. Bn.)
*Pionierzüge* (Eng. Pls.)

### Pol.-Reiter Ersatz Schwadron, Posen
(Pol. Cavalry Depot Bn.)

serving the following units :—

*Pol. Reiter Abt. Stäbe* (Pol. Cavalry Depot Bn. staffs)
*Pol. Reiter Schwadronen* (Pol. Cavalry Bns.)
*Pol. Reiterzüge im GG* (Pol. Cavalry Pls. in General Gouvernement)

### Pol.-Kraftfahrschule, Wien—
(Pol. M/T School)

### —Pol. Panz. Ers. Abt.—
(Pol. Armoured Depot Bn.)

serving :—

*Pol. Panz. Komp.* (Pol. Armoured Coys.)

### Pol.-Schule f. Technik u. Verkehr, Berlin—

### —Pol. Kraftfahrer Ersatz Abt.—
(Pol. M/T Depot Bn.)

serving the following units :—

*Pol. Kradschützen-Komp.* (Pol. M/C Coys.)
*Kraftfahrstaffeln b.d. Pol. Regt. u. Pol. Btl.* (M/T Columns of the Pol. Regts. and Pol. Bns.)
*Kradmeldegruppen* (Despatch Rider Units)
*Werkstattzüge* (Workshop Pls.)

### Pol.-Sanitäts Ersatz Abt., Berlin
(Pol. Medical Depot Bn.)

serving :—

All medical personnel

### Pol.-Nachrichten Ersatz Komp., Krakau
(Pol. Sigs. Depot Coy.)

serving :—

All *Orpo* Sigs. Coys., except Pol. Mtn. Sigs. Coys.

### Pol.-Gebirgs Nachrichten Komp. 181
(Pol. Mtn. Sigs. Coy.)

serving :—

All *Orpo* Mtn. Sigs. Coys.

* In August 1943 these *Pol.-Lehr. Batl.* were renamed " *Waffenschulen* " (Weapon Training Schools)

# WEAPONS USED BY THE ORDNUNGSPOLIZEI (ORPO)

## Pistolen (Pistols)

All pistols are semi-automatic weapons; magazines hold 7–8 cartridges.

| Designation of weapon | Calibre mm | Remarks |
|---|---|---|
| Pistole 08 (M.08) | 9 | |
| Steyr-Pistole M12 (Faustpistole M12) | 9 | New models to take 08 pistol ammunition in existence |
| Sauer & Sohn Pistolen (S & S—S & S BM —S & S M38) | 7.65 | S & S BM called *Behördenmodell* (Authorities' Model) |
| Walther Polizei Pistolen (W PP—W PPK) | 7.65 | |
| Mauser Pistolen (M—MnA) | 7.65 | MnA for Modell neuer Art (New Model) |
| Pistole 27 (M27) | 7.65 | |
| Dreyse-Pistole (Dr.) | 7.65 | |
| Steyr-Pistole 34 (Steyr) | 7.65 | |

## Gewehre und Karabiner (Rifles)

All rifles are bolt action weapons; magazines hold 5 cartridges.

| | Calibre mm | |
|---|---|---|
| Karabiner 98K | 7.92 | |
| M 95 Stutzen (ö) | 8 | Using M93 ammunition |
| M 95 " S " Stutzen (ö) | 8 | Using M30 " S " ammunition ; both are of Austrian (ö) origin and constructed on the " Mannlicher System " |

The following rifles of foreign origin may be encountered :

98(p), 29(p), 24(j), 24(t), 33(t)     p-polish ; j-jugoslav ; t-czech.

## Maschinenpistolen (MP) (Submachine Guns)

All MPs are automatic weapons ; magazines hold 20 to 32 cartridges ; take 08 pistol ammunition.

| | Calibre mm | |
|---|---|---|
| MP 18. I & MP 28. II | 9 | 20 cartridge magazine |
| MP 34 | 9 | 32 cartridge magazine ; old models take 9 mm Steyr-Pistol ammunition. |
| MP 35 Bgm. (Bergmann) | 9 | 20 or 32 cartridge magazine |
| MP 40 (Schmeisser) | 9 | 32 cartridge magazine ; folding skeleton stock |
| MP E (Erma) | 9 | 20 or 32 cartridge magazine |

## Maschinengewehre—MG (leicht oder schwer)

(Machine guns—light or heavy)

| Designation of weapon | Calibre mm | Remarks |
|---|---|---|
| MG 08 (" Maxim ") and MG 08/15 (" Maxim ") | 7.9 | Drum- or belt-fed ; water-cooled ; mounted on cradle or bipod ; 600 rounds per min. |
| MG 34 | 7.9 | Drum- or belt-fed ; air-cooled ; bipod or tripod-mounted ; 700 to 900 rounds per min. ; drum and belt each hold 50 rounds |
| MG 42 | 7.9 | Drum- or belt-fed ; air-cooled ; mounted on bipod or tripod ; 1,000 to 1,300 rounds per min. ; drum and belt each hold 50 rounds |
| MG 26(t) and MG 30 (t) | 7.92 | (t-czech) ; 20 cartridge-magazine ; air-cooled ; gas operated ; bipod-mounted ; 600 rounds per min. |
| MG 37(t) | 7.92 | Belt-fed ; air-cooled, gas-operated ; tripod-mounted ; 750 rounds per min. (similar to MG 26(t) ) |

## Panzerabwehrkanonen (Pak) (Anti-tank Guns (A/T))

Pak 37 mm ; Pak 50 mm ; Pak 75 mm may chiefly be encountered. Many others, particularly of foreign origin, in use, as :

25 mm(f) ; 75 mm(f) ;    (f-french)
76.2 mm(r)    (r-russian)

## Infantry Support Weapons

*Leichtes Infanteriege schütz* 75 mm (light Infantry Howitzer)

*Infanterie Kanonen- haubitze* (r) 76.2 mm (r) (Infantry Howitzer)

*Leichter Granatwerfer* 50 mm (l.Gr.W.) (light mortar)

*Mittlerer Granatwerfer* 81 mm (m.Gr.W.) (medium mortar)

## Armoured Vehicles

*Polizei-Panzerkampfwagen (System Steyr-Daimler-Puch)*

(Police-Armoured Scout Cars)

Twelve-wheeled armoured car with tank turret. Mounts two MG 34 or 42, and the 20 mm *Kampfwagen Kanone* 35 (Kw.-K35) (System Solothurn).

*Französischer Renault-Panzerkampfwagen*

(French Renault Tank)

Mounts a 37 mm french, short-barrelled, automatic gun (3.7 cm Kw K (f) ).

## Reizstoffpistolen (Gas Pistols)

For firing of tear-gas ammunition.

| Designation of weapon | Calibre mm | Remarks |
|---|---|---|
| *Reizstoffpatronen :* | | |
| Type A | | Only for indoors use |
| Type B | | Only for outdoors use |
| *Reizstoffhandgranate:* | | Use similar to the potato-masher type |

## Miscellaneous

*Kleinkaliberbüchse (KK.-Büchse DSM) "Deutsches Sportmodell"*

Calibre 5.46 mm ; a practice and sporting carabine, built similarly to the 98K.

Hand grenades of various types are in use.

Bayonets, sabre and daggers are worn.

# ORGANISATION OF A
# TYPICAL POLICE BATTALION (MOT)

Pol-Btl Stab
16 Offrs ﹢ Men (H.Q)

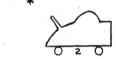

Strassenpanzerwagenzug
(Armoured Car Pl)
17 Offrs ﹢ Men

Kradschützen-Zug
(M/C Pl)
35 Offrs ﹢ Men

Nachrichten-Zug
(Sigs Pl)
19 Offrs ﹢ Men

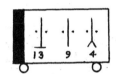

1. Pol-Komp
(1ST Police Coy)
150 Offrs ﹢ Men

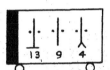

2. Pol-Komp
(2ND Police Coy)
150 Offrs ﹢ Men

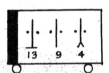

3. Pol-Komp
(3RD Police Coy)
150 Offrs ﹢ Men

Panzerjägerzug
(A/T Pl)
26 Offrs ﹢ Men

Leichter Infanterie-Geschützzug
(Light Inf Howitzer Pl)
26 Offrs ﹢ Men

Kraftfahrstaffel
(M/T Column)
97 Offrs ﹢ Men

Sanitätsstaffel
(Medical Detachment)
7 Offrs ﹢ Men

## LEGEND

| Symbol | German | English |
|---|---|---|
| ⊥ | Maschinenpistole (MP) | Sub Machine Gun |
| ⊥ | Leichtes Maschinen-Gewehr (LMG) | Light Machine Gun |
| ⊥ | Schweres Maschinen-Gewehr (SMG) | Heavy Machine Gun |
| ⊥ | Leichtes Infanterie-Geschütz (L.IG Kal 7.5cm) | Light Inf How 75mm |
| ⊤ | Panzerjägerkanone (Pak Kal 3.7cm) | A/T Gun 37mm |

\* Indicates units which may be attached from Regt

# ANNEXE F

## ORDER OF BATTLE OF THE GEHEIME STAATSPOLIZEI

**PART ONE : STAPO LEITSTELLEN**
(Regional Headquarters of the Gestapo)

**PART TWO : STAPO STELLEN**
(Sub-regional Headquarters of the Gestapo)

**PART THREE : STAPO AUSSENDIENSTSTELLEN**
(Larger Branch Offices of the Gestapo)

**PART FOUR : GRENZPOLIZEI**
(Frontier Police)
    (a) Stapo-Grenzpolizei-Kommissariate (Frontier Police Commissariats)
    (b) Stapo-Grenzpolizei-Posten (Frontier Police Outposts)

**PART FIVE : GESTAPO PRISONS AND CAMPS**

**PART SIX : NAZI PARTY HONORARY ASSISTANTS TO THE SIPO**

**PART SEVEN : COMMUNICATIONS**
    (a) Teletype Network of the Sipo and SD
    (b) Amendments to the Teletype Network of the Sipo and SD
    (c) Official Abbreviations and Terms used in (a) and (b)
    (d) Network of immobile Police Wireless Stations in Greater Germany
    (e) Code used by the Internationale Kriminalpolizeiliche Kommission
    (f) Wireless Stations of the Sipo and SD
    (g) Directives on the use of Sipo and SD Wireless Stations

A

# ANNEXE F : PART ONE

## STAPO-LEITSTELLEN

### (Regional HQ's of the Gestapo)

**BERLIN**

**Area :**
Gross-Berlin and Provinz
Mark Brandenburg
(*Reg. Bez.* Potsdam and Frankfurt/Oder)

**In direct control of :**
Gross-Berlin (*Reichshauptstadt* Berlin)

**Address :**
C 2, Grunerstr. 12
Tel : 510023 (T/P and *Polfunk* via PP Berlin)

**Chief :**
*SS-OSBF, ORuKR.* BOCK

**Deputy :**
*SS-SBF, RR.* KÜCK

**Under :**
*B.d.S.* Berlin

**Supervising :**
*St.* Potsdam (for *Reg. Bez.* Potsdam)
*St.* Frankfurt/Oder (for *Reg. Bez.* Frankfurt/Oder)

**Branch Offices :**
*Grepo* Berlin-Tempelhof (Airport)

**BRESLAU**

**Area :**
*Provinz* Niederschlesien (*Reg. Bez.* Breslau, Liegnitz)

**In direct control of :**
*Reg. Bez.* Breslau and also, since 1943, for the duration of the war, *Reg. Bez.* Liegnitz.

**Address :**
Museumstr. 2–4 or Anger 10
Tel : 22211 (and T/P)

**Chief :**
*SS-OSBF, ORR. Dr.* SCHARPWINKEL

**Under :**
*B.d.S.* Breslau

**Branch Offices :**
*AuDSt.* Glatz, Glogau, Görlitz, Gross-Wartenberg, Guhrau, Hirschberg, Liegnitz, Militsch, Waldenburg
*Stapo* Sagan
*Arbeitserziehungslager* Rattwitz (*Krs.* Ohlau)

**BRÜNN**

(Prior to 1944 listed as *Stapo Stelle*)

**Area :**
Mähren

**In direct control of :**
Area Mähren

**Address :**
Eichhornerstr. 70
Tel : 19988 (and T/P)
Former Address : Mozartgasse 3

**Chief :**
*SS-OSBF, Ru.KR. Dr.* RENNAU
Predecessor : *SS-OSBF, ORR.* NÖLLE

**Under :**
*B.d.S.* Prag

**Branch Offices :**
*AuDSt.* Iglau, Kremsier, Mährisch Ostrau, Mährisch Weisskirchen, Olmütz, Prerau, Prossnitz, Ungarisch-Hradisch, Wsetin.
*Greko* Zlin
*Grepo* Bila, Bilnitz, Blumenbach, Göding, Landshut, Oberlitz, Welka/near Strassnitz
*Arbeitserziehungslager* Gross-Kunzendorf, Witkowitz

**DANZIG**

**Area :**
*Reichsgau* Danzig-Westpreussen (*Reg. Bez.* Danzig, Bromberg and Marienwerder)

**In direct control of :**
*Reg. Bez.* Danzig, also, since 1943, for the duration of the war, *Landkreise* Marienberg, Marienwerder, Rosenberg and Stuhm of *Reg. Bez.* Marienwerder

**Address :**
Neugarten 27
Tel : 21051/56 (and T/P)

**Chief :**
*SS-OSBF, RR. Dr.* VENEDIGER

**Under :**
*B.d.S.* Danzig

**Supervising :**
*St.* Bromberg (for *Reg. Bez.* Bromberg)

**Branch offices :**
*AuDSt.* Elbing, Dirschau, Konitz, Marienwerder
*Greko* Gotenhafen controlling :
*Grepo* Gotenhafen-Hafen, Helaheide (on Island of Hela) Danzig-Hafen.

**DRESDEN**

**Area :**
Land Sachsen

**In direct control of :**
Former *Reg. Bez.* Dresden-Bautzen

**Address :**
A 24, Bismarckstr. 16/18
Tel : 44021 (and T/P)

**Chief :**
*SS-SBF, ORR.* Willy MÜLLER

**Under :**
*B.d.S.* Dresden

**Supervising :**
*St.* Chemnitz, Leipzig

**Branch offices :**
*AuDSt.* Bautzen

**DÜSSELDORF**

**Area :**
Rheinprovinz (*Reg. Bez.* Düsseldorf, Aachen, Koblenz, Köln, Trier)

**In direct control of :**
*Reg. Bez.* Düsseldorf

**Address :**
Ratingen, Mühlheimerstr. 47
Former Address : Prinz Georg St. 98
Tel : 2521/22 (and T/P via *Stapo* Dortmund)

**Chief :**
*SS-OSBF, ORR.* NOSSKE
Predecessor : *SS-OSBF, ORR. Dr.* ALBATH

**Other Personalities :**
*PR.* KINZEL (Former Chief *Abt.* I), *KK.*
SCHMIDT (Chief *Abt.* III), *SS-Ustuf KOS.*
RIECKMAN, *SS-Ustuf KOS.* POLIKEIT,
*PR.* MÜHLEN, *KK.* BROSIG

**Under :**
*B.d.S.* Düsseldorf

**Supervising :**
*St.*-Köln (for *Reg. Bez.* Köln and also, since
1943, for the duration of the war, *Reg. Bez.*
Aachen)
*St.* Koblenz (for *Reg. Bez.* Koblenz and also,
since 1943, for the duration of the war,
*Reg. Bez.* Trier)

**Branch offices :**
*AuDSt.* Duisburg, Essen, Hamborn, Krefeld,
Mülheim/Ruhr, München-Gladbach/Rheydt,
Oberhausen, Remscheid, Solingen, Velbert,
Wuppertal.
*Greko* Emmerich controlling :
*Grepo* Emmerich-Bahnhof, Elten-Babberich,
Emmerich-Hafen, Lobith
*Greko* Kaldenkirchen/Rheinland controlling :
*Grepo* Kaldenkirchen-Bahnhof, Kaldenkirchen-
Schwanenhaus
*Greko* Kleve controlling :
*Grepo* Geldern, Goch, Kranenburg-Bahnhof,
Wyler-Wylerberg

## HAMBURG

**Area :**
Hamburg, *Reg. Bez.* Lüneburg and Schleswig

**In direct control of :**
*Hansestadt* Hamburg and *Reg. Bez.* Lüneburg

**Address :**
Dammtorstr. 25
Former Address : Stadthausbrücke 8
Tel : 341000, 341612 (and T/P)

**Chief :**
*SS-OSBF, ORR.* BLOMBERG
Predecessor : *SS-OSBF, ORR. Dr.* KREUZER

**Other Personalities :**
*KR.* Karl HINTZE (Deputy Chief in 1943),
*KR.* BIELEFELD (Sect. I), *PR.* BECKER-
DORF (Pers. Dept.), *KR.* BEHRMANN
(Sect. II), *KS.* JURK (Sect. IIA), *KR. P.*
KRAUS (Sect. IIA), *KK.* WANGEMANN
(Sect. IIB), *KI.* KREUZKAMP (Sect. IIF),
*KS.* Willi BARKEY (Sect. IIG), *KOS.* G.
KOHLMANN (Sect. IIH), *KK.* HAUER-
WASS (Sect. III).

**Under :**
*B.d.S.* Hamburg

**Supervising :**
*St.* Kiel (for *Reg. Bez.* Schleswig)

**Branch offices :**
*AuDSt.* Celle, Fallingbostel, Hamburg-Bergedorf,
Hamburg-Harburg, Lüneburg, Soltau, Stadt
des KdF-Wagens near Fallersleben
*Greko* Hamburg

## HANNOVER

**Area :**
*Reg. Bez.* Hannover, Hildesheim, Osnabrück

**In direct control of :**
*Reg. Bez.* Hannover and also, since 1943, for
the duration of the war, *Reg. Bez.* Hildesheim

**Address :**
Ruehmkorffstr. 20
Tel : 60031 and 60269
Former Address : Schlageterstr. 52 and Oster-
mannstr. 14
Tel : 86181

**Chief :**
*SS-OSBF, ORR. u.KR.* RENTSCH
Deputy : *SS-SBF, RR. u. KR.* STÜWER

**Under :**
*B.d.S.* Braunschweig

**Branch offices :**
*AuDSt.* Göttingen, Hildesheim, Nienburg,
Nordhorn

## KARLSRUHE

**Area :**
*Land* Baden

**In direct control of :**
*Land* Baden

**Address :**
Reichsstr. 24
Tel : 8582/85 (and T/P)

**Chief :**
*SS-OSBF, ORR.* GMEINER
Predecessor : *SS-SBF, RR. Dr.* SCHICK

**Under :**
*B.d.S.* Stuttgart

**Branch offices :**
*AuDSt.* Baden-Baden, Freiburg/Breisgau,
Heidelberg, Mannheim, Offenburg
*Greko* Konstanz, controlling :
*Grepo* Konstanz-Kreuzlingertor
*Greko* Lörrach controlling :
*Grepo* Lörrach-Stetten/Strasse and Lörrach-
Stetten-Bahnhof, Grenzacherhorn, Weil am
Rhein-Bahnhof
*Greko* Singen/Hohentwiel controlling :
*Grepo* Singen-Bahnhof, Gottmadingen-Bahn-
hof
*Greko* Waldshut controlling :
*Grepo* Waldshut-Brücke, Erzingen
*Greko* Kehl/Rhein, Müllheim/Baden
*Stapo* Ettlingen, Mosbach, Pforzheim, Rastatt,
Villingen.

## KATTOWITZ

(Prior to 1944 listed as *Stapo Stelle*)

**Area :**
*Reg. Bez.* Kattowitz, Oppeln, Troppau

**In direct control of :**
*Reg. Bez.* Kattowitz

**Address :**
Bernhardstr. 49 (Strasse der SA)
Tel : 32923/27 (and T/P)

**Chief :**
*SS-OSBF, ORR. Dr.* THÜMMLER
Predecessor : *SS-OSBF, ORR. Dr.* MILDNER

**Under :**
*B.d.S.* Breslau

**Supervising :**
*St.* Oppeln (for *Reg. Bez.* Oppeln)
*St.* Troppau (for *Reg. Bez.* Troppau)

**Branch offices :**
*AuDSt.* Auschwitz, Beuthen, Bielitz, Gleiwitz,
Rybnik, Sosnowitz
*Greko* Teschen
*Grepo* Mosty

## KÖNIGSBERG

**Area :**
*Provinz* Ostpreussen (*Reg. Bez.* Königsberg,
Allenstein, Gumbinnen, Zichenau)

In direct control of :
Reg. Bez. Königsberg and also, since 1943, for the duration of the war, Reg. Bez. Allenstein

Address :
Lindenstr. 7–15
Former Address : General-Litzmann-Str. 3–7
Tel : 64331/36 (and T/P)

Chief :
SS-OSBF, ORR. FREYTAG

Under :
B.d.S. Königsberg

Supervising :
St. Tilsit (for Reg. Bez. Gumbinnen)
St. Zichenau-Schröttersburg (for Reg. Bez. Zichenau)

Branch offices :
AuDSt. Allenstein, Braunsberg/Ostpr., Lötzen, Neidenburg, Ortelsburg (also Greko), Rastenburg
Greko Lyck, Ortelsburg (also AuDSt), Pillau
Grepo Devau-Flughafen, Gehlenburg
Stapo Johannisburg/Ostpr.

## MAGDEBURG

(prior to 1944 listed as Stapo Stelle)

Area :
Provinzen Magdeburg, Halle-Merseburg, Land Anhalt

In direct control of :
Provinz Magdeburg, Land Anhalt

Address :
Klosterkirchhof 1
Tel : 33745/48 (and T/P)

Chief :
SS-OSBF, ORR. MOHR
Former Chief : SS-OSBF, ORR. BISCHOFF

Under :
B.d.S. Braunschweig

Supervising :
St. Halle/Saale (for Provinz Halle-Merseburg)

Branch office :
AuDSt. Dessau

## MÜNCHEN

Area :
Reg. Bez. Oberbayern, Schwaben.

In direct control of :
Reg. Bez. Oberbayern and also, since 1943, for the duration of the war, Reg. Bez. Schwaben.

Address :
Dietlindenstr. 32–43
Former Address : Briennerstr. 50
Tel : 28341/45

Chief :
SS-OSBF, ORR. SCHAEFER

Deputy :
SS-SBF, KDir. STRAUB

Under :
B.d.S. München

Branch office :
AuDSt. Augsburg
Grepo München-Riem (Airport)

## MÜNSTER/Westf.

Area :
Reg. Bez. Münster, Minden, Arnsberg and, for the duration of the war, Länder Lippe und Schaumburg-Lippe.

In direct control of :
Reg. Bez. Münster, Osnabrück and, for the duration of the war, Reg. Bez. Minden and the Länder Lippe und Schaumburg-Lippe.

Address :
Gutenbergstr. 17
Tel : 41854/56 (and T/P)

Chief :
SS-OSBF, ORR. LANDGRAF

Deputy :
SS-SBF, RR. ANDRES

Under :
B.d.S. Düsseldorf

Supervising :
St. Dortmund (für Reg. Bez. Arnsberg)

Branch offices :
AuDSt. Bielefeld, Bottrop, Buer, Gelsenkirchen, Gladbeck, Meppen, Osnabrück, Paderborn, Recklinghausen
Greko Gronau/Westf. controlling :
Grepo Glanerbrücke, Gronau-Bahnhof
Greko Bentheim controlling :
Grepo Bahnhof Bentheim, Nordhorn-Frensdorferhaar, Springbiel
Greko Borken/Westf. controlling :
Grepo Bocholt-Hemden, Borken-Bahnhof

## NÜRNBERG-FÜRTH

Area :
Reg. Bez. Ober-und Mittelfranken, Niederbayern-Oberpfalz, Mainfranken and Eger.

In direct control of :
Reg. Bez. Ober-und Mittelfranken, and also, since 1943, for the duration of the war, Reg. Bez. Mainfranken.

Address :
Ludwigstr. 36
Tel : 25541 and 27741 (and T/P)

Chief :
SS-SBF, RuKR. Dr. OTTO

Under :
B.d.S. Nürnberg

Supervising :
St. Karlsbad (for Reg. Bez. Eger)
St. Regensburg (for Reg. Bez. Nieder-Bayern-Oberpfalz)

Branch office :
AuDSt. Würzburg

## POSEN

Area :
Reichsgau Wartheland (Reg. Bez. Posen, Hohensalza and Litzmannstadt).

In direct control of :
Reg. Bez. Posen and also, since 1943, for the duration of the war, Kreise Altburgund, Dietfurt, Hohensalza, Gnesen, Mogilno of Reg. Bez. Hohensalza.

Address :
Ritterstr. 21a
Tel : 4365, 8261 (and T/P)

Chief :
SS-OSBF, ORR. STOSSBERG
Deputy : SS-SBF, RR.u.KR. KLEIN

Head of AuDSt. Posen :
SS-Hstuf, KR. ACHTERBERG

Head of the Personnel Department and office administration :
SS-Hstuf, PR. BORCHERT

Under :
B.d.S. Posen

Supervising :
St. Litzmannstadt (for Reg. Bez. Litzmannstadt)

**Branch offices :**
*AuDSt.* Posen, Gnesen, Hohensalza, Jarotschin, Kosten, Lissa, Samter
*Arbeitserziehungslager* Posen-Lenzingen and Hohensalza

## PRAG
(prior to 1944 listed as *Stapo Stelle*)

**Area :**
Böhmen (Bohemia)

**In direct control of :**
Böhmen

**Address :**
Bredauergasse 20
Tel : 30041 (and T/P)

**Chief :**
*SS-OSBF, ORR. Dr.* GERKE

**Under :**
*B.d.S.* Prag

**Branch offices :**
*AuDSt.* Beneschau, Budweis, Jitschin, Jungbunzlau, Kladno, Klattau, Kolin, Königgrätz, Pardubitz, Pilsen, Tabor
*Grepo* Prag (Airport)
*Polizeigefängnis* Theresienstadt
*Arbeitserziehungslager* Hradischko, Plan/Leinsitz, Miroschau/Pilsen-Land

## REICHENBERG (SÜD)
(prior to 1944 listed as *Stapo Stelle*)

**Area :**
*Reg. Bez.* Aussig

**In direct control of :**
*Reg. Bez.* Aussig

**Address :**
Lerchenfeldgasse 3
Tel : 2554, 4665, 4666 (and T/P)

**Chief :**
*SS-SBF, RR.* DENK
Predecessor : *SS-OSBF, ORR.* SCHRÖDER

**Under :**
*B.d.S.* Dresden

**Branch offices :**
*AuDSt.* Aussig, Brüx, Komotau, Leitmeritz, Teplitz-Schönau, Trautenau, Warnsdorf
*Greko* Böhmisch Leipa, Gablonz

## STETTIN

**Area :**
*Provinz* Pommern (*Reg. Bez.* Stettin, Köslin, Schneidemühl)

**In direct control of :**
*Reg. Bez.* Stettin and also, since 1943, for the duration of the war, *Reg. Bez.* Köslin and Schneidemühl

**Address :**
Augustastr. 47
Tel : 35231 (and T/P)

**Chief :**
*SS-OSBF, ORR.* Bruno MÜLLER
Deputy : *SS-OSBF, ORR.* LIPHARDT (*m.d.F.b.*)

**Under :**
*B.d.S.* Stettin

**Branch offices :**
*AuDSt.* Bütow, Dramburg, Flatow, Greifswald, Köslin, Kolberg, Neustettin, Schneidemühl, Stolp (also *Greko*), Woldenberg/Neumark
*Greko* Kolberg, Stettin, Swinemünde
*Greko* Stralsund controlling :
    *Grepo* Sassnitz
*Greko* Stolp controlling :
    *Grepo* Stolpmünde
*Arbeitserziehungslager* Hägerswelle/Stettin-Pölitz

## STUTTGART
(prior to 1944 listed as *Stapo Stelle*)

**Area :**
*Land* Württemberg and *Reg. Bez.* Sigmaringen

**In direct control of :**
*Land* Württemberg and *Reg. Bez.* Sigmaringen

**Address :**
Wilhelm-Murr-Str. 10
Tel : 28141, 29741/5 (and T/P)

**Chief :**
*SS-OSBF, ORu.KR.* MUSSGAY

**Under :**
*B.d.S.* Stuttgart

**Branch offices :**
*AuDSt.* Heilbronn/Neckar, Oberndorf/Neckar, Sigmaringen, Ulm
*Greko* Friedrichshafen
*Grepo* Stuttgart-Echterdingen (Airport)
*Stapo* Ellwangen, Tübingen
*Arbeitserziehungslager :* Oberndorf-Aistaig, Rudersberg/Schorndorf

## WIEN

**Area :**
*Reichsgaue* Wien, Niederdonau, Oberdonau, Steiermark, Kärnten, Salzburg, Tirol-Vorarlberg

**In direct control of :**
*Reichsgaue* Wien and Niederdonau

**Address :**
Morzinplatz 4
Tel : A 17580 (and T/P)

**Chief :**
*SS-BF, GenMaj. d. Pol.* HUBER (also *B.d.S.* in Wkr. XVII)

**Under :**
*B.d.S.* Wien

**Supervising :**
*St.* Graz (for *Reichsgau* Steiermark)
*St.* Innsbruck (for *Reichsgau* Tirol-Vorarlberg)
*St.* Klagenfurt (for *Reichsgau* Kärnten)
*St.* Linz/Donau (for *Reichsgau* Oberdonau)

**Branch offices :**
*AuDSt.* Sankt Pölten, Wiener Neustadt, Znaim
*Greko* Eisenstadt controlling :
    *Grepo* Bruck/Leitha, Kittsee, Sauerbrunn and Nebenstelle Zwettl
*Greko* Lundenburg controlling :
    *Grepo* Lundenburg-Bahnhof
*Greko* Wien controlling :
    *Grepo* Aspern (Airport), Engerau, Marchegg, Wien-Reichsbrücke

# ANNEXE F: PART TWO

## STAPO-STELLEN

### (Sub-regional HQ's of the Gestapo)

### BRAUNSCHWEIG

**In direct control of :**
*Land* Braunschweig and *Landkreis* Gifhorn of *Reg. Bez.* Lüneburg

**Address :**
Loeperstr. 52
Tel : 8044 (and T/P)
Former addresses : Steinstr. 2, Leopoldstr. 24/25

**Chief :**
*SS-SBF, ORR. Dr.* Wilhelm Friedrich KUHL

**Under supervision of :**
*B.d.S.* Braunschweig
*LSt.* None

**Branch offices :**
*AuDSt.* Bad Harzburg, Goslar (suspended), Watenstedt, Salzgitter

### BREMEN

**In direct control of :**
*Hansestadt* Bremen and also, since 1943, for the duration of the war, *Land* Oldenburg and *preuss. Reg. Bez.* Aurich, Stade and Island of Helgoland

**Address :**
Am Wall 197–199
Tel : 22471/74 (and T/P)

**Chief :**
*SS-SBF, RR. Dr.* ZIMMERMANN or *Dr.* DÖRNTE

**Under supervision of :**
*B.d.S.* Hamburg
*LSt.* None

**Branch offices :**
*AuDSt.* Delmenhorst, Oldenburg (also *Greko*), Stade, Verden/Aller, Wesermünde, Wilhelmshaven
*Greko* Bremen-Hafen, Cuxhaven, Nordenham, Oldenburg
*Greko* Emden
*Grepo* Bunderneuland, Emden-Aussenhafen, Weener
*Stapo* Aurich, Weener

### BROMBERG

**In direct control of :**
*Reg. Bez.* Bromberg, and *Kreise* Briesen, Graudenz, Leipe, Neumark, Rippin and Strasburg of *Reg. Bez.* Marienwerder

**Address :**
Flosstr. 5
Tel : 2751/2 (and T/P)

**Chief :**
*SS-OSBF, ORR.* RUX

**Under supervision of :**
*B.d.S.* Danzig
*LSt.* Danzig

**Branch offices :**
*AuDSt.* Graudenz, Rippin/Westpr., Schwetz (discontinued), Thorn

### CHEMNITZ

**In direct control of :**
Former *Reg. Bez.* Chemnitz and Zwickau

**Address :**
Kassbergstr. 22a
Tel : 34151/55 (and T/P)

**Chief :**
*SS-SBF, RR.* SCHOENESEIFFEN
Predecessor : *SS-SBF, ORR. Dr.* THÜMMLER

**Under supervision of :**
*B.d.S.* Dresden
*LSt.* Dresden

**Branch offices :**
Plauen/Vogtland, Zwickau

### DARMSTADT

**In direct control of :**
*Land* Hessen

**Address :**
Wilhelminen-Platz (Neues Palais)
Tel : 7651/53 (and T/P)
Former address : Wilhelm Gläsing Str. 21

**Chief :**
*SS-SBF, RR.* GIRKE
Predecessor : *SS-SBF, RR.* MOHR

**Under supervision of :**
*B.d.S.* Wiesbaden
*LSt.* None

**Branch offices :**
*AuDSt.* Giessen, Mainz, Offenbach/Main (discontinued)

### DORTMUND

**In direct control of :**
*Reg. Bez.* Arnsberg

**Address :**
Bergstr. 76
Former Address : Benninghoferstr. 16
Tel : 40651/55 (and T/P)

**Chief :**
*SS-SBF, RR.* ROTH
Predecessor : *SS-SBF, RR.* ILLMER

**Under supervision of :**
*B.d.S.* Düsseldorf
*LSt.* Münster

**Branch offices :**
*AuDSt.* Bochum, Hagen/Westf, Hamm, Meschede, Siegen
*Arbeitserziehungslager* Hunswinkel near Lüdenscheid/Westf.

### FRANKFURT/Main

**In direct control of :**
*Provinz* Nassau

**Address :**
Lindenstr. 27
Tel : 30361, 70261 (and T/P)
Former address : Bürgerstr. 22

**Chief :**
SS-SBF, RR. BREDER
Predecessor : SS-OSBF, RR. POCHE

**Under supervision of :**
B.d.S. Kassel
LSt. None

**Branch offices :**
AuDSt. Limburg/Lahn, Wetzlar, Wiesbaden

## FRANKFURT/Oder

**In direct control of :**
Reg. Bez. Frankfurt/Oder

**Address :**
Jüdenstr. 17
Tel : 2870/1 (and T/P)
Former address : Grosse Schárnstr. (Regierungs-
gebäude) or Halbestadt 43a

**Chief :**
SS-OSBF, ORR. RICHTER

**Under supervision of :**
B.d.S. Berlin
LSt. Berlin

**Branch offices :**
AuDSt. Cottbus, Landsberg/Warthe, Schwiebus
(also reported as Greko), Sommerfeld

## GRAUDENZ

suspended as Stapo Stelle and downgraded to
Aussendienstelle in October, 1943 (see St. Bromberg)

## GRAZ

**In direct control of :**
Reichsgau Steiermark

**Address :**
Parkring 4
Tel : 83060 (and T/P)

**Chief :**
SS-OSBF, ORR. Dr. GROSKOPF
Predecessor : SS-SBF, RR. Dr. MACHULE

**Under supervision of :**
B.d.S. Salzburg
LSt. Wien

**Branch offices :**
AuDSt. Leoben
Greko Fürstenfeld controlling :
. Grepo Hl. Kreuz i.L, Jennersdorf, Rechnitz
Greko Leibnitz controlling :
Grepo Radkersburg, Mureck, Spielfeld and
Nebenstelle Eibiswalde

## HALLE/Saale

**In direct control of :**
Province Halle-Merseburg

**Address :**
Dreyhauptstr. 2
Tel : 27681 (and T/P)

**Chief :**
SS-SBF, ORR. KOLITZ
Predecessor : SS-SBF, RR. Dr. BRAUNE

**Under supervision of :**
B.d.S. Dresden
LSt. Magdeburg

**Branch offices :**
AuDSt. Bitterfeld, Eisleben, Merseburg, Torgau,
Weissenfels, Wittenberg, Zeitz (suspended)

## HOHENSALZA

suspended as Stapo Stelle and downgraded to
Aussendienststelle in October, 1943.

## INNSBRUCK

**In direct control of :**
Reichsgau Tirol-Vorarlberg

**Address :**
Herrengasse I
Tel : 2159, 2107, 1230/31 (and T/P)

**Chief :**
SS-SBF, RR. HOFFMANN

**Other Personalities :**
POI. ROSMANER (Chief of Section I)
SS-Hstuf RADLHERR (Section I)
SS-Hstuf HILLIGES (formerly Chief of Section
II ; last reported in Italy)
SS-Ostuf SCHMIDT (Chief of Section II)
SS-Ostuf BUSCH (Chief of Section III)
SS-Ostuf, KI. KRAMER (Section III)
SS-Ostuf, OA. SPICAR (Section III)

**Under supervision of :**
B.d.S. Salzburg
LSt. Wien

**Branch offices :**
Greko Bregenz controlling :
Grepo Feldkirch, Höchst, Lustenau and
Auffanglager Innsbruck-Reichenau
Greko Brenner-Gries controlling :
Grepo Brenner-Bahnhof, Brenner-Strasse,
. Nauders (Tirol)

## KARLSBAD

**In direct control of :**
Reg. Bez. Eger

**Address :**
Obere Schillerstr. 26
Tel : 4981 (and T/P)

**Chief :**
SS-SBF, RR. Dr. LITTOW
Predecessor : SS-OSBF, ORR. GMEINER
(transferred to Stapo-LSt Karlsruhe)

**Under supervision of :**
B.d.S. Nürnberg
LSt. Nürnberg

**Branch offices :**
AuDSt. Brüx, Eger, Marienbad, Mies, Saaz
Greko Saaz]

## KASSEL

**In direct control of :**
Provinz Kurhessen

**Address :**
Barracke Goetheanlage
Former Address : Wilhelmshöher Allee 32
Tel : 36675/77 (and T/P)

**Chief :**
SS-OSBF, ORR. Dr. NEDWED

**Under supervision of :**
B.d.S. Kassel
LSt. None

**Branch offices :**
AuDSt. Fulda, Hanau

## KIEL

**In direct control of :**
Reg. Bez. Schleswig without Island Helgoland

**Address :**
Düppelstr. 23
Tel : 8790 (and T/P)

**Chief :**
SS-OSBF, ORR. HENSCHKE
, Deputy : SS-SBF, RR. F. SCHMIDT (m.d.F.b.)
(trfd. from RSHA I)

Under supervision of :
B.d.S. Hamburg
LSt. Hamburg

Branch offices :
AuDSt. Fehmarn (Burg), Heide, Itzehoe, Neu-
münster, Oldenburg/Holstein
Greko Kiel controlling :
Grepo Brunsbüttelkoog, Holtenau-Schleuse,
Westerland/Sylt, Laboe
Greko Flensburg controlling :
Grepo Böglum, Flensburg-Bahnhof, Flens-
burg-Hafen, Harrislee-Land, Kupfermühle,
Süderlügum and Nebenstelle Niebüll
Greko Lübeck controlling :
Grepo Lübeck-Hafen, Lübeck-Travemünde,
and Nebenstelle Neustadt/Holstein

### KLAGENFURT

In direct control of :
Reichsgau Kärnten

Address :
Burg
Tel : 1700, 1705 (and T/P)
Former address : Arnulfplatz I

Chief :
SS-OSBF, ORR. Dr. CHRISTMANN(?)
Predecessor : SS-SBF, RR. Dr. WEIMANN

Under supervision of :
B.d.S. Salzburg
LSt. Wien

Branch offices :
AuDSt. Prüvali, Radmannsdorf, Spittal/Drau
Greko Lienz/Drau, controlling :
Grepo Sillian
Greko Villach controlling :
Grepo Arnoldstein, Thörl-Maglern

### KOBLENZ

In direct control of :
Reg. Bez. Koblenz and, since 1943, for the
duration of the war, Reg. Bez. Trier

Address :
Im Vogelsang I
Tel : 2291 (and T/P)

Chief :
SS-OSBF, ORR. Dr. Kurt CHRISTMANN
Predecessor : SS-OSBF, ORR. SENS

Under supervision of :
B.d.S. Wiesbaden
LSt. Düsseldorf

Branch offices :
AuDSt. Prüm, Trier, Wittlich
AuSt. Idar-Oberstein
Arbeitserziehungslager Hinzert

### KÖLN

In direct control of :
Reg. Bez. Köln and, for the duration of the war,
Reg. Bez. Aachen

Address :
Godesberg, Karl Finkenburgstr. 19
Former Address : Appellhof Platz 23 -5
Tel : 70681/82 (and T/P)

Chief :
SS-SBF, RR. SPRINZ (transferred, successor
unknown)

Under supervision of :
B.d.S. Düsseldorf
LSt. Düsseldorf

Branch offices :
AuDSt. Aachen, Bonn
Greko Aachen controlling :
Grepo Aachen-Westbahnhof, Horbach, Vaal-
serquartier
Greko Eupen controlling :
Grepo Baelen, Heinrichskapelle, Herbesthal-
Bahnhof
Greko Heinsberg/Rheinland controlling :
Grepo Dalheim, Tüddern
Greko Herzogenrath controlling :
Grepo Herzogenrath-Aachenerstr., Herzogen-
rath-Bahnhof, Kohlscheid
Greko Malmedy

### KÖSLIN

suspended as Stapo Stelle and downgraded to
Aussendienststelle in October, 1943 (see LSt.
Stettin)

### LEIPZIG

In Direct Control of :
Former Reg. Bez. Leipzig

Address :
Karl-Heine Str. 12
Tel : 44641, 41283, 45163, 42603 (and T/P)
Former address : Wächterstr. 5 (Pol. Präsidium)

Chief :
SS-SBF, RR. Dr. KAUSSMANN or SS-OSF,
ORR. HEGENSCHEIDT
Predecessor : SS-SBF, KDir. FISTLER

Under supervision of :
B.d.S. Dresden
LSt. Dresden

### LINZ/Donau

In direct control of :
Reichsgau Oberdonau

Address :
Langgasse 13
Tel : 26281 (and T/P)
Former address : Gesellenhausstr. I

Chief :
SS-OSBF, ORR. Dr. BAST (transferred
successor unknown)
Predecessor : SS-OSBF, ORR. LEITZMANN

Under supervision of :
B.d.S. Wien
LSt. Wien

Branch offices :
AuDSt. Steyr
Stapo Bad Ischl
Greko Krummau/Moldau

### LITZMANNSTADT

In direct control of :
Reg. Bez. Litzmannstadt

Address :
Gardestr. 1–7
Tel : 25270 (and T/P)

Chief :
SS-OSBF, ORR. Dr. BRADFISCH

Under supervision of :
B.d.S. Posen
LSt. Posen

Branch offices :
AuDSt. Kalisch, Konin, Lentschütz, Leslau,
Schieratz
Greko Welun
Grepo Litzmannstadt

## OPPELN

**In direct control of :**
*Reg. Bez.* Oppeln

**Address :**
Moltkestr. 43
Tel : 3368, 3360 (and T/P)

**Chief :**
*SS-SBF, ORR.* STÜBER

**Under supervision of :**
*B.d.S.* Breslau
*LSt.* Kattowitz

**Branch offices :**
*AuDSt.* Heydebreck-O/S, Neisse, Neustadt-O/S,
Ratibor, Rosenberg
*Greko* Loben, Lublinitz
*Grepo* Blachstädt, Warthenau
*Arbeitserziehungslager* Blechhammer

## POTSDAM

**In direct control of :**
*Reg. Bez.* Potsdam

**Address :**
Priesterstr. 11/12
Tel : 4416 (and T/P)

**Chief :**
*SS-OSBF, OR.u.KR.* HELLER
Deputy : *SS-SBF, RR.* SENNE

**Under supervision of :**
*B.d.S.* Berlin
*LSt.* Berlin

**Branch offices :**
*AuDSt.* Brandenburg/Havel, Eberswalde,
Jüterbog, Wittenberge, Zossen
*Arbeitserziehungslager* Fehrbellin

## REGENSBURG

**In direct control of :**
*Reg. Bez.* Niederbayern und Oberpfalz

**Address :**
Minoritenweg I (Polizeidirektion)
Tel : 5145 (T/P and *Polfunk* via PD)

**Chief :**
*SS-OSBF, Pol. Dir.* POPP

**Under supervision of :**
*B.d.S.* Nürnberg
*LSt.* Nürnberg-Fürth

**Branch offices :**
*AuDSt.* Markt Eisenstein, Grafenwöhr

## SAARBRÜCKEN

**In direct control of :**
*Reichsgau* Westmark without *Zivilverwaltungsgebiet* Lothringen

**Address :**
Grüner Hof 21
Former address : Schlossplatz 14–15
Tel : 26681/85 (and T/P)

**Chief :**
*SS-OSBF, ORR. Dr.* L. SPANN
Predecessor : *SS-SBF, RR.* RENTSCH

**Under supervision of :**
*B.d.S.* Metz
*LSt.* None.

**Branch offices :**
*AuDSt.* Kaiserslautern, Ludwigshafen, Merzig,
Neunkirchen, Neustadt/Weinstr.
*AuSt.* Saarlautern, St. Ingbert/Saar
*Greko* Landau/Pfalz

## SALZBURG

**In direct control of :**
*Reichsgau* Salzburg

**Address :**
Hofstallgasse 5
Tel : 1306/7

**Chief :**
*SS-OSBF, ORR. Dr.* HUEBER

**Under supervision of :**
*B.d.S.* Salzburg
*LSt.* Wien

## SCHNEIDEMÜHL

Suspended as *Stapo Stelle* and downgraded to
*AuDSt.*, October, 1943 (see *LSt.* Stettin)

## SCHWERIN/Meckl.

**In direct control of :**
*Land* Mecklenburg

**Address :**
Weinbergstr. I
Tel : 3446/48 (and T/P)

**Chief :**
*SS-SF, RDir.* OLDACH

**Under supervision of :**
*B.d.S.* Stettin
*LSt.* None

**Branch offices :**
*AuDSt.* Neustrelitz
*Greko* Rostock controlling :
*Grepo* Warnemünde
*Greko* Wismar
*Stapo* Malchin, Stavenhagen

## TILSIT

**In direct control of :**
*Reg. Bez.* Gumbinnen

**Address :**
SA-Strasse 67
Tel : 2991 (and T/P)

**Chief :**
*SS-SBF, RR. Dr.* JAHR
Predecessor : *SS-SBF, RR.* BÖHME

**Under supervision of :**
*B.d.S.* Königsberg
*LSt.* Königsberg

**Branch offices :**
*AuDSt.* Heydekrug, Insterburg
*Greko* Eydtkau controlling :
*Grepo* Schirwindt
*Greko* Memel controlling :
*Grepo* Bajohren-Krottingen, Memel-Hafen
*Greko* Sudauen
*Greko* Tilsit controlling :
*Grepo* Laugzargen-Tauroggen, Schmallening-
ken
*Grepo* Gabergischken-Langallen, Jonaten-Kol-
leschen über Heydekrug

## TRIER

Suspended as *Stapo Stelle* and downgraded to
*AuDSt.* Oct. 1943 (see St. Koblenz)

## TROPPAU

**In direct control of :**
*Reg. Bez.* Troppau

**Address :**
Konrad-Henlein-Platz 5
Tel : 714, 721 (and T/P)

**Chief :**
SS-SBF, ORR. Dr. KULZER

**Under supervision of :**
B.d.S. Breslau
LSt. Kattowitz

**Branch offices :**
AuDSt. Landskron, Mährisch Schönberg, Neutitschein, Schönbrunn

## WEIMAR

**In direct control of :**
Land Thüringen, Reg. Bez. Erfurt and Landkreis Schmalkalden of Provinz Kurhessen

**Address :**
Kegelplatz I
Tel : 2880/81

**Chief :**
SS-SBF, ORR. vom FELDE or SS-OSBF, ORR. SCHRÖDER

**Under supervision of :**
B.d.S. Kassel
LSt. None

**Branch offices :**
AuDSt., Erfurt, Gera, Gotha, Jena, Suhl

## WILHELMSHAVEN

Suspended as Stapo Stelle and downgraded to AuDSt., October, 1943 (see LSt. Bremen)

## ZICHENAU-SCHRÖTTERSBURG

**In direct control of :**
Reg. Bez. Zichenau

**Address :**
Paul-Sohnstr. 5
Tel : 1171/75
Former addresses : Markstr. 5. Tilsiterstr. 7

**Chief :**
SS-SBF, ORR. SCHULZ
Former chief : SS-SBF, RR. Dr. PULMER

**Under supervision of :**
B.d.S. Königsberg
LSt. Königsberg

**Branch offices :**
AuDSt. Zichenau
Greko Modlin-Bugmünde controlling :
  Grepo Modlin, Ostenburg
Greko Scharfenwiese

## KdS LUXEMBURG

**In direct control of :**
Zivilverwaltungsgebiet Luxemburg

**Address :**
Einsatzkommando der Sipo und des SD in Luxemburg,
Petrussring 57
Tel : 6786/88 (and T/P)

**Kommandeur :**
SS-OSBF, ORR. HARTMANN

**Under supervision of :**
B.d.S. Wiesbaden

**Branch offices :**
AuDSt. Diekirch, Esch/Alzig
Greko Luxemburg controlling :
  Grepo Kleinbettingen, Rodingen, Steinfort

## KdS METZ

**In direct control of :**
Lothringen

**Address :**
Einsatzkommando der Sipo und des SD in Metz,
Adolf-Hitler-Str. 42
Tel : 1330

**Under supervision of :**
B.d.S. Metz

**Branch offices :**
AuDSt. Diedenhofen, Saarburg, St. Avold, Saargemünd
Greko Metz controlling :
  Grepo Almansweiler, Elfringen, Laubweiler, Mövern, Neuburg, Reichenthal, Vionville

## KdS MARBURG/DRAU

**In direct control of :**
Zivilverwaltungsgebiet Untersteiermark

**Address :**
Kommando der Sipo und des SD in Marburg
Tegethoffstr. 34
Tel : 24/84 (T/P, Polfunk, Bildfunk)

**Kommandeur :**
SS-SBF, KDir. STAGE

**Under supervision of :**
B.d.S. Salzburg

**Branch offices :**
AuDSt. Cilli, Pettau, Polstrau, Rann
Polizeigefängnis Schloss Ankenstein

## KdS STRASSBURG

**In direct control of :**
Zivilverwaltungsgebiet Elsass

**Address :**
Aussenkommando der Sipo und des SD in Strassburg,
Sängerhausstr. 11
Tel : 26135/37, 22550/52 (T/P)

**Under supervision of :**
B.d.S. Strassburg

**Branch offices :**
AuDSt. Hagenau, Kolmar, Mülhausen/Elsass
Grepo Altmünsterol, Niedersulzbach, Saal, St. Ludwig
(The above Grepos are directly subordinate to the B.d.S. Strassburg)

## KdS VELDES

**In direct control of :**
Zivilverwaltungsgebiet Oberkrain

**Address :**
Kommando der Sipo und des SD für die besetzten Gebiete Kärntens und Krains in Veldes,
Parkhotel
Tel : 204/206, T/P

**Kommandeur :**
SS-SBF, RuKR. VOGT

**Under supervision of :**
B.d.S. Salzburg

**Branch offices :**
AuDSt. Assling, Laak/Zaier, Littai, Radmannsdorf, Stein
Greko Krainburg controlling :
  Grepo Laas/Save, Ratschach-Matten, St. Veit/Save, Wochein-Feistritz
Polizeigefängnis Vigaun
Umsiedlungslager Zwischenwässern

# ANNEXE F : PART THREE

## STAPO-AUSSENDIENSTSTELLEN

### (Larger Branch Offices of the Gestapo)

*Note.*—The following Headquarters of the *Gestapo* have all been identified as *Stapo-Aussendienststellen* with the exception of a few identified as " *Aussenstellen* " and some with unknown classification (See column " Remarks ").

| Town | Address | Tel. (Existence of Teleprinter is indicated by " (T/P) ") | Branch Office of : | BdS or IdS | Remarks |
|---|---|---|---|---|---|
| Aachen | Theaterplatz 14 | 27511 (T/P) | *St.* Köln | Düsseldorf | Chief : *SS-HSF, KK.* BACH (Until 1943 listed as *Stapo-Stelle* for *Reg. Bez.* Aachen) |
| Allenstein | Freiherr-v.- Stein-Str. 3–5 | 2146/49 (T/P) | *LSt.* Königsberg | Königsberg | Chief : *KR.* WÄCHTER (Until 1943 listed as *Stapo-Stelle* for *Reg. Bez.* Allenstein) |
| Altona | Einunddreissiger Str. 66 | | | | Suspended, see Hamburg |
| Assling | Adolf-Hitler-Str. 24 | 601 | *KdS.* Veldes | Salzburg | |
| Augsburg | Prinzregenten-Str. 11 | 8453 (T/P) | *LSt.* München | München | Chief : *KK.* BRANDL (Until 1943 listed as *Stapo-Stelle* for *Reg. Bez.* Schwaben) |
| Aurich | | | *St.* Bremen | Hamburg | Classification unidentified |
| Aussig | Hugo-Wolf-Str. 4 | 2517 (T/P) | *LSt.* Reichenberg | Dresden | |
| Auschwitz | Torweg 8 | 94 (T/P) | *LSt.* Kattowitz | Breslau | |
| Baden-Baden | Kaiser-Wilhelm- Str. 1 | 1317/18 (T/P) | *LSt.* Karlsruhe | Stuttgart | |
| Bad Harzburg | Herzog-Wilhelm- Str. 91 | 910 | *St.* Braunschweig | Braunschweig | |
| Bad Ischl | | | *St.* Linz | Wien | Classification unidentified |
| Bautzen | Ortenburg | 2788 (T/P) | *LSt.* Dresden | Dresden | |
| Beneschau | Haus Nr. 386 | 146, 230 (T/P) | *LSt.* Prag | Prag | |
| Bergedorf n/Hamburg | Ernst-Mantius- Str. 8 | Hamburg 213520 | *LSt.* Hamburg | Hamburg | |
| Beuthen/OS. | Gustav-Freytag- Str. 11a | 2855/6 (T/P) | *LSt.* Kattowitz | Breslau | |
| Bielefeld | Siekerwall 9 | 6600 (T/P) | *LSt.* Münster | Düsseldorf | Chief : *KK.* DIELE (Until 1943 listed as *Stapo-Stelle* for *Reg. Bez.* Minden and the *Länder* Lippe and Schaumburg-Lippe). |
| Bielitz | Fontanestr. 6 | 1151 (T/P) | *LSt.* Kattowitz | Breslau | |
| Bitterfeld | Bismarckstr. 42 | 3444 | *St.* Halle | Dresden | |
| Bochum | Bergstr. 76 | 62251 (T/P) | *St.* Dortmund | Düsseldorf | |
| Bonn | Kreuzbergweg 5 | 8041 (T/P) | *St.* Köln | Düsseldorf | |
| Bottrop | Droste- Hülshoff-Pl. 5 | 2041 | *LSt.* Münster | Düsseldorf | |
| Brandenburg/ Havel | Neuendorferstr. 89 | 4069 | *St.* Potsdam | Berlin | |
| Braunsberg/Pr. | Hindenburgstr. 43 | 333 | *LSt.* Königsberg | Königsberg | |
| Brüx | Konrad-Henlein- Str. 36 | 797 (T/P) | *LSt.* Reichenberg | Dresden | |
| Budweis | Lannastr. 35 | 496,635 (T/P) | *LSt.* Prag | Prag | |
| Buer | Adolf-Hitler-Pl. 1 | 30751 | *LSt.* Münster | Düsseldorf | |
| Burg | See Fehmarn | | | | |
| Bütow | Konrad von Jungingen-Str. 24 | 375 (T/P) | *LSt.* Stettin | Stettin | |
| Celle | Hannoversche Str. 54 | 2525 (T/P) | *LSt.* Hamburg | Braunschweig | |
| Cilli | Grabengasse 2 | 159(T/P) | *KdS.* Marburg/ Drau | Salzburg | |
| Cottbus | Am Markt 1 | 3623, 2583 (T/P) | *St.* Frankfurt/Oder | Berlin | |
| Cuxhaven | Am Wehl 2 | 2022 | *St.* Bremen | Hamburg | |
| Delmenhorst | Adolf-Hitler-Pl. | 2833 | *St.* Bremen | Hamburg | |
| Dessau | Strasse des 30. Januar 5 | 1722 (T/P) | *LSt.* Magdeburg | Braunschweig | Chief : *SS-OSF, KK.* ROSE Former address : Friedrichstr. 27 |
| Diedenhofen | Adolf-Hitler-Pl. 6 | 520 (T/P) | *KdS.* Metz | Metz | |
| Diekirch | Alexis-Heck-Str.28 | 3252 | *KdS.* Luxemburg | Wiesbaden | |
| Dirschau | Baldauerstr. 6 | 1351 (T/P) | *LSt.* Danzig | Danzig | |
| Dramburg | | | *LSt.* Stettin | Stettin | |
| Duisburg | Düsseldorfer Str. 161 | 26301 | *LSt.* Düsseldorf | Düsseldorf | |

| Town | Address | Tel. (Existence of Teleprinter is indicated by " (T/P) ") | Branch Office of : | BdS or IdS | Remarks |
|---|---|---|---|---|---|
| Eberswalde | Eisenbahnstr. 12 | 3230 | *St.* Potsdam | Berlin | |
| Eger | Dr. Bayeuther-Str. 90 | 888/90 (T/P) | *St.* Karlsbad | Nürnberg | |
| Eisenstein (Markt) | Marktpl. 26 | 20 (T/P) | *St.* Regensburg | Nürnberg | |
| Eisleben | Hallesche Str. 21 | 2419 | *St.* Halle | Dresden | |
| Elbing | Göring-Pl. 10 | 2941 (T/P) | *LSt.* Danzig | Danzig | |
| Ellwangen/ Württembg. | Marktpl. 2 | | *LSt.* Stuttgart | Stuttgart | Identified as *Stapo-Aussenstelle* |
| Erfurt | Hindenburgstr. 7 | 25196 (T/P) | *St.* Weimar | Kassel | Chief : *KK.* HÜTTIG (Until 1943 listed as *Stapo-Stelle* for *Reg. Bez.* Erfurt). |
| Esch/Alzig | Emil-Mayrisch-Str. 39 | 2080 | *KdS.* Luxemburg | Wiesbaden | |
| Essen | Kortumstr. 46 | 44191 (T/P) | *LSt.* Düsseldorf | Düsseldorf | |
| Ettlingen | | | *LSt.* Karlsruhe | Stuttgart | Classification unidentified |
| Fallersleben | See Stadt des KdF Wagens. | | | | |
| Fallingbostel | Soltauer Str. 231 | Soltau 336 | *LSt.* Hamburg | Hamburg | |
| Fehmarn (Burg) | Burgtiefe | 605 (T/P) | *St.* Kiel | Hamburg | |
| Flatow | Adolf-Hitler-Str. 32 | 462 | *LSt.* Stettin | Stettin | |
| Freiburg/ Breisgau | Goethe-Str. 33 | 7658 (T/P) | *LSt.* Karlsruhe | Stuttgart | |
| Fulda | Heinrichstr. 8 | 2715 (T/P) | *St.* Kassel | Kassel | |
| Gelsenkirchen | Dietrich-Eckardt-Str. 21 | 25551/2 (T/P) | *LSt.* Münster | Düsseldorf | |
| Gera/Reuss | Schlosstr. 22 | 4452 (T/P) | *St.* Weimar | Kassel | Former address : Adelheidstr. 5 |
| Giessen | Neuen Bäue 23 | 4441/2 (T/P) | *St.* Darmstadt | Kassel | |
| Gladbeck/ Westf. | Horst-Wessel-Pl. 6 (Pol. Amt.) | 2441 | *LSt.* Münster | Düsseldorf | |
| Glatz | Adolf-Hitler-Str. 17 | 2134 (T/P) | *LSt.* Breslau | Breslau | |
| Gleiwitz | Teuchertstr. 20 | 3331 (T/P) | *LSt.* Kattowitz | Breslau | |
| Glogau | Steinweg 19 | 1031 (T/P) | *LSt.* Breslau | Breslau | |
| Gnesen | Kasernenstr. 12 | 144 (T/P) | *LSt.* Posen | Posen | |
| Görlitz | Augustastr. 31 | 3615 (T/P) | *LSt.* Breslau | Breslau | |
| Göttingen | Franz-Seldte-Str. 19 | 4534 | *LSt.* Hannover | Braunschweig | |
| Goslar | Breitestr. 98 | 3164/5 | *St.* Braunschweig | Braunschweig | Suspended since 25 Nov. 1941 |
| Gotha | Erfurterstr. 2 | 1790 (T/P) | *St.* Weimar | Kassel | |
| Grafenwöhr | General v. Epp-Str. 138b/1 | 65 | *St.* Regensburg | Nürnberg | |
| Graudenz | Königstr. 7 | 1023/25 (T/P) | *St.* Bromberg | Danzig | Chief : *SS-OSF, KK.* WORM (Until 1943 listed as *Stapo-Stelle* for *Reg. Bez.* Marienwerder |
| Greifswald | Wilhemstr. 37/38 | 2960 | *LSt.* Stettin | Stettin | |
| Gross-Wartenberg | | | *LSt.* Breslau | Breslau | |
| Guhrau | | | *LSt.* Breslau | Breslau | |
| Hagen/Westf. | Körnerstr. 24 | 24456 (T/P) | *St.* Dortmund | Düsseldorf | |
| Hagenau | Brunnenstubstr. 24 | 102 (T/P) | *BdS.* Strassburg | Strassburg | |
| Hamborn | August-Thyssen-Str. 39 | 26301 | *LSt.* Düsseldorf | Düsseldorf | |
| Hamm | Göring-Str. 80 | 1662 (T/P) | *St.* Dortmund | Düsseldorf | |
| Hanau | Paradepl. 2/4 | 4056 (T/P) | *St.* Kassel | Kassel | |
| Harburg, nr. Hamburg | Aussenmühlenweg 20 | Hamburg 370235 | *LSt.* Hamburg | Hamburg | |
| Heide/Holst. | Markt 67 | 2831 | *St.* Kiel | Hamburg | |
| Heidelberg | Bunsenstr. 19a | 5781 (T/P) | *LSt.* Karlsruhe | Wiesbaden | |
| Heilbronn/ Neckar | Wienerstr. 6 | 5270 (T/P) | *LSt.* Stuttgart | Stuttgart | |
| Heydebreck/ OS. | Hindenburgstr. 61 | Kosel 900 (T/P) | *St.* Oppeln | Breslau | |
| Heydekrug/ Ostpr. | Markt 16 | 278 | *St.* Tilsit | Königsberg | |
| Hildesheim | Gartenstr. 20 | 5051/2 (T/P) | *LSt.* Hannover | Braunschweig | Chief : *KK.* BAUMEISTER (Until 1943 listed as *Stapo-Stelle* for *Reg. Bez.* Hildesheim). |
| Hirschberg | Kaiser-Friedrich-Str. 18 | 3400 (T/P) | *LSt.* Breslau | Breslau | |
| Hohensalza | Adolf-Hitler-Str. 41 | 2151 (T/P) | *St.* Litzmannstadt | Posen | (Until 1943 listed as *Stapo-Stelle* for *Reg. Bez.* Hohensalza.) |
| Idar-Oberstein | Adolf-Hitler-Str. 281 | | *St.* Koblenz | Wiesbaden | Identified as *Stapo-Aussenstelle* |
| Iglau | Steingasse 50 | 480/1 (T/P) | *LSt.* Brünn | Prag | |
| Insterburg | Hindenburgstr. 58 | 424 | *St.* Tilsit | Königsberg | |
| Itzehoe | Feldschmiede 98 Dithmarscher Pl. | 2258 | *St.* Kiel | Hamburg | |

| Town | Address | Tel. (Existence of Teleprinter is indicaetd by " (T/P) ") | Branch Office of : | BdS or IdS | Remarks |
|---|---|---|---|---|---|
| Jarotschin | Hermann-Göring-Str. 19 | 20 (T/P) | LSt. Posen | Posen | |
| Jena | Kaiser-Wilhelm-Str. 2 | 3754 | St. Weimar | Kassel | |
| Jitschin | Viktoriastr. (Behördenhaus) | 214 (T/P) | LSt. Prag | Prag | |
| Johannisburg/Ostpr. | | | LSt. Königsberg | Königsberg | Classification unidentified |
| Jüterbog | Schillerstr. 55/7 | 741 | St. Potsdam | Berlin | |
| Jungbunzlau | Husgasse 212 | 406 (T/P) | LSt. Prag | Prag | |
| Kaiserslautern | | | St. Saarbrücken | Metz | |
| Kalisch | Kurzer Weg 1 | 56 (T/P) | St. Litzmannstadt | Posen | |
| Kladno | Langemarckstr. 2840 | 353/6 (T/P) | LSt. Prag | Prag | |
| Klattau | Richard-Wagner-Str. 192 | 291/4 (T/P) | LSt. Prag | Prag | |
| Königgrätz | Georgstr. 218 | Behördenamt 710/19 (T/P) | LSt. Prag | Prag | |
| Köslin | Moritzstr. 7 | 2521/23 (T/P) | LSt. Stettin | Stettin | Until 1943 listed as *Stapo-Stelle* for *Reg. Bez.* Köslin |
| Kolberg | Bahnstr. 11 | 2103 | LSt. Stettin | Stettin | |
| Kolin | Schlossgasse 28 | 362, 494 (T/P) | LSt. Prag | Prag | |
| Kolmar | Hohland Bergwald 10 | 3268 (T/P) | BdS. Strassburg | Strassburg | |
| Komotau | Deutschherrenpl. | | LSt. Reichenberg | Dresden | |
| Konin | Frhr. v. Stein-Str. 37 | 37/38 (T/P) | St. Litzmannstadt | Posen | |
| Konitz | Gotzkowskystr. 17 | 24 (T/P) | LSt. Danzig | Danzig | |
| Kosten | Adolf-Hitler-Str. 25 | 3 (T/P) | LSt. Posen | Posen | |
| Krefeld | Ürdingerstr. 62 | 27647 | LSt. Düsseldorf | Düsseldorf | |
| Kremsier | Graben 5 | | LSt. Brünn | Prag | |
| Laak a.d. Zaier | Hauptpl. 10 | 29 | KdS. Veldes | Salzburg | |
| Landsberg/Warthe | | | St. Frankfurt/Oder | Berlin | |
| Landskron | Marcus-Marcis-Str. 3 | 90 (T/P) | St. Troppau | Breslau | |
| Leitmeritz | Lange Gasse 181 | 260 (T/P) | LSt. Reichenberg | Dresden | |
| Lentschütz | Hermann-Göring-Str. 25 | 110 | St. Litzmannstadt | Posen | |
| Leoben | Strasse der Sudetendeutschen 1 | 646 (T/P) | St. Graz | Salzburg | |
| Leslau | Hermann-Göring-Str. 12 | 1071 (T/P) | St. Litzmannstadt | Po sen | |
| Liegnitz | Am Schlosspl. 1 | 1931 (T/P) | LSt. Breslau | Breslau | Chief : *POI.* WAGNER (Until 1943 listed as *Stapot-Selle* for *Reg. Bez.* Liegnitz). |
| Limburg/Lahn | Erbach 2 | 618 | St. Frankfurt/Main | Wiesbaden | |
| Lissa/Warthe | Hermann-Göring-Str. 3 | 214 (T/P) | LSt. Posen | Posen | |
| Littai | Amtsgerichts-gebäude | 16 | KdS. Veldes | Salzburg | |
| Lötzen | Angerburgerstr. (Behördenhaus) | 429 (T/P) | LSt. Königsberg | Königsberg | |
| Lüneburg | Julius-Wolff-Str. 4 | 5051 (T/P) | LSt. Hamburg | Hamburg | Chief : *SS-HSF, KR.* WESTERMANN (Until 1943 listed as *Stapo-Stelle* for *Reg Bez.* Lüneburg) |
| Ludwigshafen/Rhein | Grüner Hof 21 | 67616 | St. Saarbrücken | Metz | Former address : Uhland-str. 7, Tel : 61921 (T/P). |
| Mährisch-Ostrau | Am Heumarkt 1 | 2345 Ext. 288 (T/P) | LSt. Brünn | Prag | |
| Mähr. Schönberg | Hermann-Göring-Pl. 4 | 444 (T/P) | St. Troppau | Breslau | |
| Mähr. Weisskirchen | | | LSt. Brünn | Prag | |
| Mainz | Kaiserstr. 31 | 30047/48 (T/P) | St. Darmstadt | Wiesbaden | |
| Malchin | | | St. Schwerin | Stettin | |
| Mannheim | B 7, 3 | 41921 (T/P) | LSt. Karlsruhe | Wiesbaden | Former address : Karl-Ludwig-Str. 7 (T/P) discontinued. |
| Marienbad | Morgenzeile, Haus " Zity " | 2009 (T/P) | St. Karlsbad | Nürnberg | |
| Marienwerder | Regierungsgebäude | 2341 (T/P) | LSt. Danzig | Danzig | |
| Markt Eisenstein—see Eisenstein | | | | | |
| Meppen | Friedrichstr. 16 | 393 (T/P) | LSt. Münster or St. Bremen | Hamburg | |
| Merseburg | Karl-Str. 28 | 2121 | St. Halle | Dresden | |
| Merzig/Saar | Bahnhofstr. 15 | 8 | St. Saarbrücken | Metz | |
| Meschede | Arnsbergerstr. 2 | 775 (T/P) | St. Dortmund | Düsseldorf | |
| Mies | Ebererstr. 13 | 165 (T/P) | St. Karlsbad | Nürnberg | |
| Militsch | Andreasstr. 3 | 323 (T/P) | LSt. Breslau | Breslau | |
| Mosbach | | | LSt. Karlsruhe | Wiesbaden | Classification unidentified |
| Mülhausen/Elsass | Hermann-Cossmann-Str. 29 | 4221 (T/P) | BdS. Strassburg | Strassburg | |
| Mülheim/Ruhr | vom Bockstr. 15 | 44221 | LSt. Düsseldorf | Düsseldorf | |

F13

| Town | Address | Tel. (Existence of Teleprinter is indicated by "(T/P)") | Branch Office of : | BdS or IdS | Remarks |
|---|---|---|---|---|---|
| München-Gladbach/ Rheydt | Dietrich-Eckardt-str. 3 | 23456 | LSt. Düsseldorf | Düsseldorf | |
| Neidenburg | Behördenhaus | 318 (T/P) | LSt. Königsberg | Königsberg | |
| Neisse | Edgar-Müller-Str. 1 | 2120 | St. Oppeln | Breslau | |
| Neumünster | Wandsbeckerstr. 8 | 2700 (T/P) | St. Kiel | Hamburg | |
| Neunkirchen/ Saar | Falkensteinstr. 11 | 2755 | St. Saarbrücken | Metz | |
| Neustadt/OS. | Hoher Weg. 1 | 581 | St. Oppeln | Breslau | |
| Neustadt/ Weinstr. | Luitpoldstr. 10 | 2747 (T/P) | St. Saarbrücken | Metz | Chief : KK LICKLEDER Predecessor : KK. KAPEL (Until 1943 listed as Stapo-Stelle for Reg. Bez. Pfalz) |
| Neustettin | Schlosstr. 6 | 888 (T/P) | LSt. Stettin | Stettin | |
| Neustrelitz | Augusta-Pl. 3 | 393 | St. Schwerin | Stettin | |
| Neutitschein | Prorokgasse 8 | 175 (T/P) | St. Troppau | Breslau | |
| Nienburg/ Weser | Moltkestr. 11 | 465 (T/P) | LSt. Hannover | Braunschweig | |
| Nordhorn | | | LSt. Hannover | Düsseldorf | |
| Oberhausen | Adolf-Hitler-Pl. 2 | 24221 | LSt. Düsseldorf | Düsseldorf | |
| Oberndorf/ Neckar | Kameralstr. 20 | 303 (T/P) | LSt. Stuttgart | Stuttgart | |
| Offenbach/ Main | Kaiserstr. 88 | 80321 | St. Darmstadt | Kassel | Suspended |
| Offenburg/ Baden | Weingartenstr. 6 | 1301 (T/P) | LSt. Karlsruhe | Stuttgart | |
| Oldenburg/ Holst. | Lankenstr. 4 | 463 | St. Kiel | Hamburg | |
| Oldenburg/O. | Heiligengeiststr. 26 | 5544 (T/P) | St. Bremen | Hamburg | |
| Olmütz | Strasse Karls IV, 44 | 1200, 1400 Ext. 351/2 (T/P) | LSt. Brünn | Prag | |
| Ortelsburg | Rathaus | | LSt. Königsberg | Königsberg | |
| Osnabrück | Schloss, Str. d. SA (Former address : Schillerstr. 9) | 4341 (T/P) | LSt. Münster or St. Bremen | Hamburg | Chief : SS-HSF, Reg. Ass. RASCHER. Predecessor SS-SBF, KR. BACH (Until 1943 listed as Stapo-Stelle for Reg. Bez. Osnabrück |
| Paderborn | Ferdinandstr. 62a | 3290 (T/P) | LSt. Münster | Düsseldorf | |
| Pardubitz | Viktoriapl. 12 | 3112, 3281 (T/P) | LSt. Prag | Prag | |
| Pettau | Ungartorgasse 5a | 106 | KdS. Marburg | Salzburg | |
| Pforzheim | | | LSt. Karlsruhe | Stuttgart | Classification unidentified |
| Pilsen | Deutsches Ufer 12 (Deutsches Behörden Haus) | 2280/81 (T/P) | LSt. Prag | Prag | |
| Plauen/ Vogtland | Rähnisstr. 74 | 4940/42 (T/P) | St. Chemnitz | Dresden | Chief : SS-HSF, KLEIN Predecessor, KK. BOLTZ (Until 1943 listed as Stapo-Stelle for Reg. Bez. Zwickau). |
| Polstrau | Nr. 118 | 3 | KdS. Marburg | Salzburg | |
| Prävali | Nr. 37 | 18 | St. Klagenfurt | Salzburg | |
| Prerau | Machagasse 14 | 534 (T/P) | LSt. Brünn | Prag | |
| Prossnitz | Rejeekgasse 30 | | LSt. Brünn | Prag | |
| Prüm | Hahnstr. 6 | 388 | St. Koblenz | Wiesbaden | |
| Radmannsdorf | Megertstr. 4 | 522 | KdS. Veldes | Salzburg | |
| Rann | Adolf-Hitler-Str. 49 | 11 | KdS. Marburg | Salzburg | |
| Rastatt | | | LSt. Karlsruhe | Stuttgart | Classification unidentified |
| Rastenburg/ Ostpr. | Hotel Königsberg | 518 (T/P) | LSt. Königsberg | Königsberg | |
| Ratibor | Wilhelmstr. 13 | 2028 (T/P) | St. Oppeln | Breslau | Chief : KOS PRESS |
| Recklinghausen | Westerholterweg 27 | 4343 (T/P) | LSt. Münster | Düsseldorf | |
| Remscheid | Uhlandstr. 1 | 46033 | LSt. Düsseldorf | Düsseldorf | |
| Rippin/ Westpr. | Adolf-Hitler-Pl. 4 | 25 (T/P) | St. Bromberg | Danzig | |
| Rosenberg/OS. | Schönwälderstr. 15 | 411 | St. Oppeln | Breslau | |
| Rybnik | Grünstr. 5 | 8 (T/P) | LSt. Kattowitz | Breslau | |
| Saarburg | Bahnhofstr. 3 | 415/16 (T/P) | BdS. Metz | Metz | |
| Saargemünd | Maiglöckchenstr. 37 | 32 | BdS. Metz | Metz | |
| Saarlautern | Kaiser-Friedrich-Ring 12 | | St. Saarbrücken | Wiesbaden | Identified as Stapo-Aussenstelle |
| Saaz | Konrad-Henlein-Str. 1262 | 238 (T/P) | St. Karlsbad | Nürnberg | |
| Sagan | Nieder-Herrenmühle | | LSt. Breslau | Breslau | Classification unidentified |
| Salzgitter | Otto-Planetta-Str. 14 | 701 | St. Braunschweig | Braunschweig | (Reichswerke Hermann Göring) |
| Samter | Bahnhofstr. 31 | 87 (T/P) | LSt. Posen | Posen | |
| Schieratz | Breslauer 21 | 25 (T/P) | St. Litzmannstadt | Posen | |

| Town | Address | Tel. (Existence of Teleprinter is indicated by "(T/P)") | Branch Office of : | BdS or IdS | Remarks |
|---|---|---|---|---|---|
| Schneidemühl | Danzigerpl. 7 | 2341, 2351 (T/P) | LSt. Stettin | Stettin | Chief : *KR.* WENZEL (Until 1943 listed as *Stapo-Stelle* for *Reg. Bez.* Schneidemühl) |
| Schönbrunn | Adolf-Hitler-Str. 661 | 225 | St. Troppau | Breslau | |
| Schwetz | Bismarckstr. 7 | 26 (T/P) | St. Bromberg | Danzig | Suspended |
| Schwiebus | Adolf-Hitler-Str. 8 | 595 (T/P) | St. Frankfurt/Oder | Berlin | |
| Siegen | Unteres Schloss (Landgerichts-gebäude) | 2474, 4764 (T/P) | St. Dortmund | Düsseldorf | |
| Sigmaringen | Hedingerstr. 2 | 564 | LSt. Stuttgart | Stuttgart | |
| Solingen | Felderstr. 27/29 | 21212 | LSt. Düsseldorf | Düsseldorf | |
| Soltau/ Hannover | Wiesenstr. 9 | 459 | LSt. Hamburg | Hamburg | |
| Sommerfeld | Stadtgraben 46 | 477 | St. Frankfurt/Oder | Berlin | |
| Sosnowitz | Hauptstr. 29 | Kattowitz 62125 (T/P) | LSt. Kattowitz | Breslau | |
| Spittal/Drau | Platz der Saarpfalz 7 | 260 | St. Klagenfurt | Salzburg | |
| St. Avold | Hermann-Göring-Str. 16 | 59 | KdS. Metz | Metz | |
| St. Ingbert/ Saar | | | St. Saarbrücken | Metz | Identified as *Stapo-Aussenstelle* |
| St. Pölten | Linzerstr. 47 | 601, 683 (T/P) | LSt. Wien | Wien | |
| Stade/Elbe | Gründelstr. 8 | 2002 | St. Bremen | Hamburg | |
| Stadt des KdF Wagens (near Fallersleben) | Unter den Eichen 48–50 | Braunschweig 2484 (T/P) | LSt. Hamburg | Hamburg | |
| Stavenhagen | | | St. Schwerin | Stettin | |
| Stein | Hermann-Göring-Str. 10 | 29 | KdS. Veldes | Salzburg | |
| Steyr | Volksstr. 5 | 826 | St. Linz/Donau | Wien | |
| Stolp/Pommern | Wasserstr. 12 | 2628 (T/P) | LSt. Stettin | Stettin | |
| Suhl | Bahnhofstr. 2 | 2601 | St. Weimar | Kassel | |
| Tabor | Königgrätzerstr. 1631 | 340 (T/P) | LSt. Prag | Prag | |
| Teplitz-Schönau | Dux-Teplitz Hermann-Göring-Str. 54 | 2829 (T/P) | LSt. Reichenberg | Dresden | |
| Thorn | Hermann-Göring-Str. 39 | 2301/04 (T/P) | St. Bromberg | Danzig | |
| Torgau | Leipzigerstr. (Rathaus) | 880 | St. Halle/Salle | Dresden | |
| Trautenau | Fichtestr. 10 | 26 (T/P) | LSt. Reichenberg | Dresden | |
| Trier | Christophstr. 1 | 2255 (T/P) | St. Koblenz | Wiesbaden | Chief : *KDIR.* WENDLING Predecessor : *SS-OSBF, ORR.* HARTMANN (Trsfd. to R.S.H.A.) (Until 1943 listed as *Stapo-Stelle* for *Reg. Bez.* Trier) |
| Tübingen | — | — | LSt. Stuttgart | Stuttgart | Classification unidentified |
| Ulm/Donau | Münster-Pl. 47 (Neuer Bau) | 3198 (T/P) | LSt. Stuttgart | Stuttgart | |
| Ung. Hradisch | Komenskypl. 539 | 227 (T/P) | LSt. Brünn | Prag | |
| Velbert | Königstr. 26 | 2758/9 | LSt. Düsseldorf | Düsseldorf | |
| Verden/Aller. | Herrlichkeit 4 | 504 | St. Bremen | Hamburg | |
| Villingen | Bickenstr. 24 | | LSt. Karlsruhe | Stuttgart | Classification unidentified. |
| Waldenburg | Anlaufstr. 2 (Pol. Präs.) | 1740 Ext. 42 (T/P) | LSt. Breslau | Breslau | |
| Wandsbeck, nr. Hamburg | Löwenstr. 25 | Hamburg 288851 Ext. 3158 | LSt. Hamburg | Hamburg | Suspended, see *LSt* Hamburg |
| Warnsdorf | Lichtensteinerstr. 2380 | 84 (T/P) | LSt. Reichenberg | Dresden | |
| Watenstedt | Betonstr. | Barum 5201/ 02, (T/P) | St. Braunschweig | Braunschweig | (*Reichswerke* Hermann Göring—see also Salzgitter) |
| Wesermünde | Hohenzollernring 1 | 4240/43 (T/P) | St. Bremen | Hamburg | Chief : *KR.* HILMER (Until 1943 listed as *Stapo-Stelle* for *Reg. Bez.* Stade) |
| Wetzlar | Hausertorstr. 42 | 2539 | St. Frankfurt/ Main | Kassel | |
| Wiener Neustadt | Promenade 1 | 475, 498 (T/P) | LSt. Wien | Wien | |
| Wiesbaden | Paulinenstr. 9 | 21641/2 (T/P) | St. Frankfurt/ Main | Wiesbaden | |
| Wilhelmshaven | Am Rathauspl. 4 | 5391/93 (T/P) | St. Bremen | Hamburg | Chief : *SS-HSF, KR. Dr.* FROHMANN (Until 1943 listed as *Stapo-Stelle* for *Land* Oldenburg and *Reg. Bez.* Aurich) |
| Wittenberg | Lutherstr. 17a | 3251 | St. Halle/Saale | Dresden | |

| Town | Address | Tel. (Existence of Teleprinter is indicated by " (T/P )") | Branch Office of : | BdS or IdS | Remarks |
|---|---|---|---|---|---|
| Wittenberge | Rathaus | 405 | *St.* Potsdam | Berlin | |
| Wittlich | Kurfürstenstr. 43 | 161 | *St.* Koblenz | Wiesbaden | |
| Woldenberg/ Neumark | Am Markt 4 | 339 | *LSt.* Stettin | Stettin | |
| Wsetin | Adolf-Hitler-Pl. 31 | 265-(T/P) | *LSt.* Brünn | Prag | |
| Würzburg | Ludwigsstr. 7 | 2928, 2920 (T/P) | *LSt.* Nürnberg | Nürnberg | Chief : *SS-SBF, KR.* HEISIG (Until 1943 listed as *Stapostelle* for *Reg. Bez.* Mainfranken) |
| Wuppertal | Adolf-Hitler-Str. 390 | 21101 (T/P) | *LSt.* Düsseldorf | Düsseldorf | |
| Zeitz | Kramerstr. 5b | 2233 | *St.* Halle/Saale | Dresden | Suspended |
| Zichenau | Paul-Sohnstr. 5 | 566 (T/P) | *St.* Zichenau/ Schröttersburg | Königsberg | Former Address : Marktstr. 4 |
| Znaim | Am Ausblick 4 | 149 (T/P) | *LSt.* Wien | Wien | |
| Zossen | Rathaus | 540 | *St.* Potsdam | Berlin | |
| Zwickau/Sa. | Konradstr. 5 | 5141 (*Pol. Präs.*) (T/P) | *St.* Chemnitz | Dresden | |

# ANNEXE F: PART FOUR

## GRENZPOLIZEI

## (Frontier Police)

### (a) STAPO-GRENZPOLIZEI-KOMMISSARIATE
### (Frontier Police Commissariats)

| Town | Address | Tel. (Existence of Teleprinter is indicated by " (T/P) ") | Branch Office of : | BdS or IdS | Controlling the Branch Offices (Grepo) : |
|---|---|---|---|---|---|
| Aachen | Theaterplatz 14 | 27511 (T/P) | St. Köln | Düsseldorf | Aachen-Westbahnhof, Horbach, Vaalser-quartier. |
| Bentheim | Bahnhofstr. 21 | 328 (T/P) | LSt. Münster | Düsseldorf | Bahnhof Bentheim, Nord-horn-Frensdorferhaar, Springbiel. |
| Böhm. Leipa | | | LSt. Reichenberg | Dresden | |
| Borken-Westf. | Bocholter Str. 43 | 566 | LSt. Münster | Düsseldorf | Bocholt-Hemden, Borken-Bahnhof. |
| Bregenz | Römerstr. 7 | 491,291 (T/P) | St. Innsbruck | Salzburg | Feldkirch, Höchst, Lustenau. |
| Bremen-Hafen | Überseehafen Nr. 15 (Amtsge-bäude) | 82941/2 | St. Bremen | Hamburg | |
| Brenner (-Gries) | | Gries 8 (T/P) | St. Innsbruck | Salzburg | Brenner-Bahnhof, Bren-ner-Strasse, Nauders. |
| Cilli | Grabengasse 2 | 159 (T/P) | KdS. Marburg | Salzburg | |
| Cuxhaven | Lehmkuhle 2 | 3552 (T/P) | St. Bremen | Hamburg | |
| Eisenstadt | Landhaus | 65 (T/P) | LSt. Wien | Wien | Bruck-Leitha, Kittsee, Sauerbrunn and Nst. Zwettl. |
| Emden | Hint. d. Rahmen 13 | 3656 (T/P) | St. Bremen | Hamburg | Bundemeuland, Emden-Aussenhafen, Weener. |
| Emmerich | van Gülpenstr. 1 | 2190 (T/P) | LSt. Düsseldorf | Düsseldorf | Emmerich-Bahnhof, Em-merich-Hafen, Elten-Babberich, Lobith. |
| Eupen | Lascheterfeld 4 | 1747 (T/P) | St. Köln | Düsseldorf | Baelen, Heinrichskapelle, Herbesthal-Bahnhof. |
| Eydtkau (Eydtkuhnen) | Bahnhofsgebäude | 470 (T/P) | St. Tilsit | Königsberg | Schirwindt |
| Flensburg | Norderhofenden 1 (Pol.-Präs.) | 2590 (T/P) | St. Kiel | Hamburg | Böglum, Flensburg-Bahn-hof, Flensburg-Hafen, Harrislee-Land, Kupfer-mühle, Süderlügum, and Nst. Niebüll. |
| Friedrichshafen Bodensee | Friedrichstr. 87 (T/P) | 796, 2217 | LSt. Stuttgart | Stuttgart | |
| Fürstenfeld | Schlagelhofstr. 12 | 165 (T/P) | St. Graz | Salzburg | Hl. Kreuz i.L., Jenners-dorf, Rechnitz. |
| Gablonz | | | LSt. Reichenberg | Dresden | |
| Gotenhafen | Prinz-Eugen-Str. 8/10 | 2971 (T/P) | LSt. Danzig | Danzig | Gotenhafen-Hafen, Hela-heide, Danzig-Hafen. |
| Gronau/Westf. | Enscheder Str. 43 | 395 (T/P) | LSt. Münster | Düsseldorf | Glanerbrücke, Gronau-Bahnhof. |
| Hamburg | Johannisbollwerk 19 | 365851 | LSt. Hamburg | Hamburg | |
| Heinsberg/ Rheinld. | Hochstr. 121 | 285 (T/P) | St. Köln | Düsseldorf | Dalheim, Tüddern. |
| Herzogenrath | Aachener Str. 20 | 330 (T/P) | St. Köln | Düsseldorf | Herzogenrath-Aachener Str., Herzogenrath-Bahn-hof, Kohlscheid. |
| Kaldenkirchen/ Rheinld. | Königspfad 18 | 413 (T/P) | LSt. Düsseldorf | Düsseldorf | Kaldenkirchen-Bahnhof, Kaldenkirchen-Schwan-enhaus. |
| Kehl | | | LSt. Karlsruhe | Stuttgart | |
| Kiel | Düppelstr. 23 | 8790 (T/P) | St. Kiel | Hamburg | Brunsbüttelkoog, Holt-enau-Schleuse, Wester-land/Sylt, Laboe. |
| Kleve | Nassauer Allee 5 | 2520 (T/P) | LSt. Düsseldorf | Düsseldorf | Kranenburg-Bahnhof, Wyler-Wylerberg, Gel-dern, Goch. |
| Kolberg | | | LSt. Stettin | Stettin | |
| Konstanz | Mainaustr. 29 | 1510/11 (T/P) | LSt. Karlsruhe | Stuttgart | Konstanz-Kreuzlingertor. |
| Krainburg | Götheplatz 2 | 241 | KdS. Veldes | Salzburg | Laas/Save, Ratschach-Matten, St. Veit/Save, Wochein-Feistritz. |
| Krummau/ Moldau | Villa Spirc | | St. Linz/Donau | Wien | |
| Kutno/Posen | Graf-Spee-Str. 14 | 108 (T/P) | St. Litzmannstadt | Posen | Kutno-Bahnhof. |
| Landau/Pfalz | | | St. Saarbrücken | Metz | |
| Leibnitz | Bahnhofstr. 24 | 108 | St. Graz | Salzburg | Radkersburg, Mureck, Spielfeld and Nst. Eibiswalde. |

F17

C

| Town | Address | Tel. (Existence of Teleprinter is indicated by " (T/P) ") | Branch Office of : | BdS or IdS | Controlling the Branch Offices (Grepo) : |
|---|---|---|---|---|---|
| Lienz/Drau | Iselquai, Schweizer-gasse 2 | 202 (T/P) | St. Klagenfurt | Salzburg | Sillian. |
| Loben | Goethestr. 2 | 5 (T/P) | St. Oppeln | Breslau | Blachstädt. |
| Lörrach | Adolf-Hitler-Str. 120 | 2247 (T/P) | LSt. Karlsruhe | Stuttgart | Lörrach-Stetten/Strasse, Lörrach-Stetten/Bahnhof, Grenzacherhorn, Weil/Rhein. |
| Lübeck | Skagerrakufer | 25061 (T/P) | St. Kiel | Hamburg | Lübeck-Hafen, Lübeck-Travemünde and Nst. Neustadt/Holstein. |
| Lublinitz | | | St. Oppeln | Breslau | |
| Lundenburg | Adolf-Hitler-Platz 9 | 26 (T/P) | LSt. Wien | Wien | Lundenburg-Bahnhof. |
| Luxemburg | Petrusring 57 | 6786/88 | KdS. Luxemburg | Wiesbaden | Kleinbettingen, Rodingen, Steinfort. |
| Lyck | Kreishaus | 384 | LSt. Königsberg | Königsberg | |
| Malmedy | Hindenburgstr. 91 | 84 (T/P) | St. Köln | Düsseldorf | |
| Memel | Herderstr. 33/4 | 2175 (T/P) | St. Tilsit | Königsberg | Bajohren-Krottingen, Memel-Hafen. |
| Meppen | Friedrichstr. 16 | 393 (T/P) | LSt. Münster | Düsseldorf | |
| Metz | Adolf-Hitler-Str. 42 | 1330 | KdS. Metz | Metz | Almansweiler, Elfringen, Laubweiler, Mövern, Neuburg, Reichenthal, Vionville. |
| Modlin-Bugmünde | Freiheitsstr. 5 | Bugmünde 1 (T/P) | St. Zichenau | Königsberg | Modlin-Bahnhof, Ostenburg. |
| Müllheim/Baden | | | LSt. Karlsruhe | Stuttgart | |
| Nordenham | Hafenstr. 26 | 2181 (T/P) | St. Bremen | Hamburg | |
| Oldenburg/O | | | St. Bremen | Hamburg | |
| Ortelsburg | | | LSt. Königsberg | Königsberg | |
| Ostrolenka | | | St. Zichenau | Königsberg | |
| Pillau | Predigerstr. 6 | 437 (T/P) | LSt. Königsberg | Königsberg | |
| Rostock | Kaiser-Friedrich-Str. 8 | 7101 (T/P) | St. Schwerin | Stettin | Warnemünde |
| Saaz | Konrad-Henlein-Str. 38 | | St. Karlsbad | Nürnberg | |
| Scharfenwiese | v. Ribbentrop-Str. 70 | 34 (T/P) | St. Zichenau | Königsberg | |
| Schwiebus | Adolf-Hitler-Str. 8 | 595 (T/P) | St. Frankfurt/Oder | Berlin | |
| Singen/Hohentwiel | Robert-Wagner-Str. 60 | 2635 (T/P) | LSt. Karlsruhe | Stuttgart | Singen-Bahnhof, Gottmadingen-Bahnhof. |
| Stettin | Gr. Lastadie 101 | 35231 Ext. 8377 | LSt. Stettin | Stettin | |
| Stolp/Pommern | Wasserstr. 12 | 2628 (T/P) | LSt. Stettin | Stettin | Stolpmünde. |
| Stralsund | Alter Markt 4 | 1266 (T/P) | LSt. Stettin | Stettin | Sassnitz. |
| Sudauen | Adolf-Hitler-Str. 128 | 7 (T/P) | St. Tilsit | Königsberg | |
| Swinemünde | Hardenbergstr. 4 | 2159, 2688 (T/P) | LSt. Stettin | Stettin | |
| Teschen | Schillerstr. 8 | 1424/5 (T/P) | LSt. Kattowitz | Breslau | Mosty. |
| Tilsit | SA-Strasse 67 | 2991 (T/P) | St. Tilsit | Königsberg | Laugszargen-Tauroggen, Schmalleningken. |
| Villach | Adolf-Hitler-Pl. 7 | 5917 (T/P) | St. Klagenfurt | Salzburg | Arnoldstein, Thörl-Maglern. |
| Waldshut | Bahnhof Str. 21 | 457/8 | LSt. Karlsruhe | Stuttgart | Waldshut-Brücke, Erzingen. |
| Welun | Urbacher Str. 17 | 157 | St. Litzmannstadt | Posen | Litzmannstadt. |
| Wien | 1, Morzinpl. 4 | A 17580 | LSt. Wien | Wien | Aspern, Engerau, Marchegg, Wien-Reichsbrücke. |
| Zlin | Internat I | 401 (T/P) | LSt. Brünn | Prag | Bila, Bilnitz, Göding, Landshut, Oberlitsch. |

| Town | Address | Tel. (Existence of Teleprinter is indicated by " (T/P) ") | Controlled by *Greko* : | *LSt.* or *St.* | *BdS* or *IdS* |
|---|---|---|---|---|---|
| Aachen-Westbahnhof | | 27511 Ext. 258 | Aachen | *St.* Köln | Düsseldorf |
| Almansweiler | | 14 | Metz | *KdS.* Metz | Metz |
| Altmünsterol | Haus Nr. 47 | 3 (T/P) | — | — | Strassburg |
| Arnoldstein | Bahnhof | 5 | Villach | *St.* Klagenfurt | Salzburg |
| Aspern (Airport) | Flughafen | F 22122 | Wien | *LSt.* Wien | Wien |
| Baelen | Vervierser Str. | Eupen 1791 | Eupen | *St.* Köln | Düsseldorf |
| Bajohren-Krottingen | | Dt. Krottingen No. 31 | Memel | *St.* Tilsit | Königsberg |
| Bentheim | Bahnhofsgebäude | | Bentheim | *LSt.* Münster | Düsseldorf |
| Berlin-Tempelhof | Flughafen | 669111 | — | *LSt.* Berlin | Berlin |
| Bila | Nr. 325 | Alt-Hammer 15 | Zlin | *LSt.* Brünn | Prag |
| Bilnitz | Nr. 408 | St.-Sidonia 3 | Zlin | *LSt.* Brünn | Prag |
| Blachstädt | Lobener Str. | 28 | Loben | *St.* Oppeln | Breslau |
| Blumenbach | | | | *LSt.* Brünn | Prag |
| Bocholt-Hemden | Zollamt Hemden | 3198 | Borken/Westf. | *LSt.* Münster | Düsseldorf |
| Böglum | Zollamtsgebäude | Süderlügum 171 | Flensburg | *St.* Kiel | Hamburg |
| Borken | Bahnhof | 427 | Borken | *LSt.* Münster | Düsseldorf |
| Brenner-Bahnhof | Bahnhofsgebäude | Gries 8 | Brenner | *St.* Innsbruck | Salzburg |
| Brenner-Strasse | Amtsgeb. | Gries 8 | Brenner | *St.* Innsbruck | Salzburg |
| Bruck/Leitha | Str. d. 11. März 6 | 102 | Eisenstadt | *LSt.* Wien | Wien |
| Brunsbüttelkoog | Schleusengelände | 412 | Kiel | *St.* Kiel | Hamburg |
| Bunderneuland | — | Bunde 251 | Emden | *St.* Bremen | Hamburg |
| Dalheim | Bahnhof | 40 | Heinsberg/Rheinld. | *St.* Köln | Düsseldorf |
| Danzig-Hafen | Danzig-Neufahrwasser, Schleusenstr. 18 | 35319 | Gotenhafen | *LSt.* Danzig | Danzig |
| Devau-Flughafen | Richthofenstr. | 34011 | — | *LSt.* Königsberg | Königsberg |
| Eibiswalde (Nst.) | Adolf-Hitler-Pl. 23 | 26 | Leibnitz | *St.* Graz | Salzburg |
| Elfringen | — | 6 (T/P) | Metz | *KdS* Metz | Metz |
| Elten-Babberich | Zeveaerstr. | Elten 307 | Emmerich | *LSt.* Düsseldorf | Düsseldorf |
| Emden-Aussenhafen | — | 8130 | Emden | *St.* Bremen | Hamburg |
| Emmerich-Bahnhof | — | 2190 Ext. 15 | Emmerich | *LSt.* Düsseldorf | Düsseldorf |
| Emmerich-Hafen | Wassertor 6 | 2190 Ext. 18 | Emmerich | *LSt.* Düsseldorf | Düsseldorf |
| Engerau | Rosengasse 10 | 4 (T/P) | Wien | *LSt.* Wien | Wien |
| Erzingen | Hauptstr. | Griessen 337 | Waldshut | *LSt.* Karlsruhe | Stuttgart |
| Feldkirch | Reichsstr. 152 | 259 (T/P) | Bregenz | *St.* Innsbruck | Salzburg |
| Flensburg-Bahnhof | Reichsbahnhof | 2590 | Flensburg | *St.* Kiel | Hamburg |
| Flensburg-Hafen | Fördebrücke | 2590 | Flensburg | *St.* Kiel | Hamburg |
| Gabergischken/Memel | Langallen | | | *St.* Tilsit | Königsberg |
| Gehlenburg/Ostpr. | | | | *LSt.* Königsberg | Königsberg |
| Geldern | | | Kleve | *LSt.* Düsseldorf | Düsseldorf |
| Glanerbrücke | Zollamt | Gronau 459 | Gronau/Westf. | *LSt.* Münster | Düsseldorf |
| Goch | | | Kleve | *LSt.* Düsseldorf | Düsseldorf |
| Göding | Smetanagasse 615 | 179 | Zlin | *LSt.* Brünn | Prag |
| Gotenhafen-Hafen | Wilhelmshavener Str. 5 | 3951 | Gotenhafen | *LSt.* Danzig | Danzig |
| Gottmadingen-Bahnhof | Personenbahnhof | Singen 2879 | Singen/Hohentwiel | *LSt.* Karlsruhe | Stuttgart |
| Grenzacherhorn | Basler Str. 24 | Grenzach 327 | Lörrach | *LSt.* Karlsruhe | Stuttgart |
| Gronau-Bahnhof | Zollamt Bahnhof | Gronau 313 | Gronau/Westf. | *LSt.* Münster | Düsseldorf |
| Harrislee-Land | Zollamtsgebäude | 2899 | Flensburg | *St.* Kiel | Hamburg |
| Helaheide | Insel Hela | — | Gotenhafen | *LSt.* Danzig | Danzig |
| Hl. Kreuz i.L. | Hauptstr. 81 | 4 | Fürstenfeld | *St.* Graz | Salzburg |
| Heinrichskapelle | Zollamt, Lütticher Str. | Herbesthal 25 | Eupen | *St.* Köln | Düsseldorf |
| Herbesthal | Bahnhof | 20 (T/P) | Eupen | *St.* Köln | Düsseldorf |
| Herzogenrath-Aachenerstr. | Zollamt | 330 | Herzogenrath | *St.* Köln | Düsseldorf |
| Herzogenrath-Bahnhof | Bahnsteig II | 657 | Herzogenrath | *St.* Köln | Düsseldorf |
| Höchst | Rheinau-Höchst Eichstr. 81 | 31 | Bregenz | *St.* Innsbruck | Salzburg |
| Holtenau-Schleuse | Schleusengelände | Holtenau 389 | Kiel | *St.* Kiel | Hamburg |
| Horbach | Hindenburgstr. 196a | Aachen 21140 | Aachen | *St.* Köln | Düsseldorf |
| Jennersdorf | Nr. 356 (Zentralamtsgebäude) | 47 | Fürstenfeld | *St.* Graz | Salzburg |
| Jonaten (über Heydekrug) | | | | *St.* Tilsit | Königsberg |
| Kaldenkirchen-Bahnhof | — | 413 | Kaldenkirchen/Rheinld. | *LSt.* Düsseldorf | Düsseldorf |
| Kaldenkirchen-Schwanenhaus | — | 413 | Kaldenkirchen/Rheinld. | *LSt.* Düsseldorf | Düsseldorf |
| Kittsee | Nr. 151 | 6 | Eisenstadt | *LSt.* Wien | Wien |
| Kleinbettingen | Bahnhof | 40 | Luxemburg | *KdS.* Luxemburg | Wiesbaden |
| Kohlscheid | Roermonder Str. 205 | 594 | Herzogenrath | *St.* Köln | Düsseldorf |
| Kolleschen | see Jonaten | | | | |
| Konstanz-Kreuzlingertor | Kreuzlinger Str. 70 | 1510 | Konstanz | *LSt.* Karlsruhe | Stuttgart |
| Kranenburg | Bahnhof | 374 | Kleve | *LSt.* Düsseldorf | Düsseldorf |

| Town | Address | Tel. (Existence of Teleprinter is indicated by "(T/P)") | Controlled by *Greko* : | *LSt.* or *St.* | *BdS* or *IdS* |
|---|---|---|---|---|---|
| Kupfermühle | Zollamtsgebäude | Flensburg 927 | Flensburg | *St.* Kiel | Hamburg |
| Kutno | Bahnhof | 298 | Kutno | *St.* Litzmannstadt | Posen |
| Lass/Save | Bahnhof | — | Krainburg | *KdS.* Veldes | Salzburg |
| Laboe/Schiffs-untersuchungs-kommando | Strandstr. | Kiel 8790 | Kiel | *St.* Kiel | Hamburg |
| Landshut | Nr. 777 | 16 (T/P) | Zlin | *LSt.* Brünn | Prag |
| Langallen | see Gabergischken | | | | |
| Laubweiler | — | Neuburg 15 | Metz | *KdS.* Metz | Metz |
| Laugszargen-Tauroggen | — | 13 | Tilsit | *St.* Tilsit | Königsberg |
| Litzmannstadt | Hauptbahnhof | 25270/77 | Welun | *St.* Litzmannstadt | Posen |
| Lobith | Boterdykstr. 140 | Elten 307 | Emmerich | *LSt.* Düsseldorf | Düsseldorf |
| Lörrach-Stetten/Strasse | Adolf-Hitler-Str. | Lörrach 2247 | Lörrach | *LSt.* Karlsruhe | Stuttgart |
| Lörrach-Stetten/Bahnhof | Adolf-Hitler-Str. 24 | Lörrach 2247 | Lörrach | *LSt.* Karlsruhe | Stuttgart |
| Lübeck-Hafen | Hafenstr. 2 | 25061 | Lübeck | *St.* Kiel | Hamburg |
| Lübeck-Trave-münde | Vorderreihe 8 | 907 | Lübeck | *St.* Kiel | Hamburg |
| Lundenburg | Bahnhof | 133 (T/P) | Lundenburg | *LSt.* Wien | Wien |
| Lustenau | Bahnhof | 333 (T/P) | Bregenz | *St.* Innsbruck | Salzburg |
| Marchegg | Bahnhofsgebäude | 51 | Wien | *LSt.* Wien | Wien |
| Memel-Hafen | Holzstr. 23 | 3025 | Memel | *St.* Tilsit | Königsberg |
| Modlin | Bahnhof | Bugmünde 1 | Modlin-Bugmünde | *St.* Zichenau | Königsberg |
| Mövern | — | 38 | Metz | *KdS.* Metz | Metz |
| Mosty | Hotel Beskidenhof | 13 | Teschen | *LSt.* Kattowitz | Breslau |
| München-Riem | Flughafen (Airport) | 473551/2 | — | *LSt.* München | München |
| Mureck | Adolf-Hitler-Pl. 36 | — | Leibnitz | *St.* Graz | Salzburg |
| Nauders | Amtsgebäude | 6 | Brenner | *St.* Innsbruck | Salzburg |
| Neuburg | — | 16 (T/P) | Metz | *KdS.* Metz | Metz |
| Neustadt/Holst. (Nst.) | Am Markt 7 | 566 | Lübeck | *St.* Kiel | Hamburg |
| Niebüll (Nst.) | Böhmstr. 18 | 318 (T/P) | Flensburg | *St.* Kiel | Hamburg |
| Niedersulzbach | — | 4 | — | | Strassburg |
| Nordhorn-Frensdorferhaar | Nordhorn, Str. d. SA 8 | 264 | Bentheim | *LSt.* Münster | Düsseldorf |
| Oberlitsch | Bahnhof | 10 | Zlin | *LSt.* Brünn | Prag |
| Ostenburg | Martin-Nigglstr. 15 | 40 | Modlin-Bugmünde | *St.* Zichenau | Königsberg |
| Prag (-Flughafen) | Prag 54 Rusin | 002571 Ext. 259 | — | *LSt.* Prag | Prag. |
| Radkersburg | Grazer Torpl. 2 (Zollamt) | 51 | Leibnitz | *St.* Graz | Salzburg |
| Ratschach-Matten | Zolldienstgebäude | 4 | Krainburg | *KdS.* Veldes | Salzburg |
| Rechnitz | Bahnhofstr. 3 | 18 | Fürstenfeld | *St.* Graz | Salzburg |
| Reichenthal | — | Folkringen 5 | Metz | *KdS.* Metz | Metz |
| Rodingen | Bahnhofstr. 36 | 9150 | Luxemburg | *KdS.* Luxemburg | Wiesbaden |
| Saal | Hauptstr. 10 | 25 (T/P) | — | | Strassburg |
| Sassnitz | Hafenbahnhof | 327 (T/P) | Stralsund | *LSt.* Stettin | Stettin |
| Sauerbrunn | Kirchengasse 10 | 5 | Eisenstadt | *LSt.* Wien | Wien |
| Schirwindt (Krs. Schlossberg) | Leopold-Birmann-Str. | 58 | Eydtkau | *St.* Tilsit | Königsberg |
| Schmalleningken | — | 11 | Tilsit | *St.* Tilsit | Königsberg |
| Sillian | Sillian 26 | 17 | Lienz | *St.* Klagenfurt | Salzburg |
| Singen | Bahnhof (Personenbhf.) | 2635 | Singen/Hohentwiel | *LSt.* Karlsruhe | Stuttgart |
| Spielfeld | Bahnhof | 2 | Leibnitz | *St.* Graz | Salzburg |
| Springbiel | Grenzwachhaus | — | Bentheim | *LSt.* Münster | Düsseldorf |
| St. Veit/Save | Podgora 41 | 756 | Krainburg | *KdS.* Veldes | Salzburg |
| St. Ludwig | Rheinstr. 1a | 162 | — | | Strassburg |
| St. Veit/Save | Podgora 41 | 756 | Krainburg | *KdS.* Veldes | Salzburg |
| Steinfort | Grenzübergang Arel (Arlon) | 58 | Luxemburg | *KdS.* Luxemburg | Wiesbaden |
| Stolpmünde (Suspended) | Hitlerstr. 2 | 250 | Stolp | *LSt.* Stettin | Stettin |
| Stuttgart-Echterdingen | Flughafen (Airport) | 79435 | — | *LSt.* Stuttgart | Stuttgart |
| Süderlügum | Bahnhof | 179 | Flensburg | *St.* Kiel | Hamburg |
| Thörl-Maglern | Grenzzollstelle | 2 | Villach | *St.* Klagenfurt | Salzburg |
| Travemünde | see Lübeck | | | | |
| Tüddern | Grenzübergang | — | Heinsberg/Rheinld. | *St.* Köln | Düsseldorf |
| Vaalserquartier | Aachen-Land I Vaalser Landstr. | Aachen 21141 | Aachen | *St.* Köln | Düsseldorf |
| Vionville | — | Gravelotte 10 | Metz | *KdS.* Metz | Metz |
| Waldshut-Brücke | Zollstelle | 457 (T/P) | Waldshut | *LSt.* Karlsruhe | Stuttgart |
| Warnemünde | Fritz-Reuter-Str. 20 | 312 (T/P) | Rostock | *St.* Schwerin | Stettin |
| Warthenau | Hopfenstr. 14 | 72 | — | *St.* Oppeln | Breslau |
| Weener | Bahnhofsgebäude | 8119 | Emden | *St.* Bremen | Hamburg |
| Weil/Rhein Bahnhof | Bahnhofstr. 2 | 4230 (T/P) | Lörrach | *LSt.* Karlsruhe | Stuttgart |
| Welka/n. Strassnitz | | | | *St.* Brünn | Prag |
| Westerland/Sylt | Bomhoffstr. 22 | 271 (T/P) | Kiel | *St.* Kiel | Hamburg |
| Wien-Reichsbrücke | 2, Erzherzog-Karl-Pl. 2 | R 48238 | Wien | *LSt.* Wien | Wien |
| Wochein-Feistritz | Bahnhof | 712 | Krainburg | *KdS.* Veldes | Salzburg |
| Wyler-Wylerberg | — | Kranenburg 374 | Kleve | *LSt.* Düsseldorf | Düsseldorf |
| Zwettl (Nst.) | Landstr. 21 | 110 | Eisenstadt | *LSt.* Wien | Wien |

# ANNEXE F : PART FIVE

## GESTAPO PRISONS AND CAMPS

The following Penal Institutions, which are under immediate direction of the *Gestapo*, have been identified :

| Location | Designation | Address | Tel : (Existence of Teleprinter is indicated by " (T/P) ") | Under | *BdS* or *IdS* |
|---|---|---|---|---|---|
| Aistaig | see Oberndorf | | | | |
| Ankenstein, Schloss | Polizeigefängnis | St. Barbara i.d. Kollos | 3 | *KdS.* Marburg | Salzburg |
| Blechhammer | Arbeitserziehungslager | nr. Ehrenforst/OS. | 183 | *St.* Oppeln | Breslau |
| Farge | ditto | Bremen-Farge | 385 | *St.* Bremen | Hamburg |
| Fehrbellin | ditto | — | 142 | *St.* Potsdam | Berlin |
| Gross-Kunzendorf | ditto | nr. Mähr.-Ostrau | 3000, Ext. 21 | *LSt.* Brünn | Prag |
| Hägerwelle | ditto | Stettin-Pölitz | 28660 | *LSt.* Stettin | Stettin |
| Hinzert | ditto | nr. Beuren | 32 | *St.* Koblenz | Wiesbaden |
| Hohensalza | ditto | — | 2151, Ext. 65 | *LSt.* Posen | Posen |
| Hradischko | ditto | Post Stechowitz | Stechowitz 11 | *LSt.* Prag | Prag |
| Hunswinkel | ditto | nr. Lüdenscheid/Westf. | 4416 | *St.* Dortmund | Düsseldorf |
| Innsbruck-Reichenau (Nst.) | Auffanglager | Innsbruck | 2478 | *St.* Innsbruck | Salzburg |
| Miroschau | Arbeitserziehungslager | Bez. Pilsen-Land | 46 | *LSt.* Prag | Prag |
| Oberndorf-Aistaig | ditto | Oberndorf | 301 | *LSt.* Stuttgart | Stuttgart |
| Plan/Leinsitz | ditto | — | 27 | *LSt.* Prag | Prag |
| Posen-Lenzingen | ditto | nr. Poggenburg | 135 | *LSt.* Posen | Posen |
| Rattwitz | ditto | Krs. Ohlau | Markstaedt 228 | *LSt.* Breslau | Breslau |
| Rudersberg | ditto | nr. Schorndorf | 110 | *LSt.* Stuttgart | Stuttgart |
| Theresienstadt | Pol. Gefängnis | Kleine Festung | 14 (T/P) | *LSt.* Prag | Prag |
| Vigaun | ditto | Haus Nr. 17 | 560 | *KdS.* Veldes | Salzburg |
| Witkowitz | Arbeitserziehungslager | Eisenwerk Witkowitz | 3151, Ext. 2261 | *LSt.* Brünn | Prag |
| Zwischenwässern | Umsiedlungslager | Schloss Görtschach Nr. 1 | — | *KdS.* Veldes | Salzburg |

# ANNEXE F : PART SIX
## NAZI PARTY HONORARY ASSISTANTS TO THE SIPO
### (Ehrenamtliche Tätigkeit von Parteigenossen in der Sicherheitspolizei) —numbers called for by respective establishments (Aug. 1944)

| Headquarters of the Sipo. | Number of Nazi Party members to act as honorary (unpaid) Assistants. |
|---|---|
| BdS. Metz | 125 |
| BdS. Strassburg | 100 |
| Stapoleitst. Berlin | 200 |
| Stapost. Braunschweig | 50 |
| Stapost. Bremen | 100 |
| Stapoleitst. Breslau | 150 |
| Stapost. Bromberg | 50 |
| Stapoleitst. Brünn | 125 |
| Stapost. Chemnitz | 75 |
| Stapoleitst. Danzig | 75 |
| Stapost. Darmstadt | 75 |
| Stapost. Dortmund | 125 |
| Stapoleitst. Dresden | 100 |
| Stapoleitst. Düsseldorf | 200 |
| Stapost. Frankfurt/M. | 75 |
| Stapost. Frankfurt/O. | 50 |
| Stapost. Graz | 50 |
| Stapost. Halle | 75 |
| Stapoleitst. Hamburg | 100 |
| Stapoleitst. Hannover | 75 |
| Stapost. Innsbruck | 50 |
| Stapost. Karlsbad | 50 |
| Stapoleitst. Karlsruhe | 125 |
| Stapost. Kassel | 50 |
| Stapoleitst. Kattowitz | 150 |
| Stapost. Kiel | 75 |
| Stapost. Klagenfurt | 50 |
| Stapost. Koblenz | 75 |
| Stapost. Köln | 125 |
| Stapoleitst. Königsberg | 75 |
| Stapost. Leipzig | 75 |
| Stapost. Linz | 50 |
| Stapost. Litzmannstadt | 100 |
| Stapoleitst. Magdeburg | 100 |
| Stapoleitst. München | 150 |
| Stapoleitst. Münster | 150 |
| Stapoleitst. Nürnberg | 125 |
| Stapost. Oppeln | 75 |
| Stapoleitst. Posen | 125 |
| Stapost. Potsdam | 75 |
| Stapoleitst. Prag | 200 |
| Stapost. Regensburg | 75 |
| Stapoleitst. Reichenberg | 75 |
| Stapost. Saarbrücken | 100 |
| Stapost. Salzburg | 50 |
| Stapost. Schwerin | 50 |
| Stapoleitst. Stettin | 125 |
| Stapoleitst. Stuttgart | 125 |
| Stapost. Tilsit | 50 |
| Stapost. Troppau | 50 |
| Stapost. Weimar | 125 |
| Stapoleitst. Wien | 175 |
| Stapost. Zichenau | 50 |
| KdS. Bialystok | 75 |
| KdS. Krakau | 200 |
| KdS. Lemberg | 200 |
| KdS. Lublin | 100 |
| KdS. Marburg | 50 |
| KdS. Radom | 125 |
| KdS. Veldes | 50 |
| KdS. Warschau | 150 |
| **Total** | **6,025** |

# ANNEXE F : PART SEVEN

## COMMUNICATIONS

### (a) TELETYPE NETWORK OF THE SIPO AND SD

(1st August, 1941)

*Note :*—The following list may appear somewhat irregular but it adheres in every detail to the original German terminology and usage. Column one gives the official designation of the Headquarters (usually its geographical location but occasionally the name of the Office). Column two gives the type of office (abbreviated). When the name of the Headquarters is given in Column one the geographical location appears in Column two. Column three lists the exchanges which relay or furnish direct connection to the Headquarters listed in Column one. Headquarters listed by their former names rather than their recent designations are marked with an asterisk (*).

The original German list of abbreviations will be found at (c) of this part.

| Headquarters : | | Connecting or Relay Exchange : | Remarks : |
|---|---|---|---|
| Location, Official Designation and Classification : (*Dienststelle*) | (*Bezeichnung*) | (*Vermittlung*) | (*Bemerkung*) |
| Aachen, Nvst. | Stapost. | Koblenz | |
| Adjutantur des Chefs d. Sich. Pol. u. des SD. | | Hvst. Berlin | |
| Amsterdam | E.K. | Den Haag | |
| Arnheim | E.K. | Den Haag | |
| Allenstein, Nvst. | Stapost. | Königsberg | |
| Augsburg | Stapost. | München | |
| Auschwitz | KL. | Kattowitz | FS. an Stapost. Kattowitz |
| Agram | E.K. | Belgrad | |
| Auswärt. Amt | | Hvst. Berlin | |
| Antwerpen | E.K. | Vst. Brüssel | Hvst. Berlin |
| Aussig | ADSt. | Vst. Reichenberg | |
| Assen | ADSt. | Den Haag | |
| Athen | E.K. | Belgrad | |
| Bautzen | Stapo-ADSt. | Dresden | 7.30-19 Uhr |
| Bayreuth | SD-A. | Nürnberg | |
| Bentheim | Greko | Osnabrück | |
| Bergen | E.K. | Oslo | |
| Berlin | Stapoleitst. | Hvst. Berlin | |
| Beuthen | Stapo-ADSt. | Kattowitz | |
| Bielefeld | Stapost. | Dortmund | |
| Bonn | Stapo-ADSt. | Dortmund | |
| Bordeaux | E.K. | Paris | |
| Braunes Haus | München | München | |
| Braunschweig | Stapost. | Hannover | |
| Bregenz | Greko | Innsbruck | |
| Bremen | Stapost. | Hamburg | |
| Brennerstrasse | Grepo | Innsbruck | |
| Breslau | Stapoleitst. | Hvst. Berlin | Querv. nach **Krakau,** Posen, Dresden |
| Bromberg | Stapost. | Danzig | |
| Brünn, Nvst. | Stapoleitst. | Prag-Wien-Olmütz | |
| Brüssel | Beauftr. des Ch. d. SP. u. d. SD. | Hvst. Berlin | Querv. nach **Paris** u. Den Haag |
| Buchenwald | KL. | Hvst. Berlin | |
| Budweis | Stapo-ADSt. | Prag | |
| Bütow | Stapo-ADSt. | Köslin | |
| Bochum | ADSt. | Dortmund | |
| Bielitz | ADSt. | Kattowitz | |
| Belgrad | FSVerm. | Hvst. Berlin | |
| Celle | Stapo-ADSt. | Hannover | |
| Chalons-sur-Saone | E.K. | Dijon | Einton |
| Chemnitz | Stapost. | Dresden | |
| Cottbus | Stapo-ADSt. | Frankf./Od. | |
| Cuxhaven | Greko | Hamburg | |
| Charleroi | E.K. | Brüssel | |
| Cilli | Greko | Graz | |

| Headquarters: Location, Official Designation and Classification: (Dienststelle) | (Bezeichnung) | Connecting or Relay Exchange: (Vermittlung) | Remarks: (Bemerkung) |
|---|---|---|---|
| Dachau | KL. | München | |
| Danzig | Stapoleitst. | Hvst. Berlin | Querv. nach Königsberg u. Stettin |
| Danzig | SD-LA | Danzig | |
| Darmstadt | Stapost. | Frankf./M. | |
| Dessau | Stapost. | Hvst. Berlin | |
| Diedenhofen | E.K. | Metz | |
| Dijon | E.K. | Frankf./M. | |
| Donau | SD-LA. Wien | Wien | |
| Dortmund | Stapost. | Hvst. Berlin | Querv. nach Hamburg-Frankfurt/M-Koblenz |
| Dresden | Stapoleitst. | Hvst. Berlin | Querv. nach Reichenberg u. Breslau |
| Düsseldorf, Nvst. | Stapoleitst. | Dortmund | Querv. nach Osnabrück |
| Drontheim | E.K. | Oslo | |
| Dirschau | ADSt. | Danzig | |
| Dronhzim | | | NVSt. |
| Einwandererzentrale | Führungsstab Bln. | Hvst. Berlin | |
| Eisenstadt | Greko | Wien | |
| Eisenstein-Markt | Stapo-ADSt. | Regensburg | |
| Elbe | SD-LA. Dresden | Dresden | |
| Elbing | Stapo-ADSt. | Danzig | |
| Emden | Greko | Hamburg | |
| Emmerich | Greko | Dortmund | |
| Engerau | Grepo | Wien | |
| Erfurt | Stapost. | VSt. Weimar | |
| Essen | Stapo-ADSt. | Dortmund | |
| Eydtkau | Greko | Königsberg | |
| Enschede/Holl. | EK. ADSt. | NVSt. Den Haag | |
| Eger | ADSt. | Karlsbad | |
| Eupen | ASt. | Aachen | |
| FA | Forschungsamt | Hvst. Berlin | |
| Fehmarn (Burg) | Stapo-ADSt. | Hamburg | |
| Flensburg | Greko | Kiel | |
| Flossenbürg | KL. | NVSt. Regensburg | |
| Frankfurt/M. | Stapost. | Hvst. Berlin | Querv. nach Stuttgart, Dortmund, Koblenz, Neustadt, Paris |
| Feldkirch | Grenzpol. | Bregenz | |
| Frankfurt/Od. | Stapost. | Hvst. Berlin | |
| Freiburg-Breisgau | Stapo-ADSt. | Stuttgart | |
| Friedrichshafen | Greko | Stuttgart | |
| Fulda-Werra | SD-LA. Frankf./M. | Frankf./M. | |
| Gablonz | ADSt. | Reichenberg | |
| Gent | EK. ADSt. | Brüssel | |
| Gelsenkirchen | Stapo-ADSt. | Dortmund | |
| Giessen | Stapo-ADSt. | Frankf./M. | |
| Glatz | Stapo-ADSt. | Breslau | |
| Gleiwitz | Stapo-ADSt. | Kattowitz | |
| Glogau | Stapo-ADSt. | Breslau | |
| Gmund/Tegernsee | Dienststelle RFSS | München | |
| Görlitz | Stapo-ADSt. | Breslau | |
| Gotenhafen | Greko | Danzig | |
| Graz, Nvst. | Stapost. | Wien | |
| Graudenz | Stapost. | Danzig | |
| Grenzinspekteur I | Ost | Posen | FS. an Stapol. Posen |
| Grenzinspekteur II | Südost | Dresden | FS. an Stapol. Dresden |
| Grenzinspekteur III | West | Koblenz | FS. an Stapost. Koblenz |
| Groningen | EK. | Den Haag | |
| Grunewald | RSHA-Amt VI | Hvst. Berlin | |
| Gross-Rosen | E.L. | Breslau | |
| Gusen | KL. | Mauthausen | |
| Haag (Den Haag), Nvst. | BdSudSD. | Dortmund | Querv. nach Brüssel |
| Halle | Stapost. | Hvst. Berlin | |

| Headquarters: Location, Official Designation and Classification: (Dienststelle) | (Bezeichnung) | Connecting or Relay Exchange: (Vermittlung) | Remarks: (Bemerkung) |
|---|---|---|---|
| Hamburg | Stapoleitst. | Hvst. Berlin | Querv. nach Stettin, Dortmund |
| Hannover | Stapoleitst. | Hvst. Berlin | Querv. nach Hamburg |
| Hauptamt-SS | SS-Hauptamt | Hvst. Berlin | |
| Heeres-Gruppenkdo V | Wien (HWN) | Wien | |
| Heeresbetriebszentralamt | Berlin (HBZ) | Hvst. Berlin | |
| Heilbronn | Stapo-ADSt. | Stuttgart | |
| Heinsberg | Greko | Herzogenrath | Einton |
| Herzogenrath | Greko | Aachen | |
| Hildesheim | Stapost. | Hannover | |
| Hirschberg | Stapo-ADSt. | Breslau | |
| Hohensalza | Stapost. | Posen | |
| s'Hertogenbosch | EK. | Den Haag | |
| Herbesthal | ADSt. | Aachen | |
| Innsbruck, Nvst. | Stapost. | München | |
| Insp. d. SP. u. d. SD. | Braunschweig | Hannover | |
| Insp. d. SP. u. d. SD. | Berlin | Hvst. Berlin | |
| Insp. d. SP. u. d. SD. | Breslau | Breslau | |
| Insp. d. SP. u. d. SD. | Dresden | Dresden | |
| Insp. d. SP. u. d. SD. | Düsseldorf | Düsseldorf | |
| Insp. d. SP. u. d. SD. | Hamburg | Hamburg | |
| Insp. d. SP. u. d. SD. | Kassel | Kassel | |
| Insp. d. SP. u. d. SD. | Königsberg | Königsberg | |
| Insp. d. SP. u. d. SD. | München | München | |
| Insp. d. SP. u. d. SD. | Prag | Prag | |
| Insp. d. SP. u. d. SD. | Stettin | Stettin | |
| Insp. d. SP. u. d. SD. | Stuttgart | Stuttgart | |
| Insp. d. SP. u. d. SD. | Wien | Wien | |
| Insp. d. SP. u. d. SD. | Wiesbaden | Frankf./M. | |
| Insp. d. SP. u. d. SD. | Danzig | VSt. Danzig | |
| Insp. d. SP. u. d. SD. | Posen | VSt. Posen | |
| Insp. d. SP. u. d. SD. | Salzburg | VSt. Wien | |
| Iglau | ADSt. | Brünn | |
| Jitschin | ADSt. | Prag | |
| Jung-Bunzlau | ADSt. | Prag | |
| Kaldenkirchen | Greko | Düsseldorf | |
| Kaiserslautern | Stapo-ADSt. | Neustadt/W. | |
| Karlsbad, Nvst. | Stapost. | Dresden | Querv. nach Reichenberg |
| Kalisch | ADSt. | Posen | |
| Karlsruhe | Stapoleitst. | Neustadt/W.u. Stuttgart | |
| Kassel | Stapost. | FFM. | |
| Kattowitz | Stapost. | Breslau | |
| Kiel, Nvst. | Stapost. | Hamburg | |
| Klagenfurt Nvst. | Stapost. | Wien | |
| Koblenz | Stapost. | Hvst. Berlin | Querv. nach Frankf./M., Dortmund, Neustadt |
| Klattau | ADSt. | Prag | |
| Königshütte | ADSt. | NVSt. Kattowitz | |
| Kladno | ADSt. | Prag | |
| Kolin | Stapo-ADSt. | Prag | |
| Konstanz | Greko | Stuttgart | |
| Kommandeur SS-VT. | Oranienburg | Hvst. Berlin | |
| Kosten | Stapo-ADSt. | Posen | |
| Köln | Stapost. | Koblenz | |
| Königgrätz | Stapo-ADSt. | Pardubitz | |
| Königsberg | Stapoleitst. | Hvst. Berlin | Querv. nach Danzig |
| Köslin, Nvst. | Stapost. | Stettin | |
| Krakau | Komm. d. SP. u. d. SD. | Hvst. Berlin | Querv. nach Breslau |
| Krakau | Befehlsh. d. SP. u. d SD. | Krakau | |
| Kremsier | ADSt. | NSt. Olmütz | |
| Landsberg/W. | ADSt. | FFO. | |
| Lissa | ADSt. | Kosten | |
| Lille | ADSt. | Brüssel | |
| Lüttich | ADSt. | Brüssel | |
| Leibnitz | Greko | Graz | |
| Leipzig | Stapost. | Dresden | |

| Headquarters: Location, Official Designation and Classification: (*Dienststelle*) | (*Bezeichnung*) | Connecting or Relay Exchange: (*Vermittlung*) | Remarks: (*Bemerkung*) |
|---|---|---|---|
| Leitmeritz | ADSt. | Reichenberg | |
| Liegnitz | Stapost. | Breslau | |
| Lienz | Greko | Klagenfurt | |
| Linz | Stapost. | Wien | NVSt. |
| Litzmannstadt | Stapost. | Posen | |
| Litzmannstadt | EWZ. | Posen | |
| Lörrach | Greko | Stuttgart | |
| Lübeck | Greko | Kiel | |
| Lüneburg | Stapost. | Hamburg | |
| Lublin | Komm. d. SP. u. d. SD. | Krakau | |
| Lublinitz | Greko | Oppeln | |
| Ludwigshafen | Stapo-ADSt. | Neustadt/W. | |
| Lundenburg | Greko | Wien | |
| Luxemburg | E.K. | Trier | |
| Lyck | ADSt. | KBC. | |
| Leeuwarden | ADSt. | Den Haag. | |
| | | | |
| Malmedy | ADSt. | Aachen | |
| Mannheim | ADSt. | Neustadt | |
| Marburg | | Graz | |
| Mähr.-Ostrau | Stapo-ADSt. | Olmütz | |
| Magdeburg | Stapoleitst. | Hvst. Berlin | |
| Mainz | Stapo-ADSt. | Frankf./M. | |
| Marienwerder | Stapo-ADSt. | Danzig | |
| Markt Eisenstein | Stapo-ADSt. | NVSt. Regensburg | |
| Mauthausen | KL. | Wien-Linz | |
| Memel | Greko | Königsberg | |
| Meppen | Greko | Osnabrück | |
| Metz | Befehlsh. d. SP. u. d. SD. | FFM. | |
| Mies | Stapo-ADSt. | München | |
| Militsch | Stapo-ADSt. | Breslau | |
| Mülhausen | E.K. | Strassburg | |
| München | Stapoleitst. | Hvst. Berlin | Querv. nach Stuttgart u. Wien. |
| Münster | Stapoleitst. | Dortmund | |
| Middelburg | ADSt. | Den Haag | |
| Modlin | GPK. | Zichenau | |
| | | | |
| Narvik | ADSt. | Drontheim | |
| Nauheim (Bad) | Sonder-Kdo. | Frankf./M. | |
| Neuengamme | KL. | Hamburg | |
| Neustadt/W.,Nvst. | Stapost. | Stuttgart u. Frankf./M. | Querv. mit Saarbrücken |
| Niebüll | Grepo | Kiel | |
| Nord | SD-LA. Stettin | Stettin | |
| Nordenham | Greko | Hamburg | |
| Nordost | SD-LA. Königsberg | Königsberg | |
| Nordsee | SD-LA. Hamburg | Hamburg | |
| Nürnberg, Nvst. | Stapost. SDA. Franken | München | |
| Natzweiler | KL. | Strassburg | |
| Neustettin | SDA. | Köslin | |
| | | | |
| Oberndorf-Neckar | Stapo-ADSt. | Stuttgart | |
| Obersalzberg | Haus des Führers | München | |
| Offenbach/M. | Stapo-ADSt. | Frankf./M. | |
| Oldenburg/O. | Stapo-ADSt. | Hamburg | |
| Olmütz, Nvst. | Stapo-ADSt. | Prag u. Brünn | |
| Oppeln, Nvst. | Stapost. | Breslau | |
| Oranienburg | Kommand. SS-VT. | Hvst. Berlin | |
| Oslo | BdSP. u. d. SD. u. EK. | Hvst. Berlin | |
| Oslo | Höhere SS. u. Polf. | Oslo | |
| Oslo | Reichskommissar | Oslo | |
| Osnabrück, Nvst. | Stapost. | Hannover | |
| Ost | SD-LA. Berlin | Hvst. Berlin | |
| | | | |
| Paderborn | Stapo-ADSt. | Dortmund | |
| Pardubitz | Stapo-ADSt. | Prag | |
| Paris | Beauftr. des Ch. d. SP. u. d. SD. | Hvst. Berlin u. Frankf./M. u. Brüssel | |

| Headquarters : Location, Official Designation and Classification : (*Dienststelle*) | (*Bezeichnung*) | Connecting or Relay Exchange : (*Vermittlung*) | Remarks : (*Bermerkung*) |
|---|---|---|---|
| Pers. Stab | RFSS | Hvst. Berlin | |
| Pillau | Greko | Königsberg | |
| Pilsen | Stapo-ADSt. | Prag | |
| Plauen | Stapost. | Dresden | |
| Posen | Stapoleitst. | Hvst. Berlin | Querv. nach Breslau |
| Potsdam | Stapost. | Hvst. Berlin | |
| Prag | Stapoleitst. | Hvst. Berlin | Querv. nach Wien, Brünn, Olmütz Reichenberg |
| Prag | Befehlsh. d. SP. u. d. SD. | Prag | |
| Pretzsch | Grenzpolizeischule | Hvst. Berlin | |
| Pless | ADSt. | NVSt. Kattowitz | |
| Prossnitz | ADSt. | Olmütz | |
| Radom | Kd. SP. u. d. SD. | Krakau | |
| Ratibor | Stapo-ADSt. | Breslau | |
| Ravensbrück | KL. | Hvst. Berlin | |
| Recklinghausen | Stapo-ADSt. | Dortmund | |
| Regensburg | Stapost. | NVSt. München | |
| Reichenberg | Stapoleitst. | Hvst. Berlin | Querv. nach Dresden, Karlsbad, Troppau |
| RFSS, München | Reichsführung-SS | München | |
| RMdI. | Bln. Unter den Linden | Hvst. Berlin | |
| RKPA. | RSHA—Amt V | Hvst. Berlin | |
| Rostock | Greko | Hamburg | |
| Rzeszow | ADSt. d. Komm. Krakau | Krakau | |
| Rouen | EK. | Paris | |
| Rotterdam | EK. (ADSt.) | Den Haag | |
| Rybnik | ADSt. | Kattowitz | |
| Suwalki | Gre. Kom. | KBC. | |
| Saarbrücken | Stapost. | HVSt. | Querv. FFM. |
| Nvst. Saarbrücken | Stapost. | HVSt. | |
| Saarburg | EK. | Saarbrücken | |
| Sachsenhausen | KL. | Hvst. Berlin | |
| Salzburg | Stapost. | Wien | |
| Samter | Stapo-ADSt. | Posen | |
| Sassnitz | Grepo | Stettin | |
| Schneidemühl | Stapost. | Frankf./O. | |
| Schwerin | Stapost. | Hamburg | |
| Schwiebus | Stapo-ADSt. | Frankf./O. | |
| SD-LA. Danzig | Danzig | Danzig | |
| SD-LA. Donau | Wien | Wien | FS. nimmt Insp. Wien nimmt FS. an |
| SD-LA. Elbe | Dresden | Dresden | |
| SD-LA. Fulda-Werra | Frankf./M. | Frankf./M. | |
| SD-Grunewald | RSHA. Amt IV | Hvst. Berlin | |
| SD-LA. Nord | Stettin | Stettin | FS. nimmt Insp. Stettin |
| SD-LA. Nordost | Königsberg | Königsberg | FS. nimmt St. Kgbg. |
| SD-LA. Nordsee | Hamburg | Hamburg | FS. nimmt Insp. Hbg. |
| SD-LA. Ost | Berlin | Hvst. Berlin | FS. an Stl. Berlin |
| SD-LA. Süd | München | München | |
| SD-LA. Südost | Breslau | Breslau | FS. nimmt Insp. Bresl. |
| SD-LA. Südwest | Stuttgart | Stuttgart | FS. nimmt Insp. Stuttg. |
| SD-A. Thorn | Thorn | Danzig | |
| SD-LA. West | Düsseldorf | Düsseldorf | FS. nimmt Insp. Düsseldorf |
| Sicherungsstab | Wiesbaden | Frankf./M. | |
| SS-Hauptamt | Hauptamt-SS | Hvst. Berlin | |
| SS-OA. Nordost | Königsberg | Königsberg | |
| SS-Schule | Wewelsburg | Hannover | |
| SD-A. Pfalz | Neustadt/W. | Neustadt/W. | |
| Siegen | Stapo-ADSt. | Dortmund | |
| Stellv. General-kdo. I | Königsberg (Ast) | Königsberg | |
| Stellv. General-kdo. II | Stettin (Ast) | Stettin | |
| Stellv. General-kdo IV | Dresden (Ast) | Dresden | |
| Stellv. General-kdo V | Stuttgart (Ast) | Stuttgart | |
| Stellv. General-kdo VI | Münster | Dortmund | |
| Stellv. General-kdo VII | München | München | |
| Stellv. General-kdo VIII | Breslau | Breslau | |

| Headquarters: Location, Official Designation and Classification: (Dienststelle) | (Bezeichnung) | Connecting or Relay Exchange: (Vermittlung) | Remarks: (Bemerkung) |
|---|---|---|---|
| Stellv. General-kdo X | Hamburg | Hamburg | |
| Stellv. General-kdo XI | Hannover (Ast) | Hannover | |
| Stellv. General-kdo XII | Wiesbaden (Ast) | Frankf./M. | |
| Stettin | Stapoleitst. | Hvst. Berlin | Querv. nach Hamburg |
| Stolp/Pom. | Stapo-ADSt. | Köslin | Querv. nach Danzig |
| Stralsund | Greko | Stettin | |
| Strassburg, Nvst. | Befehlsh. d. SP. u. d. SD. | Stuttgart | |
| Stuttgart | Stapoleitst. | Hvst. Berlin | Querv. nach Frankf./M., München, Neustadt/W. |
| Stavanger | EK. u. Kdo. d. Sipo | Oslo | |
| Suwalki | GPK. | Königsberg | |
| Schröttersburg | Stapo | Zichenau | |
| St. Pölten | ADSt. | Wien | |
| Scharfenwiese | Greko | Zichenau | |
| Swinemünde | Greko | Stettin | |
| SD-A. Franken | Nürnberg | Nürnberg | |
| SD-A. Neustettin | | Köslin | |
| Sosnowitz | NVSt. Kattowitz | | |
| Saloniki | EK. | Belgrad | |
| Tegernsee-Gmund | Dienststelle RFSS | München | |
| Tilsit | Stapost. | Königsberg | |
| Travemünde | Grepo | Kiel m. Nebenstellenumsch. Lübeck | |
| Trier, Nvst. | Stapost. | Koblenz | |
| Troppau, Nvst. | Stapost. | Breslau u. Reichenberg | Querv. nach Olmütz |
| Tarnowitz | ADSt. | NVSt. Kattowitz | |
| Tabor | ADSt. | Prag | |
| Theresienstadt | ADSt. | Prag | |
| Tromsoe | ADSt. | Drontheim | |
| Ulm | Stapo-ADSt. | Stuttgart | |
| VGH | Volksgerichtshof | Hvst. Berlin | |
| Villach | Greko | Klagenfurt | |
| V.u. W.-Hauptamt | Verwalt./Wirtsch. | Hvst. Berlin | |
| Volksdeutsche Mittlestelle | | Hvst. Berlin | |
| Völkermarkt | GPK. | Klagenfurt | |
| Vierzon | NSt. | Paris | |
| Warnemünde | Grepo | Hamburg | NBSt. Umschalter Rostock |
| Waldenburg-Schl. | Stapo-ADSt. | Breslau | |
| Waldshut | Greko | Stuttgart Nst. Umschalter Lörrach | |
| Warschau | Komm. d. SP. u. d. SD. | Krakau | |
| Watenstedt | Stapo-ADSt. | Hannover Nst. Umschalter Braunschweig | |
| Weimar | Stapost. | Hvst. Berlin | |
| Wesermünde | Stapost. | Hamburg | |
| West. SD-LA. | Düsseldorf | Düsseldorf | |
| Westerland-Sylt | Grepo | Hamburg | |
| Wewelsburg | SS-Schule | Hannover | |
| Wien | Stapoleitst. | Hvst. Berlin | Querv. nach München, Prag, Brünn |
| Wiener-Neustadt | Stapo-ADSt. | Wien | |
| Wiesbaden | Stapo-ADSt. | Frankf./M. | |
| Wilhelmshaven | Stapost. | Hamburg | |
| Würzburg | Stapost. | Nürnberg | |
| Wuppertal | Stapo-ADSt. | Dortmund | |
| Wsetin | ADSt. | Olmütz | |
| Zakopane | Greko | Krakau | |
| Zichenau | Stapost. (NVSt.) | Königsberg | |
| Zlin | Greko | Olmütz | |
| Zwickau | Stapo-ADSt. | Dresden | |

The following is a consolidated list of five Amendments to the preceding list and was published by the *Chef der Sipo und des SD* on the following dates :—

$$\begin{cases} \text{30 December, 1942} \\ \text{6 February 1943} \\ \text{8 May, 1943} \\ \text{9 October, 1943} \\ \text{11 December, 1943} \end{cases}$$

There is no doubt that the Germans have issued more Amendments than those listed above ; these have not come to hand. For this reason, certain instances in the Amendments may call for a deletion of an item which is not given at all in the list of the Teletype Network of the Sipo and SD (1 August, 1941), but may have been contained in one of the Amendments not as yet available. It was, therefore, considered inadvisable to incorporate the following changes in the list under (a).

| Headquarters | | Connecting or Relay Exchange | Remarks | Date of Information |
|---|---|---|---|---|
| Location, Official Designation and Classification | | | | |
| (*Dienststelle*) | (*Bezeichnung*) | (*Vermittlung*) | (*Bemerkung*) | (*Datum*) |
| *Altmünsterol | *ADSt. | *Strassburg | | 2/1943 |
| *Amiens | *Adst. | *Paris | | 12/1943 |
| *Arnoldstein | *GPP. | *Klagenfurt | | 5/1943 |
| Baden-Baden | | { †Stuttgart / *Strassburg } | | 2/1943 |
| Belgrad, †Vst. | | | | 2/1943 |
| | | { †Berlin / *Graz } | | 10/1943 |
| *Bergen-Belsen | *K.L. | *Hannover | | 12/1943 |
| *Bozen | *EK.d.BdS, Italien | *München | | 12/1943 |
| †Braunes Haus | †München | | | 12/1943 |
| Brünn | | †Olmütz | *Querv. nach Troppau | 10/1943 |
| *Caen | *Adst. | *Rouen | | 12/1943 |
| *Carcassonne | *Adst. | *Lyon | | 12/1943 |
| Chalons s.S. | | { †Paris / *Lyon } | | 12/1943 |
| *Compiegne | *Haftlager | *Paris | | 12/1943 |
| *Cuxhaven | *Adst. | *Hamburg | | 10/1943 |
| *Czortkow | *Adst. | *Lemberg | | 12/1943 |
| Dijon | | { †Paris / *Lyon } | | 12/1943 |
| Dorpat | | { †Danzig / *Riga } | | 12/1942 |
| Dresden | | | *Querv. nach Munchen | 10/1943 |
| *Elfringen | *Grepo | *Saarbrücken | | 10/1943 |
| Freiburg | | { †Stuttgart / *Strassburg } | | 2/1943 |
| *Fulda | *Adst. | *Frankfurt/Main | | 12/1942 |
| *Gnesen | *Adst. | *Posen | | 12/1942 |
| Graz †Nvst. *Vst. | | †Wien / *Berlin } | *Querv. nach Wien | 10/1943 |
| *Hagen | *Adst. | *Dortmund | | 12/1943 |
| *Hagenau | *ADSt. | *Strassburg | | 2/1943 |
| *Hamm | *Adst. | *Dortmund | | 12/1943 |
| *Hanau | *Adst. | *Frankfurt/Main | | 5/1943 |
| *Hertogenbosch | *K.L. | *Den Haag | | 10/1943 |
| *Insp. d. Sich. Pol. u. d. SD. | *Nürnberg | *Nürnberg | | 10/1943 |
| Karlsbad | | | †Reichenberg | 12/1942 |
| Karlsruhe | | | *Querv. nach Strassburg | 2/1943 |
| Kiew, *Vst. | | { †Rowno / *Berlin } | *Querv. nach Rowno | 10/1943 |
| *Kleve | *Greko | *Dortmund | | 10/1943 |
| *Kolmar | *ADSt. | *Strassburg | | 2/1943 |
| *Konin | *Adst. | *Posen | | 12/1942 |
| *Landshut | *Grepo | *Wien | | 10/1943 |
| *Lebrechtsdorf | *UWZ-Lager | *Danzig | | 2/1943 |
| *Leibach | *E.K. | *Klagenfurt | | 12/1943 |

* Add
† Delete

| Headquarters | | Connecting or Relay Exchange | Remarks | Date of Information |
|---|---|---|---|---|
| Location, Official Designation and Classification | | | | |
| (Dienststelle) | (Bezeichnung) | (Vermittlung) | (Bemerkung) | (Datum) |
| Lemberg †Nvst. } *Vst. } | | { †Krakau } { *Berlin } | *Querv. nach Krakau | 12/1942 |
| *Leoben | *ADSt. | *Graz | | 2/1943 |
| *Leslau | *Adst. | *Posen | | 12/1942 |
| *Limoges | *EK. | *Paris | | 5/1943 |
| Lörrach | | { †Stuttgart } { *Strassburg } | | 2/1943 |
| *Lötzen | *Adst. | *Königsberg | | 5/1943 |
| *Lustenau | *Grepo | *Innsbruck | | 2/1943 |
| †Lyck | †Greko | †Königsberg | | 2/1943 |
| *Lyon, Nvst. | *KdS. | *Paris | | 2/1943 |
| Mähr. Ostrau | | { †Olmütz } { *Brünn } | | 10/1943 |
| *Maltheuern | *Arb. Erz. Lager | *Reichenberg | | 5/1943 |
| *Marburg-Lahn | *Adst. | *Frankfurt/Main | | 10/1943 |
| †Marienbad | †Stapo-Adst. | †Karlsbad | | 12/1942 |
| *Marienbad | *Adst. | *Karlsbad | | 5/1943 |
| | †Adst. | †Karlsbad | | 12/1943 |
| *Marseille | *KdS. | *Lyon | | 2/1943 |
| *Meschede | *ADSt. | *Dortmund | | 2/1943 |
| *Montpellier | *SD-Kommdst. | *Paris | | 5/1943 |
| München | | | *Querv. nach Dresden | 10/1943 |
| *München | *Kripo | *München | | 12/1943 |
| †Neidenburg | †Adst. | †Allenstein | | 5/1943 |
| *Neustettin | *ADSt. | *Koslin | | 2/1943 |
| †Offenbach/M | †Adst. | †Frankfurt/Main | | 12/1943 |
| Offenburg | | { †Stuttgart } { *Strassburg } | | 2/1943 |
| Olmütz, †Nvst. | | | | 10/1943 |
| †Ortelsburg | †ADSt. | †Köslin | | 2/1943 |
| *Paris | *Passierscheinstelle | *Paris | | 12/1943 |
| *Perpignan | *Aussenkommd. | *Lyon | | 5/1943 |
| †Pless | †Adst. | †Kattowitz | | 5/1943 |
| Prerau | | { †Olmütz } { *Brünn } | | 10/1943 |
| *Rastenburg | *ADSt. | *Königsberg | | 2/1943 |
| Reichenberg | | | †Karlsbad | 12/1942 |
| *Saal | *Greko | *Strassburg | | 2/1943 |
| Saarbrücken | | | *Querv. nach Strassburg | 2/1943 |
| *Saaz | *Adst. | *Karlsbad | | 12/1942 |
| *Sanok | *Greko | *Krakau | | 12/1943 |
| Schneidemühl | | { †Frankfurt/Oder } { *Stettin } | | 2/1943 |
| *Schwetz | *Adst. | *Danzig | | 5/1943 |
| *SD-Leitabschn., Reichenberg | *Reichenberg | *Reichenberg | | 12/1942 |
| †SD-Abschn., Thorn | †Thorn | †Danzig | | 12/1942 |
| †SD-Abschnitt, Neustettin | †Neustettin | †Köslin | | 2/1943 |
| *SD-Abschnitt, Weimar | *Weimar | *Weimar | | 10/1943 |
| *Sniatyn | *Grepo | *Lemberg | | 10/1943 |
| *Strassburg | *Kripo | *Strassburg | | 2/1943 |
| *St. Michielsgestel | *Lager | *Den Haag | | 2/1943 |
| Strassburg, †Nvst. } *Vst. } | | { †Stuttgart } { *Berlin } | *Querv. nach Stuttgart, Frankfurt/M | 2/1943 |
| *Stutthof | *K.L. | *Danzig | | 12/1942 |
| *Thorn | *Stapo-Adst. | *Danzig | | 12/1942 |
| *Toulouse | *SD-EK. | *Paris | | 5/1943 |
| Troppau | | | { †Olmütz } { *Brünn } | 10/1943 |
| *Veldes | *Kommandeur dSPudSD. | *Wien | | 12/1942 |

* Add
† Delete

F30

| Headquarters | | Connecting or Relay Exchange | Remarks | Date of Information |
|---|---|---|---|---|
| Location, Official Designation and Classification | | | | |
| (*Dienststelle*) | (*Bezeichnung*) | (*Vermittlung*) | (*Bemerkung*) | (*Datum*) |
| *Vichy | *KdS. | *Paris | | 2/1943 |
| | | { †Paris<br>{ *Lyon. } | | 12/1943 |
| *Vorbruck | *Sich.-Lager | *Strassburg | | 2/1943 |
| Waldshut | | { †Stuttgart<br>{ *Strassburg } | | 2/1943 |
| Weil/Rh. | | { †Stuttgart<br>{ *Strassburg } | | 2/1943 |
| *Wifo | *Adst. | *Weimar | | 12/1943 |
| Wsetin | | { †Olmütz<br>{ *Brünn } | | 10/1943 |
| Zlin | | { †Olmütz<br>{ *Brünn } | | 10/1943 |

\* Add
† Delete

## (c) OFFICIAL ABBREVIATIONS AND TERMS

(As used in the preceding list of the teletype network of Sipo and SD)

| *Abbreviation.* | *Term.* | *Approximation.* |
|---|---|---|
| Adjutantur des Chefs d. Sich.-Pol. u. des SD. | Adjudantur des Chefs des Sicherheitspolizei und des SD. | Offices of the Personal Adjutant of the Chief of the Security Police and of the SD |
| ADSt. or Adst. | Aussendienststelle | Larger branch office |
| ADSt. d. Komm. | Aussendienststelle des Kommissariats | Branch office of the District Commissariat |
| Amt V | Amt V of the Reichssicherheitshauptamt (RSHA); identical with Reichskriminalpolizeiamt (RKPA) | Bureau V of the National Dept. of Security, identical with the command headquarters of the Criminal Police |
| Arb. Erz. Lager | Arbeitserziehunglager | Reformatory Labour Camp (type of concentration camp) |
| Ast | Abwehrstelle | District control headquarters of the Abwehr (Military Intelligence) |
| Aussenkommd. | Aussenkommando | Outpost Headquarters |
| Auswärt. Amt | Auswärtiges Amt | Foreign Office |
| Beauftr. d. ChdSPudSD. | Beauftragter des Chefs der Sipo und des SD. | Plenipotentiary of the Chief of the Sipo and the SD |
| Beauftr. des Ch. d. SP. u. SD. | Beauftragter des Chefs der Sipo und des SD. | Plenipotentiary of the Chief of the Sipo and the SD |
| Befehlsh. d. SP. u. d. SD. | Befehlshaber der Sipo und des SD. | Commander of the Security Police and the SD |
| BdSP. u. d. SD. u. EK. | Befehlshaber der Sipo und des SD.—Einsatzkommando | Commander of the Sipo and SD —task force command |
| BdSudSD. | Befehlshaber der Sipo und des SD. | Commander of the Sipo and the SD |
| Berlin (HBZ) | Heeresbetriebszentralamt | Army office, possibly connected with Abwehr. (May be Amt III C. of Abwehr) |
| Bln (HBZ) | Heeresbetriebszentralamt | Army office, possibly connected with Abwehr. (May be Amt III C. of Abwehr) |
| Braunes Haus | Braunes Haus | Nazi Party Headquarters in Munich |
| | Einton | Single frequency wire |
| E.K. or EK. | Einsatz Kommando | Task force command |
| E.L. | Erziehungslager (?) | Type of concentration camp |
| EWZ | Einwanderer-Zentrale | Repatriation Centre of the SD for " Racial " Germans |

| Abbreviation. | Term. | Approximation. |
|---|---|---|
| FA | Forschungsamt | Research section of the RSHA |
| FFM | Frankfurt/Main | |
| FFO | Frankfurt/Oder | |
| FS | Fernschreiber | Teletype |
| FS Verm. | Fernschreibvermittlung | Teletype exchange |
| | Grenzinspekteur I, II, III (Ost, West, Südost) | Inspector of Combined Frontier Control Services. |
| GPK | Grenzpolizei-Kommissariat | Gestapo Frontier Police Commissariat |
| GPP | Grenzpolizeiposten | Gestapo Frontier Police Outpost |
| | Grenzpolizeischule | Gestapo Frontier Police School |
| Greko | Grenzpolizei-Kommissariat | Gestapo Frontier Police Commissariat |
| Gre. Kom. | Grenzpolizei-Kommissariat | Gestapo Frontier Police Commissariat |
| Grepo | Grenzpolizei Posten | Gestapo Frontier Police Post |
| | Hauptamt-SS | Central Department of the SS High Command |
| | Haus des Führers | HITLER's Berchtesgaden Residence |
| | Heeresgruppen Kommando | Army Group Operational Headquarters |
| Heeres-Gruppenkdo. V. | Heeresgruppen-Kommando V. | Headquarters of Army Group V (Vienna) |
| Höhere SS u Polf. | Höhere SS und Polizeiführer | Superior SS- and Police Commander |
| Hvst | Hauptvermittlungsstelle | Central exchange |
| Insp. d. SP. u. d. SD. | Inspekteur der Sipo und des SD | Inspector of the Sipo and the SD |
| KBC | Königsberg (?) | |
| Kdo. d. Sipo | Kommando der Sicherheits-Polizei | |
| KdSPudSD | Kommandeur der Sipo und des SD | Subdistrict Commander of the Sipo and the SD |
| KL. | Konzentrationslager | Concentration Camp |
| Kom. d. SP. u. d. SD | Kommandeur der Sipo und des SD | Subdistrict Commander of the Sipo and the SD |
| Komm. d. SP. u. d. SD. | Kommandeur der Sipo und des SD | Subdistrict Commander of the Sipo and the SD |
| Kommand. d. SP. u. d. SD. | Kommandeur der Sipo und des SD | Subdistrict Commander of the Sipo and the SD |
| Kommandeur SS-VT | Kommandeur der SS-Verfügungstruppen | SS General Service troops (now known as Waffen-SS) |
| Kommand. SS-VT | Kommandeur der SS-Verfügungstruppen | SS General Service troops (now known as Waffen-SS) |
| NBSt. | Nebenstelle | Branch teletype extension |
| Nebenstellenumsch | Nebenstellenumschalter (?) | Branch Teletype extension switchboard |
| | nimmt | " messages taken by " |
| Nst. | Nebenstelle | Branch teletype extension |
| NSt. | Nebenstelle | Branch teletype extension |
| NVSt. | Nebenvermittlungsstelle | Branch exchange |
| Nvst | Nebenvermittlungsstelle | Branch exchange |
| Pers. Stab. | Persönlicher Stab | HIMMLER's personal Staff Headquarters |
| Querv. | Querverbindung | Direct line |
| | Reichsführung-SS | SS High Command |
| | Reichskommissar | Reich Commissioner |
| RFSS | Reichsführer-SS | C. in-C. of the SS (HIMMLER) |
| RKPA | Reichskriminalpolizeiamt (Amt V des RSHA) | Command Headquarters of the Criminal Police (Identical with Bureau V of the Natl. Department of Security) |
| RMdI | Reichsministerium des Innern | Reich Ministry of the Interior |
| RSHA | Reichssicherheitshauptamt | National Department of Security |
| SD. | Sicherheitsdienst des Reichsführers-SS | Security Service of the C.-in-C. SS |

| Abbreviation. | Term. | Approximation. |
|---|---|---|
| SDA. | SD Abschnitt | Security Service Sub-regional Headquarters |
| SD-A. | SD Abschnitt | Security Service Sub-regional Headquarters |
| SD-A. | SD Abschnitt | Security Service Sub-regional Headquarters |
| SD-kommdst. | SD-Kommandostelle | SD-Command Headquarters |
| SD-LA. | SD Leitabschnitt | Security Service Regional Headquarters |
| | Sicherungsstab | Headquarters for Security and Intelligence Tasks |
| Sonder-Kdo. | Sonder-Kommando | Special SS task force Headquarters |
| | SS-Hauptamt | Department of the SS High Command |
| SS-OA | SS-Oberabschnitt | Headquarters of SS Corps Command area, almost identical with Wehrkreis (Armed Forces Military District) |
| | SS Schule | SS School |
| St. | Stapo | Secret State Police |
| Stap. ADSt. | Staatspolizei Aussendienststelle | Large branch office of a Gestapo Regional or Sub-regional Headquarters |
| Stapoleitst. | Staatspolizeileitstelle | Gestapo Regional Headquarters |
| Stapost. | Staatspolizeistelle | Gestapo Sub-regional Headquarters |
| Stellv. General Kdo. | Stellvertretendes Generalkommando | Acting Corps Command (Headquarters of Military District) |
| Stellv. Generalkdo. | Stellvertretendes Generalkommando | Acting Corps Command (Headquarters of Military District) |
| Stl. | Stapoleitstelle | Regional Headquarters of the Gestapo |
| UWZ-Lager | Lager der Umwandererzentralen | Camp for Resettlers |
| Verwalt./Wirtsch. | SS VWHA | SS Economic and Administrative Dept. (now called WVHA) |
| VGH | Volksgerichtshof | People's Court |
| | Volksdeutsche Mittelstelle | Central Agency for Resettlement and Repatriation of "Racial" Germans |
| Wien (HWN) | Heeresgruppen Kommando V. | Headquarters of Army Group V (Vienna) |
| VSt. | Vermittlungstelle | Trunk Line Exchange |
| Vst. | Vermittlungstelle | Trunk Line Exchange |
| V. u. W. Hauptamt | Verwaltungs- und Wirtschafts-hauptamt (SS VWHA) | Economic and Administration Department of the SS High Command (formerly VWHA, now WVHA) |
| | Wohnung | Residence. |

## (d) NETWORK OF IMMOBILE POLICE WIRELESS STATIONS IN GREATER GERMANY

### (Gliederung des ortsfesten deutschen Polizeifunknetzes)

As of 1 December, 1940

The following terms are used in the list :

| | |
|---|---|
| *Hauptfunkstelle* | Central Wireless Station. |
| *Leitfunkstelle* | Regional Control Wireless Station. |
| *Funkstelle* | Wireless Sub-station. |
| *Nebenleitfunkstelle* | Branch Wireless Station. |
| *Gendarmeriefunkstelle* | Rural Police Wireless Station. |

### Hauptfunkstelle : Berlin

**Leitfunkstelle Berlin**
Controlling *Funkstellen*: Frankfurt/O., Potsdam

**Leitfunkstelle Breslau**
Controlling *Funkstellen* : Beuthen, Gleiwitz, Kattowitz, Königshütte, Liegnitz, Oppeln, Sosnowitz, Troppau, Waldenburg

**Leitfunkstelle Brünn**
Controlling *Funkstellen :* Holleschau, Iglau, Mähr. Ostrau

**Leitfunkstelle Danzig**
Controlling *Funkstellen :* Bromberg, Elbing, Marienwerder, Thorn

**Leitfunkstelle Dresden**
Controlling *Funkstellen* : Altenburg, Aussig, Brüx, Chemnitz, Leipzig, Plauen, Reichenberg, Zwickau

**Leitfunkstelle Düsseldorf**
Controlling *Funkstellen* : Aachen, Duisburg, Essen, Gladbach-Rheydt, Köln, Mülheim, Oberhausen,, Remscheid, Wuppertal

**Leitfunkstelle Frankfurt/M,**
Controlling *Funkstellen* : Darmstadt, Giessen, Hanau, Koblenz, Mainz, Trier, Wiesbaden, Worms

**Leitfunkstelle Hamburg**
Controlling *Funkstellen* : Aurich, Bremen, Cuxhaven, Lüneburg, Oldenburg, Stade, Wesermünde, Wilhelmshaven

**Leitfunkstelle Hannover**
Controlling *Funkstellen* : Braunschweig, Hildesheim

**Leitfunkstelle Kiel**
Controlling *Funkstellen* : Flensburg, Lübeck, Schleswig

**Leitfunkstelle Königsberg**
Controlling *Funkstellen* : Allenstein, Gumbinnen, Memel, Pillau, Tilsit, Zichenau

**Leitfunkstelle Krakau**
Controlling *Funkstellen* : Lublin, Radom, Warschau

**Leitfunkstelle Magdeburg**
Controlling *Funkstellen* : Bitterfeld, Dessau, Halle, Merseburg, Weissenfels, Wittenberg

**Leitfunkstelle München**
Controlling *Funkstelle* : Augsburg

**Leitfunkstelle Nürnberg**
Controlling *Funkstellen* : Hof, Karlsbad, Regensburg, Würzburg

**Leitfunkstelle Posen**
Controlling *Funkstellen* : Hohensalza, Kalisch, Litzmannstadt

**Leitfunkstelle Prag**
Controlling *Funkstellen* : Klattau, Klodno, Kolin, Königsgrätz, Tabor, Pilsen

**Leitfunkstelle Recklinghausen**
Controlling *Funkstellen* : Arnsberg, Bochum, Bottrop, Dortmund, Gelsenkirchen, Gronau, Hamm, Minden, Münster, Osnabrück

**Leitfunkstelle Salzburg**
Controlling *Funkstellen* : Graz, Innsbruck, Klagenfurt, Villach
and *Gendarmeriefunkstellen* : Bludenz, Bregenz, Bruck a.d. Mur, Deutschlandsberg, Feldbach, Feldkirch, Güssing, Graz, Innsbruck, Judenburg, Klagenfurt, Leoben, Lienz, Liezen, Oberwarth, Reutte, Tamsweg, Völkermarkt, Wolfsberg

**Leitfunkstelle Stettin**
Controlling *Funkstellen* : Köslin, Rostock, Schneidemühl, Stolp, Schwerin

**Leitfunkstelle Stuttgart**
Controlling *Funkstellen* : Freiburg, Friedrichshafen, Heilbronn, Karlsruhe, Konstanz, Offenburg, Pforzheim, Sigmaringen, Ulm

**Leitfunkstelle Wien**
Controlling *Funkstellen* : Linz, Steyr, St. Pölten, Wels, Wiener-Neustadt, Znaim
and *Gendarmeriefunkstellen* : Bruck a.d. Leitha, Eisenstadt, Krems, Krummau, Neubistritz, Nikolsburg, Oberpullendorf, Ried, St. Pölten, Znaim

*Nebenleitfunkstelle* Weimar
Controlling *Funkstellen* : Kassel, Erfurt, Gera, Gotha, Jena, Suhl

**Nebenleitfunkstelle Ludwigshafen**
Controlling *Funkstellen* : Kaiserslautern, Metz, Neustadt (Weinstr.)

## (e) CODE USED BY THE INTERNATIONAL CRIMINAL POLICE COMMISSION

| No. | Code Word | German Equivalent | English Equivalent |
|---|---|---|---|
| 1 | rense | *Nachstehende Vormerkungen bestehen über . . .* | The following details are to hand re . . . |
| | | *oder* | or |
| | | *Hier ist Nachstehendes vorgemerkt über . . .* | The following details are available : |
| | qrense | *Ersuche um Bekanntgabe aller Daten, welche bekannt sind über . . .* | All information known re . . . is requested |
| | | *oder* | or |
| | | *Ersuche um Bekanntgabe, ob Vorgänge bestehen über . . .* | Inform whether there is any previous data on . . . |
| | | *oder* | or |
| | | *Ist über . . . etwas bekannt, vorgemerkt.* | Have you any information to hand re . . . |
| | nerense | *Es bestehen keinerlei Vormerkungen über . . .* | There is no information to hand re . . . |
| | | *oder* | or |
| | | *Hier liegt nichts vor über . . .* | Nothing known re . . . |
| 2 | prior | *Hier sind folgende Vorstrafen vorgemerkt.* | Details of previous convictions follow : |
| | qprior | *Ersuche um Bekanntgabe aller Vorstrafen über . . .* | Information requested on previous convictions of . . . |
| | | *oder* | or |
| | | *Sind über . . . Vorstrafen vorgemerkt ?* | Is there any information on previous convictions of . . . ? |
| | neprior | *Hier sind über . . . keine Vorstrafen vorgemerkt* | There is no information to hand as to previous convictions of . . . |
| | | *oder* | or |
| | | *. . . ist nicht vorbestraft* | . . . has not previously been convicted |
| 3 | right | *Die Angaben wurden überprüft und sind richtig.* | The statements were checked, and are correct. |
| | qright | *Ersuche um Bekanntgabe, ob die Angaben des . . . richtig sind* | Please inform whether the statements of . . . are correct ? |
| | | *oder* | or |
| | | *Sind die Angaben richtig ?* | Are the statements correct ? |
| | neright | *Die Angaben wurden überprüft und sind unrichtig.* | The statements were checked and are incorrect. |

| No. | Code Word | German Equivalent | English Equivalent |
|---|---|---|---|
| 4 | fuhom | *Flüchtig nach Mord (Totschlag)* | Fugitive following murder (manslaughter) |
| | fufur | *Flüchtig nach Diebstahl* | Fugitive following theft |
| | fufro | *Flüchtig nach Betrug* | Fugitive following fraud |
| | fumal | *Flüchtig nach Veruntreuung* | Fugitive following embezzlement |
| | furap | *Flüchtig nach Raub* | Fugitive following robbery |
| 5 | arret | *Hier ist verhaftet (angehalten)* | An arrest (detention) has been made |
| | qarret | *Ersuche zu verhaften (anhalten ?)* | Request arrest (detention) |
| | nearret | *Konnte nicht verhaftet werden* | Unable to make arrest |
| 6 | manda | *Haftbefehl liegt vor* | Warrant for arrest to hand |
| | | *oder* | or |
| | | *Steckbrief liegt vor* | Public Notice for Apprehension to hand |
| | qmanda | *Liegt dort Haftbefehl vor ?* | Have you a warrant for arrest ? |
| | | *oder* | or |
| | | *Liegt dort Steckbrief vor ?* | Do you have a Public Notice for Apprehension ? |
| | nemanda | *Steckbrief liegt nicht vor* | There is no Public Notice for Apprehension |
| | | *Haftbefehl wird nicht erlassen* | A warrant for arrest has not been put out |
| 7 | extra | *Auslieferung wird verlangt* | Extradition is requested |
| | qextra | *Ersuche um Mitteilung, ob Auslieferung verlangt wird ?* | Advise whether extradition is requested |
| | neextra | *Auslieferung wird nicht verlangt* | Extradition is not requested |
| 8 | sicher | *Es konnten folgende Gegenstände sichergestellt werden . . . .* | The following articles are in the hands of the Police : |
| | qsicher | *Ersuche um Sicherstellung des gestohlenen (veruntreuten) Gutes* | Seize the stolen (embezzled) goods |
| | | *oder* | or |
| | | *Ersuche um Sicherstellung folgender Gegenstände . . .* | Seize the following articles : |
| | nesicher | *Es konnt nicht sichergestellt werden* | Unable to seize (recover) goods |
| 9 | kuren | *Die Verfolgung (Kurrendierung) besteht noch aufrecht* | Measures for apprehension of . . . are still in force |
| | | *oder* | or |
| | | *Die Ausschreibung (Verlautbarung) besteht noch aufrecht* | The public announcement for the apprehension of . . . is still in force |
| | qkuren | *Besteht die Verfolgung (Kurrendierung) noch aufrecht ?* | Are the measures for the apprehension of . . . still in force ? |
| | | *oder* | or |
| | | *Wird . . . von dort verfolgt ?* | Is . . . wanted by you ? |
| | nekuren | *Die Verfolgung (Kurrendierung) des . . . ist nicht mehr aufrecht* | Measures for apprehension of . . . are no longer in force |
| | | *oder* | or |
| | | *. . . wird nicht verfolgt* | . . . is not wanted |
| 10 | prote | *Hier befindet sich in Schutzhaft . . .* | . . . is being held in protective custody |
| | | *oder* | |
| | | *Hier wird zu seinem Schutz angehalten* | |
| | qprote | *Ersuche in Schutzhaft zu nehmen . . .* | Hold . . . in protective custody |
| | | *oder* | or |
| | | *Ersuche schonend anzuhalten* | Detain inconspicuously |
| 11 | prend | *Wird abgeholt am . . .* | Was picked up on . . . |
| | qprend | *Ersuche Abholung des Angehaltenen zu veranlassen* | Please arrange to pick up the person held in detention |
| | neprend | *Wird nicht abgeholt (oder kann nicht abgeholt werden)* | Is not going to be picked up (or unable to pick up) |
| 12 | fande | *Fahndung wurde eingeleitet (veranlasst)* | Search for . . . was instituted |
| | qfande | *Ersuche um Einleitung der Fahndung* | Request that you institute a search for . . . |
| | nefande | *Fahndung wurde nicht eingeleitet* | Search for . . . was not instituted |
| 13 | suche | *Haus- und Personendurchsuchung wurde vorgenommen* | Search of home and persons was carried out |
| | qsuche | *Ersuche um Vornahme der Haus- und Personendurchsuchung bei . . .* | Request that you make a search of persons and home of . . . |
| | nesuche | *Haus- und Personendurchsuchung wurde nicht vorgenommen* | Search of home and persons was not carried out |

| No. | Code Word | German Equivalent | English Equivalent |
|---|---|---|---|
| 14 | perso | *Personaldaten wurden überprüft* | Personal data were checked |
| | | *oder* | or |
| | | *Identität wurde überprüft* | Identity checked |
| | qperso | *Ersuche um Überprüfung der Personaldaten* | Check up on personal data |
| | | *oder* | or |
| | | *Ersuche um Überprüfung der Identität* | Check up on identity |
| | neperso | *Personaldaten wurden nicht überprüft* | No check made on personal data |
| | | *oder* | or |
| | | *Identität wurde nicht überprüft* | No check made on identity |
| 15 | citoy | *Staatsangehörigkeit wurde überprüft und wird anerkannt* | Nationality checked and acknowledged (recognized) |
| | qcitoy | *Ersuche um Bekanntgabe, ob die Staatsangehörigkeit anerkannt wird* | Advise if nationality is acknowledged (recognized) |
| | necitoy | *Staatsangehörigkeit wird nicht anerkannt* | Nationality is not acknowledged (recognized) |
| 16 | stati | *Hält sich auf* | . . . resides at . . . |
| | qstati | *Ersuche um Bekanntgabe, ob sich . . . in . . . aufhält* | Please inform whether . . . resides at . . . |
| | nestati | *Hält sich nicht auf in . . .* | . . . does not reside at . . . |
| 17 | arriv | *Ist eingetroffen* | . . . has arrived |
| | qarriv | *Ersuche um Bekanntgabe, ob . . . eingetroffen ist in . . .* | Please inform whether . . . has arrived at |
| | | *Ist . . . in . . . eingetroffen ?* | Has . . . arrived at . . . ? |
| | nearriv | *. . . ist nicht eingetroffen in . . .* | . . . has not arrived at . . . |
| 18 | paspo | *Besitzt Reisepass ausgestellt von . . .* | Possesses passport issued by . . . |
| | qpaspo | *Ersuche um Bekanntgabe, ob dem . . . ein Reisepass ausgestellt wurde* | Please advise whether a passport was issued to . . . |
| | nepaspo | *. . . wurde kein Reisepass ausgestellt* | A passport was not issued to . . . |
| 19 | photo | *Lichtbild wurde gleichzeitig übersandt* | A photograph was forwarded at the same time |
| | qphoto | *Ersuche um Übersendung des Lichtbildes* | Request that you forward a photograph |
| | nephoto | *Lichtbild ist nicht vorhanden* | There is no photograph to hand |
| 20 | print | *Fingerabdruckblatt wurde gleichzeitig übersandt* | Fingerprint impressions were forwarded at the same time |
| | qprint | *Ersuche um Übersendung des Fingerabdruckblattes* | Request that you forward fingerprint impressions |
| | neprint | *Fingerabdruckblatt nicht vorhanden* | No fingerprint impressions to hand |
| 21 | pocku | *Als Taschendieb bekannt* | Known to be a pickpocket |
| | qpocku | *Ersuche um Mitteilung ob als Taschendieb bekannt ?* | Inform whether . . . is known to be a pickpocket |
| | nepocku | *Als Taschendieb nicht bekannt* | Not known to be a pickpocket |
| 22 | chevu | *Als Hochstapler bekannt* | Known to be an impostor |
| | qchevu | *Ersuche um Mitteilung, ob als Hochstapler bekannt ?* | Inform whether . . . is known to be an impostor ? |
| | nechevu | *Als Hochstapler nicht bekannt* | Not known to be an impostor |
| 23 | bancu | *Als Bankbetrüger (Scheck-, Wechsel-, Einlagebuchfälscher) bekannt* | Known to be a bank forger (forger of cheques, acceptances and drafts, deposit books) |
| | qbancu | *Ersuche um Mitteilung, ob als Bankbetrüger (Scheck-, Wechsel-, Einlagebuchfälscher) bekannt ?* | Inform whether . . . is known to be a bank forger (forger of cheques, acceptances and drafts, deposit books) |
| | nebancu | *Als Bankbetrüger (Scheck-, Wechsel-, Einlagebuchfälscher) nicht bekannt* | Not known to be a bank forger (forger of cheques, acceptances and drafts, deposit books) |
| 24 | monnu | *Als Geld- und Banknotenfälscher bekannt* | Known to be a forger of coins and banknotes |
| | qmonnu | *Ersuche um Mitteilung, ob als Geld- und Banknotenfälscher bekannt ?* | Inform whether . . . is known to be a forger of coins and banknotes |
| | nemonnu | *Als Geld- und Banknotenfälscher nicht bekannt* | Not known to be a forger of coins and banknotes |
| 25 | passu | *Als Passfälscher bekannt* | Known to be a forger of passports |
| | qpassu | *Ersuche um Mitteilung, ob als Passfälscher bekannt ?* | Inform whether . . . is known to be a forger of passports |
| | nepassu | *Als Passfälscher nicht bekannt* | Not known to be a forger of passports |

F36

| No. | Code Word | German Equivalent | English Equivalent |
|---|---|---|---|
| 26 | jewlu | *Als Juwelendieb bekannt* | Known to be a jewel-thief |
| | qjewlu | *Ersuche um Mitteilung, ob als Juwelendieb bekannt ?* | Inform whether . . . is known to be a jewel-thief |
| | nejewlu | *Als Juwelendieb nicht bekannt* | Not known to be a jewel-thief |
| 27 | femmu | *Als Mädchenhändler bekannt* | Known to be a white-slave trader |
| | qfemmu | *Ersuche um Mitteilung, ob als Mädchenhändler bekannt ?* | Inform whether . . . is known to be a white slave trader |
| | nefemmu | *Als Mädchenhändler nicht bekannt* | Not known to be a white-slave trader |
| 28 | stupu | *Als Rauschgifthändler bekannt* | Known to be a trader in narcotics |
| | qstupu | *Ersuche um Mitteilung, ob als Rauschgifthändler bekannt ?* | Inform whether . . . is known to be a trader in narcotics |
| | nestupu | *Als Rauschgifthändler nicht bekannt* | Not known to be a trader in narcotics |
| 29 | hotlu | *Als Hoteldieb bekannt* | Known to be a hotel-thief |
| | qhotlu | *Ersuche um Mitteilung, ob als Hoteldieb bekannt ?* | Inform whether . . . is known to be a hotel-thief |
| | nehotlu | *Als Hoteldieb nicht bekannt* | Not known to be a hotel-thief |
| 30 | repon | *Telegraphische Nachricht wird gegeben* | You will be informed by telegram |
| | qrepon | *Ersuche telegraphische Antwort auf die Depesche* | Request that you telegraph answer to wire |
| | | *oder* | *or* |
| | | *Haben Sie die Depesche beantwortet ?* | Have you replied to the wire ? |
| | nerepon | *Die Depesche kann nicht beantwortet werden* | Unable to reply to the wire |
| 31 | litte | *Die Depesche wird schriftlich beantwortet* | The telegram will be answered in writing |
| | qlitte | *Ersuche um schriftliche Antwort auf . . .* | A written answer is requested to . . . |
| | nelitte | *Schriftliche Antwort wird nicht gegeben* | A written answer will not be given |
| 32 | revoc | *Ist erledigt* | Case closed |
| | | *oder* | *or* |
| | | *Wird als gegenstandslos widerrufen* | Drop the matter—of no further interest |

F37

## (f) WIRELESS STATIONS BELONGING TO THE SIPO AND SD
### (Gliederung der Funkeinrichtungen der Sicherheitspolizei und des SD)

*Note.*—The following is a reproduction of a German table of wireless stations belonging to the *Sipo* and SD in Germany and in occupied countries, dated July, 1940. Two amendments, dated October 1940 and January 1941 respectively, have also been incorporated.

| Funkstelle (Wireless Stn.) | Standort (Location) | Posttelefon (Tel. No.) | Interne Tel. Verbindung besteht mit. (Internal telephone Circuit exists with) |
|---|---|---|---|
| Arnhem | *Einsatzkdo.* II Arnhem | | (Added October 1940) |
| Bergen | *Einsatzkdo.* IV Bergen, Museumsplatz 1 | 17 483 | |
| Berlin | *Reichssicherheitshauptamt,* (SD), Berlin SW 68, Wilhelmstr. 102 | 12 0038 App. 263 | All Bureaux of the *Reichssicherheitshauptamt, IdS, Stapo-Leitstellen, Kripo-Leitstellen, SD-Leitabschnitte* |
| Brünn | *SD-Dienststelle,* Brünn, Lehmstätte 132 | 18 937/8 | |
| Christiansand | *Einsatzkdo.* II Christiansand Ostrestrandgate Nr. 5a | 3903 | |
| Drontheim | *Einsatzkdo.* V Drontheim, Hotel Phönix | 885 | |
| Groningen | *Einsatzkdo.* I Groningen | | (Added October 1940) |
| Hamburg | *IdS,* Hamburg 36, Kaiser Wilhelmstr. 46 | 35 1722 | *Stapo-Leitstelle, Kripo-Leitstelle, SD-Leitabschnitt* |
| Grünberg (Schloss), Protektorat | *Funkschule der Sipo und des SD* | | (Added 18 January, 1941) |
| Kassel | *IdS,* Kassel, Kölnische Str. 112 | 36 607 | |
| Kornsjoe | *Dt. Grenzpolizei* | Kornsjoe-Halden 8820 | |
| Krakau | *KdS,* Krakau I, Pomorska 2 | 17 920 | |
| Lillehammer | *Aussendienststelle,* Lillehammer, Gamlevei 119 | 131 | (Added October 1940) |
| Lublin | *KdS,* Lublin, Universitätsstr. 6 | 1920/1 | |
| Mähr.-Ostrau | *SD-Dienststelle,* Mährisch-Ostrau, Parkstrasse 3 | 2605 | |
| Magnor | *Grenzpolizeiposten,* Magnor Bahnhof | Magnor 27 | (Added 18 January, 1941) |
| Meraker | *Grenzpolizeiposten,* Meraker Bahnhof | Meraker 66 | (Added 18 January, 1941) |
| Mo in Rana | *Grenzpolizeiposten,* Mo in Rana | *Über Vermittlung Orpo* | (Added 18 January, 1941) |
| Narvik | *Grenzpolizeiposten,* Narvik, Bjoermsonsgate *Feldpostnummer* 15 217 | *Über Wehrmachtsvermittlung* | (Added 18 January, 1941) |
| Oslo | *BdS,* *Funkstelle* Oslo, Fritznersgate 5 | 44 283 | |
| Posen | *SD-Leitabschnitt,* Posen, Kaiserring 15 | 1993 and 1997 | |
| Prag | *SD-Leitabschnitt,* Prag XIX, Sachsenweg 44 | 77 444 | *BdS, Stapo-Leitstelle, Kripo-Leitstelle* |
| Radom | *KdS,* Radom, Kosziuskistr. 6 | 1 306 Ammi 153 | |
| Stavanger | *Einsatzkdo* III, Stavanger, Egenesveien 93 | 5050 | |
| Warschau | *KdS,* Warschau, Aleja Szucha 25 | 80 220 | *Stapo, Kripo, SD* |
| Wien | *IdS,* Wien 50, Theresianumgasse 16/6 | Ulrich 42 520-23 | *Stapo-Leitstelle, Kripo-Leitstelle, SD-Leitabschnitt* |
| Wiesbaden | *IdS,* Wiesbaden | | |

## (g) DIRECTIVES ON THE USE OF SIPO AND SD WIRELESS STATIONS
### (Richtlinien über die Benutzung der Funkeinrichtungen der Sicherheitspolizei und des SD)

*Benutzer*

*Für die Benutzung der Funkeinrichtungen der Sicherheitspolizei und des SD durch die Ämter I bis VI des Reichssicherheitshauptamtes und die Befehlshaber, Inspekteure der Sicherheitspolizei und des SD sowie deren nachgeordnete Dienststellen wird folgendes bekanntgegeben bzw. angeordnet:*

*1. Das Funknetz der Sicherheitspolizei und des SD besteht zur Zeit aus den in der Anlage aufgeführten Funkstellen.*

*Zweck*

*2. (i) Die Funkeinrichtungen der Sicherheitspolizei und des SD haben den Zweck:*

*(a) Überall dort die Nachrichtenübermittlung der Stapo, der Kripo und des SD zu übernehmen, wo kein Fernschreiber vorhanden oder der Fernschreiber ausgefallen ist oder keine andere Nachrichtenverbindung zur Verfügung steht.*

*(b) Für einen engen Personenkreis bestimmte Nachrichten zu übermitteln (mit Stabsschlüssel).*

*(c) Auf Grund ihrer Unabhängigkeit von Drahtverbindungen eine ständige Alarmbereitschaft aufrechtzuerhalten (auch nachts).*

*(ii) Geheime Reichssachen werden grundsätzlich nur dann durch Funk befördert, wenn für sie wegen der Kürze der zur Verfügung stehenden Zeit kein anderes geeignetes Nachrichtenmittel vorhanden ist.*

*Zustellung von Funksprüchen*

*3. (i) Funksprüche von oder an ausserhalb des Hauses befindliche Dienststellen sind entweder durch Fernschreiber, über interne Telefonleitung oder durch Boten zuzuleiten. Eine Abholung oder Zustellung durch die Funkstelle erfolgt nicht.*

*(ii) Die Durchgabe von Funksprüchen über Posttelefon ist verboten. Über Posttelefon erfolgt lediglich die Benachrichtigung über den Eingang eines Funkspruches, auf die der Funkstelle mitzuteilen ist, ob der Funkspruch abgeholt wird oder auf dem üblichen Dienstwege weitergegeben werden soll.*

*(iii) Telephonisch übermittelte Funksprüche von oder an ausserhalb des Hauses befindliche Dienststellen werden auf der Funkstelle abgelegt. Eine Zusendung erfolgt nur auf Verlangen des Absenders bzw. Empfängers.*

*(iv) Dringende Funksprüche werden auch an im Hause befindliche Dienststellen telefonisch durchgesprochen, wenn eine schnelle Übermittlung auf dem gewöhnlichen Dienstweg nicht sichergestellt ist. Der Funkspruch wird in diesem Falle auf dem üblichen Dienstweg nachgesandt.*

*Aushändigungsbestätigung*

*4. Auf Verlangen wird die Aushändigung eines Funkspruchs an den Empfänger bestätigt.*

*Telegrammstil*

*5. Jeder Funkspruch soll nicht mehr als 20 Schreibmaschinenzeilen (ohne An- und Unterschrift) haben und soll im Telegramstil abgefasst sein. Betreff, Vorgang, Aktenzeichen, Tagebuchnummer usw. sind tunlichst zu vermeiden.*

*An- und Unterschriften*

*6. Funksprüche müssen mit vollen und leserlichen An- und Unterschriften versehen werden.*

*Privatfunksprüche*

*7. Private Funksprüche sind verboten.*

*8. Das Funkpersonal hat Befehl, Funksprüche, die nach Inhalt und Form gegen die vorstehenden Richtlinien verstossen, abzuweisen.*

*9. Die SD-Befehle 55/38 und 33/39 sind durch die vorstehenden Richtlinien überholt und werden hiermit aufgehoben.*

Users

The following orders concerning the use of all Security Police and Security· Service Wireless installations by Bureaux I–VI of the RSHA, the Commanders and Inspectors of the *Sipo* and SD as well as all offices and headquarters subordinated to them, are hereby made known:

1. The wireless network of the *Sipo* and SD consists at present of all wireless posts listed at (*f*) above.

Purpose

2. (i) The wireless installations of the *Sipo* and SD have the following purposes:

(*a*) To transmit communications of the Secret State Police, the Criminal Police and the Security Police in cases where no teletype facilities exist, where teleprinters are not usable or where no other signal circuits are available.

(*b*) To transmit messages intended for a limited number of recipients (cyphered).

(*c*) To maintain an ever-ready alarm and emergency service (even at night) as these installations are independent of wire circuits.

(ii) Top Secret matters (civilian classification) can only be transmitted over the wireless network when no other means of communication are available for their transmission owing to the time limit placed upon them.

Delivery of Wireless Messages

3. (i) Wireless messages originating from or addressed to offices of the organisation located outside the signal office are to be delivered either by teleprinter, house-telephone (internal circuit), or by messenger. The messages will not be fetched or delivered by the wireless station.

(ii) It is prohibited to relay wireless messages via postal telephone lines. Only the receipt of such messages may be confirmed by these means. In this manner the wireless station may be informed whether the message is to be picked up or whether it is to be sent through the usual official channels.

(iii) Wireless messages originating from or addressed to offices situated outside the transmitting station are filed at the wireless station. Delivery of the message is effected only upon request of the sender or the recipient.

(iv) Urgent wireless messages are also relayed by telephone within the office provided rapid transmission cannot be guaranteed via the usual official channels. The wireless message in such cases is sent afterwards through official channels.

Written Receipt

4. Upon request the receipt of a wireless message is signed for upon delivery by the addressee.

Telegram style

5. Each message is to contain not more than 20 typewritten lines (address and signature not included) and must be phrased in telegraphese. References to the subject matter of the message, file or official number, journal reference number, etc., are to be avoided.

Addresses and Signatures

6. Wireless messages must bear full and readable addresses and signatures.

Private messages

7. Private wireless messages are prohibited.

8. All personnel handling messages have been ordered to refuse all messages which do not conform to the above directives in contents and form.

9. The SD orders 55/38 and 33/39 are superseded by the above directives and are thus no longer valid.

# ANNEXE G

## ORDER OF BATTLE OF THE REICHSKRIMINALPOLIZEI

PART ONE :    **KRIPO-LEITSTELLEN**
        (Regional Headquarters of the Criminal Police)

PART TWO :    **KRIPO-STELLEN**
        (Sub-regional Headquarters of the Criminal Police)

PART THREE :    **KRIPO AUSSENDIENSTSTELLEN UND AUSSENPOSTEN**
        (Kripo Branch Offices)

PART FOUR :    **THREE EXAMPLES OF THE STRUCTURE OF A KRIPO REGIONAL HEADQUARTERS**
        (a)  Typical organisation of a Kripo-Leitstelle, 1938
        (b)  Organisation of Kripo-Leitstelle Köln, 1941
        (c)  Organisation of Kripo-Leitstelle Hannover, 1943

PART FIVE :    **GESCHÄFTSBEREICH DES REICHSFORSTMEISTERS**
        (Regional Organisation of the Reich Forest Administration)
        (a)  Forstverwaltungen der Länder (Forest Administration of the States)
        (b)  Jagdbehörden und -Bezirke (Headquarters of the Regional Forestry Authorities and their areas)

PART SIX :    **TABLE OF BERGBEHÖRDEN (Mining Authorities) AND THEIR CONNECTION WITH THE SIPO AND SD**

A

# KRIPO LEITSTELLEN

## BERLIN

**Area :**
Gross-Berlin and *Provinz* Mark Brandenburg (*Reg. Bez.* Potsdam and Frankfurt/Oder)

**In direct control of :**
Gross-Berlin and *Reg. Bez.* Potsdam

**Address :**
C2, Alexanderstr. 10
Tel : 510023 (T/P-*Polfunk-Bildfunk*)

**Chief :**
*SS-OSBF, ORuKR.* SCHEFE
Predecessor : *SS-SF, RuKDir.* HAERTEL (trfd. to *KPLSt.* Hamburg)

**Deputy Chief :** *SS-SBF, ORuKR. Dr.* LEO

**Other Personalities :**
*RuKR.* DRAEGER, HUCKO, *Dr.* WÄCHTER, *Dr.* ZIRPINS, ODEWALD
*KR.* BEYER, von DUEHREN, DUNKER, KNOBLAUCH, *Dr.* SCHULZE

**Under :**
*BdS.* Berlin

**Supervising :**
*KPSt.* Frankfurt/Oder (for *Reg. Bez.* Frankfurt/Oder)

**Branch offices :**
Brandenburg/Havel, Potsdam, Bernau, Eberswalde, Falkensee, Jüterbog, Hennigsdorf, Kleinmachnow, Luckenwalde, Naven, Neuruppin, Oranienburg, Perleberg, Prenzlau, Rathenow, Strausberg, Teltow, Wittenberge, Zehdenik

## BREMEN

**Area :**
Bremen, the *Kreis* Grafschaft Hoya of the *Reg. Bez.* Hannover, the *Kreise* Wesermünde, Bremervörde, Osterholz, Verden and Rotenburg of the *Reg. Bez.* Stade, the *Kreise* Wesermarsch, Oldenburg, Cloopenburg, Vechta, Friesland and Ammerland of Land Oldenburg, the *Reg. Bez.* Aurich and the Braunschweig Enclave Thedinghausen.

**In direct control of :**
As above except the *Kreise* Friesland and Ammerland of *Land* Oldenburg and the *Reg. Bez.* Aurich.

**Address :**
Am Wall 200-206
Tel : 21411, 21511, 22211 (T/P and *Polfun*

**Chief :**
*RuKR.* HAHN

**Under :**
*BdS.* Hamburg

**Supervising :**
*KPSt.* Wilhelmshaven (for the *Kreise* Friesland and Ammerland of *Land* Oldenburg and the *Reg. Bez.* Aurich)

**Branch offices :**
Oldenburg, Wesermünde, Delmenhorst, Verden (Aller)

## BRESLAU

**Area :**
*Reg. Bez.* Breslau, Liegnitz

**In direct control of :**
As above

**Address :**
Schweidnitzer Stadtgraben 5/7
Tel : 22211 (*Polfunk* and *Bildfunk*—receiver only)

**Chief :**
*SS-OSBF, ORuKR.* WIELEN

**Other Personalities :**
*SS-SBF, KR.* BOHNDORF, BRÜNNER, WILLMANN

**Under :**
*BdS.* Breslau

**Branch offices :**
Görlitz, Liegnitz, Waldenburg, Brieg, Bunzlau, Frankenstein, Glatz, Glogau, Grünberg, Hirschberg, Jauer, Landeshut, Langenbielau, Lauban, Neusalz/Oder, Oels, Ohlau, Reichenbach/Eulengebirge, Sagan, Salzbrunn (Bad), Schweidnitz, Strehlen, Striegau, Weisswasser

## DANZIG

**Area :**
*Reichsgau* Danzig-Westpreussen (*Reg. Bez.* Danzig, Bromberg, Marienwerder)

**In direct control of :**
*Reg. Bez.* Danzig and the *Kreise* Marienburg, Stuhm, Marienwerder, Rosenberg, Neumark and Graudenz of the *Reg. Bez.* Marienwerder

**Address :**
Reitbahn 4
Tel : 24141, 24241

**Chief :**
*ORuKR.* HERMANN

**Other Personalities :**
*KR.* MAY, MÜSIG

**Under :**
*BdS.* Danzig

**Supervising :**
*KPSt.* Bromberg (for *Reg. Bez.* Bromberg and the *Kreise* Leipe, Rippin, Briesen, Strasburg of the *Reg. Bez.* Marienwerder)

**Branch offices :**
Elbing, Gotenhafen, Graudenz, Marienwerder, Deutsch-Eylau, Dirschau, Konitz, Löbau/Westpr., Marienburg, Neumark/Westpr., Neustadt/Westpr., Pr. Stargard

## DRESDEN

**Area :**
*Land* Sachsen and *Reg. Bez.* Aussig

**In direct control of :**
Area Dresden-Bautzen (former *Reg. Bez.* Dresden-Bautzen)

**Address :**
A1, Schiessgasse 7
Tel : 24831 (T/P and *Polfunk*)

**Chief :**
*ORuKR.* KÖNIG

**Other Personalities :**
*RuKR.* GEBHARD, *KR.* EUBE, KLAUS, MUEHLFRIEDEL, SCHILDER, THOSS

**Under :**
*BdS.* Dresden

## Supervising :
*KPSt.* Chemnitz (for area Chemnitz)
*KPSt.* Leipzig (for area Leipzig)
*KPSt.* Reichenberg (for *Reg. Bez.* Aussig)
*KPSt.* Zwickau (for area Zwickau)

## Branch offices :
Bautzen, Bischofswerda, Coswig, Freiberg, Freital, Grossenhain, Heidenau, Kamenz, Klotzsche, Löbau, Meissen, Neugersdorf, Pirna, Radeberg, Radebeul, Riesa, Sebnitz, Zittau

# DÜSSELDORF

## Area :
*Reg. Bez.* Düsseldorf, Münster, Arnsberg and the *Landkreise* Wiedenbrück, Paderborn, Höxter, Warburg, Büren and Lipperode of the *Reg. Bez.* Minden.

## In direct control of :
The *Landkreise* Kleve, Geldern, Moers, Kempen, Krefeld, Grevenbroich-Neuss, Düsseldorf-Mettmann, Parts of the Rhein-Wupperkreis, the *Stadtkreise* Düsseldorf, Krefeld-Uerdingen, München-Gladbach, Neuss, Rheydt and Viersen of the *Reg. Bez.* Düsseldorf.

## Address :
Mackensenplatz 5/7
Tel : 10215 (T/P and *Polfunk*)

## Chief :
*SS-OSBF, ORuKR.* MOMBERG

## Other Personalities :
*RuKR. Dr.* RIESE (trfd. to Nürnberg), *RuKR.* NAUCK, *KR.* MITTELSTEINER

## Under :
*BdS.* Düsseldorf

## Supervising :
*KPSt.* Bochum
*KPSt.* Dortmund
*KPSt.* Essen
*KPSt.* Recklinghausen
*KPSt.* Wuppertal

## Branch offices :
Krefeld, M. Gladbach-Rheydt, Neuss, Dülken, Emmerich, Goch, Grevenbroich, Hilden, Homberg/Niederrh., Kamp-Lintfort, Kleve, Langenfeld, Leverkusen, Mörs, Neukirchen-Vluyn, Opladen, Ratingen, Repelen-Baerl, Rheinhausen, Viersen

# FRANKFURT/Main

## Area :
*Provinz* Nassau, *Provinz* Kurhessen without *Landkreis* Schmalkalden, *Land* Hessen and the Hess. Enclaven Steinbach, *Landkreis* Offenbach and several small wooded areas belonging to *Landkreis* Friedberg.

## In direct control of :
*Provinz* Nassau, Hess. Enclaven Steinbach, *Landkreis* Offenbach and several small wooded areas belonging to *Landkreis* Friedberg.

## Address :
Hohenzollernanlage 11
Tel : 20015 (T/P and *Polfunk*)

## Chief :
*ORuKR.* BERGER

## Other Personalities :
*KDir.* RICHTER, SCHMECHEL, THOMS

## Under :
*BdS.* Kassel

## Supervising :
*KPSt.* Darmstadt (for *Land* Hessen)
*KPSt.* Kassel (for *Provinz* Kurhessen without *Landkreis* Schmalkalden)

## Branch offices :
Bad Homburg v. d. H., Limburg a. d. Lahn, Wetzlar, Wiesbaden

# HALLE/Saale

## Area :
Prussian Provinces Halle-Merseburg and Magdeburg, *Reg. Bez.* Erfurt, *Land* Anhalt and *Land* Thüringen and the *Landkreis* Schmalkalden of *Provinz* Kurhessen

## In direct control of :
*Provinz* Halle-Merseburg

## Address :
Dreyhauptstr. 2
Tel : 7751 (T/P and *Polfunk*)

## Chief :
*SS-OSBF, KDir.* FEHL

## Under :
*BdS.* Dresden

## Supervising :
*KPSt.* Magdeburg (for *Provinz* Magdeburg)
*KPSt.* Erfurt (for *Reg. Bez.* Erfurt and the *Landkreis* Schmalkalden of Provinz Kurhessen)
*KPSt.* Dessau (for *Land* Anhalt)
*KPSt.* Weimar (for *Land* Thüringen)

## Branch offices :
Weissenfels, Wittenberg, Ammendorf, Bitterfeld, Delitzsch, Eilenburg, Eisleben, Merseburg, Mücheln, Naumburg/Saale, Schkeuditz, Schkopau, Sangerhausen, Torgau

# HAMBURG

## Area :
Hamburg, the *Reg. Bez.* Schleswig and the *Landkreise* Lauenburg, Stormarn, Pinneberg, Steinburg, Süder-Dithmarschen, Land Hadeln, Cuxhaven, Stade, Harburg, Soltau, Lüneburg, Ülzen, Dannenberg and the *Stadtkreise* Cuxhaven, Lüneburg, Kiel, Neumünster and Lübeck.

## In direct control of :
As above except *Reg. Bez.* Schleswig and the *Stadtkreise* Kiel, Neumünster and Lübeck.

## Address :
Dammtorwall 41
Tel : 444858/59 (T/P and *Polfunk*)

## Chief :
*SS-SF, RuKDir.* HAERTEL
Predecessor : *SS-OSBF, ORuKR.* GREINER

## Other Personalities :
*ORuKR.* ZECHENTER, *KDir.* BUCHELDT, DÖNNECKE, LYSS, SCHRAMM, *KR.* FREYTAG

## Under :
*BdS.* Hamburg

## Supervising :
*KPSt.* Flensburg
*KPSt.* Kiel

## Branch offices :
Cuxhaven, Elmshorn, Itzehoe, Lüneburg Pinneberg, Stade, Uelzen.

## HANNOVER

**Area :**

*Reg. Bez.* Hannover except *Landkreis* Grafschaft Hoya, *Reg. Bez.* Hildesheim and Osnabrück, the *Landkreise* Celle, Fallingbostel, Gifhorn and Burgdorf of *Reg. Bez.* Lüneburg, the *Landkreise* Halle/Westf., Bielefeld, Herford, Lübbecke, Minden/Westf. of *Reg. Bez.* Minden, *Land* Schaumburg-Lippe and *Land* Lippe-Detmold, *Land* Braunschweig except some of its Enclaves.

**In direct control of :**

As above except Braunschweig.

**Address :**

Hardenbergstr. 1
Tel : 44361, 43164

**Chief :**

*SS-OSBF, ORuKR.* LINNEMANN

**Other Personalities :**

*KR.* CIPER, PAAR

**Under :**

*BdS.* Braunschweig

**Supervising :**

*KPSt.* Braunschweig

**Branch offices :**

Brackwede, Bielefeld, Celle, Herford, Hildesheim, Osnabrück, Clausthal-Zellerfeld, Detmold, Göttingen, Hameln, Hann.-Münden, Holzminden, Lehrte, Lemgo, Lingen/Ems, Minden, Nienburg/Weser, Nordhorn, Northeim, Oeynhausen (Bad), Papenburg/Ems, Peine, Pyrmont (Bad), Salzuflen (Bad).

## KATTOWITZ

**Area :**

*Reg. Bez.* Kattowitz, Oppeln and Troppau

**In direct control of :**

*Reg. Bez.* Kattowitz

**Address :**

Hindenburgstr. 23
Tel : 35961

**Chief :**

*SS-SBF, RuKR.* RAUSCH

**Under :**

*BdS.* Breslau

**Supervising :**

*KPSt.* Oppeln (for *Reg. Bez.* Oppeln)
*KPSt.* Troppau (for *Reg. Bez.* Troppau)

**Branch offices :**

Auschwitz, Bendsburg, Beuthen, Bielitz, Dombrova, Gleiwitz, Ilkenau, Sosnowitz, Hindenburg, Jaworzno, Karwin, Krenau, Neu-Oderberg, Nikolai, Rybnick, Rydultau, Saybusch, Teschen, Tarnowitz.

## KÖLN

**Area :**

*Reg. Bez.* Köln, Koblenz, Trier and Aachen

**In direct control of :**

*Reg. Bez.* Köln

**Address :**

Am Weidenbach 10 or Reichensbergerplatz (Tel : 70561)
Tel : 210781 (T/P and *Polfunk*)

**Chief :**

*SS-OSBF, ORuKR.* SOMMER

**Other Personalities :**

*RuKR.* POSSEHL, *KR.* BERGER, FREYTAG, OPLADEN, *KRin.* PFAHL, *RR.* HÖHN, WATERMANN

**Under :**

*BdS.* Düsseldorf

**Supervising :**

*KPSt.* Aachen (for *Reg. Bez.* Aachen)
*KPSt.* Koblenz (for *Reg. Bez.* Koblenz)
*KPSt.* Trier (for *Reg. Bez.* Trier)

**Branch offices :**

Bergheim, Bonn, Beuel, Brühl, Bergisch-Gladbach, Euskirchen, Frechen, Godesberg (Bad), Gummersbach, Hermühlheim, Honnef/Rhein, Königswinter, Porz/Rhein, Rodenkirchen, Siegburg, Troisdorf, Wesseling

## KÖNIGSBERG

**Area :**

Prussian Province Ostpreussen (*Reg. Bez.* Königsberg, Allenstein, Gumbinnen and Zichenau)

**In direct control of :**

*Reg. Bez.* Königsberg and Allenstein

**Address :**

General-Litzmann-Str. 3/7
Tel : 24011 (T/P and *Polfunk*)

**Chief :**

*SS-SBF, RuKR.* Hellmuth MÜLLER

**Other Personalities :**

*KDir.* SCHECKENREUTHER, *KR.* BECKER, PENSKY

**Under :**

*BdS.* Königsberg

**Supervising :**

*KPSt.* Tilsit (for *Reg. Bez.* Gumbinnen)
*KPSt.* Zichenau (for *Reg. Bez.* Zichenau)

**Branch offices :**

Allenstein, Braunsberg, Bartenstein, Heiligenbeil, Heilsberg, Lötzen, Lyck, Ortelsburg, Osterode/Ostpr., Pillau, Rastenburg, Wormditt

## MÜNCHEN

**Area :**

*Reg. Bez.* Oberbayern (except the *Landkreise* Aichbach, Friedberg, Landsberg, Schongau, Schrobenhausen) ; *Reg. Bez.* Schwaben ; and of *Reg. Bez.* Niederbayern-Oberpfalz, the following *Kreise* :—Dingolfing, Eggenfelden, Griesbach, Landau, a.d.I., Landshut, Mainburg, Pfarrkirchen and Vilsbiburg

**In direct control of :**

As above except *Reg. Bez.* Schwaben

**Address :**

Ettstr. 2
Tel : 14321 (T/P and *Polfunk*)

**Chief :**

*SS-OSF, ORuKR.* GREINER (transfd. from Hamburg)
Predecessor : *SS-OSBF, RuKR. Dr.* POKORNY

**Other Personalities :**

*SS-SBF, KDir. Dr.* KATTO, *KR.* FUCHS, GASSNER, MEIXNER, REITMEIER, RUPPRECHT, SCHMEISSNER, *KRin.* ALBRECHT

**Under :**

*BdS.* München

**Supervising :**
KPSt. Augsburg (for *Reg. Bez.* Schwaben)

**Branch offices :**
Dachau, Freising, Garmisch-Partenkirchen, Ingolstadt, Landshut, Berchtesgaden, Reichenhall (Bad), Rosenheim, Traunstein

## NÜRNBERG-FÜRTH

**Area :**
*Reg. Bez.* Ober-and Mittelfranken (without *Landkeis* Scheinfeld), Mainfranken, the part Oberpfalz of the *Reg. Bez.* Niederbayern-Oberpfalz and *Reg. Bez.* Karlsbad (Egerland)

**In direct control of :**
As above except *Reg. Bez.* Mainfranken and *Reg. Bez.* Karlsbad (Egerland)

**Address :**
Ludwigstr. 36
Tel : 2951 (T/P and *Polfunk*)

**Chief :**
SS-SBF, RuKR. Dr. RIESE

**Other Personalities :**
KR. BEYER

**Under :**
BdS. Nürnberg

**Supervising :**
KPSt. Karlsbad
KPSt. Regensburg
KPSt. Würzburg

**Branch offices :**
Ansbach, Bamberg, Bayreuth, Coburg, Erlangen, Forchheim, Hof/Saale, Kulmbach, Marktredwitz, Schwabach, Selb

## POSEN

**Area :**
Reichsgau Wartheland
(*Reg. Bez.* Posen, Hohensalza, Litzmannstadt)

**In direct control of :**
*Reg. Bez.* Posen

**Address :**
Wilhelmsplatz 17/18
Tel : 8161 (T/P and *Polfunk*)

**Chief :**
SS-SBF, ORuKDir. KRÜGER

**Other Personalities :**
KR. PETERSEN

**Under :**
BdS. Posen

**Supervising :**
KPSt. Hohensalza (for *Reg. Bez.* Hohensalza)
KPSt. Litzmannstadt (for *Reg. Bez.* Litzmann-stadt)

**Branch offices :**
Kolmar/Wartheland, Kosten/Wartheland, Krotoschin, Lissa/Wartheland, Pleschen, Rawitsch, Samter

## PRAG

**Area :**
*Protektorat* Böhmen and Mähren

**In direct control of :**
Böhmen

**Address :**
Carl-Maria-v.-Weber-Str. 7
Tel : 22745/49

**Chief :**
SS-SF, RuKDir. SOWA

**Deputy :**
KDir. SCHMECHL

**Other Personalities :**
KDir. LISABETHS, RuKR. Dr. PAYER, KR. FEDDERSEN, HAMMER, WOLL-BRANDT

**Under :**
BdS. Prag

**Supervising :**
KPSt. Brünn (for Mähren)

**Branch offices :**
Budweis, Jitschin, Jungbunzlau, Kladno, Klattau, Kolin, Königgrätz, Pardubitz, Pilsen, Tabor

## SALZBURG

**Area :**
*Reichsgaue* Salzburg, Tirol-Vorarlberg, Kärnten, Steiermark

**In direct control of :**
Salzburg

**Address :**
Churfürststr. 1
Tel : 2521 (T/P and *Polfunk*)

**Chief :**
SS-SBF, KDir. Dr. BÖHMER (trfd. from Wien)

**Under :**
BdS. Salzburg

**Supervising :**
KPSt. Innsbruck (for RG. Tirol-Vorarlberg)
KPSt. Klagenfurt (for RG. Kärnten)
KPSt. Graz (for RG. Steiermark)

**Branch offices :**
Hallein

## STETTIN

**Area :**
Prussian Province Pommern
(*Reg. Bez.* Stettin, Köslin, Schneidemühl) and *Land* Mecklenburg

**In direct control of :**
*Reg. Bez.* Stettin and Köslin

**Address :**
Augustastr. 47
Tel : 35231 (T/P and *Polfunk*)

**Chief :**
KDir. GATZKE
Predecessor : RuKR. KROLL

**Other Personalities :**
KDir.Dr.BRASCHWITZ, ZUCKNICK, RuKR. HOLTERS, KR. BRAUNSCHMIDT, HEGER

**Under :**
BdS. Stettin

**Supervising :**
KPSt. Schneidemühl (for *Reg. Bez.* Schneidemühl)
KPSt. Schwerin (for *Land* Mecklenburg)

**Branch offices :**
Stolp, Stralsund, Anklam, Barth, Belgard, Bütow, Demmin, Gollnow, Greifenberg/Pommern, Greifenhagen, Greifswald, Kolberg, Köslin, Lauenburg/Pommern, Pasewalk, Polzin (Bad), Pyritz, Rügenwalde, Rummelsburg, Schivelbein, Schlawe, Swinemünde, Treptow/Rega, Stargard/Pommern, Torgelow

## STRASSBURG

**Area :**
*Land* Elsass

**In direct control of :**
*Land* Elsass

**Address :**
Otto-Backstr. 10
Tel : 20644/45 (T/P via *Stapo*)
or
Bitscherstr. 6
Tel : 25920/29 (T/P and *Polfunk*)

**Under :**
*BdS.* Strassburg—SS-OF, *Oberst d. Pol. Dr.*
FISCHER

**Other Personalities :**
*KDir.* DIETER (trfd. fr. Wiesbaden, February
1943), *KR.* BAUERNFEIND (trfd. fr. Berlin,
December, 1941), KLENKA

**Branch offices :** `
Mülhausen/Elsass, Altkirch, Bischweiler, Geb-
weiler, Hagenau, Hüningen-St. Ludwig,
Kolmar/Elsass, Markirch, Schlettstadt, Tann,
Zabern (Saverne)

## STUTTGART

**Area :**
*Land* Württemberg, *Land* Baden and *Reg. Bez.*
Sigmaringen, *Reichsgau* Westmark (without
Lothringen)

**In direct control of :**
*Land* Württemberg and *Reg. Bez.* Sigmaringen

**Address :**
Büchsenstr. 37
Tel : 22941, 25341

**Chief :**
*SS-SBF, ORuKR.* ELSNER

**Other Personalities :**
*RuKR. Dr.* BAUM, SCHNEIDER, WILLAS
(trfd. fr. Wien, January, 1943), *KDir.*
DINGERMANN (trfd. fr. Münster, Westf.),
*KR.* DOBRITZ, GESSNER, WIRTH

**Under :**
*BdS.* Stuttgart

**Supervising :**
*KPSt.* Karlsruhe (for *Land* Baden)
*KPSt.* Ludwigshafen
*KPSt.* Saarbrücken

**Branch offices :**
Friedrichshafen, Heilbronn/Neckar, Ulm/
Donau, Aalen, Backnang, Biberach/Riss,
Böblingen, Ebingen, Ellwangen, Bad Cann-
statt, Esslingen, Fellbach, Freudenstadt,
Geisslingen/Steige, Gmünd (Schwäbisch),
Göppingen, Heidenheim, Kirchheim, Korn-
westheim, Ludwigsburg, Nürtingen, Ravens-
burg, Reutlingen, Rottweil, Schramberg,
Hall (Schwäbisch), Schwenningen, Tailfingen,
Tübingen, Tuttlingen, Vaihingen

## WIEN

**Area :**
*Reichsgaue* Wien, Niederdonau, Oberdonau

**In direct control of :**
*Reichsgaue* Wien and Niederdonau

**Address :**
IX, Rossauerlände 5-7
Tel : A 18500 (T/P and *Polfunk*)

**Chief :**
*SS-SF, RuKDir.* KAPHENGST

**Other Personalities :**
*ORuKR. Dr.* BRICHTA (trfd. from Königsberg,
April 1943), JANKA, TRAUB, *RuKR. Dr.*
GRADL, *Dr.* INNGRAF (trfd. from Wiener-
Neustadt, October 1942), STEGERWALD, *Dr.*
STEINBACH, *Dr.* WALL (trfd. from Breslau,
November 1943), *KDir. Dr.* BÖHMER (trfd.
to Salzburg), *Dr.* ZAUCKE, *KR.* BAUER,
HERGT (trfd. from Karlsruhe, February
1942), *KRin.* GEIB

**Under :**
*BdS.* Wien

**Supervising :**
*KPSt.* Linz/Donau (for *Reichsgau* Oberdonau)

**Branch offices :**
Baden bei Wien, Berndorf, Krems, Lundenburg,
Marchegg, Neunkirchen, St. Pölten, Wiener-
Neustadt, Znaim

# KRIPO-STELLEN

## AACHEN

**In direct control of :**
*Reg. Bez.* Aachen

**Address :**
Kasernenstr. 25
Tel : 27121 (T/P and *Polfunk*)

**Chief :**
*KDir. Dr.* SCHWENKE

**Under :**
*BdS.* Düsseldorf
*KPLSt.* Köln

**Branch offices :**
Alsdorf, Düren, Eschweiler, Eupen, Jülich, Kohlscheid, Stolberg, Übach-Palenberg, Würselen

## AUGSBURG

**In direct control of :**
*Reg. Bez.* Schwaben, the *Landkreise* Aichach, Friedberg, Landsberg, Schongau and Schrobenhausen of *Reg. Bez.* Oberbayern

**Address :**
Prinz-Regenten-Platz 1
Tel : 3231 (T/P and *Polfunk* via *Orpo*)

**Chief :**
*KR.* DOBIAT

**Under :**
*BdS.* München
*KPLSt.* München

**Branch offices :**
Kaufbeuren, Kempten/Allgäu, Memmingen, Lindau, Neu-Ulm

## BOCHUM

**In direct control of :**
Ennepe-Ruhrkreis of the *Reg. Bez.* Arnsberg, *Stadtkreise* Bochum, Wanne-Eickel, Wattenscheid, Witten, Castrop-Rauxel, Herne

**Address :**
Uhlandstr. 35
Tel : 60661/68 (and *Polfunk*)

**Chief :**
*SS-Bewerber, RuKR.* OBERBECK

**Under :**
*BdS.* Düsseldorf
*KPLSt.* Düsseldorf

**Branch offices :**
Wanne-Eickel, Wattenscheid, Witten, Blankenstein, Castrop-Rauxel, Grevelsberg, Hattingen/Ruhr, Herne, Milspe-Voerde, Schwelm

## BRAUNSCHWEIG

**In direct control of :**
*Land* Braunschweig

**Address :**
Bohlweg 10
Tel : 5440 (T/P and *Polfunk*)

**Chief :**
*SS-SBF, KDir. Dr.* BARTMANN (transferred from Wien, August, 1943)
Predecessor : *SS-SBF, KDir.* VOLKMANN

**Under :**
*BdS.* Braunschweig
*KPLSt.* Hannover.

**Branch offices :**
Blankenburg, Goslar, Helmstedt, Salzgitter, Watenstedt-Salzgitter, Wolfenbüttel

## BROMBERG

**In direct control of :**
*Reg. Bez.* Bromberg and the *Kreise* Leipe, Rippin, Briesen, Strasburg (of the *Reg. Bez.* Marienwerder)

**Address :**
Potsdamerstr. 37
Tel : 2700 (T/P via *Stapo* and *Polfunk*)

**Chief :**
*SS-Bewerber KDir.* KORDA

**Under :**
*BdS.* Danzig
*KPLSt.* Danzig

**Branch offices :**
Thorn, Briesen, Gollub, Kulm, Leipe, Nakel, Rippin, Schwetz/Weichsel, Strasburg

## BRÜNN

**In direct control of :**
Mähren

**Address :**
Klacelgasse 2 or Stiftergasse 2 (Tel : 19988)
Tel : 10830 (T/P and *Polfunk*)

**Chief :**
*SS-USF, KDir.* NUSSBAUM

**Under :**
*BdS.* Prag
*KPLSt.* Prag

**Branch offices :**
Iglau, Mähr.-Ostrau, Olmütz, Zlin

## CHEMNITZ

**In direct control of :**
Area Chemnitz (former *Reg. Bez.* Chemnitz)

**Address :**
Hartmannstr. 24
Tel : 22441, 33041 (T/P and *Polfunk*)

**Chief :**
*KDir.* HOTZE

**Under :**
*BdS.* Dresden
*KPLSt.* Dresden

**Branch offices :**
Annaberg, Frankenberg, Glauchau, Hohenstein/Ernstthal, Liechtenstein, Limbach, Lugau, Meerane, Oelsnitz, Olbernhau, Siegmar-Schönau, Stollberg

## DARMSTADT

**In direct control of :**
*Land* Hessen

**Address :**
Hügelstr. 31/33
Tel : 7511/18 (T/P and *Polfunk*)

**Chief :**
*SS-Bewerber KR.* BALKE (trfd. fr. Bochum, October, 1941)

**Under :**
*BdS.* Wiesbaden
*KPLSt.* Frankfurt/Main

**Branch offices :**
Alzey, Giessen, Mainz, Worms, Bensheim, Bingen/Rh., Lampertheim, Nauheim (Bad), Neu-Isenburg, Offenbach, Rüsselsheim, Viernheim, Weinheim/Bergstr.

## DESSAU

**In direct control of :**
*Land* Anhalt

**Address :**
Wolfgangstr. 25
Tel : 4151 (T/P and *Polfunk*)

**Chief :**
SS-OSF, KR. JETZINGER
Predecessor : CIPER

**Under :**
*BdS.* Braunschweig
*KPLSt.* Halle/Saale

**Branch offices :**
Bernburg, Coswig, Dessau-Rosslau, Jessnitz/Anh., Köthen, Zerbst.

## DORTMUND

**In direct control of :**
*Reg. Bez.* Arnsberg except Ennepe-Ruhrkreis, the *Stadtkreise* Dortmund, Hamm, Hagen, Lüdenscheid, Lünen, Iserlohn and Siegen of the *Reg. Bez.* Arnsberg, the *Landkreise* Wiedenbrück, Paderborn, Höxter, Warburg, Büren, and the Enclaves Lipperode, Cappel and Grevenhagen of the *Reg. Bez.* Minden

**Address :**
Adolf-Hitler-Allee 1-3
Tel : 20821 (T/P and *Polfunk*)

**Chief :**
SS-SBF, RuKR. KLAMP

**Other Personalities :**
KR. NULLMEYER

**Under :**
*BdS.* Düsseldorf
*KPLSt.* Düsseldorf

**Branch offices :**
Hagen, Hamm, Paderborn, Siegen, Altena, Arnsberg, Gütersloh, Hemer, Hohenlimburg, Iserlohn, Kamen, Lippstadt, Lüdenscheid, Lünen, Menden, Neheim-Hüsten, Olpe, Pelkum, Plettenberg, Schwerte, Soest, Unna, Unna-Kamen, Weidenau

## ERFURT

**In direct control of :**
*Reg. Bez.* Erfurt and the *Landkreis* Schmalkalden of *Provinz* Kurhessen

**Address :**
Meister-Eckehart-Str. 2
Tel : 25261 (T/P and *Polfunk*)

**Chief :**
RuKR. LANGE

**Other Personalities :**
KR. ODENING

**Under :**
*BdS.* Kassel
*KPLSt.* Halle/Saale

**Branch offices :**
Mühlhausen, Nordhausen, Heiligenstadt, Langensalza, Schmalkalden, Sömmerda, Suhl

## ESSEN

**In direct control of :**
The *Landkreise* Rees, Dinslaken, the *Stadtkreise* Duisburg, Essen, Mülheim/Ruhr and Oberhausen of the *Reg. Bez.* Düsseldorf

**Address :**
Büscherstr. 2
Tel : 44551 (*Polfunk* via *Schupo* and T/P)

**Chief :**
SS-SBF, RuKR. DAMM

**Other Personalities :**
KR. Dr. BARTSCH

**Under :**
*BdS.* Düsseldorf
*KPLSt.* Düsseldorf

**Branch offices :**
Dinslaken, Duisburg, Mülheim/Ruhr, Oberhausen/Osterfeld, Walsum/Niederrh., Wesel

## FLENSBURG

**In direct control of :**
The *Kreise* Flensburg, Schleswig, Norderdithmarschen, Eiderstedt, Südtondern, Husum and Heide of the *Reg. Bez.* Schleswig

**Address :**
Norderhofenden 1
Tel : 2590/92 (T/P and *Polfunk*)

**Chief :**
KR. SCHNEIDER

**Under :**
*BdS.* Hamburg
*KPLSt.* Hamburg

**Branch offices :**
Heide, Husum, Schleswig, Westerland/Sylt

## FRANKFURT/Oder

**In direct control of :**
*Reg. Bez.* Frankfurt/Oder

**Address :**
Bischofstr. 11/12
Tel : 2860 and 4693 (T/P and *Polfunk*)

**Chief :**
KR. ENGEL

**Under :**
*BdS.* Berlin
*KPLSt.* Berlin

**Branch offices :**
Cottbus, Forst/Lausitz, Landsberg/Warthe, Crossen, Finsterwalde, Fürstenwalde, Guben, Küstrin, Schwiebus, Senftenberg, Sommerfeld, Sorau, Spremberg

## GRAZ

**In direct control of :**
*Reichsgau* Steiermark, except the area under the *Kdr. der Sipo u. des SD* in Marburg/Drau

**Address :**
Paulustorgasse 8
Tel : 6010 (T/P and *Polfunk*)

**Chief :**
SS-SBF, KDir. DAUMERLANG
Former Chief : SS-SBF, RuKR. CLASS

**Other Personalities :**
RuKR. Dr. KUNZ (trfd. to Innsbruck, November 1943)

**Under :**
*BdS.* Salzburg
*KPLSt.* Salzburg

**Branch offices :**
Eisenerz, Leoben

## HOHENSALZA

**In direct control of :**
*Reg. Bez.* Hohensalza

**Address :**
Bahnhofstr. 59
Tel : 2071

**Chief :**
SS-HSF, KR. KREBS
Predecessors : SS-HSF, KR. LINTHE,
SS-HSF, KR. LANGE

**Under :**
BdS. Posen
KPLSt. Posen

**Branch offices :**
Gnesen, Leslau, Konin, Kutno, Waldrode,
Warthbrücken, Zychlin

## INNSBRUCK

**In direct control of :**
Reichsgau Tirol-Vorarlberg

**Address :**
Südtiroler Platz 16
Tel : 2500 (T/P via Stapo)

**Chief :**
SS-OSBF, ORuKR. Dr. GASSER

**Other Personalities :**
RuKR. Dr. KUNZ (trfd. from Graz, November
1943)

**Under :**
BdS. Salzburg
KPLSt. Salzburg

**Branch offices :**
Feldkirch

## KARLSBAD

**In direct control of :**
Reg. Bez. Eger

**Address :**
Wałdzeile 24
Tel : 3526 (T/P and Polfunk)

**Chief :**
KDir. PETERS

**Under :**
BdS. Nürnberg
KPLSt. Nürnberg

**Branch offices :**
Asch, Eger, Falkenau, Graslitz, Marienbad, Saaz,
Weipert

## KARLSRUHE

**In direct control of :**
Land Baden

**Address :**
Karl-Friedrich-Strasse 15
Tel : 6093/95 (T/P and Polfunk)

**Chief :**
SS-SBF, RuKDir. BRASCHWITZ

**Other Personalities :**
KR. FRITZE
KR. KOLIATH

**Under :**
BdS. Stuttgart
KPLSt. Stuttgart

**Branch offices :**
Freiburg/Breisgau, Heidelberg, Konstanz,
Mannheim, Pforzheim, Baden-Baden,
Bruchsal, Kehl, Lahr/Schwarzw., Lörrach,
Offenburg, Radolfzell, Rastatt, Singen/
Hohentwiel, Schwetzingen, Villingen, Walds-
hut, Weil/Rhein, Weinheim/Bergstr.

## KASSEL

**In direct control of :**
Provinz Kurhessen except Landkreis Schmalkalden

**Address :**
Königstor 31
Tel : 35041/48 (T/P, Polfunk and Bildfunk)

**Chief :**
SS-SBF, KDir. WEBER

**Other Personalities :**
KR. LEIM
KR. SCHMIDT

**Under :**
BdS. Kassel
KPLSt. Frankfurt/Main

**Branch offices :**
Eschwege, Fulda, Hanau, Hersfeld, Marburg/
Lahn

## KIEL

**In direct control of :**
The Landkreise Segeberg, Oldenburg, Plön,
Rendsburg, Eckernförde, and Eutin of the
Reg. Bez. Schleswig ; the Stadtkreise Kiel,
Neumünster and Lübeck of the Reg. Bez.
Schleswig

**Address :**
Blumenstr. 2
Tel : 4300 (T/P, Polfunk and Bildfunk)

**Chief :**
SS-SBF, RuKR. KRÜGER-THIEMER

**Other Personalities :**
KDir. MÜLLER

**Under :**
BdS. Hamburg
KPLSt. Hamburg

**Branch offices :**
Lübeck, Neumünster, Rendsburg

## KLAGENFURT

**In direct control of :**
Reichsgau Kärnten, except the area under Kdr.
der Sipo u. des SD in Veldes

**Address :**
St. Ruprechterstr. 5
Tel : 320
Former Address : Landhaushof 3

**Chief :**
SS-HSF MEISSNER
Predecessor : KR. Friedrich SCHMIDT

**Under :**
BdS. Salzburg
KPLSt. Salzburg

**Branch offices :** Villach

## KOBLENZ

**In direct control of :**
Reg. Bez. Koblenz

**Address :**
Kaiser-Wilhelm-Ring 47/51
Tel : 2121

**Chief :**
SS-HSF, KR. MAISCH

**Other Personalities :**
KR. Dr. HALSWICK
KR. WOLFF

**Under :**
BdS. Wiesbaden
KPLSt. Köln

**Branch offices :**
Andernach, Bendorf, Idar-Oberstein, Kreuznach (Bad), Mayen, Neuwied

## LEIPZIG

**In direct control of :**
Area Leipzig (former *Reg. Bez.* Leipzig)

**Address :**
Wächterstr. 5
Tel : 30982 (T/P and *Polfunk*)

**Chief :**
*SS-SBF, RuKR. Dr.* BITTNER
*ORuKR.* v. CRIEGERN

**Other Personalities :**
*KR.* BRAEHMER
*KR.* GABLER

**Under :**
*BdS.* Dresden
*KPLSt.* Dresden

**Branch offices :**
Borna, Burgstädt, Döbeln, Grimma, Markkleeberg, Mittweida, Oschatz, Taucha, Waldheim, Wurzen

## LINZ/Donau

**In direct control of :**
*Reichsgau* Oberdonau

**Address :**
Mozartstr. 6/10
Tel : 26831 (T/P)

**Chief :**
*KDir.* MATZKE

**Other Personalities :**
*ORuKR. Dr.* SCHARINGER
*KR.* LANGENSTRASSE (trfd. from Wien, November, 1943)

**Under :**
*BdS.* Wien
*KPLSt.* Wien

**Branch offices :**
Isch (Bad), Krummau, Steyr, Wels.

## LITZMANNSTADT

**In direct control of :**
*Reg. Bez.* Litzmannstadt

**Address :**
Buschlinie 152
Tel : 19960/66 or 25360 (T/P and *Polfunk*)

**Chief :**
*SS-SBF, RuKR.* EHRLICH

**Other Personalities :**
*KR.* KAINTZIK
*KR.* MEIER
*KR.* PELLEGRINI
*KR.* SÄMANN (trfd. from Stuttgart, December, 1941)

**Under :**
*BdS.* Posen
*KPLSt.* Posen

**Branch offices :**
Brunnstadt, Frauhaus, Görnau, Kalisch, Kempen, Ostrowo, Pabianice, Schieratz, Turek, Welun

## LUDWIGSHAFEN

**In direct control of :**
*Reg. Bez. Pfalz*

**Address :**
Wittelsbachstr. 3
Tel : 61911 (T/P and *Polfunk*)

**Chief :**
*KR.* BORN

**Under :**
*BdS.* Metz
*KPLSt.* Stuttgart

**Branch offices :**
Frankenthal, Kaiserslautern, Landau, Neustadt/Weinstrasse, Pirmasens, Speyer, Zweibrücken

## MAGDEBURG

**In direct control of :**
*Provinz* Magdeburg

**Address :**
Halberstädterstr. 2
Tel : 42841 (T/P, *Polfunk* and *Bildfunk*)

**Chief :**
*SS-SBF, KDir.* SCHULZ-LEHNHARDT

**Other Personalities :**
*KR.* MORITZ

**Under :**
*BdS.* Braunschweig
*KPLSt.* Halle/Saale

**Branch offices :**
Halberstadt, Aken/Elbe, Aschersleben, Burg/Magdeburg, Calbe/Saale, Gardelegen, Genthin, Gross Ottersleben, Haldensleben, Oschersleben, Salzwedel, Schönebeck/Elbe, Stassfurt, Stendal, Tangermünde, Thale/Harz, Quedlinburg, Wernigerode

## OPPELN

**In direct control of :**
*Reg. Bez.* Oppeln

**Address :**
Moltkestr. 43
Tel : 3451 (T/P via *Stapo*)

**Chief :**
*SS-Bewerber, KDir.* REICHE

**Under :**
*BdS.* Breslau
*KPLSt.* Kattowitz

**Branch offices :**
Cosel, Gross-Strehlitz, Heydebreck, Kreuzburg, Leobschütz, Loben, Neisse, Neustadt, Ratibor, Rosenberg, Warthenau, Ziegenhals

## RECKLINGHAUSEN

**In direct control of :**
*Reg. Bez.* Münster

**Address :**
Westerholter Weg 27
Tel : 4343

**Chief :**
*SS-SBF, RuKR. Dr.* EWELER

**Other personalities :**
*KR.* KEMPE, LANGBEIN, BRUECKENHAUS

**Under :**
*BdS.* Düsseldorf
*KPLSt.* Düsseldorf

**Branch offices :**
Ahlen/Westf., Bocholt, Bockum-Hövel, Borghorst, Bork, Bottrop, Bottrop-Bay, Bottrop-Eigen, Coesfeld, Datteln, Dülmen, Emsdetten, Erkenschwick, Gelsenkirchen, Gelsenkirchen-Buer, Gelsenkirchen-Horst, Gladbeck, Gronau, Herten, Hervest-Dorsten, Hüls, Ibbenbüren, Lengerich, Marl, Recklinghausen-Süd, Recklinghausen-Suderich, Rheine, Waltrop, Werne-Lippe

## REGENSBURG

**In direct control of :**
Reg. Bez. Niederbayern and Oberpfalz with the exception of the Landkreise Beilngries, Neumarkt i.O., Mainburg, Landshut, Dingolfing, Landau a.d. Isar, Vilsbiburg, Eggenfelden, Pfarrkirchen and Griesbach.
The Landkreise Bergreichenstein, Markt-Eisenstein and Prachatitz of the Sudetenland

**Address :**
Minoritenweg 1
Tel : 5251 (T/P via Stapo and Polfunk via Pol. Direktion)

**Chief :**
KR. BURGER or KInsp. SCHMIDBAUER

**Under :**
BdS. Nürnberg
KPLSt. Nürnberg

**Branch offices :**
Amberg, Passau, Schwandorf, Straubing, Weiden

## REICHENBERG

**In direct control of :**
Reg. Bez. Aussig

**Address :**
Laufergasse 8
Tel : 3141 (T/P via Stapo and Polfunk)

**Chief :**
SS-SBF, KDir. ROSSBERG

**Under :**
BdS. Dresden
KPLSt. Dresden

**Branch offices :**
Aussig, Bilin, Böhm.-Leipa, Bruch, Brüx, Dux Gablonz, Komotau, Leitmeritz, Maltheuern, Oberleutensdorf, Teplitz-Schönau, Tetschen-Bodenbach, Trautenau, Warnsdorf

## SAARBRÜCKEN

**In direct control of :**
Saarland

**Address :**
Schlossplatz 1–2
Tel : 29261 (T/P and Polfunk)

**Chief :**
SS-HSF, KDir. DINGERMANN
Predecessor : SS-SBF, KR. KRAUSE

**Other personalities :**
KR. SCHMIDT

**Under :**
BdS. Metz
KPLSt. Stuttgart

**Branch offices :**
Brebach, Dudweiler, Forbach, Friedrichsthal, Homburg/Saar, Neunkirchen/Saar, Sulzbach/Saar, Völklingen, Saarlautern, St. Ingbert

## SCHNEIDEMÜHL

**In direct control of :**
Reg. Bez. Schneidemühl

**Address :**
Danziger Platz 6
Tel : 2341 and 2351 (T/P and Polfunk)

**Chief :**
KR. BLEY

**Under :**
BdS. Stettin
KPLSt. Stettin

**Branch offices :**
Deutsch Krone, Neustettin

## SCHWERIN

**In direct control of :**
Land Mecklenburg

**Address :**
Schelfstr. 35
Tel : 5051

**Chief :**
SS-SBF, KR. SIEDENTOPF

**Under :**
BdS. Stettin
KPLSt. Stettin

**Branch offices :**
Rostock incl. Warnemünde, Güstrow, Neu-Brandenburg, Neustrelitz, Parchim, Waren/Müritz, Wismar/Seestadt

## TILSIT

**In direct control of :**
Reg. Bez. Gumbinnen

**Address :**
SA.-Strasse 67
Tel : 2991 (T/P and Polfunk)

**Chief :**
KDir. NITSCHE

**Other personalities :**
KR. WUTH

**Under :**
BdS. Königsberg
KPLSt. Königsberg

**Branch offices :**
Insterburg, Memel, Angerburg, Goldap, Gumbinnen, Sudauen

## TRIER

**In direct control of :**
Reg. Bez. Trier

**Address :**
Eurenerstr. 6-8
Tel : 3747 (T/P via Stapo)

**Chief :**
SS-HSF, KR. ZILLMANN

**Under :**
BdS. Wiesbaden
KPLSt. Köln

## TROPPAU

**In direct control of :**
Reg. Bez. Troppau

**Address :**
Johannesgasse 4
Tel : 66, 82 and 275

**Chief :**
KR. BUNGE (trfd. from Duisburg, October, 1943)
Predecessor : RuKR. JURETZKI

**Under :**
BdS. Breslau
KPLSt. Kattowitz

**Branch offices :**
Jägerndorf, Mährisch-Schönberg, Neutitschein, Sternberg, Zwittau

## WEIMAR

**In direct control of :**
Land Thüringen

**Address :**
Sophienstr. 8-10
Tel : 6341 (T/P and Polfunk)

**Chief :**
  SS-HSF, KR. LINDNER
  Predecessor : KR. BERNER
**Under :**
  BdS. Kassel
  KPLSt. Halle/Saale
**Branch offices :**
  Apolda, Arnstadt, Altenburg, Eisenach, Gera,
  Gotha, Greiz, Ilmenau, Jena, Eisenberg,
  Meiningen, Meuselwitz, Pössneck, Rudolstadt,
  Saalfeld, Schmölln, Sondershausen, Sonne-
  berg, Weida, Zella-Mehlis, Zeulenroda

### WILHELMSHAVEN

**In direct control of :**
  Reg. Bez. Aurich and the Landkreise Friesland
  and Ammerland of Land Oldenburg
**Address :**
  Roonstr. 57 or Hindenburgstr. 29
  Tel : 2360/62 or 5231 (T/P and Polfunk)
**Chief :**
  SS-HSF, RuKR. BORRMANN
**Under :**
  BdS. Hamburg
  KPLSt. Bremen
**Branch offices :**
  Emden, Leer, Norden

### WUPPERTAL

**In direct control of :**
  The Stadtkreise Wuppertal, Remscheid and
  Solingen of the Reg. Bez. Düsseldorf
  Parts of the Rhein-Wupperkreis of the Reg. Bez.
  Düsseldorf
**Address :**
  Adolf-Hitler-Strasse 390
  Tel : 21101 (T/P and Polfunk)
**Chief :**
  KDir. BAUMANN
**Other Personalities :**
  KR. FROSIEN
**Under :**
  BdS. Düsseldorf
  KPLSt. Düsseldorf
**Branch offices :**
  Remscheid, Solingen, Haan, Langenberg, Mett-
  mann, Radevormwald, Wermelskirchen

### WÜRZBURG

**In direct control of :**
  Reg. Bez. Mainfranken and the Landkreis
  Scheinfeld of the Reg. Bez. Ober-and Mittel-
  franken and Gendarmerieposten Ostheim a.d.
  Rhön of Landkreis Meiningen (Reg. Bez.
  Weimar)
**Address :**
  Karmeliterstr. 12 or Ottostr. 1
  Tel : 4703 (T/P and Polfunk)
**Chief :**
  SS-HSF, KR. HANS
  Predecessor : KK. MARTHALER (i.V.)
**Other Personalities :**
  KK. JÄGER (trfd. from Kaiserslautern, April,
  1942)
**Under :**
  BdS. Nürnberg
  KPLSt. Nürnberg
**Branch offices :**
  Aschaffenburg, Kissingen (Bad), Kitzingen,
  Schweinfurt

### ZICHENAU

**In direct control of :**
  Reg. Bez. Zichenau
**Address :**
  Kirchenstr. 17
  Tel : 484 (T/P via Stapo)
  Former Address : Warschauerstr. 12
**Chief :**
  KInsp. TISCHINGER
  Predecessor : KR. SCHINDLER
**Under :**
  BdS. Königsberg
  KPLSt. Königsberg
**Branch offices :**
  Mielau, Plöhnen, Ostenburg, Praschnitz,
  Scharfenwiese, Schröttersburg

### ZWICKAU

**In direct control of :**
  Area Zwickau (Former Reg. Bez. Zwickau)
**Address :**
  Bahnhofstr. 2
  Tel : 5141 (T/P and Polfunk).
  Former Address : Werdauer Strasse 62
**Chief :**
  KR. KATZENBERGER
  Predecessor : RR. Dr. BASELER
**Under :**
  BdS. Dresden
  KPLSt. Dresden
**Branch offices :**
  Plauen, Aue, Auerbach, Crimmitschau, Falken-
  stein, Oelsnitz/Vogtl., Planitz, Reichenbach,
  Rodewisch, Schwarzenberg, Schneeberg,
  Werdau, Wilkau-Hasslau

### KdS LUXEMBURG

**In direct control of :**
  Zivilverwaltungsgebiet Luxemburg
**Address :**
  Einsatzkommando der Sipo und des SD in
  Luxemburg, Petrussring 57
  Tel : 6786/88 (and T/P)
**Kommandeur :**
  SS-OSBF, ORR. HARTMANN
**Under :**
  BdS. WIESBADEN
**Branch offices :**
  Esch/Alzig, Luxemburg

### KdS MARBURG/Drau

**In direct control of :**
  Zivilverwaltungsgebiet Untersteiermark
**Address :**
  Kommando der Sipo und des SD in Marburg,
  Tegethoffstr. 34
  Tel : 24-84 (T/P—Polfunk—Bildfunk)
**Kommandeur :**
  SS-SBF, KDir. STAGE
  Predecessor : SS-SBF, RuKR. VOGT
**Under :**
  BdS. Salzburg
**Branch offices :**
  Cilli, Polstrau, Rann, Trifail

## KdS METZ

**In direct control of :**
Lothringen

**Address :**
*Einsatzkommando der Sipo und des SD* in Metz,
Adolf-Hitler-Str. 42
Tel : 1330

**Under supervision of :**
*BdS*. Metz

**Branch offices :**
Diedenhofen, Saarburg, St. Avold, Saargemünd

## KdS VELDES

**In direct control of :**
*Zivilverwaltungsgebiet* Oberkrain

**Address :**
*Kommando der Sipo und des SD für die besetzten
Gebiete* Kärntens und Krains in Veldes,
Parkhotel
Tel : 204/206 (and T/P)

**Kommandeur :**
*SS-SBF, RuKR*. VOGT
Predecessor : *SS-SBF* PERSTERER

**Under :**
*BdS*. Salzburg

**Branch offices :**
Assling, Laak/Zaier, Littai, Radmannsdorf,
Stein

# KRIPO AUSSENDIENSTSTELLEN UND AUSSENPOSTEN—
## (Kripo Branch Offices)

*Note.*—An attempt has been made to arrive at the correct classification of all identified *Kripo* Branch Offices listed below, i.e. to determine on the basis of the number of inhabitants and the national importance of the town whether under the recent re-organisation (see text para. 118ff.), a particular *Kripo* office has become a *Kripo Aussendienststelle* (*AuDSt.*) or a *Kripo Aussenposten* (*AuP*). Since documentary evidence showing such classification is limited, the information in column 3 is only an indication, not a final statement. Cases marked with an asterisk (*) are, however, confirmed by documents.

| Town | Population (in 1,000 of inhabitants) | Classification | Higher Headquarters | Under BdS in Wkr. |
|---|---|---|---|---|
| Aalen, Marktplatz 4 | 16 | AuP | LSt. Stuttgart | V |
| Ahlen/Westf., Klosterstr. 15 | .26 | AuP | LSt. Düsseldorf St. Recklinghausen | VI |
| Aken, Markt 11 | 12 | AuP | LSt. Halle St. Magdeburg | XI |
| Allenstein, Rathausstr. | 50 | AuDSt. | LSt. Königsberg | I |
| Alsdorf, Hindenburgstr. 54 | 19 | AuP (*) | LSt. Köln St. Aachen | VI |
| Altena, Lüdenscheider Str. 25 | 17 | AuP | LSt. Düsseldorf St. Dortmund | VI |
| Altenburg, bei der Brüderkirche | 46 | AuDSt. | LSt. Halle St. Weimar | IX |
| Altkirch (no address) | 4 | AuP | LSt. Strassburg | V |
| Alzey, Fischmarkt 3 | 10 | AuP | LSt. Frankfurt/Main St. Darmstadt | XII |
| Amberg, Rathausplatz 1 | 32 | AuP | LSt. München St. Regensburg | XIII |
| Ammendorf, Hindenburg-str. 71 | 16 | AuP | LSt. Halle | IV |
| Annaberg, Steinweg 4 | 19 | AuP | LSt. Dresden St. Chemnitz | IV |
| Andernach, Hochstr. | 14 | AuP | LSt. Köln St. Koblenz | XII |
| Angerburg, Neue Marktstr.16 | 11 | AuP | LSt. Königsberg St. Tilsit | I |
| Anklam, Peenstr. 30–31 | 20 | AuP | LSt. Stettin | II |
| Ansbach, Martin-Luther-Platz 1 | 26 | AuP | LSt. Nürnberg | XIII |
| Apolda, Markt 1 | 28 | AuP | LSt. Halle St. Weimar | IX |
| Arnsberg, Alter Markt, 22 | 15 | AuP | LSt. Düsseldorf St. Dortmund | VI |
| Arnstadt, Rathaus | 22 | AuP | LSt. Halle St. Weimar | IX |
| Asch, Adolf-Hitler-Str. 29 | 23 | AuP | LSt. Nürnberg St. Karlsbad | XIII |
| Aschaffenburg, Schlossplatz 4 | 45 | AuDSt | LSt. Nürnberg St. Würzburg | IX |
| Aschersleben, Hohe Str. 7 | 32 | AuP | LSt. Halle St. Magdeburg | XI |
| Assling, Adolf Hitler Str. 24 | | AuDSt(*) | KdS Veldes | XVIII |
| Aue, Göthestr. 1 | 25 | AuP | LSt. Dresden St. Zwickau | IV |
| Auerbach, Bahnhofstr. 6 | 19 | AuP | LSt. Dresden St. Zwickau | IV |
| Auschwitz, Adolf-Hitler-Platz 2 | 64 | AuDSt | LSt. Kattowitz | VIII |
| Aussig, Langemarckplatz 10 | 67 | AuDSt | LSt. Dresden St. Reichenberg | IV |
| Backnang, Adolf-Hitler-Platz 6 | 13 | AuP | LSt. Stuttgart | V |
| Baden, Adolf-Hitler-Platz 1 | 24 | AuP | LSt. Wien | XVII |
| Baden-Baden, Sophienstr. 40 | 35 | AuP | LSt. Stuttgart St. Karlsruhe | V |
| Bamberg, Maximilianplatz 3 | 60 | AuDSt | LSt. Nürnberg | XIII |
| Bartenstein, Rasten-burgerstr. 12 | 13 | AuP | LSt. Königsberg | I |
| Barth, Strasse der SA 16 | 11 | AuP | LSt. Stettin | II |
| Bautzen, Ortenburg 9 | 42 | AuP | LSt. Dresden | IV |
| Bayreuth, Maxstr. 33 | 45 | AuDSt | LSt. Nürnberg | XIII |
| Belgard, Markt 16–17 | 16 | AuP | LSt. Stettin | II |

| Town | Population (in 1,000 of inhabitants) | Classification | Higher Headquarters | Under BdS in Wkr. |
|---|---|---|---|---|
| Bendorf/Rh., Stadtpark 1 | 11 | AuP | LSt. Köln St. Koblenz | XII |
| Bendsburg, Kattowitzer Str. 54a | 5 | AuDSt (*) | LSt. Kattowitz | VIII |
| Bensheim, Hauptstr. 39 | 17 | AuP | LSt. Frankfurt/M. St. Darmstadt | XII |
| Berg. Gladbach, Am Markt | 22 | AuP | LSt. Köln | VI |
| Bergheim, Adolf-Hitler-Str. 11 | 5 | AuP | LSt. Köln | VI |
| Bernau, Am Markt | 15 | AuP | LSt. Berlin | III |
| Bernburg, Rathaus | 42 | AuP | LSt. Halle St. Dessau | XI |
| Berndorf, Adolf Hitler Platz 3 | 11 | AuP | LSt. Wien | XVII |
| Beuel, Horst-Wessel-Str. 17 | 20 | AuP | LSt. Köln | VI |
| Beuthen, Reichspräsidentenplatz 17 | 101 | AuDSt | LSt. Kattowitz | VIII |
| Biberach/Riss, Hindenburgstr. 1 | 12 | AuP | LSt. Stuttgart | V |
| Bielefeld, Turnerstr. 16–18 | 130 | AuDSt | LSt. Hannover | VI |
| Bielitz, Schulgasse 1 | 54 | AuDSt | LSt. Kattowitz | VIII |
| Bilin/Mähren, Prokopigasse 9 | 9 | AuDSt | LSt. Dresden St. Reichenberg | IV |
| Bingen/Rh., Am Markt 19 | 17 | AuP | LSt. Frankfurt/M. St. Darmstadt | XII |
| Bischofswerda, Rathaus | 10 | AuP | LSt. Dresden | IV |
| Bischweiler, Bismarckpl. 7–9 | | AuP | LSt. Strassburg | V |
| Bitterfeld, Bismarckstr. 42 | 24 | AuP | LSt. Halle | IV |
| Blankenburg, Am Markt 8 | 14 | AuP | LSt. Hannover St. Braunschweig | XI |
| Blankenstein, Marktplatz 1 | | AuP | LSt. Düsseldorf St. Bochum | VI |
| Böblingen (no address) | 13 | AuP | LSt. Stuttgart | V |
| Böhm.-Leipa, Sonnengasse 231 | 12 | AuP | LSt. Dresden St. Reichenberg | IV |
| Bocholt, Schwarzstr. 70 | 35 | AuP | LSt. Düsseldorf St. Recklinghausen | VI |
| Bockum-Hövel, Vogelbrink 12 | | AuP | LSt. Düsseldorf St. Recklinghausen | VI |
| Bonn, Rathausgasse 22 | 100 | AuDSt | LSt. Köln | VI |
| Borghorst, Nordwalderstr. 20 | | AuP | LSt. Düsseldorf St. Recklinghausen | VI |
| Bork, Horst-Wessel-Platz 130 | | AuP | LSt. Düsseldorf St. Recklinghausen | VI |
| Borna, Rosengasse 2 | 15 | AuP | LSt. Dresden St. Leipzig | IV |
| Bottrop, Droste-Hülshoffstr. 5 | 83 | AuDSt (Kriminalinspektion IV of St. Recklinghausen) | LSt. Düsseldorf St. Recklinghausen | VI |
| Bottrop-Eigen, Gladbeckerstr. 215 | | AuDSt (*) | LSt. Düsseldorf St. Recklinghausen | VI |
| Bottrop-Bay, Kraneburgstr. 8 | | AuDSt (*) | LSt. Düsseldorf St. Recklinghausen | VI |
| Brackwede, Rathaus | 15 | AuP | LSt. Hannover | VI |
| Brandenburg/Havel, Neuendorferstr. 90a | 84 | AuDSt | LSt. Berlin | III |
| Braunsberg, Altstädtischer Markt 1 | 21 | AuP | LSt. Königsberg | I |
| Brebach, Adolf-Hitler-Str. 21 | | AuDSt (*) | LSt. Stuttgart St. Saarbrücken | XII |
| Brieg, Tuchhausgasse 7–9 | 31 | AuP | LSt. Breslau | VIII |
| Briesen/Westpr., Hermann-Göring-Str. 16 | 10 | AuP | LSt. Danzig St. Bromberg | XX |
| Bruch, Strasse der SA | 7 | AuDSt (*) | LSt. Dresden St. Reichenberg | IV |
| Bruchsal, Schönbornstr. 12 | 18 | AuP | LSt. Stuttgart St. Karlsruhe | V |
| Brühl, Steinweg 1 | 24 | AuP | LSt. Köln | VI |
| Brüx, Adolf-Hitler-Platz 3 | 36 | AuDSt | LSt. Dresden St. Reichenberg | IV |
| Brunnstadt, Kommandanturweg 1 | | AuP | LSt. Posen St. Litzmannstadt | XXI |

| Town | Population (in 1,000 of inhabitants) | Classification | Higher Headquarters | Under BdS in Wkr. |
|---|---|---|---|---|
| Budweis, Ottokargasse 595 | 44 | AuDSt (*) | LSt. Prag | B/M |
| Burg b. Magdeburg, Breiter Weg 28 | 30 | AuP | LSt. Halle St. Magdeburg | XI |
| Bunzlau, Rathaus | 23 | AuP | LSt. Breslau | VIII |
| Bütow, Markt 6 | 9 | AuP | LSt. Stettin | II |
| Burgstädt, Brühl 3 | 18 | AuP | LSt. Dresden St. Leipzig | IV |
| Calbe/Saale, Markt 14 | 12 | AuP | LSt. Halle St. Magdeburg | XI |
| Cannstatt, Bad (no address) under Stuttgart | | AuP | LSt. Stuttgart | V |
| Castrop-Rauxel, Zeppelinstr. 11 | 56 | AuP | LSt. Düsseldorf St. Bochum | VI |
| Celle, Bergstr. 46 | 38 | AuDSt | LSt. Hannover | XI |
| Cilli, Rathaus | 20 | AuDSt (*) | KdS Marburg/Drau | XVIII |
| Clausthal-Zellerfeld, Bahnhofstr. 2 | 11 | AuP | LSt. Hannover | XI |
| Coburg, Rathaus | 33 | AuP | LSt. Nürnberg | XIII |
| Coesfeld, Ludwig-Knickmannstr. 500 | 14 | AuP | LSt. Düsseldorf St. Recklinghausen | VI |
| Cosel, Schlosstr. | 10 | AuP | LSt. Kattowitz St. Oppeln | VIII |
| Coswig, Rathaus | 13 | AuP | LSt. Halle St. Dessau | XI |
| Coswig/Sachsen, Adolf-Hitler-Str. 20 | 10 | AuP | LSt. Dresden | IV |
| Cottbus, Neuer Markt 5 | 55 | AuDSt. | LSt. Berlin St. Frankfurt/Oder | III |
| Crimmitschau, Badergasse 2 | 27 | AuP | LSt. Dresden St. Zwickau | IV |
| Crossen, Markt 14 | 11 | AuP | LSt. Berlin St. Frankfurt/Oder | III |
| Cuxhaven, Holstenstr. 4 | 33 | AuDSt. | LSt. Hamburg | X |
| Dachau, Rathaus | 18 | AuP | LSt. München | VII |
| Datteln, Hermann-Göring-Str. 8 | 20 | AuDSt (*) | LSt. Düsseldorf St. Recklinghausen | VI |
| Delitzsch, Markt 3 | 18 | AuP | LSt. Halle | IV |
| Delmenhorst, Adolf-Hitler-Platz 6 | 38 | AuP | LSt. Bremen | X |
| Demmin, Markt 25 | 16 | AuP (*) | LSt. Stettin | II |
| Dessau-Rosslau, Am Alten Friedhof 8 | | AuP | LSt. Halle/Saale St. Dessau | XI |
| Detmold, Marktplatz 2 | 23 | AuDSt. | LSt. Hannover | VI |
| Deutsch-Eylau, Karl-Freiburgerstr. 16 | 14 | AuP | LSt. Danzig | XX |
| Deutsch Krone, Rathaus | 15 | AuDSt (*) | LSt. Stettin St. Schneidemühl | II |
| Diedenhofen, Adolf-Hitler-Platz 6 | | AuDSt | KdS. Metz | XII |
| Dinslaken, Duisburgerstr. 56 | 26 | AuP | LSt. Düsseldorf St. Essen | VI |
| Dirschau, Stadtgraben 12b | 21 | AuP | LSt. Danzig | XX |
| Döbeln, Rathaus | 25 | AuP | LSt. Dresden St. Leipzig | IV |
| Dombrowa, Graf-Reden-Str. 12 | 38 | AuDSt (*) | LSt. Kattowitz | VIII |
| Dülken, Rathaus | 16 | AuP | LSt. Düsseldorf | VI |
| Dülmen, Königswall 18 | 11 | AuP | LSt. Düsseldorf St. Recklinghausen | VI |
| Düren, Wilhelmstr. 2 | 45 | AuDSt (*) | LSt. Köln St. Aachen | VI |
| Dudweiler, Hermann-Göring-Str. 6 | | AuDSt (*) | LSt. Stuttgart St. Saarbrücken | XII |
| Duisburg, Düsseldorfstr. 162 | 435 | AuDSt. | LSt. Düsseldorf St. Essen | VI |
| Dux, Bahnhofstr. 2 | 10 | AuDSt (*) | LSt. Dresden St. Reichenberg | IV |
| Eberswalde, Breite Str. 42 | 40 | AuP | LSt. Berlin | III |
| Ebingen, Marktstr. 46 | 15 | AuP | LSt. Stuttgart | V |
| Eger, Münzgasse 1 | 35 | AuDSt. | LSt. Nürnberg St. Karlsbad | XIII |
| Eilenburg, Torgauerstr. 35 | 21 | AuP | LSt. Halle | IV |
| Eisenach, Karlstr. 1 | 53 | AuDSt | LSt. Halle St. Weimar | IX |

| Town | Population (in 1,000 of inhabitants) | Classification | Higher Headquarters | Under BdS in Wkr. |
|---|---|---|---|---|
| Eisenberg, Schloss | 11 | AuP | LSt. Halle / St. Weimar | IX |
| Eisenerz, Polizeibaracke | 12 | AuP | LSt. Salzburg / St. Graz | XVIII |
| Eisleben, Markt 22 | 23 | AuP | LSt. Halle | IV |
| Elbing, Göringplatz 10 | 85 | AuDSt | LSt. Danzig | XX |
| Ellwangen (no address) | 7 | AuP | LSt. Stuttgart | V |
| Elmshorn, Adolf-Hitler-Str. 28 | 22 | AuP | LSt. Hamburg / St. Kiel | X |
| Emden, Wilhelmstr. 2 | 35 | AuP | LSt. Bremen / St. Wilhelmshaven | X |
| Emmerich, Geistenmarkt | 16 | AuP | LSt. Düsseldorf | VI |
| Emsdetten, Isendorferstr. 51 | 17 | AuP | LSt. Düsseldorf / St. Recklinghausen | VI |
| Erkenschwick, Litzmannstr. 3 | | AuDSt (*) | LSt. Düsseldorf / St. Recklinghausen | VI |
| Erlangen, Marktplatz 1 | 36 | AuP | LSt. Nürnberg | XIII |
| Esch/Alzig, Bahnhofstr. 30 | 29 | AuDSt (*) | KdS. Luxemburg | XII |
| Eschweiler, Dürener Str. 5 | 32 | AuP (*) | LSt. Köln / St. Aachen | VI |
| Eschwege, Marktplatz 2 | 17 | AuP | LSt. Frankfurt/M. / St. Kassel | IX |
| Esslingen/Neckar, Platz der SA 7 | 50 | AuP | LSt. Stuttgart | V |
| Eupen, Aachener Str. 8 | 13 | AuP (*) | LSt. Köln / St. Aachen | VI |
| Euskirchen, Adolf-Hitler-Str. 1 | 17 | AuP | LSt. Köln | VI |
| Falkenau/Eger, Adolf-Hitler-Platz 39 | 14 | AuP | LSt. Nürnberg / St. Karlsbad | XIII |
| Falkensee, Rathaus | 3 | AuP | LSt. Berlin | III |
| Falkenstein/Vogtl., Amts-Str. 10 | 15 | AuP | LSt. Dresden / St. Zwickau | IV |
| Feldkirch, Schillerstr. 1 | 13 | AuP | LSt. Salzburg / St. Innsbruck | XVIII |
| Fellbach, Cannstatterstr. 16 | 15 | AuP | LSt. Stuttgart | V |
| Finsterwalde, Schloss Str. 7–8 | 20 | AuP | LSt. Berlin / St. Frankfurt/Oder | III |
| Forbach, Adolf-Hitler-Str. 29 | 3 | AuDSt (*) | LSt. Stuttgart / St. Saarbrücken | XII |
| Forcheim, Rathausplatz | 11 | AuP | LSt. Nürnberg | XIII |
| Forst/Lausitz, Markt 9 | 45 | AuDSt | LSt. Berlin / St. Frankfurt/Oder | III |
| Frankenberg/Sachsen, Kirchgasse 8 | | AuP | LSt. Dresden / St. Chemnitz | IV |
| Frankenstein, Rathaus | 11 | AuP | LSt. Breslau | VIII |
| Frankenthal, Rathausplatz 2 | 27 | AuP | St. Stuttgart / St. Ludwigshafen | XII |
| Frauhaus, Rathausstr. 12 | | AuP | LSt. Posen / St. Litzmannstadt | XXI |
| Frechen, Antonnieterstr. 1 | 14 | AuP | LSt. Köln | VI |
| Freiberg/Sa., Fischerstr. 2 | 36 | AuP | LSt. Dresden | IV |
| Freiburg/Breisgau, Engelstr. 3 | 110 | AuDSt | LSt. Stuttgart / St. Karlsruhe | V |
| Freising, Rathaus | 20 | AuP | LSt. München | VII |
| Freital, Obere Dresdener Str. 102 | 37 | AuP | LSt. Dresden | IV |
| Freudenstadt, Kaufhaus-Str. 2 | 11 | AuP | LSt. Stuttgart | V |
| Friedrichshafen, Friedrichstr. 87 | 25 | AuDSt (*) | LSt. Stuttgart | V |
| Friedrichsthal, Schmidt-born-Str. 13 | 14 | AuDSt (*) | LSt. Stuttgart / St. Saarbrücken | XII |
| Fürstenwalde, Rathaus-platz 2 | 29 | AuP | LSt. Berlin / St. Frankfurt/Oder | III |
| Fulda, Schlosstr. 1 | 34 | AuP | LSt. Frankfurt/M. / St. Kassel | IX |
| Gablonz/Neisse, Talstr. 33 | 29 | AuDSt (*) | LSt. Dresden / St. Reichenberg | IV |
| Gardelegen, Am Markt 12 | 12 | AuP | LSt. Halle / St. Magdeburg | XI |
| Garmisch-Partenkirchen, Adolf-Hitler-Platz | 18 | AuP | LSt. München | VII |

| Town | Population (in 1,000 of inhabitants) | Classification | Higher Headquarters | Under BdS in Wkr. |
|---|---|---|---|---|
| Gebweiler, Adolf-Hitler-Str. 63 | 12 | AuP | LSt. Strassburg | V |
| Geisslingen, Hindenburg-str. 1 | 17 | AuP | LSt. Stuttgart | V |
| Gelsenkirchen, Ahstr. 24 | 318 | AuDSt (Kriminalinspektion III of St. Recklinghausen) | LSt. Düsseldorf St. Recklinghausen | VI |
| Gelsenkirchen-Buer, Adolf-Hitler-Platz 3 | | AuDSt (Kriminalinspektion II of St. Recklinghausen) | LSt. Düsseldorf St. Recklinghausen | VI |
| Gelsenkirchen-Horst, Am Stern | | AuP | LSt. Düsseldorf St. Recklinghausen | VI |
| Genthin, Adolf-Hitler-Str. 3 | 13 | AuP | LSt. Halle St. Magdeburg | XI |
| Gera, Burgstr. 6 | 83 | AuDSt | LSt. Halle St. Weimar | IX |
| Grevelsberg, Adolf-Hitler-Str. 14 | 23 | AuP | LSt. Düsseldorf St. Bochum | VI |
| Giessen, Kirchstr. 11 | 46 | AuDSt | LSt. Frankfurt/M. St. Darmstadt | IX |
| Gladbeck, Lothringerstr. 6 | 59 | AuDSt (*) | LSt. Düsseldorf St. Recklinghausen | VI |
| Glatz, Rathaus | 22 | AuP | LSt. Breslau | VIII |
| Glauchau, Markt 4 | 34 | AuP | LSt. Dresden St. Chemnitz | IV |
| Gleiwitz, Teuchertstr. 20 | 117 | AuDSt | LSt. Kattowitz | VIII |
| Glogau, Lange Str. 44 | 34 | AuP | LSt. Breslau | VIII |
| Gmünd (Schwäbisch), Hofstatt 7 | 22 | AuP | LSt. Stuttgart | V |
| Gnesen, Neustadt 28 | 34 | AuDSt | LSt. Posen St. Hohensalza | XXI |
| Goch, Rathaus | 14 | AuP | LSt. Düsseldorf | VI |
| Godesberg, Bad, Kur-fürstenstr. 3–5 | 30 | AuP | LSt. Köln | VI |
| Goldap, Markt 2 | 13 | AuP | LSt. Königsberg St. Tilsit | I |
| Gollnow, Rathaus | 14 | AuP (*) | LSt. Stettin | II |
| Gollub, Markt 23 | 4 | AuP | LSt. Danzig St. Bromberg | XX |
| Göppingen, Pfarrstr. 29 | 30 | AuP | LSt. Stuttgart | V |
| Görlitz, Rathaus Str. 1 | 94 | AuDSt. | LSt. Breslau | VIII |
| Görnau, Adolf-Hitler-Platz 1 | | AuP | LSt. Posen St. Litzmannstadt | XXI |
| Goslar, Markt 1 | 27 | AuP | LSt. Hannover St. Braunschweig | XI |
| Gotenhafen, Litzmannplatz | 124 | AuDSt | LSt. Danzig | XX |
| Gotha, Erfurterstr. 2 | 55 | AuDSt | LSt. Halle St. Weimar | IX |
| Göttingen, Gothmarstr. 8 | 51 | AuDSt | LSt. Hannover | XI |
| Graslitz, Bürgermeisteramt | 12 | AuP | LSt. Nürnberg St. Karlsbad | XIII |
| Graudenz, Königstr. 3 | 60 | AuDSt | LSt. Danzig | XX |
| Greiffenberg, Marienstr. 53 | 11 | AuP (*) | LSt. Stettin | II |
| Greifenhagen, Wiekstr. 50 | 10 | AuP (*) | LSt. Stettin | II |
| Greifswald, Badestr. | 37 | AuP (*) | LSt. Stettin | II |
| Greiz, Brauhausgasse 7 | 39 | AuP | LSt. Halle St. Weimar | IX |
| Grevenbroich, Rathaus | 12 | AuP | LSt. Düsseldorf | VI |
| Grimma, Markt 6 | 12 | AuP | LSt. Dresden St. Leipzig | IV |
| Gronau, Hermann-Göring-Str. 21 | 19 | AuP | LSt. Düsseldorf St. Recklinghausen | VI |
| Grossenhain, Wassermarkt 21 | 16 | AuP | LSt. Dresden | IV |
| Gross Ottersleben, Hauptmann-Loepe-Str. 2 | 14 | AuP | LSt. Halle St. Magdeburg | XI |
| Gross Strehlitz, Alter Ring 1 | 12 | AuP | LSt. Kattowitz St. Oppeln | VIII |
| Grünberg/Schl., Obertorstr. 5 | 26 | AuP | LSt. Breslau | VIII |
| Guben, Klosterstr. 7-10 | 46 | AuP | LSt. Berlin St. Frankfurt/Oder | III |

| Town | Population (in 1,000 of inhabitants) | Classification | Higher Headquarters | Under BdS in Wkr. |
|---|---|---|---|---|
| Gumbinnen, Gartenstr. 2-4 | 25 | AuP | LSt. Königsberg St. Tilsit | I |
| Gummersbach, Friedrichstr. 15 | 21 | AuP | LSt. Köln | VI |
| Güstrow, Marktstr. 1 | 28 | AuP (*) | LSt. Stettin St. Schwerin | II |
| Gütersloh, Berliner Str. 23 | 33 | AuP | LSt. Düsseldorf St. Dortmund | VI |
| Haan, Kaiserstr. 85 | 12 | AuP | LSt. Düsseldorf St. Wuppertal | VI |
| Hagen, Prentzelstr. 4-6 | 152 | AuDSt | LSt. Düsseldorf St. Dortmund | VI |
| Hagenau/Elsass, Stallgasse 8 | 20 | AuP | LSt. Strassburg | V |
| Halberstadt, Domplatz 37 | 57 | AuDSt | LSt. Halle St. Magdeburg | XI |
| Haldensleben, Markt 22 | 18 | AuP | LSt. Halle St. Magdeburg | XI |
| Hallein, Burgfried 4 | 11 | AuP | LSt. Salzburg | XVIII |
| Hamm/Westf., Göringstr. 80 | 60 | AuDSt | LSt. Düsseldorf St. Dortmund | VI |
| Hameln, Osterstr. 1 | 32 | AuP | LSt. Hannover | XI |
| Hanau, Paradeplatz 2-4 | 42 | AuP | LSt. Frankfurt/M. St. Kassel | IX |
| Hann.-Münden, Marktplatz 1 | 15 | AuP | LSt. Hannover | IX |
| Hattingen/Ruhr, Rathaus-platz | 18 | AuP | LSt. Düsseldorf St. Bochum | VI |
| Heide, Markt 32 | 13 | AuP | LSt. Hamburg St. Flensburg | X |
| Heidelberg, Rohrbacherstr. 11 | 86 | AuDSt | LSt. Stuttgart St. Karlsruhe | XII |
| Heidenau, Dresdnerstr. 47 | 18 | AuP | LSt. Dresden | IV |
| Heidenheim, Schnaitheimer-str. 14 | 27 | AuP | LSt. Stuttgart | V |
| Heilbronn/Neckar, Wiener-str. 4 | 78 | AuDSt | LSt. Stuttgart | V |
| Heiligenbeil, Rathausmarkt | 12 | AuP | LSt. Königsberg | I |
| Heiligenstadt, Adolf-Hitler-Str. 50 | 10 | AuP | LSt. Halle St. Erfurt | IX |
| Heilsberg, Rathausmarkt 5 | 12 | AuP | LSt. Königsberg | I |
| Helmstedt, Am Markt | 18 | AuP | LSt. Hannover St. Braunschweig | XI |
| Hemer, Hindenburgstr. 4 | 15 | AuP | LSt. Düsseldorf St. Dortmund | VI |
| Hennigsdorf, Hauptstr. 2 | 14 | AuP | LSt. Berlin | III |
| Herford, Hindenburgplatz 1 | 42 | AuDSt | LSt. Hannover | VI |
| Hermühlheim, Luxemburgerstr. 65 | | AuP | LSt. Köln | VI |
| Herne, Adolf-Hitler-Platz 5 | 95 | AuDSt | LSt. Düsseldorf St. Bochum | VI |
| Hersfeld, Weinstr. 16 | 15 | AuP | LSt. Frankfurt/M. St. Kassel | IX |
| Herten, Hermannstr. 6 | 33 | AuDSt (*) | LSt. Düsseldorf St. Recklinghausen | VI |
| Hervest-Dorsten, Körner-str. 12 | 11 | AuP | LSt. Düsseldorf St. Recklinghausen | VI |
| Heydebreck, Ring 1 | 6 | AuP | LSt. Kattowitz St. Oppeln | VIII |
| Hilden, Mittelstr. 40 | 23 | AuP | LSt. Düsseldorf | VI |
| Hildesheim, Strasse der SA 100 | 72 | AuDSt | LSt. Hannover | XI |
| Hindenburg, Harzfeldstr. 10 | 126 | AuDSt | LSt. Kattowitz | VIII |
| Hirschberg, Adolf-Hitler-Str. 1 | 35 | AuP | LSt. Breslau | VIII |
| Hof/Bayern, Pfarrgasse 1 | 45 | AuDSt | LSt. Nürnberg | XIII |
| Hohenlimburg, Strasse der SA 12 | 17 | AuP | LSt. Düsseldorf St. Dortmund | VI |
| Hohenstein/Ernstthal, Am Markt | 18 | AuP | LSt. Dresden St. Chemnitz | IV |
| Holzminden Adolf-Hitler-Str. 10 | 14 | AuP | LSt. Hannover St. Braunschweig | XI |
| Homberg/Ndrh., Stadthaus | 27 | AuP | LSt. Düsseldorf | VI |
| Homburg/Saar, Deutsche Str. 12 | 22 | AuP | St. Stuttgart St. Saarbrücken | XII |
| Homburg, Bad, Louisenstr. 59 | 18 | AuP | LSt. Frankfurt/M. | XII |

| Town | Population (in 1,000 of inhabitants) | Classification | Higher Headquarters | Under BdS in Wkr. |
|---|---|---|---|---|
| Honnef, Markt 6 | 9 | AuP | LSt. Köln | VI |
| Hüls, Viktoria Str. 54 | 9 | AuDSt (*) | LSt. Düsseldorf St. Recklinghausen | VI |
| Hüningen-St. Ludwig Adolf-Hitler-Str. 154 | | AuP | LSt. Strassburg | V |
| Husum, Grosstr. 27 | 15 | AuP | LSt. Hamburg St. Flensburg | X |
| Ibbenbüren, Am Waldfrieden 15 | 9 | AuP | LSt. Düsseldorf St. Recklinghausen | VI |
| Idar-Oberstein, Adolf-Hitler-Str. | 26 | AuP | LSt. Köln St. Koblenz | XII |
| Iglau, Steinstr. 50 | 24 | AuDSt (*) | LSt. Prag St. Brünn | B/M |
| Ilkenau, Marktplatz | 12 | AuP | LSt. Kattowitz | VIII |
| Ilmenau, Rathaus | 17 | AuP | LSt. Halle St. Weimar | IX |
| Ingolstadt, Rathaus | 33 | AuP | LSt. München | VII |
| Insterburg, Forchestr. 2 | 48 | AuDSt | LSt. Königsberg St. Tilsit | I |
| Ischl, Bad, Horst-Wessel-Str. 11 | | AuP | LSt. Wien St. Linz/Donau | XVII |
| Iserlohn, Baarstr. 5 | 38 | AuP | LSt. Düsseldorf St. Dortmund | VI |
| Itzehoe, Am Markt 16 | 23 | AuP | LSt. Hamburg | X |
| Jägerndorf, Adolf-Hitler-Platz 1 | 25 | AuP | LSt. Kattowitz St. Troppau | VIII |
| Jauer, Ring 1 | 15 | AuP | LSt. Breslau | VIII |
| Jaworzno, Krakower Str. 247 | 20 | AuP | LSt. Kattowitz | VIII |
| Jena, Felsenkellerstr. 25 | 71 | AuDSt | LSt. Halle St. Weimar | IX |
| Jessnitz, Leopoldstr. 11 | 12 | AuP | LSt. Halle St. Dessau | XI |
| Jitschin, Cech-Gasse 677 | 10 | AuDSt (*) | LSt. Prag | B/M |
| Jungbunzlau, Hausgasse 212 | 19 | AuDSt (*) | LSt. Prag | B/M |
| Jülich, Adolf-Hitler-Platz 1 | 11 | AuP (*) | LSt. Köln St. Aachen | VI |
| Jüterbog, Rathaus | 14 | AuP | LSt. Berlin | III |
| Kaiserslautern, Ritter-von-Epp-Str. 5 | 70 | AuDSt | LSt. Stuttgart St. Ludwigshafen | XII |
| Kamp-Lintfort, Friedrich-Heinrich-Allee | 21 | AuP | LSt. Düsseldorf | VI |
| Kalisch, Brandenburgerstr. 13 | 48 | AuDSt | LSt. Posen St. Litzmannstadt | XXI |
| Kamen, Markt 1 | 13 | AuP | LSt. Düsseldorf St. Dortmund | VI |
| Kamenz/Sachsen, Markt 1 | 14 | AuP | LSt. Dresden | IV |
| Karwin, Bismarckstr. 247 | 20 | AuP | LSt. Kattowitz | VIII |
| Kaufbeuren, Kaiser-Max-Str. | 13 | AuP | LSt. München St. Augsburg | VII |
| Kehl, Schlageterplatz 3 | 12 | AuP | LSt. Stuttgart St. Karlsruhe | V |
| Kempen/Posen, Ring 2 | 7 | AuP | LSt. Posen St. Litzmannstadt | XXI |
| Kempten/Allgäu, Rathausplatz 29 | 30 | AuP | LSt. München St. Augsburg | VII |
| Kirchheim, Marktstr. 26 | 13 | AuP | LSt. Stuttgart | V |
| Kissingen, Bad, Altes Rathaus | 10 | AuP | LSt. Nürnberg St. Würzburg | XIII |
| Kitzingen, Rathaus | 14 | AuP | LSt. Nürnberg St. Würzburg | XIII |
| Kladno, Hüttengasse 20 | 21 | AuDSt (*) | LSt. Prag | B/M |
| Klattau, Rieger-Kai 138/I | 14 | AuDSt (*) | LSt. Prag | B/M |
| Kleinmachnow, Zehlendorfer Damm 54 | 12 | AuP | LSt. Berlin | III |
| Kleve, 56—er Str. 2 | 22 | AuP | LSt. Düsseldorf | VI |
| Klotzsche, Bismarckstr. 58 | 12 | AuP | LSt. Dresden | IV |
| Kohlscheid, Kaiserstr. 50 | 12 | AuP | LSt. Köln St. Aachen | VI |
| Kolberg, Markt 9 | 36 | AuP (*) | LSt. Stettin | II |
| Kolin, Tyrsgasse 223 | 15 | AuDSt (*) | LSt. Prag | B/M |
| Kolmar/Elsass, Jägergasse 6 | 37 | AuP | LSt. Strassburg | V |
| Kolmar/Posen (no address) | 7 | AuP | LSt. Posen | XXI |

| Town | Population (in 1,000 of inhabitants) | Classification | Higher Headquarters | Under BdS in Wkr. |
|---|---|---|---|---|
| Komotau, Richard-Wagner-Str. 24 | 34 | AuDSt | LSt. Dresden St. Reichenberg | IV |
| Königgrätz, Am Graben 870 | 18 | AuDSt (*) | LSt. Prag | B/M |
| Königswinter, Drachenfels-Str. 9 | 5 | AuP | LSt. Köln | VI |
| Konin, Ernst-von-Rath- Str. 15 | 11 | AuP | LSt. Posen St. Hohensalza | XXI |
| Konitz, Markt 7 | 15 | AuP | LSt. Danzig | XX |
| Konstanz, Lutherplatz 10 | 38 | AuDSt | LSt. Stuttgart St. Karlsruhe | V |
| Kornwestheim, Jakob-Sigle-Platz 1 | 12 | AuP | LSt. Stuttgart | V |
| Köslin, Neuetorstr. 35 | 33 | AuP (*) | LSt. Stettin | II |
| Kosten/Wartheland, Rathaus | 12 | AuP | LSt. Posen | XXI |
| Köthen, Rathaus | 34 | AuP | LSt. Halle St. Dessau | IV |
| Krefeld Hansaplatz 2 | 171 | AuDSt | LSt. Düsseldorf | VI |
| Krems, Otto-Planetta-Platz 2 | 28 | AuP | LSt. Wien | XVII |
| Krenau, Deutsche Str. 8 | 21 | AuP | LSt. Kattowitz | VIII |
| Kreuzburg, Adolf-Hitler-Str. 22 | 2 | AuP | LSt. Kattowitz St. Oppeln | VIII |
| Kreuznach, Bad, Hochstr. 45 | 29 | AuP | LSt. Köln St. Koblenz | XII |
| Krotoschin, Rathaus | 12 | AuP | LSt. Posen | XXI |
| Krummau/Molda, Adolf-Hitler-Platz | 8 | AuP | LSt. Wien St. Linz/Donau | XVII |
| Küstrin, Markt 114 | 24 | AuP | LSt. Berlin St. Frankfurt/Oder | III |
| Kulm/Weichsel, Adolf-Hitler-Platz | 13 | AuP | LSt. Danzig St. Bromberg | XX |
| Kulmbach, Marktplatz 1 | 13 | AuP | LSt. Nürnberg | XIII |
| Kulmsee, Wilhelmstr. 7 | 13 | AuP | LSt. Danzig St. Bromberg | XX |
| Kutno, Rathausstr. 1 | 28 | AuP | LSt. Posen St. Hohensalza | XXI |
| Laak, Hauptplatz 10 | | AuDSt (*) | KdS Veldes | XVIII |
| Lahr/Schwarzw., Friedrich-str. 17 | 18 | AuP | LSt. Stuttgart St. Karlsruhe | V |
| Lampertheim, Wilhelmstr. 60 | | AuP | LSt. Frankfurt/M St. Darmstadt | XII |
| Landau-Pfalz, Marktstr. 31 | 26 | AuP | LSt. Stuttgart St. Ludwigshafen | XII |
| Landsberg/Warthe, Schloss-Str. 41 | 48 | AuDSt | LSt. Berlin St. Frankfurt/Oder | III |
| Landeshut, Obertor 3 | 14 | AuP | LSt. Breslau | VIII |
| Landshut, Rathaus | 32 | AuP | LSt. München | VII |
| Langenberg, Hauptstr. 101 | 14 | AuP | LSt. Düsseldorf St. Wuppertal | VI |
| Langenbielau, Hindenburg-platz 1 | 20 | AuP | LSt. Breslau | VIII |
| Langenfeld, Hermann-Gör-ing-Str. 73 | 17 | AuP | LSt. Düsseldorf | VI |
| Langensalza, Markt 1 | 14 | AuP | LSt. Halle St. Erfurt | IX |
| Lauban, Langegasse 11 | 17 | AuP | LSt. Breslau | VIII |
| Lauenburg, Mauerstr. 2 | 19 | AuP | LSt. Stettin | II |
| Leer, Rathaus | 15 | AuP | LSt. Bremen St. Wilhelmshaven | X |
| Lehrte, Adolf-Hitler-Platz 1 | 12 | AuP | LSt. Hannover | XI |
| Leipe, Breite Str. 13 | 12 | AuP | LSt. Danzig St. Bromberg | XX |
| Leitmeritz, Bäckergasse 2 | 17 | AuP | LSt. Dresden St. Reichenberg | IV |
| Lemgo, Am Markt | 14 | AuP | LSt. Hannover | VI |
| Lengerich, Strasse der SA 43 | 14 | AuP | LSt. Düsseldorf St. Recklinghausen | VI |
| Leoben, Buchmüllerstr. 8 | 34 | AuDSt (*) | LSt. Salzburg St. Graz | XVIII |
| Leobschütz, Ring | 14 | AuP | LSt. Kattowitz St. Oppeln | VIII |

| Town | Population (in 1,000 of inhabitants) | Classification | Higher Headquarters | Under BdS in Wkr. |
|---|---|---|---|---|
| Leslau/Warthe, Brückenstr. 3 | 50 | AuDSt | LSt. Posen St. Hohensalza | XXI |
| Leuna, Rathausstr. 16 | | AuDSt (*) | LSt. Halle | IV |
| Leverkusen, Rathaus | 50 | AuP | LSt. Düsseldorf | VI |
| Lichtenstein, Rathaus | 12 | AuP | LSt. Dresden St. Chemnitz | IV |
| Liegnitz, Frauenstr. 3-4 | 84 | AuDSt | LSt. Breslau | VIII |
| Limbach, Schulstr. 1 | 17 | AuP | LSt. Dresden St. Chemnitz | IV |
| Limburg/Lahn, Werner-Senger-Str. 9 | 12 | AuP | LSt. Frankfurt/M | XII |
| Lindau/Bodensee, Bregenzerstr. 6 | 16 | AuP | LSt. München St. Augsburg | VII |
| Lingen, Adolf-Hitler-Platz 7 | 14 | AuP | LSt. Hannover | VI |
| Lippstadt, Adolf-Hitler-Str. 14 | 23 | AuP | LSt. Düsseldorf. St. Dortmund | VI |
| Lissa, Comeniusstr. 21 | 20 | AuP | LSt. Posen | XXI |
| Littai, Amtsgerichtsgebäude | | AuDSt (*) | KdS Veldes | XVIII |
| Loben, Ring | 11 | AuP | LSt. Kattowitz St. Oppeln | VIII |
| Löbau/Sachsen, Rathaus | 14 | AuP | LSt. Dresden | IV |
| Löbau/Westpr., SA-Str. 3 | 6 | AuP | LSt. Danzig | XX |
| Lörrach, Bahnstr. 6 | 20 | AuP | LSt. Stuttgart St. Karlsruhe | V |
| Lötzen, Am Markt 1 | 16 | AuP | LSt. Königsberg | I |
| Luckenwalde, Rathaus | 29 | AuP | LSt. Berlin | III |
| Lübeck, Grosser Bauhof 14 | 155 | AuDSt | LSt. Hamburg St. Kiel | X |
| Lüdenscheid, Rathausstr. 1 | 42 | AuP | LSt. Düsseldorf St. Dortmund | VI |
| Ludwigsburg, Vordere Schlosstr. 31 | 43 | AuP | LSt. Stuttgart | V |
| Lüneburg, Am Ochsenmarkt 1 | 35 | AuDSt | LSt. Hamburg | X |
| Lünen, Adolf-Hitler-Platz 2 | 46 | AuP | LSt. Düsseldorf St. Dortmund | VI |
| Lugau, Rathaus | 10 | AuP | LSt. Dresden St. Chemnitz | IV |
| Lundenburg, Adolf-Hitler-Platz 9 | 11 | AuP | LSt. Wien | XVII |
| Luxemburg | 225 | AuDSt | Kds. Luxemburg | XII |
| Lyck, Adolf-Hitler-Platz | 16 | AuP | LSt. Königsberg | I |
| Mährisch-Ostrau, Krankenhausgasse 35 | 13 | AuDSt (*) | LSt. Prag St. Brünn | B/M |
| Mährisch-Schönberg, Kirchengasse 2 | 16 | AuP | LSt. Kattowitz St. Troppau | VIII |
| Mainz, Klarastr. 4 | 158 | AuDSt | LSt. Frankfurt/M. St. Darmstadt | XII |
| Maltheuern, Maltheuern-Hydrierwerk | | AuDSt (*) | LSt. Dresden St. Reichenberg | IV |
| Mannheim, L6, 1 | 285 | AuDSt | LSt. Stuttgart St. Karlsruhe | XII |
| Marburg/Lahn, Reitgasse 7 | 28 | AuP | LSt. Frankfurt/M. St. Kassel | IX |
| Marchegg (no address) | 3 | AuP | LSt. Wien | XVII |
| Marienbad, Jägerstr. 45 | 12 | AuP | LSt. Nürnberg St. Karlsbad | XIII |
| Marienburg/Westpr., Altes Rathaus | 27 | AuP | LSt. Danzig | XX |
| Marienwerder, Göringstr. 21 | 20 | AuP | LSt. Danzig | XX |
| Markkleeberg, Adolf-Hitler-Str. | 18 | AuP | LSt. Dresden St. Leipzig | IV |
| Markirch, Adolf-Hitler-Str. 116 | | AuP | LSt. Strassburg | V |
| Marktredwitz, Rathaus | 12 | AuP | LSt. Nürnberg | XIII |
| Marl, Strasse der SA 22 | 35 | AuDSt (*) | LSt. Düsseldorf St. Recklinghausen | VI |
| Mayen, Göbelstr. 14 | 15 | AuP | LSt. Köln St. Koblenz | XII |
| Meerane, Marienstr. 24 | 25 | AuP | LSt. Dresden St. Chemnitz | IV |

| Town | Population (in 1,000 of inhabitants) | Classification | Higher Headquarters | Under BdS in Wkr. |
|---|---|---|---|---|
| Meiningen, Markt 3 | 22 | AuP | LSt. Halle<br>St. Weimar | IX |
| Meissen, Nickolaisteg 5 | 48 | AuP | LSt. Dresden | IV |
| Memel, Fischerstr. 12 | 41 | AuDSt | LSt. Königsberg<br>St. Tilsit | I |
| Memmingen, Marktplatz 1 | 16 | AuP | LSt. München<br>St. Augsburg | VII |
| Menden, Hauptstr. 46 | 18 | AuP | LSt. Düsseldorf<br>St. Dortmund | VI |
| Merseburg, Wilhelmstr. 12 | 38 | AuP | LSt. Halle | IV |
| Mettmann, Gartenstr. 2 | 14 | AuP | LSt. Düsseldorf<br>St. Wuppertal | VI |
| Meuselwitz, Rathaus-Str. 1 | 11 | AuP | LSt. Halle<br>St. Weimar | IX |
| Mielau (no address) | 15 | AuP | LSt. Königsberg<br>St. Zichenau | I |
| Milspe-Voerde, Bismarckstr. 9 | 12 | AuP | LSt. Düsseldorf<br>St. Bochum | VI |
| Minden, Adolf-Hitler-Platz 2 | 31 | AuDSt | LSt. Hannover | VI |
| Mittweida, Rathaus | 18 | AuP | LSt. Dresden<br>St. Leipzig | IV |
| Moers, Düsseldorferstr. | 30 | AuP | LSt. Düsseldorf | VI |
| Mücheln, Markt 19 | 10 | AuP | LSt. Halle | IV |
| Mühlhausen/Thür., Ratstr. 2 | 44 | AuDSt | LSt. Halle<br>St. Erfurt | IX |
| Mülhausen/Elsass, Belcherstr. 2 | 100 | AuDSt | LSt. Strassburg | V |
| Mülheim/Ruhr (no address) | 137 | AuDSt | LSt. Düsseldorf<br>St. Essen | VI |
| Münster/Westf., Jüdefelder Str. 56 | 141 | AuDSt | LSt. Düsseldorf<br>St. Recklinghausen | VI |
| M.-Gladbach/Rheydt, Kyffhäuserstr. 5 | 128 | AuDSt | LSt. Düsseldorf | VI |
| Nakel, Post Str. 9 | 12 | AuP | LSt. Danzig<br>St. Bromberg | XX |
| Nauen, Rathaus | | AuP | LSt. Berlin | III |
| Nauheim, Bad, Friedrichstr. 3 | 9 | AuDSt (*) | LSt. Frankfurt/M<br>St. Darmstadt | IX |
| Naumburg/Saale, Kl. Salzgraben | 37 | AuP | LSt. Halle | IV |
| Neheim-Hüsten, Kirchplatz1 | 24 | AuP | LSt. Düsseldorf<br>St. Dortmund | VI |
| Neisse, Hafenstr. 3 | 38 | AuP | LSt. Kattowitz<br>St. Oppeln | VIII |
| Neu-Brandenburg, Adolf-Hitler-Str. 20-24 | 22 | AuP (*) | LSt. Stettin<br>St. Schwerin | II |
| Neugersdorf, Liechtenstein 5 | 11 | AuP | LSt. Dresden | IV |
| Neu-Isenburg, Adolf-Hitler-Str. 55 | 15 | AuP | LSt. Frankfurt/M.<br>St. Darmstadt | IX |
| Neukirchen-Vluyn, Stadthaus | | AuP | LSt. Düsseldorf | VI |
| Neumark/Westpr., Promenade 18 | 5 | AuP | LSt. Danzig | XX |
| Neumünster, Adolf-Hitler-Str. 17 | 55 | AuDSt | LSt. Hamburg<br>St. Kiel | X |
| Neunkirchen/Niederdonau, Adolf-Hitler-Platz 1 | 11 | AuP | LSt. Wien | XVII |
| Neunkirchen/Saar, Falkensteinstr. 11 | 39 | AuDSt | St. Saarbrücken | XII |
| Neu-Oderberg, Adolf-Hitler-Platz 1 | 7 | AuP | LSt. Kattowitz | VIII |
| Neurode, Ring 1 | 10 | AuP | LSt. Breslau | VIII |
| Neuruppin, Friedrich-Wilhelm-Str. 33 | 27 | AuP | LSt. Berlin | III |
| Neusalz/Oder, Amtsstr. 7-9 | 17 | AuP | LSt. Breslau | VIII |
| Neuss, Markt 6 | 60 | AuDSt | LSt. Düsseldorf | VI |
| Neustadt/Oberschlesien, Ring | 17 | AuP | LSt. Kattowitz<br>St. Oppeln | VIII |
| Neustadt/Weinstrasse, Adolf-Hitler-Platz 1 | 24 | AuP | LSt. Stuttgart<br>St. Ludwigshafen | XII |
| Neustadt/Westpr., Adolf-Hitler-Str. 231a | 15 | AuP | LSt. Danzig | XX |

| Town | Population (in 1,000 of inhabitants) | Classification | Higher Headquarters | Under BdS in Wkr. |
|---|---|---|---|---|
| Neustettin, Rathaus | 20 | AuP (*) | LSt. Stettin<br>St. Schneidemühl | II |
| Neustrelitz, Bruchstr. 15 | 26 | AuP (*) | LSt. Stettin<br>St. Schwerin | II |
| Neutitschein, Prorokgasse 3 | 15 | AuP | LSt. Kattowitz<br>St. Troppau | VIII |
| Neu-Ulm, Maximilianstr. 2 | 15 | AuP | LSt. München<br>St. Augsburg | VII |
| Neuwied, Horst-Wessel-Str.1 | 22 | AuP | LSt. Köln<br>St. Koblenz | XII |
| Nienburg/Weser, Markplatz 1 | 13 | AuP | LSt. Hannover | X |
| Nikolai, Hermann-Göring-Str. 9 | 14 | AuP | LSt. Kattowitz | VIII |
| Norden, Am Markt | 12 | AuP | LSt. Bremen<br>St. Wilhelmshaven | X |
| Nordhausen, Adolf-Hitler-Platz 1 | 43 | AuDSt | LSt. Halle<br>St. Erfurt | IX |
| Nordhorn, Adolf-Hitler-Str. 1 | 24 | AuP | LSt. Hannover | XI |
| Northeim, Markt 14 | 12 | AuP | LSt. Hannover | XI |
| Nürtingen, Marktstr. 7 | 11 | AuP | LSt. Stuttgart | V |
| Oberhausen/Osterfeld, Adolf-Hitler-Platz 2 | 195 | AuDSt | LSt. Düsseldorf<br>St. Essen | VI |
| Oberleutensdorf/Mähren, Schlosstr. 5 | 14 | AuDSt (*) | LSt. Dresden<br>St. Reichenberg | IV |
| Oels, Ring 1 | 18 | AuP | LSt. Breslau | VIII |
| Oelsnitz/Erzg., Rathausplatz 1 | 19 | AuP | LSt. Dresden<br>St. Chemnitz | IV |
| Oelsnitz/Vogtl., Schmidtstr. 7a | 15 | AuP | LSt. Dresden<br>St. Zwickau | IV |
| Oeynhausen, Bad, Ostkorso 8 | 11 | AuP | LSt. Hannover | VI |
| Offenbach, Frankfurterstr. 99 | 85 | AuDSt | LSt. Frankfurt/M.<br>St. Darmstadt | IX |
| Offenburg, Okenstr. 21 | 20 | AuP | LSt. Stuttgart<br>St. Karlsruhe | V |
| Ohlau, Rathaus | 13 | AuP | LSt. Breslau | VIII |
| Olbernhau, Rathaus | 10 | AuP | LSt. Dresden<br>St. Chemnitz | IV |
| Oldenburg, Heiligen-Geist-Str. 14 | 78 | AuDSt | LSt. Bremen | X |
| Olmütz, Karl IV-Str. 44 | 66 | AuDSt (*) | LSt. Prag<br>St. Brünn | B/M |
| Olpe, Hindenburgstr. 27 | 7 | AuP | LSt. Düsseldorf<br>St. Dortmund | VI |
| Opladen, Rathaus | 20 | AuP | LSt. Düsseldorf | VI |
| Oranienburg, Berliner Str. 20 | 29 | AuP | LSt. Berlin | III |
| Ortelsburg, Berlinerstr. 1 | 14 | AuP | LSt. Königsberg | I |
| Oschatz, Rathaus | 16 | AuP | LSt. Dresden<br>St. Leipzig | IV |
| Oscherleben, Marktplatz 1 | 18 | AuP | LSt. Halle<br>St. Magdeburg | XI |
| Osnabrück, Markt 18 | 107 | AuDSt | LSt. Hannover | VI |
| Ostenburg (no address) | 16 | AuP | LSt. Königsberg<br>St. Zichenau | I |
| Osterode/Ostpr., Schillerstr. 3c | 20 | AuP | LSt. Königsberg | I |
| Ostrowo, Breslauerstr. 6 | 28 | AuP | LSt. Posen<br>St. Litzmannstadt | XXI |
| Pabianice, Danzigerstr. 6 | 43 | AuDSt (*) | LSt. Posen<br>St. Litzmannstadt | XXI |
| Paderborn, Grube 1 | 43 | AuDSt | LSt. Düsseldorf<br>St. Dortmund | VI |
| Papenburg/Ems, Haupt-kanal Rechts 68 | 12 | AuP | LSt. Hannover | VI |
| Parchim, Schuhmarkt 1 | 15 | AuP (*) | LSt. Stettin<br>St. Schwerin | II |
| Pardubitz, Viktoriaplatz 12 | 29 | AuDSt (*) | LSt. Prag | B/M |
| Pasewalk, Am Markt 1 | 12 | AuP (*) | LSt. Stettin | II |
| Passau, Rathaus | 26 | AuP | LSt. München<br>St. Regensburg | XIII |

| Town | Population (in 1,000 of inhabitants) | Classification | Higher Headquarters | Under BdS in Wkr. |
|---|---|---|---|---|
| Peine, Marktstr. 1 | 18 | AuP | LSt. Hannover | XI |
| Pelkum, Leo-Baumgärtnerstr. 155 | | AuP | LSt. Düsseldorf St. Dortmund | VI |
| Perleberg, Rathaus | 13 | AuP | LSt. Berlin | III |
| Pforzheim, Bahnhofstr. 26 | 79 | AuDSt | LSt. Stuttgart St. Karlsruhe | V |
| Pillau, Langgasse 2 | 12 | AuP | LSt. Königsberg | I |
| Pilsen, Viktoriastr. 20 | 115 | AuDSt (*) | LSt. Prag | B/M |
| Pinneberg, Bahnhofstr. 39 | 14 | AuP | LSt. Hamburg | X |
| Pirmasens, Hauptstr. 78 | 50 | AuDSt. | LSt. Stuttgart St. Ludwigshafen | XII |
| Pirna, Klostergässchen 1 | 36 | AuP | LSt. Dresden | IV |
| Planitz, Rathaus, Schloss | 22 | AuP | LSt. Dresden St. Zwickau | IV |
| Plauen, Blücherstr. 2 | 112 | AuDSt | St. Dresden St. Zwickau | IV |
| Pleschen, Adolf-Hitler-Platz 1 | 9 | AuP | LSt. Posen | XXI |
| Plettenberg, Rathaus | | AuP | LSt. Düsseldorf St. Dortmund | VI |
| Plöhnen (no address) | 14 | AuP | LSt. Königsberg St. Zichenau | I |
| Pössneck, Markt 1 | 16 | AuP | LSt. Halle St. Weimar | IX |
| Polstrau, Nr. 118 | | AuDSt (*) | KdS. Marburg/Drau | XVIII |
| Polzin, Bad, Rathaus | 7 | AuP | LSt. Stettin | II |
| Porz, Adolf-Hitler-Ufer | | AuP | LSt. Köln | VI |
| Potsdam, Priesterstr. 11-12 | 135 | AuDSt | LSt. Berlin | III |
| Praschnitz, Markt | 7 | AuP | LSt. Königsberg St. Zichenau | I |
| Prenzlau, Rathaus | 27 | AuP | LSt. Berlin | III |
| Preuss. Stargard, Friedrichstr. 8 | 19 | AuP | LSt. Danzig | XX |
| Pyritz, Ratstr. 2 | 11 | AuP | LSt. Stettin | II |
| Pyrmont, Bad, Rathaus | 9 | AuP | LSt. Hannover | XI |
| Quedlinburg, Markt 1 | 30 | AuP | LSt. Halle St. Magdeburg | XI |
| Radeberg, Markt 18 | 16 | AuP | LSt. Dresden | IV |
| Radebeul, Von-Otto-Str. 13a | 37 | AuP | LSt. Dresden | IV |
| Radevormwald, Bahnhofstr. 4 | 14 | AuP | LSt. Düsseldorf St. Wuppertal | VI |
| Radmannsdorf, Megertstr. 4 | | AuDSt (*) | KdS. Veldes | XVIII |
| Radolfzell (no address) | 8 | AuP | LSt. Stuttgart St. Karlsruhe | V |
| Rann, Adolf-Hitler-Str. 49 | | AuP | KdS. Marburg/Drau | XVIII |
| Rastatt, Reinhard-Heydrich-Str. 19 | 17 | AuP | LSt. Stuttgart St. Karlsruhe | V |
| Rastenburg, Adolf-Hitler-Platz 1 | 20 | AuP | LSt. Königsberg | I |
| Rathenow, Eduard-Haase-Str. 9-10 | 33 | AuP | LSt. Berlin | III |
| Ratingen, Lintorfer Str. | 20 | AuP | LSt. Düsseldorf | VI |
| Ratibor, Wilhelmstr. | 50 | AuDSt | LSt. Kattowitz St. Oppeln | VIII |
| Ravensburg, Seestr. 11 | 32 | AuP (*) | LSt. Stuttgart | V |
| Rawitsch, Kirchstr. 5 | 10 | AuP | LSt. Posen | XXI |
| Recklinghausen-Suderwich, Langemarckplatz 36 | | AuDSt (*) | LSt. Düsseldorf St. Recklinghausen | VI |
| Recklinghausen-Süd, Leo-Schlageterplatz 25 | | AuDSt (*) | LSt. Düsseldorf St. Recklinghausen | VI |
| Reichenbach/Eulengebirge, Rathaus | 17 | AuP | LSt. Breslau | VIII |
| Reichenbach/Vogtl., Albrechtstr. 6 | 32 | AuP | LSt. Dresden St. Zwickau | IV |
| Reichenhall, Wittelsbacherplatz 1 | 12 | AuP | LSt. München | VII |
| Remscheid, (no address) | 104 | AuDSt | LSt. Düsseldorf St. Wuppertal | VI |
| Rendsburg, Mühlenstr. 32 | 24 | AuP | LSt. Hamburg St. Kiel | X |
| Repelen-Baerl, Rathaus | | AuP | LSt. Düsseldorf | VI |

| Town | Population (in 1,000 of inhabitants) | Classification | Higher Headquarters | Under BdS in Wkr. |
|---|---|---|---|---|
| Reutlingen, Rebentalstr. 13 | 39 | AuP | LSt. Stuttgart | V |
| Rheine, Neuenkirchenerstr. 78 | 35 | AuP | LSt. Düsseldorf St. Recklinghausen | VI |
| Rheinhausen, Körnerplatz | 41 | AuP | LSt. Düsseldorf | VI |
| Riesa, Hindenburgplatz 12 | 30 | AuP | LSt. Dresden | IV |
| Rippin, Neuer Markt | 8 | AuP | LSt. Danzig St. Bromberg | XX |
| Rodenkirchen, Haupt Str. 28 | 7 | AuP | LSt. Köln | VI |
| Rodewisch, Wernesgrünerstr. 48 | 11 | AuP | LSt. Dresden St. Zwickau | IV |
| Rosenberg, Ring | 7 | AuP | LSt. Kattowitz St. Oppeln | VIII |
| Rosenheim, Rathaus | 22 | AuP | LSt. München | VII |
| Rostock, Seestadt, Reiferbahn (incl. Warnemünde) | 121 | AuDSt (*) | LSt. Stettin St. Schwerin | II |
| Rottweil, Adolf-Hitler-Str. 23 | 13 | AuP | LSt. Stuttgart | V |
| Rudolstadt, Ratgasse 1 | 19 | AuP | LSt. Halle St. Weimar | IX |
| Rügenwalde, Am Markt 9 | 8 | AuP | LSt. Stettin | II |
| Rüsselsheim, Frankfurter Str. 2 | 15 | AuP | LSt. Frankfurt/M St. Darmstadt | XII |
| Rummelsburg, Markt 1 | 9 | AuP | LSt. Stettin | II |
| Rybnick, Adolf-Hitler-Str. 52 | 28 | AuP | LSt. Kattowitz | VIII |
| Rydultau, Schulstr. 3 | 15 | AuP | LSt. Kattowitz | VIII |
| Saalfeld/Saale, Johannesgasse 3 | 23 | AuP | LSt. Halle St. Weimar | IV |
| Saarburg, Bahnhofstr. 3 | 6 | AuDSt (*) | KdS. Metz | XII |
| Saargemünd, Maiglöckchenstr. 37 | | AuDSt (*) | KdS. Metz | XII |
| Saarlautern, Paulusstr. 2 | 32 | AuP | LSt. Stuttgart St. Saarbrücken | XII |
| Saaz, Hans-Schemn-Platz 125 | 16 | AuP | LSt. Nürnberg St. Karlsbad | XIII |
| Sagan, (no address) | 23 | AuP | LSt. Breslau | VIII |
| Salzbrunn, Bad, Alte Poststr. 4 | 15 | AuP | LSt. Breslau | VIII |
| Salzgitter, Rathaus | | AuP | LSt. Hannover St. Braunschweig | XI |
| Salzuflen, Bad, Salzepromenade 1 | 12 | AuP | LSt. Hannover | VI |
| Salzwedel, Rathaus | 19 | AuP | LSt. Halle St. Magdeburg | XI |
| Samter, Rathaus | 10 | AuP | LSt. Posen | XXI |
| Sangerhausen, Markt 3 | 13 | AuP | LSt. Halle | IX |
| Saybusch, Bahnhofstr. 4 | 16 | AuP | LSt. Kattowitz | VIII |
| Scharfenwiese (no address) | 13 | AuP | LSt. Königsberg St. Zichenau | I |
| Schieratz, Rathausstr. 13 | 12 | AuP | LSt. Posen St. Litzmannstadt | XXI |
| Schivelbein, Mühlenstr. 3 | 10 | AuP | LSt. Stettin | II |
| Schkeuditz, Lessingstr. 2 | 15 | AuP | LSt. Halle | IV |
| Schkopau, Hallische Str. 46a | | AuDSt (*) | LSt. Halle | IV |
| Schlawe, Markt 26 | 10 | AuP | LSt. Stettin | II |
| Schleswig, Lollfuss 53 | 26 | AuP | LSt. Hamburg St. Flensburg | X |
| Schlettstadt, Rathaus | 10 | AuP | LSt. Strassburg | V |
| Schmalkalden, Marktplatz 1 | 11 | AuP | LSt. Halle St. Erfurt | IX |
| Schmölln, Rathaus | 13 | AuP | LSt. Halle St. Weimar | IX |
| Schneeberg, Rathaus | 15 | AuP | LSt. Dresden St. Zwickau | IV |
| Schönebeck/Elbe, Nicolaistr. 1 | 40 | AuP | LSt. Halle St. Magdeburg | XI |
| Schramberg, Bahnhofstr. 5 | 16 | AuP | LSt. Stuttgart | V |
| Schröttersburg (no address) | 34 | AuP | LSt. Königsberg St. Zichenau | I |
| Schwabach, Ludwigstr. 1 | 15 | AuP | LSt. Nürnberg | XIII |

| Town | Population (in 1,000 of inhabitants) | Classification | Higher Headquarters | Under BdS in Wkr. |
|---|---|---|---|---|
| Schwäb. Hall, Am Markt 9 | 15 | AuP | LSt. Stuttgart | V |
| Schwandorf, Rathausstr. 1 | 10 | AuP | LSt. München St. Regensburg | XIII |
| Schwarzenberg, Adolf-Hitler-Str. 20 | 13 | AuP | LSt. Dresden St. Zwickau | IV |
| Schweidnitz, Am Burgplan 2 | 39 | AuP | LSt. Breslau | VIII |
| Schweinfurt, Brückenstr. 39 | 49 | AuP | LSt. Nürnberg St. Würzburg | XIII |
| Schwelm, Schillerstr. | 24 | AuP | LSt. Düsseldorf St. Bochum | VI |
| Schwenningen, Oberdorfstr. 58 | 22 | AuP | LSt. Stuttgart | V |
| Schwerte, Str. der SA 31 | 19 | AuP | LSt. Düsseldorf St. Dortmund | VI |
| Schwetz/Weichsel, Hermann-Göring-Str. 3 | 11 | AuP | LSt. Danzig St. Bromberg | XX |
| Schwetzingen, Hebelstr. 1 | 11 | AuP | LSt. Stuttgart St. Karlsruhe | XII |
| Schwiebus, Stadtmauer 4 | 10 | AuP | LSt. Berlin St. Frankfurt/Oder | III |
| Sebnitz, Schlageterstr. 3 | 12 | AuP | LSt. Dresden | IV |
| Selb, Adolf-Hitler-Str. 6 | 14 | AuP | LSt. Nürnberg | XIII |
| Senftenberg, Markt 1-2 | 18 | AuP | LSt. Berlin St. Frankfurt/Oder | III |
| Siegburg, Mühlenstr. 2-4 | 21 | AuP | LSt. Köln | VI |
| Siegen, Pfarrstr. 2 | 40 | AuDSt | LSt. Düsseldorf St. Dortmund | IX |
| Siegmar-Schönau, Rathausstr. 5 | 20 | AuP | LSt. Dresden St. Chemnitz | IV |
| Singen/Hohentwiel, Hegaustr. 23 | 18 | AuP | LSt. Stuttgart St. Karlsruhe | V |
| Soest, Ludendorffplatz | 25 | AuP | LSt. Düsseldorf St. Dortmund | VI |
| Solingen (no address) | 141 | AuDSt | LSt. Düsseldorf St. Wuppertal | VI |
| Sömmerda, Marktplatz 2 | 12 | AuP | LSt. Halle St. Erfurt | IV |
| Sommerfeld, Poststr. 12 | 11 | AuP | LSt. Berlin St. Frankfurt/Oder | III |
| Sonderhausen, Markt 7 | 12 | AuP | LSt. Halle St. Weimar | IX |
| Sonnenberg/Thür., Rathaus | 20 | AuP | LSt. Halle St. Weimar | IV |
| Sorau, Rathaus | 26 | AuP | LSt. Berlin St. Frankfurt/Oder | III |
| Sosnowitz, Litzmannstr. 10 | 122 | AuDSt | LSt. Kattowitz | VIII |
| Speyer, Maximilianstr. 12-13 | 30 | AuP | LSt. Stuttgart St. Ludwigshafen | XII |
| Spremberg, Lange Str. 49 | 14 | AuP | LSt. Berlin St. Frankfurt/Oder | III |
| St. Avold, Hermann-Göring-Str. 16 | | AuDSt (*) | KdS Metz | XII |
| St. Ingbert, Kaiserstr. 86 | 23 | AuP | LSt. Stuttgart St. Saarbrücken | XII |
| St. Pölten, Linzerstr. 47 | 45 | AuDSt | LSt. Wien | XVII |
| Stade, Gründelstr. 8 | 20 | AuP | LSt. Hamburg | X |
| Stargard/Pommern, Mühlenstr. 4 | 40 | AuP (*) | LSt. Stettin | II |
| Stassfurt, Rathaus | 16 | AuP | LSt. Halle St. Magdeburg | XI |
| Stein, Hermann-Göring Str. 10 | 5 | AuDSt (*) | KdS Veldes | XVIII |
| Stendal, Bruchstr. 2 | 37 | AuP | LSt. Halle St. Magdeburg | XI |
| Sternberg, Lichtensteinpl. 9 | 12 | AuP | LSt. Kattowitz St. Troppau | VIII |
| Steyr, Berggasse 2 | 31 | AuP | LSt. Wien St. Linz/Donau | XVII |
| Stolberg/Rhld., Rathausstr. 6 | 30 | AuP (*) | LSt. Köln St. Aachen | VI |
| Stollberg/Erzgeb., Rathaus | 18 | AuP | LSt. Dresden St. Chemnitz | IV |
| Stolp, Stephanplatz 3 | 50 | AuDSt (*) | LSt. Stettin | II |

| Town | Population (in 1,000 of inhabitants) | Classification | Higher Headquarters | Under BdS in Wkr. |
|---|---|---|---|---|
| Stralsund, Alter Markt 10 | 53 | AuDSt (*) | LSt. Stettin | II |
| Straubing, Simon-Heller-Str. 3 | 29 | AuP | LSt. München St. Regensburg | XIII |
| Strasburg/Westpr., Horst-Wessel-Str. 14 | 11 | AuP | LSt. Danzig St. Bromberg | XX |
| Strausberg, Marktplatz | 12 | AuP | LSt. Berlin | III |
| Strehlen, Rathaus | 12 | AuP | LSt. Breslau | VIII |
| Striegau, Rathaus | 16 | AuP | LSt. Breslau | VIII |
| Sudauen, Adolf-Hitler-Str. 75 | 15 | AuDSt (*) | LSt. Königsberg St. Tilsit | I |
| Suhl, Strasse der SA 2 | 24 | AuP | LSt. Halle St. Erfurt | IV |
| Sulzbach/Saar, Louis-Vopeliusstr. 1 | 21 | AuP | LSt. Stuttgart St. Saarbrücken | XII |
| Swinemünde Kl. Marktstr. 17 | 30 | AuP (*) | LSt. Stettin | II |
| Tabor, Myslbeckgasse 2040 | 14 | AuDSt (*) | LSt. Prag | B/M |
| Tailfingen, Rathaus | 11 | AuP | LSt. Stuttgart | V |
| Tangermünde, Adolf-Hitler-Str. | 14 | AuP | LSt. Halle St. Magdeburg | XI |
| Tann, Adolf-Hitler-Str. 6 | 1 | AuP | LSt. Strassburg | V |
| Tarnowitz, Markgrafenstr. 24 | 23 | AuP | LSt. Kattowitz | VIII |
| Taucha, Schlosstr. 13 | 15 | AuP | LSt. Dresden St. Leipzig | IV |
| Teltow, Am Marktplatz | 12 | AuP | LSt. Berlin | III |
| Teplitz-Schönau, Adolf-Hitler-Platz 4 | 44 | AuDSt (*) | LSt. Dresden St. Reichenberg | IV |
| Teschen, Hermann-Göring-Platz 1 | 27 | AuP | LSt. Kattowitz | VIII |
| Tetschen-Bodenbach, Am Graben 29 I | 36 | AuP | LSt. Dresden St. Reichenberg | IV |
| Thale/Harz, Hans-Schemmstr. 1 | 14 | AuP | LSt. Halle St. Magdeburg | XI |
| Thorn, Stadtgraben 31 | 69 | AuDSt | LSt. Danzig St. Bromberg | XX |
| Torgau, Markt 1 | 18 | AuP | LSt. Halle | IV |
| Torgelow, Bahnhofstr. 2 | 7 | AuP | LSt. Stettin | II |
| Traunstein, Rathaus | 12 | AuP | LSt. München | VII |
| Trautenau, Schillerstr. 6 | 15 | AuP | LSt. Dresden St. Reichenberg | VIII |
| Treptow/Rega, Markt 1 | 11 | AuP (*) | LSt. Stettin | II |
| Trifail, Haus Nr. 117 | | AuDSt (*) | KdS Marburg/Drau | XVIII |
| Troisdorf, Adolf-Hitler-Str. 75 | 11 | AuP | LSt. Köln | VI |
| Tübingen, Münzgasse 13 | 30 | AuP | LSt. Stuttgart | V |
| Turek, NSKK-Strasse 1 | 9 | AuP | LSt. Posen St. Litzmannstadt | XXI |
| Tuttlingen, Bahnhofstr. 18 | 18 | AuP | LSt. Stuttgart | V |
| Übach-Palenberg, Rathaus | 10 | AuP (*) | LSt. Köln St. Aachen | VI |
| Uelzen, Adolf-Hitler-Str. 42 | 14 | AuP | LSt. Hamburg | XI |
| Ulm/Donau, Münsterplatz 47 | 74 | AuDSt | LSt. Stuttgart | V |
| Unna, Adolf-Hitler-Str. 39-40 | 20 | AuP | LSt. Düsseldorf St. Dortmund | VI |
| Vaihingen (no address) | 4 | AuP | LSt. Stuttgart | V |
| Verden (Aller), Grosse Str. 42 | 12 | AuP | LSt. Bremen | X |
| Viernheim, Adolf-Hitler-Str. 29 | 12 | AuP | LSt. Frankfurt/M. St. Darmstadt | XII |
| Viersen, Adolf-Hitler-Str. | 34 | AuP | LSt. Düsseldorf | VI |
| Villach, Adolf-Hitler-Platz 7 | 28 | AuP | LSt. Salzburg St. Klagenfurt | XVIII |
| Villingen, Bickenstr. 24 | 18 | AuP | LSt. Stuttgart St. Karlsruhe | V |
| Völklingen, Dietrich-Eckart-Str. 18 | 35 | AuP | LSt. Stuttgart St. Saarbrücken | XII |
| Waldenburg/Schl., Anlaufstr. 2 | 64 | AuDSt | LSt. Breslau | VIII |
| Waldheim, Rathaus | 13 | AuP | LSt. Dresden St. Leipzig | IV |
| Waldrode, Schmidstr. 31 | 9 | AuP | LSt. Posen St. Hohensalza | XXI |
| Waldshut, Bismarkstr. 17 | 7 | AuP | LSt. Stuttgart St. Karlsruhe | V |

| Town | Population (in 1,000 of inhabitants) | Classification | Higher Headquarters | Under BdS in Wkr. |
|---|---|---|---|---|
| Walsum, Provinzialstr. 227 | 23 | AuP | LSt. Düsseldorf St. Essen | VI |
| Waltrop, Hochstr. 100 | 11 | AuDSt (*) | LSt. Düsseldorf St. Recklinghausen | VI |
| Wanne/Eickel, Gelsenkirchener Str. 25 | 86 | AuP | LSt. Düsseldorf St. Bochum | VI |
| Waren/Müritz, Neue Markt 1 | 15 | AuP (*) | LSt. Stettin St. Schwerin | II |
| Warnsdorf, Oststr. 194 | 21 | AuP | LSt. Dresden St. Reichenberg | IV |
| Warthbrücken, Walter v. Plettenbergstr. 9 | 12 | AuP | LSt. Posen St. Hohensalza | XXI |
| Watenstedt-Salzgitter | 45 | AuDSt (*) | LSt. Hannover St. Braunschweig | XI |
| Warthenau, Adolf-Hitler-Str. 7 | 32 | AuP | LSt. Kattowitz St. Oppeln | VIII |
| Wattenscheid, Rathausstr. 3 | 61 | AuP | LSt. Düsseldorf St. Bochum | VI |
| Weida, Petersstr. 4 | 11 | AuP | LSt. Halle St. Weimar | IX |
| Weiden, Obere Bachgasse | 29 | AuP | LSt. Nürnberg St. Regensburg | XIII |
| Weidenau, Wilhelmstr. 51 | 2 | AuP | LSt. Düsseldorf St. Dortmund | VI |
| Weil/Rhein (no address) | 9 | AuP | LSt. Stuttgart St. Karlsruhe | V |
| Weinheim/Bergstrasse, Obertorstr. 9 | 19 | AuP | LSt. Stuttgart St. Karlsruhe | XII |
| Weipert, Annabergerstr. 2 | 10 | AuP | LSt. Nürnberg St. Karlsbad | XIII |
| Weissenfels, Zeitzerstr. 2 | 43 | AuDSt | LSt. Halle | IV |
| Weisswasser, Rathaus | 14 | AuP | LSt. Breslau | VIII |
| Werdau, Gedächtnisplatz 1 | 21 | AuP | LSt. Dresden St. Zwickau | IV |
| Wels, Adolf-Hitler-Platz 39 | 30 | AuP | LSt. Wien St. Linz/Donau | XVII |
| Welun, Krakower Vorstadt | 16 | AuP | LSt. Posen St. Litzmannstadt | XXI |
| Wermelskirchen, Telegrafenstr. 16-20 | 16 | AuP | LSt. Düsseldorf St. Wuppertal | VI |
| Werne/Lippe, Münsterstr. 30 | 13 | AuP | LSt. Düsseldorf St. Recklinghausen | VI |
| Wernigerode, Oberpfarrkirchhof 14 | 25 | AuP | LSt. Halle St. Magdeburg | XI |
| Wesel, Rathaus | 25 | AuP | LSt. Düsseldorf St. Essen | VI |
| Wesermünde, Am Hafen 15-17 | 113 | AuDSt | LSt. Bremen | X |
| Wesseling, Strasse des 30 Januar 22 | 5 | AuP | LSt. Köln | VI |
| Westerland-Sylt, Rathaus | 6 | AuP | LSt. Hamburg St. Flensburg | X |
| Wetzlar, Domplatz 3 | 21 | AuP | LSt. Frankfurt/M | IX |
| Wiener Neustadt, Wiener Str. 12 | 40 | AuDSt | LSt. Wien | XVII |
| Wiesbaden, Friedrichstr. 25 | 170 | AuDSt | LSt. Frankfurt/M. | XII |
| Wilkau-Hasslau, Poststr. 1 | 14 | AuP | LSt. Dresden St. Zwickau | IV |
| Witten, Poststr. 1 | 74 | AuP | LSt. Düsseldorf St. Bochum | VI |
| Wismar (Seestadt), Am Markt 11 | 37 | AuP (*) | LSt. Stettin St. Schwerin | II |
| Wittenberg, Schlosstr. 14-15 | 37 | AuDSt | LSt. Halle | IV |
| Wittenberge, Rathaus | 28 | AuP | LSt. Berlin | III |
| Wolfenbüttel, Stadtmarkt | 25 | AuP | LSt. Hannover St. Braunschweig | XI |
| Wormditt, Rathausmarkt | | AuP | LSt. Königsberg | I |
| Worms, Erenburger Str. 33 | 59 | AuDSt | LSt. Frankfurt/M. St. Darmstadt | XII |
| Würselen, Kaiserstr. 36 | 16 | AuP (*) | LSt. Köln St. Aachen | VI |
| Wurzen, Horst-Wessel-Str. 2 | 20 | AuP | LSt. Dresden St. Leipzig | IV |

| Town | Population (in 1,000 of inhabitants) | Classification | Higher Headquarters | Under BdS in Wkr. |
|---|---|---|---|---|
| Zabern (Saverne), Adolf-Hitler-Str. 80 | 9 | AuP | LSt. Strassburg | V |
| Zehdenik, Am Markt 9 | 13 | AuP | LSt. Berlin | III |
| Zeitz, Adolf-Hitler-Platz 16 | 36 | AuP | LSt. Halle | IV |
| Zerbst, Rathaus | 24 | AuP | LSt. Halle St. Dessau | IV |
| Zella-Mehlis, Rathausstr. 4 | 17 | AuP | LSt. Halle St. Weimar | IV |
| Zeulenroda, Rathaus | 13 | AuP | LSt. Halle St. Weimar | IV |
| Ziegenhalz, Ring | 10 | AuP | LSt. Kattowitz St. Oppeln | VIII |
| Zittau, Böhmische Str. 7 | 39 | AuP | LSt. Dresden | IV |
| Zlin, Internatsgebäude Nr. 2433 | 22 | AuDSt (*) | LSt. Prag St. Brünn | B/M |
| Znaim, Schillerstr. 9 | 25 | AuP | LSt. Wien | XVII |
| Zweibrücken (no address) | 31 | AuP | LSt. Stuttgart St. Ludwigshafen | XII |
| Zwittau, Adolf-Hitler-Platz 50 | 10 | AuP | LSt. Kattowitz St. Troppau | VIII |
| Zychlin, Rathausstr. 37 | 9 | AuP | LSt. Posen St. Hohensalza | XXI |

# THREE EXAMPLES OF THE STRUCTURE OF A KRIPO REGIONAL HEADQUARTERS

## (a) TYPICAL ORGANISATION OF A KRIPO-LEITSTELLE

### (Organisationsplan über die Gestaltung einer Gross-Städtischen Kriminalpolizei)

—1938

### Direktion I

| Personalien und Organisation | Personnel and Organisation |
|---|---|
| Insp. I A | |
| *Personal-, Disziplinärsachen, Urlaubsangelegenheiten, Ausbildung, Sport, Waffen, Rechtsbeiratssachen* | Personnel, disciplinary matters, leave, training, sports, arms, legal advice |
| Insp. I B | |
| *Wirtschaftsangelegenheiten, Kassensachen, Dienstreisen, Fahrkarten, Kraftwagen, Reisekosten, Belohnungen, Unterbringung* | Economic matters, financial matters, duty travel, travel warrants, M/T, travelling expenses, rewards, billeting |
| Insp. I C | |
| *Registratur, Kanzlei, Materialbeschaffung* | Registry, Chancery, supplies |
| Insp. I D | |
| *Organisation, Statistik, Ausrüstung, Fragen der Leitstelle, Bücherei, Beratungsstelle, Museum, Tagesbericht, Fahndungsnachweis, Lichtbildwerkstätte, Kriminalhunde* | Organisation, statistics, equipment, internal questions of the *Leitstelle*, library, Advisory Office, Museum, daily reports, reports on searches for wanted persons, photography laboratories, police dogs |
| Insp. I E | |
| *Fahndungs- u. Bereitschaftsdienst, Streife, Aussendienst der Abt. IV, Theaterkontrolle, KK. v. Dienst, Überwachung der Berufsverbrecher, Überführungsstelle, Polizeigefängnis* | Search for wanted persons and Emergency Service, Routine and special patrols of Section IV, control of theatres, duty officer, surveillance of professional criminals, Transit Station, Police Prison |

### Direktion II

| Gewerbs- u. Gewohnheitsmässige Straftaten | Offences by Professional and Habitual Criminals |
|---|---|
| Insp. II A | |
| *Mord und andere gemeingefährliche Verbrechen* | Murder and other dangerous crimes against the community |
|   1. *Kommissariat für Mord u. Totschlag* |   1. " Kommissariat " for murder and manslaughter |
| *2. Kommissariate für Todesermittlungssachen, Selbstmord, Vermisste* |   2. " Kommissariate " for investigations of causes of deaths, suicides and missing persons |
|   3. *Kommissariat für Leichenschauhaus* |   3. " Kommissariat " for the mortuary |
|   4. *Kommissariat für tödliche Verkehrsunfälle* |   4. " Kommissariat " for fatal traffic accidents |
| *5. Kommissariate für Brand, Katastrophen- u. Wilddiebssachen* |   5. " Kommissariate " for fires, accidents, poaching |
| Insp. II B | |
| *Gewerbsmässige Diebstähle* | Professional Acts of Theft |
| *1. Kommissariate für schwere Diebstähle* |   1. " Kommissariate " for major thefts |
| *2. Kommissariate für einfache Diebstähle* |   2. " Kommissariate " for minor thefts |
| *3. Kommissariate für Diebstähle besonderer Art, z. B. Raub, Autodiebstähle, Taschendiebstähle* |   3. " Kommissariate " for acts of theft of a special nature, e.g. robbery with violence, car thefts, pickpockets |
| Insp. II C | |
| *Gewerbsmässiger Betrug* | Professional Fraud |
| *1. Kommissariate für kfm. Betrug* |   1. " Kommissariate " for commercial fraud |
| *2. Kommissariate für Schwindeleien, z.B. Heiratsschwindel, falsche Beamte, Bauernfänger* |   2. " Kommissariate " for all types of swindles, acting under false pretences, e.g. marriage under false pretences, impersonators of officials, sharpers, quacks |
| *3. Kommissariate für Fälschungen, z.B. Falschgeld, gefälschte Urkunden u. Frachtbriefe, Falschspiele, Rauschgift* |   3. " Kommissariate " for forgeries, e.g. bad money, forged papers and bills of lading, cheating at play, cards, etc., illicit traffic in drugs |
| Insp. II D | |
| *Gewohnheitsmässige u. gemeingefährliche Sittlichkeitsverbrechen* | Sexual Offences (habitual and dangerous to the community) |
| *1. Kommissariate für Homosexuelle, Abtreibungen, Körperverletzung auf geschlechtlicher Grundlage, Verführungen* |   1. " Kommissariate " for homosexuality, abortions, physical injury (sexually), seduction |

*Number varies according to requirement of the particular *Leitstelle*.

| | |
|---|---|
| *2. Kommissariate für Überwachung der Pro-stitution, Geschlechtskrankengesetz | 2. " Kommissariate " for supervision of pro s-titution, Law on venereal diseases |
| Insp. II E | |
| Weibliche Kriminalpolizei | Female Branch of the Criminal Police |
| *1. Kommissariate für Vernehmungen u. Ermittlungen bei denen die weibliche Kriminal-polizei mitwirkt, Kinderschutz | 1. " Kommissariate " for proceedings and findings in which the Female Criminal Police collaborate ; protection of children |

## ** Direktion III

| Straftaten Nichtgewerbs- u. Gewohnheitsmässiger Art, Örtliche Kriminalpolizeiliche Tätigkeit | Offences not of a Professional or Habitual Nature, Local Activities of the Criminal Police |
|---|---|
| Insp. III A | |
| 1–4 Örtliche Kommissariate | 1–4 Local " Kommissariate " |
| Insp. III B | |
| 1–6 Örtliche Kommissariate | 1–6 Local " Kommissariate " |
| Insp. III C | |
| 1–3 Örtliche Kommissariate | 1–3 Local " Kommissariate " |
| Insp. III D | |
| 1–4 Örtliche Kommissariate | 1–4 Local " Kommissariate " |
| Insp. III E | |
| 1–4 Örtliche Kommissariate | 1–4 Local " Kommissariate " |
| Insp. III F | |
| 1–4 Örtliche Kommissariate | 1–4 Local " Kommissariate " |
| Insp. III G | |
| 1–4 Örtliche Kommissariate | 1–4 Local " Kommissariate " |
| Insp. III H | |
| 1–4 Örtliche Kommissariate | 1–4 Local " Kommissariate " |

* Number varies according to requirement of the particular *Leitstelle*

** Depending on local requirements, additional *Direktionen* may exist in particular cities

## (b) ORGANISATION OF THE KRIMINALPOLIZEI-LEITSTELLE KÖLN
### —1941

### Inspektion I

| | |
|---|---|
| 1 Kommissariat : | |
| Raub, Erpressung, Wohnungseinbrüche | Robbery, blackmail, housebreaking |
| 2 Kommissariat : | |
| Einbrüche in Geschäfte, Fabriken, Banken | Burglary of business establishments, factories, banks |
| 3 Kommissariat : | |
| Ladendiebstähle, Gepäckdiebstähle | Shoplifting, baggage thefts |
| 4 Kommissariat : | |
| Auto- u. Fahrraddiebstähle | Car and bicycle thefts |

### Inspektion II

| | |
|---|---|
| 5 Kommissariat : | |
| Betrug, Urkundenfälschung, Unterschlagung A-G | Fraud, forgery of ducuments, embezzlement A-G |
| 6 Kommissariat : | |
| Betrug, Urkundenfälschung, Unterschlagung H-P | Fraud, forgery of documents, embezzlement H-P |
| 7 Kommissariat : | |
| Betrug, Urkundenfälschung, Unterschlagung Q-Z | Fraud, forgery of documents, embezzlement Q-Z |
| 8 Kommissariat : | |
| Betrug, Urkundenfälschung, Unterschlagungen, unlauterer Wettbewerb, Beratungsstelle zum Schutze gegen Betrug | Fraud, forgery of documents, embezzlement, unfairness in competitions, Advisory Office for protection against fraud |

### Inspektion III

| | |
|---|---|
| 9 Kommissariat : | |
| Kriminaltechn. Untersuchungen, Spurensiche-rung | Criminal examination and preservation of evidence |
| 10 Kommissariat : | |
| Personenfeststellung | Personal identification |
| 11 Kommissariat : | |
| Kriminalpolizeiliches Nachrichtenwesen, Druckerei | Criminal Police Communications ; Printing Office |
| 12 Kommissariat : | |
| Personenstrafaktensammlung | Criminal dossiers |

### Inspektion IV

| | |
|---|---|
| 13 Kommissariat : | |
| Fahndungsdienst | Search for Wanted Persons |
| 14 Kommissariat : | |
| Ständige Mordkommission, Nachrichtensammel-stelle für Vermisste und unbekannte Tote | Permanent Commission on investigations of murder cases, Missing Persons and Unknown Deaths Information Centre |

| | |
|---|---|
| 15 *Kommissariat :* | |
| *Vorbeugende Verbrechensbekämpfung* | Crime Prevention |
| 16 *Kommissariat :* | |
| *Verkehrsunfälle, Brandstiftung, Katastrophen-kommando* | Traffic accidents, arson, taking command in emergencies |

### Inspektion V

| | |
|---|---|
| 17 *Kommissariat :* | |
| *Sittlichkeitsverbrechen* | Sex Crimes |
| 18 *Kommissariat :* | |
| *Rasseverrat, Abtreibung* | Transgression of the racial laws, abortion |
| 19 *Kommissariat :* | |
| *Meineid, Münzverbrechen u. -Vergehen* | Perjury, major and minor offences against currency regulations |
| 20 *Kommissariat :* | |
| *Verbrechen und Vergehen im Amte, Erpressung, weibliche Kriminalpolizei* | Abuse of official position, blackmail, Female Criminal Police |

## (c) ORGANISATION OF KRIPO-LEITSTELLE HANNOVER

### —June, 1943

#### Kriminal-Direktions-Abteilungen

| | |
|---|---|
| K.1. | |
| *Aufbau und Organisation* | Structure and Organisation |
| *Vorausbildung der Beamten* | Preliminary training of officials |
| *Versetzungen und Kommandierungen* | Transfers and assignments |
| *Gemeindliche Kripo-Abteilungen* | Municipal Criminal Police (obsolete since Sept., 1943—see text) |
| K.2. | |
| *Auszahlung von Bewegungsgeld* | Payment of expenses |
| *Ausrüstung und Bewaffnung* | Arms and equipment |
| *Bücherei und Urlaubsgewährungen* | Library.  Leave |
| K.3. | |
| *Personal Akten* | Personnel files |
| *Entlassungen und Einstellungen* | Dismissals and appointments |
| *Weiterausbildungen und Fortbildung* | Refresher Courses and Advanced Training |
| K.4. | |
| *Verteilungsstelle* | Central Office for distribution of mail, etc. |

### Inspektion K.1

| | |
|---|---|
| *Kommissariat 1.K.* | |
| *Mord, Totschlag, Raub* | Murder, manslaughter, robbery |
| *Kommissariat 2.K.* | |
| *Brand und Katastrophen* | Fire, emergencies |
| *Kommissariat 3.K.* | |
| *Einbruch, Kraftwagendiebstahl* | Burglary.  Automobile thefts |
| *Kommissariat 4.K.* | |
| *Einfacher Diebstahl einschliesslich Diebstahl v. Fahrrädern* | Minor thefts ; includes theft of bicycles |
| *Kommissariat 5.K.* | |
| *Fahndung und Vorbeugung* | Search for wanted persons and preventive measures |
| *Kontrolle von Pfandleih-Anstalten, Herbergen und Märkten* | Control of pawn-shops, hostels and markets |
| *Haftbefehle* | Warrants for arrest |

### Inspektion K. II

| | |
|---|---|
| *Kommissariat 6.K.* | |
| *Selbstmord und Fahnenflucht* | Suicide and desertion |
| *Kommissariat 7.K.* | |
| *Falschgeld* | Counterfeit money |
| *Urkundenfälschung* | Forgery of documents |
| *Renn-Betrug* | Race cheating |
| *Lotteriefälschung* | Lottery frauds |
| *Rauschgift* | Drugs |
| *Unlauterer Wettbewerb* | Unfairness in competitions |
| *Kommissariat 8.K.* | |
| *Strafakten-Verwaltung, Archive* | Criminal dossiers, archives |
| *Nachrichten-Sammelstelle* | Information Centre |
| *Fahndungs-Kartei* | Card Index on wanted persons |
| *Lichtbildstelle* | Photographs |
| *Einzel-Fingerabdrücke* | Single fingerprint impressions |
| *Zehn-Fingerabdrücke* | Ten-fingerprint impressions |
| *Kommissariat 9.K.* | |
| *Berufs-Verbrecher (B.V.)* | Professional criminals |
| *Einweisung von B.V. in Konzentrations-Lager* (KL) | Committing of professional criminals to Concentration Camps |

| | |
|---|---|
| *Letzte Überprüfung und Ausfertigung* | Final examination and decision on Concentration Camp cases |
| *Wiederholungs-Verbrecher* | Habitual criminals |
| *Zigeuner-Überwachungsstelle* | Surveillance of gypsies |
| *Kommissariat* 10.*K.* | |
| *Kriminalwache, Nachtdienst* | 24-hour duty roster ; night duty |
| *Kriminal-Bahnhofswache* | Criminal patrols at Railway Stations |
| *Auskunftei* | Information Office |
| *Fremdenanmeldungszettel-Überprüfung* | Examination of registrations made by new arrivals |

## Inspektion K. III

| | |
|---|---|
| *Kommissariat* 11.*K.* | |
| *Betrug, Stossbetrug, Untreue* | Fraud, obtaining goods under false pretences, breaking of pledges, etc. |
| *Kriegswirtschaftsvergehen und -Verbrechen* | Offences and crimes against war economy |
| *Vergehen und Verbrechen gegen die Strafordnung für den Verbrauch* | Offences and crimes against the rationing regulations |
| *Kommissariat* 12.*K.* | |
| *Abtreibung* | Abortion |
| *Mädchenhandel* | White slave traffic |
| *Blutschande* | Incest |
| *Kommissariat* 13.*K.* | |
| *Unterschlagung* | Embezzlement |
| *Schwarzhören* | Illegal listening to broadcasts |
| *Entziehung elektrischer Energie* | Illicit use of electricity |
| *Kommissariat* 14.*K.* | |
| *Prostitution* | Prostitution |
| *Geschlechtsverkehr wider die Natur* | Perversion |
| *Kommissariat* (no number) | |
| *Weibliche Kriminalpolizei (W.K.P.)* | Female Criminal Police |
| *Jugendliche und Kinder* | Juveniles and children |

# REGIONAL AUTHORITIES OF THE FORESTRY ADMINISTRATION
## —under the Reich Chief Forester, GÖRING

### (a) FORESTRY AUTHORITIES OF THE STATES
#### (Forstverwaltungen der Länder)
##### —as of 1939

**Preussen**
Der Reichsforstmeister und Preussische Landes-
forstmeister,
Berlin W 8, Leipziger Platz 11

**Bayern**
Bayer. Ministerpräs., Landesforstverwaltung,
München 43, Brieffach

**Sachsen**
Reichsstatthalter in Sachsen—Landesregierung
(Landesforstverw.),
Dresden-A. 1, Schlossplatz 1

**Württemberg**
Württ. Forstdirektion,
Stuttgart W, Militärstr. 15

**Baden**
Bad. Finanz- u. d. Wirtschaftsminister, Forstabt.,
Karlsruhe, Schlossplatz 3

**Hessen**
Reichsstatthalter in Hessen—Landesregierung
(Abt. V, Forstverw.)
Darmstadt, Neckarstr. 7

**Thüringen**
Thür. Finanzministerium (Abt. 3, Forstverw.),
Weimar

**Mecklenburg**
Meckl. Staatsministerium, Abt. Landwirtschaft,
Domänen und Forsten, Schwerin, Meckl.

**Oldenburg**
Min. der Finanzen, Forstverw., Oldenburg
(Oldb.)

**Braunschweig**
Braunschw. Finanzminister, Landesforstverw.,
Braunschweig, Postschliessfach 523.

**Anhalt**
Anhalt. Staatsministerium, Abt. Finanzen,
Landesforstverw., Dessau.

**Schaumburg-Lippe**
Schaumburg-Lippesche Landesregierung,
Forstabt.
Bückeburg, Herminenstr. 31

**Lippe**
Der Reichsstatthalter (Landesregierung Lippe)
Abt. II, Staatsforstverw., Detmold.

### (b) HEADQUARTERS OF THE REGIONAL FORESTRY AUTHORITIES AND THEIR AREAS
#### (Verzeichnis der Jagdbehörden und deren Bezirke)
##### —as of 1939

Der Reichsjägermeister : Berlin W 8,
Leipziger Platz 11

### ANHALT

**Jagdgau Anhalt**
Area :
  Land Anhalt
Gaujägermeister :
  Landforstmeister PIEPER
  Dessau, Hardenbergstr. 2
  Tel : 3953
Stabsamt d. Gaujägermeist. :
  Dessau, Bismarckstr. 22a
  Tel : 3091
    Sammel Nr.

### BADEN

Landesjägermeister :
  Landesforstmeister Wilhem HUG,
  Karlsruhe/Ba., Schlossplatz 3
  Tel : 6340-6347
Stabsamt d. Landesjägermeisters :
  Same as above

**Jagdgau Baden-Nord**
Area :
  Amtsbezirke Adelsheim, Bretten, Bruchsal,
  Buchen, Bühl, Ettlingen, Heidelberg,
  Karlsruhe, Kehl, Mannheim, Mosbach, Ober-
  kirch, Pforzheim, Rastatt, Sinsheim,
  Tauberbischofsheim, Weinheim, Wertheim,
  Wiesloch
Gaujägermeister :
  Der Landesjägermeister
Stabsamt d. Gaujägermeisters :
  See under Landesjägermeister

**Jagdgau Baden-Süd**
Area :
  Amtsbezirke Donaueschingen, Emmendingen,
  Engen, Freiburg, Konstanz, Lahr, Lörrach,
  Messkirch, Müllheim, Neustadt, Offenburg,
  Pfullendorf, Säckingen, Schopfheim, Staufen,
  Stockach, Ueberlingen, Villingen, Waldkirch,
  Waldshut, Wolfach
Gaujägermeister :
  Oberforstrat Hermann WALLI,
  Freiburg/Br., Schlossbergstr. 7,
  Tel : 6035
Stabsamt d. Gaujägermeisters :
  Same as above

### BAYERN

Landesjägermeister :
  Reichsstatthalter, General d. Inf. Franz Ritter v.
  EPP,
  München 2 NO, Prinzregentenstr. 7
  Tel : 20 209/210
Stabsamt d. Landesjägermeisters :
  München 2 NO, Prinzregentenstr. 11a
  Tel : 25 400 and 20 209/210

**Jagdgau Oberbayern**
Area :
  Reg.-Bez. Oberbayern
Gaujägermeister :
  Buchdruckereibesitzer Adolf MÜLLER,
  München, Prinzregentenstr. 11a
Stabsamt d. Gaujägermeisters :
  Same as above
  Tel : 25450

**Jagdgau Niederbayern**
Area :
  *Reg.-Bez.* Niederbayern
*Gaujägermeister* :
  Ludwig Graf v. SEYBOLTSTORFF,
  Seyboldsdorf, P. Vilsbiburg/Nb.
  Tel : Vilsbiburg 73
*Stabsamt d. Gaujägermeisters* :
  Same as above

**Jagdgau Saar-Pfalz**
Area :
  *Reg.-Bez.* Pfalz and Saarland
*Gaujägermeister* :
  Carl Freiherr v. GIENANTH,
  Eisenberg
  Tel : 50
*Stabsamt d. Gaujägermeisters* :
  Kaiserslautern, Theaterstr. 31
  Tel : Kaiserslautern 984

**Jagdgau Oberpfalz**
Area :
  *Reg.-Bez.* Oberpfalz
*Gaujägermeister* :
  Theo CRONEISS,
  Gut Schrammelhof, P. Deuerling b. Regensburg
  Tel : Regensburg 3740
*Stabsamt d. Gaujägermeisters* :
  Regensburg, Regierungsgebäude, Zimmer 134
  Tel : 2251, Nebenstelle 330

**Jagdgau Oberfranken**
Area :
  *Reg.-Bez.* Oberfranken
*Gaujägermeister* :
  *Eichungsoberinspektor* Anton SCHAEFER
  Bamberg, Weide 28
  Tel : 876
*Stabsamt d. Gaujägermeisters* :
  Same as above

**Jagdgau Mittelfranken**
Area :
  *Reg.-Bez.* Mittelfranken
*Gaujägermeister* :
  *Zollfinanzrat* Fritz SPENGLER,
  Nürnberg-W., Weidenkellerstr. 8
  Tel : 27724
*Stabsamt d. Gaujägermeisters* :
  Same as above

**Jagdgau Unterfranken**
Area :
  *Reg.-Bez.* Unterfranken
*Gaujägermeister* :
  *Geheimer Forstrat* Hans REDER,
  *Forstmeister* in Bischbrunn i. Spessart
  Tel : Esselbach 3 via Marktheidenfeld
*Stabsamt d. Gaujägermeisters* :
  Würzburg, Augustinenstr. 6
  Tel : 2974

**Jagdgau Schwaben**
Area :
  *Reg.-Bez.* Schwaben
*Gaujägermeister* :
  Gottfried KRESS,
  Augsburg, Bahnhofstr. 18/I
  Tel : 8700
*Stabsamt d. Gaujägermeisters* :
  Same as above

## BRAUNSCHWEIG

**Jagdgau Braunschweig**
Area :
  *Gebietsteile des Landes* Braunschweig

*Gaujägermeister* :
  *Staatsminister* Friedrich ALPERS,
  Braunschweig, Inselwall 11
  Tel : 7288
*Stabsamt d. Gaujägermeisters* :
  *Reichsjägerhof* Hermann GÖRING,
  Braunschweig-Riddagshausen
  Tel : Braunschweig 5858/59

## HAMBURG

**Jagdgau Hamburg**
Area :
  *Gebietsteile der Freien u. Hansestadt* Hamburg
*Gaujägermeister* :
  *SS-Gruppenführer Staatsrat* Werner LORENZ,
  Berlin
*Stabsamt d. Gaujägermeisters* :
  Hamburg 37, Isestr. 110
  Tel : 524740

## HESSEN

*Landesjägermeister* :
  *Gauleiter u. Reichsstatthalter* Jakob SPRENGER
  Darmstadt, Neckarstr. 7
  Tel : 7711, Nebenstelle 68911
*Stabsamt d. Landes jägermeisters* :
  Same as above

**Jagdgau Hessen**
Area :
  *Gebietsteile des Landes* Hessen
*Gaujägermeister* :
  *Der Landesjägermeister*

## MECKLENBURG

**Jagdgau Mecklenburg**
Area :
  *Gebietsteile des Landes* Mecklenburg
*Gaujägermeister* :
  *Oberforstmeister* Martin KLIEFOTH,
  Schwerin i. M., Staatsministerium
  Tel : 5051, Nebenanschl. 508, privat 4208
*Stamsamt d. Gaujägermeisters* :
  Schwerin i. M., Raiffeisenhaus
  Tel : 4011

## OLDENBURG

**Jagdgau Oldenburg**
Area :
  *Gebietsteile des Landes* Oldenburg
*Gaujägermeister* :
  E. RÖVER, *Reichsstatthalter in* Oldenburg u.
  Bremen,
  *Gauleiter des Gaues* Weser-Ems, Oldenburg.
  Tel : 4580
*Stabsamt d. Gaujägermeisters* :
  Oldenburg i. O., Ministerium
  Tel : Sammel Nr. 6291 (or 2781)

## PREUSSEN

**Jagdgau Gross-Berlin**
Area :
  *Verw.-Bez. der Stadt* Berlin
*Gaujägermeister* :
  E. PASSMANN,
  Berlin-Charlottenburg 9,
  Brettschneiderstr. 12
  Tel : 935198
*Stabsamt d. Gaujägermeisters* :
  Berlin W 35,
  Grossadmiral-von-Köster-Ufer 85
  Tel : 210523

**Jagdgau Hannover**
Area :
  *Reg.-Bez.* Hannover, Hildesheim, Lüneburg,
  Stade, Osnabrück, Aurich,
  *Gebiet d. Freien u. Hansestadt* Bremen

**Gaujägermeister :**
Stadtrat a. D. Dr. Gustav HEINTZE
Hannover-Kirchrode, Ostfeldstr. 32 D.
Tel : 56990
*Stabsamt d. Gaujägermeisters :*
Hannover, am Schiffgraben 57
Tel : 21695

## Jagdgau Kurhessen
Area :
*Reg.-Bez.* Kassel, except *Kr. der Herrschaft*
Schmalkalden
*Gaujägermeister :*
Major a. D. NELLE
Kassel, Herkulesstr. 83
*Stabsamt d. Gaujägermeisters :*
Kassel, Kronprinzenstr. 5
Tel : 30845

## Jagdgau Nassau
Area :
*Reg.-Bez.* Wiesbaden
*Gaujägermeister :*
*Generaldirektor* Wilhelm AVIENY
Wiesbaden, Nassaüische Landesbank
*Stabsamt d. Gaujägermeisters :*
Frankfurt a. M., Zeil 127
Tel : 27369

## Jagdgau Kurmark
Area :
*Reg. Bez.* Potsdam, Frankfurt/O, Grenzmark
Posen/Westpreussen except *Kr.* Fraustadt
*Gaujägermeister :*
*Freiherr* v. DUNGERN-OBERAU,
Berlin SW 11, Anhaltstr. 7
Tel : 192228
*Stabsamt d. Gaujägermeisters :*
Same as above

## Jagdgau Ostpreussen
Area :
*Reg.-Bez.* Königsberg, Gumbinnen, Allenstein,
Westpreussen
*Gaujägermeister :*
*Graf* FINCKENSTEIN,
Oberförsterei Garden, P. Sommerau/Westpr.
Tel : Sommerau 61
*Stabsamt d. Gaujägermeisters :*
Deutsch-Eylau, Karl-Freyburger-Str. 8

## Jagdgau Hinterpommern
Area :
*Reg.-Bez.* Köslin and the following *Kr.* of
*Reg.-Bez.* Stettin :—
Greifenhagen, Pyritz, Stargard, Saatzig,
Naugard, Cammin, Greifenberg, Regenwalde,
the part of *Kr.* Randow which lies East of the
Oder
*Gaujägermeister :*
von LETTOW-VORBECK,
Hoffelde b. Roggow über Ruhnow/Pomm.
Tel : Roggow 1
*Stabsamt d. Gaujägermeisters :*
Köslin, Schwederstr. 15
Tel : 2542

## Jagdgau Vorpommern
Area :
Following *Kr.* of *Reg.-Bez.* Stettin :—
Rügen, Stralsund, Franzburg-Barth, Grimmen,
Greifswald Stadt u. Land, Demmin,
Anklam, Usedom-Wollin, Ueckermünde,
Stettin, the part of *Kr.* Randow West of
the Oder
*Gaujägermeister :*
*Landwirt* JUHL,
Langenhanshagen b. Staatl. Horst Kr. Franz-
burg-Barth
Tel : Lüdershagen Nr. 6

*Stabsamt d. Gaujägermeisters :*
Stralsund, Ossenreyerstr. 4
Tel : Stralsund 1844

## Jagdgau Rheinland-Nord
Area :
*Reg.-Bez.* Aachen, Düsseldorf, Köln
*Gaujägermeister :*
Lothar *Graf* von u. zu HOENSBROECH,
Schloss Kellenberg über Jülich
Tel : Jülich 203
*Stabsamt d. Gaujägermeisters :*
Köln, Gereonshof 29
Tel : Köln 215010

## Jagdgau Rheinland-Süd
Area :
*Reg.-Bez.* Trier, Koblenz
*Gaujägermeister :*
*Pol.-Präs.* August Wilhelm WETTER,
Koblenz, Simmernerstr. 50
Tel : Koblenz 2920 (Pol.-Präsidium)
*Stabsamt d. Gaujägermeisters :*
Koblenz, Kaiser-Wilhelm-Ring 53 I,
Tel : 2920 (Pol.-Präsidium)

## Jagdgau Prov. Sachsen
Area :
*Reg.-Bez.* Magdeburg, Merseburg and the *Kr.*
Nordhausen-Stadt, Grafschaft Hohenstein,
Worbis, *Reg.-Bez.* Erfurt.
*Gaujägermeister :*
*Oberjägermeister* Fr. OSTERMANN
Berlin W 8, Leipziger Platz 11
*Stabsamt d. Gaujägermeisters :*
Halle/Saale, Kaiserstr. 7
Tel : 24291

## Jagdgau Schlesien
Area :
*Reg.-Bez.* Breslau, Liegnitz, Oppeln, *Kr.* Frau-
stadt v. *Reg. Bez.* Grenzmark Posen-West-
preussen
*Gaujägermeister :*
Günther Freiherr von REIBNITZ
Breslau 16, Wardeinstr. 6
Tel : 46747
*Stabsamt d. Gaujägermeisters :*
Breslau 16, Wardeinstr. 6
Tel : 46494

## Jagdgau Schleswig-Holstein
Area :
*Reg.-Bez.* Schleswig, *Freie u. Hansestadt* Lübeck
*Gaujägermeister :*
*Landrat* W. HAMKENS,
Rendsburg, Kanalufer 40
Tel : 2110
*Stabsamt d. Gaujägermeisters :*
Rendsburg, am Gerhardshain 2
Tel : 3016

## Jagdgau Westfalen
Area :
*Reg.-Bez.* Münster, Minden, Arnsberg, *Länder*
Lippe and Schaumburg-Lippe
*Gaujägermeister :*
Anton Freiherr von SCHORLEMER,
Herringhausen über Lippstadt i. W.
Tel : Benninghausen 256
*Stabsamt d. Gaujägermeisters :*
Same as above

### SACHSEN

## Jagdgau Land Sachsen
Area :
*Gebiet des Landes* Sachsen

*Gaujägermeister :*
Martin MUTSCHMANN, *Landesjägermeister*,
Dresden A-1, Schlossplatz 1
Tel : 24371
*Stabsamt d. Gaujägermeisters :*
Same as above

## THÜRINGEN

### Jagdgau Thüringen

Area :
*Gebiet des Landes* Thüringen,
*Kr. der Herrschaft* Schmalkalden (*Reg.-Bez.*
Kassel)
*Kr.* Heiligenstadt, Mühlhausen Stadt u. Land
*Reg.-Bez.* Erfurt Langensalza, Erfurt Stadt u.
Land, Weissensee, Ziegenrück, Schleusingen
*Gaujägermeister :*
*Ministerpräsident* MARSCHLER
Weimar, Thür. Staatsministerium
Tel : 1170
*Stabsamt d. Gaujägermeisters :*
Weimar, Marienstr. 7
Tel : 1170

## WÜRTTEMBERG

*Landesjägermeister :*
Dr. PFANNENSCHWARZ,
Ulm a. Do., Münsterplatz 33/2
Tel : 4866
*Stabsamt d. Landesjägermeisters :*
Same as above

### Jagdgau Württemberg-West

Area :
*Oberämter* Backnang, Besigheim, Böblingen,
Brackenheim, Calw, Esslingen, Freuden-
stadt, Heilbronn, Herrenberg, Horb,
Leonberg, Ludwigsburg, Marbach, Maul-
bronn, Nagold, Neckarsulm, Neuenbürg,
Nürtingen, Oehringen, Rottenburg, Schorn-
dorf, Stuttgart-Amt, Stuttgart-Stadt, Tüb-
ingen, Vaihingen/Enz., Waiblingen, Welz-
heim
*Gaujägermeister :*
*Oberforstrat* MAURER,
Stuttgart, Feuerbacherheide 20
*Stabsamt d. Gaujägermeisters :*
Stuttgart, Militärstr. 15, Forstdirektion
Tel : 22851–53

### Jagdgau Württemberg-Ost

Area :
*Oberämter* Aalen, Crailsheim, Ellwangen,
Gaildorf, Gerabronn, Gmünd, Hall, Künzel-
sau, Mergentheim, Biberach, Blaubeuren,
Ehingen, Geislingen, Göppingen, Heiden-
heim, Kirchheim, Laupheim, Münsingen,
Neresheim, Reutlingen, Ulm, Urach
*Gaujägermeister :*
*Forstmeister* GLÖCKLER,
Ulm a. D., Münsterplatz 33/2
Tel : 4866
*Stabsamt d. Gaujägermeisters :*
Same as above

### Jagdgau Württemberg-Süd/Hohenzollern

Area :
*Oberämter* Balingen, Leutkirch, Oberndorf,
Ravensburg, Riedlingen, Rottweil, Saulgau,
Sulz, Spaichingen, Tettnang, Tuttlingen,
Waldsee, Wangen, die Hohenzollernschen
Länder (*Reg.-Bez.* Sigmaringen)
*Gaujägermeister :*
R. HARRER,
Sigmaringen
Tel : 256
*Stabsamt d. Gaujägermeisters :*
Same as above

## OESTERREICH

*Landesjägermeister :*
Ing. Anton REINTHALLER,
*Minister für Land-Forstwirtschaft,*
Wien 1, Ministerium für Landforstwirtschaft
*Stabsamt :*
Wien 1, Opernring 5

### Jagdgau Wien

Area :
*Verwaltungsbez. Stadt* Wien
*Gaujägermeister :*
*Oberbürgermeister Dr.-Ing.* Hermann NEU-
BACHER,
Wien 1, Neues Rathaus

### Jagdgau Niederdonau

Area :
*Gebietsteile* Niederdonau *mit den Kreisen* Schreibs,
Horn, Zwettl, Waidhofen a.d. Thaya,
Neunkirchen, Mödling, Mistelbach, Wiener-
Neustadt, Bruck a.d. Leitha, Hollabrunn,
Gmünd, Gänserndorf, Baden, St. Pölten,
Lilienfeld, Melk, Amstetten, Krems, Tulln,
Pöggstall, Neusiedl am See, Oberpullendorf,
Eisenstadt, Stockerau
*Gaujägermeister :*
*Oekonomierat* CLAASS,
Paasdorf bei Mistelbach, Niederdonau
*Stabsamt :*
Wien 1, Schauflergasse 6

### Jagdgau Oberdonau

Area :
*Gebietsteile des Landes* Oberdonau
*Kreise* Braunau, Linz, Freistadt, Gmunden,
Grieskirchen, Ried im Innkreis, Kirchdorf
a.d. Krems, Perg, Schärding, Stehr, Vöckla-
bruck, Rohrbach, Wels
*Gaujägermeister :*
*Oberforstrat Ing.* Karl STARKEL
Schloss Steyr in Steyr
*Stabsamt :*
Linz a.d. Donau, Schmidtorstr. 4/1

### Jagdgau Steiermark

Area :
*Gebietsteile des Landes* Steiermark
*Kreise* Bruck a.d. Mur, Deutsch-Landsberg,
Feldbach, Graz, Gröbming, Hartberg,
Judenburg, Leibnitz, Leoben, Liezen,
Mureck, Mürzzuschlag, Voitsberg, Weiz,
Güssing, Murau
*Gaujägermeister :*
*Ing.* Ernst PICHLER,
Weiz
*Stabsamt :*
Graz VI, Radetzkystr. 7

### Jagdgau Kärnten

Area :
*Gebiete des Landes* Kärnten
*Kreise* Klagenfurt, Villach, St. Veit, Hermagor,
Spittal a.d. Drau, Völkermarkt, Wolfsberg,
Lienz
*Gaujägermeister :*
*Dr.* Werner KNAUS,
Klagenfurt,
Tarviserstr. 16
*Stabsamt :*
Klagenfurt, Adolf-Hitler-Platz 8

### Jagdgau Salzburg

Area :
*Gebietsteile des Landes* Salzburg
*Kreise* Zell am See, St. Johann im Pongau,
Tamsweg, Hallein, Salzburg
*Gaujägermeister :*
*Prof. Dr.* Eduard Paul TRATZ,
Museumsdirektor, Salzburg, Kaigasse 13

*Stabsamt :*
Salzburg, Kaigasse 13

**Jagdgau Tirol**
Area :
*Gebietsteile des Landes* Tirol u. Vorarlberg
Kreise Reutte, Landeck, Imst, Innsbruck,
Schwaz, Kufstein, Kitzbühel, Bregenz u.
Feldkirch, Bludenz
*Gaujägermeister :*
*Hofrat Ing.* Rudolf HAPPAK,
Innsbruck, Bienerstr. 17

*Stabsamt :*
Innsbruck, Wilhelm-Greil-Str. 9

**SPECIAL CASE**

**Jagdgebiet Harz**
Area :
Sangerhausen, Nordhausen, Herzberg, Oste-
rode, Seesen, Langelsheim, Goslar, Bad
Harzburg, Heudeber, Halberstadt, Aschers-
leben, Sandersleben, Mansfeld, Sangerhausen
Under the Jurisdiction of :
*KPSt.* Magdeburg

# ANNEXE G: PART SIX

## TABLE OF MINING AUTHORITIES AND THEIR CONNECTION WITH THE SIPO & SD

### (Verzeichnis der Bergbehörden und der zuständigen BdS (IdS))

#### —as of 1943

| Mining Authorities | Appropriate BdS (IdS) |
|---|---|
| O B A Breslau | Breslau |
| Controlling *Bergreviere* :— | |
| Gleiwitz-Nord, Gleiwitz-Süd, Beuthen-Nord, Beuthen-Süd, Waldenburg-Nord, Waldenburg-Süd, Görlitz, Kattowitz-Nord, Kattowitz-Süd, Sosnowitz, Königshütte, Rybnik, Karwin. | Breslau |
| O B A Halle | Dresden |
| Controlling *Bergreviere* :— | |
| Frankfurt a.d.O., Cottbus, Senftenberg. | Berlin |
| Halle (Saale), Naumburg, Zeitz, Eisleben | Dresden |
| Magdeburg | Braunschweig |
| O B A Clausthal | Braunschweig |
| Controlling *Bergreviere* :— | |
| Goslar-Süd, Goslar-Nord, Hannover | Braunschweig |
| Celle | Hamburg |
| Schmalkalden, Kassel | Kassel |
| O B A Dortmund | Düsseldorf |
| Controlling *Bergreviere* :— | |
| Hamm, Lünen, Dortmund I, Dortmund II, Witten, Castrop-Rauxel, Herne, Recklinghausen I, Recklinghausen II, Gelsenkirchen, Bochum I, Bochum II, Werden, Essen I, Essen II, Essen III, Buer, Bottrop, Dinslaken-Oberhausen, Duisburg, Krefeld | Düsseldorf |
| O B A Bonn | Düsseldorf |
| Controlling *Bergreviere* :— | |
| Sauerland, Siegen, Hellenthal | Düsseldorf |
| Dillenburg, Weilburg/Lahn, Diez, Neuenahr | Wiesbaden |
| Köln-West, Köln-Ost | Düsseldorf |
| Koblenz-Wiesbaden, Koblenz | Wiesbaden |
| Aachen-Süd, Aachen-Nord | Düsseldorf |
| O B A Saarbrücken | *BdS* Metz |
| Controlling *Bergämter* :— | |
| Saarbrücken-Mitte, Saarbrücken-Ost, Saarbrücken-West, Metz, Diedenhofen, Forbach/Lothr. | *BdS* Metz |
| *Reichsstatthalter* in Braunschweig u. Anhalt—*Landesreg.* Anhalt— | |
| Controlling *Bergrevier* :— | |
| Dessau | Braunschweig |
| O B A Karlsruhe | *IdS* Stuttgart |
| Controlling *Bergämter* :— | |
| Freiburg i. Br., Karlsruhe i. B. | *IdS* Stuttgart |
| Mülhausen i. Elsass | *BdS* Strassburg |
| O B A München | München |
| Controlling *Berginspektionen* :— | |
| München, Amberg, Bayreuth | München |
| Zweibrücken/Pfalz | *BdS* Metz |
| *Braunschweigisches Landesbergamt* | Braunschweig |
| Controlling *Bergrevier* :— | |
| Braunschweig | Braunschweig |
| *Hess. Obere Bergbehörde* Darmstadt | Wiesbaden |
| Controlling *Hessische Bergmeisterei* :— | |
| Darmstadt | Wiesbaden |

| Mining Authorities | Appropriate BdS (IdS) |
|---|---|
| Schaumburg-Lippische<br>  *Landesreg.* in Bückeburg<br>*Die Geschäfte des Bergrevierbeamten werden vom Bergrevierbeamten in*<br>  *Hannover nebenamtl. wahrgenommen.* | *Stapo. Leitstelle* Münster<br>(*Insp.* Düsseldorf)<br>*Kripo. Leitstelle* Hannover<br>(*Insp.* Braunschweig) |
| O B A für die Ostmark : Wien | Wien |
| Controlling *Bergämter* :— | |
|   Graz, Leoben, Salzburg | Salzburg |
|   Wien I | Wien |
|   Klagenfurt, Solbad Hall i. Tirol | Salzburg |
| O B A Freiberg/Sa. | Dresden |
| Controlling *Bergämter* :— | |
|   Dresden, Leipzig, Zwickau, Stollberg | Dresden |
|   Karlsbad | München |
|   Komotau | |
|   Brüx | Dresden |
|   Teplitz-Schönau | |
| Thüring. Wirtschaftsministerium Weimar | Kassel |
| Controlling *Bergämter* :— | |
|   Saalfeld, Altenburg, Weimar | Kassel |
| O B A Stuttgart | Stuttgart |
| Controlling *Bergamt* :— | |
|   Stuttgart | Stuttgart |

# ANNEXE H

## ORDER OF BATTLE OF THE SICHERHEITSDIENST

# SD-LEITABSCHNITTE

## (SD Regional Headquarters)

*Note.*—The definition " Area " refers only to the Territory under direct control of the *Leitabschnitt*, not to the larger area in which the *Leitabschnitt* has certain supervisory powers.

### BERLIN

**Area :**
*Reichshauptstadt* Berlin, *Reg. Bez.* Frankfurt/Oder (without *Landkreis* Soldin) and *Reg. Bez.* Potsdam (without *Landkreis* Prenzlau)
(37,000 qkm., 7,041,589 inhab.)

**Party Gaue concerned :**
Berlin (Berlin)
Mark Brandenburg (Berlin)

**Address :**
C2, Kaiser-Wilhelm-Strasse 22
Tel : 515261 (also T/P)

**Chief :**
*SS-OSBF* POLTE

**Under supervision of :**
*BdS* Berlin

**Branch Offices :**
*HAuSt :* Frankfurt/Oder, Potsdam
*AuSt :* Berlin I (Charlottenburg), Berlin II (Wilmersdorf), Berlin III (Südende), Berlin IV (NW 87), Berlin V (SW 68), Berlin VI (N65), Berlin VIII (Weissensee), Berlin IX (Lichtenberg), Berlin X (Neukölln), Bad Saarow, Calau, Cottbus, Eberswalde, Guben, Kirchhain, Küstrin, Landsberg, Neuruppin, Rathenow, Reppen, Schwiebus, Sorau, Templin, Wittenberge.

### BRESLAU

**Area :**
*Reg. Bez.* Breslau and Liegnitz (without *Landkreis* Hoyerswerda)
(26,981 qkm, 3,287,44 inhab.)

**Party Gau concerned :**
Niederschlesien (Breslau)

**Address :**
18, Friedrich-Hebbel-Strasse 1–3
Tel : 82471 (also T/P)

**Chief :**
*SS-OSBF Dr.* KAH

**Under supervision of :**
*BdS* Breslau

**Branch Offices :**
*HAuSt :* Breslau, Brieg, Liegnitz
*AuSt :* Glatz, Glogau, Görlitz, Hirschberg, Oels, Schweidnitz, Trebnitz, Waldenburg

### DANZIG

**Area :**
*Reichsgau* Danzig-Westpreussen (*Reg. Bez.* Bromberg, Danzig and Marienwerder)
(25,965·4 qkm—2,700,000 inhab.)

**Party Gau concerned :**
Danzig-Westpreussen (Danzig)

**Address :**
Zoppot, Adolf-Hitler-Strasse 640
Tel : 51624, 51935 (also T/P)

**Chief :**
*SS-OSBF Dr.* STEINBACHER

**Under supervision of :**
*BdS* Danzig

**Branch Offices :**
*HAuSt :* Danzig
*AuSt :* Bromberg, Dirschau, Elbing, Gotenhafen, Graudenz, Thorn

### DRESDEN

**Area :**
*Land* Sachsen and *Landkreis* Hoyerswerda of the *Reg. Bez.* Liegnitz
(15,872·2 qkm—5,291,042 inhab.)

**Party Gaue concerned :**
Sachsen (Dresden)
Niederschlesien (Breslau)

**Address :**
Gerhart-Hauptmann-Strasse 1
Tel : 45312

**Chief :**
*SS-OSBF* TSCHIERSCHKY

**Under supervision of :**
*BdS* Dresden

**Supervising :**
*Abschnitt* Halle/Saale

**Branch Offices :**
*HAuSt :* Chemnitz, Dresden, Leipzig
*AuSt :* Annaberg, Auerbach, Bautzen, Borna, Dippoldiswalde, Dresden-Land-West, Döbeln, Flöha, Freiberg, Glauchau, Grimma, Gröditz, Grossenhain, Hoyerswerda, Kamenz, Löbau, Marienberg, Meissen, Oschatz, Pirna, Plauen, Rochlitz, Schwarzenberg, Stollberg, Zittau, Zwickau

### DÜSSELDORF

**Area :**
*Reg. Bez.* Düsseldorf
(5,496·86 qkm—4,183,235 inhab.)

**Party Gaue concerned :**
Düsseldorf (Düsseldorf)
Essen (Essen)

**Address :**
Kaiserswerth, Leuchtenberger Kirchweg 73–75
T/P via *BdS* Düsseldorf

**Chief :**
*SS-OSBF* BENDT

**Under supervision of :**
*BdS* Düsseldorf

**Supervising :**
*Abschnitte* Dortmund, Köln, Münster

**Branch Offices :**
*HAuSt :* Düsseldorf, Duisburg, Essen
*AuSt :* Dinslaken, Geldern, Kleve, Krefeld, Mörs, Mülheim/Ruhr, M. Gladbach-Rheydt, Neuss, Oberhausen, Opladen, Remscheid, Solingen, Wesel, Wuppertal-Elberfeld

### HAMBURG

**Area :**
*Hansestadt* Hamburg and *Reg. Bez.* Lüneburg (without the *Stadt*- or *Landkreise* Burgdorf, Celle, Dannenberg, Fallingbostel, Gifhorn and Uelzen)
(746·04 qkm—1,711,877 inhab.)

**Party Gaue concerned :**
Hamburg (Hamburg)
Ost-Hannover (Lüneburg)

**Address :**
Neuer Jungfernstieg 16
Tel : 351722/23 and 352892 (also T/P)

**Chief :**
SS-OSBF HERFORTH
**Under supervision of :**
BdS Hamburg
**Supervising :**
Abschnitt Kiel
**Branch Offices :**
HAuSt : Lüneburg
AuSt : Hamburg-Altona, Hamburg-Bergedorf, Hamburg-Harburg, Hamburg-Innen-stadt, Hamburg-Ost, Hamburg-Wandsbek, Hamburg-West

## KARLSRUHE

Note.—Downgraded in 1943 to the status of a SD-HAuSt, but retaining its position as in-dependent Headquarters and as directing and co-ordinating agency towards subordinate branch offices. May since have been upgraded to Leit-abschnitt again.
**Area :**
Land Baden (without the Stadt- or Landkreise Heidelberg, Mannheim, Mosbach and Sinsheim) (13,051·15 qkm—1,844,425 inhab.)
**Party Gau concerned :**
Baden (Karlsruhe—Strassburg)
**Address :**
Jahnstr. 18
Tel : 2314/15 (also T/P and Polfunk)
**Chief :**
SS-HSF WENZEL
**Under supervision of :**
BdS Strassburg (Stuttgart)
KdS Strassburg
**Branch Offices :**
AuSt : Baden-Baden, Bruchsal, Bühl, Donau-eschingen, Freiburg, Karlsruhe, Kon-stanz, Lahr, Lörrach, Müllheim/Baden, Offenburg, Pforzheim, Pfullendorf, Ra-statt, Renchen, Säckingen, Singen, Stock-ach, Tauberbischofsheim, Überlingen, Villingen, Waldshut, Wolfach.

## KATTOWITZ

**Area :**
Reg. Bez. Kattowitz, Oppeln and Troppau (28,482·2 qkm—5,155,187 inhab.)
**Party Gaue concerned :**
Oberschlesien (Kattowitz)
Sudetenland (Reichenberg)
**Address :**
Strasse der SA 11
Tel : 35955/56 and 32652/53
**Chief :**
SS-SBF PODLICH
**Under supervision of :**
BdS Breslau
**Branch Offices :**
HAuSt : Gleiwitz, Oppeln, Troppau
AuSt : Beuthen-Tarnowitz, Bielitz, Freiwaldau, Freudenthal, Kattowitz, Kreuzburg, Landskron, Loben, Mährisch-Schön-berg, Neisse-Grotkau, Neustadt/Ob. Schles., Neu-Titschein, Pless, Ratibor, Rybnik, Sosnowitz, Teschen

## KÖNIGSBERG

**Area :**
Provinz Ostpreussen (without Reg. Bez. Zichenau)
(39,116 qkm—2,300,000 inhab.)
**Party Gau concerned :**
Ostpreussen (Königsberg)

**Address :**
Luisenalle 61
Tel : 21737, 24575 (also T/P via StapoLSt. Königsberg)
**Chief :**
SS-HSF Dr. SELKE (m.d.k.F.b.)
Predecessor : SS-OSBF Günther RAUSCH
**Under supervision of :**
BdS Königsberg
**Supervising :**
Abschnitt Zichenau
**Branch Offices :**
HAuSt : Allenstein, Königsberg
AuSt : Bartenstein, Braunsberg, Goldap, Gum-binnen, Insterburg, Lyck, Mohrungen, Osterode/Ostpr., Rastenburg, Sensburg, Tilsit, Treuburg

## MÜNCHEN

**Area :**
Reg. Bez. Oberbayern and Schwaben (26,291·89 qkm—2,854,587 inhab.)
**Party Gaue concerned :**
München-Oberbayern (München)
Schwaben (Augsburg)
**Address :**
Franz-Josef-Strasse 38
Tel : 34555/57 (also T/P)
**Chief :**
SS-QSBF GLITZ
**Under supervision of :**
BdS München
**Branch Offices :**
HAuSt : Augsburg, München
AuSt : Aichach, Altötting, Bad Tölz, Berchtes-gaden, Dachau, Dillingen, Donauwörth, Freising, Friedberg, Fürstenfeldbruck, Füssen, Garmisch-Partenkirchen, Günz-burg, Illertissen, Ingolstadt, Kaufbeuren, Kempten, Landsberg, Lindau, Markt-Oberdorf, Memmingen, Miesbach, Mindel-heim, Neuburg, Rosenheim, Schroben-hausen, Sonthofen, Starnberg, Traun-stein, Wasserburg, Weilheim, Wolfrats-hausen

## NÜRNBERG

**Area :**
Reg. Bez. Main-Franken (without the Stadt- or Landkreise Alzenau, Aschaffenburg, Miltenberg and Obernburg), Reg. Bez. Ober- und Mittel-franken (without the Stadt- or Landkreise Bayreuth, Bamberg, Coburg, Ebermannstadt, Forchheim, Hof, Höchstedt/Aisch, Kulmbach, Kronach, Lichtenfels, Münchberg, Naila, Peg-nitz, Rehhau, Staffelsstein and Wunsiedel), Reg. Bez. Eger
(22,278·09 qkm—2,537·951 inhab.)
**Party Gaue concerned :**
Franken (Nürnberg)
Mainfranken (Würzburg)
Sudetenland (Reichenberg)
**Address :**
Ernst vom Rath-Allee 54
Tel : 41281/84 (also T/P)
**Chief :**
SS-OSBF FRIEDRICH
**Under supervision of :**
BdS Nürnberg
**Supervising :**
Abschnitt Bayreuth
**Branch Offices :**
HAuSt : Nürnberg, Würzburg, Karlsbad
AuSt : Ansbach, Bad Kissingen, Bad Neustadt/ Saale, Brückenau, Eger/Falkenau, Fürth,

Graslitz, Hersbruck, Karlsbad, Kitzingen, Klösterle, Königshofen, Lohr, Marienbad, Marktheidenfeld, Neustadt/Aisch, Saaz, Schwabach, Schweinfurt, Wassertrüdingen, Weissenburg, Würzburg

## POSEN

**Area :**
Reg. Bez. Posen and Hohensalza (without the Stadt- or Landkreise Gasten, Hermannsbad, Konin, Kutno, Leslau and Warthbrücken) (21,567 qkm—1,755,400 inhab.)

**Party Gau concerned :**
Wartheland (Posen)

**Address :**
Kaiserring 15
Tel : 1993/97 (also T/P via StapoLSt. Posen)

**Chief :**
SS-OSBF, ORR. HÖPPNER (reported head of III A in the RSHA)

**Under supervision of :**
BdS Posen

**Supervising :**
Abschnitt Litzmannstadt

**Branch Offices :**
HAuSt : Posen
AuSt : Birnbaum, Gnesen, Grätz, Hohensalza, Jarotschin, Kolmar, Lissa, Samter, Schroda
also :
Chef d. Sipo u. d. SD, Umwandererzentrale Posen, Fritz-Reuter-Strasse 2 a
AuSt : Gnesen (f. Kr. Gnesen, Mogilno, Schroda, Wreschen), Gratz, Kolmar, Litzmannstadt, Posen, Pabianice and Hohensalza

## PRAG

**Area :**
Protektorat Böhmen und Mähren (48,914·63 qkm—7,395,547 inhab.)

**Party Gaue concerned :**
Sudetenland (Reichenberg)
Bayreuth (Bayreuth)
Oberdonau (Linz)
Niederdonau (Wien)

**Address :**
XIX, Sachsenweg 44
Tel : 77442/45 (also T/P)

**Chief :**
SS-OSBF JACOBI

**Under supervision of :**
BdS Prag

**Branch Offices :**
HAuSt : Brünn, Budweis, Iglau, Königgrätz, Mähr. Ostrau, Pilsen, Prag
AuSt : Brünn, Jitschin, Jungbunzlau, Kladno, Klattau, Kolin, Mähr. Ostrau, Olmütz, Pardubitz, Pilgrams, Prag, Strakonitz, Tabor, Trebitsch, Zlin

## REICHENBERG

(probably SD-Abschnitt only)

**Area :**
Reg. Bez. Aussig
(7,293·2 qkm—1,328,784 inhab.)

**Party Gau concerned :**
Sudetenland (Reichenberg)

**Address :**
Gablonzer Strasse 22
Tel : 4885/86 (also T/P)

**Chief :**
SS-SBF KOCH

**Under supervision of :**
BdS Dresden

**Branch Offices :**
AuSt : Aussig, Böhm. Leipa, Brüx, Gablonz, Hohenelbe, Komotau, Leitmeritz, Reichenberg/Friedland, Rumburg, Teplitz-Schönau, Tetschen, Trautenau

## STETTIN

**Area :**
Provinz Pommern (Reg. Bez. Köslin, Schneidemühl, Stettin), the Landkreise Soldin of the Reg. Bez. Frankfurt/Oder and the Landkreis Prenzlau of the Reg. Bez. Potsdam (40,723·78 qkm—2,509,764 inhab.)

**Party Gaue concerned :**
Pommern (Stettin)
Kurmark (Berlin)

**Address :**
Königsplatz 16/III
Tel : 23958/59 (also T/P)

**Chief :**
SS-SBF Dr. SCHIMMEROHN

**Under supervision of :**
BdS Stettin

**Branch Offices :**
AuSt : Greifswald, Köslin, Neustettin, Schneidemühl, Stettin, Stolp, Stralsund, Swinemünde

## STUTTGART

**Area :**
Land Württemberg and Reg. Bez. Sigmaringen (20,649·91 qkm—2,970,626 inhab.)

**Party Gau concerned :**
Württemberg-Hohenzollern (Stuttgart)

**Address :**
Reinsburgstrasse 32
Tel : 67651/53 (also T/P)

**Chief :**
SS-OSBF STEINLE

**Under supervision of :**
BdS Stuttgart

**Supervising :**
HAuSt : Karlsruhe

**Branch Offices :**
HAuSt : Stuttgart
AuSt : Aalen, Balingen, Freudenstadt, Heilbronn, Horb, Ravensburg, Rottweil, Schwäb.Hall, Sigmaringen, Spaichingen, Tübingen, Tuttlingen, Ulm/Donau

## WIEN

**Area :**
Reichsgaue Wien and Niederdonau (24,706·86 qkm—3,627,652 inhab.)

**Party Gaue concerned :**
Wien (Wien)
Niederdonau (Wien)

**Address :**
50, Theresianumgasse 16–18
Tel : U 46005 (also T/P)

**Chief :**
SS-SBF Dr. CHLAN (i.V.)

**Under supervision of :**
BdS Wien

**Supervising :**
Abschnitte Graz, Innsbruck, Klagenfurt, Linz/Donau

**Branch Offices :**
AuSt : Eisenstadt, Krems, Mistelbach, Sankt Pölten, Wiener Neustadt, Wien 1, Wien 2, Wien 3, Wien 4

# SD-ABSCHNITTE

## (Sub-regional HQ)

*NOTE :—Abschnitte* for which no supervising *Leitabschnitt* is indicated are probably independent.

### BAYREUTH

**Area :**
*Reg. Bez.* Niederbayern-Oberpfalz and the *Landkreise* Bamberg, Bayreuth, Coburg, Ebermannstadt, Forchheim, Hof, Höchstädt/Aisch, Kulmbach, Kronach, Lichtenfels, Münchberg, Naila, Pegnitz, Rehau, Staffelstein, Stadtsteinach, Wunsiedel of the *Reg. Bez.* Ober- und Mittelfranken
(29,508 qkm—2,312,254 inhab.)

**Party Gau concerned :**
Bayreuth (Bayreuth)

**Address :**
Alexanderstrasse 6
Tel : 3655/56 (also T/P)

**Chief :**
SS-SBF Dr. GLASER
Predecessor : SS-SBF Dr. JASKULSKY

**Under supervision of :**
*BdS* Nürnberg
*LAbs.* Nürnberg

**Branch Offices :**
*AuSt :* Amberg, Bamberg, Bayreuth, Bergreichenstein, Cham, Coburg, Deggendorf, Dingolfing, Forchheim, Hof/Saale, Kemnath, Kronach, Landshut, Lichtenfels, Münchberg, Nabburg, Neumarkt, Passau, Regensburg, Riedenburg, Schwandorf, Selb, Straubing, Vilshofen, Weiden, Wunsiedel, Zwiesel

### BRAUNSCHWEIG

**Area**
The *Länder* Braunschweig and Schaumburg-Lippe, *Reg. Bez.* Hannover (without *Landkreise* Grafschaft Diepholz, *Grafschaft* Hoya and Nienburg), *Reg. Bez.* Hildesheim (without *Landkreis* Münden), the *Stadt-* or *Landkreise* Burgdorf, Celle, Dannenberg, Fallingbostel, Gifhorn and Uelzen of the *Reg. Bez.* Lüneburg
(19,119.27 qkm—2,382,005 inhab.)

**Party Gaue concerned :**
Süd-Hannover-Braunschweig (Hannover)
Ost-Hannover (Lüneburg)

**Address :**
Wilhelmstrasse 21
Tel : 9080/84 (also T/P)

**Chief :**
SS-OSBF DYROFF

**Under supervision of :**
*BdS* Braunschweig

**Branch Offices :**
*HAuSt :* Hannover
*AuSt :* Alfeld, Blankenburg, Braunschweig, Bückeburg, Burgdorf, Celle, Dannenberg, Duderstadt, Einbeck, Fallingbostel, Genthin, Gifhorn, Göttingen, Goslar, Hameln, Helmstedt, Hildesheim, Holzminden, Neustadt/Rübenberge, Northeim, Osterode, Peine, Raguhn, Rinteln, Springe, Uelzen, Wolfenbüttel, Zellerfeld

### BREMEN

**Area :**
*Hansestadt* Bremen, *Land* Oldenburg, *Reg. Bez.* Aurich, *Reg. Bez.* Stade, *Reg. Bez.* Osnabrück, the *Landkreise Grafschaft* Hoya, Diepholz and Nienburg of the *Reg. Bez.* Hannover
(26,921.88 qkm—2,739,547 inhab.)

**Party Gaue concerned :**
Weser-Ems (Oldenburg)
Ost-Hannover (Lüneburg)

**Address :**
Graf-Moltke-Strasse 60
Tel : 81673 (also T/P via *StapoSt.* Bremen)

**Chief :**
SS-SBF KRÖGER

**Under supervision of :**
*BdS* Hamburg

**Branch Offices :**
*HAuSt :* Osnabrück, Wilhelmshaven
*AuSt :* Bassum, Brake, Bremen, Cloppenburg, Cuxhaven, Delmenhorst, Diepholz, Emden, Jever, Leer, Nienburg, Nordenham, Nordhorn, Oldenburg/O., Stade, Varel, Verden, Wesermünde, Wittmund

### DESSAU

(Reinstated as *SD-Abschnitt* 1 January 1944)

**Area :**
*Land* Anhalt and *Provinz* Magdeburg
(13,921.19 qkm—1,819,578 inhab.)

**Party Gau concerned :**
Magdeburg-Anhalt (Dessau)

**Address :**
Auf dem Sande 9–10
Tel : 4527, 5291 (T/P via *Stapo* Dessau)

**Chief :**
SS-HSF Karl HERMANN

**Under supervision of :**
*BdS* Braunschweig

**Branch Offices :**
*AuSt :* Bernburg, Burg, Calbe, Dessau, Gardelegen, Halberstadt, Haldensleben, Köthen, Magdeburg, Oschersleben, Osterburg, Quedlinburg, Salzwedel, Stendal, Wanzleben, Wolmirstedt, Zellerfeld, Zerbst

### DORTMUND

**Area :**
*Reg. Bez.* Arnsberg (without the *Stadt-*, or *Landkreise* Siegen and Wittgenstein)
(7,650 qkm—2,500,444 inhab.)

**Party Gau concerned :**
Westfalen-Süd (Bochum)

**Address :**
Horst-Wessel-Strasse 28
Tel : 25051/52, also T/P

**Chief :**
SS-SBF GOTTSMANN

**Under supervision of :**
*BdS* Düsseldorf
*LAbs.* Düsseldorf

**Branch Offices :**
*HAuSt :* Bochum, Dortmund
*AuSt :* Arnsberg, Brilon, Burgsteinfurt, Gelsenkirchen, Hagen, Hamm, Lippstadt, Lüdenscheid, Meschede

## FRANKFURT/Main

**Area :**
Land Hessen, Provinz Nassau, the Stadt- or Landkreise Alzenau, Aschaffenburg, Miltenberg, Obernburg of the Reg. Bez. Mainfranken, the Landkreise Siegen and Wittgenstein of the Reg. Bez. Arnsberg.
(33,717.77 qkm—6,079,644 inhab.)

**Party Gau concerned :**
Hessen-Nassau (Frankfurt/Main)

**Address :**
Schaumainkai 23
Tel : 61341/42, also T/P

**Chief :**
SS-SBF Dr. JASKULSKY

**Under supervision of :**
BdS Kassel

**Branch Offices :**
HAuSt : Darmstadt, Frankfurt/Main, Wiesbaden
AuSt : Aschaffenburg, Friedberg, Hanau, Homburg vor d. Höhe, Limburg/Lahn, Mainz, Offenbach, Rüdesheim, Siegen, Wetzlar, Worms

## GRAZ

**Area :**
Reichsgau Steiermark
(17,388 qkm—1,116,407 inhab.)

**Party Gau concerned :**
Steiermark (Graz)

**Address :**
Leechgasse 52
Tel : 83053/54 (also T/P via StapoSt. Graz)

**Chief :**
SS-OSBF Dr. ZEHLEIN
Predecessor : SS-SF LURKER

**Under supervision of :**
BdS Salzburg
LAbs. Wien

**Branch Offices :**
HAuSt : Graz-Stadt
AuSt : Bruck, Deutschlandsberg Feldbach, Fürstenfeld, Graz-Land, Hartberg, Judenburg, Leibnitz, Leoben, Liezen, Mürzzuschlag, Murau, Mureck, Oberwart, Voitsberg, Weiz

## HALLE/Saale

**Area :**
Provinz Halle-Merseburg (without the Landkreise Eckartsberga, Querfurt, and Sangerhausen)
(8,570 qkm—1,518,860 inhab.)

**Party Gaue concerned :**
Halle-Merseburg (Halle)
Thüringen (Weimar)

**Address :**
Weidenplan 12
Tel : 21448/49, 33996 (also T/P via Stapo LSt. Halle/Saale)

**Chief :**
SS-SBF BÖHLKE (i.V.)

**Under supervision of :**
BdS Dresden
LAbs. Dresden

**Branch Offices :**
AuSt : Bad Liebenwerda, Bitterfeld, Delitzsch, Eisleben, Halle, Mansfeld, Merseburg, Torgau, Weissenfels, Wittenberg, Zeitz

## INNSBRUCK

**Area :**
Reichsgaue Tirol-Vorarlberg, Salzburg
(20,378.27 qkm—793,450 inhab.)

**Party Gau concerned :**
Tirol-Vorarlberg (Innsbruck)

**Address :**
Herrengasse 3/11
Tel : 89,789 (also T/P)

**Chief :**
SS-SBF GONTHARD
Predecessor : SS-SBF KIENE

**Under supervision of :**
BdS Salzburg
LAbs. Wien

**Branch Offices :**
HAuSt : Innsbruck, Salzburg (for Party Gau Salzburg)
AuSt : Bregenz, Hallein, Kitzbühel, Kufstein, Landeck, Markt Pongau, Reutte, Schwaz, Tamsweg, Zell a.See

## KASSEL

(Reinstated as SD-Abschnitt 15 October 1943)

**Area :**
Provinz Herrschaft (without the Stadt- or Landkreise Gelnhausen, Hanau, Schlüchtern and Herrschaft Schmalkalden), Landkreis Münden of the Reg. Bez. Hildesheim
(9,200.26 qkm—981,182 inhab.)

**Party Gau concerned**
Kurhessen (Kassel)

**Address :**
Kassel-Wilhelmshöhe, Kurhausstr. 8
T/P via StapoSt. Kassel

**Chief :**
SS-HSF FRIDERICI (k.)

**Under supervision of :**
BdS Kassel

**Branch Offices :**
AuSt : Bad Wildungen, Eschwege, Frankenberg, Hersfeld, Kassel, Marburg, Witzenhausen

## KIEL

**Area :**
Reg. Bez. Schleswig
(15,682 qkm—1,600,000 inhab.)

**Party Gau concerned :**
Schleswig-Holstein (Kiel)

**Address :**
Karolinenweg 23
Tel : 8583/84 (also T/P via Stapo St. Kiel)

**Chief :**
SS-SBF Dr. ERLER

**Under supervision of :**
BdS Hamburg
LAbs. Hamburg

**Branch Offices :**
HAuSt : Kiel, Lübeck
AuSt : Bad Oldesloe, Elmshorn, Flensburg, Heide, Itzehoe, Mölln, Neumünster, Rendsburg, Schleswig, Sylt

## KLAGENFURT

**Area :**
Reichsgau Kärnten
(11,860 qkm—465,730 inhab.)

**Party Gau concerned :**
Kärnten (Klagenfurt)

**Address :**
Fromillerstr. 2
Tel : 2551/52 (also T/P via StapoSt. Klagenfurt)
Also listed under : Pernhartgasse 3

**Chief :**
SS-OSBF PERSTERER

**Under supervision of :**
BdS Salzburg
LAbs. Wien

**Branch Offices :**
AuSt : Hermagor, Klagenfurt, Lienz, Sankt
Veit, Spittal, Villach, Völkermarkt,.
Wolfsberg

## KOBLENZ

**Area :**
Reg. Bez. Koblenz and Trier
(13,957 qkm—1,560,272 inhab.)

**Party Gau concerned :**
Moselland (Koblenz)

**Address :**
SA-Ufer 3
Tel : 7325/26 (also T/P)

**Chief :**
SS-OSBF WIEBENS
Predecessors : SS-OSBF TRAUB, SS-HSF
WILBERTZ

**Under supervision of :**
BdS Wiesbaden

**Branch Offices :**
HAuSt : Trier
AuSt : Ahrweiler, Altenkirchen, Bad Kreuz-
nach, Bernkastel, Daun/Eifel, Koblenz,
Kochem, Mayen, Neuwied, Prüm,
Simmern, Wittlich, Zell/Mosel

## KÖLN

**Area :**
Reg. Bez. Aachen and Köln
(8,364.10 qkm—2,416,530 inhab.)

**Party Gau concerned :**
Köln-Aachen (Köln)

**Address :**
Bonn, Koblenzerstr. 139
Tel : 6978, 8345 (also T/P via Stapo Bonn)

**Chief :**
SS-SBF HENNICKE

**Under supervision of :**
BdS Düsseldorf
LAbs. Düsseldorf

**Branch Offices :**
HAuSt : Köln
AuSt : Aachen, Bergheim, Bonn, Düren, Erke-
lenz, Euskirchen, Gummersbach, Köln-
Deutz, Malmedy, Schleiden, Siegburg,
Wipperfürth

## LINZ/Donau

**Area :**
Reichsgau Oberdonau
(14,213.83 qkm—1,042,339 inhab.)

**Party Gau concerned :**
Oberdonau (Linz)

**Address :**
Gesellenhausstr. 5
Tel : 26701 (also T/P via StapoSt. Linz)

**Chief :**
SS-SBF GAHRMANN

**Under supervision of :**
BdS Wien
LAbs. Wien

**Branch Offices :**
HAuSt : Linz
AuSt : Braunau/Inn, Gmunden, Kirchdorf,
Krummau, Linz (Mühlviertel), Ried,
Schärding, Steyr, Vöcklabruck, Wels

## LITZMANNSTADT

**Area :**
Reg. Bez. Litzmannstadt and the Kreise Gasten
(Waldrode), Hermannsbad, Konin, Kutno,
Leslau and Warthbrücken of the Reg. Bez.
Hohensalza
(2,376,787 qkm—2,782,070 inhab.)

**Party Gau concerned :**
Wartheland (Posen)

**Address :**
Hermann-Göring-Strasse 124
Tel : 25007/09 (also T/P via StapoSt. Litzmann-
stadt and Polfunk via Pol. Präs.)

**Chief :**
SS-SBF Dr. BOLTE

**Under supervision of :**
BdS Posen
LAbs. Posen

**Branch Offices :**
HAuSt : Litzmannstadt
AuSt : Freihaus, Kalisch, Konin, Kutno,
Lentschütz, Leslau, Pabianice, Welun

## MÜNSTER/Westf.

(Reinstated as SD-Abschnitt 15 October 1943)

**Area :**
Land Lippe and Reg. Bez. Minden and Münster
(without Stadtkreis Gelsenkirchen)
(13,000 qkm—2,401,027 inhab.)

**Party Gau concerned :**
Westfalen-Nord (Münster)

**Address :**
Staufenstr. 8
Tel : Bielefeld 6650/51 (also T/P via Stapo LSt.
Münster)

**Chief :**
SS-HSF PADECKEN

**Under supervision of :**
BdS Düsseldorf
LAbs. Düsseldorf

**Branch Offices :**
HAuSt : Bielefeld
AuSt : Beckum, Bielefeld, Borken-Bocholt,
Burgsteinfurt, Detmold, Gladbeck,
Gronau, Herford, Höxter, Lüding-
hausen, Minden, Münster, Paderborn,
Recklinghausen, Tecklenburg, Waren-
dorf, Wiedenbrück

## SAARBRÜCKEN

**Area :**
Westmark without Lothringen
(7417.1 qkm—1,892,240 inhab.)

**Party Gau concerned :**
Westmark (Neustadt/Weinstrasse)

**Address :**
Viktoriastr. 10
(Also T/P)
Former address : Trillerweg 38
Tel : 26751/52, 29927/28

**Chief :**
SS-OSBF OTT

**Under supervision of :**
BdS Metz

**Branch Offices :**
HAuSt : Mannheim-Ludwigshafen, Neustadt
Weinstr.
AuSt : Kaiserslautern, Kirchheimbolanden,
Neunkirchen, Pirmasens, Saarbrücken,
Saarlautern, Zweibrücken

## SCHWERIN/Meckl.

(Reinstated as *SD-Abschnitt* 1 January 1944)

**Area :**
Land Mecklenburg
(15,721.7 qkm—900,417 inhab.)

**Party Gau concerned :**
Mecklenburg (Schwerin)

**Address :**
Schelfstr. 32
Tel : 3455 (also T/P)

**Chief :**
*SS-SBF* GRAAF

**Under supervision of :**
*BdS* Stettin

**Branch Offices :**
*AuSt :* Güstrow, Ludwigslust, Malchin, Neustrelitz, Parchim, Rostock, Stargard, Wismar

## WEIMAR

**Area :**
*Land* Thüringen, *Reg. Bez.* Erfurt, *Landkreis* Schmalkalden of the *Provinz* Kurhessen, the *Landkreise* Eckartsberga, Querfurt and Sangerhausen of the *Provinz* Halle-Merseburg
(17,781 qkm—2,640,634 inhab.) •

**Party Gaue concerned :**
Thüringen (Weimar)
Halle-Merseburg (Halle)

**Address :**
Strasse der SA 1
Tel : 2503 (also T/P)

**Chief :**
*SS-SBF* KRUSE

**Under supervision of :**
*BdS* Kassel

**Branch Offices :**
*HAuSt :* Erfurt, Jena
*AuSt :* Altenburg, Arnstadt, Eisenach, Gera, Greiz, Heiligenstadt, Hildburghausen, Langensalza, Meiningen, Mühlhausen/ Thür., Nordhausen, Rossleben, Rudolstadt, Sangerhausen, Sondershausen, Sonneberg, Suhl, Weimar

## ZICHENAU

**Area :**
*Reg. Bez.* Zichenau
(12,847 qkm—916,252 inhab.)

**Party Gau concerned :**
Ostpreussen (Königsberg)

**Address :**
Kirchenstr. 17 (Kirchplatz)
Tel : 274 (also T/P via *StapoSt.* Zichenau)

**Chief :**
*SS-SBF* Erich JAHNKE

**Under supervision of :**
*BdS* Königsberg
*LAbs.* Königsberg

**Branch Offices :**
*AuSt :* Mielau, Plöhnen, Scharfenwiese, Schröttersburg, Zichenau

## KdS LUXEMBURG

**Area :**
*Zivilverwaltungs-Gebiet* Luxemburg
(2585 qkm—291,000 inhab.)

**Address :**
*Einsatz Kommando der Sipo und des SD* in Luxemburg
Petrussring 57
Tel : 6786/88 (also T/P)

**Kommandeur :**
*SS-OSBF, ORR.* HARTMANN

**Under supervision of :**
*BdS* Wiesbaden

**Branch Offices :**
*HAuSt :* Luxemburg
*AuSt :* Diekirch, Esch

## KdS MARBURG/Drau

**Area :** .
*Zivilverwaltungs-Gebiet* Untersteiermark
(6,792 qkm—523,000 inhab.)

**Address :**
*Kommando der Sipo und des SD* in Marburg
Tegethoffstr. 34
Tel : 24/84 (also T/P, *Polfunk* and *Bildfunk*)

**Kommandeur :**
*SS-SBF, KDir.* STAGE

**Under supervision of :**
*BdS* Salzburg

**Branch Offices :**
*AuSt :* Cilli, Luttenberg, Pettau, Polstrau, Rann, Trifail

## KdS METZ

**Area :**
Lothringen

**Address :**
*Einsatz Kommando der Sipo und des SD* in Metz
Adolf-Hitler-Str. 42
Tel : 1330

**Under supervision of :**
*BdS* Metz

**Branch Offices :**
*AuSt :* Diedenhofen, Saarburg, St.Avold, Saargemünd

## KdS STRASSBURG

**Area :**
Elsass, also the *Stadt-resp. Landkreise* Heidelberg, Mannheim, Mosbach, and Sinsheim of *Land* Baden.

**Address :**
*Aussen-Kommando der Sipo und des SD* in Strassburg
Ruprechtsauer Allee 69
Tel : 25805/06

**Under supervision of :**
*BdS* Strassburg

**Branch Offices :**
*HAuSt :* Mannheim
*AuSt :* Altkirch, Hagenau, Heidelberg, Kolmar, Molsheim, Mülhausen, Schlettstadt, Tann, Weissenburg, Zabern

## KdS VELDES

**Area :**
*Zivilverwaltungs-Gebiet* Oberkrain
(3,091 qkm—187,262 inhab.)

**Address :**
*Kommando der Sipo und des SD für die besetzten Gebiete* Kärntens und Krains in Veldes
Parkhotel
Tel : 204/206 (also T/P)

**Kommandeur :**
*SS-SBF, RuKR.* VOGT
Predecessor : *SS-OSBF* PERSTERER

**Under supervision of :**
*BdS* Salzburg

**Branch Offices :**
*AuSt :* Assling, Laak/Zaier, Littai, Radmannsdorf, Stein

# ANNEXE H: PART THREE

## SD-HAUPTAUSSENSTELLEN

### (Larger Branch Offices)

*Note.*—SD-HQ marked with an asterisk (*) were downgraded in 1942/1943 from *SD-(L) Abschnitte* to *SD-Hauptaussenstellen*, but remained semi-independent and continued to report directly to the RSHA.

| Town | Address | Phone | Chief | Under *BdS* | Under (*L*)*Abs.* | Remarks |
|---|---|---|---|---|---|---|
| Allenstein* | Freiherr vom Stein-Str. 8 | 2318 (T/P via *Stapo* Allenstein) | *SS-OSF* SIEBEL | Königsberg | Königsberg | |
| Augsburg* | Frohsinnstr. 21 | 4852 (T/P via *Stapo* Augsburg) | *SS-HSF* KÖLLERER (*m.d.L.b.*) | München | München | |
| Bielefeld* | Grünstr. 14 | 14680 and 6650/1 | *SS-HSF* PADECKEN | Düsseldorf | Münster i.W. | |
| Bochum | Horst-Wessel-Str. 9/II | 61646/47 | *SS-SBF* SEVERIT | Düsseldorf | Dortmund | |
| Breslau | Gartenstr. 39/41 | 35555 | *SS-OSF* Helmut KRÜGER | Breslau | Breslau | |
| Brieg | Moltkestr. 8 | 1288 | | Breslau | Breslau | |
| Brünn | Lehmstätte 132 | 19988/437 (T/P via *Stapo* Brünn) | *SS-SBF* KOHL | Prag | Prag | |
| Budweis | Werner-Mölders-Str. 920 | 1140/20 (T/P via *StAuDSt* Budweis) | *SS-SBF* EICHLER | Prag | Prag | |
| Chemnitz* | Oststr. 65 | 45038 | *SS-OSF* MATHES | Dresden | Dresden | |
| Danzig | Rennerstiftsgasse 5 | 27083 and 27090 | *SS-HSF* Theo SCHNEIDER | Danzig | Danzig | |
| Darmstadt* | Eugen-Bracht-Weg 6 | 5288 (T/P) | *SS-OSF* SCHÖNHALS | Wiesbaden | Frankfurt/Main | |
| Dessau* | Auf dem Sande 9/10 | 4527 and 5291 | *SS-HSF* Karl HERMANN | Braunschweig | — | Reinstated as *SD-Abschnitt* 1 September, 1944 |

| | | | | | | |
|---|---|---|---|---|---|---|
| Dortmund | SS-OSF SCHRÖDER | Schwanenwall 46/III | 33115 | Düsseldorf | Dortmund | |
| Dresden | SS-HSF CLEMENS | Zirkusstr. 13 | 17086 | Dresden | Dresden | |
| Düsseldorf | SS-USF GRÜNIG (kom.) | Adolf-Hitler-Str. 35 | 12431 | Düsseldorf | Düsseldorf | |
| Duisburg | SS-HSF FONTANE | Düsseldorferstr. 160 | 25202 | Düsseldorf | Düsseldorf | |
| Erfurt | SS-SF, Pol. Präs. WICKE | Neuwerkstr. 30 | 26435 | Kassel | Weimar | |
| Essen | SS-HSF HAGE | Haumannplatz 22 | 28631 | Düsseldorf | Düsseldorf | |
| Frankfurt/Main | SS-SBF PALLAS | Bockenheimer Landstr. 2 | 78576 | Kassel | Frankfurt/Main | |
| Frankfurt/Oder | SS-SBF SCHÖTTLER | Sophienstr. 9 | 4723 | Berlin | Berlin | |
| Gleiwitz | SS-Bew. FRONZ | Wilhelmstr. 43 | 4591 | Breslau | Kattowitz | |
| Graz-Stadt | SS-SBF Dr. TOLLOWITZ | Hans-Sachs-Gasse 6 | 0193 | Salzburg | Graz | |
| Hannover | SS-HSF Rudolf SCHMIDT | Ellernstr. 7 | 37822 | Braunschweig | Braunschweig | Suspended |
| Iglau | SS-HSF RÜHL | Bräuhausgasse 10 | 497 (T/P via StADSt Iglau) | Prag | Prag | |
| Innsbruck | SS-HSF LEIBOLD | Innrain 3/I | 2487 (T/P) | Salzburg | Innsbruck | |
| Jena | SS-OSBF, Pol. Dir. SCHULZE | Löbergraben 28 | 5030 | Kassel | Weimar | |
| Karlsbad* | SS-Bew. GLAAS | Ed.-Knoll-Str. 11 | 2354/55 | Nürnberg | Nürnberg | |
| Karlsruhe* | SS-HSF WENZEL | Jahnstr. 18 | 231415 (T/P and Pol-funk) | Strassburg | (KdS Strassburg) | See also list of LAbschnitte |
| Kiel | SS-OSF DEMMIEN (i.V.) | Karolinenweg 23 | 8583/84 (T/P via Stapo Kiel) | Hamburg | Kiel | Former address : Küterstr. 5 |
| Köln | SS-HSF BUNTE | Deutscher Ring 15 | 76491 | Düsseldorf | Köln | |
| Königgrätz | SS-HSF REINER | Georgstr. 812 | 820 (T/P via StADSt Königgrätz) | Prag | Prag | |
| Königsberg/Pr. | | Hufenallee 21 | 21267 (T/P via Stapo LSt Königsberg) | Königsberg | Königsberg | |
| Leipzig* | SS-HSF WELKE | Wächterstr. 34 | 25083/84 | Dresden | Dresden | |

# ANNEXE H : PART THREE (continued)

| Town | Address | Phone | Chief | Under *BdS* | Under *(L)Abs.* | Remarks |
|---|---|---|---|---|---|---|
| Liegnitz* | Holteistr. 9 | 3218 | *SS-OSF* OBERNDÖRFER | Breslau | Breslau | |
| Linz/Donau | Gesellenhaus-Str. 5 | 2670 | *SS-OSF* STEFFEL | Wien | Linz/Donau | |
| Litzmannstadt | Hermann-Göring-Str. 124 | 25007/09 | *SS-HSF* SCHWEICHEL | Posen | Litzmannstadt | |
| Lübeck | Schlossrantzau Parade 1 | 21353 (T/P via *Stapo* Lübeck) | *SS-SBF* Hermann MÜLLER | Hamburg | Kiel | Former address : Schrangenfreiheit 22/24 |
| Lüneburg | Hindenburgstr. 107a | 3738, 5051 (T/P via *Stapo* Lüneburg) | *SS-OSF* SCHAEL | Hamburg | Hamburg | Former address : Julius Wolff Str. 4 |
| Ludwigshafen | Jägerstr. 14 | 61411 | *SS-HSF* SÜSS | Metz Wiesbaden | Saarbrücken | See also Mannheim |
| Luxemburg | Äusserer Ring 61 | 2978 | | Wiesbaden | *KdS* Luxemburg | |
| Mähr. Ostrau | Parkstr. 3 | 2348/388. (T/P via *StADSt* Mähr. Ostrau) | *SS-HSF* HENNEBERG | Prag | Prag | |
| Mannheim | Rheinstr. 5 | 40120 | *SS-HSF* SÜSS | Wiesbaden | *KdS* Strassburg | Mannheim and Ludwigshafen seem to be closely linked or merged. |
| München | Kaufingerstr. 15/I | 12000 | *SS-HSF* KAINZ | München | München | |
| Münster* | Staufenstr. 8. | Bielefeld 6650/1 | | Düsseldorf | — | Reinstated as *SD-Abschnitt* 15 October, 1943 |
| Neustadt/Weinstr. | Luitpoldstr. 10 | 3016 | | Metz Wiesbaden | Saarbrücken | |
| Nürnberg | Bucherstr. 20a | 26600 | *SS-OSF* DEININGER (k) | Nürnberg | Nürnberg | Former address : Ernst vom Rath-Allee 54 |

| Location | Address | Number | Officer | | | Notes |
|---|---|---|---|---|---|---|
| Oppeln | Hafenstr. (Regierungs-gebäude) | 3311 | SS-USF P. MÜLLER (m.d.F.b.) | Breslau | Kattowitz | Former address : Sedanstr. 6 |
| Osnabrück | Schillerstr. 9 | 3107 | SS-OSF SCHRÖDER | Hamburg | Bremen | |
| Pilsen | Pilsen-Lochotin, Plasserstr. 5 | 2280/191 (T/P via StADSt Pilsen) | SS-HSF Dr. PATIG | Prag | Prag | |
| Posen | Wilhelmplatz. 11 | 3537/38 (T/P via Stapo LSt. Posen) | SS-SBF UHLE | Posen | Posen | Code name : KOCH Hans-Georg |
| Potsdam* | Kaiser-Wilhelm-Str. 14 | 4411 | SS-HSF AHRENS | Berlin | Berlin | |
| Prag | XII, Italienische-Str. 37 | 31248 (T/P via SD-LA Prag) | SS-OSBF HÖNSCHEIDT | Prag | Prag | |
| Salzburg* | Reichenhaller-Str. 5 | 2002 | SS-HSF JAKUBZIK | Salzburg | Innsbruck | |
| Schwerin* (Meckl.) | Schelfstr. 32 | 3455 (T/P) | SS-SBF GRAAF | Stettin | — | Reinstated as SD-Abschnitt 1 January, 1944 |
| Stuttgart | Kanzleistr. 34 | 90840 | SS-USF Dr. STAHL (i.V.) | Stuttgart | Stuttgart | |
| Trier | Martinerfeld 61 | 1541 (T/P) | SS-SBF, ORR Dr. KERN | Wiesbaden | Koblenz | |
| Troppau* | Jägerndorfer-Str. 21 | 826, 1212 | SS-OSF THALACKER | Breslau | Kattowitz | |
| Wiesbaden | Humboldtstr. 5 | 21585 | SS-SBF HELLER | Wiesbaden | Frankfurt/Main | |
| Wilhelmshaven | Am Rathausplatz 4 | 5391 | SS-HSF FUSS | Hamburg | Bremen | Former address : Kirchreihe 18 |
| Würzburg* | Bismarckstr. 9 | 3811/13 (T/P via StADSt Würzburg) | SS-SBF KALLBACK | Nürnberg | Nürnberg | |

H13

# ANNEXE H: PART FOUR

## SD-AUSSENSTELLEN
### (Smaller Branch Offices)

| Town | Address | Phone | Under *BdS* | (*L*)*Abs.* | Remarks |
|------|---------|-------|-------------|-------------|---------|
| Aachen | Bismarckstr. 61 | 3071 (T/P via *StADSt* Aachen) | Düsseldorf | Köln | |
| Aalen | Kreuzstr. 3 | 840 | Stuttgart | Stuttgart | |
| Adenau/Eifel | Bürgermeisteramt | 391 | Wiesbaden | Koblenz | Suspended |
| Ahrweiler | Bad Neuenahr, Adolf-Hitler-Strasse 257 | 781 | Wiesbaden | Koblenz | Former address : Landratsamt |
| Aichach | Reckstrasse 264 | 21 | München | München | |
| Alfeld/Leine | Wilhelm-Gustloff-Strasse 42 | | Braunschweig | Braunschweig | |
| Altenburg | | | Kassel | Weimar | |
| Altenkirchen | Betzdorf-Sieg, Poststrasse 10 | Betzdorf 633 | Wiesbaden | Koblenz | |
| Altkirch | Sundgaustrasse 20 | 180 | Strassburg | *KdS* Strassburg | |
| Altötting | Marienstrasse 9/I | 6846 | München | München | |
| Amberg/Oberpfalz | Adolf-Hitler-Str. 29 | 476 | Nürnberg | Bayreuth | |
| Annaberg/Erzgeb. | Steinweg 4 | 3761 | Dresden | Dresden | |
| Ansbach | Neustadt 36/III | 2655 | Nürnberg | Nürnberg | |
| Arnsberg/Westf. | Königstrasse 23 | 341 | Düsseldorf | Dortmund | |
| Arnstadt | Kohlenmarkt 9 | 2029 | Kassel | Weimar | |
| Aschaffenburg | Danziger Str. 1 | 76 | Kassel | Frankfurt/M | |

H14

| | | | | | |
|---|---|---|---|---|---|
| Assling | Adolf-Hitler-Str. 24 | 601 | Salzburg | KdS Veldes | |
| Auerbach/Vogtl. | Nikolaistr. 11 | 2535 | Dresden | Dresden | |
| Aussig | Maternigasse 2 | 3346 | Dresden | Reichenberg | |
| Bad Kissingen | Adolf-Hitler-Str. 12 | 2796 | Nürnberg | Nürnberg | |
| Bad Kreuznach | Kurhausstr. 17 | 2039 | Wiesbaden | Koblenz | Former address : Viktoriastr. 24 *see also* Birkenfeld |
| Bad Liebenwerda | Bürgermeister, Rose Strasse | 264/267 (Landratsamt) | Dresden | Halle-Saale | |
| Bad Neustadt/Saale | Hedwig-Fichtel-Strasse 3 | 496 | Nürnberg | Nürnberg | |
| Bad Oldesloe | Wolkenweherweg 16 | 659 | Hamburg | Kiel | |
| Bad Saarow | Hindenburgdamm | 263 | Berlin | Berlin | |
| Bad Tölz/Obb. | Nockergasse 17 | 471 | München | München. | |
| Bad Wildungen | Orthenbergstr. 15 | 101 | Kassel | Kassel | |
| Baden-Baden | Baden-Baden-Lichtental, Hauptstr. 1 | 1800 | Strassburg Stuttgart | Karlsruhe | |
| Balingen | Friedrichstr. 67 | 644 | Stuttgart | Stuttgart | |
| Bamberg | Kettenbrückstr. 6 | 306 | Nürnberg | Bayreuth | |
| Bartenstein/Ostpr. | Rastenburger Str. 18 | 944 | Königsberg | Königsberg | |
| Bassum | Strasse der SA 22 | 514 | Hamburg | Bremen | |
| Bautzen | Stadthaus am Hauptmarkt | 3341 | Dresden | Dresden | |
| Bayreuth | Friedrichstr. 19 | 3657 | Nürnberg | Bayreuth | |
| Beckum/Westf. | Adolf-Hitler-Str. 67 | 3251 | Düsseldorf | Münster/W. | |

# ANNEXE H : PART FOUR (continued)

| Town | Address | Phone | Under *BdS* | *(L)Abs.* | Remarks |
|---|---|---|---|---|---|
| Berchtesgaden | Rathausplatz 1 | 2136 | München | München | |
| Bergheim/Erft | Hermann-Göring-Str. 23 | 444 | Düsseldorf | Köln | |
| Bergreichenstein | Fachschulgasse 253 | 61 | Nürnberg | Bayreuth | |
| Berlin-Charlottenburg (A I) | Berlinerstr. 81 | 346791 | Berlin | Berlin | |
| Berlin-Lichtenberg (A IX) | Rathausstr. 8 | 550239 | Berlin | Berlin | |
| Berlin-Neu-kölln (A X) | Anzengruberstr. 5 | 600302 | Berlin | Berlin | |
| Berlin-N 65 (A VI) | Müllerstr. 135 | 462821 | Berlin | Berlin | |
| Berlin-NW 87 (A IV) | Flensburgerstr. 9 | 393776 | Berlin | Berlin | |
| Berlin-Südende (A III) | Steglitzerstr. 25 | 759309 | Berlin | Berlin | |
| Berlin-SW 68 (A V) | Curthdammstr. 30 | 610456 | Berlin | Berlin | |
| Berlin-Weissensee (A VIII) | Berliner Allee 229 | 562537 | Berlin | Berlin | |
| Berlin-Wilmersdorf (A II) | Günzelstr. 54 | 875453 | Berlin | Berlin | |
| Bernburg | Wilhelmstr. 23 | 3279 | Braunschweig | Dessau | |
| Bernkastel | Schanzstr. 18 | 307 | Wiesbaden | Koblenz | |
| Beuthen-Tarnowitz | Beuthen, Braunauerplatz, Haus der SS | 4824 | Breslau | Kattowitz | |
| Bielefeld | Grünstr. 14 | 6650/1 | Düsseldorf | Münster/W. | |
| Bielitz | Giselastr. 24 | 1903 | Breslau | Kattowitz | |
| Birkenfeld/Nahe | Idar-Oberstein II, Kobachstr. 4 | | Wiesbaden | Koblenz | Suspended—duties taken over by Bad Kreuznach |

| | | | | |
|---|---|---|---|---|
| Birnbaum/Wartheland | Hubertushof, Post Bardtensee, Krs. Birnbaum | Bardtensee 3 | Posen | Posen |
| Bitterfeld | Schulstr. 2 | 3244 | Dresden | Halle/Saale |
| Blankenburg/Harz | Rathaus | 551 | Braunschweig | Braunschweig |
| Böhm. Leipa | Adalbert-Stifter-Strasse 789 | 62 | Dresden | Reichenberg |
| Bonn | Kreuzbergweg 5 | 8068 (T/P via StADSt Bonn) | Düsseldorf | Köln |
| Borken-Bocholt | Karolingerstr. 2 | 2156 | Düsseldorf | Münster/W. |
| Borna, Bez. Leipzig | Leipzigerstr. 22 | 196/197 Ext. 9 | Dresden | Dresden |
| Brake | Georgstr. 7 | | Hamburg | Bremen |
| Braunau/Inn | Franz-Ertl-Ring 13 | 107 | Wien | Linz/Donau |
| Braunsberg/Ostpr. | Sydatstr. 14 | 250 | Königsberg | Königsberg |
| Braunschweig | Wilhelmstr. 21 | 9080/84 | Braunschweig | Braunschweig |
| Bregenz | Montfortstr. 12 | 96 (T/P) | Salzburg | Innsbruck |
| Bremen, Hansestadt | Sögestr. 48 | 28588 | Hamburg | Bremen |
| Brilon | Provinzialstr. 126 | Olsberg 365/66 | Düsseldorf | Dortmund |
| Bromberg | Adolf-Hitler-Str. 24 | 2943 | Danzig | Danzig |
| Bruchsal | Schönbornstr. 14 | 2840 | Strassburg Stuttgart | Karlsruhe |
| Bruck/Mur | Grabenfeldstr. 4 | 450 | Salzburg | Graz |
| Brückenau/Unterfr. | Ludwigstr. 228 | 465 | Nürnberg | Nürnberg |
| Brünn | Postgasse 6 | 16520 (T/P via Stapo Brünn) | Prag | Prag |
| Brüx | Bahnhofstr. 15/II | 503 | Dresden | Reichenberg |
| Bückeburg | An der Kornmasch 3 | 551/552 | Braunschweig | Braunschweig |

| Town | Address | Phone | Under *BdS* | (*L*)*Abs.* | Remarks |
|---|---|---|---|---|---|
| Bühl/Baden | Adolf-Hitler-Str. Hotel Badischer Hof | 833 | Strassburg Stuttgart | Karlsruhe | |
| Burg/Magdeburg | Hauptmann-Loeper-Str. 4 | 618 | Braunschweig | Dessau | |
| Burgdorf/Hann. | Poststr. 10 | 481 | Braunschweig | Braunschweig | |
| Burgsteinfurt | Bauernschaft Sellen 102 | 420 | Düsseldorf | Münster/W. | |
| Calau/N. Laus. | Landratsamt | 244 | Berlin | Berlin | |
| Calbe/Saale | Arnstedtstr. 91 | 251 | Braunschweig | Dessau | |
| Celle | Trift 33 | 3438 | Braunschweig | Braunschweig | |
| Cham/Oberpf. | Gerhochstr. 1 | 487 | Nürnberg | Bayreuth | |
| Cilli | Roseggerstr. 10 | 136 | Salzburg | *KdS* Marburg/Drau | |
| Cloppenburg | | | Hamburg | Bremen | |
| Coburg | Ludendorfstr. 23 | 2412 | Nürnberg | Bayreuth | Former address : Strasse der SA 9 |
| Cottbus | Altes Rathaus, Room 19/20 | 3349 | Berlin | Berlin | |
| Cuxhaven | Adolf-Hitler-Str. 4 | 3418 | Hamburg | Bremen | |
| Dachau/Obb. | Schleissheimerstr. 90 | 314 | München | München | |
| Dannenberg/Elbe | Feldstr. 8 | 117 | Braunschweig | Braunschweig | |
| Daun/Eifel | Gerolstein/Eifel, Schule | Gerolstein 276 | Wiesbaden | Koblenz | |

| | Address | No. | | | Notes |
|---|---|---|---|---|---|
| Deggendorf-Plattling | Jägerstr. 243a | 204 | Nürnberg | Bayreuth | |
| Delitzsch | Schulstr. 11 | 428 | Dresden | Halle/Saale | |
| Delmenhorst | Dreilinienweg 45 | 455 | Hamburg | Bremen | |
| Dessau | Auf dem Sande 9/10 | 4527 and 5291 | Braunschweig | Dessau | |
| Detmold | Langestr. 39 | 2730 | Düsseldorf | Münster/W. | |
| Deutschlandsberg | Piberhof 171 | 110 | Salzburg | Graz | |
| Diedenhofen | Adolf-Hitler-Platz 6 | 52 (T/P) | Metz | *KdS* Metz | |
| Diekirch | Landratsamt | 3545 | Wiesbaden | *KdS* Luxemburg | |
| Diepholz | | | Hamburg | Bremen | |
| Dillingen/Donau | Wilhelm-Bauer-Str. 32 | 203 | München | München | |
| Dingolfing-Landau/Isar | Oberes Buchet 229 | 22 | München | Bayreuth | |
| Dinslaken/Niederrhein | Adolf-Hitler-Str. 111 | 2353 | Düsseldorf | Düsseldorf | |
| Dippoldiswalde | Altenberg/Sachs., Paul-Haucke-Str. 4 | Lauenstein 281 | Dresden | Dresden | |
| Dirschau | Wilhelmstr. 19 | 1478 | Danzig | Danzig | |
| Döbeln | Bahnhofstr. 35/I | 2409 | Dresden | Dresden | |
| Donaueschingen | Augustastr. 4 | 547 | Strassburg / Stuttgart | Karlsruhe | See also Neustadt /Schwarzw. |
| Donauwörth | Adolf-Hitler-Str. 467 | 118 | München | München | |
| Dresden-Land-West | Dorfhain über Thorandt 1d | Häckendorf 218 | Dresden | Dresden | |
| Duderstadt/Eichsfeld | Haberstr. 52 | 251 | Braunschweig | Braunschweig | |
| Düren/Rhld. | Schenkelstr. 13 | 2704 | Düsseldorf | Köln | Former address : Viktoriastr. 26 |
| Eberswalde | Neue Kreuzstr. 22 | 2390 | Berlin | Berlin | |

# ANNEXE H : PART FOUR (continued)

| Town | Address | Phone | Under BdS | (L)Abs. | Remarks |
|---|---|---|---|---|---|
| Eckernförde | Strasse der SA 22 | 277 | Hamburg | Kiel | Suspended |
| Eger/Falkenau | Eger, Bayreutherstr. 90 | 673 | Nürnberg | Nürnberg | |
| Einbeck | Krähengraben 1 | 202 | Braunschweig | Braunschweig | |
| Eisenach | Frauenberg 9 | 2877 | Kassel | Weimar | |
| Eisenstadt | Zentralamtsgebäude | 215 | Wien | Wien | |
| Eisleben | Hallesche Str. 61 | 2513 | Dresden | Halle/Saale | |
| Elbing | Adolf-Hitler-Str. 35 | 2577 | Danzig | Danzig | |
| Elmshorn | Stormstrasse 8 | 2081 | Hamburg | Kiel | |
| Emden | Neutorstr. 4/5 | 2912 | Hamburg | Bremen | |
| Erkelenz | Hindenburgstr. 32 | 434 | Düsseldorf | Köln | Former address : Fürbringerstr. 32 |
| Esch/Alzig | Redinger Str. 127 | 3142 | Wiesbaden | *KdS* Luxemburg | |
| Eschwege | Niederhonerstr. 54 | 2150 | Kassel | Kassel | |
| Eupen | Laschetterfeld 4 | 1749 | Düsseldorf | Köln | |
| Euskirchen | Kommernerstr. 85, Postfach 36 | 2795 | Düsseldorf | Köln | Former address : Schillerstr. 14 |
| Eutin | Am Rosengarten 3 | 641 | Hamburg | Kiel | Suspended |
| Fallingborstel | Ahlden/Aller, Eilterstr. 155 | 34 | Braunschweig | Braunschweig | |
| Feldbach | Bürgergasse 12 | 73 | Salzburg | Graz | |

| | Holm 10 | 1765 (T/P via *Stapo* Flensburg) | Hamburg | Kiel |
|---|---|---|---|---|
| Flensburg | | | | |
| Flöha | Zschopau, Viktor-Lutze-Str. 59 | Zschopau 355 | Dresden | Dresden |
| Forchheim | Hans-Schemm-Str. 6 | 4/39 | Nürnberg | Bayreuth |
| Frankenberg/Eder | Kreisbauernschaft | 344 | Kassel | Kassel |
| Freiberg/Sachs. | Wernerstr. 9 | 3041 | Dresden | Dresden |
| Freiberg/Sachs. (Kultur Aussenstelle) | Langemarckstr. 1 | 2251 | Dresden | Dresden |
| Freiburg/Breisgau | Josefstr. 3 | 7424 | Strassburg Stuttgart | Karlsruhe |
| Freihaus | Adolf-Hitler-Str. Ost 2 | 198 | Posen | Litzmannstadt |
| Freising | Wippenhauserstr. 14/I | 665 | München | München |
| Freiwaldau | Parkstr. 344 | 52 | Breslau | Kattowitz |
| Freudenstadt | Wilhelm-Murr-Str. 45 | 647 | Stuttgart | Stuttgart |
| Freudenthal | Dürergasse 4 | 21 | Breslau | Kattowitz |
| Friedberg/Bay. | Bahnhofstr. 24 | 105 | München | München |
| Friedberg/Hessen | Ludwigstr. 31 | 4653 | Kassel | Frankfurt/M. |
| Fürstenfeld | Landratsamt | 131 | Salzburg | Graz |
| Fürstenfeldbruck | General-Litzmann-Str. 6 | 316 | München | München |
| Fürth/Bayern | Schwabacherstr. 28/II | 72210 | Nürnberg | Nürnberg *Former address : Adolf-Hitler-Str. 6* |
| Füssen | Strasse der SA 12 | 55 | München | München |
| Gablonz/Neisse | Reichenbergerstr. 150 | 2437 | Dresden | Reichenberg |
| Gardelegen | Breitestr. 2 | 442 701 (during day) | Braunschweig | Dessau |

# ANNEXE H : PART FOUR (continued)

| Town | Address | Phone | Under BdS | (L)Abs. | Remarks |
|---|---|---|---|---|---|
| Garmisch-Partenkirchen | Bahnhofstr. 84/II | 3054 | München | München | |
| Geldern | Horst-Wessel-Platz 34 | 207 | Düsseldorf | Düsseldorf | |
| Gelsenkirchen | G.-Buer, Maelostr. 2 | 31436 | Düsseldorf | Dortmund | |
| Genthin (*Sitz* Altbensdorf, *Krs.* Jerichow 2) | Altbensdorf | Gr. Wusterwitz 279 | Braunschweig | Braunschweig | |
| Gera (Reuss) | Zeppelinstr. 2 (Landgericht) | 4461 | Kassel | Weimar | |
| Gifhorn | Lindenstr. 19 | 500 | Braunschweig | Braunschweig | |
| Gladbeck/Westf. | Heinz-Ötting-Str. 15 | 2412 | Düsseldorf | Münster/W. | |
| Glatz | Frankensteiner Str. 11 | 2888 (T/P) | Breslau | Breslau | |
| Glauchau | Lichtensteinerstr. 52 | 3041 | Dresden | Dresden | |
| Glogau | Martinstr. 12/13 | 2255 (T/P) | Breslau | Breslau | |
| Gmunden | Satoristr. 39 | Bad Ischl 36 | Wien | Linz/Donau | |
| Gnesen | Poststr. 7 | 162 (T/P via *Stapo*) | Posen | Posen | |
| Görlitz | Adolf-Hitler-Str. 36 | 3950 (T/P) | Breslau | Breslau | |
| Göttingen | Wagnerstr. 1 | 4449 | Braunschweig | Braunschweig | Former address : Franz-Seldte-Str. 19 |
| Goldap | Markt 2 | 481/482 | Königsberg | Königsberg | |
| Goslar | Hirschstr. 11 (Nebengebäude) | 2681 | Braunschweig | Braunschweig | |
| Gotenhafen | Adolf-Hitler-Str. 122 | 5251 | Danzig | Danzig | |

| | | | | | |
|---|---|---|---|---|---|
| Grätz | Annaplatz 13 | 94 | Posen | Posen | |
| Graslitz | Hermann-Göring-Str. 820 | 11 | Nürnberg | Nürnberg | |
| Graudenz | Bismarckstr. 99 | 1697 | Danzig | Danzig | |
| Graz-Land | Hans-Sachs-Gasse 6 | | Salzburg | Graz | |
| Greifswald | Wallstr. 19 | 2001 | Stettin | Stettin | |
| Greiz | Brauhausgasse 7 | 3351 | Kassel | Weimar | |
| Grimma | Schröderstr. 6 | 698 | Dresden | Dresden | |
| Gröditz | Am Eichenhain 5 | Riesa 841 | Dresden | Dresden | |
| Gronau | Horst-Wessel-Platz 5/7 | | Düsseldorf | Münster/W | |
| Grossenhain | Finanzamt | 341 | Dresden | Dresden | |
| Guben | Adolf-Hitler-Str. 46 | 2576 | Berlin | Berlin | Former address : Topfmarkt 10 |
| Günzburg | Hans-Weber-Str. 1 | 104 | München | München | Former address : Bleicherstr. 10 |
| Güstrow | Schwerinerstr. 17 | 2949 | Stettin | Schwerin | Former address : Parkstr. 5 |
| Gumbinnen | Königsplatz 3/I | 2549 | Königsberg | Königsberg | |
| Gummersbach | Bergneustadt, Kölnerstr. 4 | Bergneustadt 2442 | Düsseldorf | Köln | |
| Hagen/Westf. | Hochstr. 134 | 21201 | Düsseldorf | Dortmund | |
| Hagenau | Strassburgerstr. 20 | 36 | Strassburg | *KdS* Strassburg | |
| Halberstadt | Hauptmann-Loeper-Str. 61 | 1686 | Braunschweig | Dessau | |
| Haldensleben | Hagenstr. 26 | 230 | Braunschweig | Dessau | |
| Halle | Gr. Brauhausstr. 30/III | 28970 | Dresden | Halle/Saale | |

H23

| Town | Address | Phone | Under *BdS* | *(L)Abs.* | Remarks |
|---|---|---|---|---|---|
| Hallein | Burgfried 10 | 238 | Salzburg | Innsbruck | |
| Hamburg-Altona | Bahnhofstr. 19 | 420438 | Hamburg | Hamburg | |
| Hamburg-Bergedorf | Karolinenweg 19 | 212541 | Hamburg | Hamburg | |
| Hamburg-Harburg | Lüneburgerstr. 48 | 370670 | Hamburg | Hamburg | Former address: Wilsdorferstr. 20 |
| Hamburg-Innenstadt | Kaiser-Wilhelm-Str. 45 | 351722, 344322 (T/P) | Hamburg | Hamburg | |
| Hamburg-Ost | Paulstr. 11 | 331870 | Hamburg | Hamburg | Former address: Schrötteringsweg 9 |
| Hamburg-Wandsbek | Mathildenstr. 1e | 287440 | Hamburg | Hamburg | Former address: Langestr. 90 |
| Hamburg-West | Grindelberg 17 | 559510 | Hamburg | Hamburg | |
| Hameln | Karl-Dincklage-Str. 11 | 2112 | Braunschweig | Braunschweig | |
| Hamm | Osterallee 25/27 | | Düsseldorf | Dortmund | Former address: Martin Luther Str. 11a. Tel: 1969 |
| Hanau | Paradeplatz, Kaserne | 2667 | Kassel | Frankfurt/M | Former address: Hermannstr. 9 |
| Hartberg | Vorau 42 | Vorau 25 | Salzburg | Graz | |
| Heide/Holst. | Rathaus, Markt | 2833 | Hamburg | Kiel | |
| Heidelberg | Rohrbacherstr. 50 | 6363 | Wiesbaden | *KdS* Strassburg -Karlsruhe | |
| Heilbronn | Iglauerstr. 2 | 2665 | Stuttgart | Stuttgart | |

| | | | | | |
|---|---|---|---|---|---|
| Heiligenstadt/Eichsfeld | Am Graben 38 | 287 | Kassel | Weimar | |
| Helmstedt | Glockbergstr. 9 | 217 | Braunschweig | Braunschweig | |
| Herford | Hämerlingerstr. 11 | 4085 | Düsseldorf | Münster/W. | |
| Hermagor | Nr. 38 | 3 | Salzburg | Klagenfurt | |
| Hermühlheim | Hermühlheim 440 | | Düsseldorf | Köln | For Party *Kreis* Köln-Land |
| Hersbruck | Nürnbergerstr. 20 | 354 | Nürnberg | Nürnberg | |
| Hersfeld | Stift 7, Kriegsschule 3, Room 43 | 926 | Kassel | Kassel | |
| Hildburghausen | | | Kassel | Weimar | |
| Hildesheim | Am Stein 7 | 5985 | Braunschweig | Braunschweig | |
| Hirschberg/Riesengeb. | Wilhelmstr. 58 | 330 (T/P) | Breslau | Breslau | Former address: Horst-Wessel-Str. 14 |
| Höxter | Holenbergstr. 2 | 478 | Düsseldorf | Münster/W. | |
| Hof/Saale | Altstadt 41/I | 3340 | Nürnberg | Bayreuth | |
| Hohenelbe | Landratsamt | 252/255 | Dresden | Reichenberg | |
| Hohensalza | Hindenburgstr. 20 | 1137 (T/P via *Stapo*) | Posen | Posen | |
| Holzminden | Marktstr. 1 | 376 | Braunschweig | Braunschweig | |
| Homburg vor d. Höhe | Schöne Aussicht 14 | 3109 | Wiesbaden | Frankfurt/M | |
| Horb/Neckar | Rathaus | 431 | Stuttgart | Stuttgart | |
| Hoyerswerda | Werminghoff N.L., Buchwalderstr. 5 | 296 | Dresden | Dresden | |
| Illertissen/Schwaben | Schloss | 43 | München | München | |
| Ingolstadt/Donau | Münchener Str. 10 | 2837 | München | München | |
| Insterburg | Gerichtstr. 1 | 56 Ext. 34–35 | Königsberg | Königsberg | |

## ANNEXE H : PART FOUR (continued)

| Town | Address | Phone | Under BdS | (L)Abs. | Remarks |
|---|---|---|---|---|---|
| Itzehoe | Stormstr. 11 | 3121 | Hamburg | Kiel | |
| Jarotschin | Adolf-Hitler-Str. 3 | 243 (T/P via *Stapo*) | Posen | Posen | |
| Jever | Mühlenstr. 47 | 740 | Hamburg | Bremen | |
| Jitschin | Zechstr. 677 | 224 (T/P via *StADSt* Jitschin) | Prag | Prag | |
| Judenburg | Ederbastei 13 | 204 | Salzburg | Graz | |
| Jungbunzlau | Blahoslav 194 | 645 (T/P via *STADSt* Jungbunzlau) | Prag | Prag | |
| Kaiserslautern | Adolf-Hitler-Str. 53 | 1101 | Metz Wiesbaden | Saarbrücken | |
| Kalisch | Bismarckstr. 44 | 482 | Posen | Litzmannstadt | |
| Kamenz/Sachs. | Rathaus | 651 | Dresden | Dresden | |
| Karlsbad | Eduard-Knoll-Str. 11 | 2354/55 | Nürnberg | Nürnberg | |
| Karlsruhe | Nowackanlage 19 | 1004 | Strassburg Stuttgart | Karlsruhe | |
| Kassel | Kölnische Str. 112 | | Kassel | Kassel | |
| Kattowitz | Strasse der SA 11 | 35955/56 32652/53 | Breslau | Kattowitz | Former address : Markgrafenstr. 6 |
| Kaufbeuren | Ludwigstr. 2 | 241 | München | München | |
| Kemnath | Speinshart Haus 24 | Eschenbach 10 | Nürnberg | Bayreuth | Former address : Allg. Ortskrankenkasse. Tel : 45 |

H26

| | | | München | München | For Party *Kreis* |
|---|---|---|---|---|---|
| Kempten/Allgäu | Bahnhofsplatz 9/II | 3560 | München | München | |
| Kirchdorf/K. | Landratsamt | 63 | Wien | Linz/Donau | |
| Kirchhain/Nd. Laus. | An der Elster 9 | 114 | Berlin | Berlin | |
| Kirchheimbolanden | Adolf-Hitler-Str. 41 | 30 | Metz Wiesbaden | Saarbrücken | |
| Kitzbühel | St. Johann/Tirol, Brunneckerhof | 268 | Salzburg | Innsbruck | |
| Kitzingen | Adolf-Hitler-Str. 20 | 2257 | Nürnberg | Nürnberg | |
| Kladno | Hüttengasse 1374 | 555 Kl 37 (T/P via *StADSt* Kladno) 1181 | Prag | Prag | |
| Klagenfurt | Pernhartgasse 3/II | | Salzburg | Klagenfurt | |
| Klattau | Kolargasse 2 | 54 (T/P via *StADSt* Klattau) | Prag | Prag | |
| Kleve | Lindenallee 23 | 3268 | Düsseldorf | Düsseldorf | |
| Klösterle/Eger | Göthestr. 314 | 21 | Nürnberg | Nürnberg | |
| Koblenz | Rizzastr. 27 | 7326 | Wiesbaden | Koblenz | |
| Kochem | Kaisersesch/Eifel, Hindenburgstr. 87 | Kaisersesch 8 | Wiesbaden | Koblenz | |
| Köln-Deutz | Justinianstr. 2 Postfach 28 | 13810 | Düsseldorf | Köln | Köln-Rechts |
| Köslin | Regierungsstr. 10 | 3204 (T/P) | Stettin | Stettin | |
| Köthen | Heinrichstr. 36 | 2521 | Braunschweig | Dessau | |
| Kolin | Am Petersberg 231 | 362 Kl 37 (T/P via *StADSt* Kolin) | Prag | Prag | |
| Kolmar/Elsass | Schlumberger-Str. 7 | 2416 | Strassburg | *KdS* Strassburg | |
| Kolmar/Wartheland | Lindenallee 9 | 224 | Posen | Posen | |
| Komotau | Richard-Wagner-Str. 61 | 359 | Dresden | Reichenberg | |

| Town | Address | Phone | Under BdS | (L)Abs. | Remarks |
|------|---------|-------|-----------|---------|---------|
| Konin | Hermann-Göring-Str. 23 | 62 | Posen | Litzmannstadt | |
| Konstanz | Franz-Seldte-Str. 16/II | 406 | Strassburg Stuttgart | Karlsruhe | |
| Krefeld | Hochstr. 64/66 | 23903 | Düsseldorf | Düsseldorf | |
| Krems/Donau | Krems-Stein, Adolf-Hitler-Platz, Rathaus | 339 | Wien | Wien | |
| Kreuzburg/Ob. Schl. | Gartenstr. 19 | 382 | Breslau | Kattowitz | |
| Kronach | Stöhrstr. 5/II | 221 | Nürnberg | Bayreuth | |
| Krummau/Moldau | Flössberg 99 | 121 | Wien | Linz/Donau | |
| Küstrin | Schiffbauer-Str. 19 | 3437 | Berlin | Berlin | |
| Kufstein | Platz der SA 11 | 271 | Salzburg | Innsbruck | |
| Kutno | Warschauerstr. 14 | 36 | Posen | Litzmannstadt | |
| Laak/Zaier | Hauptplatz 10 | 29 | Salzburg | KdS Veldes | |
| Labiau | Königsberger-Str. 23 | 125 or 505 | Königsberg | Königsberg | Suspended. Taken over by Tilsit |
| Lahr/Baden | Obertorstr. 1 | 2749 | Strassburg Stuttgart | Karlsruhe | |
| Landeck/Tirol | Perjen-Kirchen-Str. 1 | 222 | Salzburg | Innsbruck | |
| Landsberg/Lech | Herkomerstr. 110 | 389 | München | München | |
| Landsberg/Warthe | Angerstr. 21 | 2040 | Berlin | Berlin | |
| Landshut/Isar | Altstadt 334 | 2092 | Nürnberg | Bayreuth | |

| | | | | |
|---|---|---|---|---|
| Langensalza | Langestr. 45 | 517 | Kassel | Weimar |
| Leer | Augustenstr. 28 | | Hamburg | Bremen |
| Leibnitz | Landratsamt | 9 | Salzburg | Graz |
| Leitmeritz | Langegasse 8 | 152 | Dresden | Reichenberg |
| Lentschütz | Strasse der 18 Tage 4 (Landratsamt) | 40 | Posen | Litzmannstadt |
| Leoben | Gemeindeamt | 3 | Salzburg | Graz |
| Leslau | Adolf-Hitler-Str. 11 | 1644 | Posen | Litzmannstadt |
| Lichtenfels/Bay. Ostmark | Dr. Martin-Luther-Str. 6 | 300/9 | Nürnberg | Bayreuth |
| Lienz/Drau | Messinggasse 23a | 259 | Salzburg | Klagenfurt |
| Liezen | Liezen 158 | 11 | Salzburg | Graz |
| Limburg/Lahn | Rohrweg 1p | 972 | Wiesbaden | Frankfurt/M |
| Lindau/Bodensee | Lingstr. 3 | 2730 | München | München |
| Lippstadt | Josefstr. 2 | 2829 | Düsseldorf | Dortmund |
| Lissa/Wartheland | Hindenburg-Platz 4 | 615 (T/P via *Stapo*) | Posen | Posen |
| Littai | Amtsgerichtsgebäude 16 | | Salzburg | *KdS* Veldes |
| Loben | Schulstr. 7 | 120 | Breslau | Kattowitz |
| Löbau/Sachs. | Rathaus (*Kripo*) | 2543 | Dresden | Dresden |
| Lörrach | Schwarzwaldstr. 1 | 3114 | Strassburg Stuttgart | Karlsruhe |
| Lohr/Main | Adolf-Hitler-Str. 470 | 244 | Nürnberg | Nürnberg |
| Ludwigslust | Parchim, Adolf-Hitler-Str. 34 | 645 | Stettin | Schwerin |
| Lüdenscheid | Sauerfelderstr. 16 | 3264 | Düsseldorf | Dortmund |

Former address :
Adolf-Hitler-Str. 215

# ANNEXE H : PART FOUR (continued)

| Town | Address | Phone | Under BdS | (L)Abs. | Remarks |
|---|---|---|---|---|---|
| Lüdinghausen | Tüllinghoferstr. 34 | 303 | Düsseldorf | Münster/W. | |
| Luttenberg | Hugo-Wolf-Platz 3 | 18 | Salzburg | *KdS* Marburg/ Drau | |
| Lyck | Bismarckstr. 21 | 259 | Königsberg | Königsberg | Former address : Danziger-str. 18 (T/P via *Grenzpol.* Lyck) |
| Mähr.-Ostrau | Parkstr. 3 | 2345/388 (T/P via *StADSt* Mähr.-Ostrau) | Prag | Prag | |
| Mähr.-Schönberg | Hermann-Göring-Platz 4 | 889 | Breslau | Kattowitz | |
| Magdeburg | Kantstr. 10 | 34969 | Braunschweig | Dessau | |
| Mainz | Kaiserstr. 38 | 32604 | Wiesbaden | Frankfurt/M. | |
| Malchin | Teterow, Moltkestr. 34 | 247 | Stettin | Schwerin | |
| Malmedy | Bahnhofstr. 9 | | Düsseldorf | Köln | Former address : Hochstr. 24 |
| Mansfeld | Halle/Saale, Walter-Steinbach-Str. 56 | Halle 28970 | Dresden | Halle/Saale | |
| Marburg/Lahn | Bahnhofstr. 28 | 3143 | Kassel | Kassel | |
| Marienbad | Lüderitzstr. 169/II | 2225 | Nürnberg | Nürnberg | |
| Marienberg/Sachs. | Annaberger Str. 1 | 277 | Dresden | Dresden | |
| Marktheidenfeld | Hauptstr. 9 | 62 | Nürnberg | Nürnberg | |
| Markt-Oberdorf/Schwaben | Obere Torstr. 52 | 40 | München | München | |
| Markt Pongau | Landratsamt | 101 | Salzburg | Innsbruck | |

| | | | | | |
|---|---|---|---|---|---|
| Mayen | Im Bannen 8 | 302 | Wiesbaden | Koblenz | |
| Meiningen | Bismarckstr. 6 | 2205 | Kassel | Weimar | |
| Meissen | Talstr. 9 | 2241 | Dresden | Dresden | |
| Memel | Herberstr. 33–34 | 2175/76 (T/P via *Greko* Memel) | Königsberg | Königsberg | Suspended. Duties taken over by Tilsit |
| Memmingen | Schweizerberg 5 | 2114 | München | München | |
| Merseburg | Georgstr. 5 | 3306 | Dresden | Halle/Saale | |
| Meschede | Hünnenburgstr. 27 | 541 | Düsseldorf | Dortmund | |
| Mielau | Erich-Koch-Str. 3 | 148 | Königsberg | Zichenau | |
| Miesbach | Rosenheim, Adolf-Hitler-Str. 7 | 1306 | München | München | Also see Rosenheim |
| Mindelheim | Kolleggebäude | 483 | München | München | |
| Minden/Westf. | Hahlerstr. 26 | 3582 | Düsseldorf | Münster/W. | |
| Mistelbach | Barnabitenplatz 1/24 | 33 | Wien | Wien | |
| Mölln | Adolf-Hitler-Str. 4 | 440 and 442 | Hamburg | Kiel | |
| Mörs | Urdinger Str. 11 | 3126 | Düsseldorf | Düsseldorf | |
| Mohrungen, Kreishaus Mohrungen | Neues Landratsamt | 236 | Königsberg | Königsberg | |
| Molsheim | Kanalweg 2 | 74 | Strassburg | *KdS* Strassburg | |
| Mühlhausen/Thür. | Rathaus | 3001 | Kassel | Weimar | |
| Mühlviertel | Linz, Gesellenhausstr. 5 | Linz 26701 | Wien | Linz/Donau | |
| Mülhausen/Elsass | Hermann-Cossmannstr. 29 | 4063 | Strassburg | *KdS* Strassburg | |
| Mülheim/Ruhr | Althofstr. 42 | 40931 | Düsseldorf | Düsseldorf | |
| Müllheim/Baden | Hebelstr. 30 | 304 and 444 | Strassburg Stuttgart | Karlsruhe | |

## ANNEXE H : PART FOUR (*continued*)

| Town | Address | Phone | Under *BdS* | (*L*)*Abs.* | Remarks |
|---|---|---|---|---|---|
| Münchberg | Lindenstrasse 14 | 431 and 375 | Nürnberg | Bayreuth | |
| M. Gladbach-Rheydt | Bismarckstr. 78 | 23406 | Düsseldorf | Düsseldorf | |
| Münster/Westf. | Kanalstr. 49 | 21527 (T/P via *Stapo LSt.* Münster) | Düsseldorf | Münster/W. | |
| Mürzzuschlag | Wiener Str. 2 | 152 | Salzburg | Graz | |
| Murau | Landratsamt | 1 | Salzburg | Graz | |
| Mureck | Haus Nr. 115 | 43 | Salzburg | Graz | |
| Nabburg, Schwarzenfeld/Obpf. | Bergstr. 277 | 8 | Nürnberg | Bayreuth | |
| Neisse-Grottkau | Grottkau, Ring 21 | 8140 | Breslau | Kattowitz | |
| Neuburg/Donau | SA-Platz D 13 | 148 | München | München | |
| Neumarkt/Obpf. | Sandstr. 3c | 30 | Nürnberg | Bayreuth | |
| Neumünster | Wasbekerstr. 8 | 3114 | Hamburg | Kiel | |
| Neunkirchen/Saar | Langenstrichstr. 28 | 2703 | Metz Wiesbaden | Saarbrücken | |
| Neuruppin | Friedrich-Wilhelm-Str. 78 | 2908 | Berlin | Berlin | |
| Neuss | | | Düsseldorf | Düsseldorf | |
| Neustadt/Aisch | Bambergerstr. 37 | 267 | Nürnberg | Nürnberg | |
| Neustadt/Ob. Schl. | Ring, Rathaus, Room 10 | 541 | Breslau | Kattowitz | Former Address : Weidingerstr. 37 Tel : 488 |

| | | | | | |
|---|---|---|---|---|---|
| Neustadt/Rübenberge | Stockhausenstr. 9 | 408 | Braunschweig | Braunschweig | |
| Neustadt/Schwarzwald | Hindenburgstr. 52 | 241 | Strassburg Stuttgart | Karlsruhe | Suspended. Duties taken over by Donaueschingen |
| Neustettin | Schlosstr. 6 | 634 (T/P) | Stettin | Stettin | |
| Neutrelitz | Schlosstr. 1 | 1073 | Stettin | Schwerin | |
| Neu-Titschein | Prorokgasse 8 | 291 | Breslau | Kattowitz | Former address : Adolf-Hitler-Str. 40 |
| Neuwied | Engerser Landstr. 30 | 3125 | Wiesbaden | Koblenz | |
| Nienburg | Wilhelm-Roesler-Str. 6 | 337 | Hamburg | Bremen | |
| Nordenham | Hansingstr. 41 | | Hamburg | Bremen | Suspended |
| Nordhausen | Altes Rathaus | 1500 | Kassel | Weimar | |
| Nordhorn/Kr. Grafschaft Bentheim | Veshtestr. | 665 | Hamburg | Bremen | Former address : Otmarsumerweg |
| Northeim/Hann. | Platz der SA 12 | 616 | Braunschweig | Braunschweig | |
| Oberhausen | Alsenstrasse 4 | 23435 | Düsseldorf | Düsseldorf | |
| Oberwart | Haus Nr. 32 | 43 | Salzburg | Graz | |
| Oels/Schles. | Ohlauerstr. (Landgericht) | 401 | Breslau | Breslau | |
| Offenbach/Main | Herrnstr. 16/III | 8331i | Kassel | Frankfurt/M. | |
| Offenburg/Baden | Adolf-Hitler-Str. 53 | 1313 | Strassburg Stuttgart | Karlsruhe | |
| Oldenburg/Oldenburg | Carl-Röverstr. 43 | | Hamburg | Bremen | Former Address : Achternstr. 34 Heiligengeiststr. 23 |
| Olmütz | Josef v. Engel-Str. 34 | 1400 or 1200 KI 227/29 (T/P via *StADSt* Olmütz) | Prag | Prag | |

# ANNEXE H : PART FOUR (continued)

| Town | Address | Phone | Under BdS | (L)Abs. | Remarks |
|---|---|---|---|---|---|
| Opladen | Humboldtstr. 4 | 1247 | Düsseldorf | Düsseldorf | |
| Oschatz | Alte Oschatzer Str. 2 | 146 | Dresden | Dresden | |
| Oschersleben/Bode | Schlanstedt, Kreisstr. 25 | Neuwegersleben 307 | Braunschweig | Dessau | |
| Ostenburg | Otto Schröder-Str. 188 | 35 | Königsberg | Zichenau | Suspended |
| Osterburg/Altmark | Sedanstr. 4 | 325 | Braunschweig | Dessau | |
| Osterode/Harz | Bahnhofstr. 3 | 630 | Braunschweig | Braunschweig | |
| Osterode/Ostpr. | Grollmannstr. 23 | 533 | Königsberg | Königsberg | |
| Pabianice | Ludendorff-Str. 8/9 | 100 | Posen | Litzmannstadt | |
| Paderborn | Marienplatz 18 | 2198 | Düsseldorf | Münster i.W. | |
| Parchim | Adolf-Hitler-Str. 34 | 645 | Stettin | Schwerin | |
| Pardubitz | Viktoriaplatz 12 | 3281 Kl 8821 (T/P via StADSt Pardubitz) | Prag | Prag | |
| Pasewalk | Grünstr. 11 | 490 | Stettin | Stettin | Suspended |
| Passau | Sailerwöhr 5/I | 6048 | Nürnberg | Bayreuth | |
| Peine | Hopfenstr. 13 | 2057 | Braunschweig | Braunschweig | |
| Pettau | Sarnitzgasse 11 | 88 | Salzburg | KdS Marburg/Drau | |
| Pforzheim | Schlossberg 15 | 4465 | Strassburg Stuttgart | Karlsruhe | |
| Pfullendorf | Kirchplatz 9 | 223 | Strassburg Stuttgart | Karlsruhe | |

| | | | | | |
|---|---|---|---|---|---|
| Pilgrams | Komenskigasse 244 | 10 | Prag | Prag | |
| Pirmasens | Teichstr. 10 | 2196 | Metz Wiesbaden | Saarbrücken | |
| Pirna | Liebenaustr. 2 | 2541 | Dresden | Dresden | |
| Plauen/Vogtl. | Leissnerstr. 27 | 2622 | Dresden | Dresden | |
| Pless | Adolf-Hitler-Str. 24 | 78 | Breslau | Kattowitz | |
| Plöhnen | Pultuskerstr. 16 | 50 | Königsberg | Zichenau | |
| Polstrau | Nr. 118 | 3 | Salzburg | KdS Marburg/Drau | |
| Prag | Prag II, Bolzano 5 | 38316 (T/P via SD-LA Prag) | Prag | Prag | |
| Praschnitz | Gerichtsstr. 5 | 150 | Königsberg | Zichenau | Suspended |
| Pr. Eylau | Adolf-Hitler-Str. 9/II | 393 | Königsberg | Königsberg | Suspended |
| Prüm | Kahlenberg 7 | 372 | Wiesbaden | Koblenz | Former address: Gerberweg 3. Tel: 238 |
| Pyritz | Horst-Wessel-Str. 54 | 237 | Stettin | Stettin | Suspended |
| Quedlinburg | Marktstr. 8 | 568 | Braunschweig | Dessau | |
| Radmannsdorf | Megertstr. 4 | 522 | Salzburg | KdS Veldes | |
| Raguhn | Rathaus, Adolf-Hitler-Str. 16 | 240 | Braunschweig | Braunschweig | |
| Rann | Adolf-Hitler-Str. 49 | 27 | Salzburg | KdS Marburg/Drau | |
| Rastatt | Karlstr. 8 | 2448 | Strassburg Stuttgart | Karlsruhe | |
| Rastenburg/Ostpr. | Kuhweidenweg 6 | 832 | Königsberg | Königsberg | |
| Rathenow | Berlinerstr. 1 | 3274 | Berlin | Berlin | |

| Town | Address | Phone | Under BdS | (L)Abs. | Remarks |
|------|---------|-------|-----------|---------|---------|
| Ratibor | Schrammstr. 8 | 2231 | Breslau | Kattowitz | |
| Ratzeburg | Seestr. 8 Bäkerweg 86 | 254 342 | Hamburg | Kiel | Suspended |
| Ravensburg | Herrenstr. 40 | 3638 | Stuttgart | Stuttgart | |
| Recklinghausen | Landratsamt | 3241 | Düsseldorf | Münster/W | |
| Regensburg | Minoritenweg 32/II | 5213 | Nürnberg | Bayreuth | |
| Reichenberg/Friedland | Franz-Tilk-Str. 13 | 4170 | Dresden | Reichenberg | |
| Remscheid | Hindenburgstr. 101 | 44418 | Düsseldorf | Düsseldorf | |
| Renchen | Adolf-Hitler-Str. 458 | 135 | Strassburg Stuttgart | Karlsruhe | |
| Rendsburg | Alte Kieler Landstr., Haus der Jugend | 2036 | Hamburg | Kiel | Former address : Neue Kieler Landstr. 38 |
| Reppen | Hindenburgstr. 10 | 250 | Berlin | Berlin | |
| Reutte | Siedlung Nr. 6/3 I | 122 | Salzburg | Innsbruck | |
| Ried/Innkr. | Kapuzinerberg 19 | Ried I.124 | Wien | Linz/Donau | |
| Riedenburg | Landratsamt | 25 | Nürnberg | Bayreuth | |
| Rinteln | Obernkirchen, Eilserstr. 515 | 22 | Braunschweig | Braunschweig | |
| Rochitz/Sachs. | Mittweida, Hindenburg-Str. 12 | Mittweida 2376 | Dresden | Dresden | |
| Rosenheim | Adolf-Hitler-Str. 7 | 1306 | München | München | |
| Rossleben | Hotel " Goldener Hirsch " | 391 | Kassel | Weimar | |

| Place | Address | Code | | | Notes |
|---|---|---|---|---|---|
| Rostock, Seestadt | Kaiser-Friedrich-Str. 8 | 4052 (T/P) | Stettin | Schwerin | Former address : Kaiserstr. 10 |
| Rottweil | Hochmaiengasse 16 | 567 | Stuttgart | Stuttgart | |
| Rudolstadt | Strasse der SA 40 | 621 | Kassel | Weimar | |
| Rüdesheim/Rh. | Geisenheim, Adolf-Hitler-Str. 64 | Geisenheim 465 | Wiesbaden | Frankfurt/M. | |
| Rumburg | Lichtensteinstr. 4 | 69 | Dresden | Reichenberg | |
| Rybnik | Ring 6 | 25 | Breslau | Kattowitz | |
| Saarbrücken | Victoriastr. 10 | 22718 | Metz / Wiesbaden | Saarbrücken | Former address : Trillerweg 38 |
| Saarburg | Bahnhofstr 3 | 415/16 (T/P) | Metz | *KdS* Metz | |
| Saargemünd | Maiglöckchenstr. 37 | 32 | Metz | *KdS* Metz | |
| Saarlautern | Rathaus Saarlautern | 2012/19 | Metz / Wiesbaden | Saarbrücken | |
| Saaz | Hans-Knirsch-Str. 2 | 167 | Nürnberg | Nürnberg | |
| Säckingen | Schiller Str. 10 | 508 | Strassburg / Stuttgart | Karlsruhe | |
| Salzwedel | Bahnhofstr. 8 | 1 | Braunschweig | Dessau | |
| Samter | Bahnhofstr. 16 | 109 (T/P via *Stapo*) | Posen | Posen | |
| Sangerhausen | Hüttenstr. 24 | 856 | Kassel | Weimar | |
| Schärding | Allerheiligen 38 | 164 | Wien | Linz/Donau | |
| Scharfenwiese | v. Ribbentrop-Str. 87 | 70 (T/P via *Greko*) | Königsberg | Zichenau | Former address : v. Ribbentrop-Str. 37 |
| Schleiden/Eifel | Hellenthal, Schleiden/Eifel, Bürgermeisteramt | Hellenthal 210 | Düsseldorf | Köln | |
| Schleswig | Stadtweg 56 | 3187 | Hamburg | Kiel | |

## ANNEXE H: PART FOUR (continued)

| Town | Address | Phone | Under BdS | (L)Abs. | Remarks |
|------|---------|-------|-----------|---------|---------|
| Schlettstadt | Strassburgerstr. 16 | 320 | Strassburg | *KdS* Strassburg | |
| Schneidemühl | Danziger Platz 7 | 2341 (T/P) | Stettin | Stettin | |
| Schrobenhausen | Bräuhiesengasse 10 | 125 | München | München | |
| Schroda | Kaiser-Wilhelm-Str. 1 | 69 | Posen | Posen | |
| Schröttersburg | Erich-Koch-Str. 12 | 1427 (T/P *via Stapostelle*) | Königsberg | Zichenau | Former address : Erich-Koch-Str. 35 |
| Schwabach | Albrechtstr. 8/II | 441 | Nürnberg | Nürnberg | |
| Schwäb. Hall | Am Markt 9 | 246 | Stuttgart | Stuttgart | |
| Schwandorf/Bayern | Oskar-Köster-Str. 3 | 278 and 236 | Nürnberg | Bayreuth | |
| Schwarzenberg/Erzgeb. | Markt 14 | 2822 | Dresden | Dresden | |
| Schwaz | Horst-Wessel-Str. 8 | 8 | Salzburg | Innsbruck | |
| Schweidnitz | Adolf-Hitler-Platz 14 (Landger., Room 42) | 2933 | Breslau | Breslau | Former address : Rathaus Tel : 2741 |
| Schweinfurt | Brückenstr. 8/I | 2026 | Nürnberg | Nürnberg | |
| Schwiebus | Halbe Stadt 42a. | 593 | Berlin | Berlin | |
| Selb | Schützenstr. 28 | 444 and 553 | Nürnberg | Bayreuth | |
| Sensburg | Neue Schulstr. 20 | 505 | Königsberg | Königsberg | |
| Sichelberg | Landratsamt | 118 | Königsberg | Zichenau | Suspended |
| Siegburg | Bachstr. 7 | 2361 | Düsseldorf | Köln | |

| | | | | | |
|---|---|---|---|---|---|
| Siegen | Emilienstr. 6 | 2660 | Kassel | Frankfurt/M. | |
| Sigmaringen | Sigmaringerdorf-Walke | 587 | Stuttgart | Stuttgart | |
| Simmern/Hunsrück | Schlosstr. 17 | 322 | Wiesbaden | Koblenz | |
| Singen | Romaiastr. 14 | 217 | Strassburg / Stuttgart | Karlsruhe | |
| Solingen | Strasse der SA 95 | 25533 | Düsseldorf | Düsseldorf | |
| Sondershausen | Marienstr. 10 | 170 | Kassel | Weimar | |
| Sonneberg/Thür. | Köppelsdorferstr. 43 | 2568 | Nürnberg | Weimar | Former address : Köppelsdorferstr. 86 |
| Sonthofen/Allgäu | Immenstadt, Hindenburgplatz 5 | 26 | München | München | |
| Sorau/Nd. Laus. | Claus-v. Pape-Str. 6 | 2045 | Berlin | Berlin | |
| Sosnowitz | Hauptstr. 33 | 61520 | Breslau | Kattowitz | Former address : Hauptstr. 21 |
| Spaichingen | | | Stuttgart | Stuttgart | |
| Spittal/Drau | Amtsgericht | 178 | Salzburg | Klagenfurt | |
| Springe | Bad Münder, Angerstr. 23 | 250 | Braunschweig | Braunschweig | |
| St. Avold | Hermann-Göring-Str. 16 | 59 | Metz | *KdS* Metz | |
| St. Pölten | Hesstr. 6 | 829 | Wien | Wien | |
| St. Veit/Glan | Kreisleitung der NSV, Adolf-Hitler-Platz | Treibach 9 | Salzburg | Klagenfurt | |
| Stade/Elbe | Neuburgerstr. 5 | 2 | Hamburg, | Bremen | Former address : Am Wasser-West 23 |
| Stargard/Pom. | Gr. Mühlenstr. 21 | 2605 | Stettin | Schwerin | |
| Starnberg | Vogelanger 7 | 2317 | München | München | |
| Stein | Hermann-Göring-Str. 10 | 29 | Salzburg | *KdS* Veldes | |

# ANNEXE H : PART FOUR (continued)

| Town | Address | Phone | Under *BdS* | *(L)Abs.* | Remarks |
|---|---|---|---|---|---|
| Stendal | Am Dom 2 | 282 | Braunschweig | Dessau | |
| Stettin | Am Königs Tor 6 | 31617 | Stettin | Stettin | |
| Steyr | Promenade 2 | 349 | Wien | Linz/Donau | |
| Stockach | Hauptstr. 23 | 291 | Strassburg Stuttgart | Karlsruhe | |
| Stollberg/Erzgeb. | Zwönitz/Sa., Adolf-Hitler-Str. 53 | Zwönitz 49 | Dresden | Dresden | |
| Stolp/Pom. | Bismarckstr. 4 | 3252 (T/P) | Stettin | Stettin | |
| Strakonitz | An der Burg | 360 | Prag | Prag | |
| Stralsund | Semlowerstr. 44 | 3126 (T/P) | Stettin | Stettin | |
| Straubing | Bölckestr. 13 | 2133, 2462, 2376 | Nürnberg | Bayreuth | |
| Suhl/Thür. | Rüssenstr. 2 | 2663 | Kassel | Weimar | |
| Swinemünde | Hardenbergstr. 4 | 2688 (T/P) | Stettin | Stettin | Former address : Gartenstr. 16 |
| Sylt, Keitum | Hauptstrasse | 803 | Hamburg | Kiel | |
| Tabor | Alt Taborgasse 487 | 327 (T/P via *StADSt* Tabor) | Prag | Prag | |
| Tamsweg | Landratsamt | 6 | Salzburg | Innsbruck | |
| Tann | Gutenbergstr. | 220 | Strassburg | *KdS* Strassburg | |
| Tauberbischofsheim | Königsheim über Lauda, Hauptstr. 52 | Tauberbischofs- heim 398 | Strassburg Stuttgart | Karlsruhe | |

| | Address | Number | Düsseldorf | Münster/W. | |
|---|---|---|---|---|---|
| Tecklenburg | Heinrich Himmler-Str. 2 | 180 | | Münster/W. | Former address : Landratsamt |
| Templin | Zehdenickerstr. 11 | 627 | Berlin | Berlin | |
| Teplitz-Schönau | Waisenhausgasse 4 | 3677 | Dresden | Reichenberg | |
| Teschen | Eugen Fuldaplatz 2 | 1122 | Breslau | Kattowitz | Former address : Pfarrplatz 2 |
| Tetschen | Hansastr. 341 | 117 | Dresden | Reichenberg | |
| Thorn | Graudenzerstr. 37 | 2528 | Danzig | Danzig | |
| Tilsit | Stolbeckerstr. 101e | 3356/57 (T/P via *Stapo* Tilsit) | Königsberg | Königsberg | Also see Labiau and Memel |
| Torgau | Leipzigerstr. 14 | 796 | Dresden | Halle/Saale | Former address : Laubenweg 7 |
| Traunstein | Ludwigstr. 12 | 294 | München | München | |
| Trautenau | Rinnelstr. 39 | 147 | Dresden | Reichenberg | |
| Trebitsch | | | Prag | Prag | |
| Trebnitz/Schles. | Breitestr. 14 | 521 | Breslau | Breslau | |
| Treuburg | Lazarettstr. 2 | 281 | Königsberg | Königsberg | Former address : Goldaperstr. 24a |
| Trifail | Trifail-Loke 57 | 14, Ext. 105 | Salzburg | *KdS* Marburg/Drau | |
| Tübingen | Am Marktplatz | 2341, Ext. 28 | Stuttgart | Stuttgart | |
| Tuttlingen | Rathaus | 556 | Stuttgart | Stuttgart | |
| Überlingen | Städt. Verkehrsamt | 60 | Strassburg Stuttgart | Karlsruhe | |
| Uelzen/Hann. | Bevensen, Alter Wiesenweg 21 | 436 | Braunschweig | Braunschweig | |
| Ulm/Donau | Münsterplatz (Pol. Dir. Neuer Bau) | 4862 (T/P) | Stuttgart | Stuttgart | |

# ANNEXE H : PART FOUR (continued)

| Town | Address | Phone | Under *BdS* | *(L)Abs.* | Remarks |
|------|---------|-------|-------------|-----------|---------|
| Varel | School Dangast | 324 | Hamburg | Bremen | |
| Verden/Aller | Johanniswall 2 | 355 | Hamburg | Bremen | Former address : Niedersachsenring 29 Tel : 916 |
| Villach | Adolf-Hitler-Platz 7 | 4532 | Salzburg | Klagenfurt | |
| Villingen/Schwarzw. | Hindenburgstr. 11 | By day *Finanzamt* Villingen | Strassburg Stuttgart | Karlsruhe | |
| Vilshofen/Donau | Aidenbach/Ndb., Vilshofnerstr. 73 | 22 | München | Bayreuth | |
| Vöcklabruck | Hatscheckstr., Kreisleitung | 176 | Wien | Linz/Donau | |
| Völkermarkt | Adolf-Hitler-Platz 37 | 9 | Salzburg | Klagenfurt | |
| Voitsberg/Köflach | Werkstr. 5 | 7 | Salzburg | Graz | |
| Waldenburg/Schles. | Freiburgerstr. 8 | T/P | Breslau | Breslau | Former address : Gartenstr. 3, Tel : 1025 |
| Waldshut | Bahnhofstr. 11 | 316 | Strassburg Stuttgart | Karlsruhe | |
| Wanzleben | Westeregeln, Breitestr. 14 | Egeln 364 | Braunschweig | Dessau | |
| Warendorf | Neu-Warendorf 69 | 484 | Düsseldorf | Münster/W. | |
| Wasserburg/Inn | Hofstattstr. 195 | 152 | München | München | |
| Wassertrüdingen | Adolf-Hitler-Str. 263 | 115 | Nürnberg | Nürnberg | |
| Weiden | Siechenstr. 2/II | 2208 | Nürnberg | Bayreuth | |

| | | | | | |
|---|---|---|---|---|---|
| Weilheim/Obb. | Ritter v. Epp-Platz 2 | 507 | München | München | |
| Weimar | Strasse der SA 1 | 2503 | Kassel | Weimar | |
| Weissenburg/Bayern | Dr. Dörflerstr. 10 | 483 | Nürnberg | Nürnberg | |
| Weissenburg/Elsass | Schwanenweier 15 | 35 | Strassburg | *KdS* Strassburg | |
| Weissenfels | Friedrichstr. 11 | 2128 | Dresden | Halle/Saale | |
| Weiz | Kepler Str. 463 | 18 | Salzburg | Graz | |
| Wels | Manfred v. Richthofen Str. 41 | 468 | Wien | Linz/Donau | |
| Welun | Apfel-Allee 5 | 58 | Posen | Litzmannstadt | |
| Wesel | Lipperheystr. 3 | 2732 | Düsseldorf | Düsseldorf | |
| Wesermünde | Hafenstr. 194 | 2010 | Hamburg | Bremen | |
| Wetzlar | Haussertorstr. 42 | 2539 | Kassel | Frankfurt/M. | |
| Wiedenbrück | Rheda/Westf., Steinweg 16 | 643 | Düsseldorf | Münster/W. | |
| Wien 1 | Spiegelgasse 21 | A 35033 | Wien | Wien | |
| Wien 2 | Quellenstr. 12, Kreisleitung | R 13231 | Wien | Wien | Former address : Sterneckplatz, Kreisleitung |
| Wien 3 | 14, Felberstr. 42–46, Kreisleitung | U 38508 | Wien | Wien | Former address : Schwarzenberg-Platz, Kreisleitung. See also Wien 7 |
| Wien 4 | 24, Mödling, Rathausgasse 4 | Mödling 140 | Wien | Wien | Former address : 10, Laxenburgerstr. 91/5 See also Wien 5 |
| Wien 5 | 24, Mödling, Rathausgasse 4 | Mödling 140. | Wien | Wien | Duties taken over by Wien 4 |
| Wien 7 | 14, Felberstr. 42–46, Kreisleitung | U 38508 | Wien | Wien | Duties taken over by Wien 3 |
| Wien 8 | 17, Planettaplatz, Kreisleitung | U 51681 | Wien | Wien | Suspended |

## ANNEXE H : PART FOUR (continued)

| Town | Address | Phone | Under *BdS* | *(L)Abs.* | Remarks |
|------|---------|-------|-------------|-----------|---------|
| Wien 9 | 21, Lorenz-Kellner-Gasse 15, Kreisleitung | R 49550/14 | Wien | Wien | Suspended |
| Wiener Neustadt | Martingasse 7 | 716 | Wien | Wien | |
| Wipperfürth | Hückeswagen, Islandstr. 14 | Wipperfürth 445 | Düsseldorf | Köln | |
| Wismar, Seestadt | Klusserdamm 16 | 3219 | Stettin | Schwerin | |
| Wittenberg, Lutherstadt | Schlossplatz 2 | 3546 | Dresden | Halle/Saale | |
| Wittenberge | Rathausstr. 3 | 348 | Berlin | Berlin | |
| Wittlich | Kurfürstenstr. 10 | | Wiesbaden | Koblenz | |
| Wittmund | Franz-Seldte-Str. 487 | 198 | Hamburg | Bremen | |
| Witzenhausen | Johannesberg 568 | 403 | Kassel | Kassel | |
| Wolfach | Bahnhofstr. 16 | 227 | Strassburg Stuttgart | Karlsruhe | |
| Wolfenbüttel | Herrenbreite 15 | 2073 or 2551 | Braunschweig | Braunschweig | |
| Wolfratshausen/Obb. | Sauerlacherstr. 37 | 372 | München | München | |
| Wolfsberg | Reding 78 | 135 | Salzburg | Klagenfurt | |
| Wolmirstedt | Haus d. NSDAP | 219 (by day) 254 (by night) | Braunschweig | Dessau | |
| Worms | Burckardstr. 10/III | 5904 | Wiesbaden | Frankfurt/Main | |
| Würzburg | Bismarckstr. 9 | 3811/13 | Nürnberg | Nürnberg | |
| Wunsiedel-Marktredwitz | Dammstr. 1 | 412 | Nürnberg | Bayreuth | |

| | | | | | |
|---|---|---|---|---|---|
| Wuppertal-Elberfeld | Ständestr. 45 | 51721 | Düsseldorf | Düsseldorf | |
| Zabern | Rosengärtenstr. 8 | 230 | Strassburg | *KdS* Strassburg | |
| Zeitz | Schlosstr. 12 | 2933 | Dresden | Halle/Saale | |
| Zell/Mosel | Traben-Trarbach, Untere Kaiserstr. 14 | Traben-Trarbach 452 | Wiesbaden | Koblenz | Former address : Traben-Trarbach Am Bahnhof 9 |
| Zell am See | Landhaus Wetti | 171 | Salzburg | Innsbruck | |
| Zellerfeld | Silbersaal | Clausthal-Zellerfeld 207 | Braunschweig | Braunschweig | |
| Zerbst | Langestr. 22 | 866 | Braunschweig | Dessau | |
| Zichenau | Ragniterstr. 47 | 616 (T/P via *Stapo-stelle*) | Königsberg | Zichenau | Former address : Baumstr. 16/20 |
| Zittau | Rathaus | 3264 | Dresden | Dresden | |
| Zlin | Mozartstr. 1 | 403 (T/P via *Greko* Zlin) | Prag | Prag | |
| Zweibrücken | Ehrgartenweg 19 | | Metz / Wiesbaden | Saarbrücken | |
| Zwickau/Sachsen | Konradstr. 5 | 2102 | Dresden | Dresden | |
| Zwiesel | Eisenstein, Marktplatz, 26/III | 57 | Nürnberg | Bayreuth | Former address : Bahnhofstr. 340 Angerstr. 269 |

# ANNEXE J
## SCHOOLS AND TRAINING ESTABLISHMENTS OF THE GERMAN POLICE

| Location | German Name | Translation | Remarks |
|---|---|---|---|
| Aken nr Dessau | Grenzpolizeischule | Frontier Police School | Also for Sipo and SD |
| Alexandrowo (Alexandrowka) | Gendarmerieschule | Gendarmerie School | May 1940, also Hilfs-polizei-Ausbildungs-Btl. |
| Allenstein | Gendarmerieschule | Gendarmerie School | |
| Bad Ems | Gendarmerieschule | Gendarmerie School | |
| | Polizei-Ausbildungs-Btl. | Police Training Bn | |
| Beeskow/Mk. | Feuerschutzpolizeischule | Fire Protection Police School | |
| Belzig/Mk. | Reichschule der Technischen Nothilfe | National Academy of the Technical Emergency Corps | Addr : Burg Eisenhardt |
| Bendsburg O/S (Bendzin) | Polizei Reitschule | Police Cavalry School | |
| Berlin | Polizeischule für Auslandsverwendung | Police Training School for Service Abroad | See Oranienburg |
| | also known as : | | |
| | Kolonialpolizeischule | Colonial Police School | |
| | Schule für Technik und Verkehr | School for Technical Matters and Traffic | |
| | also known as : | | |
| Berlin | Technische Polizeischule (Kraftfahr, Verkehr, Nachrichten) | Police School for Technical Training (M/T, Traffic Control, Signals) | |
| | Hauptzeugamt d. Orpo | Ordnance Depot of Orpo | Moved to Greifswald, 10th July, 1944 |
| Berlin-Spandau | Polizei Sportschule | Police Sport School | Cdr.: SS-SBF RUSSELL |
| | probably identical with : | | |
| | Polizeischule für Leibesübungen | Physical Training College for Policemen | |
| Berlin-Charlottenburg | Führerschule für Sipo und SD | Officers School for Sipo and SD | m.d.F.b. SS-OSBF HOTZEL |
| | attached to above : | | |
| | Kriminalfachschule | College for Criminology | |
| Berlin-Köpenick | Polizei Offizierschule | Police Officers School, Orpo and Schupo, Gendarmerie | Reported transferred to Oranienburg, 1st June, 1943 |
| Berlin-Schöneberg | Polizeischule für Luftschutzführer | School for ARP Police Officers | |
| | renamed in 1944 : | | |
| | Polizei-Akademie für Luftschutzführung | Police Academy for ARP Tactics | Transferred to Oranienburg, 1944 Cdr.: Oberst d. Schupo MELCHIOR |
| Berlin-Spandau | Polizei Dolmetscher Ersatzeinheit | Police Interpreters Depot Unit | French and Italian Addr : Moritzstr. 10 See also Oranienburg |
| Berlin-Spandau | Polizei Sanitätsschule | Medical School of the Orpo | Addr : Staatskrankenhaus |
| Berlin-Zehlendorf | Technische SS und Polizei-Akademie | Technical SS and Police Academy | Addr : Potsdamer Chaussee Also reported : SW11, Prinz-Albrecht-Str. Tel : 120040 Cdr.: SS-BF, Genmaj. d. Pol. Prof. Dr. GERLACH |
| Bernau | SD-Schule | SD School | Also reported for Sipo |
| | Führerschule des Sicherheitsdienstes | Officers School of the SD | Cdr.: SS-SBF NICKOL |
| Bottrop | Schutzpolizeischule | Protection Police School | |
| Brandenburg a.d.H. | Polizeischule | Police School | Existed pre-war. Not confirmed at present. |
| Breslau | Gendarmerieschule | Gendarmerie School | |
| | Hilfsgendarmerieschule | Auxiliary Gendarmerie School | |
| Brieg (Fraustadt) | Gendarmerieschule | Gendarmerie School | Cdr.: Maj. d. Gena. MICALLSEN |
| Brünn | Gendarmerieschule | Gendarmerie School | |
| | Technische SS- u. Polizei-Akademie | Technical SS and Police Academy | |

| Location | German Name | Translation | Remarks |
|---|---|---|---|
| Bunzlau | Polizei-Reserve-Schule | Police Reservist School | |
| Celle | Feuerwehrschule | School for Fire-Fighting | |
| Dahme/Mk. | Polizeiverwaltungsschule | Police Administration School | |
| Darmstadt | Gendarmerieschule | Gendarmerie School | |
| Deggingen | Gendarmerieschule (mot.) | School of the Motorised Gendarmerie | Cdr. : Maj. d. Gend. PFEIFFER |
| Dresden | Schule für Generalstabs-ausbildung der Orpo | School for General Staff Training of the Orpo | Founded late 1944. Address : Dresden-N 23 Neuländerstr. 60 Tel : 54895, 57028 |
| Dresden | Abrichteanstalt (Hundewesen) | Police Dogs Training Establishment | |
| | Kraftfahrschule (Schupo) | M/T School (Schupo) | Transferred to Suhl, December, 1943 |
| Dresden-Hellerau | Polizei Waffenschule I formerly known as : Polizei-Lehr-Btl. I | Police (Weapons) Training School I Police Training Bn I | Cdr. : Oberst d. Schupo WIRTH Adj. : Hptm. d. Schupo CHRISTIANSEN |
| Dresden-Hellerau | Schutzpolizeischule | Protection Police School | |
| Dresden-Hellerau | Taktiklehrgang für Stabsoffiziere, Juli, 1943 | Training Course in Tactics for Staff Officers, July, 1943 | |
| Eberswalde | Reichsfeuerwehrschule der Orpo renamed in August, 1943 : Offizierschule der Orpo | National School for Fire-Fighting Officers School of the Orpo | |
| Eilenburg nr Leipzig | Polizeischule für Nachrichtenwesen or Schupo-Nachrichtenschule | Protection Police Signals School | Cdr. : Oberst d. Schupo NEBEL, or Obstlt. d. Schupo KASTEN |
| Eisenstadt | Kraftfahrschule | M/T School | |
| Erfurt | Polizeischule für Nachrichtenhelferinnen (Orpo) | Police School for Women Signals Auxiliaries (Orpo) | Cdr. : Obstlt. d. Schupo FECHNER |
| Erfurt | Pz. Abt. Fahrschule (?) | Armoured Vehicle Training Unit (?) | |
| Eselstadt | Polizeischule | Police School | |
| Essegg | Polizei-Kavallerieschule | Police Cavalry School | |
| Fichtenwalde | Hilfspolizei-Ausbildungs-Btl. | Auxiliary Police Training Bn | |
| Frankenstein | Polizeischule | Police School | |
| Frankfurt/M | Schutzpolizeischule | Protection Police School | |
| Frankfurt/M | Werkluftschutzschule "Hessen" | Factory ARP School "Hessen" | Addr : Bockenheimer Anlage 36, Gutlert-Kaserne |
| Fraustadt (Schlesien) | Gendarmerieschule (mot.) | School of Motorised Gendarmerie | Probably identical with Gendarmerie School at Brieg |
| Freiburg i.B. | Gendarmerieschule | Gendarmerie School | |
| Fürstenberg | Polizeischule | Police School | Cdr. : SS-OF, Oberst d. Pol. Dr. TRUMMLER |
| | Siposchule (SD) | Sipo School (SD) | |
| | Führerschule für die Sipo | Officers School of the Sipo | Deputy Cdr. : SS-OSBF, ORR Dr. KAUSMANN See also Pretzsch |
| Fürstenfeldbruck (Bayern) | Offizierschule der Orpo | Police Officers School | |
| | Schutzpolizeischule | Protection Police School | |
| Gnesen | Schutzpolizeischule | Protection Police School | |
| | Hilfspolizeischule | Auxiliary Police School | Cdr. : Obstlt. HARTMANN |
| | Polizei Sanitätsschule | Police Medical School | |
| Grünberg (Schloss) (Protectorate) | Funkschule d. Sipo und d. SD | W/T School of Sipo and SD | |
| Grünheide nr Berlin | Zentralausbildungsinstitut für Polizeihunde also known as : Staatliche Lehr- und Versuchsanstalt für Polizeihunde | National Training Institute for Police Dogs Government Institute for Police Dog Training and Research | 500 dogs trained per year |
| Greifswald (Pommern) | Hauptzeugamt der Orpo | Main Ordnance Depot of the Orpo | Addr: Luftwaffen Kaserne |
| Den Haag | Polizei-Waffenschule III formerly known as : Polizei-Lehr-Btl. III | Police (Weapons) Training School III Police Training Bn III | Believed to have moved into the Reich, Autumn, 1944 |

| Location | German Name | Translation | Remarks |
|---|---|---|---|
| Haar n München | Polizeiverwaltungsschule | Police Administration School | See München-Haar |
| Hamburg | Schutzpolizeischule | Protection Police School | |
| Heidenheim | Schutzpolizeischule | Protection Police School | Cdr. : Obstlt. PAUST |
| | IV. Polizei-Ausbildungs-Btl. (V) | IV. Police Training Bn (V) | Asst Cdr. : Hptm. SCHOMBURG |
| Hellerau (See Dresden) | | | |
| Hildesheim | Gendarmerieschule | Gendarmerie School | Moved to Odense Cdr. : SS-SBF, Maj. d. Gend. TSCHERNITZ |
| Hollabrunn (Niederdonau) | Schutzpolizeischule | Protection Police School | |
| | Gendarmerieschule (mot.) | School of the Motorised Gendarmerie | Cdr. : Maj. d. Gend. BRANDT |
| Iglau | Polizei-Waffenschule II | Police (Weapons) Training School II | Part of School temporarily (1943/44) at Laon/France End of 1944 reported at Dresden-Moritzberg nr. Hellerau |
| | formerly known as : | | |
| | Polizei-Lehr-Btl. II | Police Training Bn II | |
| | Polizeischule für Kraftfahrwesen | Police M/T School | |
| | Polizei Kraftfahr-Ersatz-Abt. | Police M/T Training Bn | |
| Innsbruck | Polizeischule für Hochgebirgsausbildung | Police School for Alpine Training | Addr : Wiesbadenerhütte. Cdr. : Oberst LUKAS, or Oberst ALBERT |
| Jena | Polizeischule (Orpo) | Police School (Orpo) | Cdr. : Oberst (?) SPITTA |
| Karlsruhe | Abrichtanstalt (Hundewesen) | Training Establishment for Police Dogs | |
| Kassel | Polizeischule | Police School | |
| Kattowitz | Schutzpolizeischule | Protection Police School | |
| | Hilfspolizeischule | Auxiliary Police School | |
| | Hilfspolizei-Ausbildungs-Btl. | Auxiliary Police Training Bn | |
| Kehlheim | Postschutzschule | School for Postal Guards | Existed prewar. Not confirmed at present. |
| Kitzbühel (Tirol) | Polizeiskischule (Orpo) | Police Ski School (Orpo) | |
| Klattau | Nachrichten Polizeischule | Police Signals School | |
| Kobuerczin | Polizeischule für Reit- und Fahrwesen | Police Cavalry School | |
| Köln | Polizeischule II (Orpo) | Police School II (Orpo) | |
| | Gendarmerieschule (mot.) | School of the Motorised Gendarmerie | |
| Königsberg | Schutzpolizeischule | Protection Police School | |
| | Provinzialfeuerwehrschule | Provincial School for Fire-Fighting | |
| | Polizeischule (Orpo) | Police School (Orpo) | |
| Königshütte | Schutzpolizeischule | Protection Police School | |
| Laon (France) | Teil der Polizei Waffenschule II | Part of Police (Weapons) Training School II | Formerly at Iglau (until August, 1943). Believed to have returned there Cdr. : Maj. FOKENSOHN |
| Lauterbach (Rügen) | Wasserschutzpolizeischule | Waterways Protection Police School | Moved from Stettin, 19th July, 1944 |
| Lautsch | Polizeischule | Police School | |
| Lebrechtsdorf | Polizeischule (Sipo) | Police School (Sipo) | |
| Linz | Feuerwehrschule | School for Fire-Fighting | |
| Maastricht (Holland) | Polizei-Waffenschule IV | Police (Weapons) Training School IV | Dissolved, September, 1943 |
| Marburg/Lahn | Gendarmerieschule | Gendarmerie School | |
| | Hilfs-Gendarmerieschule, Neuhöffe | Auxiliary Gendarmerie School, Neuhöffe | |
| Mariaschein nr Aussig | Polizei-Offizierschule (Orpo) | Police Officers School (Orpo) | Since March, 1944, includes the Offizierschule der Orpo, Oranienburg |
| Mariaschein nr Aussig | Schutzpolizeischule | Protection Police School | Transferred to Heidenheim, March, 1944 |
| Minsk-Mazow (GG) | Gendarmerieschule | Gendarmerie School | |
| Mittenwald | Gebirgsjägerschule(?) | Mountain Gendarmerie School(?) | |
| Mödling (see Wien) | | | |

| Location | German Name | Translation | Remarks |
|---|---|---|---|
| Moritzberg nr. Dresden (see Iglau) | | | |
| Mosty-Wielky | *Polizei-Reitschule* | Police Cavalry School | |
| München | *Schutzpolizeischule* | Protection Police School | |
| München | *Abrichteanstalt (Hundewesen)* | Training Establishment for Police Dogs | |
| München-Haar | *Polizeiverwaltungsschule (Orpo)* | Police Administration School (Orpo) | |
| Münster | *Polizeischule* | Police School | Existed prewar. Not confirmed at present. |
| Obergurgl | *Polizei-Skischule* | Police Ski School | |
| Oberstein | *SS Polizeigebirgsschule* | SS-Police Mountain Training School | |
| Odense/Denmark | *Gendarmerieschule* | Gendarmerie School | Addr.: Logengebäude. Moved from Hildesheim, November 1944 |
| Oranienburg | *Polizeischule für d. Auswärtigen Einsatz (Auslandsverwendung)* | Police School for Service Abroad | Addr : Luisenplatz 4 |
| | also known as : | | |
| | *Kolonialpolizeischule* | Colonial Police School | |
| | attached to above : | | |
| | *Polizei Dolmetscher Ersatz Einheit* | Police Interpreters Depot Unit | Teaching : French, English, Italian, Hungarian, Spanish, Russian, Lithuanian, Estonian, Ukrainian |
| Oranienburg | *Offizierschule der Ordnungspolizei* | Officers School of the Orpo | Moved from Berlin-Köpenick in June, 1943, to Oranienburg, where it was in the same building as the School for Service Abroad. Transferred to Mariaschein in March, 1944. |
| Oranienburg | *Polizeischule für Luftschutzführung* | Police School for ARP Tactics | Transferred from Berlin-Schöneberg, 1944. |
| Pelplin | *Schutzpolizeischule* | Protection Police School | Cdr.: *Oberst d. Schupo* KLEINOW |
| | *Hilfspolizeischule* | Auxiliary Police School | |
| | *Hilfspolizei-Ausbildungs-Btl.* | Auxiliary Police Training Bn | |
| Porlitz | *Schutzpolizeischule* | Protection Police School | |
| Postawy | *Polizeischule für Reit- und Fahrwesen* | Police Cavalry School | |
| Prag (XIX) | *Führerschule d. Sipo und d. SD* | Officers School of Sipo and SD | |
| | *Reichsschule d. Sipo und d. SD* | National Academy of Sipo and SD | Cdr.: *SS-OSBF* RABE Deputy : *SS-SBF*, RR. GORNIG |
| Pretzsch/Elbe | *Grenzpolizeischule* | Frontier Police School | Housed in a former sanatorium in Schniedeberg. May possibly have moved to Fürstenberg. Cdr.: *SS-OF Dr.* Hans TRUMMLER |
| | *Sportschule, Sipo und SD* | Physical Training School of the Sipo and SD | |
| Proskurow (Ukraine) | *Reit- und Fahrschule d. Orpo* | Cavalry School of the Orpo | |
| Rabka (GG) | *Polizeischule* | Police School | |
| Rathenow | *Polizeischule für Reit- u. Fahrwesen (Orpo)* | Police Cavalry School (Orpo) | |
| | *Polizeischule für Veterinärhilfsdienst* | Police School for Veterinary Auxiliary Services | |
| | *Lehrschmiede d. Orpo (Hufbeschlagschule)* | Training Establishment for Blacksmiths | |
| Regensburg | *Feuerwehrschule* | School for Fire-Fighting | |
| Schepetowka | *Polizeischule* | Police School | |
| Schneidemühl | *Nebenzeugamt der Polizeischule für Technik und Verkehr* | Auxiliary Ordnance Depot of Police School for Technical Matters and Traffic Control | |

| Location | German Name | Translation | Remarks |
|---|---|---|---|
| Schöneck (Vogtland) | *Polizei Ski- und Wanderhütte* | Police Hostel for Skiing and Mountaineering | |
| Schönwalde | *Gendarmerieschule* | Gendarmerie School | |
| Schwerin | *Kriminaltechnisches Institut d. Sipo und SD* | Criminological Institute of Sipo and SD | Addr : Schloss Grabow |
| Sensburg | *Polizeischule* | Police School | Teaching following subjects : Penal Code, Police Powers, Traffic Control. |
| Skiernivice (GG) | *Polizeischule* | Police School | |
| Stettin | *Wasserschutzpolizeischule* | School of the Waterways Protection Police | Moved to Lauterbach, Isle of Rügen, 19th July, 1944 |
| Stolpmünde | *Gendarmerieschule* | Gendarmerie School | |
| Stuttgart | *Abrichteanstalt (Hundewesen)* | Police Dogs Training Establishment | |
| Sudelfeld nr Bayrish-Zell | *Polizei-Skischule* | Police Ski School | |
| Suhl | *Gendarmerieschule* | Gendarmerie School | Cdr. : *Obstlt.* DEUMICH |
| | *Polizeischule d. Kraftfahrwesens* | Police M/T School | |
| Trier | *Gendarmerieschule* | Gendarmerie School | |
| Waldau (Oberlausitz) | *Nachrichtenzeugamt d. Orpo* | Signal Supply Depot of Orpo | |
| Weichselstadt | *Polizeischule* | Police School | |
| Weimar | *Polizei Offizierschule 21* | Police Officer School 21 | |
| | *Polizeischule für d. Wirtschaftsverwaltungsdienst* | Police School for the Economic and Administration Service | Addr : Harthstr. 70 (March 1944) |
| Wendefurt (Harz) | *Polizeiverwaltungsschule* | Police Administration School | |
| Wien | *Kraftfahrschule (Schupo)* | M/T School (Schupo) | |
| Wien-Mödling | *Gendarmerieschule (mot.)* | School of the Motorised Gendarmerie | Cdr. : *Oberst d. Schupo* ALBRECHT |
| Wien-Purkersdorf | *Kraftfahr-Panzerschule d. Orpo* | Armoured Vehicles Training School | |
| Wien-Strebersdorf | *Kolonial-Polizeischule* | Colonial Police School | |
| Witow nr Zakopane | *Polizeischule für Skiausbildung* | Police School for Ski Training | |
| Zella-Mehlis | *Schiesschule* | Weapons Training School (Sipo and SD) | |

# ANNEXE K

## INDEX OF TOWNS AND POLICE HQ

---

### LIST OF ABBREVIATIONS
(not in all cases official German abbreviations)

**Column 2 : Regional Police Commanders**

(a) *HSSPf* ... ... *Höhere SS-und Polizeiführer* (Superior SS and Police Commander)
(b) *BdO* ... ... *Befehlshaber der Ordnungspolizei* (Commander of the Regular Police)
(c) *BdS* ... ... *Befehlshaber der Sicherheitspolizei und des SD* (Commander of the Security Police and Security Service)

**Column 3 : Higher Police Authorities (Höhere Polizeibehörden)**

*RSth.* ... ... ... *Reichsstatthalter* (Reich Governor)
*RPräs.* ... ... ... *Regierungspräsident* (District (Governmental) Administrative Chief)
*LdsReg.* ... ... *Landesregierung* (State Government)
*IMin.* ... ... ... *Innenminister* (Minister of the Interior)
*StMin-AI* ... ... *Staatsministerium, Abteilung Inneres* (Ministry of State, Department of Internal Affairs)
*Pol. Präs.* ... ... *Polizei Präsident* (Police President)
*Regd. Bgm.* ... ... *Regierender Bürgermeister* (Governing Mayor)

**Column 4 : National Police Administration (Staatliche Polizeiverwaltung)**

*PP* ... ... ... *Polizei Präsidium* (Police Presidency)
*PD* ... ... ... *Polizei Direktion* (Police Directorate)
*PA* ... ... ... *Polizei Amt* (Police Office)
*Z* ... ... ... *Zweigstelle* (Branch Office)

**Column 5 : Gestapo**

*Gestapo* ... ... ... *Geheime Staatspolizei* (Secret State Police)
*LSt.* ... ... ... *Leitstelle* (Regional Headquarters)
*St.* ... ... ... *Stelle* (Sub-regional Headquarters)
*AuDSt.* ... ... ... *Aussendienststelle* (Larger Branch Office)
*AuSt.* ... ... ... *Aussenstelle* (Smaller Branch Office)
*DSt.* ... ... ... *Dienststelle* (Offices of unidentified classification)
*Greko* ... ... ... *Grenzpolizei-Kommissariat* (Frontier Police-Commissariat)
*Grepo* ... ... ... *Grenzpolizei-Posten* (Frontier Police-Outpost)
*AEL.* ... ... ... *Arbeitserziehungslager* (Penal Labour Camp)
*AL.* ... ... ... *Auffanglager* (Transit and Collecting Camp)
*Pol. Gef.* ... ... ... *Polizeigefängnis* (Police Prison)
*UL.* ... ... ... *Umsiedlungslager* (Repatriation Camp)

**Column 6 : Kripo**

*Kripo* ... ... ... *Kriminalpolizei* (Criminal Police)
*LSt.* ... ... ... *Leitstelle* (Regional Headquarters)
*St.* ... ... ... *Stelle* (Sub-regional Headquarters)
*AuDSt.* ... ... *Aussendienststelle* (Larger Branch Office)
*AuP.* ... ... ... *Aussenposten* (Smaller Branch Office)

**Column 7 : SD**

*SD* ... ... ... *Sicherheitsdienst* (Security Service)
*LAbs.* ... ... ... *Leitabschnitt* (Regional Headquarters)
*Abs.* ... ... ... *Abschnitt* (Sub-regional Headquarters)
*HAuSt.* ... ... ... *Hauptaussenstelle* (Larger Branch Office)
*AuSt.* ... ... ... *Aussenstelle* (Smaller Branch Office)

**Column 8 : Miscellaneous**

*SW-Kdo.* ... ... *SW-Kommando* (Waterways Protection Police-Commands)
*SW-Abs.* ... ... *SW-Abschnitt* (Waterways Protection Police-Sectors)
*SW-Rev.* ... ... *SW-Revier* (Waterways Protection Police-Br. Wards) -US. Precincts)
*SW-Rev.Z* ... ... *SW-Revier Zweigstelle* (Waterways Protection Police-" Revier " Branches)
*SW-Station* ... ... *SW-Station* (Waterways Protection Police-Station)
*SW-Wache* ... ... *SW-Wache* (Waterways Protection Police-Squads)
*SW-Posten* ... ... *SW-Posten* (Waterways Protection Police-Posts)
*Wm.* ... ... ... *Waffenmeisterei* (Ordnance and Maintenance Shops)
*FP* ... ... ... *Feuerschutzpolizei* (Fire Protection Police)
*LS* ... ... ... *Luftschutzpolizei* (Air Raid Protection Police)

K1

A

| Town | (a) HSSPf (b) BdO (c) BdS | Higher Police Authorities (Höhere Polizei Behörden) | National Police Headquarters (Staatliche Polizei Verwaltungen) | Sicherheits Polizei | | SD | Others |
|---|---|---|---|---|---|---|---|
| | | | | Gestapo | Kripo | | |
| 1 | 2 | 3 | 4 | 5 | 6 | 7 | 8 |
| Aachen | — | RPräs. | PP { | AuDSt. Greko | St. | AuSt. | FP, Wm., LS |
| Aalen | — | — | — | — | AuP. | AuSt. | — |
| Adenau | — | — | — | — | — | AuSt.* | — |
| Ahlen | — | — | — | — | AuP. | — | — |
| Ahrweiler | — | — | — | — | — | AuSt. | — |
| Aichach | — | — | — | — | — | AuSt. | — |
| Aken | — | — | — | — | AuP. | — | — |
| Alfeld | — | — | — | — | — | AuSt. | — |
| Allenstein | — | RPräs. | — | AuDSt. | AuDSt. | HAuSt. | — |
| Almannsweiler | — | — | — | Grepo | — | — | — |
| Alsdorf | — | — | — | — | AuP. | — | — |
| Altena | — | — | — | — | AuP. | — | — |
| Altenburg | — | — | PD | — | AuDSt. | AuSt. | — |
| Altenkirchen | — | — | — | — | — | AuSt. | — |
| Altkirch | — | — | — | — | AuP. | AuSt. | — |
| Altmünsterol | — | — | — | Grepo | — | — | — |
| Altötting | — | — | — | — | — | AuSt. | — |
| Altona (Hamburg) | — | — | PA | AuDSt.* | — | AuSt | SW-Revier |
| Alzey | — | — | — | — | AuP. | — | — |
| Amberg | — | — | — | — | AuP. | AuSt. | — |
| Ammendorf | — | — | — | — | AuP. | — | — |
| Andernach | — | — | — | — | AuP. | — | — |
| Angerburg | — | — | — | — | AuP. | — | — |
| Ankenstein, Schloss | — | — | — | Pol. Gef. | — | — | — |
| Anklam | — | — | — | — | AuP. | — | — |
| Annaberg | — | — | — | — | AuP. | AuSt. | — |
| Ansbach | — | RPräs. | — | — | AuP. | AuSt. | — |
| Apolda | — | — | — | — | AuP. | — | — |
| Arnoldstein | — | — | — | Grepo | — | — | — |
| Arnsberg | — | RPräs. | — | — | AuP. | AuSt. | — |
| Arnstadt | — | — | — | — | AuP. | AuSt. | — |
| Asch | — | — | — | — | AuP. | — | — |
| Aschaffenburg | — | — | — | — | AuDSt. | AuSt. | — |
| Aschersleben | — | — | — | — | AuP. | — | — |
| Aspern (Airport) | — | — | — | Grepo | — | — | — |
| Assling | — | — | — | AuDSt. | AuDSt. | AuSt. | — |
| Aue | — | — | — | — | AuP. | — | — |
| Auerbach | — | — | — | — | AuP. | AuSt. | — |
| Augsburg | — | RPräs. | PP | AuDSt. | St. | HAuSt. | FP, Wm., LS |
| Aurich | — | RPräs. | — | DSt. | — | — | — |
| Auschwitz | — | — | — | AuDSt. | AuDSt. | — | — |
| Aussig | — | RPräs. | PP | AuDSt. | AuDSt. | AuSt. | SW-Wache, Wm., LS |
| Backnang | — | — | — | — | AuP. | — | — |
| Baden | — | — | — | — | AuP. | — | — |
| Baden-Baden | — | — | PD | AuDSt. | AuP. | AuSt. | — |
| Bad Brückenau | — | — | — | — | — | AuSt. | — |
| Bad Cannstatt | — | — | — | — | AuP. | — | — |
| Bad Godesberg | — | — | — | — | AuP. | — | — |
| Bad Harzburg | — | — | — | AuDSt. | — | — | — |
| Bad Homburg, v.d.H. | — | — | — | — | AuP. | AuSt. | — |
| Bad Ischl | — | — | — | DSt. | AuP. | — | — |
| Bad Kissingen | — | — | — | — | AuP. | AuSt. | — |
| Bad Kreuznach | — | — | — | — | AuP. | AuSt. | LS |
| Bad Liebenwerda | — | — | — | — | — | AuSt. | — |
| Bad Nauheim | — | — | — | — | AuDSt. | — | — |
| Bad Neustadt (Saale) | — | — | — | — | — | AuSt. | — |

* Offices known to have been suspended are marked by an asterisk.

| Town | (a) HSSPf (b) BdO (c) BdS | Higher Police Authorities (Höhere Polizei Behörden) | National Police Headquarters (Staatliche Polizei Verwaltungen) | Sicherheits Polizei | | SD | Others |
|---|---|---|---|---|---|---|---|
| | | | | Gestapo | Kripo | | |
| 1 | 2 | 5 | 4 | 5 | 6 | 7 | 8 |
| Bad Oeynhausen | — | — | — | — | AuP. | — | — |
| Bad Oldesloe | — | — | — | — | — | AuSt. | — |
| Bad Pyrmont | — | — | — | — | AuP. | — | — |
| Bad Saarow | — | — | — | — | — | AuSt. | — |
| Bad Salzbrunn | — | — | — | — | AuP. | — | — |
| Bad Salzuflen | — | — | — | — | AuP. | — | — |
| Bad Tölz | — | — | — | — | — | AuSt. | — |
| Bad Wildungen | — | — | — | — | — | AuSt. | — |
| Baelen | — | — | — | Grepo | — | — | — |
| Bajohren-Krottingen | — | — | — | Grepo | — | — | — |
| Balingen | — | — | — | — | — | AuSt. | — |
| Bamberg | — | — | — | — | AuDSt. | AuSt. | LS |
| Bartenstein | — | — | — | — | AuP. | AuSt. | — |
| Barth | — | — | — | — | AuP. | — | — |
| Bassum | — | — | — | — | — | AuSt. | — |
| Bautzen | — | — | — | AuDSt. | AuP. | AuSt. | — |
| Bayreuth | — | — | — | — | AuDSt. | Abs. | LS |
| Beckum | — | — | — | — | — | AuSt. | — |
| Belgard | — | — | — | — | AuP. | — | — |
| Bendorf | — | — | — | — | AuP. | — | — |
| Bendsburg | — | — | — | — | AuDSt. | — | — |
| Beneschau | — | — | — | AuDSt. | — | — | — |
| Bensheim | — | — | — | — | AuP. | — | — |
| Bentheim | — | — | — | Greko | — | — | — |
| Berchtesgaden | — | — | — | — | — | AuSt. | — |
| Bergedorf | — | — | — | AuDSt. | — | — | — |
| Bergen/Norway | — | — | — | (Kdr. d. | Sipo & | SD) | — |
| Bergheim | — | — | — | — | AuP. | AuSt. | — |
| Berg. Gladbach | — | — | — | — | AuP. | — | — |
| Bergreichenstein | — | — | — | — | — | AuSt. | — |
| †Berlin | a, b, c  a, b | Pol. Präs. | PP | LSt. | LSt. | LAbs. | FP, SW-Abs., Wm., LS |
| Berlin-Charlottenburg | — | — | — | — | — | AuSt. | — |
| Berlin-Lichtenberg | — | — | — | — | — | AuSt. | — |
| Berlin-Neukölln | — | — | — | — | — | AuSt. | — |
| Berlin-N 65 | — | — | — | — | — | AuSt. | — |
| Berlin-NW 87 | — | — | — | — | — | AuSt. | — |
| Berlin-Südende | — | — | — | — | — | AuSt. | — |
| Berlin-SW 68 | — | — | — | — | — | AuSt. | — |
| Berlin-Tempelhof | — | — | — | Grepo | — | — | — |
| Berlin-Weissensee | — | — | — | — | — | AuSt. | — |
| Berlin-Wilmersdorf | — | — | — | — | — | AuSt. | — |
| Bernau | — | — | — | — | AuP. | — | — |
| Bernburg | — | — | — | — | AuP. | AuSt. | LS |
| Berndorf | — | — | — | — | AuP. | — | — |
| Bernkastel | — | — | — | — | — | AuSt. | — |
| Beuel | — | — | — | — | AuP. | — | — |
| Beuthen | — | — | PA | AuDSt. | AuDSt. | AuSt. | FP |
| Bialystok | — | — | PP | (Kdr. d. | Sipo and | SD) | — |
| Biberach/Riss | — | — | — | — | AuP. | — | — |
| Bielefeld | — | — | — | AuDSt. | AuDSt. | HAuSt. | FP, LS |
| Bielitz | — | — | — | AuDSt. | AuDSt. | AuSt. | LS |
| Bila | — | — | — | Grepo | — | — | — |
| Bilin | — | — | — | — | AuDSt. | — | — |
| Bilnitz | — | — | — | Grepo | — | — | — |
| Bingen | — | — | — | — | AuP. | — | — |
| Birkenfeld | — | — | — | — | — | AuSt.* | — |
| Birnbaum | — | — | — | — | — | AuSt. | — |
| Bischofswerda | — | — | — | — | AuP. | — | — |
| Bischweiler | — | — | — | — | AuP. | — | — |
| Bitterfeld | — | — | PD | AuDSt. | AuP. | AuSt. | LS |
| Blachstädt | — | — | — | Grepo | — | — | — |
| Blankenburg | — | — | — | — | AuP. | AuSt. | — |

† Berlin has two *HSSPf* and two *BdO*—one of each for Berlin proper, one of each for Wkr. III.

| Town | (a) HSSPf (b) BdO (c) BdS | Higher Police Authorities (Höhere Polizei Behörden) | National Police Headquarters (Staatliche Polizei Verwaltungen) | Sicherheits Polizei | | SD | Others |
|---|---|---|---|---|---|---|---|
| | | | | Gestapo | Kripo | | |
| 1 | 2 | 3 | 4 | 5 | 6 | 7 | 8 |
| Blankenstein | — | — | — | — | AuP. | — | — |
| Blechhammer | — | — | — | AEL. | — | — | — |
| Blumenbach | — | — | — | Grepo | — | — | — |
| Bocholt | — | — | — | — | AuP. | — | — |
| Bocholt-Hemden | — | — | — | Grepo | — | — | — |
| Bochum | — | — | PP | AuDSt. | St. | HAuSt. | FP, Wm., LS |
| Bockum-Hövel | — | — | — | — | AuP. | — | — |
| Böblingen | — | — | — | — | AuP. | — | — |
| Böglum | — | — | — | Grepo | — | — | — |
| Böhmisch-Leipa | — | — | — | Greko | AuP. | AuSt. | — |
| Bonn | — | — | — | AuDSt. | AuDSt. | AuSt. | FP, SW-Wache, LS |
| Borghorst | — | — | — | — | AuP. | — | — |
| Bork | — | — | — | — | AuP. | — | — |
| Borken/Westf. | — | — | — | Greko | — | AuSt. | — |
| Borkum | — | — | — | — | — | — | LS |
| Borna | — | — | — | — | AuP. | AuSt. | — |
| Bottrop | — | — | PA | AuDSt. | AuDSt. | — | — |
| Bottrop-Boy | — | — | — | — | AuDSt. | — | — |
| Bottrop-Eigen | — | — | — | — | AuDSt. | — | — |
| Brackwede | — | — | — | — | AuP. | — | — |
| Brake | — | — | — | — | — | AuSt. | — |
| Brandenburg/Havel | — | — | — | AuDSt. | AuDSt. | — | FP, SW-Wache, LS |
| Braunau/Inn | — | — | — | — | — | AuSt. | — |
| Braunsberg/Pr. | — | — | — | AuDSt. | AuP. | AuSt. | — |
| Braunschweig | a, b, c | IMin. | PP | St. | St. | Abs. | FP, SW-Wache, Wm., LS |
| Brebach | — | — | — | — | AuDSt. | — | — |
| Bregenz | — | — | — | Greko | — | AuSt. | — |
| Bremen | — | Regd. Bgm. | PP | St. | LSt. | Abs. | FP, SW-Abs., Wm., LS |
| Bremen-Hafen | — | — | — | Greko | — | — | — |
| Bremerhaven | — | — | — | — | — | — | FP, SW-Rev. |
| Brenner (-Gries) | — | — | — | Greko | — | — | — |
| Breslau | a, b, c | RPräs. | PP | LSt. | LSt. | LAbs. | FP, SW-Kdo., Wm., LS |
| Brieg | — | — | — | — | AuP. | HAuSt. | — |
| Briesen | — | — | — | — | AuP. | — | — |
| Brilon | — | — | — | — | — | AuSt. | — |
| Bromberg | — | RPräs. | PP | St. | St. | AuSt. | FP, SW-Rev., Wm., LS |
| Bruch | — | — | — | — | AuDSt. | — | — |
| Bruchsal | — | — | — | — | AuP. | AuSt. | — |
| Bruck/Leitha | — | — | — | Grepo | — | — | — |
| Bruck/Mur | — | — | — | — | — | AuSt. | LS |
| Brühl | — | — | — | — | AuP. | — | — |
| Brünn | — | LdsReg. Mähren | PD | LSt. | St. | AuSt. | Wm., LS |
| Brüx | — | — | PP | AuDSt. | AuDSt. | AuSt. | LS |
| Brunsbüttelkoog | — | — | — | Grepo | — | — | LS |
| Brunnstadt | — | — | — | — | AuP. | — | — |
| Budweis | — | — | — | AuDSt. | AuDSt. | HAuSt. | — |
| Bückeburg | — | LdsReg. | — | — | — | AuSt. | — |
| Bühl | — | — | — | — | — | AuSt. | — |
| Bütow | — | — | — | AuDSt. | AuP. | — | — |
| Bunderneuland | — | — | — | Grepo | — | — | — |
| Bunzlau | — | — | — | — | AuP. | — | Wm. |
| Burg (Fehmarn) | — | — | — | AuDSt. | — | — | — |
| Burg (Magdeburg) | — | — | — | — | AuP. | AuSt. | — |
| Burgdorf | — | — | — | — | — | AuSt. | — |
| Burgstädt | — | — | — | — | AuP. | — | — |
| Burgsteinfurt | — | — | — | — | — | AuSt. | — |
| Calau | — | — | — | — | — | AuSt. | — |

K4

| Town | (a) HSSPf (b) BdO (c) BdS | Higher Police Authorities (Höhere Polizei Behörden) | National Police Headquarters (Staatliche Polizei Verwaltungen) | Sicherheits Polizei — Gestapo | Sicherheits Polizei — Kripo | SD | Others |
|---|---|---|---|---|---|---|---|
| 1 | 2 | 3 | 4 | 5 | 6 | 7 | 8 |
| Calbe | — | — | — | — | AuP. | AuSt. | — |
| Castrop-Rauxel | — | — | — | — | AuP. | — | — |
| Celle | — | — | — | AuDSt. | AuDSt. | AuSt. | — |
| Cham | — | — | — | — | — | AuSt. | — |
| Chemnitz | — | — | PP | St. | St. | HAuSt. | FP, Wm., LS |
| Cilli | — | — | — | Greko AuDSt. | AuDSt. | AuSt. | — |
| Clausthal-Zellerfeld | — | — | — | — | AuP. | — | — |
| Cloppenburg | — | — | — | — | — | AuSt. | — |
| Coburg | — | — | — | — | AuP. | AuSt. | LS |
| Coesfeld | — | — | — | — | AuP. | — | — |
| Copenhagen/ Dänemark | a, b, c | — | — | — | — | — | — |
| Cosel | — | — | — | — | AuP. | — | — |
| Coswig/Anhalt | — | — | — | — | AuP. | — | — |
| Coswig/Sachsen | — | — | — | — | AuP. | — | — |
| Cottbus | — | — | — | AuDSt. | AuDSt. | AuSt. | LS |
| Crimmitschau | — | — | — | — | AuP. | — | — |
| Crossen | — | — | — | — | AuP. | — | — |
| Cuxhaven | — | — | PD | AuDSt. Greko | AuDSt. | AuSt. | SW-Rev., LS |
| Dachau | — | — | — | — | AuP. | AuSt. | — |
| Dalheim | — | — | — | Grepo | — | — | — |
| Dannenberg | — | — | — | — | — | AuSt. | — |
| Danzig | a, b, c | RPräs. | PP | LSt. | LSt. | LAbs. | FP, SW-Kdo., Wm., LS |
| Darmstadt | — | RSth. | PP | St. | St. | HAuSt. | FP, Wm. |
| Datteln | — | — | — | — | AuDSt. | — | — |
| Daun | — | — | — | — | — | AuSt. | — |
| Deggendorf-Plattling | — | — | — | — | — | AuSt. | — |
| Delitzsch | — | — | — | — | AuP. | AuSt. | — |
| Delmenhorst | — | — | — | AuDSt. | AuP. | AuSt. | — |
| Demmin | — | — | — | — | AuP. | — | — |
| Dessau | — | RSth. | PP | AuDSt. | St. | Abs. | FP, SW-Station, Wm., LS |
| Dessau-Rosslau | — | — | — | — | AuP. | — | — |
| Detmold | — | RSth. | — | — | AuDSt. | AuSt. | — |
| Deutsch-Eylau | — | — | — | — | AuP. | — | — |
| Deutsch-Krone | — | — | — | — | AuP. | — | — |
| Deutschlandsberg | — | — | — | — | — | AuSt. | — |
| Devau (Airport) | — | — | — | Grepo | — | — | — |
| Diedenhofen | — | — | PA | AuDSt. | AuDSt. | AuSt. | LS |
| Diekirch | — | — | — | AuDSt. | — | AuSt. | — |
| Diepholz | — | — | — | — | — | AuSt. | — |
| Dillingen | — | — | — | — | — | AuSt. | — |
| Dingolfing-Landau | — | — | — | — | — | AuSt. | — |
| Dinslaken | — | — | — | — | AuP. | AuSt. | — |
| Dippoldiswalde | — | — | — | — | — | AuSt. | — |
| Dirschau | — | — | — | AuDSt. | AuP. | AuSt. | SW-Wache |
| Döbeln | — | — | — | — | AuP. | AuSt. | — |
| Doerpen bei Papenburg | — | — | — | — | — | — | SW-Sonderkdo. |
| Dombrowa | — | — | — | — | AuDSt. | — | — |
| Donaueschingen | — | — | — | — | — | AuSt. | — |
| Donauwörth | — | — | — | — | — | AuSt. | — |
| Dorpat | — | — | — | — | — | — | SW-Kdo. |
| Dortmund | — | — | PP | St. | St. | Abs. | FP, Wm., LS |
| Dramburg | — | — | — | AuDSt. | — | — | — |
| Dresden | a, b, c | IMin. | PP | LSt. | LSt. | LAbs. | FP, SW-Rev., Wm., LS |
| Drontheim/Norway | — | — | — | Kdr. der Sipo und des SD | | | Wm. |
| Duderstadt | — | — | — | — | — | AuSt. | — |
| Dudweiler | — | — | — | — | AuDSt. | — | — |
| Dülken | — | — | — | — | AuP. | — | — |
| Dülmen | — | — | — | — | AuP. | — | — |

| Town | (a) HSSPf (b) BdO (c) BdS | Higher Police Authorities (Höhere Polizei Behörden) | National Police Headquarters (Staatliche Polizei Verwaltungen) | Sicherheits Polizei Gestapo | Sicherheits Polizei Kripo | SD | Others |
|---|---|---|---|---|---|---|---|
| 1 | 2 | 3 | 4 | 5 | 6 | 7 | 8 |
| Düren | — | — | — | — | AuDSt. | AuSt. | — |
| Düsseldorf | a, c | RPräs. | PP | LSt. | LSt. | LAbs. | FP, SW-Wache, Wm., LS |
| Duisburg | — | — | PP | AuDSt. | AuDSt. | HAuSt. | Wm., LS, SW-Station |
| Duisburg-Hamborn | — | — | — | — | — | — | FP |
| Dux | — | — | — | — | AuDSt. | — | — |
| Eberswalde | — | — | — | AuDSt. | AuP. | AuSt. | SW-Wache, LS |
| Ebingen | — | — | PA | — | AuP. | — | — |
| Eckernförde | — | — | — | — | — | AuSt.* | — |
| Eger | — | — | — | AuDSt. | AuSt. | — | LS |
| Eibiswalde | — | — | — | Grepo | — | — | — |
| Eilenburg | — | — | — | — | AuP. | — | — |
| Einbeck | — | — | — | — | — | AuSt. | — |
| Eisenach | — | — | — | — | AuDSt. | AuSt. | LS |
| Eisenberg | — | — | — | — | AuP. | — | — |
| Eisenerz | — | — | — | — | AuDSt. | — | — |
| Eisenstadt | — | — | — | Greko | — | AuSt. | — |
| Eisenstein-Markt (Markt-Eisenstein) | — | — | — | AuDSt. | — | — | — |
| Eisleben | — | — | — | AuDSt. | AuP. | AuSt. | — |
| Elbing | — | — | PP | AuDSt. | AuDSt. | AuSt. | FP, SW-Rev., Wm., LS |
| Elfringen | — | — | — | Grepo | — | — | — |
| Ellwangen/Württbg. | — | — | — | AuSt. | AuP. | — | — |
| Elmshorn | — | — | — | — | AuP. | AuSt. | — |
| Elten Babberich/ Niederrhein | — | — | — | Grepo | — | — | — |
| Emden | — | — | — | Greko | AuP. | AuSt. | SW-Rev., LS |
| Emmerich | — | — | — | Greko | AuP. | — | SW-Wache |
| Emsdetten | — | — | — | — | AuP. | — | — |
| Engerau | — | — | — | Grepo | — | — | SW-Station |
| Erfurt | — | R Präs. | PP | AuDSt. | St. | HAuSt. | FP, Wm., LS |
| Erkelenz | — | — | — | — | — | AuSt. | — |
| Erkenschwick | — | — | — | — | AuDSt. | — | — |
| Erlangen | — | — | — | — | AuP. | AuSt. | — |
| Erzingen | — | — | — | Grepo | — | — | — |
| Esch/Luxemburg | — | — | — | AuDSt. | AuDSt. | AuSt. | — |
| Eschwege | — | — | — | — | AuP. | AuSt. | — |
| Eschweiler | — | — | — | — | AuP. | — | — |
| Essen | — | — | PP | AuDSt. | St. | HAuSt. | FP, Wm., LS |
| Esslingen | — | — | PD | — | AuDSt. | — | — |
| Ettlingen | — | — | — | DSt. | — | — | — |
| Eupen | — | — | — | Greko | AuP. | AuSt. | — |
| Euskirchen | — | — | — | — | AuP. | AuSt. | — |
| Eutin | — | — | — | — | — | AuSt.* | — |
| Eydtkau (Eydtkuhnen) | — | — | — | Greko | — | — | — |
| Falkenau/Eger | — | — | — | — | AuP. | AuSt. | |
| Falkensee | — | — | — | — | AuP. | — | — |
| Falkenstein | — | — | — | — | AuP. | — | — |
| Fallingbostel | — | — | — | AuDSt. | — | AuSt. | — |
| Farge | — | — | — | AEL. | — | — | — |
| Fehmarn/Burg | — | — | — | AuDSt. | — | — | — |
| Fehrbellin | — | — | — | AEL. | — | — | — |
| Feldbach | — | — | — | — | — | AuSt. | — |
| Feldkirch | — | — | — | Grepo | AuP. | — | — |
| Fellbach | — | — | — | — | AuP. | — | — |
| Finsterwalde | — | — | — | — | AuP. | — | — |
| Flatow | — | — | — | AuDSt. | — | — | — |
| Flensburg | — | — | PD | Greko | St. | AuSt. | FP, SW-Rev., LS |

| Town | (a) HSSPf (b) BdO (c) BdS | Higher Police Authorities (Höhere Polizei Behörden) | National Police Head-quarters (Staatliche Polizei Verwaltungen) | Sicherheits Polizei | | SD | Others |
|---|---|---|---|---|---|---|---|
| | | | | Gestapo | Kripo | | |
| 1 | 2 | 3 | 4 | 5 | 6 | 7 | 8 |
| Flöha | — | — | — | — | — | AuSt. | — |
| Forbach | — | — | — | — | AuDSt. | — | — |
| Forchheim | — | — | — | — | AuP. | AuSt. | — |
| Forst | — | — | — | — | AuDSt. | — | — |
| Frankenberg/Eder | — | — | — | — | — | AuSt. | — |
| Frankenberg/ Sachsen | — | — | — | — | AuP. | — | — |
| Frankenstein | — | — | — | — | AuP. | — | — |
| Frankenthal | — | — | — | — | AuP. | — | — |
| Frankfurt a.M. | — | — | PP | St. | LSt. | Abs. | FP, SW-Wache, Wm., LS |
| Frankfurt/Oder | — | RPräs. | PD | St. | St. | HAuSt. | FP, LS |
| Frauhaus | — | — | — | — | AuP. | — | — |
| Frechen | — | — | — | — | AuP. | — | — |
| Freiberg/Sa. | — | — | — | — | AuP. | AuSt. | — |
| Freiburg/Breisgau | — | — | PP | AuDSt. | AuDSt. | AuSt. | LS |
| Freihaus | — | — | — | — | — | AuSt. | — |
| Freising | — | — | — | — | AuP. | AuSt. | — |
| Freital | — | — | — | — | AuP. | — | — |
| Freiwaldau | — | — | — | — | — | AuSt. | — |
| Freudenstadt | — | — | — | — | AuP. | AuSt. | — |
| Freudenthal | — | — | — | — | — | AuSt. | — |
| Friedberg/Bay. | — | — | — | — | — | AuSt. | — |
| Friedberg-Bad Nauheim | — | — | PA | — | — | AuSt. | — |
| Friedrichshafen | — | — | PD | Greko | AuDSt. | — | SW-Kdo., LS |
| Friedrichsthal | — | — | — | — | AuDSt. | — | — |
| Fürstenfeld | — | — | — | Greko | — | AuSt. | — |
| Fürstenfeldbruck | — | — | — | — | — | AuSt. | — |
| Fürstenwalde | — | — | — | — | AuP. | — | — |
| Fürth | — | — | PA | — | — | AuSt. | — |
| Füssen | — | — | — | — | — | AuSt. | — |
| Fulda | — | — | — | AuDSt. | AuP. | — | — |
| Gabergischken | — | — | — | Grepo | — | — | — |
| Gablonz | — | — | PA | Greko | AuDSt. | AuSt. | — |
| Gardelegen | — | — | — | — | AuP. | AuSt. | — |
| Garmisch-Partenkirchen | — | — | — | — | AuP. | AuSt. | — |
| Gebweiler | — | — | — | — | AuP. | — | — |
| Gehlenburg/Ostpr. | — | — | — | Grepo | — | — | — |
| Geisslingen | — | — | — | — | AuP. | — | — |
| Geldern | — | — | — | Grepo | — | AuSt. | — |
| Gelsenkirchen | — | — | PA | AuDSt. | AuDSt. | AuSt. | FP |
| Gelsenkirchen-Buer | — | — | — | AuDSt. | AuDSt. | — | — |
| Genthin | — | — | — | — | AuP. | AuSt. | SW-Wache |
| Gera | — | — | PD | AuDSt. | AuDSt. | AuSt. | — |
| Gevelsberg | — | — | — | — | AuP. | — | — |
| Giessen | — | — | PD | AuDSt. | AuDSt. | — | — |
| Gifhorn | — | — | — | — | — | AuSt. | — |
| Gladbeck | — | — | PA | AuDSt. | AuDSt. | AuSt. | — |
| Glanerbrücke | — | — | — | Grepo | — | — | — |
| Glatz | — | — | — | AuDSt. | AuP. | AuSt. | — |
| Glauchau | — | — | — | — | AuP. | AuSt. | — |
| Gleiwitz | — | — | PP | AuDSt. | AuDSt. | HAuSt. | FP, SW-Wache, Wm., LS |
| Glogau | — | — | — | AuDSt. | AuP. | AuSt. | SW-Wache, LS |
| Gmunden | — | — | — | — | — | AuSt. | — |
| Gnesen | — | — | — | AuDSt. | AuDSt. | AuSt. | — |
| Goch | — | — | — | Grepo | AuP. | — | — |
| Göding | — | — | — | Grepo | — | — | — |
| Göppingen | — | — | PA | — | AuP. | — | — |
| Görlitz | — | — | — | AuDSt. | AuDSt. | AuSt. | FP, LS |
| Görnau | — | — | — | — | AuP. | — | — |

K7

| Town | (a) HSSPf (b) BdO (c) BdS | Higher Police Authorities (Höhere Polizei Behörden) | National Police Headquarters (Staatliche Polizei Verwaltungen) | Sicherheits Polizei | | SD | Others |
|---|---|---|---|---|---|---|---|
| | | | | Gestapo | Kripo | | |
| 1 | 2 | 3 | 4 | 5 | 6 | 7 | 8 |
| Göttingen | — | — | — | AuDSt. | AuDSt. | AuSt. | LS |
| Goldap | — | — | — | — | AuP. | AuSt. | — |
| Gollnow | — | — | — | — | AuP. | — | — |
| Gollub | — | — | — | — | AuP. | — | — |
| Goslar | — | — | — | AuDSt.* | AuP. | AuSt. | — |
| Gotenhafen | — | — | PP | Greko | AuDSt. | AuSt. | FP, SW-Rev., LS |
| Gotha | — | — | PD | AuDSt. | AuDSt. | AuSt. | LS |
| Gottmadingen | — | — | — | Grepo | — | — | — |
| Grafenwöhr | — | — | — | AuDSt. | — | — | — |
| Grätz | — | — | — | — | — | AuSt. | — |
| Graslitz | — | — | — | — | AuP. | AuSt. | — |
| Graudenz | — | — | PD | AuDSt. | AuDSt. | AuSt. | SW-Wache |
| Graz | — | RSth. | PP | St. | St. | Abs. | FP, Wm., LS |
| Greifenberg | — | — | — | — | AuP. | — | — |
| Greifenhagen | — | — | — | — | AuP. | — | — |
| Greifswald | — | — | — | AuDSt. | AuP. | AuSt. | — |
| Greiz | — | — | — | — | AuP. | AuSt. | — |
| Grenzacherhorn | — | — | — | Grepo | — | — | — |
| Grevenbroich | — | — | — | — | AuP. | — | — |
| Grimma | — | — | — | — | AuP. | AuSt. | — |
| Gröditz | — | — | — | — | — | AuSt. | — |
| Gronau/Westf. | — | — | — | Greko | AuP. | AuSt. | — |
| Grossenhain | — | — | — | — | AuP. | AuSt. | — |
| Grossottersleben | — | — | — | — | AuP. | — | — |
| Gross-Kunzendorf | — | — | — | AEL. | — | — | — |
| Gross-Strehlitz | — | — | — | — | AuP. | — | — |
| Gross-Wartenberg | — | — | — | AuDSt. | — | — | — |
| Grünberg | — | — | — | — | AuP. | — | — |
| Guben | — | — | — | — | AuP. | AuSt. | FP |
| Günzburg | — | — | — | — | — | AuSt. | — |
| Güstrow | — | — | — | — | AuP. | AuSt. | — |
| Gütersloh | — | — | — | — | AuP. | — | — |
| Guhrau | — | — | — | AuDSt. | — | — | — |
| Gumbinnen | — | RPräs. | — | — | AuP. | AuSt. | — |
| Gummersbach | — | — | — | — | AuP. | AuSt. | — |
| Haan | — | — | — | — | AuP. | — | — |
| Hägerwelle | — | — | — | AEL. | — | — | — |
| Hagen | — | — | — | AuDSt. | AuDSt. | AuSt. | FP, LS |
| Hagenau | — | — | — | AuDSt. | AuP. | AuSt. | — |
| Halberstadt | — | — | — | — | AuDSt. | AuSt. | FP |
| Haldensleben | — | — | — | — | AuP. | AuSt. | — |
| Halle/Saale | — | — | PP | St. | LSt. | Abs. | SW-Wache, Wm., FP, LS |
| Hallein | — | — | — | — | AuP. | AuSt. | — |
| Hamborn | — | — | — | AuDSt. | — | — | — |
| Hamburg | a, b, c | RSth. | PP | LSt. | LSt. | LAbs. | FP, SW-Gruppe, LS, Wm. |
| Hamburg-Altona | — | — | PA | AuDSt.* | — | AuSt. | SW-Rev. |
| Hamburg-Bergedorf | — | — | — | — | — | AuSt. | — |
| Hamburg-Finkenwärder | — | — | — | — | — | — | SW-Rev. |
| Hamburg-Harburg | — | — | PA | AuDSt. | — | AuSt. | SW-Rev. |
| Hamburg-Innenstadt | — | — | — | — | — | AuSt. | — |
| Hamburg-Ost | — | — | — | — | — | AuSt. | — |
| Hamburg-West | — | — | — | — | — | AuSt. | — |
| Hameln | — | — | — | — | AuP. | AuSt. | — |
| Hamm/Westf. | — | — | PD | AuDSt. | AuDSt. | AuSt. | LS |
| Hanau | — | — | PD | AuDSt. | AuP. | AuSt. | — |
| Hannover | b | RPräs. | PP | LSt. | LSt. | HAuSt. | FP, Wm., LS |
| Hann.-Münden | — | — | — | — | AuP. | — | — |
| Harrislee-Land | — | — | — | Grepo | — | — | — |

| Town | (a) HSSPf (b) BdO (c) BdS | Higher Police Authorities (Höhere Polizei Behörden) | National Police Head- quarters (Staatliche Polizei Ver- waltungen) | Sicherheits Polizei | | SD | Others |
|---|---|---|---|---|---|---|---|
| | | | | Gestapo | Kripo | | |
| 1 | 2 | 3 | 4 | 5 | 6 | 7 | 8 |
| Hartberg | — | — | — | — | — | AuSt. | — |
| Hattingen | — | — | — | — | AuP. | — | — |
| Heide | — | — | — | AuDSt. | AuP. | AuSt. | — |
| Heidelberg | — | — | PD | AuDSt. | AuDSt. | AuSt. | — |
| Heidenau | — | — | — | — | AuP. | — | — |
| Heidenheim | — | — | PA | — | AuP. | — | — |
| Heilbronn/Neckar | — | — | PD | AuDSt. | AuDSt. | AuSt. | SW-Wache, LS |
| Heiligenbeil | — | — | — | — | AuP. | — | — |
| Heiligenkreuz | — | — | — | Grepo | — | — | — |
| Heiligenstadt | — | — | — | — | AuP. | AuSt. | — |
| Heilsberg | — | — | — | — | AuP. | — | — |
| Heinrichskapelle | — | — | — | Grepo | — | — | — |
| Heinsberg | — | — | — | Greko | — | — | — |
| Helaheide | — | — | — | Grepo | — | — | — |
| Helmstedt | — | — | — | — | AuP. | AuSt. | — |
| Hemer | — | — | — | — | AuP. | — | — |
| Hennigsdorf | — | — | — | — | AuP. | — | — |
| Herbesthal | — | — | — | Grepo | — | — | — |
| Herford | — | — | — | — | AuP. | AuSt. | — |
| Hermagor | — | — | — | — | — | AuSt. | — |
| Hermühlheim | — | — | — | — | AuP. | AuSt. | — |
| Herne/Westf. | — | — | PA | — | AuDSt. | — | — |
| Hersbruck | — | — | — | — | — | AuSt. | — |
| Hersfeld | — | — | — | — | AuP. | AuSt. | — |
| Herten | — | — | — | — | AuDSt. | — | — |
| Hervest-Dorsten | — | — | — | — | AuP. | — | — |
| Herzogenrath | — | — | — | Greko | — | — | — |
| Heydebreck | — | — | — | AuDSt. | AuP. | — | — |
| Heydekrug | — | — | — | AuDSt. | — | — | — |
| Hildburghausen | — | — | — | — | — | AuSt. | — |
| Hilden | — | — | — | — | AuP. | — | — |
| Hildesheim | — | RPräs. | — | AuDSt. | AuDSt. | AuSt. | Wm., LS |
| Hindenburg | — | — | PA | — | AuDSt. | — | FP |
| Hinzert | — | — | — | AEL. | — | — | — |
| Hirschberg | — | — | — | AuDSt. | AuP. | AuSt. | — |
| Hitzacker/Elbe | — | — | — | — | — | — | SW-Wache |
| Höchst | — | — | — | Grepo | — | — | — |
| Höxter | — | — | — | — | — | AuSt. | — |
| Hof | — | — | PD | — | AuDSt. | AuSt. | — |
| Hohenelbe | — | — | — | — | — | AuSt. | — |
| Hohenlimburg | — | — | — | — | AuP. | — | — |
| Hohensalza | — | RPräs. | — | { AuDSt. AEL. | St. | AuSt. | — |
| Hohenstein/ Ernstthal | — | — | — | — | AuP. | — | — |
| Holtenau-Schleuse | — | — | — | Grepo | — | — | — |
| Holzminden | — | — | — | — | AuP. | AuSt. | — |
| Homberg | — | — | — | — | AuP. | — | — |
| Homburg/Saar | — | — | — | — | AuP. | — | — |
| Honnef | — | — | — | — | AuP. | — | — |
| Horb | — | — | — | — | — | AuSt. | — |
| Horbach | — | — | — | Grepo | — | — | — |
| Hoyerswerda | — | — | — | — | — | AuSt. | — |
| Hradischko | — | — | — | AEL. | — | — | — |
| Hunswinkel | — | — | — | AEL. | — | — | — |
| Hüls | — | — | — | — | AuP. | — | — |
| Hüningen | — | — | — | — | AuP. | — | SW-Wache |
| Husum | — | — | — | — | AuP. | — | — |
| Ibbenbüren | — | — | — | — | AuP. | — | — |
| Idar-Oberstein | — | — | — | AuSt. | AuP. | — | — |
| Iglau | — | — | PD | AuDSt. | AuDSt. | HAuSt.* | — |
| Ilkenau | — | — | — | — | AuP. | — | — |
| Illertissen | — | — | — | — | — | AuSt. | — |
| Ilmenau | — | — | — | — | AuP. | — | — |
| Ingolstadt | — | — | — | — | AuP. | AuSt. | LS |

K9                                                                                                          B

| Town | (a) HSSPf (b) BdO (c) BdS | Higher Police Authorities (Höhere Polizei Behörden) | National Police Headquarters (Staatliche Polizei Verwaltungen) | Sicherheits Polizei Gestapo | Sicherheits Polizei Kripo | SD | Others |
|---|---|---|---|---|---|---|---|
| 1 | 2 | 3 | 4 | 5 | 6 | 7 | 8 |
| Innsbruck | — | RSth. | PP | St. | St. | Abs. | FP, Wm., LS |
| Innsbruck-Reichenau | — | — | — | AL. | — | — | — |
| Insterburg | — | — | — | AuDSt. | AuDSt. | AuSt. | FP |
| Iserlohn | — | — | — | — | AuP. | — | — |
| Itzehoe | — | — | — | AuDSt. | AuP. | AuSt. | — |
| Jägerndorf | — | — | — | — | AuP. | — | — |
| Jarotschin | — | — | — | AuDSt. | — | AuSt. | — |
| Jauer | — | — | — | — | AuP. | — | — |
| Jaworzno | — | — | — | — | AuP. | — | — |
| Jena | — | — | PD | AuDSt. | AuDSt. | HAuSt. | LS |
| Jennersdorf | — | — | — | Grepo | — | — | — |
| Jessnitz | — | — | — | — | AuP. | — | — |
| Jever | — | — | — | — | — | AuSt. | — |
| Jitschin | — | — | — | AuDSt. | AuDSt. | AuSt. | — |
| Johannisburg/Ostpr. | — | — | — | DSt. | — | — | — |
| Jonaten | — | — | — | Grepo | — | — | — |
| Judenburg | — | — | — | — | — | AuSt. | — |
| Jülich | — | — | — | — | AuP. | — | — |
| Jüterbog | — | — | — | AuDSt. | AuP. | — | — |
| Jungbunzlau | — | — | — | AuDSt. | AuDSt. | AuSt. | — |
| Kaiserslautern | — | — | PD | AuDSt. | AuDSt. | AuSt. | LS |
| Kaldenkirchen | — | — | — | Greko | — | — | — |
| Kalisch | — | — | — | AuDSt. | AuDSt. | AuSt. | — |
| Kamen | — | — | — | — | AuP. | — | — |
| Kamenz | — | — | — | — | AuP. | AuSt. | — |
| Kamp-Lintfort | — | — | — | — | AuP. | — | — |
| Karlsbad | — | RPräs. | PD | St. | St. | HAuSt. | LS |
| Karlsruhe | — | IMin. | PP | LSt. | St. | HAuSt. | FP, SW-Station, Wm., LS |
| Karwin | — | — | — | — | AuP. | — | — |
| Kassel | a, b, c | RPräs. b. OPräs. | PP | St. | St. | Abs. | FP, Wm., LS |
| Kattowitz | — | RPräs. | PP | LSt. | LSt. | LAbs. | FP, Wm., LS |
| Kaufbeuren | — | — | — | — | AuP. | AuSt. | — |
| Kehl | — | — | PA | Greko | AuP. | — | — |
| Kemnath | — | — | — | — | — | AuSt. | — |
| Kempen | — | — | — | — | AuP. | — | — |
| Kempten | — | — | — | — | AuP. | AuSt. | — |
| Kiel | — | — | PP | St. | St. | Abs. | FP, SW-Kdo, LS, Wm. |
| Kirchdorf | — | — | — | — | — | AuSt. | — |
| Kirchhain | — | — | — | — | — | AuSt. | — |
| Kirchheimbolanden | — | — | — | — | — | AuSt. | — |
| Kittsee | — | — | — | Grepo | — | — | — |
| Kitzbühel | — | — | — | — | — | AuSt. | — |
| Kitzingen | — | — | — | — | AuP. | AuSt. | — |
| Kladno | — | — | — | AuDSt. | AuDSt. | AuSt. | — |
| Klagenfurt | — | RSth. | PD | St. | St. | Abs. | FP, Wm., LS |
| Klattau | — | — | — | AuDSt. | AuDSt. | AuSt. | Wm. |
| Kleinbettingen | — | — | — | Grepo | — | — | — |
| Kleinmachnow | — | — | — | — | AuP. | — | — |
| Kleve | — | — | — | Greko | AuP. | AuSt. | — |
| Klösterle | — | — | — | — | — | AuSt. | — |
| Klotzsche | — | — | — | — | AuP. | — | — |
| Koblenz | — | RPräs. | PP | St. | St. | Abs. | SW-Kdo., Wm., LS |
| Kochem | — | — | — | — | — | AuSt. | — |
| Köln | — | RPräs. | PP | St. | LSt. | Abs. | FP, SW-Station, Wm., LS |
| Köln-Deutz | — | — | — | — | — | AuSt. | — |
| Königgrätz | — | — | — | AuDSt. | AuDSt. | HAuSt. | — |

| Town | (a) HSSPf (b) BdO (c) BdS | Higher Police Authorities (Höhere Polizei Behörden) | National Police Headquarters (Staatliche Polizei Verwaltungen) | Sicherheits Polizei | | SD | Others |
|---|---|---|---|---|---|---|---|
| | | | | Gestapo | Kripo | | |
| 1 | 2 | 3 | 4 | 5 | 6 | 7 | 8 |
| Königsberg | a, b, c | RPräs. | PP | LSt. | LSt. | LAbs. | FP, SW-Kdo., Wm., LS |
| Königshofen | — | — | — | — | — | AuSt.* | — |
| Königshütte | — | — | PA | — | — | — | FP |
| Königswinter | — | — | — | — | AuP. | — | — |
| Köslin | — | RPräs. | — | AuDSt. | AuP. | AuSt. | — |
| Köthen | — | — | — | — | AuP. | AuSt. | — |
| Kohlscheid | — | — | — | Grepo | AuP. | — | — |
| Kolberg | — | — | — | { AuDSt. Greko | AuP. | — | — |
| Kolin | — | — | — | AuDSt. | AuDSt. | AuSt. | — |
| Kolmar/Elsass | — | — | — | AuDSt. | AuP. | AuSt. | FP, LS |
| Kolmar/Posen | — | — | — | — | AuP. | AuSt. | — |
| Komotau | — | — | — | AuDSt. | AuDSt. | AuSt. | — |
| Konin | — | — | — | AuDSt. | AuP. | AuSt. | — |
| Konitz | — | — | — | AuDSt. | AuP. | — | — |
| Konstanz | — | — | PA | Greko | AuDSt. | AuSt. | SW-Station |
| Kornwestheim | — | — | — | — | AuP. | — | — |
| Kosten | — | — | — | AuDSt. | AuP. | — | — |
| Krainburg | — | — | — | Greko | — | — | — |
| Kranenburg/ Niederrhein | — | — | — | Grepo | — | — | — |
| Krefeld | — | — | — | AuDSt. | AuDSt. | AuSt. | FP, LS |
| Krems | — | — | — | — | AuP. | AuSt. | — |
| Kremsier | — | — | — | AuDSt. | — | — | — |
| Krenau | — | — | — | — | AuP. | AuSt. | — |
| Kreuzburg | — | — | — | — | AuP. | AuSt. | — |
| Kronach | — | — | — | — | — | AuSt. | — |
| Krotoschin | — | — | — | — | AuP. | — | — |
| Krummau/Moldau | — | — | — | Greko | AuP. | AuSt. | — |
| Küstrin | — | — | — | — | AuP. | AuSt. | SW-Wache, LS |
| Kufstein | — | — | — | — | — | AuSt. | — |
| Kulm | — | — | — | — | AuP. | — | — |
| Kulmbach | — | — | — | — | AuP. | — | — |
| Kulmsee | — | — | — | — | AuP. | — | — |
| Kupfermühle | — | — | — | Grepo | — | — | — |
| Kutno/Posen | — | — | — | Greko | AuP. | AuSt. | — |
| Laak | — | — | — | AuDSt. | AuDSt. | AuSt. | — |
| Laas | — | — | — | Grepo | — | — | — |
| Labiau | — | — | — | — | — | AuSt.* | — |
| Laboe | — | — | — | Grepo | — | — | — |
| Lahr | — | — | PA | — | AuP. | AuSt. | — |
| Lampertheim | — | — | — | — | AuP. | — | — |
| Landau/Pfalz | — | — | — | Greko | AuP. | — | — |
| Landeck | — | — | — | — | — | AuSt. | — |
| Landeshut | — | — | — | — | AuP. | — | — |
| Landsberg/Lech | — | — | — | — | — | AuSt. | — |
| Landsberg/Warthe | — | — | — | AuDSt. | AuDSt. | AuSt. | — |
| Landshut/Isar | — | — | — | — | AuP. | AuSt. | — |
| Landshut/Mähren | — | — | — | Grepo | — | — | — |
| Landskron | — | — | — | AuDSt. | — | — | — |
| Langenberg | — | — | — | — | AuP. | — | — |
| Langenbielau | — | — | — | — | AuP. | — | — |
| Langenfeld | — | — | — | — | AuP. | — | — |
| Langensalza | — | — | — | — | AuP. | AuSt. | — |
| Langeoog | — | — | — | — | — | — | LS |
| Lauban | — | — | — | — | AuP. | — | — |
| Laubweiler | — | — | — | Grepo | — | — | — |
| Lauenburg | — | — | — | — | AuP. | — | — |
| Laugszargen- Tauroggen | — | — | — | Grepo | — | — | — |
| Leer/Ostfriesland | — | — | — | — | AuP. | AuSt. | — |
| Lehrte | — | — | — | — | AuP. | — | — |
| Leibnitz | — | — | — | Greko | — | — | — |
| Leipe | — | — | — | — | AuP. | — | — |

| Town | (a) HSSPf (b) BdO (c) BdS | Higher Police Authorities (Höhere Polizei Behörden) | National Police Head-quarters (Staatliche Polizei Ver-waltungen) | Sicherheits Polizei | | SD | Others |
|------|------|------|------|------|------|------|------|
| | | | | Gestapo | Kripo | | |
| 1 | 2 | 3 | 4 | 5 | 6 | 7 | 8 |
| Leipzig | — | — | PP | St. | HAuSt. | AuSt. | FP, Wm., LS |
| Leitmeritz | — | — | — | AuDSt. | AuP. | AuSt. | — |
| Lemgo | — | — | — | — | AuP. | — | — |
| Lengerich | — | — | — | — | AuP. | — | — |
| Lentschütz | — | — | — | AuDSt. | — | AuSt. | — |
| Leoben | — | — | PD | AuDSt. | AuDSt. | AuSt. | LS |
| Leobschütz | — | — | — | — | AuP. | — | — |
| Leslau | — | — | PD | AuDSt. | AuDSt. | AuSt. | SW-Wache, Wm. |
| Leuna | — | — | — | — | AuDSt. | — | — |
| Leverkusen | — | — | — | — | AuP. | — | LS |
| Lichtenfels | — | — | — | — | — | AuSt. | — |
| Lichtenstein | — | — | — | — | AuP. | — | — |
| Liegnitz | — | RPräs. | — | AuDSt. | AuDSt. | HAuSt. | FP, LS |
| Lienz/Drau | — | — | — | Greko | — | AuSt. | — |
| Liezen | — | — | — | — | — | AuSt. | — |
| Limbach | — | — | — | — | AuP. | — | — |
| Limburg/Lahn | — | — | — | AuDSt. | AuP. | AuSt. | — |
| Lindau | — | — | — | — | AuP. | AuSt. | — |
| Lingen | — | — | — | — | AuP. | — | — |
| Linz/Donau | — | RSth. | PP | St. | St. | Abs. | FP, SW-Rev., Wm., LS |
| Lippstadt | — | — | — | — | AuP. | AuSt. | — |
| Lissa | — | — | — | AuDSt. | AuP. | AuSt. | — |
| Littai | — | — | — | AuDSt. | AuDSt. | AuSt. | — |
| Litzmannstadt | — | RPräs. | PP | St. | St. | Abs. | FP, Wm., LS |
| Loben | — | — | — | Greko | AuP. | AuSt. | — |
| Lobith | — | — | — | Grepo | — | — | — |
| Löbau/Sachsen | — | — | — | — | AuP. | AuSt. | — |
| Löbau/Westpr. | — | — | — | — | AuP. | — | — |
| Lörrach | — | — | PA | Greko | AuP. | AuSt. | — |
| Lötzen | — | — | — | AuDSt. | AuP. | — | LS |
| Lohr/Main | — | — | — | — | — | AuSt. | — |
| Lublinitz | — | — | — | Greko | — | — | — |
| Luckenwalde | — | — | — | — | AuP. | — | — |
| Ludwigsburg | — | — | PD | — | AuP. | — | FP |
| Ludwigshafen | — | — | PP | AuDSt. | St. | HAuSt. | FP, SW-Wache, LS |
| Ludwigslust | — | — | — | — | — | AuSt. | — |
| Lübeck | — | — | PP | Greko | AuDSt. | HAuSt. | FP, SW-Rev., Wm., LS |
| Lüdenscheid | — | — | — | — | AuP. | AuSt. | — |
| Lüdinghausen | — | — | — | — | — | AuSt. | — |
| Lüneburg | — | RPräs. | PD | AuDSt. | AuDSt. | HAuSt. | — |
| Lünen | — | — | — | — | AuP. | — | — |
| Lugau | — | — | — | — | AuP. | — | — |
| Lundenburg | — | — | — | Greko | AuP. | — | — |
| Lustenau | — | — | — | Grepo | — | — | — |
| Luttenberg | — | — | — | — | — | AuSt. | — |
| Luxemburg | — | — | PD | Greko | AuDSt. | HAuSt. | LS |
| Lyck | — | — | — | Greko | AuP. | AuSt. | — |
| Mährisch-Ostrau | — | — | PD | AuDSt. | AuDSt. | HAuSt. | LS |
| Mährisch-Schönberg | — | — | — | AuDSt. | AuP. | AuSt. | — |
| Mährisch Weisskirchen | — | — | — | AuDSt. | — | — | — |
| Magdeburg | — | RPräs. b. OPräs. | PP | LSt. | St. | AuSt. | SW-Kdo., Wm., LS |
| Mainz | — | — | PP | AuDSt. | AuDSt. | AuSt. | FP, SW-Station, LS |
| Malchin | — | — | — | AuDSt. | — | AuSt. | — |
| Malmedy | — | — | — | Greko | — | AuSt. | — |
| Maltheuern | — | — | — | — | AuDSt. | — | — |
| Mannheim | — | — | PP | AuDSt. | AuDSt. | HAuSt. | FP, SW-Posten, Wm., LS |

| Town | (a) HSSPf (b) BdO (c) BdS | Higher Police Authorities (Höhere Polizei Behörden) | National Police Head-quarters (Staatliche Polizei Ver-waltungen) | Sicherheits Polizei | | SD | Others |
| | | | | Gestapo | Kripo | | |
| 1 | 2 | 3 | 4 | 5 | 6 | 7 | 8 |
|---|---|---|---|---|---|---|---|
| Mansfeld | — | — | — | — | — | AuSt. | — |
| Marburg/Drau | — | — | PD | (Kdr. d. Sipo & SD) | | | LS |
| Marburg/Lahn | — | — | — | — | AuP. | AuSt. | — |
| Marchegg | — | — | — | — | AuP. | — | — |
| Marienbad | — | — | — | AuDSt. | AuP. | AuSt. | — |
| Marienberg | — | — | — | — | — | AuSt. | — |
| Marienburg | — | — | — | — | AuP. | — | — |
| Marienwerder | — | RPräs. | — | AuDSt. | AuP. | — | — |
| Markirch | — | — | — | — | AuP. | — | — |
| Markkleeberg | — | — | — | — | AuP. | — | — |
| Marktheidenfeld | — | — | — | — | — | AuSt. | — |
| Markt-Oberdorf | — | — | — | — | — | AuSt. | — |
| Markt Pongau | — | — | — | — | — | AuSt. | — |
| Marktredwitz | — | — | — | — | AuP. | — | — |
| Marl | — | —* | — | — | AuDSt. | — | — |
| Mayen | — | — | — | — | AuP. | AuSt. | — |
| Meerane | — | — | — | — | AuP. | — | — |
| Meiningen | — | — | — | — | AuP. | AuSt. | — |
| Meissen | — | — | — | — | AuP. | AuSt. | — |
| Memel | — | — | PD | Greko | AuDSt. | AuSt.* | FP, SW-Rev., LS |
| Memmingen | — | — | — | — | AuP. | AuSt. | — |
| Menden | — | — | — | — | AuP. | — | — |
| Meppen | — | — | — | Greko AuDSt. | — | — | SW-Wache |
| Merseburg | — | RPräs. b. OPräs. | PA | AuDSt. | AuP. | AuSt. | — |
| Merzig | — | — | — | AuDSt. | — | — | — |
| Meschede | — | — | — | AuDSt. | — | AuSt. | — |
| Mettmann | — | — | — | — | AuP. | — | — |
| Metz | a, b, c | — | PP | (Kdr. d. Sipo & SD) | | | Wm., FP, LS |
| Meuselwitz | — | — | — | — | AuP. | — | — |
| Mielau | — | — | — | — | AuP. | AuSt. | — |
| Mies | — | — | — | AuDSt. | — | — | — |
| Miesbach | — | — | — | — | — | AuSt. | — |
| Militsch | — | — | — | AuDSt. | — | — | — |
| Milspe-Voerde | — | — | — | — | AuP. | — | — |
| Mindelheim | — | — | — | — | — | AuSt. | — |
| Minden | — | RPräs. | — | — | AuDSt. | AuSt. | SW-Wache, LS |
| Miroschau | — | — | — | AEL. | — | — | — |
| Mistelbach | — | — | — | — | — | AuSt. | — |
| Mittweida | — | — | — | — | AuP. | — | — |
| Modlin-Bugmünde | — | — | — | Greko | — | — | — |
| Mödling/Wien | — | — | — | — | — | — | Wm. |
| Mölln/Schleswig | — | — | — | — | — | AuSt. | — |
| Mörs | — | — | — | — | AuP. | AuSt. | — |
| Mövern | — | — | — | Grepo | — | — | — |
| Mohrungen | — | — | — | — | — | AuSt. | — |
| Molsheim | — | — | — | — | — | AuSt. | — |
| Mosbach | — | — | — | DSt. | — | — | — |
| Mosty | — | — | — | Grepo | — | — | — |
| Mücheln | — | — | — | — | AuP. | — | — |
| Mühlhausen/ Thüringen | — | — | — | — | AuDSt. | AuSt. | — |
| Mühlviertel | — | — | — | — | — | AuSt. | — |
| Mülhausen/Elsass | — | — | PP | AuDSt. | AuDSt. | AuSt. | FP, Wm., LS |
| Mülheim/Ruhr | — | — | PA | AuDSt. | AuDSt. | AuSt. | FP |
| Müllheim/Baden | — | — | — | Greko | — | AuSt. | — |
| Münchberg | — | — | — | — | — | AuSt. | — |
| München | a, b, c | RPräs. | PP | LSt. | LSt. | LAbs. | FP, Wm., LS |
| München-Gladbach-Rheydt | — | — | PP | AuDSt. | AuDSt. | AuSt. | FP, Wm., LS |
| Münster/Westf. | b | RPräs. | PP | LSt. | AuDSt. | Abs. | FP, SW-Wache, LS |
| Mürzzuschlag | — | — | — | — | — | AuSt. | — |
| Murau | — | — | — | Grepo | — | AuSt. | — |

| Town | (a) HSSPf (b) BdO (c) BdS | Higher Police Authorities (Höhere Polizei Behörden) | National Police Head-quarters (Staatliche Polizei Ver-waltungen) | Sicherheits Polizei | | SD | Others |
|---|---|---|---|---|---|---|---|
| | | | | Gestapo | Kripo | | |
| 1 | 2 | 5 | 4 | 5 | 6 | 7 | 8 |
| Mureck | — | — | — | Grepo | — | AuSt. | — |
| Nabburg | — | — | — | — | — | AuSt. | — |
| Nakel | — | — | — | — | AuP. | — | — |
| Nauders/Tirol | — | — | — | Grepo | — | — | — |
| Nauen | — | — | — | — | AuP. | — | — |
| Naumburg | — | — | — | — | AuP. | — | — |
| Neheim-Hüsten | — | — | — | — | AuP. | — | — |
| Neidenburg | — | — | — | AuD St. | — | — | — |
| Neisse | — | — | — | AuDSt. | AuP. | AuSt. | — |
| Neu-Brandenburg | — | — | — | — | AuP. | — | — |
| Neuburg/Donau | — | — | — | — | — | AuSt. | — |
| Neuburg/Lothr. | — | — | — | Grepo | — | — | — |
| Neugersdorf | — | — | — | — | AuP. | — | — |
| Neu-Isenburg | — | — | — | — | AuP. | — | — |
| Neukirchen-Vluyn | — | — | — | — | AuP. | — | — |
| Neumark | — | — | — | — | AuP. | — | — |
| Neumarkt/Obpf. | — | — | — | — | — | AuSt. | — |
| Neumünster | — | — | — | AuSt. | AuDSt. | AuSt. | FP |
| Neunkirchen/ Niederdonau | — | — | — | — | AuP. | — | — |
| Neunkirchen/Saar | — | — | — | AuDSt. | AuDSt. | AuSt. | — |
| Neu-Oderberg | — | — | — | — | AuP. | — | — |
| Neurode | — | — | — | — | AuP. | — | — |
| Neuruppin | — | — | — | — | AuP. | AuSt. | — |
| Neusalz | — | — | — | — | AuP. | — | — |
| Neuss | — | — | — | — | AuDSt. | AuSt. | — |
| Neustadt/Aisch | — | — | — | — | — | AuSt. | — |
| Neustadt/Holst. | — | — | — | Grepo | — | — | — |
| Neustadt/Ob. Schl. | — | — | — | AuDSt. | AuP. | AuSt. | — |
| Neustadt/ Rübenberge | — | — | — | — | — | AuSt. | — |
| Neustadt/Schwarzw. | — | — | — | — | — | AuSt.* | — |
| Neustadt/Weinstr. | — | — | — | AuDSt. | AuP. | HAuSt. | — |
| Neustadt/Westpr. | — | — | — | — | AuP. | — | — |
| Neustettin | — | — | — | AuDSt. | AuP. | AuSt. | — |
| Neustrelitz | — | — | — | AuDSt. | AuP. | AuSt. | — |
| Neutitschein | — | — | — | AuDSt. | AuP. | AuSt. | — |
| Neu-Ulm | — | — | — | — | AuP. | — | — |
| Neuwied | — | — | — | — | AuP. | AuSt. | LS |
| Niebüll | — | — | — | Grepo | — | — | — |
| Niedersulzbach | — | — | — | Grepo | — | — | — |
| Nienburg/Weser | — | — | — | AuDSt. | AuP. | AuSt. | — |
| Nikolai | — | — | — | — | AuP. | — | — |
| Norden | — | — | — | — | AuP. | — | — |
| Nordenham | — | — | — | Greko | — | AuSt.* | — |
| Norderney | — | — | — | — | — | — | LS |
| Nordhausen | — | — | — | — | AuDSt. | AuSt. | LS |
| Nordhorn | — | — | — | AuDSt. | AuP. | AuSt. | — |
| Nordhorn- Frensdorferhaar | — | — | — | Grepo | — | — | — |
| Northeim | — | — | — | — | AuP. | AuSt. | — |
| Nürnberg-Fürth | a, b, c | — | PP | LSt. | LSt. | LAbs. | FP, Wm., LS |
| Nürtingen | — | — | — | — | AuP. | — | — |
| Oberhausen | — | — | PP | AuD St. | AuDSt. | AuSt. | FP, Wm., LS |
| Oberleutensdorf | — | — | — | — | AuDSt. | — | — |
| Oberlitsch | — | — | — | Grepo | — | — | — |
| Oberndorf/Neckar | — | — | — | AuDSt. | — | — | — |
| Oberndorf-Aistaig | — | — | — | AEL. | — | — | — |
| Oberwart | — | — | — | — | — | AuSt. | — |
| Oels | — | — | — | — | AuP. | AuSt. | — |
| Oelsnitz/Erzg. | — | — | — | — | AuP. | — | — |
| Oelsnitz/Vogtl. | — | — | — | — | AuP. | — | — |
| Offenbach/Main | — | — | PD | AuDSt.* | AuDSt. | AuSt. | FP |
| Offenburg | — | — | PA | AuDSt. | AuP. | AuSt. | — |

K14

| Town | (a) HSSPf (b) BdO (c) BdS | Higher Police Authorities (Höhere Polizei Behörden) | National Police Head-quarters (Staatliche Polizei Ver-waltungen) | Sicherheits Polizei | | SD | Others |
|---|---|---|---|---|---|---|---|
| | | | | Gestapo | Kripo | | |
| 1 | 2 | 3 | 4 | 5 | 6 | 7 | 8 |
| Ohlau | — | — | — | — | AuP. | — | — |
| Olbernhau | — | — | — | — | AuP. | — | — |
| Oldenburg/Holstein | — | — | — | AuDSt. | — | — | — |
| Oldenburg/O. | — | IMin. | — | { AuDSt. Greko | AuDSt. | AuSt. | FP, SW-Wache, LS |
| Olmütz | — | — | PD | AuDSt. | AuDSt. | AuSt. | LS |
| Olpe | — | — | — | — | AuP. | — | — |
| Opladen | — | — | — | — | AuP. | AuSt. | — |
| Oppeln | — | RPräs. | PD | St. | St. | HAuSt. | Wm., LS |
| Oranienburg | — | — | — | — | AuP. | — | LS |
| Ortelsburg | — | — | — | { AuDSt. Greko | AuP. | — | — |
| Oschatz | — | — | — | — | AuP. | AuSt. | — |
| Oschersleben | — | — | — | — | AuP. | AuSt. | — |
| Oslo/Norway | a, b, c | — | — | — | — | — | — |
| Osnabrück | — | RPräs. | PD | AuDSt. | AuDSt. | HAuSt. | FP, LS |
| Ostenburg | — | — | — | Grepo | AuP. | AuSt.* | — |
| Osterburg | — | — | — | — | — | AuSt. | — |
| Osterode/Harz | — | — | — | — | — | AuSt. | — |
| Osterode/Ostpr. | — | — | — | — | AuP. | AuSt. | — |
| Ostrolenka | — | — | — | Greko | — | — | — |
| Ostrowo | — | — | — | — | AuP. | — | — |
| Pabianice | — | — | PA | — | AuDSt. | AuSt. | |
| Paderborn | — | — | — | AuDSt. | AuDSt. | AuSt. | |
| Papenburg | — | — | — | — | AuP. | — | |
| Parchim | — | — | — | — | AuP. | AuSt. | |
| Pardubitz | — | — | — | AuDSt. | AuDSt. | AuSt. | |
| Pasewalk | — | — | — | — | AuP. | AuSt.* | |
| Passau | — | — | — | — | AuP. | AuSt. | |
| Peine | — | — | — | — | AuP. | AuSt. | LS |
| Pelkum | — | — | — | — | AuP. | — | — |
| Perleberg | — | — | — | — | AuP. | — | — |
| Pettau | — | — | — | AuDSt. | — | AuSt. | — |
| Pforzheim | — | — | PD | DSt. | AuDSt. | AuSt. | — |
| Pfullendorf | — | — | — | — | — | AuSt. | — |
| Pilgrams | — | — | — | — | — | AuSt. | — |
| Pillau | — | — | — | Greko | AuP. | — | SW-Station, LS |
| Pilsen | — | — | PD | AuDSt. | AuDSt. | HAuSt. | LS |
| Pinneberg | — | — | — | — | AuP. | — | — |
| Pirmasens | — | — | — | — | AuDSt. | AuSt. | — |
| Pirna | — | — | — | — | AuP. | AuSt. | — |
| Plan/Leisitz | — | — | — | AEL. | — | — | — |
| Planitz | — | — | — | — | AuP. | — | — |
| Plauen | — | — | PP | AuDSt. | AuDSt. | AuSt. | FP, Wm. |
| Pleschen | — | — | — | — | AuP. | — | — |
| Pless | — | — | — | — | — | AuSt. | — |
| Plettenberg | — | — | — | — | AuP. | — | — |
| Plöhnen | — | — | — | — | AuP. | AuSt. | — |
| Pössneck | — | — | — | — | AuP. | — | — |
| Polstrau | — | — | — | AuDSt. | AuDSt. | AuSt. | — |
| Polzin | — | — | — | — | AuP. | — | — |
| Porz | — | — | — | — | AuP. | — | — |
| Posen | a, b, c | RPräs. | PP | I.St. | LSt. | LAbs. | FP, SW-Rev., Wm., LS |
| Posen-Lenzingen | — | — | — | AEL. | — | — | — |
| Potsdam | — | RPräs. | PP | St. | AuDSt. | HAuSt. | FP, SW-Rev., Wm., LS |
| Prag | a, b, c | LdsReg. | PP | LSt. | LSt. | LAbs. | FP, Wm., LS |
| Prävali | — | — | — | AuDSt. | — | — | — |
| Praschnitz | — | — | — | — | AuP. | AuSt.* | — |
| Prenzlau | — | — | — | — | AuP. | — | — |
| Prerau | — | — | — | AuDSt. | — | — | — |
| Pr. Eylau | — | — | — | — | — | AuSt.* | — |
| Preuss. Stargard | — | — | — | — | AuP. | — | — |

| Town | (a) HSSPf (b) BdO (c) BdS | Higher Police Authorities (Höhere Polizei Behörden) | National Police Head-quarters (Staatliche Polizei Verwaltungen) | Sicherheits Polizei | | SD | Others |
|---|---|---|---|---|---|---|---|
| | | | | Gestapo | Kripo | | |
| 1 | 2 | 3 | 4 | 5 | 6 | 7 | 8 |
| Prossnitz | — | — | — | AuDSt. | — | — | — |
| Prüm | — | — | — | AuDSt. | — | AuSt. | — |
| Pyritz | — | — | — | — | AuP. | AuSt.* | — |
| Quedlinburg | — | — | — | — | AuP. | AuSt. | — |
| Radeberg | — | — | — | — | AuP. | — | — |
| Radebeul | — | — | — | — | AuP. | — | — |
| Radevormwald | — | — | — | — | AuP. | — | — |
| Radkersburg | — | — | — | Grepo | — | — | — |
| Radmannsdorf/ Kärnten | — | — | — | AuDSt. | AuDSt. | AuSt. | — |
| Radolfzell | — | — | — | — | AuP. | — | — |
| Ragnit | — | — | Z | — | — | — | — |
| Raguhn | — | — | — | — | — | AuSt. | — |
| Rann | — | — | — | AuDSt. | AuP. | AuSt. | — |
| Rastatt | — | — | PA | DSt. | AuP. | AuSt. | — |
| Rastenburg | — | — | — | AuDSt. | AuP. | AuSt. | — |
| Rathenow | — | — | — | — | AuP. | AuSt. | SW-Wache |
| Ratibor | — | — | — | AuDSt. | AuDSt. | AuSt. | — |
| Ratingen | — | — | — | — | AuP. | — | — |
| Ratschach-Matten | — | — | — | Grepo | — | — | — |
| Rattwitz | — | — | — | AEL. | — | — | — |
| Ravensburg | — | — | — | — | AuP. | AuSt. | — |
| Rawitsch | — | — | — | — | AuP. | — | — |
| Recklinghausen | — | — | PP | AuDSt. | St. | AuSt. | SW-Rev., Wm., LS |
| Recklinghausen-Suderich | — | — | — | — | AuDSt. | — | — |
| Recklinghausen-Süd | — | — | — | — | Au DSt. | — | — |
| Regensburg | — | RPräs. | PD | St. | St. | AuSt. | FP, SW-Wache, Wm., LS |
| Reichenbach/ Eulengebirge | — | — | — | — | AuP. | — | — |
| Reichenbach/Vogtl. | — | — | — | — | AuP. | — | — |
| Reichenberg | — | — | PP | LSt. | St. | Abs. | — |
| Reichenhall | — | — | — | — | AuP. | — | — |
| Reichenthal | — | — | — | Grepo | — | — | — |
| Remscheid | — | — | PA | — | AuDSt. | AuSt. | FP |
| Renchen | — | — | — | — | — | AuSt. | — |
| Rendsburg | — | — | — | AuDSt. | AuP. | AuSt. | — |
| Repelen-Baerl | — | — | — | — | AuP. | — | — |
| Reppen | — | — | — | — | — | AuSt. | — |
| Reutlingen | — | — | PA | — | AuP. | — | — |
| Reutte | — | — | — | — | — | AuSt. | — |
| Rheine | — | — | — | — | AuP. | — | — |
| Rheinhausen | — | — | — | — | AuP. | — | LS |
| Ried/Innkr. | — | — | — | — | — | AuSt. | — |
| Riedenburg | — | — | — | — | — | AuSt. | — |
| Riesa | — | — | — | — | AuP. | — | LS |
| Rinteln | — | — | — | — | — | AuSt. | — |
| Rippin | — | — | — | AuDSt. | AuP. | — | — |
| Rochlitz | — | — | — | — | — | AuSt. | — |
| Rodenkirchen | — | — | — | — | AuP. | — | — |
| Rodewisch | — | — | — | — | AuP. | — | — |
| Rodingen | — | — | — | Grepo | — | — | — |
| Rosenberg | — | — | — | AuDSt. | AuP. | — | — |
| Rosenheim | — | — | — | — | AuP. | AuSt. | — |
| Rostock | — | — | PP | Greko | AuDSt. | AuSt. | FP, SW-Rev., Wm., LS |
| Rottweil | — | — | — | — | AuP. | AuSt. | — |
| Rudersberg | — | — | — | AEL. | — | — | — |
| Rudolstadt | — | — | — | — | AuP. | AuSt. | — |
| Rüdesheim | — | — | — | — | — | AuSt. | — |
| Rügenwalde | — | — | — | — | AuP. | — | — |

K16

| Town | (a) HSSPf (b) BdO (c) BdS | Higher Police Authorities (Höhere Polizei Behörden) | National Police Head-quarters (Staatliche Polizei Verwaltungen) | Sicherheits Polizei | | SD | Others |
|---|---|---|---|---|---|---|---|
| | | | | Gestapo | Kripo | | |
| 1 | 2 | 3 | 4 | 5 | 6 | 7 | 8 |
| Rüsselsheim | — | — | — | — | AuP. | — | — |
| Rumburg | — | — | — | — | — | AuSt. | — |
| Rummelsburg | — | — | — | — | AuP. | — | — |
| Rybnik | — | — | — | AuDSt. | AuP. | AuSt. | — |
| Rydultau | — | — | — | — | AuP. | — | — |
| Saal/Elsass | — | — | — | Grepo | — | — | — |
| Saalfeld | — | — | — | — | AuP. | — | — |
| Saarbrücken | a, b | RSth. | PP | St. | St. | Abs. | FP, Wm., LS |
| Saarburg | — | — | — | AuDSt. | AuDSt. | AuSt. | — |
| Saargemünd | — | — | — | AuDSt. | AuDSt. | AuSt. | — |
| Saarlautern | — | — | — | AuSt. | AuP. | AuSt. | — |
| Saaz | — | — | — | { Greko AuDSt. | AuP. | AuSt. | — |
| Säckingen | — | — | — | — | — | AuSt. | — |
| Sagan | — | — | — | DSt. | AuP. | — | — |
| Salzburg | a, b, c | RSth. | PD | St. | LSt. | HAuSt. | FP, Wm., LS SW-Wache |
| Salzgitter | — | — | — | AuDSt. | AuP. | — | — |
| Salzwedel | — | — | — | — | AuP. | AuSt. | — |
| Samter | — | — | — | AuDSt. | AuP. | AuSt. | — |
| Sangerhausen | — | — | — | — | AuP. | AuSt. | — |
| Sassnitz | — | — | — | Grepo | — | — | — |
| Sauerbrunn | — | — | — | Grepo | — | — | — |
| Saybusch | — | — | — | — | AuP. | — | — |
| Schärding | — | — | — | — | — | AuSt. | — |
| Scharfenwiese | — | — | — | Greko | AuP. | AuSt. | — |
| Schieratz | — | — | — | AuDSt. | AuP. | — | — |
| Schirwindt | — | — | — | Grepo | — | — | — |
| Schivelbein | — | — | — | — | AuP. | — | — |
| Schkeuditz | — | — | — | — | AuP. | — | — |
| Schkopau | — | — | — | — | AuDSt. | — | — |
| Schlawe | — | — | — | — | AuP. | — | — |
| Schleiden | — | — | — | — | — | AuSt. | — |
| Schleswig | — | RPräs. | — | — | AuP. | AuSt. | — |
| Schlettstadt | — | — | — | — | AuP. | AuSt. | — |
| Schmalkalden | — | — | — | — | AuP. | — | — |
| Schmalleningken | — | — | — | Grepo | — | — | — |
| Schmölln | — | — | — | — | AuP. | — | — |
| Schneeberg | — | — | — | — | AuP. | — | — |
| Schneidemühl | — | RPräs. | — | AuDSt. | St. | AuSt. | — |
| Schönbrunn | — | — | — | AuDSt. | — | — | — |
| Schönebeck | — | — | — | — | AuP. | — | LS |
| Schramberg | — | — | PA | — | AuP. | — | — |
| Schrobenhausen | — | — | — | — | — | AuSt. | — |
| Schroda | — | — | — | — | — | AuSt. | — |
| Schröttersburg | — | — | — | — | AuP. | AuSt. | — |
| Schwabach | — | — | — | — | AuP. | AuSt. | — |
| Schwäbisch Gmünd | — | — | PA | — | AuP. | — | — |
| Schwäbisch Hall | — | — | — | — | AuP. | AuSt. | — |
| Schwandorf | — | — | — | — | AuP. | AuSt. | — |
| Schwarzenberg | — | — | — | — | — | AuSt. | — |
| Schwaz | — | — | — | — | AuP. | AuSt. | — |
| Schweidnitz | — | — | — | — | AuP. | AuSt. | LS |
| Schweinfurt | — | — | — | — | AuP. | — | — |
| Schwelm | — | — | PA | — | AuP. | — | — |
| Schwerin | — | StMin. AI. | — | St. | St. | Abs. | FP |
| Schwerte | — | — | — | — | AuP. | — | — |
| Schwetz | — | — | — | AuDSt.* | AuP. | — | — |
| Schwetzingen | — | — | — | — | AuP. | — | — |
| Schwiebus | — | — | — | { Greko AuDSt. | AuP. | AuSt. | — |
| Sebnitz | — | — | — | — | AuP. | — | — |
| Selb | — | — | — | — | AuP. | AuSt. | — |
| Senftenberg | — | — | — | — | AuP. | — | — |

c

| Town | (a) HSSPf (b) BdO (c) BdS | Higher Police Authorities (Höhere Polizei Behörden) | National Police Headquarters (Staatliche Polizei Verwaltungen) | Sicherheits Polizei | | SD | Others |
|---|---|---|---|---|---|---|---|
| | | | | Gestapo | Kripo | | |
| 1 | 2 | 3 | 4 | 5 | 6 | 7 | 8 |
| Sensburg | — | — | — | — | — | AuSt. | — |
| Sichelberg | — | — | — | — | — | AuSt.* | — |
| Siegburg | — | — | — | — | AuP. | AuSt. | — |
| Siegen | — | — | — | AuDSt. | AuDSt. | AuSt. | LS |
| Siegmar-Schönau | — | — | — | — | AuP. | — | |
| Sigmaringen | — | RPräs. | — | AuDSt. | — | AuSt. | — |
| Sillian | — | — | — | Grepo | — | — | — |
| Simmern | — | — | — | — | — | AuSt. | — |
| Singen/Hohentwiel | — | — | — | Greko | AuP. | AuSt. | — |
| Sömmerda | — | — | — | — | AuP. | — | — |
| Soest | — | — | — | — | AuP. | — | — |
| Solingen | — | — | PA | AuDSt. | AuDSt. | AuSt. | — |
| Soltau | — | — | — | AuDSt. | — | — | — |
| Sommerfeld | — | — | — | AuDSt. | AuP. | — | — |
| Sondershausen | — | — | — | — | AuP. | AuSt. | — |
| Sonneberg | — | — | — | — | AuP. | AuSt. | — |
| Sonthofen | — | — | — | — | — | AuSt. | — |
| Sorau | — | — | — | — | AuP. | AuSt. | — |
| Sosnowitz | — | — | PP | AuDSt. | AuDSt. | AuSt. | FP, LS |
| Spaichingen | — | — | — | — | — | AuSt. | — |
| Spandau | — | — | — | — | — | — | SW-Rev. |
| Speyer | — | — | — | — | AuP. | — | — |
| Spielfeld | — | — | — | Grepo | — | — | — |
| Spittal/Drau | — | — | — | AuDSt. | — | AuSt. | — |
| Spremberg | — | — | — | — | AuP. | — | — |
| Springbiel | — | — | — | Grepo | — | — | — |
| Springe | — | — | — | — | — | AuSt. | — |
| St. Avold | — | — | — | AuDSt. | AuDSt. | AuSt. | — |
| St. Ingbert/Saar | — | — | — | AuSt. | AuP. | — | — |
| St. Ludwig | — | — | — | Grepo | — | — | — |
| St. Pölten | — | — | PD | AuDSt. | AuDSt. | AuSt. | LS |
| St. Veit/Glan | — | — | — | — | — | AuSt. | — |
| St. Veit/Save | — | — | — | Grepo | — | — | — |
| Stade | — | RPräs. | — | AuDSt. | AuP. | AuSt. | — |
| Stadt des KdF Wagens | — | — | — | AuDSt. | — | — | — |
| Stargard | — | — | — | — | AuP. | AuSt. | — |
| Starnberg | — | — | — | — | — | AuSt. | — |
| Stassfurt | — | — | — | — | AuP. | — | — |
| Stavanger/Norway | — | — | — | (Kdr. d. Sipo & SD) | | | — |
| Stavenhagen | — | — | — | AuDSt. | — | — | — |
| Stein/Steineralpen | — | — | — | AuDSt. | AuDSt. | AuSt. | — |
| Stendal | — | — | — | — | AuP. | AuSt. | LS |
| Sternberg | — | — | — | — | AuP. | — | — |
| Stettin | a, b, c | RPräs. | PP | LSt. | LSt. | LAbs. | FP, SW-Abs.-kdo., Wm., LS |
| Steyr | — | — | PA | AuDSt. | AuP. | AuSt. | LS |
| Stockach | — | — | — | — | — | AuSt. | — |
| Stolberg/Rhld. | — | — | — | — | AuP. | — | — |
| Stollberg/Erzgeb. | — | — | — | — | AuP. | AuSt. | — |
| Stolp | — | — | — | { Greko AuDSt. | AuDSt. | AuSt. | — |
| Stolpmünde | — | — | — | Grepo | — | — | — |
| Strakonitz | — | — | — | — | — | AuSt. | — |
| Stralsund | — | — | — | Greko | AuDSt. | AuSt. | FP, SW-Station, LS |
| Strasburg/Westpr. | — | — | — | — | AuP. | — | — |
| Strassburg | a, b, c | PP | — | — | LSt. (Kdr. d. Sipo & SD) | — | FP, SW-Station, Wm., LS |
| Straubing | — | — | — | — | AuP. | AuSt. | — |
| Strausberg | — | — | — | — | AuP. | — | — |
| Strehlen | — | — | — | — | AuP. | — | — |
| Striegau | — | — | — | — | AuP. | — | — |
| Stuttgart | a, b, c | IMin. | PP | LSt. | LSt. | LAbs. | FP, Wm., LS |
| Süderlügum | — | — | — | Grepo | — | — | — |

| Town | (a) HSSPf (b) BdO (c) BdS | Higher Police Authorities (Höhere Polizei Behörden) | National Police Head-quarters (Staatliche Polizei Verwaltungen) | Sicherheits Polizei — Gestapo | Sicherheits Polizei — Kripo | SD | Others |
|---|---|---|---|---|---|---|---|
| 1 | 2 | 3 | 4 | 5 | 6 | 7 | 8 |
| Suhl | — | — | PD | AuDSt. | AuP. | AuSt. | LS |
| Sulzbach | — | — | — | — | AuDSt. | — | — |
| Suwalki (Sudauen) | — | — | — | Greko | AuDSt. | — | — |
| Swinemünde | — | — | — | Greko | AuP. | AuSt. | SW-Station, LS |
| Sylt | — | — | — | — | — | AuSt. | — |
| Tabor | — | — | — | AuDSt. | AuDSt. | AuSt. | — |
| Tailfingen | — | — | — | — | AuP. | — | — |
| Tamsweg | — | — | — | — | — | AuSt. | — |
| Tangermünde | — | — | — | — | AuP. | — | — |
| Tann | — | — | — | — | AuP. | AuSt. | — |
| Tarnowitz | — | — | — | — | AuP. | — | — |
| Tauberbischofsheim | — | — | — | — | — | AuSt. | — |
| Taucha | — | — | — | — | AuP. | — | — |
| Tecklenburg | — | — | — | — | — | AuSt. | — |
| Teltow | — | — | — | — | AuP. | — | — |
| Templin | — | — | — | — | — | AuSt. | — |
| Teplitz-Schönau | — | — | PA | AuDSt. | AuDSt. | AuSt. | — |
| Teschen | — | — | — | Greko | AuP. | AuSt. | — |
| Tetschen | — | — | — | — | — | AuSt. | — |
| Tetschen-Bodenbach | — | — | — | — | AuP. | — | — |
| Thale | — | — | — | — | AuP. | — | — |
| Theresienstadt | — | — | — | Pol.Gef. | — | — | — |
| Thörl-Maglern | — | — | — | Grepo | — | — | — |
| Thorn | — | — | PD | AuDSt. | AuDSt. | AuSt. | FP, SW-Station |
| Tilsit | — | — | PD | St. | St. | AuSt. | FP, SW-Rev., Wm. |
| Torgau | — | — | — | AuDSt. | AuP. | AuSt. | — |
| Torgelow | — | — | — | — | AuP. | — | — |
| Traunstein | — | — | — | — | AuP. | AuSt. | — |
| Trautenau | — | — | — | AuDSt. | AuP. | AuSt. | — |
| Travemünde | — | — | — | Grepo | — | — | — |
| Trebitsch | — | — | — | — | — | AuSt. | — |
| Trebnitz | — | — | — | — | — | AuSt. | — |
| Treptow | — | — | — | — | AuP. | — | — |
| Treuburg | — | — | — | — | — | AuSt. | — |
| Trier | — | RPräs. | PD | AuDSt. | St. | HAuSt. | LS |
| Trifail | — | — | — | — | AuDSt. | AuSt. | — |
| Tromsö/Norway | — | — | — | (Kdr. d. | Sipo & | SD) | — |
| Troppau | — | RPräs. | PD | St. | St. | HAuSt. | — |
| Tübingen | — | — | PA | DSt. | AuP. | AuSt. | — |
| Tüddern | — | — | — | Grepo | — | — | — |
| Turek | — | — | — | — | AuP. | — | — |
| Tuttlingen | — | — | PA | — | AuP. | AuSt. | — |
| Übach-Palenberg | — | — | — | — | AuP. | — | — |
| Überlingen | — | — | — | — | — | AuSt. | — |
| Uelzen | — | — | — | — | AuP. | AuSt. | — |
| Ulm/Donau | — | — | PD | AuDSt. | AuDSt. | AuSt. | LS |
| Ungarisch-Hradisch | — | — | — | AuDSt. | — | — | — |
| Unna | — | — | — | — | AuP. | — | — |
| Vaalserquartier | — | — | — | Grepo | — | — | — |
| Vaihingen | — | — | — | — | AuP. | — | — |
| Varel | — | — | — | — | — | AuSt. | — |
| Velbert | — | — | — | AuDSt. | — | — | — |
| Veldes | — | — | — | (Kdr. d. | Sipo & | SD) | — |
| Verden | — | — | — | AuDSt. | AuP. | AuSt. | — |
| Viernheim | — | — | — | — | AuP. | — | — |
| Viersen | — | — | — | — | AuP. | — | — |
| Vigaun | — | — | — | Pol.Gef. | — | — | — |
| Villach | — | — | PA | Greko | AuP. | AuSt. | LS |

| Town | (a) HSSPf (b) BdO (c) BdS | Higher Police Authorities (Höhere Polizei Behörden) | National Police Head-quarters (Staatliche Polizei Ver-waltungen) | Sicherheits Polizei | | SD | Others |
|---|---|---|---|---|---|---|---|
| | | | | Gestapo | Kripo | | |
| 1 | 2 | 3 | 4 | 5 | 6 | 7 | 8 |
| Villingen | — | — | — | DSt. | AuP. | AuSt. | — |
| Vilshofen | — | — | — | — | | AuSt. | — |
| Vionville | — | — | — | Grepo | — | — | — |
| Vöcklabruck | — | — | — | — | — | AuSt. | — |
| Völkermarkt | — | — | — | — | — | AuSt. | — |
| Völklingen | — | — | — | — | AuP. | — | — |
| Voitsberg | — | — | — | — | — | AuSt. | — |
| Waldenburg/ Schlesien | — | — | PP | AuDSt. | AuDSt. | AuSt. | Wm., LS |
| Waldheim | — | — | — | — | AuP. | — | — |
| Waldrode | — | — | — | — | AuP. | — | — |
| Waldshut | — | — | PA | Greko | AuP. | AuSt. | — |
| Walsum | — | — | — | — | AuP. | — | — |
| Waltrop | — | — | — | — | AuDSt. | — | — |
| Wandsbek (Hamburg) | — | — | PA | AuDSt.* | — | AuSt. | — |
| Wanne-Eickel | — | — | — | — | AuP. | — | — |
| Wanzleben | — | — | — | — | — | AuSt. | — |
| Waren/Müritz | — | — | — | — | AuP. | — | — |
| Warendorf | — | — | — | — | — | AuSt. | — |
| Warnemünde | — | — | — | Grepo | — | — | — |
| Warnsdorf | — | — | — | AuDSt. | AuP. | — | — |
| Warthbrücken | — | — | — | — | AuP. | — | — |
| Warthenau | — | — | — | Grepo | AuP. | — | — |
| Wasserburg | — | — | — | — | — | AuSt. | — |
| Wassertrüdingen | — | — | — | — | — | AuSt. | — |
| Watenstedt- Salzgitter | — | — | PA | AuDSt. | AuDSt. | — | — |
| Wattenscheid | — | — | — | — | AuP. | — | — |
| Weener | — | — | — | Grepo | — | — | — |
| Weida | — | — | — | — | AuP. | — | — |
| Weiden | — | — | — | — | AuP. | AuSt. | — |
| Weidenau | — | — | — | — | AuP. | — | — |
| Weil/Rhein | — | — | — | Grepo | AuP. | — | — |
| Weilheim | — | — | — | — | — | AuSt. | — |
| Weimar | — | IMin. | PP | St. | St. | Abs. | Wm. |
| Weinheim/Bergstr. | — | — | — | — | AuP. | — | — |
| Weipert | — | — | — | — | AuP. | — | — |
| Weissenburg/Bayern | — | — | — | — | — | AuSt. | — |
| Weissenburg/Elsass | — | — | — | — | — | AuSt. | — |
| Weissenfels | — | — | PP | — | AuDSt. | AuSt. | LS |
| Weisswasser | — | — | — | — | AuP. | AuSt. | — |
| Weiz | — | — | — | — | — | AuSt. | — |
| Welka/near Strassnitz | — | — | — | Grepo | — | — | — |
| Wels | — | — | PA | — | AuP. | AuSt. | — |
| Welun | — | — | — | Greko | AuP. | AuSt. | — |
| Werdau | — | — | — | — | AuP. | — | — |
| Wermelskirchen | — | — | — | — | AuP. | — | — |
| Werne | — | — | — | — | AuP. | — | — |
| Wernigerode | — | — | — | — | AuP. | — | — |
| Wesel | — | — | — | — | AuP. | AuSt. | — |
| Wesermünde | — | — | PP | AuDSt. | AuDSt. | AuSt. | FP, SW-Rev., LS |
| Wesseling | — | — | — | — | AuP. | — | — |
| Westerland/Sylt | — | — | — | Grepo | AuP. | — | LS |
| Wetzlar | — | — | — | AuDSt. | AuP. | — | — |
| Wiedenbrück | — | — | — | — | — | AuSt. | — |
| Wien | a, b, c | RSth. | PP | LSt. | LSt. | LAbs. AuSt. (6) | SW-Kdo., Wm., LS, FP |
| Wien (Winterhafen) | — | — | — | — | — | | SW-Rev. |
| Wiener-Neustadt | — | — | PD | AuDSt. | AuDSt. | AuSt. | LS |
| Wiesbaden | a, b, c | RPräs. b. OPräs. | PP | AuDSt. | AuDSt. | HAuSt. | FP, Wm., LS |
| Wilhelmshaven | — | — | PP | AuDSt. | St. | HAuSt. | FP, Wm., LS |

K20

| Town | (a) HSSPf (b) BdO (c) BdS | Higher Police Authorities (Höhere Polizei Behörden) | National Police Headquarters (Staatliche Polizei Verwaltungen) | Sicherheits Polizei | | SD | Others |
| | | | | Gestapo | Kripo | | |
| 1 | 2 | 3 | 4 | 5 | 6 | 7 | 8 |
| --- | --- | --- | --- | --- | --- | --- | --- |
| Wilkau-Hasslau | — | — | — | — | AuP. | — | — |
| Wipperfürth | — | — | — | — | — | AuSt. | — |
| Wismar | — | — | — | — | AuP. | AuSt. | LS |
| Witkowitz | — | — | — | AEL. | — | — | — |
| Witten | — | — | — | — | AuP. | — | — |
| Wittenberg | — | — | PD | — | AuDSt. | AuSt. | SW-Wache, FP, LS |
| Wittenberge | — | — | — | AuDSt. | AuP. | AuSt. | — |
| Wittlich | — | — | — | AuDSt. | — | AuSt. | — |
| Wittmund | — | — | — | — | — | AuSt. | — |
| Witzenhausen | — | — | — | — | — | AuSt. | — |
| Wochheim-Feistritz | — | — | — | Grepo | — | — | — |
| Woldenberg/Neumark | — | — | — | AuDSt. | — | — | — |
| Wolfach | — | — | — | — | — | AuSt. | — |
| Wolfenbüttel | — | — | — | — | AuP. | AuSt. | — |
| Wolfratshausen | — | — | — | — | — | AuSt. | — |
| Wolfsberg | — | — | — | — | — | AuSt. | — |
| Wolmirstedt | — | — | — | — | — | AuSt. | — |
| Wormditt | — | — | — | — | — | AuP. | — |
| Worms | — | — | PD | — | AuDSt. | AuSt. | — |
| Wsetin | — | — | — | AuDSt. | — | — | — |
| Würselen | — | — | — | — | AuP. | — | — |
| Würzburg | — | RPräs. | PP | AuDSt. | St. | HAuSt. | Wm., LS |
| Wunsiedel | — | — | — | — | — | AuSt. | — |
| Wuppertal | — | — | PP | AuDSt. | St. | AuSt. | FP, Wm., LS |
| Wurzen | — | — | — | — | AuP. | — | — |
| Wyler | — | — | — | Grepo | — | — | — |
| Zabern | — | — | — | — | AuP. | AuSt. | — |
| Zehdenik | — | — | — | — | AuP. | — | — |
| Zeitz | — | — | Z | AuDSt.* | AuP. | AuSt. | — |
| Zell am See | — | — | — | — | — | AuSt. | — |
| Zell/Mosel | — | — | — | — | — | AuSt. | — |
| Zella-Mehlis | — | — | PA | — | AuP. | — | — |
| Zellerfeld | — | — | — | — | — | AuSt. | — |
| Zerbst | — | — | — | — | AuP. | AuSt. | — |
| Zeulenroda | — | — | — | — | AuP. | — | — |
| Zichenau | — | RPräs. | — | St. | St. | Abs. | — |
| Ziegenhals | — | — | — | — | AuP. | — | — |
| Zittau | — | — | — | — | AuP. | AuSt. | — |
| Zlin | — | — | — | Greko | AuDSt. | AuSt. | — |
| Znaim | — | — | PD | AuDSt. | AuP. | — | — |
| Zossen | — | — | — | AuDSt. | — | — | — |
| Zweibrücken | — | — | PA | — | AuP. | — | — |
| Zwettl | — | — | — | Grepo | — | — | — |
| Zwickau | — | — | PP | AuDSt. | St. | AuSt. | FP, Wm., LS |
| Zwiesel | — | — | — | — | — | AuSt. | — |
| Zwischenwässern | — | — | — | UL. | — | — | — |
| Zwittau | — | — | — | — | AuP. | — | — |
| Zychlin | — | — | — | — | AuP. | — | — |

# ANNEXE L

## ABBREVIATIONS

NOTE.—The following is a list of all German abbreviations used in this book with their German meaning and English translation or glossary.

| Abbreviation | German | English translation or glossary |
|---|---|---|
| abg. | abgeordnet | temporarily transferred to a position at another place |
| abg. | abgekürzt | abbreviated |
| abg. | abgeändert | altered |
| ABP | Auslandsbriefprüfstelle | Censorship office for foreign mail |
| Abs. | Abschnitt | Sector, district<br>In the SS : Regional division of Germany and its HQ<br>In the SD : Sub. Regional HQ and its area |
| Abschn. | see Abs. | |
| Abt. | Abteilung | Section, sub-section, battalion |
| Abt.W | Wirtschaftsabteilung | Section for Administration and Supply |
| Abwesenh. | Abwesenheit | Absence |
| a.D. | ausser Dienst | retired : on inactive list |
| a.D. | an der Donau | on the Danube |
| AD | Allgemeiner Dienst | General Service (of the TN) |
| a.d. | an der | on the |
| a.d.H. | an der Havel | on the Havel |
| a.Do. | an der Donau | on the Danube |
| a.d.O. | an der Oder | on the Oder |
| AE | Arbeitserziehungslager | Literally : Penal Labour camp ; a type of concentration camp |
| AEG | Allgemeine Elektrizitäts Gesellschaft | One of the largest German producers of electrical equipment |
| AG | Agent | Agent (term applied only to non-German agents) |
| allg. | allgemein | general |
| allgem. | allgemein | general |
| a.M. | am Main | on the Main |
| Angel. | Angelegenheit(en) | matter(s) ; subject(s) |
| Anh. | Anhalt | German *Land* and city |
| a.O. | an der Oder | on the Oder |
| AO ; Ic/AO | Abwehroffizier | C.I. officer |
| apl. | ausserplanmässig | supernumerary to establishment |
| a.Pr. | auf Probe | on probation ; on trial |
| Art. | Artillerie | Artillery |
| Asst. | Assistent | Assistant |
| Ast. | Abwehrstelle | M.I. Regional HQ. |
| AuDSt. | Aussendienststelle | Large branch office of *Kripo*, *Gestapo*, or SD. (also abbreviated *ADSt.*) |
| auftrw. | auftragsweise | temporarily assigned ; by authority ; upon the order of |
| Ausb. | Ausbildung | training |
| AuSt. | Aussenstelle | Smaller branch office of *Gestapo* and SD, sometimes also of *Kripo* (sometimes abbreviated *ASt.*) |
| a.W. | auf Widerruf | subject to change ; good until further notice |
| b. | bei(m) | on, near |
| b. | beauftragt | authorized ; commissioned ; in charge |
| B ; Ba ; Bad. | Baden | German *Land* |
| Bayr. ; bayr. | Bayerisch | Bavarian |
| BB-Schein | Betriebsberechtigungsschein | Certificate authorizing the purchase of gasoline |
| BD | Bereitschaftsdienst | Emergency service branch (of the TN) |
| B.d.O. or BdO | Befehlshaber der Ordnungspolizei | Commander of the *Orpo* in a *Wehrkreis* or similar territory |
| B.d.S ; BdS ; BdSuSD | Befehlshaber der Sicherheitspolizei und des Sicherheitsdienstes | Commander of *Sipo* and SD in a *Wehrkreis* or similar territory |
| Befh. | Befehlshaber | Commander |
| Ber. | Bereich | Sphere ; region ; area |
| bes. | besetzt | occupied |

| Abbreviation | German | English translation or glossary |
|---|---|---|
| Bez. | *Bezirk* | District ; sub-region |
| Bez.-F. | *Bezirksführer* | Obsolete designation of rank in the TN with the equivalent rank of Lt.-Col. |
| BF | *Brigadeführer* | Rank of Major-General in the SS (also abbreviated Brigf.) |
| B.-F. | *Bereitschaftsführer* | Rank in the TN with the equivalent rank of Major |
| BG | *Bezirksgruppe* | Sub-district ; sub-region in the TN. |
| Bh. | see Befh. | |
| Br. | Breisgau | Region in the southern part of *Land* Baden |
| Braunschw. | Braunschweig | Brunswick ; German *Land* and city |
| Brigf. | *Brigadeführer* | Rank of Major-General in the SS |
| Btl. | *Bataillon* | Battalion |
| BVG | *Bezirksverwaltungsgericht* | District Administrative Court |
| Bz. | see Bez. | |
| BZ | *Bereitschaftszug* | Emergency platoon |
| Bzp. | *Bahnschutzpolizei* | Railway Protection Police |
| C | *Centrum* | Centre ; designation for central district for large German towns, *e.g.*, Berlin |
| CdO | *Chef der Ordnungspolizei* | Chief of the Orpo (WÜNNENBERG) |
| CdS | *Chef der Sicherheitspolizei und des SD* | Chief of the *Sipo* and the SD (KALTENBRUNNER) |
| CdZ | *Chef der Zivilverwaltung* | Head of Civil Administration |
| Ch.d.Dt.P. ; ChdDtP ; ChdDtPol. | *Chef der Deutschen Polizei* | C.inC. of the German Police (HIMMLER) |
| d. | *der, die, des, dem, den* | the, of the ; to the |
| Dienstst. | *Dienststelle* | office ; HQ (generic term) ; branch office |
| Dipl. Ing. | *Diplom Ingenieur* | Engineer possessing an academic diploma |
| Dir. | *Direktor* | Director |
| Dirig. | *Dirigent* | High official |
| Do. | *Donau* | Danube |
| d.Res. ; d.R. | *der Reserve* | of the Reserve ; not on active list |
| Dr. | *Doktor* | Doctor (of Medicine, Law, Economics, etc.) |
| DSt. | see *Dienstst.* | |
| DStrK. | *Dienststrafkammer* | Service disciplinary chamber or court |
| Dt. | *Deutsch* | German |
| EAPl. | *Einheitsaktenplan* | Standard filing system |
| Einw.Meld.W. | *Einwohner Meldewesen* | Police Registry, Bureau of Census |
| EK | *Einsatzkommando* | Combined mobile *Sipo* and SD unit |
| Erg. | *Ergänzung* | Supplement |
| Ern. | *Ernährung* | Food ; nutrition |
| Ers. | *Ersatz* | Replacement |
| etc. | *und so weiter* | and so on |
| europ. | *europäisch* | European |
| EWGG | *Einsatz-Wehrmachtgebührnisgesetz* | Law governing army pay in the field |
| f. | *für* | for |
| F. | *Führer* | Leader |
| FP | *Feuerschutzpolizei* | Fire Protection Police |
| Freiw. | *Freiwillig* | voluntary |
| Freiw.Btl. | *Polizei-Freiwilligen-Bataillone* | Police Volunteer Battalions made up of foreigners and " Racial Germans " |
| Frhr. | *Freiherr* | Baron ; Count ; aristocratic title |
| Frl. | *Fräulein* | Miss |
| FS | *Fernschreiber* | Teleprinter ; teletype |
| FSchP. | see FP | |
| FSPol. | see FP | |
| F.u.E.Dienst | *Feuer- und Entgiftungsdienst* | Fire fighting and Decontamination Service of the *Luftschutzpolizei* |
| Gaultr. | *Gauleiter* | Chief of a Party *Gau*, *i.e.*, Nazi Party Administrative Region of Germany |
| GauOVwR | *Gauoberverwaltungsrat* | Senior Administrative Councillor of a Party *Gau* |
| G.B.V. | *Generalbevollmächtigter für die Verwaltung* | General Plenipotentiary for Administration (HIMMLER) |
| Geh. | *Geheim* | Secret |
| Geh.KdoS. | *Geheime Kommandosache* | Literally : Secret Command matters ; a very high security classification |
| Geh.RchS. | *Geheime Reichssache* | Literally : Secret matter of National Importance ; highest Security classification |

| Abbreviation | German | English translation or glossary |
|---|---|---|
| Geh.RR. | Geheimer Regierungsrat | Special title of administrative official with the approximate equivalent rank of Major |
| gen. | genannt | called ; named ; known as |
| Gen. | General | General |
| Gend. | Gendarmerie | Rural Police |
| Genlt. ; GenLt. | Generalleutnant | Equivalent to Major-General |
| Genmaj. ; GenMaj. | Generalmajor | Equivalent to Brigadier-General |
| Gestapa | Geheimes Staatspolizeiamt | National HQ of the Secret State Police, *i.e.*: Amt IV of the RSHA |
| Gestapo | Geheime Staatspolizei | Secret State Police |
| gew. | gewöhnlich | ordinary |
| GF | Gruppenführer | Rank of Lieutenant-General in the SS (also abbreviated *Gruf.*) |
| Gf.-F. | Gefolgschaftsführer | Obsolete designation of rank in the TN with the equivalent rank of 1st Lieutenant |
| GFP | Geheime Feldpolizei | Secret Field Police |
| GG | Generalgouvernement | Government General |
| Gm.-F. | Gemeinschaftsführer | Obsolete designation of rank in the TN with the equivalent rank of 2/Lt. |
| GP | Grenzpolizei | Frontier Police (Branch of the *Gestapo*) |
| GPA | Grenzpolizeiamt | Frontier Police Office |
| Gr. | Gross | great |
| Greko | Grenzpolizeikommissariat | Frontier Police Commissariat of the *Gestapo* |
| Gren. | Grenadier | Infantry(man) |
| Grepo | Grenzpolizei-Posten | Frontier Police Outpost of the *Gestapo* |
| Grepo | Grenzpolizei | Frontier Police (Branch of the *Gestapo*) |
| H. | Havel | A river near Berlin |
| (H) | hauptamtlich | full time ; fully paid ; professional |
| Hastuf ; Hstuf. | Hauptsturmführer | Rank of Captain in the SS |
| HAuSt. or HASt. | Hauptaussenstelle | Large type branch office of the SD |
| HB.-F. | Hauptbereitschaftsführer | Obsolete designation of rank in TN with the equivalent of a Major |
| hess. | hessisch | Hessian |
| Hess. | Hessen | German *Land* |
| Hipo | Hilfspolizei | Auxiliary Police |
| HJ | Hitler Jugend | Hitler Youth Organisation |
| Homburg v.d.H. | Homburg vor der Höhe | Homburg near Frankfurt/Main |
| Hptm. | Hauptmann | Captain |
| Hschaf. | Hauptscharführer | Rank of senior NCO in the SS with equivalent of S/Sjt. |
| HSF | Hauptsturmführer | Captain in the SS (also abbreviated *Hastuf* or *Hstuf.*) |
| HSSPf. | Höherer SS- und Polizeiführer | Superior SS and Police Commander, Commanding Officer of all SS and Police forces in a *Wehrkreis* or similar territory |
| i. | im, in | in |
| I. | Inspektor or Inspekteur | Inspector |
| i.B. | im Breisgau (see also Br.) | |
| i.B. | in Baden (see also Ba.) | |
| IB | Internationales Büro | International Bureau |
| ID | see JD | |
| IdO | Inspekteur der Ordnungspolizei | Inspector of *Orpo* in a *Wehrkreis* or similar territory ; obsolete rank now replaced by BdO (viz.) |
| I.d.S. ; IdSuSD ; IdSPuSD | Inspekteur der Sicherheitspolizei und des Sicherheitsdienstes | Inspector of *Sipo* and SD in a *Wehrkreis* or similar territory |
| IKPK | Internationale Kriminalpolizeiliche Kommission | International Criminal Police Commission |
| Inf. | Infanterie | Infantry |
| Ing. | Ingenieur | Engineer |
| InK. | see JnK. | |
| InL. | see JnL. | |
| Insp. | Inspektor or Inspekteur | Inspector |
| Insp. | Inspektion | Inspectorate |
| In Vet | see JnVet | |
| InWG | see JnWG | |
| i.O. | in Oldenburg | German *Land* |
| i.V. | in Vetretung | acting for ; acting on behalf of |
| J-Dienst ; JD | Instandsetzungsdienst (*TN*) | Repair, Demolition and Rescue Service (of the TN) |

| Abbreviation | German | English translation or glossary |
|---|---|---|
| JnK | *Inspektion für das Kraftfahr- und Verkehrswesen* | Inspectorate of M/T and Traffic Control |
| JnL | *Inspektion für die Luftschutzpolizei und den Luftschutzeinsatz* | Inspectorate of Air Raid Protection and Air Raid Protection Police |
| JnVet | *Inspektion für das Veterinärwesen* | Inspectorate of Police Veterinary Services |
| JnWG | *Inspektion für Waffen und Geräte* | Inspectorate of Arms and Equipment |
| K | *Kommissariat* | Sub-Section of a *Kripo* HQ. |
| K | *Kraftfahrwesen* | M/T |
| K | *Kriegs-* | war- ; wartime |
| (k) | *kommissarisch* | temporarily put in charge |
| Ka. | *Polizeikasse* | Cashier's Office in a National Police Administration HQ ; Police paymaster's office ; Police finance office |
| KA | *Kriminalassistent* | Official of the *Sipo* with the approximate equivalent rank of Sjt. |
| KAA | *Kriminalassistentenanwärter* | Candidate for *Kriminalassistent ;* rank of official in the *Sipo* with the approximate equivalent of Cpl. |
| Ka.F. | *Kameradschaftsführer* | Obsolete designation of rank in the TN with the equivalent rank of 2/Lt. ; Cpl. in the HJ. |
| Kas. | *Kaserne* | Barracks |
| Kav. | *Kavallerie* | Cavalry |
| KD | see KDir. | |
| KdF | *Kraft durch Freude* | Strength through Joy Movement |
| KDir. | *Kriminaldirektor* | Rank of official of the *Sipo* with the approximate equivalent rank of Major |
| Kdo. | *Kommando* | Command ; Detachment ; Detail |
| KdO | *Kommandeur der Ordnungspolizei* | Sub-regional commander of the Orpo |
| Kdr. | *Kommandeur* | Commander |
| KdS ; KdSPuSD ; Kdr.d.Sipo u.d.SD | *Kommandeur der Sicherheitspolizei und des Sicherheitsdienstes* | Sub-regional commander of *Sipo* and SD ; Chief of a *Sipo* and SD-(*Einsatz-*) Kommando |
| Kfm. | *kaufmännisch* | commercial |
| KI or KJ | *Kriminalinspektor* | Rank of official of the *Sipo* with the approximate equivalent rank of Lt. |
| KK ; KKom. | *Kriminalkommissar* | Rank of official of the *Sipo* with the approximate equivalent rank of Lt. |
| Kl. ; kl. | *klein* | little ; small |
| KL | *Konzentrationslager* | Concentration camp (official abbreviation) |
| KOA | *Kriminaloberassistent* | Rank of official of the *Sipo* with the approximate equivalent rank of S/Sjt. |
| KOI or KOJ | *Kriminaloberinspektor* | Rank of official of the *Sipo* with the approximate equivalent rank of Captain |
| Kom. | *Kommissar* | Commissar ; commissioner |
| komm. | *kommissarisch* | temporarily put in charge |
| Komp. | *Kompanie* | Company |
| KOS | *Kriminalobersekretär* | Rank of official of the *Sipo* with the approximate equivalent rank of 2/Lt. |
| KPAuDSt. | *Kriminalpolizei-Aussendienststelle* | Large branch office of the Criminal Police |
| KPAuP. | *Kriminalpolizei-Aussenposten* | Small branch office of the Criminal Police |
| KPLSt. | *Kriminalpolizei-Leitstelle* | Criminal Police Regional HQ. |
| KPSt. | *Kriminalpolizeistelle* | Criminal Police Sub-Regional HQ. |
| Kr. | *Kreis* | District ; (US : County) |
| KR | *Kriminalrat* | Rank of official of the *Sipo* with the approximate equivalent rank of Major |
| Kreishptmsch. | *Kreishauptmannschaft* | Administrative District HQ and unit |
| KrimDir. | see KDir. | |
| KRin | *Kriminalrätin* | Rank of female official of the *Sipo* with the approximate equivalent rank of Major |
| Kripo | *Kriminalpolizei* | Criminal Police |
| KS | *Kriminalsekretär* | Rank of official of the *Sipo* with the approximate equivalent rank of RSM |
| KTI | *Kriminaltechnisches Institut* | Criminological Institute |
| KTU | *Kriminaltechnische Untersuchungsstelle* | Criminal Research Branch |
| KVA | *Kriegsverwaltungsabteilung* | Branch or section of the Military Administration in occupied countries |
| KWHW | *Kriegswinterhilfswerk* | Wartime Winter Relief Work |
| KZ | *Konzentrationslager* | Concentration Camp (official abbreviation : KL) |
| LAbs. | *Leitabschnitt* | Regional HQ of the SD |

| Abbreviation | German | English translation or glossary |
|---|---|---|
| Landw. | *Landwirtschaft* | Agriculture |
| Lapo | *(Kasernierte) Landespolizei* | Literally: State Police; usually: Militarized Barrack Police Forces of the *Länder*, since 1935 taken over by the Reich and incorporated into the *Wehrmacht* |
| LD | *Luftschutzdienst* | Air Raid Protection Service (of the TN) |
| Lds.Pol. | see Lapo | |
| Lds.Pol.Beh. | *Landespolizeibehörden* | State Police Authorities; obsolete term for "*Höhere Polizeibehörden*" (Higher Police Authorities) |
| Leit. | *Leitender* | governing; leading; executive |
| Leitst. | see LSt. | |
| L.-F. | *Landesführer* | Rank in the TN with the equivalent of Colonel |
| LG | *Landesgruppe* | Territorial division of the TN equivalent to *Wehrkreis* |
| LIG | *Leichtes Infanterie-Geschütz* | Light Infantry Howitzer |
| LMG | *Leichtes Maschinen-Gewehr* | Light Machine Gun |
| LR | *Landrat* | Rural Councillor; chief executive and administrator of a *Landkreis* |
| LRA | *Landratsamt* | Office of a *Landrat* |
| LS | *Luftschutz* | ARP |
| LSt. | *Leitstelle* | Regional HQ of *Kripo* and *Gestapo* |
| LSt. | *Ladestelle* | Loading Place |
| Lt. | *Leitend(er)* | governing; leading; executive |
| Lt. | *Leutnant* | 2/Lt. |
| Ltr. | *Leiter* | Chief |
| LtRDir. | *Leitender Regierungsdirektor* | Title of an executive assistant in a high government office |
| Lvst. | *Leitvermittlungsstelle* | Main trunk line exchange |
| M. | Mecklenburg | German *Land* |
| M. | Main | German river |
| m. | *Meter* | metre; metres |
| Mähr.-Ostrau | Mährisch-Ostrau | Moravska Ostrawa, town in Czechoslovakia |
| Maj. | *Major* | Major |
| MBliV | *Ministerialblatt für die innere Verwaltung* | better known as: *Ministerialblatt des Reichs- und Preuss. Innenministeriums*, Official Gazette of the Reich and Prussian Ministry of the Interior |
| m.d.F.b. | *mit der Führung beauftragt* | temporarily charged with the conduct of affairs |
| m.d.F.d.G.b. | *mit der Führung der Geschäfte beauftragt* | temporarily charged with the conduct of affairs |
| MdI | *Ministerium d.Innern* | (Reich) Ministry of the Interior |
| M.d.R. | *Mitglied des Reichstages* | Member of the *Reichstag* (German Parliament) |
| m.d.vertretungsw.F.b. | *mit der vertretungsweisen Führung beauftragt* | temporarily charged with the conduct of affairs |
| m.d.W.d.G.b. | *mit der Wahrnehmung der Geschäfte beauftragt* | temporarily charged with the conduct of affairs |
| Meckl. | Mecklenburg | German *Land* |
| Meist. | *Meister* | Master; rank in the Protection Police and Gendarmerie with the equivalent of RSM |
| M.Gladbach | München-Gladbach | Rhineland town |
| Mil.; milit. | *Militär; militärisch* | Army; military |
| Min. | *Ministerium* | Ministry |
| Min. | *Minister* | Minister |
| MinR. | *Ministerialrat* | Rank of administrative official in a Ministry with the approximate equivalent of Colonel |
| MinDir. | *Ministerialdirektor* | Executive official in a Ministry with the approximate equivalent of Lt.-General |
| MinDirig. | *Ministerialdirigent* | Executive official in a Ministry with the approximate equivalent of Maj.-General |
| Mk. | *Mark* | Region; Province; also type |
| MKP | *Marine-Küstenpolizei* | Naval Coastal Police |
| mot. | *motorisiert* | motorized |
| MP | *Maschinenpistole* | Sub Machine Gun |
| N | *Nord* | North |
| N; Na. | *Nachrichten* | Signals |
| Nachr. | *Nachrichten* | Signals |
| Nb. | Niederbayern | Former *Regierungsbezirk* of Bavaria |

| Abbreviation | German | English translation or glossary |
|---|---|---|
| ND | *Nachrichtendienst* | Intelligence and Information Service; usually used in the meaning of enemy secret service organisations |
| ND | *Niederdonau* | German *Reichsgau*, district of former Austria |
| Nebenamtl. | *Nebenamtlich* | part time |
| Nebenanschl. | *Nebenanschluss* | Extension |
| NfDB ; N.f.D.B. | *Nur für Deutsche Behörden* | Security classification of documents with the approximate equivalent of " Restricted " |
| NfdD. | *Nur für den Dienstgebrauch* | Security classification of documents with the approximate equivalent of " Restricted " |
| Niederrh. | Niederrhein | Lower Rhine |
| Niederschl. | Niederschlesien | Prussian province of Lower Silesia |
| NO | *Nordost* | North-East |
| Nr. | *Nummer* | Number |
| NSÄB | *Nationalsozialistischer Ärztebund* | National Socialist Medical League |
| NSDAP | *Nationalsozialistische Deutsche Arbeiter Partei* | National Socialist Party |
| NSFO | *Nationalsozialistischer Führungsoffizier* | National Socialist Indoctrination officer |
| NSKK | *Nationalsozialistisches Kraftfahr Korps* | National Socialist Motor Corps |
| Nst. | *Nebenstelle* | Subsidiary office (of the *Gestapo*) |
| NW | *Nordwest* | North-West |
| | | |
| O. | *Ober-* | higher |
| O. | *Osten* | East |
| O. | Oder | German river |
| O. | Oldenburg | German *Land* |
| Oa. | *(SS-) Oberabschnitt* | Territorial division of Germany for the purpose of SS- administration |
| OA | *Oberassistent* | Rank in the administration |
| Ob. | *Ober-* | Higher |
| OBA | *Oberbergamt* | Regional mining authority |
| OBauR. | *Oberbaurat* | Rank of administrative official in the Construction and Engineering Dept., with the approximate equivalent of Lt.-Col. |
| Ob.d.L. | *Oberbefehlshaber der Luftwaffe* | C.inC. of the German Air Force |
| Oberf. | *Oberführer* | SS- rank of a Senior Colonel (Brigadier) |
| Oberstlt. | *Oberstleutnant* | Lt.-Col. |
| Oblt. | *Oberleutnant* | 1st Lt. |
| Ob.Reg.Rat | *Oberregierungsrat* | Rank of administrative official with the approximate equivalent of Lt.-Col. |
| OF ; SS-OF | *(SS-) Oberführer* | Rank of Senior Colonel (Brigadier) in the SS (also abbreviated *Oberf.*) |
| Off. | *Offizier* | Officer |
| OFinPrs. | *Oberfinanzpräsident* | High official of Finance administration |
| OG. | *Ortsgruppe* | local district branch ; local unit |
| OGF | *Obergruppenführer* | Rank of General in the SS (also abbreviated *O'Gruf* or *Ogruf.*) |
| OKH | *Oberkommando des Heeres* | German Army High Command |
| OKL | *Oberkommando der Luftwaffe* | German Air Force High Command |
| OKM | *Oberkommando der Marine* | German Navy High Command |
| Okom. | *Oberkommissar* | Obsolete rank in the *Sipo* |
| OKW | *Oberkommando der Wehrmacht* | Supreme Command of the German Armed Forces |
| Oldb. | Oldenburg | German *Land* |
| OLR | *Oberlandrat* | Rank of a senior *Landrat* (see LR) |
| OPräs ; OPrs. | *Oberpräsident* | Chief Administrator and government executive of a Prussian Province |
| OReguBauR or O.Reg.u.BauR. | *Oberregierungs- und Bau-Rat* | Rank of administrative official of the Construction and Engineering Dept., with the approximate equivalent of Lt.-Col. |
| Orpo | *Ordnungspolizei* | Regular Police ; literally : Police for the maintenance of law and order |
| ORR | *Oberregierungsrat* | Rank of administrative official with the equivalent of Lt.-Col. (also abbreviated *Ob.Reg.Rat*) |
| ORRuKR. | see ORuKR. | |
| ORuEichR. | *Oberregierungs- und Eichrat* | Rank of administrative official of the Dept. of Weights and Measures with the approximate equivalent rank of Lt.-Col. |

| Abbreviation | German | English translation or glossary |
|---|---|---|
| ORuKR ; O.R.u.K.R ; O.Reg.-u.Krim.Rat | Oberregierungs- und Kriminalrat | Executive official of the *Sipo* with the approximate equivalent rank of Lt.-Col. |
| O.S. ; OS. | Oberschlesien | Prussian Province of Upper Silesia |
| OSBF | Obersturmbannführer | Rank of Lt.-Col. in the SS (also abbreviated *Ostubaf.*) |
| Oschaf. | Oberscharführer | NCO in the SS with the equivalent of Sjt. |
| OSchlR | Oberschulrat | Rank of administrative official in the Dept. for the supervision of schools |
| OSF | Obersturmführer | Rank of 1/Lt. in the SS (also abbreviated *Ostuf.*) |
| Ostpr. | Ostpreussen | Prussian Province of East Prussia |
| Ostubaf | Obersturmbannführer | Rank of Lt.-Col. in the SS |
| Ostuf | Obersturmführer | Rank of 1/Lt. in the SS |
| OT | Organisation " Todt " | Organization " Todt " |
| OVA | Oberversicherungsamt | Government Main Insurance Office |
| OVwR. | Oberverwaltungsrat | Rank of administrative official |
| P. | Post | Post office ; postal service ; mail |
| P. | Präsidialgeschäftsstelle | Office of the chief of a *Staatliche Polizeiverwaltung* |
| PA | Polizeiamt | Smallest type *Staatliche Polizeiverwaltung* |
| PA | Polizeiassistent | Rank of civil servant in the Administrative Police with the equivalent of a Sjt. |
| PA | Personal Angelegenheiten | Personnel matters ; often used for Card Indexes on Personnel or Personalities |
| Pak. | Panzerabwehrkanone | Anti-tank gun |
| Panz.Jäg.Komp. | Panzerjägerkompanie | Anti-tank company |
| pers. | persönlich | in person |
| Pers.Ref. | Persönlicher Referent | Specialist adviser and assistant to the chief of an office |
| PI or PJ | Polizeiinspektor | Rank of civil servant in the Administrative Police with the approximate equivalent of a Lt. |
| POI or POJ | Polizeioberinspektor | Rank of civil servant in the Administrative Police with the approximate equivalent of a Capt. |
| Pol. | Polizei | Police |
| Pol.Amtm. | Polizei-Amtmann | Rank of Administrative Police official with the approximate equivalent of Capt. |
| Pol.Beschaff.Amt | Polizei-Beschaffungsamt | Police Supply Depot |
| Pol.Dir. | Polizei-Direktor | Head of a *Polizei-Direktion*, a medium sized *Staatliche Polizeiverwaltung* |
| Pol.Gef. | Polizei-Gefängnis | Police prison |
| PolORntmstr. | Polizeioberrentmeister | Rank of civil servant in the Finance and Accounting Branch of the Administrative Police with the approximate equivalent rank of Capt. |
| Pol.Präs. | Polizei-Präsidium | Large type *Staatliche Polizeiverwaltung* |
| Pol.Präs. | Polizei-Präsident | Head of a *Polizei-Präsidium* |
| PolR. | see PR | |
| PolVO | Polizeiverordnung | Police Order |
| Pomm. | Pommern | Prussian Province of Pomerania |
| PORm. | see *PolORntmstr.* | |
| POS | Polizeiobersekretär | Rank of civil servant in the Administrative Police with the equivalent of a 2/Lt. |
| PP | Polizei-Präsidium | Large type *Staatliche Polizeiverwaltung* |
| Pr. | Preussen | Prussia |
| Pr. | *Preussisch* | Prussian |
| PR | Polizeirat | Rank of civil servant in the Administrative Police with the approximate equivalent rank of a Major |
| Präs. | Präsident | President ; chairman |
| Präs. | Präsidium | Office of the President |
| Präs.Gesch.St. | Präsidial-Geschäftsstelle | Office of the Chief of a *Staatliche Polizeiverwaltung* |
| preuss. | *preussisch* | Prussian |
| Prof. | Professor | Professor |
| Prov. | Provinz | Province, sub-division of Prussia |
| ProvR. | Provinzialrat | Provincial Councillor, rank of civil servant in the government of a Prussian Province |
| Prs. | Präsident | President, chairman |
| PS | Polizeisekretär | Rank of civil servant in the Administrative Police with the equivalent rank of an RSM |
| Pü. | Postüberwachung | Control of mail (by the *Gestapo*) |

| Abbreviation | German | English translation or glossary |
|---|---|---|
| PV | Polizeiverwaltung | Police administration |
| PVG | Polizeiverwaltungsgesetz | Police Administration Law |
| Pz. | Panzer | Armour |
| Pz.Gren. | Panzer Grenadier | (Member of) armoured infantry |
| qkm. | Quadratkilometer | sq. km. |
| RA | Regierungsassessor | Rank of official with approximate equivalent of Capt.; candidate for Higher Civil Service |
| RAB Kdo. | Reichsautobahn-Kommando | Dept. or unit in charge of National Highways |
| RAmtm. | Regierungsamtmann | Rank of administrative Government official with the approximate equivalent rank of Captain |
| RATN | Reichsamt Technische Nothilfe | National Dept. of the Technical Emergency Corps, also known as "Amt Technische Nothilfe." |
| RBFD | Reichsbahnfahndungsdienst | National Railway Criminal Investigation Service |
| Rchskom. | Reichskommissar | Reich Commissioner; rank of chief civil administrator of an occupied country or of a special governmental bureau |
| RdErl. | Runderlass | Circular (Order) |
| RDF | Reichsverein Deutscher Feuerwehringenieure | National League of German Fire Protection Engineers |
| RDir. | Regierungsdirektor | Rank of administrative official in a regional government with the approximate equivalent rank of Colonel |
| Rechn. | Rechnung | Bill; invoice |
| Rechn.A. | Rechnungsamt | Finance office |
| RegAss. | see RA | |
| Reg.Bez. | Regierungsbezirk | Administrative district (of Prussia, Bavaria, Danzig-Westpreussen, Wartheland, Sudetenland) |
| Reg.Dir. | see RDir. | |
| Reg.u.Krim.Dir. | see RuKDir. | |
| Reg.u.Krim.Rat | see RuKR | |
| Reichsm.f.Ern.u. Landw. | Reichsministerium für Ernährung und Landwirtschaft | Reich Ministry of Food and Agriculture |
| Reichssth. | Reichsstatthalter | Reich Governor |
| Rev. | Revier | British: Police ward or station US: Police precinct |
| Rev.Lt. | Revierleutnant | Wartime rank of 2/Lt. in the Schupo in charge of a Revier |
| RFM | Reichsfinanzministerium | Reich Finance Ministry |
| RFSS | Reichsführer-SS | Commander in Chief of the SS |
| RFSSu.Ch.d.Dt.Pol. i.RM.d.I. | Reichsführer-SS und Chef der deutschen Polizei im Reichsministerium des Innern | C.inC. of SS and Police in the Reich Ministry of the Interior (HIMMLER) |
| RFV | Reichsfinanzverwaltung | Reich Finance Administration |
| RG. | Reichsgau | An Administrative region of the Reich, formed out of the annexed territories of Austria, Sudeten, Poland |
| RG. | Reichsgesetz | Reich Law or Decree |
| RG. | Reichsgericht | Supreme Court |
| RGBl | Reichsgesetzblatt | Reich Legal Gazette |
| Rgt. | Regiment | Regiment |
| Rh. | Rhein | Rhine |
| RKPA | Reichskriminalpolizeiamt | National HQ of the Reich Criminal Police, identical with Amt V of the RSHA |
| RLB | Reichsluftschutzbund | Reich Association for Air Raid Protection |
| RM | Reichsminister | Reich Minister |
| RM | Reichsministerium | Reich Ministry |
| RM | Reichsmark | German currency |
| RMdI. | Reichsministerium des Innern | Reich Ministry of the Interior |
| RMdLuObdL | Reichsminister der Luftfahrt und Oberbefehlshaber der Luftwaffe | Reich Minister of Aviation and Supreme Commander of the GAF |
| RPrs. | Regierungspräsident | District or governmental administrative chief in charge of a Reg.Bez. |
| RPrs.b.OPrs. | Regierungspräsident beim Oberpräsident | Deputy to the Oberpräsident (i.e., Chief of a Prussian Province) acting as Regierungspräsident |
| RR. | Regierungsrat | Administrative official with the approximate equivalent rank of Major |

| Abbreviation | German | English translation or glossary |
|---|---|---|
| RRuKR | see RuKR | |
| RSHA | *Reichssicherheitshauptamt* | National Dept. of Security |
| RStGB | *Reichsstrafgesetzbuch* | Reich Penal Code |
| Rsth. | *Reichsstatthalter* | Reich Governor ; Hitler's representative in a German *Land* or *Reichsgau* |
| RuKD | see RuKDir. | |
| RuKDir. | *Regierungs-und Kriminaldirektor* | Executive official of the *Sipo* with the approximate equivalent rank of Col. |
| RuKR | *Regierungs- und Kriminalrat* | Executive official of the *Sipo* with the approximate equivalent rank of Major |
| RuPrMdI | *Reichs- und Preussischer Minister(ium) des Innern* | Reich and Prussian Minister (Ministry) of the Interior |
| Rv. | *Rechnungsrevisor* | Rank of civil servant in the Finance and Accounting Branch of the Administrative Police with the approximate equivalent of Capt. |
| RViPrs. | *Regierungsvizepräsident* | Deputy *Regierungspräsident* |
| RVK | *Reichsverteidigungskommissar* | Reich Defence Commissioner, identical with Party *Gauleiter* |
| RVM | *Reichsverkehrsministerium* | Reich Ministry of Transport |
| RWM | *Reichswirtschaftsministerium* | Reich Ministry of Economics |
| Sa. | Sachsen | Saxony, German *Land* |
| SA | *Sturmabteilungen* | Brown shirts ; Nazi Party ; Storm Troopers |
| SAN | *Sanitätsdienst(e)* | Medical Service(s) |
| SBF | *Sturmbannführer* | Rank of Major in the SS (also abbreviated : *Stubaf.*) |
| Sch. | *Schutzpolizei* | Protection Police |
| Schaf. | *Scharführer* | Rank of NCO in the SS with the equivalent of L/Sjt. |
| Schuma | *Schutzmannschaften* | Militarized Police Units formed out of foreign elements and " racial Germans " |
| Schupo | *Schutzpolizei* | Protection Police |
| Schwarzw. | Schwarzwald | Black Forest |
| SD | *Sicherheitsdienst (des Reichsführers-SS)* | Security Service (of the C.inC. SS) the Nazi Party Intelligence system |
| SDdRFSS | see SD | |
| Sekr. | *Sekretär* | Secretary |
| SF | *Standartenführer* | Rank of Colonel in the SS (also abbreviated : *Staf.*) |
| SHD | *Sicherheits- und Hilfsdienst* | Security and Assistance Service, forerunner of the *Luftschutzpolizei* (ARP Police) |
| Sigm. | Sigmaringen | Prussian *Reg.Bez.* |
| Sipo | *Sicherheitspolizei* | Security Police (combined *Kripo* and *Gestapo*) |
| SMG | *Schweres Maschinen-Gewehr* | Heavy Machine Gun |
| SP | see Sipo | |
| SPuSD | *Sicherheitspolizei und Sicherheitsdienst* | Security Police and Security Service |
| SRD | *(HJ-)Streifendienst* | Patrol Service of the Hitler Youth Movement |
| SS | *Schutzstaffeln* | Nazi Party Elite Guard |
| SS-Oa | see Oa | |
| SSPf. | *SS- und Polizeiführer* | Sub-District Commander of SS and Police |
| SS-WVHA | *SS-Wirtschafts- und Verwaltungshauptamt* | SS- Economic and Administrative Department |
| St. | *Stelle* | Place ; HQ |
| St. | *Stab* | Staff ; HQ-staff |
| St. | *Sankt* | Saint |
| staatl. | *staatlich* | appertaining to State government |
| Stabsoff. | *Stabsoffizier* | Staff officer |
| ständ. | *ständig(er)* | permanent |
| ständ.Vertr.d.RM f.d.Bes.Ostgebiete | *ständiger Vertreter des Reichsministers für die besetzten Ostgebiete* | Permanent Deputy of the Reich Minister for Occupied Eastern Territories |
| Stapo | *Staatspolizei* | State Police, *i.e.*, Political Police |
| Std.Rat | *Studienrat* | Rank of High School teacher or educational expert |
| Stellv ; Stellvertr. | *Stellvertreter* | Deputy |
| StPO | *Strafprozessordnung* | Code of Criminal Procedure |
| Str. | *Strasse* | Street |
| Sttsmin. | *Staatsministerium* | State Ministry |
| SttsR. | *Staatsrat* | High official of the Reich Government comparable to Under-secretary |
| Stubaf | *Sturmbannführer* | Rank of Major in the SS |

| Abbreviation | German | English translation or glossary |
|---|---|---|
| SW | *Wasserschutzpolizei* | Waterways Protection Police |
| SW | *Süd-West* | South-West |
| TA | *Technischer Assistent* | Technical Assistant ; rank in the Technical Service of the Sipo |
| TD | *Technischer Dienst* | Technical Service Branch (of the TN) |
| Techn.Akad. | *Technische Akademie* | Technical Academy |
| Tel. | *Telefon* | Telephone |
| Teno | see TN | |
| Th. ; Thür. | Thüringen | Thuringia, German *Land* |
| TN | *Technische Nothilfe* | Technical Emergency Corps |
| TNVR | *Technische Nothilfe Verfügungs-reserve* | Technical Emergency Corps Reserve for special employment |
| TOS | *Technischer Obersekretär* | Rank of official in the Technical Service Branch of the *Gestapo* |
| u. | *und* | and |
| ü. | *über* | over ; above ; across |
| UG | *Untergruppe* | local sub-division or unit of an *Ortsgruppe* (local unit of the TN) |
| Uk-Stellung | *Unabkömmlichkeits-Stellung* | Deferment from military service on vocational grounds ; literally : (professional) indispensability |
| Uschaf | *Unterscharführer* | Rank of NCO in the SS with the equivalent of Cpl. |
| USF | *Untersturmführer* | Rank of 2/Lt. in the SS (also abbreviated : *Ustuf*) |
| Ustuf | see USF | |
| usw. | *und so weiter* | etc. |
| v. | *von* | Designation preceding surname indicating degree of aristocracy |
| verst. | *verstärkt* | reinforced |
| Ver.St.von Amerika | Vereinigte Staaten von Amerika | United States of America |
| Vertr. | *Vertreter* | Deputy |
| vertr. | *vertraulich* | confidential |
| vertrw. ; vertretungsw. | *vertretungsweise* | acting ; temporary |
| Verw. | *Verwaltung* | Administration |
| Vet. | *Veterinär* | Veterinary |
| VG | *Versorgungsgericht* | Court for pension and allowance claims of government employees |
| VGAD | *Verstärkter Grenzaufsichtsdienst* | Reinforced Frontier Control Service |
| VO | *Verordnung* | Decree |
| Vogtl. | Vogtland | Part of Saxony |
| Vomi ; VoMi | *Volksdeutsche Mittelstelle* | Department for the repatriation of " racial " Germans |
| Vors. | *Vorsitzender* | Chairman |
| VS | *Verschlussachen* | Classified material ; classified documents |
| vtrw. | see Vertrw. | |
| VwGDir. | *Verwaltungsgerichtsdirektor* | Director of the Administrative Court |
| W. | *West* | West |
| W. | Westfalen | Westphalia |
| WE | *Weltanschauung* | Ideology |
| WE | *Weltanschauliche Erziehung* | Ideological indoctrination |
| Wehrd. | *Wehrdienst* | (absent for) Service in the Forces |
| Wehrm. | *Wehrmacht* | German Armed Forces |
| Westf. | Westfalen | Westphalia |
| Westpr. | Westpreussen | West Prussia |
| Wirtsch. | *Wirtschaft* | Economics ; supplies |
| WKP | *Weibliche Kriminalpolizei* | Female Criminal Police |
| Wkr. ; Wks. | *Wehrkreis* | Military District |
| WSchP. | *Wasserschutzpolizei* | Waterways Protection Police |
| WSS | *Waffen-SS* | Armed SS |
| Württ. ; Württbg. | Württemberg | German *Land* |
| z. | *zu(r)* | to |
| ZABP | *Zentrale für die Auslands-Brief-prüfstellen* | Central Censorship Office |
| z.B. | *zum Beispiel* | for example |
| z.b.V. | *zur besonderen Verwendung* | for special employment |
| z.D. | *zum Dienst* | re-assigned |
| z.Pr. | *zur Probe ; zur Probedienstleitung* | on trial ; on probation |
| Zstr. | *Zivilstreifen* | Patrols in plain clothes |

| Abbreviation | German | English translation or glossary |
|---|---|---|
| ZstrF. | Fusszivilstreifen | Patrols in civilian clothes on foot |
| Zstr. mot. | Motorisierte Zivilstreifen | Patrols in civilian clothes (motorized) |
| ZstrR. | Radzivilstreifen | Patrols in civilian clothes (on bicycles) |
| Zü. | Zugüberwachung | Train control (by the *Gestapo*) |
| z.V. | zur Verwendung (Verfügung) | available ; for special employment |
| z.Z. | zur Zeit | at present |

# ANNEXE M

PLATES

**Part One:** **UNIFORMS of the GERMAN POLICE**

**Part Two:** **PERSONAL IDENTITY DOCUMENTS**

FIG. 111
Schupo sentry at gate of SS und Polizeiführer's
H.Q. at Rovno (1942)

FIG. 112
Schupo (in shako) using police call box
(Berlin—Autumn, 1943).

FIG. 113
Traffic policeman on duty
(Berlin—Autumn, 1943)

FIG. 114
Schupo major (Russian front—1942).

FIG. 115
Schupo major (left) and N.C.O. (right).

FIG. 116
Gendarmerie motor cyclist.

FIG. 117
Feuerschupo
*Note* SS flash on steel helmet and piping to cuffs.

FIG. 118

SHD despatch rider in foreground with Feuerschupo in background.

*Note.*—D.R.'s armbands, viz. Sicherheits—u. Hilfsdienst above left cuff and Melder (despatch rider) above elbow. The D.R.'s connection with the Luftwaffe is indicated by the Luftwaffe number plate (WL, i.e. Wechrmacht Luftwaffe) on mudguard of motor cycle.

FIG. 119
Senior Teno officers in conference.

FIG. 120
Teno in field grey.
*Note* Hoheitsabzeichen on left sleeve, Teno
armband above left cuff and cogwheel on
collar patch.

FIG. 121
Teno Scharführer
*Note* shoulder strap, Wehrmachtsarmbinde above left
elbow and Teno armband above left cuff.

HILFSPOLIZEI

Fig. 122
Hilfspolizei armband.

SIPO (SD)
Uniforms (black)

Fig. 123

Fig. 124

Untersturmführer of the Sicherheitsdienst instructing cadets at the Führerschule der Sicherheitspolizei—
at Berlin—Charlottenburg, 1937.

# OFFICERS OF THE ORDNUNGSPOLIZEI

## SHOULDER STRAPS OF GENERALS, ETC.

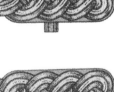
General der Polizei

Generalmajor der Ordnungspolizei (retired)

Generalarzt der Polizei

Ministerialdirektor (Administrative Official with the rank of General-leutnant der Polizei)

Officials of the Feuerschutzpolizei with General's rank

## SHOULDER STRAPS OF OFFICERS

Major der Wasserschutzpolizei

Major der Gendarmerie

Major der Schupo der Gemeinden

Major (retired)

Oberstleutnant

Oberst

Leutnant der Wasserschupo

Oberleutnant der Gendarmerie

Hauptmann der Schupo der Gemeinden

Leutnant der Schupo des Reiches

Oberleutnant der Schupo des Reiches

Hauptmann der Schupo des Reiches

## COLLAR PATCHES OF GENERALS, ETC.

Administrative officials with General's rank

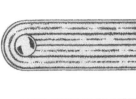
Generale der Ordnungspolizei (and officials of equivalent rank)

## COLLAR PATCHES OF OFFICERS

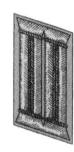
Gendarmerie

Schutzpolizei der Gemeinden

Schutzpolizei des Reiches

PLATE II

# OFFICIALS OF OFFICERS' RANK

## SHOULDER STRAPS

Oberstarzt der Polizei

Oberstabsapotheker der Polizei

Oberstveterinär der Polizei

Oberstabsveterinär der Polizei

Ministerialrat

 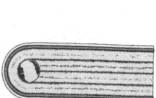

Regierungsrat

Amtrat, Pol.-Amtmann, Pol.-rat

Oberbaurat

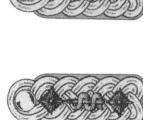  

Stabsarzt der Polizei

Oberarzt der Polizei

Stabszahnarzt der Polizei

Stabsveterinär der Polizei

Oberveterinär der Polizei

Pol.-Oberinspektor

Pol.-Inspektor

Pol.-Sekretär

Baurat (with one or two years' service)

## COLLAR PATCHES

Pol.-Medizinalbeamte

Pol.-Veterinärbeamte

Pol.-Verwaltungsbeamte

Feuerschutzpolizei

Administrative official of the Hauptamt Orpo with rank of Captain and above

PLATE III

# SENIOR NCOs OF THE ORPO AND OFFICIALS OF EQUIVALENT RANK

## SHOULDER STRAPS

Pol.-Assistent (with rank of Hauptwachtmeister)

Meister of the Feuerschupo

Oberwachtmeister of the Verkehrsdienst

Wachtmeister of the Wasserschutzpolizei (with more than 4 years' service)

Bezirks-oberwachtmeister of the Gendarmerie

Hauptwachtmeister of the Schupo der Gemeinden

Wachtmeister (with less than 4 years' service)

Wachtmeister (with more than 4 years' service)

Oberwachtmeister

Revier-oberwachtmeister

Hauptwachtmeister and Oberjunker

Meister

Obermeister (Obsolete)

Inspektor (obsolete)

## COLLAR PATCHES

### SENIOR N.C.O.s

Pol.-Assistent

Feuerschutzpolizei

Gendarmerie

Schutzpolizei der Gemeinden

Schutzpolizei des Reiches

### JUNIOR N.C.O.s

Feuerschutzpolizei

Gendarmerie

Schutzpolizei der Gemeinden

Schutzpolizei des Reiches

## SERVICE INSIGNIA

Sigrunen (Backing is black when worn on white uniform)

Southern Cross (See Text, para. 56)

Crossed lances for mounted officials of the Schupo and the Gendarmerie

Asculaepean staff for medical officials of the Wasserschutzpolizei

Asculaepean staff for medical officials of the Schupo der Gemeinden

Horseshoe for qualified farriery officials

Steering wheel for officials of the Kraftfahrdienst

Blitz for officials of the Fernmeldedienst

# CAP BADGES

PLATE IV

## CAP BADGES

Badge for Shako, etc. (gold for generals and
equivalent officials)

Tschakonationale (National cockade ;
material varies according to rank)

Badge for forage caps
(yellow for Wasserschutzpolizei)

Badge for peaked cap (for Generals, also for
Wasserschutzpolizei and Verkehrsdienst ;
quality of metal varies)

Badge for peaked cap (for all uniforms
other than the preceding)

PLATE V

# SLEEVE INSIGNIA

Sleeve Insignia for Generals and officials of
equivalent rank (In aluminium for lower
ranking officers, except Wasserschutzpolizei)

Sleeve Insignia for Wasserschutzpolizei
(Material varies according to rank)

Sleeve Insignia for senior NCO's of the
Gendarmerie (Colour varies for other
branches)

## Motorisierte Gendarmerie

Armband for officers and inspectors of the Mot. Gendarmerie

## Motorisierte Gendarmerie

Armband for senior NCO's of the Mot.    Gendarmerie

# TYPES OF UNIFORM

DIENSTANZUG

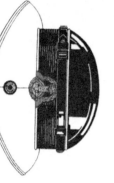

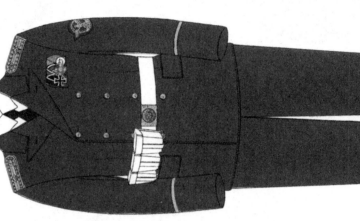

Oberstleutnant der Feuerschutzpol

PARADEANZUG

Revieroberwachtmeister der Wasser-schutzpolizei

DIENST (BERG)-ANZUG

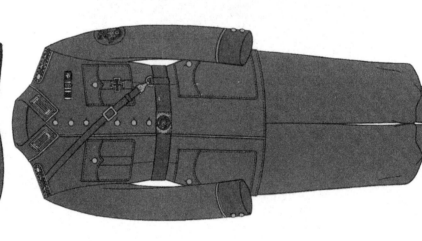

Hauptwachtmeister der Gendarmerie

DIENSTANZUG

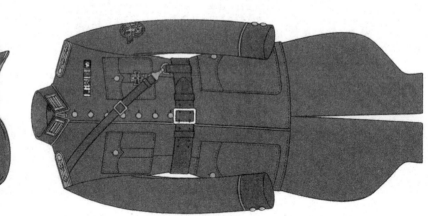

Hauptmann der Gendarmerie

PLATE VI<sup>A</sup>

# TYPES OF UNIFORM

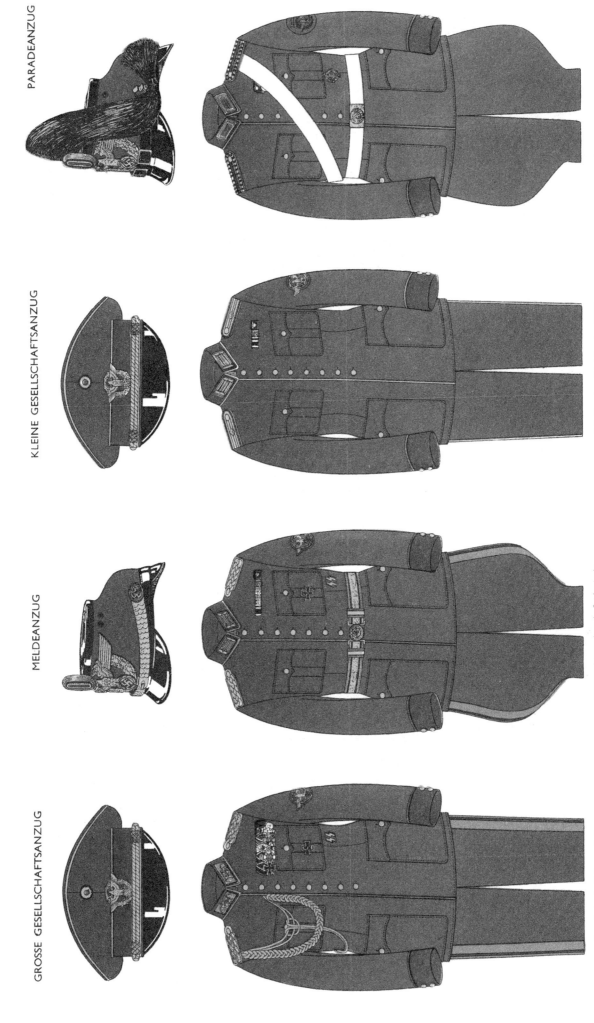

PARADEANZUG

KLEINE GESELLSCHAFTSANZUG

MELDEANZUG

GROSSE GESELLSCHAFTSANZUG

Oberwachtmeister der Schupo des Reiches

Polizei-inspektor (Administrative official)

Major der Schutzpolizei des Reiches in the
Hauptamt Orpo

Generalmajor der Ordnungspolizei

PLATE VII

# GREATCOATS AND TUNICS

Greatcoat for Orpo Generals

Greatcoat (Officer's) for Wasserschutzpolizei

White tunic (Officer's)

Tunic for branches other than Wasserschutzpolizei

Greatcoat for OR (EM) other than Wasserschutzpolizei

Greatcoat for OR (EM) other than Wasserschutzpolizei

Tunic for Wasserschutzpolizei

# HEADGEAR

PLATE VIII

hite cap (Officer's) for the Schupo des Reiches

Cap for Gendarmerie, with Officer's chin- strap cords

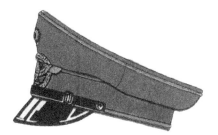

Cap for Gendarmerie with leather chin-strap

Cap for Wasserschutzpolizei with Officer's chin-strap cords

Cap for Wasserschutzpolizei, with leather chin-strap

Forage cap for Senior NCO's of the Schupo der Gemeinden

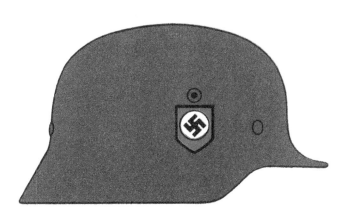

Steel helmet (right side)

Hoheitsabzeichen (left side)

Crash helmet for motor cyclists   (brown for Gendarmerie, otherwise black)

Fig. 125

## SOLDBUCH ZUGLEICH PERSONALAUSWEIS
### (Paybook and Identity Document)
#### Issued to Orpo and affiliated organisations

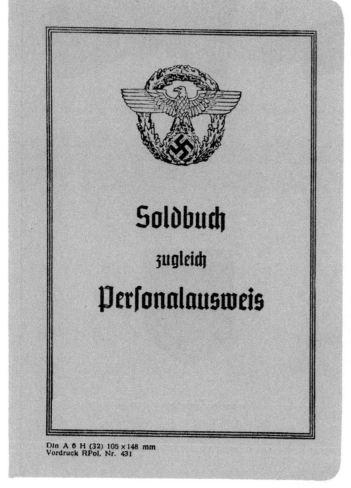

FRONT COVER

INSIDE FRONT COVER

| Lfd. Nr. | Art der Änderung | Tag Monat Jahr | Pol.-Einheit | Eigenhändige Unterschrift des Pol.-Führers | Dienstgrad und Dienststellung |
|---|---|---|---|---|---|
| | | | | | |
| | | | | | |
| | | | | | |
| | | | | | |
| | | | | | |
| | | | | | |

Bescheinigungen über die Richtigkeit der Zusätze und Berichtigungen zu den Angaben auf S. 1 und 2

Religion

Größe

Gesicht

Bart

Besondere Kennzeichen (z. B. Brillenträger)

Standl. Beruf

Gestalt

Haar

Augen

Schuhgröße

Kopfweite

Gasmaskengröße

Blutgruppe

Die Richtigkeit der vorstehenden, nicht umrandeten Angaben, der eigenhändige Unterschrift des Buchinhabers, der Eintragungen zu Lfd. Nr. ......... auf S. 7 und der Lfd. Nr.

............ bis ............ auf S. 8 sowie der umrandeten Angaben auf S. 9 „Gebührnisse" bescheinigt!

Ort ..........................

oder OU., den ..................... 19...

(Dienstsiegel)

Kommando der Wasserschutzpolizei
Rhein
(Bezeichnung der Pol.-Einheit)

(Eigenhändige Unterschrift des Führers
der Pol.-Einheit, Kommandeur o.sw.)

(Dienstgrad und Dienststellung)

---

31

## Beurlaubungen

1 Vom ......... bis ......... nach .........

Grund .........

Reisebeihilfe ist — nicht — gewährt.

Ort .........

oder OU., den ......... 19...

(Dienstsiegel)

......................................................
(Unterschrift des Führers der Pol.-Einh.)

(Dienstgrad)

2. Vom ......... bis ......... nach .........

Grund .........

Reisebeihilfe ist — nicht — gewährt.

Ort .........

oder OU., den ......... 19...

(Dienstsiegel)

......................................................
(Unterschrift des Führers der Pol.-Einh.)

(Dienstgrad)

---

3

Mitgemachte Gefechte

---

1

# Soldbuch

für den ...........................
(Dienstgrad, Amtsbezeichnung)

Besoldungsgruppe: ..................... (für Aktive)

Vergütungsgruppe: ..................... (für Pol.-Res.)

(Datum — neuer Dienstgrad)

ab ......... { Besold.-Gr. / Vergüt.-Gr.

ab ......... { Besold.-Gr. / Vergüt.-Gr.

ab ......... { Besold.-Gr. / Vergüt.-Gr.

ab ......... { Besold.-Gr. / Vergüt.-Gr.

ab ......... { Besold.-Gr. / Vergüt.-Gr.

............................................
(Vor- und Zuname)

............................................
(Vor- und Zuname vom Buchinhaber, eigenhändig geschrieben)

geboren am ......... in .........
(Ort, Kreis, Verwaltungsbezirk)

Erkennungsmarke: .........

Din. A 6 H (32) 105x148 mm
Vordruck RPol. Nr. 431

---

7

Der Buchinhaber besitzt Orden und Ehrenzeichen:

1. .........
2. .........
3. .........
4. .........
5. .........
6. .........
7. .........
8. .........
9. .........
10. .........

## Familienstand und Anschriften
### der nächsten lebenden Angehörigen.

Der Buchinhaber ist .................... und hat ........ Kinder
(ledig, verheiratet, geschieden, verwitwet)

1. Ehefrau ........................................ (Vorname)

    ........................................ (Mädchenname)

    Wohnort ........................................

    Kreis, Verwalt.-Bez. ........................................

    Straße, Hausnummer ........................................

2. Eltern:

    Vater ........................................ (Vorname)

    ........................................ (Zuname)

    Stand, Beruf ........................................

    Mutter ........................................ (Vorname)

    ........................................ (Mädchenname)

    Wohnort ........................................

    Kreis, Verwalt.-Bez. ........................................

    Straße, Hausnummer ........................................

*) 3. Verwandte oder Braut:

    Vor- und Zuname ........................................

    Wie verwandt oder ob Braut ........................................

    Stand, Beruf ........................................

    Wohnort ........................................

    Kreis, Verwalt.-Bez. ........................................

    Straße, Hausnummer ........................................

---
*) Zu 3. nur ausfüllen, wenn 1. und 2. nicht ausgefüllt sind.

---

Zuständige Heimatbehörde (in deren Kassenanschlag sich die
Planstelle des Buchinhabers befindet bzw. Erfassungs-Dienststelle bei Pol.-Reservisten)

*Der Oberpräsident der Rheinprovinz*
*Kommando der Wasserschutzpolizei*
*"Rhein"*

*) ........................................ (Datum)

ab ........................................

ab ........................................

ab ........................................

ab ........................................

Zuständige Ersatz-Einheit:

*) ........................................ (Datum)

ab ........................................

ab ........................................

ab ........................................

ab ........................................

Zuständige Einsatzpolizeieinheit:

*) ........................................ (Datum)

ab ........................................

ab ........................................

ab ........................................

ab ........................................

---
*) Wenn durch Versetzung und Abordnung Aenderung erforderlich wird,
leserlich bleibend durchstreichen und darunter die nunmehr zuständige
Heimatbehörde usw. eintragen.

---

### Beachten!

#### Bestimmungen.

1. Das Buch dient dem Polizeiangehörigen als Personalausweis
bei Eisenbahnfahrten, Kommandos, Urlaub, Post- und Gebührnisempfang. (Bei Postempfang muß noch ein mit Lichtbild ver-
sehener Ausweis vorgelegt werden.)

2. Der Polizeiangehörige hat das Buch stets bei sich zu tragen.
Aufbewahrung im Gepäck, im Quartier usw. ist unzulässig.
Sorgsame Aufbewahrung liegt im eigenen Interesse des Buch-
inhabers.

3. Berechtigten Kontrollorganen ist das Buch zur Einsichtnahme
auszuhändigen. Abnahme des Buches ist nicht zuzulassen.
Abgabe des Buches muß jedoch erfolgen, wenn der Buchinhaber vorläufig festgenommen worden ist.

4. In Beherbergungsstätten u. dergl. darf Seite 1 und 2 des Buches
vorgezeigt, das Buch jedoch nicht aus der Hand gegeben werden.
Außer Angabe der Heimatanschrift sind jede weiteren Angaben
verboten.

5. Das Buch ist eine Urkunde. Zu Eintragungen in ihm sind nur
die zuständigen Dienststellen befugt. Eigenmächtige Eintragungen oder Änderungen, außer der eigenhändigen Eintragung
der Unterschrift des Buchinhabers, werden als Urkundenfälschung bestraft.

6. Das Buch muß von den Dienststellen ordnungsmäßig geführt
werden. Der Buchinhaber hat selbst dafür zu sorgen, daß alle
Veränderungen in den zustehenden Gebührnissen bei Beförde-

---

rungen oder Versetzungen sofort durch die für die Eintragungen
zuständigen Dienststellen eingetragen werden.

7. Der Verlust des Buches ist ungesäumt der Polizeieinheit oder
der Dienststelle, wo sich der Buchinhaber gerade befindet, zu
melden; die Ausstellung eines neuen Buches ist zu erbitten.

8a. Bei einer anderen als seiner Polizeieinheit (ausgenommen Lazarett u. dergl.) darf der Buchinhaber Gebührnisse nur dann
empfangen, wenn auf S. 25 ff. des Buches ein Marschbefehl
eingetragen worden ist.

b. Falls ein solcher Marschbefehl nicht eingetragen ist und sich der
Buchinhaber in der Zwangslage befindet, die Zahlstelle einer
anderen Polizeieinheit unbedingt in Anspruch nehmen zu
müssen, kann der Buchinhaber um Zahlung eines Reisekosten-
vorschusses bitten.

9. Der Buchinhaber ist trotz der bestehenden Kontrolle durch die
maßgebenden Dienststellen verpflichtet, selbst zu überwachen,
daß ihm Gebührnisse nicht doppelt oder zuviel gezahlt werden.
Er hat besonders die Bestimmungen auf S. 11/12 zu beachten.

10. Die nach Ziff. 8 zahlende Dienststelle hat die Identität des Buchinhabers soweit möglich eingehend zu prüfen (Unterschrift auf
S. 1, Einsicht in andere Ausweise usw.), die Gebührnisse (Art u. für welchen Zeitraum), auf S. 25 ff. einzutragen und
das in Ziff. 28 Abschn. XIV PDV. 33 Angeordnete sofort zu
veranlassen.

SS **Soldbuch** zugleich Personalausweis

(SS Paybook and Identity Document)

Now issued to the Police

**Bestimmungen**

**auf Seiten 39/40 des Soldbuches beachten!**

(Wenn zu den einzelnen Teilen des Soldbuches weitere Blätter erforderlich werden, sind sie hinter Seite 40 einzuheften und mit Seitenzahlen zu versehen. Am Schlusse des zu ergänzenden Teiles ist auf die neue Fortsetzungsseitenzahl hinzuweisen.)

**Lichtbild des Inhabers**

(Stempel)

(Stempel)

DIN A 9  37 × 52 mm

(Eigenhändige Unterschrift des Inhabers)

C/0164

INSIDE

**SS**

**Soldbuch**

zugleich

Personalausweis

FRONT COVER

## ⚡⚡-Soldbuch
### zugleich Personalausweis

Nr. ................................

für ................................

.................... den ....................
        (Dienstgrad)

ab .................... ....................
   (Datum)         (neuer Dienstgrad)

ab ....................

ab ....................

ab ....................

........................................
(Vor- und Zuname)

Alle bürgerlichen und militärischen Dienststellen werden ersucht, ihn ungehindert passieren zu lassen und ihm nötigenfalls Schutz und Hilfe zu gewähren.

Inhaber ist zum Führen von Schußwaffen auf Grund gesetzlicher Vorschrift berechtigt.

Dieser Personalausweis berechtigt nicht zum Erwerb von Waffen.

Bezeichnung und Nummer der

Erkennungsmarke ....................

Blutgruppe ....................

Gasmaskengröße ....................

Wehrnummer ....................

1

---

**Personalbeschreibung**

geb. am .................... in .................... (Ort, Kreis, Verw.-Bezirk)

Religion .................... Stand, Beruf ....................

Größe .................... Gestalt ....................

Gesicht .................... Haar ....................

Bart .................... Augen ....................

Besondere Kennzeichen (z. B. Brillenträger): ....................

Schuhzeuglänge .................... Schuhzeugweite ....................

........................................
(Vor- und Zuname, eigenhändige Unterschrift des Inhabers)

Die Richtigkeit der nicht umrandeten Angaben auf Seite 1 und 2 und der eigenhändigen Unterschrift des Inhabers bescheinigt

**Aussig** den ....................

(Dienststempel)          (Ausfertigende Heimatbehörde, Pol.-Einheit)
                         (Unterschrift, Dienstgrad und Dienststellung)

2

---

**Bescheinigungen**

über die Richtigkeit der Zusätze und Berichtigungen auf Seiten 1 und 2

| Lfd. Nr. | Art der Änderung | auf Seite | Datum | Dienststelle, Pol.-Einheit | Unterschrift | Dienstgrad und Dienststellung |
|---|---|---|---|---|---|---|
| | | | | | | |
| | | | | | | |
| | | | | | | |
| | | | | | | |

3

---

**Anschriften der nächsten lebenden Angehörigen**

des ........................................
        (Vor- und Zuname)

1. Ehefrau: Vor- und Mädchenname ....................
   (ggf. Vermerk „ledig")

   Wohnort (Kreis) ....................

   Straße, Haus-Nr. ....................

2. Eltern: des Vaters, Vor- und Zuname ....................

   Stand oder Gewerbe ....................

   der Mutter, Vor- u. Mädchenname ....................

   Wohnort (Kreis) ....................

   Straße, Haus-Nr. ....................

3. Verwandte oder Braut*)

   Vor- und Zuname ....................

   Stand oder Gewerbe ....................

   Wohnort (Kreis) ....................

   Straße, Haus-Nr. ....................

*) Ausfüllung nur, wenn weder 1. noch 2. ausgefüllt sind.

7

---

**Mitgemachte Gefechte**

6

---

**Beurlaubungen über fünf Tage**

1. Von .................... bis .................... nach ....................

   Grund: ....................

   .................... den ....................

   (Dienststempel)          (Unterschrift des Komp.-, Truppenführers usw.)

2. Von .................... bis .................... nach ....................

   Grund: ....................

   .................... den ....................

   (Dienststempel)          (Unterschrift des Komp.-, Truppenführers usw.)

3. Von .................... bis .................... nach ....................

   Grund: ....................

   .................... den ....................

   (Dienststempel)          (Unterschrift des Komp.-, Truppenführers usw.)

4. Von .................... bis .................... nach ....................

   Grund: ....................

   .................... den ....................

   (Dienststempel)          (Unterschrift des Komp.-, Truppenführers usw.)

35

Zuständige Heimatbehörde (in deren Kassenanschlag sich die Planstelle des Buchinhabers befindet bzw. Erfassungs-Dienststelle bei Pol.-Reservisten)

Für Freiwillige der Deutschen Polizei: Zuständige Personalbehörde:

**Aussig**

\*) ...................................................
(Datum)

ab ...................................................

ab ...................................................

ab ...................................................

ab ...................................................

Zuständige Ersatz-Einheit:

\*) ...................................................
(Datum)

ab ...................................................

ab ...................................................

ab ...................................................

ab ...................................................

Zuständige Einsatzpolizeieinheit:

\*) ...................................................
(Datum)

ab ...................................................

ab ...................................................

ab ...................................................

ab ...................................................

\*) Wenn durch Versetzung und Abordnung Änderung erforderlich wird, leserlich bleibend durchstreichen und darunter die nunmehr zuständige Heimatbehörde usw. eintragen.

4

---

Der Soldbuchinhaber besitzt Orden und Ehrenzeichen:

1. ...................................................

2. ...................................................

3. ...................................................

4. ...................................................

5. ...................................................

6. ...................................................

7. ...................................................

8. ...................................................

9. ...................................................

10. ...................................................

5

---

## Beachten!

### Bestimmungen.

1. Das Soldbuch dient dem Polizeiangehörigen als Personalausweis bei Eisenbahnfahrten, Kommandos, Urlaub, Post- und Gebührnisempfang.

2. Der Polizeiangehörige hat das Soldbuch stets bei sich zu tragen. Aufbewahrung im Gepäck, im Quartier usw. ist unzulässig. Sorgsame Aufbewahrung liegt im eigenen Interesse des Soldbuchhabers.

3. Berechtigten Kontrollorganen ist das Soldbuch zur Einsichtnahme auszuhändigen. Abnahme des Soldbuches ist nicht zuzulassen. Abgabe des Soldbuches muß jedoch erfolgen, wenn der Soldbuchinhaber vorläufig festgenommen worden ist.

4. In Beherbergungsstätten u. dergl. darf Seite 1 und 2 des Soldbuches vorgezeigt, das Buch jedoch nicht aus der Hand gegeben werden. Außer Angabe der Heimatanschrift sind alle weiteren Angaben verboten.

5. Das Soldbuch ist eine Urkunde. Zu Eintragungen in ihm sind nur die zuständigen Dienststellen befugt. Eigenmächtige Eintragungen oder Änderungen, außer der eigenhändigen Eintragung der Unterschrift des Soldbuchinhabers, werden als Urkundenfälschung bestraft.

6. Das Soldbuch muß von den Dienststellen ordnungsmäßig geführt werden. Der Soldbuchinhaber hat selbst dafür zu sorgen, daß alle Veränderungen in den zustehenden Gebührnissen bei Beförderungen oder Versetzungen sofort durch die für die Eintragungen zuständigen Dienststellen eingetragen werden.

39

---

7. Der Verlust des Soldbuches ist ungesäumt der Polizeieinheit oder der Dienststelle, wo sich der Soldbuchinhaber gerade befindet, zu melden; die Ausstellung eines neuen Soldbuches ist zu erbitten.

8. Bei einer anderen als seiner Polizeieinheit (ausgenommen Lazarett u. dergl.) darf der Soldbuchinhaber Gebührnisse n u r d a n n empfangen, w e n n ein Marschbefehl mit den vorgeschriebenen Vermerken über die Gebührnisabfindung vorgelegt wird.

9. Der Soldbuchinhaber ist trotz der bestehenden Kontrolle durch die maßgebenden Dienststellen verpflichtet, selbst zu überwachen, daß ihm Gebührnisse nicht doppelt oder zuviel gezahlt werden.

10. Die nach Ziff. 8 zahlende Dienststelle hat die Identität des Soldbuchinhabers soweit möglich eingehend zu prüfen (Unterschrift auf S. 1, Einsicht in andere Ausweise usw.), die Zahlung der Gebührnisse (Art u. für welchen Zeitraum) auf S. 31 ff. einzutragen und der zuständigen Verwaltung von der Zahlung Kenntnis zu geben.

40

Fig. 127

## POLIZEI-DIENSTPASS
(Police Service Record)

NOTE: — The light green portions of this reproduction in the original document have anti-erasure background markings

INSIDE FRONT COVER

FRONT COVER

## Name des Paßinhabers

(Rufname, Familienname)

(Sämtliche Vornamen des Inhabers)
(Rufname, Familienname)

### Personalbeschreibung

Gestalt .........................
Haar .........................
Augen .........................

Größe .........................
Gesicht .........................
Bart .........................
Besondere Kennzeichen .........................
Kopfweite .........................  Schuhgröße .........................
Gasmaskengröße .........................

Paß ist ausgestellt ......................... den .........................

(Unterschrift, Zivilberuf, Dienststellung)

---

## I. Angaben zur Person

| | | |
|---|---|---|
| 1 | Familienname | |
| 2 | Vornamen (Rufname unterstreichen) | |
| 3 | Geburtstag, -monat, -jahr | |
| 4 | Geburtsort, Kreis, Reg.-Bezirk | |
| 5 | Religion | |
| 6 | Familienstand | |
| 7 | Kinder (Knaben / Mädchen) | |
| 8 | Unterschrift | |

---

## noch I. Angaben zur Person

| | | Genaue Berufsangabe: Berufsgruppe / Berufsgast |
|---|---|---|
| 9 | Beruf | Arbeitsbuch Nr. / Zuständiges Arbeitsamt |
| 10 | Schulbildung | |
| 11 | Kenntnisse in Fremdsprachen | |
| 12 | Berufliche, technische usw. Fähigkeiten | |
| 13 | Welche Angehörigen sind bei Tod usw. zu benachrichtigen? | |

---

## noch III. Polizeidienst

Lehrgänge — Sonderausbildungen

| Art | Zeitdauer von / bis | Ergebnis |
|---|---|---|
| | | |

---

## noch III. Polizeidienst

Abgemachte Unternehmungen

| Tag, Monat, Jahr | Ortsangabe, Truppenteil |
|---|---|
| | |

---

## noch III. Polizeidienst

Verwundungen und ernstere Erkrankungen (Dienstunfall oder Beschädigung im Dienst) und dadurch verminderte Dienstfähigkeit

| Tag, Monat, Jahr | Verwundungen, Erkrankungen (Dienstunfall, Beschädigung im Dienst) | a) Verwendungsfähigkeit  b) Krankenpapiere liegen bei: |
|---|---|---|
| | | |

## noch I. Angaben zur Person

### Nachträge

_____
_____
_____
_____
_____
_____
_____
_____
_____
_____
_____
_____
_____
_____
_____

## noch I. Angaben zur Person

Mitgliedschaft zur NSDAP., ihren Gliederungen und angeschlossenen Verbänden

NSDAP. seit _____ Mitgl.-Nr. _____ als _____
HJ. „_____ „_____ „_____
SA. „_____ „_____ „_____
SS. „_____ „_____ „_____
NSKK. „_____ „_____ „_____
NSFK. „_____ „_____ „_____
NSKOV. „_____ „_____ „_____
NSV. „_____ „_____ „_____
_____ „_____ „_____ „_____

Ehrenzeichen der NSDAP.

_____
_____
_____

SS - Dienstgrade (Ernennungen):

am _____ zum _____
„_____ „_____
„_____ „_____
„_____ „_____
„_____ „_____

## noch III. Polizeidienst

### Orden und Ehrenzeichen (einschl. II.)

## noch III. Polizeidienst

### Beschäftigung (Versetzungen, Abordnungen, Verwendungen)

| a) Dienststelle b) Führung | Art der Verwendung (Tätigkeit) | vom | bis |
|---|---|---|---|
| 1. a) | | | |
| b) | | | |
| 2. a) | | | |
| b) | | | |
| 3. a) | | | |
| b) | | | |
| 4. a) | | | |
| b) | | | |
| 5. a) | | | |
| b) | | | |

## noch III. Polizeidienst

### Ausscheiden

am _____ (Tag, Monat, Jahr)

als _____ (Dienstgrad)

nach _____ (Dienstleistungszeit)

durch _____ (letzte Dienststelle)

Grund _____ (Angabe des gesetzlichen Grundes)

(Dienststelle)

(Dienstsiegel)

(Unterschrift)

(Amtsbez. Dienststellung)

---

## 8

## II. Reichsarbeits- und Wehrdienst

Reichsarbeitsdienst von _____ bis _____

Formation _____

Letzter Dienstgrad _____

Wehrdienst (einschl. Feldgendarmerie) Truppenteil

von _____ bis _____

Letzter Dienstgrad _____

Jetziges Wehrverhältnis _____

Frontkämpfer _____

Verwundungen _____

Vorbez. und Oberschaden keine Seite 3a

## III. Polizeidienst

Diensteintritt in die _____ als _____

Übernahme, Versetzung usw. in andere Polizeiparten

am _____ durch _____ in die _____ als _____

Beamtenverhältnis auf Widerruf besteht seit _____

Lebenszeit _____

Beförderungen und Ernennungen

am _____ zum _____

1) Nur Dienstgrade eintragen, also: Schutzpolizei des Reiches, der Gemeinden, Gendarmerie, Feuerschutzpolizei, Bat.-Polizei, Verwaltungspolizei usw. 2) Zutreffendes Jahr. 3) Nur etwaigen Nachf. der Landespartie eintragen. 4) Art der Übernahme (Einstellung, Versetzung usw.). 5) Siehe 1).

---

## ...nigung

### Zusätze und Berichtigungen

| Datum | Dienststelle | Unterschrift | Dienstgrad |
|---|---|---|---|
| | | | |
| | | | |
| | | | |

## Bescheinigung

über die Richtigkeit der

| Lfd. Nr. | Art der Änderung | auf Seite |
|---|---|---|
| | | |
| | | |

Fig. 128

# DIENSTAUSWEIS—FEUERWEHRDIENST
## (Service Identification Certificate—Fire Fighting Services)

**FRONT COVER**

Dienstausweis

Nr. .................

....................................................
(Name des Inhabers)

....................................................
(Dienstgrad)

....................................................
(Wohnort)

....................................................
(Kreis)

Vordr. R. Pol. Nr. 387 DIN A 6. 105×148 mm    F.A.B.

**INSIDE**

Der ............................................
(Dienstgrad)

............................................
(Name)

gehört zur ............................................

............................................

Durch Verfügung des ............................................

in ............................................ vom ..................

ist der Inhaber zum Hilfspolizeibeamten bestellt. Die Bestellung gilt nur für die sich aus dem Feuerwehrdienst ergebende Tätigkeit.

Alle bürgerlichen und militärischen Dienststellen werden ersucht, ihn ungehindert passieren zu lassen und ihm nötigenfalls Schutz und Hilfe zu gewähren.

--------------------
(Behörde)

--------------------
(Name)

--------------------
(Amtsbezeichnung)

Stempel

**INSIDE**

Gültigkeitsvermerke:

| Gültig für das Kalenderjahr | Beglaubigt durch: | |
|---|---|---|
| | Name und Amtsbezeichnung | Stempel: |
| | | |
| | | |
| | | |
| | | |
| | | |

**BACK COVER**

Lichtbild des Inhabers

(Eigenhändige Unterschrift des Inhabers)

Fig. 129

## MITGLIEDS-AUSWEIS—FREIW. FEUERWEHR
### (Membership Card—Voluntary Fire Brigade)

FRONT COVER

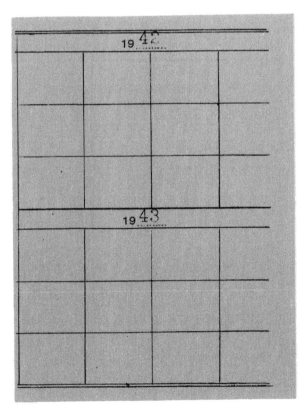

INSIDE

INSIDE

BACK COVER

Fig. 130

# AUSWEIS DER FEUERWEHRSCHAREN
## IM HJ-STREIFENDIENST
(Identity Card of the Fire Fighting Squads in the Hitler Youth Patrol
Service)

FRONT COVER

BACK COVER

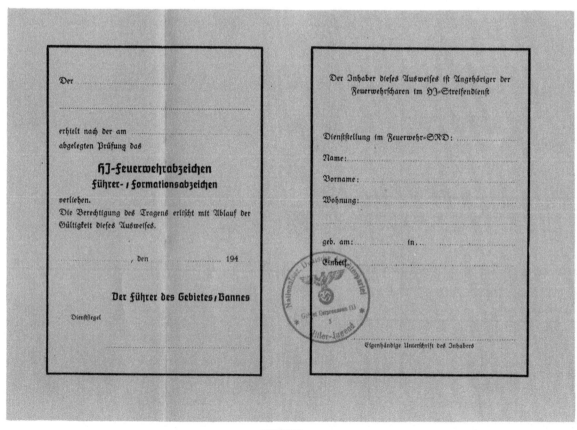

INSIDE

# FTSCHUTZDIENSTBUCH ZUGLEICH PERSONALAUSWEIS
(ARP Service Pass and Personal Document of Identity)

FRONT COVER

INSIDE

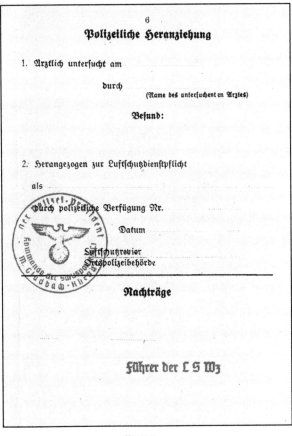

INSIDE

Fig. 132

## AUSWEIS FÜR RLB-AMTSTRÄGER
(Identity Card for Officials of the Reich Association for ARP)

FRONT COVER

Der Amtsträger des Reichsluftschutz=
bundes

......................................................
(Dienstgrad, Name, Anschrift)

ist durch die Polizei beauftragt, innerhalb

des Ortspolizeibezirks ..................................

— Bereiches des Polizeireviers Nr. ...............

— Bereiches der — des — RLB — Unter=

gruppe ...............—RLB—Blocks ............ *)

die Durchführung

des behelfsmäßigen Luftschutzraum=

baues einschließlich

der wohnlichen Ausstattung, insbe=

sondere Beheizung, und

der Schaffung der Brandmauerdurch=

brüche,

der Verdunklung,

*) Nichtzutreffendes ist zu streichen.

INSIDE

der Entrümpelung,

der Beschaffung von Selbstschutzge=

räten

zu überprüfen und zur Behebung festge=

stellter Mängel aufzufordern. Außerdem

ist dem RLB=Amtsträger von der Polizei

der auf der Rückseite bezeichnete Auftrag

erteilt worden. Er genießt bei der Durch=

führung dieser Aufgaben den besonderen

Schutz der Polizei und erhöhten Straf=

rechtschutz.

......................................................
(Ort und Datum)

(Siegel)

......................................................
(Unterschrift)

INSIDE

Dem umseitig genannten Amtsträger

des Reichsluftschutzbundes ist von der

Polizei folgender Auftrag erteilt worden:

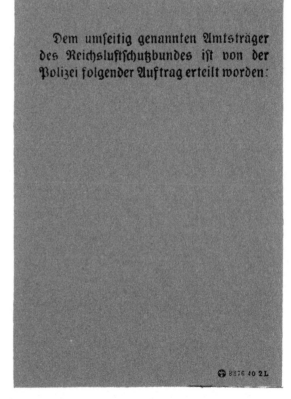

8876 40 2L

BACK COVER

Fig. 133

## MITGLIEDSAUSWEIS—REICHSLUFTSCHUTZBUND
(Membership Certificate of the Reich Association for ARP)

# Reichsluftschutzbund

Landesgruppe Niederjachsen        Bezirksgruppe Magdeburg=Anhalt
### Ortsgruppe Magdeburg=Nord

**Zur Beachtung!**
Diese Mitgliedskarte bleibt Eigen=
tum des RLB., sie ist beim Aus=
tritt zurückzugeben.
Die Beiträge sind zu Beginn des
Monats fällig.
Auszug aus den Satzungen.
§ 2, Abf. 2, Zweck.
Der RLB. hat die Aufgabe, im
Rahmen der behördlichen Vorschrif=
ten die erforderlichen Maßnahmen
auf folgenden Gebieten durchzu=
führen:
a) Aufklärung und Werbung für
den Luftschutz in der Bevölkerung.
b) Vorbereitung und Durchführung
des Selbstschutzes der Bevölkerung.
§ 3, Geschäftsjahr.
Das Geschäftsjahr läuft vom 1. 4.
eines jeden Jahres bis zum 31. 3.
des nächsten Jahres

Wohnungsänderungen sind d. Orts=
gruppe sofort schriftlich aufzugeben

## Mitgliedsausweis Nr.

Herrn
für Frau
Fräulein

Beruf: _____ Geb.=Dat. _____

Wohnort: _____ Str. _____

Monats
Jahres _____ =beitrag _____ RM. Eintritt _____

Der Ortsgruppenführer

Unterjchrift des Mitgliedes

Fig. 134

**BESCHEINIGUNG—REICHSLUFTSCHUTZBUND**

(Certificate of the Reich Association for ARP)

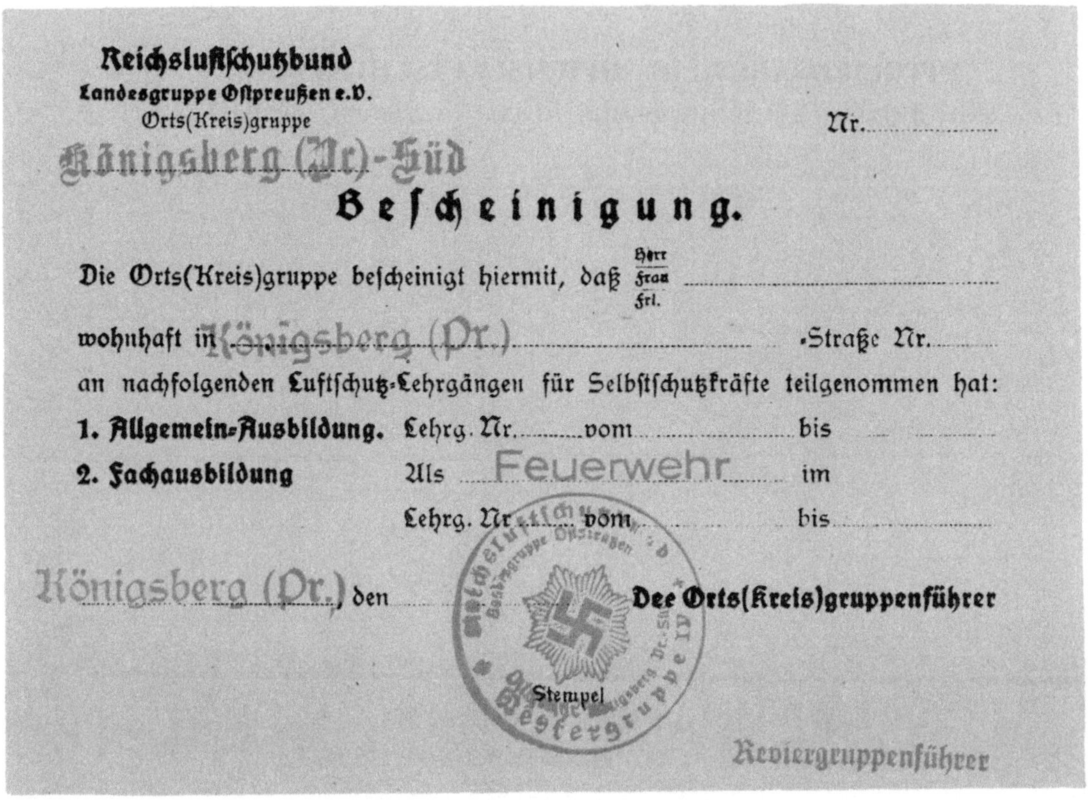

**Reichsluftschutzbund**
**Landesgruppe Ostpreußen e.V.**
Orts(Kreis)gruppe

Königsberg (Pr)-Süd

Nr. ..............

**Bescheinigung.**

Die Orts(Kreis)gruppe bescheinigt hiermit, daß Herr / Frau / Frl. ..............................

wohnhaft in Königsberg (Pr.) .............................. -Straße Nr. ..........

an nachfolgenden Luftschutz-Lehrgängen für Selbstschutzkräfte teilgenommen hat:

**1. Allgemein-Ausbildung.** Lehrg. Nr. .......... vom .............. bis ..............

**2. Fachausbildung** Als Feuerwehr im

Lehrg. Nr. .......... vom .............. bis ..............

Königsberg (Pr.), den .............................. **Der Orts(Kreis)gruppenführer**

Stempel

Reviergruppenführer

FRONT

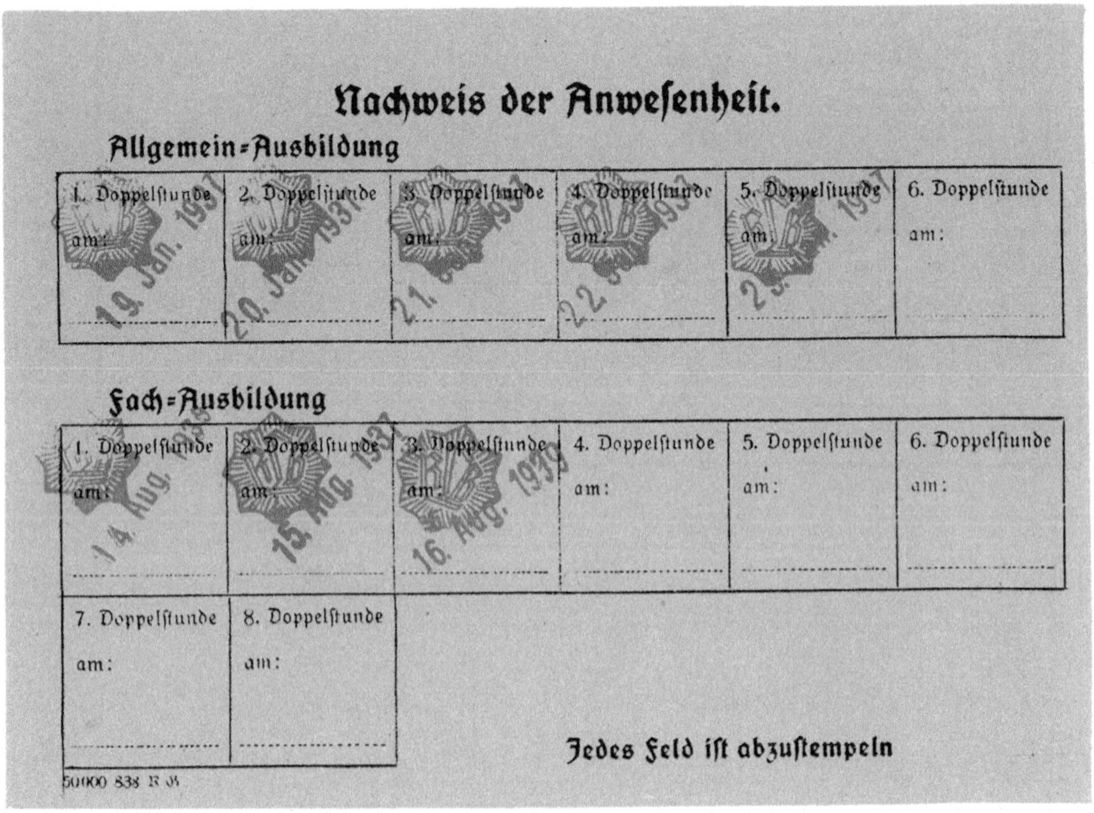

**Nachweis der Anwesenheit.**

**Allgemein-Ausbildung**

| | | | | | |
|---|---|---|---|---|---|
| 1. Doppelstunde am: 19. Jan. 1937 | 2. Doppelstunde am: 20. Jan. 1937 | 3. Doppelstunde am: 21. ... 193 | 4. Doppelstunde am: 22. ... 193 | 5. Doppelstunde am: 2... 1937 | 6. Doppelstunde am: |

**Fach-Ausbildung**

| | | | | | |
|---|---|---|---|---|---|
| 1. Doppelstunde am: 14. Aug. 193 | 2. Doppelstunde am: 15. Aug. 193 | 3. Doppelstunde am: 16. Aug. 193 | 4. Doppelstunde am: | 5. Doppelstunde am: | 6. Doppelstunde am: |
| 7. Doppelstunde am: | 8. Doppelstunde am: | | | | |

**Jedes Feld ist abzustempeln**

50000 838 R 38

BACK

Fig. 135

# AUSWEIS—TECHNISCHE NOTHILFE
## (Identity Card of the TENO)

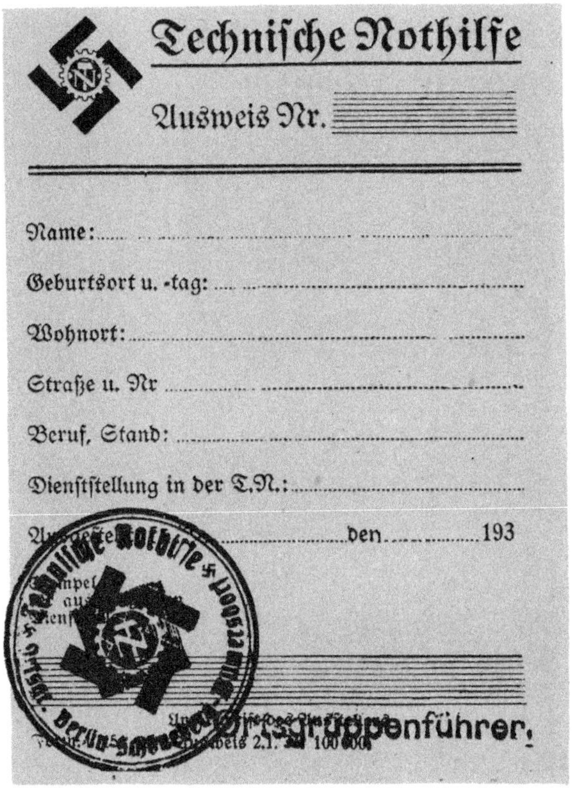

**Technische Nothilfe**

Ausweis Nr.

Name:

Geburtsort u. -tag:

Wohnort:

Straße u. Nr

Beruf, Stand:

Dienststellung in der T.N.:

den 193

Ortsgruppenführer.

FRONT COVER

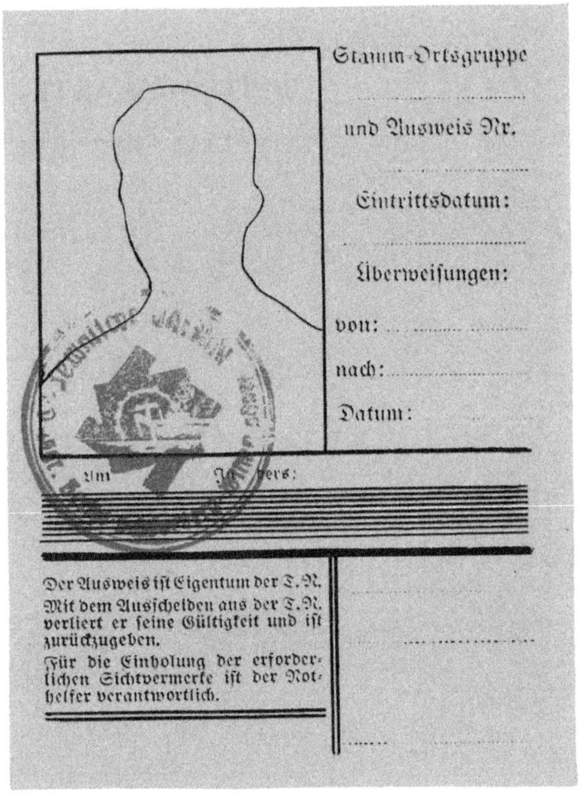

Stamm-Ortsgruppe

und Ausweis Nr.

Eintrittsdatum:

Überweisungen:

von:

nach:

Datum:

Um ers:

Der Ausweis ist Eigentum der T.N.
Mit dem Ausscheiden aus der T.N.
verliert er seine Gültigkeit und ist
zurückzugeben.
Für die Einholung der erforderlichen Sichtvermerke ist der Nothelfer verantwortlich.

INSIDE

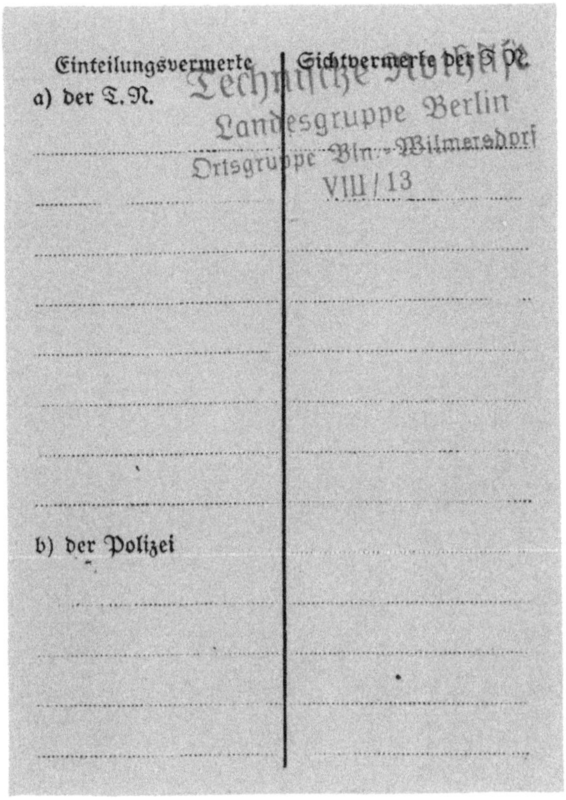

Einteilungsvermerke   Sichtvermerke der K. Pl.
a) der T.N.

Technische Nothilfe
Landesgruppe Berlin
Ortsgruppe Bln.-Wilmersdorf
VIII / 13

b) der Polizei

INSIDE

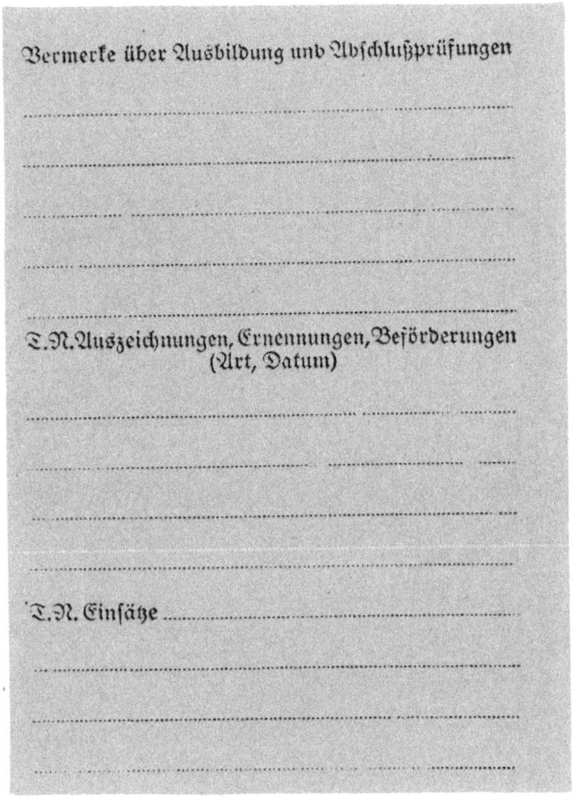

Vermerke über Ausbildung und Abschlußprüfungen

T.N.Auszeichnungen, Ernennungen, Beförderungen
(Art, Datum)

T.N. Einsätze

BACK COVER

Fig. 136

**BEITRAGSKARTE—TECHNISCHE NOTHILFE**

(Receipt for dues—TENO)

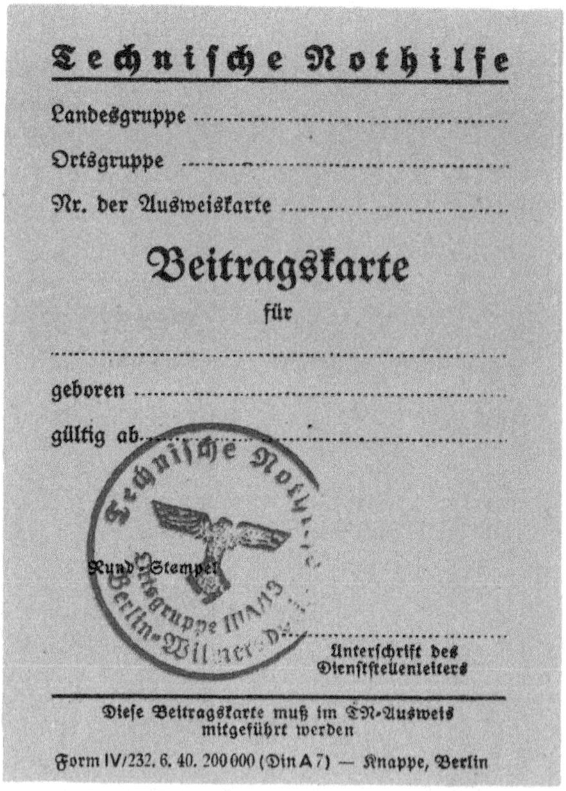

Technische Nothilfe

Landesgruppe ..............................

Ortsgruppe ..............................

Nr. der Ausweiskarte ..............................

Beitragskarte

für

..............................

geboren ..............................

gültig ab ..............................

Rund-Stempel

..............................

Unterschrift des Dienststellenleiters

Diese Beitragskarte muß im TN-Ausweis mitgeführt werden

Form IV/232. 6. 40. 200 000 (Din A 7) — Knappe, Berlin

Fig. 137

## TN-UNTERFUHRER-AUSWEIS

(Identity Card for NCO'S of the TENO)

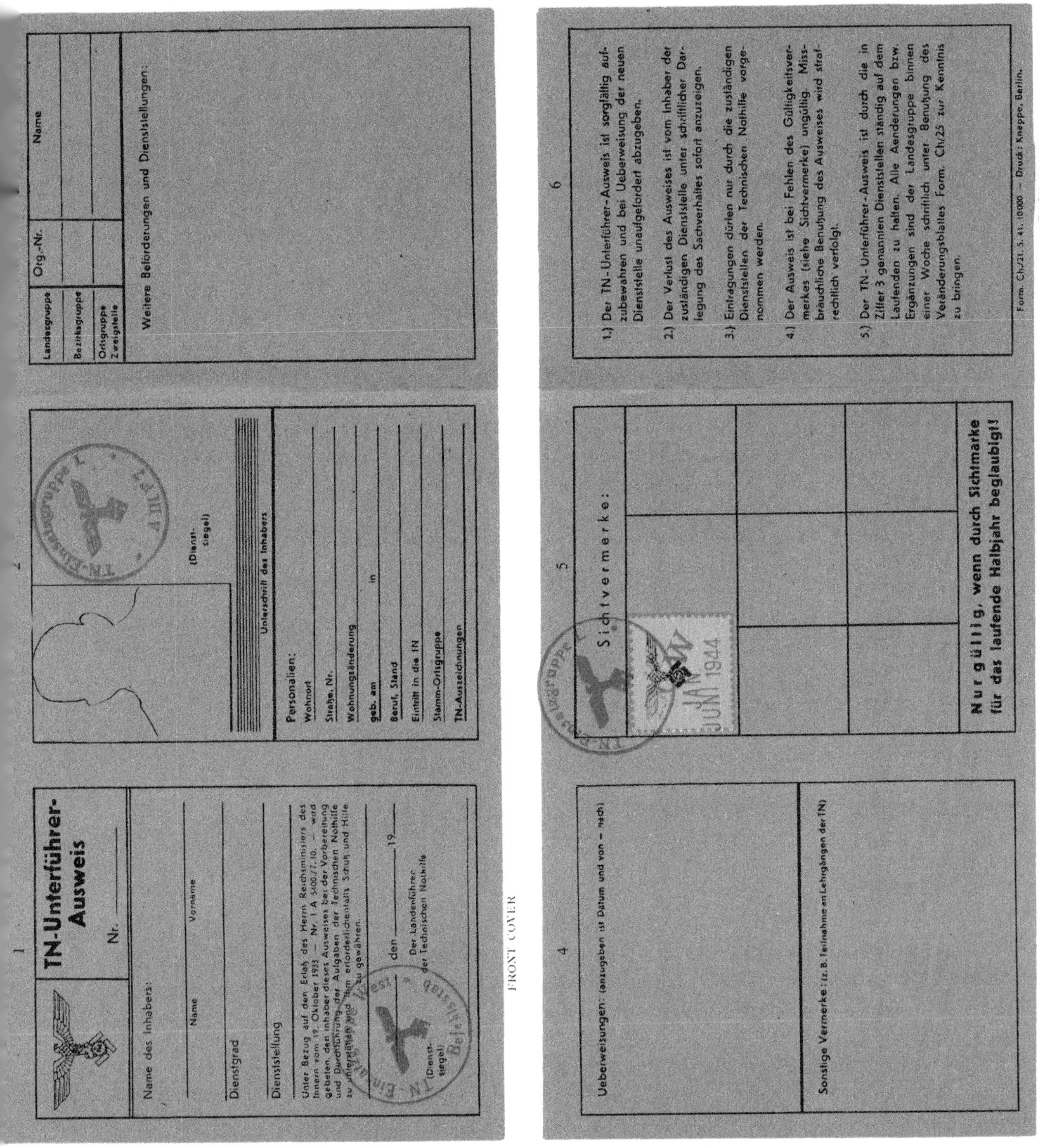
1

TN-Unterführer-Ausweis

Nr. ________

Name des Inhabers:

Name Vorname

Dienstgrad

Dienststellung

Unter Bezug auf den Erlaß des Herrn Reichsministers des Innern vom 19. Oktober 1933 — Nr. I A 5400/7.10. — wird gebeten, den Inhaber dieses Ausweises bei der Vorbereitung und Durchführung der Aufgaben der Technischen Nothilfe zu unterstützen und ihm erforderlichenfalls Schutz und Hilfe zu gewähren.

(Dienst-siegel)

den ________ 19____

Der Landenführer der Technischen Nothilfe

2

(Dienst-siegel)

Unterschrift des Inhabers

Personalien:

Wohnort

Straße, Nr.

Wohnungsänderung

geb. am in

Beruf, Stand

Eintritt in die TN

Stamm-Ortsgruppe

TN-Auszeichnungen

| Landesgruppe | Org.-Nr. | Name |
|---|---|---|
| Bezirksgruppe | | |
| Ortsgruppe Zweigstelle | | |

Weitere Beförderungen und Dienststellungen:

FRONT COVER

4

Ueberweisungen: (anzugeben ist Datum und von — nach)

Sonstige Vermerke: (z. B. Teilnahme an Lehrgängen der TN)

5

Sichtvermerke:

JAN JUNI 1944

Nur gültig, wenn durch Sichtmarke für das laufende Halbjahr beglaubigt!

6

1.) Der TN-Unterführer-Ausweis ist sorgfältig aufzubewahren und bei Ueberweisung der neuen Dienststelle unaufgefordert abzugeben.

2.) Der Verlust des Ausweises ist vom Inhaber der zuständigen Dienststelle unter schriftlicher Darlegung des Sachverhaltes sofort anzuzeigen.

3.) Eintragungen dürfen nur durch die zuständigen Dienststellen der Technischen Nothilfe vorgenommen werden.

4.) Der Ausweis ist bei Fehlen des Gültigkeitsvermerkes (siehe Sichtvermerke) ungültig. Missbräuchliche Benutzung des Ausweises wird strafrechtlich verfolgt.

5.) Der TN-Unterführer-Ausweis ist durch die in Ziffer 3 genannten Dienststellen ständig auf dem Laufenden zu halten. Alle Aenderungen bzw. Ergänzungen sind der Landesgruppe binnen einer Woche schriftlich unter Benutzung des Veränderungsblattes Form. Ch/25 zur Kenntnis zu bringen.

Form. Ch/21. 5. 41. 10000 — Druck: Kneppe, Berlin.

BACK COVER

Fig. 138

# DIENSTAUSWEIS—HILFSPOLIZEI
## (Official Service Pass—Auxiliary Police)

1

**Dienstausweis**

**Nr.**

.......................................
(Name des Inhabers)

.......................................
(Dienstgrad)

DIN A 7d (71 × 105 mm). Vordr. K. Pol. Nr. 159

FRONT COVER

— 2 —

......................., am .............. 194......

Inhaber dieses Ausweises

.......................................
(Vor- und Zuname)

geboren am .............. in ..............

ist Hilfspolizeibeamter der

.......................................

Er ist berechtigt, Waffen zu tragen.

**Der Kommandeur:**

(Stempel)

.......................................
(Dienstgrad)

INSIDE

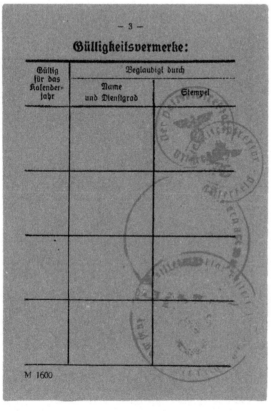

— 3 —

**Gültigkeitsvermerke:**

| Gültig für das Kalenderjahr | Beglaubigt durch | |
|---|---|---|
| | Name und Dienstgrad | Stempel |
| | | |
| | | |
| | | |
| | | |

M 1600

INSIDE

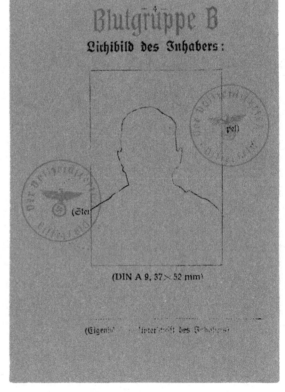

Blutgruppe B

Lichtbild des Inhabers:

(Stempel)

(DIN A 9, 37 × 52 mm)

(Eigenhändige Unterschrift des Inhabers)

BACK COVER

Fig. 139

**WEHRMANNSCHAFTSPASS**
(Identity Pass of the Internal Defence Formation)

FRONT COVER

Fig. 140

# AUSWEIS—STADTWACHT
### (Identity Pass—Auxiliary Urban Police)

Der Bürgermeister der Stadt

## Ausweis Nr.

für den Stadtwachtangehörigen

(Eigenhändige Unterschrift)

FRONT

Inhaber dieses Ausweises

(Vor- und Zuname)

geb:

ist Angehöriger der

## Stadtwacht

in

Er ist Hilfspolizeibeamter und berechtigt, im Dienste Waffen zu tragen.

, den

Der Bürgermeister als Ortspolizeiverwalter:

REVERSE SIDE

Fig. 141

**AUSWEIS—HJ.-STREIFENDIENST**

(Identity Pass—Hitler Youth Patrol Service)

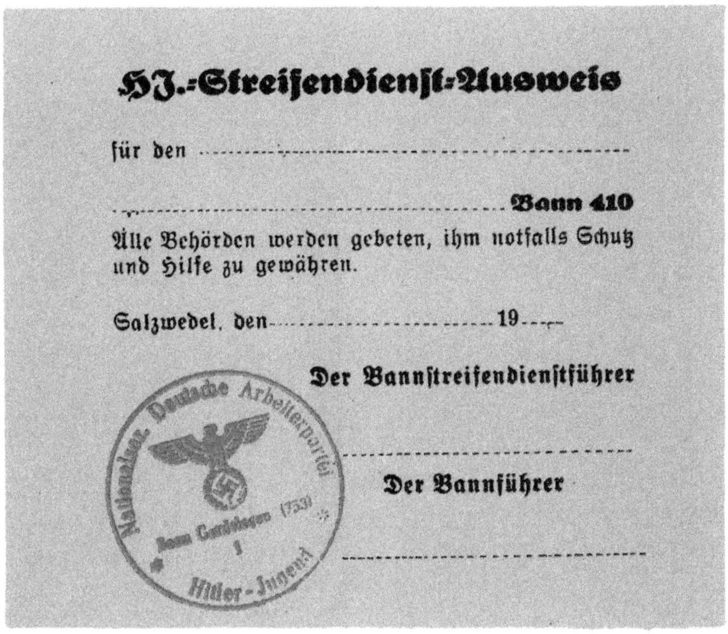

**HJ.-Streifendienst-Ausweis**

für den ..................................................

.................................................. **Bann 410**

Alle Behörden werden gebeten, ihm notfalls Schutz und Hilfe zu gewähren.

Salzwedel, den ........................ 19....

**Der Bannstreifendienstführer**

..................................................

**Der Bannführer**

..................................................

Nationalsoz. Deutsche Arbeiterpartei

Hitler-Jugend

FRONT

Fig. 142

**NSKK.-PASS**

(Identity Book of the National Socialist Motor Corps)

FRONT COVER

National = Sozialistisches Kraftfahr = Korps

# NSKK.=Paß

Nr. ▨▨▨▨▨▨▨▨

Nationalsoz. Kraftfahrkorps
Ausgestellt von: Motor-Sturm 2/M 41 Gera
Einheit

Motorgruppe Thüringen

Der NSKK.=Paß ist ungültig, wenn nicht die Beitrags=
und Versicherungsmarke für den laufenden Kalendermonat
eingeklebt ist (Seite 20—24). Es ist dann anzunehmen,
daß der Inhaber inzwischen aus dem NSKK. ausgeschie=
den ist und sich mißbräuchlich des Passes weiterbedient.

Form. 94                    1

INSIDE

---

Der Paßinhaber ist auf dem neben=
stehenden Lichtbild dargestellt und hat
die unter dem Lichtbild befindliche
Unterschrift eigenhändig vollzogen.

Unterschrift des Führers und Dienststempel
der ausstellenden Einheit

.................., den .................

## N S K K.
### Motorsturm 2/M 41

Sturmführer

### Besondere Kennzeichen

Gestalt:................... Größe:..........

Gesicht:...................................

Farbe der Augen:..........................

Farbe der Haare:..........................

Besondere Kennzeichen:....................

..........................................

2

Vor= und Zuname (Rufname unterstrichen)

..........................................

Dienstgrad und Dienststellung am Tage der Ausstellung

..........................................

..........................................

Beruf ....................................

geb. am ..................................

zu .......................................

Partei=Mitgl. Nr. ........................

Eintritt in die Partei ...................

Eintritt in die SA. bezw. MSA. ...........

Eintritt in das NSKK. ....................

Eintritt in die HJ. ......................

Übertritt in die SA. .....................

Übertritt in das NSKK. ...................

3

INSIDE

Fig. 143

**AUSWEISKARTE—BAHNPOLIZEI**
(Identity Card—State Railway Police)

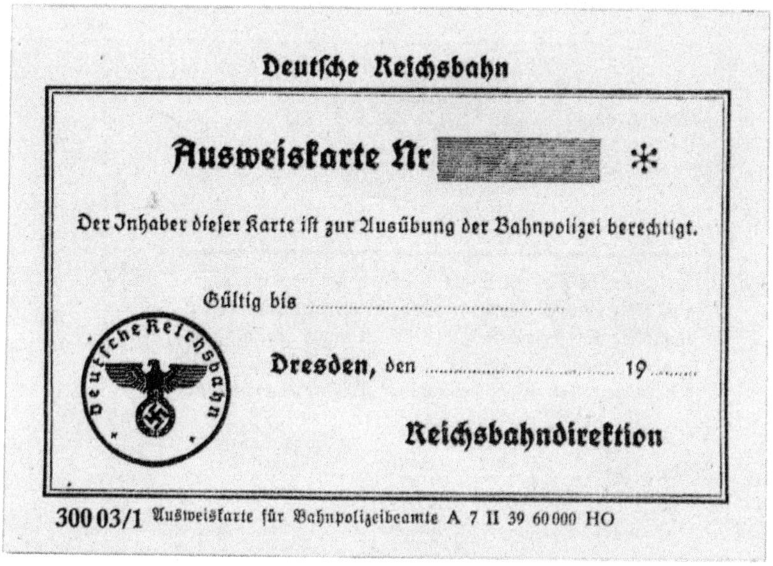

Deutsche Reichsbahn

**Ausweiskarte Nr** ▓▓▓▓▓▓ ✳

Der Inhaber dieser Karte ist zur Ausübung der Bahnpolizei berechtigt.

Gültig bis ............................................

Dresden, den ........................... 19........

**Reichsbahndirektion**

300 03/1 Ausweiskarte für Bahnpolizeibeamte A 7 II 39 60000 HO

FRONT

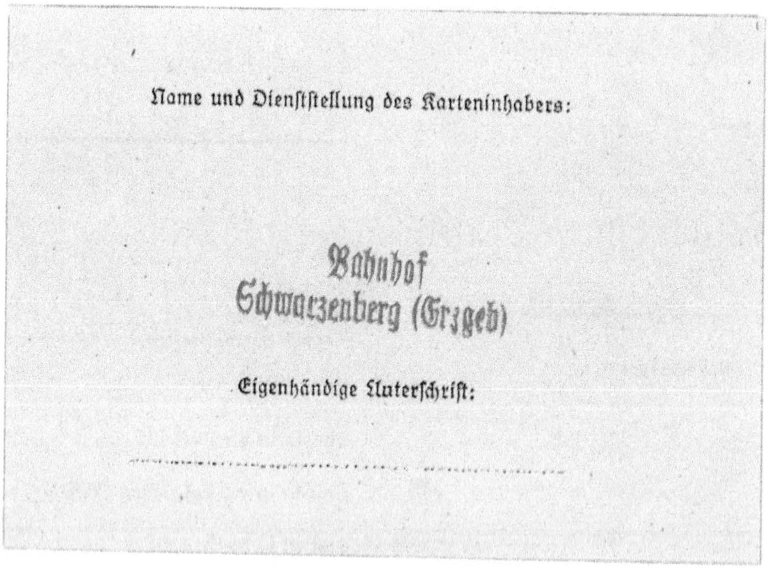

Name und Dienststellung des Karteninhabers:

Bahnhof
Schwarzenberg (Erzgeb)

Eigenhändige Unterschrift:

.....................................................

REVERSE SIDE

**SS SOLDBUCH ZUGLEICH PERSONALAUSWEIS**
S Paybook and Identity Document for the Sipo and the SD)

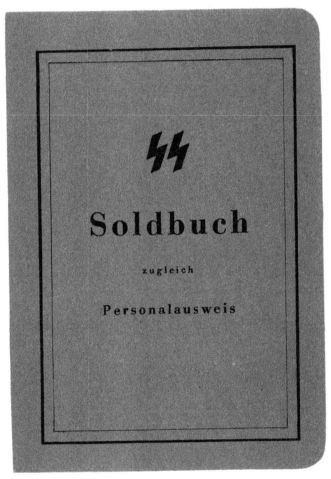

FRONT COVER

*SS*-Soldbuch
zugleich Personalausweis

Nr. ▭

für

den ................................................
　　　　　　　　　(Dienstgrad)

| ab........................ | (neuer Dienstgrad) |
|---|---|
| (Datum) | |
| ab........................ | |
| ab........................ | |

................................................
(Vor- und Zuname)

Beschriftung und Nummer der

　　Erkennungsmarke ................................................

　　Blutgruppe ................................................

　　Gasmaskengröße ................................................

　　Wehrnummer ................................................

**Bestell-Nr. W *SS* 433⁹.** Metten & Co, Berlin SW61

1

Fortsetzung zu Seite 4

B. **Zum Feldheer abgesandt von¹)**

| | Ersatztruppenteil | Kompanie | Nr. der Truppen-stammrolle |
|---|---|---|---|
| a | | | |
| b | | | |
| c | | | |

| C. | Feldtruppenteil²) | Kompanie | Nr. der Kriegs-stammrolle |
|---|---|---|---|
| a | | | |
| b | | | |
| c | | | |

| D. | Jetzt zuständiger Ersatztruppenteil²) | Standort |
|---|---|---|
| | | |
| | | |
| | | |

(Meldung dortselbst nach Rückkehr vom Feldheer oder Lazarett, zuständig
für Ersatz an Bekleidung und Ausrüstung.)

¹) Vom Ersatztruppenteil einzutragen, von dem der Soldbuchinhaber zum Feldheer abgesandt wird.
²) Vom Feldtruppenteil einzutragen und bei Versetzungen von einem zum
anderen Feldtruppenteil derart abzuändern, daß die alten Angaben nur
durchstrichen werden, also leserlich bleiben.

25

geboren am ........................ in ........................

(Ort, Kreis, Verwaltungsbezirk)

Religion ........................ Stand, Beruf ........................

## Personalbeschreibung

Größe ........................ Gestalt ........................

Gesicht ........................ Haar ........................

Bart ........................ Augen ........................

Besondere Kennzeichen (z. B. Brillenträger) ........................

........................

Schuhzeuglänge ........................ Schuhzeugweite ........................

........................

(Vor- und Zuname, eigenhändige Unterschrift des Inhabers)

Die Richtigkeit der nicht umrandeten Angaben auf Seite 1 und 2 und der eigenhändigen Unterschrift des Inhabers bescheinigt:

**Straßburg,** den **28. 9. 44** ........................ 194....

**Befehlshaber der Sicherheitspolizei und des S.D. Straßburg Elf.**

(Kennzeichen der Dienststelle)

........................

(Eigenhändige Unterschrift, Dienstgrad u. Dienststellung d. Vorges.)

2

---

### Bescheinigungen

über die Richtigkeit der Zusätze und Berichtigungen auf Seite 1 und 2

| Lfd. Nr. | Art der Änderung | auf Seite | Datum | Truppenteil | Unterschrift | Dienstgrad und Dienststellung |
|---|---|---|---|---|---|---|
| | | | | | | |
| | | | | | | |
| | | | | | | |
| | | | | | | |
| | | | | | | |

3

---

## Orden und Ehrenzeichen

| Datum | Art der Auszeichnung | Urkunde erhalten | Bestätigung (Komp.- usw. Führer) |
|---|---|---|---|
| | | | |
| | | | |
| | | | |
| | | | |
| | | | |
| | | | |
| | | | |
| | | | |
| | | | |
| | | | |
| | | | |

30

---

## Beurlaubungen über 5 Tage

1. Vom ........ bis ........ nach ........................

   Grund: ........................

   ........ den ........................ 194....

   (Dienststempel)

   ........................
   (Unterschrift des Komp.-, Truppenführers usw.)

2. Vom ........ bis ........ nach ........................

   Grund: ........................

   ........ den ........................ 194....

   (Dienststempel)

   ........................
   (Unterschrift des Komp.-, Truppenführers usw.)

3. Vom ........ bis ........ nach ........................

   Grund: ........................

   ........ den ........................ 194....

   (Dienststempel)

   ........................
   (Unterschrift des Komp.-, Truppenführers usw.)

4. Vom ........ bis ........ nach ........................

   Grund: ........................

   ........ den ........................ 194....

   (Dienststempel)

   ........................
   (Unterschrift des Komp.-, Truppenführers usw.)

31

**A.** Zuletzt zuständige Wehrersatzdienststelle..................

**B.** Zum Feldheer abgesandt von¹)

|   | Ersatztruppenteil | Kompanie | Nr. der Truppen-stammrolle |
|---|---|---|---|
| a |   |   |   |
| b |   |   |   |
| c |   |   |   |

**C.**

|   | Feldtruppenteil²) | Kompanie | Nr. der Kriegs-stammrolle |
|---|---|---|---|
| a |   |   |   |
| b |   |   |   |
| c |   |   |   |

**D.**

| Jetzt zuständiger Ersatztruppenteil²) | Standort |
|---|---|
|   |   |
|   |   |
|   |   |
|   |   |

(Meldung dortselbst nach Rückkehr vom Feldheer oder Lazarett, zuständig für Ersatz an Bekleidung und Ausrüstung.)

¹) Vom Ersatztruppenteil einzutragen, von dem der Soldbuchinhaber zum Feldheer abgesandt wird.
²) Vom Feldtruppenteil einzutragen und bei Versetzungen von einem zum anderen Feldtruppenteil derart abzuändern, daß die alten Angaben nur durchstrichen werden, also leserlich bleiben.

Weiterer Raum für Eintragungen auf Seite 25.

4

---

### Anschriften der nächsten lebenden Angehörigen

des ..................
　　　　　　(Vor- und Zuname)

1. **Ehefrau:** Vor- und Mädchenname ..................

..................
　　　　　　(gegebenenfalls Vermerk „ledig")

Wohnort (Kreis)..................

Straße, Haus-Nr. ..................

2. **Eltern:** des Vaters Vor- und Zuname ..................

Stand oder Gewerbe ..................

der Mutter Vor- und Mädchenname ..................

Wohnort (Kreis)..................

Straße, Haus-Nr. ..................

3. **Verwandte oder Braut:*)** ..................

Vor- und Zuname ..................

Stand oder Gewerbe ..................

Wohnort (Kreis)..................

Straße, Haus-Nr. ..................

*) Ausfüllung nur, wenn weder 1 noch 2 ausgefüllt sind.

5

---

INSIDE BACK COVER　　　　　　　　　　OUTSIDE BACK COVER

---

**DIENSTAUSWEIS—SIPO UND SD**

(Identity Card of the Security Police and Security Service)

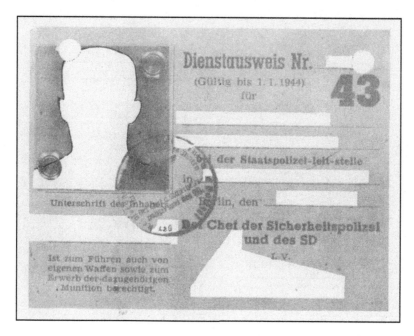

FRONT

**DIENSTAUSWEIS—SIPO UND SD**

(Identity Card of the Security Police and Security Service)

Note:  Red markings are in effect an intricate anti-erasure background in red and orange on white.

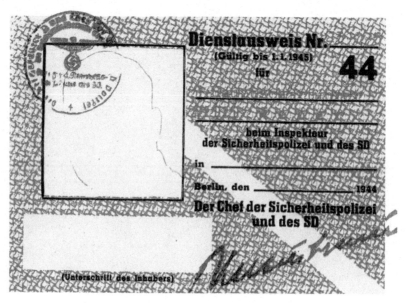

FRONT

# AUSWEIS—SS DER NSDAP IM SICHERHEITSDIENST
(Identity Card for NCO'S of the SS of the NSDAP in the Security
Service)

## Schutzstaffeln der N.S.D.A.P.

### SS-Unterführer-Ausweis Nr.

Pg. .........................................................

Mitglieds-Nr. .........................................

ist SS. .....................................................

im Sicherheitsdienst des Reichsführers-SS

Eigenhändige Unterschrift

FRONT

Befördert: ....................    Ernannt: ..................

Berlin, den ............................... 193....

Der Reichsführer der Schutzstaffeln:

Der Chef des Sicherheitshauptamtes:

i. V. ...............................................

Schutzstaffeln d. NSDAP.

19    40

Gültig für        Okt./Dez.

Ausweis nur gültig mit zeitlich richtiger Beglaubigungsmarke

REVERSE SIDE

**ERKENNUNGSMARKE—GESTAPO**

(Identity Disc—Secret State Police)

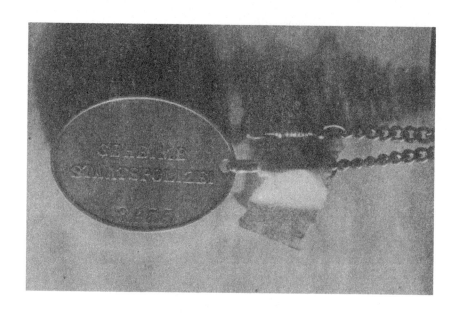

Fig. 149

# AUSWEIS—GEHEIME FELDPOLIZEI
## (Identity Pass—Secret Field Police)

## Geheime Feldpolizei
### Ausweis Nr.

.......................................
(Dienststelle)

für den .......................................

**Inhaber der**
**Kennkarte Nr.** .......................................

Lichtbild in Uniform
ohne Kopfbedeckung

.......................................
(Eigenhändige Unterschrift,
Vor- und Zuname)

Lichtbild in Zivil
ohne Kopfbedeckung

Dienststempel

Hauptquartier, den .......................................

.......................................
(Unterschrift des Befehlshabers)

FRONT

I. **Die Angehörigen der GFP sind befugt:**
   a) zum Durchschreiten jeder militärischen Absperrung und zum Betreten militärischer Dienstgebäude;
   b) zu Festnahmen, Durchsuchungen und Beschlagnahmen;
   c) zur Sicherstellung von Heeresgut;
   d) zu jeglicher Personenfeststellung (jeden Dienstgrades).

II. **Die Angehörigen der GFP sind berechtigt:**
   a) zur jederzeitigen Benutzung aller militärischen Nachrichtenmittel;
   b) zur Benutzung jeglicher Wehrmachtsfahrzeuge, soweit Platz vorhanden

III. **die Angehörigen der GFP führen ihren Dienst in Uniform oder Zivilkleidung aus.**

IV. **Die Truppe, alle Kommando- und Verwaltungsbehörden sowie jeder Wehrmachtsangehörige sind der GFP gegenüber zur Hilfeleistung verpflichtet.**

Dieser Ausweis ist im Dienst stets mitzuführen, sorgfältig aufzubewahren, vor Mißbrauch durch andere zu schützen. Verlust ist unverzüglich dem AOK (Ic/AO) unter Angabe der vermutlichen Verluststelle zu melden.

REVERSE SIDE

Fig. 150)

**PERSONALBUCH—VGAD**

(Personal Identification Book of the Reinforced Frontier Patrol Service)

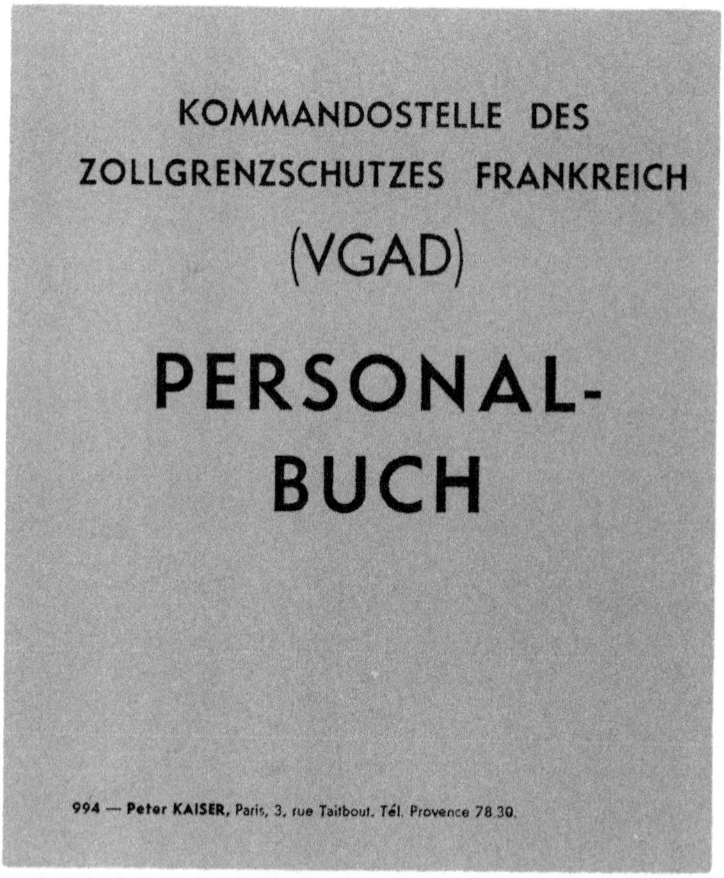

KOMMANDOSTELLE DES
ZOLLGRENZSCHUTZES FRANKREICH

(VGAD)

# PERSONAL-
# BUCH

994 — Peter KAISER, Paris, 3, rue Taitbout. Tél. Provence 78.30.

FRONT COVER

Fig. 151

# DIENSTAUSWEIS—REICHSFINANZVERWALTUNG
## (Service Identity Card—Reich Finance Administration)

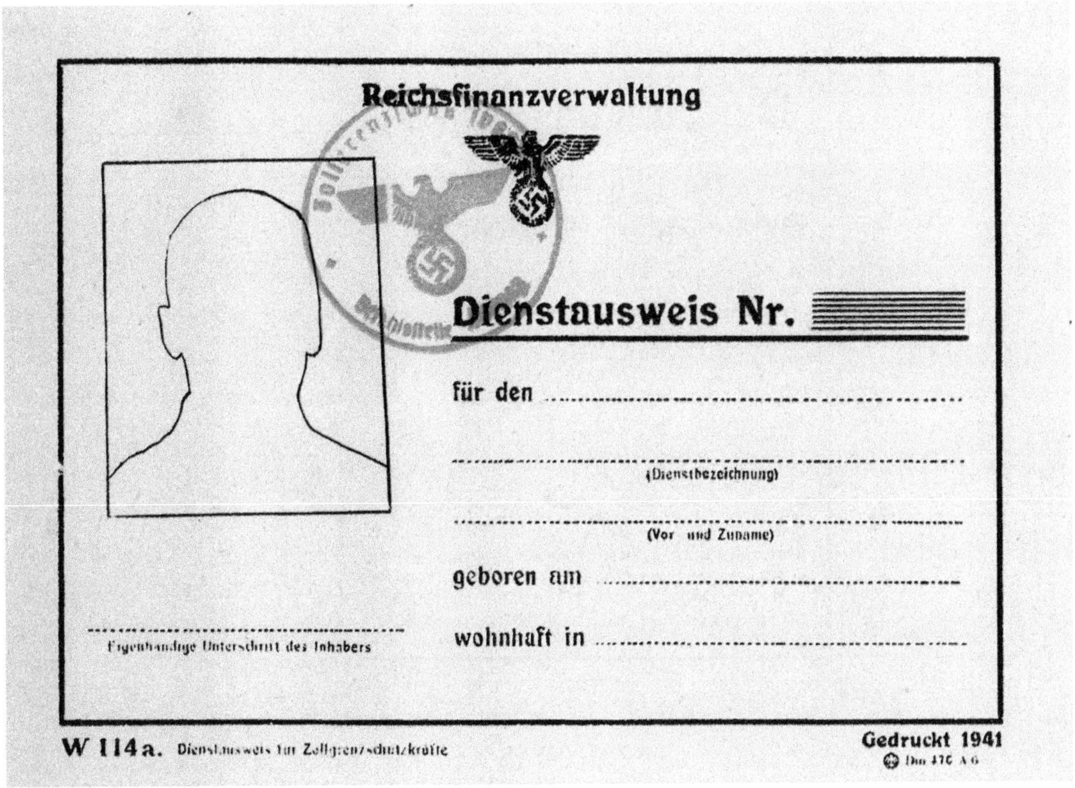

**Reichsfinanzverwaltung**

**Dienstausweis Nr.** ▦▦▦▦

für den ...............................................................

.............................................................................
(Dienstbezeichnung)

.............................................................................
(Vor und Zuname)

geboren am ........................................................

.............................................................
Eigenhändige Unterschrift des Inhabers

wohnhaft in ........................................................

W 114a. Dienstausweis für Zollgrenzschutzkräfte

Gedruckt 1941

FRONT

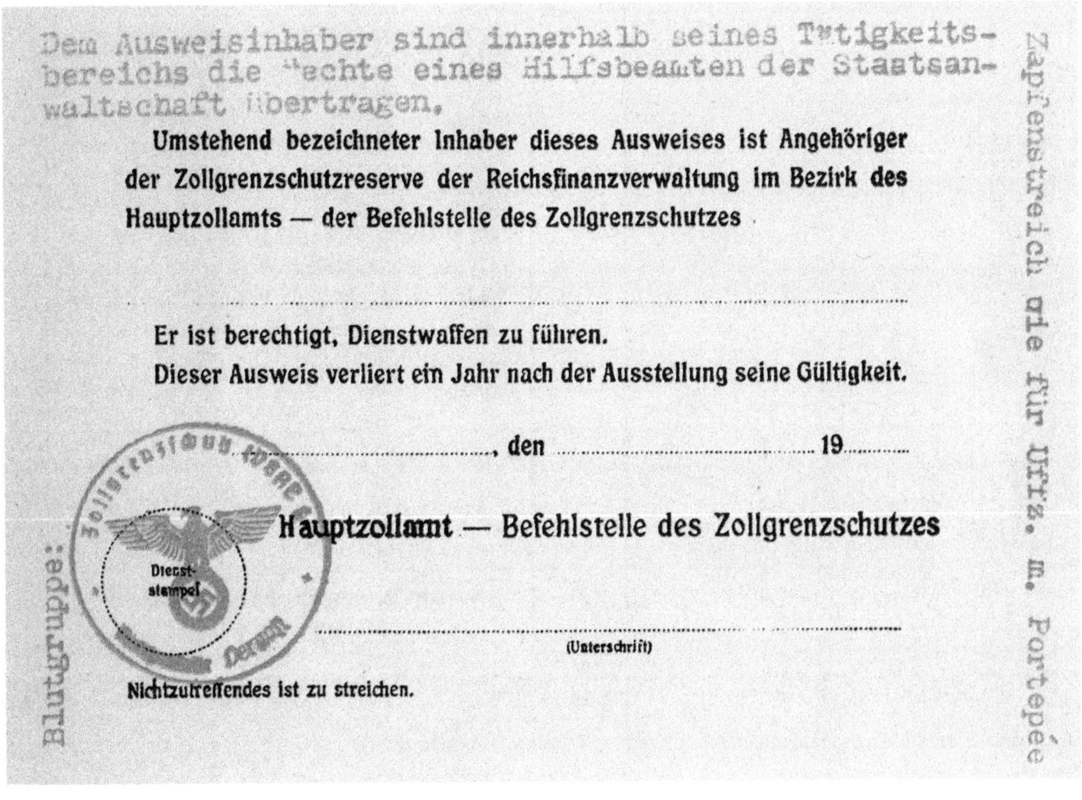

Dem Ausweisinhaber sind innerhalb seines Tätigkeits-
bereichs die Rechte eines Hilfsbeamten der Staatsanwaltschaft übertragen.

Umstehend bezeichneter Inhaber dieses Ausweises ist Angehöriger

der Zollgrenzschutzreserve der Reichsfinanzverwaltung im Bezirk des

Hauptzollamts — der Befehlstelle des Zollgrenzschutzes

Er ist berechtigt, Dienstwaffen zu führen.

Dieser Ausweis verliert ein Jahr nach der Ausstellung seine Gültigkeit.

......................................., den ...............................19.............

**Hauptzollamt — Befehlstelle des Zollgrenzschutzes**

Dienst-
stempel

.............................................................
(Unterschrift)

Blutgruppe:

Nichtzutreffendes ist zu streichen.

Zapfenstreich wie für Uffz. m. Portepee

REVERSE SIDE

Fig. 152

# BERECHTIGUNGSSCHEIN
### (Permit—issued by the Wasserpolizeibehörde)

Regierungsbezirk Aurich

**Wasserstraßenamt Leer**     Nr. ............ 19........

## Berechtigungsschein
### zur Führung eines
### Dampf- oder Motorfahrzeugs

auf der Ems, der Leda und in dem
Hafen Emden

———

(Dieser Berechtigungsschein gilt nur für Fahrzeuge,
für deren Führung nicht durch die Verordnung über
die Besetzung von Kauffahrteischiffen mit Kapitänen
und Schiffsoffizieren vom 29. Juni 1931 ein Schiffer-,
Steuermanns- oder Kapitänspatent verlangt wird.)

**FRONT COVER**

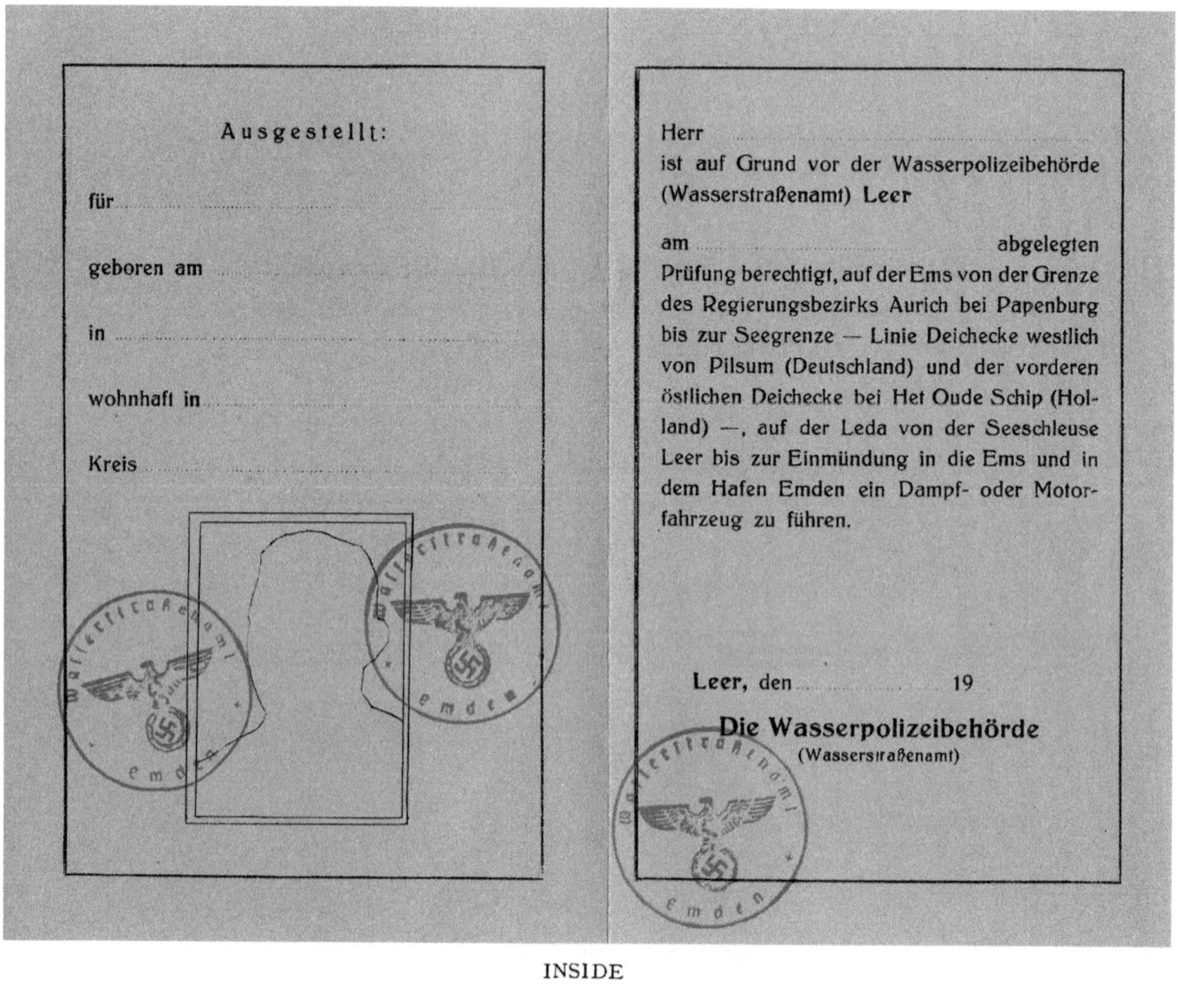

Ausgestellt:

für ........................................

geboren am ........................................

in ........................................

wohnhaft in ........................................

Kreis ........................................

Herr ........................................

ist auf Grund vor der Wasserpolizeibehörde
(Wasserstraßenamt) **Leer**

am ........................ abgelegten
Prüfung berechtigt, auf der Ems von der Grenze
des Regierungsbezirks Aurich bei Papenburg
bis zur Seegrenze — Linie Deichecke westlich
von Pilsum (Deutschland) und der vorderen
östlichen Deichecke bei Het Oude Schip (Holland) —, auf der Leda von der Seeschleuse
Leer bis zur Einmündung in die Ems und in
dem Hafen Emden ein Dampf- oder Motor-
fahrzeug zu führen.

Leer, den ........................ 19

**Die Wasserpolizeibehörde**
(Wasserstraßenamt)

**INSIDE**

Fig. 153

# KENNKARTE—DEUTSCHES REICH
## (Identity Card)

FRONT COVER                    BACK COVER

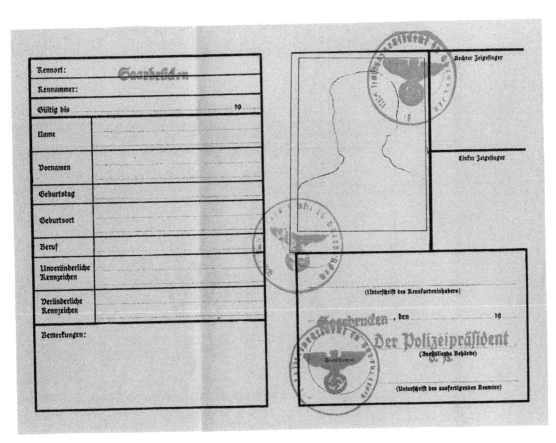

INSIDE

Fig. 154  AUSWEIS DER DEUTSCHEN VOLKSLISTE

(Blue Certificate of Registration for "Racial Germans")

INSIDE

FRONT COVER

Fig. 155   AUSWEIS DER DEUTSCHEN VOLKSLISTE

(Green Certificate of Registration for "Racial Germans")

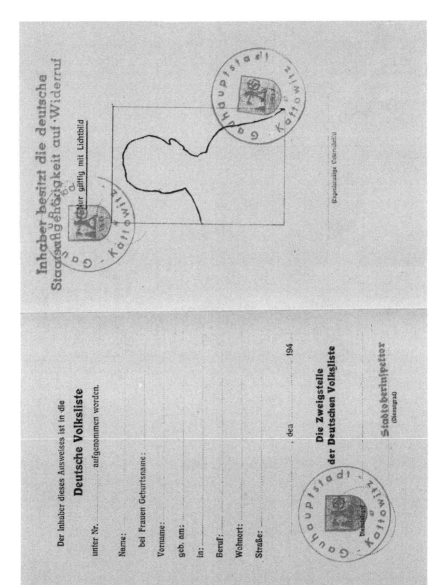

INSIDE

FRONT COVER

Fig. 156

**ANMELDUNG BEI DER POLIZEILICHEN MELDEBEHÖRDE**

(Police Registration on taking up residence)

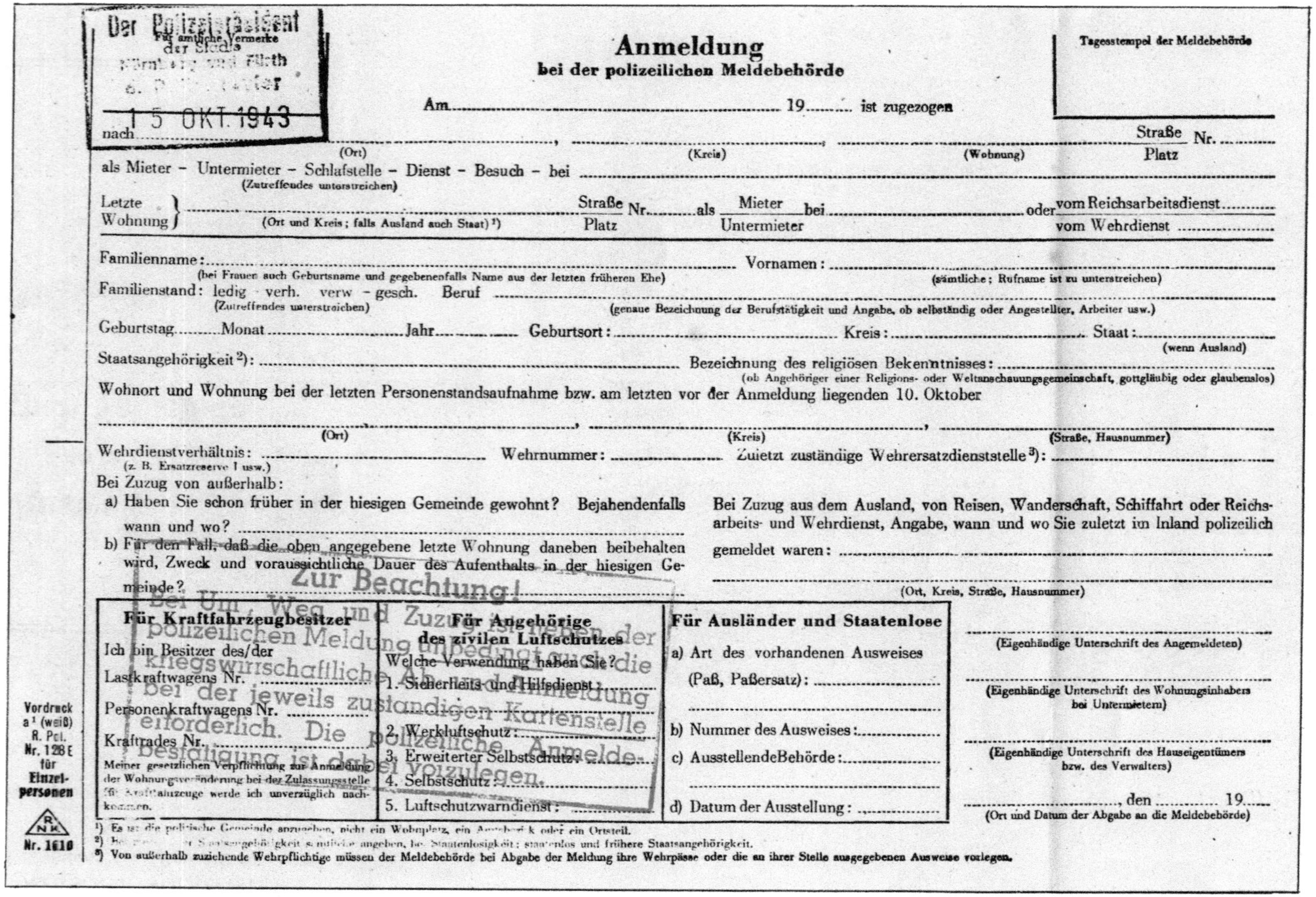

Der Polizeipräsident der Stadt Nürnberg und Fürth
Für amtliche Vermerke
15 OKT. 1943

**Anmeldung**
**bei der polizeilichen Meldebehörde**

Tagesstempel der Meldebehörde

Am .................................... 19........ ist zugezogen

nach .................................... (Ort), .................................... (Kreis), .................................... (Wohnung) Straße/Platz Nr. ..........

als Mieter – Untermieter – Schlafstelle – Dienst – Besuch – bei .................................... (Zutreffendes unterstreichen)

Letzte Wohnung } .................................... (Ort und Kreis; falls Ausland auch Staat)[1] Straße/Platz Nr. ........ als Mieter/Untermieter bei .................... oder vom Reichsarbeitsdienst/vom Wehrdienst ..........

Familienname: .................................... (bei Frauen auch Geburtsname und gegebenenfalls Name aus der letzten früheren Ehe) Vornamen: .................................... (sämtliche; Rufname ist zu unterstreichen)

Familienstand: ledig - verh. verw - gesch. (Zutreffendes unterstreichen) Beruf .................................... (genaue Bezeichnung der Berufstätigkeit und Angabe, ob selbständig oder Angestellter, Arbeiter usw.)

Geburtstag ........ Monat .................... Jahr .......... Geburtsort: .................... Kreis: .................... Staat: .......... (wenn Ausland)

Staatsangehörigkeit[2]: .................................... Bezeichnung des religiösen Bekenntnisses: .................... (ob Angehöriger einer Religions- oder Weltanschauungsgemeinschaft, gottgläubig oder glaubenslos)

Wohnort und Wohnung bei der letzten Personenstandsaufnahme bzw. am letzten vor der Anmeldung liegenden 10. Oktober

.................................... (Ort), .................................... (Kreis), .................................... (Straße, Hausnummer)

Wehrdienstverhältnis: .................... (z. B. Ersatzreserve I usw.) Wehrnummer: .................... Zuletzt zuständige Wehrersatzdienststelle[3]: ....................

Bei Zuzug von außerhalb:

a) Haben Sie schon früher in der hiesigen Gemeinde gewohnt? Bejahendenfalls wann und wo? ....................................

b) Für den Fall, daß die oben angegebene letzte Wohnung daneben beibehalten wird, Zweck und voraussichtliche Dauer des Aufenthalts in der hiesigen Gemeinde? ....................................

Bei Zuzug aus dem Ausland, von Reisen, Wanderschaft, Schiffahrt oder Reichsarbeits- und Wehrdienst, Angabe, wann und wo Sie zuletzt im Inland polizeilich gemeldet waren: ....................................

.................................... (Ort, Kreis, Straße, Hausnummer)

**Für Kraftfahrzeugbesitzer**

Ich bin Besitzer des/der
Lastkraftwagens Nr. ..........
Personenkraftwagens Nr. ..........
Kraftrades Nr. ..........

Meiner gesetzlichen Verpflichtung zur Anmeldung der Wohnungsveränderung bei der Zulassungsstelle für Kraftfahrzeuge werde ich unverzüglich nachkommen.

**Für Angehörige des zivilen Luftschutzes**

Welche Verwendung haben Sie?
1. Sicherheits- und Hilfsdienst: ..........
2. Werkluftschutz: ..........
3. Erweiterter Selbstschutz: ..........
4. Selbstschutz: ..........
5. Luftschutzwarndienst: ..........

**Für Ausländer und Staatenlose**

a) Art des vorhandenen Ausweises (Paß, Paßersatz): ..........
b) Nummer des Ausweises: ..........
c) Ausstellende Behörde: ..........
d) Datum der Ausstellung: ..........

Zur Beachtung! Bei Um-, Weg- und Zuzug ist neben der polizeilichen Meldung unbedingt auch die kriegswirtschaftliche Ab- und Anmeldung bei der jeweils zuständigen Kartenstelle erforderlich. Die polizeiliche Anmeldebestätigung ist dabei vorzulegen.

.................................... (Eigenhändige Unterschrift des Angemeldeten)

.................................... (Eigenhändige Unterschrift des Wohnungsinhabers bei Untermietern)

.................................... (Eigenhändige Unterschrift des Hauseigentümers bzw. des Verwalters)

.................... den .......... 19.... (Ort und Datum der Abgabe an die Meldebehörde)

Vordruck a[1] (weiß) R. Pol. Nr. 128 E für Einzelpersonen

RNK Nr. 1610

1) Es ist die politische Gemeinde anzugeben, nicht ein Wohnplatz, ein Amtsbezirk oder ein Ortsteil.

2) Bei [illegible] Staatsangehörigkeit s. [illegible] angeben, bei Staatenlosigkeit: staatenlos und frühere Staatsangehörigkeit.

3) Von außerhalb zuziehende Wehrpflichtige müssen der Meldebehörde bei Abgabe der Meldung ihre Wehrpässe oder die an ihrer Stelle ausgegebenen Ausweise vorlegen.

Fig. 157

**ABMELDUNG BEI DER POLIZEILICHEN MELDEBEHÖRDE**

(Police Registration on leaving the district)

Abmeldung
bei der polizeilichen Meldebehörde

Die Meldung ist erfolgt
2 8 MRZ 1943

FRONT

# Auszug aus der Reichsmeldeordnung vom 6. Januar 1938

(Reichsgesetzbl. I Nr. 3 S. 13)

Wer eine Wohnung bezieht, hat sich binnen einer Woche nach dem Beziehen der Wohnung bei der Meldebehörde anzumelden. Bei Zuzug aus einer anderen Gemeinde hat er dabei die Bestätigung über seine Abmeldung vorzulegen, falls er nicht seine bisherige Wohnung daneben beibehält. Wer seine bisherige Wohnung daneben beibehält, muß dies bei der Anmeldung angeben.

Wohnung ist jeder Wohnraum, auch die Schlafstelle (§ 2).

Wer aus einer Wohnung auszieht, hat sich binnen einer Woche bei der Meldebehörde unter Angabe seiner neuen Wohnung oder, wenn er noch keine neue Wohnung besitzt, unter Angabe seines Verbleibs abzumelden (§ 3).

Bei Umzügen innerhalb der Gemeinde ist eine Abmeldung nicht erforderlich, sondern nur die Anmeldung in der neuen Wohnung. Bestehen in der Gemeinde besondere örtliche Meldestellen, so muß die Anmeldung bei der für die neue Wohnung zuständigen Meldestelle erstattet werden (§ 3 Abs. 2 und § 8 Abs. 2).

Die Meldung (An- oder Abmeldung) ist von dem Ein- oder Ausziehenden als dem Hauptmeldepflichtigen zu erstatten. Für Kinder bis zum vollendeten 15. Lebensjahr, die im elterlichen Hausstand wohnen, ist der Haushaltsvorstand meldepflichtig; wohnt das Kind nicht im elterlichen Hausstand, so ist der Wohnungsgeber meldepflichtig. Bei Entmündigten liegt dem gesetzlichen Vertreter die Meldepflicht ob (§ 4).

Der Hauptmeldepflichtige muß den von ihm wahrheitsgemäß ausgefüllten und von ihm selbst, vom Hauseigentümer, gegebenenfalls auch vom Wohnungsgeber, unterschriebenen Meldeschein — den Anmeldeschein in zwei, den Abmeldeschein in drei Ausfertigungen — persönlich bei der Meldebehörde unter Vorlage von Ausweispapieren abgeben (§ 5 Abs. 1 und § 11 Abs. 2). Das dritte Stück des Abmeldescheins erhält der Meldepflichtige nach Abstempelung zurück.

Die höhere Verwaltungsbehörde kann auch für den Anmeldeschein die Einreichung eines dritten Stücks vorschreiben (§ 13 Abs. 2). Im Falle dieser Anordnung erhält der Meldepflichtige das dritte Stück nach Abstempelung als Bestätigung der erstatteten Meldung zurück, falls ihm nicht von der Meldebehörde eine besondere Meldebestätigung (§ 11) erteilt wird.

Bei einem Wohnungswechsel, der sich auf den ganzen Haushalt erstreckt, sind Ehefrau und Kinder, solange sie mit dem Haushaltsvorstand in gemeinsamer Wohnung wohnen und seinen Namen führen, auf dem Meldeschein des Haushaltsvorstands mit zu melden. Im übrigen ist jede Person auf einem besonderen Meldeschein zu melden.

Bei der Abgabe der Meldung bei der Meldebehörde kann sich der am persönlichen Erscheinen verhinderte Meldepflichtige unter Angabe der Behinderungsgründe durch ein erwachsenes Familienmitglied und als Untermieter durch den Wohnungsgeber, als Mieter durch den Hauseigentümer (Verwalter) oder dessen erwachsene Familienmitglieder vertreten lassen.

Bei einem Wohnungswechsel, der sich auf den ganzen Haushalt erstreckt, kann der Haushaltsvorstand, im Behinderungsfall ein erwachsenes Familienmitglied die zum Haushalt gehörigen und mit umziehenden Personen bei der Abgabe der Meldung vertreten. Zum Haushalt zählen neben den Familienangehörigen auch Personen, die auf Grund eines Dienst-, Arbeits-, Vertrags- oder Verwandtschaftsverhältnisses in den Haushalt aufgenommen sind (§ 5).

Der Meldepflichtige hat auf Verlangen der Meldebehörde die erforderlichen Auskünfte zu geben, die notwendigen Ausweise vorzulegen sowie auch auf Anordnung persönlich zu erscheinen (§ 9).

Verweigern Wohnungsgeber oder Hauseigentümer (Verwalter) ihre Unterschrift, so hat der Meldepflichtige den Meldeschein mit dem schriftlichen Vermerk „Unterschrift verweigert" der Meldebehörde vorzulegen (§ 5 Abs. 4).

Außer dem Hauptmeldepflichtigen (dem Ein- oder Ausziehenden) sind der Wohnungsgeber und der Hauseigentümer (Verwalter) meldepflichtig, der letztere neben dem Wohnungsgeber auch für Untermieter (§ 4 Abs. 2).

Bei Einzug eines Mieters oder Untermieters haben Wohnungsgeber und Hauseigentümer (Verwalter) ihrer Meldepflicht genügt, wenn sie den Meldeschein des Zuziehenden unterschrieben und sich durch Einsicht in die Meldebestätigung (§ 11) davon überzeugt haben, daß die Meldung bei der Meldebehörde tatsächlich erstattet ist (§ 6).

Verweigert oder unterläßt der Hauptmeldepflichtige die Anmeldung, so genügen Wohnungsgeber und Hauseigentümer ihrer Meldepflicht, wenn sie das der Meldebehörde anzeigen (§ 6 Abs. 2).

Den Auszug eines Mieters muß der Hauseigentümer (Verwalter), den Auszug eines Untermieters der Wohnungsgeber der Meldebehörde innerhalb einer Woche schriftlich mitteilen, wobei sie sich des hierfür vorgesehenen Postkartenvordrucks bedienen können (§ 7 Abs. 1). Die Mitteilung des Wohnungsgebers ist vom Hauseigentümer (Verwalter) mit zu unterschreiben. Im Falle des Fortzugs aus der Gemeinde bedarf es dieser Meldung nicht, falls Hauseigentümer und Wohnungsgeber den Abmeldeschein unterschrieben und sich durch Einsicht in den abgestempelten Abmeldeschein davon überzeugt haben, daß die Abmeldung bei der Meldebehörde tatsächlich erstattet ist (§ 7 Abs. 2).

Wer in einer Gemeinde des Inlands nach § 12 gemeldet ist und besuchsweise in einer anderen Gemeinde bei Verwandten oder Bekannten wohnt, braucht sich erst nach Ablauf von sechs Wochen nach seiner Ankunft in der Besuchsgemeinde anzumelden. Reist er innerhalb dieser Frist ab, so ist er der Meldung entbunden (§ 12).

Die unverheirateten Angehörigen der Wehrmacht und der ℋ-Verfügungstruppe sowie die männlichen Angehörigen des Reichsarbeitsdienstes sind von der Meldepflicht befreit, solange sie in einer Kaserne oder einer anderen Unterkunft der Wehrmacht, der ℋ-Verfügungstruppe oder des Reichsarbeitsdienstes wohnen.

Die Genannten müssen sich vor Antritt des Militärdienstes, des Arbeitsdienstes oder des Dienstes in der ℋ-Verfügungstruppe bei der für ihre letzte Wohnung zuständigen Meldebehörde unter Vorlage ihres Gestellungsbefehls oder Angabe ihrer Formation oder des für die Reichsarbeitsdienstunterkunft zuständigen Reichsarbeitsdienst-Meldeamts abmelden. Nach Beendigung ihrer Dienstzeit oder bei vorherigem Verlassen der bezeichneten Unterkünfte müssen sie sich bei der für ihre neue Wohnung zuständigen Meldebehörde, bei Rückkehr in ihre frühere Wohnung bei der dortigen Meldebehörde wieder anmelden (§ 14 Ziffern 1 und 2).

Bei kurzfristig dienenden Militärpflichtigen bedarf es der Abmeldung und der neuen Anmeldung nicht, sofern sie ihre Wohnung beibehalten.

———

Anmerkung. Nach der Verordnung über zusätzliche Bestimmungen zur Reichsmeldeordnung vom 6. September 1939 (RGBl. I S. 1688) ist die Frist zur Anmeldung beim Beziehen einer Wohnung, sowie die Meldefrist beim Ausziehen aus einer Wohnung von einer Woche auf drei Tage herabgesetzt worden. Ausländer haben sich binnen 24 Stunden bei der Meldebehörde an- bzw. abzumelden.

# INDEX

Note.—This index refers to Parts One to Eight of the text only and does not cover any of the Annexes. All references concerning the Annexes should be looked for in the Table of Contents. Ranks which appear in the text are listed in the index; all others are listed in the Table of Ranks (para. 170).

The numbers of this index refer to paragraphs, with bold print indicating the paragraph which deals with the particular subject in special detail.

ii

iv

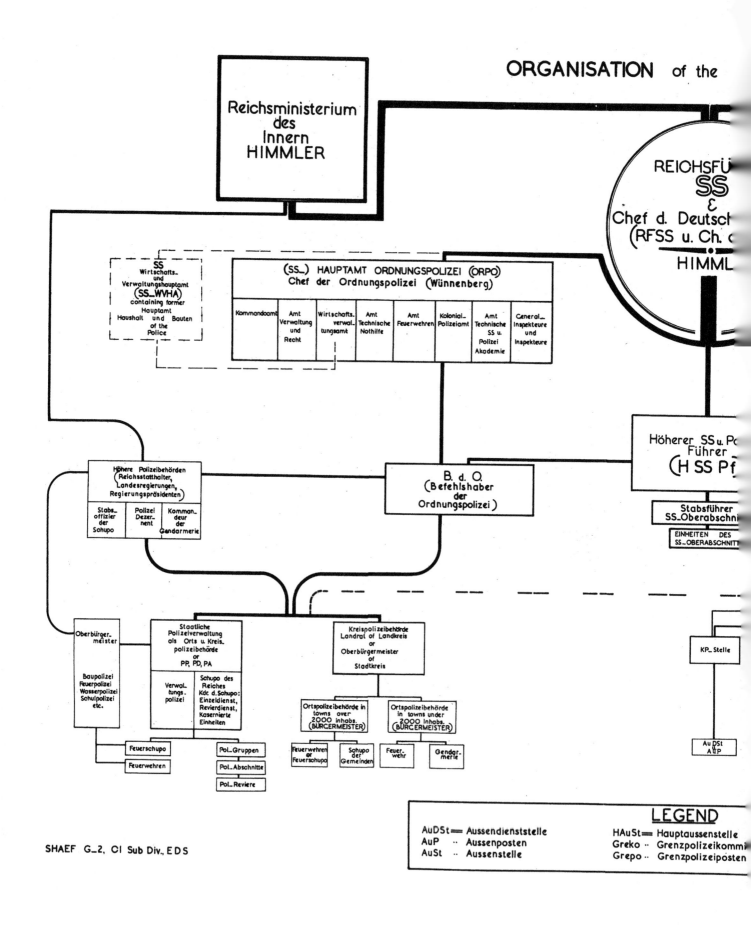

ORGANISATION of the

Reichsministerium des Innern HIMMLER

REICHSFÜ... SS & Chef d. Deutsc... (RFSS u. Ch. ... HIMML...

SS Wirtschafts_ und Verwaltungshauptamt (SS_WVHA) containing former Hauptamt Haushalt und Bauten of the Police

(SS_) HAUPTAMT ORDNUNGSPOLIZEI (ORPO)
Chef der Ordnungspolizei (Wünnenberg)

| Kommandoamt | Amt Verwaltung und Recht | Wirtschafts_ verwal_ tungsamt | Amt Technische Nothilfe | Amt Feuerwehren | Kolonial_ Polizeiamt | Amt Technische SS u. Polizei Akademie | General_ Inspekteure und Inspekteure |

Höhere Polizeibehörden (Reichsstatthalter, Landesregierungen, Regierungspräsidenten)

| Stabs_ offizier der Schupo | Polizei Dezer_ nent | Komman_ deur der Gendarmerie |

B. d. O.
(Befehlshaber der Ordnungspolizei)

Höherer SS u. Po... Führer ... (H SS Pf...

Stabsführer SS_Oberabschni...

EINHEITEN DES SS_OBERABSCHNITT...

Oberbürger_ meister

Baupolizei Feuerpolizei Wasserpolizei Schulpolizei etc.

Staatliche Polizeiverwaltung als Orts u. Kreis_ polizeibehörde or PP, PD, PA

| Verwal_ tungs_ polizei | Schupo des Reiches Kdr. d. Schupo: Einzeldienst, Revierdienst, Kasernierte Einheiten |

Kreispolizeibehörde Landrat of Landkreis or Oberbürgermeister of Stadtkreis

KP_ Stelle

Ortspolizeibehörde in towns over 2000 Inhabs. (BÜRGERMEISTER)

Ortspolizeibehörde in towns under 2000 Inhabs. (BÜRGERMEISTER)

| Feuerschupo |
| Feuerwehren |

| Pol_ Gruppen |
| Pol_ Abschnitte |
| Pol_ Reviere |

| Feuerwehren or Feuerschupo | Schupo der Gemeinden |

| Feuer_ wehr | Gendar_ merie |

AuDSt AuP

LEGEND

AuDSt = Aussendienststelle
AuP    „  Aussenposten
AuSt   „  Aussenstelle

HAuSt = Hauptaussenstelle
Greko „ Grenzpolizeikommi...
Grepo „ Grenzpolizeiposten

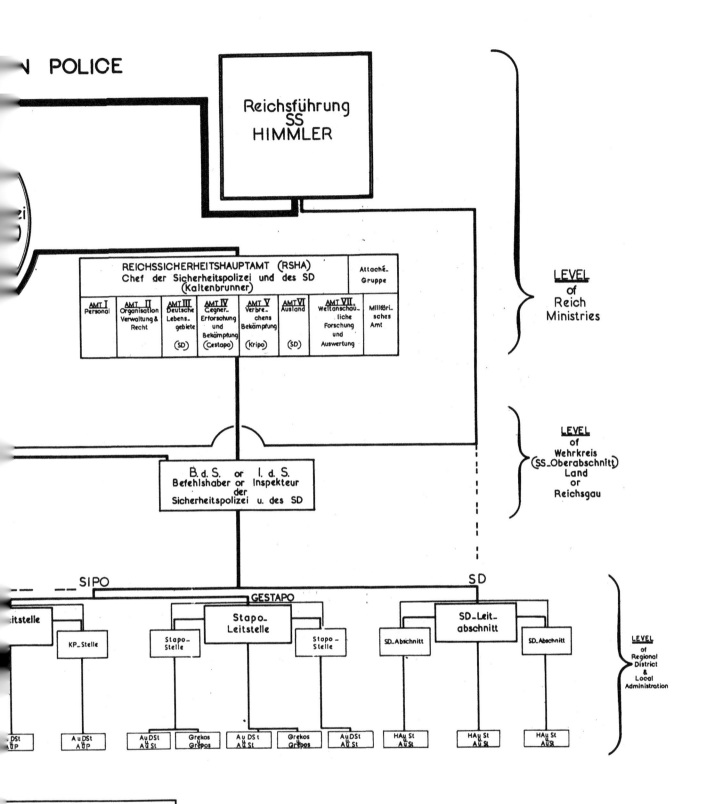

POLICE

Reichsführung
SS
HIMMLER

LEVEL
of
Reich
Ministries

REICHSSICHERHEITSHAUPTAMT (RSHA)
Chef der Sicherheitspolizei und des SD
(Kaltenbrunner)

| AMT I Personal | AMT II Organisation Verwaltung & Recht | AMT III Deutsche Lebens_ gebiete (SD) | AMT IV Gegner_ Erforschung und Bekämpfung (Gestapo) | AMT V Verbre_ chens Bekämpfung (Kripo) | AMT VI Ausland (SD) | AMT VII Weltanschau_ liche Forschung und Auswertung | Militäri_ sches Amt |

Attaché_ Gruppe

LEVEL
of
Wehrkreis
(SS_Oberabschnitt)
Land
or
Reichsgau

B. d. S. or I. d. S.
Befehlshaber or Inspekteur
der
Sicherheitspolizei u. des SD

SIPO                                                                SD

GESTAPO

| _itstelle | KP_Stelle | Stapo_ Stelle | Stapo_ Leitstelle | Stapo_ Stelle | SD_Abschnitt | SD_Leit_ abschnitt | SD_Abschnitt |

LEVEL
of
Regional
District
&
Local
Administration

| _DSt AuP | Au DSt AuP | Au DSt Au St | Grekos Gripos | Au DSt Au St | Grekos Gripos | Au DSt Au St | HAu St u AuSt | HAu St u AuSt | HAu St u AuSt |

PA =  Polizeiamt
PD  ..  Polizeidirektion
PP  ..  Polizeipräsidium

For ENGLISH see OVERLEAF

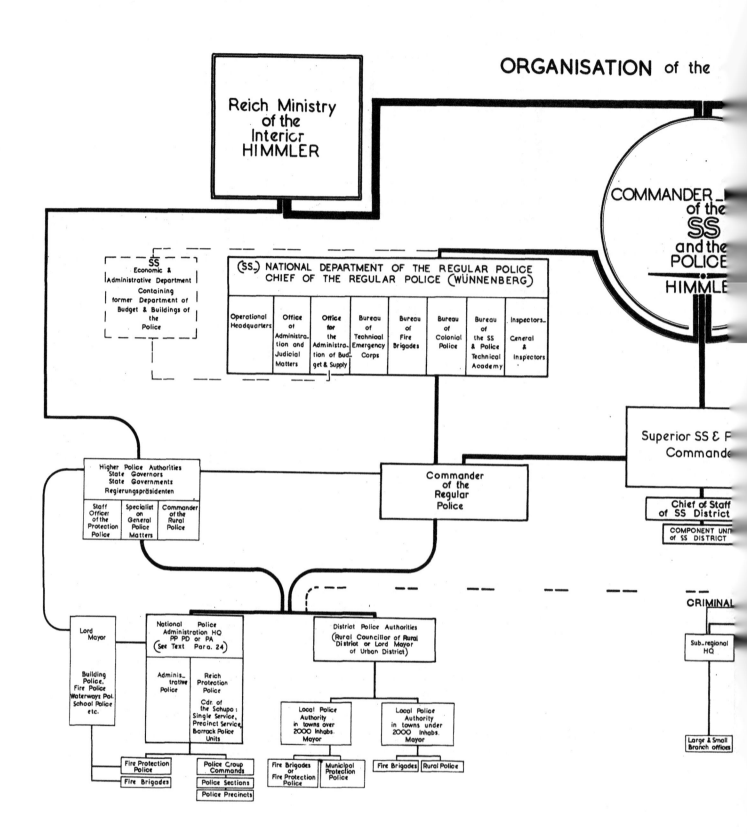

ORGANISATION of the

Reich Ministry of the Interior HIMMLER

COMMANDER of the SS and the POLICE HIMMLER

SS Economic & Administrative Department Containing former Department of Budget & Buildings of the Police

(SS.) NATIONAL DEPARTMENT OF THE REGULAR POLICE CHIEF OF THE REGULAR POLICE (WÜNNENBERG)

| Operational Headquarters | Office of Administration and Judicial Matters | Office for the Administration of Budget & Supply | Bureau of Technical Emergency Corps | Bureau of Fire Brigades | Bureau of Colonial Police | Bureau of the SS & Police Technical Academy | Inspectors General & Inspectors |

Superior SS & Police Commander

Higher Police Authorities State Governors State Governments Regierungspräsidenten

| Staff Officer of the Protection Police | Specialist on General Police Matters | Commander of the Rural Police |

Commander of the Regular Police

Chief of Staff of SS District

COMPONENT UNIT of SS DISTRICT

CRIMINAL

Lord Mayor

Building Police, Fire Police Waterways Pol. School Police etc.

National Police Administration HQ PP PD or PA (See Text Para. 24)

| Administrative Police | Reich Protection Police Cdr. of the Schupo: Single Service, Precinct Service, Barrack Police Units |

District Police Authorities (Rural Councillor of Rural District or Lord Mayor of Urban District)

Sub-regional HQ

Fire Protection Police

Fire Brigades

Police Group Commands

Police Sections

Police Precincts

Local Police Authority in towns over 2000 Inhabs. Mayor

Fire Brigades or Fire Protection Police

Municipal Protection Police

Local Police Authority in towns under 2000 Inhabs. Mayor

Fire Brigades

Rural Police

Large & Small Branch offices

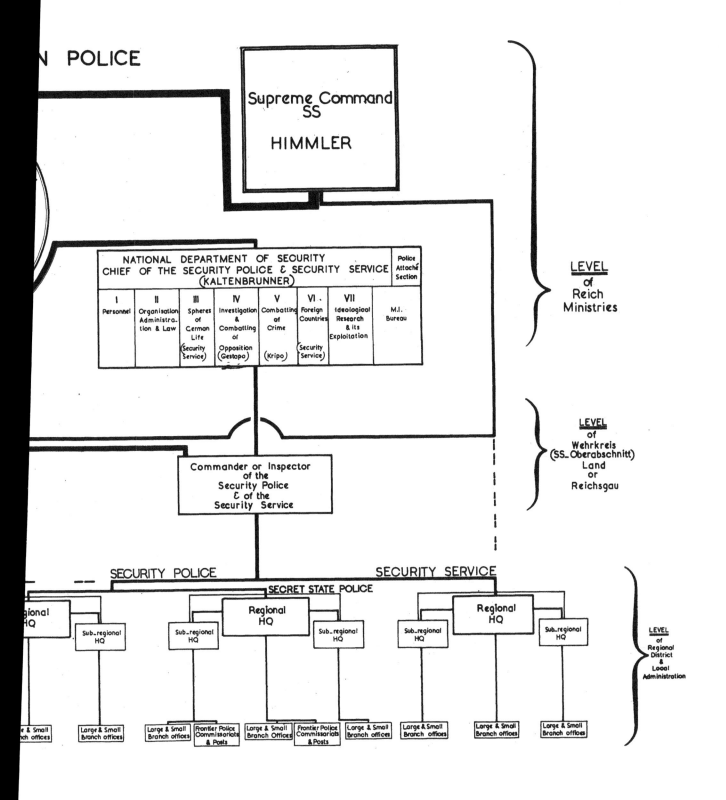

POLICE

Supreme Command
SS

HIMMLER

| NATIONAL DEPARTMENT OF SECURITY CHIEF OF THE SECURITY POLICE & SECURITY SERVICE (KALTENBRUNNER) | | | | | | | Police Attaché Section |
|---|---|---|---|---|---|---|---|
| I Personnel | II Organisation Administration & Law | III Spheres of German Life (Security Service) | IV Investigation & Combatting of Opposition (Gestapo) | V Combatting of Crime (Kripo) | VI Foreign Countries (Security Service) | VII Ideological Research & its Exploitation | M.I. Bureau |

LEVEL
of
Reich
Ministries

Commander or Inspector
of the
Security Police
& of the
Security Service

LEVEL
of
Wehrkreis
(SS_Oberabschnitt)
Land
or
Reichsgau

SECURITY POLICE          SECURITY SERVICE

SECRET STATE POLICE

Regional HQ

Regional HQ

Regional HQ

Sub-regional HQ

Sub-regional HQ

Sub-regional HQ

Sub-regional HQ

Sub-regional HQ

Sub-regional HQ

LEVEL
of
Regional
District
&
Local
Administration

Large & Small Branch offices

Large & Small Branch offices

Large & Small Branch offices

Frontier Police Commissariats & Posts

Large & Small Branch Offices

Frontier Police Commissariats & Posts

Large & Small Branch offices

Large & Small Branch offices

Large & Small Branch offices

Large & Small Branch offices

CPSIA information can be obtained
at www.ICGtesting.com
Printed in the USA
BVOW07s0352090517
483145BV00044B/50/P

9 781843 425946